View a guided tour of MyAccountingLab at
http://www.myaccountinglab.com/support/tours

For Students

Interactive Tutorial Exercises

■ Homework and practice exercises with additional algorithmic–generated problems for more practice.

■ Personalized interactive learning—guided solutions and learning aids for point-of-use help and immediate feedback.

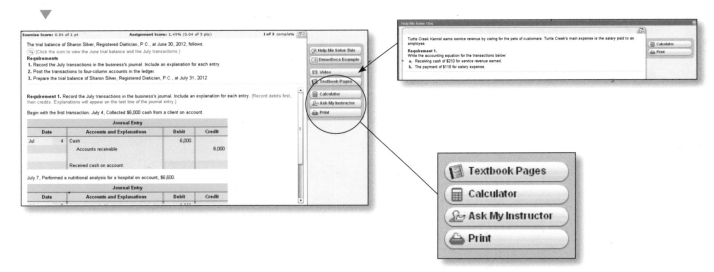

Study Plan for Self-Paced Learning

■ Assists students in monitoring their own progress by offering them a customized study plan based on their test results.

■ Includes regenerated exercises with new values for unlimited practice and guided multimedia learning aids for extra guidance.

Financial Accounting

Ninth Edition

Financial Accounting

Ninth Edition

Walter T. Harrison Jr.
Baylor University

Charles T. Horngren
Stanford University

C. William (Bill) Thomas
Baylor University

PEARSON

Boston   Columbus   Indianapolis   New York   San Francisco   Upper Saddle River
Amsterdam   Cape Town   Dubai   London   Madrid   Milan   Munich   Paris   Montréal   Toronto
Delhi   Mexico City   São Paulo   Sydney   Hong Kong   Seoul   Singapore   Taipei   Tokyo

VP/Editorial Director: Sally Yagan
Editor in Chief: Donna Battista
Acquisitions Editor: Lacey Vitetta
Director of Editorial Services: Ashley Santora
Senior Editorial Project Manager: Karen Kirincich
Editorial Assistant: Jane Avery
Editorial Assistant: Lauren Zanedis
Director of Marketing: Maggie Moylan Leen
Marketing Assistant: Ian Gold
Marketing Assistant: Kimberly Lovato
Senior Managing Editor: Nancy Fenton
Senior Production Project Manager: Roberta Sherman
Manufacturing Buyer: Carol Melville
Art Director: Anthony Gemmellaro

Text Designer: Anthony Gemmellaro
Cover Designer: Anthony Gemmellaro
Photo Researcher: Bill Smith Group
Cover Art: © Fotolia
Lead Media Project Manager: Sarah Peterson
Media Production Project Manager: John Cassar
Supplements Project Manager: Vonda Keator
Composition: GEX Publishing Services
Full-Service Project Management:
  GEX Publishing Services
Printer/Binder: Courier Kendallville
Cover Printer: Lehigh-Phoenix Color/Hagerstown
Typeface: Adobe Jensen Pro 10/12

Credits and acknowledgments borrowed from other sources and reproduced, with permission, in this textbook appear on the appropriate page within text.

All real company data presented in chapters 1–13 has been based on the most recent information reported by each company.

Library of Congress Cataloging-in-Publication Data
Harrison, Walter T.
  Financial accounting / Walter T. Harrison Jr., Charles T. Horngren, C. William (Bill) Thomas. — 9th ed.
    p. cm.
  Includes index.
  ISBN 978-0-13-275112-4 (casebound)
  1. Accounting. I. Horngren, Charles T. II. Thomas, C. William. III. Title.
  HF5636.H37 2013
  657--dc23
                  2011046912

10 9 8 7 6 5 4 3 2 1

www.pearsonhighered.com

ISBN 10: 0-13-275125-9
ISBN 13: 978-0-13-275125-4

In memory of *Charles T. Horngren* 1926–2011

Whose vast contributions to the teaching and learning of accounting impacted and will continue to impact generations of accounting students and professionals.

For our wives,
Nancy, Joan, and Mary Ann

BRIEF CONTENTS

CONTENTS

Chapter 4

Internal Control & Cash   230

Spotlight: Cooking the Books: EPIC Products Takes a Hit   230

Chapter 5

Short-Term Investments & Receivables   283

Spotlight: Receivables and Short-Term Investments are Double PepsiCo's Inventories!   283

Chapter 6

Chapter 7

Chapter 8

**Long-Term Investments & the Time Value
of Money   463**

Chapter 9

Liabilities   517

Chapter 10

Chapter 11

Chapter 12

The Statement of Cash Flows   697

Chapter 13

Financial Statement Analysis   771

Visual Walk-Through

Helping Students Nail the Accounting Cycle

The concepts and mechanics the students learn in the critical accounting cycle chapters are used consistently and repetitively—and with clear-cut details and explanations—throughout the remainder of the text, minimizing confusion.

NEW! **User-Oriented Approach** focuses students' attention on the meaning and relevance of information in the financial statements by adding new ratios to assist in evaluating liquidity, turnover, and profitability.

NEW! **Focus on Analysis** company, RadioShack Corporation. We collaborated with company executives to help us develop relevant analytical problems using its financial information.

NEW! **Challenge Problems** have been added to every chapter helping students develop higher-order critical thinking and problem-solving skills.

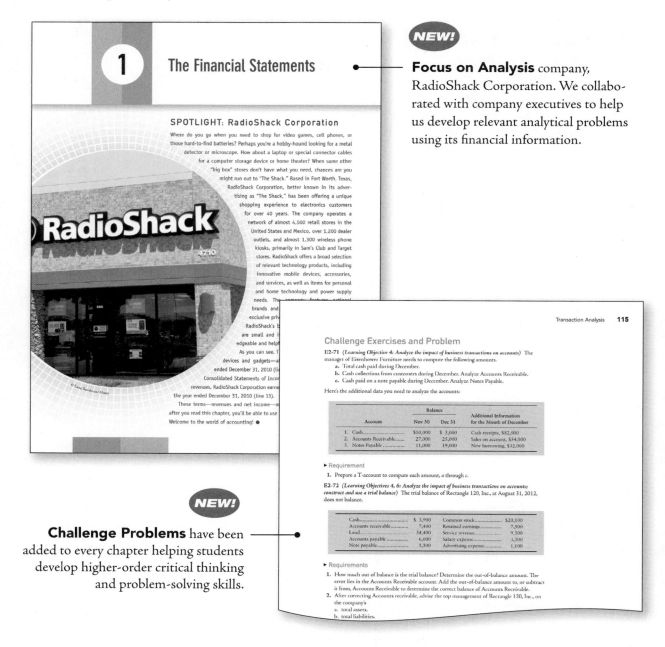

Stockholders' (Owners') Equity

The owners' claims to the assets of a corporation are called *stockholders' equity, shareholders' equity,* or simply *owners' equity.* A corporation such as Apple, Inc., uses Common Stock, Retained Earnings, and Dividends accounts to record the company's stockholders' equity. In a proprietorship, there is a single capital account. For a partnership, each partner has a separate owner's equity account.

Common Stock. The Common Stock account shows the owners' investment in the corporation. Apple, Inc., receives cash and issues common stock to its stockholders. A company's common stock is its most basic element of equity. All corporations have common stock.

STOP & THINK. . .

Name two things that **(1)** increase Apple, Inc.'s stockholders' equity and **(2)** decrease Apple's stockholders' equity.

Answer:

(1) Increases in equity: Sale of stock and net income (revenue greater than expenses).

(2) Decreases in equity: Dividends and net loss (expenses greater than revenue).

Stop & Think sections relate concepts to everyday life so students can see the immediate relevance.

Retained Earnings. The Retained Earnings account shows the cumulative net income earned by Apple, Inc., over the company's lifetime, minus its cumulative net losses and dividends.

Dividends. Dividends are optional; they are decided (declared) by the board of directors. After profitable operations, the board of directors of Apple, Inc., may (or may not) declare and pay a cash dividend. The corporation may keep a separate account titled *Dividends,* which indicates a decrease in Retained Earnings.

Revenues. The increase in stockholders' equity from delivering goods or services to customers is called *revenue.* The company uses as many revenue accounts as needed. Apple, Inc., uses a Sales Revenue account for revenue earned by selling its products. Apple has a Service Revenue account for the revenue it earns by providing services to customers. A lawyer provides legal services for clients and also uses a Service Revenue account. A business that loans money to an outside party needs an Interest Revenue account. If the business rents a building to a tenant, the business needs a Rent Revenue account.

DECISION GUIDELINES

DECISION FRAMEWORK FOR MAKING ETHICAL JUDGMENTS

Weighing tough ethical judgments in business and accounting requires a decision framework. Answering the following four questions will guide you through tough decisions:

Decision	Guidelines
1. What is the issue?	1. The issue will usually deal with making a judgment about an accounting measurement or disclosure that results in economic consequences, often to numerous parties.
2. Who are the stakeholders, and what are the consequences of the decision to each?	2. Stakeholders are anyone who might be impacted by the decision—you, your company, and potential users of the information (investors, creditors, regulatory agencies). Consequences can be economic, legal, or ethical in nature.
3. Weigh the alternatives.	3. Analyze the impact of the decision on all stakeholders, using economic, legal, and ethical criteria. Ask "Who will be helped or hurt, whose rights will be exercised or denied, and in what way?"
4. Make the decision and be prepared to deal with the consequences.	4. Exercise the courage to either defend the decision or to change it, depending on its positive or negative impact. How does your decision make you feel afterward?

To simplify, we might ask three questions:

1. Is the action legal? If not, steer clear, unless you want to go to jail or pay monetary damages to injured parties. If the action is legal, go on to questions (2) and (3).
2. Who will be affected by the decision and how? Be as thorough about this analysis as possible, and analyze it from all three standpoints (economic, legal, and ethical).
3. How will this decision make me feel afterward? How would it make me feel if my family reads about it in the newspaper?

In later chapters throughout the book, we will apply this model to decisions.

Decision Guidelines in the End-of-Chapter material summarize the chapter's key terms, concepts, and formulas in the context of business decisions.

---

 with Inventory

Crazy Eddie

It is one thing to make honest mistakes in accounting for inventory, but quite another to use inventory to commit fraud. The two most common ways to "cook the books" with inventory are

1. inserting fictitious inventory—thus overstating quantities—and
2. deliberately overstating unit prices used in the computation of ending inventory amounts.

Either one of these tricks has exactly the same effect on income as inventory errors, discussed in the previous section. The difference is that honest inventory errors are often corrected as soon as they are detected, thus minimizing their impact on income. In contrast, deliberate overstatement of inventories tends to be repeated over and over again throughout the course of months, or even years, thus causing the misstatement to grow ever higher until it is discovered. By that time, it can be too late for the company.

Crazy Eddie, Inc.,[1] was a retail consumer electronics store in 1987, operating 43 retail outlets in the New York City area, with $350 million in reported sales and reported profits of $10.5 million. Its stock was a Wall Street "darling," with a collective market value of $600 million. The only problem was that the company's reported profits had been grossly overstated since 1984, the year that the company went public.

Eddie Antar, the company's founder and major stockholder, became preoccupied with the price of his company's stock in 1984. Antar realized that the company, in an extremely competitive retail market in the largest city in the United States, had to keep posting impressive operating profits in order to maintain the upward trend in the company's stock price.

Within the first six months, Antar ordered a subordinate to double count about $2 million of inventory in the company's stores and warehouses. Using Exhibits 6-15 and 6-16, you can see that the impact of this inventory overstatement went straight to the "bottom line," overstating profits by the same amount. Unfortunately, the company's auditors failed to detect the inventory overstatement. The following year, emboldened by the audit error, Antar ordered

[1]Michael C. Knapp, *Contemporary Auditing: Real Issues and Cases,* 6th edition, Mason, Ohio: Thomson Southwestern, 2009.

Cooking the Books highlight real fraud cases in relevant sections through the text, giving student's real-life business context.

Coverage on time value of money is incorporated into Chapter 8—Long-Term Investments—highlighting its importance in measuring fair value of certain long-term assets and liabilities.

EXHIBIT 8-11 | Intel Corporation Investing Activities on the Statement of Cash Flows

Intel Corporation
Consolidated Statement of Cash Flows (Partial, Adapted)

(In billions)	2010
Cash flows provided by (used for) investing activities:	
Sales of available-for-sale investments	$ 13.1
Purchases of available-for-sale investments	(17.7)
Additions to property, plant, and equipment	(5.2)
Sales of equity-method investments	0.2
Other uses of cash	(0.9)
Net cash (used for) investing activities	$(10.5)

Explain the Impact of the Time Value of Money on Certain Types of Investments

Explain the impact of the time value of money on certain types of investments

Which would you rather have: $1,000 received today, or $1,000 received a year from now? A logical person would answer: "I'd rather have the cash now, because if I get it now, I can invest it at some interest rate so that a year in the future I'll have more." The term *future value* means the sum of money that a given current investment will be "worth" at a specified time in the future assuming a certain interest rate. The term *time value of money* refers to the fact that money earns interest over time. *Interest* is the cost of using money. To borrowers, interest is the fee paid to the lender for the period of the loan. To lenders, interest is the revenue earned from allowing someone else to use our money for a period of time.

Whether making investments or borrowing money long term, we must always recognize the interest we receive or pay. Otherwise, we overlook an important part of the transaction. Suppose you invest $4,545 in corporate bonds that pay 10% interest each year. After one year, the value of your investment has grown to $5,000, as shown in the following diagram:

EXHIBIT 8-12 | Future Value of an Investment

Present Value			Future Value
Time 0			1 year
	Roll forward (accumulate)		
$4,545			$5,000
	Present value × (1 + Interest rate) = Future Value		
	$4,545 × 1.10		

The Revenue Principle

Apply the revenue and expense recognition principles

The **revenue principle** deals with two issues:

1. When to record revenue (make a journal entry)

2. The amount of revenue to record

When should you record revenue? After it has been earned—and not before. In most cases, revenue is earned when the business has delivered a good or service to a customer. It has done everything required to earn the revenue by transferring the good or service to the customer.

Global View

Revenue recognition has been one of the areas in which a number of differences have existed between U.S. GAAP and IFRS for years. U.S. GAAP has been highly detailed and has varied by industry. For example, the rules for timing and the amount of revenue in the computer software industry have differed substantially from those in the construction industry. By contrast, IFRS has been far less detailed, leaving more room for interpretation on the part of the company. In 2011, the FASB and IASB finished a joint research project that resolved most of these differences, resulting in a consistent, converged, and simplified global revenue recognition standard. The effective date for the new standard on revenue recognition will be sometime in 2012. This book deals with the retail industry, where businesses purchase and sell largely finished goods and render services in a straightforward way. Fortunately, in the retail industry, U.S. GAAP and IFRS have historically been consistent with respect to general principles of revenue recognition, so the issuance of the new standard will not substantially change the rules by which revenue is recognized in the retail industry.

Exhibit 3-1 shows two situations that provide guidance on when to record revenue for Starbucks Corporation. Situation 1 illustrates when not to record revenue. No transaction has occurred, so Starbucks Corporation records nothing. Situation 2 illustrates when revenue should be recorded—after a transaction has occurred.

The *amount* of revenue to record is the cash value of the goods or services transferred to the customer. The event that triggers revenue recognition for the sale of goods is the *transfer of control of the goods* to the purchaser. In the case of services, the event that triggers revenue recognition is the *substantial completion of an obligation to perform a service* for the buyer. For example, suppose that in

Global View information on IFRS is introduced, where appropriate, throughout the chapters.

▶ Requirements

1. What is the ethical issue?
2. Who are the stakeholders? What are the possible consequences to each?
3. Analyze the alternatives from the following standpoints: (a) economic, (b) legal, and (c) ethical.
4. What would you do? How would you justify your decision? How would it make you feel afterward?

Part b. Now assume the same facts that were just provided, except that you have received your final grade for the course and the grade is a B. You are confident that you "aced" the final. In fact, you stayed to the very end of the period, and checked every figure twice! You are confident that the instructor must have made a mistake grading the final.

▶ Requirements

1. What is the ethical issue?
2. Who are the stakeholders and what are the consequences to each?
3. Analyze the alternatives from the following standpoints: (a) economic, (b) legal, and (c) ethical.
4. What would you do? How would you justify your decision? How would it make you feel?

Part c. How is this situation like a financial accounting misstatement? How is it different?

Focus on Financials: | Amazon.com, Inc.

(*Learning Objectives 3, 4: Record transactions; compute net income*) Refer to **Amazon.com, Inc.**'s financial statements in Appendix A at the end of the book. Assume that Amazon.com completed the following selected transactions during 2010.

a. Made company sales (revenue) of $34,204 million, all on account (debit accounts receivable).
b. Collected cash on accounts receivable $33,605.
c. Purchased inventories on account, $27,592 million (credit accounts payable).
d. Incurred cost of sales in the amount of $26,561 million. Debit the Cost of sales (expense) account. Credit the Inventories account.
e. Paid accounts payable in cash, $25,146.
f. Paid operating expenses of $6,237 million in cash.
g. Collected non-operating income (net) in cash, $91 million.
h. Paid income taxes, $352 million in cash (debit provision for income taxes).
i. Accounted for income from other investment activity net of taxes in the amount of $7 million. Debit other assets. Credit the account entitled Equity

New and updated End-of-Chapter problems, exercises, and Focus on Financials analysis questions

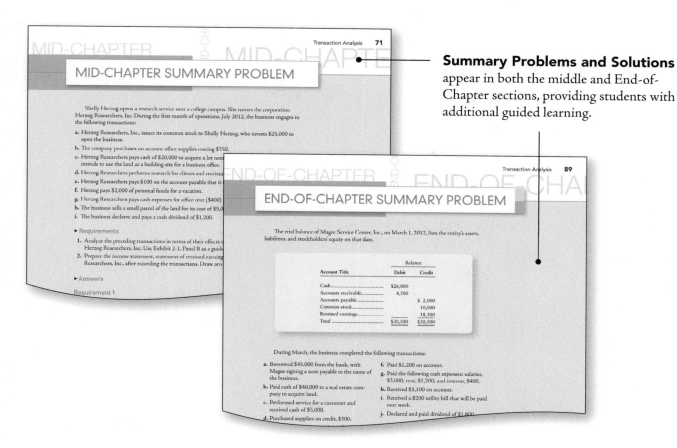

MID-CHAPTER SUMMARY PROBLEM

Shelly Herzog opens a research service near a college campus. She names the corporation Herzog Researchers, Inc. During the first month of operations, July 2012, the business engages in the following transactions:

a. Herzog Researchers, Inc., issues its common stock to Shelly Herzog, who invests $25,000 to open the business.

b. The company purchases on account office supplies costing $350.

c. Herzog Researchers pays cash of $20,000 to acquire a lot next [...] intends to use the land as a building site for a business office.

d. Herzog Researchers performs research for clients and receives [...]

e. Herzog Researchers pays $100 on the account payable that it [...]

f. Herzog pays $2,000 of personal funds for a vacation.

g. Herzog Researchers pays cash expenses for office rent ($400) [...]

h. The business sells a small parcel of the land for its cost of $5,0 [...]

i. The business declares and pays a cash dividend of $1,200.

▶ **Requirements**

1. Analyze the preceding transactions in terms of their effects [...] Herzog Researchers, Inc. Use Exhibit 2-1, Panel B as a guide [...]

2. Prepare the income statement, statement of retained earning [...] Researchers, Inc., after recording the transactions. Draw arr [...]

▶ **Answers**

Requirement 1

END-OF-CHAPTER SUMMARY PROBLEM

The trial balance of Magee Service Center, Inc., on March 1, 2012, lists the entity's assets, liabilities, and stockholders' equity on that date.

Account Title	Balance Debit	Balance Credit
Cash	$26,000	
Accounts receivable	4,500	
Accounts payable		$ 2,000
Common stock		10,000
Retained earnings		18,500
Total	$30,500	$30,500

During March, the business completed the following transactions:

a. Borrowed $45,000 from the bank, with Magee signing a note payable in the name of the business.

b. Paid cash of $40,000 to a real estate company to acquire land.

c. Performed service for a customer and received cash of $5,000.

d. Purchased supplies on credit, $300.

f. Paid $1,200 on account.

g. Paid the following cash expenses: salaries, $3,000; rent, $1,500; and interest, $400.

h. Received $3,100 on account.

i. Received a $200 utility bill that will be paid next week.

j. Declared and paid dividend of $1,800.

Summary Problems and Solutions appear in both the middle and End-of-Chapter sections, providing students with additional guided learning.

 NEW!

EXCEL in MyAccountingLab - *Coming Spring 2012*

+ Now students can get real-world Excel practice in their classes.

+ Instructors have the option to assign students End-of-Chapter questions that can be completed in an Excel-simulated environment.

+ Questions will be auto-graded, reported to, and visible in the grade book.

+ Excel remediation will be available to students.

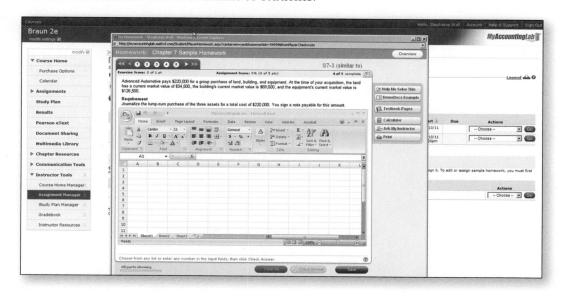

ACKNOWLEDGMENTS

A special thank you to Becky Jones and Betsy Willis for their dedication throughout the project. Thank you to C. Andrew Lafond, The College of New Jersey for his help with accuracy checking.

In revising previous editions of *Financial Accounting*, we had the help of instructors from across the country who have participated in online surveys, chapter reviews, and focus groups. Their comments and suggestions for both the text and the supplements have been a great help in planning and carrying out revisions, and we thank them for their contributions.

Reviewers

Elizabeth Ammann, Lindenwood University
Brenda Anderson, Brandeis University
Florence Atiase, University of Texas at Austin
Patrick Bauer, DeVry University, Kansas City
Amy Bourne, Oregon State University
Rada Brooks, University of California, Berkeley
Elizabeth Brown, Keene State College
Scott Bryant, Baylor University
Marci Butterfield, University of Utah
C. Catherine Chiang, Elon University
Lawrence Chui, Ph.D., CPA, Opus College of Business,
    University of St. Thomas
Dr. Paul Clikeman, University of Richmond
Sue Counte, Saint Louis Community College-Meramec
Julia Creighton, American University
Sue Cullers, Buena Vista University
Kreag Danvers, Clarion University
Betty David, Francis Marion University
Peter DiCarlo, Boston College
Allan Drebin, Northwestern University
Carolyn Dreher, Southern Methodist University
Emily Drogt, Grand Valley State University
Dr. Andrew Felo, Penn State Great Valley
Dr. Mary Fischer, Professor of Accounting, The University of
    Texas at Tyler
Dr. Caroline Ford, Baylor University
Clayton Forester, University of Minnesota
Timothy Gagnon, Northeastern University
Lisa Gillespie, Loyola University, Chicago
Marvin Gordon, University of Illinois at Chicago
Anthony Greig, Purdue University
Penny Hanes, Associate Professor, Mercyhurst College
Dr. Heidi Hansel, Kirkwood Community College
Michael Haselkorn, Bentley University
Mary Hollars, Vincennes University
Constance Malone Hylton, George Mason University
Grace Johnson, Marietta College
Celina Jozsi, University of South Florida
John Karayan, Woodbury University
Irene Kim, The George Washington University
Robert Kollar, Duquesne University
Elliott Levy, Bentley University
Joseph Lupino, Saint Mary's College of California
Anthony Masino, Queens University / NC Central
Lizbeth Matz, University of Pittsburgh, Bradford

Allison McLeod, University of North Texas
Cynthia J. Miller, Gatton College of Business & Economics, Von
    Allmen School of Accountancy, University of Kentucky
Mary Miller, University of New Haven
Scott Miller, Gannon University
Dr. Birendra (Barry) K. Mishra, University of California, Riverside
Lisa Nash, Vincennes University
Rosemary Nurre, College of San Mateo
Stephen Owen, Hamilton College
Rama Ramamurthy, College of William and Mary
Barb Reeves, Cleary University
Anwar Salimi, California State Polytechnic University, Pomona
Philippe Sammour, Eastern Michigan University
Albert A Schepanski, University of Iowa
Virginia Smith, Saint Mary's College of California
Lily Sieux, California State University, East Bay
Vic Stanton, Stanford University
Gloria J. Stuart, Georgia Southern University
Martin Taylor, University of Texas at Arlington
Vincent Turner, California State Polytechnic University,
    Pomona
Craig Weaver, University of California, Riverside
Betsy Willis, Baylor University, Waco, TX
Dr. Jia Wu, University of Massachusetts, Dartmouth
Yanfeng Xue, George Washington University
Barbara Yahvah, University of Montana-Helena

Supplements

Sandra A. Augustine, CPA Hilbert College, Hamburg NY
Courtney Baillie, Ph.D., Nebraska Wesleyan University
Lawrence Chui, Ph.D., CPA, Opus College of Business,
    University of St. Thomas
Darlene A. Deeg, C.P.A., M.S.T., University of Michigan–
    Dearborn
Becky Jones, Baylor University
Jamie McCracken, Assistant Professor of Business, Saint
    Mary-of-the-Woods College
Delvan Roehling, Ivy Tech Community College
Deborah J. Stephen, Visiting Assistant Professor of Accounting,
    Point Park University
Betsy B. Willis, Baylor University, Waco, TX

Past Reviewer Participants

Shawn Abbott, College of the Siskiyous, CA
Linda Abernathy, Kirkwood Community College

Sol Ahiarah, SUNY College at Buffalo (Buffalo State)

M. J. Albin, University of Southern Mississippi

Gary Ames, Brigham Young University, Idaho

Kim Anderson, Indiana University of Pennsylvania

Walter Austin, Mercer University, Macon GA

Brad Badertscher, University of Iowa

Sandra Bailey, Oregon Institute of Technology

Barbara A. Beltrand, Metropolitan State University, MN

Jerry Bennett, University of South Carolina–Spartanburg

Peg Beresewski, Robert Morris College, IL

Lucille Berry, Webster University, MO

John Bildersee, New York University, Stern School

Brenda Bindschatel, Green River Community College

Candace Blankenship, Belmont University, TN

Charlie Bokemeier, Michigan State University

Patrick Bouker, North Seattle Community College

Scott Boylan, Washington and Lee University, VA

Robert Braun, Southeastern Louisiana University

Linda Bressler, University of Houston Downtown

Michael Broihahn, Barry University, FL

Carol Brown, Oregon State University

Helen Brubeck, San Jose State University, CA

Marcus Butler, University of Rochester, NY

Mark Camma, Atlantic Cape Community College, NJ

Kay Carnes, Gonzaga University, WA

Brian Carpenter, University of Scranton, PA

Sandra Cereola, James Madison University, VA

Kam Chan, Pace University

Hong Chen, Northeastern Illinois University

Freddy Choo, San Francisco State University, CA

Charles Christy, Delaware Tech and Community College, Stanton Campus

Shifei Chung, Rowan University, NJ

Bryan Church, Georgia Tech at Atlanta

Carolyn Clark, Saint Joseph's University, PA

Charles Coate, St. Bonaventure University, NY

Dianne Conry, University of California State College Extension–Cupertino

Ellen D. Cook, University of Louisiana at Lafayette

John Coulter, Western New England College

Donald Curfman, McHenry County College, IL

Alan Czyzewski, Indiana State University

Laurie Dahlin, Worcester State College, MA

Bonita Daly, University of Southern Maine

Patricia Derrick, George Washington University

Bettye Rogers-Desselle, Prairie View A&M University, TX

Charles Dick, Miami University

Barbara Doughty, New Hampshire Community Technical College

Carol Dutton, South Florida Community College

James Emig, Villanova University, PA

Ellen Engel, University of Chicago

Alan Falcon, Loyola Marymount University, CA

Janet Farler, Pima Community College, AZ

Andrew Felo, Penn State Great Valley

Ken Ferris, Thunderbird College, AZ

Lou Fowler, Missouri Western State College

Terrie Gehman, Elizabethtown College, PA

Lucille Genduso, Nova Southeastern University, FL

Frank Gersich, Monmouth College, IL

Bradley Gillespie, Saddleback College, CA

Brian Green, University of Michigan at Dearborn

Ronald Guidry, University of Louisiana at Monroe

Konrad Gunderson, Missouri Western State College

William Hahn, Southeastern College, FL

Jack Hall, Western Kentucky University

Gloria Halpern, Montgomery College, MD

Kenneth Hart, Brigham Young University, Idaho

Al Hartgraves, Emory University

Thomas Hayes, University of North Texas

Larry Hegstad, Pacific Lutheran University, WA

Candy Heino, Anoka-Ramsey Community College, MN

Anit Hope, Tarrant County College, TX

Thomas Huse, Boston College

Fred R. Jex, Macomb Community College, MI

Beth Kern, Indiana University, South Bend

Hans E. Klein, Babson College, MA

Willem Koole, North Carolina State University

Emil Koren, Hillsborough Community College, FL

Dennis Kovach, Community College of Allegheny County–North Campus

Ellen Landgraf, Loyola University Chicago

Howard Lawrence, Christian Brothers University, TN

Barry Leffkov, Regis College, MA

Chao-Shin Liu, Notre Dame

Barbara Lougee, University of California, Irvine

Heidemarie Lundblad, California State University, Northridge

Anna Lusher, West Liberty State College, WV

Harriet Maccracken, Arizona State University

Carol Mannino, Milwaukee School of Engineering

Herb Martin, Hope College, MI

Aziz Martinez, Harvard University, Harvard Business School

Bruce Maule, College of San Mateo

Michelle McEacharn, University of Louisiana at Monroe

Nick McGaughey, San Jose State University, CA

Cathleen Miller, University of Michigan–Flint

Mark Miller, University of San Francisco, CA

Frank Mioni, Madonna University, MI

Theodore D. Morrison III, Wingate University, NC

Bruce L. Oliver, Rochester Institute of Technology

Charles Pedersen, Quinsigamond Community College, MA

Richard J. Pettit, Mountain View College

George Plesko, Massachusetts Institute of Technology

David Plumlee, University of Utah

Gregory Prescott, University of South Alabama

Craig Reeder, Florida A&M University

Darren Roulstone, University of Chicago

Norlin Rueschhoff, Notre Dame

Angela Sandberg, Jacksonville State University, AL

George Sanders, Western Washington University, WA

Betty Saunders, University of North Florida

William Schmul, Notre Dame
Arnie Schnieder, Georgia Tech at Atlanta
Gim Seow, University of Connecticut
Itzhak Sharav, CUNY–Lehman Graduate School of Business
Allan Sheets, International Business College
Alvin Gerald Smith, University of Northern Iowa
James Smith, Community College of Philadelphia
Beverly Soriano, Framingham State College, MA
Carolyn R. Stokes, Frances Marion University, SC
J. B. Stroud, Nicholls State University, LA
Al Taccone, Cuyamaca College, CA
Diane Tanner, University of North Florida

Howard Toole, San Diego State University
Marcia Veit, University of Central Florida
Bruce Wampler, Louisiana State University, Shreveport
Suzanne Ward, University of Louisiana at Lafayette
Frederick Weis, Claremont McKenna College, CA
Frederick Weiss, Virginia Wesleyan College
Ronald Woan, Indiana University of Pennsylvania
Allen Wright, Hillsborough Community College, FL
Myung Yoon, Northeastern Illinois University
Lin Zeng, Northeastern Illinois University
Tony Zordan, University of St. Francis, IL

About the Authors

Walter T. Harrison, Jr. is professor emeritus of accounting at the Hankamer School of Business, Baylor University. He received his BBA from Baylor University, his MS from Oklahoma State University, and his PhD from Michigan State University.

Professor Harrison, recipient of numerous teaching awards from student groups as well as from university administrators, has also taught at Cleveland State Community College, Michigan State University, the University of Texas, and Stanford University.

A member of the American Accounting Association and the American Institute of Certified Public Accountants, Professor Harrison has served as chairman of the Financial Accounting Standards Committee of the American Accounting Association, on the Teaching/Curriculum Development Award Committee, on the Program Advisory Committee for Accounting Education and Teaching, and on the Notable Contributions to Accounting Literature Committee.

Professor Harrison has lectured in several foreign countries and published articles in numerous journals, including *Journal of Accounting Research, Journal of Accountancy, Journal of Accounting and Public Policy, Economic Consequences of Financial Accounting Standards, Accounting Horizons, Issues in Accounting Education,* and *Journal of Law and Commerce.*

He is co-author of *Financial & Managerial Accounting,* second edition, 2009 and *Accounting,* eighth edition, 2009 (with Charles T. Horngren and M. Suzanne Oliver), published by Pearson Prentice Hall. Professor Harrison has received scholarships, fellowships, and research grants or awards from PricewaterhouseCoopers, Deloitte & Touche, the Ernst & Young Foundation, and the KPMG Foundation.

Charles T. Horngren is the Edmund W. Littlefield professor of accounting, emeritus, at Stanford University. A graduate of Marquette University, he received his MBA from Harvard University and his PhD from the University of Chicago. He is also the recipient of honorary doctorates from Marquette University and DePaul University.

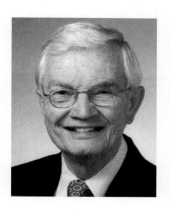

A certified public accountant, Horngren served on the Accounting Principles Board for six years, the Financial Accounting Standards Board Advisory Council for five years, and the Council of the American Institute of Certified Public Accountants for three years. For six years he served as a trustee of the Financial Accounting Foundation, which oversees the Financial Accounting Standards Board and the Government Accounting Standards Board.

Horngren is a member of the Accounting Hall of Fame.

A member of the American Accounting Association, Horngren has been its president and its director of research. He received its first annual Outstanding Accounting Educator Award.

The California Certified Public Accountants Foundation gave Horngren its Faculty Excellence Award and its Distinguished Professor Award. He is the first person to have received both awards.

The American Institute of Certified Public Accountants presented its first Outstanding Educator Award to Horngren.

Horngren was named Accountant of the Year, in Education, by the national professional accounting fraternity, Beta Alpha Psi.

Professor Horngren is also a member of the Institute of Management Accountants, from whom he has received its Distinguished Service Award. He was a member of the institute's Board of Regents, which administers the Certified Management Accountant examinations.

Horngren is the author of these other accounting books published by Pearson Prentice Hall: *Cost Accounting: A Managerial Emphasis,* thirteenth edition, 2008 (with Srikant Datar and George Foster); *Introduction to Financial Accounting,* ninth edition, 2006 (with Gary L. Sundem and John A. Elliott); *Introduction to Management Accounting,* fourteenth edition, 2008 (with Gary L. Sundem and William Stratton); *Financial & Managerial Accounting,* second edition, 2009 and *Accounting,* eighth edition, 2009 (with Walter T. Harrison, Jr. and M. Suzanne Oliver).

Horngren is the consulting editor for Pearson Prentice Hall's Charles T. Horngren Series in Accounting.

Charles William (Bill) Thomas is the J. E. Bush Professor of Accounting and a Master Teacher at Baylor University. A Baylor University alumnus, he received both his BBA and MBA there and went on to earn his PhD from The University of Texas at Austin.

With primary interests in the areas of financial accounting and auditing, Bill Thomas has served as the J.E. Bush Professor of Accounting since 1995. He has been a member of the faculty of the Accounting and Business Law Department of the Hankamer School of Business since 1971, and served as chair of the department from 1983 until 1995. He was recognized as an Outstanding Faculty Member of Baylor University in 1984 and Distinguished Professor for the Hankamer School of Business in 2002. Dr. Thomas has received several awards for outstanding teaching, including the Outstanding Professor in the Executive MBA Programs in 2001, 2002, and 2006. In 2004, he received the designation as Master Teacher.

Thomas is the author of textbooks in auditing and financial accounting, as well as many articles in auditing, financial accounting and reporting, taxation, ethics and accounting education. His scholarly work focuses on the subject of fraud prevention and detection, as well as ethical issues among accountants in public practice. His most recent publication of national prominence is "The Rise and Fall of the Enron Empire" which appeared in the April 2002 *Journal of Accountancy*, and which was selected by Encyclopedia Britannica for inclusion in its *Annals of American History*. He presently serves as both technical and accounting and auditing editor of *Today's CPA*, the journal of the Texas Society of Certified Public Accountants, with a circulation of approximately 28,000.

Thomas is a certified public accountant in Texas. Prior to becoming a professor, Thomas was a practicing accountant with the firms of KPMG, LLP, and BDO Seidman, LLP. He is a member of the American Accounting Association, the American Institute of Certified Public Accountants, and the Texas Society of Certified Public Accountants.

Financial Accounting

Ninth Edition

1 The Financial Statements

SPOTLIGHT: RadioShack Corporation

Where do you go when you need to shop for video games, cell phones, or those hard-to-find batteries? Perhaps you're a hobby-hound looking for a metal detector or microscope. How about a laptop or special connector cables for a computer storage device or home theater? When some other "big box" stores don't have what you need, chances are you might run out to "The Shack." Based in Fort Worth, Texas, RadioShack Corporation, better known in its advertising as "The Shack," has been offering a unique shopping experience to electronics customers for over 40 years. The company operates a network of almost 4,500 retail stores in the United States and Mexico, over 1,200 dealer outlets, and almost 1,300 wireless phone kiosks, primarily in Sam's Club and Target stores. RadioShack offers a broad selection of relevant technology products, including innovative mobile devices, accessories, and services, as well as items for personal and home technology and power supply needs. The company features national brands and wireless carriers, as well as exclusive private brands. And perhaps one of RadioShack's best features is that its stores are small and its sales associates are knowledgeable and helpful.

As you can see, The Shack sells lots of electronic devices and gadgets—about $4.5 billion for the year ended December 31, 2010 (line 1 of RadioShack Corporation's Consolidated Statements of Income on the next page). On these revenues, RadioShack Corporation earned net income of $206 million for the year ended December 31, 2010 (line 13).

These terms—revenues and net income—may be foreign to you now. But after you read this chapter, you'll be able to use these and other business terms. Welcome to the world of accounting! ●

© Lana Sundman/Alamy

		Year Ended December 31, 2010	Year Ended December 31, 2009
	RadioShack Corporation and Subsidiaries **Consolidated Statements of Income (Adapted)** **(In millions)**		
	Revenues		
1	Net sales and operating revenues	$4,472	$4,276
2	Cost of products sold	2,462	2,314
3	Gross profit	2,010	1,962
4	Operating expenses		
5	Selling, general and administrative	1,555	1,508
6	Depreciation and amortization	76	84
7	Other operating expenses	4	1
8	Operating expenses	1,635	1,593
9	Income from operations	375	369
10	Other income and (expense), net	(39)	(41)
11	Income before income taxes	336	328
12	Income tax expense	(130)	(123)
13	Net income	$ 206	$ 205

Each chapter of this book begins with an actual financial statement. In this chapter, it's the Consolidated Statements of Income of RadioShack Corporation for the two years ended December 31, 2010. The core of financial accounting revolves around the basic financial statements:

- ▸ Income statement (sometimes known as the statement of operations)
- ▸ Statement of retained earnings (usually included in statement of stockholders' equity)
- ▸ Balance sheet (sometimes known as the statement of financial position)
- ▸ Statement of cash flows

Financial statements are the business documents that companies use to report the results of their activities to various user groups, which can include managers, investors, creditors, and regulatory agencies. In turn, these parties use the reported information to make a variety of decisions, such as whether to invest in or loan money to the company. To learn accounting, you must learn to focus on decisions. In this chapter we explain generally accepted accounting principles, their underlying assumptions and concepts, and the bodies responsible for issuing accounting standards. We discuss the judgment process that is necessary to make good accounting decisions. We also discuss the contents of the four basic financial statements that report the results of those decisions. In later chapters, we will explain in more detail how to construct the financial statements, as well as how user groups typically use the information contained in them to make business decisions.

1. **Explain** why accounting is the language of business

2. **Explain and apply** underlying accounting concepts, assumptions, and principles

3. **Apply** the accounting equation to business organizations

4. **Evaluate** business operations through the financial statements

5. **Construct** financial statements and **analyze** the relationships among them

6. **Evaluate** business decisions ethically

Learning Objectives

For more practice and review of accounting cycle concepts, use ACT, the Accounting Cycle Tutorial, online at **www.myaccountinglab.com**. Margin logos like this one, directing you to the appropriate ACT section and material, appear throughout Chapters 1, 2, and 3. When you enter the tutorial, you'll find three buttons on the opening page of each chapter module. Here's what the buttons mean: **Tutorial** gives you a review of the major concepts, **Application** gives you practice exercises, and **Glossary** reviews important terms.

RadioShack Corporation's managers make lots of decisions. Which product is selling fastest—cell phones, batteries, GPS systems? Are camcorders more profitable than laptop computers or component cables? Should RadioShack expand into Europe or Asia? Accounting information helps companies make these decisions.

Take a look at RadioShack Corporation's Consolidated Statements of Income on page 2. Focus on net income (line13). Net income (profit) is the excess of revenues over expenses. You can see that RadioShack Corporation earned $206 million profit in the year ended December 31, 2010. That's good news because it means that RadioShack Corporation had $206 million more revenues than expenses for the year.

RadioShack Corporation's Consolidated Statements of Income convey more interesting news. Net sales and operating revenues (line 1) grew by about 4.6% from 2009 to 2010 (from $4,276 million to $4,472 million). However, net income for 2010 ($206 million) increased by less than 0.5% over net income for the previous year (about $205 million). RadioShack Corporation's sales have grown, but income has not.

Suppose you have $5,000 to invest. What information would you need before deciding to invest that money in RadioShack Corporation? Let's see how accounting works.

Explain Why Accounting is the Language of Business

Accounting is an information system. It measures business activities, processes data into reports, and communicates results to decision makers. Accounting is "the language of business." The better you understand the language, the better you can manage your finances as well as those of your business.

Accounting produces financial statements, which report information about a business entity. The financial statements measure performance and communicate where a business stands in financial terms. In this chapter we focus on RadioShack Corporation. After completing this chapter, you'll begin to understand financial statements.

Don't confuse bookkeeping and accounting. Bookkeeping is a mechanical part of accounting, just as arithmetic is a part of mathematics. Exhibit 1-1 on page 4 illustrates the flow of accounting information and helps illustrate accounting's role in business. The accounting process begins and ends with people making decisions.

1

Explain why accounting is the language of business

EXHIBIT 1-1 | The Flow of Accounting Information

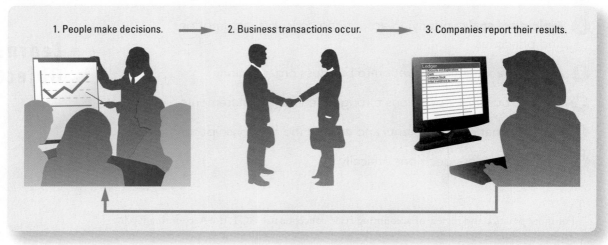

1. People make decisions. → 2. Business transactions occur. → 3. Companies report their results.

Who Uses Accounting Information?

Decision makers use many types of information. A banker decides who gets a loan. RadioShack Corporation decides where to locate a new store. Let's see how decision makers use accounting information.

- *Individuals.* People like you manage their personal bank accounts, decide whether to rent an apartment or buy a house, and budget the monthly income and expenditures of their businesses. Accounting provides the necessary information to allow individuals to make these decisions.
- *Investors and Creditors.* Investors and creditors provide the money to finance RadioShack Corporation. Investors want to know how much income they can expect to earn on an investment. Creditors want to know when and how RadioShack Corporation is going to pay them back. These decisions also require accounting information.
- *Regulatory Bodies.* All kinds of regulatory bodies use accounting information. For example, the Internal Revenue Service (IRS) and various state and local governments require businesses, individuals, and other types of organizations to pay income, property, excise, and other taxes. The U.S. Securities and Exchange Commission (SEC) requires companies whose stock is traded publicly to provide it with many kinds of periodic financial reports. All of these reports contain accounting information.
- *Nonprofit Organizations.* Nonprofit organizations—churches, hospitals, and charities such as Habitat for Humanity and the Red Cross—base many of their operating decisions on accounting data. In addition, these organizations have to file periodic reports of their activities with the IRS and state governments, even though they may owe no taxes.

Two Kinds of Accounting: Financial Accounting and Management Accounting

Both *external* and *internal users* of accounting information exist. We can therefore classify accounting into two branches.

Financial accounting provides information for decision makers outside the entity, such as investors, creditors, government agencies, and the public. This information must be relevant for the needs of decision makers and must faithfully give an accurate picture of the entity's economic activities. This textbook focuses on financial accounting.

Management accounting provides information for managers of RadioShack Corporation. Examples of management accounting information include budgets, forecasts, and projections that are used in making strategic decisions of the entity. Internal information must still be accurate and relevant for the decision needs of managers. Management accounting is covered in a separate course that usually follows this one.

Organizing a Business

Accounting is used in every type of business. A business generally takes one of the following forms:

- ▶ Proprietorship
- ▶ Partnership
- ▶ Limited-liability company (LLC)
- ▶ Corporation

Exhibit 1-2 compares ways to organize a business.

EXHIBIT 1-2 | The Various Forms of Business Organization

	Proprietorship	Partnership	LLC	Corporation
1. *Owner(s)*	Proprietor—one owner	Partners—two or more owners	Members	Stockholders—generally many owners
2. *Personal liability of owner(s) for business debts*	Proprietor is personally liable	General partners are personally liable; limited partners are not	Members are *not* personally liable	Stockholders are *not* personally liable

Proprietorship. A **proprietorship** has a single owner, called the proprietor. Dell Computer started out in the college dorm room of Michael Dell, the owner. Proprietorships tend to be small retail stores or solo providers of professional services—physicians, attorneys, or accountants. Legally, the business *is* the proprietor, and the proprietor is personally liable for all the business's debts. But for accounting purposes, a proprietorship is a distinct entity, separate from its proprietor. Thus, the business records should not include the proprietor's personal finances.

Partnership. A **partnership** has two or more parties as co-owners, and each owner is a partner. Individuals, corporations, partnerships, or other types of entities can be partners. Income and loss of the partnership "flows through" to the partners, and they recognize it based on their agreed-upon percentage interest in the business. The partnership is not a taxpaying entity. Instead, each partner takes a proportionate share of the entity's taxable income and pays tax according to that partner's individual or corporate rate. Many retail establishments, professional service firms (law, accounting, etc.), real estate, and oil and gas exploration companies operate as partnerships. Many partnerships are small or medium-sized, but some are gigantic, with thousands of partners. Partnerships are governed by agreement, usually spelled out in writing in the form of a contract between the partners. General partnerships have mutual agency and unlimited liability, meaning that each partner may conduct business in the name of the entity and can make agreements that legally bind all partners without limit for the partnership's debts. Partnerships are therefore quite risky, because an irresponsible partner can create large debts for the other general partners without their knowledge or permission. This feature of general partnerships has spawned the creation of limited-liability partnerships (LLPs).

A *limited-liability partnership* is one in which a wayward partner cannot create a large liability for the other partners. In LLPs, each partner is liable for partnership debts only up to the extent of his or her investment in the partnership, plus his or her proportionate share of the liabilities. Each LLP, however, must have one general partner with unlimited liability for all partnership debts.

Limited-Liability Company (LLC). A **limited-liability company** is one in which the business (and not the owner) is liable for the company's debts. An LLC may have one owner or many owners, called *members*. Unlike a proprietorship or a general partnership, the members of an LLC do *not* have unlimited liability for the LLC's debts. An LLC pays no business income tax. Instead, the LLC's income "flows through" to the members, and they pay income tax at their own tax rates, just as they would if they were partners. Today, many multiple-owner businesses are organized as LLCs, because members of an LLC effectively enjoy limited liability while still being taxed like members of a partnership.

Corporation.   A **corporation** is a business owned by the **stockholders**, or **shareholders**, who own **stock** representing shares of ownership in the corporation. One of the major advantages of doing business in the corporate form is the ability to raise large sums of capital from issuance of stock to the public. All types of entities (individuals, partnerships, corporations, or other types) may be shareholders in a corporation. Even though proprietorships and partnerships are more numerous, corporations transact much more business and are larger in terms of assets, income, and number of employees. Most well-known companies, such as RadioShack, Amazon.com, Google, General Motors, Toyota, and Apple, Inc., are corporations. Their full names include *Corporation* or *Incorporated* (abbreviated *Corp.* and *Inc.*) to indicate that they are corporations—for example, RadioShack Corporation and Starbucks Corporation. A few bear the name *Company*, such as Ford Motor Company.

A corporation is formed under state law. Unlike proprietorships and partnerships, a corporation is legally distinct from its owners. The corporation is like an artificial person and possesses many of the same rights that a person has. The stockholders have no personal obligation for the corporation's debts. So, stockholders of a corporation have limited liability, as do limited partners and members of an LLC. However, unlike partnerships or LLCs, a corporation pays a business income tax as well as many other types of taxes. Furthermore, the shareholders of a corporation are effectively taxed twice on distributions received from the corporation (called dividends). Thus, one of the major disadvantages of the corporate form of business is *double taxation of distributed profits.*

Ultimate control of a corporation rests with the stockholders, who generally get one vote for each share of stock they own. Stockholders elect the **board of directors**, which sets policy and appoints officers. The board elects a chairperson, who holds the most power in the corporation and often carries the title chief executive officer (CEO). The board also appoints the president as chief operating officer (COO). Corporations also have vice presidents in charge of sales, accounting, and finance (the chief financial officer or CFO), and other key areas.

Explain and Apply Underlying Accounting Concepts, Assumptions, and Principles

2

Explain and apply underlying accounting concepts, assumptions, and principles

Accountants follow professional guidelines for measurement and disclosure of financial information. These are called **generally accepted accounting principles (GAAP)**. In the United States, the **Financial Accounting Standards Board (FASB)** formulates GAAP. The **International Accounting Standards Board (IASB)** sets global—or International—Financial Reporting Standards (IFRS), as discussed in a later section.

Exhibit 1-3 gives an overview of the joint conceptual framework of accounting developed by the FASB and the IASB. Financial reporting standards (whether U.S. or international), at the bottom, follow the conceptual framework. The overall *objective* of accounting is to provide financial information about the reporting entity that is useful to existing and potential investors, lenders, and other creditors in making decisions.

To be useful, information must have the fundamental qualitative characteristics. Those include

► relevance and
► faithful representation.

To be relevant, information must be capable of making a difference to the decision maker, having predictive or confirming value. In addition, the information must be *material*, which means it must be important enough to the informed user so that, if it were omitted or erroneous, it would make a difference in the user's decision. Only information that is material needs to be separately *disclosed* (listed or discussed) in the financial statements. If not, it does not need separate disclosure but may be combined with other information. To faithfully represent, the information must be complete, neutral (free from bias), and without material error (accurate). Accounting information must focus on the *economic substance* of a transaction, event, or circumstance, which may or may not always be the same as its legal form. Faithful representation makes the information *reliable* to users.

EXHIBIT 1-3 | Conceptual Foundations of Accounting

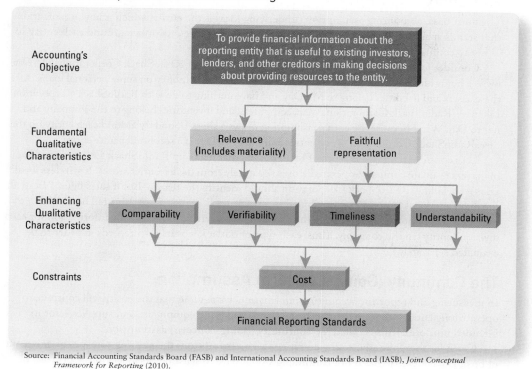

Source: Financial Accounting Standards Board (FASB) and International Accounting Standards Board (IASB), *Joint Conceptual Framework for Reporting* (2010).

Accounting information must also have a number of *enhancing qualitative characteristics.* These include

► comparability,
► verifiability,
► timeliness, and
► understandability.

Comparability means that the accounting information for a company must be prepared in such a way as to be capable of being both compared with information from other companies in the same period and *consistent* with similar information for that company in previous periods. *Verifiability* means that the information must be capable of being checked for accuracy, completeness, and reliability. The process of verifying information is often done by *internal* as well as *external auditors.* Verifiability enhances the reliability of information, and thus makes the information more representative of economic reality. *Timeliness* means that the information must be made available to users early enough to help them make decisions, thus making the information more relevant to their needs. *Understandability* means that the information must be sufficiently transparent so that it makes sense to reasonably informed users of the information (investors, creditors, regulatory agencies, and managers).

Accounting information is costly to produce. A primary constraint in the decision to disclose accounting information is that the *cost of disclosure should not exceed the expected benefits* to users. Management of an entity is primarily responsible for preparing accounting information. Managers must exercise judgment in determining whether the information is necessary for complete understanding of underlying economic facts and not excessively costly to provide.

This course will expose you to GAAP as well as to relevant international financial reporting standards (IFRS). We summarize GAAP in Appendix D and IFRS in Appendix E. In the following section, we briefly summarize some of the basic assumptions and principles that underlie the application of these standards.

The Entity Assumption

The most basic accounting assumption (underlying idea) is the **entity**, which is any organization that stands apart as a separate economic unit. Sharp boundaries are drawn around each entity so as not to confuse its affairs with those of others.

Consider Julian C. Day, chairman of the board and CEO of RadioShack Corporation. Mr. Day owns a home and several automobiles. In addition, he may owe money on some personal loans. All these assets and liabilities belong to Mr. Day and have nothing to do with RadioShack Corporation. Likewise, RadioShack Corporation's cash, computers, and inventories belong to the company and not to Day. Why? Because the entity assumption draws a sharp boundary around each entity; in this case, RadioShack Corporation is one entity, and Julian C. Day is a second, separate entity.

Let's consider the various types of retail outlets that make up RadioShack Corporation. Top managers evaluate company-operated stores separately from dealer outlet stores. If wireless kiosk sales were falling, RadioShack Corporation should identify the reason. But if sales figures from all the retail and kiosk outlets were combined in a single total, managers couldn't tell how differently each unit was performing. To correct the problem, managers need accounting information for each division (entity) in the company. Thus, each type of outlet keeps its own records in order to be evaluated separately.

The Continuity (Going-Concern) Assumption

In measuring and reporting accounting information, we assume that the entity will continue to operate long enough to use existing assets—land, buildings, equipment, and supplies—for its intended purposes. This is called the **continuity (going-concern) assumption**.

Consider the alternative to the **going-concern assumption**: the quitting concern, or going out of business. An entity that is not continuing would have to sell all of its assets in the process. In that case, the most *relevant* measure of the value of the assets would be their current fair market values (the amount the company would receive for the assets when sold). But going out of business is the exception rather than the rule. Therefore, the continuity assumption says that a business should stay in business long enough to recover the cost of those assets by allocating that cost through a process called *depreciation* to business operations over the assets' economic lives.

The Historical Cost Principle

The **historical cost principle** states that assets should be recorded at their *actual cost*, measured on the date of purchase as the amount of cash paid plus the dollar value of all non-cash consideration (other assets, privileges, or rights) also given in exchange. For example, suppose RadioShack Corporation purchases a building for a new store. The building's current owner is asking for $600,000 for the building. The management of RadioShack Corporation believes the building is worth $585,000, and offers the present owner that amount. Two real estate professionals appraise the building at $610,000. The two parties compromise and agree on a price of $590,000 for the building. The historical cost principle requires RadioShack Corporation to initially record the building at its actual cost of $590,000—not at $585,000, $600,000, or $610,000, even though those amounts were what some people believed the building was worth. At the point of purchase, $590,000 is both the *relevant* amount for the building's worth and the amount that *faithfully represents* a reliable figure for the price the company paid for it.

The *historical cost principle* and the *continuity assumption* (discussed previously), also maintain that RadioShack Corporation's accounting records should continue to use historical cost to value the asset for as long as the business holds it. Why? Because cost is a *verifiable* measure that is relatively *free from bias*. Suppose that RadioShack Corporation owns the building for six years. Real estate prices increase during this period. As a result, at the end of the period, the building can be sold for $650,000. Should RadioShack Corporation increase the carrying value of the building on the company's books to $650,000? No. According to the historical cost principle, the building remains on RadioShack Corporation's books at its historical cost of $590,000. According to the continuity assumption, RadioShack intends to stay in business and keep the building, not to sell it, so its historical cost is the most relevant and the most faithful representation of its carrying value. It is also the most easily verifiable (auditable) amount. Should the company decide to sell the building later at a price above or below its carrying value, it will record the cash received, remove the carrying value of the building from the books, and record a gain or a loss for the difference at that time.

The historical cost principle is not used as pervasively in the United States as it once was. Accounting is moving in the direction of reporting more and more assets and liabilities at their fair values. **Fair value** is the amount that the business could sell the asset for, or the amount that the business could pay to settle the liability. The FASB has issued guidance for companies to report many assets and liabilities at fair values. Moreover, in recent years, the FASB has agreed to align GAAP with International Financial Reporting Standards (IFRS). These standards generally allow for more liberal measurement of different types of assets with fair values than GAAP, which may cause more assets to be revalued periodically to fair market values. We will discuss the trend toward globalization of accounting standards in a later part of this chapter, and we will illustrate it in later chapters throughout the book.

The Stable-Monetary-Unit Assumption

In the United States, we record transactions in dollars because that is our medium of exchange. British accountants record transactions in pounds sterling, Japanese in yen, and Europeans in euros.

Unlike a liter or a mile, the value of a dollar changes over time. A rise in the general price level is called *inflation*. During inflation, a dollar will purchase less food, less toothpaste, and less of other goods and services. When prices are stable—there is little inflation—a dollar's purchasing power is also stable.

Under the **stable-monetary-unit assumption**, accountants assume that the dollar's purchasing power is stable over time. We ignore inflation, and this allows us to add and subtract dollar amounts as though the dollar over successive years has a consistent amount of purchasing power. This is important because businesses that report their financial information publicly usually report comparative financial information (that is, the current year along with one or more prior years). If we could not assume a stable monetary unit, assets and liabilities denominated in prior years' dollars would have to be adjusted to current year price levels. Since inflation is considered to be relatively minor over time, those adjustments do not have to be made.

Global View

International Financial Reporting Standards (IFRS) We live in a global economy! The global credit crisis of 2008 originated in the United States but rapidly spread throughout the world. U.S. investors can easily trade stocks on the Hong Kong, London, and Brussels stock exchanges over the Internet. Each year, American companies such as Starbucks, The Gap Inc., McDonald's, Microsoft, and Disney conduct billions of dollars of business around the globe.

Conversely, foreign companies such as Nokia, Samsung, Toyota, and Nestlé conduct billions of dollars of business in the United States. American companies have merged with foreign companies to create international conglomerates such as Pearson (publisher of this textbook) and Anheuser-Busch InBev. No matter where your career starts, it is very likely that it will eventually take you into global markets.

Until recently, one of the major challenges of conducting global business has been the fact that different countries have adopted different accounting standards for business transactions. Historically, the major developed countries in the world (United States, United Kingdom, Japan, Germany, etc.) have all had their own versions of GAAP. As investors seek to compare financial results across entities from different countries, they have had to restate and convert accounting data from one country to the next in order to make them comparable. This takes time and can be expensive.

The solution to this problem lies with the IASB, which has developed International Financial Reporting Standards (IFRS). These standards are now being used by most countries around the world. For years, accountants in the United States did not pay much attention to IFRS because our GAAP was considered to be the strongest single set of accounting standards in the world. In addition, the application of GAAP for public companies in the United States is overseen carefully by the U.S. Securities and Exchange Commission (SEC), a body which at present has no global counterpart.

Nevertheless, in order to promote consistency in global financial reporting, the SEC has announced a plan to require all U.S. public companies to adopt some version of IFRS. U.S. adoption of IFRS is tentatively scheduled in stages, beginning with the largest companies, starting in approximately 2015.

The advantage to adopting a uniform set of high-quality global accounting standards is that financial statements from a U.S. company (say, Hershey Corporation in Pennsylvania) will be comparable to those of a foreign company (say, Nestlé in Switzerland). Using these standards, it will be easier for investors and businesspeople to evaluate information of various companies in the same industries from across the globe, and companies will only have to prepare one set of financial statements, instead of multiple versions. Thus, in the long run, a uniform set of high-quality global accounting standards should significantly reduce costs of doing business globally.

These are impressive goals, but what do these changes mean for U.S. GAAP? It could mean that U.S. GAAP will be replaced by international standards within the next decade. More likely, it will mean that U.S. GAAP will continue to exist and will become a domestic interpretation of IFRS for companies that are based in the United States.

Does this mean that the accounting information you are studying in this textbook will soon become outdated? Fortunately, no. For one thing, the vast majority of the introductory material you learn from this textbook, including the underlying conceptual framework outlined in the previous section, is *already* part of IFRS as well. The most commonly used accounting practices are essentially the same under both U.S. GAAP and IFRS. Additionally, the FASB is working hand-in-hand with the IASB toward *convergence* of standards: that is, gradually adjusting both sets of standards to more closely align them over time so that, when transition to IFRS in the United States occurs, it will occur smoothly. Over the past few years, all newly issued U.S. accounting standards have conformed U.S. practices to IFRS.

As of the publication of this text, there are still some areas of disagreement between GAAP and IFRS. For example, certain widely accepted U.S. practices, such as the use of the last-in, first-out (LIFO) inventory costing method (discussed in Chapter 6), are disallowed under IFRS. Other differences exist as well. These differences must be resolved before IFRS can be fully adopted in the United States.

In general, the main difference between U.S. GAAP and IFRS is that U.S. GAAP has become rather "rules-based" over its long history, while IFRS (not in existence as long) allows more professional judgment on the part of companies. In many areas, the international regulations allow accountants and managers to apply the rules in ways they think is best. For example, revenue recognition is one area where IFRS provides significantly less guidance and allows more judgment than U.S. GAAP. Another major difference between IFRS and U.S. GAAP lies in the valuation of long-term assets (plant assets and intangibles) and liabilities. In U.S. GAAP, the historical cost principle tells us to value assets at historical cost. In contrast, IFRS prefers more of a fair-value approach, which reports assets and liabilities on the balance sheet at their up-to-date values, rather than at historical cost. This may seem like a big difference, but U.S. GAAP already allows for a partial fair-value approach with rules such as lower-of-cost-or-market, accounting for the impairment of long-term assets, and adjusting certain investments to fair values. We cover these concepts in more depth in later chapters.

In past years, there have been many more lawsuits over accounting disputes in the United States than in other countries. This has led to more detailed U.S. accounting rules so that American accountants and managers have clear guidelines to follow. Once IFRS is adopted, U.S. GAAP may be used as "secondary" guidance in instances where IFRS is vague. As of the date of this text, it's unclear exactly how the eventual interaction between IFRS and U.S. GAAP will play out.

There are also terminology differences between IFRS and GAAP. Americans may have to get used to some new words that replace old familiar ones. The underlying concepts probably won't change, but there will probably be new terms and phrasings. Portions of the income statement and balance sheet may also be rearranged, as IFRS presentation is slightly different than the financial statements of U.S. GAAP. The information would still be on the same financial statement, but it might appear in a new location.

Of course, everyone focuses on what is different, not on what stays the same. What will we have to adjust as the United States adopts international standards? Throughout the remainder of this textbook, in chapters that cover concepts where major differences between GAAP and IFRS exist, we will discuss those differences. Because this is an introductory textbook in financial accounting, our discussion will be brief in order to focus on the changes that are relevant for this course. Appendix E includes a table, cross-referenced by chapter, that summarizes all of these differences, as well as their impacts on financial statements once IFRS is fully adopted.

You can expect to hear more about the adoption of IFRS, as well as global harmonization of accounting standards, in the future. When you do, the most important things to remember will be that these changes will be beneficial for financial statement users in the long run, and that most of what you learned in this accounting course will still apply. Remember that there are far more areas of common ground than of disagreement. Whatever may come, your knowledge of international accounting principles will benefit you in the future. The globalization of the world economy provides a wonderful opportunity for you to succeed in the business world.

Apply the Accounting Equation to Business Organizations

RadioShack Corporation's financial statements tell us how the business is performing and where it stands. But how do we arrive at the financial statements? Let's examine the *elements of financial statements*, which are the building blocks on which these statements rest.

3

Apply the accounting equation to business organizations

Assets and Liabilities

The financial statements are based on the **accounting equation**. This equation presents the resources of a company and the claims to those resources.

▶ **Assets** are economic resources that are expected to produce a benefit in the future. RadioShack Corporation's cash, merchandise inventory, and equipment are examples of assets.

Claims on assets come from two sources:

▶ **Liabilities** are "outsider claims." They are debts that are payable to outsiders, called *creditors*. For example, a creditor who has loaned money to RadioShack Corporation has a claim— a legal right—to a part of RadioShack Corporation's assets until the company repays the debt.

▶ **Owners' equity** (also called **capital**, or **stockholders' equity** for a corporation) represents the "insider claims" of a business. Equity means ownership, so RadioShack Corporation's stockholders' equity is the stockholders' interest in the assets of the corporation.

The accounting equation shows the relationship among assets, liabilities, and owners' equity. Assets appear on the left side and liabilities and owners' equity on the right. As Exhibit 1-4 shows, the two sides must be equal:

EXHIBIT 1-4 | The Accounting Equation

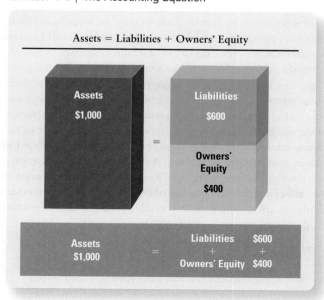

What are some of RadioShack Corporation's assets? The first asset is **cash** and cash equivalents, the liquid assets that are the medium of exchange. Another important asset is merchandise inventory (often called inventories)—the electronics items—that RadioShack Corporation's stores sell. RadioShack Corporation also has assets in the form of **property, plant, and equipment**, or **fixed assets**. These are the long-lived assets the company uses to do business—store equipment, buildings, computers, and so on.

RadioShack Corporation's liabilities include a number of payables, such as accounts payable and federal and state income taxes payable. The word *payable* always signifies a liability. An account payable is a liability for goods or services purchased on credit and supported by the credit standing of the purchaser. Accounts payable typically have to be paid within the next operating cycle (one year). **Long-term debt** is a liability that's payable beyond one year from the date of the financial statements. The **current portion** of long-term debt is the amount due within the next year, and it has to be disclosed separately.

Owners' Equity

The owners' equity of any business is its assets minus its liabilities. We can write the accounting equation to show that owners' equity is what's left over when we subtract liabilities from assets.

$$\text{Assets} - \text{Liabilities} = \text{Owners' Equity}$$

A corporation's equity—called stockholders' equity—has two main subparts:

▶ Paid-in capital
▶ Retained earnings

The accounting equation can be written as

$$\text{Assets} = \text{Liabilities} + \text{Stockholders' Equity}$$
$$\text{Assets} = \text{Liabilities} + \text{Paid-in Capital} + \text{Retained Earnings}$$

▶ **Paid-in capital** is the amount the stockholders have invested in the corporation. The basic component of paid-in capital is **common stock**, which the corporation issues to the stockholders as evidence of their ownership. All corporations have common stock.
▶ **Retained earnings** is the amount earned by income-producing activities and kept for use in the business. Three major types of transactions affect retained earnings: revenues, expenses, and dividends.
▶ **Revenues** are inflows of resources that increase retained earnings by delivering goods or services to customers. For example, a RadioShack store's sale of a GPS system brings in revenue and increases RadioShack Corporation's retained earnings.
▶ **Expenses** are resource outflows that decrease retained earnings due to operations. For example, the wages that RadioShack pays employees are an expense and decrease retained earnings. Expenses represent the costs of doing business; they are the opposite of revenues. Expenses include cost of goods sold, building rent, salaries, and utility payments. Expenses also include the depreciation of display cases, racks, shelving, and other equipment.
▶ **Dividends** decrease retained earnings, because they are distributions to stockholders of assets (usually cash) generated by net income. A successful business may pay dividends to shareholders as a return on their investments. Remember: **Dividends are not expenses. Dividends never affect net income. Instead of being subtracted from revenues to compute net income, dividends are recorded as direct reductions of retained earnings.**

Businesses strive for **profits**, the excess of revenues over expenses.

▶ When total revenues exceed total expenses, the result is called **net income**, **net earnings**, or **net profit**.
▶ When expenses exceed revenues, the result is a **net loss**.

▶ Net income or net loss is the "bottom line" on an income statement. RadioShack Corporation's bottom line reports net income for the year ended December 31, 2010, of $206 million (line 13 on the Consolidated Statements of Income on page 2).

Exhibit 1-5 shows the relationships among the following:

▶ Retained earnings
▶ Revenues − Expenses = Net income (or net loss)
▶ Dividends

EXHIBIT 1-5 │ The Components of Retained Earnings

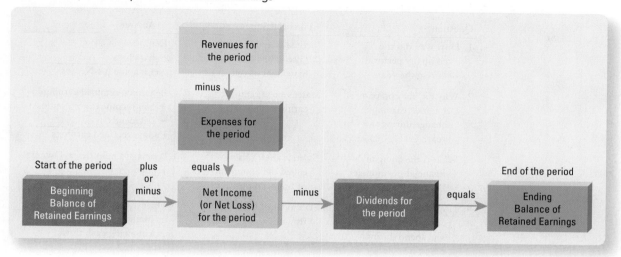

The owners' equity of proprietorships and partnerships is different from that of corporations. Proprietorships and partnerships don't identify paid-in capital and retained earnings separately. Instead, they use a single heading: Capital. Examples include Randall Waller, Capital— for a proprietorship; and Powers, Capital, and Salazar, Capital—for a partnership.

STOP & THINK. . .

(1) If the assets of a business are $240,000 and the liabilities are $80,000, how much is the owners' equity?

(2) If the owners' equity in a business is $160,000 and the liabilities are $130,000, how much are the assets?

(3) A company reported monthly revenues of $129,000 and expenses of $85,000. What is the result of operations for the month?

(4) If the beginning balance of retained earnings is $100,000, revenue is $75,000, expenses total $50,000, and the company pays a $10,000 dividend, what is the ending balance of retained earnings?

- -

Answer:

(1) $160,000 ($240,000 − $80,000)

(2) $290,000 ($160,000 + $130,000)

(3) Net income of $44,000 ($129,000 − $85,000); revenues minus expenses

(4) $115,000 [$100,000 beginning balance + net income $25,000 ($75,000 − $50,000) − dividends $10,000]

Evaluate Business Operations Through the Financial Statements

The financial statements present a company to the public in financial terms. Each financial statement relates to a specific date or time period. What would investors want to know about RadioShack Corporation at the end of its fiscal year? Exhibit 1-6 lists four questions that decision makers may ask. Each answer comes from one of the financial statements.

EXHIBIT 1-6 | Information Reported in the Financial Statements

Question	Financial Statement	Answer
1. How well did the company perform during the year?	Income statement (also called the Statement of operations)	Revenues − Expenses ———————— Net income (or Net loss)
2. Why did the company's retained earnings change during the year?	Statement of retained earnings	Beginning retained earnings + Net income (or − Net loss) − Dividends ———————— Ending retained earnings
3. What is the company's financial position at December 31?	Balance sheet (also called the Statement of financial position)	Assets = Liabilities + Owners' Equity
4. How much cash did the company generate and spend during the year?	Statement of cash flows	Operating cash flows ± Investing cash flows ± Financing cash flows ———————— Increase (decrease) in cash

To learn how to use financial statements, let's work through RadioShack Corporation's statements for 2010. The following diagram shows how the data flow from one financial statement to the next. The order is important.

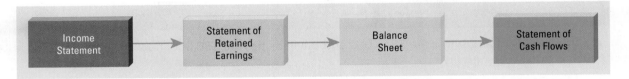

We begin with the income statement in Exhibit 1-7.

The Income Statement Measures Operating Performance

The **income statement**, or **statement of operations**, reports revenues and expenses for the period. The bottom line is net income or net loss *for the period.* At the top of Exhibit 1-7 is the company's name: RadioShack Corporation and Subsidiaries. On the second line is the term: "Consolidated Statements of Income."

RadioShack Corporation is actually made up of several corporations that are owned by a common group of shareholders. Commonly controlled corporations like this are required to combine, or consolidate, all of their revenues, expenses, assets, liabilities, and stockholders' equity and to report them all as one.

The dates of RadioShack Corporation's Consolidated Statements of Income are "Years Ended December 31, 2010 and December 31, 2009. RadioShack Corporation uses a *calendar year* as its accounting year. In contrast, some retailers use a *fiscal year* consisting of the 52 weeks ending closest to January 31 as the accounting year. This is because the holiday season is the busiest time

EXHIBIT 1-7 | RadioShack Corporation and Subsidiaries Consolidated Statements of Income

		Year Ended December 31, 2010	Year Ended December 31, 2009
	RadioShack Corporation and Subsidiaries Consolidated Statements of Income (Adapted) (In millions)		
	Revenues		
1	Net sales and operating revenues	$4,472	$4,276
2	Cost of products sold	2,462	2,314
3	Gross profit	2,010	1,962
4	Operating expenses		
5	Selling, general and administrative	1,555	1,508
6	Depreciation and amortization	76	84
7	Other operating expenses	4	1
8	Operating expenses	1,635	1,593
9	Income from operations	375	369
10	Other income and (expense), net	(39)	(41)
11	Income before income taxes	336	328
12	Income tax expense	(130)	(123)
13	Net income	$ 206	$ 205

of the year and includes Christmas, while January is typically the slowest month of the year for retailers, allowing the company time to get its books in order. Companies often adopt a fiscal year that ends at the low point of their operations. Wal-Mart and The Gap Inc. use fiscal years such as this. Whole Foods Markets, Inc., uses a fiscal year consisting of the 52 weeks ending closest to September 30. FedEx's fiscal year-end falls on May 31. About 60% of the largest companies, such as RadioShack Corporation, use a fiscal year corresponding to the calendar year.

RadioShack Corporation and Subsidiaries' Consolidated Statements of Income in Exhibit 1-7 report operating results for two years, 2010 and 2009, to show trends for revenues, expenses, and net income. To avoid clutter, RadioShack reports its results in millions of dollars. During 2010, RadioShack increased total revenues (line 1) from $4,276 million to $4,472 million. Net income rose from $205 million to $206 million (line 13). RadioShack stores sold more electronics in 2010, but at a higher cost, resulting in only slightly higher profits. Focus on 2010 (we show 2009 for comparative purposes). An income statement reports two main categories:

► Revenues and gains
► Expenses and losses

We measure net income as follows:

$$\text{Net Income} = \text{Total Revenues and Gains} - \text{Total Expenses and Losses}$$

In accounting, the word *net* refers to an amount after a subtraction. *Net* income is the profit left over after subtracting expenses and losses from revenues and gains. **Net income is the single most important item in the financial statements.**

Revenues. RadioShack Corporation has only one type of revenue: net sales, which means sales revenue after subtracting all the goods customers have returned to the company. All retailers must accept some returned goods from customers due to product defects, or items that customers do not want for other reasons. Sometimes entities also report "other revenue," which may come from sources such as interest on investments. The category "other" generally notes that the amount is not sufficiently material to label separately on an ongoing basis.

Expenses. Not all expenses have the word *expense* in their title. For example, RadioShack Corporation's largest expense is for Cost of products sold (line 2). Other titles of this expense are *cost of goods sold* and *cost of sales*. In this line, RadioShack Corporation includes the direct cost of the items sold, as well as some depreciation costs. For example, suppose a home audio component costs RadioShack $30. Assume RadioShack sells the component for $75. Sales revenue is $75, and cost of goods sold is $30. Cost of goods sold is the major expense of merchandising entities such as RadioShack, Best Buy, Wal-Mart, and Whole Foods Markets.

RadioShack Corporation has some other expenses:

▶ Selling, general and administrative expenses (line 5) are the costs of everyday operations that are not directly related to merchandise purchases and occupancy. Many expenses may be included in this category, including sales commissions paid to employees, catalog production, mailing costs, warehousing expenses, depreciation, credit card fees, executive salaries, and other home-office expenses. These expenses amounted to $1,555 million in fiscal 2010.

▶ Net interest expense (included as "other income and expense" in line 10) was $39 million for 2010. Interest represents RadioShack's net cost of borrowing money. It actually includes interest income of $2.6 million offset by interest expense of $41.9 million. Companies are allowed to offset items like interest income and interest expense against each other and show only the difference (in this case the larger item is interest expense, and so the net amount appears as an expense).

▶ Income tax expense (line 12) is the expense levied on RadioShack's income by the federal government. This is often one of a corporation's largest expenses. RadioShack's income tax expense for fiscal 2010 is a whopping $130 million (38.6% of its net income before taxes)!

RadioShack Corporation reports Income from operations (line 9) of $375 million and Net income (line 13) of $206 million in 2010. Some investors use operating income to measure operating performance. Others use the "bottom-line" net income. A company whose net income from operations is consistently growing is regarded by the financial markets as a healthy and high-quality company. In the long run, that company's stock price should increase. We will explain this trend in greater detail in Chapter 11.

Now let's examine the statement of retained earnings in Exhibit 1-8.

The Statement of Retained Earnings Shows What a Company Did with Its Net Income

Retained earnings means exactly what the term implies, which is that portion of net income the company has kept over a period of years. If, historically, revenue exceeds expenses, the result will be a positive balance in retained earnings. On the other hand, if, historically, expenses have exceeded sales revenues, the accumulation of these losses will result in an accumulated **deficit** in retained earnings (usually shown in parentheses). Net income or net loss (lines 2 and 5 in Exhibit 1-8) flows from the income statement (line 13 of Exhibit 1-7) to the **statement of retained earnings.**

EXHIBIT 1-8 | RadioShack Corporation and Subsidiaries Consolidated Statements of Retained Earnings

	RadioShack Corporation and Subsidiaries Consolidated Statements of Retained Earnings (Adapted) (In millions)	
1	Retained earnings, December 31, 2008	$ 2,150
2	Net income, 2009	205
3	Cash dividends in 2009	(31)
4	Retained earnings, December 31, 2009	$ 2,324
5	Net income, 2010	206
6	Retirement of treasury stock	(1,002)
7	Cash dividends in 2010	(26)
8	Retained earnings, December 31, 2010	$ 1,502

Net income increases retained earnings, and net losses and dividends decrease retained earnings. A positive balance in retained earnings indicates that a corporation has been able to accumulate resources over its lifetime in order to expand, as well as to return a portion of its assets in the form of dividends to shareholders.

Let's review RadioShack Corporation's Consolidated Statements of Retained Earnings for the two year period ending December 31, 2010. At the beginning of 2009, RadioShack Corporation had $2,150 in retained earnings (line 1). During 2009, the company earned net income of $205 million (line 2) and paid dividends of $31 million to shareholders (line 3). It ended 2009 with a retained earnings balance of $2,324, which carried over and became the beginning balance of retained earnings in 2010 (line 4).

During 2010, the company earned net income of $206 million (line 5). As shown on line 6, it then bought and retired $1,002 million worth of its own stock (called treasury stock). We will explain in Chapter 10 why companies do this. The company again paid dividends to shareholders in the amount of $26 million (line 7) in 2010, to end the year with a retained earnings balance of $1,502 million (line 8).

Which item on the statement of retained earnings comes directly from the income statement? It is net income. Lines 2 and 5 of the retained earnings statement come directly from line 13 of the income statement (Exhibit 1-7) for 2009 and 2010, respectively. Take a moment to trace this amount from one statement to the other.

Give yourself a pat on the back. You're already learning how to analyze financial statements!

After a company earns net income, the board of directors decides whether to pay a dividend to the stockholders. Corporations are not obligated to pay dividends unless their boards decide to pay (i.e., declare) them. Usually, companies who are in a development stage or growth mode elect not to pay dividends, opting instead to plow the money back into the company to expand operations or purchase property, plant, and equipment. However, established companies like RadioShack Corporation usually have enough accumulated retained earnings (and cash) to pay dividends. Dividends decrease retained earnings because they represent a distribution of a company's assets (usually cash) to its stockholders.

The Balance Sheet Measures Financial Position

A company's **balance sheet**, also called the **statement of financial position**, reports three items: assets (line 9), liabilities (line 17), and stockholders' equity (line 23). RadioShack Corporation's Consolidated Balance Sheets, shown in Exhibit 1-9, are dated at the *moment in time* when the accounting periods end (December 31, 2010, and December 31, 2009).

Assets. There are two main categories of assets: current and long-term. **Current assets** are assets that are expected to be converted to cash, sold, or consumed during the next 12 months or within the business's operating cycle if longer than a year. Current assets include Cash and cash equivalents, Short-term investments, Accounts and Notes receivable, Merchandise inventory, and other current assets like Prepaid expenses. RadioShack's current assets at December 31, 2010, total $1,778 million (line 5). Let's examine each current asset that RadioShack Corporation holds.

► All companies have cash. Cash is the liquid asset that's the medium of exchange, and *cash equivalents* include money-market accounts or other financial instruments that are easily convertible to cash. RadioShack Corporation owns $569 million in cash and cash equivalents at December 31, 2010 (line 1). This is down from $908 million at December 31, 2009. We will explain this further when we discuss the statement of cash flows later.

► *Short-term investments* include stocks and bonds of other companies that RadioShack intends to sell within the next year. RadioShack's only short-term investments are counted as cash equivalents.

► *Accounts receivable* are amounts the company expects to collect from customers. *Notes receivable* are amounts a company expects to collect from a party who has signed a promissory note to that company and therefore owes it money. RadioShack owns $377 million in Accounts and notes receivable as of December 31, 2010 (line 2, up from $322 million at the end of 2009). Accounts receivable are reported at the *net* amount, which means *after* an estimate of the amount uncollectible has been deducted. We'll discuss accounts receivable and the allowance for doubtful accounts further in Chapter 5.

EXHIBIT 1-9 | RadioShack Corporation and Subsidiaries Consolidated Balance Sheets

RadioShack Corporation and Subsidiaries
Consolidated Balance Sheets (Adapted)
(In millions)

			December 31,	
		Assets	2010	2009
		Current assets:		
1		Cash and cash equivalents	$ 569	$ 908
2		Accounts and notes receivable, net	377	322
3		Inventories	724	671
4		Other current assets	108	114
5		Total current assets	1,778	2,015
6		Property and equipment, net	274	282
7		Goodwill, net	41	39
8		Other assets, net	82	93
9		Total assets	$2,175	$2,429
		Liabilities and Stockholders' Equity		
10		Current maturities of long-term debt	$ 308	$ —
11		Accounts payable	272	263
12		Accrued expenses and other current liabilities	318	361
13		Income taxes payable	10	31
14		Total current liabilities	908	655
15		Long-term debt	332	628
16		Other non-current liabilities	93	98
17		Total liabilities	1,333	1,381
		Stockholders' equity:		
18		Common stock	146	191
19		Additional paid-in capital	147	162
20		Retained earnings	1,502	2,324
21		Treasury stock, at cost	(949)	(1,622)
22		Accumulated other comprehensive loss	(4)	(7)
23		Total stockholders' equity	842	1,048
24		Total liabilities and stockholders' equity	$2,175	$2,429

► Cash and cash equivalents, marketable securities, and Accounts and notes receivable are the most liquid assets, in that order.

► *Inventories* (line 3) are the company's most important, and largest, current assets. RadioShack Corporation's inventories at December 31, 2010, total $724 million (about 41% of total current assets and 33% of total assets). *Inventory* is a common abbreviation for *merchandise inventory*, and the two terms are used interchangeably.

► *Other current assets* (line 4) may include *prepaid expenses,*which represent amounts paid in advance for advertising, rent, insurance, and supplies. These are current assets because the company will benefit from these expenditures within the next year. RadioShack Corporation owns $108 million in other current assets as of December 31, 2010.

► An asset always represents a future benefit.

The main categories of *long-term (non-current) assets* are *Property and equipment* (also called *plant assets*, line 6), and intangible assets such as *Goodwill* (line 7). Long-term assets may also include *other investments* that are expected to benefit the company for long periods of time.

► *Property and equipment* includes RadioShack's land, buildings, computers, store fixtures, and equipment. RadioShack reports property and equipment on one line, *net*, meaning that the historical acquisition cost of the assets has been reduced by *accumulated depreciation*. Accumulated depreciation represents the amount of the historical cost of plant assets that that has been allocated to expense in the income statement over time as the asset has been used in producing revenue. Thus, accumulated depreciation represents the used-up portion of the plant asset. We subtract accumulated depreciation from the cost of Property and equipment to determine its net book value ($274 million on line 6). We will discuss the concept of depreciation further in later chapters.

▶ *Intangibles* are assets with no physical form, such as patents, trademarks, and goodwill. RadioShack Corporation has recorded $41 million in goodwill on line 7 of its December 31, 2010, balance sheet from a past purchase of another company. We discuss goodwill and other intangible assets in Chapter 7.

▶ *Long-term investments* are those investments the company does not intend to sell within the next year. RadioShack Corporation doesn't own any long-term investments.

▶ *Other asset, net* (line 8) is a catchall category for assets that are difficult to classify. RadioShack Corporation owns about $82 million of these assets as of December 31, 2010. These primarily represent long-term tax benefits, due to differences between the way the company keeps its books for financial reporting purposes versus tax purposes.

▶ Overall, RadioShack Corporation reports total assets of $2,175 million at December 31, 2010 (line 9).

Liabilities. Liabilities are also divided into current and long-term categories. **Current liabilities** (lines 10–14) are debts generally payable within one year. Chief among the current liabilities are Current maturities of long-term debt, Accounts payable, Accrued expenses, and Federal and state income taxes payable. *Long-term liabilities* are payable after one year.

▶ *Current maturities of long-term debt* represent the portion of long-term liabilities (usually notes payable) that the company will have to pay off within the next year. Notice on line 15 that, at the end of 2009, the company had about $628 million in long-term debt, of which none was due and payable within 12 months. However, during 2010, $308 million of that amount became due within 12 months, causing the company to reclassify that portion of total debt to current liabilities. This means that, sometime during 2011, RadioShack Corporation is going to have to pay $308 million of its long-term debt in cash. We'll talk about this more in Chapter 9.

▶ *Accounts payable* (line 11) of $272 million represents amounts owed to RadioShack's vendors and suppliers for purchases of inventory.

▶ *Accrued expenses and other current liabilities* (line 12). Included in this $318 million are interest payable on borrowed money, accrued liabilities for salaries, utilities, and other expenses that RadioShack Corporation has not yet paid.

▶ *Income taxes payable* are tax debts owed to the government. RadioShack owes $10 million of federal and state income taxes as of December 31, 2010 (line 13).

▶ At December 31, 2010, RadioShack Corporation's current liabilities total $908 million (line 14). The company also owes $425 million in long-term liabilities (the sum of lines 15 and 16). These liabilities include long-term debt and other payables due after one year.

▶ At the end of 2010, total liabilities are $1,333 million (line 17). This represents about 61% of total assets and indicates a moderately strong financial position.

Stockholders' Equity. The accounting equation states that

$$\text{Assets} - \text{Liabilities} = \text{Owners' Equity}$$

The assets (resources) and the liabilities (debts) of RadioShack Corporation are fairly easy to understand. Owners' equity is harder to pin down. Owners' equity is simple to calculate, but what does it *mean*?

RadioShack Corporation calls its owners' equity *Stockholders' equity* (line 23), and this title is descriptive. Remember that a company's owners' equity represents the stockholders' ownership of the business's assets. RadioShack's stockholders' equity consists of the following:

▶ *Common Stock* (line 18), represented by shares issued to stockholders for about $146 million through December 31, 2010. This amount represents the face amount (par value) of the stock. Par value is an artificial amount set by the company for the stock. Par value is explained in Chapter 10.

- *Additional paid-in capital* (line 19) represents amounts of cash received on initial sale of the company's stock in excess of the par value. This amounts to about $147 million at December 31, 2010.
- *Retained earnings* (line 20) are $1,502 and $2,324 at December 31, 2010, and 2009, respectively. We saw these figures on the statement of retained earnings in Exhibit 1-8 (lines 4 and 8). Retained earnings' final resting place is the balance sheet.
- RadioShack Corporation's stockholders' equity holds two other items. *Treasury Stock* (line 21) represents amounts paid by the company to repurchase its own stock. *Accumulated other comprehensive income (loss)* represents items of gain or loss that are allowed by the FASB to bypass the income statement and be recorded directly into stockholders' equity. We will discuss the reasons for this in Chapters 8 and 11. For now, focus on the two main components of stockholders' equity: common stock and retained earnings.
- At December 31, 2010, RadioShack Corporation has Total stockholders' equity of $842 million (line 23). We can now prove that RadioShack Corporation's total assets equal total liabilities and equity at December 31, 2010 (amounts in millions):

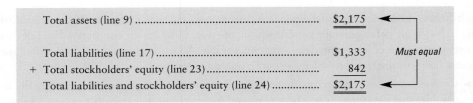

Total assets (line 9)	$2,175
Total liabilities (line 17)	$1,333
+ Total stockholders' equity (line 23)	842
Total liabilities and stockholders' equity (line 24)	$2,175

Must equal

The statement of cash flows is the fourth required financial statement.

The Statement of Cash Flows Measures Cash Receipts and Payments

Companies engage in three basic types of activities:

- **Operating activities**
- **Investing activities**
- **Financing activities**

The **statement of cash flows** reports cash receipts and cash payments in each of these categories:

- *Companies operate by selling goods and services to customers.* **Operating activities** result in net income or net loss, and they either increase or decrease cash. The income statement of RadioShack Corporation reveals whether the company is profitable. The statement of cash flows reports whether operations increased the company's cash balances. Operating activities are most important, and they should be the company's main source of cash. Continuing negative cash flow from operations can lead to bankruptcy.
- *Companies invest in long-term assets.* RadioShack Corporation buys store fixtures and equipment, for which it must often spend cash. When these assets wear out, the company might sell them, which often increases cash. Both purchases and sales of long-term assets are investing cash flows. Investing cash flows are the next most important after operations.
- *Companies need money for financing.* Financing includes issuing stock, paying dividends, borrowing, and repayments of borrowed funds. RadioShack Corporation issues stock to its shareholders and borrows from banks. These are cash receipts. The company may also pay loans, pay dividends, and repurchase its own stock. These payments are examples of financing cash flows.

Overview. Each category of cash flows—operating, investing, and financing—either increases or decreases cash. On a statement of cash flows, cash receipts appear as positive amounts. Cash payments are negative and enclosed by parentheses.

In Exhibit 1-10, which shows RadioShack Corporation's Consolidated Statements of Cash Flows, operating activities provided cash of $155 million in fiscal 2010 (line 4). Notice that this is $51 million less than net income ($206 million in line 2), caused primarily by significant payments in accounts payable and accrued expenses from the previous year. 2010's investing activities (purchase of property, plant, and equipment) used cash of about $80 million (line 6). That signals expansion.

EXHIBIT 1-10 | Radioshack Corporation and Subsidiaries Consolidated Statements of Cash Flows

		RadioShack Corporation and Subsidiaries Consolidated Statements of Cash Flows (Adapted) (In millions)	Years Ended December 31,	
			2010	**2009**
1		Cash flows from operating activities:		
2		Net income	$ 206	$ 205
3		Adjustments to reconcile to cash provided by operations	(51)	41
4		Net cash provided by operating activities	$ 155	$ 246
5		Cash flows from investing activities		
6		Additions to property, plant and equipment	(80)	(81)
7		Cash flows from financing activities:		
8		Purchases of treasury stock	(399)	
9		Payment of dividends	(26)	(31)
10		Repayment of borrowings		(43)
11		Other changes in financing activities	11	2
12		Net cash provided by (used in) financing activities	(414)	(72)
13		Increase (decrease) in cash and cash equivalents	(339)	93
14		Cash and cash equivalents, beginning of year	908	815
15		Cash and cash equivalents, end of year	$ 569	$ 908

Financing activities used another $414 million (line 12). Of this amount, RadioShack Corporation used $399 million in cash to repurchase treasury stock during the year and paid another $26 million in dividends (line 9).

Overall, RadioShack Corporation's cash decreased by about $339 million during 2010 (line 13) and ended the year at $569 million (line 15). Trace ending cash back to the balance sheet in Exhibit 1-9 (line 1). Cash links the statement of cash flows to the balance sheet. You've just performed more financial-statement analysis!

Let's now summarize the relationships that link the financial statements.

Construct the Financial Statements and Analyze the Relationships Among Them

5

Construct financial statements and **analyze** the relationships among them

Exhibit 1-11 summarizes the relationships among the financial statements of ABC Company for 2012. These statements are summarized with all amounts assumed for the illustration. Study the exhibit carefully because these relationships apply to all organizations. Specifically, note the following:

1. The income statement for the year ended December 31, 2012
    a. Reports revenues and expenses of the year. Revenues and expenses are reported *only* on the income statement.
    b. Reports net income if total revenues exceed total expenses. If expenses exceed revenues, there is a net loss.

2. The statement of retained earnings for the year ended December 31, 2012
    a. Opens with the beginning retained earnings balance.
    b. Adds net income (or subtracts net loss). Net income comes directly from the income statement (arrow ① in Exhibit 1-11).
    c. Subtracts dividends.
    d. Reports the retained earnings balance at the end of the year.

3. The balance sheet at December 31, 2012, end of the accounting year
    a. Reports assets, liabilities, and stockholders' equity at the end of the year. Only the balance sheet reports assets and liabilities.
    b. Reports that assets equal the sum of liabilities plus stockholders' equity. This balancing feature follows the accounting equation and gives the balance sheet its name.
    c. Reports retained earnings, which comes from the statement of retained earnings (arrow ② in Exhibit 1-11).

4. The statement of cash flows for the year ended December 31, 2012
    a. Reports cash flows from operating, investing, and financing activities. Each category results in net cash provided (an increase) or used (a decrease).
    b. Reports whether cash increased (or decreased) during the year. The statement shows the ending cash balance, as reported on the balance sheet (arrow ③ in Exhibit 1-11).

Accounting Cycle Tutorial Glossary

Accounting Cycle Tutorial Quiz

EXHIBIT 1-11 | Relationships Among the Financial Statements

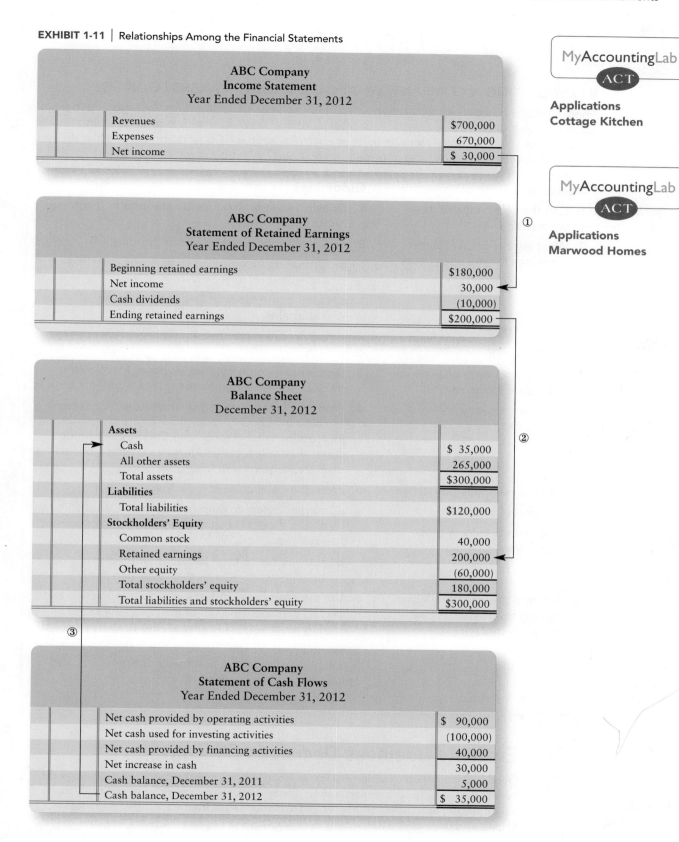

**ABC Company
Income Statement
Year Ended December 31, 2012**

Revenues	$700,000
Expenses	670,000
Net income	$ 30,000

**ABC Company
Statement of Retained Earnings
Year Ended December 31, 2012**

Beginning retained earnings	$180,000
Net income	30,000
Cash dividends	(10,000)
Ending retained earnings	$200,000

**ABC Company
Balance Sheet
December 31, 2012**

Assets	
Cash	$ 35,000
All other assets	265,000
Total assets	$300,000
Liabilities	
Total liabilities	$120,000
Stockholders' Equity	
Common stock	40,000
Retained earnings	200,000
Other equity	(60,000)
Total stockholders' equity	180,000
Total liabilities and stockholders' equity	$300,000

**ABC Company
Statement of Cash Flows
Year Ended December 31, 2012**

Net cash provided by operating activities	$ 90,000
Net cash used for investing activities	(100,000)
Net cash provided by financing activities	40,000
Net increase in cash	30,000
Cash balance, December 31, 2011	5,000
Cash balance, December 31, 2012	$ 35,000

DECISION GUIDELINES

IN EVALUATING A COMPANY, WHAT DO DECISION MAKERS LOOK FOR?

These Decision Guidelines illustrate how people use financial statements. Decision Guidelines appear throughout the book to show how accounting information aids decision making.

Suppose you are considering an investment in RadioShack Corporation stock. How do you proceed? Where do you get the information you need? What do you look for?

Decision	Guidelines
1. Can the company sell its products?	1. Sales revenue on the income statement. Are sales growing or falling?
2. What are the main income measures to watch for trends?	2. a. Gross profit (Sales – Cost of goods sold) b. Operating income (Gross profit – Operating expenses) c. Net income (bottom line of the income statement) All three income measures should be increasing over time.
3. What percentage of sales revenue ends up as profit?	3. Divide net income by sales revenue. Examine the trend of the net income percentage from year to year.
4. Can the company collect its receivables?	4. From the balance sheet, compare the percentage increase in accounts receivable to the percentage increase in sales. If receivables are growing much faster than sales, collections may be too slow, and a cash shortage may result.
5. Can the company pay its a. current liabilities? b. current and long-term liabilities?	5. From the balance sheet, compare a. current assets to current liabilities. Current assets should be somewhat greater than current liabilities. b. total assets to total liabilities. Total assets must be somewhat greater than total liabilities.
6. Where is the company's cash coming from? How is cash being used?	6. On the cash-flows statement, operating activities should provide the bulk of the company's cash during most years. Otherwise, the business will fail. Examine investing cash flows to see if the company is purchasing long-term assets—property, plant, and equipment and intangibles (this signals growth).

Evaluate Business Decisions Ethically

Good business requires decision making, which in turn requires the exercise of good judgment, both at the individual and corporate levels. For example, you may work for or eventually run a company like **Starbucks** that has decided to devote 5 cents from every cup of coffee sold to helping save the lives of AIDS victims in Africa. Can that be profitable in the long run?

6

Evaluate business decisions ethically

Perhaps as an accountant, you may have to decide whether to record a $50,000 expenditure for a piece of equipment as an asset on the balance sheet or an expense on the income statement. Alternatively, as a sales manager for a company like IBM, you may have to decide whether $25 million of goods and services delivered to customers in 2012 would be more appropriately recorded as revenue in 2012 or 2013. As mentioned earlier, the transition from U.S. GAAP to IFRS *will require increased emphasis on judgment*, because IFRS contains fewer rules than U.S. GAAP. Depending on the type of business, the facts and circumstances surrounding accounting decisions may not always make them clear cut, and yet the decision may determine whether the company shows a profit or a loss in a particular period! What are the factors that influence business and accounting decisions, and how should these factors be weighed? Generally, three factors influence business and accounting decisions: *economic, legal, and ethical.*

The *economic* factor states that the decision being made should *maximize the economic benefits* to the decision maker. Based on economic theory, every rational person faced with a decision will choose the course of action that maximizes his or her own welfare, without regard to how that decision impacts others. In summary, the combined outcome of each person acting in his or her own self-interest will maximize the benefits to society as a whole.

The *legal* factor is based on the proposition that free societies are governed by laws. Laws are written to provide clarity and to prevent abuse of the rights of individuals or society. Democratically enacted laws both contain and express society's collective moral standards. Legal analysis involves applying the relevant laws to each decision, and then choosing the action that complies with those laws. A complicating factor for a global business may be that what is legal in one country might not be legal in another. In that case, it is usually best to abide by the laws of the most restrictive country.

The *ethical* factor recognizes that while certain actions might be both economically profitable and legal, they may still not be right. Therefore, most companies, and many individuals, have established standards for themselves to enforce a higher level of conduct than that imposed by law. These standards govern how we treat others and the way we restrain our selfish desires. This behavior and its underlying beliefs are the essence of ethics. **Ethics** are shaped by our cultural, socioeconomic, and religious backgrounds. An *ethical analysis* is needed to guide judgment for making decisions.

The decision rule in an ethical analysis is to choose the action that fulfills ethical duties—responsibilities of the members of society to each other. The challenge in an ethical analysis is to identify specific ethical duties and stakeholders to whom you owe these duties. As with legal issues, a complicating factor in making global ethical decisions may be that what is considered ethical in one country is not considered ethical in another.

Among the questions you may ask in making an ethical analysis are the following:

▶ *Which options are most honest, open, and truthful?*
▶ *Which options are most kind, compassionate, and build a sense of community?*
▶ *Which options create the greatest good for the greatest number of stakeholders?*
▶ *Which options result in treating others as I would want to be treated?*

Ethical training starts at home and continues throughout our lives. It is reinforced by the teaching that we receive in our church, synagogue, or mosque; the schools we attend; and by the persons and companies we associate with.

A thorough understanding of ethics requires more study than we can accomplish in this book. However, remember that when you are making accounting decisions, you should not check your ethics at the door!

DECISION GUIDELINES

DECISION FRAMEWORK FOR MAKING ETHICAL JUDGMENTS

Weighing tough ethical judgments in business and accounting requires a decision framework. Answering the following four questions will guide you through tough decisions:

Decision	Guidelines
1. What is the issue?	**1.** The issue will usually deal with making a judgment about an accounting measurement or disclosure that results in economic consequences, often to numerous parties.
2. Who are the stakeholders, and what are the consequences of the decision to each?	**2.** Stakeholders are anyone who might be impacted by the decision—you, your company, and potential users of the information (investors, creditors, regulatory agencies). Consequences can be economic, legal, or ethical in nature.
3. Weigh the alternatives.	**3.** Analyze the impact of the decision on all stakeholders, using economic, legal, and ethical criteria. Ask "Who will be helped or hurt, whose rights will be exercised or denied, and in what way?"
4. Make the decision and be prepared to deal with the consequences.	**4.** Exercise the courage to either defend the decision or to change it, depending on its positive or negative impact. How does your decision make you feel afterward?

To simplify, we might ask three questions:

1. Is the action legal? If not, steer clear, unless you want to go to jail or pay monetary damages to injured parties. If the action is legal, go on to questions (2) and (3).
2. Who will be affected by the decision and how? Be as thorough about this analysis as possible, and analyze it from all three standpoints (economic, legal, and ethical).
3. How will this decision make me feel afterward? How would it make me feel if my family reads about it in the newspaper?

In later chapters throughout the book, we will apply this model to different accounting decisions.

In the business setting, ethics work best when modeled "from the top." Ethisphere Institute (www.ethisphere.com) has recently established the Business Ethics Leadership Alliance (BELA), aimed at "reestablishing ethics as the foundation of everyday business practices." BELA members agree to embrace and uphold four core values that incorporate ethics and integrity into all their practices: (1) Legal compliance, (2) Transparency, (3) Conflict identification, and (4) Accountability. Each year, Ethisphere Institute publishes a list of the World's Most Ethical Companies. The 2010 list includes corporations like UPS, Starbucks, The Gap Inc., and Target. Excerpts from many of these companies' financial statements will be featured in later chapters of this text. As you begin to make your decisions about future employers, put these companies on your list! It's easier to act ethically when those you work for recognize the importance of ethics in business practices. These companies have learned from experience that, in the long run, ethical conduct pays big rewards—not only socially, morally, and spiritually, but economically as well!

END-OF-CHAPTER SUMMARY PROBLEM

Genie Car Wash, Inc., began operations on April 1, 2012. During April, the business provided services for customers. It is now April 30, and investors wonder how well Genie performed during its first month. The investors also want to know the company's financial position at the end of April and its cash flows during the month.

The following data are listed in alphabetical order. Prepare the Genie Car Wash financial statements at the end of April 2012.

Accounts payable	$ 1,800	Land	$18,000
Accounts receivable	2,000	Payments of cash:	
Adjustments to reconcile net income to net cash provided by operating activities	(3,900)	Acquisition of land	40,000
		Dividends	2,100
		Rent expense	1,100
Cash balance at beginning of April	0	Retained earnings at beginning	
Cash balance at end of April	?	of April	0
Cash receipts:		Retained earnings at end of April	?
Issuance (sale) of stock to owners	50,000	Salary expense	1,200
Sale of land	22,000	Service revenue	10,000
Common stock	50,000	Supplies	3,700
		Utilities expense	400

▶ Requirements

1. Prepare the income statement, the statement of retained earnings, and the statement of cash flows for the month ended April 30, 2012, and the balance sheet at April 30, 2012. Draw arrows linking the statements.

2. Answer the following questions:
   a. How well did Genie perform during its first month of operations?
   b. Where does Genie stand financially at the end of April?

▶ Answers

Requirement 1

Financial Statements of Genie Car Wash, Inc.

Genie Car Wash, Inc.
Income Statement
Month Ended April 30, 2012

Revenue:		
Service revenue		$10,000
Expenses:		
Salary expense	$1,200	
Rent expense	1,100	
Utilities expense	400	
Total expenses		2,700
Net income		$ 7,300

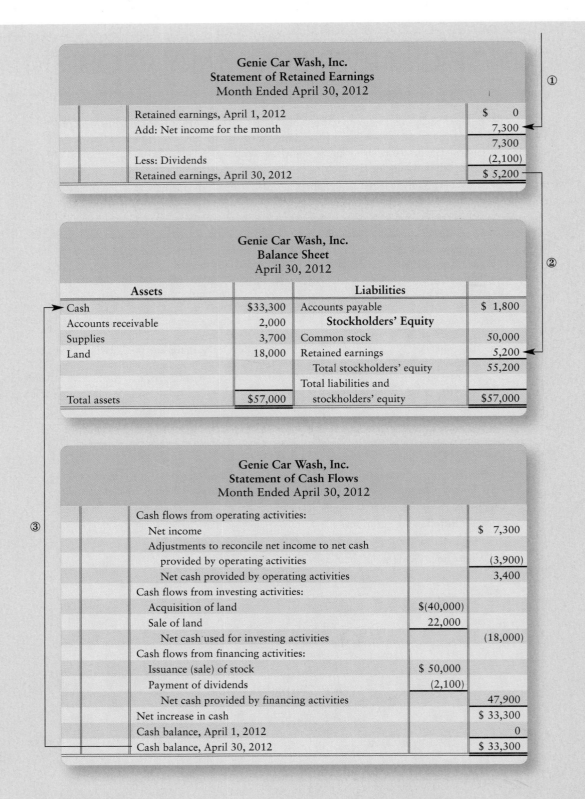

Genie Car Wash, Inc.
Statement of Retained Earnings
Month Ended April 30, 2012   ①

Retained earnings, April 1, 2012	$ 0
Add: Net income for the month	7,300
	7,300
Less: Dividends	(2,100)
Retained earnings, April 30, 2012	$ 5,200

Genie Car Wash, Inc.
Balance Sheet
April 30, 2012   ②

Assets		Liabilities	
Cash	$33,300	Accounts payable	$ 1,800
Accounts receivable	2,000	**Stockholders' Equity**	
Supplies	3,700	Common stock	50,000
Land	18,000	Retained earnings	5,200
		Total stockholders' equity	55,200
		Total liabilities and	
Total assets	$57,000	stockholders' equity	$57,000

Genie Car Wash, Inc.
Statement of Cash Flows
Month Ended April 30, 2012

③

Cash flows from operating activities:		
Net income		$ 7,300
Adjustments to reconcile net income to net cash		
provided by operating activities		(3,900)
Net cash provided by operating activities		3,400
Cash flows from investing activities:		
Acquisition of land	$(40,000)	
Sale of land	22,000	
Net cash used for investing activities		(18,000)
Cash flows from financing activities:		
Issuance (sale) of stock	$ 50,000	
Payment of dividends	(2,100)	
Net cash provided by financing activities		47,900
Net increase in cash		$ 33,300
Cash balance, April 1, 2012		0
Cash balance, April 30, 2012		$ 33,300

Requirement 2

1. Genie performed rather well in April. Net income was $7,300—very good in relation to service revenue of $10,000. The company was able to pay cash dividends of $2,100.

2. Genie ended April with cash of $33,300. Total assets of $57,000 far exceed total liabilities of $1,800. Stockholders' equity of $55,200 provides a good cushion for borrowing. The business's financial position at April 30, 2012, is strong.

REVIEW | The Financial Statements

Quick Check (Answers are given on page 54)

1. All of the following statements are true except one. Which statement is false?
   a. Bookkeeping is only a part of accounting.
   b. A proprietorship is a business with several owners.
   c. Professional accountants are held to a high standard of ethical conduct.
   d. The organization that formulates generally accepted accounting principles in the United States is the Financial Accounting Standards Board.

2. The valuation of assets on the balance sheet is generally based on
   a. current fair market value as established by independent appraisers.
   b. what it would cost to replace the asset.
   c. historical cost.
   d. selling price.

3. The accounting equation can be expressed as
   a. Assets + Liabilities = Owners' Equity
   b. Assets − Liabilities = Owners' Equity
   c. Owners' Equity − Assets = Liabilities
   d. Assets = Liabilities − Owners' Equity

4. The nature of an asset is best described as
   a. something owned by a business that has a ready market value.
   b. something with physical form that's valued at cost in the accounting records.
   c. an economic resource representing cash or the right to receive cash in the future.
   d. an economic resource that's expected to benefit future operations.

5. Which financial statement covers a period of time?
   a. Balance sheet
   b. Income statement
   c. Statement of cash flows
   d. Both b and c

6. How would net income be most likely to affect the accounting equation?
   a. Increase liabilities and decrease stockholders' equity
   b. Increase assets and increase liabilities
   c. Decrease assets and decrease liabilities
   d. Increase assets and increase stockholders' equity

7. During the year, ChemClean, Inc., has $140,000 in revenues, $75,000 in expenses, and $3,000 in dividend payments. Stockholders' equity changed by
   a. +$62,000.
   b. +$68,000.
   c. −$62,000.
   d. +$65,000.

8. ChemClean, Inc., in question 7 had
   a. net income of $62,000.
   b. net loss of $75,000.
   c. net income of $140,000.
   d. net income of $65,000.

9. Valor Corporation holds cash of $5,000 and owes $29,000 on accounts payable. Valor has accounts receivable of $40,000, inventory of $36,000, and land that cost $50,000. How much are Valor's total assets and liabilities?

	Total assets	Liabilities
a.	$126,000	$29,000
b.	$29,000	$131,000
c.	$131,000	$29,000
d.	$131,000	$84,000

10. Which item(s) is (are) reported on the balance sheet?
    a. Accounts payable
    b. Retained earnings
    c. Inventory
    d. All of the above

11. During the year, Diaz Company's stockholders' equity increased from $46,000 to $62,000. Diaz earned net income of $20,000. How much in dividends did Diaz declare during the year?
    a. $16,000
    b. $5,000
    c. $4,000
    d. $-0-

12. Hall Company had total assets of $360,000 and total stockholders' equity of $120,000 at the beginning of the year. During the year, assets increased by $60,000 and liabilities increased by $35,000. Stockholders' equity at the end of the year is
    a. $95,000.
    b. $150,000.
    c. $145,000.
    d. $155,000.

13. Which of the following is a true statement about International Financial Reporting Standards?
    a. They are converging gradually with U.S. standards.
    b. They are not needed for U.S. businesses since the United States already has the strongest accounting standards in the world.
    c. They are more exact (contain more rules) than U.S. generally accepted accounting principles.
    d. They are not being applied anywhere in the world yet, but soon they will be.

14. Which of the following is the most accurate statement regarding ethics as applied to decision making in accounting?
    a. Ethics has no place in accounting, since accounting deals purely with numbers.
    b. It is impossible to learn ethical decision making, since it is just something you decide to do or not to do.
    c. Ethics involves making difficult choices under pressure and should be kept in mind in making every decision, including those involving accounting.
    d. Ethics is becoming less and less important as a field of study in business.

Accounting Vocabulary

accounting (p. 3) The information system that measures business activities, processes that information into reports and financial statements, and communicates the results to decision makers.

accounting equation (p. 11) The most basic tool of accounting: Assets = Liabilities + Owners' Equity.

asset (p. 11) An economic resource that is expected to be of benefit in the future.

balance sheet (p. 17) List of an entity's assets, liabilities, and owners' equity as of a specific date. Also called the *statement of financial position*.

board of directors (p. 6) Group elected by the stockholders to set policy for a corporation and to appoint its officers.

capital (p. 11) Another name for the *owners' equity* of a business.

common stock (p. 12) The most basic form of capital stock.

continuity assumption (p. 8) See going-concern assumption.

corporation (p. 6) A business owned by stockholders. A corporation is a legal entity, an "artificial person" in the eyes of the law.

current asset (p. 17) An asset that is expected to be converted to cash, sold, or consumed during the next 12 months, or within the business's normal operating cycle if longer than a year.

current liability (p. 19) A debt due to be paid within one year or within the entity's operating cycle if the cycle is longer than a year.

deficit (p. 16) Negative balance in retained earnings caused by net losses over a period of years.

dividends (p. 12) Distributions (usually cash) by a corporation to its stockholders.

entity (p. 8) An organization or a section of an organization that, for accounting purposes, stands apart from other organizations and individuals as a separate economic unit.

ethics (p. 25) Standards of right and wrong that transcend economic and legal boundaries. Ethical standards deal with the way we treat others and restrain our own actions because of the desires, expectations, or rights of others, or because of our obligations to them.

expenses (p. 12) Decrease in retained earnings that results from operations; the cost of doing business; opposite of revenues.

fair value (p. 9) The amount that a business could sell an asset for, or the amount that a business could pay to settle a liability.

financial accounting (p. 4) The branch of accounting that provides information to people outside the firm.

financial statements (p. 2) Business documents that report financial information about a business entity to decision makers.

S1-7 (*Learning Objective 1: Explain accounting language*) Accounting definitions are precise, and you must understand the vocabulary to properly use accounting. Sharpen your understanding of key terms by answering the following questions:

1. How do the assets and owners' equity of Apple, Inc., differ from each other? Which one (assets or owners' equity) must be at least as large as the other? Which one can be smaller than the other?
2. How are Apple, Inc.'s liabilities and owners' equity similar? Different?

S1-8 (*Learning Objective 1: Explain accounting language*) Consider Wal-Mart, a large retailer. Classify the following items as an Asset (A), a Liability (L), or Stockholders' Equity (S) for Wal-Mart:

a. ____ Accounts payable		g. ____ Accounts receivable	
b. ____ Common stock		h. ____ Long-term debt	
c. ____ Supplies		i. ____ Merchandise inventory	
d. ____ Retained earnings		j. ____ Notes payable	
e. ____ Land		k. ____ Accrued expenses payable	
f. ____ Prepaid expenses		l. ____ Equipment	

S1-9 (*Learning Objective 1: Explain accounting language*)

1. Identify the two basic categories of items on an income statement.
2. What do we call the bottom line of the income statement?

S1-10 (*Learning Objective 4: Construct an income statement*) Split Second Wireless, Inc., began 2012 with total assets of $100 million and ended 2012 with assets of $190 million. During 2012, Split Second earned revenues of $97 million and had expenses of $26 million. Split Second paid dividends of $16 million in 2012. Prepare the company's income statement for the year ended December 31, 2012, complete with an appropriate heading.

S1-11 (*Learning Objective 4: Construct a statement of retained earnings*) CellPhone Corp. began 2012 with retained earnings of $290 million. Revenues during the year were $360 million, and expenses totaled $250 million. CellPhone declared dividends of $44 million. What was the company's ending balance of retained earnings? To answer this question, prepare CellPhone's statement of retained earnings for the year ended December 31, 2012, complete with its proper heading.

S1-12 (*Learning Objective 4: Construct a balance sheet*) At December 31, 2012, Landy Products has cash of $12,000, receivables of $8,000, and inventory of $44,000. The company's equipment totals $88,000. Landy owes accounts payable of $13,000 and long-term notes payable of $80,000. Common stock is $15,300.

Prepare Landy's balance sheet at December 31, 2012, complete with its proper heading. Use the accounting equation to compute retained earnings.

S1-13 (*Learning Objective 4: Construct a statement of cash flows*) Yidas Medical, Inc., ended 2011 with cash of $30,000. During 2012, Yidas earned net income of $80,000 and had adjustments to reconcile net income to net cash provided by operations totaling $11,000 (this is a negative amount).

Yidas paid $32,000 to purchase equipment during 2012. During 2012, the company paid dividends of $25,000.

Prepare Yidas' statement of cash flows for the year ended December 31, 2012, complete with its proper heading.

S1-14 (*Learning Objectives 1, 4: Explain accounting language; construct financial statements*) Suppose you are analyzing the financial statements of Grant Medical, Inc. Identify each item with its appropriate financial statement, using the following abbreviations: Income statement (IS), Statement of retained earnings (SRE), Balance sheet (BS), and Statement of cash flows (SCF). Three items appear on two financial statements, and one item shows up on three statements.

a. ____ Dividends		h. ____ Cash	
b. ____ Salary expense		i. ____ Net cash used for financing activities	
c. ____ Inventory			
d. ____ Sales revenue		j. ____ Accounts payable	
e. ____ Retained earnings		k. ____ Common stock	
f. ____ Net cash provided by operating activities		l. ____ Interest revenue	
		m. ____ Long-term debt	
g. ____ Net income		n. ____ Increase or decrease in cash	

S1-15 (*Learning Objectives 2, 4: Apply accounting concepts; evaluate business activity*) Apply your understanding of the relationships among the financial statements to answer these questions.

    a. How can a business earn large profits but have a small balance of retained earnings?

    b. Give two reasons why a business can have a steady stream of net income over a six-year period and still experience a cash shortage.

    c. If you could pick a single source of cash for your business, what would it be? Why?

    d. How can a business be unprofitable several years in a row and still have plenty of cash?

Exercises

MyAccountingLab

> All of the A and B exercises can be found within MyAccountingLab, an online homework and practice environment. Your instructor may ask you to complete these exercises using MyAccountingLab.

Group A

E1-16A (*Learning Objectives 3, 4: Apply the accounting equation; evaluate business operations*) Compute the missing amount in the accounting equation for each company (amounts in billions):

	Assets	Liabilities	Owners' Equity
Perfect Cleaners	$?	$15	$18
Ernie's Bank	35	?	22
Hudson Gift and Cards	27	17	?

Which company appears to have the strongest financial position? Explain your reasoning.

E1-17A (*Learning Objectives 3, 4: Apply the accounting equation; evaluate business operations*) CoffeeShop Doughnuts has current assets of $280 million; property, plant, and equipment of $430 million; and other assets totaling $170 million. Current liabilities are $170 million and long-term liabilities total $300 million.

▶ Requirements

1. Use these data to write CoffeeShop Doughnuts' accounting equation.
2. How much in resources does CoffeeShop have to work with?
3. How much does CoffeeShop owe creditors?
4. How much of the company's assets do the CoffeeShop stockholders actually own?

E1-18A (*Learning Objectives 3, 4: Apply the accounting equation; evaluate business operations*) Swit, Inc.'s comparative balance sheet at January 31, 2013, and 2012, reports the following (in millions):

	2013	2012
Total assets	$48	$28
Total liabilities	17	5

▶ Requirements

Three situations about Swit's issuance of stock and payment of dividends during the year ended January 31, 2013, follow. For each situation, use the accounting equation and the statement of retained earnings to compute the amount of Swit's net income or net loss during the year ended January 31, 2013.

1. Swit issued $1 million of stock and paid no dividends.
2. Swit issued no stock but paid dividends of $4 million.
3. Swit issued $33 million of stock and paid dividends of $8 million.

E1-19A (*Learning Objective 3: Apply the accounting equation*) Answer these questions about two companies.

1. Diamond, Inc., began the year with total liabilities of $95,000 and total stockholders' equity of $35,000. During the year, total assets increased by 5%. How much are total assets at the end of the year?
2. NorthWest Airlines Ltd. began the year with total assets of $100,000 and total liabilities of $52,000. Net income for the year was $27,000, and dividends were zero. How much is stockholders' equity at the end of the year?

E1-20A (*Learning Objective 5: Identify financial statement by type of information*)
Assume Beat, Inc., is expanding into Norway. The company must decide where to locate and how to finance the expansion. Identify the financial statement where these decision makers can find the following information about Beat, Inc. In some cases, more than one statement will report the needed data.

a. Common stock
b. Income tax payable
c. Dividends
d. Income tax expense
e. Ending balance of retained earnings
f. Total assets
g. Long-term debt
h. Revenue

i. Cash spent to acquire the building
j. Selling, general, and administrative expenses
k. Adjustments to reconcile net income to net cash provided by operations
l. Ending cash balance
m. Current liabilities
n. Net income

E1-21A (*Learning Objectives 3, 5: Apply the accounting equation; construct a balance sheet*)
Amounts of the assets and liabilities of Mary Burke Banking Company, as of August 31, 2012, are given as follows. Also included are revenue and expense figures for the year ended on that date (amounts in millions):

Total revenue	$ 31.4	Investment assets	$169.3
Receivables	0.3	Property and equipment, net	1.6
Current liabilities	155.4	Other expenses	6.6
Common stock	14.2	Retained earnings, beginning	9.3
Interest expense	0.1	Retained earnings, ending	?
Salary and other employee expenses	17.4	Cash	2.8
Long-term liabilities	2.6	Other assets	14.2

▶ Requirement

1. Construct the balance sheet of Mary Burke Banking Company at August 31, 2012. Use the accounting equation to compute ending retained earnings.

E1-22A (*Learning Objective 5: Construct an income statement and a statement of retained earnings*) This exercise should be used with Exercise 1-21A. Refer to the data of Mary Burke Banking Company in Exercise 1-21A.

▶ Requirements

1. Prepare the income statement of Mary Burke Banking Company for the year ended January 31, 2012.
2. What amount of dividends did Mary Burke declare during the year ended January 31, 2012? Hint: Prepare a statement of retained earnings.

E1-23A *(Learning Objective 5: Construct a statement of cash flows)* Glass, Inc., began 2012 with $83,000 in cash. During 2012, Glass earned net income of $430,000, and adjustments to reconcile net income to net cash provided by operations totaled $75,000, a positive amount. Investing activities used cash of $420,000, and financing activities provided cash of $11,000. Glass ended 2012 with total assets of $580,000 and total liabilities of $230,000.

▶ Requirement

1. Prepare Glass, Inc.'s statement of cash flows for the year ended December 31, 2012. Identify the data items given that do not appear on the statement of cash flows. Also identify the financial statement that reports the unused items.

E1-24A *(Learning Objective 5: Construct an income statement and a statement of retained earnings)* Assume the Dogan Copy Center ended the month of July 2012 with these data:

Payments of cash:			
Acquisition of equipment	$460,000	Cash balance, July 1, 2012.........	$ 0
Dividends...............................	4,700	Cash balance, July 31, 2012.......	10,300
Retained earnings		Cash receipts:	
July 1, 2012	0	Issuance (sale) of stock	
Retained earnings		to owners	105,300
July 31, 2012	?	Rent expense............................	2,700
Utilities expense	10,500	Common stock..........................	105,300
Adjustments to reconcile		Equipment................................	460,000
net income to net cash		Office supplies...........................	14,700
provided by operations...........	2,700	Accounts payable	17,400
Salary expense..........................	160,000	Service revenue.........................	540,200

▶ Requirement

1. Prepare the income statement and the statement of retained earnings of Dogan Copy Center, Inc., for the month ended July 31, 2012.

E1-25A *(Learning Objective 5: Construct a balance sheet)* Refer to the data in Exercise 1-24A.

▶ Requirement

1. Prepare the balance sheet of Dogan Copy Center, Inc., for July 31, 2012.

E1-26A *(Learning Objective 5: Construct a statement of cash flows)* Refer to the data in Exercises 1-24A and 1-25A.

▶ Requirement

1. Prepare the statement of cash flows of Dogan Copy Center, Inc., for the month ended July 31, 2012. Using Exhibit 1-11 as a model, show with arrows the relationships among the income statement, statement of retained earnings, balance sheet, and statement of cash flows.

E1-27A *(Learning Objective 4: Evaluate business operations through the financial statements)* This exercise should be used in conjunction with Exercises 1-24A through 1-26A.

The owner of Dogan Copy Center seeks your advice as to whether he should cease operations or continue the business. Complete the report giving him your opinion of net income, dividends, financial position, and cash flows during his first month of operations. Cite specifics from the financial statements to support your opinion. Conclude your memo with advice on whether to stay in business or cease operations.

Group B

E1-28B (*Learning Objectives 3, 4: Apply the accounting equation; evaluate business operations*)
Compute the missing amount in the accounting equation for each company (amounts in billions):

	Assets	Liabilities	Owners' Equity
Fresh Produce	$?	$20	$17
Margie's Bank	30	?	12
Flowers and Gifts	21	6	?

Which company appears to have the strongest financial position? Explain your reasoning.

E1-29B (*Learning Objectives 3, 4: Apply the accounting equation; evaluate business operations*)
Hombran Doughnuts has current assets of $270 million; property, plant, and equipment of
$400 million; and other assets totaling $160 million. Current liabilities are $160 million and
long-term liabilities total $340 million.

▶ Requirements

1. Use these data to write Hombran's accounting equation.
2. How much in resources does Hombran have to work with?
3. How much does Hombran owe creditors?
4. How much of the company's assets do the Hombran stockholders actually own?

E1-30B (*Learning Objectives 3, 4: Apply the accounting equation; evaluate business operations*)
Most, Inc.'s comparative balance sheet at January 31, 2013, and 2012, reports the following
(in millions):

	2013	2012
Total assets	$35	$31
Total liabilities	12	7

▶ Requirements

Three situations about Most's issuance of stock and payment of dividends during the year ended
January 31, 2013, follow. For each situation, use the accounting equation and the statement of
retained earnings to compute the amount of Most's net income or net loss during the year ended
January 31, 2013.
1. Most issued $4 million of stock and paid no dividends.
2. Most issued no stock but paid dividends of $4 million.
3. Most issued $10 million of stock and paid dividends of $50 million.

E1-31B (*Learning Objective 3: Apply the accounting equation*) Answer these questions about
two companies.
1. Emerald, Inc., began the year with total liabilities of $80,000 and total stockholders' equity of
$80,000. During the year, total assets increased by 25%. How much are total assets at the end
of the year?
2. JetWestAirlines Ltd. began the year with total assets of $130,000 and total liabilities of
$37,000. Net income for the year was $28,000, and dividends were zero. How much is
stockholders' equity at the end of the year?

E1-32B *(Learning Objective 5: Identify financial statement by type of information)*
Assume Neil, Inc., is expanding into Germany. The company must decide where to locate and how to finance the expansion. Identify the financial statement where these decision makers can find the following information about Neil, Inc. In some cases, more than one statement will report the needed data.

    a. Income tax expense
    b. Net income
    c. Current liabilities
    d. Common stock
    e. Income tax payable
    f. Ending balance of retained earnings
    g. Revenue
    h. Ending cash balance
    i. Dividends
    j. Total Assets
    k. Long-term debt
    l. Selling, general, and administrative expenses
    m. Cash spent to acquire the building
    n. Adjustments to reconcile net income to net cash provided by operations

E1-33B *(Learning Objectives 3, 5: Apply the accounting equation; construct a balance sheet)* Amounts of the assets and liabilities of Jill Carlson Banking Company, as of May 31, 2012, are as follows. Also included are revenue and expense figures for the year ended on that date (amounts in millions):

Total revenue	$ 34.7	Investment assets	$169.5
Receivables	0.8	Property and equipment, net	1.2
Current liabilities	152.6	Other expenses	6.6
Common stock	14.8	Retained earnings, beginning	8.7
Interest expense	0.7	Retained earnings, ending	?
Salary and other employee expenses	17.3	Cash	2.3
Long-term liabilities	2.7	Other assets	14.6

▶ Requirement

1. Prepare the balance sheet of Jill Carlson Banking Company at May 31, 2012. Use the accounting equation to compute ending retained earnings.

E1-34B *(Learning Objective 5: Construct an income statement and a statement of retained earnings)* This exercise should be used with Exercise 1-33B.

▶ Requirements

1. Prepare the income statement of Jill Carlson Banking Company for the year ended May 31, 2012.
2. What amount of dividends did Jill Carlson declare during the year ended May 31, 2012? Hint: Prepare a statement of retained earnings.

E1-35B *(Learning Objective 5: Construct a statement of cash flows)* Groovy, Inc., began 2012 with $95,000 in cash. During 2012, Groovy earned net income of $360,000, and adjustments to reconcile net income to net cash provided by operations totaled $60,000, a positive amount. Investing activities used cash of $410,000, and financing activities provided cash of $5,000. Groovy ended 2012 with total assets of $570,000 and total liabilities of $410,000.

▶ Requirement

1. Prepare Groovy, Inc.'s statement of cash flows for the year ended December 31, 2012. Identify the data items given that do not appear on the statement of cash flows. Also identify the financial statement that reports each unused items.

E1-36B (*Learning Objective 5: Construct an income statement and a statement of retained earnings*) Assume a Croyden Copy Center ended the month of July 2013 with these data:

Payments of cash:			Cash balance, July 1, 2013.........	$ 0
Acquisition of equipment.......	$410,000		Cash balance, July 31, 2013.......	11,100
Dividends..............................	4,800		Cash receipts:	
Retained earnings			Issuance (sale) of stock	
July 1, 2013	0		to owners	48,800
Retained earnings			Rent expense.............................	2,500
July 31, 2013	?		Common stock..........................	48,800
Utilities expense	10,500		Equipment................................	410,000
Adjustments to reconcile			Office supplies...........................	14,800
net income to net cash			Accounts payable	17,300
provided by operations...........	2,500		Service revenue..........................	544,600
Salary expense...........................	157,000			

▶ Requirement

1. Prepare the income statement and the statement of retained earnings of Croyden Copy Center, Inc., for the month ended July 31, 2013.

E1-37B (*Learning Objective 5: Construct a balance sheet*) Refer to the data in Exercise 1-36B.

▶ Requirement

1. Prepare the balance sheet of Croyden Copy Center, Inc., at July 31, 2013.

E1-38B (*Learning Objective 5: Construct a statement of cash flows*) Refer to the data in Exercises 1-36B and 1-37B.

▶ Requirement

1. Prepare the statement of cash flows of Croyden Copy Center, Inc., for the month ended July 31, 2013. Using Exhibit 1-11 as a model, show with arrows the relationships among the income statement, statement of retained earnings, balance sheet, and statement of cash flows.

E1-39B (*Learning Objective 4: Evaluate business operations through the financial statements*) This exercise should be used in conjunction with Exercises 1-36B through 1-38B.

The owner of Croyden Copy Center now seeks your advice as to whether he should cease operations or continue the business. Complete the report giving him your opinion of net income, dividends, financial position, and cash flows during his first month of operations. Cite specifics from the financial statements to support your opinion. Conclude your memo with advice on whether to stay in business or cease operations.

Quiz

Test your understanding of the financial statements by answering the following questions. Select the best choice from among the possible answers given.

Q1-40 The *primary* objective of financial reporting is to provide information
a. on the cash flows of the company.
b. to the federal government.
c. useful for making investment and credit decisions.
d. about the profitability of the enterprise.

Q1-41 Which type of business organization provides the least amount of protection for bankers and other creditors of the company?
a. Partnership
b. Proprietorship
c. Corporation
d. Both a and b

Q1-42 Assets are usually reported at their
a. current market value.
b. appraised value.
c. historical cost.
d. none of the above (fill in the blank).

Q1-43 During May, assets increased by $28,000, and liabilities increased by $9,000. Stockholders' equity must have
a. decreased by $19,000.
b. increased by $19,000.
c. increased by $37,000.
d. decreased by $37,000.

Q1-44 The amount a company expects to collect from customers appears on the
a. statement of cash flows.
b. balance sheet in the stockholders' equity section.
c. income statement in the expenses section.
d. balance sheet in the current assets section.

Q1-45 All of the following are current assets except
a. Accounts Receivable.
b. Cash.
c. Inventory.
d. Sales Revenue.

Q1-46 Revenues are
a. increases in retained earnings resulting from selling products or performing services.
b. decreases in liabilities resulting from paying off loans.
c. increases in paid-in capital resulting from the owners investing in the business.
d. all of the above.

Q1-47 The financial statement that reports revenues and expenses is called the
a. income statement.
b. balance sheet.
c. statement of cash flows.
d. statement of retained earnings.

Q1-48 Another name for the balance sheet is the
a. statement of financial position.
b. statement of operations.
c. statement of profit and loss.
d. statement of earnings.

Q1-49 Mason Corporation began the year with cash of $35,000 and a computer that cost $62,000. During the year Mason earned sales revenue of $55,000 and had the following expenses: salaries, $58,000; rent, $21,000; and utilities, $6,000. At year-end Mason's cash balance was down to $18,000. How much net income (or net loss) did Mason experience for the year?
a. ($30,000)
b. $55,000
c. $38,000
d. ($17,000)

Q1-50 Best Instruments had retained earnings of $200,000 at December 31, 2011. Net income for 2012 totaled $105,000, and dividends for 2012 were $45,000. How much retained earnings should Best report at December 31, 2012?
a. $200,000
b. $305,000
c. $245,000
d. $260,000

Q1-51 Net income appears on which financial statement(s)?

a. Income statement

b. Statement of retained earnings

c. Balance sheet

d. Both a and b

Q1-52 Cash paid to purchase a building appears on the statement of cash flows among the

a. Stockholders' equity.

b. Investing activities.

c. Financing activities.

d. Operating activities.

Q1-53 The stockholders' equity of Verkovsky Company at the beginning and end of 2012 totaled $21,000 and $23,000, respectively. Assets at the beginning of 2012 were $25,000. If the liabilities of Verkovsky Company increased by $12,000 in 2012, how much were total assets at the end of 2012? Use the accounting equation.

a. $16,000

b. $35,000

c. $37,000

d. $39,000

Q1-54 Murphy Company had the following on the dates indicated:

	12/31/12	12/31/11
Total assets	$750,000	$530,000
Total liabilities	33,000	24,000

Murphy had no stock transactions in 2012; thus, the change in stockholders' equity for 2012 was due to net income and dividends. If dividends were $80,000, how much was Murphy's net income for 2012? Use the accounting equation and the statement of retained earnings.

a. $291,000

b. $211,000

c. $220,000

d. $371,000

Problems

> All of the following A and B problems can be found within MyAccountingLab, an online homework and practice environment. Your instructor may ask you to complete these problems using MyAccountingLab.

MyAccountingLab

Group A

P1-55A (*Learning Objectives 1, 2, 5: Explain accounting vocabulary; explain and apply accounting concepts, assumptions, and principles; construct financial statements*) Assume that the A division of Harrold Corporation experienced the following transactions during the year ended December 31, 2013:

a. Suppose division A supplied copy services for a customer for the discounted price of $250,000. Under normal conditions, it would have provided these services for $295,000. Other revenues totaled $57,000.

b. Salaries cost the division $29,000 to provide these services. The division had to pay employees overtime occasionally. Ordinarily the salary cost for these services would have been $17,900.

c. All other expenses, excluding income taxes, totaled $242,000 for the year. Income tax expense was 34% of income before tax.

d. The A division has two operating subdivisions: basic retail and special contracts. Each subdivision is accounted for separately to indicate how well each is performing. However, the A division combines the statements of all subdivisions to show results for the A division as a whole.

e. Inflation affects the amounts that the A division must pay for copy machines. To show the effects of inflation, net income would drop by $1,000.

f. If the A division were to go out of business, the sale of its assets would bring in $125,000 in cash.

▶ Requirements

1. Prepare the A division's income statement for the year ended December 31, 2013.
2. For items a through f, explain the accounting concept, assumption, or principle that provides guidance in accounting for the item. State how you have applied the concept, assumption, or principle in preparing the income statement.

P1-56A (*Learning Objectives 3, 4: Apply the accounting equation; evaluate business operations*) Compute the missing amount (?) for each company—amounts in millions.

	Ruby Corp.	Lars Co.	Barb Inc.
Beginning			
Assets......................................	$78	$40	$?
Liabilities	45	14	1
Common stock....................	4	3	6
Retained earnings...............	?	23	7
Ending			
Assets......................................	$?	$59	$17
Liabilities	47	26	?
Common stock....................	4	?	6
Retained earnings...............	33	?	?
Income statement			
Revenues.............................	$220	$?	$21
Expenses	214	160	?
Net income.........................	?	?	?
Statement of retained earnings			
Beginning RE	$29	$23	$ 7
+ Net income........................	?	10	3
− Dividends..........................	(2)	(3)	(1)
= Ending RE.........................	$33	$30	$ 9

At the end of the year, which company has the

▶ highest net income?

▶ highest percent of net income to revenues?

P1-57A (*Learning Objectives 1, 3, 4, 5: Explain accounting language; apply the accounting equation; evaluate business operations; construct a balance sheet*) The manager of ImageMaker, Inc., prepared the company's balance sheet as of March 31, 2012, while the accountant was ill. The balance sheet contains numerous errors. In particular, the manager knew that the balance sheet should balance, so he plugged in the stockholders' equity amount needed to achieve this balance. The stockholders' equity amount is *not* correct. All other amounts are accurate.

Image Maker, Inc.
Balance Sheet
March 31, 2012

Assets		Liabilities	
Cash	$ 10,500	Notes receivable	$ 16,000
Equipment	35,000	Interest expense	2,100
Accounts payable	4,500	Office supplies	600
Utilities expense	2,000	Accounts receivable	2,400
Advertising expense	900	Note payable	53,000
Land	83,000	Total	74,100
Salary expense	2,800	**Stockholders' Equity**	
		Stockholders' equity	64,600
Total assets	$138,700	Total liabilities	$138,700

▶ Requirements

1. Prepare the correct balance sheet and date it properly. Compute total assets, total liabilities, and stockholders' equity.
2. Is ImageMaker actually in better (or worse) financial position than the erroneous balance sheet reports? Give the reason for your answer.
3. Identify the accounts listed on the incorrect balance sheet that should not be reported on the balance sheet. State why you excluded them from the correct balance sheet you prepared for Requirement 1. On which financial statement should these accounts appear?

P1-58A (*Learning Objectives 2, 4, 5: Apply underlying accounting concepts; evaluate business operations; construct a balance sheet*) Carla Hilton is a realtor. She organized the business as a corporation on December 16, 2013. The business received $55,000 cash from Hilton and issued common stock. Consider the following facts as of December 31, 2013.
   a. Hilton has $16,000 in her personal bank account and $66,000 in the business bank account.
   b. Hilton owes $6,000 on a personal charge account with Clothing Outlet.
   c. Hilton acquired business furniture for $45,000 on December 24. Of this amount, the business owes $32,000 on accounts payable at December 31.
   d. Office supplies on hand at the real estate office total $7,000.
   e. Hilton's business owes $45,000 on a note payable for some land acquired for a total price of $118,000.
   f. Hilton's business spent $21,000 for a YourHome Realty franchise, which entitles her to represent herself as an agent. YourHome Realty is a national affiliation of independent real estate agents. This franchise is a business asset.
   g. Hilton owes $100,000 on a personal mortgage on her personal residence, which she acquired in 2003 for a total price of $400,000.

▶ Requirements

1. Prepare the balance sheet of the real estate business of Carla Hilton Realtor, Inc., at December 31, 2013.
2. Does it appear that the realty business can pay its debts? How can you tell?
3. Identify the personal items given in the preceding facts that should not be reported on the balance sheet of the business.

P1-59A (*Learning Objectives 4, 5: Construct and analyze an income statement, a statement of retained earnings and a balance sheet; evaluate business operations*) The assets and liabilities of Post Oak, Inc., as of December 31, 2012, and revenues and expenses for the year ended on that date follow.

Land....................................	$ 9,000	Equipment..........................	$ 36,000
Note payable.......................	34,000	Interest expense..................	5,100
Property tax expense...........	2,100	Interest payable..................	1,200
Rent expense.......................	11,000	Accounts payable...............	8,000
Accounts receivable.............	30,000	Salary expense....................	30,000
Service revenue....................	147,000	Building.............................	123,000
Supplies..............................	2,300	Cash..................................	20,000
Utilities expense	3,700	Common stock..................	5,000

Beginning retained earnings was $114,000, and dividends totaled $37,000 for the year.

▶ Requirements

1. Prepare the income statement of Post Oak, Inc., for the year ended December 31, 2012.
2. Prepare the company's statement of retained earnings for the year.
3. Prepare the company's balance sheet at December 31, 2012.
4. Analyze Post Oak, Inc., by answering these questions:
   a. Was Post Oak profitable during 2012? By how much?
   b. Did retained earnings increase or decrease? By how much?
   c. Which is greater, total liabilities or total equity? Who owns more of Post Oak's assets, creditors of the company or the Post Oak's stockholders?

P1-60A (*Learning Objectives 4, 5: Construct a statement of cash flows; evaluate business operations*) The following data come from the financial statements of The Big Wave Company for the year ended May 31, 2013 (in millions):

Purchases of property,		Other investing cash	
plant, and equipment	$ 3,505	payments............................	$ 155
Net income..........................	3,040	Accounts receivable...............	900
Adjustments to reconcile net		Payment of dividends.............	290
income to net cash provided		Common stock.......................	4,810
by operating activities	2,350	Issuance of common stock......	180
Revenues.............................	59,000	Sales of property, plant,	
Cash, beginning of year........	230	and equipment	65
end of year	1,915	Retained earnings..................	12,980
Cost of goods sold...............	37,600		

▶ Requirements

1. Prepare a cash flow statement for the year ended May 31, 2013. Not all items given appear on the cash flow statement.
2. What activities provided the largest source of cash? Is this a sign of financial strength or weakness?

P1-61A (*Learning Objective 5: Construct financial statements*) Summarized versions of Nachos Corporation's financial statements are given for two recent years.

	2012	2011
Income Statement	(In Thousands)	
Revenues...	$ k	$15,500
Cost of goods sold......................................	11,070	a
Other expenses...	1,230	1,180
Income before income taxes	1,590	1,810
Income taxes (35% tax rate)	l	634
Net income...	$ m	$ b
Statement of Retained Earnings		
Beginning balance	$ n	$ 2,690
Net income...	o	c
Dividends...	(96)	(70)
Ending balance...	$ p	$ d
Balance Sheet		
Assets:		
Cash...	$ q	$ e
Property, plant, and equipment..................	1,500	1,750
Other assets...	r	10,381
Total assets	$ s	$13,251
Liabilities:		
Current liabilities	$ t	$ 5,640
Notes payable and long-term debt..............	4,400	3,370
Other liabilities	90	110
Total liabilities....................................	$ 9,200	$ f
Stockholders' Equity:		
Common stock..	$ 225	$ 225
Retained earnings.......................................	u	g
Other stockholders' equity	190	110
Total stockholders' equity.....................	v	4,131
Total liabilities and stockholders' equity	$ w	$ h
Cash Flow Statement		
Net cash provided by operating activities................	$ x	$ 850
Net cash used in investing activities.........................	(240)	(450)
Net cash used in financing activities.........................	(560)	(550)
Increase (decrease) in cash....................................	(80)	i
Cash at beginning of year.......................................	y	1,270
Cash at end of year	$ z	$ j

▶ Requirement

1. Determine the missing amounts denoted by the letters.

Group B

P1-62B (*Learning Objectives 1, 2, 5: Explain accounting vocabulary; explain and apply accounting concepts, assumptions, and principles; construct financial statements*) Assume that the A division of Truett Corporation experienced the following transactions during the year ended December 31, 2013:

    a. Suppose division A supplied copy services for a customer for the discounted price of $260,000. Under normal conditions, it would have provided these services for $315,000. Other revenues totaled $51,000.

    b. Salaries cost the division $28,000 to provide these services. The division had to pay employees overtime occasionally. Ordinarily the salary cost for these services would have been $17,700.

    c. All other expenses, excluding income taxes, totaled $249,000 for the year. Income tax expense was 40% of income before tax.

    d. The A division has two operating subdivisions: basic retail and special contracts. Each division is accounted for separately to indicate how well each is performing. However, the A division combines the statements of all subdivisions to show results for the A division as a whole.

    e. Inflation affects the amounts that the A division must pay for copy machines. To show the effects of inflation, net income would drop by $6,000.

    f. If the A division were to go out of business, the sale of its assets would bring in $140,000 in cash.

▶ Requirements

    1. Prepare the A division's income statement for the year ended December 31, 2013.

    2. For items a through f, explain the accounting concept, assumption, or principle that provides guidance in accounting for the item described. State how you have applied the concept, assumption, or principle in preparing the income statement.

P1-63B (*Learning Objectives 3, 4: Apply the accounting equation; evaluate business operations*) Compute the missing amount (?) for each company—amounts in millions.

	Topaz Corp.	Loiselle Co.	Berger Inc.
Beginning			
Assets...............................	$84	$45	$?
Liabilities	48	21	3
Common stock.................	6	5	4
Retained earnings..............	?	19	3
Ending			
Assets...............................	$?	$65	$11
Liabilities	50	32	?
Common stock.................	6	?	4
Retained earnings..............	32	?	?
Income statement			
Revenues...........................	$223	$?	$27
Expenses	216	156	?
Net income........................	?	?	?
Statement of retained earnings			
Beginning RE	$30	$19	$ 3
+ Net income......................	?	11	2
− Dividends.........................	(5)	(2)	(2)
= Ending RE........................	$32	$28	$ 3

Which company has the

    ▶ highest net income?

    ▶ highest percent of net income to revenues?

P1-64B (*Learning Objectives 1, 3, 4, 5: Explain accounting language; apply the accounting equation; evaluate business operations; construct a balance sheet*) The manager of Salem News, Inc., prepared the company's balance sheet as of April 30, 2012, while the accountant was ill. The balance sheet contains numerous errors. In particular, the manager knew that the balance sheet should balance, so he plugged in the stockholders' equity amount needed to achieve this balance. The stockholders' equity amount is *not* correct. All other amounts are accurate.

Assets		Liabilities	
News Salem, Inc. **Balance Sheet** **April 30, 2012**			
Cash	$ 11,000	Notes receivable	$ 15,200
Equipment	35,600	Interest expense	2,400
Accounts payable	4,000	Office supplies	800
Utilities expense	1,600	Accounts receivable	2,600
Advertising expense	1,000	Note payable	55,500
Land	84,000	Total	76,500
Salary expense	2,500	**Stockholders' Equity**	
		Stockholders' equity	63,200
Total assets	$139,700	Total liabilities	$139,700

▶ Requirements

1. Prepare the correct balance sheet and date it properly. Compute total assets, total liabilities, and stockholders' equity.
2. Is Salem News in better (or worse) financial position than the erroneous balance sheet reports? Give the reason for your answer.
3. Identify the accounts that should *not* be reported on the balance sheet. State why you excluded them from the correct balance sheet you prepared for Requirement 1. On which financial statement should these accounts appear?

P1-65B (*Learning Objectives 2, 4, 5: Apply underlying accounting concepts; evaluate business operations; construct a balance sheet*) Reva Hamlet is a realtor. She organized her business as a corporation on September 16, 2013. The business received $90,000 from Hamlet and issued common stock. Consider these facts as of September 30, 2013.

    a. Hamlet has $20,000 in her personal bank account and $71,000 in the business bank account.

    b. Hamlet owes $9,000 on a personal charge account with Strawberries Music Store.

    c. Hamlet acquired business furniture for $50,000 on September 25. Of this amount, the business owes $37,000 on accounts payable at September 30.

    d. Office supplies on hand at the real estate office total $5,000.

    e. Hamlet's business owes $41,000 on a note payable for some land acquired for a total price of $112,000.

    f. Hamlet's business spent $26,000 for a Hometown Realty franchise, which entitles her to represent herself as an agent. Hometown Realty is a national affiliation of independent real estate agents. This franchise is a business asset.

    g. Hamlet owes $120,000 on a personal mortgage on her personal residence, which she acquired in 2003 for a total price of $380,000.

▶ Requirements

1. Prepare the balance sheet of the real estate business of Reva Hamlet Realtor, Inc., at September 30, 2013.
2. Does it appear that the realty business can pay its debts? How can you tell?
3. Identify the personal items given in the preceding facts that should not be reported on the balance sheet of the business.

P1-66B (*Learning Objectives 4, 5: Construct and analyze an income statement, a statement of retained earnings, and a balance sheet; evaluate business operations*) The assets and liabilities of Post Fir as of December 31, 2012, and revenues and expenses for the year ended on that date follow.

Land..................................	$ 8,200	Equipment..........................	$ 35,000
Note payable......................	31,000	Interest expense.................	4,650
Property tax expense...........	2,400	Interest payable.................	1,000
Rent expense......................	13,000	Accounts payable..............	9,000
Accounts receivable.............	26,500	Salary expense....................	34,000
Service revenue...................	143,000	Building.............................	125,000
Supplies.............................	1,900	Cash..................................	14,000
Utilities expense	2,700	Common stock..................	5,350

Beginning retained earnings was $114,000, and dividends totaled $36,000 for the year.

▶ Requirements

1. Prepare the income statement of Post Fir, Inc., for the year ended December 31, 2012.
2. Prepare the company's statement of retained earnings for the year.
3. Prepare the company's balance sheet at December 31, 2012.
4. Analyze Post Fir, Inc., by answering these questions:
   a. Was Post Fir profitable during 2012? By how much?
   b. Did retained earnings increase or decrease? By how much?
   c. Which is greater, total liabilities or total equity? Who owns more of Post Fir's assets, creditors of the company or Post Fir's stockholders?

P1-67B (*Learning Objectives 4,5: Construct a statement of cash flows; evaluate business operations*) The following data come from the financial statements of The Water Fun Company at the year ended May 31, 2013 (in millions).

Purchases of property, plant, and equipment	$ 3,520	Other investing cash payments...........................	$ 160
Net income..........................	3,050	Accounts receivable...............	800
Adjustments to reconcile net income to net cash provided by operating activities	2,370	Payment of dividends	265
		Common stock......................	4,840
		Issuance of common stock......	205
Revenues.............................	59,200	Sales of property, plant, and equipment	35
Cash, beginning of year........	270	Retained earnings..................	12,900
end of year	1,985		
Cost of goods sold...............	37,550		

▶ Requirements

1. Prepare a cash flow statement for the year ended May 31, 2013. Not all the items given appear on the cash flow statement.
2. Which activities provided the largest source of cash? Is this a sign of financial strength or weakness?

P1-68B (*Learning Objective 5: Construct financial statements*) Summarized versions of Sanchez Corporation's financial statements follow for two recent years.

	2013	2012
Income Statement	(In Thousands)	
Revenues..	$ k	$15,000
Cost of goods sold..	11,090	a
Other expenses...	1,210	1,160
Income before income taxes	1,580	1,860
Income taxes (35% tax rate)	l	651
Net income..	$ m	$ b
Statement of Retained Earnings		
Beginning balance	$ n	$ 2,650
Net income..	o	c
Dividends..	(94)	(140)
Ending balance...	$ p	$ d
Balance Sheet		
Assets:		
Cash..	$ q	$ e
Property, plant, and equipment............................	1,900	1,925
Other assets..	r	9,854
Total assets	$ s	$13,209
Liabilities:		
Current liabilities	$ t	$ 5,620
Notes payable and long-term debt........................	4,500	3,360
Other liabilities	110	130
Total liabilities	$ 9,250	$ f
Stockholders' Equity:		
Common stock..	$ 200	$ 200
Retained earnings..	u	g
Other stockholders' equity	160	180
Total stockholders' equity	v	4,099
Total liabilities and stockholders' equity	$ w	$ h
Cash Flows Statement		
Net cash provided by operating activities................	$ x	$ 975
Net cash used in investing activities.........................	(200)	(325)
Net cash used in financing activities........................	(560)	(500)
Increase (decrease) in cash...................................	(90)	i
Cash at beginning of year....................................	y	1,280
Cash at end of year	$ z	$ j

► Requirement

1. Complete Sanchez Corporation's financial statements by determining the missing amounts denoted by the letters.

APPLY YOUR KNOWLEDGE

Decision Cases

Case 1. (*Learning Objectives 1, 4: Explain accounting language; evaluate business operations through financial statements*) Two businesses, Blue Skies Corp. and Open Road, Inc., have sought business loans from you. To decide whether to make the loans, you have requested their balance sheets.

Blue Skies Corp.			
Balance Sheet			
August 31, 2013			
Assets		**Liabilities**	
Cash	$ 5,000	Accounts payable	$ 50,000
Accounts receivable	10,000	Notes payable	80,000
Furniture	15,000	Total liabilities	130,000
Land	75,000	**Stockholders' Equity**	
Equipment	45,000	Stockholders' equity	20,000
Total assets	$150,000	Total liabilities and stockholders' equity	$150,000

Open Road, Inc.			
Balance Sheet			
August 31, 2013			
Assets		**Liabilities**	
Cash	$ 5,000	Accounts payable	$ 6,000
Accounts receivable	10,000	Note payable	9,000
Merchandise inventory	15,000	Total liabilities	15,000
Building	35,000	**Stockholders' Equity**	
		Stockholders' equity	50,000
		Total liabilities and	
Total assets	$65,000	stockholders' equity	$65,000

▶ Requirement

1. Using only these balance sheets, to which entity would you be more comfortable lending money? Explain fully, citing specific items and amounts from the respective balance sheets. (Challenge)

Case 2. *(Learning Objectives 4, 5: Correct errors; construct financial statements; evaluate business operations through financial statements)* A year out of college, you have $10,000 to invest. A friend has started Grand Prize Unlimited, Inc., and she asks you to invest in her company. You obtain the company's financial statements, which are summarized at the end of the first year as follows:

Grand Prize Unlimited, Inc.
Income Statement
Year Ended December 31, 2012

Revenues	$100,000
Expenses	80,000
Net income	$ 20,000

Grand Prize Unlimited, Inc.
Balance Sheet
December 31, 2012

Cash	$ 6,000	Liabilities	$ 60,000
Other assets	100,000	Stockholders' Equity	46,000
Total assets	$106,000	Total liabilities and stockholders' equity	$106,000

Visits with your friend turn up the following facts:
  a. Grand Prize Unlimited delivered $140,000 of services to customers during 2012 and collected $100,000 from customers for those services.
  b. Grand Prize recorded a $50,000 cash payment for software as an asset. This cost should have been an expense.
  c. To get the business started, your friend borrowed $10,000 from her parents at the end of 2011. The proceeds of the loan were used to pay salaries for the first month of 2012. Since the loan was from her parents, your friend did not reflect the loan or the salaries in the accounting records.

► Requirements
  1. Prepare corrected financial statements.
  2. Use your corrected statements to evaluate Grand Prize Unlimited's results of operations and financial position. (Challenge)
  3. Will you invest in Grand Prize Unlimited? Give your reason. (Challenge)

Ethical Issue

(*Learning Objective 6: Evaluate ethical decisions*) You are studying frantically for an accounting exam tomorrow. You are having difficulty in this course, and the grade you make on this exam can make the difference between receiving a final grade of B or C. If you receive a C, it will lower your grade point average to the point that you could lose your academic scholarship. An hour ago, a friend, also enrolled in the course but in a different section under the same professor, called you with some unexpected news. In her sorority test files, she has just found a copy of an old exam from the previous year. In looking at the exam, it appears to contain questions that come right from the class notes you have taken, even the very same numbers. She offers to make a copy for you and bring it over.

You glance at your course syllabus and find the following: "You are expected to do your own work in this class. Although you may study with others, giving, receiving, or obtaining information pertaining to an examination is considered an act of academic dishonesty, unless such action is authorized by the instructor giving the examination. Also, divulging the contents of an essay or objective examination designated by the instructor as an examination is considered an act of academic dishonesty. Academic dishonesty is considered a violation of the student honor code, and will subject the student to disciplinary procedures, which can include suspension from the university." Although you have heard a rumor that fraternities and sororities have cleared their exam files with professors, you are not sure.

▶ Requirements

1. What is the ethical issue in this situation?
2. Who are the stakeholders? What are the possible consequences to each?
3. Analyze the alternatives from the following standpoints: (a) economic, (b) legal, and (c) ethical.
4. What would you do? How would you justify your decision? How would your decision make you feel afterward?
5. How is this similar to a business situation?

Focus on Financials: | Amazon.com, Inc.

(*Learning Objectives 3, 4: Apply the accounting equation; evaluate business operations*) This and similar cases in succeeding chapters are based on the consolidated financial statements of **Amazon.com, Inc.** As you work with Amazon.com, Inc., throughout this course, you will develop the ability to use the financial statements of actual companies.

▶ Requirements

Refer to the Amazon.com, Inc., consolidated financial statements in Appendix A at the end of the book.

1. Go on the Internet and do some research on Amazon.Com, Inc. and its industry. Use one or more popular websites like http://finance.yahoo.com or http://www.google.com/finance. Write a paragraph (about 100 words) that describes the industry, some current developments, and a projection for future growth.
2. Read Part I, Item 1 (Business) of Amazon.com, Inc.'s annual report. What do you learn here and why is it important?
3. Name at least one of Amazon.com, Inc.'s competitors. Why is this information important in evaluating Amazon.com, Inc.'s financial performance?
4. Suppose you own stock in Amazon.com, Inc. If you could pick one item on the company's Consolidated Statements of Operations to increase year after year, what would it be? Why is this item so important? Did this item increase or decrease during fiscal 2010? Is this good news or bad news for the company?
5. What was Amazon.com, Inc.'s largest expense each year? In your own words, explain the meaning of this item. Give specific examples of items that make up this expense. The chapter gives another title for this expense. What is it?

6. Use the Consolidated Balance Sheets of Amazon.com, Inc., in Appendix A to answer these questions: At the end of fiscal 2010, how much in total resources did Amazon.com, Inc., have to work with? How much did the company owe? How much of its assets did the company's stockholders actually own? Use these amounts to write Amazon.com, Inc.'s accounting equation at December 31, 2010.
7. How much cash did Amazon.com, Inc., have at the beginning of the most recent year? How much cash did Amazon.com have at the end of the year?

Focus on Analysis: | RadioShack Corporation

(**Learning Objectives 3, 4: Apply the accounting equation; evaluate business operations**) This and similar cases in each chapter are based on the consolidated financial statements of **RadioShack Corporation**, given in Appendix B at the end of this book. As you work with RadioShack Corporation, you will develop the ability to analyze the financial statements of actual companies.

▶ Requirements

1. Go on the Internet and do some research on RadioShack Corporation and its industry. Use one or more popular websites like http://finance.yahoo.com or http://www.google.com/finance. Write a paragraph (about 100 words) that describes the industry, some current developments, and a projection for where the industry is headed.
2. Read Note 1—(Description of Business) of RadioShack Corporation's annual report. What do you learn here and why is it important?
3. Name two of RadioShack Corporation's competitors. Why is this information important in evaluating RadioShack Corporation's financial performance?
4. Write RadioShack Corporation's accounting equation at December 31, 2010 (express all items in millions and round to the nearest $1 million). Does RadioShack Corporation's financial condition look strong or weak? How can you tell?
5. What was the result of RadioShack Corporation's operations during 2010? Identify both the name and the dollar amount of the result of operations for 2010. Does an increase (or decrease) signal good news or bad news for the company and its stockholders?
6. Examine retained earnings in the Consolidated Statements of Shareholders' Equity. What caused retained earnings to increase during 2010?
7. Which statement reports cash as part of RadioShack Corporation's financial position? Which statement tells *why* cash increased (or decreased) during the year? What two individual items caused RadioShack Corporation's cash to change the most during 2010?

Group Projects

Project 1. As instructed by your professor, obtain the annual report of a well-known company.

▶ Requirements

1. Take the role of a loan committee of Bank of America, a large banking company headquartered in Charlotte, North Carolina. Assume a company has requested a loan from Bank of America. Analyze the company's financial statements and any other information you need to reach a decision regarding the largest amount of money you would be willing to lend. Go as deeply into the analysis and the related decision as you can. Specify the following:
   a. The length of the loan period—that is, over what period will you allow the company to pay you back?
   b. The interest rate you will charge on the loan. Will you charge the prevailing interest rate, a lower rate, or a higher rate? Why?
   c. Any restrictions you will impose on the borrower as a condition for making the loan.

Note: The long-term debt note to the financial statements gives details of the company's existing liabilities.

2. Write your group decision in a report addressed to the bank's board of directors. Limit your report to two double-spaced word-processed pages.
3. If your professor directs, present your decision and your analysis to the class. Limit your presentation to 10 to 15 minutes.

Project 2. You are the owner of a company that is about to "go public"—that is, issue its stock to outside investors. You wish to make your company look as attractive as possible to raise $1 million of cash to expand the business. At the same time, you want to give potential investors a realistic picture of your company.

▶ Requirements

1. Design a booklet to portray your company in a way that will enable outsiders to reach an informed decision as to whether to buy some of your stock. The booklet should include the following:
   a. Name and location of your company.
   b. Nature of the company's business (be as detailed as possible).
   c. How you plan to spend the money you raise.
   d. The company's comparative income statement, statement of retained earnings, balance sheet, and statement of cash flows for two years: the current year and the preceding year. Make the data as realistic as possible with the intent of receiving $1 million.
2. Word-process your booklet, not to exceed five pages.
3. If directed by your professor, make a copy for each member of your class. Distribute copies to the class and present your case with the intent of interesting your classmates in investing in the company. Limit your presentation to 10 to 15 minutes.

MyAccountingLab | For online homework, exercises, and problems that provide you with immediate feedback, please visit **www.myaccountinglab.com**.

Quick Check Answers

1. *b*

2. *c*

3. *b [This is not the typical way the accounting equation is expressed (Assets = Liabilities + Owners' Equity), but it may be rearranged this way].*

4. *d*

5. *d*

6. *d*

7. *a ($140,000 − $75,000 − $3,000 = $62,000)*

8. *d ($140,000 − $75,000 = $65,000)*

9. *c [Total assets = $131,000 ($5,000 + $40,000 + $36,000 + $50,000). Liabilities = $29,000.]*

10. *d*

11. *c $46,000 + Net income ($20,000) − Dividends = $62,000; Dividends = $4,000*

12. *c*

	Assets	=	Liabilities	+	Equity
Beginning	$360,000	=	$240,000*	+	$120,000
Increase	60,000	=	35,000	+	25,000*
Ending	$420,000*	=	$275,000*	+	$145,000*

*Must solve for these amounts

13. *a*

14. *c*

Demo Doc

The Accounting Equation and Financial Statement Preparation

To make sure you understand this material, work through the following demonstration "Demo Doc" with detailed comments to help you see the concept within the framework of a worked-through problem.

Learning Objectives 3, 4, 5

David Richardson is the only shareholder of DR Painting, Inc., a painting business near a historical housing district. At March 31, 2012, DR Painting had the following information:

Cash	$27,300
Accounts receivable	1,400
Supplies	1,800
Truck	20,000
Accounts payable	1,000
Common stock	40,000
Retained earnings (March 1)	5,000
Retained earnings (March 31)	?
Dividends	1,500
Service revenue	7,000
Salary expense	1,000

▶ Requirements

1. Prepare the income statement and statement of retained earnings for the month of March 2012 and the balance sheet of the business at March 31, 2012. Use Exhibits 1-7, 1-8, and 1-9 (pp. 15, 16, and 18) in the text as a guide.

2. Write the accounting equation of the business.

Demo Doc Solutions

▶ Requirement 1

Prepare the income statement, statement of retained earnings, and balance sheet of the business. Use Exhibits 1-7, 1-8, and 1-9 (pp. 15, 16, and 18) in the text as a guide.

Part 1	Part 2	Demo Doc Complete

Income Statement

The income statement is the first statement to prepare because the other financial statements rely upon the net income number calculated on the income statement.

The income statement reports the profitability of the business. To prepare an income statement, begin with the proper heading. A proper heading includes the name of the company (DR Painting, Inc.), the name of the statement (Income Statement), and the time period covered (Month Ended March 31, 2012). Notice that we are reporting income for a period of time, rather than at a single date.

The income statement lists all revenues and expenses. It uses the following formula to calculate net income:

$$\text{Revenues} - \text{Expenses} = \text{Net income}$$

First, you should list revenues. Second, list the expenses. After you have listed and totaled the revenues and expenses, subtract the total expenses from total revenues to determine net income or net loss. A positive number means you earned net income (revenues exceeded expenses). A negative number indicates that expenses exceeded revenues, and this is a net loss.

DR Painting's total Service Revenue for the month was $7,000. The only expense is Salary Expense of $1,000. On the income statement, these would be reported as follows:

DR Painting, Inc.
Income Statement
Month Ended March 31, 2012

Revenue:		
Service revenue		$7,000
Expenses:		
Salary expense	$1,000	
Total expenses		1,000
Net income		$6,000

Note that the result is a net income of $6,000 ($7,000 − $1,000 = $6,000). You will also report net income on the statement of retained earnings, which comes next.

Statement of Retained Earnings

The statement of retained earnings shows the changes in Retained Earnings for a period of time. To prepare a statement of retained earnings, begin with the proper heading. A proper heading includes the name of the company (DR Painting, Inc.), the name of the statement (Statement of Retained Earnings), and the time period covered (Month Ended March 31, 2012). As with the income statement, we are reporting the changes in Retained Earnings for a period of time, rather than at a single date.

Net income is used on the statement of retained earnings to calculate the new balance in Retained Earnings. This calculation uses the following formula:

Beginning Retained Earnings
+ Net Income (or − Net Loss)
− Dividends
= Ending Retained Earnings

Start the body of the statement of retained earnings with the Retained Earnings at the beginning of the period (March 1). Then list net income. Observe that the amount of net income comes directly from the income statement. Following net income you will list the dividends declared and paid, which reduce Retained Earnings. Finally, total all amounts and compute the Retained Earnings at the end of the period.

The beginning Retained Earnings of $5,000 was given in the problem. Net income of $6,000 comes from the income statement and is added. Dividends of $1,500 are deducted. On the statement of retained earnings, these amounts are reported as follows:

DR Painting, Inc. Statement of Retained Earnings Month Ended March 31, 2012	
Beginning retained earnings	$ 5,000
Add: Net income	6,000
	11,000
Less: Dividends	(1,500)
Retained earnings, March 31, 2012	$ 9,500

Note that Retained Earnings has a balance of $9,500 at March 31, 2012. You will also report Retained Earning's ending balance on the balance sheet, which you prepare last.

Balance Sheet

The balance sheet reports the financial position of the business at a moment in time. To prepare a balance sheet, begin with the proper heading. A proper heading includes the name of the company (DR Painting, Inc.), the name of the statement (Balance Sheet), and the time of the ending balances (March 31, 2012). Unlike the income statement and statement of retained earnings, we are reporting the financial position of the company at a specific date rather than for a period of time.

The balance sheet lists all assets, liabilities, and equity of the business, with the accounting equation verified at the bottom.

To prepare the body of the balance sheet, begin by listing assets. Then list all the liabilities and stockholders' equity. Notice that the balance sheet is organized in the same order as the accounting equation. The amount of Retained Earnings comes directly from the ending balance on your statement of retained earnings. You should then total both sides of the balance sheet to make sure that they are equal. If they are not equal, then you must correct an error.

In this case, assets accounts include cash of $27,300, accounts receivable of $1,400, $1,800 worth of supplies, and the truck valued at $20,000. The only liability is accounts payable of $1,000. Stockholders' equity consists of common stock of $40,000 and the updated retained earnings of $9,500 from the statement of retained earnings.

DR Painting, Inc.
Balance Sheet
March 31, 2012

Assets		Liabilities	
Cash	$27,300	Accounts payable	$ 1,000
Accounts receivable	1,400	**Stockholders' Equity**	
Supplies	1,800	Common stock	40,000
Truck	20,000	Retained earnings	9,500
		Total stockholders' equity	49,500
		Total liabilities and	
Total assets	$50,500	stockholders' equity	$50,500

Assets   =   Liabilities + Stockholders' Equity

▶ Requirement 2

Write the accounting equation of the business.

Part 1	Part 2	Demo Doc Complete

In this case, asset accounts total $50,500. Liabilities total $1,000—the balance of Accounts Payable, and stockholder's equity is $49,500. This gives us a total for liabilities and equity of $50,500 ($1,000 + $49,500).

The accounting equation is as follows:

Assets of $50,500 = Liabilities of $1,000 + Stockholders' Equity of $49,500

Part 1	Part 2	Demo Doc Complete

2 Transaction Analysis

SPOTLIGHT: Apple, Inc.

How do you manage information in your busy life? You may use any of thousands of applications ("Apps") on Apple's iPhone for texting, listening to music, or checking the weather or sports scores. You may use an iPad for reading your favorite books or playing your favorite game. The iPhone, iPod, and iPad, in addition to the company's popular Macbook and iMac notebook computers, have generated billions of dollars in profits for the company.

Apple, Inc., is U.S.-based multinational corporation that designs and manufactures consumer electronics. The company launched over 30 years ago with the name Apple Computer, Inc., but because it has expanded its product line so much in the last few years, it dropped the "computer" from its name in 2007. The company's best-known hardware products include Mac computers, as well as the iPod, iPhone, and IPad. Apple software includes the Mac OS X operating system, the iTunes media browser, the iLife suite of multimedia and creativity software, the iWork suite of productivity software, and Final Cut Studio, a suite of professional audio and film-industry software products. The company operates more than 300 retail stores worldwide and an online store where hardware and software products are sold.

How does Apple determine its revenues, expenses, and net income? Like all other companies, Apple has a comprehensive accounting system. Apple's income statement (statement of operations) is given at the start of this chapter. The income statement shows that during fiscal year 2010, Apple made over $65 billion of sales and earned net income of $14 billion. Where did those figures come from? In this chapter, we'll show you. ●

iPad

Starting at $499

© Mira/Alamy

Apple, Inc. Statement of Operations (Adapted) Fiscal Year Ended September 25, 2010		
(In billions)		**2010**
Net sales		$65.2
Cost of goods sold		39.5
Gross profit		25.7
Operating expenses:		
Research and development expense		1.8
Selling, general, and administrative expense		5.5
Total operating expenses		7.3
Operating income (loss)		18.4
Other income		.1
Income before income taxes		18.5
Income tax expense		4.5
Net income		$14.0

Chapter 1 introduced the financial statements. Chapter 2 will show you how companies actually record the transactions that eventually become part of the financial statements.

Learning Objectives

1 **Explain** what a transaction is

2 **Define** "account," and **list** and **differentiate** between different types of accounts

3 **Show** the impact of business transactions on the accounting equation

4 **Analyze** the impact of business transactions on accounts

5 **Record** (journalize and post) transactions in the books

6 **Construct and use** a trial balance

MyAccountingLab
ACT

For more practice and review of accounting cycle concepts, use ACT, the Accounting Cycle Tutorial, online at www.myaccountinglab.com. Margin logos like this one, directing you to the appropriate ACT section and material, appear throughout Chapters 1,2, and 3. When you enter the tutorial, you'll find three buttons on the opening page of each chapter module. Here's what the buttons mean: **Tutorial** gives you a review of the major concepts, **Application** gives you practice exercises, and **Glossary** reviews important terms.

Explain What a Transaction Is

1

Explain what a transaction is

Business activity is all about transactions. A **transaction** is any event that has a financial impact on the business and can be measured reliably. For example, Apple, Inc., pays programmers to create iTunes® software. Apple sells computers, borrows money, and repays the loan—three separate transactions.

But not all events qualify as transactions. iTunes® may be featured in *Showtime Magazine* and motivate you to buy an Apple iPod. The magazine article may create lots of new business for Apple. But no transaction occurs until someone actually buys an Apple product. A transaction must occur before Apple records anything.

Transactions provide objective information about the financial impact on a company. Every transaction has two sides:

▶ You give something.

▶ You receive something in return.

In accounting we always record both sides of a transaction. And we must be able to measure the financial impact of the event on the business before recording it as a transaction.

Define "Account," and List and Differentiate Between Different Types of Accounts

As we saw in Chapter 1, the accounting equation expresses the basic relationships of accounting:

$$\text{Assets} = \text{Liabilities} + \text{Stockholders' (Owners') Equity}$$

2

Define "account," and **list** and **differentiate** between different types of accounts

For each asset, each liability, and each element of stockholders' equity, we use a record called the account. An **account** is the record of all the changes in a particular asset, liability, or stockholders' equity during a period. The account is the basic summary device of accounting. Before launching into transaction analysis, let's review the accounts that a company such as Apple, Inc., uses.

Assets

Assets are economic resources that provide a future benefit for a business. Most firms use the following asset accounts:

Cash. Cash means money and any medium of exchange including bank account balances, paper currency, coins, certificates of deposit, and checks.

Accounts Receivable. Apple, Inc., like most other companies, sells its goods and services and receives a promise for future collection of cash. The Accounts Receivable account holds these amounts.

Notes Receivable. Apple may receive a note receivable from a customer, who signed the note promising to pay Apple. A note receivable is similar to an account receivable, but a note receivable is more binding because the customer signed the note. Notes receivable usually specify an interest rate.

Inventory. Apple's most important asset is its inventory—the hardware and software Apple sells to customers. Other titles for this account include *Merchandise* and *Merchandise Inventory*.

Prepaid Expenses. Apple pays certain expenses in advance, such as insurance and rent. A prepaid expense is an asset because the payment provides a *future* benefit for the business. Prepaid Rent, Prepaid Insurance, and Supplies are prepaid expenses.

Land. The Land account shows the cost of the land Apple uses in its operations.

Buildings. The costs of Apple's office buildings, manufacturing plants, and the like appear in the Buildings account.

Equipment, Furniture, and Fixtures. Apple has a separate asset account for each type of equipment, for example, Manufacturing Equipment and Office Equipment. The Furniture and Fixtures account shows the cost of these assets, which are similar to equipment.

Liabilities

Recall that a *liability* is a debt. A payable is always a liability. The most common types of liabilities include the following:

Accounts Payable. The Accounts Payable account is the direct opposite of Accounts Receivable. Apple's promise to pay a debt arising from a credit purchase of inventory or from a utility bill appears in the Accounts Payable account.

Notes Payable. A note payable is the opposite of a note receivable. The Notes Payable account includes the amounts Apple must *pay* because Apple signed notes promising to pay a future amount. Notes payable, like notes receivable, also carry interest.

Accrued Liabilities. An **accrued liability** is a liability for an expense you have not yet paid. Interest Payable and Salary Payable are accrued liability accounts for most companies. Income Tax Payable is another accrued liability.

Stockholders' (Owners') Equity

The owners' claims to the assets of a corporation are called *stockholders' equity, shareholders' equity,* or simply *owners' equity.* A corporation such as Apple, Inc., uses Common Stock, Retained Earnings, and Dividends accounts to record the company's stockholders' equity. In a proprietorship, there is a single capital account. For a partnership, each partner has a separate owner's equity account.

Common Stock. The Common Stock account shows the owners' investment in the corporation. Apple, Inc., receives cash and issues common stock to its stockholders. A company's common stock is its most basic element of equity. All corporations have common stock.

STOP & THINK. . .

Name two things that **(1)** increase Apple, Inc.'s stockholders' equity and **(2)** decrease Apple's stockholders' equity.

- -

Answer:
(1) Increases in equity: Sale of stock and net income (revenue greater than expenses).
(2) Decreases in equity: Dividends and net loss (expenses greater than revenue).

Retained Earnings. The Retained Earnings account shows the cumulative net income earned by Apple, Inc., over the company's lifetime, minus its cumulative net losses and dividends.

Dividends. Dividends are optional; they are decided (declared) by the board of directors. After profitable operations, the board of directors of Apple, Inc., may (or may not) declare and pay a cash dividend. The corporation may keep a separate account titled *Dividends,* which indicates a decrease in Retained Earnings.

Revenues. The increase in stockholders' equity from delivering goods or services to customers is called *revenue.* The company uses as many revenue accounts as needed. Apple, Inc., uses a Sales Revenue account for revenue earned by selling its products. Apple has a Service Revenue account for the revenue it earns by providing services to customers. A lawyer provides legal services for clients and also uses a Service Revenue account. A business that loans money to an outsider needs an Interest Revenue account. If the business rents a building to a tenant, the business needs a Rent Revenue account.

Expenses. The cost of operating a business is called *expense.* Expenses *decrease* stockholders' equity, the opposite effect of revenues. A business needs a separate account for each type of expense, such as Cost of Goods Sold, Salary Expense, Rent Expense, Advertising Expense, Insurance Expense, Utilities Expense, and Income Tax Expense. Businesses strive to minimize expenses and thereby maximize net income.

Show the Impact of Business Transactions on the Accounting Equation

Example: Genie Car Wash, Inc.

To illustrate the accounting for transactions, let's return to Genie Car Wash, Inc. In Chapter 1's End-of-Chapter Problem, Kyle Nielson opened Genie Car Wash, Inc., in April 2012.

We consider 11 events and analyze each in terms of its effect on Genie Car Wash. We begin by using the accounting equation. In the second half of the chapter, we record transactions using the journal and ledger of the business.

Transaction 1. Nielson and a few friends invest $50,000 to open Genie Car Wash, and the business issues common stock to the stockholders. The effect of this transaction on the accounting equation of Genie Car Wash, Inc., is a receipt of cash and issuance of common stock, as follows:

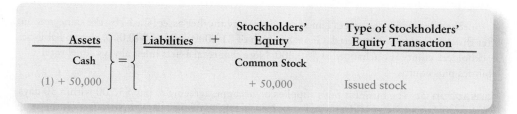

Every transaction's net amount on the left side of the equation must equal the net amount on the right side. The first transaction increases both the cash and the common stock of the business. To the right of the transaction we write "Issued stock" to show the reason for the increase in stockholders' equity.

Every transaction affects the financial statements of the business, and we can prepare financial statements after one, two, or any number of transactions. For example, Genie Car Wash could report the company's balance sheet after its first transaction, shown here.

Genie Car Wash, Inc.				
Balance Sheet				
April 1, 2012				
Assets		**Liabilities**		
Cash	$50,000	None		
		Stockholders' Equity		
		Common stock		$50,000
		Total stockholders' equity		50,000
		Total liabilities and		
Total assets	$50,000	stockholders' equity		$50,000

This balance sheet shows that the business holds cash of $50,000 and owes no liabilities. The company's equity (ownership) is denoted as *Common Stock* on the balance sheet. A bank would look favorably on this balance sheet because the business has $50,000 cash and no debt—a strong financial position.

As a practical matter, most entities report their financial statements at the end of the accounting period—not after each transaction. But an accounting system can produce statements whenever managers need to know where the business stands.

3 **Show** the impact of business transactions on the accounting equation

Transaction 2. Genie purchases land for a new location and pays cash of $40,000. The effect of this transaction on the accounting equation is as follows:

	Assets				=	Liabilities	+	Stockholders' Equity	Type of Stockholders' Equity Transaction
	Cash	+		Land				Common Stock	
(1)	50,000							50,000	Issued stock
(2)	− 40,000			+ 40,000					
Bal	10,000			40,000				50,000	
		50,000						50,000	

The purchase increases one asset (Land) and decreases another asset (Cash) by the same amount. After the transaction is completed, Genie has cash of $10,000, land of $40,000, and no liabilities. Stockholders' equity is unchanged at $50,000. Note that total assets must always equal total liabilities plus equity.

Transaction 3. The business buys supplies on account, agreeing to pay $3,700 within 30 days. This transaction increases both the assets and the liabilities of the business. Its effect on the accounting equation follows.

	Assets						=	Liabilities	+	Stockholders' Equity
	Cash	+	Supplies	+	Land			Accounts Payable	+	Common Stock
Bal	10,000				40,000					50,000
(3)			+ 3,700					+ 3,700		
Bal	10,000		3,700		40,000			3,700		50,000
			53,700						53,700	

The new asset is Supplies, and the liability is an Account Payable. Genie signs no formal promissory note, so the liability is an account payable, not a note payable.

Transaction 4. Genie earns $7,000 of service revenue by providing services for customers. The business collects the cash. The effect on the accounting equation is an increase in the asset Cash and an increase in Retained Earnings, as follows:

	Assets						=	Liabilities	+	Stockholders' Equity			Type of Stockholders' Equity Transaction
	Cash	+	Supplies	+	Land			Accounts Payable	+	Common Stock	+	Retained Earnings	
Bal	10,000		3,700		40,000			3,700		50,000			
(4)	+ 7,000											+ 7,000	Service revenue
Bal	17,000		3,700		40,000			3,700		50,000		7,000	
			60,700							60,700			

To the right we record "Service revenue" to show where the $7,000 of increase in Retained Earnings came from.

Transaction 5. Genie performs service on account, which means that Genie lets some customers pay later. Genie earns revenue but doesn't receive the cash immediately. In transaction 5, Genie cleans a fleet of UPS delivery trucks, and UPS promises to pay Genie $3,000 within one month. This promise is an account receivable—an asset—of Genie Car Wash. The transaction record follows.

		Assets			=	Liabilities	+	Stockholders' Equity			Type of Stockholders' Equity Transaction
	Cash +	Accounts Receivable +	Supplies +	Land		Accounts Payable	+	Common Stock +	Retained Earnings		
Bal	17,000		3,700	40,000		3,700		50,000	7,000		
(5)		+ 3,000							+ 3,000		Service revenue
Bal	17,000	3,000	3,700	40,000		3,700		50,000	10,000		
		63,700						63,700			

It's performing the service that earns the revenue—not collecting the cash. Therefore, Genie records revenue when it performs the service—regardless of whether Genie receives cash now or later.

Transaction 6. During the month, Genie Car Wash pays $2,700 for the following expenses: equipment rent, $1,100; employee salaries, $1,200; and utilities, $400. The effect on the accounting equation is as follows:

		Assets			=	Liabilities	+	Stockholders' Equity			Type of Stockholders' Equity Transaction
	Cash +	Accounts Receivable +	Supplies +	Land		Accounts Payable	+	Common Stock +	Retained Earnings		
Bal	17,000	3,000	3,700	40,000		3,700		50,000	10,000		
(6)	− 1,100								− 1,100		Rent expense
	− 1,200								− 1,200		Salary expense
	− 400								− 400		Utilities expense
Bal	14,300	3,000	3,700	40,000		3,700		50,000	7,300		
		61,000						61,000			

The expenses decrease Genie's Cash and Retained Earnings. List each expense separately to keep track of its amount.

Transaction 7. Genie pays $1,900 on account, which means to make a payment toward an account payable. In this transaction Genie pays the store from which it purchased supplies in transaction 3. The transaction decreases Cash and also decreases Accounts Payable as follows:

	Assets							Liabilities	+	Stockholders' Equity		
	Cash	+	Accounts Receivable	+	Supplies	+	Land	Accounts Payable	+	Common Stock	+	Retained Earnings
Bal	14,300		3,000		3,700		40,000	= 3,700		50,000		7,300
(7)	− 1,900							− 1,900				
Bal	12,400		3,000		3,700		40,000	1,800		50,000		7,300
			59,100							59,100		

Transaction 8. Kyle Nielson, the major stockholder of Genie Car Wash, paid $30,000 to remodel his home. This event is a personal transaction of the Nielson family. It is not recorded by the Genie Car Wash business. We focus solely on the business entity, not on its owners. This transaction illustrates the entity assumption from Chapter 1.

Transaction 9. In transaction 5, Genie performed services for UPS on account. The business now collects $1,000 from UPS. We say that Genie *collects the cash on account*, which means that Genie will record an increase in Cash and a decrease in Accounts Receivable. This is not service revenue because Genie already recorded the revenue in transaction 5. The effect of collecting cash on account is as follows:

	Assets							Liabilities	+	Stockholders' Equity		
	Cash	+	Accounts Receivable	+	Supplies	+	Land	Accounts Payable	+	Common Stock	+	Retained Earnings
Bal	12,400		3,000		3,700		40,000	= 1,800		50,000		7,300
(9)	+ 1,000		− 1,000									
Bal	13,400		2,000		3,700		40,000	1,800		50,000		7,300
			59,100							59,100		

Transaction 10. Genie sells some land for $22,000, which is the same amount that Genie paid for the land. Genie receives $22,000 cash, and the effect on the accounting equation is as follows:

	Assets						Liabilities	+	Stockholders' Equity		
	Cash	+	Accounts Receivable	+	Supplies	+	Land		Accounts Payable	+	Common Stock	+	Retained Earnings
Bal	13,400		2,000		3,700		40,000	=	1,800		50,000		7,300
(10)	+ 22,000						− 22,000						
Bal	35,400		2,000		3,700		18,000		1,800		50,000		7,300
				59,100							59,100		

Note that the company did not sell all its land; Genie still owns $18,000 worth of land.

Transaction 11. Genie Car Wash declares a dividend and pays the stockholders $2,100 cash. The effect on the accounting equation is as follows:

	Assets					Liabilities	+	Stockholders' Equity			Type of Stockholders' Equity Transaction
	Cash +	Accounts Receivable +	Supplies +	Land		Accounts Payable	+	Common Stock	+	Retained Earnings	
Bal	35,400	2,000	3,700	18,000	=	1,800		50,000		7,300	
(11)	− 2,100									− 2,100	Dividends
Bal	33,300	2,000	3,700	18,000		1,800		50,000		5,200	
		57,000						57,000			

The dividend decreases both the Cash and the Retained Earnings of the business. *However, dividends are not an expense.*

Transactions and Financial Statements

Exhibit 2-1 summarizes the 11 preceding transactions. Panel A gives the details of the transactions, and Panel B shows the transaction analysis. As you study the exhibit, note that every transaction maintains the equality:

$$\text{Assets} = \text{Liabilities} + \text{Stockholders' Equity}$$

Exhibit 2-1 provides the data for Genie Car Wash's financial statements:

EXHIBIT 2-1 | Transaction Analysis: Genie Car Wash, Inc.

PANEL A—Transaction Details

(1) Received $50,000 cash and issued stock to the owners
(2) Paid $40,000 cash for land
(3) Bought $3,700 of supplies on account
(4) Received $7,000 cash from customers for service revenue earned
(5) Performed services for a customer on account, $3,000
(6) Paid cash expenses: rent, $1,100; employee salary, $1,200; utilities, $400

(7) Paid $1,900 on the account payable created in transaction 3
(8) Major stockholder paid personal funds to remodel home, *not* a transaction of the business
(9) Received $1,000 on account
(10) Sold land for cash at the land's cost of $22,000
(11) Declared and paid a dividend of $2,100 to the stockholders

PANEL B—Transaction Analysis

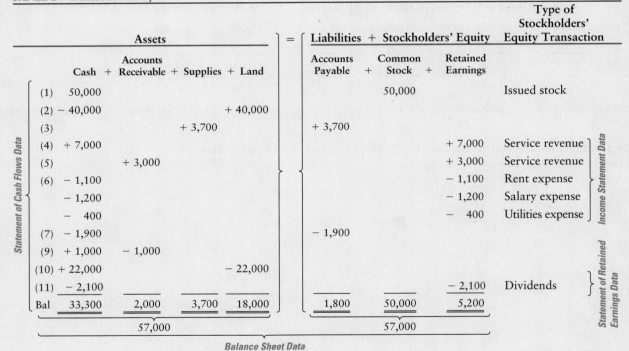

		Assets			=	Liabilities	+	Stockholders' Equity		Type of Stockholders' Equity Transaction
	Cash +	Accounts Receivable +	Supplies +	Land		Accounts Payable +	Common Stock +	Retained Earnings		
(1)	50,000						50,000			Issued stock
(2)	− 40,000			+ 40,000						
(3)			+ 3,700			+ 3,700				
(4)	+ 7,000							+ 7,000		Service revenue
(5)		+ 3,000						+ 3,000		Service revenue
(6)	− 1,100							− 1,100		Rent expense
	− 1,200							− 1,200		Salary expense
	− 400							− 400		Utilities expense
(7)	− 1,900					− 1,900				
(9)	+ 1,000	− 1,000								
(10)	+ 22,000			− 22,000						
(11)	− 2,100							− 2,100		Dividends
Bal	33,300	2,000	3,700	18,000		1,800	50,000	5,200		

Statement of Cash Flows Data

57,000

57,000

Income Statement Data

Statement of Retained Earnings Data

Balance Sheet Data

- *Income statement* data appear as revenues and expenses under Retained Earnings. The revenues increase retained earnings; the expenses decrease retained earnings.
- The *balance sheet* data are composed of the ending balances of the assets, liabilities, and stockholders' equities shown at the bottom of the exhibit. The accounting equation shows that total assets ($57,000) equal total liabilities plus stockholders' equity ($57,000).
- The *statement of retained earnings* repeats net income (or net loss) from the income statement. Dividends are subtracted. Ending retained earnings is the final result.
- Data for the *statement of cash flows* are aligned under the Cash account. Cash receipts increase cash, and cash payments decrease cash.

Exhibit 2-2 shows the Genie Car Wash financial statements at the end of April, the company's first month of operations. Follow the flow of data to observe the following:

1. The income statement reports revenues, expenses, and either a net income or a net loss for the period. During April, Genie earned net income of $7,300. Compare Genie's income statement with that of Apple, Inc., at the beginning of the chapter. The income statement includes only two types of accounts: revenues and expenses.

2. The statement of retained earnings starts with the beginning balance of retained earnings (zero for a new business). Add net income for the period (arrow ①), subtract dividends, and compute the ending balance of retained earnings ($5,200).

3. The balance sheet lists the assets, liabilities, and stockholders' equity of the business at the end of the period. Included in stockholders' equity is retained earnings, which comes from the statement of retained earnings (arrow ②).

EXHIBIT 2-2 | Financial Statements of Genie Car Wash, Inc.

Genie Car Wash, Inc.
Income Statement
Month Ended April 30, 2012

Revenues		
Service revenue ($7,000 + $3,000)		$10,000
Expenses		
Salary expense	$1,200	
Rent expense	1,100	
Utilities expense	400	
Total expenses		2,700
Net income		$ 7,300

Genie Car Wash, Inc.
Statement of Retained Earnings
Month Ended April 30, 2012

Retained earnings, April 1, 2012	$ 0
Add: Net income for the month	7,300
	7,300
Less: Dividends	(2,100)
Retained earnings, April 30, 2012	$ 5,200

①

Genie Car Wash, Inc.
Balance Sheet
April 30, 2012

Assets		Liabilities	
Cash	$33,300	Accounts payable	$ 1,800
Accounts receivable	2,000	**Stockholders' Equity**	
Supplies	3,700	Common stock	50,000
Land	18,000	Retained earnings	5,200
		Total stockholders' equity	55,200
		Total liabilities and	
Total assets	$57,000	stockholders' equity	$57,000

②

Let's put into practice what you have learned thus far.

MID-CHAPTER SUMMARY PROBLEM

Shelly Herzog opens a research service near a college campus. She names the corporation Herzog Researchers, Inc. During the first month of operations, July 2012, the business engages in the following transactions:

a. Herzog Researchers, Inc., issues its common stock to Shelly Herzog, who invests $25,000 to open the business.

b. The company purchases on account office supplies costing $350.

c. Herzog Researchers pays cash of $20,000 to acquire a lot next to the campus. The company intends to use the land as a building site for a business office.

d. Herzog Researchers performs research for clients and receives cash of $1,900.

e. Herzog Researchers pays $100 on the account payable that it created in transaction b.

f. Herzog pays $2,000 of personal funds for a vacation.

g. Herzog Researchers pays cash expenses for office rent ($400) and utilities ($100).

h. The business sells a small parcel of the land for its cost of $5,000.

i. The business declares and pays a cash dividend of $1,200.

▶ Requirements

1. Analyze the preceding transactions in terms of their effects on the accounting equation of Herzog Researchers, Inc. Use Exhibit 2-1, Panel B as a guide.

2. Prepare the income statement, statement of retained earnings, and balance sheet of Herzog Researchers, Inc., after recording the transactions. Draw arrows linking the statements.

▶ Answers

Requirement 1

PANEL B—Analysis of Transactions

	Cash	+	Office Supplies	+	Land	=	Accounts Payable	+	Common Stock	+	Retained Earnings	Type of Stockholders' Equity Transaction
(a)	+ 25,000								+ 25,000			Issued stock
(b)			+ 350				+ 350					
(c)	− 20,000				+ 20,000							
(d)	+ 1,900										+ 1,900	Service revenue
(e)	− 100						− 100					
(f)	Not a transaction of the business											
(g)	− 400										− 400	Rent expense
	− 100										− 100	Utilities expense
(h)	+ 5,000				− 5,000							
(i)	− 1,200										− 1,200	Dividends
Bal	10,100		350		15,000		250		25,000		200	
			25,450						25,450			

Requirement 2

Herzog Researchers, Inc.
Income Statement
Month Ended July 31, 2012

Revenues			
Service revenue			$1,900
Expenses			
Rent expense		$400	
Utilities expense		100	
Total expenses			500
Net income			$1,400

Herzog Researchers, Inc.
Statement of Retained Earnings
Month Ended July 31, 2012

Retained earnings, July 1, 2012		$ 0
Add: Net income for the month		1,400
		1,400
Less: Dividends		(1,200)
Retained earnings, July 31, 2012		$ 200

Herzog Researchers, Inc.
Balance Sheet
July 31, 2012

Assets		Liabilities	
Cash	$10,100	Accounts payable	$ 250
Office supplies	350	**Stockholders' Equity**	
Land	15,000	Common stock	25,000
		Retained earnings	200
		Total stockholders' equity	25,200
		Total liabilities and	
Total assets	$25,450	stockholders' equity	$25,450

The analysis in the first half of this chapter can be used, but it is cumbersome. Apple, Inc., has hundreds of accounts and millions of transactions. The spreadsheet to account for Apple's transactions would be huge! In the second half of this chapter we discuss double-entry accounting as it is actually used in business.

Analyze the Impact of Business Transactions on Accounts

All business transactions include two parts:

► You give something.
► You receive something in return.

Accounting is, therefore, based on a double-entry system, which records the *dual effects* on the entity. *Each transaction affects at least two accounts.* For example, Genie Car Wash's receipt of $50,000 cash and issuance of stock increased both Cash and Common Stock. It would be incomplete to record only the increase in Cash or only the increase in Common Stock.

The T-Account

An account can be represented by the letter T. We call this a *T-account*. The vertical line in the letter divides the account into its two sides: left and right. The account title appears at the top of the T. For example, the Cash account can appear as follows:

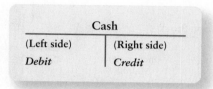

The left side of each account is called the **debit** side, and the right side is called the **credit** side. Often, students are confused by the words *debit* and *credit*. To become comfortable using these terms, remember that for every account

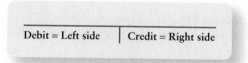

Every business transaction involves both a debit and a credit. You should remember that *debit* means "left-hand side" and *credit* means "right-hand side."

Increases and Decreases in the Accounts: The Rules of Debit and Credit

The type of account determines how we record increases and decreases. *The rules of debit and credit follow* in Exhibit 2-3.

► Increases in *assets* are recorded on the left (debit) side of the account. Decreases in *assets* are recorded on the right (credit) side. You receive cash and debit the Cash account. You pay cash and credit the Cash account.

► Conversely, increases in *liabilities* and *stockholders' equity* are recorded by credits. Decreases in *liabilities* and *stockholders' equity* are recorded by debits.

EXHIBIT 2-3 | Accounting Equation and the Rules of Debit and Credit

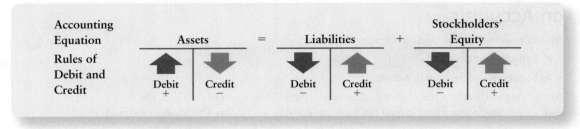

To illustrate the ideas diagrammed in Exhibit 2-3 let's review the first transaction. Genie Car Wash received $50,000 and issued (gave) stock. Which accounts are affected? The Cash account and the Common Stock account will hold these amounts:

EXHIBIT 2-4 | The Accounting Equation After Genie Car Wash's First Transaction

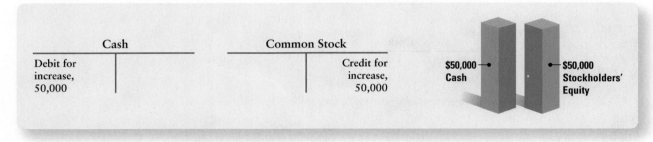

The amount remaining in an account is called its *balance*. This first transaction gives Cash a $50,000 debit balance and Common Stock a $50,000 credit balance. Exhibit 2-4 shows this relationship.

Genie's second transaction is a $40,000 cash purchase of land. This transaction decreases Cash with a credit and increases Land with a debit, as shown in the following T-accounts (focus on Cash and Land):

	Cash			Common Stock	
Bal	50,000	Credit for decrease, 40,000		Bal	50,000
Bal	10,000				

Land	
Debit for increase, 40,000	
Bal	40,000

After this transaction, Cash has a $10,000 debit balance, Land has a debit balance of $40,000, and Common Stock has a $50,000 credit balance, as shown in Exhibit 2-5.

EXHIBIT 2-5 | The Accounting Equation After Genie Car Wash's First Two Transactions

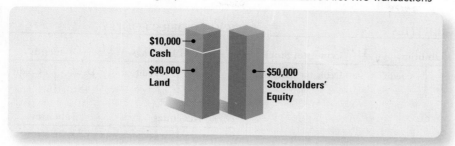

Additional Stockholders' Equity Accounts: Revenues and Expenses

Stockholders' equity also includes the two categories of income statement accounts, Revenues and Expenses:

▶ *Revenues* are increases in stockholders' equity that result from delivering goods or services to customers.

▶ *Expenses* are decreases in stockholders' equity due to the cost of operating the business.

Therefore, the accounting equation may be expanded as shown in Exhibit 2-6. Revenues and expenses appear in parentheses because their net effect—revenues minus expenses—equals net income, which increases stockholders' equity. If expenses exceed revenues, there is a net loss, which decreases stockholders' equity.

We can now express the final form of the rules of debit and credit, as shown in Exhibit 2-7. *You should not proceed until you have learned these rules.* For example, you must remember that

▶ a debit increases an asset account.

▶ a credit decreases an asset account.

EXHIBIT 2-6 | Expansion of the Accounting Equation

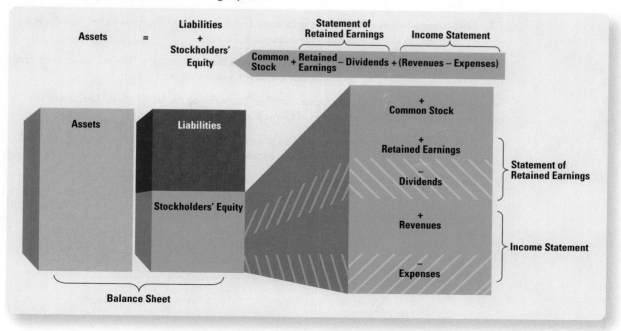

EXHIBIT 2-7 | Final Form of the Rules of Debit and Credit

ASSETS	=	LIABILITIES	+	STOCKHOLDERS' EQUITY

Assets		Liabilities		Common Stock		Retained Earnings		Dividends	
Debit	Credit	Debit	Credit	Debit	Credit	Debit	Credit	Debit	Credit
+	−	−	+	−	+	−	+	+	−

						Revenues		Expenses	
						Debit	Credit	Debit	Credit
						−	+	+	−

Liabilities and stockholders' equity are the opposite.

> ▶ A credit increases a liability or stockholders' equity account.
>
> ▶ A debit decreases a liability or stockholders' equity account.

Dividends and Expense accounts are exceptions to the rule. Dividends and Expenses are equity accounts that are increased by a debit. Dividends and Expense accounts are negative (or *contra*) equity accounts.

Revenues and Expenses are often treated as separate account categories because they appear on the income statement. Exhibit 2-7 shows Revenues and Expenses below the other equity accounts.

Record (Journalize and Post) Transactions in the Books

⑤

Record (journalize and post) transactions in the books

Accountants use a chronological record of transactions called a **journal**, also known as the *book of original entry*. The journalizing process follows three steps:

1. Specify each account affected by the transaction and classify each account by type (asset, liability, stockholders' equity, revenue, or expense).

2. Determine whether each account is increased or decreased by the transaction. Use the rules of debit and credit to increase or decrease each account.

3. Record the transaction in the journal, including a brief explanation. The debit side is entered on the left margin, and the credit side is indented to the right.

Step 3 is also called "booking the journal entry" or "journalizing the transaction." Let's apply the steps to journalize the first transaction of Genie Car Wash.

> **Step 1** The business receives cash and issues stock. Cash and Common Stock are affected. Cash is an asset, and Common Stock is equity.
>
> **Step 2** Both Cash and Common Stock increase. Debit Cash to record an increase in this asset. Credit Common Stock to record an increase in this equity account.
>
> **Step 3** Journalize the transaction as follows:

JOURNAL

Date	Accounts and Explanation	Debit	Credit
Apr 2	Cash	50,000	
	Common Stock		50,000
	Issued common stock.		

When analyzing a transaction, first pinpoint the effects (if any) on cash. Did cash increase or decrease? Typically, it is easiest to identify cash effects. Then identify the effects on the other accounts.

EXHIBIT 2-8 | The Ledger (Asset, Liability, and Stockholders' Equity Accounts)

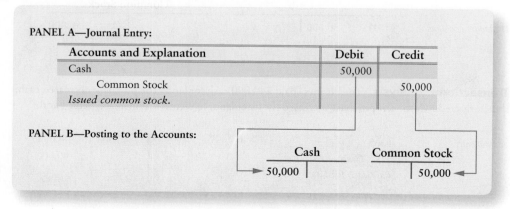

Copying Information (Posting) from the Journal to the Ledger

The journal is a chronological record of all company transactions listed by date. But the journal does not indicate how much cash or accounts receivable the business has.

The **ledger** is a grouping of all the T-accounts, with their balances. For example, the balance of the Cash T-account shows how much cash the business has. The balance of Accounts Receivable shows the amount due from customers. Accounts Payable shows how much the business owes suppliers on open account, and so on.

In the phrase "keeping the books," *books* refers to the journals as well as the accounts in the ledger. In most accounting systems, the ledger is computerized. Exhibit 2-8 shows how the asset, liability, and stockholders' equity accounts are grouped in the ledger.

Entering a transaction in the journal does not get the data into the ledger. Data must be copied to the ledger—a process called **posting**. Debits in the journal are always posted as debits in the accounts, and likewise for credits. Exhibit 2-9 shows how Genie Car Wash's stock issuance transaction is posted to the accounts.

EXHIBIT 2-9 | Journal Entry and Posting to the Accounts

PANEL A—Journal Entry:

Accounts and Explanation	Debit	Credit
Cash	50,000	
Common Stock		50,000
Issued common stock.		

PANEL B—Posting to the Accounts:

Cash		Common Stock	
50,000			50,000

EXHIBIT 2-10 | Flow of Accounting Data

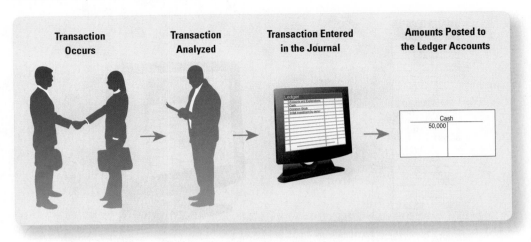

The Flow of Accounting Data

Exhibit 2-10 summarizes the flow of accounting data from the business transaction to the ledger. Let's continue the example of Genie Car Wash, Inc., and account for the same 11 transactions we illustrated earlier. Here we use the journal and the accounts. Each journal entry posted to the accounts is keyed by date or by transaction number. This linking allows you to locate any information you may need.

Transaction 1 Analysis. Genie Car Wash, Inc., received $50,000 cash from the stockholders and in turn issued common stock to them. The journal entry, accounting equation, and ledger accounts follow.

Journal entry	Cash	50,000	
	Common Stock		50,000
	Issued common stock.		

	Assets	=	Liabilities	+	Stockholders' Equity
Accounting equation	50,000	=	0	+	50,000

	Cash		Common Stock	
The ledger accounts	(1) 50,000		(1) 50,000	

Transaction 2 Analysis. The business paid $40,000 cash for land. The purchase decreased cash; therefore, credit Cash. The purchase increased the asset land; to record this increase, debit Land.

Journal entry	Land	40,000	
	Cash		40,000
	Paid cash for land.		

Accounting equation	Assets	=	Liabilities	+	Stockholders' Equity
	+ 40,000 − 40,000	=	0	+	0

The ledger accounts	Cash			Land	
	(1) 50,000	(2) 40,000	(2) 40,000		

Transaction 3 Analysis.
The business purchased supplies for $3,700 on account payable. The purchase increased Supplies, an asset, and Accounts Payable, a liability.

Journal entry			
Supplies		3,700	
Accounts Payable			3,700
Purchased office supplies on account.			

Accounting equation	Assets	=	Liabilities	+	Stockholders' Equity
	+ 3,700	=	+ 3,700	+	0

The ledger accounts	Supplies		Accounts Payable	
	(3) 3,700			(3) 3,700

Transaction 4 Analysis.
The business performed services for clients and received cash of $7,000. The transaction increased cash and service revenue. To record the revenue, credit Service Revenue.

Journal entry			
Cash		7,000	
Service Revenue			7,000
Performed services for cash.			

Accounting equation	Assets	=	Liabilities	+	Stockholders' Equity	+	Revenues
	+ 7,000	=	0			+	7,000

The ledger accounts	Cash		Service Revenue	
	(1) 50,000	(2) 40,000		(4) 7,000
	(4) 7,000			

Transaction 5 Analysis. Genie performed services for UPS on account. UPS did not pay immediately, so Genie billed UPS for $3,000. The transaction increased accounts receivable; therefore, debit Accounts Receivable. Service revenue also increased, so credit the Service Revenue account.

Journal entry

Accounts Receivable	3,000	
Service Revenue		3,000
Performed services on account.		

Accounting equation

Assets	=	Liabilities	+	Stockholders' Equity	+	Revenues
+ 3,000	=	0			+	3,000

The ledger accounts

Accounts Receivable		Service Revenue	
(5) 3,000		(4) 7,000	
		(5) 3,000	

Transaction 6 Analysis. The business paid $2,700 for the following expenses: equipment rent, $1,100; employee salary, $1,200; and utilities, $400. Credit Cash for the sum of the expense amounts. The expenses increased, so debit each expense account separately.

Journal entry

Rent Expense	1,100	
Salary Expense	1,200	
Utilities Expense	400	
Cash		2,700
Paid expenses.		

Accounting equation

Assets	=	Liabilities	+	Stockholders' Equity	−	Expenses
− 2,700	=	0			−	2,700

The ledger accounts

Cash			Rent Expense	
(1) 50,000	(2) 40,000	(6) 1,100	
(4) 7,000	(6) 2,700		

Salary Expense		Utilities Expense	
(6) 1,200		(6) 400	

Transaction 7 Analysis. The business paid $1,900 on the account payable created in transaction 3. Credit Cash for the payment. The payment decreased a liability, so debit Accounts Payable.

Journal entry	Accounts Payable		1,900	
	Cash			1,900
	Paid cash on account.			

	Assets	=	Liabilities	+	Stockholders' Equity
Accounting equation	− 1,900	=	− 1,900	+	0

The ledger accounts

	Cash					Accounts Payable		
(1)	50,000	(2)	40,000	(7)	1,900	(3)		3,700
(4)	7,000	(6)	2,700					
		(7)	1,900					

Transaction 8 Analysis. Kyle Nielson, the major stockholder of Genie Car Wash, remodeled his personal residence. This is not a transaction of the car-wash business, so the business does not record the transaction.

Transaction 9 Analysis. The business collected $1,000 cash on account from the client in transaction 5. Cash increased, so debit Cash. The asset accounts receivable decreased; therefore, credit Accounts Receivable.

Journal entry	Cash		1,000	
	Accounts Receivable			1,000
	Collected cash on account.			

	Assets	=	Liabilities	+	Stockholders' Equity
Accounting equation	+ 1,000	=	0	+	0
	− 1,000				

The ledger accounts

	Cash					Accounts Receivable		
(1)	50,000	(2)	40,000	(5)	3,000	(9)		1,000
(4)	7,000	(6)	2,700					
(9)	1,000	(7)	1,900					

Transaction 10 Analysis. The business sold land for its cost of $22,000, receiving cash. The asset cash increased; debit Cash. The asset land decreased; credit Land.

Journal entry	Cash	22,000	
	Land		22,000
	Sold land.		

Accounting equation

Assets	=	Liabilities	+	Stockholders' Equity
+ 22,000	=	0	+	0
− 22,000				

The ledger accounts

	Cash					Land		
(1)	50,000	(2)	40,000	(2)	40,000	(10)	22,000
(4)	7,000	(6)	2,700				
(9)	1,000	(7)	1,900				
(10)	22,000						

Transaction 11 Analysis. Genie Car Wash paid its stockholders cash dividends of $2,100. Credit Cash for the payment. The transaction also decreased stockholders' equity and requires a debit to an equity account. Therefore, debit Dividends.

Journal entry	Dividends	2,100	
	Cash		2,100
	Declared and paid dividends.		

Accounting equation

Assets	=	Liabilities	+	Stockholders' Equity	−	Dividends
− 2,100	=	0			−	2,100

The ledger accounts

	Cash					Dividends	
(1)	50,000	(2)	40,000	(11)	2,100	
(4)	7,000	(6)	2,700			
(9)	1,000	(7)	1,900			
(10)	22,000	(11)	2,100			

MyAccountingLab
ACT
Accounting Cycle Tutorial Application 1 — Xpert Drving School

MyAccountingLab
ACT
Accounting Cycle Tutorial Application 2 — Small Business Services

Accounts After Posting to the Ledger

Exhibit 2-11 shows the accounts after all transactions have been posted to the ledger. Group the accounts under assets, liabilities, and equity.

Each account has a balance, denoted as Bal, which is the difference between the account's total debits and its total credits. For example, the Accounts Payable's balance of $1,800 is the difference between the credit ($3,700) and the debit ($1,900). Cash has a debit balance of $33,300.

A horizontal line separates the transaction amounts from the account balance. If an account's debits exceed its total credits, that account has a debit balance, as for Cash. If the sum of the credits is greater, the account has a credit balance, as for Accounts Payable.

EXHIBIT 2-11 | Genie Car Wash's Ledger Accounts After Posting

| Assets | = | Liabilities | + | Stockholders' Equity |

Cash

(1)	50,000	(2)	40,000
(4)	7,000	(6)	2,700
(9)	1,000	(7)	1,900
(10)	22,000	(11)	2,100
Bal	33,300		

Accounts Receivable

| (5) | 3,000 | (9) | 1,000 |
| Bal | 2,000 | | |

Supplies

| (3) | 3,700 | | |
| Bal | 3,700 | | |

Land

| (2) | 40,000 | (10) | 22,000 |
| Bal | 18,000 | | |

Accounts Payable

| (7) | 1,900 | (3) | 3,700 |
| | | Bal | 1,800 |

Common Stock

| | | (1) | 50,000 |
| | | Bal | 50,000 |

Revenue

Service Revenue

		(4)	7,000
		(5)	3,000
		Bal	10,000

Dividends

| (11) | 2,100 | | |
| Bal | 2,100 | | |

Expenses

Rent Expense

| (6) | 1,100 | | |
| Bal | 1,100 | | |

Salary Expense

| (6) | 1,200 | | |
| Bal | 1,200 | | |

Utilities Expense

| (6) | 400 | | |
| Bal | 400 | | |

Construct and Use a Trial Balance

A **trial balance** lists all accounts with their balances—assets first, then liabilities and stockholders' equity. The trial balance summarizes all the account balances for the financial statements and *shows whether total debits equal total credits*. A trial balance may be taken at any time, but the most common time is at the end of the period. Exhibit 2-12 is the trial balance of Genie Car Wash, Inc., after all transactions have been journalized and posted at the end of April.

The trial balance *facilitates the preparation of the financial statements*. It is possible to prepare an income statement, statement of retained earnings, and balance sheet from the data shown in a trial balance such as the one in Exhibit 2-12. For Genie Car Wash, Inc., the financial statements would

6

Construct and **use** a trial balance

Accounting Cycle Tutorial Glossary

Accounting Cycle Tutorial Glossary Quiz

EXHIBIT 2-12 | Trial Balance

Genie Car Wash, Inc.
Trial Balance
April 30, 2012

Account Title	Balance Debit	Balance Credit
Cash	$33,300	
Accounts receivable	2,000	
Supplies	3,700	
Land	18,000	
Accounts payable		$ 1,800
Common stock		50,000
Dividends	2,100	
Service revenue		10,000
Rent expense	1,100	
Salary expense	1,200	
Utilities expense	400	
Total	$61,800	$61,800

appear exactly as shown in Exhibit 2-2 on page 70. However, the financial statements are normally not constructed at this point, because they do not yet contain end-of-period adjustments, which are covered in Chapter 3.

Analyzing Accounts

You can often tell what a company did by analyzing its accounts. This is a powerful tool for a manager who knows accounting. For example, if you know the beginning and ending balance of Cash, and if you know total cash receipts, you can compute your total cash payments during the period.

In our chapter example, suppose Genie Car Wash began May with cash of $1,000. During May Genie received cash of $8,000 and ended the month with a cash balance of $3,000. You can compute total cash payments by analyzing Genie's Cash account as follows:

Cash			
Beginning balance	1,000		
Cash receipts	8,000	Cash payments	$x = 6,000$
Ending balance	3,000		

Or, if you know Cash's beginning and ending balances and total payments, you can compute cash receipts during the period—for any company!

You can compute either sales on account or cash collections on account by analyzing the Accounts Receivable account as follows (using assumed amounts):

Accounts Receivable			
Beginning balance	6,000		
Sales on account	10,000	Collections on account	11,000
Ending balance	5,000		

Also, you can determine how much you paid on account by analyzing Accounts Payable as follows (using assumed amounts):

Accounts Payable			
		Beginning balance	9,000
Payments on account	4,000	Purchases on account	6,000
		Ending balance	11,000

Please master this powerful technique. It works for any company and for your own personal finances! You will find this tool very helpful when you become a manager.

Correcting Accounting Errors

Accounting errors can occur even in computerized systems. Input data may be wrong, or they may be entered twice or not at all. A debit may be entered as a credit, and vice versa. You can detect the reason or reasons behind many out-of-balance conditions by computing the difference between total debits and total credits. Then perform one or more of the following actions:

1. Search the records for a missing account. Trace each account back and forth from the journal to the ledger. A $200 transaction may have been recorded incorrectly in the journal or posted incorrectly to the ledger. Search the journal for a $200 transaction.

2. Divide the out-of-balance amount by 2. A debit treated as a credit, or vice versa, doubles the amount of error. Suppose Genie Car Wash added $300 to Cash instead of subtracting $300. The out-of-balance amount is $600, and dividing by 2 identifies $300 as the amount of the transaction. Search the journal for the $300 transaction and trace to the account affected.

3. Divide the out-of-balance amount by 9. If the result is an integer (no decimals), the error may be a

   ▸ *slide* (writing $400 as $40). The accounts would be out of balance by $360 ($400 − $40 = $360). Dividing $360 by 9 yields $40. Scan the trial balance in Exhibit 2-12 for an amount similar to $40. Utilities Expense (balance of $400) is the misstated account.
   ▸ *transposition* (writing $2,100 as $1,200). The accounts would be out of balance by $900 ($2,100 − $1,200 = $900). Dividing $900 by 9 yields $100. Trace all amounts on the trial balance back to the T-accounts. Dividends (balance of $2,100) is the misstated account.

Chart of Accounts

As you know, the ledger contains the accounts grouped under these headings:

1. **Balance sheet accounts: Assets, Liabilities, and Stockholders' Equity**

2. **Income statement accounts: Revenues and Expenses**

Organizations use a **chart of accounts** to list all their accounts and account numbers. Account numbers usually have two or more digits. Asset account numbers may begin with 1, liabilities with 2, stockholders' equity with 3, revenues with 4, and expenses with 5. The second, third, and higher digits in an account number indicate the position of the individual account within the category. For example, Cash may be account number 101, which is the first asset account. Accounts Payable may be number 201, the first liability. All accounts are numbered by using this system.

Organizations with many accounts use lengthy account numbers. For example, the chart of accounts of Apple, Inc., may use five-digit account numbers. The chart of accounts for Genie Car Wash appears in Exhibit 2-13. The gap between account numbers 111 and 141 leaves room to add another category of receivables, for example, Notes Receivable, which may be numbered 121.

Appendix C to this book gives two expanded charts of accounts that you will find helpful as you work through this course. The first chart lists the typical accounts that a *service* corporation, such as Genie Car Wash, would have after a period of growth. The second chart is for a *merchandising* corporation, one that sells a product instead of a service.

EXHIBIT 2-13 | Chart of Accounts—Genie Car Wash, Inc.

Balance Sheet Accounts		
Assets	**Liabilities**	**Stockholders' Equity**
101 Cash	201 Accounts Payable	301 Common Stock
111 Accounts Receivable	231 Notes Payable	311 Dividends
141 Office Supplies		312 Retained Earnings
151 Office Furniture		
191 Land		

	Income Statement Accounts (Part of Stockholders' Equity)	
	Revenues	**Expenses**
	401 Service Revenue	501 Rent Expense
		502 Salary Expense
		503 Utilities Expense

EXHIBIT 2-14 | Normal Balances of the Accounts

Assets	Debit	
Liabilities		Credit
Stockholders' Equity—overall		Credit
Common stock....................................		Credit
Retained earnings.............................		Credit
Dividends...	Debit	
Revenues..		Credit
Expenses	Debit	

The Normal Balance of an Account

An account's *normal balance* falls on the side of the account—debit or credit—where increases are recorded. The normal balance of assets is on the debit side, so assets are *debit-balance accounts*. Conversely, liabilities and stockholders' equity usually have a credit balance, so these are *credit-balance accounts*. Exhibit 2-14 illustrates the normal balances of all the assets, liabilities, and stockholders' equities, including revenues and expenses.

As explained earlier, stockholders' equity usually contains several accounts. Dividends and expenses carry debit balances because they represent decreases in stockholders' equity. In total, the equity accounts show a normal credit balance.

Account Formats

So far we have illustrated accounts in a two-column T-account format, with the debit column on the left and the credit column on the right. Another format has four *amount* columns, as illustrated for the Cash account in Exhibit 2-15. The first pair of amount columns are for the debit and credit amounts of individual transactions. The last two columns are for the account balance. This four-column format keeps a running balance in the two right columns.

Analyzing Transactions Using Only T-Accounts

Businesspeople must often make decisions without the benefit of a complete accounting system. For example, the managers of Apple, Inc., may consider borrowing $100,000 to buy equipment. To see how the two transactions [(a) borrowing cash and (b) buying equipment] affect Apple, the manager can go directly to T-accounts, as follows:

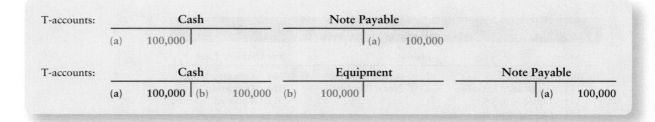

EXHIBIT 2-15 | Account in Four-Column Format

Account: Cash					Account No. 101
				Balance	
Date	Item	Debit	Credit	Debit	Credit
2012					
Apr 2		50,000		50,000	
3			40,000	10,000	

This informal analysis shows immediately that Apple will add $100,000 of equipment and a $100,000 note payable. Assuming that Apple began with zero balances, the equipment and note payable transactions would result in the following balance sheet (date assumed for illustration only):

Apple, Inc. Balance Sheet September 12, 2012			
Assets		**Liabilities**	
Cash	$ 0	Note payable	$100,000
Equipment	100,000		
		Stockholders' Equity	0
		Total liabilities and	
Total assets	$100,000	stockholders' equity	$100,000

Companies don't actually keep records in this shortcut fashion. But a decision maker who needs information quickly may not have time to journalize, post to the accounts, take a trial balance, and prepare the financial statements. A manager who knows accounting can analyze the transaction and make the decision quickly.

Now apply what you've learned. Study the Decision Guidelines, which summarize the chapter.

MyAccountingLab
ACT

**Accounting Cycle
Tutorial Application
Constanza Architect**

DECISION GUIDELINES

HOW TO MEASURE RESULTS OF OPERATIONS AND FINANCIAL POSITION

Any entrepreneur must determine whether the venture is profitable. To do this, he or she needs to know its results of operations and financial position. If Steve Jobs, who founded Apple, Inc., wants to know whether the business is making money, the Guidelines that follow will help him.

Decision	Guidelines
Has a transaction occurred?	If the event affects the entity's financial position and can be reliably recorded—Yes
	If either condition is absent—No
Where to record the transaction?	In the *journal*, the chronological record of transactions
How to record an increase or decrease in the following accounts?	Rules of *debit* and *credit*:

	Increase	Decrease
Assets	Debit	Credit
Liabilities	Credit	Debit
Stockholders' equity	Credit	Debit
Revenues	Credit	Debit
Expenses	Debit	Credit

Decision	Guidelines
Where to store all the information for each account?	In the *ledger*, the book of accounts
Where to list all the accounts and their balances?	In the *trial* balance
Where to report the following: results of operations?	In the income statement (Revenues − Expenses = Net income or net loss)
financial position?	In the balance sheet (Assets = Liabilities + Stockholders' equity)

ND-OF-CHAPTER END-OF CHAP

END-OF-CHAPTER SUMMARY PROBLEM

The trial balance of Magee Service Center, Inc., on March 1, 2012, lists the entity's assets, liabilities, and stockholders' equity on that date.

	Balance	
Account Title	Debit	Credit
Cash...	$26,000	
Accounts receivable................	4,500	
Accounts payable		$ 2,000
Common stock.......................		10,000
Retained earnings...................		18,500
Total	$30,500	$30,500

During March, the business completed the following transactions:

a. Borrowed $45,000 from the bank, with Magee signing a note payable in the name of the business.

b. Paid cash of $40,000 to a real estate company to acquire land.

c. Performed service for a customer and received cash of $5,000.

d. Purchased supplies on credit, $300.

e. Performed customer service and earned revenue on account, $2,600.

f. Paid $1,200 on account.

g. Paid the following cash expenses: salaries, $3,000; rent, $1,500; and interest, $400.

h. Received $3,100 on account.

i. Received a $200 utility bill that will be paid next week.

j. Declared and paid dividend of $1,800.

▶ Requirements

1. Open the following accounts, with the balances indicated, in the ledger of Magee Service Center, Inc. Use the T-account format.
   - Assets—Cash, $26,000; Accounts Receivable, $4,500; Supplies, no balance; Land, no balance
   - Liabilities—Accounts Payable, $2,000; Note Payable, no balance
   - Stockholders' Equity—Common Stock, $10,000; Retained Earnings, $18,500; Dividends, no balance
   - Revenues—Service Revenue, no balance
   - Expenses—(none have balances) Salary Expense, Rent Expense, Interest Expense, Utilities Expense

2. Journalize the preceding transactions. Key journal entries by transaction letter.

3. Post to the ledger and show the balance in each account after all the transactions have been posted.

4. Prepare the trial balance of Magee Service Center, Inc., at March 31, 2012.

5. To determine the net income or net loss of the entity during the month of March, prepare the income statement for the month ended March 31, 2012. List expenses in order from the largest to the smallest.

▶ Answers

Requirement 1

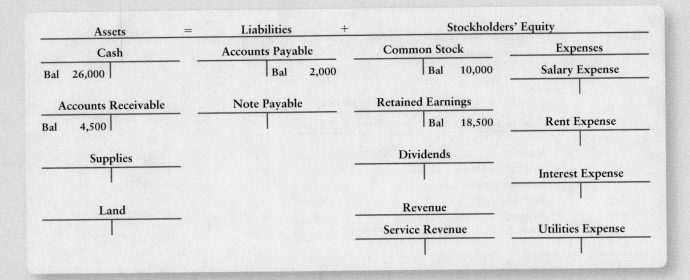

Requirement 2

Accounts and Explanation	Debit	Credit	Accounts and Explanation	Debit	Credit
a. Cash..	45,000		g. Salary Expense	3,000	
Note Payable		45,000	Rent Expense	1,500	
Borrowed cash on note payable.			Interest Expense	400	
b. Land..	40,000		Cash		4,900
Cash		40,000	Paid cash expenses.		
Purchased land for cash.			h. Cash...	3,100	
c. Cash..	5,000		Accounts Receivable		3,100
Service Revenue		5,000	Received on account.		
Performed service and received cash.			i. Utilities Expense...........................	200	
d. Supplies....................................	300		Accounts Payable....................		200
Accounts Payable................		300	Received utility bill.		
Purchased supplies on account.			j. Dividends.....................................	1,800	
e. Accounts Receivable..................	2,600		Cash		1,800
Service Revenue		2,600	Declared and paid dividends.		
Performed service on account.					
f. Accounts Payable	1,200				
Cash		1,200			
Paid on account.					

Requirement 3

Assets	=	Liabilities	+	Stockholders' Equity

Cash

Bal	26,000	(b)	40,000
(a)	45,000	(f)	1,200
(c)	5,000	(g)	4,900
(h)	3,100	(j)	1,800
Bal	31,200		

Accounts Receivable

Bal	4,500	(h)	3,100
(e)	2,600		
Bal	4,000		

Supplies

| (d) | 300 | |
| Bal | 300 | |

Land

| (b) | 40,000 | |
| Bal | 40,000 | |

Accounts Payable

(f)	1,200	Bal	2,000
		(d)	300
		(i)	200
		Bal	1,300

Note Payable

| | | (a) | 45,000 |
| | | Bal | 45,000 |

Common Stock

| | Bal | 10,000 |

Retained Earnings

| | Bal | 18,500 |

Dividends

| (j) | 1,800 | |
| Bal | 1,800 | |

Revenue

Service Revenue

	(c)	5,000
	(e)	2,600
	Bal	7,600

Expenses

Salary Expense

| (g) | 3,000 | |
| Bal | 3,000 | |

Rent Expense

| (g) | 1,500 | |
| Bal | 1,500 | |

Interest Expense

| (g) | 400 | |
| Bal | 400 | |

Utilities Expense

| (i) | 200 | |
| Bal | 200 | |

Requirement 4

Magee Service Center, Inc.
Trial Balance
March 31, 2012

Account Title	Debit	Credit
Cash	$31,200	
Accounts receivable	4,000	
Supplies	300	
Land	40,000	
Accounts payable		$ 1,300
Notes payable		45,000
Common stock		10,000
Retained earnings		18,500
Dividends	1,800	
Service revenue		7,600
Salary expense	3,000	
Rent expense	1,500	
Interest expense	400	
Utilities expense	200	
Total	$82,400	$82,400

Requirement 5

		Magee Service Center, Inc. Income Statement Month Ended March 31, 2012		
Revenues				
Service revenue				$7,600
Expenses				
Salary expense			$3,000	
Rent expense			1,500	
Interest expense			400	
Utilities expense			200	
Total expenses				5,100
Net income				$2,500

REVIEW | Transaction Analysis

Quick Check (Answers are given on page 121.)

1. A debit entry to an account

   a. increases liabilities.

   b. increases assets.

   c. increases stockholders' equity.

   d. both a and c.

2. Which account types normally have a credit balance?

   a. Revenues

   b. Liabilities

   c. Expenses

   d. Both a and b

3. An attorney performs services of $1,100 for a client and receives $400 cash with the remainder on account. The journal entry for this transaction would

   a. debit Cash, credit Accounts Receivable, credit Service Revenue.

   b. debit Cash, debit Service Revenue, credit Accounts Receivable.

   c. debit Cash, debit Accounts Receivable, credit Service Revenue.

   d. debit Cash, credit Service Revenue.

4. Accounts Payable had a normal beginning balance of $1,000. During the period, there were debit postings of $600 and credit postings of $500. What was the ending balance?

   a. $900 debit

   b. $1,100 credit

   c. $900 credit

   d. $11,100 debit

5. The list of all accounts with their balances is the

   a. journal.

   b. trial balance.

   c. chart of accounts.

   d. balance sheet.

6. The basic summary device of accounting is the

   a. account.

   b. ledger.

   c. journal.

   d. trial balance.

7. The beginning Cash balance was $3,000. At the end of the period, the balance was $2,000. If total cash paid out during the period was $27,000, the amount of cash receipts was

   a. $22,000.
   b. $28,000.

   c. $32,000.
   d. $26,000.

8. In a double-entry accounting system,

   a. liabilities, owners' equity, and revenue accounts all have normal debit balances.
   b. a debit entry is recorded on the left side of a T-account.
   c. half of all the accounts have a normal credit balance.
   d. both a and c are correct.

9. Which accounts appear on which financial statement?

Balance sheet	Income statement
a. Receivables, land, payables	Revenues, supplies
b. Cash, revenues, land	Expenses, payables
c. Cash, receivables, payables	Revenues, expenses
d. Expenses, payables, cash	Revenues, receivables, land

10. A doctor purchases medical supplies of $640 and pays $290 cash with the remainder on account. The journal entry for this transaction would be which of the following?

    a. Supplies
      Accounts Payable
      Cash

    b. Supplies
      Cash
        Accounts Payable

    c. Supplies
      Accounts Receivable
      Cash

    d. Supplies
      Accounts Payable
      Cash

11. Which is the correct sequence for recording transactions and preparing financial statements?

    a. Ledger, trial balance, journal, financial statements
    b. Journal, ledger, trial balance, financial statements
    c. Financial statements, trial balance, ledger, journal
    d. Ledger, journal, trial balance, financial statements

12. The error of posting $500 as $50 can be detected by

    a. totaling each account's balance in the ledger.
    b. dividing the out-of-balance amount by 2.
    c. dividing the out-of-balance amount by 9.
    d. examining the chart of accounts.

Accounting Vocabulary

account (p. 61) The record of the changes that have occurred in a particular asset, liability, or stockholders' equity during a period. The basic summary device of accounting.

accrued liability (p. 62) A liability for an expense that has not yet been paid by the company.

cash (p. 61) Money and any medium of exchange that a bank accepts at face value.

chart of accounts (p. 85) List of a company's accounts and their account numbers.

credit (p. 73) The right side of an account.

debit (p. 73) The left side of an account.

journal (p. 76) The chronological accounting record of an entity's transactions.

ledger (p. 77) The book of accounts and their balances.

posting (p. 77) Copying amounts from the journal to the ledger.

transaction (p. 60) Any event that has a financial impact on the business and can be measured reliably.

trial balance (p. 83) A list of all the ledger accounts with their balances.

ASSESS YOUR PROGRESS

Short Exercises

S2-1 (*Learning Objective 2: Differentiate between different types of accounts*) Bill Hooper opened a software consulting firm that immediately paid $6,000 for a computer. Was Hooper's computer an expense of the business? If not, explain.

S2-2 (*Learning Objective 4: Analyze the impact of business transactions on accounts*) Smith Software began with cash of $11,000. Smith then bought supplies for $2,400 on account. Separately, Smith paid $5,500 for a computer. Answer these questions.
  a. How much in total assets does Smith have?
  b. How much in liabilities does Smith owe?

S2-3 (*Learning Objectives 1, 4: Explain what a transaction is; analyze the impact of business transactions on accounts*) Faith Varitek, MD, opened a medical practice. The business completed the following transactions:

Apr 1	Varitek invested $27,000 cash to start her medical practice. The business issued common stock to Varitek.
	1	Purchased medical supplies on account totaling $8,800.
	2	Paid monthly office rent of $3,500.
	3	Recorded $8,300 revenue for service rendered to patients, received cash of $2,200, and sent bills to patients for the remainder.

After these transactions, how much cash does the business have to work with? Use a T-account to show your answer.

S2-4 (*Learning Objectives 3, 4: Show the impact of business transactions on the accounting equation; analyze the impact of business transactions on accounts*) Refer to Short Exercise 2-3. Which of the transactions of Faith Varitek, MD, increased the total assets of the business? For each transaction, identify the asset that was increased.

S2-5 (*Learning Objectives 1, 3: Explain what a transaction is; show the impact of transactions on the accounting equation*) Roma Design specializes in imported clothing. During March, Roma completed a series of transactions. For each of the following items, give an example of a transaction that has the described effect on the accounting equation of Roma Design.
  a. Increase one asset and decrease another asset.
  b. Decrease an asset and decrease owners' equity.
  c. Decrease an asset and decrease a liability.
  d. Increase an asset and increase owners' equity.
  e. Increase an asset and increase a liability.

S2-6 (*Learning Objective 5: Record (journalize) transactions*) After operating for several months, architect Edmund Roberge completed the following transactions during the latter part of March:

Mar 15	Borrowed $31,000 from the bank, signing a note payable.
	22	Performed service for clients on account totaling $8,900.
	28	Received $5,600 cash on account from clients.
	29	Received a utility bill of $900, an account payable that will be paid during April.
	31	Paid monthly salary of $2,600 to employee.

Journalize the transactions of Edmund Roberge, Architect. Include an explanation with each journal entry.

S2-7 (*Learning Objectives 3, 5: Show the impact of transactions on the accounting equation; record (journalize and post) transactions in the books*) Architect Aaron Ashton purchased supplies on account for $1,700. Later Ashton paid $425 on account.

1. Journalize the two transactions on the books of Aaron Ashton, architect. Include an explanation for each transaction.
2. Open a T-account for Accounts Payable and post to Accounts Payable. Compute the balance and denote it as Bal.
3. How much does the Ashton business owe after both transactions? In which account does this amount appear?

S2-8 (*Learning Objective 5: Record (journalize and post) transactions in the books*) Tolman Unlimited performed service for a client who could not pay immediately. Tolman expected to collect the $4,700 the following month. A month later, Tolman received $3,000 cash from the client.

1. Record the two transactions on the books of Tolman Unlimited. Include an explanation for each transaction.
2. Post to these T-accounts: Cash, Accounts Receivable, and Service Revenue. Compute each account balance and denote as Bal.

S2-9 (*Learning Objective 6: Construct and use a trial balance*) Assume that Old Harbor reported the following summarized data at December 31, 2012. Accounts appear in no particular order; dollar amounts are in millions.

Other liabilities	$ 1	Revenues	$19
Cash	4	Other assets	10
Expenses	14	Accounts payable	3
Stockholders' equity	5		

Prepare the trial balance of Old Harbor at December 31, 2012. List the accounts in their proper order. How much was Old Harbor's net income or net loss?

S2-10 (*Learning Objective 6: Use a trial balance*) Darlington, Inc.'s trial balance follows.

Darlington, Inc.
Trial Balance
December 31, 2012

Account Title	Balance	
	Debit	Credit
Cash	$ 4,500	
Accounts receivable	18,000	
Supplies	2,500	
Equipment	21,000	
Land	45,000	
Accounts payable		$ 25,000
Note payable		22,000
Common stock		15,000
Retained earnings		11,000
Service revenue		53,600
Salary expense	25,000	
Rent expense	9,000	
Utilities expense	1,600	
Total	$126,600	$126,600

Compute these amounts for the business:

1. Total assets
2. Total liabilities
3. Net income or net loss during December

S2-11 (*Learning Objective 6: Use a trial balance*) Refer to Darlington, Inc.'s trial balance in Short Exercise 2-10. The purpose of this exercise is to help you learn how to correct three common accounting errors.

> **Error 1.** Slide. Suppose the trial balance lists Land as $4,500 instead of $45,000. Recompute column totals, take the difference, and divide by 9. The result is an integer (no decimals), which suggests that the error is either a transposition or a slide.
>
> **Error 2.** Transposition. Assume the trial balance lists Accounts Receivable as $81,000 instead of $18,000. Recompute column totals, take the difference, and divide by 9. The result is an integer (no decimals), which suggests that the error is either a transposition or a slide.
>
> **Error 3.** Mislabeling an item. Assume that Darlington, Inc., accidentally listed Accounts Receivable as a credit balance instead of a debit. Recompute the trial balance totals for debits and credits. Then take the difference between total debits and total credits, and divide the difference by 2. You get back to the original amount of Accounts Receivable.

S2-12 (*Learning Objective 2: Define accounting terms*) Accounting has its own vocabulary and basic relationships. Match the accounting terms at the left with the corresponding definition or meaning at the right.

_____ 1. Debit	**A.** Always an asset
_____ 2. Expense	**B.** Side of an account where increases are recorded
_____ 3. Net income	**C.** Record of transactions
_____ 4. Ledger	**D.** The cost of operating a business; a decrease in stockholder's equity
_____ 5. Posting	
_____ 6. Normal balance	**E.** Grouping of accounts
_____ 7. Payable	**F.** Copying data from the journal to the ledger
_____ 8. Journal	**G.** Revenues – Expenses
_____ 9. Receivable	**H.** Always a liability
_____ 10. Owners' equity	**I.** Left side of an account
	J. Assets – Liabilities

S2-13 (*Learning Objective 4: Analyze the impact of business transactions on accounts*) Eighth Investments, Inc., began by issuing common stock for cash of $100,000. The company immediately purchased computer equipment on account for $60,000.

1. Set up the following T-accounts of Eighth Investments, Inc.: Cash, Computer Equipment, Accounts Payable, and Common Stock.
2. Record the first two transactions of the business directly in the T-accounts without using a journal.
3. Show that total debits equal total credits.

Exercises

> All of the A and B exercises can be found within MyAccountingLab, an online homework and practice environment. Your instructor may ask you to complete these exercises using MyAccountingLab.

MyAccountingLab

Group A

E2-14A (*Learning Objectives 1, 4: Explain what a transaction is; analyze the impact of transactions on accounts*) Assume Casual Wear opened a store in San Francisco, starting with cash and common stock of $98,000. Nicole Marchildon, the store manager, then signed a note payable to purchase land for $94,000 and a building for $122,000. Marchildon also paid $58,000 for equipment and $15,000 for supplies to use in the business.

Suppose the home office of Casual Wear requires a weekly report from store managers. Write Marchildon's memo to the home office to report on her purchases. Include the store's balance sheet as the final part of your memo. Prepare a T-account to compute the balance for Cash.

E2-15A (*Learning Objective 4: Analyze the impact of business transactions on accounts*) The following selected events were experienced by either Fact Finders, Inc., a corporation, or Peter Flip, the major stockholder. State whether each event (1) increased, (2) decreased, or (3) had no effect on the total assets of the business. Identify any specific asset affected.

a. Received $8,500 cash from customers on account.
b. Flip used personal funds to purchase a flat screen TV for his home.
c. Sold land and received cash of $71,000 (the land was carried on the company's books at $71,000).
d. Borrowed $56,000 from the bank.
e. Made cash purchase of land for a building site, $93,000.
f. Received $22,000 cash and issued stock to a stockholder.
g. Paid $68,000 cash on accounts payable.
h. Purchased equipment and signed a $104,000 promissory note in payment.
i. Purchased merchandise inventory on account for $16,500.
j. The business paid Flip a cash dividend of $7,000.

E2-16A (*Learning Objective 3: Show the impact of business transactions on the accounting equation*) Bob Morin opened a medical practice specializing in surgery. During the first month of operation (August), the business, titled Bob Morin, Professional Corporation (P.C.), experienced the following events:

Aug	6	Morin invested $39,000 in the business, which in turn issued its common stock to him.
	9	The business paid cash for land costing $29,000. Morin plans to build an office building on the land.
	12	The business purchased medical supplies for $1,700 on account.
	15	Bob Morin, P.C., officially opened for business.
	15–31	During the rest of the month, Morin treated patients and earned service revenue of $7,600, receiving cash for half the revenue earned.
	15–31	The business paid cash expenses: employee salaries, $1,300; office rent, $700; utilities, $500.
	31	The business sold supplies to another physician for cost of $700.
	31	The business borrowed $12,000, signing a note payable to the bank.
	31	The business paid $800 on account.

▶ Requirements

1. Analyze the effects of these events on the accounting equation of the medical practice of Bob Morin, P.C.
2. After completing the analysis, answer these questions about the business.
   a. How much are total assets?
   b. How much does the business expect to collect from patients?
   c. How much does the business owe in total?
   d. How much of the business's assets does Morin really own?
   e. How much net income or net loss did the business experience during its first month of operations?

E2-17A (*Learning Objective 5: Record (journalize) transactions in the books*) Refer to Exercise 2-16A.

▶ Requirement

1. Record the transactions in the journal of Bob Morin, P.C. List the transactions by date and give an explanation for each transaction.

E2-18A (*Learning Objective 5: Record (journalize) transactions in the books*) Doherty Tree Cellular, Inc., completed the following transactions during April 2012, its first month of operations:

Apr	1	Received $19,800 and issued common stock.
	2	Purchased $200 of office supplies on account.
	4	Paid $14,300 cash for land to use as a building site.
	6	Performed service for customers and received cash of $2,600.
	9	Paid $100 on accounts payable.
	17	Performed service for UFax on account totaling $1,900.
	23	Collected $100 from UFax on account.
	30	Paid the following expenses: salary, $1,900; rent, $1,300.

▶ Requirement

1. Record the transactions in the journal of Doherty Tree Cellular, Inc. Key transactions by date and include an explanation for each entry.

E2-19A (*Learning Objectives 4, 5, 6: Analyze the impact of business transactions on accounts; record (post) transactions in the books; construct and use a trial balance*) Refer to Exercise 2-18A.

▶ Requirements

1. After journalizing the transactions of Exercise 2-18A, post the entries to the ledger, using T-accounts. Key transactions by date. Date the ending balance of each account April 30.
2. Prepare the trial balance of Doherty Tree Cellular, Inc., at April 30, 2012.
3. How much are total assets, total liabilities, and total stockholders' equity on April 30?

E2-20A (*Learning Objectives 1, 4, 5: Explain what a transaction is; analyze the impact of business transactions on the accounts; record (journalize) transactions*) The first seven transactions of Everett Advertising, Inc., have been posted to the company's accounts as follows:

Cash				Supplies		Equipment		Land	
(1)	9,800	(3)	4,000	(4) 400	(5) 110	(6) 5,300		(3) 32,000	
(2)	7,000	(6)	5,300						
(5)	110	(7)	150						

Accounts Payable				Note Payable		Common Stock	
(7)	150	(4)	400	(2)	7,000	(1)	9,800
				(3)	28,000		

▶ Requirement

1. Prepare the journal entries that served as the sources for the seven transactions. Include an explanation for each entry. As Everett moves into the next period, how much cash does the business have? How much does Everett owe in total liabilities?

E2-21A (*Learning Objective 6: Construct and use a trial balance*) The accounts of Deluxe Patio Service, Inc., follow with their normal balances at June 30, 2012. The accounts are listed in no particular order.

Account	Balance	Account	Balance
Common stock..................	$ 8,800	Dividends..........................	$ 5,500
Accounts payable..............	4,800	Utilities expense	1,800
Service revenue..................	22,500	Accounts receivable...........	15,300
Land...................................	29,200	Delivery expense	300
Note payable.....................	11,500	Retained earnings..............	21,600
Cash..................................	9,300	Salary expense..................	7,800

▶ Requirements

1. Prepare the company's trial balance at June 30, 2012, listing accounts in proper sequence, as illustrated in the chapter. For example, Accounts Receivable comes before Land. List the expense with the largest balance first, the expense with the next largest balance second, and so on.
2. Prepare the financial statement for the month ended June 30, 2012, that will tell the company the results of operations for the month.

E2-22A (*Learning Objective 6: Construct and use a trial balance*) The trial balance of Garvey, Inc., at September 30, 2012, does not balance:

Cash.......................................	$ 4,300	
Accounts receivable...............	12,700	
Inventory...............................	17,300	
Supplies.................................	400	
Land.......................................	51,000	
Accounts payable		$11,500
Common stock.......................		47,100
Service revenue......................		33,900
Salary expense.......................	2,000	
Rent expense.........................	1,200	
Utilities expense	1,000	
Total......................................	$89,900	$92,500

The accounting records hold the following errors:
  a. Recorded a $100 cash revenue transaction by debiting Accounts Receivable. The credit entry was correct.
  b. Posted a $1,000 credit to Accounts Payable as $100.
  c. Did not record utilities expense or the related account payable in the amount of $500.
  d. Understated Common Stock by $200.
  e. Omitted Insurance Expense of $3,700 from the trial balance.

▶ Requirement

1. Prepare the correct trial balance at September 30, 2012, complete with a heading. Journal entries are not required.

E2-23A (*Learning Objective 4: Analyze the impact of business transactions on accounts*) Set up the following T-accounts: Cash, Accounts Receivable, Office Supplies, Office Furniture, Accounts Payable, Common Stock, Dividends, Service Revenue, Salary Expense, and Rent Expense. Record the following transactions directly in the T-accounts without using a journal. Use the letters to identify the transactions.

    a. Lynn Dover opened a law firm by investing $12,500 cash and office furniture valued at $9,400. Organized as a professional corporation, the business issued common stock to Dover.

    b. Paid monthly rent of $1,100.

    c. Purchased office supplies on account, $900.

    d. Paid employees' salaries of $1,600.

    e. Paid $500 of the account payable created in Transaction c.

    f. Performed legal service on account, $8,000.

    g. Declared and paid dividends of $2,200.

E2-24A *(Learning Objective 6: Construct and use a trial balance)* Refer to Exercise 2-23A.

  1. After recording the transactions in Exercise 2-23A, and assuming they all occurred in the month of May 2012, prepare the trial balance of Lynn Dover, Attorney, at May 31, 2012. Use the T-accounts that have been prepared for the business.

  2. How well did the business perform during its first month? Compute net income (or net loss) for the month.

Group B

E2-25B *(Learning Objectives 1, 4: Explain what a transaction is; analyze the impact of transactions on accounts)* Assume M. Crue opened a store in San Francisco, starting with cash and common stock of $104,000. Sharon Saboda, the store manager, then signed a note payable to purchase land for $95,000 and a building for $125,000. Saboda also paid $55,000 for equipment and $14,000 for supplies to use in the business.

    Suppose the home office of M. Crue requires a weekly report from store managers. Write Saboda's memo to the head office to report on her purchases. Include the store's balance sheet as the final part of your memo. Prepare a T-account to compute the balance for Cash.

E2-26B *(Learning Objective 4: Analyze the impact of business transactions on accounts)* The following selected events were experienced by either Simply Sensible, Inc., a corporation, or Bill Griggs, the major stockholder. State whether each event (1) increased, (2) decreased, or (3) had no effect on the total assets of the business. Identify any specific asset affected.

    a. Received $27,000 cash and issued stock to a stockholder.

    b. Purchased equipment for $78,000 cash.

    c. Paid $16,000 cash on accounts payable.

    d. Griggs used personal funds to purchase a pool table for his home.

    e. Purchased land for a building site and signed an $87,000 promissory note to the bank.

    f. Received $19,000 cash from customers for services performed.

    g. Sold land and received a note receivable of $61,000 (the land was carried on the company's books at $61,000).

    h. Earned $30,000 in revenue for services performed. The customer promises to pay Simply Sensible in one month.

    i. Purchased supplies on account for $3,000.

    j. The business paid Griggs a cash dividend of $6,000.

E2-27B (*Learning Objective 3: Show the impact of business transactions on the accounting equation*) Gary Smith opened a medical practice specializing in surgery. During the first month of operation (July), the business, titled Gary Smith, Professional Corporation (P.C.), experienced the following events:

Jul	6	Smith invested $41,000 in the business, which in turn issued its common stock to him.
	9	The business paid cash for land costing $27,000. Smith plans to build an office building on the land.
	12	The business purchased medical supplies for $2,100 on account.
	15	Gary Smith, P.C., officially opened for business.
	15–31	During the rest of the month, Smith treated patients and earned service revenue of $8,100, receiving cash for half the revenue earned.
	15–31	The business paid cash expenses: employee salaries, $1,500; office rent, $1,100; utilities, $1,200.
	31	The business sold supplies to another physician for cost of $800.
	31	The business borrowed $19,000, signing a note payable to the bank.
	31	The business paid $1,500 on account.

► Requirements

1. Analyze the effects of these events on the accounting equation of the medical practice of Gary Smith, P.C.
2. After completing the analysis, answer these questions about the business.
   a. How much are total assets?
   b. How much does the business expect to collect from patients?
   c. How much does the business owe in total?
   d. How much of the business's assets does Smith really own?
   e. How much net income or net loss did the business experience during its first month of operations?

E2-28B (*Learning Objective 5: Record (journalize) transactions in the books*) Refer to Exercise 2-27B.

► Requirement

1. Record the transactions in the journal of Gary Smith, P.C. List the transactions by date and give an explanation for each transaction.

E2-29B (*Learning Objective 5: Record (journalize) transactions in the books*) Double Tree Cellular, Inc., completed the following transactions during September 2012, its first month of operations:

Sep	1	Received $19,900 and issued common stock.
	2	Purchased $400 of office supplies on account.
	4	Paid $14,000 cash for land to use as a building site.
	6	Performed services for customers and received cash of $2,900.
	9	Paid $300 on accounts payable.
	17	Performed services for U Purchase on account totaling $1,200.
	23	Collected $100 from U Purchase on account.
	30	Paid the following expenses: salary, $1,200; rent, $800.

► Requirement

1. Record the transactions in the journal of Double Tree Cellular, Inc. Key transactions by date and include an explanation for each entry.

E2-30B (*Learning Objectives 4, 5, 6: Analyze the impact of business transactions on accounts; record (post) transactions in the books; construct and use a trial balance*) Refer to Exercise 2-29B.

▶ Requirements

1. Post the entries to the ledger, using T-accounts. Key transactions by date. Date the ending balance of each account September 30.
2. Prepare the trial balance of Double Tree Cellular, Inc., at September 30, 2012.
3. How much are total assets, total liabilities, and total shareholders' equity on September 30?

E2-31B (*Learning Objectives 1, 4, 5: Explain what a transaction is; analyze the impact of business transactions on accounts; record (journalize) transactions in the books*) The first seven transactions of Gallagher Advertising, Inc., have been posted to the company's accounts as follows:

	Cash					Supplies				Equipment			Land	
(1)	10,100	(3)	7,000	(4)	800	(5)	130	(6)	5,700		(3)	35,000		
(2)	7,300	(6)	5,700											
(5)	130	(7)	140											

	Accounts Payable				Note Payable			Common Stock	
(7)	140	(4)	800		(2)	7,300		(1)	10,100
					(3)	28,000			

▶ Requirement

1. Prepare the journal entries that served as the sources for the seven transactions. Include an explanation for each entry. As Gallagher moves into the next period, how much cash does the business have? How much does Gallagher owe in total liabilities?

E2-32B (*Learning Objective 6: Construct and use a trial balance*) The accounts of Custom Pool Service, Inc., follow with their normal balances at June 30, 2012. The accounts are listed in no particular order.

Account	Balance	Account	Balance
Common stock.................	$ 8,300	Dividends..........................	$ 5,800
Accounts payable..............	4,100	Utilities expense	1,700
Service revenue.................	22,300	Accounts receivable...........	15,200
Land.................................	29,600	Delivery expense	900
Note payable....................	11,500	Retained earnings..............	24,700
Cash.................................	9,200	Salary expense..................	8,500

▶ Requirements

1. Prepare the company's trial balance at June 30, 2012, listing accounts in proper sequence, as illustrated in the chapter. For example, Accounts Receivable comes before Land. List the expense with the largest balance first, the expense with the next largest balance second, and so on.
2. Prepare the financial statement for the month ended June 30, 2012, that will tell the company the results of operations for the month.

E2-33B (*Learning Objective 6: Construct and use a trial balance*) The trial balance of Doyle, Inc., at September 30, 2012, does not balance.

Cash...	$ 4,600	
Accounts receivable...............	13,200	
Inventory................................	17,100	
Supplies..................................	800	
Land..	58,000	
Accounts payable		$12,400
Common stock.......................		47,400
Service revenue......................		38,500
Salary expense.......................	1,900	
Rent expense..........................	1,100	
Utilities expense	1,100	
Total.......................................	$97,800	$98,300

The accounting records hold the following errors:

   a. Recorded a $600 cash revenue transaction by debiting Accounts Receivable. The credit entry was correct.

   b. Posted a $3,000 credit to Accounts Payable as $300.

   c. Did not record utilities expense or the related account payable in the amount of $400.

   d. Understated Common Stock by $200.

   e. Omitted Insurance Expense of $3,400 from the trial balance.

▶ Requirement

1. Prepare the correct trial balance at September 30, 2012, complete with a heading. Journal entries are not required.

E2-34B (*Learning Objective 4: Analyze the impact of business transactions on accounts*) Set up the following T-accounts: Cash, Accounts Receivable, Office Supplies, Office Furniture, Accounts Payable, Common Stock, Dividends, Service Revenue, Salary Expense, and Rent Expense. Record the following transactions directly in the T-accounts without using a journal. Use the letters to identify the transactions.

   a. Lisa Oxford opened a law firm by investing $13,000 cash and office furniture valued at $8,900. Organized as a professional corporation, the business issued common stock to Oxford.

   b. Paid monthly rent of $1,800.

   c. Purchased office supplies on account, $1,300.

   d. Paid employee salaries of $1,800.

   e. Paid $900 of the accounts payable created in Transaction c.

   f. Performed legal service on account, $8,700.

   g. Declared and paid dividends of $2,500.

E2-35B (*Learning Objective 6: Construct and use a trial balance*) Refer to Exercise 2-34B.

▶ Requirements

1. After recording the transactions in Exercise 2-34B, and assuming they all occurred in the month of March, 2012, prepare the trial balance of Lisa Oxford, Attorney, at March 31, 2012. Use the T-accounts that have been prepared for the business.

2. How well did the business perform during its first month? Compute net income (or net loss) for the month.

Serial Exercise

Exercise 2-36 begins an accounting cycle that is completed in Chapter 3.

E2-36 (*Learning Objectives 1, 4, 5, 6: Explain what a transaction is; analyze the impact of business transactions on accounts; record (journalize and post) transactions in the books; construct and use a trial balance*) Steve Ruiz, Certified Public Accountant, operates as a professional corporation (P.C.). The business completed these transactions during the first part of January, 2012:

Jan	2	Received $11,000 cash from Ruiz, and issued common stock to him.
	2	Paid monthly office rent, $700.
	3	Paid cash for a Dell computer, $3,900, with the computer expected to remain in service for five years.
	4	Purchased office furniture on account, $4,700, with the furniture projected to last for five years.
	5	Purchased supplies on account, $400.
	9	Performed tax services for a client and received cash for the full amount of $1,000.
	12	Paid utility expenses, $200.
	18	Performed consulting services for a client on account, $1,500.

▶ Requirements

1. Journalize the transactions. Explanations are not required.
2. Post to the T-accounts. Key all items by date and denote an account balance on January 18, 2012, as Bal.
3. Prepare a trial balance at January 18, 2012. In the Serial Exercise of Chapter 3, we add transactions for the remainder of January and will require a trial balance at January 31.

Quiz

Test your understanding of transaction analysis by answering the following questions. Select the best choice from among the possible answers.

Q2-37 An investment of cash into the business will
a. decrease total liabilities.
b. decrease total assets.
c. have no effect on total assets.
d. increase stockholders' equity.

Q2-38 Purchasing a laptop computer on account will
a. increase total assets.
b. have no effect on stockholders' equity.
c. increase total liabilities.
d. all of the above.

Q2-39 Performing a service on account will
a. increase stockholders' equity.
b. increase total assets.
c. increase total liabilities.
d. both a and b.

Q2-40 Receiving cash from a customer on account will
a. increase stockholders equity.
b. decrease liabilities.
c. increase total assets.
d. have no effect on total assets.

Q2-41 Purchasing computer equipment for cash will
a. increase both total assets and total liabilities.
b. decrease both total assets and stockholders' equity.
c. decrease both total liabilities and stockholders' equity.
d. have no effect on total assets, total liabilities, or stockholders' equity.

Q2-42 Purchasing a building for $95,000 by paying cash of $25,000 and signing a note payable for $70,000 will

a. decrease total assets and increase total liabilities by $25,000.
b. decrease both total assets and total liabilities by $25,000.
c. increase both total assets and total liabilities by $70,000.
d. increase both total assets and total liabilities by $95,000.

Q2-43 What is the effect on total assets and stockholders' equity of paying the telephone bill as soon as it is received each month?

Total assets	Stockholders' equity
a. Decrease	Decrease
b. Decrease	No effect
c. No effect	No effect
d. No effect	Decrease

Q2-44 Which of the following transactions will increase an asset and increase a liability?
a. Purchasing office equipment for cash
b. Issuing stock
c. Buying equipment on account
d. Payment of an account payable

Q2-45 Which of the following transactions will increase an asset and increase stockholders' equity?
a. Collecting cash from a customer on an account receivable
b. Borrowing money from a bank
c. Performing a service on account for a customer
d. Purchasing supplies on account

Q2-46 Where do we first record a transaction?
a. Ledger
b. Journal
c. Trial balance
d. Account

Q2-47 Which of the following is not an asset account?
a. Salary Expense
b. Service Revenue
c. Common Stock
d. None of the above accounts is an asset.

Q2-48 Which statement is false?
a. Revenues are increased by credits.
b. Assets are increased by debits.
c. Liabilities are decreased by debits.
d. Dividends are increased by credits.

Q2-49 The journal entry to record the receipt of land and a building and issuance of common stock
a. debits Land and Building and credits Common Stock.
b. debits Land and credits Common Stock.
c. debits Land, Building, and Common Stock.
d. debits Common Stock and credits Land and Building.

Q2-50 The journal entry to record the purchase of supplies on account
a. credits Supplies and debits Accounts Payable.
b. debits Supplies Expense and credits Supplies.
c. credits Supplies and debits Cash.
d. debits Supplies and credits Accounts Payable.

Q2-51 If the credit to record the purchase of supplies on account is not posted,
a. stockholders' equity will be understated.
b. assets will be understated.
c. liabilities will be understated.
d. expenses will be overstated.

Q2-52 The journal entry to record a payment on account will
a. debit Accounts Payable and credit Retained Earnings.
b. debit Cash and credit Expenses.
c. debit Accounts Payable and credit Cash.
d. debit Expenses and credit Cash.

Q2-53 If the credit to record the payment of an account payable is not posted,
a. expenses will be understated.
b. liabilities will be understated.
c. cash will be understated.
d. cash will be overstated.

Q2-54 Which statement is false?
a. A trial balance lists all the accounts with their current balances.
b. A trial balance can be taken at any time.
c. A trial balance can verify the equality of debits and credits.
d. A trial balance is the same as a balance sheet.

Q2-55 A business's receipt of a $105,000 building, with a $90,000 mortgage payable, and issuance of $15,000 of common stock will
a. increase stockholders' equity by $15,000.
b. increase assets by $15,000.
c. increase stockholders' equity by $105,000.
d. decrease assets by $90,000.

Q2-56 Bigtex, a new company, completed these transactions. What will Bigtex's total assets equal?
1. Stockholders invested $45,000 cash and inventory worth $22,000.
2. Sales on account, $11,000.
    a. $56,000
    b. $59,000
    c. $45,000
    d. $78,000

Problems

All of the A and B problems can be found within MyAccountingLab, an online homework and practice environment. Your instructor may ask you to complete these problems using MyAccountingLab.

MyAccountingLab

Group A

P2-57A *(Learning Objective 6: Construct and use a trial balance)* The trial balance of Dorman Specialties, Inc., follows.

Dorman Specialties, Inc.
Trial Balance
December 31, 2012

Cash	$ 20,000	
Accounts receivable	45,000	
Prepaid expenses	3,000	
Equipment	235,000	
Building	104,000	
Accounts payable		$102,000
Note payable		82,000
Common stock		55,000
Retained earnings		162,000
Dividends	18,000	
Service revenue		180,000
Rent expense	59,000	
Advertising expense	12,000	
Wage expense	76,000	
Supplies expense	9,000	
Total	$581,000	$581,000

Abby Ricardo, your best friend, is considering investing in Dorman Specialties, Inc. Abby seeks your advice in interpreting this information. Specifically, she asks how to use this trial balance to compute the company's total assets, total liabilities, and net income or net loss for the year.

▶ Requirement

1. Write a short note to answer Abby's questions. In your note, state the amounts of Dorman Specialties' total assets, total liabilities, and net income or net loss for the year. Also show how you computed each amount.

P2-58A *(Learning Objectives 3, 4: Show the impact of business transactions on the accounting equation; analyze the impact of business transactions on accounts)* The following amounts summarize the financial position of Martin Resources, Inc., on May 31, 2012:

		Assets				=	Liabilities	+	Stockholders' Equity		
	Cash	+	Accounts Receivable	+ Supplies +	Land	=	Accounts Payable	+	Common Stock	+	Retained Earnings
Bal	1,400		1,300		11,600		8,000		3,500		2,800

During June 2012, Martin Resources completed these transactions:

 a. The business received cash of $9,000 and issued common stock.
 b. Performed services for a customer and received cash of $6,800.
 c. Paid $4,700 on accounts payable.
 d. Purchased supplies on account, $1,200.
 e. Collected cash from a customer on account, $400.
 f. Consulted on the design of a computer system and billed the customer for services rendered, $2,400.
 g. Recorded the following business expenses for the month: (1) paid office rent—$1,400; (2) paid advertising—$900.
 h. Declared and paid a cash dividend of $1,700.

▶ Requirements

1. Analyze the effects of the preceding transactions on the accounting equation of Martin Resources, Inc.
2. Prepare the income statement of Martin Resources, Inc., for the month ended June 30, 2012. List expenses in decreasing order by amount.
3. Prepare the entity's statement of retained earnings for the month ended June 30, 2012.
4. Prepare the balance sheet of Martin Resources, Inc., at June 30, 2012.

P2-59A *(Learning Objectives 4, 5: Analyze the impact of business transactions on accounts; record (journalize and post) transactions in the books)* This problem can be used in conjunction with Problem 2-58A. Refer to Problem 2-58A.

▶ Requirements

1. Journalize the June transactions of Martin Resources, Inc. Explanations are not required.
2. Prepare T-Accounts for each account. Insert in each T-account its May 31 balance as given (example: Cash $1,400). Then, post the June transactions to the T-Accounts.
3. Compute the balance in each account.

P2-60A *(Learning Objectives 1, 3, 5: Explain what a transaction is; show the impact of business transactions on the accounting equation; record (journalize) transactions in the books)* Carlson Real Estate Co. experienced the following events during the organizing phase and its first month of operations. Some of the events were personal for the stockholders and did not affect the business. Others were transactions of the business.

Nov	4	Cody Carlson, the major stockholder of a real estate company, received $103,000 cash from an inheritance.
	5	Carlson deposited $58,000 cash in a new business bank account titled Carlson Real Estate Co. The business issued common stock to Carlson.
	6	The business paid $100 cash for letterhead stationery for the new office.
	7	The business purchased office equipment. The company paid cash of $10,000 and agreed to pay the account payable for the remainder, $6,500, within three months.
	10	Carlson sold FDR stock, which he had owned for several years, receiving $72,500 cash from his stockbroker.
	11	Carlson deposited the $72,500 cash from sale of the FDR stock in his personal bank account.
	12	A representative of a large company telephoned Carlson and told him of the company's intention to transfer $11,500 of business to Carlson.
	18	Carlson finished a real estate deal for a client and submitted his bill for services, $5,500. Carlson expects to collect from the client within two weeks.
	21	The business paid half its account payable on the equipment purchased on November 7.
	25	The business paid office rent of $1,400.
	30	The business declared and paid a cash dividend of $2,400.

▶ Requirements

1. Classify each of the preceding events as one of the following:
   a. A business-related event but not a transaction to be recorded by Carlson Real Estate Co.
   b. A business transaction for a stockholder, not to be recorded by Carlson Real Estate Co.
   c. A business transaction to be recorded by Carlson Real Estate Co.
2. Analyze the effects of the preceding events on the accounting equation of Carlson Real Estate Co.
3. Record the transactions of the business in its journal. Include an explanation for each entry.

P2-61A (*Learning Objectives 4, 5: Analyze the impact of business transactions on accounts; record (journalize and post) transactions in the books*) During December, Desimone Auction Co. completed the following transactions:

Dec	1	Desimone received $23,000 cash and issued common stock to the stockholders.
	5	Paid monthly rent, $1,900.
	9	Paid $7,000 cash and signed a $28,000 note payable to purchase land for an office site.
	10	Purchased supplies on account, $1,100.
	19	Paid $700 on account.
	22	Borrowed $19,000 from the bank for business use. Desimone signed a note payable to the bank in the name of the business.
	31	Service revenue earned during the month included $14,000 cash and $6,000 on account.
	31	Paid employees' salaries ($2,500), advertising expense ($1,300), and utilities expense ($1,700).
	31	Declared and paid a cash dividend of $2,500.

Desimone's business uses the following accounts: Cash, Accounts Receivable, Supplies, Land, Accounts Payable, Notes Payable, Common Stock, Dividends, Service Revenue, Salary Expense, Rent Expense, Advertising Expense, and Utilities Expense.

► Requirements

1. Journalize each transaction of Desimone Auction Co. Explanations are not required.
2. Post to these T-accounts: Cash, Accounts Payable, and Notes Payable.
3. After these transactions, how much cash does the business have? How much in total liabilities does it owe?

P2-62A *(Learning Objectives 4, 5, 6: Analyze the impact of business transactions on accounts; record (journalize and post) transactions in the books; construct and use a trial balance)* During the first month of operations, Cloutier Heating and Air Conditioning, Inc., completed the following transactions:

Mar	2	Cloutier received $37,000 cash and issued common stock to the stockholders.
	3	Purchased supplies, $300, and equipment, $3,000, on account.
	4	Performed services for a customer and received cash, $1,500.
	7	Paid cash to acquire land, $28,000.
	11	Performed services for a customer and billed the customer, $1,100. Cloutier expects to collect within one month.
	16	Paid for the equipment purchased March 3 on account.
	17	Paid the telephone bill, $110.
	18	Received partial payment from customer on account, $550.
	22	Paid the water and electricity bills, $130.
	29	Received $1,000 cash for servicing the heating unit of a customer.
	31	Paid employee salary, $1,900.
	31	Declared and paid dividends of $2,200.

► Requirements

1. Record each transaction in the journal. Key each transaction by date. Explanations are not required.
2. Post the transactions to the T-accounts, using transaction dates as posting references. Label the ending balance of each account Bal, as shown in the chapter.
3. Prepare the trial balance of Cloutier Heating and Air Conditioning, Inc., at March 31 of the current year.
4. The manager asks you how much in total resources the business has to work with, how much it owes, and whether March was profitable (and by how much).

P2-63A *(Learning Objectives 4, 6: Analyze the impact of business transactions on accounts; construct and use a trial balance)* During the first month of operations (October 2012), Self Music Services Corporation completed the following selected transactions:

a. The business received cash of $25,000 and a building valued at $51,000. The corporation issued common stock to the stockholders.
b. Borrowed $34,300 from the bank; signed a note payable.
c. Paid $31,000 for music equipment.
d. Purchased supplies on account, $200.
e. Paid employees' salaries, $2,200.
f. Received $1,400 for music services performed for customers.
g. Performed services for customers on account, $2,800.
h. Paid $100 of the account payable created in Transaction d.
i. Received a $700 bill for utility expense that will be paid in the near future.
j. Received cash on account, $1,900.
k. Paid the following cash expenses: (1) rent, $1,100; (2) advertising, $500.

► Requirements

1. Record each transaction directly in the T-accounts without using a journal. Use the letters to identify the transactions.
2. Prepare the trial balance of Self Music Services Corporation at October 31, 2012.

Group B

P2-64B (*Learning Objective 6: Construct and use a trial balance*) The trial balance of Famous Specialties, Inc., follows:

Famous Specialties, Inc.
Trial Balance
December 31, 2012

Cash	$ 27,000	
Accounts receivable	40,000	
Prepaid expenses	6,000	
Equipment	239,000	
Building	97,000	
Accounts payable		$104,000
Note payable		85,000
Common stock		75,000
Retained earnings		112,000
Dividends	16,000	
Service revenue		160,000
Rent expense	24,000	
Advertising expense	10,000	
Wage expense	73,000	
Supplies expense	4,000	
Total	$536,000	$536,000

Rachel Sill, your best friend, is considering making an investment in Famous Specialties, Inc. Rachel seeks your advice in interpreting the company's information. Specifically, she asks how to use this trial balance to compute the company's total assets, total liabilities, and net income or net loss for the year.

► Requirement

1. Write a short note to answer Rachel's questions. In your note, state the amounts of Famous Specialties' total assets, total liabilities, and net income or net loss for the year. Also show how you computed each amount.

P2-65B (*Learning Objectives 3, 4: Show the impact of business transactions on the accounting equation; analyze the impact of business transactions on accounts*) The following amounts summarize the financial position of Davis Resources on May 31, 2012:

		Assets				=	Liabilities	+	Stockholders' Equity	
	Cash	+	Accounts Receivable	+ Supplies +	Land	=	Accounts Payable	+	Common Stock	+ Retained Earnings
Bal	1,050		1,350		11,700		7,900		3,600	2,600

During June, 2012, the business completed these transactions:

a. The business received cash of $8,900 and issued common stock.
b. Performed services for a customer and received cash of $6,300.
c. Paid $4,100 on accounts payable.
d. Purchased supplies on account, $700.
e. Collected cash from a customer on account, $200.
f. Consulted on the design of a computer system and billed the customer for services rendered, $2,400.
g. Recorded the following expenses for the month: (1) paid office rent—$1,300; (2) paid advertising—$1,000.
h. Declared and paid a cash dividend of $2,000.

▶ Requirements

1. Analyze the effects of the preceding transactions on the accounting equation of Davis Resources, Inc.
2. Prepare the income statement of Davis Resources, Inc., for the month ended June 30, 2012. List expenses in decreasing order by amount.
3. Prepare the statement of retained earnings of Davis Resources, Inc., for the month ended June 30, 2012.
4. Prepare the balance sheet of Davis Resources, Inc., at June 30, 2012.

P2-66B (*Learning Objectives 4, 5: Analyze the impact of business transactions on accounts; record (journalize and post) transactions in the books*) This problem can be used in conjunction with Problem 2-65B. Refer to Problem 2-65B.

▶ Requirements

1. Journalize the transactions of Davis Resources, Inc. Explanations are not required.
2. Prepare T-accounts for each account. Insert in each T-account its May 31 balance as given (example: Cash $1,050). Then, post the June transactions to the T-accounts.
3. Compute the balance in each account.

P2-67B (*Learning Objectives 1, 3, 5: Explain what a transaction is; show the impact of business transactions on the accounting equation; record (journalize) transactions in the books*) Jones Real Estate Co. experienced the following events during the organizing phase and its first month of operations. Some of the events were personal for the stockholders and did not affect the business. Others were transactions of the business.

Nov	4	Evan Jones, the major stockholder of a real estate company, received $107,000 cash from an inheritance.
	5	Jones deposited $54,000 cash in a new business bank account titled Jones Real Estate Co. The business issued common stock to Jones.
	6	The business paid $1,000 cash for letterhead stationery for the new office.
	7	The business purchased office equipment. The company paid cash of $9,500 and agreed to pay the account payable for the remainder, $7,500, within three months.
	10	Jones sold CDM stock, which he owned for several years, receiving $73,000 cash from his stockbroker.
	11	Jones deposited the $73,000 cash from sale of the CDM stock in his personal bank account.
	12	A representative of a large company telephoned Jones and told him of the company's intention to transfer $14,500 of business to Jones.
	18	Jones finished a real estate deal for a client and submitted his bill for services, $4,500. Jones expects to collect from the client within two weeks.
	21	The business paid half its account payable for the equipment purchased on November 7.
	25	The business paid office rent of $1,000.
	30	The business declared and paid a cash dividend of $1,800.

▶ Requirements

1. Classify each of the preceding events as one of the following:
   a. A business-related event but not a transaction to be recorded by Jones Real Estate Co.
   b. A business transaction for a stockholder, not to be recorded by Jones Real Estate Co.
   c. A business transaction to be recorded by the Jones Real Estate Co.
2. Analyze the effects of the preceding events on the accounting equation of Jones Real Estate Co.
3. Record the transactions of the business in its journal. Include an explanation for each entry.

P2-68B (*Learning Objectives 4, 5: Analyze the impact of business transactions on accounts; record (journalize and post) transactions in the books*) During December, Blanton Auction Co. completed the following transactions:

Dec	1	Blanton received $25,000 cash and issued common stock to the stockholders.
	5	Paid monthly rent, $1,600.
	9	Paid $8,500 cash and signed a $36,000 note payable to purchase land for an office site.
	10	Purchased supplies on account, $1,000.
	19	Paid $650 on account.
	22	Borrowed $20,000 from the bank for business use. Blanton signed a note payable to the bank in the name of the business.
	31	Service revenue earned during the month included $13,500 cash and $5,000 on account.
	31	Paid employees' salaries ($2,700), advertising expense ($1,700), and utilities expense ($1,100).
	31	Declared and paid a cash dividend of $4,000.

Blanton's business uses the following accounts: Cash, Accounts Receivable, Supplies, Land, Accounts Payable, Notes Payable, Common Stock, Dividends, Service Revenue, Salary Expense, Rent Expense, Advertising Expense, and Utilities Expense.

► Requirements

1. Journalize each transaction of Blanton Auction Co. Explanations are not required.
2. Post to these T-accounts: Cash, Accounts Payable, and Notes Payable.
3. After these transactions, how much cash does the business have? How much does it owe in total liabilities?

P2-69B (*Learning Objectives 4, 5, 6: Analyze the impact of business transactions on accounts; record (journalize and post) transactions in the books; construct and use a trial balance*) During the first month of operations, Johnson Plumbing, Inc., completed the following transactions:

Mar	2	Johnson received $35,000 cash and issued common stock to the stockholders.
	3	Purchased supplies, $200, and equipment, $3,200, on account.
	4	Performed services for a client and received cash, $1,400.
	7	Paid cash to acquire land, $24,000.
	11	Performed services for a customer and billed the customer, $800. Johnson expects to collect within one month.
	16	Paid for the equipment purchased March 3 on account.
	17	Paid the telephone bill, $150.
	18	Received partial payment from customer on account, $400.
	22	Paid the water and electricity bills, $170.
	29	Received $1,500 cash for repairing the pipes of a customer.
	31	Paid employee salary, $1,800.
	31	Declared and paid dividends of $2,100.

► Requirements

1. Record each transaction in the journal. Key each transaction by date. Explanations are not required.
2. Post the transactions to the T-accounts, using transaction dates as posting references.
3. Prepare the trial balance of Johnson Plumbing, Inc., at March 31 of the current year.
4. The manager asks you how much in total resources the business has to work with, how much it owes, and whether March was profitable (and by how much).

P2-70B (*Learning Objectives 4, 6: Analyze the impact of business transactions on accounts; construct and use a trial balance*) During the first month of operations (February 2012), Starr Entertainment Corporation completed the following selected transactions:

a. The business received cash of $19,000 and a building valued at $53,000. The corporation issued common stock to the stockholders.
b. Borrowed $41,100 from the bank; signed a note payable.
c. Paid $37,000 for music equipment.
d. Purchased supplies on account, $300.
e. Paid employees' salaries, $2,000.
f. Received $1,600 for music service performed for customers.
g. Performed service for customers on account, $2,900.
h. Paid $200 of the account payable created in Transaction d.
i. Received a $900 bill for utilities expense that will be paid in the near future.
j. Received cash on account, $1,100.
k. Paid the following cash expenses: (1) rent, $1,000; (2) advertising, $800.

► Requirements

1. Record each transaction directly in the T-accounts without using a journal. Use the letters to identify the transactions.
2. Prepare the trial balance of Starr Entertainment Corporation at February 29, 2012.

Challenge Exercises and Problem

E2-71 (*Learning Objective 4: Analyze the impact of business transactions on accounts*) The manager of Eisenhower Furniture needs to compute the following amounts.

 a. Total cash paid during December.

 b. Cash collections from customers during December. Analyze Accounts Receivable.

 c. Cash paid on a note payable during December. Analyze Notes Payable.

Here's the additional data you need to analyze the accounts:

	Balance		
Account	Nov 30	Dec 31	Additional Information for the Month of December
1. Cash..................................	$10,000	$ 5,000	Cash receipts, $82,000
2. Accounts Receivable.......	27,000	25,000	Sales on account, $54,000
3. Notes Payable	11,000	19,000	New borrowing, $32,000

▶ Requirement

 1. Prepare a T-account to compute each amount, *a* through *c*.

E2-72 (*Learning Objectives 4, 6: Analyze the impact of business transactions on accounts; construct and use a trial balance*) The trial balance of Rectangle 120, Inc., at August 31, 2012, does not balance.

Cash....................................	$ 3,900	Common stock....................	$20,100
Accounts receivable.............	7,400	Retained earnings................	7,500
Land....................................	34,400	Service revenue....................	9,500
Accounts payable	6,000	Salary expense.....................	3,300
Note payable.......................	5,500	Advertising expense.............	1,100

▶ Requirements

 1. How much out of balance is the trial balance? Determine the out-of-balance amount. The error lies in the Accounts Receivable account. Add the out-of-balance amount to, or subtract it from, Accounts Receivable to determine the correct balance of Accounts Receivable.

 2. After correcting Accounts receivable, advise the top management of Rectangle 120, Inc., on the company's

 a. total assets.

 b. total liabilities.

 c. net income or net loss for August.

E2-73 (*Learning Objective 4: Analyze the impact of business transactions on accounts*) This question concerns the items and the amounts that two entities, Burlington Co. and Gardner Hospital, should report in their financial statements.

During November, Gardner provided Burlington with medical exams for Burlington employees and sent a bill for $44,000. On December 7, Burlington sent a check to Gardner for $30,000. Burlington began November with a cash balance of $53,000; Gardner began with cash of $0.

▶ Requirements

 1. For this situation, show everything that both Burlington and Gardner will report on their November and December income statements and on their balance sheets at November 30 and December 31.

 2. After showing what each company should report, briefly explain how the Burlington and Gardner data relate to each other.

P2-74 *(Learning Objectives 3, 4, 5: Analyze the impact of errors and compute correct amounts)* All-Star Advertising creates, plans, and handles advertising needs in the Tri-State area. Recently, All-Star had to replace an inexperienced office worker in charge of bookkeeping because of some serious mistakes that had been uncovered in the accounting records. You have been hired to review these transactions to determine any corrections that might be necessary. In all cases, the bookkeeper made an accurate description of the transaction.

May 1	Accounts receivable		300	
	Service revenue			300
	Collected an account receivable.			
2	Rent expense		5,000	
	Cash			5,000
	Paid monthly rent, $5,000.			
5	Cash		1,000	
	Accounts receivable			1,000
	Collected cash for services provided.			
10	Supplies		2,500	
	Accounts payable			2,500
	Purchased office equipment on account.			
16	Dividends		2,000	
	Cash			2,000
	Paid salaries.			
25	Accounts receivable		1,500	
	Cash			1,500
	Paid for supplies purchased earlier on account.			

▶ Requirements

1. For each of the preceding entries, indicate the effect on cash, total assets, and net income. The answer for the first transaction has been provided as an example.

Date	Effect on Cash	Effect on Total Assets	Effect on Net Income
May 1	Understated $300	Correct	Overstated $300

2. What is the correct balance of cash if the balance of cash on the books before correcting the preceding transactions was $5,500?
3. What is the correct amount of total assets if the total assets on the books before correcting the preceding transactions was $25,000?
4. What is the correct net income for May if the reported income before correcting the preceding transactions was $10,000?

APPLY YOUR KNOWLEDGE

Decision Cases

Case 1. (*Learning Objectives 4, 6: Analyze the impact of transactions on business accounts; construct and use a trial balance; measure net income or loss; decide whether to continue a business*) A friend named Jay Barlow has asked what effect certain transactions will have on his company. Time is short, so you cannot apply the detailed procedures of journalizing and posting. Instead, you must analyze the transactions without the use of a journal. Barlow will continue the business only if he can expect to earn monthly net income of at least $5,000. The following transactions occurred this month:

a. Barlow deposited $5,000 cash in a business bank account, and the corporation issued common stock to him.
b. Borrowed $5,000 cash from the bank and signed a note payable due within 1 year.
c. Paid $1,300 cash for supplies.
d. Purchased advertising in the local newspaper for cash, $1,800.
e. Purchased office furniture on account, $4,400.
f. Paid the following cash expenses for 1 month: employee salary, $2,000; office rent, $1,200.
g. Earned revenue on account, $7,000.
h. Earned revenue and received $2,500 cash.
i. Collected cash from customers on account, $1,200.
j. Paid on account, $1,000.

▶ Requirements

1. Set up the following T-accounts: Cash, Accounts Receivable, Supplies, Furniture, Accounts Payable, Notes Payable, Common Stock, Service Revenue, Salary Expense, Advertising Expense, and Rent Expense.
2. Record the transactions directly in the accounts without using a journal. Key each transaction by letter.
3. Construct a trial balance for Barlow Networks, Inc., at the current date. List expenses with the largest amount first, the next largest amount second, and so on.
4. Compute the amount of net income or net loss for this first month of operations. Why or why not would you recommend that Barlow continue in business?

Case 2. (*Learning Objective 4: Analyze the impact of transactions on business accounts; correct erroneous financial statements; decide whether to expand a business*) Sophia Loren opened an Italian restaurant. Business has been good, and Loren is considering expanding the restaurant. Loren, who knows little accounting, produced the following financial statements for Little Italy, Inc., at December 31, 2012, the end of the first month of operations:

Little Italy, Inc.
Income Statement
Month Ended December 31, 2012

Sales revenue	$42,000
Common stock	10,000
Total revenue	52,000
Accounts payable	$ 8,000
Advertising expense	5,000
Rent expense	6,000
Total expenses	19,000
Net income	$33,000

Little Italy, Inc.
Balance Sheet
December 31, 2012

Assets	
Cash	$12,000
Cost of goods sold (expense)	22,000
Food inventory	5,000
Furniture	10,000
Total Assets	$49,000
Liabilities	
None	
Owners' Equity	$49,000

In these financial statements all *amounts* are correct, except for Owners' Equity. Loren heard that total assets should equal total liabilities plus owners' equity, so she plugged in the amount of owners' equity at $49,000 to make the balance sheet come out even.

▶ Requirement

1. Sophia Loren has asked whether she should expand the restaurant. Her banker says Loren may be wise to expand if (a) net income for the first month reached $10,000 and (b) total assets are at least $35,000. It appears that the business has reached these milestones, but Loren doubts whether her financial statements tell the true story. She needs your help in making this decision. Prepare a corrected income statement and balance sheet. (Remember that Retained Earnings, which was omitted from the balance sheet, should equal net income for the first month; there were no dividends.) After preparing the statements, give Sophia Loren your recommendation as to whether she should expand the restaurant.

Ethical Issues

Issue 1. Scruffy Murphy is the president and principal stockholder of Scruffy's Bar & Grill, Inc. To expand, the business is applying for a $250,000 bank loan. To get the loan, Murphy is considering two options for beefing up the owners' equity of the business:

      Option 1. Issue $100,000 of common stock for cash. A friend has been wanting to invest in the company. This may be the right time to extend the offer.

      Option 2. Transfer $100,000 of Murphy's personal land to the business, and issue common stock to Murphy. Then, after obtaining the loan, Murphy can transfer the land back to himself and zero out the common stock.

▶ Requirements

Use the ethical decision model in Chapter 1 to answer the following questions:

1. What is the ethical issue?
2. Who are the stakeholders? What are the possible consequences to each?
3. Analyze the alternatives from the following standpoints: (a) economic, (b) legal, and (c) ethical.
4. What would you do? How would you justify your decision? How would your decision make you feel afterward?

Issue 2. Part a. You have received your grade in your first accounting course, and to your amazement, it is an A. You feel the instructor must have made a big mistake. Your grade was a B going into the final, but you are sure that you really "bombed" the exam, which is worth 30% of the final grade. In fact, you walked out after finishing only 50% of the exam, and the grade report says you made 99% on the exam!

▶ Requirements

1. What is the ethical issue?
2. Who are the stakeholders? What are the possible consequences to each?
3. Analyze the alternatives from the following standpoints: (a) economic, (b) legal, and (c) ethical.
4. What would you do? How would you justify your decision? How would it make you feel afterward?

Part b. Now assume the same facts that were just provided, except that you have received your final grade for the course and the grade is a B. You are confident that you "aced" the final. In fact, you stayed to the very end of the period, and checked every figure twice! You are confident that the instructor must have made a mistake grading the final.

▶ Requirements

1. What is the ethical issue?
2. Who are the stakeholders and what are the consequences to each?
3. Analyze the alternatives from the following standpoints: (a) economic, (b) legal, and (c) ethical.
4. What would you do? How would you justify your decision? How would it make you feel?

Part c. How is this situation like a financial accounting misstatement? How is it different?

Focus on Financials: | Amazon.com, Inc.

(*Learning Objectives 3, 4: Record transactions; compute net income*)   Refer to **Amazon.com, Inc.**'s financial statements in Appendix A at the end of the book. Assume that Amazon.com completed the following selected transactions during 2010.

a. Made company sales (revenue) of $34,204 million, all on account (debit accounts receivable).
b. Collected cash on accounts receivable $33,605.
c. Purchased inventories on account, $27,592 million (credit accounts payable).
d. Incurred cost of sales in the amount of $26,561 million. Debit the Cost of sales (expense) account. Credit the Inventories account.
e. Paid accounts payable in cash, $25,146.
f. Paid operating expenses of $6,237 million in cash.
g. Collected non-operating income (net) in cash, $91 million.
h. Paid income taxes, $352 million in cash (debit provision for income taxes).
i. Accounted for income from other investment activity net of taxes in the amount of $7 million. Debit other assets. Credit the account entitled Equity Method Investment Activity.
j. Paid cash for Fixed assets, $1,124 million; paid cash for other assets, $504 million (the changes in this account will not be fully accounted for in this problem).

▶ Requirements

1. Set up T-accounts for beginning balances of Cash ($3,444 million); Accounts Receivable, net and other (debit balance of $988 million); Inventories (debit balance $2,171 million); Other Assets (debit balance of $1,474); Fixed Assets, net (debit balance of $1,290); Accounts Payable (credit balance of $5,605); Net Sales ($0 balance); Cost of Sales ($0 balance); Operating expenses ($0 balance); Non-operating income (expense), net ($0 balance); Provision for income taxes ($0 balance); Equity method investment activity, net of tax ($0 balance).
2. Journalize Amazon.com's transactions a–j. Explanations are not required.
3. Post to the T-accounts, and compute the balance for each account. Key postings by transaction letters a–j.
4. For each of the following accounts, compare your computed balance to Amazon.com, Inc.'s actual balance as shown on its 2010 Consolidated Statement of Operations or Consolidated Balance Sheet in Appendix A. Your amounts should agree to the actual figures.
   a. Cash
   b. Accounts Receivable, net and other
   c. Inventories
   d. Fixed Assets, net (assume no other activity in fixed assets than given in the problem)

      e. Accounts Payable

      f. Net Sales

      g. Cost of Sales

      h. Operating Expenses

      i. Non-operating Income (expenses), net

      j. Provision for Income Taxes

      k. Equity Method Investment Activity, net of tax

5. Use the relevant accounts from Requirement 4 to prepare a summary income statement for Amazon.com, Inc., for 2010. Compare the net income you computed to Amazon.com, Inc.'s actual net income. The two amounts should be equal.

Focus on Analysis: | RadioShack Corporation

(*Learning Objective 4: Analyze financial statements*) Refer to the **RadioShack Corporation** financial statements in Appendix B at the end of the book. Suppose you are an investor considering buying RadioShack Corporation common stock. The following questions are important: **Show amounts in millions.**

1. Explain whether RadioShack Corporation had more sales revenue or collected more cash from customers during 2010. Why? Show computation. (Challenge)

2. Investors are vitally interested in a company's sales and profits and its trends of sales and profits over time. Consider RadioShack Corporation sales and net income (net loss) during the period from 2008 through 2010. Compute the percentage increase or decrease in net sales and also in net income (net loss) from 2008 to 2010. Which item grew faster during this two-year period—net sales or net income (net loss)? Can you offer a possible explanation for these changes? (Challenge)

Group Projects

Project 1. You are promoting a rock concert in your area. Your purpose is to earn a profit, so you need to establish the formal structure of a business entity. Assume you organize as a corporation.

▶ Requirements

1. Make a detailed list of 10 factors you must consider as you establish the business.

2. Describe 10 of the items your business must arrange to promote and stage the rock concert.

3. Identify the transactions that your business can undertake to organize, promote, and stage the concert. Journalize the transactions, and post to the relevant T-accounts. Set up the accounts you need for your business ledger. Refer to the chart of accounts in Appendix C at the end of the book if needed.

4. Prepare the income statement, statement of retained earnings, and balance sheet immediately after the rock concert—that is, before you have had time to pay all the business bills and to collect all receivables.

5. Assume that you will continue to promote rock concerts if the venture is successful. If it is unsuccessful, you will terminate the business within three months after the concert. Discuss how to evaluate the success of your venture and how to decide whether to continue in business.

Project 2. Contact a local business and arrange with the owner to learn what accounts the business uses.

▶ Requirements

1. Obtain a copy of the business's chart of accounts.

2. Prepare the company's financial statements for the most recent month, quarter, or year. You may use either made-up account balances or balances supplied by the owner.

If the business has a large number of accounts within a category, combine related accounts and report a single amount on the financial statements. For example, the company may have several cash accounts. Combine all cash amounts and report a single Cash amount on the balance sheet.

    You will probably encounter numerous accounts that you have not yet learned. Deal with these as best you can. The charts of accounts given in Appendix C at the end of the book can be helpful.

For online homework, exercises, and problems that provide you with immediate feedback, please visit **www.myaccountinglab.com**.

MyAccountingLab

Quick Check Answers

1. *b*	5. *b*	9. *c*
2. *d*	6. *a*	10. *d*
3. *c*	7. *d* ($3,000 + x − 27,000 =	11. *b*
4. *c* ($1,000 + 500 − 600)	2,000; $x = 26,000$)	12. *c*
	8. *b*	

Demo Doc

Debit/Credit Transaction Analysis

To make sure you understand this material, work through the following demonstration "Demo Doc" with detailed comments to help you see the concept within the framework of a worked-through problem.

Learning Objectives 1, 2, 3, 4

On September 1, 2012, Michael Moe incorporated Moe's Mowing, Inc., a company that provides mowing and landscaping services. During the month of September, the business incurred the following transactions:

a. To begin operations, Michael deposited $10,000 cash in the business's bank account. The business received the cash and issued common stock to Michael.

b. The business purchased equipment for $3,500 on account.

c. The business purchased office supplies for $800 cash.

d. The business provided $2,600 of services to a customer on account.

e. The business paid $500 cash toward the equipment previously purchased on account in transaction b.

f. The business received $2,000 in cash for services provided to a new customer.

g. The business paid $200 cash to repair equipment.

h. The business paid $900 cash in salary expense.

i. The business received $2,100 cash from a customer on account.

j. The business paid cash dividends of $1,500.

▶ Requirements
1. Create blank T-accounts for the following accounts: Cash, Accounts Receivable, Supplies, Equipment, Accounts Payable, Common Stock, Dividends, Service Revenue, Salary Expense, and Repair Expense.

2. Journalize the transactions and then post to the T-accounts. Use the table in Exhibit 2-16 to help with the journal entries.

EXHIBIT 2-16 | The Rules of Debit and Credit

	Increase	Decrease
Assets	debit	credit
Liabilities	credit	debit
Stockholders' Equity	credit	debit
Revenues	credit	debit
Expenses	debit	credit
Dividends	debit	credit

3. Total each T-account to determine its balance at the end of the month.

4. Prepare the trial balance of Moe's Mowing, Inc., at September 30, 2012.

Demo Doc Solutions

▶ Requirement 1

Create blank T-accounts for the following accounts: Cash, Accounts Receivable, Supplies, Equipment, Accounts Payable, Common Stock, Dividends, Service Revenue, Salary Expense, and Repair Expense.

Part 1	Part 2	Part 3	Part 4	Demo Doc Complete

Opening a T-account means drawing a blank account that looks like a capital "T" and putting the account title across the top. T-accounts show the additions and subtractions made to each account. For easy reference, the accounts are grouped into assets, liabilities, stockholders' equity, revenue, and expenses (in that order).

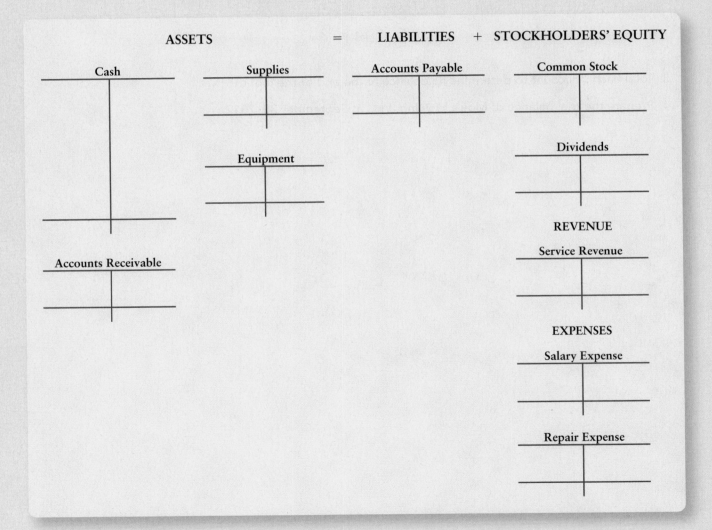

▶ Requirement 2

Journalize the transactions and show how they are recorded in T-accounts.

Part 1	**Part 2**	Part 3	Part 4	Demo Doc Complete

a. To begin operations, Michael deposited $10,000 cash in the business's bank account. The business received the cash and issued common stock to Michael.

First, we must determine which accounts are affected by the transaction.

The business received $10,000 cash from its principal stockholder (Michael Moe). In exchange, the business issued common stock to Michael. So, the accounts involved are Cash and Common Stock.

Remember that we are recording the transactions of Moe's Mowing, Inc., not the transactions of Michael Moe, the person. Michael and his business are two entirely separate accounting entities.

The next step is to determine what type of accounts these are. Cash is an asset; Common Stock is part of equity.

Next, we must determine if these accounts increased or decreased. From the business's point of view, Cash (an asset) has increased. Common Stock (equity) has also increased.

Now we must determine if these accounts should be debited or credited. According to the rules of debit and credit (see Exhibit 2-16 on p. 123), an increase in assets is a debit, while an increase in equity is a credit.

So, Cash (an asset) increases, which requires a debit. Common Stock (equity) also increases, which requires a credit.

The journal entry follows.

a.	Cash (Asset ↑; debit)	10,000	
	Common Stock (Equity ↑; credit)		10,000
	Issued common stock.		

The total dollar amounts of debits must always equal the total dollar amounts of credits.

Remember to use the transaction letters as references. This will help as we post entries to the T-accounts.

Each T-account has two sides—one for recording debits and the other for recording credits. To post the transaction to a T-account, simply transfer the amount of each debit to the correct account as a debit (left-side) entry, and transfer the amount of each credit to the correct account as a credit (right-side) entry.

This transaction includes a debit of $10,000 to cash. This means that $10,000 is posted to the left side of the Cash T-account. The transaction also includes a credit of $10,000 to Common Stock. This means that $10,000 is posted to the right side of the Common Stock account, as follows:

	Cash			Common Stock	
a.	10,000			a.	10,000

Now the first transaction has been journalized and posted. We repeat this process for every journal entry. Let's proceed to the next transaction.

b. The business purchased equipment for $3,500 on account.

The business received equipment in exchange for a promise to pay for the $3,500 cost at a future date. So the accounts involved in the transaction are Equipment and Accounts Payable.

Equipment is an asset and Accounts Payable is a liability.

The asset Equipment has increased. The liability Accounts Payable has also increased.

Looking at Exhibit 2-16, an increase in assets (in this case, the increase in Equipment) is a debit, while an increase in liabilities (in this case, Accounts Payable) is a credit.

The journal entry follows.

b.		Equipment (Asset ↑; debit)		3,500	
		Accounts Payable (Liability ↑; credit)			3,500
		Purchased equipment on account.			

$3,500 is then posted to the debit (left) side of the Equipment T-account. $3,500 is posted to the credit (right) side of Accounts Payable, as follows:

	Equipment			Accounts Payable	
b.	3,500			b.	3,500

c. The business purchased office supplies for $800 cash.

The business purchased supplies, paying cash of $800. So the accounts involved in the transaction are Supplies and Cash.

Supplies and Cash are both assets.

Supplies (an asset) has increased. Cash (an asset) has decreased.

Looking at Exhibit 2-16, an increase in assets is a debit, while a decrease in assets is a credit.

So the increase to Supplies (an asset) is a debit, while the decrease to Cash (an asset) is a credit.

The journal entry follows:

c.		Supplies (Asset ↑; debit)		800	
		Cash (Asset ↓; credit)			800
		Purchased supplies for cash.			

$800 is then posted to the debit (left) side of the Supplies T-account. $800 is posted to the credit (right) side of the Cash account, as follows:

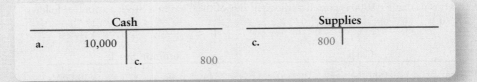

	Cash			Supplies	
a.	10,000			c.	800
		c. 800			

Notice the $10,000 already on the debit side of the Cash account. This came from transaction a.

d. The business provided $2,600 of services to a customer on account.

The business rendered service for a customer and received a promise from the customer to pay $2,600 cash next month. So the accounts involved in the transaction are Accounts Receivable and Service Revenue.

Accounts Receivable is an asset and Service Revenue is revenue.

Accounts Receivable (an asset) has increased. Service Revenue (revenue) has also increased.

Looking at Exhibit 2-16, an increase in assets is a debit, while an increase in revenue is a credit.

So the increase to Accounts Receivable (an asset) is a debit, while the increase to Service Revenue (revenue) is a credit.

The journal entry follows.

d.	Accounts Receivable (Asset ↑; debit)	2,600	
	Service Revenue (Revenue ↑; credit)		2,600
	Provided services on account.		

$2,600 is posted to the debit (left) side of the Accounts Receivable T-account. $2,600 is posted to the credit (right) side of the Service Revenue account, as follows:

Accounts Receivable		Service Revenue	
d. 2,600			d. 2,600

e. The business paid $500 cash toward the equipment previously purchased on account in transaction b.

The business paid some of the money that it owed on the purchase of equipment in transaction b. The accounts involved in the transaction are Accounts Payable and Cash.

Accounts Payable is a liability that has decreased. Cash is an asset that has also decreased.

Remember that Accounts Payable shows the amount the business must pay in the future (a liability). When the business pays these creditors, Accounts Payable will decrease because the business will then owe less (in this case, Accounts Payable drops from $3,500—in transaction b—to $3,000).

Looking at Exhibit 2-16, a decrease in liabilities is a debit, while a decrease in assets is a credit.

So Accounts Payable (a liability) decreases, which is a debit. Cash (an asset) decreases, which is a credit.

e.	Accounts Payable (Liability ↓; debit)	500	
	Cash (Asset ↓; credit)		500
	Partial payment on account.		

$500 is posted to the debit (left) side of the Accounts Payable T-account. $500 is posted to the credit (right) side of the Cash account, as follows:

Cash				Accounts Payable			
a.	10,000					b.	3,500
		c.	800	e.	500		
		e.	500				

Again notice the amounts already in the T-accounts from previous transactions. The reference letters show which transaction caused each amount to appear in the T-account.

f. The business received $2,000 in cash for services provided to a new customer.

The business received $2,000 cash in exchange for mowing and landscaping services rendered to a customer. The accounts involved in the transaction are Cash and Service Revenue.

Cash is an asset that has increased, and Service Revenue is revenue, which has also increased.

Looking at Exhibit 2-16, an increase in assets is a debit, while an increase in revenue is a credit.

So the increase to Cash (an asset) is a debit. The increase to Service Revenue (revenue) is a credit.

f.		Cash (Asset ↑; debit)	2,000	
		Service Revenue (Revenue ↑; credit)		2,000
		Provided services for cash.		

$2,000 is then posted to the debit (left) side of the Cash T-account. $2,000 is posted to the credit (right) side of the Service Revenue account, as follows:

Cash				Service Revenue			
a.	10,000					d.	2,600
		c.	800			f.	2,000
		e.	500				
f.	2,000						

Notice how we keep adding onto the T-accounts. The values from previous transactions remain in their places.

g. The business paid $200 cash to repair equipment.

The business paid $200 cash to have equipment repaired. Because the benefit of the repairs has already been used, the repairs are recorded as Repair Expense. Because the repairs were paid in cash, the Cash account is also involved.

Repair Expense is an expense that has increased and Cash is an asset that has decreased.

Looking at Exhibit 2-16, an increase in expenses calls for a debit, while a decrease in an asset requires a credit.

So Repair Expense (an expense) increases, which is a debit. Cash (an asset) decreases, which is a credit.

g.	Repair Expense (Expense ↑ ; debit)	200	
	Cash (Asset ↓ ; credit)		200
	Paid for repairs.		

$200 is then posted to the debit (left) side of the Repair Expense T-account. $200 is posted to the credit (right) side of the Cash account, as follows:

	Cash					Repair Expense	
a.	10,000				g.	200	
		c.	800				
		e.	500				
f.	2,000						
		g.	200				

h. The business paid $900 cash for salary expense.

The business paid employees $900 in cash. Because the benefit of the employees' work has already been used, their salaries are recorded as Salary Expense. Because the salaries were paid in cash, the Cash account is also involved.

Salary Expense is an expense that has increased, and Cash is an asset that has decreased.

Looking at Exhibit 2-16, an increase in expenses is a debit, while a decrease in an asset is a credit.

In this case, Salary Expense (an expense) increases, which is a debit. Cash (an asset) decreases, which is a credit.

h.	Salary Expense (Expense ↑; debit)	900	
	Cash (Asset ↓; credit)		900
	Paid salary.		

$900 is posted to the debit (left) side of the Salary Expense T-account. $900 is posted to the credit (right) side of the Cash account, as follows:

Cash						Salary Expense		
a.	10,000				h.	900		
		c.	800					
		e.	500					
f.	2,000							
		g.	200					
		h.	900					

i. The business received $2,100 cash from a customer on account.

The business received cash of $2,100 from a customer for services previously provided in transaction d. The accounts affected by this transaction are Cash and Accounts Receivable.

Cash and Accounts Receivable are both assets.

The asset Cash has increased, and the asset Accounts Receivable has decreased.

Remember, Accounts Receivable shows the amount of cash the business has coming from customers. When the business receives cash from these customers, Accounts Receivable will decrease, because the business will have less to receive in the future (in this case, it reduces from $2,600—in transaction d—to $500).

Looking at Exhibit 2-16, an increase in assets is a debit, while a decrease in assets is a credit.

So Cash (an asset) increases, which is a debit. Accounts Receivable (an asset) decreases, which is a credit.

i.	Cash (Asset ↑; debit)	2,100	
	Accounts Receivable (Asset ↓; credit)		2,100
	Received cash on account.		

$2,100 is posted to the debit (left) side of the Cash T-account. $2,100 is posted to the credit (right) side of the Accounts Receivable account, as follows:

	Cash		
a.	10,000		
		c.	800
		e.	500
f.	2,000		
		g.	200
		h.	900
i.	2,100		

	Accounts Receivable		
d.	2,600		
		i.	2,100

j. The business declared and paid cash dividends of $1,500.

The business paid Michael dividends from the earnings it had retained on his behalf. This caused Michael's ownership interest (equity) to decrease. The accounts involved in this transaction are Dividends and Cash.

Dividends has increased and Cash is an asset that has decreased.

Looking at Exhibit 2-16, an increase in dividends is a debit, while a decrease in an asset is a credit.

Remember that dividends are a negative element of stockholders' equity. Therefore, when dividends increase, stockholders' equity decreases. So in this case, Dividends decreases equity with a debit. Cash (an asset) decreases with a credit.

j.	Dividends (Dividends ↑; debit) ↓SE	1,500	
	Cash (Asset ↓; credit)		1,500
	Paid dividends.		

$1,500 is posted to the debit (left) side of the Dividends T-account. $1,500 is posted to the credit (right) side of the Cash account, as follows:

	Cash		
a.	10,000		
		c.	800
		e.	500
f.	2,000		
		g.	200
		h.	900
i.	2,100		
		j.	1,500

	Dividends	
j.	1,500	

Now we can summarize all of the journal entries during the month.

Ref.		Accounts and Explanation	Debit	Credit
a.		Cash	10,000	
		Common Stock		10,000
		Issued common stock.		
b.		Equipment	3,500	
		Accounts Payable		3,500
		Purchased equipment on account.		
c.		Supplies	800	
		Cash		800
		Purchased supplies for cash.		
d.		Accounts Receivable	2,600	
		Service Revenue		2,600
		Provided services on account.		
e.		Accounts Payable	500	
		Cash		500
		Partial payment on account.		
f.		Cash	2,000	
		Service Revenue		2,000
		Provided services for cash.		
g.		Repair Expense	200	
		Cash		200
		Paid for repairs.		
h.		Salary Expense	900	
		Cash		900
		Paid salary.		
i.		Cash	2,100	
		Accounts Receivable		2,100
		Received cash on account.		
j.		Dividends	1,500	
		Cash		1,500
		Paid dividends.		

▶ Requirement 3

Total each T-account to determine its balance at the end of the month.

Part 1	Part 2	**Part 3**	Part 4	Demo Doc Complete

To compute the balance in a T-account (total the T-account), add up the numbers on the debit/ left side of the account and (separately) add the credit/right side of the account. The difference between the total debits and the total credits is the account's balance, which is placed on the side that holds the larger total. This gives the balance in the T-account.

For example, for the Cash account, the numbers on the debit/left side total $10,000 + $2,000 + $2,100 = $14,100. The credit/right side = $800 + $500 + $200 + $900 + $1,500 = $3,900. The difference is $14,100 − $3,900 = $10,200. At the end of the period, Cash has a debit balance of $10,200. We put the $10,200 at the bottom of the debit side because that was the side that showed the bigger total ($14,100). This is called a debit balance.

An easy way to think of totaling T-accounts is as follows:

Beginning balance in a T-account
+ Increases to the T-account
− Decreases to the T-account
T-account balance (net total)

T-accounts after posting all transactions and totaling each account are as follows:

▶ Requirement 4

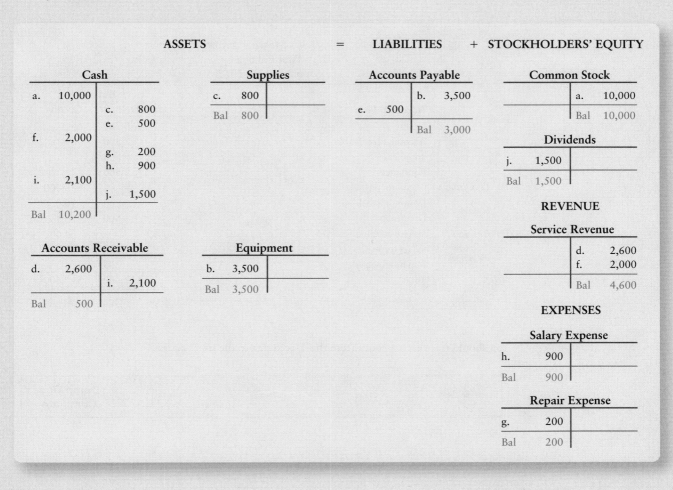

| Part 1 | Part 2 | Part 3 | **Part 4** | Demo Doc Complete |

The trial balance lists all the accounts along with their balances. This listing is helpful because it summarizes all the accounts in one place. Otherwise one must plow through all the T-accounts to find the balance of Accounts Payable, Salary Expense, or any other account.

The trial balance is an *internal* accounting document that accountants and managers use to prepare the financial statements. It's not like the income statement and balance sheet, which are presented to the public.

Data for the trial balance come directly from the T-accounts that we prepared in Requirement 3. A debit balance in a T-account remains a debit in the trial balance, and likewise for credits. For example, the T-account for Cash shows a debit balance of $10,200, and the trial balance lists Cash the same way. The Accounts Payable T-account shows a $3,000 credit balance, and the trial balance lists Accounts Payable correctly.

The trial balance for Moe's Mowing at September 30, 2012, appears as follows. Notice that we list the accounts in their proper order—assets, liabilities, stockholder's equity, revenues, and expenses.

Moe's Mowing, Inc.
Trial Balance
September 30, 2012

	Account Title	Debit	Credit
Assets	Cash	$10,200	
	Accounts receivable	500	
	Supplies	800	
	Equipment	3,500	
Liabilities	Accounts payable		$ 3,000
Equity	Common stock		10,000
	Dividends	1,500	
Revenues	Service revenue		4,600
Expenses	Salary expense	900	
	Repair expense	200	
	Total	$17,600	$17,600

You should trace each account from the T-accounts to the trial balance.

| Part 1 | Part 2 | Part 3 | Part 4 | Demo Doc Complete |

3

Accrual Accounting & Income

SPOTLIGHT: Starbucks Corporation

Starbucks has changed coffee from a breakfast drink to an experience. The corporation began in Seattle, Washington, in 1985 and now has almost 17,000 locations in 50 countries around the world.

As you can see from Starbucks' Consolidated Statement of Earnings on the next page, the company sold over $10.7 billion of coffee and related products during the 2010 fiscal year. The company translated that revenue into about $946 million in profits. That's a lot of coffee!

But at Starbucks, it's about more than coffee. From the aromas and music to the wi-fi connection, having a latte, frappucino, or caramel macchiato at Starbucks is designed to be a friendly, "socially connected" experience. It's also about a Shared Planet™. An integral part of the company's mission and values is to do business in a way that demonstrates a strong commitment to people and to the environment. The company has developed standards for environmentally, socially, and economically responsible coffee-buying to help assure better prices for farmers who do business with Starbucks. Starbucks works with Conservation International to encourage coffee growers to use sustainable farming practices that help protect the environment. The company has developed reusable and recyclable cups. It also sponsors employee programs that contribute hundreds of thousands of service hours to the communities where Starbucks stores operate. Starbucks is even committed to building "green" buildings that reduce its environmental footprint. All of these ethical practices cost money, which can be hard to justify during difficult economic times. But Starbucks is committed to using its resources for good as well as for gain. Think about that when you buy your next latte. ●

© Meccasky/Dreamstime.com

Starbucks Corporation Consolidated Statement of Earnings (Adapted) Year Ended October 3, 2010	
(In millions)	
Revenues:	
Net operating revenues	$10,707
Other income	20
Total net revenues	10,727
Expenses:	
Cost of sales (cost of goods sold)	4,458
Store operating expenses	3,551
Other operating expenses	144
Depreciation and amortization expenses	570
General and administrative expenses	569
Total operating expenses	9,292
Income before income tax	1,435
Income tax expense	489
Net income	$ 946

This chapter completes our coverage of the accounting cycle.
It gives the basics of what you need before tackling individual topics such as receivables, inventory, and cash flows.

Learning Objectives

1. **Explain** how accrual accounting differs from cash-basis accounting
2. **Apply** the revenue and expense recognition principles
3. **Adjust** the accounts
4. **Construct** the financial statements
5. **Close** the books
6. **Analyze** and evaluate a company's debt-paying ability

For more practice and review of accounting cycle concepts, use ACT, the accounting Cycle Tutorial, online at www.myaccountinglab.com. Margin logos like this one, directing you to the appropriate ACT section and material, appear throughout Chapters 1, 2, and 3. When you enter the tutorial, you'll find three buttons on the opening page of each chapter module. Here's what the buttons mean: **Tutorial** gives you a review of the major concepts, **Application** gives you practice exercises, and **Glossary** reviews important terms.

Explain How Accrual Accounting Differs From Cash-Basis Accounting

1

Explain how accrual accounting differs from cash-basis accounting

Managers want to earn a profit. Investors search for companies whose stock prices will increase. Banks seek borrowers who'll pay their debts. Accounting provides the information these people use for decision making. Accounting can be based on either the

► accrual basis, or the
► cash basis.

Accrual accounting records the impact of a business transaction as it occurs. When the business performs a service, makes a sale, or incurs an expense, the accountant records the transaction even if the business receives or pays no cash.

Cash-basis accounting records only cash transactions—cash receipts and cash payments. Cash receipts are treated as revenues, and cash payments are handled as expenses.

Generally accepted accounting principles (GAAP) require accrual accounting. The business records revenues as the revenues are earned and expenses as the expenses are incurred—not necessarily when cash changes hands. Consider a sale on account. Which transaction increases your wealth—making an $800 sale on account, or collecting the $800 cash? Making the sale increases your wealth by $300 because you gave up inventory that cost you $500 and you got a receivable worth $800. Collecting cash later merely swaps your $800 receivable for $800 cash—no gain on this transaction. Making the sale—not collecting the cash—increases your wealth.

The basic defect of cash-basis accounting is that the cash basis ignores important information. That makes the financial statements incomplete. The result? People using the statements make decisions based on incomplete information, which can lead to mistakes.

Suppose your business makes a sale *on account*. The cash basis does not record the sale because you received no cash. You may be thinking, "Let's wait until we collect cash and then record the sale. After all, we pay the bills with cash, so let's ignore transactions that don't affect cash."

What's wrong with this argument? There are two defects—one on the balance sheet and the other on the income statement.

Balance-Sheet Defect. If we fail to record a sale on account, the balance sheet reports no account receivable. Why is this so bad? The receivable represents a claim to receive cash in the future, which is a real asset, and it should appear on the balance sheet. Without this information, assets are understated on the balance sheet.

Income-Statement Defect. A sale on account provides revenue that increases the company's wealth. Ignoring the sale understates revenue and net income on the income statement.

The take-away lessons from this discussion are as follows:

▶ Companies that use the cash basis of accounting do not follow GAAP. Their financial statements omit important information.

▶ All but the smallest businesses use the accrual basis of accounting.

Accrual Accounting and Cash Flows

Accrual accounting is more complex—and, in terms of the Conceptual Foundations of Accounting (Exhibit 1-3), is a more faithful representation of economic reality—than cash-basis accounting. To be sure, accrual accounting records cash transactions, such as the following:

CASH FLOW

▶ Collecting cash from customers
▶ Receiving cash from interest earned
▶ Paying salaries, rent, and other expenses
▶ Borrowing money
▶ Paying off loans
▶ Issuing stock

But accrual accounting also records *noncash* transactions, such as the following:

▶ Sales on account
▶ Purchases of inventory on account
▶ Accrual of expenses incurred but not yet paid
▶ Depreciation expense
▶ Usage of prepaid rent, insurance, and supplies
▶ Earning of revenue when cash was collected in advance

Accrual accounting is based on a framework of additional concepts and principles to those we discussed in Chapter 1. We turn now to the time-period concept, the revenue principle, and the expense recognition principle.

The Time-Period Concept

The only way for a business to know for certain how well it performed is to shut down, sell the assets, pay the liabilities, and return any leftover cash to the owners. This process, called liquidation, means going out of business. Ongoing companies can't wait until they go out of business to measure income! Instead, they need regular progress reports. Accountants, therefore, prepare financial statements for specific periods. The **time-period concept** ensures that accounting information is reported at regular intervals.

The basic accounting period is one year, and virtually all businesses prepare annual financial statements. Around 60% of large companies—including Amazon.com, RadioShack Corporation, eBay, and YUM! Brands—use the calendar year from January 1 through December 31.

A *fiscal* year ends on a date other than December 31. Most retailers, including Wal-Mart, The Gap Inc. and JCPenney, use a fiscal year that ends on or near January 31 because the low point in their business activity falls in January, after Christmas. Starbucks Corporation uses a fiscal year that ends on or near September 30.

Companies also prepare financial statements for interim periods of less than a year, such as a month, a quarter (three months), or a semiannual period (six months). Most of the discussions in this text are based on an annual accounting period.

Apply the Revenue and Expense Recognition Principles

The Revenue Principle

The **revenue principle** deals with two issues:

1. When to record revenue (make a journal entry)

2. The amount of revenue to record

When should you record revenue? After it has been earned—and not before. In most cases, revenue is earned when the business has delivered a good or service to a customer. It has done everything required to earn the revenue by transferring the good or service to the customer.

2

Apply the revenue and expense recognition principles

Global View   Revenue recognition has been one of the areas in which a number of differences have existed between U.S. GAAP and IFRS for years. U.S. GAAP has been highly detailed and has varied by industry. For example, the rules for timing and the amount of revenue in the computer software industry have differed substantially from those in the construction industry. By contrast, IFRS has been far less detailed, leaving more room for interpretation on the part of the company. In 2011, the FASB and IASB finished a joint research project that resolved most of these differences, resulting in a consistent, converged, and simplified global revenue recognition standard. The effective date for the new standard on revenue recognition will be sometime in 2012. This book deals with the retail industry, where businesses purchase and sell largely finished goods and render services in a straightforward way. Fortunately, in the retail industry, U.S. GAAP and IFRS have historically been consistent with respect to general principles of revenue recognition, so the issuance of the new standard will not substantially change the rules by which revenue is recognized in the retail industry.

Exhibit 3-1 shows two situations that provide guidance on when to record revenue for Starbucks Corporation. Situation 1 illustrates when not to record revenue. No transaction has occurred, so Starbucks Corporation records nothing. Situation 2 illustrates when revenue should be recorded—after a transaction has occurred.

The *amount* of revenue to record is the cash value of the goods or services transferred to the customer. The *event* that triggers revenue recognition for the sale of goods is the *transfer of control of the goods* to the purchaser. In the case of services, the event that triggers revenue recognition is the *substantial completion of an obligation to perform a service* for the buyer. For example, suppose that in

EXHIBIT 3-1 | When to Record Revenue

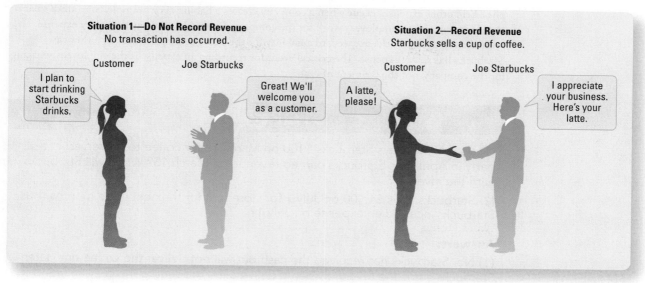

order to promote business, Starbucks runs a promotion and sells lattes for the discount price of $2 per cup. Ordinarily Starbucks would charge $4 for this drink. How much revenue should Starbucks record? The answer is $2—the cash value of the transaction. The amount of the sale, $2, is the amount of revenue earned—not the regular price of $4. The event that triggers revenue recognition on the part of Starbucks is the point when the customer takes control (and in this case, possession) of the product.

By contrast, suppose that a plumbing company signs a contract to perform plumbing services for a customer who is remodeling a home. The value of the services is $50,000. In signing the contract, the plumbing company becomes obligated to complete the plumbing services by a certain date. Revenue may not be recognized until the plumbing company has substantially completed its obligation and has finished performing the services for the customer.

The Expense Recognition Principle

The **expense recognition principle** is the basis for recording expenses. Expenses are the costs of assets used up, and of liabilities created, in earning revenue. Expenses have no future benefit to the company. The expense recognition principle includes two steps:

1. Identify all the expenses incurred during the accounting period.

2. Measure the expenses, and recognize them in the same period in which any related revenues are earned.

To *recognize* expenses along with related revenues means to subtract expenses from related revenues to compute net income or net loss. Exhibit 3-2 illustrates the expense recognition (sometimes referred to as matching) principle.

EXHIBIT 3-2 | The Expense Recognition Principle

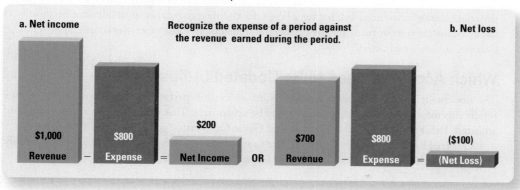

Some expenses are paid in cash. Other expenses arise from using up an asset such as supplies. Still other expenses occur when a company creates a liability. For example, Starbucks' salary expense occurs when employees work for the company. Starbucks may pay the salary expense immediately, or Starbucks may record a liability for the salary to be paid later. In either case, Starbucks has salary expense. The critical event for recording an expense is the employees' working for the company, not the payment of cash.

STOP & THINK...

(1) A customer pays Starbucks $100 on March 15 for coffee to be served at a party in April. Has Starbucks earned revenue on March 15? When will Starbucks earn the revenue?

(2) Starbucks pays $4,500 on July 1 for store rent for the next three months. Has Starbucks incurred an expense on July 1?

- -

Answers:

(1) No. Starbucks has received the cash but will not deliver the coffee until later. Starbucks earns the revenue when it delivers the product to the customer and the customer assumes control over it.

(2) No. Starbucks has paid cash for rent in advance. No expense has yet been incurred because the company has not yet occupied the space. This prepaid rent is an asset because Starbucks has acquired the use of a store location in the future.

Ethical Issues in Accrual Accounting

Accrual accounting provides some ethical challenges that cash accounting avoids. For example, suppose that in 2012, Starbucks Corporation prepays a $3 million advertising campaign to be conducted by a large advertising agency. The advertisements are scheduled to run during September, October, and November. In this case, Starbucks is buying an asset, a prepaid expense.

Suppose Starbucks pays for the advertisements on September 1 and the ads start running immediately. Under accrual accounting, Starbucks should record one-third of the expense ($1 million) during the year ended September 30, 2012, and two-thirds ($2 million) during 2013.

Suppose fiscal 2012 is a great year for Starbucks—net income is better than expected. Starbucks' top managers believe that fiscal 2013 will not be as profitable. In this case, the company has a strong incentive to expense the full $3 million during fiscal 2012 in order to report all the advertising expense in the fiscal 2012 income statement. This unethical action would keep $2 million of advertising expense off the fiscal 2013 income statement and make 2013's net income look $2 million better.

Adjust the Accounts

3

Adjust the accounts

At the end of the period, the business reports its financial statements. This process begins with the trial balance introduced in Chapter 2. We refer to this trial balance as unadjusted because the accounts are not yet ready for the financial statements. In most cases, the simple label "Trial Balance" means "unadjusted."

Which Accounts Need to Be Updated (Adjusted)?

The stockholders need to know how well Genie Car Wash is performing. The financial statements report this information, and all accounts must be up-to-date. That means some accounts must be adjusted. Exhibit 3-3 gives the trial balance of Genie Car Wash, Inc., at June 30, 2012.

This trial balance is unadjusted. That means it's not completely up-to-date. It's not quite ready for preparing the financial statements for presentation to the public.

EXHIBIT 3-3 | Unadjusted Trial Balance

Genie Car Wash, Inc. Unadjusted Trial Balance June 30, 2012		
Cash	$24,800	
Accounts receivable	2,200	
Supplies	700	
Prepaid rent	3,000	
Equipment	24,000	
Accounts payable		$13,100
Unearned service revenue		400
Common stock		20,000
Retained earnings		18,800
Dividends	3,200	
Service revenue		7,000
Salary expense	900	
Utilities expense	500	
Total	$59,300	$59,300

Cash, Equipment, Accounts Payable, Common Stock, and Dividends are up-to-date and need no adjustment at the end of the period. Why? Because the day-to-day transactions provide all the data for these accounts.

Accounts Receivable, Supplies, Prepaid Rent, and the other accounts are another story. These accounts are not yet up-to-date on June 30. Why? Because certain transactions have not yet been recorded. Consider Supplies. During June, Genie Car Wash used cleaning supplies to wash cars. But Genie didn't make a journal entry for supplies used every time it washed a car. That would waste time and money. Instead, Genie waits until the end of the period and then records the supplies used up during the entire month.

The cost of supplies used up is an expense. An adjusting entry at the end of June updates both Supplies (an asset) and Supplies Expense. We must adjust all accounts whose balances are not yet up-to-date.

Categories of Adjusting Entries

Accounting adjustments fall into three basic categories: deferrals, depreciation, and accruals.

Deferrals. A **deferral** is an adjustment for payment of an item or receipt of cash in advance. Starbucks purchases supplies for use in its operations. During the period, some supplies (assets) are used up and become expenses. At the end of the period, an adjustment is needed to decrease the Supplies account for the supplies used up. This is Supplies Expense. Prepaid rent, prepaid insurance, and all other prepaid expenses require deferral adjustments.

There are also deferral adjustments for liabilities. Companies such as Starbucks may collect cash from a grocery-store chain in advance of earning the revenue. When Starbucks receives cash up front, Starbucks has a liability to provide coffee for the customer. This liability is called Unearned Sales Revenue. Then, when Starbucks delivers the goods to the customer, it earns Sales Revenue. This earning process requires an adjustment at the end of the period. The adjustment decreases the liability and increases the revenue for the revenue earned. Publishers such as Time, Inc., and your cell-phone company collect cash in advance. They too must make adjusting entries for revenues earned later.

Depreciation. **Depreciation** allocates the cost of a plant asset to expense over the asset's useful life. Depreciation is the most common long-term deferral. Starbucks buys buildings and equipment. As Starbucks uses the assets, it records depreciation for wear-and-tear and obsolescence. The accounting adjustment records Depreciation Expense and decreases the asset's book value over its life. The process is identical to a deferral-type adjustment; the only difference is the type of asset involved.

Accruals. An **accrual** is the opposite of a deferral. For an accrued *expense*, Starbucks records the expense before paying cash. For an accrued *revenue*, Starbucks records the revenue before collecting cash.

Salary Expense can create an accrual adjustment. As employees work for Starbucks Corporation, the company's salary expense accrues with the passage of time. At September 30, 2012, Starbucks owed employees some salaries to be paid after year end. At September 30, Starbucks recorded Salary Expense and Salary Payable for the amount owed. Other examples of expense accruals include interest expense and income tax expense.

An accrued revenue is a revenue that the business has earned and will collect next year. At year end, Starbucks must accrue the revenue. The adjustment debits a receivable and credits a revenue. For example, accrual of interest revenue debits Interest Receivable and credits Interest Revenue.

Let's see how the adjusting process actually works for Genie Car Wash at June 30. We start with prepaid expenses.

Prepaid Expenses

A **prepaid expense** is an expense paid in advance. Therefore, prepaid expenses are assets because they provide a future benefit for the owner. Let's do the adjustments for prepaid rent and supplies.

Prepaid Rent. Companies pay rent in advance. This prepayment creates an asset for the renter, who can then use the rented item in the future. Suppose Genie Car Wash prepays three months' store rent ($3,000) on June 1. The entry for the prepayment of three months' rent debits Prepaid Rent as follows:

Jun 1	Prepaid Rent ($1,000 × 3)	3,000	
	Cash		3,000
	Paid three months' rent in advance.		

The accounting equation shows that one asset increases and another decreases. Total assets are unchanged.

Assets	=	Liabilities	+	Stockholders' Equity
3,000	=	0	+	0
− 3,000				

After posting, the Prepaid Rent account appears as follows:

Prepaid Rent	
Jun 1 3,000	

Throughout June, the Prepaid Rent account carries this beginning balance, as shown in Exhibit 3-3 (p. 141). The adjustment transfers $1,000 from Prepaid Rent to Rent Expense as follows:*

Adjusting entry a

Jun 30	Rent Expense ($3,000 × 1/3)	1,000	
	Prepaid Rent		1,000
	To record rent expense.		

*See Exhibit 3-8, (p. 152), for a summary of adjustments a–g.

Both assets and stockholders' equity decrease.

Assets	=	Liabilities	+	Stockholders' Equity	−	Expenses
− 1,000	=	0				− 1,000

After posting, Prepaid Rent and Rent Expense appear as follows:

Prepaid Rent					Rent Expense		
Jun 1	3,000	Jun 30	1,000 →		Jun 30	1,000	
Bal	2,000				Bal	1,000	

This adjusting entry illustrates application of the expense recognition principle. We record an expense in order to measure net income.

Supplies. Supplies are another type of prepaid expense. On June 2, Genie Car Wash paid cash of $700 for cleaning supplies:

Jun 2	Supplies	700	
	Cash		700
	Paid cash for supplies.		

Assets	=	Liabilities	+	Stockholders' Equity
700	=	0	+	0
− 700				

The cost of the supplies Genie used is supplies expense. To measure June's supplies expense, the business counts the supplies on hand at the end of the month. The count shows that $400 of supplies remain. Subtracting the $400 of supplies on hand from the supplies available ($700) measures supplies expense for the month ($300), as follows:

Asset Available During the Period	−	Asset on Hand at the End of the Period	=	Asset Used (Expense) During the Period
$700	−	$400	=	$300

The June 30 adjusting entry debits the expense and credits the asset, as follows:

Adjusting entry b

Jun 30	Supplies Expense ($700 − $400)	300	
	Supplies		300
	To record supplies expense.		

Assets	=	Liabilities	+	Stockholders' Equity	−	Expenses
− 300	=	0				− 300

After posting, the Supplies and Supplies Expense accounts appear as follows. The adjustment is highlighted for emphasis.

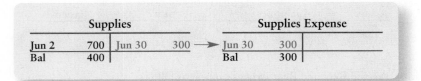

Supplies				Supplies Expense	
Jun 2	700	Jun 30	300 →	Jun 30	300
Bal	400			Bal	300

At the start of July, Supplies has this $400 balance, and the adjustment process is repeated each month.

STOP & THINK...

At the beginning of the month, supplies were $5,000. During the month, $7,000 of supplies were purchased. At month's end, $3,000 of supplies are still on hand. What is the

- adjusting entry?
- ending balance in the Supplies account?

- -

Answer:

Supplies Expense ($5,000 + $7,000 − $3,000)	9,000	
Supplies		9,000
Ending balance of supplies = $3,000 (the supplies still on hand)		

Depreciation of Plant Assets

Plant assets are long-lived tangible assets, such as land, buildings, furniture, and equipment. All plant assets except land decline in usefulness, and this decline is an expense. Accountants spread the cost of each plant asset, except land, over its useful life. Depreciation is the process of allocating cost to expense for a long-term plant asset.

To illustrate depreciation, consider Genie Car Wash. Suppose that on June 3 Genie purchased car-washing equipment on account for $24,000:

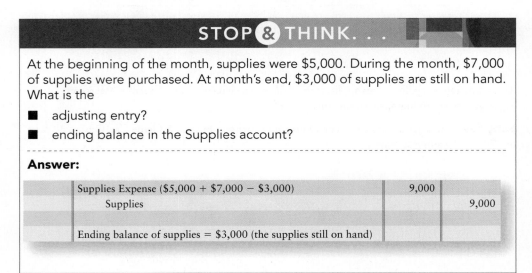

Jun 3	Equipment	24,000	
	Accounts Payable	.	24,000
	Purchased equipment on account.		

Assets	=	Liabilities	+	Stockholders' Equity
24,000	=	24,000	+	0

After posting, the Equipment account appears as follows:

Equipment	
Jun 3	24,000

Genie records an asset when it purchases equipment. Then, as the asset is used, a portion of the asset's cost is transferred to Depreciation Expense. The machine is being used to produce revenue. The cost of the machine should be allocated (matched) against that revenue. This is another illustration of the expense recognition principle. Computerized systems program the depreciation for automatic entry each period.

Genie's equipment will remain useful for five years and then be worthless. One way to compute the amount of depreciation for each year is to divide the cost of the asset ($24,000 in our example) by its expected useful life (five years). This procedure—called the straight-line depreciation method—gives annual depreciation of $4,800. The depreciation amount is an estimate. (Chapter 7 covers plant assets and depreciation in more detail.)

$$\text{Annual depreciation} = \$24,000/5 \text{ years} = \$4,800 \text{ per year}$$

Depreciation for June is $400.

$$\text{Monthly depreciation} = \$4,800/12 \text{ months} = \$400 \text{ per month}$$

The Accumulated Depreciation Account. Depreciation expense for June is recorded as follows:

			Adjusting entry c
Jun 30	Depreciation Expense—Equipment	400	
	Accumulated Depreciation—Equipment		400
	To record depreciation.		

Total assets decrease by the amount of the expense:

Assets	=	Liabilities	+	Stockholders' Equity	−	Expenses
− 400	=	0				− 400

The Accumulated Depreciation account (not Equipment) is credited to preserve the original cost of the asset in the Equipment account. Managers can then refer to the Equipment account if they ever need to know how much the asset cost.

The **Accumulated Depreciation** account shows the sum of all depreciation expense from using the asset. Therefore, the balance in the Accumulated Depreciation account increases over the asset's life.

Accumulated Depreciation is a contra asset account—an asset account with a normal credit balance. A **contra account** has two distinguishing characteristics:

1. It always has a companion account.

2. Its normal balance is opposite that of the companion account.

In this case, Accumulated Depreciation is the contra account to Equipment, so Accumulated Depreciation appears directly after Equipment on the balance sheet. A business carries an accumulated depreciation account for each depreciable asset, for example, Accumulated Depreciation—Building and Accumulated Depreciation—Equipment.

After posting, the plant asset accounts of Genie Car Wash are as follows—with the adjustment highlighted:

Equipment				Accumulated Depreciation—Equipment			Depreciation Expense—Equipment	
Jun 3	24,000			Jun 30	400	Jun 30	400	
Bal	24,000			Bal	400	Bal	400	

Book Value. The net amount of a plant asset (cost minus accumulated depreciation) is called that asset's **book value (of a plant asset)**, or carrying amount. Exhibit 3-4 shows how Genie would report the book value of its equipment and building at June 30 (the building data are assumed for this illustration).

EXHIBIT 3-4 | Plant Assets on the Balance Sheet of Genie Car Wash, Inc.

Genie Car Wash Plant Assets at June 30		
Equipment	$24,000	
Less: Accumulated Depreciation	(400)	$23,600
Building	$50,000	
Less: Accumulated Depreciation	(200)	49,800
Book value of plant assets		$73,400

At June 30, the book value of equipment is $23,600; the book value of the building is $49,800.

STOP & THINK...

What will be the book value of Genie's equipment at the end of July?

Answer:
$24,000 − $400 − $400 = $23,200.

Exhibit 3-5 shows how Starbucks Corporation reports property, plant, and equipment in its 2010 annual report. Lines 1 to 6 list specific assets and their cost. Line 7 shows the cost of all Starbucks' plant assets. Line 8 gives the amount of accumulated depreciation, and line 9 shows the assets' book value of $2,417 million.

Accrued Expenses

Businesses may incur expenses before they pay cash. Consider an employee's salary. Starbucks' expense and payable grow as the employee works, so the liability is said to accrue. Another example is interest expense on a note payable. Interest accrues as the clock ticks. The term **accrued expense** refers to a liability that arises from an expense that has not yet been paid.

Companies don't record accrued expenses daily or weekly. Instead, they wait until the end of the period and use an adjusting entry to update each expense (and related liability) for the financial statements. Let's look at salary expense.

EXHIBIT 3-5 | Starbucks Corporation's Reporting of Property, Plant, and Equipment (Adapted, in millions)

1	Land...	$ 58
2	Buildings	266
3	Leasehold improvements.....................................	3,436
4	Store equipment	1,048
5	Roasting equipment	291
6	Furniture, fixtures, and other	790
7	Property, plant, and equipment, at cost..............	5,889
8	Less: Accumulated depreciation	(3,472)
9	Property, plant, and equipment, net	$ 2,417

Most companies pay their employees at set times. Suppose Genie Car Wash pays its employee a monthly salary of $1,800, half on the 15th and half on the last day of the month. The following calendar for June has the paydays circled:

June						
Sun.	Mon.	Tue.	Wed.	Thur.	Fri.	Sat.
						1
2	3	4	5	6	7	8
9	10	11	12	13	14	(15)
16	17	18	19	20	21	22
23	24	25	26	27	28	29
(30)						

Assume that if a payday falls on a Sunday, Genie pays the employee on the following Monday. During June, Genie paid its employees the first half-month salary of $900 and made the following entry:

Jun 15	Salary Expense	900	
	Cash		900
	To pay salary.		

Assets	=	Liabilities	+	Stockholders' Equity	−	Expenses
− 900	=	0				− 900

After posting, the Salary Expense account appears as follows:

Salary Expense	
Jun 15 900	

The trial balance at June 30 (Exhibit 3-3, p. 141) includes Salary Expense with its debit balance of $900. Because June 30, the second payday of the month, falls on a Sunday, the second half-month amount of $900 will be paid on Monday, July 1. At June 30, therefore, Genie adjusts for additional salary expense and salary payable of $900 as follows:

Adjusting entry d

Jun 30	Salary Expense	900	
	Salary Payable		900
	To accrue salary expense.		

An accrued expense increases liabilities and decreases stockholders' equity:

Assets	=	Liabilities	+	Stockholders' Equity	−	Expenses
0	=	900				− 900

After posting, the Salary Payable and Salary Expense accounts appear as follows (adjustment highlighted):

Salary Payable				Salary Expense		
	Jun 30	900		Jun 15	900	
	Bal	900		Jun 30	900	
				Bal	1,800	

The accounts now hold all of June's salary information. Salary Expense has a full month's salary, and Salary Payable shows the amount owed at June 30. All accrued expenses are recorded this way—debit the expense and credit the liability.

Computerized systems contain a payroll module. Accrued salaries can be automatically journalized and posted at the end of each period.

Accrued Revenues

Businesses often earn revenue before they receive the cash. A revenue that has been earned but not yet collected is called an **accrued revenue**.

Assume that FedEx hires Genie on June 15 to wash FedEx delivery trucks each month. Suppose FedEx will pay Genie $600 monthly, with the first payment on July 15. During June, Genie will earn half a month's fee, $300, for work done June 15 through June 30. On June 30, Genie makes the following adjusting entry:

Adjusting entry e

Jun 30	Accounts Receivable ($600 × 1/2)	300	
	Service Revenue		300
	To accrue service revenue.		

Revenue increases both total assets and stockholders' equity:

Assets	=	Liabilities	+	Stockholders' Equity	+	Revenues
300	=	0				+ 300

Recall that Accounts Receivable has an unadjusted balance of $2,200, and Service Revenue's unadjusted balance is $7,000 (Exhibit 3-3, p. 141). This June 30 adjusting entry has the following effects (adjustment highlighted):

Accounts Receivable		Service Revenue	
2,200			7,000
Jun 30 300			Jun 30 300
Bal 2,500			Bal 7,300

All accrued revenues are accounted for similarly—debit a receivable and credit a revenue.

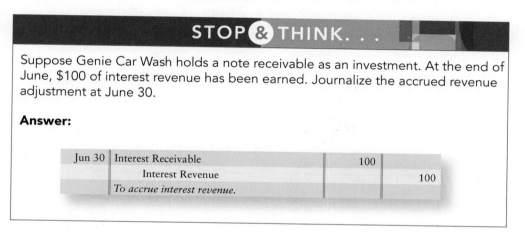

STOP & THINK. . .

Suppose Genie Car Wash holds a note receivable as an investment. At the end of June, $100 of interest revenue has been earned. Journalize the accrued revenue adjustment at June 30.

Answer:

Jun 30	Interest Receivable	100	
	Interest Revenue		100
	To accrue interest revenue.		

Unearned Revenues

Some businesses collect cash from customers before earning the revenue. This creates a liability called **unearned revenue**. Only when the job is completed does the business earn the revenue. Suppose **Home Depot** engages Genie Car Wash to wash Home Depot trucks, agreeing to pay Genie $400 monthly, beginning immediately. If Genie collects the first amount on June 15, then Genie records this transaction as follows:

Jun 15	Cash	400	
	Unearned Service Revenue		400
	Received cash for revenue in advance.		

Assets	=	Liabilities	+	Stockholders' Equity
400	=	400	+	0

After posting, the liability account appears as follows:

Unearned Service Revenue	
	Jun 15 400

Unearned Service Revenue is a liability because Genie is obligated to perform services for Home Depot. The June 30 unadjusted trial balance (Exhibit 3-3, p. 141) lists Unearned Service Revenue with a $400 credit balance. During the last 15 days of the month, Genie will earn one-half of the $400, or $200. On June 30, Genie makes the following adjustment:

			Adjusting entry f
Jun 30	Unearned Service Revenue ($400 × 1/2)	200	
	Service Revenue		200
	To record unearned service revenue that has been earned.		

Assets	=	Liabilities	+	Stockholders' Equity	+	Revenues
0	=	− 200				+ 200

This adjusting entry shifts $200 of the total amount received ($400) from liability to revenue. After posting, Unearned Service Revenue is reduced to $200, and Service Revenue is increased by $200, as follows (adjustment highlighted):

Unearned Service Revenue				Service Revenue		
Jun 30	200	Jun 15	400			7,000
		Bal	200	Jun 30		300
				Jun 30		200
				Bal		7,500

All revenues collected in advance are accounted for this way. An unearned revenue is a liability, not a revenue.

One company's prepaid expense is the other company's unearned revenue. For example, Home Depot's prepaid expense is Genie Car Wash's liability for unearned revenue.

Exhibit 3-6 diagrams the distinctive timing of prepaids and accruals. Study prepaid expenses all the way across. Then study unearned revenues across, and so on.

EXHIBIT 3-6 | Prepaid and Accrual Adjustments

PREPAIDS—Cash First

	First			Later		
Prepaid expenses	*Pay cash and record an asset:*			*Record an expense and decrease the asset:*		
	Prepaid Expense......	XXX		Expense..............................	XXX	
	Cash..............		XXX	Prepaid Expense.........		XXX
Unearned revenues	*Receive cash and record unearned revenue:*			*Record revenue and decrease unearned revenue:*		
	Cash........................	XXX		Unearned Revenue	XXX	
	Unearned Revenue		XXX	Revenue		XXX

ACCRUALS—Cash Later

	First			Later		
Accrued expenses	*Accrue expense and a payable:*			*Pay cash and decrease the payable:*		
	Expense..................	XXX		Payable.............................	XXX	
	Payable...........		XXX	Cash..............................		XXX
Accrued revenues	*Accrue revenue and a receivable:*			*Receive cash and decrease the receivable:*		
	Receivable...............	XXX		Cash..............................	XXX	
	Revenue		XXX	Receivable.................		XXX

The authors thank Professors Darrel Davis and Alfonso Oddo for suggesting this exhibit.

Summary of the Adjusting Process

Two purposes of the adjusting process are to

► measure income, and
► update the balance sheet.

Therefore, every adjusting entry affects at least one of the following:

► Revenue or expense—to measure income
► Asset or liability—to update the balance sheet

Exhibit 3-7 summarizes the standard adjustments.

EXHIBIT 3-7 | Summary of Adjusting Entries

	Type of Account	
Category of Adjusting Entry	**Debit**	**Credit**
Prepaid expense..................	Expense	Asset
Depreciation.......................	Expense	Contra asset
Accrued expense.................	Expense	Liability
Accrued revenue.................	Asset	Revenue
Unearned revenue...............	Liability	Revenue

Exhibit 3-8 summarizes the adjustments of Genie Car Wash, Inc., at June 30—the adjusting entries we've examined over the past few pages.

► Panel A repeats the data for each adjustment.
► Panel B gives the adjusting entries.
► Panel C on the following page shows the accounts after posting the adjusting entries. The adjustments are keyed by letter.

EXHIBIT 3-8 | The Adjusting Process of Genie Car Wash, Inc.

PANEL A—Information for Adjustments at June 30, 2012	PANEL B—Adjusting Entries	D	C
(a) Prepaid rent expired, $1,000.	(a) Rent Expense .... Prepaid Rent .... *To record rent expense.*	1,000	1,000
(b) Supplies used, $300.	(b) Supplies Expense .... Supplies... *To record supplies used.*	300	300
(c) Depreciation on equipment, $400.	(c) Depreciation Expense—Equipment .... Accumulated Depreciation—Equipment *To record depreciation.*	400	400
(d) Accrued salary expense, $900.	(d) Salary Expense .... Salary Payable .... *To accrue salary expense.*	900	900
(e) Accrued service revenue, $300.	(e) Accounts Receivable.................................... Service Revenue.................................... *To accrue service revenue.*	300	300
(f) Amount of unearned service revenue that has been earned, $200.	(f) Unearned Service Revenue.......................... Service Revenue.................................... *To record unearned revenue that has been earned.*	200	200
(g) Accrued income tax expense, $600.	(g) Income Tax Expense .... Income Tax Payable.............................. *To accrue income tax expense.*	600	600

PANEL C—Ledger Accounts

Assets	Liabilities	Stockholders' Equity

Assets

Cash

Bal 24,800	

Accounts Receivable

	2,200	
(e)	300	
Bal	2,500	

Supplies

	700	(b)	300
Bal	400		

Prepaid Rent

	3,000	(a)	1,000
Bal	2,000		

Equipment

Bal 24,000	

Accumulated Depreciation— Equipment

	(c)	400
	Bal	400

Liabilities

Accounts Payable

	Bal 13,100

Salary Payable

	(d)	900
	Bal	900

Unearned Service Revenue

(f)	200		400
		Bal	200

Income Tax Payable

	(g)	600
	Bal	600

Stockholders' Equity

Common Stock

	Bal 20,000

Retained Earnings

	Bal 18,800

Dividends

Bal 3,200	

Revenue

Service Revenue

		7,000
	(e)	300
	(f)	200
	Bal	7,500

Expenses

Rent Expense

(a)	1,000	
Bal	1,000	

Salary Expense

	900	
(d)	900	
Bal	1,800	

Supplies Expense

(b)	300	
Bal	300	

Depreciation Expense—Equipment

(c)	400	
Bal	400	

Utilities Expense

Bal	500	

Income Tax Expense

(g)	600	
Bal	600	

Exhibit 3-8 includes an additional adjusting entry that we have not yet discussed—the accrual of income tax expense. Like individual taxpayers, corporations are subject to income tax. They typically accrue income tax expense and the related income tax payable as the final adjusting entry of the period. Genie Car Wash accrues income tax expense with adjusting entry g, as follows:

Adjusting entry g

Jun 30	Income Tax Expense	600	
	Income Tax Payable		600
	To accrue income tax expense.		

The income tax accrual follows the pattern for accrued expenses.

The Adjusted Trial Balance

This chapter began with the unadjusted trial balance (see Exhibit 3-3, p. 141). After the adjustments are journalized and posted, the accounts appear as shown in Exhibit 3-8, Panel C. A useful step in preparing the financial statements is to list the accounts, along with their adjusted balances, on an **adjusted trial balance**. This document lists all the accounts and their final balances in a single place. Exhibit 3-9 shows the adjusted trial balance of Genie Car Wash, Inc.

EXHIBIT 3-9 | Adjusted Trial Balance

	Trial Balance		Adjustments		Adjusted Trial Balance		
Account Title	**Debit**	**Credit**	**Debit**	**Credit**	**Debit**	**Credit**	
Cash	24,800				24,800		
Accounts receivable	2,200		(e) 300		2,500		
Supplies	700			(b) 300	400		
Prepaid rent	3,000			(a) 1,000	2,000		
Equipment	24,000				24,000		
Accumulated depreciation—equipment				(c) 400		400	**Balance Sheet** *(Exhibit 3-12)*
Accounts payable		13,100				13,100	
Salary payable				(d) 900		900	
Unearned service revenue		400	(f) 200			200	
Income tax payable				(g) 600		600	
Common stock		20,000				20,000	
Retained earnings		18,800				18,800	**Statement of Retained Earnings** *(Exhibit 3-11)*
Dividends	3,200				3,200		
Service revenue		7,000		(e) 300		7,500	
				(f) 200			
Rent expense			(a) 1,000		1,000		
Salary expense	900		(d) 900		1,800		**Income Statement** *(Exhibit 3-10)*
Supplies expense			(b) 300		300		
Depreciation expense			(c) 400		400		
Utilities expense	500				500		
Income tax expense			(g) 600		600		
	59,300	59,300	3,700	3,700	61,500	61,500	

Genie Car Wash, Inc.
Preparation of Adjusted Trial Balance
June 30, 2012

Note how clearly the adjusted trial balance presents the data. The Account Title and the Trial Balance data come from the trial balance. The two Adjustments columns summarize the adjusting entries. The Adjusted Trial Balance columns then give the final account balances. Each adjusted amount in Exhibit 3-9 is the unadjusted balance plus or minus the adjustments. For example, Accounts Receivable starts with a balance of $2,200. Add the $300 debit adjustment to get Accounts Receivable's ending balance of $2,500. Spreadsheets are designed for this type of analysis.

Construct the Financial Statements

Construct the financial statements

The June financial statements of Genie Car Wash can be prepared from the adjusted trial balance. At the far right, Exhibit 3-9 shows how the accounts are distributed to the financial statements.

► The income statement (Exhibit 3-10) lists the revenue and expense accounts.
► The statement of retained earnings (Exhibit 3-11) shows the changes in retained earnings.
► The balance sheet (Exhibit 3-12) reports assets, liabilities, and stockholders' equity.

The arrows in Exhibits 3-10, 3-11, and 3-12 (all on the following page) show the flow of data from one statement to the next.

Why is the income statement prepared first and the balance sheet last?

1. The income statement reports net income or net loss, the result of revenues minus expenses. Revenues and expenses affect stockholders' equity, so net income is then transferred to retained earnings. The first arrow (1) tracks net income.
2. Retained Earnings is the final balancing element of the balance sheet. To solidify your understanding, trace the $18,500 retained earnings figure from Exhibit 3-11 to Exhibit 3-12. Arrow 2 tracks retained earnings.

EXHIBIT 3-10 | Income Statement

Genie Car Wash, Inc.
Income Statement
Month Ended June 30, 2012

Revenue:		
Service revenue		$7,500
Expenses:		
Salary expense	$1,800	
Rent expense	1,000	
Utilities expense	500	
Depreciation expense	400	
Supplies expenses	300	4,000
Income before tax		3,500
Income tax expense		600
Net income		$2,900

EXHIBIT 3-11 | Statement of Retained Earnings

Genie Car Wash, Inc.
Statement of Retained Earnings
Month Ended June 30, 2012

Retained earnings, May 31, 2012	$18,800
Add: Net income	2,900
	21,700
Less: Dividends	(3,200)
Retained earnings, June 30, 2012	$18,500

①

EXHIBIT 3-12 | Balance Sheet

Genie Car Wash, Inc.
Balance Sheet
June 30, 2012

②

Assets			Liabilities	
Cash		$24,800	Accounts payable	$13,100
Accounts receivable		2,500	Salary payable	900
Supplies		400	Unearned service revenue	200
Prepaid rent		2,000	Income tax payable	600
Equipment	$24,000		Total liabilities	14,800
Less: Accumulated			**Stockholders' Equity**	
depreciation	(400)	23,600	Common stock	20,000
			Retained earnings	18,500
			Total stockholders' equity	38,500
			Total liabilities and	
Total assets		$53,300	stockholders' equity	$53,300

MID-CHAPTER SUMMARY PROBLEM

The given trial balance of Goldsmith Company pertains to December 31, 2012, which is the end of its year-long accounting period. Data needed for the adjusting entries include the following:

a. Supplies on hand at year end, $2,000.

b. Depreciation on furniture and fixtures, $20,000.

c. Depreciation on building, $10,000.

d. Salaries owed but not yet paid, $5,000.

e. Accrued service revenue, $12,000.

f. Of the $45,000 balance of unearned service revenue, $32,000 was earned during the year.

g. Accrued income tax expense, $35,000.

▶ Requirements

1. Open the ledger accounts with their unadjusted balances. Show dollar amounts in thousands, as shown for Accounts Receivable:

Accounts Receivable
370

2. Journalize the Goldsmith Company adjusting entries at December 31, 2012. Key entries by letter, as in Exhibit 3-8 (p. 152).

3. Post the adjusting entries.

4. Prepare an adjusted trial balance, as shown in Exhibit 3-9 (p. 154).

5. Prepare the income statement, the statement of retained earnings, and the balance sheet. (At this stage, it is not necessary to classify assets or liabilities as current or long term.) Draw arrows linking these three financial statements.

Goldsmith Company
Trial Balance
December 31, 2012

Cash	$ 198,000	
Accounts receivable	370,000	
Supplies	6,000	
Furniture and fixtures	100,000	
Accumulated depreciation—furniture and fixtures		$ 40,000
Building	250,000	
Accumulated depreciation—building		130,000
Accounts payable		380,000
Salary payable		
Unearned service revenue		45,000
Income tax payable		
Common stock		100,000
Retained earnings		193,000
Dividends	65,000	
Service revenue		286,000
Salary expense	172,000	
Supplies expense		
Depreciation expense—furniture and fixtures		
Depreciation expense—building		
Income tax expense		
Miscellaneous expense	13,000	
Total	$1,174,000	$1,174,000

▶ Answers

Requirements 1 and 3

(Amounts in thousands)

Assets

Cash
Bal 198	

Accounts Receivable
370	
(e) 12	
Bal 382	

Supplies
6	(a) 4
Bal 2	

Furniture and Fixtures
Bal 100	

Accumulated Depreciation—Furniture and Fixtures
	40
	(b) 20
	Bal 60

Building
Bal 250	

Accumulated Depreciation—Building
	130
(c)	10
	Bal 140

Liabilities

Accounts Payable
	Bal 380

Salary Payable
	(d) 5
	Bal 5

Unearned Service Revenue
(f) 32	45
	Bal 13

Income Tax Payable
	(g) 35
	Bal 35

Stockholders' Equity

Common Stock
	Bal 100

Retained Earnings
	Bal 193

Dividends
Bal 65	

Revenues

Service Revenue
	286
(e)	12
(f)	32
	Bal 330

Expenses

Salary Expense
172	
(d) 5	
Bal 177	

Supplies Expense
(a) 4	
Bal 4	

Depreciation Expense—Furniture and Fixtures
(b) 20	
Bal 20	

Depreciation Expense—Building
(c) 10	
Bal 10	

Income Tax Expense
(g) 35	
Bal 35	

Miscellaneous Expense
Bal 13	

Requirement 2

(a)	Dec 31	Supplies Expense ($6,000 − $2,000)	4,000	
		Supplies		4,000
		To record supplies used.		
(b)	31	Depreciation Expense—Furniture and Fixtures	20,000	
		Accumulated Depreciation—Furniture and Fixtures		20,000
		To record depreciation expense on furniture and fixtures.		
(c)	31	Depreciation Expense—Building	10,000	
		Accumulated Depreciation—Building		10,000
		To record depreciation expense on building.		
(d)	31	Salary Expense	5,000	
		Salary Payable		5,000
		To accrue salary expense.		
(e)	31	Accounts Receivable	12,000	
		Service Revenue		12,000
		To accrue service revenue.		
(f)	31	Unearned Service Revenue	32,000	
		Service Revenue		32,000
		To record unearned service revenue that has been earned.		
(g)	31	Income Tax Expense	35,000	
		Income Tax Payable		35,000
		To accrue income tax expense.		

Requirement 4

Goldsmith Company
Preparation of Adjusted Trial Balance
December 31, 2012

(Amounts in thousands) Account Title	Trial Balance Debit	Trial Balance Credit	Adjustments Debit		Adjustments Credit		Adjusted Trial Balance Debit	Adjusted Trial Balance Credit
Cash	198						198	
Accounts receivable	370		(e)	12			382	
Supplies	6				(a)	4	2	
Furniture and fixtures	100						100	
Accumulated depreciation—furniture and fixtures		40			(b)	20		60
Building	250						250	
Accumulated depreciation—building		130			(c)	10		140
Accounts payable		380						380
Salary payable					(d)	5		5
Unearned service revenue		45	(f)	32				13
Income tax payable					(g)	35		35
Common stock		100						100
Retained earnings		193						193
Dividends	65						65	
Service revenue		286			(e)	12		330
					(f)	32		
Salary expense	172		(d)	5			177	
Supplies expense			(a)	4			4	
Depreciation expense—furniture and fixtures			(b)	20			20	
Depreciation expense—building			(c)	10			10	
Income tax expense			(g)	35			35	
Miscellaneous expense	13						13	
	1,174	1,174		118		118	1,256	1,256

Requirement 5

Goldsmith Company
Income Statement
Year Ended December 31, 2012

(Amounts in thousands)		
Revenue:		
Service revenue		$330
Expenses:		
Salary expense	$177	
Depreciation expense—furniture and fixtures	20	
Depreciation expense—building	10	
Supplies expense	4	
Miscellaneous expenses	13	224
Income before tax		106
Income tax expense		35
Net income		$ 71

①

Goldsmith Company
Statement of Retained Earnings
Year Ended December 31, 2012

(Amounts in thousands)	
Retained earnings, December 31, 2011	$193
Add: Net income	71
	264
Less: Dividends	(65)
Retained earnings, December 31, 2012	$199

②

Goldsmith Company
Balance Sheet
December 31, 2012

(Amounts in thousands) Assets			Liabilities	
Cash		$198	Accounts payable	$380
Accounts receivable		382	Salary payable	5
Supplies		2	Unearned service revenue	13
Furniture and fixtures	$100		Income tax payable	35
Less: Accumulated			Total liabilities	433
depreciation	(60)	40		
			Stockholders' Equity	
Building	$250		Common stock	100
Less: Accumulated			Retained earnings	199
depreciation	(140)	110	Total stockholders' equity	299
			Total liabilities and	
Total assets		$732	stockholders' equity	$732

Close the Books

5

Close the books

It is now June 30, the end of the month. Kyle Nielson, the manager, will continue Genie Car Wash into July, August, and beyond. But wait—the revenue and the expense accounts still hold amounts for June. At the end of each accounting period, it is necessary to close the books.

Closing the books means to prepare the accounts for the next period's transactions. The **closing entries** set the revenue, expense, and dividends balances back to zero at the end of the period. The idea is the same as setting the scoreboard back to zero after a game.

Closing is easily handled by computers. Recall that the income statement for a particular year reports only one year's income. For example, net income for Starbucks Corporation in fiscal 2010 relates exclusively to the year ended October 3, 2010. At each year end, Starbucks accountants close the company's revenues and expenses for that year.

Temporary Accounts. Because revenues and expenses relate to a limited period, they are called **temporary accounts**. The Dividends account is also temporary. The closing process applies only to temporary accounts (revenues, expenses, and dividends).

Permanent Accounts. Let's contrast the temporary accounts with the **permanent accounts**: assets, liabilities, and stockholders' equity. The permanent accounts are not closed at the end of the period because they carry over to the next period. Consider Cash, Receivables, Equipment, Accounts Payable, Common Stock, and Retained Earnings. Their ending balances at the end of one period become the beginning balances of the next period.

Closing entries transfer the revenue, expense, and dividends balances to Retained Earnings. Here are the steps to close the books of a company such as Starbucks Corporation or Genie Car Wash:

1. Debit each revenue account for the amount of its credit balance. Credit Retained Earnings for the sum of the revenues. Now the sum of the revenues is in Retained Earnings.

2. Credit each expense account for the amount of its debit balance. Debit Retained Earnings for the sum of the expenses. The sum of the expenses is now in Retained Earnings.

3. Credit the Dividends account for the amount of its debit balance. Debit Retained Earnings. This entry places the dividends amount in the debit side of Retained Earnings. Remember that dividends are not expenses. Dividends never affect net income.

After closing the books, the Retained Earnings account of Genie Car Wash appears as follows (data from page 155):

Retained Earnings			
		Beginning balance	18,800
Expenses	4,600	Revenues	7,500
Dividends	3,200		
		Ending balance	18,500

Assume that Genie Car Wash closes the books at the end of June. Exhibit 3-13 presents the complete closing process for the business. Panel A gives the closing journal entries, and Panel B shows the accounts after closing.

Classifying Assets and Liabilities Based on Their Liquidity

On the balance sheet, assets and liabilities are classified as current or long term to indicate their relative liquidity. **Liquidity** measures how quickly an item can be converted to cash. Cash is the most liquid asset. Accounts receivable are relatively liquid because cash collections usually follow quickly. Inventory is less liquid than accounts receivable because the company must first sell the goods. Equipment and buildings are even less liquid because these assets are held for use and not for sale. A balance sheet lists assets and liabilities in the order of relative liquidity.

EXHIBIT 3-13 | Journalizing and Posting the Closing Entries

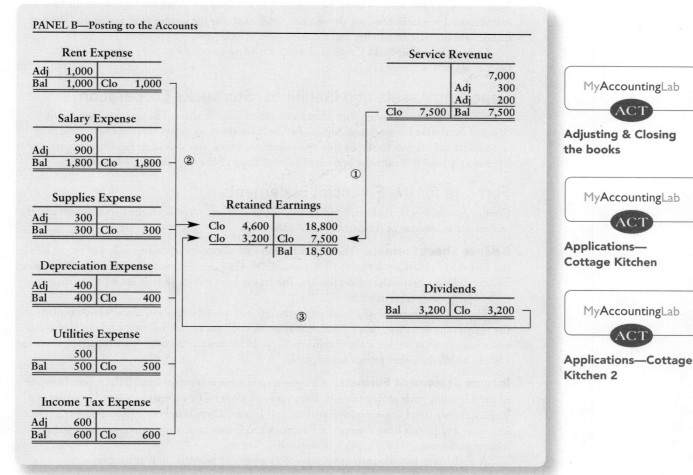

PANEL A—Journalizing the Closing Entries   Page 5

			Closing Entries		
①	Jun 30	Service Revenue.............................		7,500	
		Retained Earnings			7,500
②	30	Retained Earnings		4,600	
		Rent Expense			1,000
		Salary Expense			1,800
		Supplies Expense			300
		Depreciation Expense..............			400
		Utilities Expense.....................			500
		Income Tax Expense			600
③	30	Retained Earnings		3,200	
		Dividends................................			3,200

PANEL B—Posting to the Accounts

Rent Expense

Adj	1,000		
Bal	1,000	Clo	1,000

Salary Expense

		900	
Adj	900		
Bal	1,800	Clo	1,800

Supplies Expense

Adj	300		
Bal	300	Clo	300

Depreciation Expense

Adj	400		
Bal	400	Clo	400

Utilities Expense

	500		
Bal	500	Clo	500

Income Tax Expense

Adj	600		
Bal	600	Clo	600

Service Revenue

			7,000
		Adj	300
		Adj	200
Clo	7,500	Bal	7,500

Retained Earnings

Clo	4,600		18,800
Clo	3,200	Clo	7,500
		Bal	18,500

Dividends

Bal	3,200	Clo	3,200

Adj = Amount posted from an adjusting entry
Clo = Amount posted from a closing entry
Bal = Balance
As arrow ② in Panel B shows, we can make a compound closing entry for all the expenses.

MyAccountingLab
ACT
Adjusting & Closing the books

MyAccountingLab
ACT
Applications—Cottage Kitchen

MyAccountingLab
ACT
Applications—Cottage Kitchen 2

Current Assets. As we saw in Chapter 1, **current assets** are the most liquid assets. They will be converted to cash, sold, or consumed during the next 12 months or within the business's normal operating cycle if longer than a year. The **operating cycle** is the time span during which cash is paid for goods and services, and these goods and services are sold to bring in cash.

For most businesses, the operating cycle is a few months. Cash, Short-Term Investments, Accounts Receivable, Merchandise Inventory, and Prepaid Expenses are the current assets.

Long-Term Assets. **Long-term assets** are all assets not classified as current assets. One category of long-term assets is plant assets, often labeled Property, Plant, and Equipment. Land, Buildings, Furniture and Fixtures, and Equipment are plant assets. Of these, Genie Car Wash has only Equipment. Long-Term Investments, Intangible Assets, and Other Assets (a catchall category for assets that are not classified more precisely) are also long-term.

Current Liabilities. As we saw in Chapter 1, **current liabilities** are debts that must be paid within one year or within the entity's operating cycle if longer than a year. Accounts Payable, Notes Payable due within one year, Salary Payable, Unearned Revenue, Interest Payable, and Income Tax Payable are current liabilities.

Bankers and other lenders are interested in the due dates of an entity's liabilities. The sooner a liability must be paid, the more pressure it creates. Therefore, the balance sheet lists liabilities in the order in which they must be paid. Balance sheets usually report two liability classifications, current liabilities and long-term liabilities.

Long-Term Liabilities. All liabilities that are not current are classified as **long-term liabilities**. Many notes payable are long term. Some notes payable are paid in installments, with the first installment due within one year, the second installment due the second year, and so on. The first installment is a current liability and the remainder is long term.

Let's see how Starbucks Corporation reports these asset and liability categories on its balance sheet.

Reporting Assets and Liabilities: Starbucks Corporation

Exhibit 3-14 on the following page shows a classified balance sheet: The Consolidated Balance Sheet of Starbucks Corporation. A **classified balance sheet** separates current assets from long-term assets and current liabilities from long-term liabilities. You should be familiar with most of Starbucks' accounts. Study the Starbucks balance sheet all the way through—line by line.

Formats for the Financial Statements

Companies can format their financial statements in different ways. Both the balance sheet and the income statement can be formatted in two basic ways.

Balance Sheet Formats. The **report format** lists the assets at the top, followed by the liabilities and stockholders' equity below. The Consolidated Balance Sheet of Starbucks Corporation in Exhibit 3-14 illustrates the report format. The report format is more popular, with approximately 60% of large companies using it.

The **account format** lists the assets on the left and the liabilities and stockholders' equity on the right in the same way that a T-account appears, with assets (debits) on the left and liabilities and equity (credits) on the right. Exhibit 3-12 (p. 155) shows an account-format balance sheet for Genie Car Wash. Either format is acceptable.

Income Statement Formats. A **single-step income statement** lists all the revenues together under a heading such as Revenues, or Revenues and Gains. The expenses are listed together in a single category titled Expenses, or Expenses and Losses. There is only one step, the subtraction of Expenses and Losses from the sum of Revenues and Gains, in arriving at net income. Starbucks' income statement (p. 136) appears in single-step format.

A **multi-step income statement** reports a number of subtotals to highlight important relationships between revenues and expenses. Exhibit 3-15 shows Starbucks' income statement in multi-step format. Gross profit, income from operations, income before tax, and net income are highlighted for emphasis.

In particular, income from operations ($1,415 million) is separated from "Other income," which Starbucks did not earn by selling coffee. The other income was mainly interest revenue and other investment income. Most companies consider it important to report their operating income separately from nonoperating income such as interest and dividends.

Most companies' income statements do not conform to either a pure single-step format or a pure multi-step format. Business operations are too complex for all companies to conform to rigid reporting formats. We will discuss the components of the income statement in more detail in Chapter 11.

EXHIBIT 3-14 | Classified Balance Sheet of Starbucks Corporation

Starbucks Corporation
Consolidated Balance Sheet (Adapted)
October 3, 2010

(In millions)	
Assets	
Current assets:	
Cash and cash equivalents	$1,164
Short-term investments	286
Accounts receivable	303
Inventories	543
Prepaid expenses and other current assets	460
Total current assets	2,756
Long-term investments	533
Property, plant, and equipment, net	2,417
Intangible assets	333
Other assets	347
Total assets	$6,386
Liabilities and Shareholders' Equity	
Current liabilities:	
Accounts payable	$ 283
Accrued expenses payable	673
Other accrued liabilities	409
Unearned revenue	414
Total current liabilities	1,779
Long-term debt	550
Other long-term liabilities	375
Total liabilities	2,704
Shareholders' equity:	
Common stock	146
Retained earnings	3,471
Other equity	65
Total shareholders' equity	3,682
Total liabilities and shareholders' equity	$6,386

EXHIBIT 3-15 | Starbucks Corporation Income Statement in Multi-Step Format

Starbucks Corporation
Consolidated Statement of Earnings (Adapted)
Year Ended October 3, 2010

		Millions
Net operating revenues		$10,707
Cost of sales (Cost of goods sold)		4,458
Gross profit		6,249
Store operating expenses	$3,551	
Other operating expenses	144	
Depreciation and amortization expenses	570	
General and administrative expenses	569	
Total operating expenses		4,834
Income from operations		1,415
Other income		20
Income before income taxes		1,435
Income tax expense		489
Net income		$ 946

Analyze and Evaluate a Company's Debt-Paying Ability

As we've seen, accounting provides information for decision making. A bank considering lending money must predict whether the borrower can repay the loan. If the borrower already has a lot of debt, the probability of repayment may be low. If the borrower owes little, the loan may go through. To analyze a company's financial position, decision makers use data and ratios computed from various items in the financial statements. Let's see how this process works.

Net Working Capital

Net working capital is computational data that represents operating liquidity. Its computation is simple:

$$\text{Net working capital} = \text{Total current assets} - \text{Total current liabilities}$$

For Starbucks Corporation (amounts in millions on page 165),

$$\text{Net working capital} = \$2,756 - \$1,779 = \$977$$

Generally, to be considered sufficiently liquid, entities should have a sufficient excess of current assets over current liabilities. The amount of that excess is usually expressed in terms of the current ratio discussed below, and the amount considered "sufficient" varies with the industry. Starbucks Corporation's current assets exceed its current liabilities by \$977 million, meaning that after the company pays all of its current liabilities, it will still have almost \$1 billion in cash and other assets that can be converted into cash. Thus, Starbucks Corporation is considered highly "liquid."

Current Ratio

Another means of expressing operating liquidity through the relationship between current assets and current liabilities is the **current ratio**, which divides total current assets by total current liabilities.

$$\text{Current ratio} = \frac{\text{Total current assets}}{\text{Total current liabilities}}$$

For Starbucks Corporation (amounts in millions on page 165),

$$\text{Current ratio} = \frac{\text{Total current assets}}{\text{Total current liabilities}} = \frac{\$2,756}{\$1,779} = 1.55$$

Like net working capital, the current ratio measures the company's ability to pay current liabilities with current assets. A company prefers a high current ratio, which means that the business has plenty of current assets to pay current liabilities. An increasing current ratio from period to period indicates improvement in financial position.

As a rule of thumb, a strong current ratio is 1.50, which indicates that the company has \$1.50 in current assets for every \$1.00 in current liabilities. A company with a current ratio of 1.50 would probably have little trouble paying its current liabilities. Most successful businesses operate with current ratios between 1.20 and 1.50. A current ratio of less than 1.00 is considered low. That would mean that current liabilities exceed current assets.

Starbucks' current ratio of 1.55 indicates a strong current ratio position. The company makes most sales for cash. It has 55% more cash, cash equivalents, and short term investments than the amount needed to pay off accounts payable, accrued expenses, and other accrued liabilites, which are the liabilities that must be met with cash immediately.

Debt Ratio

Still another measure of debt-paying ability is the **debt ratio**, which is the ratio of total liabilities to total assets.

$$\text{Debt ratio} = \frac{\text{Total liabilities}}{\text{Total assets}}$$

For Starbucks (amounts in millions on page 165),

$$\text{Debt ratio} = \frac{\text{Total liabilities}}{\text{Total assets}} = \frac{\$2,704}{\$6,386} = 0.42$$

The debt ratio indicates the proportion of a company's assets that is financed with debt. This ratio measures a business's ability to pay both current and long-term debts (total liabilities).

A low debt ratio is safer than a high debt ratio. Why? Because a company with few liabilities has low required debt payments. This company is unlikely to get into financial difficulty. By contrast, a business with a high debt ratio may have trouble paying its liabilities, especially when sales are low and cash is scarce.

Starbucks' debt ratio of 42% (0.42) is low compared to most companies in the United States. The norm for the debt ratio ranges from 60% to 70%. Starbucks' debt ratio indicates low risk for the company.

When a company fails to pay its debts, some of its creditors might be in a position to take the company away from its owners. Most bankruptcies result from high debt ratios. Companies that continue in this pattern are often forced out of business.

How Do Transactions Affect the Ratios?

Companies such as Starbucks are keenly aware of how transactions affect their ratios. Lending agreements often require that a company's current ratio not fall below a certain level. Another loan requirement is that the company's debt ratio may not rise above a threshold, such as 0.70. When a company fails to meet one of these conditions, it is said to default on its lending agreements. The penalty can be severe: the lender can require immediate payment of the loan. Starbucks has little enough debt that the company is not in danger of default. But many companies are. To help keep debt ratios within normal limits, companies might adopt one or more of the following strategies:

▶ Increase revenue and decrease costs, thus increasing current assets, net income, and retained earnings without increasing liabilities
▶ Sell stock, thus increasing cash and stockholder equity
▶ Choose to borrow less money

Let's use Starbucks Corporation to examine the effects of some transactions on the company's current ratio and debt ratio. As shown in the preceding section, Starbucks' ratios are as follows (dollar amounts in millions):[1]

$$\text{Current ratio} = \frac{\$2,756}{\$1,779} = 1.549 \qquad \text{Debt ratio} = \frac{\$2,704}{\$6,386} = 0.423$$

The managers of any company would be concerned about how inventory purchases, payments on account, expense accruals, and depreciation would affect its ratios. Let's see how Starbucks

---

[1]Because of the relatively small amounts of these particular illustrative transactions compared to the original components, we have chosen to carry debt ratio computations to three decimals in order to illustrate the impact of individual transactions on the debt ratio. The larger the individual transaction in comparison with the original components (for example, see the End-of-Chapter Summary Problem), the less necessary this will be.

would be affected by some typical transactions. For each transaction, the journal entry helps identify the effects on the company.

    a. Issued stock and received cash of $50 million.

Journal entry:	Cash	50	
	Common Stock		50

Cash, a current asset, affects both the current ratio and the debt ratio as follows:

$$\text{Current ratio} = \frac{\$2,756 + \$50}{\$1,779} = 1.577 \qquad \text{Debt ratio} = \frac{\$2,704}{\$6,386 + \$50} = 0.420$$

The issuance of stock improves both ratios slightly.

    b. Paid cash to purchase buildings for $20 million.

Journal entry:	Buildings	20	
	Cash		20

Cash, a current asset, decreases, but total assets stay the same. Liabilities are unchanged.

$$\text{Current ratio} = \frac{\$2,756 - \$20}{\$1,779} = 1.538 \qquad \text{Debt ratio} = \frac{\$2,704}{\$6,386 + \$20 - \$20} = 0.423; \text{ no change}$$

A cash purchase of a building hurts the current ratio, but doesn't affect the debt ratio.

    c. Made a $30 million sale on account to a grocery chain.

Journal entry:	Accounts Receivable	30	
	Sales Revenue		30

The increase in Accounts Receivable increases current assets and total assets, as follows: [1]

$$\text{Current ratio} = \frac{\$2,756 + \$30}{\$1,779} = 1.566 \qquad \text{Debt ratio} = \frac{\$2,704}{\$6,386 + \$30} = 0.421$$

A sale on account improves both ratios slightly.

    d. Collected the account receivable, $30 million.

Journal entry:	Cash	30	
	Accounts Receivable		30

This transaction has no effect on total current assets, total assets, or total liabilities. Both ratios are unaffected.

e. Accrued expenses at year end, $40 million.

Journal entry:

Expenses	40	
Expenses Payable		40

$$\text{Current ratio} = \frac{\$2,756}{\$1,779 + \$40} = 1.515 \qquad \text{Debt ratio} = \frac{\$2,704 + \$40}{\$6,386} = 0.430$$

Most expenses hurt both ratios.

f. Recorded depreciation, $80 million.

Journal entry:

Depreciation Expense	80	
Accumulated Depreciation		80

No current accounts are affected, so only the debt ratio is affected.

$$\text{Current ratio} = \frac{\$2,756}{\$1,779} = 1.549 \qquad \text{Debt ratio} = \frac{\$2,704}{\$6,386 - \$80} = 0.429$$

Depreciation decreases total assets and therefore hurts the debt ratio.

g. Earned interest revenue and collected cash, $40 million.
Cash, a current asset, affects both the current ratio and the debt ratio as follows:

Journal entry:

Cash	40	
Interest Revenue		40

$$\text{Current ratio} = \frac{\$2,756 + \$40}{\$1,779} = 1.572 \qquad \text{Debt ratio} = \frac{\$2,704}{\$6,386 + \$40} = 0.421$$

A revenue improves both ratios.

Now, let's wrap up the chapter by seeing how to use net working capital, the current ratio, and the debt ratio for decision making. The Decision Guidelines feature offers some clues.

DECISION GUIDELINES

EVALUATE DEBT-PAYING ABILITY USING NET WORKING CAPITAL, THE CURRENT RATIO, AND THE DEBT RATIO

In general, a larger amount of net working capital is preferable to a smaller amount. Similarly, a *high* current ratio is preferable to a low current ratio. *Increases* in net working capital and increases in the current ratio improve financial position. By contrast, a *low* debt ratio is preferable to a high debt ratio. Improvement is indicated by a *decrease* in the debt ratio.

No single ratio gives the whole picture about a company. Therefore, lenders and investors use many ratios to evaluate a company. Let's apply what we have learned. Suppose you are a loan officer at Bank of America, and Starbucks Corporation has asked you for a $20 million loan to launch a new blend of coffee. How will you make this loan decision? The Decision Guidelines show how bankers and investors use two key ratios.

USING NET WORKING CAPITAL AND THE CURRENT RATIO

Decision	Guidelines
How can you measure a company's ability to pay current liabilities with current assets?	Net working capital = Total current assets − Total current liabilities $$\text{Current ratio} = \frac{\text{Total current assets}}{\text{Total current liabilities}}$$
Who uses net working capital and the current ratio for decision making?	*Lenders and other creditors*, who must predict whether a borrower can pay its current liabilities. *Stockholders*, who know that a company that cannot pay its debts is not a good investment because it may go bankrupt. *Managers*, who must have enough cash to pay the company's current liabilities.
What is a good value of net working capital and the current ratio?	There is no correct answer for this. It depends on the industry as well as the individual entity's ability to generate cash quickly and primarily from operations. An entity with strong operating cash flow can operate successfully with a low amount of net working capital as long as cash comes in through operations at least as fast as accounts payable become due. A current ratio of, say, 1.10–1.20 is sometimes sufficient. An entity with relatively slow cash flow from operations needs a higher current ratio of, say, 1.30–1.50. Traditionally, a current ratio of 2.00 was considered ideal. Recently, acceptable values have decreased as companies have been able to operate more efficiently; today, a current ratio of 1.50 is considered strong. Although not ideal, cash-rich companies like Starbucks can operate with a current ratio below 1.0.

USING THE DEBT RATIO

Decision	**Guidelines**
How can you measure a company's ability to pay total liabilities?	$$\text{Debt ratio} = \frac{\text{Total liabilities}}{\text{Total assets}}$$
Who uses the debt ratio for decision making?	*Lenders and other creditors*, who must predict whether a borrower can pay its debts.
	Stockholders, who know that a company that cannot pay its debts is not a good investment because it may go bankrupt.
	Managers, who must have enough assets to pay the company's debts.
What is a good value of the debt ratio?	Depends on the industry:
	A company with strong cash flow can operate successfully with a high debt ratio of, say, 0.70–0.80.
	A company with weak cash flow needs a lower debt ratio of, say, 0.50–0.60.
	Traditionally, a debt ratio of 0.50 was considered ideal. Recently, values have increased as companies have been able to operate more efficiently; today, a normal value of the debt ratio is around 0.60–0.70.

END-OF-CHAPTER SUMMARY PROBLEM

Refer to the Mid-Chapter Summary Problem that begins on page 156. The adjusted trial balance appears on page 160.

▶ Requirements

1. Make Goldsmith Company's closing entries at December 31, 2012. Explain what the closing entries accomplish and why they are necessary. Show amounts in thousands.
2. Post the closing entries to Retained Earnings and compare Retained Earnings' ending balance with the amount reported on the balance sheet on page 161. The two amounts should be the same.

3. Prepare Goldsmith Company's classified balance sheet to identify the company's current assets and current liabilities. (Goldsmith has no long-term liabilities.) Use the account format. Then compute the company's net working capital, current ratio, and debt ratio at December 31, 2012.

4. The top management of Goldsmith Company has asked you for a $500,000 loan to expand the business. Goldsmith proposes to pay off the loan over a 10-year period. Recompute Goldsmith's debt ratio assuming you make the loan. Use the company financial statements plus the ratio values to decide whether to grant the loan at an interest rate of 8%, 10%, or 12%. Goldsmith's cash flow is strong. Give the reasoning underlying your decision.

▶ Answers

Requirement 1

2012			(In thousands)	
Dec 31	Service Revenue..	330		
	Retained Earnings		330	
31	Retained Earnings	259		
	Salary Expense		177	
	Depreciation Expense—			
	Furniture and Fixtures.............................		20	
	Depreciation Expense—Building		10	
	Supplies Expense		4	
	Income Tax Expense		35	
	Miscellaneous Expense...............................		13	
31	Retained Earnings	65		
	Dividends...		65	

Explanation of Closing Entries

The closing entries set the balance of each revenue, expense, and dividend account back to zero for the start of the next accounting period. We must close these accounts because their balances relate only to one accounting period.

Requirement 2

Retained Earnings			
			193
Clo	259	Clo	330
Clo	65		
		Bal	199

The balance in the Retained Earnings account agrees with the amount reported on the balance sheet, as it should.

Requirement 3

Goldsmith Company
Balance Sheet
December 31, 2012

(Amounts in thousands) Assets			Liabilities	
Current assets:			Current liabilities:	
Cash		$198	Accounts payable	$380
Accounts receivable		382	Salary payable	5
Supplies		2	Unearned service revenue	13
Total current assets		582	Income tax payable	35
Furniture and fixtures	$100		Total current liabilities	433
Less: Accumulated			**Stockholders' Equity**	
depreciation	(60)	40	Common stock	100
Building	$ 250		Retained earnings	199
Less: Accumulated			Total stockholders' equity	299
depreciation	(140)	110	Total liabilities and	
Total assets		$732	stockholders' equity	$732

$$\text{Net working capital} = \$582 - \$433 = \$149$$

$$\text{Current ratio} = \frac{\$582}{\$433} = 1.34 \qquad \text{Debt ratio} = \frac{\$433}{\$732} = 0.59$$

Requirement 4

$$\begin{array}{l}\text{Debt ratio assuming} \\ \text{the loan is made}\end{array} = \frac{\$433 + \$500}{\$732 + \$500} = \frac{\$933}{\$1,232} = .76$$

Decision: Make the loan at 10%.

Reasoning: Prior to the loan, the company's financial position and cash flow are strong. The current ratio is in a middle range, and the debt ratio is not too high. Net income (from the income statement) is high in relation to total revenue. Therefore, the company should be able to repay the loan.

The loan will increase the company's debt ratio from 59% to 76%, which is more risky than the company's financial position at present. On this basis, a midrange interest rate appears reasonable—at least as the starting point for the negotiation between Goldsmith Company and the bank.

REVIEW | Accrual Accounting & Income

Quick Check (Answers are given on page 214.)

1. On November 1, RosebriarApartments received $3,600 from a tenant for four months' rent. The receipt was credited to Unearned Rent Revenue. What adjusting entry is needed on December 31?

   a. Unearned Rent Revenue   1,800
        Rent Revenue   1,800

   b. Cash   900
        Rent Revenue   900

   c. Unearned Rent Revenue   900
        Rent Revenue   900

   d. Rent Revenue   900
        Unearned Rent Revenue   900

2. The following normal balances appear on the *adjusted* trial balance of Kittery National Company:

Equipment...	$90,000
Accumulated depreciation, equipment................	12,000
Depreciation expense, equipment......................	3,000

   The book value of the equipment is

   a. $66,000.   c. $78,000.
   b. $87,000.   d. $75,000.

3. Sullivan, Inc., purchased supplies for $1,500 during 2012. At year end, Sullivan had $400 of supplies left. The adjusting entry should

   a. debit Supplies Expense $1,100.   c. debit Supplies $400.
   b. credit Supplies $400.   d. debit Supplies $1,100.

4. The accountant for Zero Corp. failed to make the adjusting entry to record depreciation for the current year. The effect of this error is which of the following?

   a. Assets and expenses are understated; net income is understated.
   b. Net income is overstated and liabilities are understated.
   c. Assets, net income, and stockholders' equity are all overstated.
   d. Assets are overstated; stockholders' equity and net income are understated.

5. Interest earned on a note receivable at December 31 equals $225. What adjusting entry is required to accrue this interest?

   a. Interest Receivable   225
        Interest Revenue   225

   b. Interest Payable   225
        Interest Expense   225

   c. Interest Expense   225
        Cash   225

   d. Interest Expense   225
        Interest Payable   225

6. If a real estate company fails to accrue commission revenue,

   a. liabilities are overstated, and owners' equity is understated.
   b. assets are understated, and net income is understated.
   c. net income is understated, and stockholders' equity is overstated.
   d. revenues are understated, and net income is overstated.

7. All of the following statements are true except one. Which statement is false?

   a. The expense recognition principle directs accountants to identify and measure all expenses incurred and deduct them from revenues earned during the same period.

   b. Accrual accounting produces better information than cash-basis accounting.

   c. A fiscal year ends on some date other than December 31.

   d. Adjusting entries are required for a business that uses the cash basis.

8. The account Unearned Revenue is a(n)

   a. revenue.

   b. asset.

   c. liability.

   d. expense.

9. Adjusting entries

   a. are needed to measure the period's net income or net loss.

   b. do not debit or credit cash.

   c. update the accounts.

   d. All of the above

10. An adjusting entry that debits an expense and credits a liability is which type?

    a. Accrued expense

    b. Prepaid expense

    c. Depreciation expense

    d. Cash expense

    Use the following data for questions 11 and 12.

    Here are key figures from the balance sheet of Sicily, Inc., at the end of 2012 (amounts in thousands):

	December 31, 2012
Total assets (of which 30% are current)	$7,000
Current liabilities	700
Bonds payable (long-term)	1,300
Common stock	1,200
Retained earnings	3,800
Total liabilities and stockholders' equity	7,000

11. Sicily's current ratio at the end of 2012 is

    a. 10.00.

    b. 0.55.

    c. 1.05.

    d. 3.00.

12. Sicily's debt ratio at the end of 2012 is (all amounts are rounded)

    a. 1.05%.

    b. 14%.

    c. 29%.

    d. 10%.

13. On a trial balance, which of the following would indicate that an error has been made?

    a. Service Revenue has a debit balance.

    b. Accumulated Depreciation has a credit balance.

    c. Salary Expense has a debit balance.

    d. All of the above indicate errors.

14. The entry to close Management Fee Revenue would be which of the following?

    a. Management Fee Revenue
            Retained Earnings

    b. Management Fee Revenue does not need to be closed

    c. Retained Earnings
            Management Fee Revenue

    d. Management Fee Revenue
            Service Revenue

15. Which of the following accounts is not closed?
    a. Dividends
    b. Interest Revenue
    c. Accumulated Depreciation
    d. Depreciation Expense

16. FedEx earns service revenue of $750,000. How does this transaction affect FedEx's ratios?
    a. Hurts both ratios
    b. Improves both ratios
    c. Improves the current ratio and doesn't affect the debt ratio
    d. Hurts the current ratio and improves the debt ratio

17. Suppose Red Hill Corporation borrows $10 million on a 10-year note payable. How does this transaction affect Red Hill's current ratio and debt ratio?
    a. Improves the current ratio and hurts the debt ratio
    b. Hurts the current ratio and improves the debt ratio
    c. Improves both ratios
    d. Hurts both ratios

Accounting Vocabulary

account format (p. 164) A balance-sheet format that lists assets on the left and liabilities and stockholders' equity on the right.

accrual (p. 142) An expense or a revenue that occurs before the business pays or receives cash. An accrual is the opposite of a deferral.

accrual accounting (p. 137) Accounting that records the impact of a business event as it occurs, regardless of whether the transaction affected cash.

accrued expense (p. 146) An expense incurred but not yet paid in cash.

accrued revenue (p. 148) A revenue that has been earned but not yet received in cash.

accumulated depreciation (p. 145) The cumulative sum of all depreciation expense from the date of acquiring a plant asset.

adjusted trial balance (p. 153) A list of all the ledger accounts with their adjusted balances.

book value (of a plant asset) (p. 146) The asset's cost minus accumulated depreciation.

cash-basis accounting (p. 137) Accounting that records only transactions in which cash is received or paid.

classified balance sheet (p. 164) A balance sheet that shows current assets separate from long-term assets and current liabilities separate from long-term liabilities.

closing the books (p. 162) The process of preparing the accounts to begin recording the next period's transactions. Closing the accounts consists of journalizing and posting the closing entries to set the balances of the revenue, expense, and dividends accounts to zero. Also called closing the accounts.

closing entries (p. 162) Entries that transfer the revenue, expense, and dividends balances from these respective accounts to the Retained Earnings account.

contra account (p. 145) An account that always has a companion account and whose normal balance is opposite that of the companion account.

current asset (p. 163) An asset that is expected to be converted to cash, sold, or consumed during the next 12 months or within the business's normal operating cycle if longer than a year.

current liability (p. 164) A debt due to be paid within one year or within the entity's operating cycle if the cycle is longer than a year.

current ratio (p. 166) Current assets divided by current liabilities. Measures a company's ability to pay current liabilities with current assets.

debt ratio (p. 167) Ratio of total liabilities to total assets. States the proportion of a company's assets that is financed with debt.

deferral (p. 141) An adjustment for which the business paid or received cash in advance. Examples include prepaid rent, prepaid insurance, and supplies.

depreciation (p. 141) Allocation of the cost of a plant asset to expense over its useful life.

expense recognition principle (p. 139) The basis for recording expenses. Directs accountants to identify all expenses incurred during the period, to measure the expenses, and to match them against the revenues earned during that same period.

liquidity (p. 162) Measure of how quickly an item can be converted to cash.

long-term asset (p. 164) An asset that is not a current asset.

long-term liability (p. 164) A liability that is not a current liability.

multi-step income statement (p. 164) An income statement that contains subtotals to highlight important relationships between revenues and expenses.

net working capital (p. 166) A measure of liquidity; Current assets − current liabilities.

operating cycle (p. 163) Time span during which cash is paid for goods and services that are sold to customers who pay the business in cash.

permanent accounts (p. 162) Asset, liability, and stockholders' equity accounts that are not closed at the end of the period.

plant assets (p. 144) Long-lived assets, such as land, buildings, and equipment, used in the operation of the business. Also called fixed assets.

prepaid expense (p. 142) A category of miscellaneous assets that typically expire or get used up in the near future. Examples include prepaid rent, prepaid insurance, and supplies.

report format (p. 164) A balance-sheet format that lists assets at the top, followed by liabilities and stockholders' equity below.

revenue principle (p. 138) The basis for recording revenues; tells accountants when to record revenue and the amount of revenue to record.

single-step income statement (p. 164) An income statement that lists all the revenues together under a heading such as Revenues or Revenues and Gains. Expenses appear in a separate category called Expenses or perhaps Expenses and Losses.

temporary accounts (p. 162) The revenue and expense accounts that relate to a limited period and are closed at the end of the period are temporary accounts. For a corporation, the Dividends account is also temporary.

time-period concept (p. 138) Ensures that accounting information is reported at regular intervals.

unearned revenue (p. 149) A liability created when a business collects cash from customers in advance of earning the revenue. The obligation is to provide a product or a service in the future.

ASSESS YOUR PROGRESS

Short Exercises

S3-1 (*Learning Objective 1: Explain how accrual accounting differs from cash-basis accounting*) Western Corporation made sales of $850 million during 2012. Of this amount, Western collected cash for all but $27 million. The company's cost of goods sold was $290 million, and all other expenses for the year totaled $325 million. Also during 2012, Western paid $380 million for its inventory and $255 million for everything else. Beginning cash was $75 million. Western's top management is interviewing you for a job and they ask two questions:

  a. How much was Western's net income for 2012?
  b. How much was Western's cash balance at the end of 2012?

You will get the job only if you answer both questions correctly.

S3-2 (*Learning Objective 1: Explain how accrual accounting differs from cash-basis accounting*) Duneside Corporation began 2012 owing notes payable of $4.1 million. During 2012 Duneside borrowed $1.7 million on notes payable and paid off $1.6 million of notes payable from prior years. Interest expense for the year was $0.8 million, including $0.3 million of interest payable accrued at December 31, 2012.

Show what Duneside should report for these facts on the following financial statements:

1. Income statement
   a. Interest expense
2. Balance sheet
   a. Notes payable
   b. Interest payable

S3-3 (*Learning Objectives 1, 2: Explain how accrual accounting differs from cash-basis accounting; apply the revenue and expense recognition principles*) As the controller of Emblem Consulting, you have hired a new employee, whom you must train. She objects to making an adjusting entry for accrued salaries at the end of the period. She reasons, "We will pay the salaries soon. Why not wait until payment to record the expense? In the end, the result will be the same." Write a reply to explain to the employee why the adjusting entry is needed for accrued salary expense.

S3-4 (*Learning Objective 2: Apply the revenue and expense recognition principles*) A large auto manufacturer sells large fleets of vehicles to auto rental companies, such as Budget and Hertz. Suppose Budget is negotiating with the auto manufacturer to purchase 827 vehicles. Write a short paragraph to explain to the auto manufacturer when the company should, and should not, record this sales revenue and the related expense for cost of goods sold. Mention the accounting principles that provide the basis for your explanation.

S3-5 (*Learning Objective 2: Apply the expense recognition principle*) Write a short paragraph to explain in your own words the concept of depreciation as used in accounting.

S3-6 (*Learning Objective 2: Apply the revenue and expense recognition principles*) Identify the accounting concept or principle that gives the most direction on how to account for each of the following situations:

  a. Salary expense of $38,000 is accrued at the end of the period to measure income properly.
  b. March has been a particularly slow month, and the business will have a net loss for the second quarter of the year. Management is considering not following its customary practice of reporting quarterly earnings to the public.
  c. A physician performs a surgical operation and bills the patient's insurance company. It may take three months to collect from the insurance company. Should the physician record revenue now or wait until cash is collected?
  d. A construction company is building a highway system, and construction will take four years. When should the company record the revenue it earns?
  e. A utility bill is received on December 27 and will be paid next year. When should the company record utility expense?

S3-7 (*Learning Objective 3: Adjust the accounts*) Answer the following questions about prepaid expenses:

  a. On October 1, Up & Down Travel prepaid $3,000 for six months' rent. Give the adjusting entry to record rent expense at October 31. Include the date of the entry and an explanation. Then post all amounts to the two accounts involved, and show their balances at October 31. Up & Down Travel adjusts the accounts only at October 31, the end of its fiscal year.
  b. On October 1, Up & Down Travel paid $950 for supplies. At October 31, Up & Down Travel has $400 of supplies on hand. Make the required journal entry at October 31. Then post all amounts to the accounts and show their balances at October 31.

S3-8 (*Learning Objectives 1, 3: Explain how accrual accounting differs from cash-basis accounting; adjust the accounts for depreciation*) Suppose that on January 1 Foreton Golf Company paid cash of $50,000 for computers that are expected to remain useful for five years. At the end of five years, the computers' values are expected to be zero.

  1. Make journal entries to record (a) purchase of the computers on January 1 and (b) annual depreciation on December 31. Include dates and explanations, and use the following accounts: Computer Equipment; Accumulated Depreciation—Computer Equipment; and Depreciation Expense—Computer Equipment.
  2. Post to the accounts and show their balances at December 31.
  3. What is the computer equipment's book value at December 31?

S3-9 (*Learning Objective 2: Apply the revenue and expense recognition principles*) During 2012, Transit Airlines paid salary expense of $42.4 million. At December 31, 2012, Transit accrued salary expense of $2.2 million. Transit then paid $2.2 million to its employees on January 3, 2013, the company's next payday after the end of the 2012 year. For this sequence of transactions, show what Transit would report on its 2012 income statement and on its balance sheet at the end of 2012.

S3-10 (*Learning Objective 3: Adjust the accounts for interest expense*) Cheap Travel borrowed $60,000 on October 1 by signing a note payable to Community Bank. The interest expense for each month is $250. The loan agreement requires Cheap to pay interest on December 31.

1. Make Cheap's adjusting entry to accrue monthly interest expense at October 31, at November 30, and at December 31. Date each entry and include its explanation.
2. Post all three entries to the Interest Payable account. You need not take the balance of the account at the end of each month.
3. Record the payment of three months' interest at December 31.

S3-11 (*Learning Objective 3: Adjust the accounts for interest revenue*) Return to the situation in Short Exercise 3-10. Here you are accounting for the same transactions on the books of Community Bank, which lent the money to Cheap Travel.

1. Make Community Bank's adjusting entry to accrue monthly interest revenue at October 31, at November 30, and at December 31. Date each entry and include its explanation.
2. Post all three entries to the Interest Receivable account. You need not take the balance of the account at the end of each month.
3. Record the receipt of three months' interest at December 31.

S3-12 (*Learning Objectives 1, 3: Explain how accrual accounting differs from cash-basis accounting; adjust the accounts for unearned revenue*). Write a paragraph to explain why unearned revenues are liabilities instead of revenues. In your explanation, use the following actual example: *The World Star*, a national newspaper, collects cash from subscribers in advance and later delivers newspapers to subscribers over a one-year period. Explain what happens to the unearned revenue over the course of a year as *The World Star* delivers papers to subscribers. Into what account does the earned subscription revenue go as *The World Star* delivers papers? Give the journal entries that *The World Star* would make to (a) collect $60,000 of subscription revenue in advance and (b) record earning $40,000 of subscription revenue. Include an explanation for each entry, as illustrated in the chapter.

S3-13 (*Learning Objectives 3, 4: Adjust the accounts for prepaid expenses; construct the financial statements*) Dove Golf Co. prepaid three years' rent ($18,000) on January 1, 2012. At December 31, 2012, Dove prepared a trial balance and then made the necessary adjusting entry at the end of the year. Dove adjusts its accounts once each year—on December 31.

What amount appears for Prepaid Rent on

    a. Dove's *unadjusted* trial balance at December 31, 2012?
    b. Dove's *adjusted* trial balance at December 31, 2012?

What amount appears for Rent Expense on

    c. Dove's *unadjusted* trial balance at December 31, 2012?
    d. Dove's *adjusted* trial balance at December 31, 2012?

S3-14 (*Learning Objective 3: Adjust the accounts for accrued and unearned revenue*) Bantley, Inc., collects cash from customers two ways:

    a. **Accrued revenue.** Some customers pay Bantley after Bantley has performed service for the customer. During 2012, Bantley made sales of $55,000 on account and later received cash of $35,000 on account from these customers.
    b. **Unearned revenue.** A few customers pay Bantley in advance, and Bantley later performs the service for the customer. During 2012, Bantley collected $9,000 cash in advance and later earned $7,000 of this amount.

Journalize the following for Bantley:

    a. Earning service revenue of $55,000 on account and then collecting $35,000 on account
    b. Receiving $9,000 in advance and then earning $7,000 as service revenue

S3-15 (*Learning Objective 4: Construct the financial statements*) Suppose Sparrow Sporting Goods Company reported the following data at March 31, 2012, with amounts in thousands:

Retained earnings, March 31, 2011	$ 21,500	Cost of goods sold	$136,000
Accounts receivable	28,000	Cash	20,800
Net revenues	175,500	Property and equipment, net	6,300
Total current liabilities	55,100	Common stock	22,500
All other expenses	29,000	Inventories	35,000
Other current assets	5,000	Long-term liabilities	7,500
Other assets	22,000	Dividends	0

Use these data to prepare Sparrow Sporting Goods Company's income statement for the year ended March 31, 2012; statement of retained earnings for the year ended March 31, 2012; and classified balance sheet at March 31, 2012. Use the report format for the balance sheet. Draw arrows linking the three statements.

S3-16 (*Learning Objective 5: Close the books*) Use the Sparrow Sporting Goods Company data in Short Exercise 3-15 to make the company's closing entries at March 31, 2012. Then set up a T-account for Retained Earnings and post to that account. Compare Retained Earnings' ending balance to the amount reported on Sparrow's statement of retained earnings and balance sheet. What do you find?

S3-17 (*Learning Objective 6: Analyze and evaluate liquidity and debt paying ability*) Sparrow Sporting Goods reported the following data at March 31, 2012, with amounts adapted in thousands:

Sparrow Sporting Goods Company
Income Statement
For the Year Ended March 31, 2012

(Amounts in thousands)	
Net revenues	$175,500
Cost of goods sold	136,000
All other expenses	29,000
Net income	$ 10,500

Sparrow Sporting Goods Company
Statement of Retained Earnings
For the Year Ended March 31, 2012

(Amounts in thousands)	
Retained earnings, March 31, 2011	$21,500
Add: Net income	10,500
Retained earnings, March 31, 2012	$32,000

Sparrow Sporting Goods Company
Balance Sheet
March 31, 2012

(Amounts in thousands)	
Assets	
Current:	
Cash	$ 20,800
Accounts receivable	28,000
Inventories	35,000
Other current assets	5,000
Total current assets	88,800
Property and equipment, net	6,300
Other assets	22,000
Total assets	$117,100
Liabilities	
Total current liabilites	$ 55,100
Long-term liabilities	7,500
Total liabilities	62,600
Stockholders' Equity	
Common stock	22,500
Retained earnings	32,000
Total stockholders' equity	54,500
Total liabilities and stockholders' equity	$117,100

1. Compute Sparrow's net working capital.
2. Compute Sparrow's current ratio. Round to two decimal places.
3. Compute Sparrow's debt ratio. Round to two decimal places.

Do these values and ratios look strong, weak, or middle-of-the-road?

S3-18 (*Learning Objective 6: Analyze and evaluate liquidity and debt-paying ability*) Refer to the Sparrow Sporting Goods Company data in Short Exercise 3-17.

At March 31, 2012, Sparrow Sporting Goods Company's current ratio was 1.61 and their debt ratio was 0.53. Compute Sparrow's (a) net working capital (b) current ratio and (c) debt ratio after each of the following transactions (all amounts in thousands, as in the Sparrow financial statements):

1. Sparrow earned revenue of $10,000 on account.
2. Sparrow paid off accounts payable of $10,000.

When calculating the revised ratios, treat each of the above scenarios independently. Round ratios to two decimal places.

Exercises

Group A

E3-19A (*Learning Objective 1: Explain how accrual accounting differs from cash-basis accounting*) During 2012, Consolidated Corporation made sales of $4,300 (assume all on account) and collected cash of $4,500 from customers. Operating expenses totaled $1,200, all paid in cash. At year end, 2012, Consolidated customers owed the company $900. Consolidated owed creditors $1,000 on account. All amounts are in millions.

1. For these facts, show what Consolidated reported on the following financial statements:
   ▶ Income statement
   ▶ Balance sheet
2. Suppose Consolidated had used the cash basis of accounting. What would Consolidated have reported for these facts?

E3-20A (*Learning Objective 1: Explain how accrual accounting differs from cash-basis accounting*) During 2012, Tundra Sales, Inc., earned revenues of $530,000 on account. Tundra collected $540,000 from customers during the year. Expenses totaled $440,000, and the related cash payments were $420,000. Show what Tundra would report on its 2012 income statement under the

   a. cash basis.
   b. accrual basis.

Compute net income under both bases of accounting. Which basis measures net income better? Explain your answer.

E3-21A (*Learning Objectives 1, 2: Explain how accrual accounting differs from cash-basis accounting; apply the revenue and expense recognition principles*) During 2012, Barron Network, Inc., which designs network servers, earned revenues of $840 million. Expenses totaled $500 million. Barron collected all but $26 million of the revenues and paid $580 million on its expenses. Barron's top managers are evaluating 2012, and they ask you the following questions:

   a. Under accrual accounting, what amount of revenue should Barron Network report for 2012? Is the revenue the $840 million earned or is it the amount of cash actually collected? How does the revenue principle help to answer these questions?
   b. Under accrual accounting, what amount of total expense should Barron Network report for 2012—$500 million or $580 million? Which accounting principle helps to answer this question?
   c. Which financial statement reports revenues and expenses? Which statement reports cash receipts and cash payments?

E3-22A (*Learning Objectives 1, 3: Explain how accrual accounting differs from cash-basis accounting; adjust the accounts*) An accountant made the following adjustments at December 31, the end of the accounting period:

   a. Prepaid insurance, beginning, $400. Payments for insurance during the period, $1,200. Prepaid insurance, ending, $700.
   b. Interest revenue accrued, $1,600.
   c. Unearned service revenue, beginning, $1,100. Unearned service revenue, ending, $500.
   d. Depreciation, $4,800.
   e. Employees' salaries owed for three days of a five-day work week; weekly payroll, $18,000.
   f. Income before income tax, $21,000. Income tax rate is 25%.

▶ Requirements

1. Journalize the adjusting entries.
2. Suppose the adjustments were not made. Compute the overall overstatement or understatement of net income as a result of the omission of these adjustments.

E3-23A *(Learning Objectives 2, 3: Apply the revenue and expense recognition principles; adjust the accounts)* Bird-Watcher, Inc., experienced four situations for its supplies. Compute the amounts that have been left blank for each situation. For situations 1 and 2, journalize the needed transaction. Consider each situation separately.

	Situation			
	1	2	3	4
Beginning supplies.....................................	$ 500	$ 400	$1,000	$1,000
Payments for supplies during the year.......	?	800	?	400
Total amount to account for	2,200	?	?	1,400
Ending supplies	(500)	(500)	(700)	?
Supplies Expense.......................................	$1,700	$?	$1,300	$ 900

E3-24A *(Learning Objective 3: Adjust the accounts)* Morton Motor Company faced the following situations. Journalize the adjusting entry needed at December 31, 2012, for each situation. Consider each fact separately.

a. The business has interest expense of $9,600 that it must pay early in January 2013.
b. Interest revenue of $4,900 has been earned but not yet received.
c. On July 1, when the business collected $12,000 rent in advance, it debited Cash and credited Unearned Rent Revenue. The tenant was paying for two years' rent.
d. Salary expense is $1,900 per day—Monday through Friday—and the business pays employees each Friday. This year, December 31 falls on a Thursday.
e. The unadjusted balance of the Supplies account is $3,200. The total cost of supplies on hand is $1,400.
f. Equipment was purchased at the beginning of this year at a cost of $80,000. The equipment's useful life is five years. There is no residual value. Record depreciation for this year and then determine the equipment's book value.

[handwritten margin notes:]
Unearned Revenue
Prepaid Expense
Accrued Expense
Prepaid Expense
Plant Asset

E3-25A *(Learning Objective 3: Adjust the T-accounts)* The accounting records of Fairmount Publishing Company include the following unadjusted balances at August 31: Accounts Receivable, $1,500; Supplies, $500; Salary Payable, $0; Unearned Service Revenue, $600; Service Revenue, $4,200; Salary Expense, $1,900; Supplies Expense, $0.

Fairmount's accountant develops the following data for the August 31 adjusting entries:

a. Supplies on hand, $300
b. Salary owed to employees, $400
c. Service revenue accrued, $900
d. Unearned service revenue that has been earned, $500

Open the foregoing T-accounts with their beginning balances. Then record the adjustments directly in the accounts, keying each adjustment amount by letter. Show each account's adjusted balance. Journal entries are not required.

E3-26A (*Learning Objective 4: Construct the financial statements*) The adjusted trial balance of Honeyglazed Hams, Inc., follows.

Honeyglazed Hams, Inc.
Adjusted Trial Balance
December 31, 2012

(Amounts in thousands) Account	Adjusted Trial Balance	
	Debit	Credit
Cash	$ 3,700	
Accounts receivable	1,700	
Inventories	1,600	
Prepaid expenses	1,600	
Property, plant and equipment	6,800	
Accumulated depreciation		$ 2,800
Other assets	9,500	
Accounts payable		7,900
Income tax payable		500
Other liabilities		2,400
Common stock		4,600
Retained earnings (beginning, December 31, 2011)		4,700
Dividends	1,500	
Sales revenue		40,900
Cost of goods sold	25,000	
Selling, administrative, and general expenses	10,300	
Income tax expense	2,100	
Total	$63,800	$63,800

▶ **Requirement**

1. Prepare Honeyglazed Hams, Inc.'s income statement and statement of retained earnings for the year ended December 31, 2012, and its balance sheet on that date.

E3-27A (*Learning Objectives 3, 4: Adjust the accounts; construct the financial statements*) The adjusted trial balances of Verne Corporation at March 31, 2012, and March 31, 2011, include these amounts (in millions):

	2012	2011
Receivables..	$370	$220
Prepaid insurance	170	150
Accrued liabilities payable (for other operating expenses)	700	600

Verne completed these transactions during the year ended March 31, 2012.

Collections from customers	$20,400
Payment of prepaid insurance	440
Cash payments for other operating expenses...............	4,300

Compute the amount of sales revenue, insurance expense, and other operating expenses to report on the income statement for the year ended March 31, 2012.

E3-28A (*Learning Objectives 1, 3: Explain how accrual accounting differs from cash-basis accounting; compute adjusted financial statement amounts*) Bennett, the British wireless phone service provider, collects cash in advance from customers. All amounts are in millions of pounds sterling (£), the British monetary unit. Assume Bennett collected £430 in advance during 2012 and at year end still owed customers phone service worth £80.

▶ Requirements

1. Show what Bennett will report for 2012 on its income statement and balance sheet.
2. Use the same facts for Bennett as in Requirement 1. Further, assume Bennett reported unearned service revenue of £65 back at the end of 2011. Show what Bennett will report for 2012 on the same financial statements. Explain why your answer here differs from your answer to Requirement 1.

E3-29A (*Learning Objective 5: Close the books*) Prepare the closing entries from the following selected accounts from the records of North Shore Corporation at December 31, 2012:

Cost of services sold............	$11,000	Service revenue.......................	$23,900
Accumulated depreciation...	41,100	Depreciation expense	4,100
Selling, general, and		Other revenue	400
administrative expenses....	6,400	Dividends.............................	300
Retained earnings,		Income tax expense...............	500
December 31, 2011..........	2,600	Income tax payable	1,200

How much net income did North Shore earn during 2012? Prepare a T-account for Retained Earnings to show the December 31, 2012, balance of Retained Earnings.

E3-30A (*Learning Objectives 3, 5: Adjust the accounts, close the books*) The unadjusted trial balance and income statement amounts from the December 31 adjusted trial balance of Anderson Production Company follow.

Anderson Production Company

Account	Unadjusted Trial Balance		From the Adjusted Trial Balance	
Cash	14,100			
Prepaid rent	800			
Equipment	42,000			
Accumulated depreciation		3,400		
Accounts payable		5,100		
Salary payable				
Unearned service revenue		9,100		
Income tax payable				
Notes payable, long-term		16,000		
Common stock		8,600		
Retained earnings		8,500		
Dividends	1,400			
Service revenue		13,200		19,500
Salary expense	4,300		4,600	
Rent expense	1,300		1,600	
Depreciation expense			700	
Income tax expense			1,500	
Total	63,900	63,900	8,400	19,500

▶ Requirement

1. Journalize the adjusting and closing entries of Anderson Production Company at December 31. There was only one adjustment to Service Revenue.

E3-31A (*Learning Objectives 4, 6: Construct the financial statements; analyze and evaluate liquidity and debt-paying ability*) Refer to Exercise 3-30A.

▶ Requirements

1. Use the data in the partial worksheet to prepare Anderson Production Company's classified balance sheet at December 31 of the current year. Use the report format. First you must compute the adjusted balance for several of the balance-sheet accounts.
2. Compute Anderson Production Company's net working capital, current ratio, and debt ratio at December 31. A year ago, net working capital was $5,000, the current ratio was 1.55, and the debt ratio was 0.30. Indicate whether the company's ability to pay its debts—both current and total—improved or deteriorated during the current year.

E3-32A (*Learning Objective 6: Analyze and evaluate liquidity and debt-paying ability*) Johnston Company reported these ratios at December 31, 2012 (dollar amounts in millions):

$$\text{Current ratio} = \frac{\$50}{\$40} = 1.25$$

$$\text{Debt ratio} = \frac{\$40}{\$70} = 0.57$$

Johnston Company completed these transactions during 2013:

a. Purchased equipment on account, $5
b. Paid long-term debt, $6
c. Collected cash from customers in advance, $5
d. Accrued interest expense, $2
e. Made cash sales, $6

Determine whether each transaction improved or hurt Johnston's current ratio and debt ratio.

Group B

E3-33B (*Learning Objective 1: Explain how accrual accounting differs from cash-basis accounting*) During 2012, Orion Corporation made sales of $4,400 (assume all on account) and collected cash of $4,600 from customers. Operating expenses totaled $1,300, all paid in cash. At year end, 2012, Orion customers owed the company $700. Orion owed creditors $1,200 on account. All amounts are in millions.

1. For these facts, show what Orion reported on the following financial statements:
   ▶ Income statement
   ▶ Balance sheet
2. Suppose Orion had used the cash basis of accounting. What would Orion have reported for these facts?

E3-34B (*Learning Objective 1: Explain how accrual accounting differs from cash-basis accounting*) During 2012, Valley Sales, Inc., earned revenues of $500,000 on account. Valley collected $510,000 from customers during the year. Expenses totaled $450,000, and the related cash payments were $410,000. Show what Valley would report on its 2012 income statement under the

a. cash basis.
b. accrual basis.

Compute net income under both bases of accounting. Which basis measures net income better? Explain your answer.

E3-35B (*Learning Objectives 1, 2: Explain how accrual accounting differs from cash-basis accounting; apply the revenue and expense recognition principles*) During 2012, Gibson Network, Inc., which designs network servers, earned revenues of $780 million. Expenses totaled $530 million. Gibson collected all but $25 million of the revenues and paid $560 million on its expenses. Gibson's top managers are evaluating 2012, and they ask you the following questions:

    a. Under accrual accounting, what amount of revenue should Gibson Network report for 2012? Is it the revenue of $780 million earned or is it the amount of cash actually collected? How does the revenue principle help to answer these questions?

    b. Under accrual accounting, what amount of total expense should Gibson report for 2012—$530 million or $560 million? Which accounting principle helps to answer this question?

    c. Which financial statement reports revenues and expenses? Which statement reports cash receipts and cash payments?

E3-36B (*Learning Objectives 1, 3: Explain how accrual accounting differs from cash-basis accounting; adjust the accounts*) An accountant made the following adjustments at December 31, the end of the accounting period:

    a. Prepaid insurance, beginning, $300. Payments for insurance during the period, $900. Prepaid insurance, ending, $500.

    b. Interest revenue accrued, $1,300.

    c. Unearned service revenue, beginning, $1,200. Unearned service revenue, ending, $300.

    d. Depreciation, $4,400.

    e. Employees' salaries owed for three days of a five-day work week; weekly payroll, $17,000.

    f. Income before income tax, $26,000. Income tax rate is 25%.

▶ Requirements

    1. Journalize the adjusting entries.

    2. Suppose the adjustments were not made. Compute the overall overstatement or understatement of net income as a result of the omission of these adjustments.

E3-37B (*Learning Objectives 2, 3: Apply the revenue and expense recognition principles; adjust the accounts*) Paradise, Inc., experienced four situations for its supplies. Compute the amounts that have been left blank for each situation. For situations 1 and 2, journalize the needed transaction. Consider each situation separately.

	Situation			
	1	2	3	4
Beginning supplies....................................	$ 400	$ 600	$ 1,100	$ 900
Payments for supplies during the year.......	?	1,100	?	600
Total amount to account for	2,000	?	?	1,500
Ending supplies	(200)	(300)	(1,000)	?
Supplies Expense......................................	$1,800	$?	$ 1,600	$1,200

E3-38B (*Learning Objective 3: Adjust the accounts*) Forrest Company faced the following situations. Journalize the adjusting entry needed at December 31, 2012, for each situation. Consider each fact separately.

    a. The business has interest expense of $9,000 that it must pay early in January 2013.

    b. Interest revenue of $4,300 has been earned but not yet received.

    c. On July 1, when the business collected $13,900 rent in advance, it debited Cash and credited Unearned Rent Revenue. The tenant was paying for two years' rent.

d. Salary expense is $1,300 per day—Monday through Friday—and the business pays employees each Friday. This year, December 31 falls on a Wednesday.

e. The unadjusted balance of the Supplies account is $2,900. The total cost of supplies on hand is $1,600.

f. Equipment was purchased at the beginning of this year at a cost of $140,000. The equipment's useful life is five years. There is no residual value. Record depreciation for this year and then determine the equipment's book value.

E3-39B (*Learning Objective 3: Adjust the T-accounts*) The accounting records of Belmont Publishing Company include the following unadjusted balances at August 31: Accounts Receivable, $1,400; Supplies, $300; Salary Payable, $0; Unearned Service Revenue, $1,000; Service Revenue, $4,600; Salary Expense, $2,400; Supplies Expense, $0.

Belmont' accountant develops the following data for the August 31 adjusting entries:

a. Supplies on hand, $100
b. Salary owed to employees, $700
c. Service revenue accrued, $500
d. Unearned service revenue that has been earned, $200

Open the foregoing T-accounts with their beginning balances. Then record the adjustments directly in the accounts, keying each adjustment amount by letter. Show each account's adjusted balance. Journal entries are not required.

E3-40B (*Learning Objective 4: Construct the financial statements*) The adjusted trial balance of Honeybee Hams, Inc., follows.

Honeybee Hams, Inc.
Adjusted Trial Balance
December 31, 2012

(Amounts in thousands) Account	Adjusted Trial Balance Debit	Credit
Cash	$ 3,400	
Accounts receivable	1,900	
Inventories	1,700	
Prepaid expenses	1,700	
Property, plant and equipment	6,700	
Accumulated depreciation		$ 2,500
Other assets	9,700	
Accounts payable		7,700
Income tax payable		600
Other liabilities		2,400
Common stock		4,500
Retained earnings (beginning, December 31, 2011)		4,600
Dividend	1,400	
Sales revenue		42,200
Cost of goods sold	25,500	
Selling, administrative, and general expenses	10,000	
Income tax expense	2,500	
Total	$64,500	$64,500

▶ Requirement

1. Prepare Honeybee Hams, Inc.'s income statement and statement of retained earnings for the year ended December 31, 2012, and its balance sheet on that date. Draw the arrows linking the three statements.

E3-41B (*Learning Objectives 3, 4: Adjust the accounts; construct the financial statements*) The adjusted trial balances of King Corporation at March 31, 2012, and March 31, 2011, include these amounts (in millions):

	2012	2011
Receivables...	$320	$210
Prepaid insurance...	200	160
Accrued liabilities payable (for other operating expenses).....	730	640

King completed these transactions during the year ended March 31, 2012.

Collections from customers...	$20,900
Payment of prepaid insurance	470
Cash payments for other operating expenses..............	4,200

Compute the amount of sales revenue, insurance expense, and other operating expenses to report on the income statement for the year ended March 31, 2012.

E3-42B (*Learning Objectives 1, 3: Explain how accrual accounting differs from cash-basis accounting; compute adjusted financial statement amounts*) Terra, the British wireless phone service provider, collects cash in advance from customers. All amounts are in millions of pounds sterling (£), the British monetary unit. Assume Terra collected £380 in advance during 2012 and at year end still owed customers phone service worth £95.

▶ Requirements

1. Show what Terra will report for 2012 on its income statement balance sheet.
2. Use the same facts for Terra as in Requirement 1. Further, assume Terra reported unearned service revenue of £75 back at the end of 2011. Show what Terra will report for 2012 on the same financial statements. Explain why your answer here differs from your answer to Requirement 1.

E3-43B (*Learning Objective 5: Close the books*) Prepare the closing entries from the following selected accounts from the records of North Pole Corporation at December 31, 2012:

Cost of services sold............	$11,400	Service revenue........................	$24,300
Accumulated depreciation...	41,200	Depreciation expense	4,500
Selling, general, and		Other revenue	200
administrative expenses....	6,000	Dividends..............................	400
Retained earnings,		Income tax expense................	600
December 31, 2011.........	2,200	Income tax payable	500

How much net income did North Pole earn during 2012? Prepare a T-account for Retained Earnings to show the December 31, 2012, balance of Retained Earnings.

E3-44B (*Learning Objectives 3, 5: Adjust the accounts; close the books*) The unadjusted trial balance and income statement amounts from the December 31 adjusted trial balance of Durkin Production Company follow.

		Durkin Production Company			
	Account	Unadjusted Trial Balance		From the Adjusted Trial Balance	
	Cash	14,200			
	Prepaid rent	1,500			
	Equipment	44,000			
	Accumulated depreciation		3,500		
	Accounts payable		4,700		
	Salary payable				
	Unearned service revenue		8,400		
	Income tax payable				
	Notes payable, long-term		17,000		
	Common stock		8,700		
	Retained earnings		11,400		
	Dividends	1,100			
	Service revenue		13,300		19,600
	Salary expense	4,700		5,600	
	Rent expense	1,500		2,300	
	Depreciation expense			600	
	Income tax expense			1,200	
	Total	67,000	67,000	9,700	19,600

▶ Requirement

1. Journalize the adjusting and closing entries of Durkin Production Company at December 31. There was only one adjustment to Service Revenue.

E3-45B (*Learning Objectives 4, 6: Construct the financial statements; analyze and evaluate liquidity and debt-paying ability*) Refer to Exercise 3-44B.

▶ Requirements

1. Use the data in the partial worksheet to prepare Durkin Production Company's classified balance sheet at December 31 of the current year. Use the report format. First you must compute the adjusted balance for several of the balance-sheet accounts.
2. Compute Durkin Production Company's net working capital, current ratio and debt ratio at December 31. A year ago, the net working capital was $7,000, the current ratio was 1.70, and the debt ratio was 0.40. Indicate whether the company's ability to pay its debts—both current and total—improved or deteriorated during the current year.

E3-46B (*Learning Objective 6: Analyze and evaluate liquidity and debt-paying ability*) Bart Morris Company reported these ratios at December 31, 2012 (dollar amounts in millions):

$$\text{Current ratio} = \frac{\$60}{\$50} = 1.20$$

$$\text{Debt ratio} = \frac{\$70}{\$90} = 0.78$$

Bart Morris Company completed these transactions during 2013:

    a. Purchased equipment on account, $8
    b. Paid long-term debt, $5
    c. Collected cash from customers in advance, $4
    d. Accrued interest expense, $4
    e. Made cash sales, $8

Determine whether each transaction improved or hurt Morris' current ratio and debt ratio.

Serial Exercise

Exercise 3-47 continues the Steve Ruiz, Certified Public Accountant, P.C., situation begun in Exercise 2-36 of Chapter 2.

E3-47 (*Learning Objectives 3, 4, 5, 6: Adjust the accounts; close the books; construct the financial statements; analyze and evaluate liquidity and debt-paying ability*) Refer to Exercise 2-36 of Chapter 2. Start from the trial balance and the posted T-accounts that Steve Ruiz, Certified Public Accountant, Professional Corporation (P.C.), prepared for his accounting practice at January 18. A professional corporation is not subject to income tax. Later in January, the business completed these transactions:

Jan 21	Received $2,400 in advance for tax work to be performed over the next 30 days.	
21	Hired a secretary to be paid on the 15th day of each month.	
26	Paid $400 for the supplies purchased on January 5.	
28	Collected $1,500 from the client on January 18.	
31	Declared and paid dividends of $1,200.	

▶ Requirements

1. Journalize the transactions of January 21 through 31.
2. Post the January 21 to 31 transactions to the T-accounts, keying all items by date.
3. Prepare a trial balance at January 31.
4. At January 31, Ruiz gathers the following information for the adjusting entries:
    a. Accrued service revenue, $2,000
    b. Earned $800 of the service revenue collected in advance on January 21
    c. Supplies on hand, $200
    d. Depreciation expense equipment, $65; furniture, $78
    e. Accrued expense for secretary's salary, $500

Make these adjustments in the adjustments columns and complete the adjusted trial balance at January 31.

5. Journalize and post the adjusting entries. Denote each adjusting amount as Adj and an account balance as Bal.
6. Prepare the income statement and statement of retained earnings of Steve Ruiz, Certified Public Accountant, P.C., for the month ended January 31 and the classified balance sheet at that date.
7. Journalize and post the closing entries at January 31. Denote each closing amount as Clo and an account balance as Bal.
8. Compute the net working capital, current ratio, and the debt ratio of Steve Ruiz, Certified Public Accountant, P.C., and evaluate these values as indicative of a strong or weak financial position.

Quiz

Test your understanding of accrual accounting by answering the following questions. Select the best choice from among the possible answers given.

Questions 48–50 are based on the following facts: Fred Harris began a music business in July 2012. Harris prepares monthly financial statements and uses the accrual basis of accounting. The following transactions are Harris Company's only activities during July through October:

Jul	14	Bought music on account for $25, with payment to the supplier due in 90 days.
Aug	3	Performed a job on account for Jimmy Jones for $40, collectible from Jones in 30 days. Used up all the music purchased on July 14.
Sep	16	Collected the $40 receivable from Jones.
Oct	22	Paid the $25 owed to the supplier from the July 14 transaction.

Q3-48 In which month should Harris record the cost of the music as an expense?

a. July

b. August

c. September

d. October

Q3-49 In which month should Harris report the $40 revenue on its income statement?

a. July

b. August

c. September

d. October

Q3-50 If Harris Company uses the *cash* basis of accounting instead of the accrual basis, in what month will Harris report revenue and in what month will it report expense?

Revenue	**Expense**
a. August	August
b. September	July
c. September	October
d. August	October

Q3-51 In which month should revenue be recorded?

a. In the month that the invoice is mailed to the customer

b. In the month that goods are ordered by the customer

c. In the month that cash is collected from the customer

d. In the month that goods are shipped to the customer

Q3-52 On January 1 of the current year, Alladin Company paid $2,100 rent to cover six months (January–June). Alladin recorded this transaction as follows:

Journal Entry			
Date	Accounts	Debit	Credit
Jan 1	Prepaid Rent	2,100	
	Cash		2,100

Alladin adjusts the accounts at the end of each month. Based on these facts, the adjusting entry at the end of January should include

a. a credit to Prepaid Rent for $350.

b. a credit to Prepaid Rent for $1,750.

c. a debit to Prepaid Rent for $350.

d. a debit to Prepaid Rent for $1,750.

Q3-53 Assume the same facts as in question 3-52. Alladin's adjusting entry at the end of February should include a debit to Rent Expense in the amount of

a. $0.

b. $350.

c. $700.

d. $1,750.

Q3-54   What effect does the adjusting entry in question 3-53 have on Alladin's net income for February?

a. Increase by $350

b. Decrease by $350

c. Decrease by $700

d. Increase by $700

Q3-55   An adjusting entry recorded June salary expense that will be paid in July. Which statement best describes the effect of this adjusting entry on the company's accounting equation?

a. Assets are not affected, liabilities are increased, and stockholders' equity is decreased.

b. Assets are decreased, liabilities are increased, and stockholders' equity is decreased.

c. Assets are decreased, liabilities are not affected, and stockholders' equity is decreased.

d. Assets are not affected, liabilities are increased, and stockholders' equity is increased.

Q3-56   On April 1, 2012, Residential Insurance Company sold a one-year insurance policy covering the year ended March 31, 2013. Residential collected the full $3,000 on April 1, 2012. Residential made the following journal entry to record the receipt of cash in advance:

Journal Entry			
Date	Accounts	Debit	Credit
Apr 1	Cash	3,000	
	Unearned Revenue		3,000

Nine months have passed, and Residential has made no adjusting entries. Based on these facts, the adjusting entry needed by Residential at December 31, 2012, is

a.	Insurance Revenue	2,250	
	Unearned Revenue		2,250
b.	Unearned Revenue	2,250	
	Insurance Revenue		2,250
c.	Unearned Revenue	750	
	Insurance Revenue		750
d.	Insurance Revenue	750	
	Unearned Revenue		750

Q3-57   The Unearned Revenue account of Lorelai Incorporated began 2012 with a normal balance of $5,000 and ended 2012 with a normal balance of $15,000. During 2012, the Unearned Revenue account was credited for $22,000 that Lorelai will earn later. Based on these facts, how much revenue did Lorelai earn in 2012?

a. $5,000

b. $22,000

c. $27,000

d. $12,000

Q3-58   What is the effect on the financial statements of recording depreciation on equipment?

a. Net income and assets are decreased, but stockholders' equity is not affected.

b. Net income, assets, and stockholders' equity are all decreased.

c. Assets are decreased, but net income and stockholders' equity are not affected.

d. Net income is not affected, but assets and stockholders' equity are decreased.

Q3-59   For 2012, Bryant Company had revenues in excess of expenses. Which statement describes Bryant' closing entries at the end of 2012?

a. Revenues will be debited, expenses will be credited, and retained earnings will be credited.

b. Revenues will be credited, expenses will be debited, and retained earnings will be debited.

c. Revenues will be credited, expenses will be debited, and retained earnings will be credited.

d. Revenues will be debited, expenses will be credited, and retained earnings will be debited.

Q3-60   Which of the following accounts would *not* be included in the closing entries?

a. Depreciation Expense

b. Accumulated Depreciation

c. Service Revenue

d. Retained earnings

Q3-61 A major purpose of preparing closing entries is to

a. zero out the liability accounts.
b. close out the Supplies account.
c. adjust the asset accounts to their correct current balances.
d. update the Retained Earnings account.

Q3-62 Selected data for the Austin Company follow:

Current assets.............	$ 29,700		Current liabilities	$ 25,100
Long-term assets	188,500		Long-term liabilities	113,000
Total revenues.............	195,000		Total expenses.................	176,000

Based on these facts, what are Austin's current ratio and debt ratio?

	Current ratio	**Debt ratio**
a.	1.108 to 1	0.222 to 1
b.	8.693 to 1	0.845 to 1
c.	1.580 to 1	0.633 to 1
d.	1.183 to 1	0.633 to 1

Q3-63 Unadjusted net income equals $8,000. Calculate what net income will be after the following adjustments:

1. Salaries payable to employees, $510
2. Interest due on note payable at the bank, $125
3. Unearned revenue that has been earned, $800
4. Supplies used, $200

Q3-64 Salary Payable at the beginning of the month totals $20,000. During the month salaries of $122,000 were accrued as expense. If ending Salary Payable is $6,000, what amount of cash did the company pay for salaries during the month?

a. $130,000
b. $142,000
c. $122,000
d. $136,000

Problems

> All of the A and B problems can be found within MyAccountingLab, an online homework and practice environment. Your instructor may ask you to complete these problems using MyAccountingLab.

MyAccountingLab

Group A

P3-65A (*Learning Objective 1: Explain how accrual accounting differs from cash-basis accounting*) Cova Corporation earned revenues of $40 million during 2013 and ended the year with net income of $6 million. During 2013, Cova collected $25 million from customers and paid cash for all of its expenses plus an additional $3 million for amounts payable at December 31, 2012. Answer these questions about Cova's operating results, financial position, and cash flows during 2013:

▶ Requirements

1. How much were Cova's total expenses? Show your work.
2. Identify all the items that Cova will report on its 2013 income statement. Show each amount.
3. Cova began 2013 with receivables of $10 million. All sales are on account. What was the company's receivables balance at the end of 2013? Identify the appropriate financial statement, and show how Cova should report ending receivables in the 2013 annual report.

4. Cova began 2013 owing accounts payable of $7 million. All expenses are incurred on account. During 2013 Cova paid $37 million on account. How much in accounts payable did the company owe at the end of 2013? Identify the appropriate financial statement and show how Cova should report accounts payable in its 2013 annual report.

P3-66A *(Learning Objective 1: Explain how accrual accounting differs from cash-basis accounting)* Masters Consulting had the following selected transactions in July:

Jul 1	Prepaid insurance for July through November, $2,000.	
4	Purchased office furniture for cash, $1,000.	
5	Performed services and received cash, $800.	
8	Paid advertising expense, $700.	
11	Performed service on account, $3,400.	
19	Purchased computer on account, $2,000.	
24	Collected for July 11 service.	
26	Paid account payable from July 19.	
29	Paid salary expense, $1,500.	
31	Adjusted for July insurance expense (see July 1).	
31	Earned revenue of $1,000 that was collected in advance back in June.	

▶ Requirements

1. Show how each transaction would be handled using the cash basis and the accrual basis.
2. Compute July income (loss) before tax under each accounting method.
3. Indicate which measure of net income or net loss is preferable. Use the transactions on July 11 and July 24 to explain.

P3-67A *(Learning Objective 3: Adjust the accounts)* Journalize the adjusting entry needed on December 31, end of the current accounting period, for each of the following independent cases affecting Green Corp. Include an explanation for each entry.

a. Details of Prepaid Insurance are shown in the account:

Prepaid Insurance		
Jan 1 Bal	1,050	
Mar 31	4,800	

Green prepays insurance on March 31 each year. At December 31, $1,200 is still prepaid.
b. Green pays employees each Friday. The amount of the weekly payroll is $5,800 for a five-day work week. The current accounting period ends on Tuesday.
c. Green has a note receivable. During the current year, Green has earned accrued interest revenue of $600 that it will collect next year.
d. The beginning balance of supplies was $2,300. During the year, Green purchased supplies costing $6,100, and at December 31 supplies on hand total $2,100.
e. Green is providing services for Manatee Investments, and the owner of Manatee paid Green $12,100 as the annual service fee. Green recorded this amount as Unearned Service Revenue. Green estimates that it has earned 60% of the total fee during the current year.
f. Depreciation for the current year includes Office Furniture, $3,000, and Equipment, $6,300. Make a compound entry.

P3-68A *(Learning Objectives 3, 4: Adjust the accounts; construct the financial statements)* Consider the unadjusted trial balance of Lady, Inc., at July 31, 2012, and the related month-end adjustment data.

	Trial Balance		Adjustments		Adjusted Trial Balance	
Account	Debit	Credit	Debit	Credit	Debit	Credit
Cash	8,800					
Accounts receivable	1,600					
Prepaid rent	3,000					
Supplies	2,100					
Furniture	90,000					
Accumulated depreciation		3,000				
Accounts payable		3,200				
Salary payable						
Common stock		14,000				
Retained earnings		75,060				
Dividends	3,900					
Service revenue		17,000				
Salary expense	2,400					
Rent expense						
Utilities expense	460					
Depreciation expense						
Supplies expense						
Total	112,260	112,260				

Lady, Inc.
Trial Balance Work Sheet
July 31, 2012

Adjustment data at July 31, 2012:

a. Accrued service revenue at July 31, $1,700.
b. Prepaid rent expired during the month. The unadjusted prepaid balance of $3,000 relates to the period July 1, 2012, through September, 2013.
c. Supplies used during July, $1,630.
d. Depreciation on furniture for the month. The estimated useful life of the furniture is five years.
e. Accrued salary expense at July 31 for Monday, Tuesday, and Wednesday. The five-day weekly payroll of $5,000 will be paid on Friday.

▶ Requirements

1. Using Exhibit 3-9 as an example, prepare the adjusted trial balance of Lady, Inc., at July 31, 2012. Key each adjusting entry by letter.
2. Prepare the monthly income statement, the statement of retained earnings, and the classified balance sheet. Draw arrows linking the three statements.

P3-69A (*Learning Objective 3: Adjust the accounts*) Valley Apartments, Inc.'s unadjusted and adjusted trial balances at April 30, 2012, follow.

Valley Apartments, Inc.
Adjusted Trial Balance
April 30, 2012

Account	Trial Balance Debit	Trial Balance Credit	Adjusted Trial Balance Debit	Adjusted Trial Balance Credit
Cash	$ 8,200		$ 8,200	
Accounts receivable	6,300		6,830	
Interest receivable			500	
Note receivable	4,900		4,900	
Supplies	1,200		800	
Prepaid insurance	2,400		1,000	
Building	69,000		69,000	
Accumulated depreciation		$ 9,100		$ 11,000
Accounts payable		6,800		6,800
Wages payable				700
Unearned rental revenue		1,700		1,300
Common stock		19,000		19,000
Retained earnings		41,000		41,000
Dividends	3,800		3,800	
Rental revenue		19,700		20,630
Interest revenue		800		1,300
Depreciation expense			1,900	
Supplies expense			400	
Utilities expense	100		100	
Wage expense	1,600		2,300	
Property tax expense	600		600	
Insurance expense			1,400	
Total	$98,100	$98,100	$101,730	$101,730

► Requirements

1. Make the adjusting entries that account for the differences between the two trial balances.
2. Compute Valley's total assets, total liabilities, net income, and total equity.

P3-70A *(Learning Objectives 4, 6: Construct the financial statements; analyze and evaluate debt-paying ability)* The adjusted trial balance of Simpson Corporation at March 31, 2012, follows.

Simpson Corporation Adjusted Trial Balance March 31, 2012		
Account	**Debit**	**Credit**
Cash	$ 1,700	
Accounts receivable	8,800	
Supplies	2,000	
Prepaid rent	1,700	
Equipment	36,000	
Accumulated depreciation		$ 4,600
Accounts payable		3,100
Interest payable		700
Unearned service revenue		800
Income tax payable		2,400
Note payable		18,400
Common stock		3,000
Retained earnings		2,000
Dividends	23,000	
Service revenue		105,500
Depreciation expense	1,300	
Salary expense	39,800	
Rent expense	10,100	
Interest expense	2,700	
Insurance expense	4,000	
Supplies expense	2,400	
Income tax expense	7,000	
Total	$140,500	$140,500

▶ **Requirements**

1. Prepare Simpson Corporation's 2012 income statement, statement of retained earnings, and balance sheet. List expenses (except for income tax) in decreasing order on the income statement, and show total liabilities on the balance sheet. Draw arrows linking the three financial statements.
2. Simpson's lenders require that the company maintain a debt ratio no higher than 0.60. Compute Simpson's debt ratio at March 31, 2012, to determine whether the company is in compliance with this debt restriction. If not, suggest a way that Simpson could have avoided this difficult situation.

P3-71A *(Learning Objective 5: Close the books, and evaluate retained earnings)* The accounts of Mountain Lodge Service, Inc., at March 31, 2012, are listed in alphabetical order.

Accounts payable	$14,100	Interest expense	$ 300
Accounts receivable	16,600	Note payable, long term	5,700
Accumulated depreciation—		Other assets	13,700
equipment	6,700	Prepaid expenses	5,000
Advertising expense	11,000	Retained earnings,	
Cash	7,500	March 31, 2011	19,500
Common stock	10,000	Salary expense	17,900
Current portion of note		Salary payable	2,500
payable	400	Service revenue	94,100
Depreciation expense	1,000	Supplies	3,700
Dividends	32,500	Supplies expense	5,000
Equipment	42,500	Unearned service revenue	3,700

▶ Requirements

1. All adjustments have been journalized and posted, but the closing entries have not yet been made. Journalize Mountain Lodge's closing entries at March 31, 2012.
2. Set up a T-account for Retained Earnings and post to that account. Then compute Mountain Lodge's net income for the year ended March 31, 2012. What is the ending balance of Retained Earnings?
3. Did Retained Earnings increase or decrease during the year? What caused the increase or the decrease?

P3-72A *(Learning Objectives 4, 6: Construct the financial statements; analyze and evaluate liquidity and debt-paying ability)* Refer back to Problem 3-71A.

▶ Requirements

1. Use the Mountain Lodge data in Problem 3-71A to prepare the company's classified balance sheet at March 31, 2012. Show captions for total assets, total liabilities, and total liabilities and stockholders' equity.
2. Compute Mountain Lodge's net working capital, current ratio, and debt ratio at March 31, 2012, rounding to two decimal places. At March 31, 2011, net working capital was $11,800, the current ratio was 1.20, and the debt ratio was 0.25. Did Mountain Lodge's ability to pay both current and total debts improve or deteriorate during fiscal 2012? Evaluate Mountain Lodge's debt position as strong or weak and give your reason.

P3-73A *(Learning Objective 6: Analyze and evaluate liquidity and debt-paying ability)* This problem demonstrates the effects of transactions on the current ratio and the debt ratio of Harrington Company. Harrington's condensed and adapted balance sheet at December 31, 2012, follows.

	(In millions)
Total current assets	$15.8
Properties, plant, equipment, and other assets	16.3
	$32.1
Total current liabilities	$ 8.6
Total long-term liabilities	5.3
Total stockholders' equity	18.2
	$32.1

Assume that during the first quarter of the following year, 2013, Harrington completed the following transactions:

a. Paid half the current liabilities.

b. Borrowed $2.0 million on long-term debt.

c. Earned revenue, $2.4 million, on account.

d. Paid selling expense of $0.7 million.

e. Accrued general expense of $0.5 million. Credit General Expense Payable, a current liability.

f. Purchased equipment for $4.0 million, paying cash of $1.5 million and signing a long-term note payable for $2.5 million.

g. Recorded depreciation expense of $0.4 million.

▶ Requirements

1. Compute Harrington's current ratio and debt ratio at December 31, 2012. Round to two decimal places.

2. Consider each transaction separately. Compute Harrington's current ratio and debt ratio after each transaction during 2013—that is, seven times. Round ratios to two decimal places.

3. Based on your analysis, you should be able to readily identify the effects of certain transactions on the current ratio and the debt ratio. Test your understanding by completing these statements with either "increase" or "decrease":

a. Revenues usually _____ the current ratio.

b. Revenues usually _____ the debt ratio.

c. Expenses usually _____ the current ratio. (*Note:* Depreciation is an exception to this rule.)

d. Expenses usually _____ the debt ratio.

e. If a company's current ratio is greater than 1.0, as it is for Harrington, paying off a current liability will always _____ the current ratio.

f. Borrowing money on long-term debt will always _____ the current ratio and the debt ratio.

Group B

P3-74B (*Learning Objective 1: Explain how accrual accounting differs from cash-basis accounting*) Cherokee Corporation earned revenues of $37 million during 2012 and ended the year with net income of $7 million. During 2012, Cherokee collected cash of $20 million from customers and paid cash for all of its expenses plus an additional $5 million on account for amounts payable at December 31, 2011. Answer these questions about Cherokee's operating results, financial position, and cash flows during 2012:

▶ Requirements

1. How much were Cherokee's total expenses? Show your work.

2. Identify all the items that Cherokee will report on its 2012 income statement. Show each amount.

3. Cherokee began 2012 with receivables of $11 million. All sales are on account. What was Cherokee's receivables balance at the end of 2012? Identify the appropriate financial statement and show how Cherokee will report its ending receivables balance in the company's 2012 annual report.

4. Cherokee began 2012 owing accounts payable of $6 million. All expenses are incurred on account. During 2012, Cherokee paid $35 million on account. How much in accounts payable did Cherokee owe at the end of 2012? Identify the appropriate financial statement and show how Cherokee will report accounts payable in its 2012 annual report.

P3-75B (*Learning Objective 1: Explain how accrual accounting differs from cash-basis accounting*)
Healthy Hearts Consulting had the following selected transactions in December:

Dec	1	Prepaid insurance for December through April, $3,500.
	4	Purchased office furniture for cash, $900.
	5	Performed services and received cash, $500.
	8	Paid advertising expense, $200.
	11	Performed service on account, $3,100.
	19	Purchased computer on account, $1,800.
	24	Collected for December 11 service.
	26	Paid account payable from December 19.
	29	Paid salary expense, $800.
	31	Adjusted for December insurance expense (see December 1).
	31	Earned revenue of $400 that was collected in advance back in November.

▶ Requirements

1. Show how each transaction would be handled using the cash basis and the accrual basis.
2. Compute December income (loss) before tax under each accounting method.
3. Indicate which measure of net income or net loss is preferable. Use the transactions on December 11 and December 24 to explain.

P3-76B (*Learning Objective 3: Adjust the accounts*) Journalize the adjusting entry needed on December 31, the end of the current accounting period, for each of the following independent cases affecting Woods Corp. Include an explanation for each entry.

a. Details of Prepaid Insurance are shown in the account:

Prepaid Insurance	
Jan 1 Bal	800
Mar 31	3,600

Woods prepays insurance on March 31 each year. At December 31, $900 is still prepaid.
b. Woods pays employees each Friday. The amount of the weekly payroll is $6,200 for a five-day work week. The current accounting period ends on Monday.
c. Woods has a note receivable. During the current year, Woods has earned accrued interest revenue of $500 that it will collect next year.
d. The beginning balance of supplies was $2,700. During the year, Woods purchased supplies costing $6,400, and at December 31 supplies on hand total $2,300.
e. Woods is providing services for Blue Whale Investments, and the owner of Blue Whale paid Woods $11,900 as the annual service fee. Woods recorded this amount as Unearned Service Revenue. Woods estimates that it has earned 70% of the total fee during the current year.
f. Depreciation for the current year includes Office Furniture, $3,500, and Equipment, $5,800. Make a compound entry.

P3-77B (*Learning Objectives 3, 4: Adjust the accounts; construct the financial statements*)
Consider the unadjusted trial balance of Princess, Inc., at August 31, 2012, and the related month-end adjustment data.

Princess, Inc.
Trial Balance Work Sheet
August 31, 2012

Account	Trial Balance Debit	Trial Balance Credit	Adjustments Debit	Adjustments Credit	Adjusted Trial Balance Debit	Adjusted Trial Balance Credit
Cash	8,300					
Accounts receivable	1,900					
Prepaid rent	2,100					
Supplies	2,400					
Furniture	63,000					
Accumulated depreciation		3,700				
Accounts payable		4,000				
Salary payable						
Common stock		13,000				
Retained earnings		53,430				
Dividends	4,300					
Service revenue		11,000				
Salary expense	2,600					
Rent expense						
Utilities expense	530					
Depreciation expense						
Supplies expense						
Total	85,130	85,130				

Adjustment data at August 31, 2012, include the following:

a. Accrued advertising revenue at August 31, $2,100.
b. Prepaid rent expired during the month. The unadjusted prepaid balance of $2,100 relates to the period August 2012 through October 2012.
c. Supplies used during August, $2,090.
d. Depreciation on furniture for the month. The furniture's expected useful life is three years.
e. Accrued salary expense at August 31 for Monday, Tuesday, and Wednesday. The five-day weekly payroll is $5,100 and will be paid on Friday.

▶ Requirements

1. Using Exhibit 3-9 as an example, prepare the adjusted trial balance of Princess, Inc., at August 31, 2012. Key each adjusting entry by letter.
2. Prepare the monthly income statement, the statement of retained earnings, and the classified balance sheet. Draw arrows linking the three statements.

P3-78B (*Learning Objective 3: Adjust the accounts*) Crossway Apartments, Inc.'s unadjusted and adjusted trial balances at April 30, 2012, follow:

Crossway Apartments, Inc.
Adjusted Trial Balance
April 30, 2012

Account	Trial Balance Debit	Trial Balance Credit	Adjusted Trial Balance Debit	Adjusted Trial Balance Credit
Cash	$ 8,400		$ 8,400	
Accounts receivable	6,300		6,800	
Interest receivable			400	
Note receivable	5,300		5,300	
Supplies	1,300		600	
Prepaid insurance	2,400		900	
Building	63,000		63,000	
Accumulated depreciation		$ 8,800		$10,200
Accounts payable		6,300		6,300
Wages payable				1,200
Unearned rental revenue		2,000		1,800
Common stock		14,000		14,000
Retained earnings		46,200		46,200
Dividends	3,500		3,500	
Rental revenue		15,000		15,700
Interest revenue		300		700
Depreciation expense			1,400	
Supplies expense			700	
Utilities expense	400		400	
Wage expense	1,300		2,500	
Property tax expense	700		700	
Insurance expense			1,500	
Total	$92,600	$92,600	$96,100	$96,100

▶ Requirements

1. Make the adjusting entries that account for the differences between the two trial balances.
2. Compute Crossway's total assets, total liabilities, net income, and total equity.

P3-79B *(Learning Objectives 4, 6: Construct the financial statements; analyze and evaluate debt-paying ability)* The adjusted trial balance of Nicholl Corporation at May 31, 2012, follows:

		Account	Debit	Credit
		Nicholl Corporation		
		Adjusted Trial Balance		
		May 31, 2012		
		Cash	$ 1,500	
		Accounts receivable	8,600	
		Supplies	2,200	
		Prepaid rent	1,800	
		Equipment	37,300	
		Accumulated depreciation		$ 4,100
		Accounts payable		3,700
		Interest payable		500
		Unearned service revenue		900
		Income tax payable		2,100
		Note payable		18,800
		Common stock		7,000
		Retained earnings		4,000
		Dividends	20,000	
		Service revenue		97,800
		Depreciation expense	1,200	
		Salary expense	40,200	
		Rent expense	10,300	
		Interest expense	2,600	
		Insurance expense	3,600	
		Supplies expense	2,500	
		Income tax expense	7,100	
		Total	$138,900	$138,900

► Requirements

1. Prepare Nicholl's 2012 income statement, statement of retained earnings, and balance sheet. List expenses (except for income tax) in decreasing order on the income statement, and show total liabilities on the balance sheet.
2. Nicholl's lenders require that the company maintain a debt ratio no higher than 0.60. Compute Nicholl's debt ratio at May 31, 2012, to determine whether the company is in compliance with this debt restriction. If not, suggest a way Nicholl could have avoided this difficult situation.

P3-80B (*Learning Objective 5: Close the books, evaluate retained earnings*) The accounts of Cool River Service, Inc., at March 31, 2012, are listed in alphabetical order.

Accounts payable	$14,400	Interest expense	$ 400
Accounts receivable	17,000	Note payable, long term	5,600
Accumulated depreciation—		Other assets	14,000
equipment	6,900	Prepaid expenses	5,500
Advertising expense	11,400	Retained earnings,	
Cash	7,400	March 31, 2011	20,000
Common stock	13,200	Salary expense	17,700
Current portion of note		Salary payable	2,600
payable	700	Service revenue	91,500
Depreciation expense	2,000	Supplies	3,000
Dividends	32,500	Supplies expense	4,800
Equipment	42,800	Unearned service revenue	3,600

▶ Requirements

1. All adjustments have been journalized and posted, but the closing entries have not yet been made. Journalize Cool River's closing entries at March 31, 2012.
2. Set up a T-account for Retained Earnings and post to that account. Then compute Cool River's net income for the year ended March 31, 2012. What is the ending balance of Retained Earnings?
3. Did Retained Earnings increase or decrease during the 2012 fiscal year? What caused the increase or decrease?

P3-81B (*Learning Objectives 4, 6: Construct the financial statements; analyze and evaluate liquidity and debt-paying ability*) Refer back to Problem 3-80B.

▶ Requirements

1. Prepare the company's classified balance sheet in report form at March 31, 2012. Show captions for total assets, total liabilities, and total liabilities and stockholders' equity.
2. Compute Cool River's net working capital, current ratio, and debt ratio at March 31, 2012, rounding to two decimal places. At March 31, 2011, the net working capital was $11,000, the current ratio was 1.30, and the debt ratio was 0.35. Did Cool River's ability to pay both current and total liabilities improve or deteriorate during fiscal 2012? Evaluate Cool River's debt position as strong or weak and give your reason.

P3-82B (*Learning Objective 6: Analyze and evaluate liquidity and debt-paying ability*) This problem demonstrates the effects of transactions on the current ratio and the debt ratio of Hiaport Company. Hiaport's condensed and adapted balance sheet at December 31, 2011, follows.

	(In millions)
Total current assets	$15.4
Properties, plant, equipment, and other assets	15.8
	$31.2
Total current liabilities	$ 9.4
Total long-term liabilities	5.5
Total shareholders' equity	16.3
	$31.2

Assume that during the first quarter of the following year, 2012, Hiaport completed the following transactions:

a. Paid half of the current liabilities.
b. Borrowed $3.0 million on long-term debt.
c. Earned revenue of $2.4 million, on account.

d. Paid selling expense of $0.6 million.
e. Accrued general expense of $0.3 million. Credit General Expense Payable, a current liability.
f. Purchased equipment for $4.9 million, paying cash of $2.0 million and signing a long-term note payable for $2.9 million.
g. Recorded depreciation expense of $0.9 million.

▶ Requirements

1. Compute Hiaport's current ratio and debt ratio at December 31, 2011. Round to two decimal places.
2. Consider each transaction separately. Compute Hiaport's current ratio and debt ratio after each transaction during 2012—that is, seven times. Round ratios to two decimal places.
3. Based on your analysis, you should be able to readily identify the effects of certain transactions on the current ratio and the debt ratio. Test your understanding by completing these statements with either "increase" or "decrease."
   a. Revenues usually _____ the current ratio.
   b. Revenues usually _____ the debt ratio.
   c. Expenses usually _____ the current ratio. (*Note:* Depreciation is an exception to this rule.)
   d. Expenses usually _____ the debt ratio.
   e. If a company's current ratio is greater than 1.0, as for Hiaport, paying off a current liability will always _____ the current ratio.
   f. Borrowing money on long-term debt will always _____ the current ratio and _____ the debt ratio.

Challenge Exercises and Problems

E3-83 (*Learning Objective 6: Analyze and evaluate liquidity and debt-paying ability*) Valley Forge Corporation reported the following current accounts at December 31, 2011 (amounts in thousands):

Cash	$1,500
Receivables	5,900
Inventory	2,700
Prepaid expenses	1,000
Accounts payable	2,600
Unearned revenue	1,600
Accrued expenses payable	1,900

During January 2012, Valley Forge completed these selected transactions:

▶ Sold services on account, $9,000
▶ Depreciation expense, $400
▶ Paid for expenses, $7,300
▶ Collected from customers on account, $8,100
▶ Accrued expenses, $500
▶ Paid on account, $1,400
▶ Used up prepaid expenses, $700

Compute Valley Forge's net working capital and current ratio at December 31, 2011, and again at January 31, 2012. Did the net working capital and current ratio improve or deteriorate during January 2012? Comment on the level of the company's net working capital and current ratio.

E3-84 (*Learning Objectives 3, 4: Adjust the accounts; compute financial statement amounts*) The accounts of Gleneagles Company prior to the year-end adjustments follow.

Cash..	$ 7,300	Common stock...........................	$ 14,000
Accounts receivable.................	7,500	Retained earnings........................	46,000
Supplies.....................................	4,600	Dividends....................................	16,000
Prepaid insurance.....................	3,500	Service revenue...........................	161,000
Building......................................	110,000	Salary expense.............................	37,000
Accumulated depreciation—		Depreciation expense—	
building...............................	15,600	building.....................................	
Land..	53,000	Supplies expense.........................	
Accounts payable	6,100	Insurance expense	
Salary payable...........................		Advertising expense.....................	7,300
Unearned service revenue	5,500	Utilities expense	2,000

Adjusting data at the end of the year include the following:

a. Unearned service revenue that has been earned, $1,650
b. Accrued service revenue, $32,200
c. Supplies used in operations, $3,100
d. Accrued salary expense, $3,500
e. Prepaid insurance expired, $1,500
f. Depreciation expense—building, $2,600

Rorie St.Pierre, the principal stockholder, has received an offer to sell Gleneagles Company. He needs to know the following information within one hour:

a. Net income for the year covered by these data
b. Total assets
c. Total liabilities
d. Total stockholders' equity
e. Proof that Total assets = Total liabilities + Total stockholders' equity after all items are updated

▶ Requirement

1. Without opening any accounts, making any journal entries, or using a work sheet, provide Mr. St. Pierre with the requested information. The business is not subject to income tax.

P3-85 *(Learning Objective 4: Construct a balance sheet from given financial data)* Express Detail, Inc. provides mobile car washing and detailing to its customers. The Income Statement for the month ended January 31, 2012, the Balance Sheet for December 31, 2011, and details of postings to the cash account in the general ledger for the month of January 2012 follow:

Express Detail, Inc.
Income Statement
Month Ended January 31, 2012

Revenue:		
Detailing revenue	$29,400	
Gift certificates redeemed	600	$30,000
Expenses:		
Salary expense	$12,000	
Depreciation expense—equipment	6,000	
Supplies expense	4,000	
Advertising	2,000	24,000
Net income		$ 6,000

Express Detail, Inc.
Balance Sheet
December 31, 2011

Assets			Liabilities	
Cash		$ 1,300	Accounts payable	$ 5,000
Accounts receivable		2,000	Salary payable	1,000
Supplies		1,500	Unearned gift certificate revenue	800
Equipment	$30,000		Total liabilities	6,800
Less: Accumulated			**Stockholders' Equity**	
depreciation	(6,000)	24,000	Common stock	10,000
			Retained earnings	12,000
			Total stockholders' equity	22,000
			Total liabilities and	
Total assets		$28,800	stockholders' equity	$28,800

Cash

Bal 12/31/2011	1,300		
Cash collections from customers	31,000	Salaries paid	12,500
Issuance of common stock	8,000	Dividends paid	500
		Purchase of equipment	5,000
		Payments of accounts payable	5,500
		Advertising paid	1,500
Bal 1/31/2012	?		

The following additional information is also available:

1. $1,000 of the cash collected from customers in January 2012 was for gift certificates for detailing services to be performed in the future. As of January 31, 2012, $1,200 of gift certificates were still outstanding.
2. $3,500 of supplies were purchased on account.
3. Employees are paid monthly during the first week after the end of the pay period.

► Requirement

1. Based on these statements, prepare the Balance Sheet for January 31, 2012.

APPLY YOUR KNOWLEDGE

Decision Cases

Case 1. *(Learning Objectives 3, 6: Adjust the accounts; analyze and evaluate liquidity)* The unadjusted trial balance of Good Times, Inc., at January 31, 2012, does not balance. The list of accounts and their balances is given below. The trial balance needs to be prepared and adjusted before the financial statements at January 31, 2012, can be prepared. The manager of Good Times also needs to know the business's current ratio.

Cash	$ 8,000
Accounts receivable	4,200
Supplies	800
Prepaid rent	1,200
Land	43,000
Accounts payable	12,000
Salary payable	0
Unearned service revenue	700
Note payable, due in three years	23,400
Common stock	5,000
Retained earnings	9,300
Service revenue	9,100
Salary expense	3,400
Rent expense	0
Advertising expense	900
Supplies expense	0

▶ Requirements

1. How much *out of balance* is the trial balance? Notes Payable (the only error) is understated.
2. Good Times needs to make the following adjustments at January 31:
   a. Supplies of $400 were used during January.
   b. The balance of Prepaid Rent was paid on January 1 and covers the whole year 2012. No adjustment was made on January 31.
   c. At January 31, Good Times owed employees $1,000.
   d. Unearned service revenue of $500 was earned during January.
   Prepare a corrected, adjusted trial balance. Give Notes Payable its correct balance.
3. After the error is corrected and after these adjustments are made, compute the current ratio of Good Times, Inc. If your business had this current ratio, could you sleep at night?

Case 2. (*Learning Objectives 4, 6: Construct the financial statements; analyze and evaluate liquidity and debt-paying ability*) On October 1, 2012, Lou Marks opened Eagle Restaurant, Inc. Marks is now at a crossroads. The October financial statements paint a glowing picture of the business, and Marks has asked you whether he should expand the business. To expand the business, Marks wants to be earning net income of $10,000 per month and have total assets of $50,000. Marks believes he is meeting both goals.

To start the business, Marks invested $25,000, not the $15,000 amount reported as "Common stock" on the balance sheet. The business issued $25,000 of common stock to Marks. The book-keeper "plugged" the $15,000 "Common stock" amount into the balance sheet (entered the amount necessary without any support) to make it balance. The bookkeeper made some other errors too. Marks shows you the following financial statements that the bookkeeper prepared:

Eagle Restaurant, Inc.
Income Statement
Month Ended October 31, 2012

Revenues:		
Investments by owner	$25,000	
Unearned banquet sales revenue	3,000	
		$28,000
Expenses:		
Wages expense	$ 5,000	
Rent expense	4,000	
Dividends	3,000	
Depreciation expense—fixtures	1,000	
		13,000
Net income		$15,000

Eagle Restaurant, Inc.
Balance Sheet
October 31, 2012

Assets		Liabilities	
Cash	$ 8,000	Accounts payable	$ 7,000
Prepaid insurance	1,000	Sales revenue	32,000
Insurance expense	1,000	Accumulated depreciation—	
Food inventory	5,000	fixtures	1,000
Cost of goods sold (expense)	12,000		40,000
Fixtures (tables, chairs, etc.)	24,000	**Stockholders' Equity**	
Dishes and silverware	4,000	Common stock	15,000
	$55,000		$55,000

▶ Requirement

1. Prepare corrected financial statements for Eagle Restaurant, Inc.: Income Statement, Statement of Retained Earnings, and Balance Sheet. Then, based on Marks' goals and your corrected statements, recommend to Marks whether he should expand the restaurant.

Case 3. (*Learning Objectives 3, 4: Adjust the accounts; construct the financial statements; evaluate a business based on financial statements*). Stanley Williams has owned and operated SW Advertising, Inc., since it began 10 years ago. Recently, Williams mentioned that he would consider selling the company for the right price.

Assume that you are interested in buying this business. You obtain its most recent monthly trial balance, which follows. Revenues and expenses vary little from month to month, and June is a typical month. Your investigation reveals that the trial balance does not include the effects of monthly revenues of $4,000 and expenses totaling $1,100. If you were to buy SW Advertising, you would hire a manager so you could devote your time to other duties. Assume that your manager would require a monthly salary of $5,000.

SW Advertising, Inc. Trial Balance June 30, 2012		
Cash	$ 12,000	
Accounts receivable	6,900	
Prepaid expenses	3,200	
Plant assets	125,000	
Accumulated depreciation		$ 81,500
Land	158,000	
Accounts payable		13,800
Salary payable		
Unearned advertising revenue		58,700
Common stock		50,000
Retained earnings		93,000
Dividends	9,000	
Advertising revenue		22,000
Rent expense		
Salary expense	4,000	
Utilities expense	900	
Depreciation expense		
Supplies expense		
Total	$319,000	$319,000

▶ Requirements

1. Assume that the most you would pay for the business is 16 times the amount of monthly net income *you could expect to earn* from it. Compute this possible price.
2. Williams states that the least he will take for the business is two times its stockholders' equity on June 30. Compute this amount.
3. Under these conditions, how much should you offer Williams? Give your reason. (Challenge)

Ethical Issues

Issue 1. Cross Timbers Energy Co. is in its third year of operations, and the company has grown. To expand the business, Cross Timbers borrowed $15 million from Bank of Fort Worth. As a condition for making this loan, the bank required that Cross Timbers maintain a current ratio of at least 1.50 and a debt ratio of no more than 0.50.

Business recently has been worse than expected. Expenses have brought the current ratio down to 1.47 and the debt ratio up to 0.51 at December 15. Lane Collins, the general manager, is considering the result of reporting this current ratio to the bank. Collins is considering recording this year some revenue on account that Cross Timbers will earn next year. The contract for this job has been signed, and Cross Timbers will deliver the natural gas during January of next year.

▶ Requirements

1. Journalize the revenue transaction (without dollar amounts), and indicate how recording this revenue in December would affect the current ratio and the debt ratio.
2. Analyze this transaction according to the decision framework for making ethical judgments in Chapter 1:
   a. What is the issue?
   b. Who are the stakeholders and what are the alternatives? Weigh them from the standpoint of economic, legal, and ethical implications.
   c. What decision would you make?
3. Propose for Cross Timbers a course of action that is ethical.

Issue 2. The net income of Solas Photography Company decreased sharply during 2012. Lisa Almond, owner of the company, anticipates the need for a bank loan in 2013. Late in 2012, Almond instructed Brad Lail, the accountant and a personal friend of yours, to record a $10,000 sale of portraits to the Almond family, even though the photos will not be shot until January 2013. Almond also told Lail *not* to make the following December 31, 2012, adjusting entries:

Salaries owed to employees $10,000
Prepaid insurance that has expired 1,000

▶ Requirements

1. Compute the overall effect of these transactions on the company's reported income for 2012. Is reported net income overstated or understated?
2. Why did Almond take these actions? Are they ethical? Give your reason, identifying the parties helped and the parties harmed by Almond's action. Consult the Decision Framework for Making Ethical Judgments in Chapter 1. Which factor (economic, legal, or ethical) seems to be taking precedence? Identify the stakeholders and the potential consequences to each.
3. As a personal friend of Brad's, what advice would you give him?

Focus on Financials: | Amazon.com, Inc.

(Learning Objectives 3, 4, 6: Adjust the accounts; construct financial statements, evaluate debt-paying ability) **Amazon.com, Inc.**—like all other businesses—adjusts accounts prior to year end to get correct amounts for the financial statements. Examine Amazon.com, Inc.'s Consolidated Balance Sheets in Appendix A, and pay particular attention to "accrued expenses and other."

▶ Requirements

1. Why does a company have accrued expenses payable at year end?
2. Open a T-account for "Accrued Expenses and Other." Insert Amazon.com, Inc.'s balance (in millions) at December 31, 2009.
3. Journalize the following transactions for the year ended December 31, 2010. Key entries by letter, and show amounts in millions. Explanations are not required.
   a. Paid off the beginning balance of "Accrued Expenses and Other"
   b. Recorded operating expenses, other than cost of sales, of $6,237 million, paying $3,916 million in cash and accruing the remainder
4. Post these entries to "Accrued Expenses and Other" and show that the ending balance of the account agrees with the corresponding amount reported in Amazon.com, Inc.'s December 31, 2010, Consolidated Balance Sheets.
5. Compute net working capital, the current ratio, and the debt ratio for Amazon.com, Inc., at December 31, 2009, and December 31, 2010. Did the amount of working capital and ratio values improve, deteriorate, or hold steady during 2010? Do Amazon.com, Inc.'s ratio values indicate relative financial strength or weakness?

Focus on Analysis: | RadioShack Corporation

(*Learning Objective 1: Explain accruals and deferrals*) Refer to the consolidated financial statements of **RadioShack Corporation** in Appendix B. During 2010, the company had numerous accruals and deferrals. As a new member of RadioShack's accounting staff, it is your job to explain the effects of accruals and deferrals on net income for 2010. The accrual and deferral data follow, along with questions that RadioShack Corporation stockholders have raised (all amounts in millions):

1. Examine RadioShack's comparative balance sheets at December 31, 2010, and 2009. Ending net receivables for 2009 (beginning balance for 2010) were $322.5 million. Ending net receivables for 2010 were $377.5 million. Which of these amounts did RadioShack Corporation earn in 2009? Which amount is included in RadioShack Corporation's 2010 net income? Explain the make-up of the parties who owed RadioShack Corporation and the amounts as of December 31, 2010.

2. In Note 3, Supplemental Balance Sheet Disclosures, examine the details of the account entitled "other current assets, net." What do you think is meant by "deferred income taxes"? Why is this recorded as a current asset? The beginning balance is $69 million and the ending balance is $61 million. Construct a journal entry that might account for the $8 million change.

3. In Note 3 (Supplemental Balance Sheet Disclosures), focus on Property, Plant and Equipment, net. Notice that accumulated depreciation stood at $799 million at the end of 2009 and at $820 million at year end 2010. Assume that depreciation expense for 2010 was $70. Explain what must have happened to account for the remainder of the change in the accumulated depreciation account during 2010. (Challenge)

4. In Note 3 (Supplemental Balance Sheet Disclosures) focus on Accrued Expenses and Other Current Liabilities. RadioShack Corporation reports an account titled Advertising (meaning accrued advertising payable). This account carried a credit balance of $31.4 million at the end of 2009 and $26.9 million at the end of 2010. What type of account is Accrued Advertising Payable? What year's income statement did the $26.9 million accrued advertising affect? What year's income statement did the $31.4 million accrued advertising affect? Did the company's advertising expense increase, decrease, or stay the same from 2009 to 2010?

Group Project

Matt Trozo formed a lawn service company as a summer job. To start the business on May 1, he deposited $2,500 in a new bank account in the name of Trozzo Lawn Service, Inc. consisting of a $1,500 loan from his father and $1,000 of his own money. The corporation issued 100 shares of common stock to Trozo.

He rented lawn equipment, purchased supplies, and hired high school students to mow and trim customers' lawns. At the end of each month, Trozo mailed bills to his customers. On August 31, Trozo was ready to dissolve the business and return to Regal University for the fall semester. Because he had been so busy, he had kept few records other than his checkbook and a list of amounts owed by customers.

At August 31, Trozo's checkbook shows a balance of $2,640, and his customers still owe him $600. During the summer, he collected $5,600 from customers. His checkbook lists payments for supplies totaling $400, and he still has gasoline, weedeater cord, and other supplies that cost a total of $50. He paid his employees wages of $1,900, and he still owes them $200 for the final week of the summer.

Trozo rented some equipment from Ludwig Tool Company. On May 1, he signed a six-month lease on mowers and paid $600 for the full lease period. Ludwig will refund the unused portion of the prepayment if the equipment is in good shape. To get the refund, Trozo has kept the mowers in excellent condition. In fact, he had to pay $300 to repair a mower that ran over a hidden tree stump.

To transport employees and equipment to jobs, Trozo used a trailer that he bought for $300. He figures that the summer's work used up one-third of the trailer's service potential. The business checkbook lists an expenditure of $460 for dividends paid to Trozo during the summer. Also, Trozo paid his father back during the summer.

▶ Requirements

1. Prepare the income statement of Trozo Lawn Service, Inc., for the four months May through August. The business is not subject to income tax.
2. Prepare the classified balance sheet of Trozo Lawn Service, Inc., at August 31.
3. Prepare a simple cash flow statement, showing cash flows from the following 3 areas:
   a. Operations: Collections from customers, less payments for supplies, wages, rent, and repairs (show each separately)
   b. Investing activities: purchase of trailer
   c. Financing activities: borrowing from father, issuance of stock, repayment of loan, and payment of dividends
   d. Payments for supplies, wages, rent, and repairs
4. Evalute Matt Trozo's profitability, liquidity, and cash flows for the summer. Would you say he was successful in his lawn business? Why or why not?

MyAccountingLab

> For online homework, exercises, and problems that provide you with immediate feedback, please visit **www.myaccountinglab.com**.

Quick Check Answers

1. *a*	7. *d*	13. *a*
2. *c*	8. *c*	14. *a*
3. *a*	9. *d*	15. *c*
4. *c*	10. *a*	16. *b*
5. *a*	11. *d*	17. *a*
6. *b*	12. *c*	

Demo Doc

Preparation of Adjusting Entries, Closing Entries, and Financial Statements

To make sure you understand this material, work through the following demonstration "Demo Doc" with detailed comments to help you see the concept within the framework of a worked-through problem.

Learning Objectives 2–5

Cloud Break Consulting, Inc., has the following information at June 30, 2012:

		Balance	
Account Title		**Debit**	**Credit**
	Cloud Break Consulting, Inc.		
	Unadjusted Trial Balance		
	June 30, 2012		
Cash		$131,000	
Accounts receivable		104,000	
Supplies		4,000	
Prepaid rent		27,000	
Land		45,000	
Building		300,000	
Accumulated depreciation—building			$155,000
Accounts payable			159,000
Unearned service revenue			40,000
Common stock			50,000
Retained earnings			52,000
Dividends		7,000	
Service revenue			450,000
Salary expense		255,000	
Rent expense		25,000	
Miscellaneous expense		8,000	
Total		$906,000	$906,000

June 30 is Cloud Break's fiscal year end; accordingly, it must make adjusting entries for the following items:

a. Supplies on hand at year-end, $1,000.

b. Nine months of rent totaling $27,000 were paid in advance on April 1, 2012. Cloud Break has recorded no rent expense yet.

c. Depreciation expense has not been recorded on the building for the 2012 fiscal year. The building has a useful life of 25 years.

d. Employees work Monday through Friday. The weekly payroll is $5,000 and is paid every Friday. June 30, 2012, falls on a Thursday.

e. Service revenue of $15,000 must be accrued.

f. Cloud Break received $40,000 in advance for consulting services to be provided evenly from January 1, 2012, through August 31, 2012. Cloud Break has recorded none of this revenue.

► Requirements

1. Open the T-accounts with their unadjusted balances.

2. Journalize Cloud Break's adjusting entries at June 30, 2012, and post the entries to the T-accounts.

3. Total each T-account in the ledger.

4. Journalize and post Cloud Break's closing entries.

5. Prepare Cloud Break's income statement and statement of retained earnings for the year ended June 30, 2012, and the balance sheet at June 30, 2012. Draw arrows linking the three financial statements.

Demo Doc Solutions

► Requirement 1

Open the T-accounts with their unadjusted balances.

Part 1	Part 2	Part 3	Part 4	Part 5	Demo Doc Complete

Remember from Chapter 2 that opening a T-account means drawing a blank account that looks like a capital "T" and putting the account title across the top. To help find the accounts later, they are grouped into assets, liabilities, stockholders' equity, revenues, and expenses (in that order). If the account has a starting balance, it **must** appear on the correct side.

Remember that debits are always on the left side of the T-account and credits are always on the right side. This is true for *every* account.

The correct side on which to enter each account's starting balance is the side of *increase* in the account. This is because we expect all accounts to have a *positive* balance (that is, more increases than decreases).

For assets, an increase is a debit, so we would expect all assets (except contra assets such as Accumulated Depreciation) to have a debit balance. For liabilities and stockholders' equity, an increase is a credit, so we would expect all liabilities and equities (except Dividends) to have a credit balance. By the same reasoning, we expect revenues to have credit balances and expenses and dividends to have debit balances.

The unadjusted balances appearing in the T-accounts are simply the amounts from the starting trial balance.

ASSETS

Cash
Bal   131,000 |

Accounts Receivable
Bal 104,000 |

Supplies
Bal   4,000 |

Prepaid Rent
Bal   27,000 |

Land
Bal   45,000 |

Building
Bal   300,000 |

Accumulated Depreciation—Building
| Bal 155,000

LIABILITIES

Accounts Payable
| Bal   159,000

Unearned Service Revenue
| Bal   40,000

STOCKHOLDERS' EQUITY

Common Stock
| Bal   50,000

Retained Earnings
| Bal   52,000

Dividends
Bal   7,000 |

REVENUE

Service Revenue
| Bal   450,000

EXPENSES

Salary Expense
Bal 255,000 |

Rent Expense
Bal   25,000 |

Miscellaneous Expense
Bal   8,000 |

Journalize Cloud Break's adjusting entries at June 30, 2012, and post the entries to the T-accounts.

Part 1	**Part 2**	Part 3	Part 4	Part 5	Demo Doc Complete

a. Supplies on hand at year-end, $1,000.

On June 30, 2012, the unadjusted balance in the Supplies account was $4,000. However, a count shows that only $1,000 of supplies actually remains on hand. The supplies that are no longer there have been used. When assets/benefits are used, an expense is created.

Cloud Break will need to make an adjusting journal entry in order to report the correct amount of supplies on the balance sheet.

Look at the Supplies T-account:

Supplies			
	4,000	Used up	X
Bal	1,000		

The supplies have decreased because they have been used up. The amount of the decrease is **X** = $4,000 − $1,000 = $3,000.

$3,000 of supplies expense must be recorded to show the value of supplies that have been used.

a.	Jun 30	Supplies Expense ($4,000 − $1,000) (Expense ↑; debit)	3,000	
		Supplies (Asset ↓; credit)		3,000
		To record supplies expense.		

After posting, Supplies and Supplies Expense hold their correct ending balances:

	ASSETS				EXPENSES		
	Supplies				Supplies Expense		
	4,000			a.	3,000		
		a.	3,000	Bal	3,000		
Bal	1,000						

b. Nine months of rent (totaling $27,000) were paid in advance on April 1, 2012. Cloud Break has recorded no rent expense yet.

A prepayment for something, such as for rent or insurance, creates a *future* benefit (an asset) because the business is now entitled to receive the prepaid goods or services. Once those goods or services are received (in this case, once Cloud Break has occupied the building being rented), the benefit expires, and the prepaid cost becomes an expense.

Cloud Break prepaid $27,000 for nine months of rent on April 1. This means that Cloud Break pays $27,000/9 = $3,000 a month for rent. At June 30, Prepaid Rent is adjusted for the amount of the asset that has been used up. Because Cloud Break has occupied the building being rented for three months (April, May, and June), three months of the prepayment have been used. The amount of rent used is 3 × $3,000 = $9,000. Because that portion of the past benefit (asset) has expired, it becomes an expense (in this case, the adjustment transfers $9,000 from Prepaid Rent to Rent Expense).

This means that Rent Expense must be increased (a debit) and Prepaid Rent (an asset) must be decreased (a credit), with the following journal entry:

b.	Jun 30	Rent Expense (Expense ↑; debit)	9,000	
		Prepaid Rent (Asset ↓; credit)		9,000
		To record rent expense.		

Posting places $9,000 in each account, as follows:

ASSETS			EXPENSES		
Prepaid Rent			**Rent Expense**		
27,000			25,000		
	b.	9,000	b.	9,000	
Bal	18,000		Bal	34,000	

c. **Depreciation expense has not been recorded on the building for the 2012 fiscal year. The building has a useful life of 25 years.**

Depreciation expense per year is calculated as follows:

$$\text{Depreciation expense per year} = \frac{\text{Original cost of asset}}{\text{Useful life of asset (in years)}}$$

The cost principle compels us to keep the original cost of a plant asset in that asset account. Because there is $300,000 in the Building account, we know that this is the original cost of the building. We are told in the question that the building's useful life is 25 years.

$$\text{Depreciation expense per year} = \$300,000/25 \text{ years} = \$12,000 \text{ per year}$$

We will record depreciation of $12,000 in an adjusting journal entry. The journal entry for depreciation expense is *always* the same. Only the dollar amount changes. There is always an increase to Depreciation Expense (a debit) and an increase to the contra asset account of Accumulated Depreciation (a credit).

The book value of the building is its original cost (the amount in the Building T-account) minus the accumulated depreciation on the building.

Book value of plant assets:	
Building..	$300,000
Less: Accumulated depreciation	(167,000)
Book value of the building	$133,000

c.	Jun 30	Depreciation Expense—Building (Expense ↑; debit)	12,000	
		Accumulated Depreciation—Building		
		(Contra Asset ↑; credit)		12,000
		To record depreciation on building.		

ASSETS			EXPENSES	
ASSET		**CONTRA ASSET**		

| | | Accumulated Depreciation— | | Depreciation Expense— |
| **Building** | | **Building** | | **Building** |

Building		Accumulated Depreciation—Building		Depreciation Expense—Building	
300,000			155,000	c.	12,000
		c.	12,000		
Bal	300,000	Bal	167,000	Bal	12,000

d. Employees work Monday through Friday. The weekly payroll is $5,000 and is paid every Friday. June 30, 2012, falls on a Thursday.

Salary is an accrued expense. That is, it's a liability that comes from an *expense* that hasn't been paid yet. Most employers pay their employees *after* the work has been done, so the work is a past benefit to the employer. This expense (Salary Expense, in this case) grows until payday.

Cloud Break's employees are paid $5,000 for five days of work. That means they earn $5,000/5 = $1,000 per day. By the end of the day on Thursday, June 30, they have earned $1,000/day × 4 days = $4,000 of salary.

If the salaries have not been paid, then they are pay*able* (or in other words, they are *owed*) and must be recorded as some kind of payable account. You might be tempted to use Accounts Payable, but this account is usually reserved for *bills* received. But employees don't bill employers for their paychecks. The appropriate payable account for salaries is Salary Payable.

The accrual of salary expense creates an increase to Salary Expense (a debit) and an increase to the liability Salary Payable (a credit) of $4,000.

EXPENSES			LIABILITIES		
Salary Expense			Salary Payable		
	255,000			d.	4,000
d.	4,000				
Bal	259,000			Bal	4,000

d.	Jun 30	Salary Expense (Expense ↑; debit)	4,000	
		Salary Payable (Liability ↑; credit)		4,000
		To accrue salary expense.		

e. Service revenue of $15,000 must be accrued.

Accrued revenue is another way of saying "accounts receivable" (or receipt in the future). When *accrued* revenue is recorded, it means that accounts receivable are also recorded (that is, the business gave goods or services to customers, but the business has not yet received the cash). The business is entitled to these receivables because the revenue has been earned.

Service Revenue must be increased by $15,000 (a credit) and the Accounts Receivable asset must be increased by $15,000 (a debit).

e.	Jun 30	Accounts Receivable (Asset ↑; debit)	15,000	
		Service Revenue (Revenue ↑; credit)		15,000
		To accrue service revenue.		

ASSETS		REVENUES	
Accounts Receivable		**Service Revenue**	
104,000			450,000
e. 15,000			e. 15,000
Bal 119,000			Bal 465,000

f. Cloud Break received $40,000 in advance for consulting services to be provided evenly from January 1, 2012, through August 31, 2012. Cloud Break has recorded none of this revenue.

Cloud Break received cash in advance for work to be performed in the future. By accepting the cash, Cloud Break also accepted the obligation to perform that work (or provide a refund). In accounting, an obligation is a liability. We call this liability "unearned revenue" because it *will* be revenue (after the work is performed) but it is not revenue *yet*.

The $40,000 collected in advance is still in the Unearned Service Revenue account. However, some of the revenue has been earned as of June 30. Six months of the earnings period have passed (January through June), so Cloud Break has earned six months of the revenue.

The entire revenue-earning period is eight months (January through August), so the revenue earned per month is $40,000/8 = $5,000. The six months of revenue that Cloud Break has earned through the end of June totals $30,000 (6 × $5,000).

So Unearned Service Revenue, a liability, must be decreased by $30,000 (a debit). Because that portion of the revenue is now earned, Service Revenue is increased by $30,000 (a credit).

f.	Jun 30	Unearned Service Revenue (Liability ↓; debit)	30,000	
		Service Revenue (Revenue ↑; credit)		30,000
		To record the earning of service revenue that was		
		collected in advance.		

Essentially, the $30,000 has been shifted from "unearned revenue" to "earned" revenue.

LIABILITIES			REVENUES		
Unearned Service Revenue			**Service Revenue**		
		40,000			450,000
f.	30,000			e.	15,000
				f.	30,000
	Bal	10,000		Bal	495,000

Now we can summarize all of the adjusting journal entries:

Ref.	Date	Accounts and Explanation	Debit	Credit
	2012			
a.	Jun 30	Supplies Expense ($4,000 − $1,000)	3,000	
		Supplies		3,000
		To record supplies expense.		
b.	30	Rent Expense	9,000	
		Prepaid Rent		9,000
		To record rent expense.		
c.	30	Depreciation Expense—Building	12,000	
		Accumulated Depreciation—Building		12,000
		To record depreciation on building.		
d.	30	Salary Expense	4,000	
		Salary Payable		4,000
		To accrue salary expense.		
e.	30	Accounts Receivable	15,000	
		Service Revenue		15,000
		To accrue service revenue.		
f.	30	Unearned Service Revenue	30,000	
		Service Revenue		30,000
		To record the earning of service revenue that was collected in advance.		

Total each T-account in the ledger.

Part 1	Part 2	**Part 3**	Part 4	Part 5	Demo Doc Complete

After posting all of these entries and totaling all of the T-accounts, we have the following:

ASSETS

Cash

Bal	131,000		

Accounts Receivable

	104,000		
e.	15,000		
Bal	119,000		

Supplies

	4,000		
		a.	3,000
Bal	1,000		

Prepaid Rent

	27,000		
		b.	9,000
Bal	18,000		

Land

Bal	45,000		

Building

Bal	300,000		

Accumulated Depreciation—Building

			155,000
		c.	12,000
		Bal	167,000

LIABILITIES

Accounts Payable

		Bal	159,000

Salary Payable

		d.	4,000
		Bal	4,000

Unearned Service Revenue

			40,000
f.	30,000		
		Bal	10,000

STOCKHOLDERS' EQUITY

Common Stock

		Bal	50,000

Retained Earnings

		Bal	52,000

Dividends

Bal	7,000		

REVENUE

Service Revenue

			450,000
		e.	15,000
		f.	30,000
		Bal	495,000

EXPENSES

Salary Expense

	255,000		
d.	4,000		
Bal	259,000		

Supplies Expense

a.	3,000		
Bal	3,000		

Rent Expense

	25,000		
b.	9,000		
Bal	34,000		

Depreciation Expense— Building

c.	12,000		
Bal	12,000		

Miscellaneous Expense

Bal	8,000		

Journalize and post Cloud Break's closing entries.

Part 1	Part 2	Part 3	**Part 4**	Part 5	Demo Doc Complete

We prepare closing entries to (1) clear out the revenue, expense, and dividends accounts to a zero balance in order to get them ready for the next period. They must begin the next period empty so that we can evaluate each period's income separately from all other periods. We also need to (2) update the Retained Earnings account by transferring all revenues, expenses, and dividends into it.

The Retained Earnings balance is calculated each year using the following formula:

Beginning retained earnings
+ Net income (or − Net loss)
− Dividends declared
= Ending retained earnings

You can see this in the Retained Earnings T-account as well:

	Retained Earnings
	Beginning retained earnings
	Net income
Dividends	
	Ending retained earnings

This formula is the key to preparing the closing entries. We will use this formula, but we will do it *inside* the Retained Earnings T-account.

From the trial balance given in the problem, we know that beginning Retained Earnings is $52,000. The first component of the formula is already in the T-account.

The next component is net income, which is *not* yet in the Retained Earnings account. There is no T-account with net income in it, but we can place all the components of net income into the Retained Earnings account and come out with the net income number at the bottom. Remember:

Revenues − Expenses = Net income

This means that we need to get all of the revenues and expenses into the Retained Earnings account.

a. **We start with our revenue T-account (service revenue as shown).**

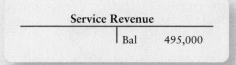

Service Revenue	
	Bal 495,000

In order to clear out all the income statement accounts so that they are empty to begin the next year, the first step is to *debit* each revenue account for the amount of its *credit* balance. Service Revenue has a *credit* balance of $495,000, so to bring that to zero, we need to *debit* Service Revenue for $495,000.

This means that we have part of our first closing entry:

1.		Service Revenue	495,000	
		???		495,000

What is the credit side of this entry? The reason we started with Service Revenue was to help calculate net income in the Retained Earnings account. So the other side of the entry must go to Retained Earnings:

1.		Service Revenue	495,000	
		Retained Earnings		495,000

b. **The second step is to *credit* each expense account for the amount of its *debit* balance to bring each expense account to zero. In this case, we have five different expenses:**

Salary Expense			Supplies Expense	
Bal	259,000		Bal	3,000

Rent Expense			Depreciation Expense—Building	
Bal	34,000		Bal	12,000

Miscellaneous Expense	
Bal	8,000

The sum of all the expenses will go to the debit side of the Retained Earnings account:

2.		Retained Earnings	316,000	
		Salary Expense		259,000
		Supplies Expense		3,000
		Rent Expense		34,000
		Depreciation Expense—Building		12,000
		Miscellaneous Expense		8,000

The last component of the Retained Earnings formula is dividends. There is a Dividends account:

Dividends	
Bal	7,000

c. **The final step in the closing process is to transfer Dividends to the debit site of the Retained Earnings account.** The Dividends account has a *debit* balance of $7,000, so to bring that to zero, we need to *credit* Dividends by $7,000. The balancing debit will go to Retained Earnings:

3.	Retained Earnings	7,000	
	Dividends		7,000

This entry subtracts Dividends from Retained Earnings. Retained Earnings now holds the following data:

			Retained Earnings		
				52,000	**Beginning retained earnings**
Expenses	2.	316,000	1.	495,000	Revenue } Net income
Dividends	3.	7,000			
			Bal	224,000	**Ending retained earnings**

The formula to update Retained Earnings has now been re-created inside the Retained Earnings T-account.

The following accounts are included in the closing process:

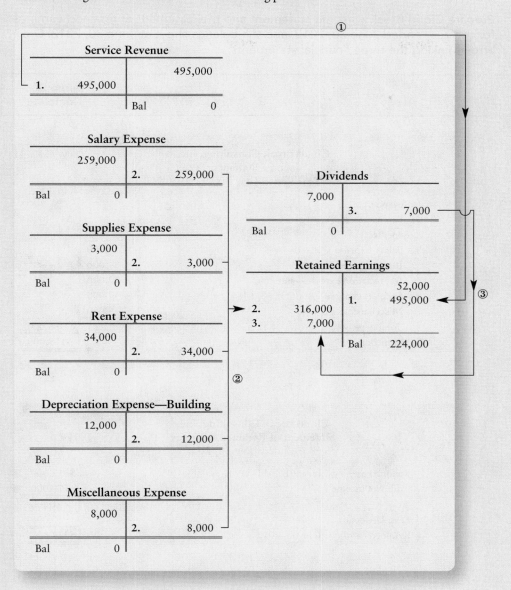

Notice that all temporary accounts (Service Revenues, Various expenses, and Dividends), now have zero balances.

► Requirement 5

Prepare Cloud Break's income statement and the statement of retained earnings for the year ended June 30, 2012, and the balance sheet at June 30, 2012. Draw arrows linking the three financial statements.

Part 1	Part 2	Part 3	Part 4	**Part 5**	Demo Doc Complete

Cloud Break Consulting, Inc.
Income Statement
Year Ended June 30, 2012

Revenue:		
Service revenue		$495,000
Expenses:		
Salary expense	$259,000	
Rent expense	34,000	
Depreciation expense—building	12,000	
Supplies expense	3,000	
Miscellaneous expense	8,000	
Total expenses		316,000
Net income		$179,000

Cloud Break Consulting, Inc.
Statement of Retained Earnings
Year Ended June 30, 2012

Retained earnings, June 30, 2011	$ 52,000
Add: Net income	179,000
	231,000
Less: Dividends	(7,000)
Retained earnings, June 30, 2012	$224,000

Cloud Break Consulting, Inc.
Balance Sheet
June 30, 2012

Assets			Liabilities	
Cash		$131,000	Accounts payable	$159,000
Accounts receivable		119,000	Salary payable	4,000
Supplies		1,000	Unearned service revenue	10,000
Prepaid rent		18,000	Total liabilities	173,000
Land		45,000	**Stockholders' Equity**	
Building	$300,000		Common stock	50,000
Less: Accumulated			Retained earnings	224,000
depreciation	(167,000)	133,000	Total stockholders' equity	274,000
			Total liabilities and	
Total assets		$447,000	stockholders' equity	$447,000

Relationships among the Financial Statements

The arrows in these statements show how the financial statements relate to each other. Follow the arrow that takes the ending balance of Retained Earnings to the balance sheet.

1. **Net income from the income statements is reported as an increase to Retained Earnings on the statement of retained earnings. A net loss would be reported as a decrease to Retained Earnings.**

2. **Ending Retained Earnings from the statement of retained earnings is transferred to the balance sheet. The ending Retained Earnings is the final balancing amount for the balance sheet.**

Part 1	Part 2	Part 3	Part 4	Part 5	Demo Doc Complete

Internal Control & Cash

SPOTLIGHT: Cooking the Books: EPIC Products Takes a Hit

The following is adapted from a true story:

"I've never been so shocked in my life!" exclaimed Mike Cassell, manager of the **EPIC Products** office in Palo Alto, California. "I never thought this could happen to us. We are such a close-knit organization where everyone trusts everyone else. Why, people at EPIC feel like family! I feel betrayed, violated."

Cassell had just returned from the trial of Erica Price, who had been convicted of embezzling over $600,000 from EPIC over a six-year period. Price had been one of EPIC's most trusted employees for 10 years. A single mom with two teenage daughters, Price had pulled herself up by her own bootstraps, putting herself through community college where she had obtained an associate's degree in accounting. Cassell had hired her as a part-time bookkeeper at EPIC while Price was in college to help her out. She had done such a good job that, when she completed her degree, Cassell asked her to stay on and assigned her the additional role of cashier, in charge of accumulating the daily cash receipts from customers and taking them to the night depository at the bank each day after work. Through the years, he also awarded her what he considered good raises, compensating her at a rate that was generally higher than other employees with her education and experience levels.

Price rapidly became the company's "go-to" financial employee. She was eager to learn, dependable, responsible. In 10 years she never took a day of vacation, choosing instead to take advantage of the company's policy that allowed employees to draw additional compensation for vacation accrued but not taken at the end of each year. Cassell grew to depend on Price more and more each month, as the business grew to serve over 1,000 customers.

© iStockPhoto

Price's increased involvement on the financial side of the business freed Cassell to spend his time working on new business, spending less and less time on financial matters. Cassell had noticed that, in the past few years, Price had begun to wear better clothes and drive a shiny late-model convertible around town. Both of her teenagers also drove late-model automobiles, and the family had recently moved into a new home in an upscale subdivision of the city. Cassell had been pleased that he had contributed to Price's success. But in recent months, Cassell was becoming worried because, in spite of increasing revenues, the cash balances and cash flows from operations at EPIC had been steadily deteriorating, sometimes causing the company difficulty in paying its bills on time.

Price, on the other hand, had felt underappreciated and underpaid for all of her hard work. Having learned the system well, and observing that no one was monitoring her, Price fell into a simple but deadly trap. As cashier, she was in charge of receiving customer payments that came in by mail. Unknown to Cassell, Price had been **lapping** accounts receivable, an embezzlement scheme nicknamed "robbing Peter to pay Paul." Price began by misappropriating (stealing) some of the customers' checks, endorsing them, and depositing them to her own bank account. To cover up the shortage in a particular customer's account, Price would apply the collections received later from another customer's account. She would do this just before the monthly statements were mailed to the first customer, so that the customer wouldn't notice when he or she received the statement that someone else's payment was being applied to the amount owed EPIC. Of course, this left the second customer's account short, so Price had to misapply the collection from a third customer to straighten out the discrepancy in the second customer's account. She did this for many customers, over a period of many months, boldly stealing more and more each month. With unlimited access to both cash and customer accounts, and with careful planning and constant diligence, Price became very proficient at juggling entries in the books to keep anyone from discovering her scheme. This embezzlement went on for six years, allowing Price to misappropriate $622,000 from the company. The customer accounts that were misstated due to the fraud eventually had to be written off.

What tipped off Cassell to the embezzlement? Price was involved in an automobile accident and couldn't work for two weeks. The employee covering for Price was swamped with telephone calls from customers wanting to discuss unexplained differences in their billing statements for amounts they could prove had been paid. The ensuing investigation pointed straight to Price, and Cassell turned the case over to the authorities. ●

The excerpt from the EPIC Products balance sheet on the following page reports the company's assets. Focus on the top line, Cash and cash equivalents. At December 31, 2012, EPIC reported cash of $6,260. Due to Price's scheme, the company had been cheated of $622,000 over several years that it could have used to buy new equipment, expand operations, or pay off debts.

EPIC Products has now revamped its internal controls. The company has hired a separate person, with no access to cash, to keep customer accounts receivable records. The company now uses a **lockbox system** for all checks received by mail. They are sent to EPIC's bank lock box, where they are gathered by a bank employee and immediately deposited. The remittance advices accompanying the checks are electronically scanned and forwarded to EPIC's accounts receivable bookkeeper where they are used as the source documents for posting amounts collected from customers. A summary of cash received goes to Cassell, who reviews it for reasonableness and compares it with the daily bank deposit total. Another employee, who has neither cash handling nor customer bookkeeping responsibilities, reconciles EPIC's monthly bank statement, and reconciles the total cash deposited per the daily listings with the total credits to customer accounts receivable. Now Cassell requires every employee to take time off for earned vacation, and rotates other employees through those positions while those employees are away.

EPIC Products, Inc.
Balance Sheet (Partial, Adapted)

Assets	December 31, 2012
Cash and cash equivalents	$ 6,260
Cash pledged as collateral	2,000
Accounts receivable	8,290
Inventories	36,200
Prepaid expenses	1,400
Investments	10,000
Equipment and facilities (net of accumulated depreciation of $2,400)	13,170
Other assets	3,930
Total assets	$81,250

Lapping is a type of fraud known as misappropriation of assets. Although it doesn't take a genius to accomplish, lapping requires some *motivation*, and is usually *rationalized* by distorted and unethical thinking. The *opportunity* to commit this type and other types of frauds arises through a weak internal control system. In this case, Price's access to cash and the customer accounts receivable, along with Cassell's failure to monitor Price's activities, proved to be the deadly combination that provided the opportunity for this fraud.

This chapter begins with a discussion of fraud, its types, and common characteristics. We then discuss internal controls, which are the primary means by which fraud as well as unintentional financial statement errors are prevented. We also discuss how to account for cash. These three topics—fraud, internal control, and cash—go together. Internal controls help prevent fraud. Cash is the asset that is most often misappropriated through fraud.

1 **Describe** fraud and its impact

2 **Explain** the objectives and components of internal control

3 **Design** and **use** a bank reconciliation

4 **Evaluate** internal controls over cash receipts and cash payments

5 **Construct** and **use** a cash budget

Learning Objectives

Describe Fraud and Its Impact

1

Describe fraud and its impact

Fraud is an intentional misrepresentation of facts, made for the purpose of persuading another party to act in a way that causes injury or damage to that party. For example, in the chapter-opening story, Erica Price intentionally misappropriated money from EPIC and covered it up by making customer accounts look different than they actually were. In the end, her actions caused $622,000 in damages to EPIC.

Fraud is a huge problem and is getting bigger, not only in the United States, but across the globe. Recent surveys of large and medium-sized companies in the United States and Canada revealed the following:

- ▶ Over 75% of businesses surveyed had experienced fraud.
- ▶ Over 50% of companies had experienced six or more instances of fraud in only one year.
- ▶ In 2007, companies lost an average of $2.4 million each to fraud (up from $1.7 million each in 2005).
- ▶ One out of every five American workers indicated personal awareness of fraud in the workplace.

Since small businesses and those in countries outside the United States and Canada were omitted from these surveys, we can be sure that the actual incidence of fraud is even higher! Another recent survey taken by the Association for Certified Fraud Examiners (ACFE) reveals that occupational fraud and abuse in America alone results in losses equal to about 6% of total business revenue. When applied to the U.S. gross domestic product, this means that about $600 billion per year is lost due to fraud, an astonishing $4,500 per employee! If you think that fraud occurs only in the for-profit sector, think again. About 13.4% of the ACFE survey cases are not-for-profit organizations, amounting to about $50 billion in fraud through not-for-profit organizations each year.

Fraud has literally exploded with the expansion of e-commerce via the Internet. In addition, studies have shown that the percentage of losses related to fraud from transactions originating in "third world" or developing countries via the Internet is even higher than in economically-developed countries.

What are the most common types of fraud? What causes fraud? What can be done to prevent it?

There are many types of fraud. Some of the most common types are insurance fraud, check forgery, Medicare fraud, credit card fraud, and identity theft. Following are the two most common types of fraud that impact financial statements:

- ▶ **Misappropriation of assets** *This type of fraud is committed by employees of an entity who steal money from the company and cover it up* through erroneous entries in the books. The EPIC case is an example. Other examples of asset misappropriation include employee theft of inventory, bribery or kickback schemes in the purchasing function, or employee overstatement of expense reimbursement requests.
- ▶ **Fraudulent financial reporting** *This type of fraud is committed by company managers who make false and misleading entries in the books,* making financial results of the company appear to be better than they actually are. The purpose of this type of fraud is to deceive investors and creditors into investing or loaning money to the company that they might not otherwise have invested or loaned.

Both of these types of fraud involve making false or misleading entries in the books of the company. We call this *cooking the books.* Of these two types, asset misappropriation is the most common, but fraudulent financial reporting is by far the most expensive. Perhaps the two most notorious recent cases involving fraudulent financial reporting in the United States involved **Enron Corporation** in 2001 and

WorldCom Corporation in 2002. These two scandals alone rocked the U.S. economy and impacted financial markets across the world. Enron (discussed in Chapter 8) committed fraudulent financial reporting by overstating profits through bogus sales of nonexistent assets with inflated values. When Enron's banks found out, they stopped loaning the company money to operate, causing it to go out of business almost overnight. WorldCom (discussed in Chapter 7) reported expenses as plant assets and overstated both profits and assets. The company's internal auditor blew the whistle on WorldCom, resulting in the company's eventual collapse. Sadly, the same international accounting firm, Arthur Andersen, LLP, had audited both companies' financial statements. Because of these and other failed audits, the once mighty firm of Arthur Andersen was forced to close its doors in 2002.

Each of these frauds, and many others revealed about the same time, involved losses in billions of dollars and thousands of jobs when the companies went out of business. Widespread media coverage sparked adverse market reaction, loss of confidence in the financial reporting system, and losses through declines in stock values that ran in the trillions of dollars! We will discuss some of these cases throughout the remaining chapters of the text as examples of how accounting principles were deliberately misapplied, through cooking the books, in environments characterized by *weak internal controls*.

Exhibit 4-1 explains in graphic form the elements that make up virtually every fraud. We call it the **fraud triangle**.

EXHIBIT 4-1 | The Fraud Triangle

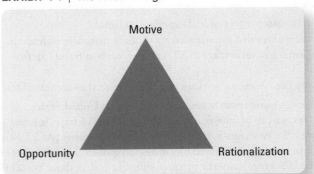

The first element in the fraud triangle is *motive*. This usually results from either critical need or greed on the part of the person who commits the fraud (the perpetrator). Sometimes it is a matter of just never having enough (because some persons who commit fraud are already rich by most people's standards). Other times the perpetrator of the fraud might have a legitimate financial need, such as a medical emergency, but he or she uses illegitimate means to meet that need. A recent article in the *Wall Street Journal* indicated that employee theft was on the rise due to economic hard times. In any case, the prevailing attitude on the part of the perpetrator is, "I want it, and someone else has it, so I'm going to do whatever I have to do to get it."

The second element in the fraud triangle is *opportunity*. As in the case of EPIC, the opportunity to commit fraud usually arises through weak internal controls. It might be a breakdown in a key element of controls, such as improper *segregation of duties* and/or *improper access to assets*. Or it might result from a weak *control environment*, such as a domineering CEO, a weak or conflicted board of directors, or lax ethical practices, allowing top management to override whatever controls the company has placed in operation for other transactions.

The third element in the triangle is *rationalization*. The perpetrator engages in distorted thinking, such as "I deserve this;" "Nobody treats me fairly;" "No one will ever know;" "Just this once, I won't let it happen again;" or "Everyone else is doing it."

Fraud and Ethics

As we pointed out in our decision model for making ethical accounting and business judgments introduced in Chapter 1, the decision to engage in fraud is an act with economic, legal, and ethical implications. The perpetrators of fraud usually do so for their own short-term *economic gain*, while others incur *economic losses* that may far outstrip the gains of the fraudsters. Moreover, fraud is defined by state, federal, and international law as *illegal*. Those who are caught and found guilty of fraud ultimately face penalties which include imprisonment, fines, and monetary damages. Finally, from an *ethical* standpoint, fraud violates the rights of many for the temporary betterment of a few, and for the ultimate betterment of no one. At the end of the day, everyone loses! **Fraud is the ultimate unethical act in business!**

Explain the Objectives and Components of Internal Control

The primary way that fraud, as well as unintentional errors, is prevented, detected, or corrected in an organization is through a proper system of internal control. **Internal control** is a plan of organization and a system of procedures implemented by company management and the board of directors designed to accomplish the following five objectives:

1. *Safeguard assets.* A company must safeguard its assets against waste, inefficiency, and fraud. As in the case of EPIC, if management fails to safeguard assets such as cash or inventory, those assets will slip away.

2. *Encourage employees to follow company policy.* Everyone in an organization—managers and employees—needs to work toward the same goals. A proper system of controls provides clear policies that result in fair treatment of both customers and employees.

3. *Promote operational efficiency.* Companies cannot afford to waste resources. They work hard to make a sale, and they don't want to waste any of the benefits. If the company can buy something for $30, why pay $35? Effective controls minimize waste, which lowers costs and increases profits.

4. *Ensure accurate, reliable accounting records.* Accurate records are essential. Without proper controls, records may be unreliable, making it impossible to tell which part of the business is profitable and which part needs improvement. A business could be losing money on every product it sells—unless it keeps accurate records for the cost of its products.

5. *Comply with legal requirements.* Companies, like people, are subject to laws, such as those of regulatory agencies like the SEC, the IRS, and state, local, and international governing bodies. When companies disobey the law, they are subject to fines, or in extreme cases, their top executives may even go to prison. Effective internal controls help ensure compliance with the law and avoidance of legal difficulties.

How critical are internal controls? They're so important that the U.S. Congress has passed a law to require public companies—those that sell their stock to the public—to maintain a system of internal controls and to require that their auditors examine those controls and issue audit reports as to their reliability. Exhibit 4-2 is EPIC Products' Management Discussion of Financial Responsibility.

②

Explain the objectives and components of internal control

EXHIBIT 4-2 | EPIC Products, Inc., Management's Discussion of Financial Responsibility

> **Management's Discussion of Financial Responsibility**
>
> EPIC Products regularly reviews its framework of internal controls, which includes the company's policies, procedures, and organizational structure. Corrective actions are taken to address any control deficiencies, and improvements are implemented as appropriate.

The Sarbanes-Oxley Act (SOX)

As the Enron and WorldCom scandals unfolded, many people asked, "How can these things happen? If such large companies that we have trusted commit such acts, how can we trust any company to be telling the truth in its financial statements? Where were the auditors?" To address public concerns, Congress passed the Sarbanes-Oxley Act of 2002 (SOX). SOX revamped corporate governance in the United States and profoundly affected the way that accounting and auditing is done in public companies. Here are some of the SOX provisions:

1. Public companies must issue an internal control report, and the outside auditor must evaluate and report on the soundness of the company's internal controls.

2. A special body, the Public Company Accounting Oversight Board, has been created to oversee the audits of public companies.

3. An accounting firm may not both audit a public client and also provide certain consulting services for the same client.

4. Stiff penalties await violators—25 years in prison for securities fraud; 20 years for an executive making false sworn statements.

The former CEO of WorldCom was convicted of securities fraud and sentenced to 25 years in prison. The top executives of Enron were also sent to prison. You can see that internal controls and related matters can have serious consequences.

Exhibit 4-3 diagrams the shield that internal controls provide for an organization. Protected by this shield, which provides protection from fraud, waste, and inefficiency, companies can do business in a trustworthy manner that ensures public confidence—an extremely important element in maintaining the stability of financial markets around the world.

EXHIBIT 4-3 | The Shield of Internal Control

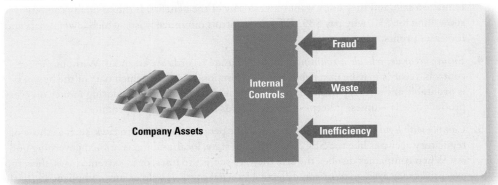

How does a business achieve good internal controls? The next section identifies the components of internal control.

The Components of Internal Control

Internal control can be broken down into five components:

- ▶ Control environment
- ▶ Risk assessment
- ▶ Information system
- ▶ Control procedures
- ▶ Monitoring of controls

Exhibit 4-4 (p. 237) diagrams the components of internal control.

Control Environment. The control environment, symbolized by the roof over the building in Exhibit 4-4, is the "tone at the top" of the business. It starts with the owner and the top managers. They must behave honorably to set a good example for company employees. The owner must demonstrate the importance of internal controls if he or she expects employees to take the controls seriously. A key ingredient in the control environment of many companies is a corporate code of ethics, modeled by top management, which includes such provisions as prohibition against giving or taking bribes or kickbacks from customers or suppliers, prohibition of transactions that involve conflicts of interest, and provisions that encourage good citizenship and corporate social responsibility.

EXHIBIT 4-4 | The Components of Internal Control

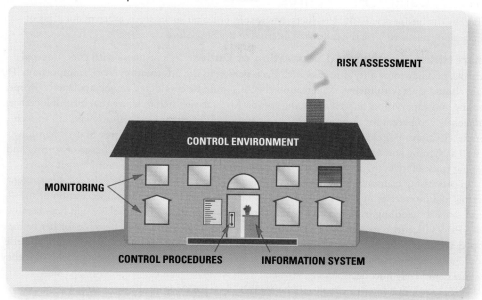

Risk Assessment. Symbolized by the smoke rising from the chimney, assessment of risks that a company faces offers hints of where mistakes or fraud might arise. A company must be able to identify its business risks, as well as to establish procedures for dealing with those risks to minimize their impacts on the company. For example, Kraft Foods faces the risk that its food products may harm people. American Airlines' planes may crash. And all companies face the risk of bankruptcy. The managements of companies, supported by their boards, have to identify these risks and do what they can to prevent those risks from causing financial or other harm to the company, its employees, its owners, and its creditors.

Information System. Symbolized by the door of the building, the information system is the means by which accounting information enters and exits. The owner of a business needs accurate information to keep track of assets and measure profits and losses. Every system within the business that processes accounting data should have the ability to capture transactions as they occur, record (journalize) those transactions in an accurate and timely manner, summarize (post) those transactions in the books (ledgers), and report those transactions in the form of account balances or footnotes in the financial statements.

Control Procedures. Also symbolized by the door, control procedures built into the control environment and information system are the means by which companies gain access to the five objectives of internal controls discussed previously. Examples include proper separation of duties, comparison and other checks, adequate records, proper approvals, and physical safeguards to protect assets from theft. The next section discusses internal control procedures.

Monitoring of Controls. Symbolized by the windows of the building, monitoring provides "eyes and ears," so that no one person or group of persons can process a transaction completely without being seen and checked by another person or group. With modern computerized systems, much of the monitoring of day-to-day activity is done through controls programmed into a company's information technology. Computer programs dealing with such systems as cash receipts and cash disbursements can be automatically programmed to generate *exception reports* for transactions that exceed certain pre-defined guidelines (such as disbursements in excess of $15,000 in a payroll) for special management scrutiny. In addition, companies hire auditors to monitor their controls. Internal auditors monitor company controls from the inside to safeguard the company's assets, and external auditors test the controls from the outside to ensure that the accounting records are accurate and reliable. Audits are discussed more thoroughly in the next section.

Internal Control Procedures

Whether the business is EPIC Products, Microsoft, or a Starbucks store, every major class of transactions needs to have the following *internal control procedures*.

Smart Hiring Practices and Separation of Duties. In a business with good internal controls, no important duty is overlooked. Each person in the information chain is important. The chain should start with hiring. Background checks should be conducted on job applicants. Proper training and supervision, as well as paying competitive salaries, helps ensure that all employees are sufficiently competent for their jobs. Employee responsibilities should be clearly laid out in position descriptions. For example, the **treasurer**'s department should be in charge of cash handling, as well as signing and approving checks. Warehouse personnel should be in charge of storing and keeping track of inventory. With clearly assigned responsibilities, all important jobs get done.

In processing transactions, smart management *separates three key duties: asset handling, record keeping, and transaction approval.* For example, in the case of EPIC Products, separation of the duties of cash handling from record keeping for customer accounts receivable would have removed Erica Price's incentive to engage in fraud, because it would have made it impossible for her to have lapped accounts receivable if another employee had been keeping the books. Ideally, someone else should also review customer accounts for collectibility and be in charge of writing them off if they become completely uncollectible.

The accounting department should be completely separate from the operating departments, such as production and sales. What would happen if sales personnel, who were compensated based on a percentage of the amount of sales they made, approved the company's sales transactions to customers? Sales figures could be inflated and might not reflect the eventual amount collected from customers.

At all costs, accountants must not handle cash, and cash handlers must not have access to the accounting records. If one employee has both cash-handling and accounting duties, that person can steal cash and conceal the theft. This is what happened at EPIC Products.

For companies that are *too small* to hire separate persons to do all of these functions, the key to good internal control is *getting the owner involved*, usually by approving all large transactions, making bank deposits, or reconciling the monthly bank account.

Comparisons and Compliance Monitoring. No person or department should be able to completely process a transaction from beginning to end without being cross-checked by another person or department. For example, some division of the treasurer's department should be responsible for depositing daily cash receipts in the bank. The **controller**'s department should be responsible for recording customer collections to individual customer accounts receivable. A third employee (perhaps the person in the controller's department who reconciles the bank statement) should compare the treasurer department's daily records of cash deposited with totals of collections posted to individual customer accounts by the accounting department.

One of the most effective tools for monitoring compliance with management's policies is the use of **operating budgets** and **cash budgets**. A **budget** is a quantitative financial plan that helps control day-to-day management activities. Management may prepare these budgets on a yearly, quarterly, monthly, or more frequent basis. Operating budgets are budgets of future periods' net income. They are prepared by line item of the income statement. Cash budgets, discussed in depth later in this chapter, are budgets of future periods' cash receipts and cash disbursements. Often these budgets are "rolling," being constantly updated by adding a time period a year away while dropping the time period that has just passed. Computer systems are programmed to prepare exception reports for data that are out of line with expectations. This data can include variances for each account from budgeted amounts. Department managers are required to explain the variances, and to take corrective actions in their operating plans to keep the budgets in line with expectations. This is an example of the use of **exception reporting**.

To validate the accounting records and monitor compliance with company policies, most companies have an audit. An **audit** is an examination of the company's financial statements and its accounting system, including its controls.

Audits can be internal or external. *Internal auditors* are employees of the business. They ensure that employees are following company policies and that operations are running efficiently. Internal auditors also determine whether the company is following legal requirements.

External auditors are completely independent of the business. They are hired to determine whether or not the company's financial statements agree with generally accepted accounting principles. Auditors examine the client's financial statements and the underlying transactions in order to form a professional opinion on the accuracy and reliability of the company's financial statements.

Adequate Records. *Accounting records* provide the details of business transactions. The general rule is that all major groups of transactions should be supported by either hard copy documents or electronic records. Examples of documents include sales invoices, shipping records, customer remittance advices, purchase orders, vendor invoices, receiving reports, and canceled (paid) checks. Documents should be pre-numbered to assure completeness of processing and proper transaction cutoff, and to prevent theft and inefficiency. A gap in the numbered document sequence draws attention to the possibility that transactions might have been omitted from processing.

Limited Access. To complement segregation of duties, company policy should limit access to assets only to those persons or departments that have custodial responsibilities. For example, access to cash should be limited to persons in the treasurer's department. Cash receipts might be processed through a lock-box system. Access to inventory should be limited to persons in the company warehouse where inventories are stored, or to persons in the shipping and receiving functions. Likewise, the company should limit access to records to those persons who have record keeping responsibilities. All manual records of the business should be protected by lock and key, and electronic records should be protected by passwords. Only authorized persons should have access to certain records. Individual computers in the business should be protected by user identification and password. Electronic data files should be encrypted (processed through a special code) to prevent their recognition if accessed by a "hacker" or other unauthorized person.

Proper Approvals. No transaction should be processed without management's general or specific approval. The bigger the transaction, the more specific approval it should have. For individual small transactions, management might delegate approval to a specific department, such as in the following examples:

► Sales to customers on account should all be approved by a separate *credit department* that reviews all customers for creditworthiness before goods are shipped to customers on credit. This helps assure that the company doesn't make sales to customers who cannot afford to pay their bills.

► Purchases of all items on credit should be approved by a separate *purchasing department* that specializes in that function. Among other things, a purchasing department should only buy from approved vendors, on the basis of competitive bids, to assure that the company gets the highest quality products for the most competitive prices.

► All personnel decisions, including hiring, firing, and pay adjustments, should be handled by a separate *human resources (HR) department* that specializes in personnel-related matters.

Very large (material) transactions should generally be approved by top management, and may even go to the board of directors.

What's an easy way to remember the basic control procedures for any class of transactions? Look at the first letters of each of the headings in this section:

Smart hiring practices and **S**eparation of duties
Comparisons and compliance monitoring
Adequate records
Limited access to both assets and records
Proper approvals (either general or specific) for each class of transaction

So, if you can remember SCALP and how to apply each of these attributes, you can have great controls in your business!

Information Technology

Accounting systems are relying less on manual procedures and more on information technology (IT) than ever before for record keeping, asset handling, approval, and monitoring, as well as for physically safeguarding the assets. For example, retailers such as Target Stores and Macy's control inventory by attaching an *electronic sensor* to merchandise. The cashier must remove the sensor before the customer can walk out of the store. If a customer tries to leave the store with the sensor attached, an alarm sounds. According to Checkpoint Systems, these devices reduce theft by as much as 50%. *Bar codes* speed checkout at retail stores, performing multiple operations in a single step. When the sales associate scans the merchandise at the register, the computer records the sale, removes the item from inventory, and computes the amount of cash tendered.

© David R. Frazier/Photolibrary, Inc./Photo Researchers, Inc.

When a company employs sophisticated IT, the basic attributes of internal control (SCALP) do not change, but the procedures by which these attributes are implemented change substantially. For example, segregation of duties is often accomplished by separating mainframe computer departments from other user departments (i.e., controller, sales, purchasing, receiving, credit, HR, treasurer) and restricting access to the IT department only to authorized personnel. Within the computer department, programmers should be separated from computer operators and data librarians. Access to sensitive data files is protected by **password** and data encryption. Electronic records must be saved routinely, or they might be written over or erased. Comparisons of data (such as cash receipts with total credits to customer accounts) that might otherwise be done by hand are performed by the computer. Computers can monitor inventory levels by item, generating a purchase order for inventory when it reaches a certain level.

The use of computers has the advantage of speed and accuracy (when programmed correctly). However, a computer that is *not* programmed correctly can corrupt *all* the data, making it unusable. It is therefore important to hire experienced and competent people to run the IT department, to restrict access to sensitive data and the IT department only to authorized personnel, to check data entered into and retrieved from the computer for accuracy and completeness, and to test and retest programs on a regular basis to assure data integrity and accuracy.

Safeguard Controls

Businesses keep important documents in *fireproof vaults*. *Burglar alarms* safeguard buildings, and *security cameras* safeguard other property. *Loss-prevention specialists* train employees to spot suspicious activity.

Employees who handle cash are in a tempting position. Many businesses purchase **fidelity bonds** on cashiers. The bond is an insurance policy that reimburses the company for any losses due to employee theft. Before issuing a fidelity bond, the insurance company investigates the employee's background.

Mandatory vacations and *job rotation* improve internal control. Companies move employees from job to job. This improves morale by giving employees a broad view of the business. Also, knowing someone else will do your job next month keeps you honest. EPIC Products didn't rotate employees to different jobs, and it cost the company $622,000.

Internal Controls for E-Commerce

E-commerce creates its own risks. Hackers may gain access to confidential information such as account numbers and passwords.

E-commerce pitfalls include the following:

- ▶ Stolen credit card numbers
- ▶ Computer viruses and Trojan Horses
- ▶ Phishing expeditions

Stolen Credit Card Numbers. Suppose you buy CDs from EMusic.com. To make the purchase, your credit card number must travel through cyberspace. Wireless networks (Wi-Fi) are creating new security hazards.

Amateur hacker Carlos Salgado, Jr., used his home computer to steal 100,000 credit card numbers with a combined limit exceeding $1 billion. Salgado was caught when he tried to sell the numbers to an undercover FBI agent.

Computer Viruses and Trojan Horses. A **computer virus** is a malicious program that (a) enters program code without consent and (b) performs destructive actions in the victim's computer files or programs. A **Trojan Horse** is a malicious computer program that hides inside a legitimate program and works like a virus. Viruses can destroy or alter data, make bogus calculations, and infect files. Most firms have found a virus in their system at some point.

Suppose the U.S. Department of Defense takes bids for a missile system. Raytheon and Lockheed-Martin are competing for the contract. A hacker infects Raytheon's system and alters Raytheon's design. Then the government labels the Raytheon design as flawed and awards the contract to Lockheed.

Phishing Expeditions. Thieves **phish** by creating bogus Web sites, such as AOL4Free.com and BankAmerica.com. The neat-sounding Web site attracts lots of visitors, and the thieves obtain account numbers and passwords from unsuspecting people. The thieves then use the data for illicit purposes.

Security Measures

To address the risks posed by e-commerce, companies have devised a number of security measures, including

- encryption and
- firewalls.

Encryption. The server holding confidential information may not be secure. One technique for protecting customer data is encryption. **Encryption** rearranges messages by a mathematical process. The encrypted message can't be read by those who don't know the code. An accounting example uses check-sum digits for account numbers. Each account number has its last digit equal to the sum of the previous digits. For example, consider Customer Number 2237, where $2 + 2 + 3 = 7$. Any account number that fails this test triggers an error message.

Firewalls. **Firewalls** limit access into a local network. Members can access the network but nonmembers can't. Usually several firewalls are built into the system. Think of a fortress with multiple walls protecting the company's computerized records in the center. At the point of entry, passwords, personal identification numbers (PINs), and signatures are used. More sophisticated firewalls are used deeper in the network. Start with Firewall 1, and work toward the center.

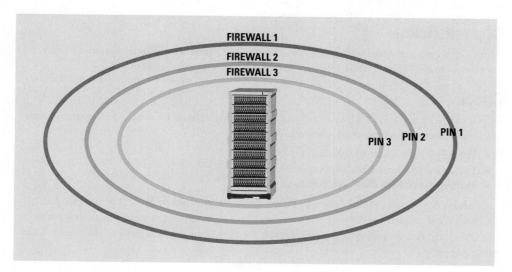

The Limitations of Internal Control—Costs and Benefits

Unfortunately, most internal controls can be overcome. Collusion—two or more people working together—can beat internal controls. Consider EPIC Products, discussed in the chapter opening. Even if Cassell were to hire a new person to keep the books, if that person had a relationship with

Price and they conspired with each other, they could design a scheme to lap accounts receivable, the same as Price did, and split the take. Other ways to circumvent a good system of internal controls include management override, human limitations such as fatigue and negligence, and gradual deterioration over time due to neglect. Because of the cost/benefit principle, discussed in the next paragraph, internal controls are not generally designed to detect these types of breakdowns. The best a company can do in this regard is to exercise care in hiring honest persons who have no conflicts of interest with existing employees and to exercise constant diligence in monitoring the system to assure it continues to work properly.

The stricter the internal control system, the more it costs. An overly complex system of internal control can strangle the business with red tape. How tight should the controls be? Internal controls must be judged in light of their costs and benefits. Here is an example of a good cost/benefit relationship: A part-time security guard at a **Wal-Mart** store costs about $28,000 a year. On average, each part-time guard prevents about $50,000 of theft. The net savings to Wal-Mart is $22,000. Most people would say the extra guard is well worth the cost!

Design and Use a Bank Reconciliation

3

Design and **use** a bank reconciliation

Cash is the most liquid asset because it's the medium of exchange. Cash is easy to conceal and relatively easy to steal. As a result, most businesses create specific controls for cash.

Keeping cash in a bank account helps control cash because banks have established practices for safeguarding customers' money. The documents used to control a bank account include the following:

▶ Signature card
▶ Bank statement
▶ Deposit ticket
▶ Bank reconciliation
▶ Check

Signature Card

Banks require each person authorized to sign on an account to provide a *signature card*. This protects against forgery.

Deposit Ticket

Banks supply standard forms such as *deposit tickets*. The customer fills in the amount of each deposit. As proof of the transaction, the customer keeps a deposit receipt.

Check

To pay cash, the depositor can write a **check**, which tells the bank to pay the designated party a specified amount. There are three parties to a check:

▶ The maker, who signs the check
▶ The payee, to whom the check is paid
▶ The bank on which the check is drawn

Exhibit 4-5 shows a check drawn by EPIC Products, the maker. The check has two parts, the check itself and the **remittance advice** below. This optional attachment, which may often be scanned electronically, tells the payee the reason for the payment and is used as the source document for posting to proper accounts.

EXHIBIT 4-5 | Check with Remittance Advice

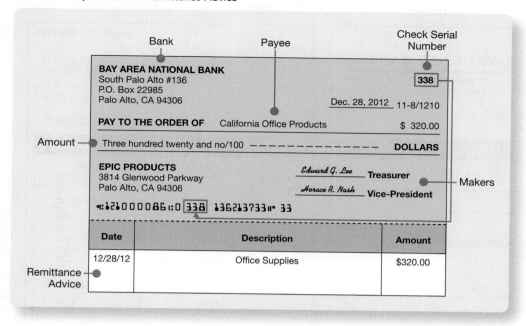

Bank Statement

Banks send monthly statements to customers. A **bank statement** reports what the bank did with the customer's cash. The statement shows the account's beginning and ending balances, cash receipts, and payments. Included with the statement is a list, and often visual images, of the maker's *canceled checks* (or the actual paid checks). Exhibit 4-6 is the December bank statement of the Palo Alto office of EPIC Products.

Electronic funds transfer (**EFT**) moves cash by electronic communication. It is cheaper to pay without having to mail a check, so many businesses and individuals pay their mortgages, rent, utilities, and insurance by EFT.

Bank Reconciliation

There are two records of a business's cash:

1. The Cash account in the company's general ledger. Exhibit 4-7, on page 245, shows that EPIC Products' ending cash balance is $3,340.

2. The bank statement, which shows the cash receipts and payments transacted through the bank. In Exhibit 4-6, the bank shows an ending balance of $5,900 for EPIC.

The books and the bank statement usually show different cash balances. Differences arise because of a time lag in recording transactions—two examples follow:

▸ When you write a check or use your bank debit card, you immediately deduct it in your checkbook. But the bank does not subtract the check or EFT from your account until the bank pays the item a few days later. And you immediately add the cash receipt for all your deposits or EFT credits. But it may take a day or two for the bank to add deposits or EFT credits to your balance.

▸ Your EFT payments and cash receipts are recorded by the bank before you learn of them.

EXHIBIT 4-6 | Bank Statement

| | **BANK STATEMENT** |

BAY AREA NATIONAL BANK
SOUTH PALO ALTO #136 P.O. BOX 22985 PALO ALTO, CA 94306

EPIC Products
3814 Glenwood Parkway
Palo Alto, CA 94306

CHECKING ACCOUNT 136–213733

DECEMBER 31, 2012

BEGINNING BALANCE	TOTAL DEPOSITS	TOTAL WITHDRAWALS	SERVICE CHARGES	ENDING BALANCE
6,550	4,370	5,000	20	5,900

— TRANSACTIONS —

DEPOSITS	DATE	AMOUNT
Deposit	12/04	1,150
Deposit	12/08	190
EFT—Receipt of cash dividend	12/17	900
Bank Collection	12/26	2,100
Interest	12/31	30

CHARGES	DATE	AMOUNT
Service Charge	12/31	20

CHECKS

Number	Amount	Number	Amount	Number	Amount
307	100	333	150	335	100
332	3,000	334	100	336	1,100

OTHER DEDUCTIONS	DATE	AMOUNT
NSF	12/04	50
EFT—Insurance	12/20	400

To ensure accurate cash records, you need to update your cash record—either online or after you receive your bank statement. The result of this updating process creates a **bank reconciliation**, which you must prepare. The bank reconciliation explains all differences between your cash records and your bank balance. The person who prepares the bank reconciliation should have no other cash duties. Otherwise, he or she can steal cash and manipulate the reconciliation to conceal the theft.

Preparing the Bank Reconciliation

Exhibit 4-8 on page 246 illustrates a typical bank reconciliation. It lists items that account for differences between the bank balance and the book balance. We call the cash record (also known as a "checkbook") the "Books."

Bank Side of the Reconciliation

1. Items to show on the *Bank* side of the bank reconciliation include the following:
   a. **Deposits in transit** (outstanding deposits). You have recorded these deposits, but the bank has not. Add deposits in transit on the bank reconciliation.

EXHIBIT 4-7 | Cash Records of EPIC Products

General Ledger:

ACCOUNT Cash

Date	Item	Debit	Credit	Balance
2012				
Dec 1	Balance			6,550
2	Cash receipt	1,150		7,700
7	Cash receipt	190		7,890
31	Cash payments		6,150	1,740
31	Cash receipt	1,600		3,340

Cash Payments:

Check No.	Amount	Check No.	Amount
332	$3,000	337	$ 280
333	510	338	320
334	100	339	250
335	100	340	490
336	1,100	Total	$6,150

    b. Outstanding checks. You have recorded these checks, but the bank has not yet paid them. Subtract outstanding checks.

    c. Bank errors. Correct all bank errors on the Bank side of the reconciliation. For example, the bank may erroneously subtract from your account a check written by someone else.

Book Side of the Reconciliation

2. Items to show on the *Book* side of the bank reconciliation include the following:

    a. Bank collections. Bank collections are cash receipts that the bank has recorded for your account. But you haven't recorded the cash receipt yet. Many businesses have their customers pay directly to their bank. This is called a *lock-box system* and reduces theft. An example is a bank collecting an account receivable for you. Add bank collections on the bank reconciliation.

    b. Electronic funds transfers. The bank may receive or pay cash on your behalf. An EFT may be a cash receipt or a cash payment. Add EFT receipts and subtract EFT payments.

    c. Service charge. This cash payment is the bank's fee for processing your transactions. Subtract service charges.

    d. Interest revenue on your checking account. On certain types of bank accounts, you earn interest if you keep enough cash in your account. The bank statement tells you of this cash receipt. Add interest revenue.

    e. Nonsufficient funds (NSF) checks. These are cash receipts from customers for which there are not sufficient funds in the bank to cover the amount. NSF checks (sometimes called hot checks) are treated as cash payments on your bank reconciliation. Subtract NSF checks.

    f. The cost of printed checks. This cash payment is handled like a service charge. Subtract this cost.

    g. Book errors. Correct all book errors on the Book side of the reconciliation. For example, you may have recorded a $150 check that you wrote as $510.

Bank Reconciliation Illustrated. The bank statement in Exhibit 4-6 shows that the December 31 bank balance of EPIC Products is $5,900 (upper right corner). However, the company's Cash account has a balance of $3,340, as shown in Exhibit 4-7. This situation calls for a

EXHIBIT 4-8 | Bank Reconciliation

PANEL A—Reconciling Items

Bank side:

1. Deposit in transit, $1,600.
2. Bank error: The bank deducted $100 for a check written by another company. Add $100 to the bank balance.
3. Outstanding checks—total of $1,340.

Check No.	Amount
337	$280
338	320
339	250
340	490

Book side:

4. EFT receipt of your dividend revenue earned on an investment, $900.
5. Bank collection of your account receivable, $2,100.
6. Interest revenue earned on your bank balance, $30.
7. Book error: You recorded check no. 333 for $510. The amount you actually paid on account was $150. Add $360 to your book balance.
8. Bank service charge, $20.
9. NSF check from a customer, $50. Subtract $50 from your book balance.
10. EFT payment of insurance expense, $400.

PANEL B—Bank Reconciliation

EPIC Products
Bank Reconciliation
December 31, 2012

Bank			Books		
Balance, December 31		$5,900	Balance, December 31		$3,340
Add:			Add:		
1. Deposit in transit		1,600	4. EFT receipt of dividend revenue		900
2. Correction of bank error		100	5. Bank collection of account		
		7,600	receivable		2,100
			6. Interest revenue earned on		
			bank balance		30
			7. Correction of book error—		
			overstated our check no. 333		360
Less:					6,730
3. Outstanding checks					
No. 337	$280		Less:		
No. 338	320		8. Service charge	$ 20	
No. 339	250		9. NSF check	50	
No. 340	490	(1,340)	10. EFT payment of insurance expense	400	(470)
Adjusted bank balance		$6,260	Adjusted book balance		$6,260

These amounts should agree.

SUMMARY OF THE VARIOUS RECONCILING ITEMS:

BANK BALANCE—ALWAYS

- *Add* deposits in transit.
- *Subtract* outstanding checks.
- *Add* or *subtract* corrections of bank errors.

BOOK BALANCE—ALWAYS

- *Add* bank collections, interest revenue, and EFT receipts.
- *Subtract* service charges, NSF checks, and EFT payments.
- *Add* or *subtract* corrections of book errors.

bank reconciliation. Exhibit 4-8, panel A, lists the reconciling items for easy reference, and panel B shows the completed reconciliation.

Journalizing Transactions from the Bank Reconciliation.   The bank reconciliation is an accountant's tool separate from the journals and ledgers. It does *not* account for transactions in the journal. To get the transactions into the accounts, we must make journal entries and post to the ledger. All items on the *Book* side of the bank reconciliation require journal entries.

The bank reconciliation in Exhibit 4-8 requires EPIC Products to make journal entries to bring the Cash account up-to-date. The numbers in red correspond to the reconciling items listed in Exhibit 4-8, Panel A.

4.	Dec 31	Cash	900	
		Dividend Revenue		900
		Receipt of dividend revenue earned on investment.		
5.	31	Cash	2,100	
		Accounts Receivable		2,100
		Account receivable collected by bank.		
6.	31	Cash	30	
		Interest Revenue		30
		Interest earned on bank balance.		
7.	31	Cash	360	
		Accounts Payable		360
		Correction of check no. 333.		
8.	31	Miscellaneous Expense[1]	20	
		Cash		20
		Bank service charge.		
9.	31	Accounts Receivable	50	
		Cash		50
		NSF check returned by bank.		
10.	31	Insurance Expense	400	
		Cash		400
		Payment of monthly insurance.		

[1]Miscellaneous Expense is debited for the bank service charge because the service charge pertains to no particular expense category.

The entry for the NSF check (entry 9) needs explanation. Upon learning that a customer's $50 check to us was not good, we must credit Cash to update the Cash account. Unfortunately, we still have a receivable from the customer, so we must debit Accounts Receivable to reinstate our receivable.

Online Banking

Online banking allows you to pay bills and view your account electronically. You don't have to wait until the end of the month to get a bank statement. With online banking you can reconcile transactions at any time and keep your account current whenever you wish. Exhibit 4-9 shows a page from the account history of Toni Anderson's bank account.

EXHIBIT 4-9 | Online Banking—Account History

Account History for Toni Anderson Checking # 5401-632-9 as of Close of Business 07/27/2012

Account Details

Current Balance $4,136.08

Date ↓	Description	Withdrawals	Deposits	Balance
	Current Balance			**$4,136.08**
07/27/12	DEPOSIT		1,170.35	
07/26/12	28 DAYS INTEREST		2.26	
07/25/12	Check #6131 View Image	443.83		
07/24/12	Check #6130 View Image	401.52		
07/23/12	EFT PYMT CINGULAR	61.15		
07/22/12	EFT PYMT CITICARD PAYMENT	3,172.85		
07/20/12	Check #6127 View Image	550.00		
07/19/12	Check #6122 View Image	50.00		
07/16/12	Check #6116 View Image	2,056.75		
07/15/12	Check #6123 View Image	830.00		
07/13/12	Check #6124 View Image	150.00		
07/11/12	ATM 4900 SANGER AVE	200.00		
07/09/12	Check #6119 View Image	30.00		
07/05/12	Check #6125 View Image	2,500.00		
07/04/12	ATM 4900 SANGER AVE	100.00		
07/01/12	DEPOSIT		9,026.37	

AAIFAOAO

FDIC
EQUAL HOUSING LENDER

E-Mail

The account history—like a bank statement—lists deposits, checks, EFT payments, ATM withdrawals, and interest earned on your bank balance. It also often lists the running balance in the account (the updated balance after each addition and subtraction).

STOP & THINK...

The bank statement balance is $4,500 and shows a service charge of $15, interest earned of $5, and an NSF check for $300. Deposits in transit total $1,200; outstanding checks are $575. The bookkeeper recorded as $152 a check of $125 in payment of an account payable. This created a book error of $27 (positive amount to correct the error).

(1) What is the adjusted bank balance?

(2) What was the book balance of cash before the reconciliation?

Answers:

(1) $5,125 ($4,500 + $1,200 − $575).

(2) $5,408 ($5,125 + $15 − $5 + $300 − $27). The adjusted book and bank balances are the same. The answer can be determined by working backward from the adjusted balance.

Using the Bank Reconciliation to Control Cash. The bank reconciliation can be a powerful control device. Tim Kayworth is a CPA in Houston, Texas. He owns several apartment complexes that are managed by his aunt. His aunt signs up tenants, collects the monthly rents, arranges maintenance work, hires and fires employees, writes the checks, and performs the bank reconciliation. In short, she does it all. This concentration of duties in one person is evidence of weak internal control. Kayworth's aunt could be stealing from him, and as a CPA he is aware of this possibility.

Kayworth trusts his aunt because she is a member of the family. Nevertheless, Kayworth exercises some controls over his aunt's management of his apartments. Kayworth periodically drops by the apartments to see whether the maintenance staff is keeping the property in good condition. To control cash, Kayworth occasionally examines the bank reconciliation that his aunt has performed. Kayworth would know immediately if his aunt were writing checks to herself. By examining the copy of each check, Kayworth establishes control over cash payments.

Kayworth has a simple method for controlling cash receipts. He knows the occupancy level of his apartments. He also knows the monthly rent he charges. Kayworth multiplies the number of apartments—say 20—by the monthly rent (which averages $500 per unit) to arrive at expected monthly rent revenue of $10,000. By tracing the $10,000 revenue to the bank statement, Kayworth can tell if all his rent money went into his bank account. To keep his aunt on her toes, Kayworth lets her know that he periodically audits her work.

Control activities such as these are critical. If there are only a few employees, separation of duties may not be feasible. The manager must control operations, or the assets will slip away.

MID-CHAPTER SUMMARY PROBLEM

The cash account of Ayers Associates at February 28, 2012, follows.

Cash			
Feb 1	Bal 3,995	Feb 3	400
6	800	12	3,100
15	1,800	19	1,100
23	1,100	25	500
28	2,400	27	900
Feb 28	Bal 4,095		

Ayers Associates received the bank statement on February 28, 2012 (negative amounts are in parentheses):

Bank Statement for February 2012		
Beginning balance		$3,995
Deposits:		
Feb 7	$ 800	
15	1,800	
24	1,100	3,700
Checks (total per day):		
Feb 8	$ 400	
16	3,100	
23	1,100	(4,600)
Other items:		
Service charge		(10)
NSF check from M. E. Crown		(700)
Bank collection of note receivable for the company		1,000
EFT—monthly rent expense		(330)
Interest revenue earned on account balance		15
Ending balance		$3,070

Additional data:
Ayers deposits all cash receipts in the bank and makes all payments by check.

▶ Requirements
1. Prepare the bank reconciliation of Ayers Associates at February 28, 2012.
2. Journalize the entries based on the bank reconciliation.

▶ Answers

Requirement 1

Ayers Associates
Bank Reconciliation
February 28, 2012

Bank:		
Balance, February 28, 2012		$ 3,070
Add: Deposit of February 28 in transit		2,400
		5,470
Less: Outstanding checks issued on Feb 25 ($500)		
and Feb 27 ($900)		(1,400)
Adjusted bank balance, February 28, 2012		$ 4,070
Books:		
Balance, February 28, 2012		$ 4,095
Add: Bank collection of note receivable		1,000
Interest revenue earned on bank balance		15
		5,110
Less: Service charge	$ 10	
NSF check	700	
EFT—Rent expense	330	(1,040)
Adjusted book balance, February 28, 2012		$ 4,070

Requirement 2

Feb 28	Cash	1,000	
	Note Receivable		1,000
	Note receivable collected by bank.		
28	Cash	15	
	Interest Revenue		15
	Interest earned on bank balance.		
28	Miscellaneous Expense	10	
	Cash		10
	Bank service charge.		
28	Accounts Receivable	700	
	Cash		700
	NSF check returned by bank.		
28	Rent Expense	330	
	Cash		330
	Monthly rent expense.		

Evaluate Internal Controls over Cash Receipts and Cash Payments

④ **Evaluate** internal controls over cash receipts and cash payments

Cash requires some specific internal controls because cash is relatively easy to steal and it's easy to convert to other forms of wealth. Moreover, all transactions ultimately affect cash. That's why cash is called the "eye of the needle." Let's see how to control cash receipts.

All cash receipts should be deposited for safekeeping in the bank—quickly. Companies receive cash over the counter and through the mail. Each source of cash has its own security measures.

Cash Receipts over the Counter

Exhibit 4-10 illustrates the purchase of products in a grocery store. The point-of-sale terminal provides control over the cash receipts, while also recording the sale and relieving inventory for the appropriate cost of the goods sold. Consider a **Whole Foods Market** store. For each transaction, the Whole Foods sales associate issues a receipt to the customer as proof of purchase. The cash drawer opens when the sales associate enters a transaction, and the machine electronically transmits a record of the sale to the store's main computer. At the end of each shift, the sales associate delivers his or her cash drawer to the office, where it is combined with cash from all other terminals and delivered by armored car to the bank for deposit, as explained in the next section. Later, a separate employee in the accounting department reconciles the electronic record of the sales per terminal to the record of the cash turned in. These measures, coupled with oversight by a manager, discourage theft.

Point-of-sale terminals also provide effective control over inventory. For example, in a restaurant, these devices track sales by menu item and total sales by cash, type of credit card, gift card redeemed, etc. They create the daily sales journal for that store, which, in turn, interfaces with the general ledger. Managers can use records produced by point-of-sale terminals to check inventory levels and compare them against sales records for accuracy. For example, in a restaurant, an effective way to monitor sales of expensive wine is for a manager to perform a quick count of the bottles on hand at the end of the day and compare it with the count at the end of the previous day, plus the record of any purchased. The count at the end of the previous day, plus the record of bottles purchased, minus the count at the end of the current day should equal the amount sold as recorded by the point-of-sale terminals in the restaurant.

An effective control for many chain retail businesses, such as restaurants, grocery stores, or clothing stores, to prevent unauthorized access to cash as well as to allow for more efficient management of cash, is the use of "depository bank accounts." Cash receipts for an individual store are deposited into a local bank account (preferably delivered by armored car for security reasons) on a daily basis. The corporate headquarters arranges for its centralized bank to draft the local depository accounts on a frequent (perhaps daily) basis to get the money concentrated into the company's centralized account, where it can be used to pay the corporation's bills. Depository accounts are "one-way" accounts where the local management may only make deposits; it has no authority to write checks on the account or take money out of the store's account.

EXHIBIT 4-10 | Cash Receipts over the Counter

© Catherine Yeulet/iStockphoto

Cash Receipts by Mail

Many companies receive cash by mail. Exhibit 4-11 shows how companies control cash received by mail. All incoming mail is opened by a mailroom employee. The mailroom then sends all customer checks to the treasurer, who has the cashier deposit the money in the bank. The remittance advices go to the accounting department for journal entries to Cash and customer accounts receivable. As a final step, the controller compares the following records for the day:

► Bank deposit amount from the treasurer
► Debit to Cash from the accounting department

The debit to Cash should equal the amount deposited in the bank. All cash receipts are safe in the bank, and the company books are up-to-date.

EXHIBIT 4-11 | Cash Receipts by Mail

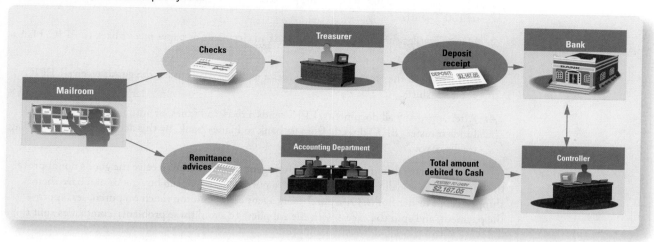

To prevent unauthorized access to cash, many companies use a bank lock-box system rather than risk processing checks through the mailroom. Customers send their checks by return mail directly to a post office box controlled by the company's bank. The bank sends a detailed record of cash received, by customer, to the company for use in posting collections to accounts receivable. Internal control is tight because company personnel never touch incoming cash. The lock-box system also gets the cash to the bank in a more timely manner, allowing the company to put the cash to work faster than would be possible if it were processed by the company's mailroom.

Controls over Payment by Check

Companies make most payments by check or electronic funds transfer (EFT). As we have seen, a company needs good separation of duties between (a) operations and (b) writing checks or authorizing EFTs for cash payments. Payment by check or EFT is an important internal control, as follows:

- The check or EFT provides a record of the payment.
- The check must be signed by an authorized official. The EFT must be approved by an authorized official.
- Before signing the check or authorizing the EFT, the official should study the evidence supporting the payment.

Controls over Purchase and Payment.   To illustrate the internal control over cash payments by check, suppose EPIC Products buys some of its inventory from Hanes Textiles. The purchasing and payment process follows these steps, as shown in Exhibit 4-12. Start with the box for EPIC Products on the left side.

EXHIBIT 4-12 | Cash Payments by Check or EFT

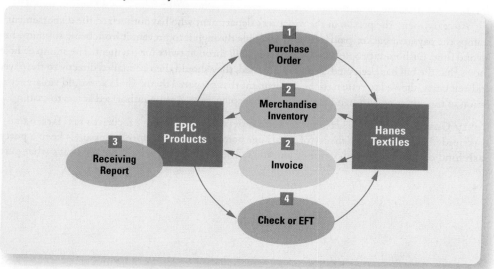

1. EPIC faxes or e-mails an electronic *purchase order* to Hanes Textiles. EPIC says, "Please send us 100 T-shirts."

2. Hanes Textiles ships the goods and sends an electronic or paper *invoice* back to EPIC. Hanes sent the goods.

3. EPIC receives the *inventory* and prepares a *receiving report* to list the goods received. EPIC got its T-shirts.

4. After approving all documents, EPIC sends a *check* to Hanes, or authorizes an electronic funds transfer (EFT) directly from its bank to Hanes' bank. By this action, EPIC says, "Okay, we'll pay you."

For good internal control, the purchasing agent should neither receive the goods nor approve the payment. If these duties aren't separated, a purchasing agent can buy goods and have them shipped to his or her home. Or a purchasing agent can spend too much on purchases, approve the payment, and split the excess with the supplier. To avoid these problems, companies split the following duties among different employees:

▶ Purchasing goods
▶ Receiving goods
▶ Approving and paying for goods

Exhibit 4-13 shows EPIC's payment packet of documents. Before signing the check or approving the EFT, the treasurer's department should examine the packet to prove that all the documents agree. Only then does the company know that

1. it received the goods ordered.

2. it is paying only for the goods received.

EXHIBIT 4-13 | Payment Packet

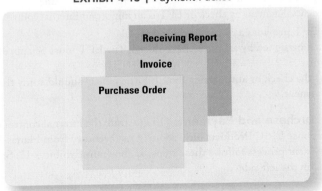

After payment, the person in the treasurer's department who has authorized the disbursement stamps the payment packet "paid" or punches a hole through it to prevent it from being submitted a second time. Dishonest people have tried to run a bill through twice for payment. The stamp or hole shows that the bill has been paid. If checks are used, they should then be mailed directly to the payee without being allowed to return to the department that prepared them. To do so would violate separation of the duties of cash handling and record keeping, as well as unauthorized access to cash.

Petty Cash. It would be wasteful to write separate checks for an executive's taxi fare, name tags needed right away, or delivery of a package across town. Therefore, companies keep a **petty cash** fund on hand to pay such minor amounts. The word "petty" means small. That's what petty cash is—a small cash fund kept by a single employee for the purpose of making such on-the-spot minor purchases.

The petty cash fund is opened with a particular amount of cash. A check for that amount is then issued to the custodian of the petty cash fund, who is solely responsible for accounting for it. Assume that on February 28 **Cisco Systems**, the worldwide leader in networks for the Internet, establishes a petty cash fund of $500 in a sales department by writing a check to the designated custodian. The custodian of the petty cash fund cashes the check and places $500 in the fund, which may be a cash box or other device.

For each petty cash payment, the custodian prepares a petty cash voucher to list the item purchased. The sum of the cash in the petty cash fund plus the total of the paid vouchers in the cash box should equal the opening balance at all times—in this case, $500. The Petty Cash account keeps its $500 balance at all times. Maintaining the Petty Cash account at this balance, supported by the fund (cash plus vouchers), is how an **imprest system** works. The control feature is that it clearly identifies the amount for which the custodian is responsible.

In recent years, banks have instituted the practice of *debit cards*, which are used to make cash purchases of relatively small amounts. A company employee who needs to make a small purchase may obtain permission from a supervisor to use a company debit card. Supervisors require receipts for all such purchases and compare them with EFT amounts on the bank statement. Debit cards are taking the place of petty cash systems in many companies.

Construct and Use a Cash Budget

As mentioned earlier in the chapter, a budget is a financial plan that helps coordinate business activities. Managers control operations with an operating budget. They also control cash receipts and cash payments, as well as ending cash balances, through use of a cash budget.

How, for example, does EPIC Products decide when to invest in new inventory-tracking technology? How will EPIC decide how much to spend? Will borrowing be needed, or can EPIC finance the purchase with internally generated cash? What do ending cash balances need to be in order to provide a "safety margin" so the company won't unexpectedly run out of cash? A cash budget for a business works on roughly the same concept as a personal budget. By what process do you decide how much to spend on your education? On an automobile? On a house? All these decisions depend to some degree on the information that a cash budget provides.

A *cash budget helps a company or an individual manage cash by planning receipts and payments during a future period.* The company must determine how much cash it will need and then decide whether or not operations will bring in the needed cash. Managers proceed as follows:

5

Construct and **use** a cash budget

1. Start with the entity's cash balance at the beginning of the period. This is the amount left over from the preceding period.

2. Add the budgeted cash receipts and subtract the budgeted cash payments.

3. The beginning balance plus receipts and minus payments equals the expected cash balance at the end of the period.

4. Compare the cash available before new financing to the budgeted cash balance at the end of the period. Managers know the minimum amount of cash they need (the budgeted balance). If the budget shows excess cash, managers can invest the excess. But if the cash available falls below the budgeted balance, the company will need additional financing. The company may need to borrow the shortfall amount. The budget is a valuable tool for helping the company plan for the future.

The budget period can span any length of time—a day, a week, a month, or a year. Exhibit 4-14 shows a cash budget for EPIC Products, Inc., for the year ended December 31, 2012. Study it carefully, because at some point you will use a cash budget.

EPIC Products' cash budget in Exhibit 4-14 begins with $6,260 of cash at the end of the previous year (line 1). Then add budgeted cash receipts and subtract budgeted payments for the current year. In this case, EPIC expects to have $3,900 of cash available at year-end (line 10). EPIC managers need to maintain a cash balance of at least $5,000 (line 11). Line 12 shows that EPIC must arrange $1,100 of financing in order to achieve its goals for 2012.

EXHIBIT 4-14 | Cash Budget

		EPIC Products, Inc. Cash Budget For the Year Ended December 31, 2012		
1		Cash balance, December 31, 2011		$ 6,260
		Budgeted cash receipts:		
2		Collections from customers		55,990
3		Dividends on investments		1,200
4		Sale of store fixtures		5,700
				69,150
		Budgeted cash payments:		
5		Purchases of inventory	$33,720	
6		Operating expenses	11,530	
7		Expansion of store	12,000	
8		Payment of long-term debt	5,000	
9		Payment of dividends	3,000	65,250
10		Cash available (needed) before new financing		$ 3,900
11		Budgeted cash balance, December 31, 2012		(5,000)
12		Cash available for additional investments, or		
		(New financing needed)		$ (1,100)

Reporting Cash on the Balance Sheet

Most companies have numerous bank accounts, but they usually combine all cash amounts into a single total called "Cash and Cash Equivalents." **Cash equivalents** include liquid assets such as time deposits, certificates of deposit, and high-grade government securities. These are interest-bearing accounts that can be withdrawn with no penalty, or interest-bearing securities. Slightly less liquid than cash, cash equivalents are sufficiently similar to be reported along with cash. The balance sheet of EPIC Products reported the following:

	EPIC Products, Inc. Balance Sheet (Excerpts, adapted) For the Year Ended December 31, 2012	
	Assets	
	Cash and cash equivalents	$6,260
	Cash pledged as collateral	2,000

Compensating Balance Agreements

The Cash account on the balance sheet reports the liquid assets available for day-to-day use. None of the Cash balance is restricted in any way.

Any restricted amount of cash should *not* be reported as Cash on the balance sheet. For example, on the EPIC Products balance sheet, *cash pledged as collateral* is reported separately because that cash is not available for day-to-day use. Instead, EPIC has pledged the cash as security (collateral) for a loan. If EPIC fails to pay the loan, the lender can take the pledged cash. For this reason, the pledged cash is less liquid.

Also, banks often lend money under a compensating balance agreement. The borrower agrees to maintain a minimum balance in a checking account at all times. This minimum balance becomes a long-term asset and is therefore not cash in the normal sense.

Suppose EPIC Products borrowed $10,000 at 8% from First Interstate Bank and agreed to keep 20% ($2,000) on deposit at all times. The net result of the compensating balance agreement is that EPIC actually borrowed only $8,000. And by paying 8% interest on the full $10,000, EPIC's actual interest rate is really 10%, as shown here:

$10,000 × .08 = $800 interest
$800/$8,000 = .10 interest rate

END-OF-CHAPTER SUMMARY PROBLEM

Assume the following situation for PepsiCo, Inc.: PepsiCo ended 2012 with cash of $200 million. At December 31, 2012, Bob Detmer, the CFO of PepsiCo, is preparing the budget for 2013.

During 2013, Detmer expects PepsiCo to collect $26,400 million from customers and $80 million from interest earned on investments. PepsiCo expects to pay $12,500 million for its inventories and $5,400 million for operating expenses. To remain competitive, PepsiCo plans to spend $2,200 million to upgrade production facilities and an additional $350 million to acquire other companies. PepsiCo also plans to sell older assets for approximately $300 million and to collect $220 million of this amount in cash. PepsiCo is budgeting dividend payments of $550 million during the year. Finally, the company is scheduled to pay off $1,200 million of long-term debt plus the $6,600 million of current liabilities left over from 2012.

Because of the growth planned for 2013, Detmer budgets the need for a minimum cash balance of $300 million.

▶ Requirement

1. How much must PepsiCo borrow during 2013 to keep its cash balance from falling below $300 million? Prepare the 2013 cash budget to answer this important question.

▶ Answer

PepsiCo, Inc. Cash Budget For the Year Ended December 31, 2013		
(In millions)		
Cash balance, December 31, 2012		$ 200
Estimated cash receipts:		
Collections from customers		26,400
Receipt of interest		80
Sales of assets		220
		26,900
Estimated cash payments:		
Purchases of inventory	$12,500	
Payment of operating expenses	5,400	
Upgrading of production facilities	2,200	
Acquisition of other companies	350	
Payment of dividends	550	
Payment of long-term debt and other liabilities ($1,200 + $6,600)	7,800	(28,800)
Cash available (needed) before new financing		$ (1,900)
Budgeted cash balance, December 31, 2013		(300)
Cash available for additional investments, or (New financing needed)		$ (2,200)

PepsiCo. must borrow $2,200 million.

REVIEW | Internal Control and Cash

Quick Check (Answers are given on page 282.)

1. Internal control has its own terminology. On the left are some key internal control concepts. On the right are some key terms. Match each internal control concept with its term by writing the appropriate letter in the space provided. Not all letters are used.

   ___h___ Internal control cannot always safeguard against this problem.
   ___g___ This is often mentioned as the cornerstone of a good system of internal control.
   ___c___ Pay employees enough to require them to do a good job.
   ___i___ This procedure limits access to sensitive data.
   ___f___ This type of insurance policy covers losses due to employee theft.
   ___a___ Trusting your employees can lead you to overlook this procedure.
   ___b___ This is the most basic purpose of internal control.

   a. Supervision
   b. Safeguarding assets
   c. Competent personnel
   d. Firewalls
   e. External audits
   f. Fidelity bond
   g. Separation of duties
   h. Collusion
   i. Encryption

2. Each of the following is an example of a control procedure, *except*
   a. Sound personnel procedures   c. A sound marketing plan
   b. Limited access to assets   d. Separation of duties

3. Which of the following is an example of poor internal control?
   a. Rotate employees through various jobs.
   b. The accounting department compares goods received with the related purchase order.
   c. Employees must take vacations.
   d. The mailroom clerk records daily cash receipts in the journal.

Libby Corporation has asked you to prepare its bank reconciliation at the end of the current month. Answer questions 4–8 using the following code letters to indicate how the item described would be reported on the bank reconciliation.

   a. Add to the bank balance
   b. Deduct from the book balance
   c. Does not belong on the bank reconciliation
   d. Add to the book balance
   e. Deduct from the bank balance

4. A check for $753 written by Libby during the current month was erroneously recorded as a $375 payment.

5. A $600 deposit made on the last day of the current month did not appear on this month's bank statement.

6. The bank statement showed interest earned of $50.

7. The bank statement included a check from a customer that was marked NSF.

8. The bank statement showed that the bank had credited Libby's account for a $500 deposit made by Lubbock Company.

9. Which of the following reconciling items does not require a journal entry?
   a. Deposit in transit   c. Bank service charge
   b. Bank collection of note receivable   d. NSF check

10. A check was written for $462 to purchase supplies. The check was recorded in the journal as $426. The entry to correct this error would
    a. increase Supplies, $36.   c. decrease Supplies, $36.
    b. decrease Cash, $36.   d. both a and b.

11. A cash budget helps control cash by
    a. developing a plan for increasing sales.
    b. ensuring accurate cash records.
    c. helping to determine whether additional cash is available for investments or new financing is needed.
    d. all of the above.

Accounting Vocabulary

audit (p. 238) A periodic examination of a company's financial statements and the accounting systems, controls, and records that produce them. Audits may be either external or internal. External audits are usually performed by certified public accountants (CPAs).

bank collections (p. 245) Collection of money by the bank on behalf of a depositor.

bank reconciliation (p. 244) A document explaining the reasons for the difference between a depositor's records and the bank's records about the depositor's cash.

bank statement (p. 243) Document showing the beginning and ending balances of a particular bank account listing the month's transactions that affected the account.

budget (p. 238) A quantitative expression of a plan that helps managers coordinate the entity's activities.

cash budget (p. 238) A budget that projects the entity's future cash receipts and cash disbursements.

cash equivalent (p. 256) Investments such as time deposits, certificates of deposit, or high-grade government securities that are considered so similar to cash that they are combined with cash for financial disclosure purposes on the balance sheet.

check (p. 242) Document instructing a bank to pay the designated person or business the specified amount of money.

computer virus (p. 241) A malicious program that enters a company's computer system by e-mail or other means and destroys program and data files.

controller (p. 238) The chief accounting officer of a business.

deposits in transit (p. 244) A deposit recorded by the company but not yet by its bank.

electronic fund transfer (EFT) (p. 243) System that transfers cash by electronic communication rather than by paper documents.

encryption (p. 241) Mathematical rearranging of data within an electronic file to prevent unauthorized access to information.

exception reporting (p. 238) Identifying data that is not within "normal limits" so that managers can follow up and take corrective action. Exception reporting is used in operating and cash budgets to keep company profits and cash flow in line with management's plans.

fidelity bond (p. 240) An insurance policy taken out on employees who handle cash.

firewall (p. 241) An electronic barrier, usually provided by passwords, around computerized data files to protect local area networks of computers from unauthorized access.

fraud (p. 233) An intentional misrepresentation of facts, made for the purpose of persuading another party to act in a way that causes injury or damage to that party.

fraud triangle (p. 234) The three elements that are present in almost all cases of fraud. These elements are motive, opportunity, and rationalization on the part of the perpetrator.

fraudulent financial reporting (p. 233) Fraud perpetrated by management by preparing misleading financial statements.

imprest system (p. 255) A way to account for petty cash by maintaining a constant balance in the petty cash account, supported by the fund (cash plus payment tickets) totaling the same amount.

internal control (p. 235) Organizational plan and related measures adopted by an entity to safeguard assets, encourage adherence to company policies, promote operational efficiency, and ensure accurate and reliable accounting records.

lapping (p. 231) A fraudulent scheme to steal cash through misappropriating certain customer payments and posting payments from other customers to the affected accounts to cover it up. Lapping is caused by weak internal controls (i.e., not segregating the duties of cash handling and accounts receivable bookkeeping, allowing the bookkeeper improper access to cash, and not appropriately monitoring the activities of those who handle cash).

lock-box system (p. 231) A system of handling cash receipts by mail whereby customers remit payment directly to the bank, rather than through the entity's mail system.

misappropriation of assets (p. 233) Fraud committed by employees by stealing assets from the company.

nonsufficient funds (NSF) check (p. 245) A "hot" check, one for which the payer's bank account has insufficient money to pay the check. NSF checks are cash receipts that turn out to be worthless.

operating budget (p. 238) A budget of future net income. The operating budget projects a company's future revenue and expenses. It is usually prepared by line item of the company's income statement.

outstanding checks (p. 245) A check issued by the company and recorded on its books but not yet paid by its bank.

password (p. 240) A special set of characters that must be provided by the user of computerized program or data files to prevent unauthorized access to those files.

petty cash (p. 254) Fund containing a small amount of cash that is used to pay minor amounts.

phishing (p. 241) Creating bogus Web sites for the purpose of stealing unauthorized data, such as names, addresses, social security numbers, bank account, and credit card numbers.

remittance advice (p. 242) An optional attachment to a check (sometimes a perforated tear-off document and sometimes capable of being electronically scanned) that indicates the payer, date, and purpose of the cash payment. The remittance advice is often used as the source documents for posting cash receipts or payments.

treasurer (p. 238) In a large company, the individual in charge of the department that has final responsibility for cash handling and cash management. Duties of the treasurer's department include cash budgeting, cash collections, writing checks, investing excess funds, and making proposals for raising additional cash when needed.

Trojan Horse (p. 241) A malicious program that hides within legitimate programs and acts like a computer virus.

ASSESS YOUR PROGRESS

Short Exercises

S4-1 (*Learning Objective 1: Define fraud*) Define "fraud." List and briefly discuss the three major components of the "fraud triangle."

S4-2 (*Learning Objective 2: Describe components of internal control*) List the components of internal control. Briefly describe each component.

S4-3 (*Learning Objective 2: Explain the objectives of internal control*) Explain why separation of duties is often described as the cornerstone of internal control for safeguarding assets. Describe what can happen if the same person has custody of an asset and also accounts for the asset.

S4-4 (*Learning Objective 2: Explain the components of internal control*) Identify the other control procedures usually found in a company's system of internal control besides separation of duties, and tell why each is important.

S4-5 (*Learning Objective 1: Describe fraud over e-commerce*) How do computer viruses, Trojan Horses, and phishing expeditions work? How can these e-commerce pitfalls hurt you? Be specific.

S4-6 (*Learning Objective 2: Explain the objectives of internal control*) Cash may be a small item on the financial statements. Nevertheless, internal control over cash is very important. Why is this true?

S4-7 (*Learning Objectives 2, 4: Explain the objectives of internal control; evaluate controls over cash payments*) Peacock Company requires that all documents supporting a check be cancelled by punching a hole through the packet. Why is this practice required? What might happen if it were not?

S4-8 (*Learning Objective 3: Design and use a bank reconciliation*) The Cash account of Rampart Corp. reported a balance of $2,540 at October 31. Included were outstanding checks totaling $900 and an October 31 deposit of $400 that did not appear on the bank statement. The bank statement, which came from Tri Bank, listed an October 31 balance of $3,675. Included in the bank balance was an October 30 collection of $670 on account from a customer who pays the bank directly. The bank statement also shows a $30 service charge, $20 of interest revenue that Rampart earned on its bank balance, and an NSF check for $25.

Prepare a bank reconciliation to determine how much cash Rampart actually has at October 31.

S4-9 (*Learning Objective 3: Design and use a bank reconciliation*) After preparing Rampart Corp.'s bank reconciliation in Short Exercise 4-8, make the company's journal entries for transactions that arise from the bank reconciliation. Date each transaction October 31, and include an explanation with each entry.

S4-10 (*Learning Objective 3: Design and use a bank reconciliation*) Brenda Small manages Harris Manufacturing. Small fears that a trusted employee has been stealing from the company. This employee receives cash from clients and also prepares the monthly bank reconciliation. To check up on the employee, Small prepares her own bank reconciliation, as follows:

Harris Manufacturing Bank Reconciliation October 31, 2012			
Bank		**Books**	
Balance, October 31	$4,150	Balance, October 31	$3,980
Add:		Add:	
Deposits in transit	300	Bank collections	450
		Interest revenue	35
Less:		Less:	
Outstanding checks	(760)	Service charge	(65)
Adjusted bank balance	$3,690	Adjusted book balance	$4,400

Does it appear that the employee has stolen from the company? If so, how much? Explain your answer. Which side of the bank reconciliation shows the company's true cash balance?

S4-11 (*Learning Objective 4: Evaluate internal control over cash receipts*) Gretchen Cilla sells memberships to the Denver Symphony Association in Denver, Colorado. The Symphony's procedure requires Cilla to write a patron receipt for all memberships sold. The receipt forms are prenumbered. Cilla is having personal financial problems, and she stole $600 received from a customer. To hide her theft, Cilla destroyed the company copy of the receipt that she gave the patron. What will alert manager Sabrina Sims that something is wrong?

S4-12 (*Learning Objective 4: Evaluate internal control over cash payments*) Answer the following questions about internal control over cash payments:

1. Payment by check carries three controls over cash. What are they?
2. Suppose a purchasing agent receives the goods that he purchases and also approves payment for the goods. How could a dishonest purchasing agent cheat his company? How do companies avoid this internal control weakness?

S4-13 (*Learning Objective 5: Use a cash budget*) Briefly explain how a cash budget works and what it accomplishes with its last few lines of data.

S4-14 (*Learning Objective 5: Construct a cash budget*) Cooper Apple Growers (CAG) is a major food cooperative. Suppose CAG begins 2011 with cash of $8 million. CAG estimates cash receipts during 2011 will total $103 million. Planned payments will total $86 million. To meet daily cash needs next year, CAG must maintain a cash balance of at least $20 million. Prepare the organization's cash budget for 2011.

S4-15 (*Learning Objective 1: Describe fraud and its impact*) Grace Rocker, an accountant for Dill Limited, discovers that her supervisor, Bob Doon, made several errors last year. Overall, the errors overstated the company's net income by 20%. It is not clear whether the errors were deliberate or accidental. What should Rocker do?

Exercises

MyAccountingLab

> All of the Group A and Group B exercises can be found within MyAccountingLab, an online homework and practice environment. Your instructor may ask you to complete these exercises using MyAccountingLab.

Group A

E4-16A (*Learning Objectives 1, 2: Describe fraud and its impact; identify internal controls*) Identify the internal control weakness in the following situations. State how the person can hurt the company.

a. John Munson works as a security guard at VALID parking in Denver. Munson has a master key to the cash box where customers pay for parking. Each night Munson prepares the cash report that shows (a) the number of cars that parked on the lot and (b) the day's cash receipts. Lily Cruise, the VALID treasurer, checks Munson's figures by multiplying the number of cars by the parking fee per car. Cruise then deposits the cash in the bank.

b. Eloise Fulton is the purchasing agent for Milton Sports Equipment. Fulton prepares purchase orders based on requests from division managers of the company. Fulton faxes the purchase order to suppliers who then ship the goods to Milton. Fulton receives each incoming shipment and checks it for agreement with the purchase order and the related invoice. She then routes the goods to the respective division managers and sends the receiving report and the invoice to the accounting department for payment.

E4-17A (*Learning Objective 4: Evaluate internal control*) The following situations describe two cash payment situations and two cash receipt situations. In each pair, one set of internal controls is better than the other. Evaluate the internal controls in each situation as strong or weak, and give the reason for your answer.

Cash payments:

    a. Tom Mick Construction policy calls for construction supervisors to request the equipment needed for their jobs. The home office then purchases the equipment and has it shipped to the construction site.

    b. Quarry, Inc., policy calls for project supervisors to purchase the equipment needed for jobs. The supervisors then submit the paid receipts to the home office for reimbursement. This policy enables supervisors to get the equipment quickly and keep construction jobs moving.

Cash receipts:

    a. At Colt Auto Parts, cash received by mail goes straight to the accountant, who debits Cash and credits Accounts Receivable to record the collections from customers. The Colt accountant then deposits the cash in the bank.

    b. Cash received by mail at Soft Dermatology Clinic goes to the mail room, where a mail clerk opens envelopes and totals the cash receipts for the day. The mail clerk forwards customer checks to the cashier for deposit in the bank and forwards the remittance advices to the accounting department for posting credits to customer accounts.

E4-18A (*Learning Objectives 1, 2, 4: Describe fraud and its impact; explain the objectives and components of internal control; evaluate internal controls*) Billy Flack served as executive director of Downtown Columbia, an organization created to revitalize Columbia, South Carolina. Over the course of 11 years, Flack embezzled $444,000. How did Flack do it? By depositing subscriber cash receipts in his own bank account, writing Downtown Columbia checks to himself, and creating phony entities that Downtown Columbia wrote checks to.

    Downtown Columbia was led by a board of directors comprised of civic leaders. Flack's embezzlement went undetected until Downtown Columbia couldn't pay its bills.

    Give four ways Flack's embezzlement could have been prevented.

E4-19A (*Learning Objective 3: Design and use a bank reconciliation*) The following items appear on a bank reconciliation:

    1. ____ Service charge
    2. ____ Book error: We debited Cash for $100. The correct debit was $1,000.
    3. ____ NSF check
    4. ____ Bank collection of a note receivable on our behalf
    5. ____ Deposits in transit
    6. ____ Bank error: The bank credited our account for a deposit made by another bank customer.
    7. ____ Outstanding checks

Classify each item as (a) an addition to the bank balance, (b) a subtraction from the bank balance, (c) an addition to the book balance, or (d) a subtraction from the book balance.

E4-20A (*Learning Objective 3: Prepare a bank reconciliation*) D. J. Harris' checkbook lists the following:

Date	Check No.	Item	Check	Deposit	Balance
1/1					$ 530
4	622	Moe's Cafe	$ 15		515
9		Dividends received		$ 115	630
13	623	Good Year Tire Co.	45		585
14	624	Jiffy Lube	18		567
18	625	Cash	60		507
26	626	Shandon Baptist Church	90		417
28	627	Everygreen Apartments	270		147
31		Paycheck		1,225	1,372

The January bank statement shows

Balance			$530
Add: Deposits			115
Debit checks:	No.	Amount	
	622	$15	
	623	45	
	624	81*	
	625	60	(201)
Other charges:			
NSF check		$25	
Service charge		10	(35)
Balance			$409

*This is the correct amount for check number 624.

▶ **Requirement**

1. Prepare Harris' bank reconciliation at January 31.

E4-21A (*Learning Objective 3: Use a bank reconciliation*) Frank White operates a roller skating center. He has just received the monthly bank statement at November 30 from Citizen National Bank, and the statement shows an ending balance of $570. Listed on the statement are an EFT rent collection of $335, a service charge of $8, two NSF checks totaling $120, and a $10 charge for printed checks. In reviewing his cash records, White identifies outstanding checks totaling $601 and a November 30 deposit in transit of $1,765. During November, he recorded a $270 check for the salary of a part-time employee as $27. White's Cash account shows a November 30 cash balance of $1,780. How much cash does White actually have at November 30?

E4-22A (*Learning Objective 3: Design and use a bank reconciliation*) Use the data from Exercise 4-21A to make the journal entries that White should record on November 30 to update his Cash account. Include an explanation for each entry.

E4-23A (*Learning Objective 4: Evaluate internal control over cash receipts*) McIntosh stores use point-of-sale terminals as cash registers. The register shows the amount of each sale, the cash received from the customer, and any change returned to the customer. The machine also produces a customer receipt but keeps no record of transactions. At the end of the day, the clerk counts the cash in the register and gives it to the cashier for deposit in the company bank account.

Write a memo to convince the store manager that there is an internal control weakness over cash receipts. Identify the weakness that gives an employee the best opportunity to steal cash, and state how to prevent such a theft.

E4-24A (*Learning Objective 4: Evaluate internal control over cash payments*) Flat Flyers Company manufactures a popular line of remote airplanes. Flat Flyers employs 125 workers and keeps their employment records on time sheets that show how many hours the employee works each week. On Friday the shop foreman collects the time sheets, checks them for accuracy, and delivers them to the payroll department for preparation of paychecks. The treasurer signs the paychecks and returns the checks to the payroll department for distribution to the employees.

Identify the main internal control weakness in this situation, state how the weakness can hurt Flat Flyers, and propose a way to correct the weakness.

E4-25A (*Learning Objective 5: Construct and use a cash budget*) Gale Communications, Inc., is preparing its cash budget for 2012. Gale ended 2011 with cash of $85 million, and managers need to keep a cash balance of at least $78 million for operations.

Collections from customers are expected to total $11,335 million during 2012, and payments for the cost of services and products should reach $6,169 million. Operating expense payments are budgeted at $2,553 million.

During 2012, Gale expects to invest $1,822 million in new equipment and sell older assets for $157 million. Debt payments scheduled for 2012 will total $578 million. The company forecasts net income of $893 million for 2012 and plans to pay dividends of $358 million.

Prepare Gale Communications' cash budget for 2012. Will the budgeted level of cash receipts leave Gale with the desired ending cash balance of $78 million, or will the company need additional financing? If so, how much?

E4-26A (*Learning Objective 5: Use cash budgeting*) Assume Victor's Vans borrowed $15 million from Jay's Bank and agreed to (a) pay an interest rate of 7.2% and (b) maintain a compensating balance amount equal to 5.3% of the loan. Determine Victor's Vans' actual effective interest rate on this loan.

Group B

E4-27B (*Learning Objectives 1, 2: Describe fraud and its impact; evaluate internal controls*) Identify the internal control weakness in the following situations. State how the person can hurt the company.

  a. Jay Mott works as a security guard at TOWN parking in Des Moines. Mott has a master key to the cash box where customers pay for parking. Each night Mott prepares the cash report that shows (a) the number of cars that parked on the lot and (b) the day's cash receipts. Lucy Casey, the TOWN treasurer, checks Mott's figures by multiplying the number of cars by the parking fee per car. Casey then deposits the cash in the bank.

  b. Ava Austin is the purchasing agent for Idle Sports Equipment. Austin prepares purchase orders based on requests from division managers of the company. Austin faxes the purchase order to suppliers who then ship the goods to Idle. Austin receives each incoming shipment and checks it for agreement with the purchase order and the related invoice. She then routes the goods to the respective division managers and sends the receiving report and the invoice to the accounting department for payment.

E4-28B (*Learning Objective 4: Evaluate internal control*) The following situations describe two cash payment situations and two cash receipt situations. In each pair, one set of internal controls is better than the other. Evaluate the internal controls in each situation as strong or weak, and give the reason for your answer.

Cash payments:

  a. Mark Moon Construction policy calls for construction supervisors to request the equipment needed for their jobs. The home office then purchases the equipment and has it shipped to the construction site.

  b. Best Buildings, Inc., policy calls for project supervisors to purchase the equipment needed for jobs. The supervisors then submit the paid receipts to the home office for reimbursement. This policy enables supervisors to get the equipment quickly and keep construction jobs moving.

Cash receipts:

  a. At Cunnigham Auto Parts, cash received by mail goes straight to the accountant, who debits Cash and credits Accounts Receivable to record the collections from customers. The Cunningham accountant then deposits the cash in the bank.

  b. Cash received by mail at Healthy Heart Clinic goes to the mail room, where a mail clerk opens envelopes and totals the cash receipts for the day. The mail clerk forwards customer checks to the cashier for deposit in the bank and forwards the remittance slips to the accounting department for posting credits to customer accounts.

E4-29B (*Learning Objectives 1, 2, 4: Describe fraud and its impact; explain the objectives and components of internal control; evaluate internal controls*) Scott Smart served as executive director of Downtown Huntsville, an organization created to revitalize Huntsville, Alabama. Over the course of 14 years, Smart embezzled $236,000. How did Smart do it? He did it by depositing subscriber cash receipts in his own bank account, writing Downtown Huntsville checks to himself, and creating phony entities that Downtown Huntsville wrote checks to.

Downtown Huntsville was led by a board of directors comprised of civic leaders. Smart's embezzlement went undetected until Downtown Huntsville couldn't pay its bills.

Give four ways Smart's embezzlement could have been prevented.

E4-30B (*Learning Objective 3: Design and use a bank reconciliation*) The following items appear on a bank reconciliation.

Classify each item as (a) an addition to the bank balance, (b) a subtraction from the bank balance, (c) an addition to the book balance, or (d) a subtraction from the book balance.

1. ___ Outstanding checks
2. ___ Bank error: The bank credited our account for a deposit made by another bank customer.
3. ___ Service charge
4. ___ Deposits in transit
5. ___ NSF check
6. ___ Bank collection of a note receivable on our behalf
7. ___ Book error: We debited Cash for $400. The correct debit was $4,000.

E4-31B (*Learning Objective 3: Prepare a bank reconciliation*) D. J. Hardy's checkbook and August bank statement show the following:

Date	Check No.	Item	Check	Deposit	Balance
8/1					$ 535
4	622	Sun Cafe	$ 20		515
9		Dividends received		$ 110	625
13	623	Goodsense Co.	35		590
14	624	FastMobil	58		532
18	625	Cash	60		472
26	626	First Baptist Church	75		397
28	627	Willow Tree Apartments	265		132
31		Paycheck		1,220	1,352

Balance				$535	
Add: Deposits				110	
Debit checks:	No.	Amount			
	622	$20			
	623	35			
	624	85*			
	625	60		(200)	
Other charges:					
NSF check			$30		
Service charge			10	(40)	
Balance				$405	

*This is the correct amount for check number 624.

▶ Requirement

1. Prepare Hardy's bank reconciliation at August 31.

E4-32B (*Learning Objective 3: Use a bank reconciliation*) Evan Neal operates a roller skating center. He has just received the monthly bank statement at January 31 from Citizen National Bank, and the statement shows an ending balance of $575. Listed on the statement are an EFT rent collection of $330, a service charge of $9, two NSF checks totaling $115, and an $11 charge for printed checks. In reviewing his cash records, Neal identifies outstanding checks totaling $606 and a January 31 deposit in transit of $1,775. During January, he recorded a $280 check for the salary of a part-time employee as $28. Neal's Cash account shows a January 31 cash balance of $1,801. How much cash does Neal actually have at January 31?

E4-33B (*Learning Objective 3: Design and use a bank reconciliation*) Use the data from Exercise 4-32B to make the journal entries that Neal should record on January 31 to update his Cash account. Include an explanation for each entry.

E4-34B (*Learning Objective 4: Evaluate internal control over cash receipts*) Roper stores use point-of-sale terminals as cash registers. The register shows the amount of each sale, the cash received from the customer, and any change returned to the customer. The machine also produces a customer receipt but keeps no record of transactions. At the end of the day, the clerk counts the cash in the register and gives it to the cashier for deposit in the company bank account.

Write a memo to convince the store manager that there is an internal control weakness over cash receipts. Identify the weakness that gives an employee the best opportunity to steal cash and state how to prevent such a theft.

E4-35B (*Learning Objective 4: Evaluate internal control over cash payments*) Fast Pass Company manufactures a popular brand of footballs. Fast Pass employs 142 workers and keeps its employment records on time sheets that show how many hours the employee works each week. On Friday the shop foreman collects the time sheets, checks them for accuracy, and delivers them to the payroll department for preparation of paychecks. The treasurer signs the paychecks and returns the checks to the payroll department for distribution to the employees.

Identify the main internal control weakness in this situation, state how the weakness can hurt Fast Pass, and propose a way to correct the weakness.

E4-36B (*Learning Objective 5: Construct and use a cash budget*) Donn Communications, Inc., is preparing its cash budget for 2012. Donn ended 2011 with cash of $88 million, and managers need to keep a cash balance of at least $79 million for operations.

Collections from customers are expected to total $11,323 million during 2012, and payments for the cost of services and products should reach $6,185 million. Operating expense payments are budgeted at $2,557 million.

During 2012, Donn expects to invest $1,823 million in new equipment and sell older assets for $151 million. Debt payments scheduled for 2012 will total $611 million. The company forecasts net income of $884 million for 2012 and plans to pay dividends of $316 million.

Prepare Donn Communications' cash budget for 2012. Will the budgeted level of cash receipts leave Donn with the desired ending cash balance of $79 million, or will the company need additional financing? If so, how much?

E4-37B (*Learning Objective 5: Use cash budgeting*) Assume Slippy Slides borrowed $17 million from West Side Bank and agreed to (a) pay an interest rate of 7.0% and (b) maintain a compensating balance amount equal to 5.1% of the loan. Determine Slippy Slides' actual effective interest rate on this loan.

Quiz

Test your understanding of internal control and cash by answering the following questions. Answer each question by selecting the best choice from among the answers given.

Q4-38 All of the following are objectives of internal control except
a. To safeguard assets
b. To maximize net income
c. To ensure accurate and reliable accounting records
d. To comply with legal requirements

Q4-39 All of the following are internal control procedures except
a. Electronic devices
b. Assignment of responsibilities
c. Internal and external audits
d. Sarbanes-Oxley reforms

Q4-40 Requiring that an employee with no access to cash do the accounting is an example of which characteristic of internal control?
a. Monitoring of controls
b. Competent and reliable personnel
c. Assignment of responsibility
d. Separation of duties

Q4-41 All of the following are controls for cash received over the counter except
a. The customer should be able to see the amounts entered into the cash register.
b. The cash drawer should open only when the sales clerk enters an amount on the keys.
c. The sales clerk must have access to the cash register tape.
d. A printed receipt must be given to the customer.

Q4-42 In a bank reconciliation, an outstanding check is
a. deducted from the bank balance.
b. deducted from the book balance.
c. added to the bank balance.
d. added to the book balance.

Q4-43 In a bank reconciliation, a bank collection of a note receivable is
a. deducted from the book balance.
b. deducted from the bank balance.
c. added to the bank balance.
d. added to the book balance.

Q4-44 In a bank reconciliation, an EFT cash payment is
a. added to the bank balance.
b. deducted from the book balance.
c. added to the book balance.
d. deducted from the bank balance.

Q4-45 If a bookkeeper mistakenly recorded a $72 deposit as $27, the error would be shown on the bank reconciliation as a
a. $45 deduction from the book balance.
b. $27 deduction from the book balance.
c. $27 addition to the book balance.
d. $45 addition to the book balance.

Q4-46 If a bank reconciliation included a deposit in transit of $790, the entry to record this reconciling item would include a
a. credit to prepaid insurance for $790.
b. debit to cash for $790.
c. credit to cash for $790.
d. no entry is required.

Q4-47 In a bank reconciliation, interest revenue earned on your bank balance is
a. deducted from the book balance.
b. added to the bank balance.
c. added to the book balance.
d. deducted from the bank balance.

Q4-48 Before paying an invoice for goods received on account, the controller or treasurer should ensure that
a. the company is paying for the goods it ordered.
b. the company is paying for the goods it actually received.
c. the company has not already paid this invoice.
d. all of the above.

Q4-49 Scrumptious Crumpets Bakery is budgeting cash for 2012. The cash balance at December 31, 2011, was $14,000. Scrumptious Crumpets Bakery budgets 2012 cash receipts at $81,000. Estimated cash payments include $44,000 for inventory, $34,000 for operating expenses, and $25,000 to expand the store. Scrumptious Crumpets Bakery needs a minimum cash balance of $13,000 at all times. Scrumptious Crumpets Bakery expects to earn net income of $76,000 during 2012. What is the final result of the company's cash budget for 2012?
a. Must arrange new financing for $21,000
b. Pay off $42,000 of debt.
c. $21,000 available for additional investments
d. $42,000 available for additional investments

Problems

MyAccountingLab

All of the Group A and Group B problems can be found within MyAccountingLab, an online homework and practice environment. Your instructor may ask you to complete these problems using MyAccountingLab.

Group A

P4-50A (*Learning Objectives 1, 4: Describe fraud and its impact; evaluate internal controls*)
Irish Imports is an importer of silver, brass, and furniture items from Ireland. Kathleen O'Shea is the general manager of Irish Imports. O'Shea employs two other people in the business. Molly Fitzpatrick serves as the buyer for Irish Imports. In her work, Fitzpatrick travels throughout Ireland to find interesting new products. When Fitzpatrick finds a new product, she arranges for Irish Imports to purchase and pay for the item. She helps the Irish artisans prepare their invoices and then faxes the invoices to O'Shea in the company office.

O'Shea operates out of an office in Boston, Massachusetts. The office is managed by Maura Riley, who handles the mail, keeps the accounting records, makes bank deposits, and prepares the monthly bank reconciliation. Virtually all of Irish Imports' cash receipts arrive by mail—from sales made to Target, Pier 1 Imports, and Macy's.

Riley also prepares checks for payment based on invoices that come in from the suppliers who have been contacted by Fitzpatrick. To maintain control over cash payments, O'Shea examines the paperwork and signs all checks.

► Requirement

1. Identify all the major internal control weaknesses in Irish Imports' system and how the resulting action could hurt Irish Imports. Also state how to correct each weakness.

P4-51A (*Learning Objectives 2, 4: Explain the components of internal control; evaluate internal controls*) Each of the following situations reveals an internal control weakness:

a. In evaluating the internal control over cash payments of Farley Manufacturing, an auditor learns that the purchasing agent is responsible for purchasing diamonds for use in the company's manufacturing process, approving the invoices for payment, and signing the checks. No supervisor reviews the purchasing agent's work.

b. Leah Royce owns an architectural firm. Royce's staff consists of 16 professional architects, and Royce manages the office. Often, Royce's work requires her to travel to meet with clients. During the past six months, Royce has observed that when she returns from a business trip, the architecture jobs in the office have not progressed satisfactorily. Royce learns that when she is away, two of her senior architects take over office management and neglect their normal duties. One employee could manage the office.

c. James Dorf has been an employee of the City of Marion for many years. Because the city is small, Dorf performs all accounting duties, in addition to opening the mail, preparing the bank deposit, and preparing the bank reconciliation.

► Requirements

1. Identify the missing internal control characteristic in each situation.
2. Identify each firm's possible problem.
3. Propose a solution to the problem.

P4-52A (*Learning Objective 3: Design and use a bank reconciliation*) The cash data of Durkin Automotive for April 2012 follow:

Cash					Account No. 101
Date	Item	Jrnl. Ref.	Debit	Credit	Balance
Apr 1	Balance				7,300
30		CR6	9,069		16,369
30		CP11		9,850	6,519

Cash Receipts (CR)		Cash Payments (CP)	
Date	Cash Debit	Check No.	Cash Credit
Apr 2	$2,719	3113	$1,524
8	507	3114	1,601
10	1,661	3115	1,830
16	827	3116	43
22	415	3117	839
29	892	3118	120
30	2,048	3119	425
Total	$9,069	3120	987
		3121	177
		3122	2,304
		Total	$9,850

Durkin received the following bank statement on April 30, 2012:

Bank Statement for April 2012

Beginning balance			$ 7,300
Deposits and other additions:			
Apr 1		$ 625 EFT	
4		2,719	
9		507	
12		1,661	
17		827	
22		415	
23		1,375 BC	8,129
Checks and other deductions:			
Apr 7		$1,524	
13		1,380	
14		455 US	
15		1,601	
18		43	
21		397 EFT	
26		839	
30		120	
30		10 SC	(6,369)
Ending balance			$ 9,060

Explanation: BC—bank collection, EFT—electronic funds transfer, US—unauthorized signature, SC—service charge

Additional data for the bank reconciliation include the following:

a. The EFT deposit was a receipt of monthly rent. The EFT debit was a monthly insurance payment.
b. The unauthorized signature check was received from a customer.
c. The correct amount of check number 3115, a payment on account, is $1,380. (Durkin's accountant mistakenly recorded the check for $1,830.)

▶ Requirements

1. Prepare the Durkin Automotive bank reconciliation at April 30, 2012.
2. Describe how a bank account and the bank reconciliation help the general manager control Durkin's cash.

P4-53A (*Learning Objective 3: Design and use a bank reconciliation*) The November 30 bank statement of Donald Engineering Associates has just arrived from Kansas First Bank. To prepare the Donald bank reconciliation, you gather the following data:

a. Donald's Cash account shows a balance of $7,684.83 on November 30.
b. The November 30 bank balance is $8,457.95.
c. The bank statement shows that Donald earned $16.38 of interest on its bank balance during November. This amount was added to Donald's bank balance.
d. Donald pays utilities ($750) and insurance ($240) by EFT.

e. The following Donald checks did not clear the bank by November 30:

Check No.	Amount
237	$404.80
288	74.82
291	34.89
293	173.25
294	238.00
295	47.75
296	105.78

f. The bank statement includes a deposit of $903.10, collected on account by the bank on behalf of Donald.

g. The bank statement lists a $7.50 bank service charge.

h. On November 30, the Donald treasurer deposited $381.75, which will appear on the December bank statement.

i. The bank statement includes a $415.00 deposit that Donald did not make. The bank added $415.00 to Donald's account for another company's deposit.

j. The bank statement includes two charges for returned checks from customers. One is a $193.75 check received from a customer with the imprint "Unauthorized Signature." The other is a nonsufficient funds check in the amount of $67.65 received from another customer.

▶ Requirements

1. Prepare the bank reconciliation for Donald Engineering Associates.

2. Journalize the November 30 transactions needed to update Donald's Cash account. Include an explanation for each entry.

P4-54A (*Learning Objectives 2, 4: Explain components of internal control; evaluate internal control over cash receipts*) Healthy Hair Care makes all sales on credit. Cash receipts arrive by mail, usually within 30 days of the sale. Kathy Mulberry opens envelopes and separates the checks from the accompanying remittance advices. Mulberry forwards the checks to another employee, who makes the daily bank deposit but has no access to the accounting records. Mulberry sends the remittance advices, which show the amount of cash received, to the accounting department for entry in the accounts receivable. Mulberry's only other duty is to grant allowances to customers. (An *allowance* decreases the amount that the customer must pay.) When Mulberry receives a customer check for less than the full amount of the invoice, she records the allowance in the accounting records and forwards the document to the accounting department.

▶ Requirement

1. You are a new employee of Healthy Hair Care. Write a memo to the company president identifying the internal control weakness in this situation. State how to correct the weakness.

P4-55A (*Learning Objective 5: Construct and use a cash budget*) Nathan Farmer, chief financial officer of Bosworth Wireless, is responsible for the company's budgeting process. Farmer's staff is preparing the Bosworth cash budget for 2013. A key input to the budgeting process is last year's statement of cash flows, which follows (amounts in thousands):

Bosworth Wireless
Statement of Cash Flows
2012

(In thousands)	
Cash Flows from Operating Activities	
Collections from customers	$ 61,000
Interest received	400
Purchases of inventory	(46,000)
Operating expenses	(13,200)
Net cash provided by operating activities	2,200
Cash Flows from Investing Activities	
Purchases of equipment	(4,500)
Purchases of investments	(800)
Sales of investments	900
Net cash used for investing activities	(4,400)
Cash Flows from Financing Activities	
Payment of long-term debt	(200)
Issuance of stock	1,400
Payment of cash dividends	(500)
Net cash provided by financing activities	700
Cash	
Increase (decrease) in Cash	(1,500)
Cash, beginning of year	2,900
Cash, end of year	$ 1,400

▶ Requirements

1. Prepare the Bosworth Wireless cash budget for 2013. Date the budget simply "2013" and denote the beginning and ending cash balances as "beginning" and "ending." Assume the company expects 2013 to be the same as 2012, but with the following changes:
   a. In 2013, the company expects a 15% increase in collections from customers and a 24% increase in purchases of inventory.
   b. There will be no sales of investments in 2013.
   c. Bosworth plans to issue no stock in 2013.
   d. Bosworth plans to end the year with a cash balance of $3,550.

Group B

P4-56B (*Learning Objectives 1, 4: Describe fraud and its impact; evaluate internal controls*) European Imports is an importer of silver, brass, and furniture items from Spain. Eloise Stiles is the general manager of European Imports. Stiles employs two other people in the business. Michelle Woods serves as the buyer for European Imports. In her work, Woods travels throughout Spain to find interesting new products. When Woods finds a new product, she arranges for European Imports to purchase and pay for the item. She helps the Spanish artisans prepare their invoices and then faxes the invoices to Stiles in the company office.

Stiles operates out of an office in Brooklyn, New York. The office is managed by Doreen Davis, who handles the mail, keeps the accounting records, makes bank deposits, and prepares the monthly bank reconciliation. Virtually all of European Imports' cash receipts arrive by mail—from sales made to Target, Crate and Barrel, and Williams-Sonoma.

Davis also prepares checks for payment based on invoices that come in from the suppliers who have been contacted by Woods. To maintain control over cash payments, Stiles examines the paperwork and signs all checks.

▶ Requirement

1. Identify all the major internal control weaknesses in European Imports' system and how the resulting action could hurt European Imports. Also state how to correct each weakness.

P4-57B (*Learning Objectives 2, 4: Explain the components of internal control; evaluate internal controls*) Each of the following situations reveals an internal control weakness:

Situation a. In evaluating the internal control over cash payments of Yankee Manufacturing, an auditor learns that the purchasing agent is responsible for purchasing diamonds for use in the company's manufacturing process, approving the invoices for payment, and signing the checks. No supervisor reviews the purchasing agent's work.

Situation b. Rachel Williams owns an architectural firm. Williams' staff consists of 19 professional architects, and Williams manages the office. Often, Williams' work requires her to travel to meet with clients. During the past six months, Williams has observed that when she returns from a business trip, the architecture jobs in the office have not progressed satisfactorily. Williams learns that when she is away, two of her senior architects take over office management and neglect their normal duties. One employee could manage the office.

Situation c. Mike Dolan has been an employee of the City of Southport for many years. Because the city is small, Dolan performs all accounting duties, in addition to opening the mail, preparing the bank deposit, and preparing the bank reconciliation.

▶ Requirements

1. Identify the missing internal control characteristic in each situation.
2. Identify each firm's possible problem.
3. Propose a solution to the problem.

P4-58B (*Learning Objective 3: Design and use a bank reconciliation*) The cash data of Duffy Automotive for October 2012 follow:

Cash					Account No. 101
Date	**Item**	**Jrnl. Ref.**	**Debit**	**Credit**	**Balance**
Oct 1	Balance				7,750
31		CR 6	9,230		16,980
31		CP 11		10,305	6,675

Cash Receipts (CR)		Cash Payments (CP)	
Date	**Cash Debit**	**Check No.**	**Cash Credit**
Oct 2	$2,787	3113	$ 1,506
8	586	3114	1,838
10	1,695	3115	1,930
16	845	3116	95
22	413	3117	819
29	896	3118	174
30	2,008	3119	488
Total	$9,230	3120	972
		3121	165
		3122	2,318
		Total	$10,305

Duffy received the following bank statement on October 31, 2012:

Bank Statement for October 2012

Beginning balance			$ 7,750
Deposits and other additions:			
Oct 1		$ 750 EFT	
4		2,787	
9		586	
12		1,695	
17		845	
22		413	
23		1,350 BC	8,426
Checks and other deductions:			
Oct 7		$1,506	
13		1,390	
14		417 US	
15		1,838	
18		95	
21		312 EFT	
26		819	
30		174	
30		25 SC	(6,576)
Ending balance			$ 9,600

Explanation: BC—bank collection, EFT—electronic funds transfer, US—unauthorized signature, SC—service charge

Additional data for the bank reconciliation include the following:

a. The EFT deposit was a receipt of monthly rent. The EFT debit was a monthly insurance expense.
b. The unauthorized signature check was received from a customer.
c. The correct amount of check number 3115, a payment on account, is $1,390. (Duffy's accountant mistakenly recorded the check for $1,930.)

▶ Requirements

1. Prepare the Duffy Automotive bank reconciliation at October 31, 2012.
2. Describe how a bank account and the bank reconciliation help the general manager control Duffy's cash.

P4-59B (*Learning Objective 3: Design and use a bank reconciliation*) The April 30 bank statement of Durkin Engineering Associates has just arrived from Maine First Bank. To prepare the Durkin bank reconciliation, you gather the following data:

a. Durkin's Cash account shows a balance of $7,795.12 on April 30.
b. The April 30 bank balance is $8,501.15.
c. The bank statement shows that Durkin earned $16.55 of interest on its bank balance during April. This amount was added to Durkin's bank balance.
d. Durkin pays utilities ($780) and insurance ($290) by EFT.

e. The following Durkin checks did not clear the bank by April 30:

Check No.	Amount
237	$405.15
288	73.87
291	35.47
293	167.88
294	238.00
295	48.10
296	103.54

f. The bank statement includes a deposit of $932.87, collected on account by the bank on behalf of Durkin.

g. The bank statement lists a $5.50 bank service charge.

h. On April 30, the Durkin treasurer deposited $382.25, which will appear on the May bank statement.

i. The bank statement includes a $398.00 deposit that Durkin did not make. The bank added $398.00 to Durkin's account for another company's deposit.

j. The bank statement includes two charges for returned checks from customers. One is a $187.50 check received from a customer with the imprint "Unauthorized Signature." The other is a nonsufficient funds check in the amount of $68.15 received from another customer.

▶ Requirements

1. Prepare the bank reconciliation for Durkin Engineering Associates.

2. Journalize the April 30 transactions needed to update Durkin's Cash account. Include an explanation for each entry.

P4-60B (*Learning Objectives 2, 4: Explain components of internal control; evaluate internal control over cash receipts*) Radiant Hair Care makes all sales on credit. Cash receipts arrive by mail, usually within 30 days of the sale. Ella Neil opens envelopes and separates the checks from the accompanying remittance advices. Neil forwards the checks to another employee, who makes the daily bank deposit but has no access to the accounting records. Neil sends the remittance advices, which show the amount of cash received, to the accounting department for entry in the accounts receivable. Neil's only other duty is to grant allowances to customers. (An *allowance* decreases the amount that the customer must pay.) When Neil receives a customer check for less than the full amount of the invoice, she records the allowance in the accounting records and forwards the document to the accounting department.

▶ Requirement

1. You are a new employee of Radiant Hair Care. Write a memo to the company president identifying the internal control weakness in this situation. State how to correct the weakness.

P4-61B (*Learning Objective 5: Construct and use a cash budget*) David Doyle, chief financial officer of Madison Wireless, is responsible for the company's budgeting process. Doyle's staff is preparing the Madison cash budget for 2013. A key input to the budgeting process is last year's statement of cash flows, which follows (amount in thousands):

Madison Wireless Statement of Cash Flows 2012	
(In thousands)	
Cash Flows from Operating Activities	
Collections from customers	$ 66,000
Interest received	100
Purchases of inventory	(50,000)
Operating expenses	(13,400)
Net cash provided by operating activities	2,700
Cash Flows from Investing Activities	
Purchases of equipment	(4,800)
Purchases of investments	(400)
Sales of investments	400
Net cash used for investing activities	(4,800)
Cash Flows from Financing Activities	
Payment of long-term debt	(600)
Issuance of stock	1,500
Payment of cash dividends	(200)
Net cash provided by financing activities	700
Cash	
Increase (decrease) in Cash	(1,400)
Cash, beginning of year	2,700
Cash, end of year	$ 1,300

▶ Requirements

1. Prepare the Madison Wireless cash budget for 2013. Date the budget simply "2013" and denote the beginning and ending cash balances as "beginning" and "ending." Assume the company expects 2013 to be the same as 2012, but with the following changes:
   a. In 2013, the company expects a 12% increase in collections from customers and a 25% increase in purchases of inventory.
   b. There will be no sales of investments in 2013.
   c. Madison plans to issue no stock in 2013.
   d. Madison plans to end the year with a cash balance of $3,650.

Challenge Exercises and Problem

E4-62 (*Learning Objectives 1, 4: Describe fraud and its impact; evaluate internal control*) Sharon Hall, the owner of Sharon's Party Picks, has delegated management of the business to Lola Oster, a friend. Hall drops by to meet customers and check up on cash receipts, but Oster buys the merchandise and handles cash payments. Business has been very good lately, and cash receipts have kept pace with the apparent level of sales. However, for a year or so, the amount of cash on hand has been too low. When asked about this, Oster explains that suppliers are charging more for goods than in the past. During the past year, Oster has taken two expensive vacations, and Hall wonders how Oster can afford these trips on her $52,000 annual salary and commissions.

List at least three ways Oster could be defrauding Hall of cash. In each instance, also identify how Hall can determine whether Oster's actions are ethical. Limit your answers to the store's cash payments. The business pays all suppliers by check (no EFTs).

E4-63 (*Learning Objective 5: Construct and use a cash budget*) Dave Dern, the chief financial officer, is responsible for The Grand Design's cash budget for 2013. The budget will help Dem determine the amount of long-term borrowing needed to end the year with a cash balance of $135,000. Dern's assistants have assembled budget data for 2013, which the computer printed in alphabetical order. Not all the data items reproduced below are used in preparing the cash budget.

(Assumed Data)	(In thousands)
Actual cash balance, December 31, 2012	$ 145
Budgeted total assets	22,677
Budgeted total current assets	7,576
Budgeted total current liabilities	4,360
Budgeted total liabilities	11,588
Budgeted total stockholders' equity	11,089
Collections from customers	20,400
Dividend payments	307
Issuance of stock	632
Net income	1,213
Payment of long-term and short-term debt	990
Payment of operating expenses	2,849
Purchases of inventory items	14,245
Purchase of property and equipment	1,588

▶ Requirements

1. Construct the cash budget of The Grand Design, Inc.
2. Compute The Grand Design's budgeted current ratio and debt ratio at December 31, 2013. Based on these ratio values, and on the cash budget, would you lend $95,000 to The Grand Design? Give the reason for your decision.

P4-64 (*Learning Objective 3: Use a bank reconciliation to detect fraud*) The president of The Pembrook Company has recently become concerned that the bookkeeper has embezzled cash from the company. He asks you, confidentially, to look over the bank reconciliation that the bookkeeper has prepared to see if you discover any discrepancies between the books and the bank statement. He provides you with the Cash account from the general ledger, the bank statement, and the bank reconciliation as of December 31. You learn from the November bank reconciliation that the following checks were outstanding on November 30: No 1560 for $185, No. 1880 for $565, No. 1882 for $122, and No. 1883 for $468. There was one deposit in transit on November 30 for $1,252. An examination of the actual deposit slips revealed no bank errors.

Pembrook Company Bank Reconciliation December 31					
Bank			**Books**		
Balance, 12/31		$ 3,668	Balance, 12/31		$ 9,455
Add:			Add:		
Deposits in transit		3,150	EFT receipt from customer		52
		6,818	Interest revenue		6
Less:					9,513
Outstanding checks			Less:		
No. 1560	$185		Book error	$3,000	
No. 1901	842		NSF check	135	
No. 1902	168	(1,195)	EFT payment of utilities	755	(3,890)
Adjusted bank balance		$ 5,623	Adjusted book balance		$ 5,623

General Ledger
Cash

Bal 12/1	7,354		
Cash receipt 12/7	1,300	No. 1880	565
Cash receipt 12/15	4,193	No. 1882	122
Cash receipt 12/23	5,425	No. 1883	468
Cash receipt 12/30	650	No. 1884	1,284
		No. 1885	1,388
		No. 1886	700
		No. 1887	2,478
		No. 1888	1,030
		No. 1889	422
		No. 1901	842
		No. 1902	168
Bal 12/31	9,455		

Bank Statement for December 31

Bal 12/1			$ 3,787
Deposits			
Dec 1		$ 1,252	
8		1,300	
16		4,193	
24		2,425	
31		6	
31		52	
Total deposits			9,228
Checks and other debits:			
No. 1880		565	
No. 1882		122	
No. 1883		468	
No. 1884		1,284	
No. 1885		1,388	
No. 1886		700	
No. 1887		2,478	
No. 1888		1,030	
No. 1889		422	
NSF		135	
EFT		755	
Total checks and other debits			(9,347)
Bal 12/31			$ 3,668

Explanation: BC—bank collection, EFT—electronic funds transfer, US—unauthorized signature, SC—service charge

▶ Requirement

1. Prepare a corrected bank reconciliation. Show the unexplained difference as an adjustment to the book balance. Include in your analysis the amount of the theft and how the bookkeeper attempted to conceal the theft.

APPLY YOUR KNOWLEDGE

Decision Cases

Case 1. (*Learning Objectives 1, 3, 4: Describe fraud; use a bank reconciliation; evaluate internal controls*) Environmental Concerns, Inc., has poor internal control. Recently, Oscar Benz, the manager, has suspected the bookkeeper of stealing. Details of the business's cash position at September 30 follow.

a. The Cash account shows a balance of $10,402. This amount includes a September 30 deposit of $3,794 that does not appear on the September 30 bank statement.

b. The September 30 bank statement shows a balance of $8,224. The bank statement lists a $200 bank collection, an $8 service charge, and a $36 NSF check. The accountant has not recorded any of these items.

c. At September 30, the following checks are outstanding:

Check No.	Amount
154	$116
256	150
278	853
291	990
292	206
293	145

d. The bookkeeper receives all incoming cash and makes the bank deposits. He also reconciles the monthly bank statement. Here is his September 30 reconciliation:

Balance per books, September 30..............		$10,402
Add: Outstanding checks		1,460
Bank collection..............................		200
Subtotal...		12,062
Less: Deposits in transit...........................	$3,794	
Service charge	8	
NSF check.......................................	36	(3,838)
Balance per bank, September 30................		$ 8,224

▶ Requirement

1. Benz has requested that you determine whether the bookkeeper has stolen cash from the business and, if so, how much. He also asks you to explain how the bookkeeper attempted to conceal the theft. To make this determination, you perform a proper bank reconciliation. There are no bank or book errors. Benz also asks you to evaluate the internal controls and to recommend any changes needed to improve them.

Case 2. (*Learning Objectives 1, 4: Describe fraud and its impact; evaluate internal control*) This case is based on an actual situation experienced by one of the authors. Gilead Construction, headquartered in Topeka, Kansas, built a motel in Kansas City. The construction foreman, Slim Pickins, hired the workers for the project. Pickins had his workers fill out the necessary tax forms and sent the employment documents to the home office.

Work on the motel began on May 1 and ended in December. Each Thursday evening, Pickins filled out a time card that listed the hours worked by each employee during the five-day work-week ended at 5 p.m. on Thursday. Pickins faxed the time sheets to the home office, which prepared the payroll checks on Friday morning. Pickins drove to the home office after lunch on Friday, picked up the payroll checks, and returned to the construction site. At 5 p.m. on Friday, Pickins distributed the paychecks to the workers.

    a. Describe in detail the internal control weakness in this situation. Specify what negative result could occur because of the internal control weakness.

    b. Describe what you would do to correct the internal control weakness.

Ethical Issues

For each of the following situations, answer the following questions:

1. What is the ethical issue in this situation?
2. What are the alternatives?
3. Who are the stakeholders? What are the possible consequences to each? Analyze from the following standpoints: (a) economic, (b) legal, and (c) ethical.
4. Place yourself in the role of the decision maker. What would you do? How would you justify your decision?

Issue 1. Sunrise Bank recently appointed the accounting firm of Smith, Godfroy, and Hannaford as the bank's auditor. Sunrise quickly became one of Smith, Godfroy, and Hannaford's largest clients. Subject to banking regulations, Sunrise must provide for any expected losses on notes receivable that Sunrise may not collect in full.

During the course of the audit, Smith, Godfroy, and Hannaford determined that three large notes receivable of Sunrise seem questionable. Smith, Godfroy, and Hannaford discussed these loans with Susan Carter, controller of Sunrise. Carter assured the auditors that these notes were good and that the makers of the notes will be able to pay their notes after the economy improves.

Smith, Godfroy, and Hannaford stated that Sunrise must record a loss for a portion of these notes receivable to account for the likelihood that Sunrise may never collect their full amount. Carter objected and threatened to dismiss Smith, Godfroy, and Hannaford if the auditor demands that the bank record the loss. Smith, Godfroy, and Hannaford wants to keep Sunrise as a client. In fact, Smith, Godfroy, and Hannaford was counting on the revenue from the Sunrise audit to finance an expansion of the firm.

Issue 2. Barry Galvin is executive vice president of Community Bank. Active in community affairs, Galvin serves on the board of directors of The Salvation Army. The Salvation Army is expanding rapidly and is considering relocating. At a recent meeting, The Salvation Army decided to buy 250 acres of land on the edge of town. The owner of the property is Olga Nadar, a major depositor in Community Bank. Nadar is completing a bitter divorce, and Galvin knows that Nadar is eager to sell her property. In view of Nadar's difficult situation, Galvin believes Nadar would accept a low offer for the land. Realtors have appraised the property at $3.6 million.

Issue 3. Community Bank has a loan receivable from IMS Chocolates. IMS is six months late in making payments to the bank, and Jan French, a Community Bank vice president, is assisting IMS to restructure its debt.

French learns that IMS is depending on landing a contract with Snicker Foods, another Community Bank client. French also serves as Snicker Foods' loan officer at the bank. In this capacity, French is aware that Snicker is considering bankruptcy. No one else outside Snicker Foods knows this. French has been a great help to IMS and IMS's owner is counting on French's expertise in loan workouts to advise the company through this difficult process. To help the bank collect on this large loan, French has a strong motivation to alert IMS of Snicker's financial difficulties.

Focus on Financials: | Amazon.com, Inc.

(*Learning Objectives 2, 3: Prepare a bank reconciliation; analyze internal controls*) Refer to the **Amazon.com, Inc.**, consolidated financial statements in Appendix A at the end of this book. The cash and cash equivalents section of the Consolidated Balance Sheet shows a balance of $3,777 as of December 31, 2010, and is made up of many different bank accounts, as well as time deposits, certificates of deposit, and perhaps government securities that are equivalent to cash. Suppose Amazon.com's year-end bank statement for the operating bank account, dated December 31, 2010, has just arrived at company headquarters. Further assume the bank statement shows Amazon.com's cash balance at $324 million and that Amazon.com, Inc.'s operating bank account has a balance of $316 million on the books (since this is only one of many bank accounts, it will not be possible to match it to the $3,777 that is shown.)

1. You must determine the correct balance for cash in the operating bank account on December 31, 2010. Suppose you uncover the following reconciling items (all amounts are assumed and are stated in millions):
   a. Interest earned on bank balance, $1
   b. Outstanding checks, $8
   c. Bank collections of various items, $2
   d. Deposits in transit, $3

   Prepare a bank reconciliation to show how Amazon.com, Inc., arrived at the correct amount of cash in the operating bank account at December 31, 2010. Journal entries are not required.

2. Study Amazon.com, Inc.'s Management's Report on Internal Control over Financial Reporting in Item 9A of its annual report, paragraph 2. Indicate how that report links to specific items of internal control discussed in this chapter. (Challenge)

Focus on Analysis: | RadioShack Corporation

(*Learning Objectives 2, 5: Analyze internal controls and cash flows*) Refer to the RadioShack Corporation Consolidated Financial Statements in Appendix B at the end of this book.

1. Focus on cash and cash equivalents. Why did cash change during 2010? The statement of cash flows holds the answer to this question. Analyze the seven largest *individual* items on the statement of cash flows (not the summary subtotals such as "net cash provided by operating activities"). For each of the seven individual items, state how RadioShack Corporation's action affected cash. Show amounts in millions and round to the nearest $1 million. (Challenge)

2. RadioShack Corporation's Report of Management describes the company's internal controls. Show how the management report corresponds to the objectives of internal control included in this chapter. (Challenge)

Group Project

You are promoting a rock concert in your area. Assume you organize as a corporation, with each member of your group purchasing $10,000 of the corporation's stock. Therefore, each of you is risking some hard-earned money on this venture. Assume it is April 1 and that the concert will be performed on June 30. Your promotional activities begin immediately, and ticket sales start on May 1. You expect to sell all of the firm's assets, pay all the liabilities, and distribute all remaining cash to the group members by July 31.

▶ Requirements

Write an internal control manual that will help to safeguard the assets of the business. The manual should address the following aspects of internal control:

1. Assign responsibilities among the group members.
2. Authorize individuals, including group members and any outsiders that you need to hire to perform specific jobs.
3. Separate duties among the group and any employees.
4. Describe all documents needed to account for and safeguard the business's assets.

MyAccountingLab

> **For online homework, exercises, and problems that provide you with immediate feedback, please visit www.myaccountinglab.com**

Quick Check Answers

1. *h, g, c, both i and d, f, a, b* Unused: *e*	4. b	8. *e*
	5. *a*	9. *a*
2. *c*	6. *d*	10. *d*
3. *d*	7. *b*	11. *c*

5 Short-Term Investments & Receivables

SPOTLIGHT: Receivables and Short-Term Investments are Double PepsiCo's Inventories!

What comes to mind when you think of **PepsiCo**? Do you think of a soft drink or a snack chip? PepsiCo's two main products are soft drinks and snack foods. PepsiCo also owns Frito Lay, the snack-food company. That might lead you to believe that inventories are the company's largest current asset. However, as of December 31, 2010, short-term investments and receivables account for about 38% of PepsiCo's current assets—more than double inventories.

Take a look at PepsiCo's comparative balance sheets for 2010 and 2009 on the following page. Does it surprise you that receivables are PepsiCo's largest current asset? It turns out that receivables are the largest current asset for lots of companies, including **FedEx** and **The Boeing Company**.

Another important current asset is short-term investments. As you can see from PepsiCo's 2010 balance sheet, PepsiCo had about $426 million in short-term investments at the end of 2010. You'll notice that short-term investments are listed on the balance sheet immediately after cash and before receivables. It is interesting that, since 2007 (not shown), short-term investments have decreased to $426 million from $1,540 million (more than threefold), while cash and cash equivalents have increased from $910 million to $5,943 million (more than sixfold)! This is typical for many Fortune 500 companies as they emerge from the worst economic recession in 75 years, which was caused in part by a banking crisis in which credit became harder to obtain and in part by markets characterized by instability. This has caused many companies to convert their short-term investments to cash and cash equivalents, hoarding cash in order to have it more readily available for company needs. ●

© Shaun Lowe/iStockphoto.com

PepsiCo, Inc.
Balance Sheets (Excerpt, Adapted)
December 31, 2010 and 2009

(In millions)	2010	2009
ASSETS		
Current Assets		
Cash and cash equivalents	$ 5,943	$ 3,943
Short-term investments	426	192
Accounts and notes receivable, net	6,323	4,624
Inventories	3,372	2,618
Prepaid expenses and other current assets	1,505	1,194
Total Current Assets	$17,569	$12,571

This chapter shows how to account for short-term investments and receivables. We cover short-term investments along with receivables to emphasize their relative liquidity. Short-term investments are the next-most-liquid current assets after cash. (Recall that *liquid* means "close to cash.") We begin our discussion with short-term investments.

Learning Objectives

1. **Account for** short-term investments

2. **Apply** GAAP for proper revenue recognition

3. **Account for and control** accounts receivable

4. **Evaluate** collectibility using the allowance for uncollectible accounts

5. **Account for** notes receivable

6. **Show** how to speed up cash flow from receivables

7. **Evaluate** liquidity using two new ratios

Account for Short-Term Investments

1 **Account for** short-term investments

Short-term investments are also called **marketable securities**. These are investments in marketable securities easily convertible to cash that a company plans to hold for one year or less. They allow the company to invest cash for a short period of time and earn a return until the cash is needed.

Short-term investments are the next-most-liquid asset after cash. This is why we report short-term investments in marketable securities immediately after cash and before receivables on the balance sheet. Investments in marketable securities fall into one of three categories:

Three Categories of Investments in Securities		
Trading Securities	**Available-for-Sale Securities**	**Held-to-Maturity Securities**
Covered in this section of the chapter	Covered in Chapter 8	Covered in Chapter 8

The investor, such as PepsiCo, expects to sell a trading security within a very short time—a few months at most. Therefore, all trading securities are included in current assets. The other two categories of securities can be either current or long-term, depending on how long management intends to hold them. However, available-for-sale and held-to-maturity securities are usually classified as long-term, unless they mature in the current period. We reserve discussion of these securities until Chapter 8.

Trading Securities

The purpose of owning a **trading security** is to hold it for a short time and then sell it for more than its cost. Trading securities can be in the form of stock or debt securities of another company. Suppose PepsiCo purchases **IBM** stock, intending to sell the stock within a few months. If the fair market value of the IBM stock increases, PepsiCo will have a gain; if IBM's stock price drops, PepsiCo will have a loss. Along the way, PepsiCo will receive dividend revenue from IBM.

Suppose PepsiCo buys the IBM stock on November 18, 2012, paying $100,000 cash. PepsiCo records the purchase of the investment at cost:

2012			
Nov 18	Investment in IBM stock	100,000	
	Cash		100,000
	Purchased investment.		

Investment in IBM Stock	
100,000	

Assume that PepsiCo receives a cash dividend of $4,000 from IBM. PepsiCo records the dividend revenue as follows:

2012			
Nov 27	Cash	4,000	
	Dividend Revenue		4,000
	Received cash dividend.		

Assets	=	Liabilities	+	Stockholders' Equity	+	Revenues
+ 4,000	=				+	4,000

Unrealized Gains and Losses. PepsiCo's fiscal year ends on December 31, and PepsiCo prepares financial statements. The IBM stock has risen in value, and on December 31, PepsiCo's investment has a current fair value of $102,000. Fair (market) value is the amount for which the owner can sell the securities. PepsiCo has an *unrealized gain* on the investment:

▶ *Gain* because the fair value ($102,000) of the securities is greater than PepsiCo's cost of the securities ($100,000). A gain has the same effect as a revenue.
▶ *Unrealized gain* because PepsiCo has not yet sold the securities.

Trading securities are reported on the balance sheet at their current fair value, because fair (market) value is the amount the investor can receive by selling the securities. Prior to preparing financial statements on December 31, PepsiCo adjusts the investment in IBM securities to its current fair value with this year-end journal entry:

2012			
Dec 31	Investment in IBM stock	2,000	
	Unrealized Gain on Investments		2,000
	Adjusted investment to fair value.		

Investment in IBM Stock		Unrealized Gain on Investments	
100,000			
2,000			2,000
102,000			

After the adjustment, PepsiCo's Short-Term Investments account, reflecting its investment in IBM stock, is ready to be reported on the balance sheet—at current fair value of $102,000.

If PepsiCo's investment in IBM stock had decreased in value, say to $95,000, then PepsiCo would have reported an unrealized loss. A *loss* has the same effect as an expense. In that case, PepsiCo would have made a different entry at December 31. For an *unrealized* loss of $5,000, the entry would have been as follows:

Unrealized Loss on Investments	5,000	
Investment in IBM Stock		5,000
Adjusted investment to fair value.		

Investment in IBM Stock		Unrealized Loss on Investments	
100,000	5,000	5,000	
95,000			

Reporting on the Balance Sheet and the Income Statement

The Balance Sheet. Short-term investments are current assets. They appear on the balance sheet immediately after cash because short-term investments are almost as liquid as cash. Report trading investments at their *current fair (market) value.*

Income Statement. Investments in debt and equity securities earn interest revenue and dividend revenue. Investments also create gains and losses. For trading investments, these items are reported on the income statement as Other revenue, gains, and (losses), as shown in Exhibit 5-1.

Realized Gains and Losses. A *realized* gain or loss occurs only when the investor sells an investment. This gain or loss is different from the unrealized gain that we just reported for PepsiCo. The result may be one of the following:

► Realized gain = Sale price is *greater than* the Investment carrying amount
► Realized loss = Sale price is *less than* the Investment carrying amount

EXHIBIT 5-1 | Reporting Short-Term Investments and Related Revenues, Gains, and Losses

Balance sheet		Income statement	
Current assets:........................		Revenues...........................	$ XXX
Cash..................................	$ XXX	Expenses	XXX
Short-term investments, at		Other revenue, gains	
fair value........................	102,000	and (losses):	
Accounts receivable...............	XXX	Interest revenue...........	XXX
		Dividend revenue	4,000
		Unrealized gain on	
		investment...............	2,000
		Net income...................	$ XXX

Suppose PepsiCo sells its IBM stock during 2013. The sale price is $98,000, and PepsiCo makes this journal entry:

2013			
Jan 19	Cash	98,000	
	Loss on Sale of Investments	4,000	
	Investment in IBM Stock		102,000
	Sold investments at a loss.		

Investment in IBM Stock		Loss on Sale of Investments	
100,000		4,000	
2,000	102,000		

Accountants rarely use the word "realized" in the account title. A gain (or a loss) is understood to be a realized gain (or loss) arising from a sale transaction. Unrealized gains and losses are clearly labeled as *unrealized*. PepsiCo would report Gain (or Loss) on Sale of investments among the "Other" items of the income statement, as shown in Exhibit 5-1.

Ethics and the Current Ratio

Lending agreements often require the borrower to maintain a current ratio at some specified level, say 1.50 or greater. What happens when the borrower's current ratio falls below 1.50? The consequences can be severe:

▶ The lender can call the loan for immediate payment.
▶ If the borrower cannot pay, then the lender may take over the company.

Suppose it's December 10 and it looks like Health Corporation of America's (HCA's) current ratio will end the year at a value of 1.48. That would put HCA in default on the lending agreement and create a bad situation. With three weeks remaining in the year, how can HCA improve its current ratio?

Recall that the current ratio is computed as follows:

$$\text{Current ratio} = \frac{\text{Total current assets}}{\text{Total current liabilities}}$$

There are several strategies for increasing the current ratio, such as the following:

1. Launch a major sales effort. The increase in cash and receivables will more than offset the decrease in inventory, total current assets will increase, and the current ratio will improve.

2. Pay off some current liabilities before year-end. Both current assets in the numerator and current liabilities in the denominator will decrease by the same amount. The proportionate impact on current liabilities in the denominator will be greater than the impact on current assets in the numerator, and the current ratio will increase. This strategy increases the current ratio when the current ratio is already above 1.0, as for HCA and PepsiCo.

3. A third strategy is questionable, and it reveals one of the accounting games that unethical companies sometimes play. Suppose HCA has some long-term investments (investments that HCA plans to hold for longer than a year—these are long-term assets). Before year-end, HCA might choose to reclassify these long-term investments as current assets. The reclassification of these investments increases HCA's current assets, and that increases the current ratio. This strategy would be acceptable if HCA does in fact plan to sell the investments within the next year. But the strategy would be unethical and dishonest if HCA in fact plans to keep the investments for longer than a year.

From this example you can see that accounting is not cut-and-dried or all black-and-white. It takes good judgment—which includes ethics—to become a successful accountant.

MID-CHAPTER SUMMARY PROBLEM

The largest current asset on Waverly Corporation's balance sheet is Short-Term Investments. The investments consist of stock in other corporations and cost Waverly $8,660. At the balance sheet date, the fair value of these securities is $9,000 (amounts in millions).

Suppose Waverly holds the stock investments in the hope of selling at a profit within a few months. How will Waverly classify the investments? What will Waverly report on the balance sheet at December 31, 2012? What will Waverly report on its 2012 income statement? Show a T-account for Short-Term Investments.

▶ Answer

These investments in trading securities are *current assets* as reported on the 2012 balance sheet, and Waverly's 2012 income statement will report as follows (amounts in millions):

Balance sheet		Income statement	
Current assets:		Other revenue and expense:	
Cash....................................	$ XX	Unrealized gain on investments	
Short-term investments,		($9,000 − $8,660)	$ 340
at fair value.....................	9,000		

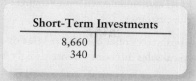

Short-Term Investments

| 8,660 | |
| 340 | |

Suppose Waverly sells the investment in securities for $8,700 in 2013. Journalize the sale and then show the Short-Term Investments T-account as it appears after the sale.

▶ Answer

	(In millions)	
Cash..	8,700	
Loss on Sale of Investments.........	300	
Short-Term Investments		9,000
Sold investments at a loss.		

Short-Term Investments

| 8,660 | |
| 340 | 9,000 |

Apply GAAP for Proper Revenue Recognition

A study of accounts and notes receivable would not be complete without a brief review of the principles of revenue recognition, which is the basis for accounts and notes receivable. Recall from the discussion of the revenue principle in Chapter 3 that revenue should be recognized when it is earned, and not before. Revenue recognition is proper when the seller of goods and services has done everything required to earn the revenue by transferring the good or service to the customer, and when the customer has assumed ownership and control over goods or the service provider has substantially completed the service. In addition, the price of the goods or services is fixed or determinable, and collection is reasonably assured. The amount of the revenue to be recognized is the cash value of the goods or services transferred from the seller to the buyer. For example, assume PepsiCo, Inc., delivers a truckload of beverages to a Publix Supermarket in Florida. On the truck are 500 12-pack cases of soft drinks, each of which PepsiCo sells to Publix for $3. The amount of PepsiCo's sale to Publix is $1,500. At the point when PepsiCo delivers the beverages to the store, and Publix Supermarkets assumes ownership of them, PepsiCo, Inc., may record the following transaction:

Accounts Receivable	1,500	
Sales Revenue		1,500

The timing and amount of revenue recognized is determined by the shipping terms and payment incentives offered to the buyer by the seller.

Shipping Terms, Sales Discounts, and Sales Returns

Shipping Terms. The proper time to recognize sales revenue is when ownership of goods changes hands between the seller and the buyer. This point is determined by the **shipping terms** in the sales contract. When goods are shipped **FOB (free on board)** *shipping point*, ownership

2

Apply GAAP for proper revenue recognition

changes hands and revenue is recognized at the point when the goods leave the seller's shipping dock. When goods are shipped **FOB** *destination*, ownership changes hands and revenue is recognized at the point of delivery to the customer.

Sales Discounts. Sometimes businesses offer customers **sales discounts** for early payment in order to speed up cash flow. A typical sales discount incentive might be stated as follows:

$$2/10, n/30$$

This expression means that the seller is willing to discount the order by 2% if the buyer pays the invoice within 10 days. After that time, the seller withdraws the discount offer. Regardless, the buyer *must* pay within 30 days. In the case of PepsiCo, Inc.'s sale to Publix, if Publix pays the invoice within 10 days, it is entitled to a $30 discount, making the full amount due to settle PepsiCo, Inc.'s invoice $1,470 rather than $1,500. The transaction to record the collection of this sale would be as follows:

Cash	1,470	
Sales Discount	30	
Accounts Receivable		1,500

Companies with plenty of cash often take advantage of early payment discounts on their purchases, thus adding to their reported profits and cash flows.

Sales Returns and Allowances. Retailers and consumers have a right to return unsatisfactory or damaged merchandise for a refund or exchange. This is called **sales returns and allowances.** Retailers keep track of sales returns over time to make sure they are not excessive. Returned merchandise means lost profits. For example, suppose that of the 500 cases of beverages PepsiCo, Inc., sells to Publix, 3 cases are returned (or PepsiCo grants Publix an allowance) because they are damaged in shipment. PepsiCo, Inc., would record the following entry[1]:

Sales Returns and Allowances	9	
Accounts Receivable		9

Retailers, wholesalers, and manufacturers typically disclose sales revenue at the *net* amount, which means after sales discounts and sales returns and allowances have been subtracted. Using hypothetical data for discounts and returns, PepsiCo, Inc.'s net sales (revenue) for 2010, compared with the last 2 years, is as follows:

PepsiCo, Inc.
(2010, Adapted)

Gross revenue	$59,000
− Sales discounts	(900)
− Sales returns and allowances	(262)
= Net revenue	$57,838

	2010	2009	2008
Net revenue (in millions)	$57,838	$43,232	$43,251

---

[1]In this example, we ignore the cost of the product to PepsiCo, Inc., which is accounted for both at the point of sale and the point of return. We will discuss this further when we cover inventories and cost of goods sold in Chapter 6.

Account for and Control Accounts Receivable

Receivables are the third most liquid asset—after cash and short-term investments. Most of the remainder of this chapter shows how to account for receivables.

3

Account for and control accounts receivable

Types of Receivables

Receivables are monetary claims against others. Receivables are acquired mainly by selling goods and services (accounts receivable) and by lending money (notes receivable). The journal entries to record the receivables can be shown as follows:

Performing a Service on Account		Lending Money on a Note Receivable	
Accounts Receivable...................	XXX	Note Receivable	XXX
Service Revenue.......................	XXX	Cash..	XXX
Performed a service on account.		*Loaned money to another company.*	

The two major types of receivables are accounts receivable and notes receivable. A business's *accounts receivable* are the amounts collectible from customers from the sale of goods and services. Accounts receivable, which are *current assets*, are sometimes called *trade receivables* or merely *receivables*.

The Accounts Receivable account in the general ledger serves as a *control account* that summarizes the total amount receivable from all customers. Companies also keep a *subsidiary record* of accounts receivable with a separate account for each customer, illustrated as follows:

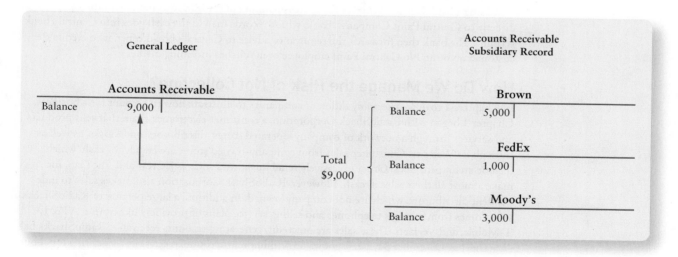

Notes receivable are more formal contracts than accounts receivable. For a note, the borrower signs a written promise to pay the lender a definite sum at the **maturity** date, plus interest. This is why notes are also called *promissory notes*. The note may require the borrower to pledge *security* for the loan. This means that the borrower gives the lender permission to claim certain assets, called *collateral*, if the borrower fails to pay the amount due. We cover the details of notes receivable starting on page 301.

Other receivables is a miscellaneous category for all receivables other than accounts receivable and notes receivable. Examples include loans to employees and to related companies.

Internal Controls over Cash Collections on Account

Businesses that sell on credit receive most of their cash receipts from collections of accounts receivable. Internal control over collections on account is important. Chapter 4 discusses control procedures for cash receipts, but another element of internal control deserves emphasis here—the separation of cash-handling and cash-accounting duties. Consider the following case:

> Central Paint Company is a small, family-owned business that takes pride in the loyalty of its workers. Most employees have been with Central for 10 or more years. The company makes 90% of its sales on account and receives most of its cash by mail.
>
> The office staff consists of a bookkeeper and an office supervisor. The bookkeeper maintains the general ledger and a subsidiary record of individual customer accounts receivable. The bookkeeper also makes the daily bank deposit.
>
> The supervisor prepares monthly financial statements and any special reports the company needs. The supervisor also takes sales orders from customers and serves as office manager.

Can you identify the internal control weakness here? The problem is that the bookkeeper makes the bank deposit. Remember the EPIC case in Chapter 4? With this cash-handling duty, the bookkeeper could lap accounts receivable. Alternatively, he or she could steal an incoming customer check and write off the customer's account as uncollectible. The customer doesn't complain because the bookkeeper wrote off the customer's account, and Central therefore stops pursuing collection.

How can this weakness be corrected? The supervisor—not the bookkeeper—could open incoming mail and make the daily bank deposit. The bookkeeper should *not* be allowed to handle cash. Only the remittance advices should be forwarded to the bookkeeper to credit customer accounts receivable. Removing cash handling from the bookkeeper and keeping the accounts away from the supervisor separates duties and strengthens internal control.

Using a bank lockbox achieves the same separation of duties. Customers send their payments directly to Central Paint Company's bank, which records cash as the cash goes into Central's bank account. The bank then forwards the remittance advice to Central's bookkeeper, who credits the customer account. No Central Paint employee even touches incoming cash.

How Do We Manage the Risk of Not Collecting?

In Chapters 1 to 4, we use many different companies to illustrate how to account for a business. Chapter 1 began with RadioShack Corporation, a consumer electronics chain that sells products and services through a network of company-operated stores, distributors, and kiosks, as well as through its Web site. Consumer sales from company-owned stores are largely for cash, which include credit card sales. Other exclusively retail businesses such as J. Crew and The Gap, Inc., make almost all their sales in cash. However, RadioShack Corporation also makes sales to independent distributors, which are not company-owned. In addition, a large portion of RadioShack's sales comes from wireless telephones and selling service plans of providers like Sprint, AT&T, T-Mobile, and Verizon. These sales are on credit, generating accounts receivable. RadioShack's balance sheet at December 31, 2010, shows $377 million in accounts receivable, accounting for about 22% of its current assets. Chapter 2's opening vignette featured Apple, Inc., Chapter 3 featured Starbucks Corporation, and this chapter features PepsiCo. All of these companies hold substantial amounts of receivables.

By selling on credit, companies run the risk of not collecting some receivables. Unfortunately, some customers don't pay their debts. The prospect of failing to collect from a customer provides the biggest challenge in accounting for receivables. The Decision Guidelines address this challenge.

DECISION GUIDELINES

MANAGING AND ACCOUNTING FOR RECEIVABLES

Here are the management and accounting issues a business faces when the company extends credit to customers. For each issue, the Decision Guidelines propose a plan of action. Let's look at a business situation: Suppose you open a health club near your college. Assume you will let customers use the club and bill them for their monthly dues. What challenges will you encounter by extending credit to customers?

The main issues in *managing* receivables, along with plans of action, are as follows:

Issues	Plan of Action
1. What are the benefits and the costs of extending credit to customers?	1. Benefit—Increase in sales. Cost—Risk of not collecting.
2. Run a credit check on prospective customers.	2. Extend credit only to creditworthy customers.
3. Design the internal control system to separate duties.	3. Separate cash-handling and accounting duties to keep employees from stealing the cash collected from customers.
4. Keep a close eye on customer payment habits. Send second and third statements to slow-paying customers, if necessary.	4. Pursue collection from customers to maximize cash flow.

The main issues in accounting for receivables, and the related plans of action, are (amounts are assumed) as follows:

Issues

1. Measure and report receivables on the balance sheet at net realizable value, the amount we expect to collect. This is the appropriate amount to report for receivables.

2. Measure and report the expense associated with failure to collect receivables. This expense is called *uncollectible-account expense* and is reported on the income statement.

Plan of Action

Report receivables at net realizable value:

Balance sheet

Receivables.................................	$1,000
Less: Allowance for uncollectibles..............	(80)
Receivables, net..........................	$ 920

Measure the expense of not collecting from customers:

Income statement

Sales (or service) revenue............................	$8,000
Expenses:	
Uncollectible-account expense.................	190

These guidelines lead to our next topic, accounting for uncollectible receivables.

Evaluate Collectibility Using the Allowance for Uncollectible Accounts

A company gets an account receivable only when it sells its product or service on credit (on account). You'll recall that the entry to record the earning of revenue on account is (amount assumed) as follows:

Accounts Receivable	1,000	
Sales Revenue (or Service Revenue)		1,000
Earned revenue on account.		

Evaluate collectibility using the allowance for uncollectible accounts

Ideally, the company would collect cash for all of its receivables. But unfortunately the entry to record cash collections on account is for only $950.

Cash	950	
Accounts Receivable		950
Collections on account.		

You can see that companies rarely collect all of their accounts receivable. So companies must account for their uncollectible accounts—$50 in this example. Selling on credit creates both a benefit and a cost:

▶ *Benefit*: Customers who cannot pay cash immediately can buy on credit, so sales and profits increase.

▶ *Cost*: The company cannot collect from some customers. Accountants label this cost **uncollectible-account expense, doubtful-account expense**, or **bad-debt expense**.

PepsiCo reports receivables as follows on its 2010 balance sheet (in millions):

Accounts and notes receivable, net (in millions) $6,323

The word "net" implies that a small amount has been subtracted from total accounts and notes receivable, representing the amount that PepsiCo does *not* expect to collect. In PepsiCo, Inc.'s case, this amount is insignificant (immaterial), so it is not separately disclosed in either the line item of the financial statements or the footnotes. The net amount of the receivables ($6,323 million) is the amount that PepsiCo *does* expect to collect. This is called the *net realizable value* because it's the amount of cash PepsiCo expects to realize in cash receipts.

Uncollectible-account expense is an operating expense in the selling, general and administrative category along with salaries, rent, and utilities. To measure uncollectible-account expense, accountants use the allowance method or, in certain limited cases, the direct write-off method (p. 300).

Allowance Method

The best way to measure bad debts is by the **allowance method**. This method records collection losses based on estimates developed from the company's collection experience. PepsiCo doesn't wait to see which customers will not pay. Instead, PepsiCo records the estimated amount as Uncollectible-Account Expense and also sets up **Allowance for Uncollectible Accounts**. Other titles for this account are **Allowance for Doubtful Accounts** and *Allowance for Bad Debts*. This is a contra account to Accounts Receivable. The allowance shows the amount of the receivables the business expects *not* to collect.

In Chapter 3 we used the Accumulated Depreciation account to show the amount of a plant asset's cost that has been expensed—the portion of the asset that's no longer a benefit to the company. Allowance for Uncollectible Accounts serves a similar purpose for Accounts Receivable. The allowance shows how much of the receivable has been expensed. You'll find this diagram helpful (amounts are assumed):

Equipment.........................	$100,000	Accounts receivable...................	$10,000
Less: Accumulated		Less: Allowance for	
depreciation	(40,000)	uncollectible accounts	(900)
Equipment, net..................	60,000	Accounts receivable, net............	9,100

Focus on Accounts Receivable. Customers owe this company $10,000, but it expects to collect only $9,100. The *net realizable value* of the receivables is therefore $9,100. Another way to report these receivables is as follows:

Accounts receivable, less allowance of $900.................	$9,100

You can work backward to determine the full amount of the receivable, $10,000 (net realizable value of $9,100 plus the allowance of $900).

The income statement reports Uncollectible-Account Expense among the operating expenses, as follows (using assumed figures):

Income statement (partial):

Expenses:

    Uncollectible-account expense:................ $2,000

STOP & THINK. . .

Refer to the PepsiCo balance sheet on page 284. Assume that the balance in PepsiCo's allowance for doubtful accounts was $100 million. At December 31, 2010, how much in total did customers owe PepsiCo? How much did PepsiCo expect *not* to collect? How much did PepsiCo expect to collect? What was the net realizable value of PepsiCo's receivables?

Answer:

	Millions
Customers owed PepsiCo...	$6,423 ($6,323 + $100)
PepsiCo expected not to collect the allowance of	(100)
PepsiCo expected to collect—net realizable value........	$6,323

Notice that, to determine the *total* (*gross*) amount customers owed, you have to add the amount of the allowance back to the "net realizable value" ($6,323 + $100 = $6,423). Although this amount is not shown in the financial statements, it is useful for analysis purposes, as shown in the following section.

The best way to estimate uncollectibles uses the company's history of collections from customers. There are two basic ways to estimate uncollectibles:

► Percent-of-sales method
► Aging-of-receivables method

Percent-of-Sales. The **percent-of-sales method** computes uncollectible-account expense as a percent of revenue. This method takes an *income-statement approach* because it focuses on the amount of expense to be reported on the income statement. Assume it is December 31, 2010, and PepsiCo's accounts have these balances *before the year-end adjustments* (amounts in millions):

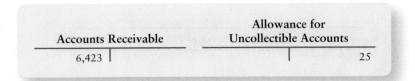

Accounts Receivable	Allowance for Uncollectible Accounts
6,423	25

Customers owe PepsiCo $6,423, and the Allowance amount on the books is $25. But PepsiCo's top managers know that the company will fail to collect more than $25. Suppose PepsiCo's credit department estimates that uncollectible-account expense is 1/10 of 1% (0.001) of total revenues, which were $57,000. The entry that records uncollectible-account expense for the year also updates the allowance as follows (using PepsiCo figures):

2010			
Dec 31	Uncollectible-Account Expense		
	($57,000 × .001)	57	
	Allowance for Uncollectible Accounts		57
	Recorded expense for the year.		

The expense decreases PepsiCo's assets, as shown by the accounting equation.

Assets	=	Liabilities	+	Stockholders' Equity	−	Expenses
− 57	=	0			−	57

The percent-of-sales method employs the expense recognition (matching) concept to estimate, probably on a monthly or quarterly basis, the amount of cost that has been incurred in order to earn a certain amount of revenue, and to recognize both in the same time period.

Accounts Receivable		Allowance for Uncollectible Accounts		Uncollectible-Account Expense	
6,423			25	57	
		Adj	57		
		End Bal	82		

Net accounts receivable, $6,341

Using the percent-of-sales method, the net realizable value of accounts receivable, or the amount ultimately expected to be collected from customers, would be $6,341 ($6,423 − $82). This method will usually result in a different amount of estimated uncollectible accounts expense and net realizable value than the aging method, discussed next.

Aging-of-Receivables. The other popular method for estimating uncollectibles is called **aging-of-receivables.** The aging method is a *balance-sheet approach* because it focuses on what should be the most relevant and faithful representation of accounts receivable as of the balance sheet date. In the aging method, individual receivables from specific customers are analyzed based on how long they have been outstanding.

Suppose it is December 31, 2010, and PepsiCo's receivables accounts show the following before the year-end adjustment (amounts in millions):

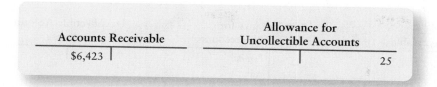

Accounts Receivable	Allowance for Uncollectible Accounts
$6,423	25

These accounts are not yet ready for the financial statements because the allowance balance is not realistic.

PepsiCo's computerized accounting package ages the company's accounts receivable. Exhibit 5-2 shows a representative aging schedule at December 31, 2010. PepsiCo's gross receivables total $6,423. Of this amount, the aging schedule shows that the company will *not* collect $100 (lower right corner).

EXHIBIT 5-2 | Aging the Accounts Receivable of PepsiCo

	Age of Account (Dollar amounts rounded to the nearest million)				
Customer	1–30 Days	31–60 Days	61–90 Days	Over 90 Days	Total Balance
Wal-Mart					
Publix					
Totals	$5,559	$ 600	$ 200	$ 64	$6,423
Estimated percent uncollectible	× 1.1%	× 2%	× 7%	× 20%	
Allowance for Uncollectible Accounts balance should be	$ 61* +	$ 12 +	$ 14 +	$ 13* =	$ 100

*Rounded to the nearest million

The aging method will bring the balance of the allowance account ($25) to the needed amount as determined by the aging schedule ($100). The lower right corner of the aging schedule gives the needed balance in the allowance account. To update the allowance, PepsiCo would make this adjusting entry at year-end:

2010			
Dec 31	Uncollectible-Account Expense	75	
	Allowance for Uncollectible Accounts		
	($100 − $25)		75
	Recorded expense for the year.		

The expense decreases PepsiCo's assets and net income, as shown by the accounting equation.

Assets	=	Liabilities	+	Stockholders' Equity	−	Expenses
− 75	=	0			−	75

Now the balance sheet can report the amount that PepsiCo actually expects to collect from customers: $6,323 ($6,423 − $100). This is the net realizable value of PepsiCo's accounts receivable.

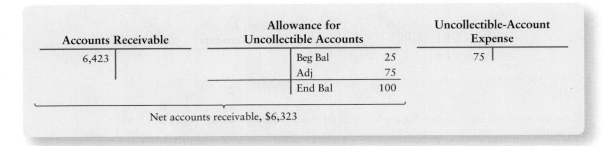

Writing Off Uncollectible Accounts. Assume that at the beginning of 2012, a division of PepsiCo had these accounts receivable (amounts in thousands):

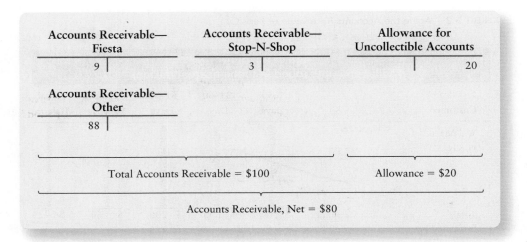

Suppose that early in 2012, PepsiCo's credit department determines that PepsiCo cannot collect from customers Fiesta and Stop-N-Shop. PepsiCo then writes off the receivables from these customers with the following entry:

2012			
Jan 31	Allowance for Uncollectible Accounts	12	
	Accounts Receivable—Fiesta		9
	Accounts Receivable—Stop-N-Shop		3
	Wrote off uncollectible receivables.		

After the write-off, PepsiCo's accounts show these amounts:

Accounts Receivable—Fiesta		Accounts Receivable—Stop-N-Shop		Allowance for Uncollectible Accounts	
9	9	3	3	12	20
					8

Accounts Receivable—Other

88

Total Accounts Receivable = $88   Allowance = $8

Accounts Receivable, Net = $80

The accounting equation shows that the write-off of uncollectibles has no effect on PepsiCo's total assets, no effect on current assets, and no effect on net accounts receivable. Notice that Accounts Receivable, Net is still $80. There is no effect on net income either. Why is there no effect on net income? Net income is unaffected because the write-off of uncollectibles affects no expense account. If the company uses the allowance method as discussed in the previous section, expenses would have been properly recognized in the period they were incurred, which is the same period in which the related sales took place.

Assets	=	Liabilities	+	Stockholders' Equity
+ 12	=	0	+	0
− 12				

Combining the Percent-of-Sales and the Aging Methods. Most companies use the percent-of-sales and aging-of-accounts methods together, as follows:

▶ For *interim statements* (monthly or quarterly), companies use the percent-of-sales method because it is easier to apply. The percent-of-sales method focuses on the uncollectible-account *expense*, but that is not enough.

▶ At the end of the year, companies use the aging method to ensure that Accounts Receivable is reported at *net realizable value* on the balance sheet. The aging method focuses on the amount of the receivables that is uncollectible.

▶ Using the two methods together provides good measures of both the *expense* and the *asset*. Exhibit 5-3 compares the two methods.

EXHIBIT 5-3 │ Comparing the Percent-of-Sales and Aging Methods for Estimating Uncollectibles

THE ALLOWANCE METHOD: TWO APPROACHES

Percent-of-Sales		Aging-of-Receivables	

Adjusts Allowance for Uncollectible Accounts **BY**

Adjusts Allowance for Uncollectible Accounts **TO**

The Amount of UNCOLLECTIBLE-ACCOUNT EXPENSE	The Amount of UNCOLLECTIBLE ACCOUNTS RECEIVABLE

Direct Write-Off Method

There is another, less preferable way to account for uncollectible receivables. Under the **direct write-off method**, the company waits until a specific customer's receivable proves uncollectible. Then the accountant writes off the customer's account and records Uncollectible-Account Expense, as follows (using assumed data):

2012			
Jan 31	Uncollectible-Account Expense	12	
	Accounts Receivable—Fiesta		9
	Accounts Receivable—Stop-N-Shop		3
	Wrote off bad accounts by direct write-off method.		

The direct write-off method is not considered generally accepted accounting for financial statement purposes. It is considered defective for two reasons:

1. It uses no allowance for uncollectibles. As a result, receivables are always reported at their full amount, which is more than the business expects to collect. *Assets on the balance sheet may be overstated.*

2. It fails to recognize the expense of uncollectible accounts in the same period in which the related sales revenue is earned. In this example, PepsiCo made the sales to Fiesta and Stop-N-Shop in 2011 and should have recorded the uncollectible-account expense during 2011, not in 2012 when it wrote off the accounts.

Because of these deficiencies, PepsiCo and virtually all other large companies use the allowance method for preparing their financial statements.

The direct write-off method is the *required* method of accounting for uncollectible accounts for federal income tax purposes. It is one of several sources of timing differences that may arise between net income for financial reporting purposes and net income for federal income tax purposes. We will discuss other differences between book and taxable income in later chapters.

Computing Cash Collections from Customers

A company earns revenue and then collects the cash from customers. For PepsiCo and most other companies, there is a time lag between earning the revenue and collecting the cash. Collections from customers are the single most important source of cash for any business. You can compute a company's collections from customers by analyzing its Accounts Receivable account. Receivables typically hold only five items, as reflected in the five elements of the following Accounts Receivable account balance (amounts assumed):

Accounts Receivable			
Beg Bal (left over from last period)	200	Write-offs of uncollectibles	100**
Sales (or service) revenue	1,800*	Collections from customers	X = 1,500†
End Bal (carries over to next period)	400		

*The journal entry that places revenue into the receivable account is

Accounts Receivable	1,800	
Sales (or Service) Revenue		1,800

**The journal entry for write-offs is

Allowance for Uncollectibles	100	
Accounts Receivable		100

†The journal entry that places collections into the receivable account is

Cash	1,500	
Accounts Receivable		1,500

Suppose you know all these amounts *except* collections from customers. You can compute collections by solving for X in the T-account.[2] Often write-offs are unknown and must be omitted. Then the computation of collections becomes an approximation.

Account for Notes Receivable

As stated earlier, notes receivable are more formal than accounts receivable. Notes receivable due within one year or less are current assets. Notes due beyond one year are *long-term receivables* and are reported as long-term assets. Some notes receivable are collected in installments. The portion due within one year is a current asset and the remainder is long term. PepsiCo may hold a $20,000 note receivable from a customer, but only the $6,000 that the customer must pay within one year is a current asset of PepsiCo.

Before launching into the accounting for notes receivable, let's define some key terms:

Creditor. The party to whom money is owed. The creditor is also called the *lender*.
Debtor. The party that borrowed and owes money on the note. The debtor is also called the *maker* of the note or the *borrower*.
Interest. Interest is the cost of borrowing money. The interest is stated in an annual percentage rate.
Maturity date. The date on which the debtor must pay the note.
Maturity value. The sum of principal and interest on the note.
Principal. The amount of money borrowed by the debtor.
Term. The length of time from when the note was signed by the debtor to when the debtor must pay the note.

There are two parties to a note:

▶ The *creditor* has a note receivable.
▶ The *debtor* has a note payable.

5 Account for notes receivable

---

[2]An equation may help you solve for X. The equation is $200 + $1,800 − X − $100 = $400. X = $1,500.

Exhibit 5-4 is a typical promissory note.

EXHIBIT 5-4 | Promissory Note

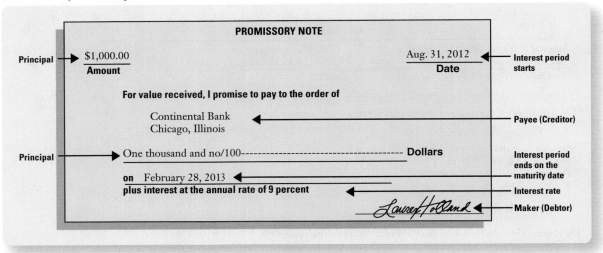

The **principal** amount of the note ($1,000) is the amount borrowed by the debtor, lent by the creditor. This six-month note receivable runs from August 31, 2012, to February 28, 2013, when Lauren Holland (the maker) promises to pay Continental Bank (the creditor) the principal of $1,000 plus 9% interest. Interest is revenue to the creditor (Continental Bank, in this case).

Accounting for Notes Receivable

Consider the promissory note in Exhibit 5-4. After Lauren Holland signs the note, Continental Bank gives her $1,000 cash. The bank's entries follow, assuming a December 31 year-end for Continental Bank:

2012			
Aug 31	Note Receivable—L. Holland	1,000	
	Cash		1,000
	Made a loan.		

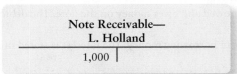

Note Receivable—L. Holland	
1,000	

The bank gave one asset, cash, in return for another asset, a note receivable, so total assets did not change.

Continental Bank earns interest revenue during September, October, November, and December. At December 31, the bank accrues 9% interest revenue for four months as follows:

2012			
Dec 31	Interest Receivable ($1,000 \times .09 \times 4/12$)	30	
	Interest Revenue		30
	Accrued interest revenue.		

The bank's assets and revenues increase.

Continental Bank reports these amounts in its financial statements at December 31, 2012:

Balance sheet	
Current assets:	
Note receivable	$1,000
Interest receivable..............	30
Income statement	
Interest revenue	$ 30

The bank collects the note on February 28, 2013, and records the following:

2013			
Feb 28	Cash	1,045	
	Note Receivable—L. Holland		1,000
	Interest Receivable		30
	Interest Revenue ($1,000 × .09 × 2/12)		15
	Collected note at maturity.		

This entry zeroes out Note Receivable and Interest Receivable and also records the interest revenue earned in 2013.

Note Receivable— L. Holland	
1,000	1,000

In its 2013 financial statements, the only item that Continental Bank will report is the interest revenue of $15 that was earned in 2013. There's no note receivable or interest receivable on the balance sheet because those items were zeroed out when the bank collected the note at maturity.

Three aspects of the interest computation deserve mention:

1. Interest rates are always for an annual period, unless stated otherwise. In this example, the annual interest rate is 9%. At December 31, 2012, Continental Bank accrues interest revenue for four months. The interest computation is as follows:

Principal	×	**Interest Rate**	×	**Time**	=	**Amount of Interest**
$1,000	×	.09	×	4/12	=	$30

2. The time element (4/12) is the fraction of the year that the note has been in force during 2012.

3. Interest is often computed for a number of days. For example, suppose you loaned out $10,000 on April 10. The note receivable runs for 90 days and specifies interest at 8%.

   a. Interest starts accruing on April 11 and runs for 90 days, ending on the due date, July 9, as follows:

Month	Number of Days That Interest Accrues
April	20
May	31
June	30
July	9
Total	90

   b. The interest computation is
      $10,000 × .08 × 90/365 = $197

Some companies sell goods and services on notes receivable (versus selling on accounts receivable). This often occurs when the payment term extends beyond the customary accounts receivable period of 30 to 60 days.

Suppose that on March 20, 2011, PepsiCo sells a large amount of food to Wal-Mart. PepsiCo gets Wal-Mart's three-month promissory note plus 10% annual interest. At the outset, PepsiCo would debit Notes Receivable and credit Sales Revenue.

A company may also accept a note receivable from a trade customer whose account receivable is past due. The company then debits Notes Receivable and credits Accounts Receivable. We would say the company "received a note receivable on account." Now let's examine some strategies to speed up cash flow.

Show How to Speed Up Cash Flow from Receivables

Show how to speed up cash flow from receivables

All companies want speedy cash receipts. Rapid cash flow means companies have the ability to pay off current liabilities faster, as well as to finance new products, research, and development. Thus, companies such as PepsiCo develop strategies to shorten the credit cycle and collect cash more quickly. For example, they might offer sales discounts for early payment, as discussed earlier. They might also charge interest on customer accounts that exceed a certain age. They adopt more effective credit and collection procedures. In recent years, as electronic banking has become more popular, a common strategy has been to emphasize credit card or bankcard sales.

Credit Card or Bankcard Sales

The merchant sells merchandise and lets the customer pay with a credit card, such as Discover or American Express, or with a bankcard, such as VISA or MasterCard. This strategy may dramatically increase sales, but the added revenue comes at a cost, which is typically about 2% to 3% of the total amount of the sale. Let's see how credit cards and bankcards work from the seller's perspective.

Suppose Dell, Inc., sells computers for $5,000, and the customer pays with a VISA card. Dell records the sale as follows:

Cash	4,900	
Credit Card Discount Expense	100	
Sales Revenue		5,000
Recorded bankcard sales.		

Assets	=	Liabilities	+	Stockholders' Equity	+	Revenues	−	Expenses
+ 4,900	=	0	+			+ 5,000		− 100

Dell enters the transaction in the credit card machine. The machine, linked to a VISA server, automatically credits Dell's account for a discounted portion, say $4,900, of the $5,000 sale amount. Two percent ($100) goes to VISA. To Dell, the credit card discount expense is an operating expense similar to interest expense.

Selling (Factoring) Receivables

PepsiCo makes some large sales to grocery chains on account, debiting Accounts Receivable and crediting Sales Revenue. PepsiCo might then sell these accounts receivable to another business, called a *factor*. The factor earns revenue by paying a discounted price for the receivable and then hopefully collecting the full amount from the customer. The benefit to PepsiCo is the immediate receipt of cash. The biggest disadvantage of factoring is that it is often quite expensive, when compared to the costs of retaining the receivable on the books and ultimately collecting the full amount. In addition, the company that factors its receivables loses control over the collection process. For these reasons, factoring is often not used by companies who have other less costly means to raise cash, such as short-term borrowing from banks. Factoring may be used by start-up companies with insufficient credit history to obtain loans at a reasonable cost, by companies with weak credit history, or by companies that are already saddled with a significant amount of debt.

To illustrate selling, or *factoring*, accounts receivable, suppose a company wishes to speed up cash flow and therefore sells $100,000 of accounts receivables, receiving cash of $95,000. The company would record the sale of the receivables as follows:

Cash	95,000	
Financing Expense	5,000	
Accounting Receivable		100,000
Sold accounts receivable.		

Again, Financing Expense is an operating expense, with the same effect as a loss. Some companies may debit a Loss account. Discounting a note receivable is similar to selling an account receivable. However, the credit is to Notes Receivable (instead of Accounts Receivable).

Notice the high price (5% of the face amount, or $5,000) the company has had to pay in order to collect the cash immediately, as opposed to waiting 30–60 days to collect the full amount. Therefore, if the company can afford to wait, it will probably not engage in factoring in order to collect the full amount of the receivables.

Reporting on the Statement of Cash Flows

Receivables and short-term investments appear on the balance sheet as assets. We saw these in PepsiCo's balance sheet at the beginning of the chapter. We've also seen how to report the related revenues, expenses, gains, and losses on the income statement. Because receivable and investment transactions affect cash, their effects must also be reported on the statement of cash flows.

Receivables bring in cash when the business collects from customers. These transactions are reported as *operating activities* on the statement of cash flows because they result from sales. Investment transactions show up as *investing activities* on the statement of cash flows. Chapter 12 shows how companies report their cash flows on the statement of cash flows. In that chapter, we will see exactly how to report cash flows related to receivables and investment transactions.

⑦

Evaluate liquidity
using two new ratios

Evaluate Liquidity Using Two New Ratios

Investors and creditors use ratios to evaluate the financial health of a company. We introduced the current ratio in Chapter 3. Other ratios, including the **quick** (or *acid-test*) **ratio** and the number of days' sales in receivables, help investors measure liquidity.

Quick (Acid-test) Ratio

The balance sheet lists assets in the order of relative liquidity:

1. Cash and cash equivalents

2. Short-term investments

3. Accounts (or notes) receivable

PepsiCo's balance sheet in the chapter-opening story lists these accounts in order.

Managers, stockholders, and creditors care about the liquidity of a company's assets. The current ratio measures ability to pay current liabilities with current assets. A more stringent measure of ability to pay current liabilities is the **quick** (or *acid-test*) **ratio**:

PepsiCo 2010

(Dollars in millions, taken from PepsiCo balance sheet)

$$\text{Quick (acid-test) ratio} = \frac{\text{Cash} + \frac{\text{Short-term}}{\text{investments}} + \frac{\text{Net current}}{\text{receivables}}}{\text{Total current liabilities}} = \frac{\$5,943 + \$426 + \$6,323}{\$15,892} = 0.80$$

The higher the quick ratio, the easier it is to pay current liabilities. PepsiCo's quick ratio of 0.80 means that it has $0.80 of quick assets to pay each $1 of current liabilities. This ratio value is considered reasonably good, but not excellent. Traditionally, companies have wanted a quick ratio of at least 1.0 to be safe. The ratio needs to be high enough for safety, but not too high. After all, cash and the other liquid assets don't earn very high rates of return, as inventory and plant assets do.

What is an acceptable quick ratio? The answer depends on the industry. Auto dealers can operate smoothly with a quick ratio of 0.20, roughly one-fourth of PepsiCo's ratio value. How can auto dealers survive with so low a quick ratio? The auto manufacturers help finance their dealers' inventory. Most dealers, therefore, have a financial safety net provided through the manufacturers. During the recent business recession, General Motors' sales slumped and the company ran dangerously low of cash. One of the many consequences of GM's cash shortage was that it deprived dealerships of these safety nets and put them in jeopardy of bankruptcy and insolvency. You can see the "domino effect" of arrangements like this, and why a number of GM dealerships were forced to close even after GM received about $25 billion in "bailout money" from the United States government.

Days' Sales in Receivables

After a business makes a credit sale, the *next* step is collecting the receivable. **Days' sales in receivables**, also called *days sales outstanding* (DSO) or the *collection period*, tells a company how long it takes to collect its average level of receivables. Shorter is better because cash is coming in quickly. The longer the collection period, the less cash is available to pay bills and expand.

Days' sales in receivables can be computed in two logical steps. First, compute average daily sales (or average revenue for one day). Then divide average daily sales into average receivables for the period. We show days' sales in receivables for PepsiCo.

(Dollars in millions, taken from PepsiCo's financial statements) Days' Sales in Receivables		PepsiCo
1. $\dfrac{\text{Average daily sales}}{} = \dfrac{\text{Net sales}}{\text{365 days}}$		$\dfrac{\$57,838}{\text{365 days}} = \$158 \text{ per day}$
2. $\dfrac{\text{Days' sales in average receivables}}{} = \dfrac{\text{Average receivables *}}{\text{Average daily sales}}$		$\dfrac{\$5,474*}{\$158 \text{ per day}} = 35 \text{ days}$
*Average net receivables $= \dfrac{\text{Beginning net receivables} + \text{Ending net receivables}}{2}$		$= \dfrac{\$4,624 + \$6,323}{2} = \$5,474$

Net sales come from the income statement, and the receivables amounts are taken from the balance sheet. Average receivables is the simple average of the beginning and ending balance.

It takes PepsiCo 35 days to collect its average level of receivables. To evaluate PepsiCo's collection period of 35 days, we need to compare 35 days to the credit terms that PepsiCo offers customers when the company makes a sale, as well as the number of days on average that creditors typically allow PepsiCo to pay them without penalty. Suppose PepsiCo makes sales on "net 30" terms, which means that customers should pay PepsiCo within 30 days of the sale. PepsiCo's collection period of 35 days is pretty good in comparison to the ideal measure of 30 days. After all, some customers drag out their payments. And, as we've seen, some customers don't pay at all. On the other hand, if PepsiCo's short-term creditors expect payment of their accounts payable within 30 days, PepsiCo might be forced to borrow cash at banks in order to pay its creditors on time, which could prove to be expensive.

Companies watch their collection periods closely. Whenever collections slow down, the business must find other sources of financing, such as borrowing or selling receivables. During recessions, customers pay more slowly, and a longer collection period may be unavoidable.[3]

---

[3]Another ratio, **accounts receivable turnover**, captures the same information as days' sales in receivables. Receivable turnover is computed as follows: Net sales/Average net accounts receivable. During 2010, PepsiCo had a receivable turnover rate of 10.57 ($57,838/$5,474 = 10.57). Days sales in average receivables can then be computed by dividing 365 by the receivable turnover (365/10.57 = 34.53, rounded to 35). You can see that this method merely rearranges the equations in the body of the text, "going through the back door" to achieve the same result. The authors prefer days' sales in receivables to receivables turnover because days' sales in receivable can be compared directly to the company's credit sale terms.

END-OF-CHAPTER

END-OF-CHAPTER SUMMARY PROBLEM

Superior Technical Resources' (STR's) balance sheet at December 31, 2012, reported the following:

	(In millions)
Accounts receivable.....................................	$382
Allowance for doubtful accounts...............	(52)

STR uses both the percent-of-sales and the aging approaches to account for uncollectible receivables.

▶ **Requirements**

1. How much of the December 31, 2012, balance of accounts receivables did STR expect to collect? Stated differently, what was the net realizable value of STR's receivables?

2. Journalize, without explanations, 2013 entries for STR:

   a. Estimated doubtful-account expense of $40 million, based on the percent-of-sales method, all during the year.

   b. Write-offs of uncollectible accounts receivable totaling $58 million. Prepare a T-account for Allowance for Doubtful Accounts and post to this account. Show its unadjusted balance at December 31, 2013.

   c. December 31, 2013, aging of receivables, which indicates that $47 million of the total receivables of $409 million is uncollectible at year-end. Post to Allowance for Doubtful Accounts, and show its adjusted balance at December 31, 2013.

3. Show how STR's receivables and the related allowance will appear on the December 31, 2013, balance sheet.

4. Show what STR's income statement will report for the foregoing transactions.

▶ **Answers**

Requirement 1

	(In millions)
Net realizable value of receivables ($382 − $52)	$330

Requirement 2

		(In millions)	
a.	Doubtful-Account Expense	40	
	Allowance for Doubtful Accounts		40
b.	Allowance for Doubtful Accounts	58	
	Accounts Receivable		58

Allowance for Doubtful Accounts

		Dec 31, 2012	52
2013 Write-offs	58	2013 Expense	40
		Unadjusted balance at Dec 31, 2013	34

c.	Doubtful-Account Expense ($47 − $34)	13	
	Allowance for Doubtful Accounts		13

Allowance for Doubtful Accounts

	Dec 31, 2013 Unadj bal	34
	2013 Expense	13
	Dec 31, 2013 Adj bal	47

Requirement 3

	(In millions)
Accounts receivable.....................................	$409
Allowance for doubtful accounts...............	(47)

Requirement 4

	(In millions)
Expenses: Doubtful-account expense for 2013 ($40 + $13)	$53

REVIEW | Receivables and Investments

Quick Check (Answers are given on page 336.)

1. Rolling Green Tennis Academy held investments in trading securities valued at $45,000 at December 31, 2012. These investments cost Rolling Green $38,000. What is the appropriate amount for Rolling Green to report for these investments on the December 31, 2012, balance sheet?

a. $7,000 gain
b. 38,000

c. $45,000
d. Cannot be determined from the data given

2. Return to Rolling Green Tennis Academy in question 1. What should appear on the Rolling Green income statement for the year ended December 31, 2012, for the trading securities?

a. $38,000
b. $45,000

c. $7,000 unrealized gain
d. Cannot be determined from the data given

Use the following information to answer questions 3–7.
Anderson Company had the following information in 2012.

Accounts receivable 12/31/12	$13,000
Allowance for uncollectible accounts 12/31/12 (before adjustment)	750
Credit sales during 2012	47,000
Cash sales during 2012	14,000
Collections from customers on account during 2012	50,000

3. Uncollectible accounts are determined by the percent-of-sales method to be 2% of credit sales. How much is uncollectible-account expense for 2012?

   a. $1,220

   b. $940

   c. $1,000

   d. $260

4. Uncollectible-account expense for 2012 is $940. What is the adjusted balance in the Allowance account at year-end for 2012?

   a. $2,160

   b. $940

   c. $750

   d. $1,690

5. If uncollectible accounts are determined by the aging-of-receivables method to be $1,140, the uncollectible account expense for 2012 would be

   a. $390.

   b. $1,140.

   c. $1,890.

   d. $750.

6. Using the aging-of-receivables method, the balance of the Allowance account after the adjusting entry would be

   a. $390.

   b. $1,890.

   c. $750.

   d. $1,140.

7. Using the aging-of-receivables method, the net realizable value of accounts receivable on the 12/31/12 balance sheet would be

   a. $11,110.

   b. $12,250.

   c. $13,000.

   d. $11,860.

8. Accounts Receivable has a debit balance of $2,900, and the Allowance for Uncollectible Accounts has a credit balance of $100. A $70 account receivable is written off. What is the amount of net receivables (net realizable value) after the write-off?

   a. $2,730

   b. $2,830

   c. $2,800

   d. $2,870

9. Rosewood Corporation began 2012 with Accounts Receivable of $450,000. Sales for the year totaled $1,600,000. Rosewood ended the year with accounts receivable of $525,000. Rosewood's bad-debt losses are minimal. How much cash did Rosewood collect from customers in 2012?

   a. $1,525,000

   b. $2,125,000

   c. $1,675,000

   d. $1,600,000

10. Mars Company received a four-month, 7%, $6,000 note receivable on March 1. The adjusting entry on March 31 will

   a. debit Interest Receivable $35.

   b. credit Interest Revenue $35.

   c. both a and b.

   d. credit Interest Revenue $420.

11. What is the maturity value of a $40,000, 10%, six-month note?

   a. $42,000

   b. $44,000

   c. $38,000

   d. $40,000

12. If the adjusting entry to accrue interest on a note receivable is omitted, then

    a. liabilities are understated, net income is overstated, and stockholders' equity is overstated.

    b. assets, net income, and stockholders' equity are understated.

    c. assets, net income, and stockholders' equity are overstated.

    d. assets are overstated, net income is understated, and stockholders' equity is understated.

13. Net sales total $547,500. Beginning and ending accounts receivable are $38,000 and $46,000, respectively. Calculate days' sales in receivables.

    a. 31 days   **c.** 25 days

    b. 28 days   **d.** 23 days

14. From the following list of accounts, calculate the quick ratio.

Cash.............................	$ 3,000	Accounts payable...........................	$9,000
Accounts receivable..............	10,000	Salary payable................................	3,000
Inventory.......................	14,000	Notes payable (due in two years)	11,000
Prepaid insurance................	2,000	Short-term investments...................	7,000

    a. 1.6   **c.** 2.2

    b. 3.0   **d.** 1.7

Accounting Vocabulary

acid-test ratio (p. 306) Ratio of the sum of cash plus short-term investments plus net current receivables to total current liabilities. Tells whether the entity can pay all its current liabilities if they come due immediately. Also called the *quick ratio*.

accounts receivable turnover (p. 307) Net sales divided by average net accounts receivable.

aging-of-receivables (p. 296) A way to estimate bad debts by analyzing individual accounts receivable according to the length of time they have been receivable from the customer.

Allowance for Doubtful Accounts (p. 294) Another name for *Allowance for Uncollectible Accounts*.

Allowance for Uncollectible Accounts (p. 294) The estimated amount of collection losses. Another name for *Allowance for Doubtful Accounts*.

allowance method (p. 294) A method of recording collection losses based on estimates of how much money the business will not collect from its customers.

bad-debt expense (p. 294) Another name for *uncollectible-account expense*.

creditor (p. 301) The party to whom money is owed.

days' sales in receivables (p. 306) Ratio of average net accounts receivable to one day's sales. Indicates how many days' sales remain in Accounts Receivable awaiting collection. Also called the *collection period*.

debtor (p. 301) The party who owes money.

direct write-off method (p. 300) A method of accounting for bad debts in which the company waits until a customer's account receivable proves uncollectible and then debits Uncollectible-Account Expense and credits the customer's Account Receivable.

doubtful-account expense (p. 294) Another name for *uncollectible-account expense*.

FOB (p. 289) Acronym for "free on board"; used in quoting shipping terms. See also *shipping terms*.

interest (p. 301) The borrower's cost of renting money from a lender. Interest is revenue for the lender and expense for the borrower.

marketable securities (p. 284) Another name for *short-term investments*.

maturity (p. 291) The date on which a debt instrument must be paid.

maturity date (p. 301) The date on which the debtor must pay the note.

maturity value (p. 301) The sum of principal and interest on the note.

percent-of-sales method (p. 295) Computes uncollectible-account expense as a percentage of net sales. Also called the *income statement approach* because it focuses on the amount of expense to be reported on the income statement.

principal (p. 302) The amount borrowed by a debtor and lent by a creditor.

quick ratio (p. 306) Another name for *acid-test ratio*.

receivables (p. 291) Monetary claims against a business or an individual, acquired mainly by selling goods or services and by lending money.

sales discount (p. 290) Percentage reduction of sales price by the seller as an incentive for early payment before the due date. A typical way to express sales discount is "2/10, n/30." This means the seller will grant a 2% discount if the invoice is paid within 10 days, and the entire amount is due within 30 days.

sales return and allowance (p. 290) Merchandise returned for credit or refunds for services provided.

shipping terms (p. 289) Terms provided by the seller of merchandise that dictate the date on which title transfers to the buyer. A typical way to express shipping terms is through FOB terms. For example, "FOB destination" means title to the goods passes to the buyer when the goods are delivered and the buyer assumes control over them. "FOB shipping point" means title passes on the date the goods are shipped from the seller's warehouse.

short-term investments (p. 284) Investments that a company plans to hold for one year or less. Also called *marketable securities*.

term (p. 301) The length of time from inception to maturity.

trading securities (p. 285) Stock investments that are to be sold in the near future with the intent of generating profits on the sale.

uncollectible-account expense (p. 294) Cost to the seller of extending credit. Arises from the failure to collect from credit customers. Also called *doubtful-account expense* or *bad-debt expense*.

ASSESS YOUR PROGRESS

Short Exercises

S5-1 (*Learning Objective 1: Report trading investments*) Answer these questions about investments.

1. What is the amount to report on the balance sheet for a trading security?
2. Why is a trading security always a current asset? Explain.

S5-2 (*Learning Objective 1: Account for short-term investments*) Newfield Corp. holds a portfolio of trading securities. Suppose that on October 15, Newfield paid $85,000 for an investment in Turok shares to add to its portfolio. At December 31, the market value of Turok shares is $96,000. For this situation, show everything that Newfield would report on its December 31 balance sheet and on its income statement for the year ended December 31.

S5-3 (*Learning Objective 1: Account for short-term investments*) Siegal Investments purchased Demer shares as a trading security on December 16 for $109,000.

1. Suppose the Demer shares decreased in value to $100,000 at December 31. Make the Siegal journal entry to adjust the Short-Term Investment account to market value.
2. Show how Siegal would report the short-term investment on its balance sheet and the unrealized gain or loss on its income statement.

S5-4 (*Learning Objective 3: Apply internal controls to the collection of receivables*) Sharon Peel keeps the Accounts Receivable T-account of Ace & Pool, a partnership. What duty will a good internal control system withhold from Peel? Why?

S5-5 (*Learning Objective 2: Apply GAAP for proper revenue recognition*) On December 23, 2012, Big Sky Sports Manufacturing sells a truckload of sporting goods to the Sports R Us store in Amarillo, Texas. The terms of the sale are FOB destination. The truck runs into bad weather on the way to Amarillo and doesn't arrive until January 2, 2013. Big Sky Sports Manufacturing's invoice totals $126,000 including sales tax. The company's year-end is December 31. What should Big Sky Sports Manufacturing reflect in its 2012 income statement for this sale?

S5-6 (*Learning Objective 2: Apply GAAP for proper revenue recognition*) Refer to the facts in S5-5. The sales terms on the invoice are 2/10, net 30. What does this mean? What is Sports R Us' potential savings, if any? How much time does the company have to take advantage of these savings?

S5-7 (*Learning Objective 2: Apply GAAP for proper revenue recognition*) Refer to the facts in S5-5. Suppose that, when store personnel uncrate the shipment of merchandise, they find that a shipment of clothing worth $5,000 is defective. They notify Big Sky of the problem and return the shipment to the company. What entry will Big Sky make?

S5-8 (*Learning Objective 3: Apply internal controls to accounts receivable*) As a recent college graduate, you land your first job in the customer collections department of City Publishing. Zeke Pitt, the manager, asked you to propose a system to ensure that cash received from customers by mail is handled properly. Draft a short memorandum to explain the essential element in your proposed plan. State why this element is important.

S5-9 (*Learning Objective 4: Evaluate collectibility using the allowance for uncollectible accounts*) During its first year of operations, Chocolate Passion, Inc., had sales of $361,000, all on account. Industry experience suggests that Chocolate Passion's uncollectibles will amount to 2% of credit sales. At December 31, 2012, accounts receivable total $35,000. The company uses the allowance method to account for uncollectibles.

1. Make Chocolate Passion's journal entry for uncollectible-account expense using the percent-of-sales method.
2. Show how Chocolate Passion should report accounts receivable on its balance sheet at December 31, 2012.

S5-10 (*Learning Objectives 3, 4: Account for accounts receivable and uncollectible accounts*) During 2013, Chocolate Passion completed these transactions:

1. Sales revenue on account, $1,030,000
2. Collections on account, $895,000
3. Write-offs of uncollectibles, $15,000
4. Uncollectible-account expense, 2% of sales revenue

Journalize Chocolate Passion's 2013 transactions. Explanations are not required.

S5-11 (*Learning Objectives 3, 4: Account for account receivable and uncollectible accounts*) Use the information from the journal entries of Chocolate Passion, Inc., to answer the following questions:

Journal Entry			
	Accounts	Debit	Credit
1.	Accounts Receivable	1,030,000	
	Sales Revenue		1,030,000
2.	Cash	895,000	
	Accounts Receivable		895,000
3.	Allowance for Uncollectible Accounts	15,000	
	Accounts Receivable		15,000
4.	Uncollectible-Account Expense	20,600	
	Allowance for Uncollectible Accounts		20,600

▶ Requirements

1. Start with Accounts Receivable's beginning balance ($35,000), and then post to the Accounts Receivable T-account. How much do Chocolate Passion's customers owe the company at December 31, 2013?
2. Start with the Allowance account's beginning credit balance ($7,220), and then post to the Allowance for Uncollectible Accounts T-account. How much of the receivables at December 31, 2013, does Chocolate Passion expect *not* to collect?
3. At December 31, 2013, how much cash does Chocolate Passion expect to collect on its accounts receivable?

S5-12 (*Learning Objectives 3, 4: Account for accounts receivable and uncollectible accounts*) Gulig and Doherty, a law firm, started 2012 with accounts receivable of $26,000 and an allowance for uncollectible accounts of $2,000. The 2012 service revenues on account totaled $183,000, and cash collections on account totaled $133,000. During 2012, Gulig and Doherty wrote off uncollectible accounts receivable of $2,500. At December 31, 2012, the aging of accounts receivable indicated that Gulig and Doherty will not collect $1,790 of its accounts receivable.

Journalize Gulig and Doherty's (a) service revenue, (b) cash collections on account, (c) write-offs of uncollectible receivables, and (d) uncollectible-account expense for the year. Explanations are not required. Prepare a T-account for Allowance for Uncollectible Accounts to show your computation of uncollectible-account expense for the year.

S5-13 (*Learning Objectives 3, 4: Account for accounts receivable and uncollectible accounts*) Perform the following accounting for the receivables of Garvey and Pullman, a law firm, at December 31, 2012.

▶ Requirements

1. Start with the beginning balances for these T-accounts:
   ▶ Accounts Receivable, $101,000
   ▶ Allowance for Uncollectible Accounts, $9,000
   Post the following 2012 transactions to the T-accounts:
   a. Service revenue of $696,000, all on account
   b. Collections on account, $718,000
   c. Write-offs of uncollectible accounts, $13,000
   d. Uncollectible-account expense (allowance method), $11,000

2. What are the ending balances of Accounts Receivable and Allowance for Uncollectible Accounts?
3. Show how Garvey and Pullman will report accounts receivable on its balance sheet at December 31, 2012.

S5-14 (*Learning Objectives 2, 3, 4, 5, 6: Apply GAAP for revenue recognition; account for accounts receivable, uncollectible accounts, and notes receivable; show how to speed up cash flow from receivables*) Answer these questions about receivables and uncollectibles. For the true-false questions, explain any answers that turn out to be false.

1. True or false? Credit sales increase receivables. Collections and write-offs decrease receivables.
2. True or false? A proper way to express credit terms is "FOB shipping point."
3. Which receivables figure—the *total* amount that customers *owe* the company, or the *net* amount the company expects to collect—is more interesting to investors as they consider buying the company's stock? Give your reason.
4. Show how to determine net sales revenue.
5. Show how to determine net accounts receivable.
6. True or false? The direct write-off method of accounting for uncollectibles understates assets.
7. Carolina Bank lent $150,000 to Sumter Company on a six-month, 6% note. Which party has interest receivable? Which party has interest payable? Interest expense? Interest revenue? How much interest will these organizations record one month after Sumter Company signs the note?
8. When Carolina Bank accrues interest on the SumterCompany note, show the directional effects on the bank's assets, liabilities, and equity (increase, decrease, or no effect).
9. True or False? Credit card sales increase accounts receivable.
10. True or False? Companies with strong liquidity usually factor receivables.

S5-15 (*Learning Objective 5: Account for notes receivable*) Highland Bank & Trust Company lent $150,000 to Sherman Summers on a three-month, 8% note. Record the following for the bank (explanations are not required):

   a. Lending the money on February 10.
   b. Collecting the principal and interest at maturity. Specify the date.

S5-16 (*Learning Objective 5: Account for notes receivable*)

1. Compute the amount of interest during 2012, 2013, and 2014 for the following note receivable: On May 31, 2012, TMRN Bank lent $220,000 to Bob Morrison on a two-year, 8% note.
2. Which party has a (an)
   a. note receivable?
   b. note payable?
   c. interest revenue?
   d. interest expense?
3. How much in total would TMRN Bank collect if Bob Morrison paid off the note early—say, on November 30, 2012?

S5-17 (*Learning Objective 5: Account for notes receivable*) On August 31, 2012, Nancy Totten borrowed $5,000 from First Interstate Bank. Totten signed a note payable, promising to pay the bank principal plus interest on August 31, 2013. The interest rate on the note is 7%. The accounting year of First Interstate Bank ends on June 30, 2013. Journalize First Interstate Bank's (a) lending money on the note receivable at August 31, 2012, (b) accrual of interest at June 30, 2013, and (c) collection of principal and interest at August 31, 2013, the maturity date of the note.

S5-18 (*Learning Objective 5: Account for notes receivable*) Using your answers to Short Exercise 5-17, show how the First Interstate Bank will report the following:

a. Whatever needs to be reported on its classified balance sheet at June 30, 2013.
b. Whatever needs to be reported on its income statement for the year ended June 30, 2013.
c. Whatever needs to be reported on its classified balance sheet at June 30, 2014. Ignore Cash.
d. Whatever needs to be reported on its income statement for the year ended June 30, 2014.

S5-19 (*Learning Objective 7: Evaluate liquidity using the quick (acid-test) ratio and days' sales in receivables*) Lakeland Clothiers reported the following amounts in its 2013 financial statements. The 2012 amounts are given for comparison.

		2013		2012
Current assets:				
Cash..................................		$ 9,600		$ 9,600
Short-term investments................		14,500		10,500
Accounts receivable.....................	$82,000		$78,000	
Less: Allowance for				
uncollectibles......................	(7,200)	74,800	(6,200)	71,800
Inventory..................................		193,000		194,000
Prepaid insurance........................		2,100		2,100
Total current assets.....................		294,000		288,000
Total current liabilities..................		101,000		110,000
Net sales....................................		803,000		731,000

▶ Requirements

1. Compute Lakeland's quick (acid-test) ratio at the end of 2013. Round to two decimal places. How does the quick (acid-test) compare with the industry average of 0.95?
2. Compare days' sales in receivables for 2013 with the company's credit terms of net 30 days.

S5-20 (*Learning Objectives 3, 4, 7: Account for accounts receivable and uncollectible accounts; evaluate liquidity using ratios*) Farmore Medical Service reported the following items (amounts in thousands):

Unearned revenues (current)	$ 600	Service revenue	$23,650
Allowance for		Other assets	1,740
doubtful accounts	300	Property, plant, and equipment	25,350
Other expenses	12,560	Operating expense	11,650
Accounts receivable	4,460	Cash	290
Accounts payable	2,225	Notes payable (long term)	18,730

▶ Requirements

1. Classify each item as (a) income statement or balance sheet and as (b) debit balance or credit balance.
2. How much net income (or net loss) did Farmore report for the year?
3. Compute Farmore's quick (acid-test) ratio. Round to two decimal places. Evaluate Farmore Medical Service's liquidity position.

Exercises

All of A and B exercises can be found within MyAccountingLab, an online homework and practice environment. Your instructor may ask you to complete these exercises using MyAccountingLab.

Group A

E5-21A (*Learning Objective 1: Apply GAAP for short-term investments*) Eastern Corporation, the investment banking company, often has extra cash to invest. Suppose Eastern buys 1,000 shares of Dream, Inc., stock at $57 per share. Assume Eastern expects to hold the Dream stock for one month and then sell it. The purchase occurs on December 15, 2012. At December 31, the market price of a share of Dream stock is $58 per share.

▶ Requirements

1. What type of investment is this to Eastern? Give the reason for your answer.
2. Record Eastern's purchase of the Dream stock on December 15 and the adjustment to market value on December 31.
3. Show how Eastern would report this investment on its balance sheet at December 31 and any gain or loss on its income statement for the year ended December 31, 2012.

E5-22A (*Learning Objective 1: Apply GAAP for short-term investments*) Norton Corporation reports short-term investments on its balance sheet. Suppose a division of Norton completed the following short-term investment transactions during 2012:

2012	
Dec 12	Purchased 900 shares of Armor, Inc., stock for $38,700. Norton plans to sell the stock at a profit in the near future.
21	Received a cash dividend of $0.72 per share on the Armor, Inc., stock.
31	Adjusted the investment in Armor, Inc., stock. Current market value is $50,400. Norton still plans to sell the stock in early 2013.
2013	
Jan 16	Sold the Armor, Inc., stock for $54,300.

► Requirement

1. Prepare T-accounts for Cash, Short-Term Investment, Dividend Revenue, Unrealized Gain (Loss) on Investment, and Gain on Sale of Investment. Show the effects of Norton's investment transactions. Start with a cash balance of $98,000; all the other accounts start at zero.

E5-23A (*Learning Objectives 2, 3: Apply GAAP for sales, sales discount, and sales returns; account for accounts receivable*) Unique Interiors reported the following transactions in July:

Jul 2	Sold merchandise on account to Erin Bailey, $800, terms 2/10, n/30.
10	Sold merchandise on account to Alise O'Brien, $1,500, terms 2/10, n/30.
12	Collected payment from Erin Bailey for the Jul 2 sale.
15	Alise returned $500 of the merchandise purchased on Jul 10.
20	Collected payment from Alise O'Brien for the balance of the Jul 10 sale.

► Requirements

1. Record the foregoing transactions in the journal of Unique Interiors.
2. Prepare a computation of net sales for the month of July.

E5-24A (*Learning Objective 4: Apply GAAP for uncollectible receivables*) At December 31, 2012, Warm Weather Travel has an Accounts Receivable balance of $91,000. Allowance for Doubtful Accounts has a credit balance of $840 before the year-end adjustment. Service Revenue for 2012 was $600,000. Warm Weather estimates that doubtful-account expense for the year is 1% of sales. Make the year-end entry to record Doubtful-Account Expense. Show how Accounts Receivable and Allowance for Doubtful Accounts are reported on the balance sheet.

E5-25A (*Learning Objectives 2, 3, 4: Apply GAAP for revenue recognition, accounts receivable, and uncollectible receivables*) On November 30, High Peaks Party Planners had a $34,000 balance in Accounts Receivable and a $3,000 credit balance in Allowance for Uncollectible Accounts. During December, the store made credit sales of $159,000. December collections on account were $130,000, and write-offs of uncollectible receivables totaled $2,700. Uncollectible-accounts expense is estimated as 1% of revenue.

► Requirements

1. Journalize sales, collections, write-offs of uncollectibles, and uncollectible-accounts expense by the allowance method during December. Explanations are not required.
2. Show the ending balances in Accounts Receivable, Allowance for Uncollectible Accounts, and *Net* Accounts Receivable at December 31. How much does the store expect to collect?
3. Show how the store will report accounts receivable and net sales on its December 31 balance sheet and income statement.

E5-26A (*Learning Objective 4: Apply direct write-off method for uncollectible receivables*) Refer to Exercise 5-25A.

► Requirements

1. Record Uncollectible-Account Expense for December by the direct write-off method.
2. What amount of accounts receivable would High Peaks report on its December 31 balance sheet under the direct write-off method? Does it expect to collect the full amount?

E5-27A (*Learning Objective 4: Apply GAAP to uncollectible receivables*) At December 31, 2012, before any year-end adjustments, the Accounts Receivable balance of Stenner's Electronics is $180,000. The Allowance for Doubtful Accounts has an $11,600 credit balance. Stenner's Electronics prepares the following aging schedule for Accounts Receivable:

	Age of Accounts			
Total Balance	1–30 Days	31–60 Days	61–90 Days	Over 90 Days
$180,000	$70,000	$50,000	$40,000	$20,000
Estimated uncollectible	0.5%	2.0%	8.0%	50.0%

▶ Requirements

1. Based on the aging of Accounts Receivable, is the unadjusted balance of the allowance account adequate? Too high? Too low?
2. Make the entry required by the aging schedule. Prepare a T-account for the allowance.
3. Show how Stenner's Electronics will report Accounts Receivable on its December 31 balance sheet.

E5-28A (*Learning Objective 4: Applying GAAP for uncollectible accounts*) Assume Oak Leaf Foods, Inc., experienced the following revenue and accounts receivable write-offs:

Month	Service Revenue	Accounts Receivable Write-Offs in Month			
		March	April	May	Totals
March	$ 6,750	$51	$ 88		$139
April	6,950		104	$ 33	137
May	7,050			113	113
	$20,750	$51	$192	$146	$389

Suppose Oak Leaf estimates that 3% of revenues will become uncollectible.

▶ Requirement

1. Journalize service revenue (all on account), bad-debt expense, and write-offs during May. Include explanations.

E5-29A (*Learning Objective 5: Apply GAAP for notes receivable*) Record the following note receivable transactions in the journal of Arabian Realty. How much interest revenue did Arabian earn this year? **Use a 365-day year** for interest computations, and round interest amounts to the nearest dollar. Arabian Realty has an October 31 fiscal year-end.

Aug	1	Loaned $10,000 cash to Candace Smith on a one-year, 7% note.
Oct	6	Performed service for Putt Pro, receiving a 90-day, 6% note for $15,000.
	16	Received a $2,000, six-month, 11% note on account from Vernon, Inc.
	31	Accrued interest revenue for the year.

E5-30A *(Learning Objective 5: Apply GAAP for notes receivable)* Assume Queen City Credit Union completed these transactions:

2012		
May	1	Loaned $90,000 to Lois Frank on a one-year, 9% note.
Dec	31	Accrued interest revenue on the Frank note.
2013		
May	1	Collected the maturity value of the note from Frank (principal plus interest).

Show what the company would report for these transactions on its December 31, 2012, and 2013 balance sheets and income statements. Use a 12-month (rather than 365-day) year for interest computations.

E5-31A *(Learning Objectives 6, 7: Show how to speed up cash flow from receivables; evaluate liquidity through ratios)* Algonquin, Inc., reported the following items at December 31, 2012, and 2011:

Balance Sheets (Summarized)

	Year End 2012	Year End 2011		Year End 2012	Year End 2011
Current assets:			**Current liabilities:**		
Cash	$ 6,000	$ 12,000	Accounts payable	$ 15,000	$ 16,500
Marketable securities	22,000	11,000	Other current liabilities	107,000	109,000
Accounts receivable, net	56,000	70,000	Long-term liabilities	15,000	16,000
Inventory	193,000	189,000			
Other current assets	3,000	3,000	Stockholders' equity	143,000	143,500
Long-term assets					
Total assets	$280,000	$285,000	Total liabilities and equity	$280,000	$285,000

Income Statement (partial):	2012
Sales revenue	$728,000

▶ Requirements

1. Compute Algonquin's (a) quick (acid-test) ratio and (b) days' sales in average receivables for 2012. Evaluate each ratio value as strong or weak. Algonquin sells on terms of net 30 days.
2. Recommend two ways for Algonquin to speed up its cash flow from receivables.

E5-32A *(Learning Objectives 6, 7: Show how to speed up cash flow from receivables; evaluate liquidity through ratios)* Creative Co., Inc., the electronics and appliance chain, reported these figures in millions of dollars:

	2013	2012
Net sales	$570,000	$604,500
Receivables at end of year	3,810	4,310

▶ Requirements

1. Compute Creative's days' sales in receivables, or days' sales outstanding (DSO) during 2013.
2. Is Creative's DSO long or short? Nerad Networks takes 39 days to collect its average level of receivables. Fast Freight, the overnight shipper, takes 33 days. What causes Creative's collection period to be so different?

Group B

E5-33B (*Learning Objective 1: Apply GAAP for short-term investments*) Summer Corporation, the investment banking company, often has extra cash to invest. Suppose Summer buys 700 shares of Musica, Inc., stock at $59 per share. Assume Summer expects to hold the Musica stock for one month and then sell it. The purchase occurs on December 15, 2012. At December 31, the market price of a share of Musica stock is $62 per share.

▶ Requirements

1. What type of investment is this to Summer? Give the reason for your answer.
2. Record Summer's purchase of the Musica stock on December 15 and the adjustment to market value on December 31.
3. Show how Summer would report this investment on its balance sheet at December 31 and any gain or loss on its income statement for the year ended December 31, 2012.

E5-34B (*Learning Objective 1: Apply GAAP for short-term investments*). Southern Corporation reports short-term investments on its balance sheet. Suppose a division of Southern completed the following short-term investment transactions during 2012:

2012	
Dec 12	Purchased 700 shares of Trad, Inc., stock for $24,500. Southern plans to sell the stock at a profit in the near future.
21	Received a cash dividend of $0.98 per share on the Trad, Inc., stock.
31	Adjusted the investment in Trad, Inc., stock. Current market value is $26,600. Southern still plans to sell the stock in early 2013.
2013	
Jan 16	Sold the Trad, Inc., stock for $27,200.

▶ Requirement

1. Prepare T-accounts for Cash, Short-Term Investment, Dividend Revenue, Unrealized Gain (Loss) on Investment, and Gain on Sale of Investment. Show the effects of Southern's investment transactions. Start with a cash balance of $96,000; all the other accounts start at zero.

E5-35B (*Learning Objectives 2, 3: Apply GAAP for sales, sales discount, and sales returns; account for accounts receivable*) Drake Designs reported the following transactions in November:

Nov 8	Sold merchandise on account to Jennifer Grant, $500, terms 2/10, n/30.
15	Sold merchandise on account to Art Glass, $1,200, terms 2/10, n/30.
16	Art Glass returned $500 of the merchandise purchased on Nov 15.
18	Collected payment from Jennifer Grant for the Nov 8 sale.
25	Collected payment from Art Glass for the balance of the Nov 15 sale.

► Requirements

1. Record the foregoing transactions in the journal of Drake Designs.
2. Prepare a computation of net sales for the month of November.

E5-36B (*Learning Objective 4: Apply GAAP for uncollectible receivables*) At December 31, 2012, Get Away Travel has an Accounts Receivable balance of $89,000. Allowance for Doubtful Accounts has a credit balance of $810 before the year-end adjustment. Service Revenue for 2012 was $700,000. Get Away Travel estimates that Doubtful-Account Expense for the year is 2% of sales. Make the December 31 entry to record Doubtful-Account Expense. Show how the Accounts Receivable and the Allowance for Doubtful Accounts are reported on the balance sheet.

E5-37B (*Learning Objectives 2, 3, 4: Apply GAAP for revenue recognition, accounts receivable, and uncollectible receivables*) On September 30, Premier Party Planners had a $28,000 balance in Accounts Receivable and a $3,000 credit balance in Allowance for Uncollectible Accounts. During October, the store made credit sales of $163,000. October collections on account were $127,000, and write-offs of uncollectible receivables totaled $2,400. Uncollectible-account expense is estimated as 3% of revenue.

► Requirements

1. Journalize sales, collections, write-offs of uncollectibles, and uncollectible-account expense by the allowance method during October. Explanations are not required.
2. Show the ending balances in Accounts Receivable, Allowance for Uncollectible Accounts, and *Net* Accounts Receivable at October 31. How much does the store expect to collect?
3. Show how the store will report Accounts Receivable and net sales on its October 31 balance sheet and income statement.

E5-38B (*Learning Objective 4: Apply direct write-off method for uncollectible receivables*) Refer to Exercise 5-37B.

► Requirements

1. Record Uncollectible-Account Expense for October by the direct write-off method.
2. What amount of accounts receivable would Premier report on its October 31 balance sheet under the direct write-off method? Does it expect to collect the full amount?

E5-39B (*Learning Objective 4: Apply GAAP for uncollectible receivables*) At December 31, 2012, before any year-end adjustments, the Accounts Receivable balance of TM Manufacturing is $130,000. The Allowance for Doubtful Accounts has a $8,000 credit balance. TM Manufacturing prepares the following aging schedule for Accounts Receivable:

Total Balance	Age of Accounts			
	1–30 Days	31–60 Days	61–90 Days	Over 90 Days
$130,000	$50,000	$40,000	$30,000	$10,000
Estimated uncollectible	0.5%	5.0%	6.0%	60.0%

► Requirements

1. Based on the aging of Accounts Receivable, is the unadjusted balance of the Allowance account adequate? Too high? Too low?
2. Make the entry required by the aging schedule. Prepare a T-account for the allowance.
3. Show how TM Manufacturing will report Accounts Receivable on its December 31 balance sheet.

E5-40B (*Learning Objective 4: Apply GAAP for uncollectible receivables*) Assume Beech Tree Foods, Inc., experienced the following revenue and accounts receivable write-offs:

Month	Service Revenue	March	April	May	Totals
			Accounts Receivable Write-Offs in Month		
March	$ 6,800	$55	$ 84		$139
April	7,000		100	$ 31	131
May	7,100			111	111
	$20,900	$55	$184	$142	$381

Suppose Beech Tree estimates that 4% of revenues will become uncollectible.

▶ Requirement

1. Journalize service revenue (all on account), bad-debt expense, and write-offs during May. Include explanations.

E5-41B (*Learning Objective 5: Applying GAAP for notes receivable*) Record the following note receivable transactions in the journal of Coral Realty. How much interest revenue did Coral earn this year? **Use a 365-day year** for interest computations, and round interest amounts to the nearest dollar. Assume that Coral Realty has a July 31 fiscal year-end.

May	1	Loaned $19,000 cash to Carl Fajar on a one-year, 8% note.
Jul	6	Performed service for Fairway, receiving a 90-day, 10% note for $13,000.
	16	Received a $5,000, six-month, 13% note on account from Weston, Inc.
	31	Accrued interest revenue for the year.

E5-42B (*Learning Objective 5: Applying GAAP for notes receivable*) Assume Thrifty-One Credit Union completed these transactions:

2012		
Sep	1	Loaned $75,000 to Lily Heart on a one-year, 11% note.
Dec	31	Accrued interest revenue on the Heart note.
2013		
Sep	1	Collected the maturity value of the note from Heart (principal plus interest).

Show what the company would report for these transactions on its December 31, 2012, and 2013 balance sheets and income statements. Use a 12-month (rather than 365-day) year for interest computations.

E5-43B (*Learning Objectives 6, 7: Show how to speed up cash flow from receivables; evaluate liquidity through ratios*) Seminole, Inc., reported the following items at December 31, 2012, and 2011:

Balance Sheets (Summarized)

Current assets:	Year End 2012	Year End 2011	Current liabilities:	Year End 2012	Year End 2011
Cash	$ 2,000	$ 8,000	Accounts payable	$ 18,000	$ 19,500
Marketable securities	24,000	13,000	Other current liabilities	104,000	105,000
Accounts receivable, net	57,000	71,000	Long-term liabilities	14,000	16,000
Inventory	196,000	192,000			
Other current assets	5,000	5,000	Stockholders' equity	148,000	148,500
Long-term assets					
Total assets	$284,000	$289,000	Total liabilities and equity	$284,000	$289,000

Income Statement (partial):	2012				
Sales revenue	$731,000				

▶ Requirements

1. Compute Seminole's (a) quick (acid-test) ratio and (b) days' sales in average receivables for 2012. Evaluate each ratio value as strong or weak. Seminole sells on terms of net 30 days.
2. Recommend two ways for Seminole to improve its cash flow from receivables.

E5-44B (*Learning Objectives 6, 7: Show how to speed up cash flow from receivables; evaluate liquidity through ratios*) Unique Co., Inc., the electronics and appliance chain, reported these figures in millions of dollars:

	2013	2012
Net sales...	$570,500	$602,000
Receivables at end of year	3,870	4,210

▶ Requirements

1. Compute Unique's days' sales in receivables or days' sales outstanding (DSO) during 2013.
2. Is Unique's DSO long or short? Zion Networks takes 39 days to collect its average level of receivables. QuickShip, the overnight shipper, takes 33 days. What causes Unique's collection period to be so different?

Quiz

Test your understanding of receivables by answering the following questions. Select the best choice from among the possible answers given.

Q5-45 All America Bank, the nationwide banking company, owns many types of investments. Assume that All America Bank paid $650,000 for trading securities on December 5. Two weeks later, All America Bank received a $45,000 cash dividend. At December 31, these trading securities were quoted at a market price of $655,000. All America Bank's December income statement should report

a. unrealized loss of $5,000.

b. unrealized loss of $3,000.

c. unrealized gain of $50,000.

d. unrealized gain of $5,000.

Q5-46 Refer to the All America Bank data in Quiz question 5-45. At December 31, All America Bank's balance sheet should report

a. short-term investment of $655,000.

b. unrealized gain of $5,000.

c. short-term investment of $650,000.

d. dividend revenue of $45,000.

Q5-47 Under the allowance method for uncollectible receivables, the entry to record uncollectible-account expense has what effect on the financial statements?

a. Decreases owners' equity and increases liabilities

b. Decreases net income and decreases assets

c. Increases expenses and increases owners' equity

d. Decreases assets and has no effect on net income

Q5-48 Maverson Company uses the aging method to adjust the allowance for uncollectible accounts at the end of the period. At December 31, 2012, the balance of accounts receivable is $220,000, and the allowance for uncollectible accounts has a credit balance of $3,000 (before adjustment). An analysis of accounts receivable produced the following age groups:

Current	$170,000
60 days past due..........................	41,000
Over 60 days past due................	9,000
	$220,000

Based on past experience, Maverson estimates that the percentage of accounts that will prove to be uncollectible within the three age groups is 2%, 8%, and 20%, respectively. Based on these facts, the adjusting entry for uncollectible accounts should be made in the amount of

a. $12,480.

b. $5,480.

c. $11,480.

d. $8,480.

Q5-49 Refer to Question 5-48. The net receivables on the balance sheet is _____.

Q5-50 Linus Company uses the percent-of-sales method to estimate uncollectibles. Net credit sales for the current year amount to $100,000, and management estimates 2% will be uncollectible. Allowance for doubtful accounts prior to adjustment has a credit balance of $3,000. The amount of expense to report on the income statement will be

a. $5,000.

b. $1,500.

c. $6,000.

d. $2,000.

Q5-51 Refer to question 5-50. The balance of Allowance for Doubtful Accounts, after adjustment, will be

a. $5,000.

b. $2,000.

c. $1,000.

d. $1,500.

Q5-52 Refer to Quiz questions 5-50 and 5-51. The following year, Linus Company wrote off $2,000 of old receivables as uncollectible. What is the balance in the Allowance account now?

Questions 5-53 through 5-57 use the following data:

On August 1, 2012, Azores, Inc., sold equipment and accepted a six-month, 11%, $30,000 note receivable. Azores' year-end is December 31.

Q5-53 How much interest revenue should Azores accrue on December 31, 2012?

a. $1,650

b. $1,375

c. $3,300

d. $1,100

Q5-54 If Azores, Inc., fails to make an adjusting entry for the accrued interest,

a. net income will be understated and liabilities will be overstated.

b. net income will be understated and assets will be understated.

c. net income will be overstated and assets will be overstated.

d. net income will be overstated and liabilities will be understated.

Q5-55 How much interest does Azores, Inc., expect to collect on the maturity date (February 1, 2013)?

a. $1,650

b. $1,375

c. $3,300

d. $1,100

Q5-56 Which of the following accounts will Azores credit in the journal entry at maturity on February 1, 2013, assuming collection in full?

a. Interest Receivable

b. Interest Payable

c. Note Payable

d. Cash

Q5-57 Write the journal entry on the maturity date (February 1, 2013).

Q5-58 Which of the following is included in the calculation of the quick (acid-test) ratio?

a. Prepaid expenses and cash

b. Cash and accounts receivable

c. Inventory and short-term investments

d. Inventory and prepaid expenses

Q5-59 A company with net sales of $1,095,000, beginning net receivables of $90,000, and ending net receivables of $114,000 has days' sales in accounts receivable of

a. 34 days.

b. 37 days.

c. 31 days.

d. 40 days.

Q5-60 A company sells on credit terms of "2/10, n/30" and has days' sales in account receivable of 30 days. Its days' sales in receivables is

a. too low.

b. too high.

c. about right.

d. not able to be evaluated from the data given.

Problems

All of the A and B problems can be found within MyAccountingLab, an online homework and practice environment. Your instructor may ask you to complete these problems using MyAccountingLab.

MyAccountingLab

Group A

P5-61A (*Learning Objective 1: Apply GAAP to short-term investments*) During the fourth quarter of 2012, Spring, Inc., generated excess cash, which the company invested in trading securities as follows:

2012	
Nov 16	Purchased 1,300 common shares as an investment in trading securities, paying $8 per share.
Dec 16	Received cash dividend of $0.22 per share on the trading securities.
Dec 31	Adjusted the trading securities to fair value of $7 per share.

► Requirements

1. Open T-accounts for Cash (including its beginning balance of $19,000), Short-Term Investments, Dividend Revenue, and Unrealized Gain (Loss) on Investment.
2. Journalize the foregoing transactions and post to the T-accounts.
3. Show how to report the short-term investment on Spring's balance sheet at December 31.
4. Show how to report whatever should appear on Spring's income statement for the year ended December 31, 2012.
5. Spring sold the trading securities for $9,850 on January 14, 2013. Journalize the sale.

P5-62A *(Learning Objective 3: Apply controls to cash receipts from customers)* Lance Products, Inc., makes all sales on account. Selena Camp, accountant for the company, receives and opens incoming mail. Company procedure requires Camp to separate customer checks from the remittance slips, which list the amounts that Camp posts as credits to customer accounts receivable. Camp deposits the checks in the bank. At the end of each day, she computes the day's total amount posted to customer accounts and matches this total to the bank deposit slip. This procedure ensures that all receipts are deposited in the bank.

► Requirement

1. As a consultant hired by Lance Products, Inc., write a memo to management evaluating the company's internal controls over cash receipts from customers. If the system is effective, identify its strong features. If the system has flaws, propose a way to strengthen the controls.

P5-63A *(Learning Objectives 2, 3, 4: Apply GAAP for revenue, receivables, collections, and uncollectibles using the percent-of-sales method)* This problem takes you through the accounting for sales, receivables, and uncollectibles for Quick Mail Corp., the overnight shipper. By selling on credit, the company cannot expect to collect 100% of its accounts receivable. At July 31, 2012, and 2013, respectively, Quick Mail Corp. reported the following on its balance sheet (in millions of dollars):

| | May 31, | |
	2013	2012
Accounts receivable..	$3,690	$3,430
Less: Allowance for uncollectible accounts..............	(119)	(160)
Accounts receivable, net..	$3,571	$3,270

During the year ended July 31, 2013, Quick Mail Corp. earned service revenue and collected cash from customers. Assume uncollectible-account expense for the year was 4% of service revenue and that Quick Mail wrote off uncollectible receivables. At year-end, Quick Mail ended with the foregoing July 31, 2013, balances.

► Requirements

1. Prepare T-accounts for Accounts Receivable and Allowance for Uncollectible Accounts and insert the July 31, 2012, balances as given.
2. Journalize the following assumed transactions of Quick Mail Corp. for the year ended July 31, 2013 (explanations are not required):
   a. Service revenue on account, $32,480 million
   b. Collections from customers on account, $30,880 million
   c. Uncollectible-account expense, 4% of service revenue
   d. Write-offs of uncollectible accounts receivable, $1,340 million
3. Post your entries to the Accounts Receivable and the Allowance for Uncollectible Accounts T-accounts.
4. Compute the ending balances for Accounts Receivable and the Allowance for Uncollectible Accounts and compare your balances to the actual July 31, 2013, amounts. They should be the same.
5. Show what Quick Mail would report on its income statement for the year ended July 31, 2013.

P5-64A (*Learning Objective 4: Apply GAAP for uncollectible receivables*) The September 30, 2013, records of Up-To-Date Communications include these accounts:

Accounts Receivable.....................................	$243,000
Allowance for Doubtful Accounts..............	(8,100)

During the year, Up-To-Date Communications estimates doubtful-account expense at 1% of credit sales. At year-end (December 31), the company ages its receivables and adjusts the balance in Allowance for Doubtful Accounts to correspond to the aging schedule. During the last quarter of 2013, the company completed the following selected transactions:

Nov 30	Wrote off as uncollectible the $1,600 account receivable from Cheap Carpets and the $400 account receivable from Retired Antiques.
Dec 31	Adjusted the Allowance for Doubtful Accounts and recorded doubtful-account expense at year-end, based on the aging of receivables, which follows.

	Age of Accounts			
Accounts Receivable	1–30 Days	31–60 Days	61–90 Days	Over 90 Days
$231,000	$139,000	$53,000	$20,000	$19,000
Estimated percent uncollectible	0.2%	2%	15%	35%

▶ Requirements

1. Record the transactions in the journal. Explanations are not required.
2. Prepare a T-account for Allowance for Doubtful Accounts with the appropriate beginning balances. Post the entries from Requirement 1 to that account.
3. Show how Up-To-Date Communications will report its accounts receivable in a comparative balance sheet for 2012 and 2013. Use the three-line reporting format. At December 31, 2012, the company's Accounts Receivable balance was $211,000, and the Allowance for Doubtful Accounts stood at $4,700.

P5-65A (*Learning Objectives 1, 4, 7: Apply GAAP for short-term investments and uncollectible receivables; evaluate liquidity through ratios*) Assume Adams & Murray, the accounting firm, advises Pappadeaux Seafood that its financial statements must be changed to conform to GAAP. At December 31, 2012, Pappadeaux's accounts include the following:

Cash...	$ 59,000
Short-term investment in trading securities, at cost	27,000
Accounts receivable..	37,000
Inventory..	60,000
Prepaid expenses	17,000
Total current assets	$200,000
Accounts payable	$ 61,000
Other current liabilities	36,000
Total current liabilities..	$ 97,000

The accounting firm advised Pappadeaux of the following:

▶ Cash includes $18,000 that is deposited in a compensating balance account that is tied up until 2014.

▶ The market value of the trading securities is $13,000. Pappadeaux purchased the investments a couple of weeks ago.

▶ Pappadeaux has been using the direct write-off method to account for uncollectible receivables. During 2012, Pappadeaux wrote off bad receivables of $8,000. Adams & Murray determines that uncollectible-account expense should be 3% of service revenue, which totaled $590,000 in 2012. The aging of Pappadeaux's receivables at year-end indicated uncollectibles of $9,700.

▶ Pappadeaux reported net income of $90,000 in 2012.

▶ Requirements

1. Restate Pappadeaux's current accounts to conform to GAAP. (Challenge)
2. Compute Pappadeaux's current ratio and quick (acid-test) ratio both before and after your corrections.
3. Determine Pappadeaux's correct net income for 2012. (Challenge)

P5-66A *(Learning Objective 4: Apply GAAP for notes receivable)* Yummy Foods completed the following selected transactions.

2012	
Oct 31	Sold goods to Bob's Foods, receiving a $36,000, three-month, 6% note.
Dec 31	Made an adjusting entry to accrue interest on the Bob's Foods note.
2013	
Jan 31	Collected the Bob's Foods note.
Feb 18	Received a 90-day, 7.75%, $6,800 note from Dutton Market on account.
19	Sold the Dutton Market note to Chelmsford Bank, receiving cash of $6,600. (Debit the difference to financing expense.)
Nov 11	Lent $15,400 cash to Sauble Provisions, receiving a 90-day, 9.75% note.
Dec 31	Accrued the interest on the Sauble Provisions note.

▶ Requirements

1. Record the transactions in Yummy Foods' journal. Round interest amounts to the nearest dollar. Explanations are not required.
2. Show what Yummy Foods will report on its comparative classified balance sheet at December 31, 2013, and December 31, 2012.

P5-67A (*Learning Objectives 6, 7: Show how to speed up cash flow from receivables; evaluate liquidity using ratios*) The comparative financial statements of True Beauty Pools, Inc., for 2013, 2012, and 2011 included the following select data:

	(In millions)		
	2013	2012	2011
Balance sheet			
Current assets:			
Cash..	$ 80	$ 60	$ 40
Short-term investments	135	155	110
Receivables, net of allowance for doubtful accounts of $7, $6, and $4, respectively	270	260	230
Inventories	365	330	300
Prepaid expenses........................	70	15	55
Total current assets....................	$ 920	$ 820	$ 735
Total current liabilities...................	$ 590	$ 630	$ 690
Income statement			
Net sales	$5,850	$5,110	$4,210

▶ Requirements

1. Compute these ratios for 2013 and 2012:
   a. Current ratio
   b. Quick (acid-test) ratio
   c. Days' sales in receivables
2. Which ratios improved from 2012 to 2013 and which ratios deteriorated? Is this trend favorable or unfavorable?
3. Recommend two ways for True Beauty Pools to improve cash flows from receivables.

Group B

P5-68B (*Learning Objective 1: Apply GAAP for short-term investments*) During the fourth quarter of 2012, California, Inc., generated excess cash, which the company invested in trading securities, as follows:

2012	
Nov 17	Purchased 1,200 common shares as an investment in trading securities, paying $11 per share.
Dec 19	Received cash dividend of $0.46 per share on the trading securities.
Dec 31	Adjusted the trading securities to fair value of $9 per share.

▶ Requirements

1. Open T-accounts for Cash (including its beginning balance of $21,000), Short-Term Investment, Dividend Revenue, and Unrealized Gain (Loss) on Investment.
2. Journalize the foregoing transactions and post to the T-accounts.
3. Show how to report the short-term investment on California's balance sheet at December 31.
4. Show how to report whatever should appear on California's income statement for the year ended December 31, 2012.
5. California sold the trading securities for $11,928 on January 11, 2013. Journalize the sale.

P5-69B (*Learning Objective 3: Apply controls to cash receipts from customers*) Mini Computer Solutions makes all sales on account, so virtually all cash receipts arrive in the mail. Luke Hill, the company president, has just returned from a trade association meeting with new ideas for the business. Among other things, Hill plans to institute stronger internal controls over cash receipts from customers.

▶ Requirement

1. Take the role of Luke Hill, the company president. Write a memo to employees outlining procedures to ensure that all cash receipts are deposited in the bank and that the total amounts of each day's cash receipts are posted to customer accounts receivable.

P5-70B (*Learning Objectives 2, 3, 4: Apply GAAP for revenue, receivables, collections, and uncollectibles using the percent-of-sales method*) This problem takes you through the accounting for sales, receivables, and uncollectibles for Ship Fast Corp, the overnight shipper. By selling on credit, the company cannot expect to collect 100% of its accounts receivable. At July 31, 2012, and 2013, respectively, Ship Fast Corp. reported the following on its balance sheet (in millions of dollars):

| | July 31, | |
	2013	2012
Accounts receivable..	$3,695	$3,436
Less: Allowance for uncollectible accounts...............	(121)	(159)
Accounts receivable, net...	$3,574	$3,277

During the year ended July 31, 2013, Ship Fast Corp. earned sales revenue and collected cash from customers. Assume uncollectible-account expense for the year was 5% of service revenue, and Ship Fast wrote off uncollectible receivables. At year-end, Ship Fast ended with the foregoing July 31, 2013, balances.

▶ Requirements

1. Prepare T-accounts for Accounts Receivable and Allowance for Uncollectible Accounts, and insert the July 31, 2012, balances as given.
2. Journalize the following transactions of Ship Fast for the year ended July 31, 2013. (Explanations are not required.)
   a. Service revenue on account, $32,484 million
   b. Collections from customers on account, $30,563 million
   c. Uncollectible-account expense, 5% of service revenue
   d. Write-offs of uncollectible accounts receivable, $1,662 million
3. Post to the Accounts Receivable and Allowance for Uncollectible Accounts T-accounts.
4. Compute the ending balances for Accounts Receivable and Allowance for Uncollectible Accounts and compare your balances to the actual July 31, 2013, amounts. They should be the same.
5. Show what Ship Fast should report on its income statement for the year ended July 31, 2013.

P5-71B (*Learning Objective 4: Apply GAAP for uncollectible receivables*) The September 30, 2013, records of Media Communications include these accounts:

Accounts Receivable..................................	$242,000
Allowance for Doubtful Accounts..............	(8,300)

During the year, Media Communications estimates doubtful-account expense at 1% of credit sales. At year-end, the company ages its receivables and adjusts the balance in Allowance for Doubtful Accounts to correspond to the aging schedule. During the last quarter of 2013, the company completed the following selected transactions:

Nov 30	Wrote off as uncollectible the $1,500 account receivable from Brown Carpets and the $500 account receivable from Rare Antiques.
Dec 31	Adjusted the Allowance for Doubtful Accounts and recorded doubtful-account expense at year-end, based on the aging of receivables, which follows.

	Age of Accounts			
Accounts Receivable	1–30 Days	31–60 Days	61–90 Days	Over 90 Days
$230,000	$135,000	$40,000	$14,000	$41,000
Estimated percent uncollectible	0.3%	3%	12%	25%

▶ Requirements

1. Record the transactions in the journal. Explanations are not required.
2. Prepare a T-account for Allowance for Doubtful Accounts with the appropriate beginning balance. Post the entries from Requirement 1 to that account.
3. Show how Media Communications will report its accounts receivable in a comparative balance sheet for 2013 and 2012. Use the three-line reporting format. At December 31, 2012, the company's Accounts Receivable balance was $212,000, and the Allowance for Doubtful Accounts stood at $4,300.

P5-72B (*Learning Objectives 1, 4, 7: Apply GAAP for short-term investments and uncollectible receivables; evaluate liquidity through ratios*) Assume Cline & Nichols, the accounting firm, advises Derbyshire Seafood that its financial statement must be changed to conform to GAAP. At December 31, 2012, Derbyshire's accounts include the following:

Cash	$ 50,000
Short-term trading securities, at cost	20,000
Accounts receivable	41,000
Inventory	57,000
Prepaid expenses	16,000
Total current assets	$184,000
Accounts payable	$ 60,000
Other current liabilities	40,000
Total current liabilities	$100,000

The accounting firm advised Derbyshire of the following:

▶ Cash includes $19,000 that is deposited in a compensating balance account that will be tied up until 2014.
▶ The market value of the trading securities is $12,000. Derbyshire purchased the trading securities a couple of weeks ago.
▶ Derbyshire has been using the direct write-off method to account for uncollectible receivables. During 2012, Derbyshire wrote off bad receivables of $6,500. Cline & Nichols determines that uncollectible-account expense should be 3% of service revenue, which totaled $630,000 in 2012. The aging of Derbyshire's receivables at year-end indicated uncollectibles of $12,400.
▶ Derbyshire reported net income of $94,000 for 2012.

▶ Requirements

1. Restate Derbyshire's current accounts to conform to GAAP. (Challenge)
2. Compute Derbyshire's current ratio and quick (acid-test) ratio both before and after your corrections.
3. Determine Derbyshire's correct net income for 2012. (Challenge)

P5-73B (*Learning Objective 5: Apply GAAP for notes receivable*) Easy Nutrition completed the following selected transactions:

2012		
Oct 31	Sold goods to Basic Foods, receiving a $38,000, three-month, 5.00% note.	
Dec 31	Made an adjusting entry to accrue interest on the Basic Foods note.	
2013		
Jan 31	Collected the Basic Foods note.	
Feb 18	Received a 90-day, 8.50%, $7,400 note from Daphne's Market on account.	
19	Sold the Daphne's Market note to GlenCove Bank, receiving cash of $7,200. (Debit the difference to financing expense.)	
Nov 11	Lent $15,800 cash to Sincere Provisions, receiving a 90-day, 9.00% note.	
Dec 31	Accrued the interest on the Sincere Provisions note.	

▶ Requirements

1. Record the transactions in Easy Nutrition's journal. Round all amounts to the nearest dollar. Explanations are not required.
2. Show what Easy Nutrition will report on its comparative classified balance sheet at December 31, 2013, and December 31, 2012.

P5-74B (*Learning Objectives 6, 7: Show how to speed up cash flow from receivables; evaluate liquidity through ratios*) The comparative financial statements of Lakeland Pools, Inc., for 2013, 2012, and 2011 included the following select data:

	(In millions)		
	2013	**2012**	**2011**
Balance sheet			
Current assets:			
Cash..	$ 90	$ 70	$ 40
Short-term investments	130	165	105
Receivables, net of allowance for doubtful accounts of $7, $6, and $4, respectively	290	260	250
Inventories	365	325	315
Prepaid expenses	55	30	40
Total current assets	$ 930	$ 850	$ 750
Total current liabilities....................	$ 550	$ 610	$ 650
Income statement			
Net sales	$5,860	$5,120	$4,230

▶ Requirements

1. Compute these ratios for 2013 and 2012:
   a. Current ratio
   b. Quick (acid-test) ratio
   c. Days' sales in receivables
2. Which ratios improved from 2012 to 2013 and which ratios deteriorated? Is this trend favorable or unfavorable?
3. Recommend two ways for Lakeland Pools, Inc., to improve cash flow from receivables.

Challenge Exercises and Problem

E5-75 (*Learning Objective 6: Show how to speed up cash from receivables*) Retro Shirt Company sells on credit and manages its own receivables. Average experience for the past three years has been as follows:

	Cash	Credit	Total
Sales	$250,000	$250,000	$500,000
Cost of goods sold	125,000	125,000	250,000
Uncollectible-account expense	—	12,000	12,000
Other expenses	82,500	82,500	165,000

Jed Rivers, the owner, is considering whether to accept bankcards (VISA, MasterCard). Rivers expects total sales to increase by 10% but cash sales to remain unchanged. If Rivers switches to bankcards, the business can save $8,000 on other expenses, but VISA and MasterCard charge 3% on bankcard sales. Rivers figures that the increase in sales will be due to the increased volume of bankcard sales.

▶ Requirement

1. Should Retro Shirt Company start selling on bankcards? Show the computations of net income under the present plan and under the bankcard plan.

E5-76 (*Learning Objectives 3, 4: Apply GAAP for receivables and uncollectible receivables*) Suppose Overpriced, Inc., reported net receivables of $2,582 million and $2,269 million at January 31, 2013, and 2012, after subtracting allowances of $71 million and $67 million at these respective dates. Overpriced earned total revenue of $26,667 million (all on account) and recorded doubtful-account expense of $8 million for the year ended January 31, 2013.

▶ Requirement

1. Use this information to measure the following amounts for the year ended January 31, 2013:
   a. Write-offs of uncollectible receivables
   b. Collections from customers

P5-77 (*Learning Objectives 2, 3, 4: Analyze accounts receivable*) The balance sheet of Gemini, Inc., a world leader in the design and sale of telescopic equipment, reported the following information on its balance sheets for 2012 and 2011 (figures are in thousands):

(In thousands)	December 31, 2012	December 31, 2011
Accounts receivable (net of allowance of $1,000 and $930)	$8,300	$8,500

In 2012, Gemini recorded $16,500 in sales (all on account), of which $900 was returned for credit. Gemini offers its customers credit terms of 2/10, n/30. Seventy-five percent of collections on accounts receivable were made within the discount period. Gemini wrote off uncollectible accounts receivable in the amount of $130 during 2012.

▶ Requirements

1. Compute the amount of uncollectible accounts expense recorded by Gemini in 2012.
2. Compute Gemini's cash collections from customers in 2012.
3. Open T-accounts for Accounts Receivable and Allowance for Uncollectible Accounts. Enter the beginning balances into each of these accounts. Prepare summary journal entries in the T-accounts to record the following for 2012:
   a. Sales
   b. Collections
   c. Sales returns
   d. Write-offs of uncollectible accounts
   e. Uncollectible-Accounts Expense

APPLY YOUR KNOWLEDGE

Decision Cases

Case 1. (*Learning Objectives 2, 3, 4: Apply GAAP for revenue, accounts receivable, and uncollectible receivables*) A fire during 2012 destroyed most of the accounting records of Clearview Cablevision, Inc. The only accounting data for 2012 that Clearview can come up with are the following balances at December 31, 2012. The general manager also knows that bad-debt expense should be 5% of service revenue.

Accounts receivable	$180,000
Less: Allowance for bad debts.................................	(22,000)
Total expenses, excluding bad-debt expense............	670,000
Collections from customers......................................	840,000
Write-offs of bad receivables...................................	30,000
Accounts receivable, December 31, 2011	110,000

Prepare a summary income statement for Clearview Cablevision, Inc., for the year ended December 31, 2012. The stockholders want to know whether the company was profitable in 2012. Use a T-account for Accounts Receivable to compute service revenue.

Case 2. (*Learning Objectives 4, 7: Apply GAAP for uncollectible receivables; evaluate liquidity through ratios*) Suppose you work in the loan department of Superior Bank. Dean Young, owner of Dean Young Beauty Aids, has come to you seeking a loan for $500,000 to expand operations. Young proposes to use accounts receivable as collateral for the loan and has provided you with the following information from the company's most recent financial statements:

	2013	2012	2011
	(In thousands)		
Sales..	$1,475	$1,001	$902
Cost of goods sold.............................	876	647	605
Gross profit..	599	354	297
Other expenses..................................	518	287	253
Net profit or (loss) before taxes.........	$ 81	$ 67	$ 44
Accounts receivable...........................	$ 128	$ 107	$ 94
Allowance for doubtful accounts.......	13	11	9

► Requirement

1. Analyze the trends of sales, days' sales in receivables, and cash collections from customers for 2013 and 2012. Would you make the loan to Young? Support your decision with facts and figures.

Ethical Issue

Sunnyvale Loan Company is in the consumer loan business. Sunnyvale borrows from banks and loans out the money at higher interest rates. Sunnyvale's bank requires Sunnyvale to submit quarterly financial statements to keep its line of credit. Sunnyvale's main asset is Notes Receivable. Therefore, Uncollectible-Account Expense and Allowance for Uncollectible Accounts are important accounts for the company.

Kimberly Burnham, the company's owner, prefers that net income reflect a steady increase in a smooth pattern, rather than an increase in some periods and a decrease in other periods. To report smoothly increasing net income, Burnham underestimates Uncollectible-Account Expense in some periods. In other periods, Burnham overestimates the expense. She reasons that the income overstatements roughly offset the income understatements over time.

▶ Requirements

1. What is the ethical issue in this situation?
2. Who are the stakeholders? What are the possible consequences to each?
3. Analyze the alternatives from the following standpoints: (a) economic, (b) legal, (c) ethical.
4. What would you do? How would you justify your decision?

Focus on Financials: | Amazon.com, Inc.

(*Learning Objectives 1, 2: Account for short-term investments; Apply GAAP for proper revenue recognition*). Refer to **Amazon.com, Inc.'s** Consolidated financial statements in Appendix A at the end of this book.

1. Examine the account "marketable securities" in the consolidated balance sheet.
   a. What does this account consist of?
   b. Why do you think the company has made these investments?
   c. What percentage change has occurred in short-term investments from December 31, 2009, to December 31, 2010? What management business strategy might this reveal?
   d. Using the financial statement footnotes for reference, explain how Amazon.com, Inc., accounts for marketable securities. What footnote contains this information?
   e. Has the company profited from holding its portfolio of marketable securities during the year ended December 31, 2010? How do you know?
2. Using the "Description of Business" section of Note 1 as a reference, describe how Amazon.com, Inc., recognizes revenue.
3. The fourth account listed on Amazon.com's Consolidated Balance Sheet is called "accounts receivable, net and other." What does the "net" mean? The "other"?
4. Refer to Note 1. What kinds of accounts receivable are included in Amazon.com, Inc.'s receivables?
5. How much is the allowance for doubtful accounts in 2010 and 2009?
6. Evaluate Amazon.com, Inc.'s liquidity as of December 31, 2010, and compare it with 2009. What other information might be helpful in evaluating these statistics?

Focus on Analysis: | RadioShack Corporation

(*Learning Objectives 2, 3: Apply GAAP for revenue recognition; account for and control accounts receivable*) This case is based on **RadioShack Corporation's** consolidated balance sheets, consolidated statements of income, and Note 2 of its financial statements (Significant Accounting Policies) in Appendix B at the end of this book.

1. Describe RadioShack Corporation's revenue recognition policy. From what sources do they earn most of their revenue?
2. Since RadioShack is a consumer retail business, most of its retail sales are cash sales. However, accounts receivable still comprise about 21% ($377/$1,779) of its current assets. What customers do business with RadioShack on account? Why is this necessary? What is the average payment term for these receivables?
3. Compute the following for 2010:
   a. Average daily sales.
   b. Days' sales to collection for accounts receivable.
   c. Compare 3(b) with the average payment term for accounts receivable. Did the company perform better or worse than its normal payment terms for its credit customers?
4. Evaluate RadioShack Corporation's liquidity as of December 31, 2010, and compare it with 2009. What other information might be helpful in evaluating these statistics?

Group Project

Jillian Michaels and Dee Childress worked for several years as sales representatives for Xerox Corporation. During this time, they became close friends as they acquired expertise with the company's full range of copier equipment. Now they see an opportunity to put their expertise to work and fulfill lifelong desires to establish their own business. Navarro Community College, located in their city, is expanding, and there is no copy center within five miles of the campus. Business in the area is booming, office buildings and apartments are springing up, and the population of the Navarro section of the city is growing.

Michaels and Childress want to open a copy center, similar to FedEx Kinko's, near the Navarro campus. A small shopping center across the street from the college has a vacancy that would fit their needs. Michaels and Childress each have $35,000 to invest in the business, but they forecast the need for $200,000 to renovate the store and purchase some of the equipment they will need. Xerox Corporation will lease two large copiers to them at a total monthly rental of $6,000. With enough cash to see them through the first six months of operation, they are confident they can make the business succeed. The two women work very well together, and both have excellent credit ratings. Michaels and Childress must borrow $130,000 to start the business, advertise its opening, and keep it running for its first six months.

▶ Requirements

Assume two roles: (1) Michaels and Childress, the partners who will own Navarro Copy Center; and (2) loan officers at Synergy Bank.

1. As a group, visit a copy center to familiarize yourselves with its operations. If possible, interview the manager or another employee. Then write a loan request that Michaels and Childress will submit to Synergy Bank with the intent of borrowing $130,000 to be paid back over three years. The loan will be a personal loan to the partnership of Michaels and Childress, not to Navarro Copy Center. The request should specify all the details of Michaels' and Childress' plan that will motivate the bank to grant the loan. Include a budget for each of the first six months of operation of the proposed copy center.
2. As a group, interview a loan officer in a bank. Write Synergy Bank's reply to the loan request. Specify all the details that the bank should require as conditions for making the loan.
3. If necessary, modify the loan request or the bank's reply in order to reach agreement between the two parties.

MyAccountingLab

> For online homework, exercises, and problems that provide you with immediate feedback, please visit **www.myaccountinglab.com**.

Quick Check Answers

1. c
2. c
3. b ($47,000 × .02)
4. d ($750 + $940)
5. a ($1,140 − $750)
6. d
7. d ($13,000 − $1,140)
8. c ($2,900 − $70) − ($100 − $70)

9. a ($450,000 + $1,600,000 − $525,000)
10. c ($6,000 × .07 × 4/12 × 1/4)
11. a ($40,000 + ($40,000 × .10 × 6/12)
12. b
13. b [($38,000 + $46,000)/2] ÷ ($547,500/365)
14. d ($3,000 + $10,000 + $7,000) ÷ ($9,000 + $3,000)

© Getty Images

6 Inventory & Cost of Goods Sold

SPOTLIGHT: Williams-Sonoma, Inc.

You've just graduated from college, taken a job, and you're moving into an apartment. The place is unfurnished, so you'll need everything: furniture, rugs, dishes, pots, pans, and everything that goes with them. Where will you find these things? Williams-Sonoma, Inc., stores, its subsidiaries (Pottery Barn, Pottery Barn Bed and Bath, and West Elm), and its e-commerce Web sites may get some of your business.

Williams-Sonoma, Inc., is a specialty retailer of high-style products for the home. As of its 2010 fiscal year (January 31, 2011), the company operated 592 stores in 44 states, Washington, D.C., and Canada.

Williams-Sonoma, Inc.'s Consolidated Balance Sheets for fiscal 2010 and 2009 are summarized on the following page. You can see that as of January 31, 2011, merchandise inventory is Williams-Sonoma's second-largest current asset (cash is the largest). That's not surprising since Williams-Sonoma, like other retailers, attracts customers with the latest styles in home furnishings that they can purchase and take home immediately. A closer look at the company's balance sheet shows that the company increased its merchandise inventory levels by about $47 million between fiscal 2009 and 2010. Why would it do that? As of the end of fiscal 2009, the specialty retail industry had just weathered its worst economic recession in 70 years. One way that companies like Williams-Sonoma conserve cash during hard economic times is to cut their investments in inventories, especially those products that don't sell fast. When the economy began to recover in 2010, the company started increasing inventory levels in anticipation of increased sales volume.

We also present Williams-Sonoma's Consolidated Statements of Earnings for the comparative fiscal years 2010 and 2009. A few quick computations will show that during fiscal 2010 net revenues increased by $401 million compared with fiscal 2009. The corresponding increase in cost of goods sold (related to inventories, as we will see later) was $131 million. The company also incurred an additional $68 million in selling, general, and administrative expenses. As a result, the company's pre-tax earnings increased by about $203 million. In short, as revenues increased, the company was able to hold the line on costs, resulting in even more bottom line profits. ●

Williams-Sonoma, Inc.
Consolidated Balance Sheets (Adapted)
Fiscal years 2010 and 2009

(In thousands)	2010	2009
ASSETS		
Current assets		
Cash and cash equivalents	$ 640,915	$ 513,943
Accounts receivable, net	41,565	44,187
Merchandise inventories, net	513,381	466,124
Prepaid expenses	57,945	54,886
Other current assets	93,788	101,053
Total current assets	1,347,594	1,180,193
Property and equipment, net	730,556	829,027
Other non-current assets	53,612	69,949
Total assets	$2,131,762	$2,079,169
LIABILITIES AND STOCKHOLDERS' EQUITY		
Current liabilities	$ 611,716	$ 563,482
Long-term liabilities	261,183	304,092
Total liabilities	872,899	867,574
Stockholders' equity	1,258,863	1,211,595
Total liabilities and stockholders' equity	$2,131,762	$2,079,169

Williams-Sonoma, Inc.
Consolidated Statements of Earnings (Adapted)
Fiscal years 2010 and 2009

(In thousands)	2010	2009
Net revenues	$3,504,158	$3,102,704
Cost of goods sold	2,130,299	1,999,467
Gross margin (gross profit)	1,373,859	1,103,237
Selling, general, and administrative expenses	1,050,445	981,795
Interest expense, net	(354)	(1,153)
Earnings before income taxes	323,060	120,289
Income taxes	122,833	42,847
Net earnings	$ 200,227	$ 77,442

You can see that cost of goods sold is by far Williams-Sonoma's largest expense. The title *Cost of Goods Sold* perfectly describes that expense. In short,

▶ Williams-Sonoma buys inventory, an asset carried on the books at cost.

▶ the goods that Williams-Sonoma sells are no longer Williams-Sonoma's assets. The cost of inventory that's sold gets shifted into the expense account Cost of Goods Sold.

Merchandise inventory is the heart of a merchandising business, and cost of goods sold is the most important expense for a company that sells goods rather than services. Gross profit (or gross margin) is the difference between net sales and cost of goods sold. **This chapter covers the accounting for inventory and cost of goods sold.** It also shows you how to analyze financial statements. Here we focus on inventory, cost of goods sold, and gross profit.

1 ***Show*** how to account for inventory

2 ***Apply and compare*** various inventory cost methods

3 ***Explain and apply*** underlying GAAP for inventory

4 ***Compute and evaluate*** gross profit (margin) and inventory turnover

5 ***Use*** the cost-of-goods-sold (COGS) model to make management decisions

6 ***Analyze*** effects of inventory errors

Learning Objectives

Show How to Account for Inventory

We begin by showing how the financial statements of a merchandiser such as Williams-Sonoma, Inc., or The Gap, Inc., differ from those of service entities such as FedEx and Century 21 Real Estate. The financial statements in Exhibit 6-1 (p. 340) highlight how service entities differ from merchandisers (dollar amounts are assumed).

1

Show how to account for inventory

The basic concept of accounting for merchandise inventory can be illustrated with an example. Suppose Pottery Barn (a subsidiary company of Williams-Sonoma, Inc.) has in stock three chairs that cost $300 each. Pottery Barn marks the chairs up by $200 and sells two of the chairs for $500 each.

▶ Pottery Barn's balance sheet reports the one chair that the company still holds in inventory.

▶ The income statement reports the cost of the two chairs sold, as shown in Exhibit 6-2 (p. 340).

Here is the basic concept of how we identify **inventory**, the asset, from **cost of goods sold**, the expense.

The cost of the inventory sold shifts from asset to expense when the seller delivers the goods to the buyer.

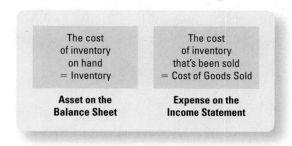

The cost of inventory on hand = Inventory	The cost of inventory that's been sold = Cost of Goods Sold
Asset on the Balance Sheet	**Expense on the Income Statement**

EXHIBIT 6-1 | Contrasting a Service Company with a Merchandising Company

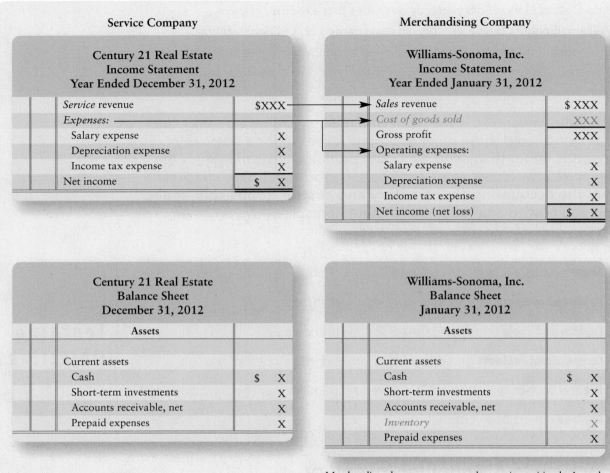

Merchandisers have two accounts that service entities don't need:
- Cost of goods sold on the income statement
- Inventory on the balance sheet

EXHIBIT 6-2 | Inventory and Cost of Goods Sold When Inventory Cost is Constant

Balance Sheet (partial)		Income Statement (partial)	
Current assets		Sales revenue	
Cash......................................	$XXX	(2 chairs @ sale price of $500 each)	$1,000
Short-term investments	XXX	Cost of goods sold	
Accounts receivable..............................	XXX	(2 chairs @ cost of $300 each)...............	600
Inventory (1 chair @ cost of $300)	300	Gross profit..	$ 400
Prepaid expenses	XXX		

Sale Price vs. Cost of Inventory

Note the difference between the sale price of inventory and the cost of inventory. In our example,

► Sales revenue is based on the *sale price* of the inventory sold ($500 per chair).
► Cost of goods sold is based on the *cost* of the inventory sold ($300 per chair).
► Inventory on the balance sheet is based on the *cost* of the inventory still on hand ($300 per chair).

Exhibit 6-2 shows these items.

Gross profit, also called **gross margin**, is the excess of sales revenue over cost of goods sold. It is called *gross* profit because operating expenses have not yet been subtracted. Exhibit 6-3 shows actual inventory and cost of goods sold data adapted from the financial statements of Williams-Sonoma.

EXHIBIT 6-3 | Williams-Sonoma, Inc., Inventory and Cost of Goods Sold

Williams-Sonoma, Inc.
Consolidated Balance Sheet (Adapted)
January 31, 2011

Assets (In millions)	
Current assets	
Cash and cash equivalents	$641
Accounts receivable, net	42
Merchandise inventories, net	513

Williams-Sonoma, Inc.
Consolidated Statement of Income (Adapted)
Year Ended January 31, 2011

(In millions)	
Net revenues	$3,504
Cost of goods sold	2,130
Gross margin (gross profit)	$1,374

Williams-Sonoma, Inc.'s inventory of $513 million represents

$$\begin{array}{c} \text{Inventory} \\ \text{(balance sheet)} \end{array} = \begin{array}{c} \text{Number of units of} \\ \text{inventory } on \text{ } hand \end{array} \times \begin{array}{c} \text{Cost per unit} \\ \text{of inventory} \end{array}$$

Williams-Sonoma's cost of goods sold ($2,130 million) represents

$$\begin{array}{c} \text{Cost of goods sold} \\ \text{(income statement)} \end{array} = \begin{array}{c} \text{Number of units of} \\ \text{inventory } sold \end{array} \times \begin{array}{c} \text{Cost per unit} \\ \text{of inventory} \end{array}$$

Let's see what "units of inventory" and "cost per unit" mean.

Number of Units of Inventory. The number of inventory units on hand is determined from the accounting records, backed up by a physical count of the goods at year-end. Companies do not include in their inventory any goods they hold on **consignment** because those goods belong to another company. But they do include their own inventory that is out on consignment and held for sale by another company. As discussed in Chapter 5, companies include inventory in transit from suppliers or in transit to customers that, according to shipping terms, legally belong to them as of the year-end. Shipping terms, otherwise known as *FOB (free on board) terms*, indicate who owns the goods at a particular time and, therefore, who must pay for the shipping costs. When the vendor invoice specifies *FOB shipping point* (the most common business practice), legal title to the goods passes from the seller to the purchaser when the inventory leaves the seller's place of business. The purchaser therefore owns the goods while they are in transit and must pay the transportation costs. In the case of goods purchased FOB shipping point, the company purchasing the goods must include goods in transit from suppliers as units in inventory as of the year-end. In the case of goods purchased *FOB destination*, title to the goods does not pass from the seller to the purchaser until the goods arrive at the purchaser's receiving dock. Therefore, these goods are not counted in year-end inventory of the purchasing company. Rather, the cost of these goods is included in inventory of the seller until the goods reach their destination.

Cost Per Unit of Inventory. The cost per unit of inventory poses a challenge because companies purchase goods at different prices throughout the year. Which unit costs go into ending inventory? Which unit costs go to cost of goods sold?

The next section shows how different accounting methods determine amounts on the balance sheet and the income statement. First, however, you need to understand how inventory accounting systems work.

Accounting for Inventory in the Perpetual System

There are two main types of inventory accounting systems: the periodic system and the perpetual system. The **periodic inventory system**, discussed in more detail in Appendix 6A, is used for inexpensive goods. A fabric store or a lumber yard won't keep a running record of every bolt of fabric or every two-by-four. Instead, these stores count their inventory periodically—at least once a year—to determine the quantities on hand. Businesses such as restaurants and hometown nurseries also use the periodic system because the accounting cost of a periodic system is low.

A **perpetual inventory system** uses computer software to keep a running record of inventory on hand. This system achieves control over goods such as Pottery Barn furniture, automobiles, jewelry, apparel, and most other types of inventory. Most businesses use the perpetual inventory system.

Even with a perpetual system, the business still counts the inventory on hand annually. The physical count establishes the correct amount of ending inventory for the financial statements and also serves as a check on the perpetual records. Here is a quick summary of the two main inventory accounting systems.

Perpetual Inventory System	Periodic Inventory System
• Used for all types of goods	• Used for inexpensive goods
• Keeps a running record of all goods bought, sold, and on hand	• Does *not* keep a running record of all goods bought, sold, and on hand
• Inventory counted at least once a year	• Inventory counted at least once a year

How the Perpetual System Works. Let's use an everyday situation to show how a perpetual inventory system works. When you check out of a Wal-Mart, a RadioShack, or a Pottery Barn store, the clerk scans the bar codes on the labels of the items you buy. Exhibit 6-4 illustrates

EXHIBIT 6-4 | Bar Code for Electronic Scanner

0 7 2 5 1 2 0 6 5 8 1 5

a typical bar code. Suppose you are buying a desk lamp from Pottery Barn. The bar code on the product label holds lots of information. The optical scanner reads the bar code, and the computer records the sale and updates the inventory records.

Recording Transactions in the Perpetual System.
All accounting systems record each purchase of inventory. When Pottery Barn makes a sale, two entries are needed in the perpetual system:

▸ The company records the sale—debits Cash or Accounts Receivable and credits Sales Revenue for the sale price of the goods.

▸ Pottery Barn also debits Cost of Goods Sold and credits Inventory for the cost of the inventory sold.

Exhibit 6-5 shows the accounting for inventory in a perpetual system. Panel A gives the journal entries and the T-accounts, and Panel B shows the income statement and the balance sheet. All amounts are assumed. (Appendix 6A illustrates the accounting for these same transactions for a periodic inventory system.)

EXHIBIT 6-5 | Recording and Reporting Inventory—Perpetual System (Amounts Assumed)

PANEL A—Recording Transactions and the T-accounts (All amounts are assumed)

Journal Entry

1.	Inventory	560,000	
	Accounts Payable		560,000
	Purchased inventory on account.		
2.	Accounts Receivable	900,000	
	Sales Revenue		900,000
	Sold inventory on account.		
	Cost of Goods Sold	540,000	
	Inventory		540,000
	Recorded cost of goods sold.		

Inventory

Beginning balance	100,000*		
Purchases	560,000	Cost of goods sold	540,000
Ending balance	120,000		

*Beginning inventory was $100,000

Cost of Goods Sold

Cost of goods sold	540,000

PANEL B—Reporting in the Financial Statements

Income Statement (partial)

Sales revenue	$900,000
Cost of goods sold	540,000
Gross profit	$360,000

Ending Balance Sheet (partial)

Current assets:	
Cash	$ XXX
Short-term investments	XXX
Accounts receivable	XXX
Inventory	120,000
Prepaid expenses	XXX

In Exhibit 6-5, the first entry to Inventory summarizes a lot of detail. The cost of the inventory, $560,000, is the *net* amount of the purchases, determined as follows (using assumed amounts):

Purchase price of the inventory	$600,000
+ **Freight in** (the cost to transport the goods from the seller to the buyer)	4,000
− **Purchase returns** for unsuitable goods returned to the seller	(25,000)
− **Purchase allowances** granted by the seller	(5,000)
− **Purchase discounts** for early payment by the buyer	(14,000)
= Net purchases of inventory—Cost to the buyer	$560,000

Freight in is the transportation cost, paid by the buyer, under terms FOB shipping point, to move goods from the seller to the buyer. Freight in is accounted for as part of the cost of inventory. A **purchase return** is a decrease in the cost of inventory because the buyer returned the goods to the seller (vendor). A **purchase allowance** also decreases the cost of inventory because the buyer got an allowance (a deduction) from the amount owed. These terms are the "flip side" of the seller's *sales return* and *sales allowance* discussed in Chapter 5. To document approval of purchase returns, management issues a **debit memorandum**, meaning that accounts payable are reduced (debited) for the amount of the return. The offsetting credit is to inventory as the goods are shipped back to the seller (vendor). Purchase discounts and allowances are usually documented on the final invoice received from the vendor. Throughout this book, we often refer to net purchases simply as Purchases.

A **purchase discount** (the "flip side" of a *sales discount* discussed in Chapter 5) is a decrease in the buyer's cost of inventory earned by paying quickly. Many companies offer payment terms of "2/10 n/30." This means the buyer can take, and the seller grants, a 2% discount for payment within 10 days, with the final amount due within 30 days. Another common credit term is "net 30," which tells the customer to pay the full amount within 30 days. In summary,

Net purchases = Purchases
− Purchase returns and allowances
− Purchase discounts
+ Freight in

Net sales for the seller are computed exactly the same as net purchases, but with no freight in, as follows:

Net sales = Sales revenue
− Sales returns and allowances
− Sales discounts

Freight out paid by the *seller*, under shipping terms FOB destination, is not part of the cost of inventory. Instead, freight out is delivery expense. It's the seller's expense of delivering merchandise to customers.

Apply and Compare Various Inventory Cost Methods

Inventory is the first asset for which a manager can decide which accounting method to use. The accounting method selected affects the profits to be reported, the amount of income tax to be paid, and the values of the ratios derived from the financial statements.

Apply and compare various inventory cost methods

What Goes into Inventory Cost?

The cost of inventory on Williams-Sonoma, Inc's balance sheet represents all the costs that the company incurred to bring its inventory to the point of sale. The following cost principle applies to all assets:

> **The cost of any asset, such as inventory, is the sum of all the costs incurred to bring the asset to its intended use, less any discounts.**

As we have seen, inventory's cost includes its basic purchase price, plus freight in, insurance while in transit, and any fees or taxes paid to get the inventory ready to sell, less returns, allowances, and discounts.

After a Pottery Barn chair is sitting in the showroom, other costs, such as advertising and sales commissions, are *not* included as the cost of inventory. Advertising, sales commissions, and delivery costs are selling expenses that go in the income statement, rather than in the balance sheet.

Apply the Various Inventory Costing Methods

Determining the cost of inventory is easy when the unit cost remains constant, as in Exhibit 6-2. But the unit cost usually changes. For example, prices often rise. The desk lamp that cost Pottery Barn $10 in January may cost $14 in June and $18 in October. Suppose Pottery Barn sells 1,000 lamps in November. How many of those lamps cost $10, how many cost $14, and how many cost $18?

To compute cost of goods sold and the cost of ending inventory still on hand, we must assign unit cost to the items. Accounting uses four generally accepted inventory methods:

1. **Specific unit cost**

2. **Average cost**

3. **First-in, first-out (FIFO) cost**

4. **Last-in, first-out (LIFO) cost**

A company can use any of these methods. The methods can have very different effects on reported profits, income taxes, and cash flow. Therefore, companies select their inventory method with great care.

Specific Unit Cost. Some businesses deal in unique inventory items, such as automobiles, antique furniture, jewels, and real estate. These businesses cost their inventories at the specific cost of the particular unit. For instance, a Toyota dealer may have two vehicles in the showroom—a "stripped-down" model that cost the dealer $19,000 and a "loaded" model that cost the dealer $30,000. If the dealer sells the loaded model, the cost of goods sold is $30,000. The stripped-down auto will be the only unit left in inventory, and so ending inventory is $19,000.

The **specific-unit-cost method** is also called the *specific identification method*. This method is too expensive to use for inventory items that have common characteristics, such as bushels of wheat, gallons of paint, or auto tires.

The other inventory accounting methods—average, FIFO, and LIFO—are fundamentally different. These other methods do not use the specific cost of a particular unit. Instead, they assume different flows of inventory costs. To illustrate average, FIFO, and LIFO costing, we use a common set of data, given in Exhibit 6-6.

EXHIBIT 6-6 | Inventory Data Used to Illustrate the Various Inventory Costing Methods

Inventory		
Beg bal	(10 units @ $10)	100
Purchases:		Cost of goods sold
No. 1	(25 units @ $14)	350 (40 units @ ?) ?
No. 2	(25 units @ $18)	450
End bal	(20 units @ ?)	?

In Exhibit 6-6, Pottery Barn began the period with 10 lamps that cost $10 each; the beginning inventory was therefore $100. During the period, Pottery Barn bought 50 more lamps, sold 40 lamps, and ended the period with 20 lamps.

Goods Available		Number of Units	Total Cost
Goods available	=	10 + 25 + 25 = 60 units	$100 + $350 + $450 = $900
Cost of goods sold	=	40 units	?
Ending inventory	=	20 units	?

The big accounting questions are as follows:

1. What is the cost of goods sold for the income statement?

2. What is the cost of the ending inventory for the balance sheet?

The answers to these questions depend on which inventory method Pottery Barn uses. Pottery Barn, like other Williams-Sonoma, Inc., companies, actually uses the average-cost method, so let's look at average costing first.

Average Cost. The **average-cost method**, sometimes called the **weighted-average method**, is based on the average cost of inventory during the period. Average cost per unit is determined as follows (data from Exhibit 6-6):

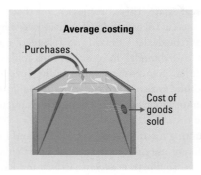

Average costing

$$\text{Average cost per unit} = \frac{\text{Cost of goods available*}}{\text{Number of units available*}} = \frac{\$900}{60} = \$15$$

*Goods available = Beginning inventory + Purchases

Cost of goods sold = Number of units sold × Average cost per unit
= 40 units × $15 = $600

Ending inventory = Number of units on hand × Average cost per unit
= 20 units × $15 = $300

The following T-account shows the effects of average costing:

Inventory (at Average Cost)					
Beg bal	(10 units @ $10)	100			
Purchases:					
No. 1	(25 units @ $14)	350			
No. 2	(25 units @ $18)	450	Cost of goods sold (40 units @ average cost of $15 per unit)		600
End bal	(20 units @ average cost of $15 per unit)	300			

FIFO Cost. Under the FIFO method, the first costs into inventory are the first costs assigned to cost of goods sold—hence the name **first-in, first-out**. The diagram near the bottom of the page shows the effect of FIFO costing. The following T-account shows how to compute FIFO cost of goods sold and ending inventory for the Pottery Barn lamps (data from Exhibit 6-6):

Inventory (at FIFO cost)					
Beg bal	(10 units @ $10)	100			
Purchases:			Cost of goods sold (40 units):		
No. 1	(25 units @ $14)	350	(10 units @ $10)	100	
No. 2	(25 units @ $18)	450	(25 units @ $14)	350	} 540
			(5 units @ $18)	90	
End bal	(20 units @ $18)	360			

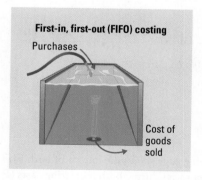

First-in, first-out (FIFO) costing

Purchases

Cost of goods sold

Under FIFO, the cost of ending inventory is always based on the latest costs incurred—in this case $18 per unit.

LIFO Cost. LIFO (**last-in, first-out**) costing is the opposite of FIFO. Under LIFO, the last costs into inventory go immediately to cost of goods sold, as shown in the diagram on the following page. Compare LIFO and FIFO, and you will see a vast difference.

The following T-account shows how to compute the LIFO inventory amounts for the Pottery Barn lamps (data from Exhibit 6-6):

Inventory (at LIFO cost)						
Beg bal	(10 units @ $10)	100	Cost of goods sold (40 units):			
Purchases:						
No. 1	(25 units @ $14)	350	(25 units @ $18)	450	}	660
No. 2	(25 units @ $18)	450	(15 units @ $14)	210		
End bal	(10 units @ $10) } 240					
	(10 units @ $14)					

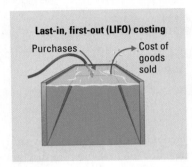

Last-in, first-out (LIFO) costing

Purchases → Cost of goods sold

Under LIFO, the cost of ending inventory is always based on the oldest costs—from beginning inventory plus the early purchases of the period—$10 and $14 per unit.

Compare the Effects of FIFO, LIFO, and Average Cost on Cost of Goods Sold, Gross Profit, and Ending Inventory

When inventory unit costs change, the various inventory methods produce different cost-of-goods sold figures. Exhibit 6-7 summarizes the income effects (sales − cost of goods sold = gross profit) of the three inventory methods (remember that prices are rising). Study Exhibit 6-7 carefully, focusing on cost of goods sold and gross profit.

EXHIBIT 6-7 | Income Effects of the FIFO, LIFO, and Average Inventory Methods

	FIFO	LIFO	Average
Sales revenue (assumed)	$1,000	$1,000	$1,000
Cost of goods sold	- 540 (lowest)	660 (highest)	600
Gross profit	$ 460 (highest)	$ 340 (lowest)	$ 400

Exhibit 6-8 on the following page shows the impact of both FIFO and LIFO costing methods on cost of goods sold and inventories during both increasing costs (Panel A) and decreasing costs (Panel B). Study this exhibit carefully; it will help you *really* understand FIFO and LIFO.

Financial analysts search the stock markets for companies with good prospects for income growth. Analysts sometimes need to compare the net income of a company that uses LIFO with the net income of a company that uses FIFO. Appendix 6B, page 398, shows how to convert a LIFO company's net income to the FIFO basis in order to compare the companies.

EXHIBIT 6-8 | Cost of Goods Sold and Ending Inventory—FIFO and LIFO; Increasing Costs and Decreasing Costs

<u>PANEL A—When Inventory Costs Are Increasing</u>

	Cost of Goods Sold (COGS)	Ending Inventory (EI)
FIFO	FIFO COGS is lowest because it's based on the oldest costs, which are low. Gross profit is, therefore, the highest.	FIFO EI is highest because it's based on the most recent costs, which are high.
LIFO	LIFO COGS is highest because it's based on the most recent costs, which are high. Gross profit is, therefore, the lowest.	LIFO EI is lowest because it's based on the oldest costs, which are low.

<u>PANEL B—When Inventory Costs Are Decreasing</u>

	Cost of Goods Sold (COGS)	Ending Inventory (EI)
FIFO	FIFO COGS is highest because it's based on the oldest costs, which are high. Gross profit is, therefore, the lowest.	FIFO EI is lowest because it's based on the most recent costs, which are low.
LIFO	LIFO COGS is lowest because it's based on the most recent costs, which are low. Gross profit is, therefore, the highest.	LIFO EI is highest because it's based on the oldest costs, which are high.

Keeping Track of Perpetual Inventories under LIFO and Weighted-Average Cost Methods

The LIFO cost flow assumption does not follow the logical flow of goods. Therefore, when costs are changing, it is physically impossible to apply LIFO unit costs to units purchased and sold as the transactions are happening using a perpetual inventory accounting system. Similarly, for large companies with millions of purchases and sales transactions, although it might be physically possible to do so, keeping track of perpetual inventories using weighted-average cost can be quite challenging, requiring sophisticated computer software to make constant updates to both changing quantities and changing unit prices on a daily basis. Therefore, many companies that use these methods keep track of perpetual inventories in quantities only during the period, making adjusting journal entries at the end of the period to apply either LIFO or weighted-average cost to both ending inventory and cost of goods sold. The details of this topic are reserved for more advanced accounting courses.

The Tax Advantage of LIFO

The Internal Revenue Service requires all U.S. companies to use the same method of pricing inventories for tax purposes that they use for financial reporting purposes. Thus, the choice of inventory methods directly affects income taxes, which must be paid in cash. When prices are rising, LIFO results in the *lowest taxable income* and thus the *lowest income taxes*. Let's use the gross profit data of Exhibit 6-7 to illustrate.

	FIFO	LIFO
Gross profit (from Exhibit 6-7)	$460	$340
Operating expenses (assumed).................	260	260
Income before income tax	$200	$ 80
Income tax expense (40%)	$ 80	$ 32

Income tax expense is lowest under LIFO by $48 ($80 − $32). **This is the most attractive feature of LIFO—low income tax payments**, which is why about one-third of all U.S. companies use LIFO. During periods of inflation, companies that can justify it may switch to LIFO for its tax and cash-flow advantages.

Let's compare the FIFO and LIFO inventory methods from a couple of different standpoints.

1. Measuring Cost of Goods Sold. How well does each method match inventory expense— cost of goods sold—against revenue? LIFO results in the most realistic net income figure because LIFO assigns the most recent inventory costs to expense. In contrast, FIFO matches old inventory costs against revenue—a poor measure of expense. FIFO income is therefore less realistic than LIFO income.

2. Measuring Ending Inventory. Which method reports the most up-to-date inventory cost on the balance sheet? FIFO. LIFO can value inventory at very old costs because LIFO leaves the oldest prices in ending inventory.

LIFO and Managing Reported Income. LIFO allows managers to manipulate net income by timing their purchases of inventory. When inventory prices are rising rapidly and a company wants to show less income (in order to pay less taxes), managers can buy a large amount of inventory near the end of the year. Under LIFO, these high inventory costs go straight to cost of goods sold. As a result, net income is decreased.

If the business is having a bad year, management may wish to report higher income. The company can delay the purchase of high-cost inventory until next year. This avoids decreasing current-year income. In the process, the company draws down inventory quantities, a practice known as *LIFO inventory liquidation*.

LIFO Liquidation. When LIFO is used and inventory quantities fall below the level of the previous period, the situation is called a *LIFO liquidation*. To compute cost of goods sold, the company must dip into older layers of inventory cost. Under LIFO, and when prices are rising, that action shifts older, lower costs into cost of goods sold. The result is higher net income. Managers try to avoid a LIFO liquidation because it increases income taxes.

International Perspective Many U.S. companies that currently use LIFO must use another method in foreign countries. Why? LIFO is not allowed in Australia, the United Kingdom, and some other British commonwealth countries. Virtually all countries permit FIFO and the average cost method.

These differences can create comparability problems for financial analysts when comparing a U.S. company against a foreign competitor. As discussed earlier, Appendix 6B illustrates how analysts convert reported income for a company that uses LIFO to report income under FIFO.

International Financial Reporting Standards (IFRS) also do not permit the use of LIFO, although they do permit FIFO and other methods. When U.S. GAAP and IFRS are fully integrated in a few years, U.S. companies that use LIFO will be forced to convert their inventory pricing to another method. As we discussed earlier in the chapter, in periods of rising prices, the use of LIFO inventories results in the lowest amount of reported income and, thus, the lowest amount of income taxes. If, as stated previously, about a third of U.S. companies continue to use LIFO through the next few years, conversion of inventories to methods other than LIFO may substantially increase income for them. This change has potentially far-reaching implications. For example, if the Internal Revenue Service continues to require companies to use the same inventory pricing methods for income tax purposes and financial statement purposes, conversion of LIFO inventories to another method will greatly increase the tax burden on many U.S. companies, including small and medium-sized businesses that can least afford it.

The disallowance of LIFO inventories under IFRS is only one of several rather thorny issues that must be resolved before the United States can adopt IFRS. Resolution of these differences will likely have political as well as financial implications. We will cover other key differences between GAAP and IFRS in later chapters. Appendix E summarizes all of these differences.

MID-CHAPTER SUMMARY PROBLEM

Suppose a division of **Texas Instruments** that sells computer microchips has these inventory records for January 2013:

Date	Item	Quantity	Unit Cost	Total cost
Jan 1	Beginning inventory	100 units	$ 8	$ 800
6	Purchase	60 units	9	540
21	Purchase	150 units	9	1,350
27	Purchase	90 units	10	900

Company accounting records show sales of 310 units for revenue of $6,770. Operating expense for January was $1,900.

▶ Requirements

1. Prepare the January income statement, showing amounts for LIFO, average, and FIFO cost. Label the bottom line "Operating income." Round average cost per unit to three decimal places and all other figures to whole-dollar amounts. Show your computations.

2. Suppose you are the financial vice president of Texas Instruments. Which inventory method will you use if your motive is to

   a. minimize income taxes?

   b. report the highest operating income?

   c. report operating income between the extremes of FIFO and LIFO?

   d. report inventory on the balance sheet at the most current cost?

   e. attain the best measure of net income for the income statement?

   State the reason for each of your answers.

▶ Answers
Requirement 1

Texas Instruments Incorporated
Income Statement for Microchip
Month Ended January 31, 2013

	LIFO	Average	FIFO
Sales revenue	$6,770	$6,770	$6,770
Cost of goods sold	2,870	2,782	2,690
Gross profit	3,900	3,988	4,080
Operating expenses	1,900	1,900	1,900
Operating income	$2,000	$2,088	$2,180

Cost of goods sold computations:

LIFO: (90 @ $10) + (150 @ $9) + (60 @ $9) + (10 @ $8) = $2,870
Average: 310 × $8.975* = $2,782
FIFO: (100 @ $8) + (60 @ $9) + (150 @ $9) = $2,690

$$*\frac{(\$800 + \$540 + \$1,350 + \$900)}{(100 + 60 + 150 + 90)} = \$8.975$$

Requirement 2

a. Use LIFO to minimize income taxes. Operating income under LIFO is lowest when inventory unit costs are increasing, as they are in this case (from $8 to $10). (If inventory costs were decreasing, income under FIFO would be lowest.)

b. Use FIFO to report the highest operating income. Income under FIFO is highest when inventory unit costs are increasing, as in this situation.

c. Use the average-cost method to report an operating income amount between the FIFO and LIFO extremes. This is true in this situation and in others when inventory unit costs are increasing or decreasing.

d. Use FIFO to report inventory on the balance sheet at the most current cost. The oldest inventory costs are expensed as cost of goods sold, leaving in ending inventory the most recent (most current) costs of the period.

e. Use LIFO to attain the best measure of net income. LIFO produces the best current expense recognition by matching the most current expense with current revenue. The most recent (most current) inventory costs are expensed as cost of goods sold.

Explain and Apply Underlying GAAP for Inventory

Several accounting principles have special relevance to inventories:

- ► Consistency
- ► Disclosure
- ► Representational faithfulness

3

Explain and apply
underlying GAAP for
inventory

> **EXCERPT FROM NOTE 6 OF THE FINANCIAL STATEMENTS**
> . . . American-Saudi changed its method of accounting for the cost of crude oil . . . from the FIFO method to the LIFO method. The company believes that the LIFO method better matches current costs with current revenues. . . . The change decreased the Company's net income . . . by $3 million. . . .

Disclosure Principle

The **disclosure principle** holds that a company's financial statements should report enough information for outsiders to make informed decisions about the company. The company should report *relevant* and *representationally faithful* information about itself. That means properly disclosing inventory accounting methods, as well as the substance of all material transactions impacting the existence and proper valuation of inventory, using *comparable* methods from period to period. The financial statements typically contain a footnote describing the inventory pricing method used, as well as the fact that inventory was valued at the lower of that method or market. The lower-of-cost-or-market rule is described later. Without knowledge of the accounting method and without clear, complete disclosures in the financial statements, a banker could make an unwise lending decision. Suppose the banker is comparing two companies—one using LIFO and the other, FIFO. The FIFO company reports higher net income but only because it uses FIFO. Without knowing this, the banker could loan money to the wrong business.

Lower-of-Cost-or-Market Rule

The **lower-of-cost-or-market rule** (abbreviated as **LCM**) is based on the principles of relevance and representational faithfulness. LCM requires that inventory be reported in the financial statements at whichever is lower—the inventory's historical cost or its market value. Applied to inventories, *market value* generally means *current replacement cost* (that is, how much the business would have to pay now to replace its inventory). If the replacement cost of inventory falls below its historical cost, the business must write down the value of its goods to market value, which is the most relevant and representationally faithful measure of its true worth to the business. **The business reports ending inventory at its LCM value on the balance sheet**. All this can be done automatically by a computerized accounting system. How is the write-down accomplished?

Suppose Williams-Sonoma, Inc., paid $3,000 for inventory on September 26. By January 31, its fiscal year-end, the inventory can be replaced for $2,000. Williams-Sonoma's year-end balance sheet must report this inventory at LCM value of $2,000. Exhibit 6-9 on the following page presents the effects of LCM on the balance sheet and the income statement. Before any LCM effect, cost of goods sold is $9,000. An LCM write-down decreases Inventory and increases Cost of Goods Sold, as follows:

Cost of Goods Sold	1,000	
Inventory		1,000
Wrote inventory down to market value.		

EXHIBIT 6-9 | Lower-of-Cost-or-Market (LCM) Effects on Inventory and Cost of Goods Sold

Balance Sheet

Current assets:

Cash	$ XXX
Short-term investments	XXX
Accounts receivable...	XXX
Inventories, at market	
(which is lower than $3,000 cost)	2,000
Prepaid expenses	XXX
Total current assets	$X,XXX

Income Statement

Sales revenue	$21,000
Cost of goods sold ($9,000 + $1,000)	10,000
Gross profit..	$11,000

If the market value of Williams-Sonoma's inventory had been above cost, it would have made no adjustment for LCM. In that case, simply report the inventory at cost, which is the lower of cost or market.

Companies disclose LCM in notes to their financial statements, as shown next for Williams-Sonoma, Inc.:

NOTE 1: ACCOUNTING POLICIES
- *Inventories.* Inventories are . . . stated at the *lower of average cost or market.* [Emphasis added.]

LCM is not optional. It is required by GAAP.

Global View

Another IFRS Difference IFRS defines "market" differently than U.S. GAAP. Under IFRS, "market" is always defined as "net realizable value," which, for inventories, is current market value. Once IFRS is adopted in the United States, inventory write-downs may become less common than they are now, due to the fact that selling prices are usually greater than replacement cost.

Under U.S. GAAP, once the LCM rule is applied to write inventories down to replacement cost, the write-downs may never be reversed. In contrast, under IFRS, some LCM write-downs may be reversed, and inventory may be subsequently written up again, not to exceed original cost. This may cause more fluctuation in the reported incomes of companies that sell inventories than we currently see.

Inventory and the Detailed Income Statement

Exhibit 6-10 provides an example of a detailed income statement, complete with all the discounts and expenses in their proper places. Study it carefully.

EXHIBIT 6-10 | Detailed Income Statement

New Jersey Technology, Inc.
Income Statement
Year Ended December 31, 2013

Sales revenue	$100,000	
Less: Sales discounts	(2,000)	
Sales returns and allowances	(3,000)	
Net sales		$95,000*
Cost of goods sold		45,000
Gross profit		50,000
Operating expenses:		
Selling:		
Sales commission expense	$ 5,000	
Freight out (delivery expense)	1,000	
Other expenses (detailed)	6,000	12,000
Administrative:		
Salary expense	$ 2,000	
Depreciation expense	2,000	
Other expenses (detailed)	4,000	8,000
Income before income tax		30,000
Income tax expense (40%)		12,000
Net income		$18,000

*Most companies report only the net sales figure, $95,000.

Compute and Evaluate Gross Profit (Margin) and Inventory Turnover

Owners, managers, and investors use ratios to evaluate a business. Two ratios relate directly to inventory: gross profit percentage and the rate of inventory turnover.

Gross Profit Percentage

Gross profit—sales minus cost of goods sold—is a key indicator of a company's ability to sell inventory at a profit. Merchandisers strive to increase **gross profit percentage**, also called the **gross margin percentage**. Gross profit percentage is markup stated as a percentage of sales. Gross profit percentage is computed as follows for Williams-Sonoma, Inc. Data (in millions) for the year ended January 31, 2011, are taken from Exhibit 6-3 (p. 341).

$$\text{Gross profit percentage} = \frac{\text{Gross profit}}{\text{Net sales revenue}} = \frac{\$1,374}{\$3,504} = 0.392 = 39.2\%$$

The gross profit percentage is watched carefully by managers and investors. A 39.2% gross margin means that each dollar of sales generates about $0.39 of gross profit. On average, cost of goods sold consumes $0.61 of each sales dollar for Williams-Sonoma, Inc. For most firms, the gross profit percentage changes little from year to year, so a small downturn may signal trouble, and an upturn by a small percentage can mean millions of dollars in additional profits. Williams-Sonoma's trend in gross profit for fiscal years 2008 through 2010 was 33.8%, 35.6%,

4

Compute and evaluate gross profit (margin) and inventory turnover

and 39.2%, respectively. These figures reflect healthy increases in gross profit over the three-year period. However, Williams-Sonoma's gross profit in 2007 was 39.8%. In 2008 and 2009, a severe economic recession hit retail sales hard. In order to sell inventories, many retailers had to cut selling prices, thus reducing gross profit. In the latter part of 2009, the economy began to turn around, and gross margins began to improve again, but it took three years for gross profit to return to its 2007 levels.

Williams-Sonoma's gross profit percentage of 39.2% is greater than that of Wal-Mart Stores, Inc., (24.7%) but smaller than the gross profit percentage of Nordstrom, Inc. (39.9%). Both Williams-Sonoma and Nordstrom handle higher-priced merchandise than Wal-Mart, thus resulting in higher gross profit. Exhibit 6-11 graphs the gross profit percentages for these three companies.

EXHIBIT 6-11 | Gross Profit Percentages of Three Leading Retailers

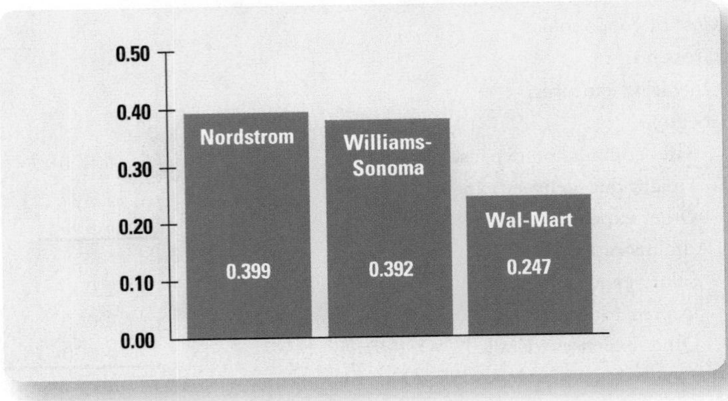

Inventory Turnover

Williams-Sonoma, Inc., strives to sell its inventory as quickly as possible because the goods generate no profit until they're sold. The faster the sales, the higher the income, and vice versa for slow-moving goods. Ideally, a business could operate with zero inventory, but most businesses, especially retailers, must keep some goods on hand. **Inventory turnover**, the ratio of cost of goods sold to average inventory, indicates how rapidly inventory is sold. The fiscal 2010 computation for Williams-Sonoma, Inc., follows (data in millions from the Consolidated Balance Sheets and Statements of Income, page 338):

$$\text{Inventory turnover} = \frac{\text{Cost of goods sold}}{\text{Average inventory}} = \frac{\text{Cost of goods sold}}{\left(\begin{array}{c}\text{Beginning} \\ \text{inventory}\end{array} + \begin{array}{c}\text{Ending} \\ \text{inventory}\end{array}\right) \div 2}$$

$$= \frac{\$2,130}{(\$466 + \$513)/2} = \begin{array}{l}\text{4.35 times per year} \\ \text{(every 84 days)}\end{array}$$

The inventory turnover statistic shows how many times the company sold (or turned over) its average level of inventory during the year. Inventory turnover varies from industry to industry.

Exhibit 6-12 graphs the rates of inventory turnover for the same three companies. Let's compare Williams-Sonoma's turnover with that of Nordstrom and Wal-Mart department stores. You can see that both Nordstrom and Wal-Mart turn inventory over faster than Williams-Sonoma. Both Nordstrom and Wal-Mart are department stores. They sell a variety of products (Nordstrom sells clothing and Wal-Mart sells virtually every kind of consumer item) that sell faster than the specialty home furnishings of Williams-Sonoma, Inc. Thus, both Nordstrom and Wal-Mart, Inc., report higher dollar amounts of gross profit and net income than Williams-Sonoma.

EXHIBIT 6-12 | Inventory Turnover Rates of Three Leading Retailers

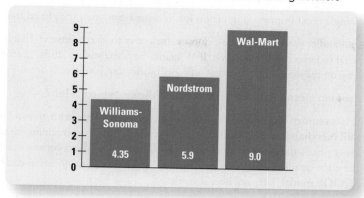

STOP & THINK...

Examine Exhibits 6-11 and 6-12. What do those ratio values say about the merchandising (pricing) strategies of Nordstrom, Inc., and Wal-Mart Stores, Inc.?

Answer:

It's obvious that Nordstrom sells high-end merchandise. Nordstrom's gross profit percentage is higher than Wal-Mart's. However, Wal-Mart has a much faster rate of inventory turnover. The lower the price, the faster the turnover, and vice versa.

Use the COGS Model to Make Management Decisions

Exhibit 6-13 presents the **cost-of-goods-sold (COGS) model.** Some may view this model as related to the periodic inventory system. But the COGS model is used by all companies, regardless of their accounting systems. The model is extremely powerful because it captures all the inventory information for an entire accounting period. Study this model carefully (all amounts are assumed).

5

Use the COGS model to make management decisions

EXHIBIT 6-13 | The Cost-of-Goods-Sold (COGS) Model

Cost of goods sold:	
Beginning inventory	$1,200
+ Purchases	6,300
= Goods available.....................	7,500
− Ending inventory...................	(1,500)
= Cost of goods sold.................	$6,000

Williams-Sonoma, Inc., uses a perpetual inventory accounting system. Let's see how the company can use the COGS model to manage the business effectively.

Computing Budgeted Purchases

1. What's the single most important question for Williams-Sonoma, Inc., to address?

    ▶ What merchandise should Williams-Sonoma, Inc., offer to its customers? This is a *marketing* question that requires market research. If Williams-Sonoma and its affiliated stores continually stock up on the wrong merchandise, sales will suffer and profits will drop.

2. What's the second most important question for Williams-Sonoma, Inc.?

    ▶ How much inventory should Williams-Sonoma, Inc., buy? **This is an accounting question faced by all merchandisers.** If Williams-Sonoma, Inc., buys too much merchandise, it will have to lower prices, the gross profit percentage will suffer, and the company may lose money. Buying the right quantity of inventory is critical for success. This question can be answered with the COGS model. Let's see how it works.

We must rearrange the COGS formula. Then we can help a Williams-Sonoma store manager know how much inventory to buy, as follows (using amounts from Exhibit 6-13):

1	Cost of goods sold (based on the plan for the next period)	$6,000
2	+ Ending inventory (based on the plan for the next period)	1,500
3	= Goods available as planned	7,500
4	− Beginning inventory (actual amount left over from the prior period)	(1,200)
5	= Purchases (how much inventory the manager needs to buy)	$6,300

In this case the manager should buy $6,300 of merchandise to work his plan for the upcoming period.

Estimating Inventory by the Gross Profit Method

Often a business must *estimate* the value of its goods. For example, suppose a fire destroys the warehouse, all inventory, and all records. The insurance company requires an estimate of the loss. In this case, the business must estimate the cost of ending inventory because the records have been destroyed.

The **gross profit method**, also known as the **gross margin method**, is widely used to estimate ending inventory. This method uses the familiar COGS model (amounts are assumed).

For the gross-profit method, we rearrange *ending inventory* and *cost of goods sold* as follows:

Beginning inventory	$ 4,000
+ Purchases	16,000
= Goods available	20,000
− Ending inventory	(5,000)
= Cost of goods sold	$15,000

Beginning inventory	$ 4,000
+ Purchases	16,000
= Goods available	20,000
− Cost of goods sold	(15,000)
= Ending inventory	$ 5,000

Suppose a fire destroys some of Williams-Sonoma's inventory. To collect insurance, the company must estimate the cost of the ending inventory lost. Using its *actual gross profit rate* of 39%, you can estimate the cost of goods sold. Then subtract cost of goods sold from goods available to estimate the amount of ending inventory. Exhibit 6-14 shows the calculations for the gross profit method, with new amounts assumed for the illustration.

You can also use the gross profit method to test the overall reasonableness of an ending inventory amount. This method also helps to detect large errors.

EXHIBIT 6-14 | Gross Profit Method of Estimating Inventory

Beginning inventory	$ 38,000
Purchases	72,000
Goods available...	110,000
Estimated cost of goods sold:	
Net sales revenue $100,000	
Less estimated gross profit of 39% .... (39,000)	
Estimated cost of goods sold	61,000
Estimated cost of *ending inventory* lost.............	$ 49,000

STOP & THINK...

Beginning inventory is $70,000, net purchases total $365,000, and net sales are $500,000. With a normal gross profit rate of 40% of sales (cost of goods sold = 60%), how much is ending inventory?

Answer:

$135,000 = [$70,000 + $365,000 − (0.60 × $500,000)]

Analyze Effects of Inventory Errors

Inventory errors sometimes occur. An error in ending inventory creates errors for two accounting periods. In Exhibit 6-15, start with period 1 in which ending inventory is *overstated* by $5,000 and cost of goods sold is therefore *understated* by $5,000. Then compare period 1 with period 3, which is correct. *Period 1 should look exactly like period 3.*

Inventory errors counterbalance in two consecutive periods. Why? Recall that period 1's ending inventory becomes period 2's beginning amount. Thus, the period 1 error carries over into period 2. Trace the ending inventory of $15,000 from period 1 to period 2. Then compare periods 2 and 3. *All three periods should look exactly like period 3.* The Exhibit 6-15 amounts in color are incorrect.

Analyze effects of inventory errors

EXHIBIT 6-15 | Inventory Errors: An Example

	Period 1 Ending Inventory Overstated by $5,000		Period 2 Beginning Inventory Overstated by $5,000		Period 3 Correct	
Sales revenue.....................................		$100,000		$100,000		$100,000
Cost of goods sold:						
Beginning inventory	$10,000		$15,000		$10,000	
Purchases	50,000		50,000		50,000	
Cost of goods available	60,000		65,000		60,000	
Ending inventory...........................	(15,000)		(10,000)		(10,000)	
Cost of goods sold		45,000		55,000		50,000
Gross profit....................................		$ 55,000		$ 45,000		$ 50,000
			$100,000			

The authors thank Professor Carl High for this example.

Beginning inventory and ending inventory have opposite effects on cost of goods sold (beginning inventory is added; ending inventory is subtracted). Therefore, after two periods, an inventory error washes out (counterbalances). Notice that total gross profit is correct for periods 1 and 2 combined ($100,000) even though each year's gross profit is off by $5,000. The correct gross profit is $50,000 for each period, as shown in Period 3.

We must have accurate information for all periods. Exhibit 6-16 summarizes the effects of inventory accounting errors.

EXHIBIT 6-16 | Effects of Inventory Errors

Inventory Error	Period 1		Period 2	
	Cost of Goods Sold	Gross Profit and Net Income	Cost of Goods Sold	Gross Profit and Net Income
Period 1				
Ending inventory **overstated**	Understated	Overstated	Overstated	Understated
Period 1				
Ending inventory **understated**	Overstated	Understated	Understated	Overstated

Cooking the Books with Inventory

Crazy Eddie

It is one thing to make honest mistakes in accounting for inventory, but quite another to use inventory to commit fraud. The two most common ways to "cook the books" with inventory are

1. inserting fictitious inventory—thus overstating quantities—and

2. deliberately overstating unit prices used in the computation of ending inventory amounts.

Either one of these tricks has exactly the same effect on income as inventory errors, discussed in the previous section. The difference is that honest inventory errors are often corrected as soon as they are detected, thus minimizing their impact on income. In contrast, deliberate overstatement of inventories tends to be repeated over and over again throughout the course of months, or even years, thus causing the misstatement to grow ever higher until it is discovered. By that time, it can be too late for the company.

Crazy Eddie, Inc.,[1] was a retail consumer electronics store in 1987, operating 43 retail outlets in the New York City area, with $350 million in reported sales and reported profits of $10.5 million. Its stock was a Wall Street "darling," with a collective market value of $600 million. The only problem was that the company's reported profits had been grossly overstated since 1984, the year that the company went public.

Eddie Antar, the company's founder and major stockholder, became preoccupied with the price of his company's stock in 1984. Antar realized that the company, in an extremely competitive retail market in the largest city in the United States, had to keep posting impressive operating profits in order to maintain the upward trend in the company's stock price.

Within the first six months, Antar ordered a subordinate to double count about $2 million of inventory in the company's stores and warehouses. Using Exhibits 6-15 and 6-16, you can see that the impact of this inventory overstatement went straight to the "bottom line," overstating profits by the same amount. Unfortunately, the company's auditors failed to detect the inventory overstatement. The following year, emboldened by the audit error, Antar ordered

[1]Michael C. Knapp, *Contemporary Auditing: Real Issues and Cases*, 6th edition, Mason, Ohio: Thomson Southwestern, 2009.

subordinates (now accomplices) to bump the overstatement to $9 million. In addition, he ordered employees to destroy incriminating documents to conceal the inventory shortage. When auditors asked for these documents, employees told them they had been lost. Antar also ordered that the company scrap its sophisticated computerized perpetual inventory system and return to an outdated manual system that was easier to manipulate. The auditors made the mistake of telling Antar which company stores and warehouses they were going to visit in order to observe the year-end physical count of inventory. Antar shifted sufficient inventory to those locations just before the counts to conceal the shortages. By 1988, when the fraud was discovered, the inventory shortage (overstatement) was larger than the total profits the company had reported since it went public in 1984.

In June 1989, Crazy Eddie, Inc., filed for Chapter 11 bankruptcy protection. Later that year, the company closed its stores and sold off its assets. Eddie Antar became a fugitive from justice, moved to Israel, and took an assumed name. He was arrested in 1992, extradited to the United States, and convicted on 17 counts of fraudulent financial reporting in 1993. He was ordered to pay $121 million in restitution to former stockholders and creditors.

A series of missteps by the courts led to a plea bargain agreement in 1996, a condition of which was Antar's admittance, for the first time, that he had defrauded investors by manipulating the company's accounting records. One of the prosecuting attorneys was quoted as saying, "Crazy Eddie wasn't crazy, just crooked."

The following Decision Guidelines summarize the situations that call for (a) a particular inventory system and (b) the motivation for using each costing method.

DECISION GUIDELINES

ACCOUNTING FOR INVENTORY

Suppose a Williams-Sonoma store stocks two basic categories of merchandise:
- ▶ Furniture pieces, such as tables and chairs
- ▶ Small items of low value, near the checkout stations, such as cupholders and bottle openers

Jacob Stiles, the store manager, is considering how accounting will affect the business. Let's examine several decisions Stiles must make to properly account for the store's inventory.

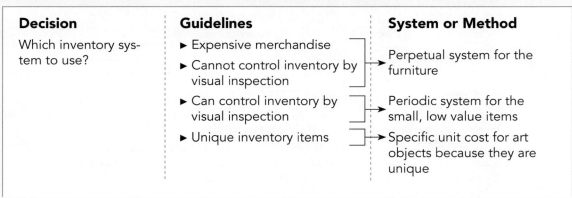

Decision	Guidelines	System or Method
Which inventory system to use?	▶ Expensive merchandise ▶ Cannot control inventory by visual inspection	Perpetual system for the furniture
	▶ Can control inventory by visual inspection	Periodic system for the small, low value items
	▶ Unique inventory items	Specific unit cost for art objects because they are unique

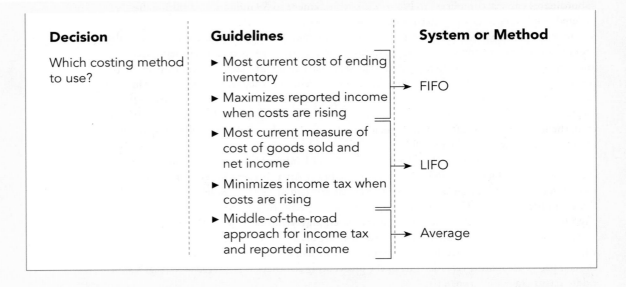

Decision	Guidelines	System or Method
Which costing method to use?	▸ Most current cost of ending inventory ▸ Maximizes reported income when costs are rising	FIFO
	▸ Most current measure of cost of goods sold and net income ▸ Minimizes income tax when costs are rising	LIFO
	▸ Middle-of-the-road approach for income tax and reported income	Average

END-OF-CHAPTER SUMMARY PROBLEM

Town & Country Gift Ideas began 2012 with 60,000 units of inventory that cost $36,000. During 2012, Town & Country purchased merchandise on account for $352,500 as follows:

Purchase 1	(100,000 units costing)	$ 65,000
Purchase 2	(270,000 units costing)	175,500
Purchase 3	(160,000 units costing)	112,000

Cash payments on account totaled $326,000 during the year.

Town & Country's sales during 2012 consisted of 520,000 units of inventory for $660,000, all on account. The company uses the FIFO inventory method.

Cash collections from customers were $630,000. Operating expenses totaled $240,500, of which Town & Country paid $211,000 in cash. Town & Country credited Accrued Liabilities for the remainder. At December 31, Town & Country accrued income tax expense at the rate of 35% of income before tax.

▸ Requirements

1. Make summary journal entries to record Town & Country's transactions for the year, assuming the company uses a perpetual inventory system.

2. Determine the FIFO cost of Town & Country's ending inventory at December 31, 2012, two ways:

   a. Use a T-account.

   b. Multiply the number of units on hand by the unit cost.

3. Show how Town & Country would compute cost of goods sold for 2012. Follow the FIFO example on page 347.

4. Prepare Town & Country's income statement for 2012. Show totals for the gross profit and income before tax.

5. Determine Town & Country's gross profit percentage, rate of inventory turnover, and net income as a percentage of sales for the year. In Town & Country's industry, a gross profit percentage of 40%, an inventory turnover of six times per year, and a net income percentage of 7% are considered excellent. How well does Town & Country compare to these industry averages?

▶ **Answers**

Requirement 1

Inventory ($65,000 + $175,500 + $112,000)	352,500	
Accounts Payable		352,500
Accounts Payable	326,000	
Cash		326,000
Accounts Receivable	660,000	
Sales Revenue		660,000
Cost of Goods Sold (see Requirement 3)	339,500	
Inventory		339,500
Cash	630,000	
Accounts Receivable		630,000
Operating Expenses	240,500	
Cash		211,000
Accrued Liabilities		29,500
Income Tax Expense (see Requirement 4)	28,000	
Income Tax Payable		28,000

Requirement 2

Inventory			
Beg bal	36,000		
Purchases	352,500	Cost of goods sold	339,500
End bal	49,000		

Number of units in ending inventory (60,000 + 100,000 + 270,000 + 160,000 − 520,000)	70,000
Unit cost of ending inventory at FIFO ($112,000 ÷ 160,000 from Purchase 3)....	× $ 0.70
FIFO cost of ending inventory.......................	$49,000

Requirement 3

Cost of goods sold (520,000 units):	
60,000 units costing..	$ 36,000
100,000 units costing..	65,000
270,000 units costing..	175,500
90,000 units costing $0.70 each*	63,000
Cost of goods sold...	$339,500

*From Purchase 3: $112,000/160,000 units = $0.70 per unit.

Requirement 4

Town & Country Gift Ideas
Income Statement
Year Ended December 31, 2012

Sales revenue	$660,000
Cost of goods sold	339,500
Gross profit	320,500
Operating expenses	240,500
Income before tax	80,000
Income tax expense (35%)	28,000
Net income	$ 52,000

Requirement 5

		Industry Average
Gross profit percentage:	$320,500 ÷ $660,000 = 48.6%	40%
Inventory turnover:	$\dfrac{\$339,500}{(\$36,000 + \$49,000)/2} = 8$ times	6 times
Net income as a percent of sales:	$52,000 ÷ $660,000 = 7.9%	7%

Town & Country's statistics are better than the industry averages.

REVIEW | Inventory & Cost of Goods Sold

Quick Check (Answers are given on page 393.)

1. Which statement is true?

   a. Gross profit is the excess of sales revenue over cost of goods sold.

   b. The Sales account is used to record only sales on account.

   c. A service company purchases products from suppliers and then sells them.

   d. The invoice is the purchaser's request for collection from the customer.

2. Sales discounts should appear in the financial statements

   a. as an addition to sales.

   b. among the current liabilities.

   c. as an addition to inventory.

   d. as an operating expense.

   e. as a deduction from sales.

3. How is inventory classified in the financial statements?

   a. As a liability

   b. As a revenue

   c. As an asset

   d. As a contra account to Cost of Goods Sold

   e. As an expense

   Questions 4–6 use the following data of Bluefish, Inc.:

	Units	Unit Cost	Total Cost	Units Sold
Beginning inventory	25	$4	$100	
Purchase on Apr 25	41	5	205	
Purchase on Nov 16	17	10	170	
Sales	45	?	?	

4. Bluefish uses a FIFO inventory system. Cost of goods sold for the period is

   a. $200.　　　　　　　　　　　　c. $450.

   b. $257.　　　　　　　　　　　　d. $310.

5. Bluefish's LIFO cost of ending inventory would be

   a. $217.　　　　　　　　　　　　c. $165.

   b. $275.　　　　　　　　　　　　d. $450.

6. Bluefish's average cost of ending inventory is

   a. $165.　　　　　　　　　　　　c. $217.

   b. $275.　　　　　　　　　　　　d. $450.

7. When applying the lower-of-cost-or-market rule to inventory, "market" generally means

   a. original cost, less physical deterioration.　　　c. replacement cost.

   b. original cost.　　　　　　　　　　　　　　　d. resale value.

8. During a period of rising prices, the inventory method that will yield the highest net income and asset value is

   a. LIFO.　　　　　　　　　　　　c. FIFO.

   b. average cost.　　　　　　　　　d. specific identification.

9. Which statement is true?

   a. Application of the lower-of-cost-or-market rule often results in a lower inventory value.

   b. An error overstating ending inventory in 2011 will understate 2011 net income.

   c. When prices are rising, the inventory method that results in the lowest ending inventory value is FIFO.

   d. The inventory method that best matches current expense with current revenue is FIFO.

10. The ending inventory of Sag Harbor Co. is $46,000. If beginning inventory was $70,000 and goods available totaled $115,000, the cost of goods sold is

    a. $45,000.
    b. $70,000.
    c. $69,000.

    d. $139,000.
    e. none of the above.

11. Bell Company had cost of goods sold of $160,000. The beginning and ending inventories were $8,000 and $23,000, respectively. Purchases for the period must have been

    a. $183,000.
    b. $145,000.
    c. $168,000.

    d. $191,000.
    e. $175,000.

Use the following information for questions 12–14.

Putter Company had an $18,000 beginning inventory and a $21,000 ending inventory. Net sales were $200,000; purchases, $95,000; purchase returns and allowances, $6,000; and freight in, $8,000.

12. Cost of goods sold for the period is

    a. $91,000.
    b. $100,000.
    c. $94,000.

    d. $111,000.
    e. none of the above.

13. What is Putter's gross profit percentage (rounded to the nearest percentage)?

    a. 47%
    b. 9%

    c. 53%
    d. None of the above

14. What is Putter's rate of inventory turnover?

    a. 4.9 times
    b. 4.5 times

    c. 4.8 times
    d. 9.5 times

15. Beginning inventory is $100,000, purchases are $240,000, and sales total $430,000. The normal gross profit is 45%. Using the gross profit method, how much is ending inventory?

    a. $96,500
    b. $193,500
    c. $103,500

    d. $190,000
    e. None of the above

16. An overstatement of ending inventory in one period results in

    a. no effect on net income of the next period.

    b. an understatement of net income of the next period.

    c. an understatement of the beginning inventory of the next period.

    d. an overstatement of net income of the next period.

Accounting Vocabulary

average-cost method (p. 346) Inventory costing method based on the average cost of inventory during the period. Average cost is determined by dividing the cost of goods available by the number of units available. Also called the *weighted-average method*.

consignment (p. 342) An inventory arrangement where the seller sells inventory that belongs to another party. The seller does not include consigned merchandise on hand in its balance sheet, because the seller does not own this inventory.

cost of goods sold (p. 339) Cost of the inventory the business has sold to customers.

cost-of-goods-sold model (p. 357) Formula that brings together all the inventory data for the entire accounting period: Beginning inventory + Purchases = Goods available. Then, Goods available − Ending inventory = Cost of goods sold.

debit memorandum (p. 344) A document issued to the seller (vendor) when an item of inventory that is unwanted or damaged is returned. This document authorizes a reduction (debit) to accounts payable for the amount of the goods returned.

disclosure principle (p. 353) A business's financial statements must report enough information for outsiders to make knowledgeable decisions about the business. The company should report relevant, reliable, and comparable information about its economic affairs.

first-in, first-out (FIFO) cost (method) (p. 347) Inventory costing method by which the first costs into inventory are the first costs out to cost of goods sold. Ending inventory is based on the costs of the most recent purchases.

gross margin (p. 341) Another name for *gross profit*.

gross margin method (p. 358) Another name for the *gross profit method*.

gross margin percentage (p. 355) Another name for the *gross profit percentage*.

gross profit (p. 341) Sales revenue minus cost of goods sold. Also called *gross margin*.

gross profit method (p. 358) A way to estimate inventory based on a rearrangement of the cost-of-goods-sold model: Beginning inventory + Net purchases = Goods available − Cost of goods sold = Ending inventory. Also called the *gross margin method*.

gross profit percentage (p. 355) Gross profit divided by net sales revenue. Also called the *gross margin percentage*.

inventory (p. 339) The merchandise that a company sells to customers.

inventory turnover (p. 356) Ratio of cost of goods sold to average inventory. Indicates how rapidly inventory is sold.

last-in, first-out (LIFO) cost (method) (p. 347) Inventory costing method by which the last costs into inventory are the first costs out to cost of goods sold. This method leaves the oldest costs—those of beginning inventory and the earliest purchases of the period—in ending inventory.

lower-of-cost-or-market (LCM) rule (p. 353) Requires that an asset be reported in the financial statements at whichever is lower—its historical cost or its market value (current replacement cost for inventory).

periodic inventory system (p. 342) An inventory system in which the business does not keep a continuous record of the inventory on hand. Instead, at the end of the period, the business makes a physical count of the inventory on hand and applies the appropriate unit costs to determine the cost of the ending inventory.

perpetual inventory system (p. 342) An inventory system in which the business keeps a continuous record for each inventory item to show the inventory on hand at all times.

purchase allowance (p. 344) A decrease in the cost of purchases because the seller has granted the buyer a subtraction (an allowance) from the amount owed.

purchase discount (p. 344) A decrease in the cost of purchases earned by making an early payment to the vendor.

purchase return (p. 344) A decrease in the cost of purchases because the buyer returned the goods to the seller.

specific-unit-cost method (p. 345) Inventory cost method based on the specific cost of particular units of inventory.

weighted-average method (p. 346) Another name for the *average-cost method*.

ASSESS YOUR PROGRESS

Short Exercises

S6-1 (*Learning Objective 1: Show how to account for inventory transactions*) Journalize the following assumed transactions for The Soda Pop Company. Show amounts in billions.
- **a.** Cash purchases of inventory, $4.5 billion
- **b.** Sales on account, $18.9 billion
- **c.** Cost of goods sold (perpetual inventory system), $3.9 billion
- **d.** Collections on account, $18.7 billion

S6-2 (*Learning Objective 1: Show how to account for inventory transactions*) Bridget Krumb, Inc., purchased inventory costing $125,000 and sold 80% of the goods for $190,000. All purchases and sales were on account. Krumb later collected 25% of the accounts receivable.

1. Journalize these transactions for Krumb, which uses the perpetual inventory system.
2. For these transactions, show what Krumb will report for inventory, revenues, and expenses on its financial statements. Report gross profit on the appropriate statement.

S6-3 (*Learning Objective 2: Apply the average, FIFO, and LIFO methods*) Championship Sporting Goods started March with an inventory of 9 sets of golf clubs that cost a total of $1,350. During March, Charmpionship purchased 27 sets of clubs for $4,320. At the end of the month, Championship had 8 sets of golf clubs on hand. The store manager must select an inventory costing method, and he asks you to tell him both cost of goods sold and ending inventory under these three accounting methods:
- **a.** Average cost (round average unit cost to the nearest cent)
- **b.** FIFO
- **c.** LIFO

S6-4 (*Learning Objective 2: Apply the average, FIFO, and LIFO methods*) Jonah's Copy Center uses laser printers. Assume Jonah started the year with 100 containers of ink (average cost of $9.50 each, FIFO cost of $8.40 each, LIFO cost of $8.10 each). During the year, Jonah purchased 700 containers of ink at $9.90 and sold 600 units for $20.50 each. Jonah paid operating expenses throughout the year, a total of $3,900. Jonah is not subject to income tax.

Prepare Jonah's income statement for the current year ended December 31 under the average, FIFO, and LIFO inventory costing methods. Include a complete statement heading.

S6-5 (*Learning Objective 2: Compare income tax effects of the inventory costing methods*) This exercise should be used in conjunction with Short Exercise 6-4. Jonah is a corporation subject to a 40% income tax. Compute Jonah's income tax expense under the average, FIFO, and LIFO inventory costing methods. Which method would you select to (a) maximize income before tax and (b) minimize income tax expense?

S6-6 (*Learning Objective 2: Compare income and income tax effects of LIFO*) Macrovision.com uses the LIFO method to account for inventory. Macrovision is having an unusually good year, with net income well above expectations. The company's inventory costs are rising rapidly. What can Macrovision do immediately before the end of the year to decrease net income? Explain how this action decreases reported income, and tell why Macrovision might want to decrease its net income.

S6-7 (*Learning Objective 3: Apply the lower-of-cost-or-market rule to inventory*) It is December 31, end of the year, and the controller of Cornell Corporation is applying the lower-of-cost-or-market (LCM) rule to inventories. Before any year-end adjustments, Cornell reports the following data:

Cost of goods sold..	$420,000
Historical cost of ending inventory, as determined by a physical count..............	65,000

Cornell determines that the replacement cost of ending inventory is $49,000. Show what Cornell should report for ending inventory and for cost of goods sold. Identify the financial statement where each item appears.

S6-8 (*Learning Objective 2: Managing income under the LIFO method*) Tolbert Trumpet Company is nearing the end of its worst year ever. With two weeks until year-end, it appears that net income for the year will have decreased by 30% from last year. Jim Tolbert, the president and principal stockholder, is distressed with the year's results. Tolbert asks you, the financial vice president, to come up with a way to increase the business's net income. Inventory quantities are a little higher than normal because sales have been slow during the last few months. Tolbert uses the LIFO inventory method, and inventory costs have risen dramatically during the latter part of the year.

Write a memorandum to Jim Tolbert to explain how the company can increase its net income for the year. Explain your reasoning in detail. Tolbert is a man of integrity, so your plan must be completely ethical.

S6-9 (*Learning Objective 2: Compare income, tax, and other effects of the inventory methods*) This exercise tests your understanding of the four inventory methods. List the name of the inventory method that best fits the description. Assume that the cost of inventory is rising.

1. _____ Generally associated with saving income taxes
2. _____ Used to account for automobiles, jewelry, and art objects
3. _____ Results in a cost of ending inventory that is close to the current cost of replacing the inventory
4. _____ Maximizes reported income
5. _____ Enables a company to buy high-cost inventory at year-end and thereby decrease reported income and income tax
6. _____ Results in an old measure of the cost of ending inventory
7. _____ Provides a middle-ground measure of ending inventory and cost of goods sold
8. _____ Enables a company to keep reported income from dropping lower by liquidating older layers of inventory
9. _____ Writes inventory down when replacement cost drops below historical cost
10. _____ Matches the most current cost of goods sold against sales revenue

S6-10 (*Learning Objective 4: Compute ratio data to evaluate operations*) Cola Company made sales of $35,376 million during 2012. Cost of goods sold for the year totaled $15,437 million. At the end of 2011, Cola's inventory stood at $1,672 million, and Cola ended 2012 with inventory of $1,908 million.

Compute Cola's gross profit percentage and rate of inventory turnover for 2012.

S6-11 (*Learning Objective 5: Estimate ending inventory by the gross profit method*) Federal Technology began the year with inventory of $315,000 and purchased $1,820,000 of goods during the year. Sales for the year are $3,920,000, and Federal's gross profit percentage is 60% of sales. Compute Federal's estimated cost of ending inventory by using the gross profit method.

S6-12 (*Learning Objective 6: Analyze the effect of an inventory error—one year only*) CWD, Inc., reported these figures for its fiscal year (amounts in millions):

Net sales..............................	$ 2,500
Cost of goods sold...............	1,160
Ending inventory.................	480

Suppose CWD later learns that ending inventory was overstated by $13 million. What are the correct amounts for (a) net sales, (b) ending inventory, (c) cost of goods sold, and (d) gross profit?

S6-13 (*Learning Objective 6: Analyze the effect of an inventory error on two years*) Office Stop's $4.8 million cost of inventory at the end of last year was understated by $1.4 million.

1. Was last year's reported gross profit of $3.7 million overstated, understated, or correct? What was the correct amount of gross profit last year?
2. Is this year's gross profit of $4.6 million overstated, understated, or correct? What is the correct amount of gross profit for the current year?

S6-14 (*Learning Objectives 3, 5: Explain underlying GAAP for inventory; evaluate management decisions*) Determine whether each of the following actions in buying, selling, and accounting for inventories is ethical or unethical. Give your reason for each answer.

1. In applying the lower-of-cost-or-market rule to inventories, Tundra Financial Industries recorded an excessively low value for its ending inventory (below both cost and market). This allowed the company to pay less income tax for the year.
2. Mercy Pharmaceuticals purchased a large amount of inventory shortly before year-end to increase the LIFO cost of goods sold and decrease reported income for the year.
3. Marsten, Inc., delayed the purchase of inventory until after December 31, 2012, to keep 2012's cost of goods sold from growing too large. The delay in purchasing inventory helped net income of 2012 to reach the level of profit demanded by the company's investors.
4. Dopler Sales Company deliberately overstated ending inventory in order to report higher profits (net income).
5. Blake Corporation deliberately overstated purchases to produce a high figure for cost of goods sold (low amount of net income). The real reason was to decrease the company's income tax payments to the government.

Exercises

MyAccountingLab

> All of the A and B exercises can be found within MyAccountingLab, an online homework and practice environment. Your instructor may ask you to complete these exercises using MyAccountingLab.

Group A

E6-15A (*Learning Objectives 1, 2: Show how to account for inventory transactions; apply the FIFO cost method*) Accounting records for Dundas Corporation yield the following data for the year ended June 30, 2012:

Inventory, June 30, 2011..	$10,000
Purchases of inventory (on account)...	46,000
Sales of inventory—83% on account; 17% for cash (cost $39,000).........	75,000
Inventory at FIFO, June 30, 2012	17,000

▶ Requirements

1. Journalize Dundas' inventory transactions for the year under the perpetual system.
2. Report ending inventory, sales, cost of goods sold, and gross profit on the appropriate financial statement.

E6-16A (*Learning Objectives 1, 2: Show how to account for inventory transactions; apply the FIFO cost method*) Ontario, Inc.'s inventory records for a particular development program show the following at January 31:

Jan 1	Beginning inventory	4 units @ $155	=	$ 620
15	Purchase.................................	7 units @ 155	=	$1,085
26	Purchase.................................	12 units @ 165	=	$1,980

At January 31, eight of these programs are on hand. Journalize the following for Ontario, Inc:

1. Total January purchases in one summary entry. All purchases were on credit.
2. Total January sales and cost of goods sold in two summary entries. The selling price was $600 per unit, and all sales were on credit. Assume that Ontario, Inc., uses the FIFO inventory method.
3. Under FIFO, how much gross profit would Ontario, Inc., earn on these transactions? What is the FIFO cost of Ontario, Inc.'s ending inventory?

E6-17A *(Learning Objective 2: Compare ending inventory and cost of goods sold by four methods)* Use the data for Ontario, Inc., in Exercise 6-16A to answer the following:

▶ Requirements

1. Compute cost of goods sold and ending inventory, using each of the following methods:
   a. Specific unit cost, with three $155 units and five $165 units still on hand at the end
   b. Average cost
   c. First-in, first-out
   d. Last-in, first-out

2. Which method produces the highest cost of goods sold? Which method produces the lowest cost of goods sold? What causes the difference in cost of goods sold?

E6-18A *(Learning Objective 2: Compare the tax advantage of LIFO over FIFO)* Use the data for Ontario, Inc., in Exercise 6-16A to illustrate Ontario, Inc.'s income tax advantage from using LIFO over FIFO. Sales revenue is $9,000, operating expenses are $1,400, and the income tax rate is 28%. How much in taxes would Ontario, Inc., save by using the LIFO method versus FIFO?

E6-19A *(Learning Objective 2: Compare ending inventory and cost of goods sold—FIFO vs. LIFO)* MusicWorld.net specializes in sound equipment. Because each inventory item is expensive, MusicWorld uses a perpetual inventory system. Company records indicate the following data for a line of speakers:

Date		Item	Quantity	Unit Cost	Sale Price
Jun	1	Balance..................	14	$42	
Jun	2	Purchase................	4	69	
Jun	7	Sale	7		$111
Jun	13	Sale	5		111

▶ Requirements

1. Determine the amounts that MusicWorld should report for cost of goods sold and ending inventory two ways:
   a. FIFO
   b. LIFO

2. MusicWorld uses the FIFO method. Prepare MusicWorld's income statement for the month ended June 30, 2012, reporting gross profit. Operating expenses totaled $340, and the income tax rate was 40%.

E6-20A *(Learning Objective 2: Compare gross profit—FIFO vs. LIFO—falling prices)* Suppose a Corse store in Kansas City, Missouri, ended May 2012 with 700,000 units of merchandise that cost an average of $6 each. Suppose the store then sold 650,000 units for $8,450,000 during June. Further, assume the store made two large purchases during June as follows:

Jun 10	100,000 units @ $5.00	=	$ 500,000
20	400,000 units @ $4.00	=	$1,600,000

▶ Requirements

1. At June 30, the store manager needs to know the store's gross profit under both FIFO and LIFO. Supply this information.
2. What caused the FIFO and LIFO gross profit figures to differ?

E6-21A (*Learning Objective 3: Apply the lower-of-cost-or-market rule to inventories*) Princeton Garden Supplies uses a perpetual inventory system. Princeton Garden Supplies has these account balances at October 31, 2012, prior to making the year-end adjustments:

Inventory		Cost of Goods Sold		Sales Revenue	
Beg bal 13,000					
End bal 14,000		Bal 70,000		Bal 115,000	

A year ago, the replacement cost of ending inventory was $13,500, which exceeded cost of $13,000. Princeton Garden Supplies has determined that the replacement cost of the October 31, 2012, ending inventory is $12,500.

▶ Requirement

1. Prepare Princeton Garden Supplies' 2012 income statement through gross profit to show how the company would apply the lower-of-cost-or-market rule to its inventories.

E6-22A (*Learning Objective 4: Compute cost of goods sold and gross profit*) Supply the missing income statement amounts for each of the following companies (amounts adapted, in millions):

Company	Net Sales	Beginning Inventory	Net Purchases	Ending Inventory	Cost of Goods Sold	Gross Profit
Baker	$106,000	$21,000	$62,000	$17,000	(a)	(b)
Lawson	137,000	26,000	(c)	23,000	(d)	44,000
Ethan	(e)	(f)	54,000	24,000	62,000	29,000
Paulus	82,000	8,000	29,000	(g)	33,000	(h)

▶ Requirement

1. Prepare the income statement for Baker Company for the year ended December 31, 2012. Use the cost-of-goods-sold model to compute cost of goods sold. Baker's operating and other expenses, as adapted, for the year were $44,000. Ignore income tax.

Note: Exercise E6-23A builds on Exercise 6-22A with a profitability analysis of these companies.

E6-23A (*Learning Objective 4: Evaluate profitability and inventory turnover*) Refer to the data in Exercise 6-22A. Compute all ratio values to answer the following questions:

▶ Which company has the highest, and which company has the lowest, gross profit percentage?
▶ Which company has the highest, and which has the lowest, rate of inventory turnover?

Based on your figures, which company appears to be the most profitable?

E6-24A (*Learning Objective 4: Compute and evaluate gross profit percentage and inventory turnover*) Burner & Brett, a partnership, had the following inventory data:

	2011	2012
Ending inventory at:		
FIFO Cost	$22,000	$ 26,000
LIFO Cost	9,000	21,000
Cost of goods sold at:		
FIFO Cost		$ 85,800
LIFO Cost		92,900
Sales revenue		139,000

Burner & Brett need to know the company's gross profit percentage and rate of inventory turnover for 2012 under

1. FIFO.
2. LIFO.

Which method produces a higher gross profit percentage? Inventory turnover?

E6-25A (*Learning Objective 5: Use the COGS model to make management decisions*) Super Toys prepares budgets to help manage the company. Super Toys is budgeting for the fiscal year ended January 31, 2012. During the preceding year ended January 31, 2011, sales totaled $9,500 million and cost of goods sold was $6,600 million. At January 31, 2011, inventory was $1,900 million. During the upcoming 2012 year, suppose Super Toys expects cost of goods sold to increase by 10%. The company budgets next year's ending inventory at $2,200 million.

▶ Requirement

1. One of the most important decisions a manager makes is how much inventory to buy. How much inventory should Super Toys purchase during the upcoming year to reach its budget?

E6-26A (*Learning Objective 5: Use the COGS model to make management decisions*) RK Company began September with inventory of $45,300. The business made net purchases of $33,300 and had net sales of $61,600 before a fire destroyed the company's inventory. For the past several years, RK's gross profit percentage has been 45%. Estimate the cost of the inventory destroyed by the fire. Identify another reason that owners and managers use the gross profit method to estimate inventory.

E6-27A (*Learning Objective 6: Analyze the effect of an inventory error*) Myrtle Bay Marine Supply reported the following comparative income statements for the years ended June 30, 2012, and 2011:

Myrtle Bay Marine Supply Income Statements For the Years Ended September 30, 2012, and 2011				
		2012		**2011**
Sales revenue		$136,000		$119,000
Cost of goods sold:				
Beginning inventory	$ 15,000		$ 11,500	
Net purchases	75,000		74,000	
Cost of goods available	90,000		85,500	
Ending inventory	(18,000)		(15,000)	
Cost of goods sold		72,000		70,500
Gross profit		64,000		48,500
Operating expenses		28,000		26,000
Net income		$ 36,000		$ 22,500

Myrtle Bay's president and shareholders are thrilled by the company's boost in sales and net income during 2012. Then the accountants for the company discover that ending 2011 inventory was understated by $7,500. Prepare the corrected comparative income statements for the two-year period, complete with a heading for the statements. How well did Myrtle Bay really perform in 2012 as compared with 2011?

Group B

E6-28B *(Learning Objectives 1, 2: Show how to account for inventory transactions; apply the FIFO cost method)* Accounting records for Thames Corporation yield the following data for the year ended March 31, 2012:

Inventory, March 31, 2011	$ 9,000
Purchases of inventory (on account)...	48,000
Sales of inventory—79% on account; 21% for cash (cost $38,000).........	72,000
Inventory at FIFO, March 31, 2012..	19,000

▶ Requirements

1. Journalize Thames' inventory transactions for the year under the perpetual system.
2. Report ending inventory, sales, cost of goods sold, and gross profit on the appropriate financial statement.

E6-29B *(Learning Objectives 1, 2: Show how to account for inventory transactions; apply the FIFO cost method)* Donovan, Inc.'s inventory records for a particular development program show the following at August 31:

Aug 1	Beginning inventory	5 units @	$170	=	$ 850
Aug 15	Purchase................................	7 units @	170	=	1,190
Aug 26	Purchase................................	13 units @	180	=	2,340

At August 31, nine of these programs are on hand. Journalize the following for Donovan:

1. Total August purchases in one summary entry. All purchases were on credit.
2. Total August sales and cost of goods sold in two summary entries. The selling price was $575 per unit, and all sales were on credit. Assume that Donovan uses the FIFO inventory method.
3. Under FIFO, how much gross profit would Donovan earn on these transactions? What is the FIFO cost of Donovan, Inc.'s ending inventory?

E6-30B *(Learning Objective 2: Compare ending inventory and cost of goods sold by four methods)* Use the data for Donovan, Inc., in Exercise 6-29B to answer the following.

▶ Requirements

1. Compute cost of goods sold and ending inventory using each of the following methods:
   a. Specific unit cost, with five $170 units and four $180 units still on hand at the end
   b. Average cost
   c. FIFO
   d. LIFO

2. Which method produces the highest cost of goods sold? Which method produces the lowest cost of goods sold? What causes the difference in cost of goods sold?

E6-31B *(Learning Objective 2: Compare the tax advantage of LIFO over FIFO)* Use the data for Donovan, Inc., in Exercise 6-29B to illustrate Donovan's income tax advantage from using LIFO over FIFO. Sales revenue is $9,200, operating expenses are $1,800, and the income tax rate is 40%. How much in taxes would Donovan save by using the LIFO method versus FIFO?

E6-32B (*Learning Objective 2: Compare ending inventory and cost of goods sold—FIFO vs. LIFO*) MusicMagic.net specializes in sound equipment. Because each inventory item is expensive, MusicMagic uses a perpetual inventory system. Company records indicate the following data for a line of speakers:

Date		Item	Quantity	Unit Cost	Sale Price
Sep	1	Balance..................	17	$59	
Sep	3	Purchase................	3	71	
Sep	8	Sale	6		$118
Sep	12	Sale	7		107

▶ Requirements

1. Determine the amounts that MusicMagic should report for cost of goods sold and ending inventory two ways:
   a. FIFO
   b. LIFO

2. MusicMagic uses the FIFO method. Prepare MusicMagic's income statement for the month ended September 30, 2012, reporting gross profit. Operating expenses totaled $320, and the income tax rate was 35%.

E6-33B (*Learning Objective 2: Compare gross profit—FIFO vs. LIFO—falling prices*) Suppose a Robak store in Denver, Colorado, ended September 2012 with 1,000,000 units of merchandise that cost an average of $7.00 each. Suppose the store then sold 950,000 units for $9,500,000 during October. Further, assume the store made two large purchases during October as follows:

Oct 8	200,000 units @ $6.00	= $1,200,000
22	600,000 units @ $5.00	= $3,000,000

▶ Requirements

1. At October 31, the store manager needs to know the store's gross profit under both FIFO and LIFO. Supply this information.
2. What caused the FIFO and LIFO gross profit figures to differ?

E6-34B (*Learning Objective 3: Apply the lower-of-cost-or-market rule to inventories*) Erie Garden Supplies uses a perpetual inventory system. Erie Garden Supplies has these account balances at August 31, 2012, prior to making the year-end adjustments:

Inventory		Cost of Goods Sold		Sales Revenue	
Beg bal 10,000					
End bal 14,000		Bal 72,000		Bal 120,000	

A year ago, the replacement cost of ending inventory was $11,500, which exceeded the cost of $10,000. Erie Garden Supplies has determined that the replacement cost of the August 31, 2012, ending inventory is $12,000.

▶ Requirement

1. Prepare Erie Garden Supplies' 2012 income statement through gross profit to show how the company would apply the lower-of-cost-or-market rule to its inventories.

E6-35B *(Learning Objective 4: Compute cost of goods sold and gross profit)* Supply the missing amounts for each of the following companies:

Company	Net Sales	Beginning Inventory	Net Purchases	Ending Inventory	Cost of Goods Sold	Gross Profit
Gerald	$100,000	$21,000	$60,000	$19,000	(a)	(b)
Evans	137,000	28,000	(c)	22,000	(d)	41,000
Dunleavy	(e)	(f)	55,000	21,000	60,000	32,000
Thomas	80,000	9,000	33,000	(g)	35,000	(h)

▶ Requirement

1. Prepare the income statement for Gerald Company for the year ended December 31, 2012. Use the cost-of-goods-sold model to compute cost of goods sold. Gerald's operating and other expenses for the year were $42,000. Ignore income tax.

Note: Exercise E6-36B builds on Exercise E6-35B with a profitability analysis of these companies.

E6-36B *(Learning Objective 4: Evaluate profitability and inventory turnover)* Refer to the data in Exercise E6-35B. Compute all ratio values to answer the following questions:
   ▶ Which company has the highest, and which company has the lowest, gross profit percentage?
   ▶ Which company has the highest, and which has the lowest, rate of inventory turnover?

Based on your figures, which company appears to be the most profitable?

E6-37B *(Learning Objective 4: Compute and evaluate gross profit percentage and inventory turnover)* Tilton & Taft, a partnership, had these inventory data:

	2011	2012
Ending inventory at:		
FIFO Cost...............	$16,000	$ 27,000
LIFO Cost...............	8,000	16,000
Cost of goods sold at:		
FIFO Cost...............		$ 85,900
LIFO Cost...............		92,300
Sales revenue...............		143,000

Tilton & Taft need to know the company's gross profit percentage and rate of inventory turnover for 2012 under
   1. FIFO.
   2. LIFO.

Which method produces a higher gross profit percentage? Inventory turnover?

E6-38B *(Learning Objective 5: Use the COGS model to make management decisions)* Fun Toys prepares budgets to help manage the company. Fun Toys is budgeting for the fiscal year ended January 31, 2012. During the preceding year ended January 31, 2011, sales totaled $9,600 million and cost of goods sold was $6,700 million. At January 31, 2011, inventory was $1,700 million. During the upcoming 2012 year, suppose Fun Toys expects cost of goods sold to increase by 10%. The company budgets next year's inventory at $2,000 million.

▶ Requirement

1. One of the most important decisions a manager makes is how much inventory to buy. How much inventory should Fun Toys purchase during the upcoming year to reach its budget?

E6-39B (*Learning Objective 5: Use the COGS model to make management decisions*) Putnam Company began April with inventory of $46,100. The business made net purchases of $31,500 and had net sales of $64,600 before a fire destroyed the company's inventory. For the past several years, Putnam's gross profit percentage has been 40%. Estimate the cost of the inventory destroyed by the fire. Identify another reason that owners and managers use the gross profit method to estimate inventory.

E6-40B (*Learning Objective 6: Analyze the effect of an inventory error*) By the Bay Marine Supply reported the following comparative income statements for the years ended June 30, 2012, and 2011:

	2012		2011	
Sales revenue		$138,000		$120,000
Cost of goods sold:				
Beginning inventory	$ 12,000		$ 9,500	
Net purchases	78,000		75,000	
Cost of goods available	90,000		84,500	
Ending inventory	(16,500)		(12,000)	
Cost of goods sold		73,500		72,500
Gross profit		64,500		47,500
Operating expenses		30,000		25,000
Net income		$ 34,500		$ 22,500

By the Bay Marine Supply
Income Statements
For the Years Ended June 30, 2012, and 2011

By the Bay's president and shareholders are thrilled by the company's boost in sales and net income during 2012. Then the accountants for the company discover that ending 2011 inventory was understated by $8,000. Prepare the corrected comparative income statements for the two-year period, complete with a heading for the statements. How well did By the Bay really perform in 2012 as compared with 2011?

Quiz

Test your understanding of accounting for inventory by answering the following questions. Select the best choice from among the possible answers given.

Q6-41 Oceanside Software began January with $3,400 of merchandise inventory. During January, Oceanside made the following entries for its inventory transactions:

Inventory	6,700	
Accounts Payable		6,700
Accounts Receivable	7,700	
Sales Revenue		7,700
Cost of Goods Sold	5,500	
Inventory		5,500

How much was Oceanside's inventory at the end of January?
a. $10,100
b. Zero

c. $4,600
d. $6,700

Q6-42 What was Oceanside's gross profit for January?
a. $5,500
c. $7,700
b. $2,200
d. $Zero

Q6-43 When does the cost of inventory become an expense?
a. When payment is made to the supplier
b. When inventory is delivered to a customer
c. When cash is collected from the customer
d. When inventory is purchased from the supplier

The next two questions use the following facts. Perfect Picture Frame Shop wants to know the effect of different inventory costing methods on its financial statements. Inventory and purchases data for June follow:

			Units	Unit Cost	Total Cost
Jun 1		Beginning inventory	2,100	$11.00	$23,100
4		Purchase	1,200	$11.50	13,800
9		Sale	(1,400)		

Q6-44 If Perfect Picture uses the FIFO method, the *cost of the ending inventory* will be
a. $15,700.
c. $13,800.
b. $21,500.
d. $15,400.

Q6-45 If Perfect Picture uses the LIFO method, *cost of goods sold* will be
a. $16,000.
c. $13,800.
b. $15,400.
d. $15,700.

Q6-46 In a period of rising prices,
a. net income under LIFO will be higher than under FIFO.
b. gross profit under FIFO will be higher than under LIFO.
c. cost of goods sold under LIFO will be less than under FIFO.
d. LIFO inventory will be greater than FIFO inventory.

Q6-47 The income statement for Nature's Way Foods shows gross profit of $153,000, operating expenses of $123,000, and cost of goods sold of $213,000. What is the amount of net sales revenue?
a. $366,000
c. $276,000
b. $489,000
d. $336,000

Q6-48 The word "market" as used in "the lower of cost or market" generally means
a. replacement cost.
c. original cost.
b. retail market price.
d. liquidation price.

Q6-49 The sum of ending inventory and cost of goods sold is
a. net purchases.
c. goods available.
b. beginning inventory.
d. gross profit.

Q6-50 The following data come from the inventory records of Dodge Company:

Net sales revenue..	$627,000
Beginning inventory	61,000
Ending inventory..	40,000
Net purchases..	430,000

Based on these facts, the gross profit for Dodge Company is
a. $197,000.
c. $166,000.
b. $190,000.
d. $176,000.

Q6-51 Ellen Donoghue Cosmetics ended the month of March with inventory of $25,000. Ellen Donoghue expects to end April with inventory of $17,000 after selling goods with a cost of $92,000. How much inventory must Donoghue purchase during April in order to accomplish these results?

a. $84,000

b. $109,000

c. $100,000

d. $134,000

Q6-52 Two financial ratios that clearly distinguish a discount chain such as Wal-Mart from a high-end retailer such as Gucci are the gross profit percentage and the rate of inventory turnover. Which set of relationships is most likely for Gucci?

Gross profit percentage	Inventory turnover
a. Low	High
b. High	High
c. Low	Low
d. High	Low

Q6-53 Sales are $580,000 and cost of goods sold is $310,000. Beginning and ending inventories are $23,000 and $38,000, respectively. How many times did the company turn its inventory over during this period?

a. 8.9 times

b. 11.7 times

c. 19.0 times

d. 10.2 times

Q6-54 Tulsa, Inc., reported the following data:

Freight in......................	$ 21,000	Sales returns..............	$ 4,000
Purchases	202,000	Purchase returns........	6,000
Beginning inventory	55,000	Sales revenue.............	490,000
Purchase discounts......	4,600	Ending inventory.......	44,000

Tulsa's gross profit percentage is

a. 54.0.

b. 50.7.

c. 53.0.

d. 46.0.

Q6-55 Turbo Tank Company had the following beginning inventory, net purchases, net sales, and gross profit percentage for the first quarter of 2012:

Beginning inventory, $56,000	Net purchases, $79,000
Net sales revenue, $95,000	Gross profit rate, 40%

By the gross profit method, the ending inventory should be

a. $78,000.

b. $97,000.

c. $57,000.

d. $135,000.

Q6-56 An error understated Rex Corporation's December 31, 2012, ending inventory by $36,000. What effect will this error have on total assets and net income for 2012?

Assets	Net income
a. Understate	No effect
b. No effect	No effect
c. No effect	Overstate
d. Understate	Understate

Q6-57 An error understated Rex Corporation's December 31, 2012, ending inventory by $36,000. What effect will this error have on net income for 2013?

a. Understate

b. No effect

c. Overstate

Problems

MyAccountingLab

> All of the A and B problems can be found within MyAccountingLab, an online homework and practice environment. Your instructor may ask you to complete these problems using MyAccountingLab.

Group A

P6-58A (*Learning Objectives 1, 2: Show how to account for inventory in a perpetual system using the average-costing method*) Better Buy purchases inventory in crates of merchandise; each crate of inventory is a unit. The fiscal year of Better Buy ends each January 31. Assume you are dealing with a single Better Buy store in San Diego, California. The San Diego store began 2012 with an inventory of 20,000 units that cost a total of $1,000,000. During the year, the store purchased merchandise on account as follows:

Jul (32,000 units at $58)	$1,856,000
Nov (52,000 units at $62)...................................	3,224,000
Dec (62,000 units at $68)...................................	4,216,000
Total purchases...	$9,296,000

Cash payments on account totaled $8,896,000. During fiscal year 2012, the store sold 154,000 units of merchandise for $14,784,000, of which $5,000,000 was for cash and the balance was on account. Better Buy uses the average-cost method for inventories. Operating expenses for the year were $2,750,000. Better Buy paid 70% in cash and accrued the rest as accrued liabilities. The store accrued income tax at the rate of 40%.

▶ Requirements

1. Make summary journal entries to record the store's transactions for the year ended January 31, 2012. Better Buy uses a perpetual inventory system.
2. Prepare a T-account to show the activity in the Inventory account.
3. Prepare the store's income statement for the year ended January 31, 2012. Show totals for gross profit, income before tax, and net income.

P6-59A (*Learning Objective 2: Apply various inventory costing methods*) Assume a Gold Medal Sports outlet store began August 2012 with 44 pairs of running shoes that cost the store $33 each. The sale price of these shoes was $61. During August, the store completed these inventory transactions:

		Units	Unit Cost	Unit Sale Price
Aug 2	Sale	15	$33	$61
9	Purchase......	79	34	
13	Sale	29	33	61
18	Sale	11	34	63
22	Sale	30	34	63
29	Purchase......	26	35	

▶ Requirements

1. The preceding data are taken from the store's perpetual inventory records. Which cost method does the store use? Explain how you arrived at your answer.
2. Determine the store's cost of goods sold for August. Also compute gross profit for August.
3. What is the cost of the store's August 31 inventory of running shoes?

P6-60A (*Learning Objective 2: Compare inventory by three methods*) Army-Navy Surplus began March with 75 tents that cost $16 each. During the month, Army-Navy Surplus made the following purchases at cost:

Mar 3	95 tents @ $18	= $1,710
17	165 tents @ $20	= 3,300
23	36 tents @ $21	= $ 756

Army-Navy Surplus sold 318 tents, and at March 31, the ending inventory consists of 53 tents. The sale price of each tent was $45.

▶ Requirements

1. Determine the cost of goods sold and ending inventory amounts for March under the average cost, FIFO cost, and LIFO cost. Round average cost per unit to four decimal places, and round all other amounts to the nearest dollar.
2. Explain why cost of goods sold is highest under LIFO. Be specific.
3. Prepare Army-Navy Surplus' income statement for March. Report gross profit. Operating expenses totaled $2,750. Army-Navy Surplus uses average costing for inventory. The income tax rate is 30%.

P6-61A (*Learning Objective 2: Compare various inventory costing methods*) The records of Lindbergh Aviation include the following accounts for inventory of aviation fuel at July 31 of the current year:

Inventory

Aug 1	Balance	720 units @ $7.10	$ 5,112
Nov 5	Purchase	400 units @ $7.20	2,880
Jan 24	Purchase 8,420 units @ $7.60	63,992
Apr 8	Purchase	480 units @ $8.60	4,128

Sales Revenue

Dec 31	9,050 units	$127,605

▶ Requirements

1. Prepare a partial income statement through gross profit under the average, FIFO, and LIFO methods. Round average cost per unit to four decimal places and all other amounts to the nearest dollar.
2. Which inventory method would you use to minimize income tax? Explain why this method causes income tax to be the lowest.

P6-62A (*Learning Objective 3: Explain GAAP and apply the lower-of-cost-or-market rule to inventories*) Great White Trade Mart has recently had lackluster sales. The rate of inventory turnover has dropped, and the merchandise is gathering dust. At the same time, competition has forced Great White's suppliers to lower the prices that Great White will pay when it replaces its inventory. It is now December 31, 2012, and the current replacement cost of Great White's ending inventory is $90,000 below what Great White actually paid for the goods, which was $240,000. Before any adjustments at the end of the period, the Cost of Goods Sold account has a balance of $810,000.

   a. What accounting action should Great White take in this situation?
   b. Give any journal entry required.
   c. At what amount should Great White report Inventory on the balance sheet?
   d. At what amount should the company report Cost of Goods Sold on the income statement?
   e. Discuss the accounting principle or concept that is most relevant to this situation.

P6-63A *(Learning Objective 4: Compute and evaluate gross margin and inventory turnover)*
Muffin Mania, Inc., and La Crème Coffee Corporation are both specialty food chains. The two
companies reported these figures, in millions:

Muffin Mania, Inc.
Income Statements (Adapted)
Years Ended December 31

(Amounts in millions)	2012	2011
Revenues:		
Net sales	$540	$705
Costs and Expenses:		
Cost of goods sold	470	595
Selling, general, and administrative expenses	61	53

Muffin Mania, Inc.
Balance Sheets (Adapted)
December 31

(Amounts in millions)	2012	2011
Assets		
Current assets:		
Cash and temporary investments	$21	$24
Receivables	25	40
Inventories	18	30

La Crème Coffee Corporation
Income Statements (Adapted)
Years Ended December 31

(Amounts in millions)	2012	2011
Net sales	$7,710	$6,400
Cost of goods sold	3,170	2,600
Selling, general, and administrative expenses	2,975	2,360

La Crème Coffee Corporation
Balance Sheets (Adapted)
December 31

(Amounts in millions)	2012	2011
Assets		
Current assets:		
Cash and temporary investments	$320	$175
Receivables, net	220	195
Inventories	630	540

▶ Requirements

1. Compute the gross profit percentage and the rate of inventory turnover for Muffin Mania and La Crème Coffee for 2012.
2. Based on these statistics, which company looks more profitable? Why? What other expense category should we consider in evaluating these two companies?

P6-64A (*Learning Objective 5: Use the COGS model to make management decisions, and estimate inventory by the gross profit method*) Assume Smith Company, a camera store, lost some inventory in a fire on August 15. To file an insurance claim, Smith Company must estimate its inventory by the gross profit method. Assume that for the past two years Smith Company's gross profit has averaged 45% of net sales. Suppose that Smith Company's inventory records reveal the following data:

Inventory, August 1..................	$ 57,200
Transactions during August:	
Purchases	490,800
Purchase discounts	15,000
Purchase returns.......................	70,800
Sales..	665,000
Sales returns.............................	12,000

▶ Requirements

1. Estimate the cost of the lost inventory using the gross profit method.
2. Prepare the August income statement for this product through gross profit. Show the detailed computations of cost of goods sold in a separate schedule.

P6-65A (*Learning Objective 5: Use the COGS model to make management decisions (amount of inventory to purchase)*) Chester's Convenience Stores' income statement for the year ended December 31, 2011 and its balance sheet as of December 31, 2011 reported the following.

Chester's Convenience Stores
Income Statement
Year Ended December 31, 2011

Sales	$964,000
Cost of sales	721,000
Gross profit	243,000
Operating expenses	109,000
Net income	$134,000

Chester's Convenience Stores
Balance Sheet
December 31, 2011

Assets		Liabilities and Capital	
Cash	$ 37,000	Accounts payable	$ 32,000
Inventories	64,000	Note payable	185,000
Land and		Total liabilities	217,000
buildings, net	273,000	Owner, capital	157,000
		Total liabilities	
Total assets	$374,000	and capital	$374,000

The business is organized as a proprietorship, so it pays no corporate income tax. The owner is budgeting for 2012. He expects sales and cost of goods sold to increase by 5%. To meet customer demand, ending inventory will need to be $83,000 at December 31, 2012. The owner hopes to earn a net income of $158,000 next year.

▶ Requirements

1. One of the most important decisions a manager makes is the amount of inventory to purchase. Show how to determine the amount of inventory to purchase in 2012.
2. Prepare the store's budgeted income statement for 2012 to reach the target net income of $158,000. To reach this goal, operating expenses must decrease by $11,850.

P6-66A (*Learning Objective 6: Analyze the effects of inventory errors*) The accounting records of J.L. Home Store show these data (in millions). The shareholders are very happy with J.L.'s steady increase in net income.

Auditors discovered that the ending inventory for 2010 was understated by $4 million and that the ending inventory for 2011 was also understated by $4 million. The ending inventory at December 31, 2012, was correct.

	2012		2011		2010	
Net sales revenue.............................		$44		$41		$38
Cost of goods sold:						
Beginning inventory...................	$ 8		$ 7		$ 6	
Net purchases	29		27		25	
Cost of goods available	37		34		31	
Less ending inventory................	(9)		(8)		(7)	
Cost of goods sold		28		26		24
Gross profit.....................................		16		15		14
Operating expenses		8		8		8
Net income......................................		$ 8		$ 7		$ 6

▶ Requirements

1. Show corrected income statements for each of the three years.
2. How much did these assumed corrections add to or take away from J.L.'s total net income over the three-year period? How did the corrections affect the trend of net income?
3. Will J.L.'s shareholders still be happy with the company's trend of net income? Give the reason for your answer.

Group B

P6-67B (*Learning Objectives 1, 2: Show how to account for inventory in a perpetual system using the average-costing method*) Fun Buy purchases inventory in crates of merchandise; each crate of inventory is a unit. The fiscal year of Fun Buy ends each June 30. Assume you are dealing with a single Fun Buy store in Nashville, Tennessee. The Nashville store began 2012 with an inventory of 23,000 units that cost a total of $1,150,000. During the year, the store purchased merchandise on account as follows:

August (28,000 units at $54).................................	$1,512,000
March (48,000 units at $58)	2,784,000
May (58,000 units at $64)	3,712,000
Total purchases..	$8,008,000

Cash payments on account totaled $7,608,000. During fiscal 2012, the store sold 153,000 units of merchandise for $14,688,000, of which $5,400,000 was for cash and the balance was on account. Fun Buy uses the average-cost method for inventories. Operating expenses for the year were $3,500,000. Fun Buy paid 50% in cash and accrued the rest as accrued liabilities. The store accrued income tax at the rate of 35%.

▶ Requirements

1. Make summary journal entries to record the store's transactions for the year ended June 30, 2012. Fun Buy uses a perpetual inventory system.
2. Prepare a T-account to show the activity in the Inventory account.
3. Prepare the store's income statement for the year ended June 30, 2012. Show totals for gross profit, income before tax, and net income.

P6-68B (*Learning Objective 2: Apply various inventory costing methods*) Assume a Tilton Sports outlet store began January 2012 with 42 pairs of running shoes that cost the store $37 each. The sale price of these shoes was $63. During January, the store completed these inventory transactions:

		Units	Unit Cost	Unit Sale Price
Jan 3	Sale	15	$37	$63
8	Purchase......	82	38	
11	Sale	27	37	63
19	Sale	6	38	65
24	Sale	29	38	65
30	Purchase......	25	39	

▶ Requirements

1. The preceding data are taken from the store's perpetual inventory records. Which cost method does the store use? Explain how you arrived at your answer.
2. Determine the store's cost of goods sold for January. Also compute gross profit for January.
3. What is the cost of the store's January 31 inventory of running shoes?

P6-69B (*Learning Objective 2: Compare inventory by three methods*) Camp Surplus began May with 67 tents that cost $25 each. During the month, Camp Surplus made the following purchases at cost:

May 6	101 tents @ $27 = $2,727
18	163 tents @ $29 = 4,727
26	41 tents @ $30 = 1,230

Camp Surplus sold 323 tents, and at May 31 the ending inventory consists of 49 tents. The sale price of each tent was $49.

▶ Requirements

1. Determine the cost of goods sold and ending inventory amounts for May under the average cost, FIFO cost, and LIFO cost. Round average cost per unit to four decimal places, and round all other amounts to the nearest dollar.
2. Explain why cost of goods sold is highest under LIFO. Be specific.
3. Prepare the Camp Surplus income statement for May. Report gross profit. Operating expenses totaled $3,250. Camp Surplus uses average costing for inventory. The income tax rate is 30%.

P6-70B (*Learning Objective 2: Compare various inventory costing methods*) The records of Shepard Aviation include the following accounts for inventory of aviation fuel at October 31 of the current year:

Inventory

Nov 1	Balance	700 units @ $7.40	$ 5,180	
Jan 8	Purchase	350 units @ $7.50	2,625	
May 21	Purchase	8,450 units @ $7.90	66,755	
Jul 7	Purchase	480 units @ $8.90	4,272	

Sales Revenue

Oct 31	9,080 units	$128,936

► Requirements

1. Prepare a partial income statement through gross profit under the average, FIFO, and LIFO methods. Round average cost per unit to four decimal places and all other amounts to the nearest whole dollar.
2. Which inventory method would you use to minimize income tax? Explain why this method causes income tax to be the lowest.

P6-71B (*Learning Objective 3: Explain GAAP and apply the lower-of-cost-or-market rule to inventories*) Saltwater Trade Mart has recently had lackluster sales. The rate of inventory turnover has dropped, and the merchandise is gathering dust. At the same time, competition has forced Saltwater's suppliers to lower the prices that Saltwater will pay when it replaces its inventory. It is now December 31, 2012, and the current replacement cost of Saltwater's ending inventory is $85,000 below what Saltwater actually paid for the goods, which was $270,000. Before any adjustments at the end of the period, the Cost of Goods Sold account has a balance of $790,000.

  a. What accounting action should Saltwater take in this situation?
  b. Give any journal entry required.
  c. At what amount should Saltwater report Inventory on the balance sheet?
  d. At what amount should the company report Cost of Goods Sold on the income statement?
  e. Discuss the accounting principle or concept that is most relevant to this situation.

P6-72B (*Learning Objective 4: Compute and evaluate gross margin and inventory turnover*) Cinnamon Roll, Inc., and Dunking Coffee Corporation are both specialty food chains. The two companies reported these figures, in millions:

Cinnamon Roll, Inc.
Income Statements (Adapted)
Years Ended December 31

(Amounts in millions)		2012	2011
Revenues:			
Net sales		$542	$704
Costs and Expenses:			
Cost of goods sold		474	592
Selling, general, and administrative expenses		67	50

Cinnamon Roll, Inc.
Balance Sheets (Adapted)
December 31

(Amounts in millions)		2012	2011
Assets			
Current assets:			
Cash and cash equivalents		$16	$26
Receivables		27	33
Inventories		20	36

Dunking Coffee Corporation
Income Statements (Adapted)
Years Ended December 31

(Amounts in millions)	2012	2011
Net sales	$7,777	$6,369
Cost of goods sold	3,180	2,600
Selling, general, and administrative expenses	3,000	2,350

Dunking Coffee Corporation
Balance Sheets (Adapted)
December 31

(Amounts in millions)	2012	2011
Assets		
Current assets:		
Cash and temporary investments	$318	$171
Receivables, net	227	194
Inventories	625	541

► Requirements

1. Compute the gross profit percentage and the rate of inventory turnover for Cinnamon Roll, Inc., and Dunking Coffee Corporation for 2012.
2. Based on these statistics, which company looks more profitable? Why? What other expense category should we consider in evaluating these two companies?

P6-73B (*Learning Objective 5: Use the COGS model to make management decisions, and estimate inventory by the gross profit method*) Assume Young Company, a music store, lost some inventory in a fire on March 15. To file an insurance claim, Young Company must estimate its ending inventory by the gross profit method. Assume that for the past two years, Young Company's gross profit has averaged 44% of net sales. Suppose Young Company's inventory records reveal the following data:

Inventory, March 1	$ 57,300
Transactions during March:	
Purchases	490,700
Purchase discounts	17,000
Purchase returns	70,000
Sales	660,000
Sales returns	13,000

► Requirements

1. Estimate the cost of the lost inventory using the gross profit method.
2. Prepare the March income statement for this product through gross profit. Show the detailed computation of cost of goods sold in a separate schedule.

P6-74B (*Learning Objective 5: Use COGS model to make management decision of the amount of inventory to purchase*) Eddie's Convenience Stores' income statement for the year ended December 31, 2011 and its balance sheet as of December 31, 2011 reported the following. The business is organized as a proprietorship, so it pays no corporate income tax. The owner is budgeting for 2012. He expects sales and cost of goods sold to increase by 10%. To meet customer demand, ending inventory will need to be $81,000 at December 31, 2012. The owner hopes to earn a net income of $152,000 next year.

Eddie's Convenience Stores
Income Statement
Year Ended December 31, 2011

Sales		$962,000
Cost of sales		724,000
Gross profit		238,000
Operating expenses		113,000
Net income		$125,000

Eddie's Convenience Stores
Balance Sheet
December 31, 2011

Assets		Liabilities and Capital	
Cash	$ 44,000	Accounts payable	$ 28,000
Inventories	69,000	Note payable	188,000
Land and		Total liabilities	216,000
buildings, net	266,000	Owner, capital	163,000
		Total liabilities	
Total assets	$379,000	and capital	$379,000

▶ Requirements

1. One of the most important decisions a manager makes is the amount of inventory to purchase. Show how to determine the amount of inventory to purchase in 2012.
2. Prepare the store's budgeted income statement for 2012 to reach the target net income of $152,000. To reach this goal, operating expenses must decrease by $3,200.

P6-75B (*Learning Objective 6: Analyze the effects of inventory errors*) The accounting records of Columbia Furniture show these data (in millions). The shareholders are very happy with Columbia's steady increase in net income.

	2012	2011	2010
Net sales revenue	$38	$35	$32
Cost of goods sold:			
Beginning inventory	$ 11	$ 10	$ 9
Net purchases	30	28	26
Cost of goods available	41	38	35
Less ending inventory	(12)	(11)	(10)
Cost of goods sold	29	27	25
Gross profit	9	8	7
Operating expenses	6	6	6
Net income	$ 3	$ 2	$ 1

Auditors discovered that the ending inventory for 2010 was understated by $1 million and that the ending inventory for 2011 was also understated by $1 million. The ending inventory at December 31, 2012, was correct.

▶ Requirements

1. Show corrected income statements for each of the three years.
2. How much did these assumed corrections add to or take away from Columbia's total net income over the three-year period? How did the corrections affect the trend of net income?
3. Will Columbia's shareholders still be happy with the company's trend of net income? Give the reason for your answer.

Challenge Exercises and Problem

E6-76 (*Learning Objective 2: Apply various inventory methods to make inventory policy decisions*) For each of the following situations, identify the inventory method that you would use; or, given the use of a particular method, state the strategy that you would follow to accomplish your goal:

a. Inventory costs are increasing. Your company uses LIFO and is having an unexpectedly good year. It is near year-end, and you need to keep net income from increasing too much in order to save on income tax.

b. Suppliers of your inventory are threatening a labor strike, and it may be difficult for your company to obtain inventory. This situation could increase your income taxes.

c. Company management, like that of Apple and Pottery Barn, prefers a middle-of-the-road inventory policy that avoids extremes.

d. Inventory costs are *decreasing*, and your company's board of directors wants to minimize income taxes.

e. Inventory costs are *increasing*, and the company prefers to report high income.

f. Inventory costs have been stable for several years, and you expect costs to remain stable for the indefinite future. (Give the reason for your choice of method.)

E6-77 (*Learning Objective 2: Measure the effect of a LIFO liquidation*) Suppose In Style Fashions, a specialty retailer, had these records for ladies' evening gowns during 2012.

Beginning inventory (44 @ $975)	$ 42,900
Purchase in February (19 @ $1,050)	19,950
Purchase in June (55 @ $1,100)	60,500
Purchase in December (31 @ $1,200)	37,200
Goods available for sale	$160,550

Assume In Style sold 117 gowns during 2012 and uses the LIFO method to account for inventory. The income tax rate is 35%.

▶ **Requirements**

1. Compute In Style's cost of goods sold for evening gowns in 2012.
2. Compute what cost of goods sold would have been if In Style had purchased enough inventory in December—at $1,200 per evening gown—to keep year-end inventory at the same level it was at the beginning of the year.

E6-78 (*Learning Objective 4: Evaluate profitability*) Z Mart, Inc., declared bankruptcy. Let's see why. Z Mart reported these figures:

Z Mart, Inc.
Statements of Income
Years Ended December 31

Millions	2012	2011	2010	2009
Sales	$36.6	$35.3	$34.3	
Cost of sales	29.4	27.6	26.8	
Selling expenses	7.5	6.3	6.0	
Other expenses	0.1	0.9	0.7	
Net income (net loss)	$ (0.4)	$ 0.5	$ 0.8	
Additional data:				
Ending inventory	$ 8.6	$ 7.2	$ 7.2	$6.4

▶ **Requirement**

1. Evaluate the trend of Z Mart's results of operations during 2010 through 2012. Consider the trends of sales, gross profit, and net income. Track the gross profit percentage (to three decimal places) and the rate of inventory turnover (to one decimal place) in each year. Also discuss the role that selling expenses must have played in Z Mart's difficulties.

P6-79 (*Learning Objectives 1, 4: Account for inventory; analyze two companies that use different inventory methods*) Arnold Financial Management believes that the biotechnology industry is a good investment and is considering investing in one of two companies. However, one company, HeartStart, Inc., uses the FIFO method of inventory, and another company, GeneTech, Inc., uses LIFO. The following information about the two companies is available from their annual reports.

HeartStart, Inc.	2011	2010
Inventory..	$ 101,000	$ 95,000
Cost of goods sold...	1,200,000	1,100,000
Sales..	2,000,000	1,850,000
Net income..	190,000	187,000
GeneTech, Inc.	**2011**	**2010**
Inventory (See Note)	$ 330,000	$ 300,000
Cost of goods sold...	3,900,000	3,800,000
Sales..	6,700,000	6,400,000
Net income..	870,000	770,000

Notes to the Financial Statement. If GeneTech had used the FIFO method, inventory would have been $20,000 at the end of 2010 and $22,000 higher at the end of 2011.

The income of the two companies is difficult to compare because GeneTech is a much larger company and uses a different inventory method. To better compare the two companies, Arnold wants you to prepare the following analysis.

▶ **Requirements**

1. Show the computation of GeneTech's cost of goods sold using the LIFO method. Refer to Appendix 6B for an illustration.
2. Prepare summary journal entries for GeneTech's purchases of inventory (assume all purchases are on account), sales (assume all are on account), and cost of goods sold. Prepare a T-account for inventory and post these transactions into the T-account.
3. Show the computation of GeneTech's cost of goods sold using the FIFO method.
4. Compute the gross profit percentage for both HeartStart and GeneTech using FIFO figures for both.
5. Compute the inventory turnover for both HeartStart and GeneTech using FIFO figures for both.
6. Which company appears stronger? Support your answer.

APPLY YOUR KNOWLEDGE

Decision Cases

Case 1. (*Learning Objective 2: Apply and compare various inventory methods, and assess the impact of a year-end purchase of inventory*) Duracraft Corporation is nearing the end of its first year of operations. Duracraft made inventory purchases of $745,000 during the year, as follows:

January	1,000 units @	$100.00 =	$100,000
July	4,000	121.25	485,000
November	1,000	160.00	160,000
Totals	6,000		$745,000

Sales for the year are 5,000 units for $1,200,000 of revenue. Expenses other than cost of goods sold and income taxes total $200,000. The president of the company is undecided about whether to adopt the FIFO method or the LIFO method for inventories. The income tax rate is 40%.

▶ Requirements

1. To aid company decision making, prepare income statements under FIFO and under LIFO.
2. Compare the net income under FIFO with net income under LIFO. Which method produces the higher net income? What causes this difference? Be specific.

Case 2. (*Learning Objectives 2, 3: Apply and compare various inventory methods; apply underlying GAAP for inventory*) The inventory costing method a company chooses can affect the financial statements and thus the decisions of the people who use those statements.

▶ Requirements

1. Company A uses the LIFO inventory method and discloses its use of the LIFO method in notes to the financial statements. Company B uses the FIFO method to account for its inventory. Company B does *not* disclose which inventory method it uses. Company B reports a higher net income than Company A. In which company would you prefer to invest? Give your reason.
2. Representational faithfulness is an accepted accounting concept. Would you want management to be faithful in representing its in accounting for inventory if you were a shareholder or a creditor of a company? Give your reason.

Ethical Issue

During 2012, Vanguard, Inc., changed to the LIFO method of accounting for inventory. Suppose that during 2013, Vanguard changes back to the FIFO method and the following year Vanguard switches back to LIFO again.

▶ Requirements

1. What would you think of a company's ethics if it changed accounting methods every year?
2. What accounting principle would changing methods every year violate?
3. Who can be harmed when a company changes its accounting methods too often? How?

Focus on Financials: | Amazon.com, Inc.

(*Learning Objectives 1, 4: Show how to account for inventories; compute and evaluate gross profit and inventory turnover*) The notes are part of the financial statements. They give details that would clutter the statements. This case will help you learn to use a company's inventory notes. Refer to **Amazon.com, Inc.**'s consolidated financial statements and related notes in Appendix A at the end of the book and answer the following questions:

1. How much was Amazon.com, Inc.'s merchandise inventory at December 31, 2010? At December 31, 2009? Does Amazon.com, Inc., include all inventory that it handles in the inventory account on its balance sheet?

2. How does Amazon.com, Inc., *value* its inventories? Which *cost* method does the company use?

3. Using the cost-of-goods-sold model, compute Amazon.com, Inc.'s purchases of inventory during the year ended December 31, 2010.

4. Did Amazon.com, Inc.'s gross profit percentage on company sales improve or deteriorate in the year ended December 31, 2010, compared to the previous year?

5. Would you rate Amazon.com, Inc.'s rate of inventory turnover for the years ended December 31, 2010, and December 31, 2009, as fast or slow in comparison to most other companies in its industry? Explain your answer.

6. Go to the SEC's Web site (www.sec.gov). Find Amazon.com, Inc.'s most recent consolidated balance sheet and consolidated statement of operations. What has happened to the company's inventory turnover and gross profit percentages since December 31, 2010? Can you explain the reasons? Where would you find the company's explanations for these changes? (Challenge)

Focus on Analysis: | RadioShack Corporation

(*Learning Objectives 1, 2, 4: Show how to account for inventory; explain GAAP for inventory; compute and evaluate gross profit and inventory turnover*) Refer to the **RadioShack Corporation** consolidated financial statements in Appendix B at the end of this book. Show amounts in millions and round to the nearest $1 million.

1. Three important pieces of inventory information are (a) the cost of inventory on hand, (b) the cost of sales, and (c) the cost of inventory purchases. Identify or compute each of these items for RadioShack Corporation at December 31, 2010.

2. Which item in Requirement 1 is most directly related to cash flow? Why? (Challenge)

3. Assume that all inventory purchases were made on account, and that only inventory purchases increased Accounts Payable. Compute RadioShack Corporation's cash payments for inventory during 2010.

4. How does RadioShack Corporation *value* its inventories? Which *costing* method does RadioShack Corporation use?

5. Did RadioShack Corporation's gross profit percentage and rate of inventory turnover improve or deteriorate in 2010 (versus 2009)? Consider the overall effect of these two ratios. Did RadioShack Corporation improve during 2010? How did these factors affect the net income for 2010? RadioShack Corporation's inventories totaled $636.3 million at the end of fiscal 2008. Round decimals to three places.

Group Project

(*Learning Objective 4: Evaluate inventory turnover ratios*) Obtain the annual reports of 10 companies, two from each of five different industries. Most companies' financial statements can be downloaded from their Web sites.

1. Compute each company's gross profit percentage and rate of inventory turnover for the most recent two years. If annual reports are unavailable or do not provide enough data for multiple-year computations, you can gather financial statement data from *Moody's Industrial Manual*.

2. For the industries of the companies you are analyzing, obtain the industry averages for gross profit percentage and inventory turnover from Robert Morris Associates, *Annual Statement Studies*; Dun and Bradstreet, *Industry Norms and Key Business Ratios*; or Leo Troy, *Almanac of Business and Industrial Financial Ratios*.

3. How well does each of your companies compare to the other company in its industry? How well do your companies compare to the average for their industry? What insight about your companies can you glean from these ratios?

4. Write a memo to summarize your findings, stating whether your group would invest in each of the companies it has analyzed.

For online homework, exercises, and problems that provide you with immediate feedback, please visit **www.myaccountinglab.com**.

MyAccountingLab

Quick Check Answers

1. *a*
2. *e*
3. *c*
4. *a* [(25 × $4) + (20 × $5)]
5. *c* (25 × $4) + ($13 × $5)
6. *c* 38 × [($100 + $205 + $170) ÷ 83]
7. *c*
8. *c*
9. *a*
10. *c* ($115,000 − $46,000)
11. *e* ($160,000 + $23,000 − $8,000)
12. *c* ($18,000 + $95,000 + $8,000 − $6,000 − $21,000)
13. *c* ($200,000 − $94,000)/$200,000
14. *c* [$94,000 ÷ ($18,000 + $21,000)/2]
15. *c* $100,000 + $240,000 − [$430,000 × (1 − 0.45)]
16. *b*

Appendix 6A

Accounting for Inventory in the Periodic System

In the periodic inventory system, the business keeps no running record of the merchandise. Instead, at the end of the period, the business counts inventory on hand and applies the unit costs to determine the cost of ending inventory. This inventory figure appears on the balance sheet and is used to compute cost of goods sold.

Recording Transactions in the Periodic System

In the periodic system, the Inventory account carries the beginning balance left over from the preceding period throughout the current period. The business records purchases of inventory in the Purchases account (an expense). Then, at the end of the period, the Inventory account must be updated for the financial statements. A journal entry removes the beginning balance by crediting Inventory and debiting Cost of Goods Sold. A second journal entry sets up the ending inventory balance, based on the physical count. The final entry in this sequence transfers the amount of Purchases to Cost of Goods Sold. These end-of-period entries can be made during the closing process.

Exhibit 6A-1 illustrates the accounting in the periodic system. After the process is complete, Inventory has its correct ending balance of $120,000, and Cost of Goods Sold shows $540,000.

EXHIBIT 6A-1 | Recording and Reporting Inventories—Periodic System (Amounts Assumed)

PANEL A—Recording Transactions and the T-accounts (All amounts are assumed)

1.	Purchases	560,000	
	Accounts Payable		560,000
	Purchased inventory on account.		
2.	Accounts Receivable	900,000	
	Sales Revenue		900,000
	Sold inventory on account.		
3.	End-of-period entries to update Inventory and record Cost of Goods Sold:		
a.	Cost of Goods Sold	100,000	
	Inventory (beginning balance)		100,000
	Transferred beginning inventory to COGS.		
b.	Inventory (ending balance)	120,000	
	Cost of Goods Sold		120,000
	Set up ending inventory based on physical count.		
c.	Cost of Goods Sold	560,000	
	Purchases		560,000
	Transferred purchases to COGS.		

The T-accounts show the following:

Inventory			Cost of Goods Sold		
100,000*		100,000	100,000		120,000
120,000			560,000		
			540,000		

*Beginning inventory was $100,000

PANEL B—Reporting in the Financial Statements

Income Statement (Partial)

Sales revenue		$900,000
Cost of goods sold:		
Beginning inventory	$ 100,000	
Purchases	560,000	
Goods available	660,000	
Ending inventory	(120,000)	
Cost of goods sold		540,000
Gross profit		$360,000

Ending Balance Sheet (Partial)

Current assets:		
Cash	$	XXX
Short-term investments		XXX
Accounts receivable		XXX
Inventory		120,000
Prepaid expenses		XXX

APPENDIX ASSIGNMENTS

Short Exercises

S6A-1 (*Record inventory transactions in the periodic system*) Flexon Technologies began the year with inventory of $580. During the year, Flexon purchased inventory costing $1,190 and sold goods for $2,900, with all transactions on account. Flexon ended the year with inventory of $650. Journalize all the necessary transactions under the periodic inventory system.

S6A-2 (*Compute cost of goods sold and prepare the income statement—periodic system*) Use the data in Short Exercise 6A-1 to do the following for Flexon Technologies:

▶ Requirements

1. Post to the Inventory and Cost of Goods Sold accounts.
2. Compute cost of goods sold by the cost-of-goods-sold model.
3. Prepare the income statement of Flexon Technologies through gross profit.

Exercises

> All of these exercises can be found within MyAccountingLab, an online homework and practice environment. Your instructor may ask you to complete these exercises using MyAccountingLab.

MyAccountingLab

Group A

E6A-3A (*Compute amounts for the GAAP inventory methods—periodic system*) Suppose Cambridge Corporation's inventory records for a particular computer chip indicate the following at October 31:

Oct	1	Beginning inventory	5 units @ $60 = $300
	8	Purchase.................................	4 units @ $60 = 240
	15	Purchase.................................	10 units @ $70 = 700
	26	Purchase.................................	1 units @ $80 = 80

The physical count of inventory at October 31 indicates that seven units of inventory are on hand.

▶ Requirements

Compute ending inventory and cost of goods sold, using each of the following methods:
1. Specific unit cost, assuming three $60 units and four $70 units are on hand
2. Average cost (round average unit cost to the nearest cent)
3. First-in, first-out
4. Last-in, first-out

E6A-4A (*Journal inventory transactions in the periodic system; compute cost of goods sold*) Use the data in Exercise 6A-3A.

▶ Requirements

Journalize the following for the periodic system:
1. Total October purchases in one summary entry. All purchases were on credit.
2. Total October sales in a summary entry. Assume that the selling price was $300 per unit and that all sales were on credit.
3. October 31 entries for inventory. Cambridge uses LIFO. Post to the Cost of Goods Sold T-account to show how this amount is determined. Label each item in the account.
4. Show the computation of cost of goods sold by the cost-of-goods-sold model.

Group B

E6A-5B (*Compare amounts for GAAP inventory methods—periodic system*) Suppose Synergy Corporation's inventory records for a particular computer chip indicate the following at December 31:

Dec	1	Beginning inventory	6 units @ $59 = $354
	8	Purchase.................................	4 units @ $59 = 236
	15	Purchase.................................	10 units @ $69 = 690
	26	Purchase.................................	5 units @ $79 = 395

The physical count of inventory at December 31 indicates that seven units of inventory are on hand.

▶ Requirements

Compute ending inventory and cost of goods sold, using each of the following methods:
1. Specific unit cost, assuming two $59 units and five $69 units are on hand
2. Average cost (round average unit cost to the nearest cent)
3. First-in, first-out
4. Last-in, first-out

E6A-6B (*Show how to account for inventory transactions in the periodic system; compute cost of goods sold*) Use the data in Exercise 6A-5B.

▶ Requirements

Journalize the following for the periodic system:
1. Total December purchases in one summary entry. All purchases were on credit.
2. Total December sales in a summary entry. Assume that the selling price was $315 per unit and that all sales were on credit.
3. December 31 entries for inventory. Synergy uses LIFO. Post to the Cost of Goods Sold T-account to show how this amount is determined. Label each item in the account.
4. Show the computation of cost of goods sold by the cost-of-goods-sold model.

Problems

MyAccountingLab

> All of these problems can be found within MyAccountingLab, an online homework and practice environment. Your instructor may ask you to complete these problems using MyAccountingLab.

Group A

P6A-7A (*Compute cost of goods sold and gross profit on sales—periodic system*) Assume a Waverly outlet store began August 2012 with 52 units of inventory that cost $13 each. The sale price of these units was $67. During August, the store completed these inventory transactions:

			Units	Unit Cost	Unit Sale Price
Aug	3	Sale	14	$13	$67
	8	Purchase......	78	14	69
	11	Sale	38	13	67
	19	Sale	7	14	69
	24	Sale	32	14	69
	30	Purchase......	20	15	70
	31	Sale	9	14	69

▶ Requirements

1. Determine the store's cost of goods sold for August under the periodic inventory system. Assume the FIFO method.
2. Compute gross profit for August.

P6A-8A (*Record transactions in the periodic system; report inventory items in the financial statements*) Accounting records for Total Desserts, Inc., yield the following data for the year ended December 31, 2012 (amounts in thousands):

Inventory, Dec 31, 2011	$ 490
Purchases of inventory (on account)	2,000
Sales of inventory—75% on account, 25% for cash	3,400
Inventory at the lower of FIFO cost or market, Dec 31, 2012	620

▶ Requirements

1. Journalize Total Desserts' inventory transactions for the year under the periodic system. Show all amounts in thousands.
2. Report ending inventory, sales, cost of goods sold, and gross profit on the appropriate financial statement (amounts in thousands). Show the computation of cost of goods sold.

Group B

P6A-9B (*Compute cost of goods sold and gross profit on sales—periodic system*) Assume a Whitewater outlet store began May 2012 with 48 units of inventory that cost $18 each. The sale price of these units was $73. During May, the store completed these inventory transactions:

		Units	Unit Cost	Unit Sale Price
May 3	Sale	18	$18	$73
8	Purchase	83	19	75
11	Sale	30	18	73
19	Sale	6	19	75
24	Sale	32	19	75
30	Purchase	17	20	76
31	Sale	11	19	75

▶ Requirements

1. Determine the store's cost of goods sold for May under the periodic inventory system. Assume the FIFO method.
2. Compute gross profit for May.

P6A-10B (*Record transactions in the periodic system; report inventory items in the financial statements*) Accounting records for Parkland Pastries, Inc., yield the following data for the year ended December 31, 2012 (amounts in thousands):

Inventory, Dec 31, 2011	$ 520
Purchases of inventory (on account)	1,180
Sales of inventory—80% on account, 20% for cash	3,100
Inventory at the lower of FIFO cost or market, Dec 31, 2012	620

▶ Requirements

1. Journalize Parkland Pastries' inventory transactions for the year under the periodic system. Show all amounts in thousands.
2. Report ending inventory, sales, cost of goods sold, and gross profit on the appropriate financial statement (amounts in thousands). Show the computation of cost of goods sold.

Appendix 6B

The LIFO Reserve—Converting a LIFO Company's Net Income to the FIFO Basis

Suppose you are a financial analyst, and it is your job to recommend stocks for your clients to purchase as investments. You have narrowed your choice to B-Mart Stores, Inc., and **The Gap, Inc.** B-Mart uses the LIFO method for inventories, and The GAP uses FIFO. The two companies' net incomes are not comparable because they use different inventory methods. To compare the two companies, you need to place them on the same footing.

The Internal Revenue Service allows companies to use LIFO for income tax purposes only if they use LIFO for financial reporting, but companies may also report an alternative inventory amount in the financial statements. Doing so presents a rare opportunity to convert a company's net income from the LIFO basis to what the income would have been if the business had used FIFO. Fortunately, you can convert B-Mart's income from the LIFO basis, as reported in the company's financial statements, to the FIFO basis. Then you can compare B-Mart and The Gap.

Like many other companies that use LIFO, B-Mart reports the FIFO cost, a LIFO Reserve, and the LIFO cost of ending inventory. The LIFO Reserve[2] is the difference between the LIFO cost of an inventory and what the cost of that inventory would be under FIFO. Assume that B-Mart reported the following amounts:

B-Mart Uses LIFO		
	(In millions)	
	2013	**2012**
From the B-Mart balance sheet:		
Inventories (approximate FIFO cost)	$ 25,056	$22,749
Less LIFO reserve	(165)	(135)
LIFO cost	24,891	22,614
From the B-Mart income statement:		
Cost of goods sold	$191,838	
Net income	8,039	
Income tax rate	35%	

Converting B-Mart's 2013 net income to the FIFO basis focuses on the LIFO Reserve because the reserve captures the difference between B-Mart's ending inventory costed at LIFO and at FIFO. Observe that during each year, the FIFO cost of ending inventory exceeded the LIFO cost. During 2013, the LIFO Reserve increased by $30 million ($165 million–$135 million). *The LIFO Reserve can increase only when inventory costs are rising.* Recall that during a period of rising costs, LIFO produces the highest cost of goods sold and the lowest net income. Therefore, for 2013, B-Mart's cost of goods sold would have been lower if the company had used the FIFO method for inventories. B-Mart's net income would have been higher, as the following computations show:

---

[2]The LIFO Reserve account is widely used in practice even though the term "reserve" is poor terminology.

If B-Mart Had Used FIFO in 2013	
	(In millions)
Cost of goods sold, as reported under LIFO..	$191,838
− Increase in LIFO Reserve ($165 − $135)...	(30)
= Cost of goods sold, if B-Mart had used FIFO..	$191,808
Lower cost of goods sold → Higher pretax income by....................................	$ 30
Minus income taxes (35%).............................	11
Higher net income under FIFO.......................	19
Net income as reported under LIFO..............	8,039
Net income B-Mart would have reported for 2013 if using FIFO......................................	$ 8,058

Now you can compare B-Mart's net income with that of The Gap, Inc. All the ratios used for the analysis—current ratio, inventory turnover, and so on—can be compared between the two companies as though they both used the FIFO inventory method.

The LIFO Reserve provides another opportunity for managers and investors to answer a key question about a company.

> **How much income tax has the company saved over its lifetime by using the LIFO method to account for inventory?**

Using B-Mart as an example, the computation at the end of 2013 is as follows (amounts in millions):

> **Income tax saved by using LIFO = LIFO Reserve × Income tax rate**
> **$58   = $165   ×   .35**

With these price changes, by the end of 2013, B-Mart has saved a total of $58 million by using the LIFO method to account for its merchandise inventory. Had B-Mart used the FIFO method, B-Mart would have almost $58 million less cash to invest in the opening of new stores.

In recent years, many companies have experienced decreases in the cost of their inventories. When prices decline, cost of goods sold under FIFO is greater (LIFO cost of goods sold is less). This makes gross profit and net income less under FIFO.

Plant Assets, Natural Resources, & Intangibles

SPOTLIGHT: FedEx Corporation

If you need a document delivered across the country overnight, FedEx can handle it. **FedEx Corporation** sets the standard for quick delivery. As you can see from the company's Consolidated Balance Sheets on the following page, FedEx moves packages using property and equipment such as aircraft, package-handling equipment, computers, and vehicles. These are FedEx's most important resources (lines 8–16). The company owns over $31 billion of property and equipment as of May 31, 2010 (line 14), which is actually $6 billion more than total assets (line 22)! How can this be? Notice that, over the estimated useful lives of these assets, the company has built up accumulated depreciation of about $17 billion (line 15), indicating that the assets are more than half used up as of that date. The net book value of FedEx's property and equipment is about $14 billion (line 16). The company also owns over $3.2 billion in goodwill and other intangible long-term assets (line 21). When you complete this chapter, you will understand better what these terms and concepts mean. ●

© Getty Images

FedEx Corporation
Consolidated Balance Sheets (Partial, Adapted)

	(In millions)	May 31,	
		2010	2009
1	ASSETS		
2	CURRENT ASSETS		
3	Cash and cash equivalents	$ 1,952	$ 2,292
4	Receivables, less allowances of $166 and $196	4,163	3,391
5	Spare parts, supplies, and fuel	389	367
6	Prepaid expenses and other	780	1,066
7	Total current assets	7,284	7,116
8	PROPERTY AND EQUIPMENT, AT COST		
9	Aircraft and related equipment	11,640	10,118
10	Package handling and ground support equipment	5,193	4,960
11	Computer and electronic equipment	4,218	4,280
12	Vehicles	3,170	3,078
13	Facilities and other	7,081	6,824
14	Total cost	31,302	29,260
15	Less: Accumulated depreciation	(16,917)	(15,843)
16	Net property and equipment	14,385	13,417
17	OTHER LONG-TERM ASSETS		
18	Goodwill	2,200	2,229
19	Prepaid pension cost	—	311
20	Intangible and other assets	1,033	1,171
21	Total other long-term assets	3,233	3,711
22	TOTAL ASSETS	$ 24,902	$ 24,244

This chapter covers the measurement and reporting principles for long-term tangible fixed assets (also known as plant assets or property and equipment) **as well as intangible assets**. Unlike inventories that are typically bought, manufactured, and sold, fixed tangible and intangible assets are used in the business to earn a profit. This chapter also briefly covers measurement and reporting principles for natural resources, which begin as long-term assets. Then, as they are extracted or depleted, their cost is transferred to the income statement as expense.

1. *Measure and account for* the cost of plant assets

2. *Distinguish* a capital expenditure from an immediate expense

3. *Measure and record* depreciation on plant assets

4. *Analyze* the effect of a plant asset disposal

5. *Apply* GAAP for natural resources and intangible assets

6. *Explain* the effect of an asset impairment on the financial statements

7. *Analyze* rate of return on assets

8. *Analyze* the cash flow impact of long-lived asset transactions

Learning Objectives

Businesses use several types of long-lived (long-term) assets. We show these assets in Exhibit 7-1, along with the expense account that is typically associated with each one. For example, buildings, airplanes, and equipment depreciate. Natural resources deplete (often through cost of goods sold), and intangible assets are amortized.

EXHIBIT 7-1 | Long-Lived Assets and Related Expense Accounts

Asset Account (Balance Sheet)	Related Expense Account (Income Statement)
Plant Assets	
Land	None
Buildings, Machinery, and Equipment	Depreciation
Furniture and Fixtures	Depreciation
Land Improvements	Depreciation
Natural Resources	Depletion (through cost of goods sold)
Intangibles	Amortization

▶ **Plant assets**, (also known as *property, plant, and equipment* or *fixed assets*), are long-lived assets that are tangible—for instance, land, buildings, and equipment. The expense associated with plant assets is called *depreciation*. Of the plant assets, land is unique. Land is not expensed over time because its usefulness does not decrease. Most companies report plant assets as property, plant, and equipment on the balance sheet. **FedEx** uses the heading Property and Equipment in its balance sheet shown on page 401 (lines 8–16).

▶ **Natural resources** such as oil and gas reserves, coal mines, or stands of timber, are accounted for as long-term assets when they are purchased or developed. As the natural resource is extracted, its cost is transferred to inventory. Later, as the inventory is sold, its cost is transferred to cost of goods sold in a manner similar to that described in Chapter 6.

▶ **Intangible assets** are useful because of the special rights they carry. They have no physical form. Patents, copyrights, and trademarks are intangible assets, as is goodwill. Accounting for intangibles is similar to accounting for plant assets. FedEx reports Goodwill and Intangible Assets on its balance sheet (lines 18 and 20).

Measure and Account for the Cost of Plant Assets

1

Measure and account for the cost of plant assets

Here is the basic working rule for measuring the cost of an asset:

The cost of any asset is the sum of all the costs incurred to bring the asset to its intended use. The cost of a plant asset includes purchase price, plus any taxes, commissions, and other amounts paid to make the asset ready for use. Because the specific costs differ for the various types of plant assets, we discuss the major groups individually.

Land

The cost of land includes its purchase price (cash plus any note payable given), brokerage commission, survey fees, legal fees, and any back property taxes that the purchaser pays. Land cost also includes expenditures for grading and clearing the land and for removing unwanted buildings.

The cost of land does *not* include the cost of fencing, paving, security systems, and lighting. These are separate plant assets—called *land improvements*—and they are subject to depreciation.

Suppose FedEx signs a $300,000 note payable to purchase 20 acres of land for a new shipping site. FedEx also pays $10,000 for real estate commission, $8,000 of back property tax, $5,000 for removal of an old building, a $1,000 survey fee, and $260,000 to pave the parking lot—all in cash. What is FedEx's cost of this land?

Purchase price of land......................		$300,000
Add related costs:		
Real estate commission	$10,000	
Back property tax......................	8,000	
Removal of building...................	5,000	
Survey fee.................................	1,000	
Total related costs......................		24,000
Total cost of land..........................		$324,000

Note that the cost to pave the parking lot, $260,000, is *not* included in the land's cost, because the pavement is a land improvement. FedEx would record the purchase of this land as follows:

Land	324,000	
Note Payable		300,000
Cash		24,000

Assets	=	Liabilities	+	Stockholders' Equity
+ 324,000				
− 24,000	=	+ 300,000	+	0

This purchase of land increases both assets and liabilities. There is no effect on equity.

Buildings, Machinery, and Equipment

The cost of constructing a building includes architectural fees, building permits, contractors' charges, and payments for material, labor, and overhead. If the company constructs its own building, the cost will also include the cost of interest on money borrowed to finance the construction.

When an existing building (new or old) is purchased, its cost includes the purchase price, brokerage commission, sales and other taxes paid, and all expenditures to repair and renovate the building for its intended purpose.

The cost of FedEx's package-handling equipment includes its purchase price (less any discounts), plus transportation from the seller to FedEx, insurance while in transit, sales and other taxes, purchase commission, installation costs, and any expenditures to test the asset before it's placed in service. The equipment cost will also include the cost of any special platforms. Then after the asset is up and running, insurance, taxes, and maintenance costs are recorded as expenses, not as part of the asset's cost.

Land Improvements and Leasehold Improvements

For a FedEx shipping terminal, the cost to pave a parking lot ($260,000) would be recorded in a separate account entitled Land Improvements. This account includes costs for such other items as driveways, signs, fences, and sprinkler systems. Although these assets are located on the land, they are subject to decay, and their cost should therefore be depreciated.

FedEx may lease some of its airplanes and other assets. The company customizes these assets for its special needs. For example, FedEx paints its logo on delivery trucks. These improvements are assets of FedEx even though the company may not own the truck. The cost of leasehold improvements should be depreciated over the term of the lease. Most companies call the depreciation on leasehold improvements *amortization*, which is a similar concept to *depreciation*.

Lump-Sum (or Basket) Purchases of Assets

Businesses often purchase several assets as a group, or a "basket," for a single lump-sum amount. For example, FedEx may pay one price for land and a building. The company must identify the cost of each asset. The total cost is divided among the assets according to their relative sales (or market) values. This technique is called the *relative-sales-value method*.

Suppose FedEx purchases land and a building in Denver. The building sits on two acres of land, and the combined purchase price of land and building is $2,800,000. An appraisal indicates that the land's market value is $300,000 and that the building's market value is $2,700,000.

FedEx first figures the ratio of each asset's market value to the total market value. Total appraised value is $2,700,000 + $300,000 = $3,000,000. Thus, the land, valued at $300,000, is 10% of the total market value. The building's appraised value is 90% of the total. These percentages are then used to determine the cost of each asset, as follows:

Asset	Market (Sales) Value		Total Market Value		Percentage of Total Market Value		Total Cost	Cost of Each Asset
Land	$ 300,000	÷	$3,000,000	=	10%	× $2,800,000		$ 280,000
Building	2,700,000	÷	3,000,000	=	90%	× $2,800,000		2,520,000
Total	$3,000,000				100%			$2,800,000

If FedEx pays cash, the entry to record the purchase of the land and building is as follows:

Land		280,000	
Building		2,520,000	
Cash			2,800,000

Assets	=	Liabilities	+	Stockholders' Equity
+ 280,000	=			
+ 2,520,000	=	0	+	0
− 2,800,000	=			

Total assets don't change—it is merely the makeup of FedEx's assets that changes.

STOP & THINK. . .

How would FedEx divide a $120,000 lump-sum purchase price for land, building, and equipment with estimated market values of $40,000, $95,000, and $15,000, respectively?

Answer:

	Estimated Market Value	Percentage of Total Market Value	×	Total Cost	=	Cost of Each Asset
Land..................	$ 40,000	26.7%*	×	$120,000	=	$ 32,040
Building............	95,000	63.3%	×	$120,000	=	75,960
Equipment.........	15,000	10.0%	×	$120,000	=	12,000
Total	$150,000	100.0%				$120,000

*$40,000/$150,000 = 0.267, and so on

Distinguish a Capital Expenditure from an Immediate Expense

2

Distinguish a capital expenditure from an immediate expense

When a company spends money on a plant asset, it must decide whether to record an asset or an expense. Examples of these expenditures range from FedEx's purchase of an airplane to replacing the tires on a FedEx truck.

Expenditures that increase the asset's capacity or extend its useful life are called **capital expenditures**. For example, the cost of a major overhaul that extends the useful life of a FedEx truck is a capital expenditure. Capital expenditures are said to be *capitalized, which means the cost is added to an asset account* and not expensed immediately. A major decision in accounting for plant assets is whether to capitalize or to expense a certain cost.

Costs that do not extend the asset's capacity or its useful life, but merely maintain the asset or restore it to working order, are recorded as expenses. For example, Repair Expense is reported on the income statement and matched against revenue. The costs of repainting a FedEx delivery truck, repairing a dented fender, and replacing tires are also expensed immediately. Exhibit 7-2 shows the distinction between capital expenditures and immediate expenses for ordinary repairs.

EXHIBIT 7-2 | Capital Expenditures vs. Immediate Expenses

Record an Asset for Capital Expenditures	Record Repair and Maintenance Expense (Not an Asset) for an Expense
Extraordinary repairs:	**Ordinary repairs:**
Major engine overhaul	Repair of transmission or other mechanism
Modification of body for new use of truck	Oil change, lubrication, and so on
Addition to storage capacity of truck	Replacement of tires and windshield, or a paint job

The distinction between a capital expenditure (a long-term asset) and an immediate expense requires judgment: Does the cost extend the asset's usefulness or its useful life? If so, record an asset. If the cost merely maintains the asset in its present condition or returns it to its prior condition, then record an expense.

Most companies expense all small (immaterial) costs (say, below $1,000) regardless of whether the costs are capital in nature. For larger (material) costs, they follow the capitalization rule stated in the previous paragraph. A conservative policy is one that avoids overstating assets and profits. A company that overstates its assets may eventually have to defend itself in court if investors or creditors lose money because of the company's improper accounting practices.

Accounting errors sometimes occur for plant asset costs. For example, a company may

▶ expense a cost that should have been capitalized. This error overstates expenses and understates net income in the year of the error.

▶ capitalize a cost that should have been expensed. This error understates expenses and overstates net income in the year of the error.

Cooking the Books by Improper Capitalization

WorldCom

It is one thing to accidentally capitalize a plant asset but quite another to do it intentionally, thus deliberately overstating assets, understating expenses, and overstating net income. One well-known company committed one of the biggest financial statement frauds in U.S. history in this way.

In 2002, WorldCom, Inc., was one of the largest telecommunications service providers in the world. The company had grown rapidly from a small, regional telephone company in 1983 to a giant corporation in 2002 by acquiring an ever-increasing number of other such companies. But 2002 was a bad year for WorldCom, as well as for many others in the "telecom" industry. The United States was reeling from the effects of a deep economic recession spawned by the "bursting dot-com bubble" in 2000 and intensified by the terrorist attacks on U.S. soil in 2001. Wall Street was looking high and low for positive signs, pressuring public companies to keep profits trending upward in order to support share prices, without much success, at least for the honest companies.

Bernard J. ("Bernie") Ebbers, WorldCom's chief executive officer, was worried. He began to press his chief financial officer, Scott Sullivan, to find a way to make the company's income statement look healthier. After all legitimate attempts to improve earnings failed, Sullivan concocted a scheme to cook the books.

Like all telecommunications companies, WorldCom had signed contracts with other telephone companies, paying them fees so that WorldCom customers could use their lines for telephone calls and Internet usage. GAAP require such fees to be expensed as incurred, rather than capitalized. Overestimating the growth of its business, WorldCom had incurred billions of dollars in such costs, about 15% more than its customers would ever use.

In direct violation of GAAP, Sullivan rationalized that the excessive amounts WorldCom had spent on line costs would eventually lead to the company's recognizing revenue in future years (thus extending their usefulness and justifying, in his mind, their classification as assets). Sullivan directed the accountants working under him to reclassify line costs as property, plant, and equipment assets, rather than as expenses, and to amortize (spread) the costs over several years rather than to expense them in the periods in which they were incurred. Over several quarters, Mr. Sullivan and his assistants transferred a total of $3.1 billion in such charges from operating expense accounts to property, plant, and equipment, resulting in the transformation of what would have been a net loss for all of 2001 and the first quarter of 2002 into a sizeable profit. It was the largest single fraud in U.S. history to that point.

Sullivan's fraudulent scheme was discovered by the company's internal audit staff during a routine spot-check of the company's records for capital expenditures. The staff members reported Sullivan's (and his staff's) fraudulent activities to the head of the company's audit committee and its external auditor, setting in motion a chain of events that resulted in Ebbers' and Sullivan's firing, and the company's eventual bankruptcy. Ebbers, Sullivan, and several of their assistants went to prison for their participation in this fraudulent scheme.

Shareholders of WorldCom lost billions of dollars in share value when the company went down, and more than 500,000 people lost their jobs.

The WorldCom scandal rocked the financial world, causing global stock markets to plummet from lack of confidence. This prompted action on the part of the U.S. Congress and President George W. Bush that eventually led to the passage of the Sarbanes-Oxley Act of 2002, the most significant piece of shareholder protection legislation since the Great Depression in the 1930s.

Measure and Record Depreciation on Plant Assets

3

Measure and record depreciation on plant assets

As we've seen in previous chapters, plant assets are reported on the balance sheet at book value, which is calculated as follows:

> Book Value of a Plant Asset = Cost − Accumulated Depreciation

Plant assets wear out, grow obsolete, and lose value over time. To account for this process, we allocate a plant asset's cost to expense over its life—a process called *depreciation*. The depreciation process follows the expense recognition principle discussed in Chapter 3. Depreciation apportions the cost of using a fixed asset over time by allocating a portion of that cost against the revenue the asset helps earn each period. Exhibit 7-3 illustrates the accounting for a Boeing 737 jet by FedEx.

EXHIBIT 7-3 | Depreciation: Allocating costs to periods in which revenues are generated

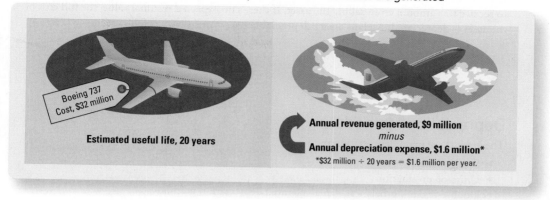

Recall that depreciation expense (not accumulated depreciation) is reported on the income statement.

Only land has an unlimited life and is not depreciated for accounting purposes. For most plant assets, depreciation is caused by one of the following:

▶ *Physical wear and tear.* For example, physical deterioration takes its toll on the usefulness of FedEx airplanes, equipment, delivery trucks, and buildings.

▶ *Obsolescence.* Computers and other electronic equipment may become *obsolete* before they deteriorate. An asset is obsolete when another asset can do the job more efficiently. An asset's useful life may be shorter than its physical life. FedEx and other companies depreciate their computers over a short period of time—perhaps four years—even though the computers will remain in working condition much longer.

Suppose FedEx buys a computer for use in tracking packages. FedEx believes it will get four years of service from the computer, which will then be worthless. Under straight-line depreciation, FedEx expenses one-quarter of the asset's cost in each of its four years of use.

You've just seen what depreciation is. Let's see what depreciation is *not*.

1. ***Depreciation is not a process of valuation.*** Businesses do *not* record depreciation based on changes in the market value of their plant assets. Instead, businesses allocate the asset's *cost* to the period of its useful life.

2. ***Depreciation does not mean setting aside cash to replace assets as they wear out.*** Any cash fund is entirely separate from depreciation.

How to Measure Depreciation

To measure depreciation for a plant asset, we must know three things about it:

1. Cost

2. Estimated useful life

3. Estimated residual value

We have discussed cost, which is a known amount. The other two factors must be estimated.

Estimated useful life is the length of service expected from using the asset. Useful life may be expressed in years, units of output, miles, or some other measure. For example, the useful life of a building is stated in years. The useful life of a FedEx airplane or delivery truck may be expressed as the number of miles the vehicle is expected to travel. Companies base estimates on their experience and trade publications.

Estimated residual value—also called *scrap value* or *salvage value*—is the expected cash value of an asset at the end of its useful life. For example, FedEx may believe that a package-handling machine will be useful for seven years. After that time, FedEx may expect to sell the machine as scrap metal. The amount FedEx believes it can get for the machine is the estimated residual value.

In computing depreciation, the estimated residual value is *not* depreciated because FedEx expects to receive this amount from selling the asset. If there's no expected residual value, the full cost of the asset is depreciated. A plant asset's **depreciable cost** is measured as follows:

$$\text{Depreciable Cost} = \text{Asset's cost} - \text{Estimated residual value}$$

Depreciation Methods

There are three main depreciation methods:

- ▶ Straight-line
- ▶ Units-of-production
- ▶ Double-declining-balance—an accelerated depreciation method

These methods allocate different amounts of depreciation to each period. However, they all result in the same total amount of depreciation, which is the asset's depreciable cost. Exhibit 7-4 presents the data we use to illustrate depreciation computations for a FedEx truck.

EXHIBIT 7-4 | Depreciation Computation Data

Data Item	Amount
Cost of truck	$41,000
Less: Estimated residual value	(1,000)
Depreciable cost	$40,000
Estimated useful life:	
Years	5 years
Units of production	100,000 units [miles]

Straight-Line Method. In the **straight-line (SL) method**, an equal amount of depreciation is assigned to each year (or period) of asset use. Depreciable cost is divided by useful life in years to determine the annual depreciation expense. Applied to the FedEx truck data from Exhibit 7-4, SL depreciation is as follows:

$$\text{Straight-line depreciation per year} = \frac{\text{Cost} - \text{Residual value}}{\text{Useful life, in years}}$$

$$= \frac{\$41,000 - \$1,000}{5}$$

$$= \$8,000$$

Assets	=	Liabilities	+	Stockholders' Equity	−	Expenses
− 8,000	=	0				− 8,000

The entry to record depreciation is as follows:

	Depreciation Expense		8,000	
	Accumulated Depreciation			8,000

Observe that depreciation decreases the asset (through Accumulated Depreciation) and also decreases equity (through Depreciation Expense). Let's assume that FedEx purchased this truck on January 1, 2011. Assume that FedEx's accounting year ends on December 31. Exhibit 7-5 gives a *straight-line depreciation schedule* for the truck. The final column of the exhibit shows the *asset's book value*, which is cost less accumulated depreciation.

EXHIBIT 7-5 | Straight-Line Depreciation Schedule for Truck

| Date | Asset Cost | Depreciation for the Year | | | | Accumulated Depreciation | Asset Book Value |
		Depreciation Rate	Depreciable Cost		Depreciation Expense		
1- 1-2011	$41,000						$41,000
12-31-2011		0.20*	× $40,000	=	$8,000	$ 8,000	33,000
12-31-2012		0.20	× 40,000	=	8,000	16,000	25,000
12-31-2013		0.20	× 40,000	=	8,000	24,000	17,000
12-31-2014		0.20	× 40,000	=	8,000	32,000	9,000
12-31-2015		0.20	× 40,000	=	8,000	40,000	1,000

*⅕ per year = .20 per year.

As an asset is used in operations,

▶ accumulated depreciation increases.
▶ the book value of the asset decreases.

You can estimate the stage of the useful life of a plant asset by calculating the ratio between accumulated depreciation on a straight-line basis and cost. For example, if accumulated depreciation is $500,000 and cost is $1,000,000, the plant asset is approximately half used up. An asset's final book value is its *residual value* ($1,000 in Exhibit 7-5). At the end of its useful life, the asset is said to be *fully depreciated*.

STOP & THINK. . .

A FedEx sorting machine that cost $10,000, has a useful life of five years, and residual value of $2,000, was purchased on January 1. What is SL depreciation for each year?

- -

Answer:

$1,600 = ($10,000 − $2,000)/5

Units-of-Production Method. In the **units-of-production (UOP) method**, a fixed amount of depreciation is assigned to each *unit of output*, or service, produced by the asset. Depreciable cost is divided by useful life—in units of production—to determine this amount. This per-unit depreciation expense is then multiplied by the number of units produced each period to compute depreciation. The UOP depreciation for the FedEx truck data in Exhibit 7-4 (p. 408) is as follows:

$$\text{Units-of-production depreciation per unit of output} = \frac{\text{Cost} - \text{Residual value}}{\text{Useful life, in units of production}}$$

$$= \frac{\$41,000 - \$1,000}{100,000 \text{ miles}} = \$0.40 \text{ per mile}$$

Assume that FedEx expects to drive the truck 20,000 miles during the first year, 30,000 during the second, 25,000 during the third, 15,000 during the fourth, and 10,000 during the fifth. Exhibit 7-6 shows the UOP depreciation schedule.

EXHIBIT 7-6 | Units-of-Production (UOP) Depreciation Schedule for Truck

| Date | Asset Cost | Depreciation for the Year | | | Accumulated Depreciation | Asset Book Value |
		Depreciation Per Unit	Number of Units	Depreciation Expense		
1- 1-2011	$41,000					$41,000
12-31-2011		$0.40* ×	20,000 =	$ 8,000	$ 8,000	33,000
12-31-2012		0.40 ×	30,000 =	12,000	20,000	21,000
12-31-2013		0.40 ×	25,000 =	10,000	30,000	11,000
12-31-2014		0.40 ×	15,000 =	6,000	36,000	5,000
12-31-2015		0.40 ×	10,000 =	4,000	40,000	1,000

*($41,000 − $1,000)/100,000 miles = $0.40 per mile.

The amount of UOP depreciation varies with the number of units the asset produces. In our example, the total number of units produced is 100,000. UOP depreciation does not depend directly on time, as do the other methods.

Double-Declining-Balance Method. An **accelerated depreciation method** writes off a larger amount of the asset's cost near the start of its useful life than the straight-line method does. **Double-declining-balance (DDB)** is the most frequently used accelerated depreciation method. It computes annual depreciation by multiplying the asset's declining book value by a constant percentage, which is two times the straight-line depreciation rate. DDB amounts are computed as follows:

- ▶ *First*, compute the straight-line depreciation rate per year. A truck with a 5-year useful life has a straight-line depreciation rate of 1/5, or 20% each year. An asset with a 10-year useful life has a straight-line depreciation rate of 1/10, or 10%, and so on.
- ▶ *Second*, multiply the straight-line rate by 2 to compute the DDB rate. For a 5-year asset, the DDB rate is 40% (20% × 2). A 10-year asset has a DDB rate of 20% (10% × 2).
- ▶ *Third*, multiply the DDB rate by the period's *beginning* asset book value (cost less accumulated depreciation). Under the DDB method, ignore the residual value of the asset in computing depreciation, except during the last year. The DDB rate for the FedEx truck in Exhibit 7-4 (p. 408) is as follows:

$$\text{DDB depreciation rate per year} = \frac{1}{\text{Useful life, in years}} \times 2$$

$$= \frac{1}{5 \text{ years}} \times 2$$

$$= 20\% \times 2 = 40\%$$

- ▶ *Fourth*, determine the final year's depreciation amount—that is, the amount needed to reduce the asset's book value to its residual value. In Exhibit 7-7, the fifth and final year's DDB depreciation is $4,314—book value of $5,314 less the $1,000 residual value. *The residual value should not be depreciated* but should remain on the books until the asset is disposed of.

EXHIBIT 7-7 | Double-Declining-Balance (DDB) Depreciation Schedule for Truck

| Date | Asset Cost | Depreciation for the Year | | | Accumulated Depreciation | Asset Book Value |
		DDB Rate	Asset Book Value	Depreciation Expense		
1- 1-2011	$41,000					$41,000
12-31-2011		0.40 ×	$41,000 =	$16,400	$16,400	24,600
12-31-2012		0.40 ×	24,600 =	9,840	26,240	14,760
12-31-2013		0.40 ×	14,760 =	5,904	32,144	8,856
12-31-2014		0.40 ×	8,856 =	3,542	35,686	5,314
12-31-2015				4,314*	40,000	1,000

*Last-year depreciation is the "plug" amount needed to reduce asset book value (far right column) to the residual amount ($5,314 − $1,000 = $4,314).

The DDB method differs from the other methods in two ways:

1. Residual value is ignored initially; first-year depreciation is computed on the asset's full cost.

2. Depreciation expense in the final year is the "plug" amount needed to reduce the asset's book value to the residual amount.

STOP & THINK. . .

What is the DDB depreciation each year for the asset in the Stop & Think on page 409?

Answers:

Yr. 1: $4,000 ($10,000 × 40%)
Yr. 2: $2,400 ($6,000 × 40%)
Yr. 3: $1,440 ($3,600 × 40%)
Yr. 4: $160 ($10,000 − $4,000 − $2,400 − $1,440 − $2,000 = $160)*
Yr. 5: $0

*The asset is not depreciated below residual value of $2,000.

Comparing Depreciation Methods

Let's compare the three methods in terms of the yearly amount of depreciation. The yearly amount varies by method, but the total $40,000 depreciable cost is the same under all methods.

| | Amount of Depreciation per Year | | |
Year	Straight-Line	Units-of-Production	Accelerated Method Double-Declining Balance
1	$ 8,000	$ 8,000	$16,400
2	8,000	12,000	9,840
3	8,000	10,000	5,904
4	8,000	6,000	3,542
5	8,000	4,000	4,314
Total	$40,000	$40,000	$40,000

GAAP requires matching an asset's depreciation against the revenue the asset produces. For a plant asset that generates revenue evenly over time, the straight-line method best meets the matching principle. The units-of-production method best fits those assets that wear out because of physical use rather than obsolescence. The accelerated method (DDB) applies best to assets that generate more revenue earlier in their useful lives and less in later years.

Exhibit 7-8 graphs annual depreciation amounts for the straight-line, units-of-production, and accelerated depreciation (DDB) methods. The graph of straight-line depreciation is flat through time because annual depreciation is the same in all periods. Units-of-production depreciation follows no particular pattern because annual depreciation depends on the use of the asset. Accelerated depreciation is greatest in the first year and less in the later years.

EXHIBIT 7-8 | Depreciation Patterns Through Time

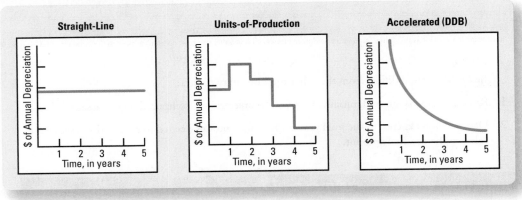

Exhibit 7-9 shows the percentage of companies that use each depreciation method from a recent survey of 600 companies conducted by the American Institute of Certified Public Accountants (AICPA).

EXHIBIT 7-9 | Depreciation Methods Used by 600 Companies

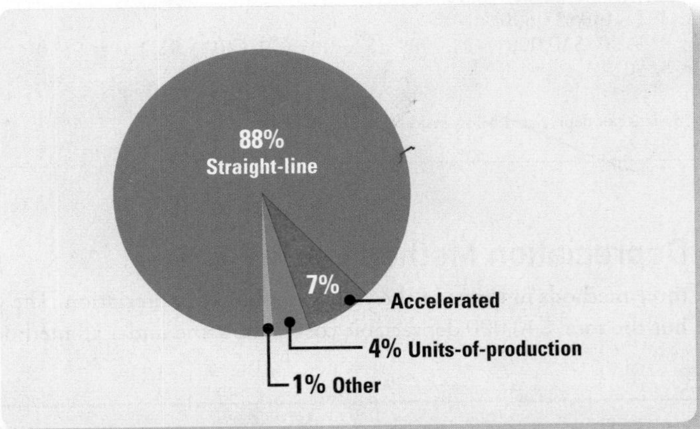

88% Straight-line

7% — Accelerated

4% Units-of-production

1% Other

For reporting in the financial statements, straight-line depreciation is the most popular method. As we shall see, however, accelerated depreciation is most popular for income-tax purposes.

MID-CHAPTER SUMMARY PROBLEM

Suppose FedEx purchased equipment on January 1, 2012, for $44,000. The expected useful life of the equipment is 10 years or 100,000 units of production, and its residual value is $4,000. Under three depreciation methods, the annual depreciation expense and the balance of accumulated depreciation at the end of 2012 and 2013 are as follows:

	Method A		Method B		Method C	
Year	Annual Depreciation Expense	Accumulated Depreciation	Annual Depreciation Expense	Accumulated Depreciation	Annual Depreciation Expense	Accumulated Depreciation
2012	$4,000	$4,000	$8,800	$ 8,800	$1,200	$1,200
2013	4,000	8,000	7,040	15,840	5,600	6,800

▶ Requirements

1. Identify the depreciation method used in each instance, and show the equation and computation for each. (Round to the nearest dollar.)
2. Assume continued use of the same method through year 2014. Determine the annual depreciation expense, accumulated depreciation, and book value of the equipment for 2012 through 2014 under each method, assuming 12,000 units of production in 2014.

▶ Answers
▶ Requirement 1

Method A: Straight-Line

$$\text{Depreciable cost} = \$40,000 (\$44,000 - \$4,000)$$
$$\text{Each year: } \$40,000 / 10 \text{ years} = \$4,000$$

Method B: Double-Declining-Balance

$$\text{Rate} = \frac{1}{10 \text{ years}} \times 2 = 10\% \times 2 = 20\%$$
$$2012: 0.20 \times \$44,000 = \$8,800$$
$$2013: 0.20 \times (\$44,000 - \$8,800) = \$7,040$$

Method C: Units-of-Production

$$\text{Depreciation per unit} = \frac{\$44,000 - \$4,000}{100,000 \text{ units}} = \$0.40$$
$$2012: \$0.40 \times 3,000 \text{ units} = \$1,200$$
$$2013: \$0.40 \times 14,000 \text{ units} = \$5,600$$

▶ Requirement 2

Method A: Straight-Line

Year	Annual Depreciation Expense	Accumulated Depreciation	Book Value
Start			$44,000
2012	$4,000	$ 4,000	40,000
2013	4,000	8,000	36,000
2014	4,000	12,000	32,000

Method B: Double-Declining-Balance

Year	Annual Depreciation Expense	Accumulated Depreciation	Book Value
Start			$44,000
2012	$8,800	$ 8,800	35,200
2013	7,040	15,840	28,160
2014	5,632	21,472	22,528

Method C: Units-of-Production

Year	Annual Depreciation Expense	Accumulated Depreciation	Book Value
Start			$44,000
2012	$1,200	$ 1,200	42,800
2013	5,600	6,800	37,200
2014	4,800	11,600	32,400

Computations for 2014

Straight-line	$40,000/10 years = $4,000
Double-declining-balance	$28,160 × 0.20 = $5,632
Units-of-production	12,000 units × $0.40 = $4,800

Other Issues in Accounting for Plant Assets

Plant assets are complex because

- ▶ they have long lives.
- ▶ depreciation affects income taxes.
- ▶ companies may have gains or losses when they sell plant assets.
- ▶ international accounting changes in the future may affect the recognition as well as the carrying values of assets.

Depreciation for Tax Purposes

FedEx and most other companies use straight-line depreciation for reporting to stockholders and creditors on their financial statements. However, for income tax purposes they also keep a separate set of depreciation records, based on accelerated depreciation methods in the Internal Revenue Code (IRC) developed by the Internal Revenue Service (IRS). This is legal, ethical, and honest. U.S. tax law not only permits but expects it. The reason that different methods are typically used for financial statement and income tax purposes is that the objectives of GAAP are different from the tax reporting objectives of the IRC. The objective of GAAP is to provide useful information for making economic decisions. The objective of the IRC is to raise sufficient revenue to pay for federal government expenditures.

Suppose you are a business manager, and the IRS allows an accelerated depreciation method. Why do FedEx managers prefer accelerated over straight-line depreciation for income-tax purposes? Accelerated depreciation provides the fastest tax deductions, thus decreasing immediate tax payments. FedEx can reinvest the tax savings back into the business. FedEx has a choice—pay taxes or buy equipment. This choice is easy.

To understand the relationships between cash flow, depreciation, and income tax, recall our depreciation example of a FedEx truck:

▶ First-year depreciation is $8,000 under straight-line and $16,400 under double-declining-balance (DDB).

▶ DDB is permitted for income tax purposes.

Assume that this FedEx office has $400,000 in revenue and $300,000 in cash operating expenses during the truck's first year and an income tax rate of 30%. The cash-flow analysis appears in Exhibit 7-10.

EXHIBIT 7-10 | The Cash-Flow Advantage of Accelerated Depreciation for Tax Purposes

		SL	Accelerated
1	Cash revenue	$400,000	$400,000
2	Cash operating expenses	300,000	300,000
3	Cash provided by operations before income tax	100,000	100,000
4	Depreciation expense (a noncash expense)	8,000	16,400
5	Income before income tax	$ 92,000	$ 83,600
6	Income tax expense (30%)	$ 27,600	$ 25,080
	Cash-flow analysis:		
7	Cash provided by operations before tax	$100,000	$100,000
8	Income tax expense	27,600	25,080
9	Cash provided by operations	$ 72,400	$ 74,920
10	Extra cash available for investment if DDB is used ($74,920 – $72,400)		$ 2,520

You can see that, for income-tax purposes, accelerated depreciation helps conserve cash for the business. That's why virtually all companies use accelerated depreciation to compute their income taxes.

There is a special depreciation method—used only for income tax purposes—called the **Modified Accelerated Cost Recovery System (MACRS)**. Under MACRS, each fixed asset is classified into one of eight classes identified by asset life (Exhibit 7-11 on the following page). Depreciation for the first four classes is computed by the double-declining-balance method. Depreciation for 15-year assets and 20-year assets is computed by the 150%-declining-balance method. Under 150% DB, annual depreciation is computed by multiplying the straight-line rate by 1.50 (instead of 2.00, as for DDB). For a 20-year asset, the straight-line rate is 0.05 per year ($1/20 = 0.05$), so the annual MACRS depreciation rate is 0.075 (0.05×1.50). The taxpayer computes annual depreciation by multiplying asset book value by 0.075, in a manner similar to how DDB works.

Most real estate is depreciated by the straight-line method (see the last two categories in Exhibit 7-11).

EXHIBIT 7-11 | Modified Accelerated Cost Recovery System (MACRS)

Class Identified by Asset Life (years)	Representative Assets	Depreciation Method
3	Race horses	DDB
5	Automobiles, light trucks	DDB
7	Equipment	DDB
10	Equipment	DDB
15	Sewage-treatment plants	150% DDB
20	Certain real estate	150% DDB
27½	Residential rental property	SL
39	Nonresidential rental property	SL

Depreciation for Partial Years

Companies purchase plant assets whenever they need them, not just at the beginning of the year. Therefore, companies must compute *depreciation for partial years*. Suppose UPS purchases a warehouse building on April 1 for $500,000. The building's estimated life is 20 years, and its estimated residual value is $80,000. UPS's accounting year ends on December 31. Let's consider how UPS computes depreciation for April through December:

► First, compute depreciation for a full year (unless you are using the units-of-production method, which automatically adjusts for partial periods by merely accounting for the number of units produced in the period).

► Second, multiply full-year depreciation by the fraction of the year that you held the asset—in this case, 9/12. Assuming the straight-line method, the year's depreciation for this UPS building is $15,750, as follows:

$$\text{Full-year depreciation} \quad \frac{\$500,000 - \$80,000}{20} = \$21,000$$

$$\text{Partial year depreciation} \quad \$21,000 \times 9/12 = \$15,750$$

What if UPS bought the asset on April 18? Many businesses record no monthly depreciation on assets purchased after the 15th of the month, and they record a full month's depreciation on an asset bought on or before the 15th.

Most companies use computerized systems to account for fixed assets. Each asset has a unique identification number, and the system will automatically calculate the asset's depreciation expense. Accumulated Depreciation is automatically updated.

Changing the Useful Life of a Depreciable Asset

After an asset is in use, managers may change its useful life on the basis of experience and new information. **Disney Enterprises, Inc.**, made such a change, called a *change in accounting estimate*. Disney recalculated depreciation on the basis of revised useful lives of several of its theme park assets. The following note in Disney Enterprises, Inc.'s financial statements reports this change in accounting estimate:

> **Note 5**
> ...[T]he Company extended the estimated useful lives of certain theme park ride and attraction assets based upon historical data and engineering studies. The effect of this change was to decrease depreciation by approximately $8 million (an increase in net income of approximately $4.2 million...).

Assume that a Disney hot dog stand cost $50,000 and that the company originally believed the asset had a 10-year useful life with no residual value. Using the straight-line method, the company would record $5,000 depreciation each year ($50,000/10 years = $5,000). Suppose Disney used the asset for four years. Accumulated depreciation reached $20,000, leaving a remaining depreciable book value (cost less accumulated depreciation less residual value) of $30,000 ($50,000 − $20,000). From its experience, management believes the asset will remain useful for an *additional* 10 years. The company would spread the remaining depreciable book value over the asset's remaining life as follows:

Asset's remaining depreciable book value	÷	(New) Estimated useful life remaining	=	(New) Annual depreciation
$30,000	÷	10 years	=	$3,000

The yearly depreciation entry based on the new estimated useful life is as follows:

Depreciation Expense—Hot Dog Stand	3,000	
Accumulated Depreciation—Hot Dog Stand		3,000

Depreciation decreases both assets and equity.

Assets	=	Liabilities	+	Stockholders' Equity	−	Expenses
− 3,000	=	0				− 3,000

Cooking the Books

Through Depreciation

Waste Management

Since plant assets usually involve relatively large amounts and relatively large numbers of assets, sometimes a seemingly subtle change in the way they are accounted for can have a tremendous impact on the financial statements. When these changes are made in order to cook the books, the results can be devastating.

Waste Management, Inc., is North America's largest integrated waste service company, providing collection, transfer, recycling, disposal, and waste-to-energy services for commercial, industrial, municipal, and residential customers from coast to coast.

Starting in 1992, six top executives of the company, including its founder and chairman of the board, its chief financial officer, its corporate controller, its top lawyer, and its vice-president of finance, decided that the company's profits were not growing fast enough to meet "earnings targets," which were tied to their executive bonuses. Among several fraudulent financial tactics these top executives employed to cook the books were (1) assigning unsupported and inflated salvage values to garbage trucks, (2) unjustifiably extending the estimated useful lives of their garbage trucks, and (3) assigning arbitrary salvage values to other fixed assets that previously had no salvage values. All of these tactics had the effect of decreasing the amount of depreciation expense in the income statements and increasing net income by a corresponding amount. While practices like this might seem relatively subtle and even insignificant when performed on an individual asset, remember that there were thousands of trash trucks and dumpsters involved, so the dollar amount grew huge in a short time. In addition, the company continued these practices for five years, overstating earnings by $1.7 billion.

The Waste Management fraud was the largest of its kind in history until the WorldCom scandal, discussed earlier in this chapter. In 1997, the company fired the officers involved and hired a new CEO who ordered a review of these practices, which uncovered the fraud. In the meantime, these dishonest executives had profited handsomely, receiving performance-based bonuses based on the company's inflated earnings, retaining their high-paying jobs, and receiving enhanced retirement benefits. One of the executives took the fraud to another level. Just 10 days before the fraud was disclosed, he enriched himself with a tax benefit by donating inflated company stock to his alma mater to fund a building in his name! Although the men involved were sued for monetary damages, none of them ever went to jail.

When the fraud was disclosed, Waste Management shareholders lost over $6 billion in the market value of their investments as the stock price plummeted by more than 33%. The company and these officers eventually settled civil lawsuits for approximately $700 million because of the fraud.

You might ask, "Where were the auditors while this was occurring?" The company's auditor was Arthur Andersen, LLP, whose partners involved on the audit engagement were eventually found to be complicit in the scheme. In fact, a few of the Waste Management officers who perpetrated the scheme had been ex-partners of the audit firm. As it turns out, the auditors actually identified many of the improper accounting practices of Waste Management. However, rather than insisting that the company fix the errors, or risk exposure, they merely "persuaded" management to agree not to repeat these practices in the future, and entered into an agreement with them to write off the accumulated balance sheet overstatement over a period of 10 years. In June 2001, the SEC fined Arthur Andersen $7 million for "knowingly and recklessly issuing false and misleading audit reports" for Waste Management from 1993 through 1996.

In October 2001, immediately on the heels of these disclosures, the notorious Enron scandal broke. Enron, as well as WorldCom, were Arthur Andersen clients at the time. The Enron scandal finally put the firm out of business. Many people feel that, had it not been for Andersen's involvement in the Waste Management affair, the SEC might have been more lenient toward the company in the Enron scandal.

The Enron scandal is discussed in Chapter 10.

Fully Depreciated Assets

A *fully depreciated asset* is one that has reached the end of its estimated useful life. Suppose FedEx has fully depreciated equipment with zero residual value (cost was $60,000). FedEx accounts will appear as follows:

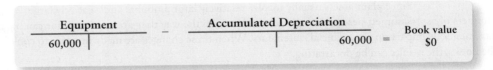

The equipment's book value is zero, but that doesn't mean the equipment is worthless. FedEx may use the equipment for a few more years, but FedEx will not record any more depreciation on a fully depreciated asset.

When FedEx disposes of the equipment, FedEx will remove both the asset's cost ($60,000) and its accumulated depreciation ($60,000) from the books. The next section shows how to account for plant asset disposals.

Analyze the Effect of a Plant Asset Disposal

Eventually, a plant asset ceases to serve a company's needs. The asset may wear out or become obsolete. Before accounting for the disposal of the asset, the business should bring depreciation up to date to

- ▶ measure the asset's final book value and
- ▶ record the expense up to the date of sale.

Analyze the effect of a plant asset disposal

Disposing of a Fully Depreciated Asset for No Proceeds

To account for disposal, remove the asset and its related accumulated depreciation from the books. Suppose the final year's depreciation expense has just been recorded for a machine that cost $60,000 and is estimated to have zero residual value. The machine's accumulated depreciation thus totals $60,000. Assuming that this asset is junked, the entry to record its disposal is as follows:

	Accumulated Depreciation—Machinery	60,000	
	Machinery		60,000
	To dispose of a fully depreciated machine.		

Assets	=	Liabilities	+	Stockholders' Equity
+ 60,000				
− 60,000	=	0	+	0

There is no gain or loss on this disposal, and there's no effect on total assets, liabilities, or equity.

If assets are disposed of for no proceeds before being fully depreciated, the company incurs a loss on the disposal in the amount of the asset's net book value. Suppose FedEx disposes of equipment that cost $60,000. This asset's accumulated depreciation is $50,000, and book value is, therefore, $10,000. Junking this equipment results in a loss equal to the book value of the asset, as follows:

	Accumulated Depreciation—Equipment	50,000	
	Loss on Disposal of Equipment	10,000	
	Equipment		60,000
	To dispose of equipment.		

Assets	=	Liabilities	+	Stockholders' Equity	−	Losses
+ 50,000						
− 60,000	=	0				− 10,000

FedEx disposed of an asset with $10,000 book value and received nothing. The result is a $10,000 loss, which decreases both total assets and equity.

The Loss on Disposal of Equipment is reported as Other income (expense) on the income statement. Losses decrease net income exactly as expenses do. Gains increase net income the same as revenues.

Selling a Plant Asset

Suppose FedEx sells equipment on September 30, 2012, for $7,300 cash. The equipment cost $10,000 when purchased on January 1, 2009, and has been depreciated straight-line. FedEx estimated a 10-year useful life and no residual value. Prior to recording the sale, FedEx accountants must update the asset's depreciation. Assume that FedEx uses the calendar year as its accounting period. Partial-year depreciation must be recorded for the asset's depreciation from January 1, 2012, to the sale date. The straight-line depreciation entry at September 30, 2012, is

Sep 30	Depreciation Expense ($10,000/10 years × 9/12)	750	
	Accumulated Depreciation—Equipment		750
	To update depreciation.		

The Equipment account and the Accumulated Depreciation account appear as follows. Observe that the equipment's book value is $6,250 ($10,000 − $3,750).

Equipment			Accumulated Depreciation		
Jan 1, 2009	10,000		Dec 31, 2009	1,000	
		−	Dec 31, 2010	1,000	= Book value
			Dec 31, 2011	1,000	$6,250
			Sep 30, 2012	750	
			Balance	3,750	

The gain on the sale of the equipment for $7,300 is $1,050, computed as follows:

Cash received from sale of the asset		$7,300
Book value of asset sold:		
Cost	$10,000	
Less: Accumulated depreciation	(3,750)	6,250
Gain on sale of the asset.................................		$1,050

The entry to record sale of the equipment is as follows:

Sep 30	Cash	7,300	
	Accumulated Depreciation—Equipment	3,750	
	Equipment		10,000
	Gain on Sale of Equipment		1,050
	To sell equipment.		

Total assets increase, and so does equity—by the amount of the gain.

Assets	=	Liabilities	−	Stockholders' Equity	+	Gains
+ 7,300						
+ 3,750	=	0			+	1,050
− 10,000						

Gains are recorded as credits on the income statement, just as revenues are. Gains and losses on asset disposals appear as Other income (expense), or Other gains (losses).

Exchanging a Plant Asset

Managers often trade in old assets for new ones. This is called a *nonmonetary exchange*. The accounting for nonmonetary exchanges is based on the *fair values of the assets involved*. Thus, the cost of an asset like plant and equipment received in a nonmonetary exchange is equal to the fair values of the assets given up (including the old asset and any cash paid). Any difference between the fair value of the old asset from its book value is recognized as gain (fair value of old asset exceeds book value) or loss (book value of old asset exceeds fair value) on the exchange.

For example, assume Papa John's Pizza's

► old delivery car cost $9,000 and has accumulated depreciation of $8,000. Thus, the old car's book value is $1,000.

Assume Papa John's trades in the old automobile for a new one with a fair market value of $15,000 and pays cash of $10,000. Thus, the implied fair value of the old car is $5,000 ($15,000 − $10,000). This amount is treated as cash paid by the seller for the old vehicle.

► The cost of the new delivery car is $15,000 (fair value of the old asset, $5,000, plus cash paid, $10,000).

The pizzeria records the exchange transaction as follows:

Delivery Auto (new)		15,000	
Accumulated Depreciation (old)		8,000	
Delivery Auto (old)			9,000
Cash			10,000
Gain on Exchange of Delivery Auto			4,000
Traded in old delivery car for new auto.			

Assets	=	Liabilities	+	Stockholders' Equity
+ 15,000				
+ 8,000	=	0	+	4,000
− 9,000				
− 10,000				

There was a net increase in total assets of $4,000 and a corresponding increase in stockholders' equity, to reflect the gain on the exchange. Notice that this amount represents the excess of the fair value of the old asset over its book value. Some special rules may apply here, but they are reserved for more advanced courses.

T-Accounts for Analyzing Plant Asset Transactions

You can perform quite a bit of analysis if you know how transactions affect the plant asset accounts. Here are the accounts with descriptions of the activity in each account.

Building (or Equipment)		Accumulated Depreciation	

Beg bal
Cost of assets
  purchased
	Cost of assets
	disposed of
		Accum deprec
		of assets
		disposed of
			Beg bal
			Depreciation expense
			  for the current period

End bal			End bal

Cash		Long-Term Debt	
Cash proceeds for assets disposed of	Cash paid for assets purchased		New Debt incurred for assets purchased

Depreciation Expense		Gain on Sale of Building (or Equipment)	
Depreciation expense for the current period			Gain on sale
		Loss on Sale of Building (or Equipment)	
		Loss on sale	

You can analyze transactions as they flow through these accounts to answer very useful questions such as the amount of cash paid to purchase new plant assets, the amount of cash proceeds from disposal of plant assets, the cost of assets purchased, and the gross cost as well as net book value of assets disposed of.

Example: Suppose you started the year with buildings that cost $100,000. During the year, you bought another building for $150,000 and ended the year with buildings that cost $180,000. What was the cost of the building you sold?

Building			
Beg bal	100,000		
Cost of assets purchased	150,000	Cost of assets sold	? = 70,000*
End bal	180,000		

*100,000 + 150,000 − 180,000

One of the most significant differences between U.S. GAAP and International Financial Reporting Standards (IFRS) is the permitted reported carrying values of property, plant, and equipment. Recall from Chapter 1 that U.S. GAAP has long advocated the historical cost principle as most appropriate for plant assets because it results in a more objective (nonbiased) and therefore more reliable (auditable) figure. It also supports the continuity assumption, which states that we expect the entity to remain in business long enough to recover the cost of its plant assets through depreciation.

In contrast, while historical cost is the primary basis of accounting under IFRS, it permits the periodic revaluation of plant assets to fair market value. The primary justification for this position is that the historical cost of plant assets purchased years ago does not properly reflect their current values. Thus, the amounts shown on the balance sheet for these assets do not reflect a relevant measure of what these assets are worth. For example, suppose a business bought a building in downtown Orlando, Florida, in 1960 for $1 million. Assume that this year that building has been appraised for $20 million. IFRS would permit the company to periodically revalue the building on its balance sheet.

The primary objection to the use of fair values on the balance sheet for plant assets is that these values are subjective and subject to change, sometimes quite rapidly. Consider, for example, residential and commercial real estate in California during the credit crisis of 2008 and 2009. The fair market values of these assets dropped by double-digit percentages in a period of less than one year. If these assets had been valued at fair market values on the books of the companies that held them, assets would have to have been adjusted accordingly, causing the balance sheet amounts to fluctuate wildly. Furthermore, if the assets had been depreciated, it is likely that both the depreciation expense and the allowance for depreciation would also have had to be adjusted more frequently.

IFRS also differs substantially from U.S. GAAP with respect to accounting for depreciation. Whereas U.S. GAAP depreciates each asset as a composite whole (a building, manufactured equipment, an aircraft, etc.) IFRS uses a "components" approach. For example, suppose a company builds and owns a building that it is using for its operations. The total cost of the building, including all components (air conditioning systems, roofing, duct work, plumbing, lighting systems, etc.) is $15 million. U.S. GAAP usually treats the building as a single composite asset within the class of buildings, with an estimated useful life of about 40 years that it depreciates using straight-line depreciation (about $375,000 per year). In contrast, IFRS does not view the building as a single composite asset, but recognizes the separate components of it—each with a different useful life and potentially accounted for with a different depreciation method. Thus, the frame of the building, the roof, air conditioning systems, duct work, plumbing, light fixtures, and all other major components of the building each might have a different useful life (most being far less than 40 years) and be depreciated using a different method over shorter periods of time. Each has to be set up on the books as a separate plant asset with separate amounts of depreciation expense and accumulated depreciation. Converting a large enterprise's accounting system to a component approach for depreciation requires a massive one-time expenditure in information technology, as well as more extensive ongoing record keeping requirements.

Apply GAAP for Natural Resources and Intangible Assets

Accounting for Natural Resources

Natural resources are long-term assets of a special type, such as iron ore, petroleum (oil), and timber. These resources are often called *wasting assets* because, in contrast to property and equipment, they are actually physically used up over time. The process by which this occurs is called **depletion**. Depletion is distinctively different from depreciation, because it involves actually tracking the flow of a natural resource from its raw state, through inventory (to the extent not sold), to cost of goods sold or some other expense on the income statement. When a natural resource is acquired or developed, the entity follows the cost principle, similarly to that used in accounting for a plant asset. When the asset is extracted, the entity follows an approach much like the units-of-production depreciation method to account for the production. If all of the resource extracted is regarded as sold (as in the case of a drilling and exploration company), the amount depleted is transferred directly from long-term assets to the income statement in the form of an expense (such as depletion expense). However, as in the case of an integrated oil company (one with both production and refining operations), if a portion of the extracted resource is not immediately sold, it becomes saleable inventory (a current asset). Then, as the inventory is sold, its cost is transferred to an expense such as cost of goods sold, as discussed in Chapter 6.

For example, an oil reserve may cost **ExxonMobil** $100,000,000 and contain an estimated 10,000,000 barrels of oil. ExxonMobil is an integrated oil company, meaning it both drills for oil and refines it, so the company retains some inventory rather than selling all it produces. Upon purchase or development of the oil (assuming the company paid cash), ExxonMobil makes the following entry:

Oil Reserve		100,000,000	
Cash			100,000,000

The depletion rate is $10 per barrel ($100,000,000/10,000,000 barrels). If 3,000,000 barrels are extracted, and 1,000,000 barrels are sold, the company's different divisions might make the following entries. First, the oil reserve (long-term asset) is depleted by $30,000,000 (3,000,000 barrels × $10 per barrel) and $30,000,000 is transferred to inventory. The depletion entry is as follows:

Oil Inventory (3,000,000 barrels × $10)		30,000,000	
Oil Reserve			30,000,000

5   **Apply** GAAP for natural resources and intangible assets

The following week, as the oil is sold, ExxonMobil makes the following entry:

	Cost of oil sold (1,000,000 barrels × $10)	10,000,000	
	Oil Inventory		10,000,000

This would assign $10 million to Cost of Sales (an expense), and leave $20 million in Oil Inventory (a current asset). The net book value of the oil reserve (the long-term asset) after these entries is $70 million ($100 million – $30 million).

Accounting for Intangible Assets

As we've seen, *intangible assets* are long-lived assets with no physical form. Intangibles are valuable because they carry special rights from patents, copyrights, trademarks, franchises, leaseholds, and goodwill. Like buildings and equipment, an intangible asset is recorded at its acquisition cost. Intangibles are the most valuable assets of high-tech companies and those that depend on research and development. The residual value of most intangibles is zero.

Intangible assets fall into two categories:

▶ Intangibles with *finite lives* that can be measured. We record amortization for these intangibles. **Amortization** expense is the title of the expense associated with intangibles. Amortization works like depreciation and is usually computed on a straight-line basis. Amortization can be credited directly to the asset account, as we shall see.

▶ Intangibles with *indefinite lives*. Record no amortization for these intangibles. Instead, check them annually for any loss in value (impairment), and record a loss when it occurs. Goodwill is the most prominent example of an intangible asset with an indefinite life.

In the following discussions, we illustrate the accounting for both categories of intangibles.

Accounting for Specific Intangibles

Each type of intangible asset is unique, and the accounting can vary from one asset to another.

Patents. Patents are federal government grants that give the holder the exclusive right for 20 years to produce and sell an invention. The invention may be a product or a process—for example, the Sony Blu-Ray disc players and the Dolby Laboratories surround-sound process. Like any other asset, a patent may be purchased. Suppose **Sony** pays $170,000 to acquire a patent on January 1, and the business believes the expected useful life of the patent is 5 years—not the entire 20-year period. Amortization expense is $34,000 per year ($170,000/5 years). Sony records the acquisition and amortization for this patent as follows:

Jan 1	Patents	170,000	
	Cash		170,000
	To acquire a patent.		

Dec 31	Amortization Expense—Patents ($170,000/5)	34,000	
	Patents		34,000
	To amortize the cost of a patent.		

You can see that we credited the Patents account directly (no Accumulated Amortization account).

Assets	=	Liabilities	+	Stockholders' Equity	−	Expenses
− 34,000	=	0				− 34,000

Amortization for an intangible decreases both assets and equity exactly as depreciation does for equipment or a building.

Copyrights. **Copyrights** are exclusive rights to reproduce and sell a book, musical composition, film, or other work of art. Copyrights also protect computer software programs, such as **Microsoft's** Windows® and Excel. Issued by the federal government, copyrights extend 70 years beyond the author's (composer's, artist's, or programmer's) life. The cost of obtaining a copyright from the government is low, but a company may pay a large sum to purchase an existing copyright from the owner. For example, a publisher may pay the author of a popular novel $1 million or more for the book copyright. Because the useful life of a copyright is usually no longer than two or three years, each period's amortization amount is a high proportion of the copyright cost.

Trademarks and Trade Names. **Trademarks** and **trade names** (or *brand names*) are distinctive identification of a product or service. The "eye" symbol that flashes across our television screens is the trademark that identifies the **CBS** television network. You are probably also familiar with **NBC's** peacock. Advertising slogans that are legally protected include **American Airlines'** "AAdvantage®" program and **Enterprise Rent-a-Car's** "We pick you up®" slogan. These are distinctive identifications of products or services, marked with the symbol ™ or ®.

Some trademarks may have a definite useful life set by contract. We should amortize the cost of this type of trademark over its useful life. But a trademark or a trade name may have an indefinite life and not be amortized.

Franchises and Licenses. **Franchises** and **licenses** are privileges granted by a private business or a government to sell a product or service in accordance with specified conditions. The Chicago Cubs baseball organization is a franchise granted to its owner by the National League. **McDonald's** restaurants and **Holiday Inn**s are popular franchises. The useful lives of many franchises and licenses are indefinite and, therefore, not amortized.

Goodwill. In accounting, **goodwill** has a very specific meaning:

> **Goodwill is defined as the excess of the cost of purchasing another company over the sum of the market values of the acquired company's net assets (assets minus liabilities).**

A purchaser is willing to pay for goodwill when the purchaser buys another company that has abnormal earning power.

FedEx operates in several foreign countries. Suppose FedEx acquires Europa Company at a cost of $10 million. Europa's assets have a market value of $9 million, and its liabilities total $2 million, so Europa's net assets total $7 million at current market value. In this case, FedEx paid $3 million for goodwill, computed as follows:

Purchase price paid for Europa Company		$10 million
Sum of the market values of Europa Company's assets	$9 million	
Less: Europa Company's liabilities	(2 million)	
Market value of Europa Company's net assets		7 million
Excess is called *goodwill*		$ 3 million

FedEx's entry to record the acquisition of Europa Company, including its goodwill, would be as follows:

	Assets (Cash, Receivables, Inventories, Plant Assets, all at market value)	9,000,000	
	Goodwill	3,000,000	
	Liabilities		2,000,000
	Cash		10,000,000

Goodwill in accounting has special features:

1. Goodwill is recorded *only* when it is purchased in the acquisition of another company. A purchase transaction provides objective evidence of the value of goodwill. Companies never record goodwill that they create for their own business.

2. According to GAAP, goodwill is not amortized because the goodwill of many entities increases in value. Rather, each year, companies with goodwill on their financial statements are required to perform a special impairment test for goodwill, similar (but not identical) to the impairment test for other long-term assets described in the next section. If the test shows that goodwill is impaired, it must be written down to the impaired value. The details of this impairment test are beyond the scope of this text and are reserved for later courses.

Accounting for Research and Development Costs

Accounting for research and development (R&D) costs is one of the most difficult issues in accounting. R&D is the lifeblood of companies such as **Procter & Gamble, General Electric, Intel,** and **Boeing.** R&D is one of these companies' most valuable intangible assets. However, in general, U.S. companies do not report R&D assets on their balance sheets. Rather, they expense R&D costs as they are incurred.

Explain the Effect of an Asset Impairment on the Financial Statements

6

Explain the effect of an asset impairment on the financial statements

Generally accepted accounting principles require that management of companies test both tangible and intangible long-term assets for impairment yearly. **Impairment** occurs when the expected future cash flows (which approximate the expected future benefits) from a long-term asset fall below the asset's net book (carrying) value (cost minus accumulated depreciation or amortization). If an asset is impaired, the company is required to adjust the carrying value downward from its book value to its **fair value.** In this case, fair value is based not on the expected future cash flows, but on the asset's estimated market value at the date of the impairment test. Exhibit 7-12 displays both the normal relationship and an impaired relationship between net book value, future cash flows, and fair value.

EXHIBIT 7-12 | Normal Relationship and Impaired Relationship Among Values of an Asset

Normal	Impaired
Largest: Future cash flows	Largest: Net book value
Middle: Fair value	Middle: Future cash flows
Smallest: Net book value	Smallest: Fair value

In a normal relationship, estimated future cash flow represents the largest of the three amounts, followed by fair value, and then net book value. An impaired relationship exists if net book value exceeds estimated future cash flows. The process of accounting for asset impairment requires two steps:

> Step 1: **Test the asset for impairment.**
>
> > ► If net book value > Estimated future cash flows, then the asset is impaired.
>
> Step 2: **If the asset is impaired under Step 1, compute the impairment loss.**
>
> > ► **Impairment Loss = Net Book Value – Fair Value**

To illustrate, let's assume that FedEx has a long-term asset with the following information as of May 31, 2010:

- ► **Net book value** $100 million
- ► **Estimated future cash flows**   80 million
- ► **Fair (market) value**   70 million

The two-stage impairment process is as follows:

> Step 1: **Impairment test: Is net book value > estimated future cash flows? (Answer: Yes, so the asset is impaired).**
>
> Step 2: **Impairment loss = Net book value – Fair value ($100 – 70)**

FedEx will make the following entry:

2010				
May 31	Impairment Loss on Long-term Asset ($100 – 70)		30	
	Long-term Asset			30

Both long-term assets and equity decrease (through the Loss account). Under U.S. GAAP, once a long-term asset has been written down because of impairment, it may never again be written back up, should it increase in value.

Assets	=	Liabilities	+	Stockholders' Equity	–	Losses
– 30	=	0				– 30

Global View

Like U.S. GAAP, IFRS also records impairments based on a two-step impairment process. The details of this process are covered in more advanced accounting courses. However, unlike U.S. GAAP, asset impairments under IFRS may be reversed in future periods for some types of long-term assets, in the event that the market price recovers. Thus, under IFRS, a company can record an impairment loss on certain long-term assets in one period, and then write the asset back up with a corresponding gain in a later period.

Accounting for research and development costs represents another prominent difference between U.S. GAAP and IFRS. Whereas under GAAP, in general, both research and development costs are expensed as incurred, under IFRS, costs associated with the creation of intangible assets are classified into research phase costs and development phase costs. Costs in the research phase are always expensed. However, costs in the development phase are capitalized if the company can demonstrate meeting all of the following six criteria:

- ► The technical feasibility of completing the intangible asset
- ► The intention to complete the intangible asset
- ► The ability to use or sell the intangible asset
- ► The future economic benefits (e.g., the existence of a market or, if for internal use, the usefulness of the intangible asset)

▶ The availability of adequate resources to complete development of the asset
▶ The ability to reliably measure the expenditure attributable to the intangible asset during its development

Thus, IFRS are generally more permissive than U.S. GAAP toward capitalization of research and development costs. Adoption of IFRS should result in generally higher reported incomes for companies that incur research and development costs in periods in which these costs are incurred.

The Financial Accounting Standards Board (FASB) is currently working on a new accounting standard aimed at eliminating the differences between U.S. GAAP and IFRS in the area of research and development costs.

Still another difference between IFRS and U.S. GAAP lies in the capitalization of internally generated intangible assets such as brand names and patents. U.S. GAAP only permits capitalization of these when they are purchased from a source outside the company. The cost of internally generated brand names and patents must be expensed on the income statement. In contrast, IFRS allows the capitalization of internally generated intangible assets like these as long as it is probable (i.e., more likely than not) that the company will receive future benefits from them. Adoption of IFRS by U.S. companies is therefore expected to result in the recognition of more intangible assets on their balance sheets than presently exist. These assets may be either amortized over the assets' estimated useful lives or tested for impairment as they are held, depending on the asset.

Analyze Rate of Return on Assets

7

Analyze rate of return on assets

Evaluating company performance is a key goal of financial statement analysis. Shareholders entrust managers with the responsibility of developing a business strategy that utilizes company assets in a manner that both effectively and efficiently generates a profit. In this chapter, we begin to develop a framework by which company performance can be evaluated. The most basic framework for this purpose is **return on assets (ROA)**.

ROA, also known as *rate* of return on assets, measures how profitably management has used the assets that stockholders and creditors have provided the company. The basic formula for the ROA ratio is as follows:

$$ROA = \frac{\text{Net income}[1]}{\text{Average total assets}}$$

where Average total assets = (Beginning total assets + Ending total assets)/2)

ROA measures how much the entity earned for each dollar of assets invested by both stockholders and creditors. Companies with high ROA have both selected assets and managed them more successfully than companies with low ROA. ROA is often computed on a divisional or product-line basis to help identify less profitable segments and improve their performance.

DuPont Analysis: A More Detailed View of ROA

To better understand why ROA increased or decreased over time, companies often perform a **DuPont Analysis**[2], which breaks ROA down into two components ratios that drive it:

$$\text{Net profit margin} = \frac{\text{Net income}}{\text{Net sales}}$$

$$\text{Total asset turnover} = \frac{\text{Net sales}}{\text{Average total assets}}$$

---

[1]For companies with significant debt, some analysts may add interest expense to net income. While it is theoretically correct to do so, in order to illustrate DuPont analysis, we do not. Adding back interest makes a material difference to ROA only when interest expense is relatively high compared to net income.

[2]The full DuPont Analysis model actually contains three components: profit margin, asset turnover, and leverage. We discuss the first two components in this chapter and add the third in Chapter 9 (Liabilities).

Net profit margin measures how much every sales dollar generates in profit. Net profit can be increased in one of three ways: (1) increasing sales volume, or the amount of goods or services sold or performed; (2) increasing sales prices; or (3) decreasing cost of goods sold and operating expenses.

Total asset turnover measures how many sales dollars are generated for each dollar of assets invested. This is a measure of how effectively and efficiently the company manages its assets. Asset turnover can be increased by (1) increasing sales in the ways just described, (2) keeping less inventory on hand, or (3) closing unproductive facilities, selling idle assets, and consolidating operations to fewer places to reduce the amount of plant assets needed.

ROA is the product of net profit margin and total asset turnover:

$$\text{ROA} = \text{Net profit margin} \times \text{Total asset turnover}$$

$$\text{ROA} = \frac{\text{Net income}}{\text{Net sales}} \times \frac{\text{Net sales}}{\text{Average total assets}} = \frac{\text{Net income}}{\text{Average total assets}}$$

By influencing the drivers of net profit margin and total asset turnover, management devises strategies to improve each one, thus increasing ROA. Successful manufacturing firms often choose between a mixture of two different strategies: *product differentiation* or *low-cost*. A company that follows a high product differentiation strategy usually spends a great deal on research and development and advertising to convince customers that the company's products (usually higher priced) are worth the investment. **Apple, Inc.,** our spotlight company in Chapters 2 and 13, follows a product differentiation strategy, introducing innovative and attractive technology in the marketplace before any other competitor, and always at a higher price. Alternatively, a low-cost strategy usually relies on efficient management of inventory and productive assets to produce a high asset turnover. **Dell, Inc.,** a competitor of Apple's, follows a low-cost strategy. Of course all companies would like to have the best of both worlds by maximizing both profit margin and asset turnover, but some companies have to settle for one or the other.

To illustrate, let's consider **Masimo Corporation,** a company that produces electronic instruments used in the health care industry. The following table contains approximate financial data adapted from Masimo's income statements and balance sheets for 2009 and 2010:

Masimo Corporation Selected (Adapted) Financial Data		
	(Amounts in thousands)	
	2009	**2010**
Net sales..................................	$350,000	$400,000
Net income...............................	52,500	75,000
Average total assets....................	350,000	300,000

Masimo Corporation DuPont Analysis				
	Net profit margin (Net income/Net sales)	× Total asset turnover × (Net sales/Average total assets)	= ROA = (Net income/Average total assets)	
2009	$\dfrac{52,500}{350,000}$	× $\dfrac{350,000}{350,000}$	=	15%
2010	$\dfrac{75,000}{400,000}$	× $\dfrac{400,000}{300,000}$	=	25%

In 2009, the company's profit margin was 15% (52,500/350,000). Its asset turnover was 1.0 (350,000/350,000), meaning that it earned $1 of sales revenue for every $1 of assets invested. In 2010, the company improved its profit margin to 18.75% (75,000/400,000) by reducing expenses and increasing sales, introducing new and unique products to the market that no other competitor had. In addition, Masimo sold unproductive plant assets, reducing total average assets from $350,000 to $300,000 and increasing asset turnover from 1.0 to 1.33. Thus, the company used both product differentiation and low-cost strategies to its benefit, increasing return on assets from 15% to 25%.

Return on assets is the first of several ratios we will introduce over the next few chapters to show how analysts dissect financial statements to get behind the numbers, discover management's strategies, and evaluate their performance. In Chapters 9 and 10 we will add the component of financial leverage and explain how it is combined with ROA to calculate return on stockholders' equity (ROE).

Analyze the Cash Flow Impact of Long-Lived Asset Transactions

Analyze the cash flow impact of long-lived asset transactions

Three main types of long-lived asset transactions appear on the statement of cash flows:

- ▶ acquisitions,
- ▶ sales, and
- ▶ depreciation (as well as amortization).

Acquisitions and sales of long-term assets are *investing* activities. Capital expenditures are examples of investing activities that appear on the statement of cash flows. The disposition of plant and other long-term assets results in a cash receipt, as illustrated in Exhibit 7-13, which excerpts data from the cash-flow statement of FedEx Corporation. Depreciation, acquisitions (capital expenditures), and sales (dispositions) of long-term capital assets are denoted in color (lines 2, 5, and 6).

EXHIBIT 7-13 | Reporting Investing Activities on FedEx's Statement of Cash Flows

		FedEx Corporation Statement of Cash Flows (Partial, Adapted) Year Ended May 31, 2010	(In millions)
		Cash Flows from Operating Activities:	
1		Net income	$ 1,184
		Adjustments to reconcile net income to net cash provided by operating activities:	
2		Depreciation and amortization	1,958
3		Other items (summarized)	(4)
4		Cash provided by operating activities	3,138
		Cash Flows from Investing Activities:	
5		Capital expenditures	(2,816)
6		Proceeds from asset dispositions	35
7		Cash (used in) investing activities	(2,781)
		Cash Flows from Financing Activities:	
8		Cash (used in) financing activities	(692)
9		Effect of exchange rate changes on cash	(5)
10		**Net (decrease) in cash and cash equivalents**	(340)
11		**Cash and cash equivalents, beginning of period**	2,292
12		**Cash and cash equivalents, end of period**	$ 1,952

Let's examine FedEx's investing activities first. During 2010, FedEx invested $2,816 million for plant and other long-term assets (line 5). FedEx also disposed of property and equipment and other long-term assets, receiving cash of $35 million (line 6). FedEx labels the cash received as "proceeds from asset dispositions."

FedEx's statement of cash flows reports Depreciation and amortization (line 2). Observe that "Depreciation and amortization" is listed as a positive item under "adjustments to reconcile net income to cash provided by operating activities." Since depreciation and amortization do not affect cash, you may be wondering why these amounts appear on the statement of cash flows. In this format, the operating activities section of the statement of cash flows starts with net income (line 1) and reconciles to cash provided by operating activities (line 4). Depreciation and amortization decrease net income but do not affect cash. Depreciation and amortization are therefore added back to net income to measure cash flow from operations. The add-back of depreciation and amortization to net income offsets the earlier subtraction of these expenses. The sum of net income plus depreciation and amortization, therefore, helps to reconcile net income (on the accrual basis) to cash flow from operations (a cash-basis amount). We revisit this topic in the full context of the statement of cash flows in Chapter 12.

FedEx's cash flows are strong. Cash provided by operating activities exceeds net income by almost $2 billion. With this excess, the company has made sizeable capital expenditures, signaling that the company has invested in new plant and equipment and other long-term assets needed to expand and run its business. However, the company has also had to borrow money to help finance these purchases. The company's net cash used in financing activities ($692 million, including debt payments of $653 million) has grown substantially over the past several years as well. This has resulted in a decline in cash and cash equivalents of $340 million in 2010. However, the company's cash position at the end of the 2010, in the amount of $1,952 million, is still very strong.

DECISION GUIDELINES

PLANT ASSETS AND RELATED EXPENSES

FedEx Corporation, like all other companies, must make some decisions about how to account for its plant assets and intangibles. Let's review some of these decisions.

Decision	Guidelines
Capitalize or expense a cost?	General rule: Capitalize all costs that provide *future* benefit for the business such as a new package-handling system. Expense all costs that provide no *future* benefit, such as a repair to an airplane.
Capitalize or expense:	
► Cost associated with a new asset?	Capitalize all costs that bring the asset to its intended use, including asset purchase price, transportation charges, and taxes paid to acquire the asset.
► Cost associated with an existing asset?	Capitalize only those costs that add to the asset's usefulness or to its useful life. Expense all other costs as maintenance or repairs.

Decision	Guidelines
Which depreciation method to use:	
▸ For financial reporting?	Use the method that best allocates the cost of an asset through depreciation expense against the revenues produced by the asset. Most companies use the straight-line method.
▸ For income tax?	Use the method that produces the fastest tax deductions (MACRS). A company can use different depreciation methods for financial reporting and for income-tax purposes. In the United States, this practice is both legal and ethical.
How to account for natural resources?	Capitalize the asset's acquisition cost and all later costs that add to the natural resource's future benefit. Record depletion by the units-of-production method by transferring the amount extracted to inventory and eventually to cost of goods sold.
How to account for intangibles?	Capitalize acquisition cost and all later costs that add to the asset's future benefit. For intangibles with finite lives, record amortization expense. For intangibles with indefinite lives, do not record amortization. But if an intangible asset loses value, record a loss in the amount of the decrease in asset value.
How to record impairments in long-term assets?	Every year, conduct a two-step impairment process for long-term assets: Step 1: Compare net book value with expected cash flows from the asset. If net book value > expected cash flows, the asset is impaired. Otherwise, the asset is not impaired. Step 2: For all impaired assets under Step 1, reduce the carrying value of the asset from net book value to fair value. Record a loss for the difference.
How profitable is the company?	Return on assets (ROA) = Net profit margin × Total asset turnover = (Net income/Net sales) × (Net sales/Average total assets)

END-OF-CHAPTER SUMMARY PROBLEM

The figures that follow appear in the *Answers to the Mid-Chapter Summary Problem*, Requirement 2, on page 414.

	Method A: Straight-Line			Method B: Double-Declining-Balance		
Year	Annual Depreciation Expense	Accumulated Depreciation	Book Value	Annual Depreciation Expense	Accumulated Depreciation	Book Value
Start			$44,000			$44,000
2012	$4,000	$ 4,000	40,000	$8,800	$ 8,800	35,200
2013	4,000	8,000	36,000	7,040	15,840	28,160
2014	4,000	12,000	32,000	5,632	21,472	22,528

▶ Requirements

1. Suppose the income tax authorities permitted a choice between these two depreciation methods. Which method would FedEx select for income-tax purposes? Why?
2. Suppose FedEx purchased the equipment described in the table on January 1, 2012. Management has depreciated the equipment by using the double-declining-balance method. On July 1, 2014, FedEx sold the equipment for $27,000 cash.

Record depreciation for 2014 and the sale of the equipment on July 1, 2014.

▶ Answers
▶ Requirement 1

For tax purposes, most companies select the accelerated method because it results in the most depreciation in the earliest years of the asset's life. Accelerated depreciation minimizes income tax payments in the early years of the asset's life. That maximizes the business's cash at the earliest possible time.

▶ Requirement 2

Entries to record depreciation to date of sale, and then the sale of the equipment, follow:

	2014			
	Jul 1	Depreciation Expense—Equipment ($5,632 × 1/2 year)	2,816	
		Accumulated Depreciation—Equipment		2,816
		To update depreciation.		
	Jul 1	Cash	27,000	
		Accumulated Depreciation—Equipment		
		($15,840 + $2,816)	18,656	
		Equipment		44,000
		Gain on Sale of Equipment		1,656
		To record sale of equipment.		

REVIEW | Plant Assets and Intangibles

Quick Check (Answers are given on page 462.)

1. Benoit, Inc., purchased a tract of land, a small office building, and some equipment for $1,800,000. The appraised value of the land was $1,144,000, the building $660,000, and the equipment $396,000. What is the cost of the land?

   a. $600,000

   b. $936,000

   c. $1,144,000

   d. None of the above

2. Which statement is false?

   a. Depreciation is based on the expense recognition principle because it apportions the cost of the asset against the revenue generated over the asset's useful life.

   b. Depreciation is a process of allocating the cost of a plant asset over its useful life.

   c. Depreciation creates a fund to replace the asset at the end of its useful life.

   d. The cost of a plant asset minus accumulated depreciation equals the asset's book value.

   Use the following data for questions 3–6.

   On October 1, 2012, Freedom Communications purchased a new piece of equipment that cost $35,000. The estimated useful life is five years and estimated residual value is $8,000.

3. What is the depreciation expense for 2012 if Freedom uses the straight-line method?

   a. $5,400

   b. $1,750

   c. $1,350

   d. $7,000

4. Assume Freedom Communications purchased the equipment on January 1, 2012. If Freedom uses the straight-line method for depreciation, what is the asset's book value at the end of 2013?

   a. $16,200

   b. $24,200

   c. $21,000

   d. $32,200

5. Assume Freedom Communications purchased the equipment on January 1, 2012. If Freedom uses the double-declining-balance method, what is depreciation for 2013?

   a. $14,000

   b. $6,480

   c. $22,400

   d. $8,400

6. Return to Freedom's original purchase date of October 1, 2012. Assume that Freedom uses the straight-line method of depreciation and sells the equipment for $22,400 on October 1, 2016. The result of the sale of the equipment is a gain (loss) of

   a. ($4,600).

   b. $1,000.

   c. $9,000.

   d. $0.

7. A company bought a new machine for $23,000 on January 1. The machine is expected to last four years and to have a residual value of $3,000. If the company uses the double-declining-balance method, accumulated depreciation at the end of year 2 will be

   a. $23,000.

   b. $20,000.

   c. $17,250.

   d. $15,000.

8. Which of the following is *not* a capital expenditure?

   a. A complete overhaul of an air-conditioning system

   b. Replacement of an old motor with a new one in a piece of equipment

   c. A tune-up of a company vehicle

   d. The cost of installing a piece of equipment

   e. The addition of a building wing

9. Which of the following assets is *not* subject to a decreasing book value through depreciation, depletion, or amortization?

   a. Natural resources
   b. Goodwill

   c. Land improvements
   d. Intangibles

10. Why would a business select an accelerated method of depreciation for tax purposes?

    a. Accelerated depreciation is easier to calculate because salvage value is ignored.
    b. MACRS depreciation follows a specific pattern of depreciation.
    c. Accelerated depreciation generates higher depreciation expense immediately, and therefore lowers tax payments in the early years of the asset's life.
    d. Accelerated depreciation generates a greater amount of depreciation over the life of the asset than does straight-line depreciation.

11. A company purchased an oil well for $210,000. It estimates that the well contains 30,000 barrels, has an eight-year life, and no salvage value. If the company extracts and sells 2,000 barrels of oil in the first year, how much in cost of sales should be recorded?

    a. $14,000
    b. $105,000

    c. $21,000
    d. $26,250

12. Which item among the following is not an intangible asset?

    a. Goodwill
    b. A copyright
    c. A trademark

    d. A patent
    e. All of the above are intangible assets.

13. An important measure of profitability is

    a. Inventory turnover.
    b. Quick (acid test) ratio.

    c. Return on assets (ROA).
    d. Net sales.

14. In 2012, total asset turnover for JBC Company has increased. This means that the

    a. company has become more effective.
    b. company has become more efficient.
    c. company has become more effective and more efficient.
    d. company has neither become more effective nor more efficient.

Accounting Vocabulary

accelerated depreciation method (p. 410) A depreciation method that writes off a relatively larger amount of the asset's cost nearer the start of its useful life than the straight-line method does.

amortization (p. 424) The systematic reduction of a lump-sum amount. Expense that applies to intangible assets in the same way depreciation applies to plant assets and depletion applies to natural resources.

capital expenditure (p. 405) Expenditure that increases an asset's capacity or efficiency or extends its useful life. Capital expenditures are debited to an asset account.

copyright (p. 425) Exclusive right to reproduce and sell a book, musical composition, film, other work of art, or computer program. Issued by the federal government, copyrights extend 70 years beyond the author's life.

depletion (p. 423) That portion of a natural resource's cost that is used up in a particular period. Depletion expense is computed in the same way as units-of-production depreciation. A depleted asset usually flows into inventory and eventually to cost of goods sold as the resource is sold.

depreciable cost (p. 408) The cost of a plant asset minus its estimated residual value.

double-declining-balance (DDB) method (p. 410) An accelerated depreciation method that computes annual depreciation by multiplying the asset's decreasing book value by a constant percentage, which is two times the straight-line rate.

DuPont Analysis (p. 428) A detailed approach to measuring rate of return on equity (see Chapter 10). In this chapter, we confine our discussion to return on assets, comprising the first two components of return on equity, calculated as follows: Net profit margin (net income before taxes/net sales) × total asset turnover (net sales/ average total assets).

estimated residual value (p. 407) Expected cash value of an asset at the end of its useful life. Also called *residual value, scrap value,* or *salvage value.*

estimated useful life (p. 407) Length of service that a business expects to get from an asset. May be expressed in years, units of output, miles, or other measures.

fair value (p. 426) The asset's estimated market value at a particular date.

franchises and **licenses** (p. 425) Privileges granted by a private business or a government to sell a product or service in accordance with specified conditions.

goodwill (p. 425) Excess of the cost of an acquired company over the sum of the market values of its net assets (assets minus liabilities).

impairment (p. 426) The condition that exists when the carrying amount of a long-lived asset exceeds the amount of the estimated cash flows from the asset. Whenever long-term assets have been impaired, they have to be written down to fair market values using a two-step process. Under U.S. GAAP, once impaired, the carrying value of a long-lived asset may never again be increased. Under IFRS, if the fair value of impaired assets recovers in the future, the values may be increased.

intangible assets (p. 402) An asset with no physical form—a special right to current and expected future benefits.

Modified Accelerated Cost Recovery System (MACRS) (p. 415) A special depreciation method used only for income-tax purposes. Assets are grouped into classes, and for a given class depreciation is computed by the double-declining-balance method, the 150%-declining balance method, or, for most real estate, the straight-line method.

natural resources (p. 402) Assets such as oil and gas reserves, coal mines, or stands of timber—accounted for as long-term assets when purchased or developed, their cost is transferred to expense through a process called depletion.

net profit margin (p.429) Computed by the formula net income/net sales. This ratio measures the portion of each net sales dollar generated in net profit.

patent (p. 424) A federal government grant giving the holder the exclusive right for 20 years to produce and sell an invention.

plant assets (p. 402) Long-lived assets, such as land, buildings, and equipment, used in the operation of the business. Also called *fixed assets or property and equipment.*

return on assets (ROA) (p. 428) Also known as *rate of return on assets.* Measures how profitably management has used the assets that stockholders and creditors have provided the company.

straight-line (SL) method (p. 408) Depreciation method in which an equal amount of depreciation expense is assigned to each year of asset use.

total asset turnover (p. 429) A measure of efficiency in usage of total assets. The ratio calculates how many times per year total assets are covered by net sales. Formula: Net sales ÷ Average total assets. Also known as *asset turnover.*

trademark, trade name (p. 425) A distinctive identification of a product or service. Also called a *brand name.*

units-of-production (UOP) method (p. 409) Depreciation method by which a fixed amount of depreciation is assigned to each unit of output produced by the plant asset.

ASSESS YOUR PROGRESS

Short Exercises

S7-1 (*Learning Objective 1: Measure the cost and book value of a company's plant assets*) Examine Riverside's assets on the next page.

Riverside Corporation Consolidated Balance Sheets (Partial, Adapted)			
		May 31,	
(In millions)		2013	2012
1	Assets		
2	Current assets		
3	Cash and cash equivalents	$ 2,088	$ 257
4	Receivables, less allowances of $144 and $125	2,770	2,623
5	Spare parts, supplies, and fuel	4,653	4,509
6	Prepaid expenses and other	467	423
7	Total current assets	9,978	7,812
8	Property and equipment, at cost		
9	Aircraft	2,392	2,392
10	Package handling and ground support equipment	12,229	12,132
11	Computer and electronic equipment	28,159	26,102
12	Vehicles	581	452
13	Facilities and other	1,432	1,589
14	Total cost	44,793	42,667
15	Less: Accumulated depreciation	(14,900)	(12,944)
16	Net property and equipment	29,893	29,723
17	Other long-term assets		
18	Goodwill	722	722
19	Prepaid pension cost	1,340	1,271
20	Intangible and other assets	329	333
21	Total other long-term assets	2,391	2,326
22	Total assets	$ 42,262	$ 39,861

1. What is Riverside's largest category of assets? List all 2013 assets in the largest category and their amounts as reported by Riverside.
2. What was Riverside's cost of property and equipment at May 31, 2013? What was the book value of property and equipment on this date? Why is book value less than cost?

S7-2 (*Learning Objective 1: Measure and record the cost of individual assets in a lump-sum purchase of assets*) Advanced Automotive pays $210,000 for a group purchase of land, building, and equipment. At the time of acquisition, the land has a current market value of $66,000, the building's current market value is $22,000, and the equipment's current market value is $132,000. Journalize the lump-sum purchase of the three assets for a total cost of $210,000. The business signs a note payable for this amount.

S7-3 (*Learning Objective 2: Distinguish a capital expenditure from an immediate expense*) Assume Worldwide Airlines repaired a Jumbo 747 aircraft at a cost of $1.1 million, which Worldwide paid in cash. Further, assume the Worldwide accountant erroneously capitalized this expense as part of the cost of the plane.

Show the effects of the accounting error on Worldwide Airlines' income statement. To answer this question, determine whether revenues, total expenses, and net income were overstated or understated by the accounting error.

S7-4 (*Learning Objective 3: Compute depreciation and book value by three methods—first year only*) Assume that at the beginning of 2011, Fast Delivery, a UPS competitor, purchased a used Jumbo 747 aircraft at a cost of $44,400,000. Fast Delivery expects the plane to remain useful for five years (6.5 million miles) and to have a residual value of $5,400,000. Fast Delivery expects to fly the plane 725,000 miles the first year, 1,225,000 miles each year during the second, third, and fourth years, and 2,100,000 miles the last year.

1. Compute Fast Delivery's depreciation for the first two years on the plane using the following methods:
   a. Straight-line
   b. Units-of-production
   c. Double-declining-balance

2. Show the airplane's book value at the end of the first year under each depreciation method.

S7-5 (*Learning Objective 3: Select the best depreciation method for income tax purposes*) This exercise uses the assumed Fast Delivery data from Short Exercise 7-4. Assume Fast Delivery is trying to decide which depreciation method to use for income tax purposes. The company can choose from among the following methods: (a) straight-line, (b) units of production, or (c) double-declining-balance.

1. Which depreciation method offers the tax advantage for the first year? Describe the nature of the tax advantage.
2. How much income tax will Fast Delivery save for the first year of the airplane's use under the method you just selected as compared with using the straight-line depreciation method? The income tax rate is 36%. Ignore any earnings from investing the extra cash.

S7-6 (*Learning Objective 3: Compute partial year depreciation, and select the best depreciation method*) Assume that on September 30, 2011, Grandair, the national airline of Germany, purchased a Jumbo aircraft at a cost of €41,000,000 (€ is the symbol for the euro). Grandair expects the plane to remain useful for five years (5,200,000 miles) and to have a residual value of €5,200,000. Grandair will fly the plane 390,000 miles during the remainder of 2011. Compute Grandair's depreciation on the plane for the year ended December 31, 2011, using the following methods:

   a. Straight-line
   b. Units-of-production
   c. Double-declining-balance

Which method would produce the highest net income for 2011? Which method produces the lowest net income?

S7-7 (*Learning Objective 3: Compute and record depreciation after a change in useful life of the asset*) Five Flags over New York paid $90,000 for a concession stand. Five Flags started out depreciating the building straight-line over 10 years with zero residual value. After using the concession stand for 5 years, Five Flags determines that the building will remain useful for only 3 more years. Record Five Flag's depreciation on the concession stand for year 6 by the straight-line method.

S7-8 (*Learning Objectives 3, 4: Compute depreciation; record a gain or loss on disposal*) On January 1, 2012, Smith Air purchased an airplane for $67,850,000. Smith Air expects the plane to remain useful for 11 years and to have a residual value of $2,950,000. Smith Air uses the straight-line method to depreciate its airplanes. Smith Air flew the plane for 5 years and sold it on January 1, 2017, for $8,000,000.

1. Compute accumulated depreciation on the airplane at January 1, 2017 (same as December 31, 2016).
2. Record the sale of the plane on January 1, 2017.

S7-9 (*Learning Objective 5: Account for the depletion of a company's natural resources*) TexAm Petroleum, the giant oil company, holds reserves of oil and gas assets. At the end of 2012, assume the cost of TexAM Petroleum's mineral assets totaled $234 billion, representing 13 billion barrels of oil in the ground.

1. Which depreciation method is similar to the depletion method that TexAM Petroleum and other oil companies use to compute their annual depletion expense for the minerals removed from the ground?
2. Suppose the company removed 800 million barrels of oil during 2013. Record this event. Show amounts in billions.
3. Assume that, of the amount removed in (2), the company sold 200 million barrels. Make the cost of sales entry.

S7-10 (*Learning Objective 5: Measure and record goodwill*) PTL, Inc., dominates the snack-food industry with its Salty Chip brand. Assume that, PTL, Inc., purchased Seacoast Snacks, Inc., for $8.2 million cash. The market value of Seacoast Snacks' assets is $12 million, and Seacoast Snacks has liabilities of $10 million.

▶ Requirements

1. Compute the cost of the goodwill purchased by PTL.
2. Explain how PTL will account for goodwill in future years.

S7-11 (*Learning Objective 7: Calculate return on assets*) In 2012, Artesia, Inc., reported $300 million in sales, $18 million in net income, and average total assets of $120 million. What is Artesia's return on assets in 2012?

S7-12 (*Learning Objective 7: Calculate return on assets*) Ochoa Optical, Inc., provides a full line of designer eyewear to optical dispensaries. Ochoa reported the following information for 2012 and 2013:

	2013	2012
Sales revenue	$500,000	$450,000
Net income	$ 45,000	$ 42,500
Average total assets	$250,000	$240,000

Compute return on assets for 2012 and 2013.

S7-13 (*Learning Objective 8: Analyze the cash flow impact of investing activities on the statement of cash flows*) During 2012, Southeast Satellite Systems, Inc., purchased two other companies for $15 million. Also during 2012, Southeast made capital expenditures of $8 million to expand its market share. During the year, Southeast sold its North American operations, receiving cash of $13 million. Overall, Southeast reported a net income of $11 million during 2012.

Show what Southeast would report for cash flows from investing activities on its statement of cash flows for 2012. Report a total amount for net cash provided by (used in) investing activities.

S7-14 (*Learning Objective 6: Explain the effect of asset impairment on financial statements*) For each of the following scenarios, indicate whether a long-term asset has been impaired (Y for yes and N for no) and, if so, the amount of the loss that should be recorded.

Asset	Book Value	Estimated Future Cash Flows	Fair value	Impaired? (Y or N)	Amount of Loss
a. Equipment	$160,000	$120,000	$100,000		
b. Trademark	$320,000	$420,000	$380,000		
c. Land	$56,000	$30,000	$28,000		
d. Factory building	$3 million	$3 million	$2 million		

Exercises

All of the A and B exercises can be found within MyAccountingLab, an online homework and practice environment. Your instructor may ask you to complete these exercises using MyAccountingLab.

MyAccountingLab

Group A

E7-15A (*Learning Objective 1: Measure the cost of plant assets*) Murphy Self Storage purchased land, paying $150,000 cash as a down payment and signing a $180,000 note payable for the balance. Murphy also had to pay delinquent property tax of $2,500, title insurance costing $5,500, and $5,000 to level the land and remove an unwanted building. The company paid $54,000 to add soil for the foundation and then constructed an office building at a cost of $750,000. It also paid $51,000 for a fence around the property, $11,000 for the company sign near the property entrance, and $2,000 for lighting of the grounds. What is the capitalized cost of each of Murphy's land, land improvements, and building?

E7-16A (*Learning Objectives 1, 4: Allocate costs to assets acquired in a lump-sum purchase; dispose of a plant asset*) Maplewood Manufacturing bought three used machines in a $204,000 lump-sum purchase. An independent appraiser valued the machines as shown in the table.

Machine No.	Appraised Value
1	$ 63,000
2	107,100
3	39,900

What is each machine's individual cost? Immediately after making this purchase, Maplewood sold machine 1 for its appraised value. What is the result of the sale? (Round decimals to three places when calculating proportions, and use your computed percentages throughout.)

E7-17A (*Learning Objective 2: Distinguish capital expenditures from expenses*) Assume Plastic Products, Inc., purchased conveyor-belt machinery. Classify each of the following expenditures as a capital expenditure or an immediate expense related to machinery:

    a. Sales tax paid on the purchase price
    b. Transportation and insurance while machinery is in transit from seller to buyer
    c. Purchase price
    d. Installation
    e. Training of personnel for initial operation of the machinery
    f. Special reinforcement to the machinery platform
    g. Income tax paid on income earned from the sale of products manufactured by the machinery
    h. Major overhaul to extend the machinery's useful life by five years
    i. Ordinary repairs to keep the machinery in good working order
    j. Lubrication of the machinery before it is placed in service
    k. Periodic lubrication after the machinery is placed in service

E7-18A (*Learning Objectives 1, 3: Measure, depreciate, and report plant assets*) During 2012, Cheng Book Store paid $483,000 for land and built a store in Georgetown. Prior to construction, the city of Georgetown charged Cheng $1,300 for a building permit, which Cheng paid. Cheng also paid $15,300 for architect's fees. The construction cost of $685,000 was financed by a long-term note payable, with interest cost of $28,220 paid at completion of the project. The building was completed June 30, 2012. Cheng depreciates the building by the straight-line method over 35 years, with estimated residual value of $336,000.

    1. Journalize transactions for the following:
        a. Purchase of the land
        b. All the costs chargeable to the building in a single entry
        c. Depreciation on the building

Explanations are not required.
    2. Report Cheng Book Store's plant assets on the company's balance sheet at December 31, 2012.
    3. What will Cheng's income statement for the year ended December 31, 2012, report for these facts?

E7-19A (*Learning Objective 3: Determine depreciation amounts by three methods*) Ralph's Pizza bought a used Toyota delivery van on January 2, 2012, for $18,600. The van was expected to remain in service for four years (35,000 miles). At the end of its useful life, Ralph's officials estimated that the van's residual value would be $2,500. The van traveled 13,500 miles the first year, 12,000 miles the second year, 3,500 miles the third year, and 6,000 miles in the fourth year. Prepare a schedule of *depreciation expense* per year for the van under the three depreciation methods discussed in this chapter. (For units-of-production and double-declining-balance, round to the nearest two decimals after each step of the calculation.)

Which method best tracks the wear and tear on the van? Which method would Ralph's prefer to use for income tax purposes? Explain in detail why Ralph's prefers this method.

E7-20A (*Learning Objectives 1, 3, 8: Report plant assets, depreciation, and investing cash flows*) Assume that in early January 2012, a Sunshine Bakery restaurant purchased a building, paying $53,000 cash and signing a $103,000 note payable. The restaurant paid another $66,000 to remodel the building. Furniture and fixtures cost $59,000, and dishes and supplies—a current asset—were obtained for $9,600.

Sunshine Bakery is depreciating the building over 20 years by the straight-line method, with estimated residual value of $56,000. The furniture and fixtures will be replaced at the end of five years and are being depreciated by the double-declining-balance method, with zero residual value. At the end of the first year, the restaurant still has dishes and supplies worth $1,200.

Show what the restaurant will report for supplies, plant assets, and cash flows at the end of the first year on its

- ▶ income statement,
- ▶ balance sheet, and
- ▶ statement of cash flows (investing only).

Note: The purchase of dishes and supplies is an operating cash flow because supplies are a current asset.

E7-21A (*Learning Objective 3: Change a plant asset's useful life*) Assume Z-1 Software Consultants purchased a building for $445,000 and depreciated it on a straight-line basis over 40 years. The estimated residual value was $90,000. After using the building for 20 years, Z-1 realized that the building will remain useful only 15 more years. Starting with the 21st year, Z-1 began depreciating the building over a revised total life of 35 years and decreased the residual value to $14,900. Record depreciation expense on the building for years 20 and 21.

E7-22A (*Learning Objectives 3, 4: Measure DDB depreciation; analyze the effect of a sale of a plant asset*) Assume that on January 2, 2012, Vincent of Vermont purchased fixtures for $8,700 cash, expecting the fixtures to remain in service for five years. Vincent has depreciated the fixtures on a double-declining-balance basis, with $1,800 estimated residual value. On September 30, 2013, Vincent sold the fixtures for $2,600 cash. Record both the depreciation expense on the fixtures for 2013 and the sale of the fixtures. Apart from your journal entry, also show how to compute the gain or loss on Vincent's disposal of these fixtures.

E7-23A (*Learning Objectives 1, 3, 4: Measure a plant asset's cost; calculate UOP depreciation; analyze the effect of a used asset trade-in*) National Truck Company is a large trucking company that operates throughout the United States. National Truck Company uses the units-of-production (UOP) method to depreciate its trucks. National Truck Company trades in trucks often to keep driver morale high and to maximize fuel economy. Consider these facts about one Mack truck in the company's fleet: When acquired in 2012, the tractor-trailer rig cost $360,000 and was expected to remain in service for 10 years or 1,000,000 miles. Estimated residual value was $50,000. During 2012, the truck was driven 75,000 miles; during 2013, 85,000 miles; and during 2014, 135,000 miles. After 39,000 miles in 2015, the company traded in the Mack truck for a less-expensive Freightliner with a sticker price of $210,000. National Truck Company paid cash of $20,000. Determine National's gain or loss on the transaction. Prepare the journal entry to record the trade-in of the old truck on the new one.

E7-24A (*Learning Objective 5: Record natural resource assets and depletion*) Boulder Mines paid $425,000 for the right to extract ore from a 250,000-ton mineral deposit. In addition to the purchase price, Boulder Mines also paid a $110 filing fee, a $2,000 license fee to the state of West Virginia, and $55,390 for a geologic survey of the property. Because the company purchased the rights to the minerals only, it expects the asset to have zero residual value when fully depleted.

During the first year of production, Boulder Mines removed 35,000 tons of ore, of which it sold 30,000 tons. Make journal entries to record (a) purchase of the mineral rights, (b) payment of fees and other costs, (c) depletion for first-year production, and (d) sales of ore.

E7-25A *(Learning Objectives 5, 6: Record intangibles, amortization, and impairment)*

1. Makon Printers incurred costs of $1,500,000 for a patent for a new laser printer. Although the patent gives legal protection for 20 years, it is expected to provide Makon Printers with a competitive advantage for only 15 years. Assuming the straight-line method of amortization, make journal entries to record (a) the purchase of the patent and (b) amortization for year 1.
2. After using the patent for 10 years, Makon Printers learns at an industry trade show that Fast Printers is designing a more-efficient printer. On the basis of this new information, Makon Printers determines that the expected future cash flows from the patent are only $400,000. Its fair value on the open market is zero. Is this asset impaired? If so, make the impairment adjusting entry.

E7-26A *(Learning Objectives 5, 6: Compute and account for goodwill; explain the effect of asset impairment)* Assume Caltron paid $20 million to purchase HarborSide.com. Assume further that HarborSide had the following summarized data at the time of the Caltron acquisition (amounts in millions):

HarborSide.com			
Assets		**Liabilities and Equity**	
Current assets	$15	Total liabilities	$28
Long-term assets	26	Stockholders' equity	13
	$41		$41

Caltron's long-term assets had a current market value of only $21 million.

▶ Requirements

1. Compute the cost of goodwill purchased by Caltron.
2. Journalize Caltron's purchase of HarborSide.
3. Explain how Caltron will account for goodwill.

E7-27A *(Learning Objective 7: Calculate return on assets)* Kroger, Inc., one of the nation's largest grocery retailers, reported the following information (adapted) for its fiscal year ended January 31, 2011:

	January 31, 2011	January 31, 2010
Net sales.....................................	$48,815	$47,220
Net earnings..............................	$ 2,010	$ 1,783
Average total assets..................	$33,699	$33,005

▶ Requirements

1. Compute profit margin for the year ended January 31, 2011.
2. Compute asset turnover for the year ended January 31, 2011.
3. Compute return on assets for the year ended January 31, 2011.

E7-28A *(Learning Objective 8: Report cash flows for plant assets)* Assume Happy Feet Corporation completed the following transactions:

a. Sold a store building for $680,000. The building cost Happy Feet $1,600,000, and at the time of the sale, its accumulated depreciation totaled $920,000.

b. Lost a store building in a fire. The building cost $360,000 and had accumulated depreciation of $210,000. The insurance proceeds received by Happy Feet totaled $190,000.

c. Renovated a store at a cost of $130,000.

d. Purchased store fixtures for $60,000. The fixtures are expected to remain in service for 10 years and then be sold for $25,000. Happy Feet uses the straight-line depreciation method.

For each transaction, show what Happy Feet would report for investing activities on its statement of cash flows. Show negative amounts in parentheses.

Group B

E7-29B (*Learning Objective 1: Measure the cost of plant assets*) Pierce Self Storage purchased land, paying $160,000 cash as a down payment and signing a $150,000 note payable for the balance. Pierce also had to pay delinquent property tax of $5,000, title insurance costing $2,000, and $3,000 to level the land and remove an unwanted building. The company paid $58,000 to add soil for the foundation and then constructed an office building at a cost of $700,000. It also paid $46,000 for a fence around the property, $16,000 for the company sign near the property entrance, and $7,000 for lighting of the grounds. What is the capitalized cost of each of Pierce's land, land improvements, and building?

E7-30B (*Learning Objectives 1, 4: Allocate costs to assets acquired in a lump-sum purchase; dispose of a plant asset*) Southwood Manufacturing bought three used machines in a $192,000 lump-sum purchase. An independent appraiser valued the machines as shown:

Machine No.	Appraised Value
1	$50,000
2	$96,600
3	$54,000

What is each machine's individual cost? Immediately after making this purchase, Southwood sold machine 3 for its appraised value. What is the result of the sale? (Round decimals to three places when calculating proportions, and use your computed percentages throughout.)

E7-31B (*Learning Objective 2: Distinguish capital expenditures from expenses*) Assume Decadent Delights, Inc., purchased conveyor-belt machinery. Classify each of the following expenditures as a capital expenditure or an immediate expense related to machinery:

a. Sales tax paid on the purchase price

b. Transportation and insurance while machinery is in transit from seller to buyer

c. Purchase price

d. Installation

e. Training of personnel for initial operation of the machinery

f. Special reinforcement to the machinery platform

g. Income tax paid on income earned from the sale of products manufactured by the machinery

h. Major overhaul to extend the machinery's useful life by four years

i. Ordinary repairs to keep the machinery in good working order

j. Lubrication of the machinery before it is placed in service

k. Periodic lubrication after the machinery is placed in service

E7-32B (*Learning Objectives 1, 3: Measure, depreciate, and report plant assets*) During 2012, Ming Book Store paid $485,000 for land and built a store in Baltimore. Prior to construction, the city of Baltimore charged Ming $1,700 for a building permit, which Ming paid. Ming also paid $15,700 for architect's fees. The construction cost of $705,000 was financed by a long-term note payable, with interest cost of $30,040 paid at completion of the project. The building was completed August 31, 2012. Ming depreciates the building by the straight-line method over 35 years, with estimated residual value of $340,000.

1. Journalize transactions for the following:
   a. Purchase of the land
   b. All the costs chargeable to the building in a single entry
   c. Depreciation on the building

Explanations are not required.

2. Report Ming Book Store's plant assets on the company's balance sheet at December 31, 2012.
3. What will Ming's income statement for the year ended December 31, 2012, report for this situation?

E7-33B (*Learning Objective 3: Determine depreciation amounts by three methods*) Deluxe Pizza bought a used Honda delivery van on January 2, 2012, for $22,000. The van was expected to remain in service for four years (113,125 miles). At the end of its useful life, Deluxe officials estimated that the van's residual value would be $3,900. The van traveled 30,000 miles the first year, 32,000 miles the second year, 18,125 miles the third year, and 33,000 miles in the fourth year. Prepare a schedule of *depreciation expense* per year for the van under the three depreciation methods discussed in this chapter. (For units-of-production and double-declining-balance, round to the nearest two decimals after each step of the calculation.)

Which method best tracks the wear and tear on the van? Which method would Deluxe prefer to use for income tax purposes? Explain in detail why Deluxe prefers this method.

E7-34B (*Learning Objectives 1, 3, 8: Report plant assets, depreciation, and investing cash flows*) Assume that in early January 2012, an Early Bird Café purchased a building, paying $54,000 cash and signing a $104,000 note payable. The restaurant paid another $65,000 to remodel the building. Furniture and fixtures cost $51,000, and dishes and supplies—a current asset—were obtained for $9,000.

Early Bird Café is depreciating the building over 20 years by the straight-line method, with estimated residual value of $50,000. The furniture and fixtures will be replaced at the end of five years and are being depreciated by the double-declining-balance method, with zero residual value. At the end of the first year, the restaurant still has dishes and supplies worth $1,300.

Show what the restaurant will report for supplies, plant assets, and cash flows at the end of the first year on its

- ▶ income statement,
- ▶ balance sheet, and
- ▶ statement of cash flows (investing only).

Note: The purchase of dishes and supplies is an operating cash flow because supplies are a current asset.

E7-35B (*Learning Objective 3: Change a plant asset's useful life*) Assume S-1 Security Consultants purchased a building for $450,000 and depreciated it on a straight-line basis over 40 years. The estimated residual value was $93,000. After using the building for 20 years, S-1 realized that the building will remain useful only 15 more years. Starting with the 21st year, S-1 began depreciating the building over the newly revised total life of 35 years and decreased the estimated residual value to $15,300. Record depreciation expense on the building for years 20 and 21.

E7-36B (*Learning Objectives 3, 4: Measure DDB depreciation; analyze the effect of a sale of a plant asset*) Assume that on January 2, 2012, Barrett of Nebraska purchased fixtures for $8,200 cash, expecting the fixtures to remain in service for five years. Barrett has depreciated the fixtures on a double-declining-balance basis, with $1,100 estimated residual value. On October 31, 2013, Barrett sold the fixtures for $2,200 cash. Record both the depreciation expense on the fixtures for 2013 and then the sale of the fixtures. Apart from your journal entry, also show how to compute the gain or loss on Barrett's disposal of these fixtures.

E7-37B (*Learning Objectives 1, 3, 4: Measure a plant asset's cost; calculate UOP depreciation; analyze the effect of a used asset trade-in*) United Truck Company is a large trucking company that operates throughout the United States. United Truck Company uses the units-of-production (UOP) method to depreciate its trucks.

United Truck Company trades in trucks often to keep driver morale high and to maximize fuel economy. Consider these facts about one Mack truck in the company's fleet: When acquired in 2012, the tractor-trailer cost $430,000 and was expected to remain in service for 10 years or 1,000,000 miles. Estimated residual value was $20,000. During 2012, the truck was driven 81,000 miles; during 2013, 111,000 miles; and during 2014, 141,000 miles. After 41,000 miles in 2015, the company traded in the Mack truck for a less-expensive Freightliner with a sticker price of $250,000. United Truck Company paid cash of $24,000. Determine United's gain or loss on the transaction. Prepare the journal entry to record the trade-in of the old truck on the new one.

E7-38B (*Learning Objective 5: Record natural resource assets and depletion*) Valley Mines paid $428,000 for the right to extract ore from a 325,000-ton mineral deposit. In addition to the purchase price, Valley Mines also paid a $130 filing fee, a $2,300 license fee to the state of West Virginia, and $66,820 for a geologic survey of the property. Because the company purchased the rights to the minerals only, it expected the asset to have zero residual value when fully depleted. During the first year of production, Valley Mines removed 50,000 tons of ore, of which it sold 40,000 tons. Make journal entries to record (a) purchase of the mineral rights, (b) payment of fees and other costs, (c) depletion for first-year production, and (d) sales of ore.

E7-39B (*Learning Objectives 5, 6: Record intangibles, amortization, and impairment*)

1. Mayflower Printers incurred costs of $1,200,000 for a patent for a new laser printer. Although the patent gives legal protection for 20 years, it is expected to provide Mayflower Printers with a competitive advantage for only 12 years. Assuming the straight-line method of amortization, make journal entries to record (a) the purchase of the patent and (b) amortization for year 1.

2. After using the patent for 8 years, Mayflower Printers learns at an industry trade show that Superb Printers is designing a more-efficient printer. On the basis of this new information, Mayflower Printers determines that the expected future cash flows from the patent are only $350,000 and that the patent is worthless on the open market. Is this asset impaired? If so, record the impairment adjusting entry.

E7-40B (*Learning Objectives 5, 6: Compute and account for goodwill and impairment*) Assume Doltron paid $19 million to purchase Northeast.com. Assume further that Northeast had the following summarized data at the time of the Doltron acquisition (amounts in millions):

Northeast.com			
Assets		**Liabilities and Equity**	
Current assets	$11	Total liabilities	$22
Long-term assets	27	Stockholders' equity	16
	$38		$38

Northeast's long-term assets had a current market value of only $25 million.

▶ Requirements

1. Compute the cost of goodwill purchased by Doltron.
2. Journalize Doltron's purchase of Northeast.
3. Explain how Doltron will account for goodwill.

E7-41B (*Learning Objective 7: Calculate return on assets*) Lowe's Companies, Inc., the second-largest home improvement retailer, reported the following information (adapted) for its fiscal year ended January 31, 2011:

	January 31, 2011	January 31, 2010
Net sales.................................	$82,189	$76,733
Net earnings............................	$ 1,116	$ 70
Average total assets..................	$23,505	$23,126

▶ Requirements

1. Compute profit margin for the year ended January 31, 2011.
2. Compute asset turnover for the year ended January 31, 2011.
3. Compute return on assets for the year ended January 31, 2011.

E7-42B (*Learning Objective 8: Report cash flows for plant assets*) Assume Shoe Mania Corporation completed the following transactions:

    a. Sold a store building for $620,000. The building had cost Shoe Mania $1,400,000, and at the time of the sale, its accumulated depreciation totaled $780,000.
    b. Lost a store building in a fire. The building cost $330,000 and had accumulated depreciation of $160,000. The insurance proceeds received by Shoe Mania totaled $100,000.
    c. Renovated a store at a cost of $140,000.
    d. Purchased store fixtures for $80,000. The fixtures are expected to remain in service for 10 years and then be sold for $15,000. Shoe Mania uses the straight-line depreciation method.

For each transaction, show what Shoe Mania would report for investing activities on its statement of cash flows. Show negative amounts in parentheses.

Quiz

Test your understanding of accounting for plant assets, natural resources, and intangibles by answering the following questions. Select the best choice from among the possible answers given.

Q7-43 A capital expenditure
a. records additional capital.
b. is a credit like capital (owners' equity).
c. is expensed immediately.
d. adds to an asset.

Q7-44 Which of the following items should be accounted for as a capital expenditure?
a. Taxes paid in conjunction with the purchase of office equipment
b. Maintenance fees paid with funds provided by the company's capital
c. Costs incurred to repair leaks in the building roof
d. The monthly rental cost of an office building

Q7-45 Suppose you buy land for $3,000,000 and spend $1,000,000 to develop the property. You then divide the land into lots as follows:

Category	Sale Price per Lot
15 Hilltop lots...............	$480,000
15 Valley lots	$270,000

How much did each hilltop lot cost you?

a. $133,333

b. $480,000

c. $96,000

d. $170,667

Q7-46 Which statement about depreciation is false?

a. Depreciation is a process of allocating the cost of an asset to expense over its useful life.

b. Obsolescence as well as physical wear and tear should be considered when determining the period over which an asset should be depreciated.

c. Depreciation should not be recorded in years in which the market value of the asset has increased.

d. A major objective of depreciation accounting is to allocate the cost of using an asset against the revenues it helps to generate.

Q7-47 At the beginning of last year, Bremond Corporation purchased a piece of heavy equipment for $34,000. The equipment has a life of five years or 100,000 hours. The estimated residual value is $4,000. Bremond used the equipment for 22,000 hours last year and 25,000 hours this year. Depreciation expense for year 2 using double-declining-balance (DDB) and units-of-production would be as follows:

	DDB	UOP
a.	$7,200	$8,500
b.	$7,200	$7,500
c.	$8,160	$8,500
d.	$8,160	$7,500

Q7-48 Denver Corporation acquired a machine for $26,000, and has recorded depreciation for 3 years using the straight-line method over a 6-year life and $2,000 residual value. At the start of the fourth year of use, Denver revised the estimated useful life to a total of 10 years. Estimated residual value declined to $0.

How much depreciation should Denver record in each of the asset's last 7 years (that is, year 4 through year 10), following the revision?

a. $13,000

b. $2,600

c. $2,000

d. Some other amount

Q7-49 Kline Company failed to record depreciation of equipment. How does this omission affect Kline's financial statements?

a. Net income is understated and assets are overstated.

b. Net income is overstated and assets are understated.

c. Net income is understated and assets are understated.

d. Net income is overstated and assets are overstated.

Q7-50 Jane's Beauty, Inc., uses the double-declining-balance method for depreciation on its computers. Which item is not needed to compute depreciation for the first year?

a. Estimated residual value

b. Original cost

c. Expected useful life in years

d. All the above are needed.

Q7-51 Which of the following costs are reported on a company's income statement and balance sheet?

Income Statement	**Balance Sheet**
a. Accumulated depreciation	Land
b. Cost of goods sold	Accumulated Deprecation
c. Gain on sale of land	Cost of goods sold
d. Goodwill	Accounts payable

Use the following information to answer questions 7-52 through 7-53.

Ringle Company purchased a machine for $9,200 on January 1, 2012. The machine has been depreciated using the straight-line method over an 8-year life and $800 residual value. Ringle sold the machine on January 1, 2014, for $7,900.

Q7-52 What is straight-line depreciation for the year ended December 31, 2012, and what is the book value on December 31, 2013?

Q7-53 What gain or loss should Ringle record on the sale?
a. Gain, $1,000
b. Loss, $1,300
c. Gain, $800
d. Gain, $1,600

Q7-54 A company purchased mineral assets costing $832,000, with estimated residual value of $68,800, and holding approximately 240,000 tons of ore. During the first year, 54,000 tons are extracted and sold. What is the amount of depletion for the first year?
a. $187,200
b. $156,620
c. $171,720
d. Cannot be determined from the data given

Q7-55 Suppose George's Delivery pays $66 million to buy Lone Star Overnight. Lone Star's assets are valued at $72 million, and its liabilities total $23 million. How much goodwill did George's Delivery purchase in its acquisition of Lone Star Overnight?
a. $17 million
b. $29 million
c. $23 million
d $43 million

Q7-56 Hydra, Inc., was reviewing its assets for impairment at the end of the current year. Information about one of its assets is as follows:

Net book value..........................	$1,000,000
Estimated future cash flows......	$ 850,000
Fair (market) value...................	$ 820,000

Hydra should report an impairment loss for the current year of
a. $0.
b. $150,000.
c. $180,000.
d. $30,000.

Q7-57 TextDat, Inc., reported sales revenue of $600,000, net income of $45,000, and average total assets of $500,000. TextDat's return on assets is
a. 7.5%.
b. 9.0%.
c. 1.1%.
d. 83.3%.

Problems

MyAccountingLab

All of the A and B problems can be found within MyAccountingLab, an online homework and practice environment. Your instructor may ask you to complete these problems using MyAccountingLab.

Group A

P7-58A (*Learning Objectives 1, 2, 3: Measure and account for plant assets; distinguish a capital expenditure from an expense; measure and record depreciation*) Assume Monroe Sales, Inc., opened an office in Jacksonville, Florida. Further assume that Monroe Sales incurred the following costs in acquiring land, making land improvements, and constructing and furnishing the new sales building:

a.	Purchase price of land, including an old building that will be used for a garage (land market value is $320,000; building market value is $80,000)...	$350,000
b.	Landscaping (additional dirt and earth moving)......................................	8,300
c.	Fence around the land..	31,400
d.	Attorney fee for title search on the land	300
e.	Delinquent real estate taxes on the land to be paid by Monroe Sales.......	5,900
f.	Company signs at entrance to the property	1,500
g.	Building permit for the sales building..	500
h.	Architect fee for the design of the sales building....................................	19,200
i.	Masonry, carpentry, and roofing of the sales building.............................	516,000
j.	Renovation of the garage building..	41,000
k.	Interest cost on construction loan for sales building..............................	9,600
l.	Landscaping (trees and shrubs)	6,900
m.	Parking lot and concrete walks on the property	52,500
n.	Lights for the parking lot and walkways..	7,800
o.	Salary of construction supervisor (85% to sales building; 10% to land improvements; and 5% to garage building renovations)..............	45,000
p.	Office furniture for the sales building..	79,800
q.	Transportation and installation of furniture..	1,200

Assume Monroe Sales depreciates buildings over 50 years, land improvements over 20 years, and furniture over 12 years, all on a straight-line basis with zero residual value.

▶ Requirements

1. Show how to account for each of Monroe Sales' costs by listing the cost under the correct account. Determine the total cost of each asset.
2. All construction was complete and the assets were placed in service on April 2. Record depreciation for the year ended December 31. Round to the nearest dollar.
3. How will what you learned in this problem help you manage a business?

P7-59A (*Learning Objectives 1, 3: Measure and account for the cost of plant assets; measure and record depreciation under DDB*) Bruno Lake Resort reported the following on its balance sheet at December 31, 2012:

Property, plant, and equipment, at cost:	
Land..	$ 147,000
Buildings	701,000
Less: Accumulated depreciation	(348,000)
Equipment..	409,000
Less: Accumulated depreciation	(263,000)

In early July 2013, the resort expanded operations and purchased additional equipment at a cost of $108,000. The company depreciates buildings by the straight-line method over 20 years with residual value of $87,000. Due to obsolescence, the equipment has a useful life of only 10 years and is being depreciated by the double-declining-balance method with zero residual value.

▶ Requirements

1. Journalize Bruno Lake Resort's plant asset purchase and depreciation transactions for 2013.
2. Report plant assets on the December 31, 2013, balance sheet.

P7-60A *(Learning Objectives 1, 3, 4: Measure and account for the cost of plant assets and depreciation; analyze and record a plant asset disposal)* Miller, Inc., has the following plant asset accounts: Land, Buildings, and Equipment, with a separate accumulated depreciation account for each of these except Land. Miller completed the following transactions:

Jan 4		Traded in equipment with accumulated depreciation of $61,000 (cost of $134,000) for similar new equipment with a cash cost of $178,000. Received a trade-in allowance of $77,000 on the old equipment and paid $101,000 in cash.
Jun 29		Sold a building that had a cost of $650,000 and had accumulated depreciation of $140,000 through December 31 of the preceding year. Depreciation is computed on a straight-line basis. The building has a 40-year useful life and a residual value of $220,000. Miller received $110,000 cash and a $394,625 note receivable.
Oct 30		Purchased land and a building for a single price of $360,000. An independent appraisal valued the land at $160,800 and the building at $241,200.
Dec 31		Recorded depreciation as follows:
		Equipment has an expected useful life of 8 years and an estimated residual value of 3% of cost. Depreciation is computed on the double-declining-balance method.
		Depreciation on buildings is computed by the straight-line method. The new building carries a 40-year useful life and a residual value equal to 30% of its cost.

▶ Requirement

1. Record the transactions in Miller, Inc.'s journal.

P7-61A *(Learning Objectives 1, 3, 8: Measure and account for the cost of a plant asset; measure depreciation by three methods; identify the cash-flow advantage of accelerated depreciation for tax purposes)* On January 7, 2012, J.B. Griffin Co. paid $240,000 for a computer system. In addition to the basic purchase price, the company paid a setup fee of $1,400, $6,500 sales tax, and $29,100 for a special platform on which to place the computer. J.B. Griffin's management estimates that the computer will remain in service for five years and have a residual value of $25,000. The computer will process 50,000 documents the first year, with annual processing decreasing by 2,500 documents during each of the next four years (that is, 47,500 documents in year 2013; 45,000 documents in year 2014; and so on). In trying to decide which depreciation method to use, the company president has requested a depreciation schedule for each of the three depreciation methods (straight-line, units-of-production, and double-declining-balance).

▶ Requirements

1. For each of the generally accepted depreciation methods, prepare a depreciation schedule showing asset cost, depreciation expense, accumulated depreciation, and asset book value.
2. J.B. Griffin reports to stockholders and creditors in the financial statements using the depreciation method that maximizes reported income in the early years of asset use. For income tax purposes, the company uses the depreciation method that minimizes income tax payments in those early years. Consider the first year J.B. Griffin Co. uses the computer. Identify the depreciation methods that meet Griffin's objectives, assuming the income tax authorities permit the use of any of the methods.
3. Cash provided by operations before income tax is $158,000 for the computer's first year. The income tax rate is 32%. For the two depreciation methods identified in Requirement 2, compare the net income and cash provided by operations (cash flow). Show which method gives the net-income advantage and which method gives the cash-flow advantage.

P7-62A *(Learning Objectives 1, 3, 4, 6, 8: Analyze plant asset transactions from a company's financial statements)* Avril, Inc., sells electronics and appliances. The excerpts that follow are adapted from Avril's financial statements for 2012 and 2011.

Balance Sheet (dollars in millions)	February 28, 2012	2011
Assets		
Total current assets	$7,987	$6,901
Property, plant, and equipment	4,831	4,197
Less: Accumulated depreciation	2,124	1,729
Goodwill..	555	512

Statement of Cash Flows (dollars in millions)	Year Ended February 28, 2012	2011
Operating activities:		
Net income	$1,148	$ 986
Noncash items affecting net income:		
Depreciation	460	458
Investing activities:		
Additions to property, plant, and equipment................	(713)	(619)

▶ Requirements

1. How much was Avril's cost of plant assets at February 28, 2012? How much was the book value of plant assets? Show computations.
2. The financial statements give three evidences that Avril purchased plant assets and goodwill during fiscal year 2012. What are they?
3. Prepare T-accounts for Property, Plant, and Equipment; Accumulated Depreciation; and Goodwill. Then show all the activity in these accounts during 2012. Label each increase or decrease and give its dollar amount. During 2012, Avril sold plant assets that had cost the company $79 million (accumulated depreciation on these assets was $65 million). Assume goodwill was not impaired during 2012.
4. (Independent of the information in Requirement 3) Avril reviews its assets for impairment annually. On February 28, 2012, the fair value of the goodwill is estimated at $450 million. Prepare the journal entry to record the impairment.

P7-63A (*Learning Objective 5: Account for natural resources*) Mid Atlantic Energy Company's balance sheet includes the asset Iron Ore. Mid Atlantic Energy paid $2.4 million cash for the right to work a mine that contained an estimated 195,000 tons of ore. The company paid $63,000 to remove unwanted buildings from the land and $73,000 to prepare the surface for mining. Mid Atlantic Energy also signed a $34,100 note payable to a landscaping company to return the land surface to its original condition after the lease ends. During the first year, Mid Atlantic Energy removed 32,500 tons of ore, of which it sold 25,000 tons on account for $33 per ton. Operating expenses for the first year totaled $246,000, all paid in cash. In addition, the company accrued income tax at the tax rate of 28%.

▶ Requirements

1. Record all of Mid Atlantic Energy's transactions for the year.
2. Prepare the company's income statement for its iron ore operations for the first year. Evaluate the profitability of the company's operations.
3. What balances should appear from these transactions on Mid Atlantic Energy's balance sheet at the end of its first year of operations?

P7-64A (*Learning Objectives 1, 4, 8: Analyze the effect of a plant asset addition and disposal; report plant asset transactions on the financial statements*) At the end of 2011, Solar Power Associates (SPA) had total assets of $17.6 billion and total liabilities of $9 billion. Included among the assets were property, plant, and equipment with a cost of $4.9 billion and accumulated depreciation of $2.6 billion.

SPA completed the following selected transactions during 2012: The company earned total revenues of $26.6 billion and incurred total expenses of $21.7 billion, which included depreciation of $1.8 billion. During the year, SPA paid $1.3 billion for new property, plant, and equipment and sold old plant assets for $0.8 billion. The cost of the assets sold was $1.6 billion, and their accumulated depreciation was $1 billion.

▶ Requirements

1. Explain how to determine whether SPA had a gain or loss on the sale of old plant assets during the year. What was the amount of the gain or loss, if any?
2. Show how SPA would report property, plant, and equipment on the balance sheet at December 31, 2012, after all the year's activity. What was the book value of property, plant, and equipment?
3. Show how SPA would report its operating activities and investing activities on its statement of cash flows for 2012. Ignore gains and losses.

P7-65A (*Learning Objective 7: Calculate return on assets*) Target Corporation operates general merchandise and food discount stores in the United States. The company reported the following information for the three years ending January 31, 2011:

		Target Corporation Income Statement (Adapted) For the years ended		
(In millions)		Jan 31, 2011	Jan 31, 2010	Jan 31, 2009
Total net revenue		$67,390	$65,357	$64,948
Cost of revenue		45,725	44,062	44,157
Selling, general and administrative		16,413	16,622	16,389
Operating income or loss		5,252	4,673	4,402
Other revenue (expense)		(757)	(801)	(866)
Income before tax		4,495	3,872	3,536
Income tax expense		(1,575)	(1,384)	(1,322)
Net income		$ 2,920	$ 2,488	$ 2,214

		Target Corporation Partial Balance Sheet (Condensed)		
(In millions)		Jan 31, 2011	Jan 31, 2010	Jan 31, 2009
Total current assets		$17,213	$18,424	$17,488
Property, plant, and equipment		25,493	25,280	25,756
Other assets		999	829	862
Total assets		$43,705	$44,533	$44,106

▶ Requirements

1. Compute profit margin for Target for the years ended January 31, 2011, and January 31, 2010.
2. Compute asset turnover for Target for the years ended January 31, 2011, and

January 31, 2010.

3. Compute return on assets for Target for the years ended January 31, 2011, and January 31, 2010.

4. What factors contributed to the change in return on assets during the year?

Group B

P7-66B *(Learning Objectives 1, 2, 3: Measure and account for plant assets; distinguish a capital expenditure from an expense, measure and record depreciation)* Assume Coffee House, Inc., opened an office in Cocoa Beach, Florida. Further assume that Coffee House incurred the following costs in acquiring land, making land improvements, and constructing and furnishing the new sales building:

a. Purchase price of land, including an old building that will be used for a garage (land market value is $330,000; building market value is $70,000)...	$360,000
b. Landscaping (additional dirt and earth moving).....................................	8,000
c. Fence around the land..	31,300
d. Attorney fee for title search on the land	600
e. Delinquent real estate taxes on the land to be paid by Coffee House	5,200
f. Company signs at entrance to the property	1,700
g. Building permit for the sales building...	200
h. Architect fee for the design of the sales building..................................	19,400
i. Masonry, carpentry, and roofing of the sales building...........................	512,000
j. Renovation of the garage building..	41,500
k. Interest cost on construction loan for sales building.............................	9,700
l. Landscaping (trees and shrubs)	6,100
m. Parking lot and concrete walks on the property	52,300
n. Lights for the parking lot and walkways	7,200
o. Salary of construction supervisor (83% to sales building; 10% to land improvements; and 7% to garage building renovations)...............	42,000
p. Office furniture for the sales building..	79,000
q. Transportation and installation of furniture...	1,400

Assume Coffee House depreciates buildings over 40 years, land improvements over 25 years, and furniture over 10 years, all on a straight-line basis with zero residual value.

▶ Requirements

1. Show how to account for each of Coffee House's costs by listing the cost under the correct account. Determine the total cost of each asset.

2. All construction was complete and the assets were placed in service on July 2. Record depreciation for the year ended December 31. Round to the nearest dollar.

3. How will what you learned in this problem help you manage a business?

P7-67B *(Learning Objectives 1, 3: Measure and account for the cost of plant assets; measure and record depreciation under DDB)* Greco Lake Resort reported the following on its balance sheet at December 31, 2012:

Property, plant, and equipment, at cost:	
Land..	$ 143,000
Buildings	702,000
Less: Accumulated depreciation	(344,000)
Equipment..	408,000
Less: Accumulated depreciation	(264,000)

In early July 2013, the resort expanded operations and purchased additional equipment at a cost of $100,000. The company depreciates buildings by the straight-line method over 20 years with residual value of $85,000. Due to obsolescence, the equipment has a useful life of only 10 years and is being depreciated by the double-declining-balance method with zero residual value.

▶ Requirements

1. Journalize Greco Lake Resort's plant asset purchase and depreciation transactions for 2013.
2. Report plant assets on the December 31, 2013, balance sheet.

P7-68B (*Learning Objectives 1, 3, 4: Measure and account for the cost of plant assets and depreciation; analyze and record a plant asset disposal*) Carney, Inc., has the following plant asset accounts: Land, Buildings, and Equipment, with a separate accumulated depreciation account for each of these except Land. Carney completed the following transactions:

Jan 3	Traded in equipment with accumulated depreciation of $68,000 (cost of $131,000) for similar new equipment with a cash cost of $178,000. Received a trade-in allowance of $73,000 on the old equipment and paid $105,000 in cash.
Jun 30	Sold a building that had a cost of $640,000 and had accumulated depreciation of $100,000 through December 31 of the preceding year. Depreciation is computed on a straight-line basis. The building has a 40-year useful life and a residual value of $240,000. Carney received $120,000 cash and a $415,000 note receivable.
Oct 31	Purchased land and a building for a single price of $320,000. An independent appraisal valued the land at $70,200 and the building at $280,800.
Dec 31	Recorded depreciation as follows:
	Equipment has an expected useful life of 4 years and an estimated residual value of 12% of cost. Depreciation is computed on the double-declining-balance method.
	Depreciation on buildings is computed by the straight-line method. The new building carries a 40-year useful life and a residual value equal to 10% of its cost.

▶ Requirement

1. Record the transactions in Carney, Inc's journal.

P7-69B (*Learning Objectives 1, 3, 8: Measure and account for the cost of a plant asset; measure depreciation by three methods; identify the cash-flow advantage of accelerated depreciation for tax purposes*) On January 4, 2012, G.L. Brown Co. paid $235,000 for a computer system. In addition to the basic purchase price, the company paid a setup fee of $1,100, $6,200 sales tax, and $37,200 for a special platform on which to place the computer. G.L. Brown management estimates that the computer will remain in service for five years and have a residual value of $24,500. The computer will process 35,000 documents the first year, with annual processing decreasing by 2,500 documents during each of the next four years (that is, 32,500 documents in 2013; 30,000 documents in 2014; and so on). In trying to decide which depreciation method to use, the company president has requested a depreciation schedule for each of the three depreciation methods (straight-line, units-of-production, and double-declining-balance).

▶ Requirements

1. For each of the generally accepted depreciation methods, prepare a depreciation schedule showing asset cost, depreciation expense, accumulated depreciation, and asset book value.
2. G.L. Brown reports to stockholders and creditors in the financial statements using the depreciation method that maximizes reported income in the early years of asset use. For income tax purposes, the company uses the depreciation method that minimizes income tax payments in those early years. Consider the first year G.L. Brown Co. uses the computer.

Identify the depreciation methods that meet Brown's objectives, assuming the income tax authorities permit the use of any of the methods.

3. Cash provided by operations before income tax is $154,000 for the computer's first year. The income tax rate is 40%. For the two depreciation methods identified in Requirement 2, compare the net income and cash provided by operations (cash flow). Show which method gives the net-income advantage and which method gives the cash-flow advantage.

P7-70B (*Learning Objectives 1, 3, 4, 6, 8: Analyze plant asset transactions from a company's financial statements*) Lily, Inc., sells electronics and appliances. The excerpts that follow are adapted from Lily's financial statements for 2012 and 2011.

Balance Sheet (dollars in millions)	February 28, 2012	2011
Assets		
Total current assets	$7,988	$6,904
Property, plant, and equipment	4,838	4,192
Less: Accumulated depreciation	2,124	1,729
Goodwill...	557	510

Statement of Cash Flows (dollars in millions)	Year Ended February 28, 2012	2011
Operating activities:		
Net income	$1,149	$ 980
Noncash items affecting net income:		
Depreciation	461	459
Investing activities:		
Additions to property, plant, and equipment...............	(723)	(615)

▶ Requirements

1. How much was Lily's cost of plant assets at February 28, 2012? How much was the book value of plant assets? Show computations.
2. The financial statements give three evidences that Lily purchased plant assets and goodwill during fiscal year 2012. What are they?
3. Prepare T-accounts for Property, Plant, and Equipment; Accumulated Depreciation; and Goodwill. Then show all the activity in these accounts during 2012. Label each increase or decrease and give its dollar amount. During 2012, Lily sold plant assets that had cost the company $77 million (accumulated depreciation on these assets was $66 million). Assume goodwill was not impaired during 2012.
4. (Independent of the information in Requirement 3) Lily reviews its assets for impairment annually. On February 28, 2012, the fair value of the goodwill is estimated at $450 million. Prepare the journal entry to record the impairment.

P7-71B (*Learning Objective 5: Account for natural resources*) Central Energy Company's balance sheet includes the asset Iron Ore. Central Energy paid $2.8 million cash for the right to work a mine that contained an estimated 215,000 tons of ore. The company paid $67,000 to remove unwanted buildings from the land and $76,500 to prepare the surface for mining. Central Energy also signed a $38,550 note payable to a landscaping company to return the land surface to its original condition after the lease ends. During the first year, Central Energy removed 34,500 tons of ore, of which it sold 25,000 tons on account for $37 per ton. Operating expenses for the first year totaled $254,000, all paid in cash. In addition, the company accrued income tax at the tax rate of 35%.

▶ Requirements

1. Record all of Central Energy's transactions for the year.
2. Prepare the company's income statement for its iron ore operations for the first year. Evaluate the profitability of the company's operations.
3. What balances should appear from these transactions on Central Energy's balance sheet at the end of its first year of operations?

P7-72B (*Learning Objectives 1, 4, 8: Analyze the effect of a plant asset addition and disposal; report plant asset transactions on the financial statements*) At the end of 2011, Creative Accounting Associates (CAA) had total assets of $17 billion and total liabilities of $9.2 billion. Included among the assets were property, plant, and equipment with a cost of $4.8 billion and accumulated depreciation of $2.8 billion.

CAA completed the following selected transactions during 2012: The company earned total revenues of $26.2 billion and incurred total expenses of $22 billion, which included depreciation of $1.3 billion. During the year, CAA paid $2 billion for new property, plant, and equipment and sold old plant assets for $0.6 billion. The cost of the assets sold was $0.9 billion, and their accumulated depreciation was $0.8 billion.

▶ Requirements

1. Explain how to determine whether CAA had a gain or loss on the sale of old plant assets during the year. What was the amount of the gain or loss, if any?
2. Show how CAA would report property, plant, and equipment on the balance sheet at December 31, 2012, after all the year's activity. What was the book value of property, plant, and equipment?
3. Show how CAA would report its operating activities and investing activities on its statement of cash flows for 2012. Ignore gains and losses.

P7-73B (*Learning Objective 7: Calculate return on assets*) Kohl's Corporation operates family oriented department stores that sell moderately priced apparel and housewares. The company reported the following information (adapted) for the three years ending January 31, 2011:

Kohl's Corporation Income Statement (Adapted)				
		Jan 31, 2011	Jan 31, 2010	Jan 31, 2009
	Net sales	$18,391	$17,178	$16,389
	Cost of merchandise sold	11,359	10,680	10,334
	Selling, general and administrative	5,118	4,786	4,519
	Operating income	1,914	1,712	1,536
	Other revenue (expense)	(132)	(124)	(111)
	Income before tax	1,782	1,588	1,425
	Provision for income tax	(668)	(597)	(540)
	Net income	$ 1,114	$ 991	$ 885

Kohl's Corporation
Partial Balance Sheet

	Jan 31, 2011	Jan 31, 2010	Jan 31, 2009
Total current assets	$ 5,645	$ 5,485	$ 3,728
Long-term investments	386	336	333
Property, plant, and equipment	7,256	7,018	6,984
Other assets	277	321	318
Total assets	$13,564	$13,160	$11,363

▶ Requirements

1. Compute profit margin for Kohl's for the years ended January 31, 2011, and January 31, 2010.
2. Compute asset turnover for Kohl's for the years ended January 31, 2011, and January 31, 2010.
3. Compute return on assets for Kohl's for the years ended January 31, 2011, and January 31, 2010.
4. What factors contributed to the change in return on assets during the year?

Challenge Exercises and Problem

E7-74 (*Learning Objectives 5, 6: Account for goodwill and impairment*) Macy's, Inc., is one the nation's premier retailers, with fiscal 2010 sales of $25 billion. The company operates about 810 Macy's department stores and furniture galleries. In 2005, Macy's acquired May Department Stores, Inc. Excerpts from the notes to the financial statements for the year ended January 31, 2009, provide details about the purchase and intangible assets.

Note 2: Acquisition

The aggregate purchase price for the merger with May (the "Merger") was approximately $11.7 billion, including approximately $5.7 billion of cash and approximately 100 million shares of Company common stock. The value of the approximately 100 million shares of Company common stock was determined based on the average market price of the Company's stock from February 24, 2005 to March 2, 2005. In connection with the Merger, the Company also assumed approximately $6.0 billion of May debt.

The May purchase price has been allocated to the assets acquired and liabilities assumed based on their fair values, and is subject to the final fair value determination of certain assets and liabilities. The following table summarizes the preliminary purchase price allocation at the date of acquisition:

	(millions)
Current assets, excluding assets of discontinued operations	$ 5,288
Assets of discontinued operations	2,264
Property and equipment	6,579
Goodwill	8,946
Intangible assets	679
Other assets	31
Total assets acquired	23,787
Total liabilities assumed	(12,038)
Total purchase price	11,749

Note 8: Goodwill

	Jan 31, 2009	Jan 31, 2008	Jan 31, 2007
Non-amortizing intangible assets (Goodwill and tradenames)	$4,157	$9,610	$9,691

During 2008, the Company recorded a goodwill impairment charge of $5,382 million based on the result of goodwill impairment testing as of January 31, 2009.

▶ Requirements

1. Prepare the entry (in millions) to record the purchase of May Department Stores.
2. Record the 2008 impairment of goodwill.

E7-75 (*Learning Objective 3: Determine the effect on net income of a change in the depreciation method*) Kerusi, Inc., has a popular line of boogie boards. Kerusi reported net income of $64 million for 2012. Depreciation expense for the year totaled $30 million. Kerusi, Inc., depreciates plant assets over eight years using the straight-line method and no residual value.

Kerusi, Inc., paid $240 million for plant assets at the beginning of 2012. At the start of 2013, Kerusi changed its method of accounting for depreciation to double-declining-balance (DDB). 2013 is expected to be the same as 2012 except for the change in depreciation method. If Kerusi had been using DDB depreciation all along, how much net income can Kerusi, Inc., expect to earn during 2013? Ignore income tax.

E7-76 (*Learning Objective 2: Distinguish a capital expenditure from an expense, and measure the financial statement effects of an expensing error*) The European Press (TEP) is a major telecommunication conglomerate. Assume that early in year 1, TEP purchased equipment at a cost of 20 million euros (€20 million). Management expects the equipment to remain in service for four years and estimated residual value to be negligible. TEP uses the straight-line depreciation method. *Through an accounting error, TEP expensed the entire cost of the equipment at the time of purchase.* Because TEP is operated as a partnership, it pays no income tax.

▶ Requirements

Prepare a schedule to show the overstatement or understatement in the following items at the end of each year over the four-year life of the equipment:

1. Total current assets
2. Equipment, net
3. Net income

P7-77 (*Learning Objective 4: Determine plant and equipment transactions for an actual company*) FedEx Corporation provides a broad portfolio of transportation, e-commerce, and business services. FedEx reported the following information in its 2009 annual report.

FedEx Corporation
Partial Consolidated Balance Sheets
(In millions)

	May 31,	
	2009	2008
Property and equipments, at cost		
Aircraft and related equipment	$10,118	$10,165
Package handling and ground support equipment	4,960	4,817
Computer and electronic equipment	4,280	5,040
Vehicles	3,078	2,754
Facilities and other	6,824	6,529
	29,260	29,305
Less accumulated depreciation and amortization	15,843	15,827
Net property and equipment	13,417	13,478

FedEx Corporation
Partial Statement of Cash Flows
(In millions)

	May 31,	
	2009	2008
Investing activities		
Capital expenditures	(2,459)	(2,947)
Business acquisitions, net of cash acquired	(3)	(4)
Proceeds from asset dispositions and other	79	54
Cash used in investing activities	(2,383)	(2,897)

Note 1: DESCRIPTION OF BUSINESS AND SUMMARY OF SIGNIFICANT ACCOUNTING POLICIES

Property and Equipment

For financial reporting purposes, we record depreciation and amortization of property and equipment on a straight-line basis over the asset's service life or related lease term, if shorter. For income tax purposes, depreciation is computed using accelerated methods when applicable. Depreciation expense, excluding gains and losses on sales of property and equipment used in operations, was $1.8 billion in 2009 and $1.8 billion in 2008.

During the fourth quarter of 2009, we recorded $202 million in property and equipment impairment charges. These charges are primarily related to our April 2009 decision to premanently remove from service 10 Airbus A310-200 aircraft and four Boeing MD10-10 aircraft owned by the company, along with certain excess aircraft engines at FedEx Express. A limited amount of our total aircraft capacity remains temporarily grounded because of network overcapacity due to the current economic environment.

▶ Requirements

1. Using the information provided from the balance sheet and statement of cash flows for FedEx, reconstruct the Property and Equipment and Accumulated Depreciation accounts. You will have to solve for the original cost of the plant and equipment sold.
2. Prepare the journal entries to record capital expenditures, depreciation expense, asset impairments, and sales of property, plant, and equipment.

APPLY YOUR KNOWLEDGE

Decision Cases

Case 1. (*Learning Objective 3: Measure profitability based on different inventory and depreciation methods*) Suppose you are considering investing in two businesses, La Petite France Bakery and Burgers Ahoy. The two companies are virtually identical, and both began operations at the beginning of the current year. During the year, each company purchased inventory as follows:

Jan	4	10,000 units at $4 =	40,000	
Apr	6	5,000 units at 5 =	25,000	
Aug	9	7,000 units at 6 =	42,000	
Nov	27	10,000 units at 7 =	70,000	
	Totals	32,000	$177,000	

During the first year, both companies sold 25,000 units of inventory.

In early January, both companies purchased equipment costing $150,000 that had a 10-year estimated useful life and a $20,000 residual value. La Petite France uses the inventory and depreciation methods that maximize reported income. By contrast, Burgers Ahoy uses the inventory and depreciation methods that minimize income tax payments. Assume that both companies' trial balances at December 31 included the following:

Sales revenue.........................	$350,000
Operating expenses	50,000

The income tax rate is 40%.

▶ Requirements

1. Prepare both companies' income statements.
2. Write an investment newsletter to address the following questions: Which company appears to be more profitable? Which company has more cash to invest in promising projects? If prices continue rising over the long term, which company would you prefer to invest in? Why? (Challenge)

Case 2. (*Learning Objectives 2, 5: Distinguish between capital expenditures and expense; account for plant assets and intangible assets*) The following questions are unrelated except that they all apply to plant assets and intangible assets:

1. The manager of Carpet World regularly debits the cost of repairs and maintenance of plant assets to Plant and Equipment. Why would she do that, since she knows she is violating GAAP?
2. The manager of Horizon Software regularly buys plant assets and debits the cost to Repairs and Maintenance Expense. Why would he do that, since he knows this action violates GAAP?
3. It has been suggested that because many intangible assets have no value except to the company that owns them, they should be valued at $1.00 or zero on the balance sheet. Many accountants disagree with this view. Which view do you support? Why?

Ethical Issue

United Jersey Bank of Princeton purchased land and a building for the lump sum of $6 million. To get the maximum tax deduction, the bank's managers allocated 80% of the purchase price to the building and only 20% to the land. A more realistic allocation would have been 60% to the building and 40% to the land.

▶ Requirements

1. What is the ethical issue in this situation?
2. Who are the stakeholders? What are the possible consequences to each?
3. Analyze the alternatives from the following standpoints: (a) economic, (b) legal, and (c) ethical.
4. What would you do? How would you justify your decision?

Focus on Financials: | Amazon.com, Inc.

(*Learning Objectives 2, 3, 6: Analyze activity in plant assets*) Refer to **Amazon.com, Inc.'s** Consolidated Financial Statements in Appendix A at the end of the book, and answer the following questions:

1. Refer to Note 1 and Note 3 of the Notes to Consolidated Financial Statements. What kinds of assets are included in fixed assets of Amazon.com, Inc?
2. Which depreciation method does Amazon.com, Inc., use for reporting to stockholders and creditors in the financial statements? What type of depreciation method does the company probably use for income tax purposes? Why is this method preferable for tax purposes?
3. Depreciation expense is embedded in operating expense accounts listed on the income statement, so you can't break out the actual figure for depreciation in that way. Refer to Note 3—Fixed Assets. How much was Amazon.com, Inc.'s depreciation expense on fixed assets during 2010? What did this figure include? How much was Amazon.com, Inc.'s accumulated depreciation on fixed assets at the end of 2010? Explain why accumulated depreciation exceeds depreciation expense for the current year.
4. How much did Amazon.com, Inc., spend on fixed assets, including internal-use software and website development, during 2010? In 2009? Evaluate the trend in these capital expenditures as to whether it conveys good news or bad news for Amazon.com, Inc. Explain.
5. Refer to Notes 1 and 4 of the Notes to Consolidated Financial Statements. What are Amazon.com, Inc.'s intangible assets? How does the company account for each of these intangibles over its lifetime?

Focus on Analysis: | RadioShack Corporation.

(*Learning Objectives 2, 4, 7: Distinguish a capital expenditure from an immediate expense; explain plant asset activity; analyze rate of return on assets*) Refer to the **RadioShack Corporation** Consolidated Financial Statements in Appendix B at the end of this book. This case leads you through an analysis of the activity in Radioshack's long-term assets, as well as the calculation of its rate of return on total assets.

1. On the statement of cash flows, how much did RadioShack Corporation pay for capital expenditures during fiscal 2010? In what section of the cash flows statement do you find this amount?
2. Explain RadioShack Corporation's policy for capitalization of fixed assets. You can find this in Note 2 of the Consolidated Financial Statements (Summary of Significant Accounting Policies).
3. Which depreciation method does RadioShack Corporation use? Over what useful life does RadioShack Corporation depreciate various types of fixed assets?
4. Were RadioShack Corporation's plant assets proportionately newer or older at the end of fiscal 2010 (versus 2009)? Explain your answer. (Challenge)
5. Using DuPont Analysis, calculate RadioShack Corporation's rate of return on total assets for 2010 and 2009. Total assets at December 31, 2008, were $2,254. Did the company perform better or worse in 2010 than in 2009?

Group Project

Visit a local business.

▶ Requirements

1. List all its plant assets.
2. If possible, interview the manager. Gain as much information as you can about the business's plant assets. For example, try to determine the assets' costs, the depreciation method the company is using, and the estimated useful life of each asset category. If an interview is impossible, then develop your own estimates of the assets' costs, useful lives, and book values, assuming an appropriate depreciation method.
3. Determine whether the business has any intangible assets. If so, list them and gain as much information as possible about their nature, cost, and estimated useful lives.
4. Write a detailed report of your findings and be prepared to present your results to the class.

MyAccountingLab

For online homework, exercises, and problems that provide you with immediate feedback, please visit **www.myaccountinglab.com.**

Quick Check Answers

1. *b* {[$1,144/($1,144 + $660 + $396)] × $1,800 = $936}
2. *c*
3. *c* ($35,000 − $8,000)/5 × 3/12 = $1,350)
4. *b* [($35,000 − $8,000)/5 × 2 = $10,800; $35,000 − $10,800 = $24,200]
5. *d* [$35,000 × .4 = $14,000; ($35,000 − $14,000) × .4 = $8,400]
6. *c* [($35,000 − $8,000)/5 × 4 = $21,600; $35,000 − $21,600 = $13,400; $22,400 − $13,400 = gain of $9,000]
7. *c* [$23,000 × 2/4 = $11,500; ($23,000 − $11,500) × 2/4 = $5,750; $11,500 + $5,750 = $17,250]
8. *c*
9. *b*
10. *c*
11. *a* [$210,000 × (2,000/30,000) = $14,000]
12. *e*
13. *c*
14. *c*

8 Long-Term Investments & the Time Value of Money

SPOTLIGHT: Intel Holds Several Different Types of Investments

After college you may start investing through a retirement or savings plan at work, and you may make some investments on your own. The reasons people invest are for current income (interest and dividends) and appreciation of the investment's value (stocks, bonds, and real estate, for example). Some very wealthy individuals invest in a wide variety of traditional and non-traditional investments in order to obtain significant influence over, or even to control, corporate entities and to maximize their wealth.

Businesses such as **Intel**, **General Electric**, and **Coca-Cola** invest for the same reasons. In this chapter you'll learn how to account for investments of many types. We use Intel Corporation as our example company because Intel has so many interesting investments. You'll also learn about the time value of money, which is an essential factor in valuing some types of long-term investments, as well as long-term liabilities (covered in Chapter 9). ●

Robert Clare/Photographer's Choice/Getty Images, Inc.

(In millions)		2010
1	Assets	
2	Current assets:	
3	Cash and cash equivalents	$ 5,498
4	Short-term investments	11,294
5	Trading assets	5,093
6	Accounts receivable, net of allowance for doubtful accounts of $28	2,867
7	Inventories	3,757
8	Other current assets	3,102
9	Total current assets	31,611
10	Property, plant and equipment, net	17,899
11	Marketable strategic equity securities	1,008
12	Other long-term investments	3,026
13	Goodwill	4,531
14	Other long-term assets	5,111
15	Total assets	$63,186

Intel Corporation
Consolidated Balance Sheet (Partial, Adapted)
December 25, 2010

What comes to mind when you think of Intel? Computer processors and microchips? Yes, Intel produces processors and computer chips. But interestingly, 32.3% [($11,294 + $5,093 + $1,008 + $3,026) /$63,186] of Intel's assets are tied up in investments in other companies. The assets section of Intel's 2010 balance sheet reports these investments on lines 4, 5, 11, and 12. Some of Intel's other asset categories also include investments.

Throughout this course, you've become increasingly familiar with the financial statements of companies such as **Intel, FedEx,** and **Starbucks**. You've seen most of the items that appear in a set of financial statements. One of your learning goals should be to develop the ability to analyze whatever you encounter in real-company statements. This chapter will help you advance toward that goal.

The first half of this chapter shows how to account for long-term investments, including a brief overview of consolidated financial statements. The second half of the chapter covers the time value of money.

Learning Objectives

① *Analyze and report* investments in held-to-maturity debt securities

② *Analyze and report* investments in available-for-sale securities

③ *Analyze and report* investments in affiliated companies using the equity method

④ *Analyze and report* controlling interests in other corporations using consolidated financial statements

⑤ *Report* investing activities on the statement of cash flows

⑥ *Explain* the impact of the time value of money on certain types of investments

Investments come in all sizes and shapes—ranging from a few shares of stock to a controlling interest in multiple corporations, or interests in other types of investments such as corporate or municipal bonds or real estate. In later chapters, we will discuss stocks and bonds from the perspective of the company that issues the securities. In this chapter, we examine *long-term investments* from the perspective of the purchaser, or investor.

To consider investments, we need to define two key terms. The entity that owns stock or bonds of a corporation or other entity is the *investor*. The corporation or other entity that issues the stock is the *investee*. A corporation or other entity, such as a municipality, that issues bonds is a *debtor*. If you own some shares of Intel common stock, you are an investor and Intel is the investee. If you own Intel bonds, you are an investor/creditor and Intel is the investee/debtor.

Stock and Bond Prices

You can log on to the Internet to learn Intel's current stock price or the current trading value of its publicly held debt. Exhibit 8-1 presents recent information about Intel's stock. During the previous 52 weeks, Intel common stock had a high price of $24.37 and a low of $17.60 per share. The annual cash dividend for the most recent full year was $0.63 per share. During the previous day, 38.1 million shares of Intel common stock were traded. At day's end, the price of the stock closed at $19.78, up $0.02 from the closing price of the preceding day.

EXHIBIT 8-1 | Stock Information for Intel Corporation

52-Week Hi	Lo	Stock (sym)	Div	Volume	Close	Net Change
$24.37	$17.60	INTC	$0.63	38,148,000	$19.78	+ $0.02

Reporting Investments on the Balance Sheet

An investment is an asset to the investor. The investment may be short-term or long-term. **Short-term investments** in marketable equity or debt securities are current assets. They can be classified as either *trading, held-to-maturity,* or *available for sale,* depending on management's intent and ability to hold them until they mature. To be listed as short-term on the balance sheet,

- ▶ the investment must be *liquid* (readily convertible to cash).
- ▶ the investor must intend either to convert the investment to cash within one year or to use it to pay a current liability.

We saw how to account for short-term investments in Chapter 5.

Investments that aren't short-term are listed as **long-term investments**, a category of noncurrent assets. Long-term investments include stocks and bonds that the investor expects to hold for longer than one year. Exhibit 8-2 on the following page shows where short-term and long-term investments appear on the balance sheet.

EXHIBIT 8-2 | Reporting Investments on the Balance sheet

Current Assets:		
Cash	$X	
Short-term investments	X	
Accounts receivable	X	
Inventories	X	
Prepaid expenses	X	
Total current assets		X
Long-term investments [or simply Investments]		X
Property, plant, and equipment		X
Intangible assets		X
Other assets		X

Assets are listed in order of liquidity. Long-term investments are less liquid than current assets but more liquid than property, plant, and equipment. Intel reports short-term investments immediately after cash (p. 464, lines 4 and 5). The company reports long-term investments in both debt securities (bonds) and equity securities (stock) in the non-current section of the balance sheet (p. 464, lines 11 and 12). We now discuss the financial reporting for each of these types of long-term investments.

Analyze and Report Investments in Held-to-Maturity Debt Securities

The major investors in debt securities such as bonds are financial institutions—pension funds, mutual funds, and insurance companies such as Intel Capital. The relationship between the issuing corporation and the investor (bondholder) may be diagrammed as follows:

Chapter 8	Chapter 9
Investor (Bondholder)	Issuing Corporation
Investment in bonds ← →	Bonds payable
Interest revenue ← →	Interest expense

If the investor company intends to hold debt securities longer than a year, but not until maturity, they are categorized as available-for-sale securities and accounted for under the fair value method, described in the next section. If the investing company intends to hold a debt security until maturity, it accounts for the security at amortized cost, as a **held-to-maturity investment**, as described in this section.

Bonds of publicly traded companies are traded on the open market, just as stocks are. Like other forms of debt, bonds pay investors interest, usually semi-annually (twice a year). The (face) interest rate of a particular bond is quoted on the face of the instrument and determines the cash amount of semiannual interest the debtor company pays. Bonds are usually issued in $1,000 face (par) denominations, but they typically do not sell at par value. The price of a bond at a particular time is quoted as a percentage of its par value. Market prices of bonds (yields) fluctuate with market interest rates. If market rates on competing instruments are higher than the face rate of interest on a particular bond, the bond sells at a discount (below 100% of par, or face value). For example, a quoted bond price of 96.5 means that the $1,000 bond is selling for 96.5% of par, or $965 (discounted from par value). If market rates are lower than the face rate of interest on the bond being considered, the bond sells at a premium (above 100% of par). For example, a quoted bond price of 102.5 means that the bond is selling for 102.5% of par, or $1,025 (a premium over par value).

Held-to-maturity investments are reported by the *amortized cost method*, which determines the carrying amount. Bond investments are initially recorded at cost (market price as a percentage × par value of bonds issued). At each semiannual interest payment date, the investor records interest revenue (1/2 the annual face interest rate × the face amount of the bond). In addition, whenever there is issue premium or discount, it is amortized by adjusting the carrying amount of the bond upward or downward toward its par or face value, with an offsetting entry being made to interest revenue. Years later, at maturity, the carrying amount will have been adjusted from the original issue amount to its par or face value, and the investor will receive the face amount upon redemption of the bond.

As an example, assume that Intel Capital purchases $10,000 of 6% CBS bonds at a price of 95.2 on April 1, 2012. Intel Capital intends to hold the bonds until their maturity date, April 1, 2016. Interest dates are semiannual, on April 1 and October 1. Because these bonds mature on April 1, 2016, they will be outstanding for four years (48 months). In this case, Intel Capital pays a discount price for the bonds (95.2% of face value), because the market rates of interest for other similar instruments are higher than 6%[1]. The initial purchase price and carrying value of the investment is $9,520 (95.2% × $10,000). Intel Capital must amortize the bonds' carrying amount from cost of $9,520 up to $10,000 over their 48-month term to maturity. Assume Intel Capital amortizes discount on the bonds by the straight-line method. Following are the entries for this bond investment on April 1 and October 1, 2012, the issue date and the first interest payment date:

2012			
Apr 1	Long-Term Investment in Bonds ($10,000 × 0.952)	9,520	
	Cash		9,520
	To purchase bond investment.		
Oct 1	Cash ($10,000 × 0.06 × 6/12)	300	
	Interest Revenue		300
	To receive semiannual interest.		
Oct 1	Long-Term Investment in Bonds [($10,000 − $9,520)/48] × 6	60	
	Interest Revenue		60
	To amortize bond investment.		

At December 31, 2012, Intel Capital's year-end adjustments are as follows:

2012			
Dec 31	Interest Receivable ($10,000 × 0.06 × 3/12)	150	
	Interest Revenue		150
	To accrue interest revenue.		
Dec 31	Long-Term Investment in Bonds [($10,000 − $9,520)/48] × 3	30	
	Interest Revenue		30
	To amortize bond investment.		

This amortization entry has two effects:

► It increases the Long-Term Investment account on its march toward maturity value, which will be $10,000 on April 1, 2016.
► It records the interest revenue earned from the increase in the carrying amount of the investment.

---

[1] We will discuss how the time value of money impacts the price of investment in the second half of this chapter.

The financial statements of Intel Capital at December 31, 2012, would report the following for this investment in bonds:

Balance sheet at December 31, 2012:	
Current assets:	
Interest receivable..	$ 150
Long-term investments in bonds ($9,520 + $60 + $30)..............	9,610
Property, plant, and equipment...	X,XXX
Income statement for the year ended December 31, 2012:	
Other revenues:	
Interest revenue ($300 + $60 + $150 + $30).........................	$ 540

By April 1, 2016, the maturity date of the bonds, the carrying value will have been adjusted to equal the face value of $10,000, and Intel Capital will redeem the bonds for this amount.

Analyze and Report Investments in Available-for-Sale Securities

②

Analyze and report investments in available-for-sale securities

Available-for-sale securities may be debt securities not held to maturity, or equity (stock) securities other than trading securities. *Cost* is used only as the initial amount for recording the purchase of these investments. At the end of each reporting period, these securities are adjusted to their current **fair values** because the company expects to sell the investments at these values at some point in the future, although not within the next year.

Accounting Methods for Long-Term Stock Investments

The accounting rules for long-term investments in equity securities (stock) depend on the percentage of ownership by the investor, as shown in Exhibit 8-3.

EXHIBIT 8-3 | Accounting Methods for Long-Term Stock Investments by Percentage of Ownership

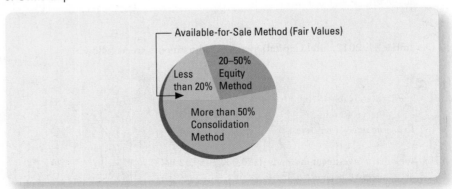

An investment less than, but up to, 20% is considered available-for-sale because the investor usually has little or no influence on the investee, in which case the strategy would be to hold the investment, making it available for sale in periods beyond the end of the fiscal year. Ownership between 20% and 50% provides the investor with the opportunity to significantly influence the investee's operating decisions and policies over the long run. An investment above 50% allows the investor a great deal of long-term influence—perhaps control—over the investee company. The methods of accounting for greater-than-20%-owned equity interests are discussed in the two sections that follow. In this section, we discuss securities accounted for as available-for-sale investments. Let's begin with an example.

Suppose Intel purchases 1,000 shares of **Hewlett-Packard** common stock at the market price of $44. Intel intends to hold this investment for longer than a year and therefore treats it as a long-term available-for-sale investment. Intel's entry to record the investment is as follows:

2012			
Oct 23	Long-Term Investment (1,000 × $44)	44,000	
	Cash		44,000
	Purchased investment.		

Assets	=	Liabilities	+	Stockholders' Equity
+ 44,000 − 44,000	=	0	+	0

Assume that Intel receives a $0.20 cash dividend on the Hewlett-Packard stock. Intel's entry to record receipt of the dividend is as follows:

2012			
Nov 14	Cash (1,000 × $0.20)	200	
	Dividend Revenue		200
	Received cash dividend.		

Assets	=	Liabilities	+	Stockholders' Equity	+	Revenues
+200	=	0	+			+200

Receipt of a *stock* dividend is different from receipt of a cash dividend. For a stock dividend, the investor records no dividend revenue. Instead, the investor makes a memorandum entry in the accounting records to denote the new number of shares of stock held as an investment. Because the number of shares of stock held has increased, the investor's cost per share decreases. To illustrate, suppose Intel receives a 10% stock dividend from Hewlett-Packard Company. Intel would receive 100 shares (10% of 1,000 shares previously held) and make this memorandum entry in its accounting records:

> **MEMORANDUM—Receipt of stock dividend: Received 100 shares of Hewlett-Packard common stock in 10% stock dividend. New cost per share is $40.00 (cost of $44,000 ÷ 1,100 shares).**

In all future transactions affecting this investment, Intel's cost per share is now $40.

The Fair Value Adjustment

GAAP requires that companies adjust their portfolios of available-for-sale securities to *fair value* as of the balance sheet date. Fair value of an asset is the amount that would be received for the securities in an "orderly sale." GAAP recognizes three different approaches:

- ▶ Level 1: Quoted prices in active markets for identical assets
- ▶ Level 2: Estimates based on other observable inputs (e.g., prices for similar assets)
- ▶ Level 3: Estimates based on unobservable estimates (the company's own estimates based on certain assumptions)

Fair value should be determined using the most reliable method available. Level 1 is preferable, because it is considered easiest to verify. If no quoted prices in active markets are available, the investor moves to levels 2 and 3, in that order, to make the fair value adjustment. Companies must disclose the aggregate amounts of fair value for both trading and available-for-sale investments determined under each of these three levels in the financial statement footnotes. In our example of the investment in Hewlitt-Packard stock, a Level 1 fair value is available, because the stock has a quoted market price as of the end of the year. Returning to our original example before the stock dividend, assume that the quoted market price of the stock is $46.50, making fair value of the 1,000 shares of Hewlett-Packard common stock $46,500 on December 31, 2012. In this case, Intel makes the following entry to adjust the investment to fair value.

2012			
Dec 31	Allowance to Adjust Investment to Market		
	($46,500 − $44,000)	2,500	
	Unrealized Gain on Investment		2,500
	Adjusted investment to fair value.		

The increase in the investment's fair value creates additional equity for the investor.

Assets	=	Liabilities	+	Stockholders' Equity
+ 2,500	=	0		+ 2,500

Allowance to Adjust Investment to Market is a companion account to Long-Term Investment. In this case, the investment's cost ($44,000) plus the allowance ($2,500) equals the investment fair value carrying amount ($46,500), as follows:

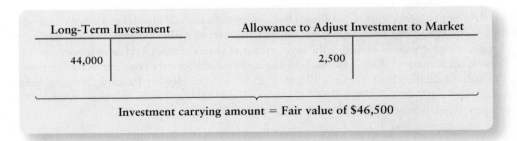

Here the allowance has a debit balance because the fair value of the investment increased. If the investment's fair value declines, the allowance is credited. In that case, the carrying amount is its cost minus the allowance.

The other side of this adjustment entry is a credit to Unrealized Gain on Investment. If the fair value of the investment declines, the company debits Unrealized Loss on Investment. *Unrealized* gains and losses result from changes in fair value, not from sales of investments. For available-for-sale investments, the unrealized gain account or the unrealized loss account is reported as an element of *other comprehensive income,* which is a change in owners' equity that bypasses net income, reported in a separate statement of comprehensive income, or in a separate section of the income statement below net income in a combined statement of income and comprehensive income.

The statement of comprehensive income is covered more thoroughly in Chapter 11. The following display shows one of the ways that Intel could report its regular net income plus comprehensive income from the unrealized gain in its combined Statement of

Income and Other Comprehensive Income at the end of 2012 (all other figures are assumed for this illustration):

Intel Corporation Consolidated Statement of Comprehensive Income Year Ended December 25, 2010		
(figures assumed, not actual)		
Revenues		$50,000
Expenses, including income tax		36,000
Net income		$14,000
Other comprehensive income:		
Unrealized gain on investments	$ 2,500	
Less Income tax 40%	(1,000)	1,500
Comprehensive income		$15,500

The preceding example assumes that the investor holds an investment in only one equity security: stock of another company. Usually companies invest in a portfolio of securities (both equity and debt securities of more than one company). In this case, the periodic adjustment to fair value must be made for the portfolio as a whole. See the "Stop & Think" exercise at the end of this section (p. 472) for an example.

Selling an Available-for-Sale Investment

The sale of an available-for-sale investment usually results in a *realized* gain or loss. When an available-for-sale asset that has been re-valued is subsequently sold, the amount of unrealized gain or loss existing on the asset at the date of sale is reversed, effectively returning the carrying value of the portion of the asset sold to its original cost. Realized gains and losses on the investment are then measured as the difference between the amount received from the sale and the cost of the investment at the date of sale.

Suppose Intel sells its entire investment in Hewlett-Packard stock for $43,000 during 2013. Intel would record the sale as follows:

2013 May 19	Unrealized gain on investments	2,500	
	Allowance to adjust investment to market		2,500
	To eliminate unrealized gain on available-for-sale investments sold		
May 19	Cash	43,000	
	Loss on Sale of Investment	1,000	
	Long-Term Investment (cost)		44,000
	Sold investment.		

Assets	=	Liabilities	+	Stockholders' Equity	−	Losses
+ 43,000 − 44,000	=	0			−	1,000

Intel would report Loss on Sale of Investments as a realized loss in "Other income" on the income statement.

STOP & THINK. . .

Suppose Intel Corporation holds the following available-for-sale securities as long-term investments at December 31, 2013:

Stock	Cost	Level 1 Fair Value
The Coca-Cola Company.........	$ 85,000	$71,000
Eastman Kodak Company........	16,000	12,000
	$101,000	$83,000

Show how Intel will report long-term investments on its December 31, 2013, balance sheet.

Answer:

Assets	
Long-term investments, at fair value	$83,000

Analyze and Report Investments in Affiliated Companies Using The Equity Method

Buying a Large Stake in Another Company

3

Analyze and report investments in affiliated companies using the equity method

An investor owning between 20% and 50% of the investee's voting stock may significantly influence the investee. Such an investor can probably affect dividend policy, product lines, and other important matters. The investor company will more than likely hold one or more seats on the Board of Directors of the investee company. As shown in Exhibit 8-3, we use the **equity method** to account for these types of investments.

Intel holds equity-method investments in IM Flash Technologies and Clearwire Corporation. These investee companies are referred to as *affiliates* because the investor has a sufficient ownership percentage in them to significantly influence their operations. Because Intel has a voice in shaping the policy and operations of IM Flash Technologies, some measure of its profits and losses should be included in Intel's income.

Accounting for Equity-Method Investments

Investments accounted for by the equity method are recorded initially at cost. Suppose Intel pays $400 million for 30% of the common stock of IM Flash Technologies. Intel's entry to record the purchase of this investment follows (in millions):

2012			
Jan 6	Long-Term Investment	400	
	Cash		400
	To purchase equity–method investment.		

Assets	=	Liabilities	+	Stockholders' Equity
+ 400	=	0	+	0
− 400				

The Investor's Percentage of Investee Income. Under the equity method, Intel, as the investor, applies its percentage of ownership—30% in our example—in recording its share of the investee's net income and dividends. If IM Flash Technologies reports net income of $250 million for the year, Intel records 30% of this amount as follows (in millions):

2012			
Dec 31	Long-Term Investment ($250 × 0.30)	75	
	Equity-Method Investment Revenue		75
	To record investment revenue.		

Assets	=	Liabilities	+	Stockholders' Equity
+ 75	=	0		+ 75

Because of the close relationship between Intel and IM Flash Technologies, Intel, the investor, increases the Investment account and records Investment Revenue when IM Flash Technolgoies, the investee, reports income. As IM Flash's stockholder equity increases, so does the Investment account on Intel's books.

Receiving Dividends Under the Equity Method. Intel records its proportionate part of cash dividends received from IM Flash. When IM Flash declares and pays a cash dividend of $100 million, Intel receives 30% of this dividend and records this entry (in millions):

2012			
Dec 31	Cash ($100 × 0.30)	30	
	Long-Term Investment		30
	To receive cash dividend on equity-method investment.		

Assets	=	Liabilities	+	Stockholders' Equity
+ 30	=	0	+	0
− 30				

The Investment account is *decreased* for the receipt of a dividend on an equity-method investment. Why? Because the dividend decreases the investee's owners' equity and thus the investor's investment.

After the preceding entries are posted, Intel's Investment account at December 31, 2012, shows Intel's equity in the net assets of IM Flash Technologies (in millions):

Long-Term Investment					
Jan 6	Purchase	400	Dec 31	Dividends	30
Dec 31	Net income	75			
Dec 31	Balance	445			

Intel would report the long-term investment on the balance sheet and the equity-method investment revenue on the income statement as follows:

	Millions
Balance sheet (partial):	
Assets	
Total current assets..	$XXX
Long-term investments, at equity........................	445
Property, plant, and equipment, net...................	XXX
Income statement (partial):	
Income from operations......................................	$XXX
Other revenue:	
Equity-method investment revenue................	75
Net income..	$XXX

Gain or loss on the sale of an equity-method investment is measured as the difference between the sale proceeds and the carrying amount of the investment. For example, Intel's sale of 20% of the IM Flash Technologies common stock for $81 million would be recorded as follows:

2013			
Feb 13	Cash	81	
	Loss on Sale of Investment	8	
	Long-Term Investment ($445 × 0.20)		89
	Sold 20% of investment.		

Assets	=	Liabilities	+	Stockholders' Equity	−	Losses
+ 81	=	0			−	8
− 89						

Summary of the Equity Method. The following T-account illustrates the accounting for equity-method investments:

Equity-Method Investment	
Original cost	Share of losses
Share of income	Share of dividends
Balance	

Analyze and Report Controlling Interests in Other Corporations Using Consolidated Financial Statements

In this section, we cover the situation in which an investing corporation buys more than 50% of the voting stock of another company, permitting the investor to actually *control* the investee. Intel's ownership of Intel Capital is an example.

4

Analyze and report controlling interests in other corporations using consolidated financial statements

Why Buy Another Company?

Most large corporations own controlling interests in other companies. A **controlling** (or **majority**) **interest** is the ownership of more than 50% of the investee's voting stock. Such an investment enables the investor to elect a majority of the members of the investee's board of directors and thus control the investee's policies such as its production, distribution (supply chain), financing and investing decisions. The investor is called the **parent company**, and the investee company is called the **subsidiary**. For example, **Intel Capital** is a subsidiary of Intel Corporation, the parent. Therefore, the stockholders of Intel control Intel Capital, as diagrammed in Exhibit 8-4.

EXHIBIT 8-4 | Ownership Structure of Intel Corporation and Intel Capital

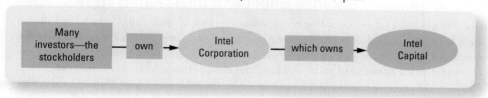

Exhibit 8-5 shows some of the subsidiaries of Intel Corporation.

EXHIBIT 8-5 | Selected Subsidiaries of Intel

Intel Capital	Intel Americas, Inc.
Componentes Intel de Costa Rica, S.A.	Intel Europe, Inc.
Intel Asia Holding Limited	Intel Kabushiki Kaisha

Consolidation Accounting

Consolidation accounting is a method of combining the financial statements of all the companies controlled by the same stockholders. This method reports a single set of financial statements for the consolidated entity, which carries the name of the parent company.

Consolidated financial statements combine the balance sheets, income statements, and cash-flow statements of the parent company with those of its subsidiaries. The result is a single set of statements as if the parent and its subsidiaries were one company. Investors can gain a better perspective on total operations than they could by examining the reports of the parent and each individual subsidiary.

In consolidated financial statements, the assets, liabilities, revenues, and expenses of each subsidiary are added to the parent's accounts. For example, the balance in Intel Capital's Cash account is added to the balance in the Intel Corporation Cash account and to the cash of all other subsidiaries. The sum of all of the cash amounts is presented as a single amount in the Intel consolidated balance sheet. Each account balance of a subsidiary, such as Intel Capital or Intel Europe, Inc., loses its identity in the consolidated statements, which bear the name of the parent, Intel Corporation. After a subsidiary's financial statements become consolidated into the parent company's statements, the subsidiary's statements are no longer available to the public.

Exhibit 8-6 diagrams a corporate structure for a parent corporation that owns controlling interests in five subsidiaries and an equity-method investment in another investee company.

EXHIBIT 8-6 | Parent Company with Consolidated Subsidiaries and an Equity-Method Investment

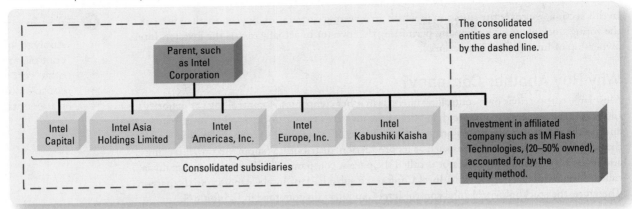

The Consolidated Balance Sheet and the Related Work Sheet

Intel owns all (100%) the outstanding voting common stock of Intel Capital. Both Intel and Intel Capital keep separate sets of books. Intel, the parent company, uses a work sheet to prepare the consolidated statements of Intel and its consolidated subsidiaries. Then Intel's consolidated balance sheet shows the combined assets and liabilities of both Intel and all its subsidiaries.

Exhibit 8-7 shows the work sheet for consolidating the balance sheets of Parent Corporation and Subsidiary Corporation. We use these hypothetical entities to illustrate the consolidation process. Consider elimination entry (a) for the parent-subsidiary ownership accounts. Entry (a) credits the parent's Investment account to eliminate its debit balance. Entry (a) also eliminates the subsidiary's stockholders' equity accounts by debiting the subsidiary's Common Stock and Retained Earnings for their full balances. Without this elimination, the consolidated financial statements would include both the parent company's investment in the subsidiary and the subsidiary company's equity. But these accounts represent the same thing—Subsidiary's equity—and so they must be eliminated from the consolidated totals. If they weren't, the same resources would be counted twice.

EXHIBIT 8-7 | Work Sheet for a Consolidated Balance Sheet

	Parent Corporation	Subsidiary Corporation	Eliminations Debit	Eliminations Credit	Parent and Subsidiary Consolidated Amounts
Assets					
Cash	12,000	18,000			30,000
Note receivable from Subsidiary	80,000	—		(b) 80,000	—
Inventory	104,000	91,000			195,000
Investment in Subsidiary	150,000	—		(a) 150,000	—
Other assets	218,000	138,000			356,000
Total	564,000	247,000			581,000
Liabilities and Stockholders' Equity					
Accounts payable	43,000	17,000			60,000
Notes payable	190,000	80,000	(b) 80,000		190,000
Common stock	176,000	100,000	(a) 100,000		176,000
Retained earnings	155,000	50,000	(a) 50,000		155,000
Total	564,000	247,000	230,000	230,000	581,000

The resulting Parent and Subsidiary consolidated balance sheet (far-right column) reports no Investment in Subsidiary account. Moreover, the consolidated totals for Common Stock and Retained Earnings are those of Parent Corporation only. Study the final column of the consolidation work sheet.

In this example, Parent Corporation has an $80,000 note receivable from Subsidiary, and Subsidiary has a note payable to Parent. The parent's receivable and the subsidiary's payable represent the same resources—all entirely within the consolidated entity. Both, therefore, must be eliminated, and entry (b) accomplishes this.

▶ The $80,000 credit in the Elimination column of the work sheet zeros out Parent's Note Receivable from Subsidiary.

▶ The $80,000 debit in the Elimination column zeros out the Subsidiary's Note Payable to Parent.

▶ The resulting consolidated amount for notes payable is the amount owed to creditors outside the consolidated entity, which is appropriate.

After the work sheet is complete, the consolidated amount for each account represents the total asset, liability, and equity amounts controlled by Parent Corporation.

STOP & THINK...

Examine Exhibit 8-7. Why does the consolidated stockholders' equity ($176,000 + $155,000) *exclude* the equity of Subsidiary Corporation?

Answer:

The stockholders' equity of the consolidated entity is that of the parent only. To include the stockholders' equity of the subsidiary as well as the investment in the subsidiary on the parent's books would be double counting.

Goodwill and Noncontrolling Interest

Goodwill and Noncontrolling (minority) Interest are two accounts that only a consolidated entity can have. As we saw in Chapter 7, goodwill is the intangible asset that represents the parent company's excess payment over and above the fair market value of assets to acquire the subsidiary. GE reports goodwill as an intangible asset on its balance sheet.

Noncontrolling (minority) interest arises when a parent company owns less than 100% of the stock of a subsidiary. For example, General Electric (GE) owns less than 100% of some of the companies it controls. The remainder of the subsidiaries' stock is noncontrolling (minority) interest to GE. Noncontrolling Interest is reported as a separate account in the stockholders' equity section of the consolidated balance sheet of the parent company. The amount of noncontrolling interest in subsidiaries' stock must be clearly identified and labeled as such. GE reports noncontrolling interest in the stockholders' equity section on its balance sheet. By contrast, Intel reports no noncontrolling interest, which suggests that Intel owns 100% of all its subsidiaries.

Income of a Consolidated Entity

The income of a consolidated entity is the net income of the parent plus the parent's proportion of the subsidiaries' net income. Suppose Parent Company owns all the stock of Subsidiary S-1 and 60% of the stock of Subsidiary S-2. During the year just ended, Parent earned net income of $330,000, S-1 earned $150,000, and S-2 had a net loss of $100,000. Parent Company would report net income of $420,000, computed as follows:

	Net Income (Net Loss) of Each Company		Parent's Ownership of Each Company		Parent's Consolidated Net Income (Net Loss)
Parent Company	$330,000	×	100%	=	$330,000
Subsidiary S-1	150,000	×	100%	=	150,000
Subsidiary S-2	(100,000)	×	60%	=	(60,000)
Consolidated net income					$420,000

with Investments and Debt

Enron Corporation

In 2000, Enron Corporation in Houston, Texas, employed approximately 22,000 people and was one of the world's leading electricity, natural gas, pulp and paper, and communications companies, with reported revenues of nearly $101 billion. *Fortune* had named Enron "America's Most Innovative Company" for six consecutive years. To many outside observers, Enron was the model corporation.

Enron's financial statements showed that the company was making a lot of money, but in reality, most of its profits were merely on paper. Rather than from operations, the great majority of the cash Enron needed to operate on a day-to-day basis came from bank loans. It was very important, therefore, that Enron keep its debt ratio (discussed in Chapter 3) as well as its return on assets (ROA, discussed in Chapter 7) at acceptable levels, so the banks would continue to view the company as creditworthy. Enron's balance sheets contained large misstatements in the liabilities and stockholders' equity sections over a period of years. Many of the offsetting misstatements were in long-term assets. Specifically, Enron owned numerous long-term investments including power plants; water rights; broadband cable; and sophisticated, complex, and somewhat dubious derivative financial instruments in such unusual things as the weather! Many of these investments actually had questionable value, but Enron had abused fair market value accounting to estimate them at grossly inflated values.

To create paper profits, Andrew Fastow, Enron's chief financial officer, created a veritable maze of "special purpose entities" (SPEs), financed with bank debt. He valued these investments using "mark-to-market" (fair value accounting), using unrealistic assumptions that created inflated asset values on the financial statements. He then "sold" the dubious investments to the SPEs to get them off Enron's books. Enron recorded millions of dollars in "profits" from these transactions. Fastow then used Enron stock to collateralize the bank debt of the SPEs, making the transactions entirely circular. Unknown to Enron's board of directors, Fastow or members of his own family owned most of these entities, making them related parties to Enron. Enron was, in fact, the owner of the assets, and was, in fact, obligated for the debts of the SPEs since those debts were collateralized with Enron stock. When Enron's fraud was discovered in late 2001, the company was forced to consolidate the assets of the SPEs, as well as all of their bank debt, into its own financial statements. The inflated assets had to be written down to impaired market values. The end result of the restatement impacted Enron's debt ratio and ROA so much that the banks refused to loan the company any more money to operate. Enron's energy trading business virtually dried up overnight, and it was bankrupt within 60 days. An estimated $60 billion in shareholder value, and 22,000 jobs, were lost. Enron's CEO, Jeffrey Skilling, its CFO, Andrew Fastow, and Board Chairman Kenneth Lay were all convicted of fraud. Skilling and Fastow both went to prison. Lay died suddenly of a heart attack before being sentenced.

Enron's audit firm, Arthur Andersen, was accused of trying to cover up its knowledge of Enron's practices by shredding documents. The firm was indicted by the U.S. Justice Department in March 2002. Because of the indictment, Andersen lost all of its public clients and was forced out of business. As a result, over 58,000 persons lost their jobs worldwide. A U.S. Supreme Court decision in 2005 eventually led to withdrawal of the indictment, but it came much too late for the once "gold plated" CPA firm. Allegations about the quality of its work on Enron, as well as other well-publicized cases such as Waste Management (p. 417) and WorldCom (p. 405), who were also clients, doomed Arthur Andersen.

DECISION GUIDELINES

ACCOUNTING METHODS FOR LONG-TERM INVESTMENTS

These guidelines show which accounting method to use for each type of long-term investment.

Intel has all types of investments—stocks, bonds, 25% interests, and controlling interests. How should Intel account for its various investments?

Type of Long-Term Investment	Accounting Method
Intel owns long-term investment in bonds (held-to-maturity investment)	Amortized cost
Intel owns a portfolio of bond and other debt securities as well as equity securities in companies (less than 20%)	Available-for-sale; fair value
Intel owns between 20% and 50% of investee/affiliate stock	Equity
Intel owns more than 50% of investee stock	Consolidation

MID-CHAPTER SUMMARY PROBLEMS

1. Identify the appropriate accounting method for each of the following situations:
   a. Investment in 25% of investee's stock
   b. 10% investment in stock
   c. Investment in more than 50% of investee's stock

2. At what amount should the following available-for-sale investment portfolio be reported on the December 31 balance sheet? All the investments are less than 5% of the investee's stock. Journalize any adjusting entry required by these data.

Stock	Investment Cost	Current Market Value
DuPont	$ 5,000	$ 5,500
ExxonMobil	61,200	53,000
Procter & Gamble	3,680	6,230

3. Investor paid $67,900 to acquire a 40% equity-method investment in the common stock of Investee. At the end of the first year, Investee's net income was $80,000, and Investee declared and paid cash dividends of $55,000. What is Investor's ending balance in its Equity-Method Investment account? Use a T-account to answer.

4. Parent company paid $85,000 for all the common stock of Subsidiary Company, and Parent owes Subsidiary $20,000 on a note payable. Complete the following consolidation work sheet.

	Parent Company	Subsidiary Company	Eliminations Debit	Eliminations Credit	Consolidated Amounts
Assets					
Cash	7,000	4,000			
Note receivable from Parent	—	20,000			
Investment in Subsidiary	85,000	—			
Other assets	108,000	99,000			
Total	200,000	123,000			
Liabilities and Stockholders' Equity					
Accounts payable	15,000	8,000			
Notes payable	20,000	30,000			
Common stock	120,000	60,000			
Retained earnings	45,000	25,000			
Total	200,000	123,000			

▶ **Answers**

1. **a.** Equity
   b. Available-for-sale
   c. Consolidation

2. Report the investments at fair value: $64,730, as follows:

Stock	Investment Cost	Current Market Value
DuPont	$ 5,000	$ 5,500
ExxonMobil	61,200	53,000
Procter & Gamble	3,680	6,230
Totals	$69,880	$64,730

Adjusting entry:

Unrealized Loss on Investments ($69,880 – $64,730)	5,150	
Allowance to Adjust Investment to Market		5,150
To adjust investments to fair value.		

3.

Equity-Method Investment			
Cost	67,900	Dividends	22,000**
Income	32,000*		
Balance	77,900		

* $80,000 × .40 = $32,000
** $55,000 × .40 = $22,000

4. Consolidation work sheet:

	Parent Company	Subsidiary Company	Eliminations Debit	Eliminations Credit	Consolidated Amounts
Assets					
Cash	7,000	4,000			11,000
Note receivable from Parent	—	20,000		(a) 20,000	—
Investment in Subsidiary	85,000	—		(b) 85,000	—
Other assets	108,000	99,000			207,000
Total	200,000	123,000			218,000
Liabilities and Stockholders' Equity					
Accounts payable	15,000	8,000			23,000
Notes payable	20,000	30,000	(a) 20,000		30,000
Common stock	120,000	60,000	(b) 60,000		120,000
Retained earnings	45,000	25,000	(b) 25,000		45,000
Total	200,000	123,000	105,000	105,000	218,000

Consolidation of Foreign Subsidiaries

Many U.S. companies conduct a large part of their business abroad. Intel, General Electric, and PepsiCo, among others, are very active in other countries. In fact, Intel earns 80% of its revenue outside the United States. Exhibit 8-8 shows the approximate percentages of international revenues for these companies.

Global View

EXHIBIT 8-8 | Extent of International Business

Company	Percentage of International Revenues
Intel..	80%
General Electric......................	53%
PepsiCo..................................	40%

Foreign Currencies and Exchange Rates

Most countries use their own national currency. An exception is the European Union nations—France, Germany, Italy, Belgium, and others, use a common currency, the *euro*, whose symbol is €. If Intel, a U.S. company, sells computer processors to software developers in France, will Intel receive U.S. dollars or euros? If the transaction is in dollars, the company in France must buy dollars to pay Intel in U.S. currency. If the transaction is in euros, then Intel will collect euros and must sell euros for dollars.

The price of one nation's currency can be stated in terms of another country's monetary unit. This measure of one currency against another is called the **foreign-currency exchange rate**. In Exhibit 8-9, the dollar value of a euro is $1.44. This means that one euro can be bought for $1.44. Other currencies are also listed in Exhibit 8-9.

EXHIBIT 8-9 | Foreign Currency Exchange Rates

Country	Monetary Unit	U.S. Dollar Value	Country	Monetary Unit	U.S. Dollar Value
Brazil............	Real (R)...............	$0.63	United Kingdom.......	Pound (£).........	$1.63
Canada.........	Dollar ($)...........	1.04	China	Yuan (元)	0.153
France	Euro (€)..............	1.44	Japan........................	Yen (¥)	0.012
Germany......	Euro (€)..............	1.44	Mexico.....................	Peso (P)	0.085

Source: *www.x-rates.com* (April 14, 2011).

We can convert the cost of an item stated in one currency to its cost in a second currency. We call this conversion a *translation*. Suppose an item costs 200 euros. To compute its cost in dollars, we multiply the euro amount by the conversion rate: 200 euros × $1.44 = $288.

Two main factors affect the price (the exchange rate) of a particular currency:

1. The ratio of a country's imports to its exports

2. The rate of return available in the country's capital markets

The Import/Export Ratio. Japanese exports often exceed Japan's imports. Customers of Japanese companies must buy yen (the Japanese unit of currency) to pay for their purchases. This strong demand drives up the price of the yen. In contrast, the United States imports more goods than it exports. Americans must sell dollars to buy the foreign currencies needed to pay for the foreign goods. As the supply of dollars increases, the price of the dollar falls.

The Rate of Return. The rate of return available in a country's capital markets affects the amount of investment funds flowing into the country. When rates of return are high in a politically stable country such as the United States, international investors buy stocks, bonds, and real estate in that country. This activity increases the demand for the nation's currency and drives up its exchange rate.

Currencies are often described as "strong" or "weak." The exchange rate of a **strong currency** is rising relative to other nations' currencies. The exchange rate of a **weak currency** is falling relative to other currencies.

The Internet Web site www.x-rates.com lists the exchange rate for the British pound as $1.63 on April 14, 2011. On April 18, that rate may rise to $1.65. We would say that the dollar has weakened against the pound. The pound has thus become more expensive, making travel and conducting business in England more expensive for Americans.

The Foreign-Currency Translation Adjustment

The process of translating a foreign subsidiary's financial statements into dollars usually creates a **foreign-currency translation adjustment**. This item appears in the consolidated financial statements of most multinational companies and is reported as part of other comprehensive income. The statement of other comprehensive income will be discussed in Chapter 11.

A translation adjustment arises due to changes in the foreign exchange rate over time. In general,

▶ *assets* and *liabilities* are translated into dollars at the current exchange rate on the date of the statements.
▶ *stockholders' equity* is translated into dollars at older, historical exchange rates. Paid-in capital accounts are translated at the historical exchange rate when the subsidiary was acquired. Retained earnings are translated at the average exchange rates applicable over the period in which interest in the subsidiary has been held.

This difference in exchange rates creates an out-of-balance condition on the balance sheet. The translation adjustment brings the balance sheet back into balance. Let's see how the translation adjustment works.

Suppose Intel has an Italian subsidiary whose financial statements are expressed in euros (the European currency). Intel must consolidate the Italian subsidiary's financials into its own statements. When Intel acquired the Italian company in 2009, a euro was worth $1.35 (assumed). When the Italian firm earned its retained income during 2009–2012, the average exchange rate was $1.30 (assumed). On the balance sheet date in 2012, a euro is worth only $1.20 (assumed). Exhibit 8-10 shows how to translate the Italian company's balance sheet into dollars.

EXHIBIT 8-10 | Translation of a Foreign Currency Balance Sheet into Dollars

Italian Imports, Inc., Accounts	Euros	Exchange Rate	Dollars
Assets	800,000	$1.20	$960,000
Liabilities	500,000	1.20	$600,000
Stockholders' equity			
Common stock	100,000	1.35	135,000
Retained earnings	200,000	1.30	260,000
Accumulated other comprehensive income:			
Foreign-currency translation adjustment			(35,000)
	800,000		$960,000

The *foreign-currency translation adjustment* is the balancing amount that brings the dollar amount of liabilities and equity of a foreign subsidiary into agreement with the dollar amount of total assets (in Exhibit 8-10, total assets equal $960,000). Only after the translation adjustment of $35,000 do total liabilities and equity equal total assets stated in dollars.

What caused the negative translation adjustment? The euro weakened after the acquisition of the Italian company.

- ▶ When Intel acquired the foreign subsidiary in 2009, a euro was worth $1.35.
- ▶ When the Italian company earned its income during 2009 through 2012, the average exchange rate was $1.30.
- ▶ On the balance sheet date in 2012, a euro is worth only $1.20.
- ▶ Thus, the Italian company's equity (assets minus liabilities) is translated into only $360,000 ($960,000 – $600,000).
- ▶ To bring stockholders' equity to $360,000 requires a $35,000 negative adjustment.

A negative translation adjustment is like a loss, reported as a negative item in the statement of other comprehensive income. Losses and gains from translation adjustments eventually are transferred to accumulated other comprehensive income in the stockholders' equity section of the balance sheet, as shown in Exhibit 8-10. The Italian firm's dollar figures in Exhibit 8-10 reflect what Intel would include in its consolidated balance sheet. The consolidation procedures would follow those illustrated in Exhibit 8-7.

Report Investing Activities on the Statement of Cash Flows

Report Investing Activities on the Statement of Cash Flows

Investing activities include many types of transactions. In Chapter 7, we covered the purchase and sale of long-term assets such as plant and equipment. In this chapter, we examine investments in stocks and bonds.

Exhibit 8-11 provides excerpts from Intel's 2010 consolidated statement of cash flows. During 2010, Intel sold available-for-sale investments and received $13.1 billion in cash. Intel purchased available-for-sale investments for $17.7 billion and sold equity-method investments for $200 million. These investing activities relate directly to the topics you studied in this chapter.

EXHIBIT 8-11 | Intel Corporation Investing Activities on the Statement of Cash Flows

Intel Corporation
Consolidated Statement of Cash Flows (Partial, Adapted)

(In billions)	2010
Cash flows provided by (used for) investing activities:	
Sales of available-for-sale investments	$ 13.1
Purchases of available-for-sale investments	(17.7)
Additions to property, plant, and equipment	(5.2)
Sales of equity-method investments	0.2
Other uses of cash	(0.9)
Net cash (used for) investing activities	$(10.5)

Explain the Impact of the Time Value of Money on Certain Types of Investments

6

Explain the impact of the time value of money on certain types of investments

Which would you rather have: $1,000 received today, or $1,000 received a year from now? A logical person would answer: "I'd rather have the cash now, because if I get it now, I can invest it at some interest rate so that a year in the future I'll have more." The term **future value** means the sum of money that a given current investment will be "worth" at a specified time in the future assuming a certain interest rate. The term *time value of money* refers to the fact that money earns interest over time. *Interest* is the cost of using money. To borrowers, interest is the fee paid to the lender for the period of the loan. To lenders, interest is the revenue earned from allowing someone else to use our money for a period of time.

Whether making investments or borrowing money long term, we must always recognize the interest we receive or pay. Otherwise, we overlook an important part of the transaction. Suppose you invest $4,545 in corporate bonds that pay 10% interest each year. After one year, the value of your investment has grown to $5,000, as shown in the following diagram:

EXHIBIT 8-12 | Future Value of an Investment

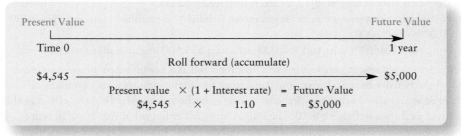

The difference between your original (present) investment ($4,545) and the future value of the investment ($5,000) is the amount of interest revenue you will earn during the year ($455). Interest becomes more important as the time period lengthens because the amount of interest depends on the span of time the money is invested. The time value of money plays a key role in measuring the value of certain long-term investments as well as long-term debt.

If the money were invested for five years, you would have to perform five calculations like the one described above. You would also have to consider the compound interest that your investment is earning. *Compound interest* is not only the interest you earn on your principal amount, but also the interest you receive on the interest you have already earned. Most business applications include compound interest.

To calculate the future value of an investment, we need three inputs: (1) the *amount of initial payment (or receipt)*, (2) the length of *time* between investment and future receipt (or *payment*), and (3) the *interest rate*. The following table shows the interest revenue earned on the original $4,545 investment each year for five years at 10%:

End of Year	Interest	Future Value
0	—	$4,545
1	$4,545 × 0.10 = $455	5,000
2	5,000 × 0.10 = 500	5,500
3	5,500 × 0.10 = 550	6,050
4	6,050 × 0.10 = 605	6,655
5	6,655 × 0.10 = 666	7,321

As shown in the table, earning 10% compounded annually, a $4,545 investment grows to $5,000 at the end of one year, to $5,500 at the end of two years, and $7,321 at the end of five years.

Present Value

Often a person knows or is able to estimate a future amount and needs to determine the related present value (PV). The term **present value** means the value on a given date of a future payment or series of future payments, discounted to reflect the time value of money. In Exhibit 8-12, present value and future value are on opposite ends of the same time line. Suppose an investment promises to pay you $5,000 at the *end* of one year. How much would you pay *now* to acquire this investment? You would be willing to pay the present value of the $5,000 future amount, which, at 10% interest, is $4,545.

Like future value, present value depends on three factors: (1) the *amount of payment (or receipt)*, (2) the length of *time* between investment and future receipt (or *payment*), and (3) the *interest rate*. The process of computing a present value is called *discounting* because the present value is *less* than the future value.

In our investment example, the future receipt is $5,000. The investment period is one year. Assume that you demand an annual interest rate of 10% on your investment. With all three factors specified, you can compute the present value of $5,000 at 10% for one year:

$$\text{Present value} = \frac{\text{Future value}}{1 + \text{Interest rate}} = \frac{\$5,000}{1.10} = \$4,545$$

By turning the data around into a future-value problem, we can verify the present-value computation:

Amount invested (present value)	$4,545
Expected earnings ($4,545 × 0.10)	455
Amount to be received one year from now (future value)	$5,000

This example illustrates that present value and future value are based on variations of the same equation:

$$\text{Future value} = \text{Present value} \times (1 + \text{Interest rate})^n$$

$$\text{Present value} = \frac{\text{Future value}}{(1 + \text{Interest rate})^n}$$

Where n = number of periods

If the $5,000 is to be received two years from now, you will pay only $4,132 for the investment, as shown in Exhibit 8-13. By turning the data around, we verify that $4,132 accumulates to $5,000 at 10% for two years:

Amount invested (present value)	$4,132
Expected earnings for first year ($4,132 × 0.10).........................	413
Value of investment after one year	4,545
Expected earnings for second year ($4,545 × 0.10)	455
Amount to be received two years from now (future value)	$5,000

$$\text{Formula: Present value} = \frac{\text{Future value}}{(1 + \text{Interest rate})^n}$$

$$4,132 = \frac{5,000}{(1 + 0.10)^2}$$

$$\text{Future value} = \text{Present value} \times (1 + \text{Interest rate})^n$$

$$5,000 = \$4,132 \times (1 + 0.10)^2$$

EXHIBIT 8-13 | Present Value: An Example

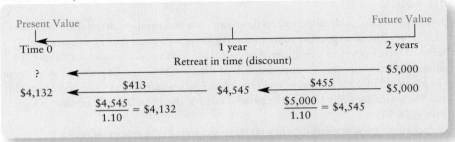

You would pay $4,132—the present value of $5,000—to receive the $5,000 future amount at the end of two years at 10% per year. The $868 difference between the amount invested ($4,132) and the amount to be received ($5,000) is the return on the investment, the sum of the two interest receipts: $413 + $455 = $868.

Present-Value Tables

We have shown the simple formula for computing present value. However, figuring present value "by hand" for investments spanning many years is time-consuming and presents too many opportunities for arithmetic errors. Present-value tables simplify our work. Let's reexamine our examples of present value by using Exhibit 8-14, Present Value of $1.

EXHIBIT 8-14 | Present Value of $1

Present Value of $1

Periods	4%	5%	6%	7%	8%	10%	12%	14%	16%
1	0.962	0.952	0.943	0.935	0.926	0.909	0.893	0.877	0.862
2	0.925	0.907	0.890	0.873	0.857	0.826	0.797	0.769	0.743
3	0.889	0.864	0.840	0.816	0.794	0.751	0.712	0.675	0.641
4	0.855	0.823	0.792	0.763	0.735	0.683	0.636	0.592	0.552
5	0.822	0.784	0.747	0.713	0.681	0.621	0.567	0.519	0.476
6	0.790	0.746	0.705	0.666	0.630	0.564	0.507	0.456	0.410
7	0.760	0.711	0.665	0.623	0.583	0.513	0.452	0.400	0.354
8	0.731	0.677	0.627	0.582	0.540	0.467	0.404	0.351	0.305
9	0.703	0.645	0.592	0.544	0.500	0.424	0.361	0.308	0.263
10	0.676	0.614	0.558	0.508	0.463	0.386	0.322	0.270	0.227
11	0.650	0.585	0.527	0.475	0.429	0.350	0.287	0.237	0.195
12	0.625	0.557	0.497	0.444	0.397	0.319	0.257	0.208	0.168
13	0.601	0.530	0.469	0.415	0.368	0.290	0.229	0.182	0.145
14	0.577	0.505	0.442	0.388	0.340	0.263	0.205	0.160	0.125
15	0.555	0.481	0.417	0.362	0.315	0.239	0.183	0.140	0.108
16	0.534	0.458	0.394	0.339	0.292	0.218	0.163	0.123	0.093
17	0.513	0.436	0.371	0.317	0.270	0.198	0.146	0.108	0.080
18	0.494	0.416	0.350	0.296	0.250	0.180	0.130	0.095	0.069
19	0.475	0.396	0.331	0.277	0.232	0.164	0.116	0.083	0.060
20	0.456	0.377	0.312	0.258	0.215	0.149	0.104	0.073	0.051

For the 10% investment for one year, we find the junction of the 10% column and row 1 in Exhibit 8-14. The figure 0.909 is computed as follows: 1/1.10 = 0.909. This work has been done for us, and only the present values are given in the table. To figure the present value for $5,000, we multiply 0.909 by $5,000. The result is $4,545, which matches the result we obtained by hand.

For the two-year investment, we read down the 10% column and across row 2. We multiply 0.826 (computed as 0.909/1.10 = 0.826) by $5,000 and get $4,130, which confirms our earlier computation of $4,132 (the difference is due to rounding in the present-value table). Using the table, we can compute the present value of any single future amount.

Present Value of an Annuity

Return to the investment example at the top of page 486. That investment provided the investor with only a single future receipt ($5,000 at the end of two years). *Annuity investments* provide multiple receipts of an equal amount at fixed intervals over the investment's duration.

Consider an investment that promises *annual* cash receipts of $10,000 to be received at the end of three years. Assume that you demand a 12% return on your investment. What is the investment's present value? That is, what would you pay today to acquire the investment? The investment spans three periods, and you would pay the sum of three present values. The computation follows.

Year	Annual Cash Receipt	Present Value of $1 at 12% (Exhibit 8-14)	Present Value of Annual Cash Receipt
1	$10,000	0.893	$ 8,930
2	10,000	0.797	7,970
3	10,000	0.712	7,120
Total present value of investment...............			$24,020

The present value of this annuity is $24,020. By paying this amount today, you will receive $10,000 at the end of each of the three years while earning 12% on your investment.

This example illustrates repetitive computations of the three future amounts, a time consuming process. One way to ease the computational burden is to add the three present values of $1 (0.893 + 0.797 + 0.712) and multiply their sum (2.402) by the annual cash receipt ($10,000) to obtain the present value of the annuity ($10,000 × 2.402 = $24,020).

An easier approach is to use a present-value-of-an-annuity table. Exhibit 8-15 shows the present value of $1 to be received periodically for a given number of periods. The present value of a three-period annuity at 12% is 2.402 (the junction of row 3 and the 12% column). Thus, $10,000 received annually at the end of each of three years, discounted at 12%, is $24,020 ($10,000 × 2.402), which is the present value.

EXHIBIT 8-15 | Present Value of Annuity of $1

Present Value of Annuity of $1

Periods	4%	5%	6%	7%	8%	10%	12%	14%	16%
1	0.962	0.952	0.943	0.935	0.926	0.909	0.893	0.877	0.862
2	1.886	1.859	1.833	1.808	1.783	1.736	1.690	1.647	1.605
3	2.775	2.723	2.673	2.624	2.577	2.487	2.402	2.322	2.246
4	3.630	3.546	3.465	3.387	3.312	3.170	3.037	2.914	2.798
5	4.452	4.329	4.212	4.100	3.993	3.791	3.605	3.433	3.274
6	5.242	5.076	4.917	4.767	4.623	4.355	4.111	3.889	3.685
7	6.002	5.786	5.582	5.389	5.206	4.868	4.564	4.288	4.039
8	6.733	6.463	6.210	5.971	5.747	5.335	4.968	4.639	4.344
9	7.435	7.108	6.802	6.515	6.247	5.759	5.328	4.946	4.608
10	8.111	7.722	7.360	7.024	6.710	6.145	5.650	5.216	4.833
11	8.760	8.306	7.887	7.499	7.139	6.495	5.938	5.453	5.029
12	9.385	8.863	8.384	7.943	7.536	6.814	6.194	5.660	5.197
13	9.986	9.394	8.853	8.358	7.904	7.103	6.424	5.842	5.342
14	10.563	9.899	9.295	8.745	8.244	7.367	6.628	6.002	5.468
15	11.118	10.380	9.712	9.108	8.559	7.606	6.811	6.142	5.575
16	11.652	10.838	10.106	9.447	8.851	7.824	6.974	6.265	5.669
17	12.166	11.274	10.477	9.763	9.122	8.022	7.120	6.373	5.749
18	12.659	11.690	10.828	10.059	9.372	8.201	7.250	6.467	5.818
19	13.134	12.085	11.158	10.336	9.604	8.365	7.366	6.550	5.877
20	13.590	12.462	11.470	10.594	9.818	8.514	7.469	6.623	5.929

Using Microsoft Excel to Calculate Present Value

While tables such as Exhibits 8-14 and 15 are helpful, they are limited to the interest rates in the columns or the periods of time in the rows. Using a computer program like Microsoft Excel provides an infinite range of interest rates and periods. For that reason, most businesspeople solve present value problems quickly and easily using Excel rather than tables.

▶ **To compute the present value of a single payment,** open an Excel spreadsheet to a blank cell. In the cell, enter the following formula:

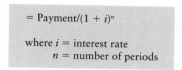

$$= \text{Payment}/(1 + i)^n$$

where i = interest rate
n = number of periods

▶ Use the ^ symbol to indicate the exponent. To illustrate, suppose you are expecting to receive a $500,000 payment four years from now, and suppose that market interest rates are 8%. You would enter the following in Excel:

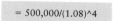

$$= 500{,}000/(1.08)^{\wedge}4$$

You should calculate a present value of $367,515.

▶ **To compute the present value of an annuity (stream of payments),** open an Excel spreadsheet to a blank cell. Click the insert function button (f_x). Then select the "Financial" category from the drop down box. The following box will appear:

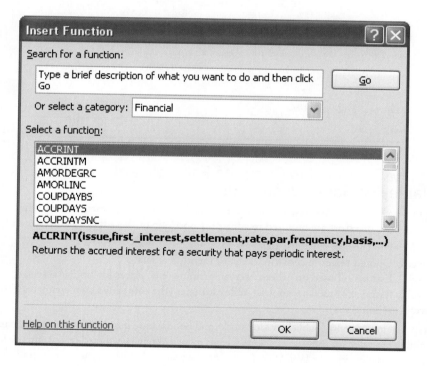

Scroll down the function list and select "PV." A description of the PV function will display beneath the function list, along with the following line: **PV(rate,nper,pmt,fv,type)**. Double-click PV, and the following box will appear.

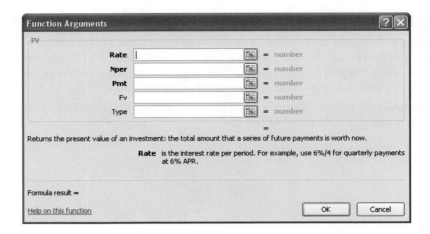

Enter the interest rate, the number of periods, and the payment (as a negative number). The present value of the annuity will appear at the bottom of the box after the "=" sign.

To illustrate, notice that we have assumed an investment that is expected to return $20,000 per year for 20 years and a market interest rate of 8%. The net present value of this annuity is $196,362.95, computed with Excel as follows:

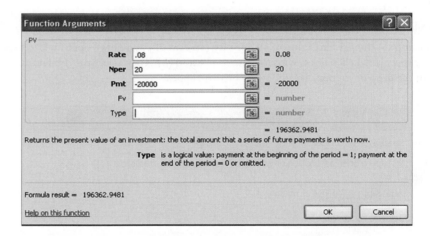

Using the PV Model to Compute Fair Value of Available-for-Sale Investments

Earlier in the chapter, we discussed GAAP for available-for-sale investments. Recall that, at the end of each year, investors are required to adjust the portfolio of these types of investments to fair values, using one of three different approaches (in this order of preference):

- ► Level 1: Quoted prices in active markets for identical assets
- ► Level 2: Estimates based on other observable inputs (e.g., prices for similar assets)
- ► Level 3: Estimates based on unobservable estimates (the company's own estimates based on certain assumptions)

Some types of investments (publicly traded stocks and bonds) have quoted prices in active markets. Determining fair value for these investments is easy: merely obtain the quoted price from the financial media (usually the Internet or *Wall Street Journal* on the year-end). Other types of non-traditional investments (e.g., notes, bonds or stocks, contracts, annuities) may not have daily quoted market prices in active markets. Therefore, the company may use financial models that predict expected cash flows from these investments over a period of time and discount those cash flows back to the balance sheet date. These are called level 2 or level 3 approaches to asset valuation. Use of these models may require a great deal of sophisticated judgment about the amount and timing of cash flows and sometimes a number of subjective estimates such as interest rates. Models such as these are quite sensitive to changes in these judgments and estimates. Let's illustrate with a simple example.

Present Value of an Investment in Bonds

The present value of a bond—its market price—is the present value of the future principal amount at maturity plus the present value of the future stated interest payments. The principal is a *single amount* to be received by the investor and paid by the debtor at maturity. The interest is an *annuity* because it occurs periodically.

Let's compute the present value of 9% five-year bonds of **Southwest Airlines** from the standpoint of an investor. The face value of the bonds is $100,000, and the face interest rate is 9% annually. Since bonds typically pay interest twice per year, these bonds pay 4 1/2% semiannually. At issuance, the market interest rate is as assumed to be 10% annually, but it is computed at 5% semiannually (again, because the bonds pay interest twice a year). Therefore, the effective (market) interest rate for each of the 10 semiannual periods is 5%. We thus use 5% in computing the present value of the maturity and of the interest. The market price of these bonds is $96,149, as follows:

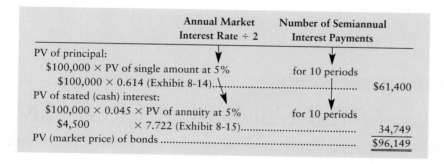

	Annual Market Interest Rate ÷ 2	Number of Semiannual Interest Payments	
PV of principal:			
$100,000 × PV of single amount at 5%		for 10 periods	
$100,000 × 0.614 (Exhibit 8-14)			$61,400
PV of stated (cash) interest:			
$100,000 × 0.045 × PV of annuity at 5%		for 10 periods	
$4,500 × 7.722 (Exhibit 8-15)			34,749
PV (market price) of bonds			$96,149

Using the Excel PV function as outlined previously, the inputs are as follows:[2]

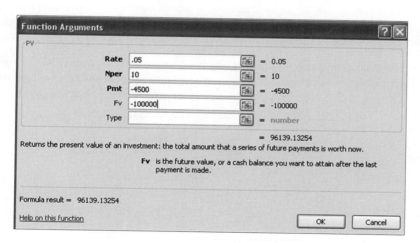

Function Arguments		? X
PV		
Rate	.05	= 0.05
Nper	10	= 10
Pmt	-4500	= -4500
Fv	-100000	= -100000
Type		= number
		= 96139.13254

Returns the present value of an investment: the total amount that a series of future payments is worth now.

   Fv   is the future value, or a cash balance you want to attain after the last payment is made.

Formula result = 96139.13254

Help on this function   OK   Cancel

The fair value of the Southwest bonds on the investor's balance sheet would be $96,149.[3]

Amounts calculated from PV table ($96,149) and EXCEL ($96,139) differ merely by rounding. We discuss accounting for these bonds from the debtor's point of view in Chapter 9 on pages 532–535. It may be helpful for you to reread this section before you study those pages.

---

[2]Assume that all payments of interest and principal occur at the end of the period, rather than the beginning. Therefore, it is appropriate to leave the Excel table field labeled "Type" blank.

[3]In the real world, bond investments in public companies are typically classified as level 1 investments, because they are usually traded in active markets with quoted prices. We use an investment in bonds here to illustrate the valuation computation for level 3 investments because bonds are easier to understand than the more complex types of level 3 investments. The process of estimating fair value using discounted cash flow models is similar for all types of investments.

Intel reports fair value of its investments in the footnotes of its 2010 financial statements as follows:

	Level 1	Level 2	Level 3	Total
Marketable equity securities	785	223		1,008
Other long-term assets	187	2,736	103	3,026

Some of the level 2 and level 3 fair value estimates use discounted cash flow projections such as the ones we have described in this section.

END-OF-CHAPTER SUMMARY PROBLEMS

1. Translate the balance sheet of the Brazilian subsidiary of **Wrangler Corporation**, a U.S. company, into dollars. When Wrangler acquired this subsidiary, the exchange rate of the Brazilian currency, the real, was $0.40. The average exchange rate applicable to retained earnings is $0.41. The real's current exchange rate is $0.43.

Before performing the translation, predict whether the translation adjustment will be positive or negative. Does this situation generate a foreign-currency translation gain or loss? Give your reasons.

	Reals
Assets	900,000
Liabilities	600,000
Stockholders' equity:	
Common stock	30,000
Retained earnings	270,000
	900,000

▶ Answer

Translation of foreign-currency balance sheet:

This situation will generate a *positive* translation adjustment, which is like a gain. The gain occurs because the real's current exchange rate, which is used to translate net assets (assets minus liabilities), exceeds the historical exchange rates used for stockholders' equity.

The calculation follows:

	Reals	Exchange Rate	Dollars
Assets...	900,000	0.43	$387,000
Liabilities	600,000	0.43	$258,000
Stockholders' equity:			
Common stock......................	30,000	0.40	12,000
Retained earnings.................	270,000	0.41	110,700
Accumulated other comprehensive income:			
Foreign-currency translation adjustment	—		6,300
	900,000		$387,000

2. You have invested in a commercial building that you are leasing to a national retail chain. The tenant has signed a 10-year noncancelable lease agreement. You expect to collect $8,000 per month for the full term of the lease. What is the present value of this investment if prevailing interest rates are 12%, compounded monthly?

► Answer

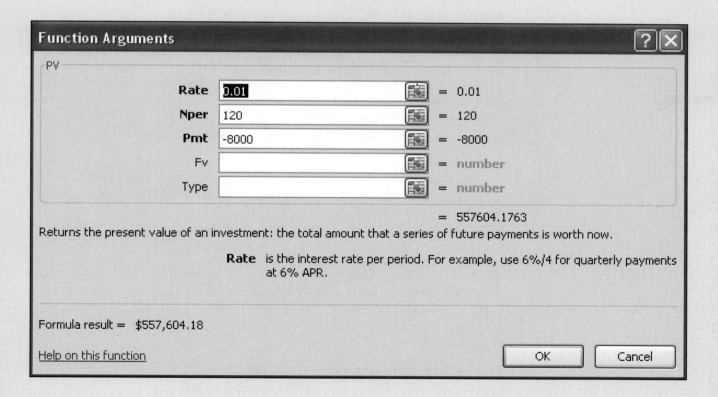

The interest compounds monthly, so it is appropriate to use 120 periods, the number of months in the lease, rather than 10 years. In addition, the yearly interest rate must be adjusted to a monthly rate of 1% (12% ÷ 12). The net present value of this lease is $557,604. Note that you cannot use Exhibit 8-15 since it does not include 1% and does not have 120 periods. The Excel PV function easily gives the result.

REVIEW | Long-Term Investments & the Time Value of Money

Quick Check (Answers are given on page 516.)

1. Mac's investment in less than 2% of Mobil's stock, which Mac expects to hold for three years and then sell, is what type of investment?

   a. Available-for-sale
   b. Equity

   c. Consolidation
   d. Trading

2. Langolis Corporation purchased an available-for-sale investment in 1,600 shares of Southwest Supplies stock for $26 per share. On the next balance-sheet date, Southwest Supplies stock is quoted at $29 per share. Langolis' *balance sheet* should report

   a. investments of $46,400.
   b. investments of $41,600.

   c. unrealized loss of $4,800.
   d. unrealized gain of $41,600.

3. Use the Langolis Corporation data in question 2. Langolis' *income statement* should report

   a. unrealized loss of $4,800.
   b. investments of $41,600.

   c. unrealized gain of $4,800.
   d. nothing, because Langolis hasn't sold the investment.

4. Langolis Corporation purchased an available-for-sale investment in 1,600 shares of Southwest Supplies for $26 per share. On the next balance sheet date, Southwest Supplies stock is quoted at $29 per share. Langolis sold the Southwest Supplies stock for $55,000 two months later. Langolis *income statement* for the period of the sale should report a(n)

   a. unrealized gain of $4,800.
   b. gain on sale of $8,600.

   c. gain on sale of $13,400.
   d. investments of $55,000.

5. Sheridan Moving & Storage Co. paid $80,000 for 25% of the common stock of Holland Co. Holland earned net income of $60,000 and paid dividends of $40,000. The carrying value of Sheridan's investment in Holland is

   a. $80,000.
   b. $140,000.

   c. $100,000.
   d. $85,000.

6. Shore, Inc., owns 80% of Rockwall Corporation, and Rockwall owns 80% of Smith Company. During 2012, these companies' net incomes are as follows before any consolidations:

   ▶ Shore, $160,000
   ▶ Rockwall, $70,000
   ▶ Smith, $40,000

   How much net income should Shore report for 2012?

   a. $241,600
   b. $270,000

   c. $248,000
   d. $160,000

7. Majestic, Inc., holds an investment in Cromwell bonds that pay interest each October 31. Majestic's *balance sheet* at December 31 should report

   a. interest expense.
   b. interest revenue.

   c. interest receivable.
   d. interest payable.

8. You are taking a vacation to Germany, and you buy euros for $1.65. On your return, you cash in your unused euros for $1.40. During your vacation,

a. the dollar rose against the euro.

b. the euro gained value.

c. the euro rose against the dollar.

d. the dollar lost value.

9. Arnold Financing leases airplanes to airline companies. Arnold has just signed a 10-year lease agreement that requires annual lease payments of $1,000,000. What is the present value of the lease using a 10% interest rate?

a. $6,145,000

b. $61,450,000

c. $3,860,000

d. $386,000

10. Sunnyside owns numerous foreign subsidiary companies. When Sunnyside consolidates its Swiss subsidiary, Sunnyside should translate the subsidiary's assets into dollars at the

a. current exchange rate.

b. historical exchange rate when Sunnyside purchased the Swiss company.

c. average exchange rate during the period Sunnyside owned the Swiss subsidiary.

d. none of the above. There's no need to translate the subsidiary's assets into dollars.

Accounting Vocabulary

available-for-sale securities (p. 468) All investments not classified as held-to-maturity or trading securities.

consolidated financial statements (p. 475) Financial statements of the parent company plus those of majority-owned subsidiaries as if the combination were a single legal entity.

controlling (majority) interest (p. 475) Ownership of more than 50% of an investee company's voting stock.

equity method (p. 472) The method used to account for investments in which the investor has 20–50% of the investee's voting stock and can significantly influence the decisions of the investee.

fair value (p. 468) The amount that a seller would receive on the sale of an investment to a willing purchaser on a given date. Securities and available-for-sale securities are valued at fair market values on the balance sheet date. Other assets may be recorded at fair market value on occasion.

foreign-currency exchange rate (p. 481) The measure of one country's currency against another country's currency.

foreign-currency translation adjustment (p. 482) The balancing figure that brings the dollar amount of the total liabilities and stockholders' equity of the foreign subsidiary into agreement with the dollar amount of its total assets.

future value (p. 484) Measures the future sum of money that a given current investment is "worth" at a specified time in the future assuming a certain interest rate.

held-to-maturity investments (p. 466) Bonds and notes that an investor intends to hold until maturity.

long-term investments (p. 465) Any investment that does not meet the criteria of a short-term investment; any investment that the investor expects to hold longer than a year or that is not readily marketable.

noncontrolling (minority) interest (p. 477) A subsidiary company's equity that is held by stockholders other than the parent company (i.e., less than 50%).

parent company (p. 475) An investor company that owns more than 50% of the voting stock of a subsidiary company.

present value (p. 485) The value on a given date of a future payment or series of future payments, discounted to reflect the time value of money.

short-term investments (p. 465) Investment that a company plans to hold for 1 year or less. Also called *marketable securities*.

strong currency (p. 482) A currency whose exchange rate is rising relative to other nations' currencies.

subsidiary (p. 475) An investee company in which a parent company owns more than 50% of the voting stock.

weak currency (p. 482) A currency whose exchange rate is falling relative to that of other nations.

ASSESS YOUR PROGRESS

Short Exercises

S8-1 (*Learning Objective 2: Analyze and report an available-for-sale investment*) Mail 4 You completed these long-term available-for-sale investment transactions during 2012:

2012	
Apr 10	Purchased 600 shares of Tycon stock, paying $17 per share. Mail 4 You intends to hold the investment for the indefinite future.
Jul 22	Received a cash dividend of $1.24 per share on the Tycon stock.
Dec 31	Adjusted the Tycon investment to its current market value of $5,500.

1. Journalize Mail 4 You's investment transactions. Explanations are not required.
2. Assume the Tycon stock is Mail 4 You's only investment. Explain how these transactions will be reflected on Mail 4 You's Income Statement and its Statement of Other Comprehensive Income.
3. Show how to report the investment and any unrealized gain or loss on Mail 4 You's balance sheet at December 31, 2012. Ignore income tax.

S8-2 (*Learning Objective 2: Account for the sale of an available-for-sale investment*) Use the data given in Short Exercise 8-1. On May 21, 2013, Mail 4 You sold its investment in Tycon stock for $23 per share.

1. Journalize the sale. No explanation is required.
2. How does the gain or loss that you recorded here differ from the gain or loss that was recorded at December 31, 2012?

S8-3 (*Learning Objective 3: Analyze and report an investment in an affiliate*) Suppose on February 1, 2012, Western Motors paid $380 million for a 35% investment in Phase Motors. Assume Phase earned net income of $40 million and paid cash dividends of $20 million during 2012.

1. What method should Western Motors use to account for the investment in Phase? Give your reason.
2. Journalize these three transactions on the books of Western Motors. Show all amounts in millions of dollars and include an explanation for each entry.
3. Post to the Long-Term Investment T-account. What is its balance after all the transactions are posted?

S8-4 (*Learning Objective 3: Account for the sale of an equity-method investment*) Use the data given in Short Exercise 8-3. Assume that in November 2013, Western Motors sold half its investment in Phase Motors. The sale price was $130 million. Compute Western Motors' gain or loss on the sale.

S8-5 (*Learning Objective 4: Define and explain controlling interests and consolidated financial statements*) Answer these questions about consolidation accounting:

1. Define "parent company." Define "subsidiary company."
2. How do consolidated financial statements differ from the financial statements of a single company?
3. Which company's name appears on the consolidated financial statements? How much of the subsidiary's shares must the parent own before reporting consolidated statements?

S8-6 (*Learning Objective 4: Explain goodwill and minority interest*) Two accounts that arise from consolidation accounting are goodwill and noncontrolling interest.

1. What is goodwill, and how does it arise? Which company reports goodwill, the parent or the subsidiary? Where is goodwill reported?
2. What is noncontrolling interest, and which company reports it, the parent or the subsidiary? Where is noncontrolling interest reported?

S8-7 (*Learning Objective 1: Analyze and report investments in held-to-maturity securities*) North Mark (NM) owns vast amounts of corporate bonds. Suppose that on June 30, 2012, NM buys $800,000 of CitiSide bonds at a price of 102. The CitiSide bonds pay cash interest at the annual rate of 7% and mature at the end of five years.

1. How much did NM pay to purchase the bond investment? How much will NM collect when the bond investment matures?
2. How much cash interest will NM receive each year from CitiSide?
3. Will NM's annual interest revenue on the bond investment be more or less than the amount of cash interest received each year? Give your reason.
4. Compute NM's annual interest revenue on this bond investment. Use the straight-line method to amortize the investment.

S8-8 (*Learning Objective 1: Record held-to-maturity investment transactions*) Return to Short Exercise 8-7, the North Mark (NM) investment in CitiSide bonds. Journalize the following on NM's books:

a. Purchase of the bond investment on June 30, 2012. NM expects to hold the investment to maturity.
b. Receipt of semiannual cash interest on December 31, 2012.
c. Amortization of the bonds on December 31, 2012. Use the straight-line method.
d. Collection of the investment's face value at the maturity date on June 30, 2017. (Assume the receipt of 2017 interest and the amortization of bonds for 2017 have already been recorded, so ignore these entries.)

S8-9 (*Learning Objective 6: Calculate present value*) Calculate the present value of the following amounts:

1. $10,000 at the end of five years at 8%
2. $10,000 a year at the end of the next five years at 8%

S8-10 (*Learning Objective 6: Calculate the present value of an investment*) Artest Lease leased a car. Artest will receive $300 a month for 60 months.

1. What is the present value of the lease if the annual interest rate in the lease in 12%? Use the PV function in Excel to compute the present value.
2. What is the present value of the lease if the car can be sold for $5,000 at the end of five years?

S8-11 (*Learning Objective 5: Report investing transactions on the statement of cash flows*) Companies divide their cash flows into three categories for reporting on the cash flow statement.

1. List the three categories of cash flows in the order they appear on the cash flow statement. Which category of cash flows is most closely related to this chapter?
2. Identify two types of transactions that companies report as cash flows from investing activities.

S8-12 *(Learning Objective 5: Using a statement of cash flows)* Excerpts from The XYZ Company statement of cash flows, as adapted, appear as follows:

The XYZ Company and Subsidiaries Consolidated Statement of Cash Flows (Adapted)		
	Years Ended December 31,	
(In millions)	**2012**	**2011**
Operating Activities		
Net cash provided by operating activities	$ 5,404	$ 1,498
Investing Activities		
Purchases of property, plant, and equipment	(1,001)	(951)
Acquisitions and investments, principally trademarks and bottling companies	(851)	(521)
Purchases of investments	(590)	(668)
Proceeds from disposals of investments	608	384
Proceeds from disposals of property, plant, and equipment	128	72
Other investing activities	183	178
Net cash used in investing activities	(1,523)	(1,506)
Financing Activities		
Issuances of debt (borrowing)	3,867	4,704
Payments of debt	(5,142)	(5,477)
Issuances of stock	220	438
Purchases of stock for treasury	(358)	(186)
Dividends	(2,298)	(2,172)
Net cash used in financing activities	(3,711)	(2,693)

As the chief executive officer of The XYZ Company, your duty is to write the management letter to your stockholders explaining XYZ's major investing activities during 2012. Compare the company's level of investment with previous years and indicate how the company financed its investments during 2012. Net income for 2012 was $5,083 million.

Exercises

All of the A and B exercises can be found within MyAccountingLab, an online homework and practice environment. Your instructor may ask you to complete these exercises using MyAccountingLab.

MyAccountingLab

Group A

E8-13A *(Learning Objective 2: Record transactions for available-for-sale securities)* Journalize the following long-term available-for-sale security transactions of Roya Brothers Department Stores:

a. Purchased 410 shares of Fordham Foods common stock at $35 per share, with the intent of holding the stock for the indefinite future
b. Received a cash dividend of $1.80 per share on the Fordham investment
c. At year-end, adjusted the investment account to fair value of $42 per share
d. Sold the Fordham stock for the price of $27 per share

E8-14A (*Learning Objective 2: Analyze and report investments in available-for-sale investments*)
Folgate Co. bought 4,000 shares of German common stock at $40; 680 shares of Chile stock at $47.75; and 1,600 shares of Sweden stock at $78—all as available-for-sale investments. At December 31, Hoover's Online reports German stock at $30.125, Chile at $50.00, and Sweden at $70.00.

▶ Requirements

1. Determine the cost and the fair value of the long-term investment portfolio at December 31.
2. Record Folgate's adjusting entry at December 31.
3. What would Folgate report on its statement of other comprehensive income and balance sheet for the information given? Make the necessary disclosures. Ignore income tax.

E8-15A (*Learning Objective 3: Account for transactions using the equity method*) McCloud Corporation owns equity-method investments in several companies. Suppose McCloud paid $1,800,000 to acquire a 40% investment in Simpson Software Company. Simpson Software reported net income of $660,000 for the first year and declared and paid cash dividends of $460,000.

▶ Requirements

1. Record the following in McCloud's journal: (a) purchase of the investment, (b) McCloud's proportion of Simpson Software's net income, and (c) receipt of the cash dividends.
2. What is the ending balance in McCloud's investment account?

E8-16A (*Learning Objective 3: Analyze gains or losses on equity-method investments*) Without making journal entries, record the transactions of Exercise 8-15A directly in the McCloud account, Long-Term Investment in Simpson Software. Assume that after all the noted transactions took place, McCloud sold its entire investment in Simpson Software for cash of $2,900,000. How much is McCloud's gain or loss on the sale of the investment?

E8-17A (*Learning Objective 3: Apply the appropriate accounting method for a 35% investment*)
Conroy Financial paid $510,000 for a 35% investment in the common stock of Timberwolf, Inc. For the first year, Timberwolf reported net income of $210,000 and at year-end declared and paid cash dividends of $135,000. On the balance-sheet date, the fair value of Conroy's investment in Timberwolf stock was $400,000.

▶ Requirements

1. Which method is appropriate for Conroy Financial to use in accounting for its investment in Timberwolf? Why?
2. Show everything that Conroy would report for the investment and any investment revenue in its year-end financial statements.

E8-18A (*Learning Objective 4: Prepare a consolidated balance sheet*)   Zeta, Inc., owns Juliet Corp. The two companies' individual balance sheets follow:

Zeta, Inc.
Consolidation Work Sheet

	Zeta, Inc.	Juliet Corp.	Elimination Debit	Elimination Credit
Cash	$ 54,000	$ 20,000		
Accounts receivable, net	75,000	52,000		
Note receivable from Zeta	—	38,000		
Inventory	56,000	80,000		
Investment in Juliet	113,000	—		
Plant assets, net	283,000	97,000		
Other assets	29,000	13,000		
Total	$610,000	$300,000		
Accounts payable	$ 49,000	$ 22,000		
Notes payable	148,000	33,000		
Other liabilities	78,000	132,000		
Common stock	112,000	80,000		
Retained earnings	223,000	33,000		
Total	$610,000	$300,000		

▶ Requirements

1. Prepare a consolidated balance sheet of Zeta, Inc. It is sufficient to complete the consolidation work sheet. Use Exhibit 8-7 as a model.
2. What is the amount of stockholders' equity for the consolidated entity?

E8-19A (*Learning Objective 1: Analyze and report held-to-maturity security transactions*)
Assume that on September 30, 2012, Protex, Inc., paid 99 for 5.5% bonds of McPhee Corporation as a long-term held-to-maturity investment. The maturity value of the bonds will be $15,000 on September 30, 2017. The bonds pay interest on March 31 and September 30.

▶ Requirements

1. What method should Protex use to account for its investment in the McPhee bonds?
2. Using the straight-line method of amortizing the bonds, journalize all of Protex's transactions on the bonds for 2012.
3. Show how Protex would report everything related to the bond investment on its balance sheet at December 31, 2012.

E8-20A (*Learning Objective 6: Calculate the present value of a bond investment*)   Brinkman Corp. purchased 10 $1,000, 5% bonds of General Electric Corporation when the market rate of interest was 4%. Interest is paid semiannually on the bonds, and the bonds will mature in six years. Using the PV function in Excel, compute the price Brinkman paid (the present value) on the bond investment.

E8-21A (*Learning Objective 4: Translate a foreign-currency balance sheet into dollars*) Translate into dollars the balance sheet of Alaska Leather Goods' German subsidiary. When Alaska Leather Goods acquired the foreign subsidiary, a euro was worth $1.03. The current exchange rate is $1.36. During the period when retained earnings were earned, the average exchange rate was $1.15 per euro.

	Euros
Assets	450,000
Liabilities	150,000
Stockholders' equity:	
Common stock....................	90,000
Retained earnings...............	210,000
	450,000

During the period covered by this situation, which currency was stronger, the dollar or the euro?

E8-22A (*Learning Objective 5: Prepare and use the statement of cash flows*) During fiscal year 2012, Sprinkle Doughnuts reported a net income of $134.9 million. Sprinkle received $1.3 million from the sale of other businesses. Sprinkle made capital expenditures of $10.1 million and sold property, plant, and equipment for $7.0 million. The company purchased long-term investments at a cost of $11.6 million and sold other long-term investments for $2.3 million.

► Requirement

1. Prepare the investing activities section of Sprinkle Doughnuts' statement of cash flows. Based solely on Sprinkle Doughnuts' investing activities, does it appear that the company is growing or shrinking? How can you tell?

E8-23A (*Learning Objective 5: Use the statement of cash flows*) At the end of the year, Blue City Properties' statement of cash flows reported the following for investment activities:

Blue City Properties
Consolidated Statement of Cash Flows (Partial)

Cash flows from Investing Activities:	
Notes receivable collected	$ 3,115,000
Purchases of short-term investments	(3,450,000)
Proceeds from sales of equipment	1,630,000*
Proceeds from sales of investments (cost of $430,000)	438,000
Expenditures for property and equipment	(1,740,000)
Net used by investing activities	$ (7,000)

*Cost $5,300,000; Accumulated depreciation, $3,670,000.

► Requirement

1. For each item listed, make the journal entry that placed the item on Blue City's statement of cash flows.

Group B

E8-24B (*Learning Objective 2: Record transactions for available-for-sale securities*) Journalize the following long-term available-for-sale investment transactions of Jeakins Brothers Department Stores:

    a. Purchased 400 shares of Chang Foods common stock at $33 per share, with the intent of holding the stock for the indefinite future.
    b. Received cash dividend of $1.90 per share on the Chang investment.
    c. At year-end, adjusted the investment account to fair value of $38 per share.
    d. Sold the Chang stock for the price of $26 per share.

E8-25B (*Learning Objective 2: Analyze and report investments in available-for-sale investments*) Western Co. bought 3,200 shares of New Brunswick common stock at $34; 600 shares of Paris stock at $46.25; and 1,000 shares of Ireland stock at $73—all as available-for-sale investments. At December 31, Hoover's Online reports New Brunswick stock at $28.125, Paris at $48.00, and Ireland at $68.00.

▶ Requirements

1. Determine the cost and the fair value of the long-term investment portfolio at December 31.
2. Record Western's adjusting entry at December 31.
3. What would Western report on its statement of other comprehensive income and balance sheet for the information given? Make the necessary disclosures. Ignore income tax.

E8-26B (*Learning Objective 3: Account for transactions using the equity method*) Potter Corporation owns equity-method investments in several companies. Suppose Potter paid $1,100,000 to acquire a 30% investment in Faulk Software Company. Faulk Software reported net income of $660,000 for the first year and declared and paid cash dividends of $400,000.

▶ Requirements

1. Record the following in Potter's journal: (a) purchase of the investment, (b) Potter's proportion of Faulk Software's net income, and (c) receipt of the cash dividends.
2. What is the ending balance in Potter's investment account?

E8-27B (*Learning Objective 3: Analyze gains or losses on equity-method investments*) Without making journal entries, record the transactions of Exercise 8-26B directly in the Potter account, Long-Term Investment in Faulk Software. Assume that after all the noted transactions took place, Potter sold its entire investment in Faulk Software for cash of $1,300,000. How much is Potter's gain or loss on the sale of the investment?

E8-28B (*Learning Objective 3: Apply the appropriate accounting method for a 45% investment*) Wilcox Financial paid $530,000 for a 45% investment in the common stock of Hornet, Inc. For the first year, Hornet reported net income of $240,000 and at year-end declared and paid cash dividends of $125,000. On the balance-sheet date, the fair value of Wilcox's investment in Hornet stock was $420,000.

▶ Requirements

1. Which method is appropriate for Wilcox Financial to use in its accounting for its investment in Hornet? Why?
2. Show everything that Wilcox would report for the investment and any investment revenue in its year-end financial statements.

E8-29B (*Learning Objective 4: Prepare a consolidated balance sheet*)   Alfa, Inc., owns Tempest Corp. These two companies' individual balance sheets follow:

Alfa, Inc.
Consolidation Work Sheet

	Alfa, Inc.	Tempest Corp.	Elimination Debit	Credit
Cash	$ 52,000	$ 20,000		
Accounts receivable, net	82,000	58,000		
Note receivable from Alfa	—	39,000		
Inventory	54,000	83,000		
Investment in Tempest	119,000	—		
Plant assets, net	288,000	98,000		
Other assets	29,000	11,000		
Total	$624,000	$309,000		
Accounts payable	$ 49,000	$ 25,000		
Notes payable	152,000	33,000		
Other liabilities	78,000	132,000		
Common stock	107,000	82,000		
Retained earnings	238,000	37,000		
Total	$624,000	$309,000		

▶ Requirements

1. Prepare a consolidated balance sheet of Alfa, Inc. It is sufficient to complete the consolidation work sheet. Use Exhibit 8-7 as a model.
2. What is the amount of stockholders' equity for the consolidated entity?

E8-30B (*Learning Objective 1: Analyze and report held-to-maturity security transactions*)   Assume that on September 30, 2012, Rentex, Inc., paid 95 for 7% bonds of Clarkson Corporation as a long-term held-to-maturity investment. The maturity value of the bonds will be $10,000 on September 30, 2017. The bonds pay interest on March 31 and September 30.

▶ Requirements

1. What method should Rentex use to account for its investment in the Clarkson bonds?
2. Using the straight-line method of amortizing the bonds, journalize all of Rentex's transactions on the bonds for 2012.
3. Show how Rentex would report everything related to the bond investment on its balance sheet at December 31, 2012.

E8-31B (*Learning Objective 6: Calculate the present value of a bond investment*)   Brinkman Corp. purchased 20, $1,000, 4% bonds of Citigroup when the market rate of interest was 3%. Interest is paid semiannually, and the bonds will mature in five years. Using the PV function in Excel, compute the price Brinkman paid (the present value) for the bond investment.

E8-32B (*Learning Objective 4: Translate a foreign-currency balance sheet into dollars*) Translate into dollars the balance sheet of Washington Leather Goods' Spanish subsidiary. When Washington Leather Goods acquired the foreign subsidiary, a euro was worth $1.02. The current exchange rate is $1.34. During the period when retained earnings were earned, the average exchange rate was $1.17 per euro.

	Euros
Assets	400,000
Liabilities	300,000
Stockholders' equity:	
Common stock....................	45,000
Retained earnings...............	55,000
	400,000

During the period covered by this situation, which currency was stronger, the dollar or the euro?

E8-33B (*Learning Objective 5: Prepare and use the statement of cash flows*) During fiscal year 2012, Capitol Cupcakes reported a net income of $132.4 million. Capitol received $1.4 million from the sale of other businesses. Capitol made capital expenditures of $10.5 million and sold property, plant, and equipment for $6.8 million. The company purchased long-term investments at a cost of $12.1 million and sold other long-term investments for $2.3 million.

▶ Requirement

1. Prepare the investing activities section of Capitol Cupcakes' statement of cash flows. Based solely on Capitol Cupcakes' investing activities, does it appear that the company is growing or shrinking? How can you tell?

E8-34B (*Learning Objective 5: Use the statement of cash flows*) At the end of the year, Providence Properties' statement of cash flows reported the following for investing activities:

Providence Properties Consolidated Statement of Cash Flows (Partial)	
Cash flows from Investing Activities:	
Notes receivable collected	$ 3,108,000
Purchases of short-term investments	(3,451,000)
Proceeds from sales of equipment	1,419,000*
Proceeds from sales of investments (cost of $410,000)	418,000
Expenditures for property and equipment	(1,741,000)
Net used by investing activities	$ (247,000)

*Cost $5,100,000; Accumulated depreciation, $3,681,000.

▶ Requirement

1. For each item listed, make the journal entry that placed the item on Providence's statement of cash flows.

Quiz

Test your understanding of long-term investments and international operations by answering the following questions. Select the best choice from among the possible answers given.

Questions 35–37 use the following data:

Assume that Fast Networks owns the following long-term available-for-sale investments:

Company	Number of Shares	Cost per Share	Year-end Fair Value per Share	Dividend per Share
Hurlburt Corp.	800	$56	$71	$1.90
Rosewood, Inc.	100	7	11	1.30
Sticks Ltd.	300	20	24	1.10

Q8-35 Fast's balance sheet should report

a. investments of $65,100.

b. unrealized loss of $13,600.

c. investments of $51,500.

d. dividend revenue of $1,980.

Q8-36 Fast's income statement should report

a. unrealized loss of $13,600.

b. dividend revenue of $1,980.

c. gain on sale of investment of $13,600.

d. investments of $51,500.

Q8-37 Suppose that, before year-end, Fast sells the Hurlburt stock for $69 per share. Journalize the sale.

Q8-38 Dividends received on an equity-method investment

a. decrease the investment account.

b. increase owners' equity.

c. increase the investment account.

d. increase dividend revenue.

Q8-39 The starting point in accounting for all investments is

a. equity value.

b. cost minus dividends.

c. cost.

d. market value on the balance-sheet date.

Q8-40 Consolidation accounting

a. reports the receivables and payables of the parent company only.

b. eliminates all liabilities.

c. combines the accounts of the parent company and those of the subsidiary companies.

d. all of the above.

Q8-41 On January 1, 2012, Microsport, Inc., purchased $120,000 face value of the 9% bonds of Service Express, Inc., at 104. The bonds mature on January 1, 2017. For the year ended December 31, 2015, Microsport received cash interest of

a. $9,800.

b. $8,800.

c. $10,800.

d. $11,800.

Q8-42 Return to Microsport, Inc.'s bond investment in the preceding question. For the year ended December 31, 2015, Microsport received cash interest of $10,800. What was the interest revenue that Microsport earned in this period?

a. $9,800

b. $9,840

c. $11,800

d. $8,800

Q8-43 The present value of $5,000 at the end of eight years at 5% interest is

a. $5,000.

b. $32,315.

c. $3,385.

d. $4,228.

Q8-44 Which of the following is not needed to compute the present value of an investment?
a. The interest rate
b. The length of time between the investment and future receipt
c. The amount of the receipt
d. The rate of inflation

Q8-45 What is the present value of bonds with a face value of $5,000; a stated interest rate of 6%; a market rate of 8%; and a maturity date four years in the future? Interest is paid semiannually.
a. $5,000
b. $4,663
c. $5,393
d. $3,947

Q8-46 Consolidation of a foreign subsidiary usually results in a
a. foreign-currency transaction gain or loss.
b. foreign-currency translation adjustment.
c. gain or loss on consolidation.
d. LIFO/FIFO difference.

Problems

> All of the A and B problems can be found within MyAccountingLab, an online homework and practice environment. Your instructor may ask you to complete these problems using MyAccountingLab.

MyAccountingLab

Group A

P8-47A (*Learning Objectives 2,3: Analyze and report various long-term investment transactions on the balance sheet and income statement*) Delaware Exchange Company completed the following long-term investment transactions during 2012:

2012	
May 12	Purchased 28,000 shares, which make up 35% of the common stock of Brentwood Corporation at total cost of $390,000.
Jul 9	Received annual cash dividend of $1.23 per share on the Brentwood investment.
Sep 16	Purchased 800 shares of Detroit, Inc., common stock as an available-for-sale investment, paying $41.75 per share.
Oct 30	Received cash dividend of $0.35 per share on the Detroit investment.
Dec 31	Received annual report from Brentwood Corporation. Net income for the year was $510,000.

At year-end, the fair value of the Detroit stock is $30,500. The fair value of the Brentwood stock is $656,000.

▶ Requirements

1. For which investment is fair value used in the accounting? Why is fair value used for one investment and not the other?
2. Show what Delaware would report on its year-end balance sheet, income statement, and statement of other comprehensive income for these investment transactions. It is helpful to use a T-account for the Long-Term Investment in Brentwood Stock account. Ignore income tax.

P8-48A (*Learning Objectives 2, 3: Analyze and report available-for-sale and equity-method investments*) The beginning balance sheet of Evita Corporation included the following:

Long-Term Investment in Reading Software (equity-method investment)................. $611,000

Evita completed the following investment transactions during the year:

Mar 16	Purchased 1,600 shares of Lawrence, Inc., common stock as a long-term available-for-sale investment, paying $12.00 per share.
May 21	Received cash dividend of $0.75 per share on the Lawrence investment.
Aug 17	Received cash dividend of $81,000 from Reading Software.
Dec 31	Received annual reports from Reading Software, net income for the year was $560,000. Of this amount Evita's proportion is 29%.

At year-end, the fair values of Evita's investments are as follows: Lawrence, $26,000; Reading, $692,000.

▶ Requirements

1. Record the transactions in the journal of Evita Corporation.
2. Post entries to the T-account for Long-Term Investment in Reading and determine its balance at December 31.
3. Show how to report the Long-Term Available-for-Sale Investments and the Long-Term Investment in Reading accounts on Evita's balance sheet at December 31.

P8-49A (*Learning Objective 4: Analyze consolidated financial statements*) This problem demonstrates the dramatic effect that consolidation accounting can have on a company's ratios. Spindler Motor Company (Spindler) owns 100% of Spindler Motor Credit Corporation (SMCC), its financing subsidiary. Spindler's main operations consist of manufacturing automotive products. SMCC mainly helps people finance the purchase of automobiles from Spindler and its dealers. The two companies' individual balance sheets are adapted and summarized as follows (amounts in billions):

	Spindler (Parent)	SMCC (Subsidiary)
Total assets	$89.8	$170.1
Total liabilities	$65.8	$156.2
Total stockholders' equity................	24.0	13.9
Total liabilities and equity................	$89.8	$170.1

Assume that SMCC's liabilities include $1.9 billion owed to Spindler, the parent company.

▶ Requirements

1. Compute the debt ratio of Spindler Motor Company considered alone.
2. Determine the consolidated total assets, total liabilities, and stockholders' equity of Spindler Motor Company after consolidating the financial statements of SMCC into the totals of Spindler, the parent company.
3. Recompute the debt ratio of the consolidated entity. Why do companies prefer not to consolidate their financing subsidiaries into their own financial statements?

P8-50A *(Learning Objective 4: Consolidate a wholly owned subsidiary)* Assume Abbey, Inc., paid $479,000 to acquire all the common stock of Bookstore Corporation, and Bookstore owes Abbey $164,000 on a note payable. Immediately after the purchase on September 30, 2012, the two companies' balance sheets follow.

	Abbey	Bookstore
Assets		
Cash...	$ 56,000	$ 28,000
Accounts receivable, net........................	169,000	86,000
Note receivable from Bookstore............	164,000	—
Inventory..	321,000	490,000
Investment in Bookstore.......................	479,000	—
Plant assets, net....................................	407,000	527,000
Total	$1,596,000	$1,131,000
Liabilities and Stockholders' Equity		
Accounts payable	$ 122,000	$ 61,000
Notes payable	409,000	289,000
Other liabilities	223,000	302,000
Common stock.......................................	561,000	253,000
Retained earnings..................................	281,000	226,000
Total	$1,596,000	$1,131,000

▶ Requirement

1. Prepare the worksheet for the consolidated balance sheet of Abbey, Inc. Use Exhibit 8-7 as a model.

P8-51A *(Learning Objective 1: Analyze and report held-to-maturity investments purchased at a premium)* Insurance companies and pension plans hold large quantities of bond investments. Discount Insurance Corp. purchased $2,100,000 of 6.0% bonds of Soucy, Inc., for 116 on January 1, 2012. These bonds pay interest on January 1 and July 1 each year. They mature on January 1, 2016. At October 31, 2012, the end of the company's fiscal year, the market price of the bonds is 109.

▶ Requirements

1. Journalize Discount's purchase of the bonds as a long-term investment on January 1, 2012, (to be held to maturity), receipt of cash interest, and amortization of the bond investment at July 1, 2012. The straight-line method is appropriate for amortizing the bond investment.
2. Journalize the accrual of interest receivable and amortization of premium on October 31, 2012 (round the answer to the nearest whole number).
3. Show all financial statement effects of this long-term bond investment on Discount Insurance Corp.'s balance sheet and income statement at October 31, 2012.

P8-52A *(Learning Objective 6: Explain the impact of the time value of money on valuation of investments)* Annual cash flows from two competing investment opportunities are given. Each investment opportunity will require the same initial investment.

	Investment	
Year	A	B
1	$10,000	$ 8,000
2	8,000	8,000
3	6,000	8,000
	$24,000	$24,000

▶ Requirement

1. Assuming a 12% interest rate, which investment opportunity would you choose?

P8-53A (*Learning Objective 4: Consolidate a foreign subsidiary*) Assume that Goss has a subsidiary company based in Japan.

► Requirements

1. Translate into dollars the foreign-currency balance sheet of the Japanese subsidiary of Goss.

	Yen
Assets.....................................	500,000,000
Liabilities	145,000,000
Stockholders' equity:	
Common stock...................	18,000,000
Retained earnings..............	337,000,000
	500,000,000

When Goss acquired this subsidiary, the Japanese yen was worth $0.0092. The current exchange rate is $0.0107. During the period when the subsidiary earned its income, the average exchange rate was $0.0095 per yen. Before you perform the foreign-currency translation calculations, indicate whether Goss has experienced a positive or a negative translation adjustment. State whether the adjustment is a gain or a loss, and show where it is reported in the financial statements.

2. To which company does the foreign-currency translation adjustment "belong"? In which company's financial statements will the translation adjustment be reported?

Group B

P8-54B (*Learning Objectives 2, 3: Analyze and report various long-term investment transactions on the balance sheet and income statement*) Georgia Exchange Company completed the following long-term investment transactions during 2012:

2012	
May 12	Purchased 21,000 shares, which make up 45% of the common stock of Portland Corporation at total cost of $340,000.
Jul 9	Received annual cash dividend of $1.26 per share on the Portland investment.
Sep 16	Purchased 1,100 shares of Sydney, Inc., common stock as an available-for-sale investment, paying $41.75 per share.
Oct 30	Received cash dividend of $0.32 per share on the Sydney investment.
Dec 31	Received annual report from Portland Corporation. Net income for the year was $500,000.

At year-end the fair value of the Sydney stock is $30,900. The fair value of the Portland stock is $653,000.

► Requirements

1. For which investment is fair value used in the accounting? Why is fair value used for one investment and not the other?

2. Show what Georgia would report on its year-end balance sheet, income statement, and statement of other comprehensive income for these investment transactions. It is helpful to use a T-account for the Long-Term Investment in Portland Stock account. Ignore income tax.

P8-55B (*Learning Objectives 2, 3: Analyze and report available-for-sale and equity-method investments*) The beginning balance sheet of Moret Corporation included the following:

Long-Term Investment in LPC Software (equity-method investment)........................	$615,000

Moret completed the following investment transactions during the year:

Mar 16	Purchased 1,800 shares of Littleton, Inc., common stock as a long-term available-for-sale investment, paying $12.50 per share.
May 21	Received cash dividend of $1.50 per share on the Littleton investment.
Aug 17	Received cash dividend of $80,000 from LPC Software.
Dec 31	Received annual reports from LPC Software; net income for the year was $510,000. Of this amount, Moret's proportion is 28%.

At year-end, the fair values of Moret's investments are are follows: Littleton, $26,400; LPC, $695,000.

▶ Requirements

1. Record the transactions in the journal of Moret Corporation.
2. Post entries to the T-account for Long-Term Investment in LPC and determine its balance at December 31.
3. Show how to report the Long-Term Available-for-Sale Investments and the Long-Term Investment in LPC accounts on Moret's balance sheet at December 31.

P8-56B (*Learning Objective 4: Analyze consolidated financial statements*) This problem demonstrates the dramatic effect that consolidation accounting can have on a company's ratios. Roto Motor Company (Roto) owns 100% of Roto Motor Credit Corporation (RMCC), its financing subsidiary. Roto's main operations consist of manufacturing automotive products. RMCC mainly helps people finance the purchase of automobiles from Roto and its dealers. The two companies' individual balance sheets are adapted and summarized as follows (amounts in billions):

	Roto (Parent)	RMCC (Subsidiary)
Total assets	$89.1	$170.3
Total liabilities	$65.8	$156.3
Total stockholders' equity	23.3	14.0
Total liabilities and equity.................	$89.1	$170.3

Assume that RMCC's liabilities include $1.5 billion owed to Roto, the parent company.

▶ Requirements

1. Compute the debt ratio of Roto Motor Company considered alone.
2. Determine the consolidated total assets, total liabilities, and stockholders' equity of Roto Motor Company after consolidating the financial statements of RMCC into the totals of Roto, the parent company.
3. Recompute the debt ratio of the consolidated entity. Why do companies prefer not to consolidate their financing subsidiaries into their own financial statements?

P8-57B (*Learning Objective 4: Consolidate a wholly owned subsidiary*) Assume Jackson, Inc., paid $351,000 to acquire all the common stock of Aiello Corporation, and Aiello owes Jackson $168,000 on a note payable. Immediately after the purchase on September 30, 2012, the two companies' balance sheets follow.

	Jackson	Aiello
Assets		
Cash..	$ 48,000	$ 32,000
Accounts receivable, net............................	179,000	88,000
Note receivable from Aiello....................	168,000	—
Inventory...	329,000	424,000
Investment in Aiello	351,000	—
Plant assets, net.....................................	407,000	477,000
Total	$1,482,000	$1,021,000
Liabilities and Stockholders' Equity		
Accounts payable	$ 134,000	$ 64,000
Notes payable	409,000	306,000
Other liabilities	215,000	300,000
Common stock..	587,000	260,000
Retained earnings..................................	137,000	91,000
Total	$1,482,000	$1,021,000

▶ Requirement

1. Prepare the work sheet for the consolidated balance sheet of Jackson, Inc. Use Exhibit 8-7 as a model.

P8-58B (*Learning Objective 1: Analyze and report held-to-maturity investments purchased at a premium*) Insurance companies and pension plans hold large quantities of bond investments. Brighton Insurance Corp. purchased $2,300,000 of 10.0% bonds of Scanlon, Inc., for 114 on January 1, 2012. These bonds pay interest on January 1 and July 1 each year. They mature on January 1, 2016. At October 31, 2012, the end of the fiscal year, the market price of the bonds is 105.

▶ Requirements

1. Journalize Brighton's purchase of the bonds as a long-term investment on January 1, 2012 (to be held to maturity), receipt of cash interest, and amortization of the bond investment at July 1, 2012. The straight-line method is appropriate for amortizing the bond investment.
2. Journalize the accrual of interest receivable and amortization of premium on October 31, 2012 (round answer to the nearest whole number).
3. Show all financial statement effects of this long-term bond investment on Brighton Insurance Corp.'s balance sheet and income statement at October 31, 2012.

P8-59B (*Learning Objective 6: Explain the impact of the time value of money on the valuation of investments*) Annual cash flows from two competing investment opportunities are given. Each investment opportunity will require the same initial investment.

	Investment	
Year	X	Y
1	$15,000	$10,000
2	10,000	10,000
3	5,000	10,000
	$30,000	$30,000

▶ Requirement

1. Assuming a 10% interest rate, which investment opportunity would you choose?

P8-60B (*Learning Objective 4: Consolidate a foreign subsidiary*) Assume that Mattson has a subsidiary company based in Japan.

▶ Requirements

1. Translate into dollars the foreign-currency balance sheet of the Japanese subsidiary of Mattson.

	Yen
Assets......................................	375,000,000
Liabilities	145,000,000
Stockholders' equity:	
Common stock....................	21,000,000
Retained earnings................	209,000,000
	375,000,000

When Mattson acquired this subsidiary, the Japanese yen was worth $0.0088. The current exchange rate is $0.0103. During the period when the subsidiary earned its income, the average exchange rate was $0.0092 per yen. Before you perform the foreign-currency translation calculations, indicate whether Mattson has experienced a positive or a negative translation adjustment. State whether the adjustment is a gain or a loss, and show where it is reported in the financial statements.

2. To which company does the foreign-currency translation adjustment "belong?" In which company's financial statements will the translation adjustment be reported?

Challenge Exercises and Problem

E8-61 (*Learning Objectives 1, 2, 3, 5: Accounting for various types of investments*) Suppose MyPlace owns the following investments at December 31, 2012:

a. 100% of the common stock of MyPlace United Kingdom, which holds assets of £600,000 and owes a total of £400,000. At December 31, 2012, the current exchange rate of the pound (£) is £1 = $1.97. The translation rate of the pound applicable to stockholders' equity is £1 = $1.63. During 2012, MyPlace United Kingdom earned net income of £75,000, and the average exchange rate for the year was £1 = $1.89. MyPlace United Kingdom paid cash dividends of £40,000 during 2012.

b. Investments that MyPlace is holding to sell. These investments cost $550,000 and declined in value by $250,000 during 2012, but they paid cash dividends of $25,000 to MyPlace. One year ago, at December 31, 2011, the fair value of these investments was $900,000.

c. 35% of the common stock of MyPlace Financing Associates. During 2012, MyPlace Financing earned net income of $900,000 and declared and paid cash dividends of $80,000. The carrying amount of this investment was $700,000 at December 31, 2011.

▶ Requirements

1. Which method is used to account for each investment?
2. By how much did each of these investments increase or decrease MyPlace's net income during 2012?
3. For investments b and c, show how MyPlace would report these investments on its balance sheet at December 31, 2012.

E8-62 (*Learning Objectives 2, 4: Explain and analyze accumulated other comprehensive income*)
Brown-Box Retail Corporation reported stockholder's equity on its balance sheet at December 31
as follows:

Brown-Box Retail Balance Sheet (Partial)	
Stockholders' equity:	
Common stock, $0.10 par value—	
1200 million shares authorized	
500 shares issued	$ 50
Additional paid-in capital	1,098
Retained earnings	6,100
Accumulated other comprehensive (loss)	(?)
Less: Treasury stock, at cost	(80)

▶ Requirements

1. Identify the two components that typically make up accumulated other comprehensive
   income.
2. For each component of accumulated other comprehensive income, describe the event that
   can cause a *positive* balance. Also describe the events that can cause a *negative* balance for
   each component.
3. At December 31, 2012, Brown-Box Retail's accumulated other comprehensive loss was
   $57 million. Then during 2013, Brown-Box Retail had a positive foreign-currency translation
   adjustment of $25 million and an unrealized loss of $15 million on available-for-sale investments. What was Brown-Box Retail's balance of accumulated other comprehensive income
   (loss) at December 31, 2013?

P8-63 (*Learning Objective 6: Calculate present values of competing investments*) Which option
is better: receive $100,000 now or $20,000, $25,000, $30,000, $25,000, and $20,000, respectively,
over the next five years?

▶ Requirements

1. Assuming a 5% interest rate, which investment opportunity would you choose?
2. If you could earn 10%, would your choice change?
3. What would the cash flow in year 5 have to be in order for you to be indifferent to the two plans?

APPLY YOUR KNOWLEDGE

Decision Cases

Case 1. (*Learning Objectives 2, 4: Make an investment decision*) Infografix Corporation's consolidated sales for 2012 were $26.6 billion, and expenses totaled $24.8 billion. Infografix operates worldwide and conducts 37% of its business outside the United States. During 2012, Infografix reported the following items in its financial statements (amounts in billions):

Foreign-currency translation adjustments...	$(202)
Unrealized holding _____ on available-for-sale investments.............	(328)

As you consider an investment in Infografix stock, some concerns arise. Answer each of the following questions:

1. What do the parentheses around the two dollar amounts signify?
2. Are these items reported as assets, liabilities, stockholders' equity, revenues, or expenses? Are they normal-balance accounts, or are they contra accounts?
3. Did Infografix include these items in net income? in retained earnings? In the final analysis, how much net income did Infografix report for 2012?
4. Should these items scare you away from investing in Infografix stock? Why or why not? (Challenge)

Case 2. (*Learning Objectives 1, 2, 5: Make an investment sale decision*) Cathy Talbert is the general manager of Barham Company, which provides data-management services for physicians in the Columbus, Ohio, area. Barham Company is having a rough year. Net income trails projections for the year by almost $75,000. This shortfall is especially important. Barham plans to issue stock early next year and needs to show investors that the company can meet its earnings targets.

Barham holds several investments purchased a few years ago. Even though investing in stocks is outside Barham's core business of data-management services, Talbert thinks these investments may hold the key to helping the company meet its net income goal for the year. She is considering what to do with the following investments:

1. Barham owns 50% of the common stock of Ohio Office Systems, which provides the business forms that Barham uses. Ohio Office Systems has lost money for the past two years but still has a retained earnings balance of $550,000. Talbert thinks she can get Ohio's treasurer to declare a $160,000 cash dividend, half of which would go to Barham.
2. Barham owns a bond investment purchased eight years ago for $250,000. The purchase price represents a discount from the bonds' maturity value of $400,000. These bonds mature two years from now, and their current market value is $380,000. Ms. Talbert has checked with a **Charles Schwab** investment representative, and Talbert is considering selling the bonds. Schwab would charge a 1% commission on the sale transaction.
3. Barham owns 5,000 shares of **Microsoft** stock valued at $53 per share. One year ago, Microsoft stock was worth only $28 per share. Barham purchased the Microsoft stock for $37 per share. Talbert wonders whether Barham should sell the Microsoft stock.

▶ Requirement

1. Evaluate all three actions as a way for Barham Company to generate the needed amount of income. Recommend the best way for Barham to achieve its net income goal.

Ethical Issue

Media One owns 18% of the voting stock of Web Talk, Inc. The remainder of the Web Talk stock is held by numerous investors with small holdings. Austin Cohen, president of Media One and a member of Web Talk's board of directors, heavily influences Web Talk's policies.

Under the fair value method of accounting for investments, Media One's net income increases as it receives dividend revenue from Web Talk. Media One pays President Cohen a bonus computed as a percentage of Media One's net income. Therefore, Cohen can control his personal bonus to a certain extent by influencing Web Talk's dividends.

A recession occurs in 2012, and Media One's income is low. Cohen uses his power to have Web Talk pay a large cash dividend. The action requires Web Talk to borrow in order to pay the dividend.

▶ Requirements

1. What are the ethical issues in the Media One case?
2. Who are the stakeholders? What are the possible consequences to each?
3. What are the alternatives for Austin Cohen to consider? Analyze each alternative from the following standpoints: (a) economic, (b) legal, (c) ethical.
4. If you were Cohen, what would you do?
5. Discuss how using the equity method of accounting for investment would decrease Cohen's potential for manipulating his bonus.

Focus on Financials: | Amazon.com, Inc.

(*Learning Objectives 2, 3, 4: Analyze investments, consolidated subsidiaries, and international operations*) The consolidated financial statements of **Amazon.com, Inc.**, are given in Appendix A at the end of this book.

1. Refer to Note 1—Description of Business and Accounting Policies, under *Investments*. Describe the method of accounting used for investments over which the company can exercise significant influence but not control. How does the company classify these investments on its balance sheet? How does the company account for these investments on its income statement?
2. Does Amazon.com have any other types of investments other than those described in (1)? How does the company account for them? Does it adjust for periodic changes in fair value of these investments? If so, where do these adjustments appear?
3. Does Amazon.com, Inc. make any fair value adjustments to its investment portfolio? Which levels of fair value does it use? Why do you think it uses these methods?
4. What are Amazon.com's principles of consolidation? Where do you find them?

Focus on Analysis: | RadioShack Corporation

(*Learning Objectives 2, 3, 4: Analyze and report available-for-sale investments; analyze consolidated statements and international operations*) This case is based on the consolidated financial statements of **RadioShack Corporation** given in Appendix B at the end of this book.

1. Read Note 4: Acquisitions. Does RadioShack Corporation own any foreign subsidiaries? How much of the subsidiary does it own? Explain the method of accounting the company uses to account for this subsidiary.
2. At December 31, 2010, did RadioShack Corporation have a cumulative net gain or a cumulative net loss from translating its foreign subsidiaries' financial statements into dollars? How can you tell?
3. Read Note 12. What are the types of investments that RadioShack Corporation reports at fair values? What level of fair values does it use (1, 2, or 3)? Describe in general how this fair value adjustment works. What judgments must financial managers of the company make in order to make these adjustments?

Group Project

Pick a stock from The *Wall Street Journal* or another database or publication. Assume that your group purchases 1,000 shares of the stock as a long-term investment and that your 1,000 shares are less than 20% of the company's outstanding stock. Research the stock in *Value Line, Moody's Investor Record,* or another source to determine whether the company pays cash dividends and, if so, how much and at what intervals.

▶ Requirements

1. Track the stock for a period assigned by your professor. Over the specified period, keep a daily record of the price of the stock to see how well your investment has performed. Each day, search the Corporate Dividend News in The *Wall Street Journal* to keep a record of any dividends you've received. End the period of your analysis with a month-end, such as September 30 or December 31.
2. Journalize all transactions that you have experienced, including the stock purchase, dividends received (both cash dividends and stock dividends), and any year-end adjustment required by the accounting method that is appropriate for your situation. Assume you will prepare financial statements on the ending date of your study.
3. Show what you will report on your company's balance sheet, income statement, and statement of cash flows as a result of your investment transactions.

MyAccountingLab

> For online homework, exercises, and problems that provide you with immediate feedback, please visit **www.myaccountinglab.com.**

Quick Check Answers

1. *a*
2. *a* (1,600 shares x $29 = $46,400)
3. *d*
4. *b* ($55,000 − $46,400)
5. *d* [$80,000 + 0.25 ($60,000 − $40,000) = $85,000]
6. *a* {$160,000 + 0.80 [$70,000 + 0.64($40,000)] = $241,600}
7. *c*
8. *a*
9. *a*
10. *a*

9 Liabilities

SPOTLIGHT: Southwest Airlines: A Success Story

Southwest Airlines has been a maverick in the airline industry from the start. In recent years, despite turmoil in the industry, Southwest has managed to stay profitable while other airlines have been in bankruptcy or close to it.

The airlines have some interesting liabilities. Southwest's Rapid Rewards program provides free flights to the company's frequent fliers. Southwest accrues frequent-flier liability for this program and reports "Accrued liabilities" on the company's consolidated balance sheet.

Southwest collects cash in advance for tickets sold and then provides flights for customers later. This creates unearned revenue that Southwest reports as "Air traffic liability." The company also has notes payable and bonds payable that it reports under "Long-term debt." ●

© Icholakov/Dreamstime.com

(In millions)				
Assets			**Liabilities and Stockholders' Equity**	
Current Assets			Current Liabilities	
Cash	$ 1,261		Accounts payable	$ 739
Other current assets	3,018		Accrued liabilities	863
Total current assets	4,279		Air traffic liability	1,198
Equipment and property, net	10,578		Current maturities of	
Other assets	606		long-term debt	505
			Total current liabilities	3,305
			Long-term debt, less current liabilities	2,875
			Other long-term liabilities	3,046
			Stockholders' Equity	6,237
Total assets	$15,463		Total liabilities and equity	$15,463

Southwest Airlines Co.
Consolidated Balance Sheet (Adapted)
December 31, 2010

This chapter shows how to account for liabilities—both current and long-term. We begin with current liabilities.

Learning Objectives

1 **Account for** current and contingent liabilities

2 **Account for** bonds payable, notes payable, and interest expense

3 **Analyze and differentiate** financing with debt vs. equity

4 **Understand** other long-term liabilities

5 **Report** liabilities

Account for Current and Contingent Liabilities

1

Account for current and contingent liabilities

Current liabilities are obligations due within one year or within the company's normal operating cycle if longer than a year. Obligations due beyond that period of time are classified as *long-term liabilities*.
Current liabilities are of two kinds:

► Known amounts
► Estimated amounts

We look first at current liabilities of a known amount.

Current Liabilities of Known Amount

Current liabilities of known amount include accounts payable, short-term notes payable, sales tax payable, accrued liabilities, payroll liabilities, unearned revenues, and current portion of long-term debt.

Accounts Payable. Amounts owed for products or services purchased on account are *accounts payable*. For example, Southwest Airlines purchases soft drinks and napkins on accounts payable. We have seen many other accounts payable examples in preceding chapters. One of a merchandiser's most common transactions is the credit purchase of inventory. **Best Buy** and **RadioShack** buy their inventory on account.

Accounts Payable Turnover. An important measure of liquidity for a retail business is **accounts payable turnover**, which measures the number of times a year a company is able to pay its accounts payable. The ratio is computed as follows:

> Accounts payable turnover (T/O) = Cost of goods sold ÷ Average accounts payable
> Turnover expressed in days = 365 ÷ T/O (computed above)

Once the turnover is computed, it is usually expressed in number of days, or **days payable outstanding (DPO)** by dividing the turnover into 365. Here are comparative ratios for accounts payable turnover for **Best Buy** and **RadioShack** from their 2010 financial statements:

(In millions)	Best Buy	RadioShack
Cost of goods sold..	$37,611	$2,462
Average accounts payable	5,085	268
Accounts payable turnover (T/O)...	7.40	9.19
Turnover in days (365 ÷ T/O), or days payable outstanding (DPO)........	49 days	40 days

Because different industries have different business models and standard business practices, it is important to compare companies with competitors in the same industry. Since **Best Buy** and **RadioShack** are both in the consumer electronics industry, purchasing many of their products from the same vendors, it is reasonable to compare them on the basis of accounts payable turnover. RadioShack pays its accounts payable in about 40 days, whereas Best Buy takes 49 days to pay its accounts payable. If you were a supplier of these two giant companies, which would you rather do business with, on the basis of this ratio? If cash collections are important to you in order to pay your own bills, the obvious answer is RadioShack, based strictly on this ratio.

What makes an accounts payable turnover ratio strong or weak in the eyes of creditors and investors? Generally, a high turnover ratio (short period in days) is better than a low turnover ratio. Companies with shorter payment periods are generally better credit risks than those with longer payment periods. However, some companies with strong credit ratings strategically follow shrewd cash management policies, withholding payment to suppliers as long as possible, while speeding up collections, in order to conserve cash. For example, Wal-Mart's accounts payable turnover is about 37 days, which is longer than a typical 30-day credit period. The company strategically stretches its payment period, which is tough on suppliers, but because of Wal-Mart's size, market share, and buying power, few suppliers can afford not to do business with the company.

To be sure, credit and sales decisions are based on far more information than accounts payable turnover, so it's wise not to oversimplify. However, combined with inventory turnover (discussed in Chapter 6) and accounts receivable turnover (discussed in Chapter 5), all expressed in days, accounts payable turnover is an important ingredient in computing the *cash conversion cycle*, which is an overall measure of liquidity. Combined with the current ratio (discussed in Chapter 3) and the quick ratio (discussed in Chapter 5), studying the cash conversion cycle helps users of financial statements determine the overall liquidity of a company. We will discuss the cash conversion cycle in more depth in Chapter 13.

Short-Term Notes Payable. **Short-term notes payable**, a common form of financing, are notes payable due within one year. **Starbucks** lists its short-term notes payable as *short-term borrowings*. Starbucks may issue short-term notes payable to borrow cash or to purchase assets. On its notes payable, Starbucks must accrue interest expense and interest payable at the end of the period. The following sequence of entries covers the purchase of inventory, accrual of interest expense, and payment of a 10% short-term note payable that's due in one year.

2012			
Jan 1	Inventory	8,000	
	Note Payable, Short-Term		8,000
	Purchase of inventory by issuing a note payable.		

This transaction increases both an asset and a liability.

Assets	=	Liabilities	+	Stockholders' Equity
+ 8,000	=	+ 8,000	+	0

The Starbucks fiscal year ends each September 30. At year-end, Starbucks must accrue interest expense at 10% for January through September:

Sep 30	Interest Expense ($8,000 × 0.10 × 9/12)	600	
	Interest Payable		600
	Accrual of interest expense at year-end.		

Liabilities increase and equity decreases because of the expense.

Assets	=	Liabilities	+	Stockholders' Equity	−	Expenses
0	=	+ 600				− 600

The balance sheet at year-end will report the Note Payable of $8,000 and the related Interest Payable of $600 as current liabilities. The income statement will report interest expense of $600.

The following entry records the note's payment at maturity on January 1, 2013:

2013			
Jan 1	Note Payable, Short-Term	8,000	
	Interest Payable	600	
	Interest Expense ($8,000 × 0.10 × 3/12)	200	
	Cash [$8,000 + ($8,000 × 0.10)]		8,800
	Payment of a note payable and interest at maturity.		

The debits zero out the payables and also record Starbucks' interest expense for October, November, and December.

Sales Tax Payable. Most states levy a sales tax on retail sales. Retailers collect the tax from customers and thus owe the state for sales tax collected. Suppose one Saturday's sales at a Home Depot store totaled $200,000. Home Depot collected an additional 5% ($10,000) of sales tax. The store would record that day's sales as follows:

Cash ($200,000 × 1.05)	210,000	
Sales Revenue		200,000
Sales Tax Payable ($200,000 × 0.05)		10,000
To record cash sales and the related sales tax.		

Assets, liabilities, and equity all increase—equity because of the revenues.

Assets	=	Liabilities	+	Stockholders' Equity	+	Revenues
+ 210,000	=	+ 10,000				+ 200,000

Accrued Liabilities (Accrued Expenses). An **accrued liability** usually results from an expense that the business has incurred but not yet paid. Therefore, an accrued expense creates a liability, which explains why it is also called an **accrued expense**.

For example, Southwest Airlines' salary expense and salary payable occur as employees work for the company. Interest expense accrues with the passage of time. There are several categories of accrued expenses:

- ▶ Salaries and Wages Payable
- ▶ Interest Payable
- ▶ Income Taxes Payable

Salaries and Wages Payable is the liability for payroll expenses not yet paid at the end of the period. This category includes salaries, wages, and payroll taxes withheld from employee paychecks. *Interest Payable* is the company's interest payable on notes payable. *Income Taxes Payable* is the amount of income tax the company still owes at year-end.

Payroll Liabilities. **Payroll**, also called *employee compensation*, is a major expense. For service organizations—such as law firms, real estate companies, and airlines—compensation is *the* major expense, just as cost of goods sold is the largest expense for a merchandising company.

Employee compensation takes many different forms. A *salary* is employee pay stated at a monthly or yearly rate. A *wage* is employee pay stated at an hourly rate. Sales employees earn a *commission*, which is a percentage of the sales the employee has made. A *bonus* is an amount over and above regular compensation. Accounting for all forms of compensation follows the pattern illustrated in Exhibit 9-1 (using assumed figures).

EXHIBIT 9-1 | Accounting for Payroll Expenses and Liabilities

Salary Expense	10,000	
Employee Income Tax Payable		1,200
FICA Tax Payable		800
Salary Payable to Employees [take-home pay]		8,000
To record salary expense.		

Every expense accrual has the same effect: Liabilities increase and equity decreases because of the expense. The accounting equation shows these effects.

Assets	=	Liabilities	+	Stockholders' Equity	−	Expenses
		+ 1,200				− 10,000
0	=	+ 800				
		+ 8,000				

Salary expense represents *gross pay* (that is, employee pay before subtractions for taxes and other deductions). Salary expense creates several payroll liabilities:

- ▶ *Employee Income Tax Payable* is the employees' income tax that has been withheld from paychecks.
- ▶ *FICA Tax Payable* includes the employees' Social Security tax and Medicare tax, which also are withheld from paychecks. (FICA stands for the Federal Insurance Contributions Act, which created the Social Security tax.)
- ▶ *Salary Payable* to employees is their net (take-home) pay.

Companies must also pay some *employer* payroll taxes and expenses for employee benefits. Accounting for these expenses is similar to the illustration in Exhibit 9-1.

Unearned Revenues. *Unearned revenues* are also called *deferred revenues* and *revenues collected in advance.* For all unearned revenue, the business has received cash from customers before earning the revenue. The company has a liability—an obligation to provide goods or services to the customer. Let's consider an example.

Southwest Airlines sells tickets and collects cash in advance. Southwest therefore reports unearned ticket revenue (which it calls Air traffic liability) for airline tickets sold in advance. At December 31, 2010, Southwest owed customers $1,198 million of air travel (see page 518). Let's see how Southwest accounts for its air traffic liability.

Assume that Southwest collects $300 for a round-trip ticket from Dallas to Los Angeles. Southwest records the cash collection and related liability as follows:

2012			
Dec 15	Cash	300	
	Air traffic liability		300
	Received cash in advance for ticket sales.		

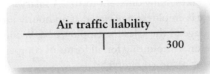

Air traffic liability	
	300

Suppose the customer flies to Los Angeles late in December. Southwest records the revenue earned as follows:

2012			
Dec 28	Air traffic liability	150	
	Ticket Revenue ($300 × 1/2)		150
	Earned revenue that was collected in advance.		

Air traffic liability			Ticket Revenue	
150	300			150
	Bal 150			

The liability decreases and the revenue increases.
At year-end, Southwest reports

▶ $150 of Air traffic liability on the balance sheet, and
▶ $150 of ticket revenue on the income statement.

The customer returns to Dallas in January 2013, and Southwest records the revenue earned with this journal entry:

2013			
Jan 4	Air traffic liability	150	
	Ticket Revenue ($300 × 1/2)		150
	Earned revenue that was collected in advance.		

Now the liability balance is zero because Southwest has earned all the revenue it collected in advance.

Air traffic liability	
150	300
150	
	Bal 0

Current Portion of Long-Term Debt. Some long-term debt must be paid in installments. The **current portion of long-term debt** (also called *current maturity* or *current installment*) is the amount of the principal that is payable within one year. At the end of each year, a company reclassifies (from long-term debt to a current liability) the amount of its long-term debt that must be paid next year.

Southwest Airlines reports Current maturities of long-term debt as a current liability. Southwest also reports a long-term liability for Long-term debt, which excludes the current maturities. *Long-term debt* refers to long-term notes payable and bonds payable, which we cover in the second half of this chapter.

Current Liabilities That Must Be Estimated

A business may know that a liability exists but not know its exact amount. The business must report the liability on the balance sheet. Estimated liabilities vary among companies. Let's look first at Estimated Warranty Payable, a liability account that most merchandisers have.

Estimated Warranty Payable. Many companies guarantee their products under *warranty* agreements. The warranty period may extend for 90 days to a year for consumer products. Automobile companies—like **General Motors, BMW,** and **Toyota**—accrue liabilities for vehicle warranties.

Whatever the warranty's life, the expense recognition (matching) principle demands that the company record the *warranty expense* in the same period that the business records sales revenue. After all, the warranty motivates customers to buy products, so the company must record warranty expense. At the time of the sale, however, the company doesn't know which products are defective. The exact amount of warranty expense cannot be known with certainty, so the business must estimate warranty expense and the related liability.

Assume that **Black & Decker**, which manufactures power tools, made sales of $100,000 subject to product warranties. Assume that in past years between 2% and 4% of products proved defective. Black & Decker could estimate that 3% of sales will require repair or replacement. In this case, Black & Decker would estimate warranty expense of $3,000 ($100,000 × 0.03) for the year and make the following entry:

	Warranty Expense	3,000	
	Estimated Warranty Payable		3,000
	To accrue warranty expense.		

```
            Estimated Warranty Payable
                          |        3,000
```

Assume that defects add up to $2,800, and Black & Decker will replace the defective products. Black & Decker then records the following:

Estimated Warranty Payable	2,800	
Inventory		2,800
To replace defective products sold under warranty.		

```
            Estimated Warranty Payable
            2,800  |  3,000
                   |  Bal    200
```

At the end of the year, Black & Decker will report Estimated Warranty Payable of $200 as a current liability. The income statement reports Warranty Expense of $3,000 for the year. Then, next year Black & Decker will repeat this process. The Estimated Warranty Payable account probably won't ever zero out.

If Black & Decker paid cash to satisfy the warranty, then the credit would be to Cash rather than to Inventory.

Vacation pay is another expense that must be estimated. And income taxes must be estimated because the final amount isn't determined until early the next year.

Contingent Liabilities

A *contingent liability* is not an actual liability. Instead, it's a potential liability that depends on the future outcome of past events. Examples of contingent liabilities are future obligations that may arise because of lawsuits, tax disputes, or alleged violations of environmental protection laws. The principle of representational faithfulness, discussed in Chapter 1, requires that companies disclose the substance of their financial positions and results of operations in a way that is as transparent and complete as possible. With liabilities, that principle implies "When in doubt, disclose. When necessary, accrue." The Financial Accounting Standards Board (FASB) provides these guidelines to account for contingent liabilities:[1]

1. *Accrue* (i.e., make an adjusting journal entry for) a contingent liability if, in management's opinion, it's *probable* that the loss (or expense) will occur *and* the *amount can be reasonably estimated*. Warranty expense, illustrated previously, is an example. Another example is a lawsuit that has been settled as of the balance sheet date but has not yet been paid.

2. *Disclose* a contingency in a financial statement note if it's *reasonably possible* (less than probable but more than remote) that a loss (or expense) will occur. Lawsuits in progress are

---

[1]The FASB is currently reconsidering its disclosure requirements for contingent liabilities. If the new requirements are adopted, entities will be required to expand and enhance disclosures of loss contingencies. Specifically, *regardless of likelihood*, entities would be required to *disclose* loss contingencies if, in the opinion of management, they could have a *severe impact* on the entity's financial position, cash flows, or results of operation. An example of such a situation is a lawsuit that could put the company out of business within the next *year*. Both quantitative (dollar amounts) and qualitative (descriptive) information would be included. In addition, for all amounts *accrued*, the entity would have to include a table and explanations that show how these accruals have changed from the previous period. These proposals are similar, but not identical to, proposed changes in IFRS requirements for loss contingencies.

a prime example. Southwest Airlines includes a note in its financial statements to report contingent liabilities from examinations of its past income tax returns by the IRS.

> **Note 17, Contingencies**
>
> The Company is subject to various legal proceedings [...] including [...] examinations by the Internal Revenue Service (IRS). The IRS regularly examines the Company's federal income tax returns and, in the course thereof, proposes adjustments to the Company's federal income tax liability reported on such returns. The Company's management does not expect that [...] any of its currently ongoing legal proceedings or [...] any proposed adjustments [...] by the IRS [...] will have a material adverse effect on the Company's financial condition, results of operations, or cash flow.

3. There is no need to report a contingent loss that is unlikely to occur. Instead, wait until an actual transaction clears up the situation. For example, suppose **Del Monte Foods** grows vegetables in Nicaragua, and the Nicaraguan government threatens to confiscate the assets of all foreign companies. Del Monte will report nothing about the contingency if the probability of a loss is considered remote.

A contingent liability may arise from lawsuits that claim wrongdoing by the company. The plaintiff may seek damages through the courts. If the court or the IRS rules in favor of Southwest, there is no liability. But if the ruling favors the plaintiff, then Southwest will have an actual liability. It would be unethical to omit these disclosures from the financial statements because investors need this information to properly evaluate a company.

The international accounting standard for loss contingencies requires accrual (i.e., journal entries) for *both* probable and possible contingent liabilities. The threshold for *probable* under IFRS is lower than the threshold under GAAP, which means that IFRS requires accrual of loss contingencies more frequently than GAAP.

The IASB is studying its existing standard with a view toward harmonizing it with the changes that are being contemplated by the FASB (discussed in the footnote on p. 524). Regardless of the outcome of the changes that are being proposed by both the IASB and FASB, it is likely that future financial statements of all companies will include *more disclosures of both quantitative and qualitative information* for contingent liabilities than are presently required.

Appendix E summarizes differences between U.S. GAAP and IFRS, cross-referenced by chapter.

Are All Liabilities Reported on the Balance Sheet?

The big danger with liabilities is that you may fail to report a large debt on your balance sheet. What is the consequence of missing a large liability? You will definitely understate your liabilities and your debt ratio. By failing to accrue interest on the liability, you'll probably overstate your net income as well. In short, your financial statements will make you look better than you really are. Any such error, if significant, hurts a company's credibility.

Contingent liabilities are very easy to overlook because they aren't actual debts. How would you feel if you owned stock in a company that failed to report a contingency that put the company out of business? If you had known of the contingency, you could have sold the stock and avoided the loss. In this case, you would hire a lawyer to file suit against the company for negligent financial reporting.

Cooking the Books with Liabilities

Crazy Eddie, Inc.

Accidentally understating liabilities is one thing, but doing it intentionally is quite another. When unethical management decides to cook the books in the area of liabilities, its strategy is to *deliberately understate recorded liabilities*. This can be done by intentionally under-recording the amount of existing liabilities or by omitting certain liabilities altogether.

Crazy Eddie, Inc., first discussed in Chapter 6, used *multiple tactics* to overstate its financial position over a period of four consecutive years. In addition to overstating inventory (thus understating cost of goods sold and overstating income), the management of the company deliberately *understated accounts payable* by issuing fictitious (false) debit memoranda from suppliers (vendors). A debit memo is issued for goods returned to a vendor, such as Sony. When a debit memorandum is issued, accounts payable are debited (reduced), thus reducing current liabilities and increasing the current ratio. Eventually, expenses are also decreased, and profits are correspondingly increased through reduction of expenses. Crazy Eddie, Inc., issued $3 million of fictitious debit memoranda in one year, making the company's current ratio and debt ratio look better than they actually were, as well as overstating profits.

Summary of Current Liabilities

Let's summarize what we've covered thus far. A company can report its current liabilities on the balance sheet as follows:

Accounting, Inc. **Balance Sheet** December 31, 2012				
Assets		**Liabilities**		
Current Assets:		Current liabilities:		
Cash		Accounts payable		
Short-term investments		Salary payable*		
Etc.		Interest payable*		
		Income tax payable*		
Property, plant, and equipment:		Unearned revenue		
Land		Estimated warranty payable*		
Etc.		Notes payable, short-term		
		Current portion of long-term debt		
Other assets		Total current liabilities		
		Long-term liabilities		
		Stockholders' Equity		
		Common stock		
		Retained earnings		
		Total liabilities and		
Total assets	$XXX	stockholders' equity		$XXX

*These items are often combined and reported in a single total as "Accrued Liabilities" or "Accrued Expenses Payable."

On its income statement this company would report the following:

▶ *Expenses* related to some of the current liabilities. Examples include Salary Expense, Interest Expense, Income Tax Expense, and Warranty Expense.
▶ *Revenue* related to the unearned revenue. Examples include Service Revenue and Sales Revenue that were collected in advance.

MID-CHAPTER SUMMARY PROBLEM

Assume that the **Estée Lauder Companies, Inc.**, faced the following liability situations at June 30, 2012, the end of the company's fiscal year. Show how Estée Lauder would report these liabilities on its balance sheet at June 30, 2012.

a. Salary expense for the last payroll period of the year was $900,000. Of this amount, employees' withheld income tax totaled $88,000 and FICA taxes were $61,000. These payroll amounts will be paid in early July.

b. On fiscal-year 2012 sales of $400 million, management estimates warranty expense of 2%. One year ago, at June 30, 2011, Estimated Warranty Payable stood at $3 million. Warranty payments were $9 million during the year ended June 30, 2012.

c. The company pays royalties on its purchased trademarks. Royalties for the trademarks are equal to a percentage of Estée Lauder's sales. Assume that sales in 2012 were $400 million and were subject to a royalty rate of 3%. At June 30, 2012, Estée Lauder owes two-thirds of the year's royalty, to be paid in July.

d. Long-term debt totals $100 million and is payable in annual installments of $10 million each. The interest rate on the debt is 7%, and the interest is paid each December 31.

▶ Answer

Liabilities at June 30, 2012:	
a. Current liabilities:	
Salary payable ($900,000 − $88,000 − $61,000)...............	$ 751,000
Employee income tax payable	88,000
FICA tax payable	61,000
b. Current liabilities:	
Estimated warranty payable...	2,000,000
[$3,000,000 + ($400,000,000 × 0.02) − $9,000,000]	
c. Current liabilities:	
Royalties payable ($400,000,000 × 0.03 × 2/3)...................	8,000,000
d. Current liabilities:	
Current installment of long-term debt	10,000,000
Interest payable ($100,000,000 × 0.07 × 6/12)...................	3,500,000
Long-term debt ($100,000,000 − $10,000,000).....................	90,000,000

Account for Bonds Payable, Notes Payable, and Interest Expense

In Chapter 8, we discussed bonds and notes from the standpoint of the investor, as held-to-maturity or available-for-sale investments (long-term assets). In this chapter, we examine bonds and notes from the flip-side, or the standpoint of the borrower, on whose balance sheets they appear as long-term liabilities. We treat bonds payable and notes payable together because the way they are accounted for is virtually the same.

Large companies such as Southwest Airlines, Home Depot, and **Toyota** cannot borrow billions from a single lender. So how do corporations borrow huge amounts? They issue (sell) bonds to the public. **Bonds payable** are groups of notes payable issued to multiple lenders, called

2

Account for bonds payable, notes payable, and interest expense

bondholders. Southwest Airlines needs airplanes and can borrow large amounts by issuing bonds to thousands of individual investors, who each lend Southwest a modest amount. Southwest receives the cash it needs, and each investor limits risk by diversifying investments—not putting all the investor's "eggs in one basket."

Bonds: An Introduction

Bonds payable are debts of the issuing company. Purchasers of bonds receive a bond's certificate, which carries the issuing company's name. The certificate also states the *principal*, which is typically stated in units of $1,000; principal is also called the bond's *face value*, *maturity value*, or *par value*. The bond obligates the issuing company to pay the debt at a specific future time called the *maturity date*.

Interest is the rental fee on borrowed money. The bond certificate states the interest rate that the issuer will pay the holder and the dates that the interest payments are due (generally twice a year). Exhibit 9-2 shows an actual bond certificate.

EXHIBIT 9-2 | Bond Certificate (Adapted)

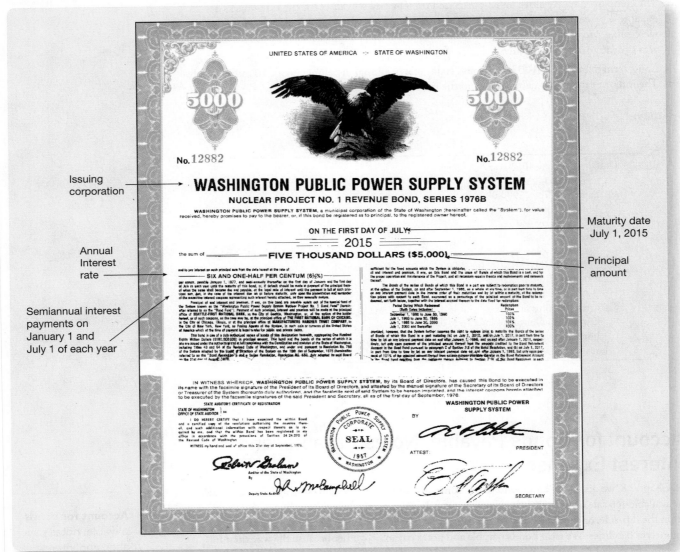

Issuing bonds usually requires the services of a securities firm, such as Merrill Lynch, to act as the underwriter of the bond issue. The **underwriter** purchases the bonds from the issuing company and resells them to its clients, or it may sell the bonds to its clients and earn a commission on the sale.

Types of Bonds. All the bonds in a particular issue may mature at the same time (**term bonds**) or in installments over a period of time (**serial bonds**). Serial bonds are like installment notes payable. Some of Southwest Airlines' long-term debts are serial in nature because they are payable in installments.

Secured, or *mortgage*, *bonds* give the bondholder the right to take specified assets of the issuer if the company *defaults*—that is, fails to pay interest or principal. *Unsecured bonds*, called **debentures**, are backed only by the good faith of the borrower. Debentures carry a higher rate of interest than secured bonds because debentures are riskier investments.

Bond Prices. Investors may buy and sell bonds through bond markets. Bond prices are quoted at a percentage of their maturity value. For example,

- a $1,000 bond quoted at 100 is bought or sold for $1,000, which is 100% of its face value.
- the same bond quoted at 101.5 has a market price of $1,015 (101.5% of face value = $1,000 × 1.015).
- a $1,000 bond quoted at 88.375 is priced at $883.75 ($1,000 × 0.88375).

Bond Premium and Bond Discount. A bond issued at a price above its face (par) value is said to be issued at a **premium**, and a bond issued at a price below face (par) value has a **discount**.

Premium on Bonds Payable has a *credit* balance and Discount on Bonds Payable carries a *debit* balance. Bond Discount is therefore a contra liability account.

As a bond nears maturity, its market price moves toward par value. Therefore, the price of a bond issued at a

- premium decreases toward maturity value.
- discount increases toward maturity value.

On the maturity date, a bond's market value exactly equals its face value because the company that issued the bond pays that amount to retire the bond.

The Time Value of Money. We discussed the time value of money in Chapter 8. You should refresh your understanding of that material at this point because we will use it extensively in accounting for bonds payable and related interest expense. Let's examine how the *time value of money* affects the pricing of bonds, using the same example provided in Chapter 8—except this time, from the issuer (or debtor)'s point of view.

Bond Interest Rates Determine Bond Prices. Bonds are always sold at their *market price*, which is the amount investors will pay for the bond. **Market price is the bond's present value**, which equals the present value of the principal payment plus the present value of the cash interest payments. Interest is usually paid semiannually (twice a year). Some companies pay interest annually or quarterly.

As discussed in Chapter 8, two interest rates work to set the price of a bond:

- The **stated interest rate**, also called the coupon rate, is the interest rate printed on the bond certificate. The stated interest rate determines the amount of cash interest the borrower pays—and the investor receives—each year. As shown in the example in Chapter 8, suppose Southwest Airlines bonds have a stated interest rate of 9%. Southwest would pay $9,000 of interest annually on $100,000 of bonds. Each semiannual payment would be $4,500 ($100,000 × 0.09 × 6/12).
- The **market interest rate**, or *effective interest rate*, is the rate that investors demand for loaning their money. The market interest rate varies by the minute.

A company may issue bonds with a stated interest rate that differs from the prevailing market interest rate. In fact, the two interest rates often differ.

Exhibit 9-3 shows how the stated interest rate and the market interest rate interact to determine the issue price of a bond payable for three separate cases.

EXHIBIT 9-3 | How Stated Interest Rates and Market Interest Rates Interact to Determine the Price of a Bond

Issue Price of Bonds Payable

Case A:

Stated interest rate on a bond payable	equals	Market interest rate	Therefore,	Price of face (par, or maturity) value
Example: 9%	=	9%	→	*Par: $1,000 bond issued for $1,000*

Case B:

Stated interest rate on a bond payable	less than	Market interest rate	Therefore,	Discount price (price below face value)
Example: 9%	<	10%	→	*Discount: $1,000 bond issued for a price below $1,000*

Case C:

Stated interest rate on a bond payable	greater than	Market interest rate	Therefore,	Premium price (price above face value)
Example: 9%	>	8%	→	*Premium: $1,000 bond issued for a price above $1,000*

Southwest Airlines may issue 9% bonds when the market rate has risen to 10%. Will the Southwest 9% bonds attract investors in this market? No, because investors can earn 10% on other bonds of similar risk. Therefore, investors will purchase Southwest bonds only at a price less than their face value. The difference between the lower price and face value is a *discount* (Exhibit 9-3). Conversely, if the market interest rate is 8%, Southwest's 9% bonds will be so attractive that investors will pay more than face value to purchase them. The difference between the higher price and face value is a *premium*.

Issuing Bonds Payable at Par (Face Value)

We start with the most straightforward situation—issuing bonds at their par value. There is no premium or discount on these bonds payable.

Suppose Southwest Airlines has $50,000 of 9% bonds payable that mature in five years. Assume that Southwest issued these bonds at par on January 1, 2012. The issuance entry is as follows:

2012			
Jan 1	Cash	50,000	
	Bonds Payable		50,000
	To issue bonds at par.		

Bonds Payable	
	50,000

Assets and liabilities increase when a company issues bonds payable.

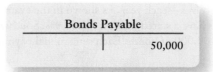

Assets	=	Liabilities	+	Stockholders' Equity
+ 50,000	=	+ 50,000	+	0

Southwest, the borrower, makes a one-time entry to record the receipt of cash and the issuance of bonds. Afterward, investors buy and sell the bonds through the bond markets. These later buy-and-sell transactions between outside investors do *not* involve Southwest at all.

Interest payments occur each January 1 and July 1. Southwest's entry to record the first semiannual interest payment is as follows:

2012			
Jul 1	Interest Expense ($50,000 × 0.09 × 6/12)	2,250	
	Cash		2,250
	To pay semiannual interest.		

The payment of interest expense decreases assets and equity. Bonds payable are not affected.

Assets	=	Liabilities	+	Stockholders' Equity	−	Expenses
− 2,250	=	0	+			− 2,250

At year-end, Southwest accrues interest expense and interest payable for six months (July through December), as follows:

2012			
Dec 31	Interest Expense ($50,000 × 0.09 × 6/12)	2,250	
	Interest Payable		2,250
	To accrue interest.		

Liabilities increase, and equity decreases.

Assets	=	Liabilities	+	Stockholders' Equity	−	Expenses
0	=	+ 2,250	+			− 2,250

On January 1, Southwest will pay the interest, debiting Interest Payable and crediting Cash. Then, at maturity, Southwest pays off the bonds as follows:

2017			
Jan 1	Bonds Payable	50,000	
	Cash		50,000
	To pay bonds payable at maturity.		

Bonds Payable	
50,000	50,000
	Bal 0

Assets	=	Liabilities	+	Stockholders' Equity
− 50,000	=	− 50,000		

Issuing Bonds Payable at a Discount

Market conditions may force a company to issue bonds at a discount. Suppose Southwest Airlines issued $100,000 of 9%, five-year bonds when the market interest rate is 10%. The market price of the bonds drops, and Southwest receives $96,149[2] at issuance. The transaction is recorded as follows:

2012			
Jan 1	Cash	96,149	
	Discount on Bonds Payable	3,851	
	Bonds Payable		100,000
	To issue bonds at a discount.		

The accounting equation shows that Southwest has a net liability of $96,149—not $100,000.

Assets	=	Liabilities	+	Stockholders' Equity
+ 96,149	=	− 3,851	+	0
		+ 100,000		

The bonds payable accounts have a net balance of $96,149 as follows:

Bonds Payable		Discount on Bonds Payable		Net carrying amount of bonds payable
	100,000	−	3,851	= $96,149

Southwest's balance sheet immediately after issuance of the bonds would report the following:

Total current liabilities		$ XXX
Long-term liabilities:		
Bonds payable, 9%, due 2017....................	$100,000	
Less: Discount on bonds payable...............	(3,851)	96,149

Discount on Bonds Payable is a contra account to Bonds Payable, a decrease in the company's liabilities. Subtracting the discount from Bonds Payable yields the *carrying amount* of the bonds. Thus, Southwest's liability is $96,149, which is the amount the company borrowed.

What Is the Interest Expense on These Bonds Payable?

Southwest pays interest on bonds semiannually, which is common practice. Each semiannual *interest payment* is set by the bond contract and therefore remains the same over the life of the bonds:

$$\text{Semiannual interest payment} = \$100,000 \times 0.09 \times 6/12$$
$$= \$4,500$$

But Southwest's *interest expense* increases as the bonds march toward maturity. Remember: These bonds were issued at a discount.

---

[2]The example in Chapter 8 shows how to determine the price of this bond.

Panel A of Exhibit 9-4 repeats the Southwest Airlines bond data we've been using. Panel B provides an amortization table that does two things:

▶ Determines the periodic interest expense (column B)
▶ Shows the bond carrying amount (column E)

Study the exhibit carefully because the amounts we'll be using come directly from the amortization table. This exhibit shows the *effective-interest method of amortization*, which is the correct way to measure interest expense.

EXHIBIT 9-4 | Debt Amortization for Bond Discount

Panel A—Bond Data

Issue date—January 1, 2012	Maturity date—January 1, 2017
Face (par or *maturity*) value—$100,000	Market interest rate at time of issue—10% annually, 5% semiannually
Stated interest rate—9%	Issue price—$96,149
Interest paid—4 1/2% semiannually, $4,500 = $100,000 × 0.09 × 6/12	

Panel B—Amortization Table

	A	B	C	D	E
Semiannual Interest Date	Interest Payment (4 1/2% of Maturity Value)	Interest Expense (5% of Preceding Bond Carrying Amount)	Discount Amortization (B − A)	Discount Account Balance (Preceding D − C)	Bond Carrying Amount ($100,000 − D)
Jan 1, 2012				$3,851	$ 96,149
Jul 1	$4,500	$4,807	$307	3,544	96,456
Jan 1, 2013	4,500	4,823	323	3,221	96,779
Jul 1	4,500	4,839	339	2,882	97,118
Jan 1, 2014	4,500	4,856	356	2,526	97,474
Jul 1	4,500	4,874	374	2,152	97,848
Jan 1, 2015	4,500	4,892	392	1,760	98,240
Jul 1	4,500	4,912	412	1,348	98,652
Jan 1, 2016	4,500	4,933	433	915	99,085
Jul 1	4,500	4,954	454	461	99,539
Jan 1, 2017	4,500	4,961*	461	-0-	100,000

*Adjusted for effect of rounding

Notes
■ Column A   The semiannual interest payments are constant—fixed by the bond contract.
■ Column B   The interest expense each period = the preceding bond carrying amount × the market interest rate.
  Interest expense increases as the bond carrying amount (E) increases.
■ Column C   The discount amortization (C) is the excess of interest expense (B) over interest payment (A).
■ Column D   The discount balance (D) decreases when amortized.
■ Column E   The bond carrying amount (E) increases from $96,149 at issuance to $100,000 at maturity.

Interest Expense on Bonds Issued at a Discount

In Exhibit 9-4, Southwest Airlines borrowed $96,149 cash but must pay $100,000 when the bonds mature. What happens to the $3,851 balance of the discount account over the life of the bond issue?

The $3,851 is additional interest expense to Southwest over and above the stated interest that Southwest pays each six months. Exhibit 9-5 graphs the interest expense and the interest payment on the Southwest bonds over their lifetime. Observe that the semiannual interest payment is fixed—by contract—at $4,500. But the amount of interest expense increases as the discount bond marches upward toward maturity.

EXHIBIT 9-5 | Interest Expense on Bonds Payable Issued at a Discount

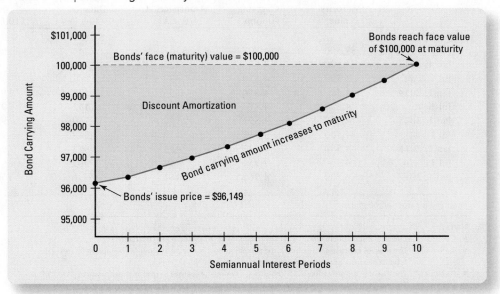

The discount is allocated to interest expense through amortization over the term of the bonds. Exhibit 9-6 illustrates the amortization of the bonds from $96,149 at the start to $100,000 at maturity. These amounts come from Exhibit 9-4, column E (p. 533).

EXHIBIT 9-6 | Amortizing Bonds Payable Issued at a Discount

Now let's see how Southwest would account for these bonds issued at a discount. In our example, Southwest issued its bonds on January 1, 2012. On July 1, Southwest makes the first semiannual interest payment. But Southwest's interest expense is greater than its payment of $4,500. Southwest's journal entry to record interest expense and the interest payment for the first six months follows (with all amounts taken from Exhibit 9-4):

2012			
Jul 1	Interest Expense	4,807	
	Discount on Bonds Payable		307
	Cash		4,500
	To pay semiannual interest and amortize bond discount.		

The credit to Discount on Bonds Payable accomplishes two purposes:

▶ It adjusts the carrying value of the bonds as they march upward toward maturity value.
▶ It amortizes the discount to interest expense.

At December 31, 2012, Southwest accrues interest and amortizes the bonds for July through December with this entry (amounts from Exhibit 9-4, page 533):

2012			
Dec 31	Interest Expense	4,823	
	Discount on Bonds Payable		323
	Interest Payable		4,500
	To accrue semiannual interest and amortize bond discount.		

At December 31, 2012, Southwest's bond accounts appear as follows:

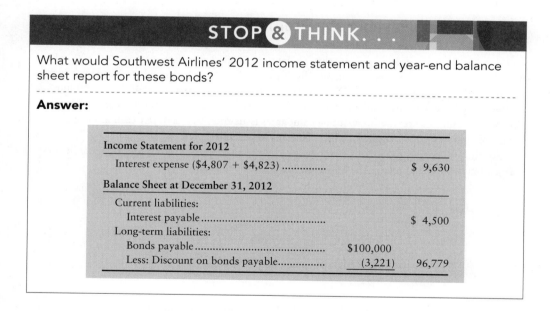

Bond carrying amount, $96,779 = $100,000 − $3,221 from Exhibit 9-4, page 533.

STOP & THINK. . .

What would Southwest Airlines' 2012 income statement and year-end balance sheet report for these bonds?

Answer:

Income Statement for 2012		
Interest expense ($4,807 + $4,823)		$ 9,630
Balance Sheet at December 31, 2012		
Current liabilities:		
Interest payable		$ 4,500
Long-term liabilities:		
Bonds payable	$100,000	
Less: Discount on bonds payable...............	(3,221)	96,779

At maturity on January 1, 2017, the discount will have been amortized to zero, and the bonds' carrying amount will be face value of $100,000. Southwest will retire the bonds by paying $100,000 to the bondholders.

Partial-Period Interest Amounts

Companies don't always issue bonds at the beginning or the end of their accounting year. They issue bonds when market conditions are most favorable, and that may be on May 16, August 1, or any other date. To illustrate partial-period interest, assume **Google, Inc.,** issues $100,000 of 8% bonds payable at 96 on August 31, 2012. The market rate of interest was 9%, and these bonds pay semiannual interest on February 28 and August 31 each year. The first few lines of Google's amortization table are as follows:

Semiannual Interest Date	4% Interest Payment	4 ½% Interest Expense	Discount Amortization	Discount Account Balance	Bond Carrying Amount
Aug 31, 2012				$4,000	$96,000
Feb 28, 2013	$4,000	$4,320	$320	3,680	96,320
Aug 31, 2013	4,000	4,334	334	3,346	96,654

Google's accounting year ends on December 31, so at year-end Google must accrue interest and amortize bond discount for four months (September through December). At December 31, 2012, Google will make this entry:

2012			
Dec 31	Interest Expense ($4,320 × 4/6)	2,880	
	Discount on Bonds Payable ($320 × 4/6)		213
	Interest Payable ($4,000 × 4/6)		2,667
	To accrue interest and amortize discount at year-end.		

The year-end entry at December 31, 2012, uses 4/6 of the upcoming semiannual amounts at February 28, 2013. This example clearly illustrates the benefit of an amortization schedule.

Issuing Bonds Payable at a Premium

Let's modify the Southwest Airlines bond example to illustrate issuance of the bonds at a premium on the interest payment date. Assume that, on January 1, 2012, Southwest issues $100,000 of five-year, 9% bonds that pay interest semiannually. If the 9% bonds are issued when the market interest rate is 8%, their issue price is $104,100.[3] The premium on these bonds is $4,100, and Exhibit 9-7 on the following page shows how to amortize the bonds by the effective-interest method. In practice, bond premiums are rare because few companies issue their bonds to pay cash interest above the market interest rate. We cover bond premiums for completeness.

Southwest's entries to record issuance of the bonds on January 1, 2012, and to make the first interest payment and amortize the bonds on July 1, are as follows:

2012			
Jan 1	Cash	104,100	
	Bonds Payable		100,000
	Premium on Bonds Payable		4,100
	To issue bonds at a premium.		

At the beginning, Southwest's liability is $104,100—not $100,000. The accounting equation makes this clear.

Assets	=	Liabilities	+	Stockholders' Equity
+ 104,100	=	+ 100,000	+	0
		+ 4,100		

---

[3]You can use the same concepts in the example in Chapter 8 to determine the price of this bond.

EXHIBIT 9-7 | Debt Amortization for Bond Premium

Panel A—Bond Data

Issue date—January 1, 2012	Maturity date—January 1, 2017
Face (par or *maturity*) value—$100,000	Market interest rate at time of issue—8% annually, 4% semiannually
Stated interest rate—9%	Issue price—$104,100
Interest paid—4 1/2% semiannually, $4,500 = $100,000 × 0.09 × 6/12	

Panel B—Amortization Table

Semiannual Interest Date	A Interest Payment (4 1/2% of Maturity Value)	B Interest Expense (4% of Preceding Bond Carrying Amount)	C Premium Amortization (A − B)	D Premium Account Balance (Preceding D − C)	E Bond Carrying Amount ($100,000 + D)
Jan 1, 2012				$4,100	$ 104,100
Jul 1	$4,500	$4,164	$336	3,764	103,764
Jan 1, 2013	4,500	4,151	349	3,415	103,415
Jul 1	4,500	4,137	363	3,052	103,052
Jan 1, 2014	4,500	4,122	378	2,674	102,674
Jul 1	4,500	4,107	393	2,281	102,281
Jan 1, 2015	4,500	4,091	409	1,872	101,872
Jul 1	4,500	4,075	425	1,447	101,447
Jan 1, 2016	4,500	4,058	442	1,005	101,005
Jul 1	4,500	4,040	460	545	100,545
Jan 1, 2017	4,500	3,955*	545	-0-	100,000

*Adjusted for effect of rounding

Notes

- Column A The semiannual interest payments are constant—fixed by the bond contract.
- Column B The interest expense each period = the preceding bond carrying amount × the market interest rate. Interest expense decreases as the bond carrying amount (E) decreases.
- Column C The premium amortization (C) is the excess of interest payment (A) over interest expense (B).
- Column D The premium balance (D) decreases when amortized.
- Column E The bond carrying amount (E) decreases from $104,100 at issuance to $100,000 at maturity.

Immediately after issuing the bonds at a premium on January 1, 2012, Southwest would report the bonds payable on the balance sheet as follows:

Total current liabilities.............................		$ XXX
Long-term liabilities:		
Bonds payable...	$100,000	
Premium on bonds payable....................	4,100	104,100

A premium is *added* to the balance of bonds payable to determine the carrying amount.

In Exhibit 9-7, Southwest borrowed $104,100 cash but must pay back only $100,000 at maturity. Amortization of the $4,100 premium will result in a reduction in Southwest's interest expense over the term of the bonds. The first interest payment on July 1, 2012, follows:

2012			
Jul 1	Interest Expense (from Exhibit 9-7)	4,164	
	Premium on Bonds Payable	336	
	Cash		4,500
	To pay semiannual interest and amortize bond premium.		

This entry shows that amortization of premium over the first six months results in reducing interest expense to $4,164 ($4,500 – $336) while the cash interest paid remains at $4,500. Exhibit 9-8 graphs Southwest's interest payments (column A from Exhibit 9-7) and interest expense (column B).

EXHIBIT 9-8 | Interest Expense on Bonds Payable Issued at a Premium

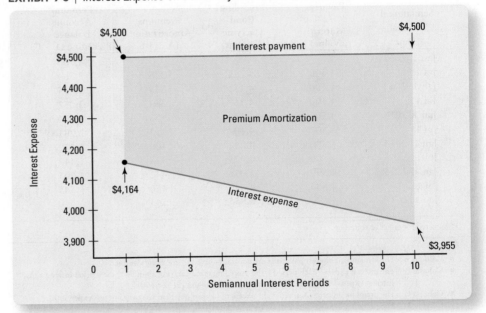

Through amortization, the premium decreases interest expense each period over the term of the bonds. Exhibit 9-9 on the following page diagrams the amortization of the bonds from the issue price of $104,100 to maturity value of $100,000. All amounts are taken from Exhibit 9-7.

EXHIBIT 9-9 | Amortizing Bonds Payable Issued at a Premium

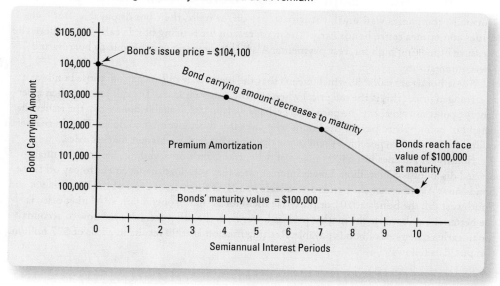

The Straight-Line Amortization Method: A Quick and Dirty Way to Measure Interest Expense

There's a less precise way to amortize bond discount or premium. The *straight-line amortization method* divides a bond discount (or premium) into equal periodic amounts over the bond's term. The amount of interest expense is the same for each interest period.

Let's apply the straight-line method to the Southwest Airlines bonds issued at a discount and illustrated in Exhibit 9-4 (p. 533). Suppose Southwest's financial vice president is considering issuing the 9% bonds at $96,149. To estimate semiannual interest expense on the bonds, the executive can use the straight-line amortization method for the bond discount, as follows:

Semiannual cash interest payment ($100,000 × 0.09 × 6/12).............	$4,500
+ Semiannual amortization of discount ($3,851 ÷ 10)...........................	385
= Estimated semiannual interest expense..	$4,885

The straight-line amortization method uses these same amounts every period over the term of the bonds.

Southwest's entry to record interest and amortization of the bond discount under the straight-line amortization method would be as follows:

2012			
Jul 1	Interest Expense	4,885	
	Discount on Bonds Payable		385
	Cash		4,500
	To pay semiannual interest and amortize bond discount.		

Generally accepted accounting principles (GAAP) permit the straight-line amortization method only when its amounts differ insignificantly from the amounts determined by the effective-interest method.

Should We Retire Bonds Payable Before Their Maturity?

Normally, companies wait until maturity to pay off, or *retire*, their bonds payable. But companies sometimes retire bonds early. The main reason for retiring bonds early is to relieve the pressure of making high interest payments. Also, the company may be able to borrow at a lower interest rate.

Some bonds are **callable**, which means that the issuer may *call*, or pay off, those bonds at a prearranged price (this is the *call price*) whenever the issuer chooses. The call price is often a percentage point or two above the par value, perhaps 101 or 102. Callable bonds give the issuer the benefit of being able to pay off the bonds whenever it is most favorable to do so. The alternative to calling the bonds is to purchase them in the open market at their current market price.

Southwest Airlines has $300 million of debenture bonds outstanding. Assume the unamortized discount is $30 million. Lower interest rates may convince management to pay off these bonds now. Assume that the bonds are callable at 101. If the market price of the bonds is 99, will Southwest call the bonds at 101 or purchase them for 99 in the open market? Market price is the better choice because the market price is lower than the call price. Let's see how to account for an early retirement of bonds payable. Retiring the bonds at 99 results in a loss of $27 million, computed as follows:

	Millions
Par value of bonds being retired	$300
Less: Unamortized discount	(30)
Carrying amount of the bonds being retired	270
Market price ($300 × 0.99)	297
Loss on retirement of bonds payable	$ 27

Gains and losses on early retirement of bonds payable are reported as Other income (loss) on the income statement.

Convertible Bonds and Notes

Some corporate bonds may be converted into the issuing company's common stock. These bonds are called **convertible bonds** (or **convertible notes**). For investors, these bonds combine the safety of (a) assured receipt of interest and principal on the bonds with (b) the opportunity for gains on the stock. The conversion feature is so attractive that investors usually accept a lower interest rate than they would on nonconvertible bonds. The lower cash interest payments benefit the issuer. If the market price of the issuing company's stock gets high enough, the bondholders will convert the bonds into stock.

Suppose Southwest Airlines has convertible notes payable of $100 million. If Southwest's stock price rises high enough, the note holders will convert the notes into the company's common stock. Conversion of the notes payable into stock will decrease Southwest's liabilities and increase its equity.

Assume the note holders convert the notes into four million shares of Southwest Airlines common stock ($1 par) on May 14. Southwest makes the following entry in its accounting records:

May 14	Notes Payable	100,000,000	
	Common Stock (4,000,000 × $1 par)		4,000,000
	Paid-in Capital in Excess of		
	Par—Common		96,000,000
	To record conversion of notes payable.		

The accounting equation shows that liabilities decrease and stockholders' equity increases.

Assets	=	Liabilities	+	Stockholders' Equity	
0	=	(100,000,000)		+ 4,000,000 + 96,000,000	

The carrying amount of the notes ($100 million) ceases to be debt and becomes stockholders' equity. Common Stock is recorded at its *par value*, which is a dollar amount assigned to each share of stock. In this case, the credit to Common Stock is $4,000,000 (4,000,000 shares × $1 par value per share). The extra carrying amount of the notes payable ($96,000,000) is credited to another stockholders' equity account, Paid-in Capital in Excess of Par—Common. We'll be using this account in various ways in the next chapter.

Analyze and Differentiate Financing with Debt Versus Equity

Managers must decide how to get the money they need to pay for assets. There are three main ways to finance operations:

► By retained earnings
► By issuing equity (stock)
► By issuing bonds (or notes) payable

Each strategy has its advantages and disadvantages.

1. *Financed by retained earnings* means that the company has enough cash from profitable operations to purchase the needed assets. There's no need to issue more stock or to borrow money. This strategy is low-risk to the company.

2. *Issuing equity (stock)* creates no liabilities or interest expense and is less risky to the issuing corporation. But issuing stock is more costly, as we shall see.

3. *Issuing bonds or notes payable* does not dilute control of the corporation. It often results in higher earnings per share because the earnings on borrowed money usually exceed interest expense. But creating more debt increases the risk of the company.

Earnings per share (EPS) is the amount of a company's net income for each share of its stock. EPS is the single most important statistic for evaluating companies because EPS is a standard measure of operating performance that applies to companies of different sizes and from different industries.

Suppose Southwest Airlines needs $500,000 for expansion. Assume Southwest has net income of $300,000 and 100,000 shares of common stock outstanding. Management is considering two financing plans. Plan 1 is to issue $500,000 of 6% bonds payable, and plan 2 is to issue 50,000 shares of common stock for $500,000. Management believes the new cash can be invested in operations to earn income of $200,000 before interest and taxes.

Exhibit 9-10 shows the relative earnings-per-share advantage of borrowing. As you can see, Southwest's EPS amount is higher if the company borrows by issuing bonds (compare lines 9 and 10). Southwest earns more on the investment ($102,000) than the interest it pays on the bonds ($30,000). This is called **trading on the equity**, or using **leverage**. It is widely used to increase earnings per share of common stock.

3

Analyze and differentiate financing with debt vs. equity

EXHIBIT 9-10 | Relative Advantage of Borrowing

	Plan 1		Plan 2	
	Borrow $500,000 at 6%		Issue 50,000 Shares of Common Stock for $500,000	
1 Net income before expansion		$300,000		$300,000
2 Expected project income before interest and income tax	$200,000		$200,000	
3 Less interest expense ($500,000 × 0.06)	(30,000)		0	
4 Expected project income before income tax	170,000		200,000	
5 Less income tax expense (40%)	(68,000)		(80,000)	
6 Expected project net income		102,000		120,000
7 Total company net income		$402,000		$420,000
8 Earnings per share after expansion:				
9 Plan 1 Borrow ($402,000/100,000 shares)		$4.02		
10 Plan 2 Issue Stock ($420,000/150,000 shares)				$2.80

In this case, borrowing results in higher earnings per share than issuing stock. Borrowing has its disadvantages, however. Interest expense may be high enough to eliminate net income and lead to losses. Also, borrowing creates liabilities that must be paid during bad years as well as good years. In contrast, a company that issues stock can omit its dividends during a bad year. The Decision Guidelines provide some help in deciding how to finance operations.

DECISION GUIDELINES

FINANCING WITH DEBT OR WITH STOCK

El Chico is the leading chain of Tex-Mex restaurants in the United States, begun by the Cuellar family in the Dallas area. Suppose El Chico is expanding into neighboring states. Take the role of Miguel Cuellar and assume you must make some key decisions about how to finance the expansion.

Decision	Guidelines
How will you finance El Chico's expansion?	Your financing plan depends on El Chico's ability to generate cash flow, your willingness to give up some control of the business, the amount of financing risk you are willing to take, and El Chico's credit rating.
Do El Chico's operations generate enough cash to meet all its financing needs?	If yes, the business needs little outside financing. There is no need to borrow.
	If no, the business will need to issue additional stock or borrow the money.
Are you willing to give up some of your control of the business?	If yes, then issue stock to other stockholders, who can vote their shares to elect the company's directors.
	If no, then borrow from bondholders, who have no vote in the management of the company.
How much leverage (financing risk) are you willing or able to take?	If much, then borrow as much as you can, and you may increase El Chico's earnings per share. But this will increase the business's debt ratio and the risk of being unable to pay its debts.
	If little, then borrow sparingly. This will hold the debt ratio down and reduce the risk of default on borrowing agreements. But El Chico's earnings per share may be lower than if you were to borrow.
How good is the business's credit rating?	The better the credit rating, the easier it is to borrow on favorable terms. A good credit rating also makes it easier to issue stock. Neither stockholders nor creditors will entrust their money to a company with a bad credit rating.

The Leverage Ratio

As discussed and illustrated above, financing with debt can be advantageous, but management of a company must be careful not to incur too much debt. Chapter 3 discussed the debt ratio, which measures the proportion of total liabilities to total assets, two elements of the fundamental accounting equation:

$$\text{Debt ratio} = \frac{\text{Total debt (liabilities)}}{\text{Total assets}}$$

We can rearrange this relationship between total assets, total liabilities, and stockholders' equity in a different manner to illustrate the impact that leverage can have on profitability. The **leverage ratio** is calculated as follows:

$$\text{Leverage ratio} = \frac{\text{Total assets}}{\text{Total stockholders' equity}}$$

Also known as the **equity multiplier**, this ratio shows a company's total assets per dollar of stockholders' equity. A leverage ratio of exactly 1.0 would mean a company has no debt, because total assets would exactly equal total stockholders' equity. This condition is almost non-existent, because virtually all companies have liabilities, and, therefore, have leverage ratios in excess of 1.0. In fact, as we have shown previously, having a healthy amount of debt can actually enhance a company's profitability, in terms of the shareholders' investment. The leverage ratio is the third element of the *DuPont Analysis* model, introduced in part with the discussion of return on assets in Chapter 7.[4] The higher the leverage ratio, the more it magnifies return on stockholders' equity (Net Income/ Average Stockholders' Equity, or ROE). If net income is positive, return on assets (ROA) is positive. The leverage ratio magnifies this positive return to make return on equity (ROE) even more positive. This is because the company is using borrowed money to earn a profit (a concept known as *trading on the equity*). However, if earnings are negative (losses), ROA is negative, and the leverage ratio makes ROE even more negative. We will discuss DuPont Analysis and ROE in more detail as we discuss Stockholders' Equity in Chapter 10. For now, let's just focus on understanding the meaning of the leverage ratio by looking at Southwest Airlines in comparison with one of its competitors, United Continental Holdings (parent company of United Airlines and Continental Airlines). Here are the leverage ratios and debt ratios for the two companies at the end of 2010:

(In millions) for 2010	Southwest	United Continental
1. Total assets	$15,463	$40,552
2. Stockholders' equity	$ 6,237	$ 1,912
3. Leverage ratio (1 ÷ 2)	2.48	21.2
4. Total debt (1 − 2)	$ 9,226	$38,640
5. Debt ratio (4 ÷ 1)	59.7%	95.3%

These figures show that Southwest has $2.48 of total assets for each dollar of stockholders' equity. This translates to a debt ratio of 59.7%, which we learned in Chapter 3 is about normal for many companies. However, United Continental has a leverage ratio of 21.2, meaning there are $21.20 of assets for each dollar of stockholders' equity. Rearranging the elements to show debt to total assets, United Continental has an astonishing ratio of 95.3%. This company is drowning in debt!

---

[4]The DuPont analysis model provides a detailed analysis of return on equity (ROE). It is the product of three elements: (Net income/Net sales) × (Net Sales/Total Assets) × (Total Assets/Total Stockholders' Equity). Notice that elements cross-cancel so that the model reduces to Net income/Stockholders' Equity. See Chapter 10 for a more complete discussion of ROE. A modified version of the model considers only the first two elements to calculate return on assets, as discussed in Chapter 7.

The Times-Interest-Earned Ratio

Analysts use a second ratio—the **times-interest-earned ratio**—to relate income to interest expense. To compute this ratio, we divide *income from operations* (also called *operating income*) by interest expense. This ratio measures the number of times that operating income can *cover* interest expense. The times-interest-earned ratio is also called the **interest-coverage** *ratio*. A high times-interest-earned ratio indicates ease in paying interest expense; a low value suggests difficulty. Let's see how our competing airlines, Southwest and United Continental, compare on the times-interest-earned ratio (dollar amounts in millions taken from the companies' 2010 financial statements):

$$\text{Times-interest-earned ratio} = \frac{\text{Operating income}}{\text{Interest expense}}$$

$$\text{Southwest} \quad \frac{\$988}{\$167} = 5.9 \text{ times}$$

$$\text{United Continental} \quad \frac{\$976}{\$798} = 1.2 \text{ times}$$

Southwest's income from operations covers its interest expense 5.9 times. In contrast, United Continental's operating earnings of $976 (slightly less than Southwest's) barely cover its huge interest charges of $798, for a coverage ratio of only 1.2 times, another signal that the company has incurred too much debt.

Understand Other Long-Term Liabilities

Leases

4

Understand other long-term liabilities

A **lease** is a rental agreement in which the tenant (**lessee**) agrees to make rent payments to the property owner (**lessor**) in exchange for the use of the asset. Leasing allows the lessee to acquire the use of a needed asset without having to make the large up-front payment that purchase agreements require. Accountants distinguish between two types of leases: operating leases and capital leases.

Types of Leases

Operating leases are sometimes short-term or cancelable. However, often operating lease agreements are noncancelable and require the lessee to commit funds to pay the lessor for use of property for years. They give the lessee the right to use the asset but provide no continuing rights to the asset. Instead, the lessor retains the usual risks and rewards of owning the leased asset. To account for an operating lease, the lessee debits Rent Expense (or Lease Expense) and credits Cash for the amount of the lease payment. Operating leases require the lessee to make rent payments, so an operating lease creates a liability even though that liability does not appear on the lessee's balance sheet. In recent years, Southwest Airlines has begun to lease most of its facilities (hangars; buildings; and equipment, including airplanes) under operating lease agreements. Following is an excerpt from Note 8 of Southwest's 2010 financial statements:

Note 8 Leases (partial)
The majority of the Company's terminal operations space, as well as 92 aircraft, were under operating leases at December 31, 2010. Future minimum lease payments under noncancelable operating leases with initial or remaining terms in excess of one year at December 31, 2010, were (in millions) as follows:

2011	$ 386
2012	414
2013	333
2014	285
2015	239
Thereafter	886
Total	$2,543

This essentially means that, although the company has merely signed rental agreements for these assets, it has an obligation over several years in an amount exceeding $2.5 billion to the companies from which it is leasing these assets. Neither the obligation nor the associated assets are included in Southwest's balance sheet. This is an example of what is called "off-balance-sheet financing."

Capital leases are often used to finance the acquisition of long-term assets. A **capital lease** is a long-term noncancelable debt. How do we distinguish a capital lease from an operating lease? The FASB provides the U.S. GAAP guidelines. To be classified as a capital lease, the lease must meet any *one* of the following criteria:

1. The lease transfers title of the leased asset to the lessee at the end of the lease term. Thus, the lessee becomes the legal owner of the leased asset.

2. The lease contains a *bargain purchase option*. The lessee can be expected to purchase the leased asset and become its legal owner.

3. The lease term is 75% or more of the estimated useful life of the leased asset. The lessee uses up most of the leased asset's service potential.

4. The present value of the lease payments is 90% or more of the market value of the leased asset. In effect, the lease payments are the same as installment payments for the leased asset.

If the lease does not meet one of these exact criteria, it is classified as an operating lease by default.

Accounting for a capital lease is much like accounting for the purchase of an asset. The lessee enters the asset into the lessee's long-term asset accounts at the present value of the future cash outflows from the lease contact, and records a long-term lease liability at the beginning of the lease term. Thus, the lessee capitalizes the asset even though the lessee may never take legal title to it, because the lease agreement, in substance, makes the lessee assume the risks and rewards of ownership of the assets and the associated obligations. In lieu of rent expense, the lessee of the capital asset records depreciation expense on the asset (as required of an owner) and interest expense on the lease obligation each period. Both of these expenses are recorded over the term of the lease obligation.

At December 31, 2010, Southwest Airlines reported its capital leases in Note 8 of its financial statements, excerpted as follows:

The Company had five and nine aircraft classified leases as December 31, 2010, and 2009, respectively. The amounts applicable to these aircraft included in property and equipment were as follows:

(In millions)	2010	2009
Flight equipment	$132	$168
Less accumulated depreciation	125	154
	$ 7	$ 14

The note shows that as of December 31, 2010, Southwest only had five aircraft classified as capital leased assets. This number was down from nine aircraft as of December 31, 2009, and from many more than that in previous years. Notice that, since accumulated depreciation almost equals the carrying value of the asset, these lease obligations are about to expire within the next year or two. After that, the company will hold no capital lease equipment, having switched to exclusively operating lease arrangements as shown above.

Do Lessees Prefer Operating Leases or Capital Leases?

Suppose you were the chief financial officer (CFO) of Southwest Airlines. Southwest leases most of its planes. Suppose the leases can be structured either as operating leases or as capital leases. Which type of lease would you prefer for Southwest? Why? Consider what would happen to Southwest's debt ratio if its operating leases in footnote 8 were capitalized and the related liabilities recognized.

Computing Southwest's debt ratio two ways (*operating* leases versus reclassifying them as *capital* leases) will make your decision clear (using Southwest's actual figures in millions):

		Operating Leases as Stated	Operating Leases Reclassified as Capital Leases	
Debt ratio $= \dfrac{\text{Total liabilities}}{\text{Total assets}} =$		$\dfrac{\$9,226}{\$15,463}$	$\dfrac{\$9,226 + \$2,543}{\$15,463 + \$2,543} =$	$\dfrac{\$11,769}{\$18,006}$
	$=$	0.597	$=$	0.654

You can see that a capital lease increases the debt ratio—by almost six percentage points for Southwest, but a lot more for United Continental and AMR (parent company of American Airlines). By contrast, notice that operating leases don't affect the debt ratio that's reported on the balance sheet. For this reason, companies prefer operating leases. It is easy to see why Southwest's long-term commitment for operating leases, as disclosed in Note 8, far outweighs that of its capital lease agreements.

Ethical Challenge. Because of the relatively mechanical nature of the accounting criteria for capitalization of leases, it is possible under existing U.S. GAAP to purposely structure a company's lease agreements so that they barely miss meeting the third criterion (75% test) or the fourth criterion (90% test) for capitalization. Many U.S. companies have taken advantage of these mechanical rules, quite legally, to their economic advantage, thus obtaining almost all the same economic benefits associated with ownership of long-term assets, but avoiding the detrimental impact that recording those assets and obligations can have on their debt ratios.

Global View

In contrast to U.S. GAAP with its mechanical, or "bright line" tests for capitalization of leases, IFRS adopts a much broader approach. Rather than rules, IFRS employs "guidance" that focuses on the overall substance of the transaction, rather than on the mechanical form, and that leaves more to the judgment of the preparer of the financial statement. If, in the judgment of the company's accountants, the lease transfers "substantially all of the risks and rewards of ownership to the lessee," IFRS says the lease should be capitalized. Otherwise, the lease should be expensed as an operating lease.

As of the date of this text, the FASB and IASB have issued a joint exposure draft of a new standard on long-term leases that will, for the great majority of such agreements, require capital lease treatment. This will essentially end the practice of operating leases and off-balance-sheet financing for leased equipment. A revised statement is expected sometime in 2012. When that happens, Southwest Airlines and many other companies with long-term operating leases for fixed assets could be forced to add billions of dollars to their long-term assets, as well as their long-term liabilities, with results as we just showed on their debt and other ratios.

Pensions and Postretirement Liabilities

Most companies have retirement plans for their employees. A **pension** is employee compensation that will be received during retirement. Companies also provide postretirement benefits, such as medical insurance for retired former employees. Because employees earn these benefits by their service, the company records pension and retirement-benefit expense while employees work for the company.

Pensions are one of the most complex areas of accounting. As employees earn their pensions and the company pays into the pension plan, the plan's assets grow. The obligation for future pension payments to employees also accumulates. At the end of each period, the company compares

- ▶ the fair market value of the assets in the retirement plans—cash and investments—with
- ▶ the plans' *projected benefit obligation*, which is the present value of promised future payments to retirees.

If the plan assets exceed the projected benefit obligation, the plan is said to be *overfunded*. In this case, the asset and obligation amounts are to be reported only in the notes to the financial statements. However, if the projected benefit obligation (the liability) exceeds plan assets, the plan is *underfunded*, and the company must report the excess liability amount as a long-term liability on the balance sheet.

Southwest Airlines' retirement plans don't create large liabilities for Southwest. To illustrate pension liabilities, let's see the pension plan of AMR Corp., the parent company of American Airlines.

At December 31, 2010, the retirement plans of AMR Corporation were underfunded. They had

- ► assets with a fair market value of $7,773 million.
- ► projected benefit obligations totaling $11,508 million.

AMR's balance sheet, therefore, included a Pension and Post-Retirement Liability of $3,735 million ($11,508 − $7,773). This liability was split between current and long-term liabilities, in accordance with the due dates for the obligations.

Report Liabilities

Reporting on the Balance Sheet

This chapter began with the liabilities reported on the consolidated balance sheets of Southwest Airlines. Exhibit 9-11 shows a standard way for Southwest to report its long-term debt.

Exhibit 9-11 includes Note 7 from Southwest's consolidated financial statements. The note gives additional details about the company's liabilities. Note 7 shows the interest rates and the maturity dates of Southwest's long-term debt. Investors need these data to evaluate the company. The note also reports

5

Report liabilities

- ► current maturities of long-term debt ($505 million) as a current liability.
- ► long-term debt (less current maturities) of $2,875 million.

Trace these amounts from the Note to the balance sheet. Working back and forth between the financial statements and the related notes is an important part of financial analysis. You now have the tools to understand the liabilities reported on an actual balance sheet.

EXHIBIT 9-11 | Reporting the Liabilities of Southwest Airlines Co.

Southwest Airlines Co. Consolidated Balance Sheet (Partial, Adapted)		Note 7 Long-term debt (In millions) (Adapted)	
Liabilities (in millions)		Term loans due 2019–20	$ 933
Current Liabilities:		10.5% notes due 2011	404
Accounts payable	$ 739	Term agreement due 2020	522
Accrued liabilities	863	French credit agreements due 2012	14
Unearned ticket revenue	1,198	6 1/2% notes due 2012	400
Current maturities of		5 1/2% notes due 2014	385
long-term debt	505 ◄	5 1/2% notes due 2016	309
Total current liabilities	3,305	5 1/2% notes due 2017	345
Long-term debt, less current maturities	2,875 ◄	French credit agreements due 2018	73
Other long-term liabilities	3,046	Other long-term debt	23
		Total long-term debt	3,408
		Less current maturities	(505)
		Less debt discounted and issuance costs	(28)
		Long-term debt	$2,875

Disclosing the Fair Value of Long-Term Debt

Generally accepted accounting principles require companies to report the fair value of their long-term debt. At December 31, 2010, Southwest Airlines' Note 11 included this excerpt (adapted, details omitted):

The estimated fair value of the Company's long-term debt was $3,108 million.

Overall, the fair value of Southwest's long-term debt is about $233 million more than its carrying amount on the books ($2,875). Fair values of publicly-traded debt are based on quoted market prices (level 1 measures, as discussed in Chapter 8), which fluctuate with interest rates and overall market conditions. Therefore, at any one time, fair values for various obligations can either exceed or be less than their carrying amounts.

Reporting Financing Activities on the Statement of Cash Flows

The Southwest Airlines consolidated balance sheet (p. 518) shows that the company finances about 60% of its operations with debt. Southwest's debt ratio is about 60%. Let's examine Southwest's financing activities as reported on its statement of cash flows. Exhibit 9-12 is an excerpt from Southwest's consolidated statement of cash flows.

EXHIBIT 9-12 | Consolidated Statement of Cash Flows (Partial, Adapted) for Southwest Airlines Co.

Southwest Airlines Co. Consolidated Statement of Cash Flows (Adapted)	
(In millions)	**Year Ended December 31, 2010**
Cash Flow from Operating Activities:	
Net cash provided by operating activities	$ 1,561
Cash Flow from Investing Activities:	
Net cash used for investing activities	$(1,265)
Cash Flow from Financing Activities:	
Payments of long-term debt and capital lease obligations	(155)
Other financing sources (net)	6
Net cash used for financing activities	(149)
Net increase in Cash	147

Southwest has provided $1.56 billion more cash from operations than it used in 2010. The company has a long history of good financial management, and it is the most liquid and profitable airline company in the industry. With the excess cash generated from operations, Southwest has invested $1.27 billion in property and equipment and investments of various types. In contrast, it has had a very quiet year from the standpoint of financing, with no new long-term debt and repayments of $155 million on existing debt. During the recession of 2008, Southwest borrowed heavily in order to finance its operations. This is evident in the long-term debt footnote in Exhibit 9-11. Much of that debt has not yet come due as of the end of 2010, but current installments on the debt have been increasing in recent years. About $2.88 billion of the debt still remains, with maturities extending to 2020. Over the next several years, the company will have to pay the debt off, as it comes due in installments, hopefully with cash provided by operations.

END-OF-CHAPTER SUMMARY PROBLEM

The **Cessna Aircraft Company** has outstanding an issue of 8% convertible bonds that mature in 2020. Suppose the bonds are dated October 1, 2012, and pay interest each April 1 and October 1.

▶ Requirements

1. Complete the following effective-interest amortization table through October 1, 2014.

   Bond Data
   Maturity (face) value—$100,000
   Stated interest rate—8%
   Interest paid—4% semiannually, $4,000 ($100,000 × 0.08 × 6/12)
   Market interest rate at the time of issue—9% annually, 4 1/2% semiannually
   Issue price—93.5

	Amortization Table				
	A	B	C	D	E
Semiannual Interest Date	Interest Payment (4% of Maturity Amount)	Interest Expense (4 1/2% of Preceding Bond Carrying Amount)	Discount Amortization (B – A)	Discount Account Balance (Preceding D – C)	Bond Carrying Amount ($100,000 – D)
10-1-12					
4-1-13					
10-1-13					
4-1-14					
10-1-14					

2. Using the amortization table, record the following transactions:

   a. Issuance of the bonds on October 1, 2012.

   b. Accrual of interest and amortization of the bonds on December 31, 2012.

   c. Payment of interest and amortization of the bonds on April 1, 2013.

   d. Conversion of one-third of the bonds payable into no-par stock on October 2, 2014. For no-par stock, transfer the bond carrying amount into the Common Stock account. There is no Additional Paid-in Capital account.

   e. Retirement of two-thirds of the bonds payable on October 2, 2014. Purchase price of the bonds was based on their call price of 102.

▶ Answers
Requirement 1

	A	B	C	D	E
Semiannual Interest Date	Interest Payment (4% of Maturity Amount)	Interest Expense (4 1/2% of Preceding Bond Carrying Amount)	Discount Amortization (B – A)	Discount Account Balance (Preceding D – C)	Bond Carrying Amount ($100,000 – D)
10-1-12				$6,500	$93,500
4-1-13	$4,000	$4,208	$208	6,292	93,708
10-1-13	4,000	4,217	217	6,075	93,925
4-1-14	4,000	4,227	227	5,848	94,152
10-1-14	4,000	4,237	237	5,611	94,389

Requirement 2

a.	2012				
	Oct 1	Cash ($100,000 × 0.935)		93,500	
		Discount on Bonds Payable		6,500	
		Bonds Payable			100,000
		To issue bonds at a discount.			
b.	Dec 31	Interest Expense ($4,208 × 3/6)		2,104	
		Discount on Bonds Payable ($208 × 3/6)			104
		Interest Payable ($4,000 × 3/6)			2,000
		To accrue interest and amortize the bonds.			
c.	2013				
	Apr 1	Interest Expense ($4,208 × 3/6)		2,104	
		Interest Payable		2,000	
		Discount on Bonds Payable ($208 × 3/6)			104
		Cash			4,000
		To pay semiannual interest, part of which was accrued, and amortize the bonds.			
d.	2014				
	Oct 2	Bonds Payable ($100,000 × 1/3)		33,333	
		Discount on Bonds Payable ($5,611 × 1/3)			1,870
		Common Stock ($94,389 × 1/3)			31,463
		To record conversion of bonds payable.			
e.	Oct 2	Bonds Payable ($100,000 × 2/3)		66,667	
		Loss on Retirement of Bonds		5,074	
		Discount on Bonds Payable ($5,611 × 2/3)			3,741
		Cash ($100,000 × 2/3 × 1.02)			68,000
		To retire bonds payable before maturity.			

REVIEW | Liabilities

Quick Check (Answers are given on page 580.)

1. Which of the following is *not* an estimated liability?

   a. Allowance for bad debts   c. Income taxes
   b. Product warranties   d. Vacation pay

2. Recording estimated warranty expense in the current year *best* follows which accounting principle?

   a. Full disclosure   d. Materiality
   b. Consistency   e. Historical cost
   c. Expense recognition (matching)

3. Accounts payable turnover for Big Red, Inc., increased from 10 to 12 during 2012. Which of the following statements best describes what this means?

   a. The company paid its accounts payable more quickly in 2012, signaling a stronger liquidity position.

   b. The company paid its accounts payable more slowly in 2013, signaling a weaker liquidity position.

   c. Inventory turned over faster in 2012, meaning sales increased.

   d. Not enough information is provided to make a conclusion.

4. Adventure Camera Co. was organized to sell a single product that carries a 45-day warranty against defects. Engineering estimates indicate that 2% of the units sold will prove defective and require an average repair cost of $45 per unit. During Adventure's first month of operations, total sales were 900 units; by the end of the month, 5 defective units had been repaired. The liability for product warranties at month-end should be

   a. $225.   d. $810.

   b. $1,035.   e. none of these.

   c. $585.

5. A contingent liability should be recorded in the accounts

   a. if the amount can be reasonably estimated.

   b. if the amount is due in cash within one year.

   c. if the related future event will probably occur.

   d. Both b and c

   e. Both a and c

6. An unsecured bond is a

   a. mortgage bond.   d. term bond.

   b. registered bond   e. serial bond.

   c. debenture bond.

7. The Discount on Bonds Payable account

   a. is a contra account to Bonds Payable.   d. is an expense account.

   b. is a miscellaneous revenue account.   e. has a normal credit balance.

   c. is expensed at the bond's maturity.

8. The discount on a bond payable becomes

   a. additional interest expense over the life of the bonds.

   b. a reduction in interest expense the year the bonds mature.

   c. a liability in the year the bonds are sold.

   d. additional interest expense the year the bonds are sold.

   e. a reduction in interest expense over the life of the bonds.

9. A bond that matures in installments is called a

   a. serial bond.   d. callable bond.

   b. zero coupon.   e. term bond.

   c. secured bond.

10. The carrying value of Bonds Payable equals

    a. Bonds Payable + Accrued Interest.

    b. Bonds Payable − Discount on Bonds Payable.

    c. Bonds Payable − Premium on Bonds Payable.

    d. Bonds Payable + Discount on Bonds Payable.

11. Dart Corporation's leverage ratio increased from 2.5 in 2011 to 3.0 in 2012. Without looking at the financial statements, which statement best describes what may have occurred?

 a. The company incurred new debt financing in 2012, making it more profitable.
 b. The company incurred new equity financing in 2012, making it less profitable.
 c. The company incurred new debt financing in 2012, but it may or may not have been more profitable.
 d. The company incurred new equity financing in 2012, but it may or may not have been more profitable.

Use this information to answer questions 12–16.
McCoy Corporation issued $100,000 of 7.5% 10-year bonds. The bonds are dated and sold on January 1, 2013. Interest payment dates are January 1 and July 1. The bonds are issued for $96,602 to yield the market interest rate of 8%. Use the effective-interest method for questions 12–15.

12. What is the amount of interest expense that McCoy Corporation will record on July 1, 2013, the first semiannual interest payment date? (All amounts rounded to the nearest dollar.)

 a. $7,500   c. $3,864
 b. $4,000   d. $3,750

13. What is the amount of discount amortization that McCoy Corporation will record on July 1, 2013, the first semiannual interest payment date?

 a. $4,000   c. $114
 b. $-0-   d. $3,864

14. What is the total cash payment for interest for each 12-month period? (All amounts are rounded to the nearest dollar.)

 a. $7,725   c. $8,000
 b. $4,000   d. $7,500

15. What is the carrying amount of the bonds on the January 1, 2014, balance sheet?

 a. $96,835   c. $96,716
 b. $96,563   d. $96,907

16. Using straight-line amortization, the carrying amount of McCoy Corporation's bonds at December 31, 2013, is

 a. $96,676.   c. $97,910.
 b. $96,942.   d. $96,563.

Accounting Vocabulary

accounts payable turnover (p. 519) The number of times per year a company pays off its accounts payable.

accrued expense (p. 521) An expense incurred but not yet paid in cash. Also called *accrued liability*.

accrued liability (p. 521) A liability for an expense that has not yet been paid. Also called *accrued expense*.

bonds payable (p. 527) Groups of notes payable issued to multiple lenders called *bondholders*.

callable bond (p. 540) Bonds that are paid off early at a specified price at the option of the issuer.

capital lease (p. 545) Lease agreement in which the lessee assumes, in substance, the risks and rewards of asset ownership.

In the United States, a lease is assumed to be a capital lease if it meets any one of four criteria: (1) The lease transfers title of the leased asset to the lessee. (2) The lease contains a bargain purchase option. (3) The lease term is 75% or more of the estimated useful life of the leased asset. (4) The present value of the lease payments is 90% or more of the market value of the leased asset.

convertible bonds (or notes) (p. 540) Bonds or notes that may be converted into the issuing company's common stock at the investor's option.

current portion of long-term debt (p. 523) The amount of the principal that is payable within one year.

days payable outstanding (DPO) (p. 519) Accounts payable turnover expressed in days (365/turnover).

debentures (p. 529) Unsecured bonds—bonds backed only by the good faith of the borrower.

discount (on a bond) (p. 529) Excess of a bond's face (par) value over its issue price.

earnings per share (EPS) (p. 541) Amount of a company's net income per share of its outstanding common stock.

equity multiplier (p. 543) Another name for *leverage ratio*.

interest-coverage ratio (p. 544) Another name for the *times-interest-earned ratio*.

lease (p. 544) Rental agreement in which the tenant (lessee) agrees to make rent payments to the property owner (lessor) in exchange for the use of the asset.

lessee (p. 544) Tenant in a lease agreement.

lessor (p. 544) Property owner in a lease agreement.

leverage (p. 541) Using borrowed funds to increase the return on equity. Successful use of leverage means earning more income on borrowed money than the related interest expense, thereby increasing the earnings for the owners of the business. Also called *trading on the equity*.

leverage ratio (p. 543) The ratio of total assets ÷ total stockholders' equity, showing the proportion of total stockholder's equity to total assets. This ratio, like the debt ratio introduced in Chapter 3, tells the mixture of a company's debt and equity financing and is useful in calculating rate of return on stockholders' equity (ROE) through the DuPont Model.

market interest rate (p. 529) Interest rate that investors demand for loaning their money. Also called *effective interest rate*.

operating lease (p. 544) A lease in which the lessee does not assume the risks or rewards of asset ownership.

payroll (p. 521) Employee compensation, a major expense of many businesses.

pension (p. 546) Employee compensation that will be received during retirement.

premium (on a bond) (p. 529) Excess of a bond's issue price over its face (par) value.

serial bonds (p. 529) Bonds that mature in installments over a period of time.

short-term notes payable (p. 519) Note payable that are due within one year.

stated interest rate (p. 529) Interest rate that determines the amount of cash interest the borrower pays and the investor receives each year.

term bonds (p. 529) Bonds that all mature at the same time for a particular issue.

times-interest-earned ratio (p. 544) Ratio of income from operations to interest expense. Measures the number of times that operating income can cover interest expense. Also called the *interest-coverage ratio*.

trading on the equity (p. 541) Earning more income on borrowed money than the related interest expense, thereby increasing the earnings for the owners of the business. Also called *leverage*—the power of which is illustrated through the *leverage ratio*.

underwriter (p. 529) Organization that purchases the bonds from an issuing company and resells them to its clients or sells the bonds for a commission, agreeing to buy all unsold bonds.

ASSESS YOUR PROGRESS

Short Exercises

S9-1 (*Learning Objective 1: Account for a short-term note payable*) Gordon Sports Authority purchased inventory costing $11,000 by signing a 12% short-term note payable. The purchase occurred on July 31, 2012. Gordon pays annual interest each year on July 31. Journalize the company's (a) purchase of inventory; (b) accrual of interest expense on April 30, 2013, which is the year-end; and (c) payment of the note plus interest on July 31, 2013. (Round your answers to the nearest whole number.) (d) Show what the company would report on its balance sheet at April 30, 2013, and on its income statement for the year ended on that date.

S9-2 (*Learning Objective 1: Analyze accounts payable turnover*) Wardlow Sales, Inc.'s comparative income statements and balance sheets show the following selected information for 2011 and 2012:

	2012	2011
Cost of goods sold	$2,700,000	$2,500,000
Average accounts payable	$ 300,000	$ 250,000

Requirements

1. Calculate the company's accounts payable turnover and days payable outstanding (DPO) for 2011 and 2012.
2. On the basis of this computation alone, has the company's liquidity position improved or deteriorated during 2012?

S9-3 (*Learning Objective 1: Account for warranty expense and estimated warranty payable*) Trail Runner USA guarantees tires against defects for five years or 55,000 miles, whichever comes first. Suppose Trail Runner USA can expect warranty costs during the five-year period to add up to 5% of sales. Assume that a Trail Runner USA dealer in Atlanta, Georgia, made sales of $564,000 during 2012. Trail Runner USA received cash for 40% of the sales and took notes receivable for the remainder. Payments to satisfy customer warranty claims totaled $18,000 during 2012.

1. Record the sales, warranty expense, and warranty payments for Trail Runner USA.
2. Post to the Estimated Warranty Payable T-account. The beginning balance was $13,000. At the end of 2012, how much in estimated warranty payable does Trail Runner USA owe to its customers?

S9-4 (*Learning Objective 1: Report warranties in the financial statements*) Refer to the data given in Short Exercise 9-3. What amount of warranty expense will Trail Runner USA report during 2012? Which accounting principle addresses this situation? Does the warranty expense for the year equal the year's cash payments for warranties? Explain the relevant accounting principle as it applies to measuring warranty expense.

S9-5 (*Learning Objective 1: Interpret a company's contingent liabilities*) Tony Chase, Inc., the motorcycle manufacturer, included the following note in its annual report:

NOTES TO CONSOLIDATED FINANCIAL STATEMENTS
7 (In Part): Commitments and Contingencies
   The Company self-insures its product liability losses in the United States up to $3.8 million (catastrophic coverage is maintained for individual claims in excess of $3.8 million up to $26.3 million). Outside the United States, the Company is insured for product liability up to $26.3 million per individual claim and in the aggregate.

---

1. Why are these *contingent* (versus *real*) liabilities?
2. In the United States, how can the contingent liability become a real liability for Tony Chase? What are the limits to the company's product liabilities in the United States?
3. How can a contingency outside the United States become a real liability for the company? How does Tony Chase's potential liability differ for claims outside the United States?

S9-6 (*Learning Objective 2: Price bonds*) Compute the price of the following bonds:

   a. $200,000 issued at 77.75
   b. $200,000 issued at 103.50
   c. $200,000 issued at 94.25
   d. $200,000 issued at 102.50

S9-7 (*Learning Objective 2: Determine bond prices at par, discount, or premium*) Determine whether the following bonds payable will be issued at par value, at a premium, or at a discount:

   a. The market interest rate is 7%. Horton Corp. issues bonds payable with a stated rate of 6 1/2%.
   b. Sharp, Inc., issued 6% bonds payable when the market rate was 5 3/4%.
   c. Houston Corporation issued 3% bonds when the market interest rate was 3%.
   d. Ontario Company issued bonds payable that pay stated interest of 8%. At issuance, the market interest rate was 8 1/4%.

S9-8 (*Learning Objective 2: Journalize basic bond payable transactions and bonds issued at par*)
Hunter Corp. issued 7-year bonds payable with a face amount of $125,000 when the market
interest rate was 8%. Assume that the accounting year of Hunter ends on December 31 and that
bonds pay interest on January 1 and July 1. Journalize the following transactions for Hunter.
Include an explanation for each entry.

    a. Issuance of the bonds payable at par on July 1, 2012
    b. Accrual of interest expense on December 31, 2012 (rounded to the nearest dollar)
    c. Payment of cash interest on January 1, 2013
    d. Payment of the bonds payable at maturity (give the date)

S9-9 (*Learning Objective 2: Issue bonds payable and amortize bonds by the effective-interest method*)
EKU, Inc., issued $560,000 of 6%, 10-year bonds payable at a price of 80.5 on March 31, 2012. The
market interest rate at the date of issuance was 9%, and the EKU bonds pay interest semiannually.

    1. Prepare an effective-interest amortization table for the bonds through the first three interest
payments. Round amounts to the nearest dollar.
    2. Record EKU, Inc.'s issuance of the bonds on March 31, 2012, and payment of the first
semiannual interest amount and amortization of the bond discount on September 30, 2012.
Explanations are not required.

S9-10 (*Learning Objective 2: Account for bonds payable; analyze data on bonds*) Use the
amortization table that you prepared for EKU's bonds in Short Exercise 9-9 to answer the
following questions:

    1. How much cash did EKU borrow on March 31, 2012? How much cash will EKU pay back
at maturity on March 31, 2022?
    2. How much cash interest will EKU pay each six months?
    3. How much interest expense will EKU report on September 30, 2012, and on March 31,
2013? Why does the amount of interest expense increase each period?

S9-11 (*Learning Objective 2: Determine bonds payable amounts; amortize bonds by the straight-line
method*) Starlight Drive-Ins Ltd. borrowed money by issuing $3,000,000 of 8% bonds payable at 97.5
on July 1, 2012. The bonds are 10-year bonds and pay interest each January 1 and July 1.

    1. How much cash did Starlight receive when it issued the bonds payable? Journalize this
transaction.
    2. How much must Starlight pay back at maturity? When is the maturity date?
    3. How much cash interest will Starlight pay each six months?
    4. How much interest expense will Starlight report each six months? Assume the straight-line
amortization method. Journalize the entries for accrual of interest on December 31, 2012,
and payment of interest on January 1, 2013.

S9-12 (*Learning Objective 3: Calculate the leverage ratio, debt ratio, and times-interest-earned,
and evaluate debt-paying ability*) Examine the following selected financial information for Best
Buy Co., Inc., and Wal-Mart Stores, Inc., as of the end of their 2010 fiscal years:

(In millions)	Best Buy Co., Inc.	Wal-Mart Stores, Inc.
1. Total assets	$17,849	$180,663
2. Stockholders' equity	$ 7,292	$ 71,247
3. Operating income	$ 2,114	$ 25,542
4. Interest expense	$ 87	$ 1,928
5. Leverage ratio		
6. Total debt		
7. Debt ratio		
8. Times interest earned		

    1. Complete the table, calculating all the requested information for the two companies.
    2. Evaluate each company's long-term debt-paying ability (strong, medium, weak).

S9-13 (*Learning Objective 3: Compute earnings-per-share effects of financing with bonds versus stock*) Wavetown Marina needs to raise $1 million to expand the company. Wavetown Marina is considering the issuance of either

- ▶ $1,000,000 of 7% bonds payable to borrow the money, or
- ▶ 100,000 shares of common stock at $10 per share.

Before any new financing, Wavetown Marina expects to earn net income of $400,000, and the company already has 100,000 shares of common stock outstanding. Wavetown Marina believes the expansion will increase income before interest and income tax by $100,000. The income tax rate is 30%.

   Prepare an analysis to determine which plan is likely to result in the higher earnings per share. Based solely on the earnings-per-share comparison, which financing plan would you recommend for Wavetown Marina?

S9-14 (*Learning Objective 3: Compute and evaluate three ratios*) Evensen Plumbing Products Ltd. reported the following data in 2012 (in millions):

	2012
Net operating revenues................	$ 29.1
Operating expenses	25.0
Operating income........................	4.1
Nonoperating items:	
Interest expense......................	(1.0)
Other	(0.2)
Net income................................	$ 2.8
Total assets	$100.0
Total stockholders' equity...........	40.0

   Compute Evensen's leverage ratio, debt ratio, and times-interest-earned ratio, and write a sentence to explain what those ratio values mean. Would you be willing to lend Evensen $1 million? State your reason.

S9-15 (*Learning Objectives 4, 5: Report liabilities, including capital lease obligations*) Regal, Inc., includes the following selected accounts in its general ledger at December 31, 2012:

Bonds payable...	$375,000
Equipment..	117,000
Current portion of bonds payable	56,000
Notes payable, long-term	125,000
Interest payable (due March 1, 2013)...	1,700
Accounts payable	33,000
Discount on bonds payable (all long-term)..	11,250
Accounts receivable...	31,000

   Prepare the liabilities section of Regal, Inc.'s balance sheet at December 31, 2012, to show how the company would report these items. Report total current liabilities and total liabilities.

Exercises

All of the A and B exercises can be found within MyAccountingLab, an online homework and practice environment. Your instructor may ask you to complete these exercises using MyAccountingLab.

MyAccountingLab

Group A

E9-16A (*Learning Objective 1: Account for warranty expense and the related liability*) The accounting records of Earthtone Ceramics included the following balances at the end of the period:

Estimated Warranty Payable		Sales Revenue		Warranty Expense	
	Beg bal 5,000		111.000		

In the past, Earthtone's warranty expense has been 8% of sales. During 2012, the business paid $7,000 to satisfy the warranty claims.

▶ Requirements

1. Journalize Earthtone's warranty expense for the period and the company's cash payments to satisfy warranty claims. Explanations are not required.
2. Show what Earthtones will report on its income statement and balance sheet for this situation.
3. Which data item from Requirement 2 will affect Earthtone's current ratio? Will Earthtone's current ratio increase or decrease as a result of this item?

E9-17A (*Learning Objective 1: Record and report current liabilities*) Worldwide Publishing completed the following transactions for one subscriber during 2012:

Oct 1	Sold a one-year subscription, collecting cash of $2,400, plus sales tax of 9%.
Nov 15	Remitted (paid) the sales tax to the state of Massachusetts.
Dec 31	Made the necessary adjustment at year-end.

▶ Requirement

1. Journalize these transactions (explanations not required). Then report any liability on the company's balance sheet at December 31, 2012.

E9-18A (*Learning Objective 1: Account for payroll expense and liabilities*) Perrin Talent Search has an annual payroll of $150,000. In addition, the company incurs payroll tax expense of 8%. At December 31, Perrin owes salaries of $7,500 and FICA and other payroll tax of $700. The company will pay these amounts early next year. Show what Perrin will report for the foregoing on its income statement and year-end balance sheet.

E9-19A (*Learning Objective 1: Record note-payable transactions*) Assume that Cranmore Company completed the following note-payable transactions.

2012		
Apr 1	Purchased delivery truck costing $85,000 by issuing a one-year, 8% note payable.
Dec 31	Accrued interest on the note payable.
2013		
Apr 1	Paid the note payable at maturity.

▶ Requirements

1. How much interest expense must be accrued at December 31, 2012? (Round your answer to the nearest whole dollar.)
2. Determine the amount of Cranmore's final payment on April 1, 2013.
3. How much interest expense will Cranmore report for 2012 and for 2013? (Round your answer to the nearest whole dollar.)

E9-20A (*Learning Objective 1: Account for income tax*) At December 31, 2012, Olsen Real Estate reported a current liability for income tax payable of $150,000. During 2013, Olsen earned income of $900,000 before income tax. The company's income tax rate during 2013 was 29%. Also during 2013, Olsen paid income taxes of $245,000.

How much income tax payable did Olsen Real Estate report on its balance sheet at December 31, 2013? How much income tax expense did Olsen report on its 2013 income statement?

E9-21A (*Learning Objectives 1, 3: Analyze current and long-term liabilities; evaluate debt-paying ability*) Geodesic Domes, Inc., builds environmentally sensitive structures. The company's 2012 revenues totaled $2,800 million. At December 31, 2012, and 2011, the company had $661 million and $600 million in current assets, respectively. The December 31, 2012, and 2011, balance sheets and income statements reported the following amounts:

At Year-end (In millions)	2012	2011
Liabilities and stockholders' equity		
Current liabilities		
Accounts payable	$ 110	$ 182
Accrued expenses	97	177
Employee compensation and benefits	45	15
Current portion of long-term debt........................	7	20
Total current liabilities.......................................	259	394
Long-term debt	1,394	1,315
Post-retirement benefits payable.............................	102	154
Other liabilities	8	20
Stockholders' equity...	1,951	1,492
Total liabilities and stockholders' equity	$3,714	$3,375
Year-end (in millions)		
Cost of goods sold...	$1,656	$1,790

▶ Requirements

1. Describe each of Geodesic Domes, Inc.'s liabilities and state how the liability arose.
2. What were the company's total assets at December 31, 2012? Evaluate the company's leverage and debt ratios at the end of 2011 and 2012. Did the company improve, deteriorate, or remain about the same over the year?
3. Accounts payable at the end of 2010 was $190 million. Calculate accounts payable turnover as a ratio and days payable outstanding (DPO) for 2011 and 2012. Calculate current ratios for 2011 and 2012 as well. Evaluate whether the company improved or deteriorated from the standpoint of ability to cover accounts payable and current liabilities over the year.

E9-22A (*Learning Objectives 1, 5: Report a contingent liability*) Smith Security Systems' revenues for 2012 totaled $25.8 million. As with most companies, Smith is a defendant in lawsuits related to its products. Note 14 of the Smith Annual Report for 2012 reported the following:

> **14. Contingencies**
> The company is involved in various legal proceedings.... It is the Company's policy to accrue for amounts related to these legal matters if it is probable that a liability has been incurred and an amount is reasonably estimable.

▶ Requirements

1. Suppose Smith's lawyers believe that a significant legal judgment against the company is reasonably possible. How should Smith report this situation in its financial statements?
2. Suppose Smith's lawyers believe it is probable that a $3 million judgment will be rendered against the company. Report this situation in Smith's financial statements. Journalize any entry requirements by GAAP. Explanations are not required.

E9-23A (*Learning Objectives 1, 5: Report current and long-term liabilities*) Assume that Banff Electronics completed these selected transactions during March 2012:

a. Sales of $2,400,000 are subject to estimated warranty cost of 4%. The estimated warranty payable at the beginning of the year was $35,000, and warranty payments for the year totaled $57,000.
b. On March 1, Banff Electronics signed a $65,000 note payable that requires annual payments of $16,250 plus 7% interest on the unpaid balance each March 2.
c. Music For You, Inc., a chain of music stores, ordered $100,000 worth of CD players. With its order, Music For You, Inc., sent a check for $100,000 in advance, and Banff shipped $85,000 of the goods. Banff will ship the remainder of the goods on April 3, 2012.
d. The March payroll of $320,000 is subject to employee withheld income tax of $30,900 and FICA tax of 7.65%. On March 31, Banff pays employees their take-home pay and accrues all tax amounts.

▶ Requirement

1. Report these items on Banff Electronics' balance sheet at March 31, 2012.

E9-24A (*Learning Objective 2: Issue bonds payable (discount), pay and accrue interest, and amortize bonds by the straight-line method*) On January 31, Doherty Logistics, Inc., issued five-year, 7% bonds payable with a face value of $8,000,000. The bonds were issued at 96 and pay interest on January 31 and July 31. Doherty Logistics, Inc., amortizes bonds by the straight-line method. Record (a) issuance of the bonds on January 31, (b) the semiannual interest payment and amortization of bond discount on July 31, and (c) the interest accrual and discount amortization on December 31.

E9-25A (*Learning Objective 2: Measure cash amounts for a bond payable (premium); amortize the bonds by the straight-line method*) Town Bank has $100,000 of 7% debenture bonds outstanding. The bonds were issued at 105 in 2012 and mature in 2032.

▶ Requirements

1. How much cash did Town Bank receive when it issued these bonds?
2. How much cash in *total* will Town Bank pay the bondholders through the maturity date of the bonds?
3. Take the difference between your answers to Requirements 1 and 2. This difference represents Town Bank's total interest expense over the life of the bonds.
4. Compute Town Bank's annual interest expense by the straight-line amortization method. Multiply this amount by 20. Your 20-year total should be the same as your answer to Requirement 3.

E9-26A (*Learning Objective 2: Issue bonds payable (discount), record interest payments and the related bond amortization using the effective-interest method*) Team Sports Ltd. is authorized to issue $5,000,000 of 5%, 10-year bonds payable. On December 31, 2012, when the market interest rate is 6%, the company issues $4,000,000 of the bonds and receives cash of $3,702,450. Team Sports Ltd. amortizes bond discount by the effective-interest method. The semiannual interest dates are June 30 and December 31.

▶ Requirements

1. Prepare a bond amortization table for the first four semiannual interest periods.
2. Record issuance of the bonds payable on December 31, 2012; the first semiannual interest payment on June 30, 2013; and the second payment on December 31, 2013.

E9-27A (*Learning Objective 2: Issue bonds payable (premium), record interest payment and the related bond amortization using the effective interest method*) On June 30, 2012, the market interest rate is 8%. First Place Sports Ltd. issues $4,000,000 of 9%, 20-year bonds payable at a price of 109.895. The bonds pay interest on June 30 and December 31. First Place Sports Ltd. amortizes bonds by the effective-interest method.

▶ Requirements

1. Prepare a bond amortization table for the first four semiannual interest periods.
2. Record the issuance of bonds payable on June 30, 2012; the payment of interest on December 31, 2012; and the payment of interest on June 30, 2013.

E9-28A (*Learning Objective 2: Create a bond amortization schedule (discount)*) Lawrence Co. issued $300,000 of 6% (0.06), 10-year bonds payable on January 1, 2012, when the market interest rate was 7% (0.07). The company pays interest annually at year-end. The issue price of the bonds was $278,929.

▶ Requirement

1. Create a spreadsheet model to prepare a schedule to amortize the bonds. Use the effective-interest method of amortization. (Round to the nearest dollar.)

E9-29A (*Learning Objectives 3, 4: Interpret an operating lease footnote*) Footnote 10 of Abercrombie and Fitch Co.'s financial statements for fiscal year 2010 (January 29, 2011) contains the following information:

At January 29, 2011, the Company was committed to noncancelable leases with remaining terms of 1 to 17 years. A summary of operating lease commitments under noncancelable leases follows (thousands):

Fiscal 2011..	$ 331,151
Fiscal 2012..	$ 319,982
Fiscal 2013..	$ 303,531
Fiscal 2014..	$ 285,337
Fiscal 2015..	$ 262,586
Thereafter	$1,110,598
Total	$2,613,185

▶ Requirements

1. Interpret the information in the footnote. What rights does the company have? What obligations?
2. Are the rights and obligations discussed in Requirement 1 reported in the liability section of the balance sheet? Why or why not? How does this impact the company's debt and leverage ratios?
3. How is this type of reporting likely to change in the future?

E9-30A (*Learning Objective 3: Evaluate debt-paying ability*) Companies that operate in different industries may have very different financial ratio values. These differences may grow even wider when we compare companies located in different countries.

Compare three leading companies on their current ratio, debt ratio, leverage ratio, and times-interest-earned ratio. Compute the ratios for Company B, Company N, and Company V.

(Amounts in millions or billions)	Company B	Company N	Company V
Income data			
Total revenues	$9,732	¥7,320	€136,146
Operating income	295	230	5,646
Interest expense	41	27	655
Net income	22	17	450
Assets and liability data			
(Amounts in millions or billions)			
Total current assets	429	5,321	144,720
Long-term assets	81	592	65,828
Total current liabilities	227	2,217	72,000
Long-term liabilities	77	2,277	111,177
Stockholders' equity	206	1,419	27,371

Based on your computed ratio values, which company looks the least risky?

E9-31A (*Learning Objective 3: Analyze alternative plans for raising money*) Prime Nation Financial Services is considering two plans for raising $600,000 to expand operations. Plan A is to borrow at 6%, and plan B is to issue 125,000 shares of common stock at $4.80 per share. Before any new financing, Prime Nation Financial Services has net income of $300,000 and 100,000 shares of common stock outstanding. Assume you own most of Prime Nation Financial Services' existing stock. Management believes the company can use the new funds to earn additional income of $500,000 before interest and taxes. Prime Nation Financial Services' income tax rate is 25%.

▶ Requirements

1. Analyze Prime Nation Financial Services' situation to determine which plan will result in higher earnings per share.
2. Which plan results in the higher earnings per share? Which plan allows you to retain control of the company? Which plan creates more financial risk for the company? Which plan do you prefer? Why? Present your conclusion in a memo to Prime Nation Financial Services' board of directors.

Group B

E9-32B (*Learning Objective 1: Account for warranty expense and the related liability*) The accounting records of Off the Wheel Ceramics included the following balances at the end of the period:

Estimated Warranty Payable		Sales Revenue		Warranty Expense	
	Beg bal 2,000		176,000		

In the past, Off the Wheel's warranty expense has been 9% of sales. During 2012, the business paid $9,000 to satisfy the warranty claims.

▶ Requirements

1. Journalize Off the Wheel's warranty expense for the period and the company's cash payments to satisfy warranty claims. Explanations are not required.
2. Show what Off the Wheel will report on its income statement and balance sheet for this situation.
3. Which data item from Requirement 2 will affect Off the Wheel's current ratio? Will Off the Wheel's current ratio increase or decrease as a result of this item?

E9-33B (*Learning Objective 1: Record and report current liabilities*) Travis Publishing completed the following transactions for one subscriber during 2012:

Oct 1	Sold a one-year subscription, collecting cash of $2,100, plus sales tax of 7%.
Nov 15	Remitted (paid) the sales tax to the state of Massachusetts.
Dec 31	Made the necessary adjustment at year-end.

▶ Requirement

1. Journalize these transactions (explanations not required). Then report any liability on the company's balance sheet at December 31, 2012.

E9-34B (*Learning Objective 1: Account for payroll expense and liabilities*) Penske Talent Search has an annual payroll of $190,000. In addition, the company incurs payroll tax expense of 8%. At December 31, Penske owes salaries of $8,000 and FICA and other payroll tax of $750. The company will pay these amounts early next year.

   Show what Penske will report for the foregoing on its income statement and year-end balance sheet.

E9-35B (*Learning Objective 1: Record note-payable transactions*) Assume that Creative Company completed the following note-payable transactions:

2012	
Oct 1	Purchased delivery truck costing $84,000 by issuing a one-year, 7% note payable.
Dec 31	Accrued interest on the note payable.
2013	
Oct 1	Paid the note payable at maturity.

▶ Requirements

1. How much interest expense must be accrued at December 31, 2012? (Round your answer to the nearest whole dollar.)
2. Determine the amount of Creative's final payment on October 1, 2013.
3. How much interest expense will Creative report for 2012 and for 2013? (Round your answer to the nearest whole dollar.)

E9-36B (*Learning Objective 1: Account for income tax*) At December 31, 2012, McKinley Real Estate reported a current liability for income tax payable of $210,000. During 2013, McKinley earned income of $1,600,000 before income tax. The company's income tax rate during 2013 was 36%. Also during 2013, McKinley paid income taxes of $350,000.

   How much income tax payable did McKinley Real Estate report on its balance sheet at December 31, 2013? How much income tax expense did McKinley report on its 2013 income statement?

E9-37B (*Learning Objectives 1, 3: Analyze current and long-term liabilities; evaluate debt-paying ability*) Green Earth Homes, Inc., builds environmentally sensitive structures. The company's 2012 revenues totaled $2,785 million. At December 31, 2012 and 2011, the company had $643 million and $610 million in current assets, respectively. The December 31, 2012 and 2011 balance sheets and income statements reported the following amounts:

At year-end (In millions)	2012	2011
Liabilities and stockholders' equity		
Current liabilities		
Accounts payable	$ 137	$ 181
Accrued expenses	163	169
Employee compensation and benefits	51	16
Current portion of long-term debt	17	10
Total Current Liabilities	368	376
Long-term debt	1,497	1,326
Post-retirement benefits payable	138	112
Other liabilities	20	22
Stockholders' equity	2,027	1,492
Total liabilities and stockholders' equity	$4,050	3,328
Year-end (in millions)		
Cost of goods sold	$1,885	$2,196

▶ Requirements

1. Describe each of Green Earth Homes, Inc.'s liabilities and state how the liability arose.
2. What were the company's total assets at December 31, 2012? Evaluate the company's leverage and debt ratios at the end of 2011 and 2012. Did the company improve, deteriorate, or remain about the same over the year?
3. Accounts payable at the end of 2010 was $195. Calculate accounts payable turnover as a ratio and days payable outstanding (DPO) for 2011 and 2012. Calculate current ratios for 2011 and 2012 as well. Evaluate whether the company improved or deteriorated from the standpoint of ability to cover accounts payable and current liabilities over the year.

E9-38B (*Learning Objectives 1, 5: Report a contingent liability*) Clark Security Systems' revenues for 2012 totaled $25.9 million. As with most companies, Clark is a defendant in lawsuits related to its products. Note 14 of the Clark Annual Report for 2012 reported the following:

> **14. Contingencies**
> The company is involved in various legal proceedings.... It is the Company's policy to accrue for amounts related to these legal matters if it is probable that a liability has been incurred and an amount is reasonably estimable.

▶ Requirements

1. Suppose Clark's lawyers believe that a significant legal judgment against the company is reasonably possible. How should Clark report this situation in its financial statements?
2. Suppose Clark's lawyers believe it is probable that a $2.0 million judgment will be rendered against the company. Report this situation in Clark's financial statements. Journalize any entry required by GAAP. Explanations are not required.

E9-39B (*Learning Objectives 1, 5: Report current and long-term liabilities*) Assume Jasper Electronics completed these selected transactions during June 2012.

a. Sales of $2,100,000 are subject to estimated warranty cost of 6%. The estimated warranty payable at the beginning of the year was $36,000, and warranty payments for the year totaled $51,000.
b. On June 1, Jasper Electronics signed a $45,000 note payable that requires annual payments of $11,250 plus 7% interest on the unpaid balance each June 2.
c. Music For You, Inc., a chain of music stores, ordered $130,000 worth of CD players. With its order, Music For You, Inc., sent a check for $130,000, and Jasper Electronics shipped $75,000 of the goods. Jasper Electronics will ship the remainder of the goods on July 3, 2012.

d. The June payroll of $300,000 is subject to employee withheld income tax of $30,300 and FICA tax of 7.65%. On June 30, Jasper Electronics pays employees their take-home pay and accrues all tax amounts.

▶ Requirement

1. Report these items on Jasper Electronics' balance sheet at June 30, 2012.

E9-40B (*Learning Objective 2: Issue bonds payable (discount); pay and accrue interest; amortize the bonds by the straight-line method*) On January 31, Dogwood Logistics, Inc., issued 10-year, 9% bonds payable with a face value of $9,000,000. The bonds were issued at 93 and pay interest on January 31 and July 31. Dogwood Logistics, Inc., amortizes bond discount by the straight-line method. Record (a) issuance of the bonds on January 31, (b) the semiannual interest payment and amortization of bond discount on July 31, and (c) the interest accrual and discount amortization on December 31.

E9-41B (*Learning Objective 2: Measure cash amounts for a bond payable (premium); amortize the bonds by the straight-line method*) Municipal Bank has $300,000 of 6% debenture bonds outstanding. The bonds were issued at 101 in 2012 and mature in 2032.

▶ Requirements

1. How much cash did Municipal Bank receive when it issued these bonds?
2. How much cash in *total* will Municipal Bank pay the bondholders through the maturity date of the bonds?
3. Take the difference between your answers to Requirements 1 and 2. This difference represents Municipal Bank's total interest expense over the life of the bonds.
4. Compute Municipal Bank's annual interest expense by the straight-line amortization method. Multiply this amount by 20. Your 20-year total should be the same as your answer to Requirement 3.

E9-42B (*Learning Objective 2: Issue bonds payable (discount), and record interest payments and the related bond amortization using the effective-interest method*) Winner Sports Ltd. is authorized to issue $4,000,000 of 12%, 10-year bonds payable. On December 31, 2012, when the market interest rate is 14%, the company issues $3,200,000 of the bonds and receives cash of $2,861,000. Winner Sports amortizes bond discount by the effective-interest method. The semiannual interest dates are June 30 and December 31.

▶ Requirements

1. Prepare a bond amortization table for the first four semiannual interest periods.
2. Record issuance of the bonds payable on December 31, 2012; the first semiannual interest payment on June 30, 2013; and the second payment on December 31, 2013.

E9-43B (*Learning Objective 2: Issue bonds payable (premium); record interest payment and the related bond amortization using the effective-interest method*) On June 30, 2012, the market interest rate is 7%. Victory Sports Ltd. issues $1,600,000 of 8%, 25-year bonds payable at a price of 111.75. The bonds pay interest on June 30 and December 31. Victory Sports Ltd. amortizes bonds by the effective-interest method.

▶ Requirements

1. Prepare a bond amortization table for the first four semiannual interest periods.
2. Record the issuance of bonds payable on June 30, 2012; the payment of interest on December 31, 2012; and the payment of interest on June 30, 2013.

E9-44B (*Learning Objective 2: Create a bond amortization schedule (discount)*) Lowell Co. issued $450,000 of 5% (0.05), 10-year bonds payable on January 1, 2010, when the market interest rate was 6% (0.06). The company pays interest annually at year-end. The issue price of the bonds was $416,880.

▶ Requirement

1. Create a spreadsheet model to prepare a schedule to amortize the bonds. Use the effective-interest method of amortization. (Round to the nearest dollar.)

E9-45B (*Learning Objectives 3, 4: Interpret an operating lease footnote*) Footnote 7 of AnnTaylor Stores Corp.'s financial statements for fiscal year 2010 contains the following information:

7. Commitments and Contingencies
Operating Leases

The Company occupies its retail stores and administrative facilities under operating leases, most of which are noncancelable. Some of the store leases grant the Company the right to extend the term for one or two additional five-year periods under substantially the same terms and conditions as the original leases. Some store leases also contain early termination options, which can be exercised by the Company under specific conditions. Most of the store leases require payment of a specified minimum rent, plus contingent rent based on a percentage of the store's net sales in excess of a specified threshold. The Company also leases certain office equipment for its corporate offices and store locations under noncancelable operating leases which generally have three-year terms.

Future minimum lease payments under noncancelable operating leases as of January 29, 2011, are as follows:

Fiscal Year	(in thousands)
2011	$ 177,337
2012	160,110
2013	149,471
2014	136,073
2015	118,096
Thereafter	306,139
Total	1,047,226
Sublease rentals	24,351
Net rentals	$1,022,875

► Requirements

1. Interpret the information in the footnote. What rights does the company have? What obligations?
2. Are the rights and obligations discussed in Requirement 1 reported in the liability section of the balance sheet? Why or why not? How does this impact the company's debt and leverage ratios?
3. How is this type of reporting likely to change in the future?

E9-46B (*Learning Objective 3: Evaluate debt-paying ability*) Companies that operate in different industries may have very different financial ratio values. These differences may grow even wider when we compare companies located in different countries.

Compare three leading companies on their current ratio, debt ratio, leverage ratio, and times-interest-earned ratio. Compute the ratios for Company F, Company K, and Company R.

(Amounts in millions or billions)	Company F	Company K	Company R
Income data			
Total revenues	$9,724	¥7,307	€136,492
Operating income	292	224	5,592
Interest expense	46	33	736
Net income	23	15	448
Assets and liability data **(Amounts in millions or billions)**			
Total current assets	434	5,383	148,526
Long-term assets	96	405	49,525
Total current liabilities	207	2,197	72,100
Long-term liabilities	107	2,318	110,107
Stockholders' equity	216	1,273	15,844

Based on your computed ratio values, which company looks the least risky?

E9-47B (*Learning Objective 4: Analyze alternative plans for raising money*) United Nation Financial Services is considering two plans for raising $900,000 to expand operations. Plan A is to borrow at 10%, and plan B is to issue 250,000 shares of common stock at $3.60 per share. Before any new financing, United Nation Financial Services has net income of $600,000 and 200,000 shares of common stock outstanding. Assume you own most of United Nation Financial Services' existing stock. Management believes the company can use the new funds to earn additional income of $800,000 before interest and taxes. United Nation Financial Services' income tax rate is 40%.

▶ Requirements

1. Analyze United Nation Financial Services' situation to determine which plan will result in the higher earnings per share.
2. Which plan results in the higher earnings per share? Which plan allows you to retain control of the company? Which plan creates more financial risk for the company? Which plan do you prefer? Why? Present your conclusion in a memo to United Nation Financial Services' board of directors.

Quiz

Test your understanding of accounting for liabilities by answering the following questions. Select the best choice from among the possible answers given.

Q9-48 For the purpose of classifying liabilities as current or noncurrent, the term *operating cycle* refers to
a. the average time period between business recessions.
b. the time period between date of sale and the date the related revenue is collected.
c. a period of one year.
d. the time period between purchase of merchandise and the conversion of this merchandise back to cash.

Q9-49 Failure to accrue interest expense results in
a. an overstatement of net income and an understatement of liabilities.
b. an understatement of net income and an overstatement of liabilities.
c. an overstatement of net income and an overstatement of liabilities.
d. an understatement of net income and an understatement of liabilities.

Q9-50 Mega Planes Warehouse operates in a state with a 6.5% sales tax. For convenience, Mega Planes Warehouse credits Sales Revenue for the total amount (selling price plus sales tax) collected from each customer. If Mega Planes Warehouse fails to make an adjustment for sales taxes,
a. net income will be understated and liabilities will be understated.
b. net income will be overstated and liabilities will be overstated.
c. net income will be understated and liabilities will be overstated.
d. net income will be overstated and liabilities will be understated.

Q9-51 What kind of account is Unearned Revenue?
a. Revenue account
b. Expense account
c. Liability account
d. Asset account

Q9-52 An end-of-period adjusting entry that debits Unearned Revenue most likely will credit
a. a revenue.
b. an asset.
c. an expense.
d. a liability.

Q9-53 Myron, Inc., manufactures and sells computer monitors with a three-year warranty. Warranty costs are expected to average 7% of sales during the warranty period. The following table shows the sales and actual warranty payments during the first two years of operations:

Year	Sales	Warranty Payments
2012	$650,000	$ 5,200
2013	850,000	42,500

Based on these facts, what amount of warranty liability should Myron, Inc., report on its balance sheet at December 31, 2013?

a. $47,700
b. $57,300

c. $105,000
d. $42,500

Q9-54 Moment's Fashions has a debt that has been properly reported as a long-term liability up to the present year (2012). Some of this debt comes due in 2012. If Moment's Fashions continues to report the current position as a long-term liability, the effect will be to

a. overstate net income.
b. understate total liabilities.

c. understate the debt ratio.
d. overstate the current ratio.

Q9-55 A bond with a face amount of $10,000 has a current price quote of 102.875. What is the bond's price?

a. $10,287.50
b. $10,102.88

c. $1,028,750
d. $1,028.75

Q9-56 Bond carrying value equals Bonds Payable

a. minus Premium on Bonds Payable.
b. plus Discount on Bonds Payable.
c. plus Premium on Bonds Payable.

d. minus Discount on Bonds Payable.
e. Both a and b
f. Both c and d

Q9-57 What type of account is *Discount on Bonds Payable* and what is its normal balance?

a. Contra liability; Credit
b. Contra liability; Debit

c. Adjusting account; Credit
d. Reversing account; Debit

Questions 58–61 use the following data:

Sunny Day Company sells $400,000 of 13%, 10-year bonds for 97 on April 1, 2012. The market rate of interest on that day is 13.5%. Interest is paid each year on April 1.

Q9-58 The entry to record the sale of the bonds on April 1 would be as follows:

a.	Cash	388,000	
	Bonds Payable		388,000
b.	Cash	400,000	
	Discount on Bonds Payable		12,000
	Bonds Payable		388,000
c.	Cash	388,000	
	Discount on Bonds Payable	12,000	
	Bonds Payable		400,000
d.	Cash	400,000	
	Bonds Payable		400,000

Q9-59 Sunny Day Company uses the straight-line amortization method. The amount of interest expense for each year will be

a. $60,000.
b. $53,200.
c. $54,000.

d. $52,000.
e. none of these.

Q9-60 Write the adjusting entry required at December 31, 2012.

Q9-61 Write the journal entry required at April 1, 2013.

Q9-62 McPherson Corporation issued $400,000 of 10%, 20-year bonds payable on January 1, 2012, for $295,000. The market interest rate when the bonds were issued was 14%. Interest is paid semiannually on January 1 and July 1. The first interest payment is July 1, 2012. Using the effective-interest amortization method, how much interest expense will McPherson record on July 1, 2012?

a. $28,000

b. $20,500

c. $14,750

d. $20,650

e. $20,000

Q9-63 Using the facts in the preceding question, McPherson's journal entry to record the interest expense on July 1, 2012, will include a

a. debit to Bonds Payable.

b. credit to Interest Expense.

c. credit to Discount on Bonds Payable.

d. debit to Premium on Bonds Payable.

Q9-64 Amortizing the discount on bonds payable

a. is necessary only if the bonds were issued at more than face value.

b. reduces the carrying value of the bond liability.

c. increases the recorded amount of interest expense.

d. reduces the semiannual cash payment for interest.

Q9-65 The journal entry on the maturity date to record the payment of $1,500,000 of bonds payable that were issued at a $70,000 discount includes

a. a debit to Discount on Bonds Payable for $70,000.

b. a credit to Cash for $1,570,000.

c. a debit to Bonds Payable for $1,500,000.

d. all of the above.

Q9-66 Is the payment of the face amount of a bond on its maturity date regarded as an operating activity, an investing activity, or a financing activity?

a. Financing activity

b. Operating activity

c. Investing activity

Problems

MyAccountingLab

All of the A and B problems can be found within MyAccountingLab, an online homework and practice environment. Your instructor may ask you to complete these problems using MyAccountingLab.

Group A

P9-67A (*Learning Objective 1: Measure and report current liabilities*) Salt Air Marine experienced these events during the current year.

> a. December revenue totaled $150,000; and, in addition, Salt Air collected sales tax of 6%. The tax amount will be sent to the state of North Carolina early in January.
>
> b. On August 31, Salt Air signed a six-month, 4% note payable to purchase a boat costing $81,000. The note requires payment of principal and interest at maturity.
>
> c. On August 31, Salt Air received cash of $3,000 in advance for service revenue. This revenue will be earned evenly over six months.
>
> d. Revenues of $800,000 were covered by Salt Air's service warranty. At January 1, estimated warranty payable was $11,300. During the year, Salt Air recorded warranty expense of $32,000 and paid warranty claims of $34,500.
>
> e. Salt Air owes $100,000 on a long-term note payable. At December 31, 6% interest for the year plus $20,000 of this principal are payable within one year.

▶ Requirement

1. For each item, indicate the account and the related amount to be reported as a current liability on the Salt Air Marine balance sheet at December 31.

P9-68A (*Learning Objective 1: Record liability-related transactions*) The following transactions of Smooth Sounds Music Company occurred during 2012 and 2013:

2012		
Mar	3	Purchased a piano (inventory) for $50,000, signing a six-month, 8% note payable.
May	31	Borrowed $85,000 on an 8% note payable that calls for annual installment payments of $17,000 principal plus interest. Record the short-term note payable in a separate account from the long-term note payable.
Sep	3	Paid the six-month, 8% note at maturity.
Dec	31	Accrued warranty expense, which is estimated at 2.5% of sales of $196,000.
	31	Accrued interest on the outstanding note payable.
2013		
May	31	Paid the first installment and interest for one year on the outstanding note payable.

▶ Requirement

1. Record the transactions in Smooth Sound's journal. Explanations are not required.

P9-69A (*Learning Objectives 1, 2: Record bond transactions (at par); report bonds payable on the balance sheet*) The board of directors of Radio Plus authorizes the issue of $7,000,000 of 9%, 25-year bonds payable. The semiannual interest dates are May 31 and November 30. The bonds are issued on May 31, 2012, at par.

▶ Requirements

1. Journalize the following transactions:
   a. Issuance of half of the bonds on May 31, 2012
   b. Payment of interest on November 30, 2012
   c. Accrual of interest on December 31, 2012
   d. Payment of interest on May 31, 2013
2. Report interest payable and bonds payable as they would appear on the Radio Plus balance sheet at December 31, 2012.

P9-70A (*Learning Objectives 1, 2, 5: Issue bonds at a discount; amortize by the straight-line method; report bonds payable and accrued interest on the balance sheet*) On February 28, 2012, Dolphin Corp. issues 6%, 10-year bonds payable with a face value of $900,000. The bonds pay interest on February 28 and August 31. Dolphin Corp. amortizes bonds by the straight-line method.

▶ Requirements

1. If the market interest rate is 5% when Dolphin Corp. issues its bonds, will the bonds be priced at par, at a premium, or at a discount? Explain.
2. If the market interest rate is 7% when Dolphin Corp. issues its bonds, will the bonds be priced at par, at a premium, or at a discount? Explain.
3. Assume that the issue price of the bonds is 96. Journalize the following bonds payable transactions.
   a. Issuance of the bonds on February 28, 2012
   b. Payment of interest and amortization of the bonds on August 31, 2012
   c. Accrual of interest and amortization of the bonds on December 31, 2012, the year end.
   d. Payment of interest and amortization of the bonds on February 28, 2013
4. Report interest payable and bonds payable as they would appear on the Dolphin Corp. balance sheet at December 31, 2012.

P9-71A (*Learning Objective 2: Account for bonds payable at a discount; amortize by the straight-line method*)

▶ Requirements

1. Journalize the following transactions of Laroux Communications, Inc.:

2012		
Jan	1	Issued $4,000,000 of 6%, 10-year bonds payable at 95. Interest payment dates are July 1 and January 1.
Jul	1	Paid semiannual interest and amortized bonds by the straight-line method on the 6% bonds payable.
Dec	31	Accrued semiannual interest expense and amortized bonds by the straight-line method on the 6% bonds payable.
2013		
Jan	1	Paid semiannual interest.
2022		
Jan	1	Paid the 6% bonds at maturity.

2. At December 31, 2012, after all year-end adjustments, determine the carrying amount of Laroux Communications bonds payable, net.
3. For the six months ended July 1, 2012, determine the following for Laroux Communications, Inc.:
    a. Interest expense
    b. Cash interest paid

What causes interest expense on the bonds to exceed cash interest paid?

P9-72A (*Learning Objectives 2, 5: Analyze a company's long-term debt; report long-term debt on the balance sheet (effective-interest method)*) The notes to the Giving Charities' financial statements reported the following data on December 31, Year 1 (end of the fiscal year):

Note 6. Indebtedness		
Bonds payable, 6% due in Year 8	$5,000,000	
Less: Discount...	(520,640)	$4,479,360
Notes payable, 5%, payable in amounts of $55,000 annual installments starting in Year 5...............		330,000

Giving Charities' amortizes bonds by the effective-interest method and pays all interest amounts at December 31.

▶ Requirements

1. Answer the following questions about Giving Charities' long-term liabilities:
    a. What is the maturity value of the 6% bonds?
    b. What is Giving Charities' annual cash interest payment on the 6% bonds?
    c. What is the carrying amount of the 6% bonds at December 31, year 1?
2. Prepare an amortization table through December 31, Year 4, for the 6% bonds. The market interest rate is 8%. (Round all amounts to the nearest dollar.) How much is Giving Charities' interest expense on the 6% bonds for the year ended December 31, Year 4?
3. Show how Giving Charities would report the 6% bonds payable and the 5% notes payable at December 31, Year 4.

P9-73A (*Learning Objectives 2, 5: Issue convertible bonds at a discount, amortize by the effective-interest method, and convert bonds; report bonds payable on the balance sheet*) On December 31, 2012, Laraboo Corp. issues 11%, 10-year convertible bonds payable with a maturity value of $4,000,000. The semiannual interest dates are June 30 and December 31. The market interest rate is 12%, and the issue price of the bonds is 94.265. Laraboo Corp. amortizes bonds by the effective-interest method.

▶ Requirements

1. Prepare an effective-interest method amortization table for the first four semiannual interest periods.
2. Journalize the following transactions:
   a. Issuance of the bonds on December 31, 2012. Credit Convertible Bonds Payable.
   b. Payment of interest and amortization of the bonds on June 30, 2013.
   c. Payment of interest and amortization of the bonds on December 31, 2013.
   d. Conversion by the bondholders on July 1, 2014, of bonds with face value of $1,600,000 into 90,000 shares of Laraboo Corp.'s $1-par common stock.
3. Show how Laraboo Corp. would report the remaining bonds payable on its balance sheet at December 31, 2014.

P9-74A (*Learning Objective 3: Differentiate financing with debt vs. equity*) Tony Sporting Goods is embarking on a massive expansion. Assume plans call for opening 20 new stores during the next two years. Each store is scheduled to be 30% larger than the company's existing locations, offering more items of inventory, and with more elaborate displays. Management estimates that company operations will provide $1 million of the cash needed for expansion. Tony must raise the remaining $6.75 million from outsiders. The board of directors is considering obtaining the $6.75 million either through borrowing or by issuing common stock.

▶ Requirement

1. Write a memo to Tony's management discussing the advantages and disadvantages of borrowing and of issuing common stock to raise the needed cash. Which method of raising the funds would you recommend?

P9-75A (*Learning Objectives 4, 5: Report liabilities on the balance sheet; calculate the leverage ratio, debt ratio, and times-interest-earned ratio*) The accounting records of Brighton Foods, Inc., include the following items at December 31, 2012:

Mortgage note payable, current portion.........................	$ 92,000	Total assets	$4,500,000
Accumulated pension benefit obligation	450,000	Accumulated depreciation, equipment	166,000
Bonds payable, long-term............	200,000	Discount on bonds payable (all long-term)	25,000
Mortgage note payable, long-term	318,000	Operating income................	370,000
Bonds payable, current portion ...	500,000	Equipment...........................	744,000
Interest expense..........................	229,000	Pension plan assets (market value).................	420,000
		Interest payable..................	75,000

▶ Requirements

1. Show how each relevant item would be reported on the Brighton Foods, Inc., classified balance sheet, including headings and totals for current liabilities and long-term liabilities.
2. Answer the following questions about Brighton's financial position at December 31, 2012:
   a. What is the carrying amount of the bonds payable (combine the current and long-term amounts)?
   b. Why is the interest-payable amount so much less than the amount of interest expense?
3. How many times did Brighton cover its interest expense during 2012?
4. Assume that all of the existing liabilities are included in the information provided. Calculate the leverage ratio and debt ratio of the company. Evaluate the health of the company from a leverage point of view. What other information would be helpful in making your evaluation?
5. Independent of your answer to (4), assume that Footnote 8 of the financial statements includes commitments for operating leases over the next 15 years in the amount of $3,000,000. If the company had to capitalize these leases in 2012, how would it change the leverage ratio and the debt ratio? How would this change impact your assessment of the company's health from a leverage point of view?

Group B

P9-76B (*Learning Objective 1: Measure and report current liabilities*) Sea Air Marine experienced these events during the current year.

    a. December revenue totaled $130,000; and, in addition, Sea Air collected sales tax of 7%. The tax amount will be sent to the state of New Hampshire early in January.

    b. On August 31, Sea Air signed a six-month, 6% note payable to purchase a boat costing $80,000. The note requires payment of principal and interest at maturity.

    c. On August 31, Sea Air received cash of $3,000 in advance for service revenue. This revenue will be earned evenly over six months.

    d. Revenues of $850,000 were covered by Sea Air's service warranty. At January 1, estimated warranty payable was $11,800. During the year, Sea Air recorded warranty expense of $34,000 and paid warranty claims of $34,800.

    e. Sea Air owes $90,000 on a long-term note payable. At December 31, 6% interest for the year plus $30,000 of this principal are payable within one year.

▶ Requirement

1. For each item, indicate the account and the related amount to be reported as a current liability on the Sea Air Marine balance sheet at December 31.

P9-77B (*Learning Objective 1: Record liability-related transactions*) The following transactions of Happy Music Company occurred during 2012 and 2013:

2012	
Mar 3	Purchased a piano (inventory) for $70,000, signing a six-month, 6% note payable.
May 31	Borrowed $70,000 on a 5% note payable that calls for annual installment payments of $14,000 principal plus interest. Record the short-term note payable in a separate account from the long-term note payable.
Sep 3	Paid the six-month, 6% note at maturity.
Dec 31	Accrued warranty expense, which is estimated at 2% of sales of $194,000.
31	Accrued interest on the outstanding note payable.
2013	
May 31	Paid the first installment and interest for one year on the outstanding note payable.

▶ Requirement

1. Record the transactions in Happy Music Company's journal. Explanations are not required.

P9-78B (*Learning Objectives 1, 2: Record bond transactions (at par); report bonds payable on the balance sheet*) The board of directors of Media Plus authorizes the issue of $8,000,000 of 6%, 20-year bonds payable. The semiannual interest dates are May 31 and November 30. The bonds are issued on May 31, 2012, at par.

▶ Requirements

1. Journalize the following transactions:
    a. Issuance of half of the bonds on May 31, 2012
    b. Payment of interest on November 30, 2012
    c. Accrual of interest on December 31, 2012
    d. Payment of interest on May 31, 2013
2. Report interest payable and bonds payable as they would appear on the Media Plus balance sheet at December 31, 2012.

P9-79B (*Learning Objectives 1, 2, 5: Issue bonds at a discount; amortize by the straight-line method; report bonds payable and accrued interest payable on the balance sheet*) On February 28, 2012, Starfish Corp. issues 10%, five-year bonds payable with a face value of $1,200,000. The bonds pay interest on February 28 and August 31. Starfish Corp. amortizes bonds by the straight-line method.

▶ Requirements

1. If the market interest rate is 9% when Starfish Corp. issues its bonds, will the bonds be priced at par, at a premium, or at a discount? Explain.
2. If the market interest rate is 11% when Starfish Corp. issues its bonds, will the bonds be priced at par, at a premium, or at a discount? Explain.
3. Assume that the issue price of the bonds is 96. Journalize the following bond transactions.
   a. Issuance of the bonds on February 28, 2012
   b. Payment of interest and amortization of the bonds on August 31, 2012
   c. Accrual of interest and amortization of the bonds on December 31, 2012, the year-end
   d. Payment of interest and amortization of the bonds on February 28, 2013
4. Report interest payable and bonds payable as they would appear on the Starfish Corp. balance sheet at December 31, 2012.

P9-80B (*Learning Objective 2: Account for bonds payable at a discount; amortize by the straight-line method*)

▶ Requirements

1. Journalize the following transactions of Lamothe Communications, Inc.:

2012		
Jan	1	Issued $3,000,000 of 8%, 10-year bonds payable at 94. Interest payment dates are July 1 and January 1.
Jul	1	Paid semiannual interest and amortized the bonds by the straight-line method on the 8% bonds payable.
Dec 31		Accrued semiannual interest expense and amortized the bonds by the straight-line method on the 8% bonds payable.
2013		
Jan	1	Paid semiannual interest.
2022		
Jan	1	Paid the 8% bonds at maturity.

2. At December 31, 2012, after all year-end adjustments, determine the carrying amount of Lamothe Communications bonds payable, net.
3. For the six months ended July 1, 2012, determine the following for Lamothe Communications Inc:
   a. Interest expense
   b. Cash interest paid

What causes interest expense on the bonds to exceed cash interest paid?

P9-81B (*Learning Objectives 2, 5: Analyze a company's long-term debt; report the long-term debt on the balance sheet (effective-interest method)*) The notes to the Thankful Charities financial statements reported the following data on December 31, Year 1 (end of the fiscal year):

Note 6. Indebtedness		
Bonds payable, 5% due in Year 8	$4,000,000	
Less: Discount..	(431,150)	$3,568,850
Notes payable, 8%, payable in $40,000 annual installments starting in Year 5...............		240,000

Thankful Charities amortizes bonds by the effective-interest method and pays all interest amounts at December 31.

► Requirements

1. Answer the following questions about Thankful Charities long-term liabilities:
   a. What is the maturity value of the 5% bonds?
   b. What is Thankful Charities' annual cash interest payment on the 5% bonds?
   c. What is the carrying amount of the 5% bonds at December 31, Year 1?
2. Prepare an amortization table through December 31, Year 4, for the 5% bonds. The market interest rate on the bonds was 7%. Round all amounts to the nearest dollar. How much is Thankful Charities' interest expense on the 5% bonds for the year ended December 31, Year 4?
3. Show how Thankful Charities would report the 5% bonds and the 8% notes payable at December 31, Year 4.

P9-82B *(Learning Objectives 2, 5: Issue convertible bonds at a discount; amortize by the effective-interest method; convert bonds; report bonds payable on the balance sheet)* On December 31, 2012, Zugaboo Corp. issues 5%, 10-year convertible bonds payable with a maturity value of $5,000,000. The semiannual interest dates are June 30 and December 31. The market interest rate is 6%, and the issue price of the bonds is 92.56. Zugaboo Corp. amortizes bonds by the effective-interest method.

► Requirements

1. Prepare an effective-interest method amortization table for the first four semiannual interest periods.
2. Journalize the following transactions:
   a. Issuance of the bonds on December 31, 2012. Credit Convertible Bonds Payable.
   b. Payment of interest and amortization of the bonds on June 30, 2013.
   c. Payment of interest and amortization of the bonds on December 31, 2013.
   d. Conversion by the bondholders on July 1, 2014, of bonds with face value of $2,000,000 into 90,000 shares of Zugaboo Corp. $1-par common stock.
3. Show how Zugaboo Corp. would report the remaining bonds payable on its balance sheet at December 31, 2014.

P9-83B *(Learning Objective 3: Differentiate financing with debt vs. equity)* Marco's Sporting Goods is embarking on a massive expansion. Assume the plans call for opening 40 new stores during the next three years. Each store is scheduled to be 35% larger than the company's existing locations, offering more items of inventory, and with more elaborate displays. Management estimates that company operations will provide $2.5 million of the cash needed for expansion. Marco must raise the remaining $7.75 million from outsiders. The board of directors is considering obtaining the $7.75 million either through borrowing or by issuing common stock.

► Requirement

1. Write a memo to Marco's management discussing the advantages and disadvantages of borrowing and of issuing common stock to raise the needed cash. Which method of raising the funds would you recommend?

P9-84B *(Learning Objectives 4, 5: Report liabilities on the balance sheet; calculate the leverage ratio, debt ratio, and times-interest-earned ratio)* The accounting records of Braintree Foods, Inc., include the following items at December 31, 2012:

Mortgage note payable, current portion	$ 97,000	Total assets	$4,200,000
Accumulated pension benefit obligation	470,000	Accumulated depreciation, equipment	162,000
Bonds payable, long-term	1,680,000	Discount on bonds payable (all long-term)	22,000
Mortgage note payable, long-term	314,000	Operating income	390,000
Bonds payable, current portion	420,000	Equipment	745,000
Interest expense	227,000	Pension plan assets (market value)	425,000
		Interest payable	74,000

▶ Requirements

1. Show how each relevant item would be reported on the Braintree Foods, Inc., classified balance sheet, including headings and totals for current liabilities and long-term liabilities.
2. Answer the following questions about Braintree's financial position at December 31, 2012:
   a. What is the carrying amount of the bonds payable (combine the current and long-term amounts)?
   b. Why is the interest-payable amount so much less than the amount of interest expense?
3. How many times did Braintree cover its interest expense during 2012?
4. Assume that all of the existing liabilities are included in the information provided. Calculate the leverage ratio and debt ratio of the company. Evaluate the health of the company from a leverage point of view. What other information would be helpful in making your evaluation?
5. Independent of your answer to (4), assume that Footnote 8 of the financial statements includes commitments for operating leases over the next 15 years in the amount of $3,000,000. If the company had to capitalize these leases in 2012, how would it change the leverage ratio and the debt ratio? How would this change impact your assessment of the company's health from a leverage point of view?

Challenge Exercises and Problem

E9-85 (*Learning Objectives 1, 3, 5: Report current and long-term liabilities; evaluate leverage*) The top management of Marquis Marketing Services examines the following company accounting records at August 29, immediately before the end of the year, August 31:

Total current assets......................	$ 324,500
Noncurrent assets........................	1,098,500
	$1,423,000
Total current liabilities................	$ 173,800
Noncurrent liabilities	247,500
Stockholders' equity....................	1,001,700
	$1,423,000

1. Suppose Marquis's management wants to achieve a current ratio of 2. How much in current liabilities should Marquis pay off within the next two days in order to achieve its goal?
2. Calculate Marquis's leverage ratio and debt ratio. Evaluate the company's debt position. Is it low, high, or about average? What other information might help you to make a decision?

E9-86 (*Learning Objectives 3, 5: Analyze the financial statement impact of refinancing*) Modern Brands recently completed a large debt refinancing. A debt refinancing occurs when a company issues new bonds payable to retire old bonds. The company debits the old bonds payable and credits the new bonds payable.

Modern Brands had $160 million of 5 1/4% bonds payable outstanding, with 20 years to maturity. Modern retired these old bonds by issuing $80 million of new 13% bonds payable to the holders of the old bonds and paying the bondholders $17 million in cash. Modern issued both groups of bonds at face value. At the time of the debt refinancing, Modern Brands had total assets of $503 million and total liabilities of $359 million. Net income for the most recent year was $6.1 million on sales of $1 billion.

▶ Requirements

1. Journalize the debt refinancing transaction.
2. Compute annual interest expense for both the old and the new bond issues.
3. Why did Modern Brands refinance the old 5 1/4% bonds payable with the new 13% bonds? Consider interest expense, net income, the leverage ratio and the debt ratio.

P9-87 (*Learning Objective 3: Understand how structuring debt transactions can affect a company*) The Coca-Cola Company reported the following comparative information at December 31, 2010, and December 31, 2009 (amounts in millions and adapted):

	2010	2009
Current assets	$21,579	$17,551
Total assets	72,921	48,671
Current liabilities	18,508	13,721
Total stockholders' equity	31,317	25,346
Net sales	35,119	30,990
Net income	11,809	6,824

▶ Requirements

1. Calculate the following ratios for 2010 and 2009:
   a. Current ratio
   b. Debt ratio
2. During 2010, The Coca Cola Company issue $1,590 million of long-term debt that was used to retire short-term debt. What would the current ratio and debt ratio have been if this transaction had not been made?
3. The Coca Cola Company reports that its lease payments under operating leases will total $965 million in the future and $205 million will occur in the next year (2011). What would the current ratio and debt ratio have been if these leases had been capitalized?

APPLY YOUR KNOWLEDGE

Decision Cases

Case 1. (*Learning Objective 3: Explore an actual bankruptcy; calculate leverage ratio, ROA, debt ratio, and times-interest-earned*) In 2002, **Enron Corporation** filed for Chapter 11 bankruptcy protection, shocking the business community: How could a company this large and this successful go bankrupt? This case explores the causes and the effects of Enron's bankruptcy.

At December 31, 2000, and for the four years ended on that date, Enron reported the following (amounts in millions):

Balance Sheet (summarized)			
Total assets			$65,503
Total liabilities			54,033
Total stockholders' equity			11,470

Income Statements (excerpts)				
	2000	1999	1998	1997
Net income	$ 979*	$893	$703	$105
Revenues	100,789			

*Operating income = $1,953
Interest expense = $838

Unknown to investors and lenders, Enron also controlled hundreds of partnerships that owed vast amounts of money. These special-purpose entities (SPEs) did not appear on the Enron financial statements. Assume that the SPEs' assets totaled $7,000 million and their liabilities stood at $6,900 million; assume a 10% interest rate on these liabilities.

During the four-year period up to December 31, 2000, Enron's stock price shot up from $17.50 to $90.56. Enron used its escalating stock price to finance the purchase of the SPEs by guaranteeing lenders that Enron would give them Enron stock if the SPEs could not pay their loans.

In 2001, the SEC launched an investigation into Enron's accounting practices. It was alleged that Enron should have been including the SPEs in its financial statements all along. Enron then restated net income for years up to 2000, wiping out nearly $600 million of total net income (and total assets) for this four-year period. Assume that $300 million of this loss applied to 2000. Enron's stock price tumbled, and the guarantees to the SPEs' lenders added millions to Enron's liabilities (assume the full amount of the SPEs' debt). To make matters worse, the assets of the SPEs lost much of their value; assume that their market value is only $500 million.

▶ Requirements

1. Compute the debt ratio that Enron reported at the end of 2000. By using the DuPont Model, which we discussed in Chapter 7 (page 428), compute Enron's Return on total assets (ROA) for 2000. For this purpose, use only total assets at the end of 2000, rather than the average of 1999 and 2000.

2. Compute Enron's leverage ratio. Now compute Enron's return on equity (ROE) by multiplying the ROA computed in part 1 by the leverage ratio. Can you see anything unusual in these ratios that might have caused you to question them? Why or why not?

3. Add the asset and liability information about the SPEs to the reported amounts provided in the table. Recompute all ratios after including the SPEs in Enron's financial statements. Also compute Enron's times-interest-earned ratio both ways for 2000. Assume that the changes to Enron's financial position occurred during 2000.

4. Why does it appear that Enron failed to include the SPEs in its financial statements? How do you view Enron after including the SPEs in the company's financial statements? (Challenge)

Case 2. *(Learning Objective 3: Analyze alternative ways of raising $5 million)* Business is going well for **Park 'N Fly**, the company that operates remote parking lots near major airports. The board of directors of this family-owned company believes that Park 'N Fly could earn an additional $1.5 million income before interest and taxes by expanding into new markets. However, the $5 million that the business needs for growth cannot be raised within the family. The directors, who strongly wish to retain family control of the company, must consider issuing securities to outsiders. The directors are considering three financing plans.

Plan A is to borrow at 6%. Plan B is to issue 100,000 shares of common stock. Plan C is to issue 100,000 shares of nonvoting, $3.75 preferred stock ($3.75 is the annual dividend paid on each share of preferred stock).[5] Park 'N Fly presently has net income of $3.5 million and 1 million shares of common stock outstanding. The company's income tax rate is 35%.

▶ Requirements

1. Prepare an analysis to determine which plan will result in the highest earnings per share of common stock.

2. Recommend a plan to the board of directors. Give your reasons.

Ethical Issues

Issue 1. **Microsoft Corporation** is the defendant in numerous lawsuits claiming unfair trade practices. Microsoft has strong incentives not to disclose these contingent liabilities. However, GAAP requires that companies report their contingent liabilities.

▶ Requirements

1. Why would a company prefer not to disclose its contingent liabilities?
2. Identify the parties involved in the decision and the potential consequences to each.

---

[5]For a discussion of preferred stock, see Chapter 10.

3. Analyze the issue of whether to report contingent liabilities from lawsuits from the following standpoints:
   a. Economic
   b. Legal
   c. Ethical
4. What impact will future changes in accounting standards, both at the U.S. level and the international level, likely have on the issue of disclosure of loss contingencies?

Issue 2. When Is A Lease a Capital Idea? Laurie Gocker, Inc., entered into a lease arrangement with Nathan Morgan Leasing Corporation for an industrial machine. Morgan's primary business is leasing. The cash purchase price of the machine is $1,000,000. Its economic life is six years.

Gocker's balance sheet reflects total assets of $10 million and total liabilities of $7.5 million. Among the liabilities is a $2.5 million long-term note outstanding at Last National Bank. The note carries a restrictive covenant that requires the company's debt ratio to be no higher than 75%. The company's revenues have been falling of late and the shareholders are concerned about profitability.

Gocker and Morgan are engaging in negotiations for terms of the lease. Some relevant other facts are as follows:
1. Morgan wants to take possession of the machine at the end of the initial lease term.
2. The term may run from four to five years, at Gocker's discretion.
3. Morgan estimates the machine will have no residual value, and Gocker will not purchase it at the end of the lease term.
4. The present value of minimum lease payments on the machine is $890,000.

▶ Requirements

1. What is (are) the ethical issue(s) in this case?
2. Who are the stakeholders? Analyze the consequences for each stakeholder from the following standpoints: (a) economic, (b) legal, and (c) ethical.
3. How should Gocker structure the lease agreement?
4. As of the date of this text, the FASB and IASB have issued a joint exposure draft of a new standard on long-term leases that will require companies to capitalize most leases like this one. How will the analysis of this case change when this standard is issued?

Focus on Financials: | Amazon.com, Inc.

(Learning Objectives 1, 2, 3, 4, 5: Analyze current and long-term liabilities; evaluate debt-paying ability) Refer to **Amazon.com, Inc.**'s consolidated financial statements in Appendix A at the end of this book.

1. Did accounts payable for Amazon.com, Inc., increase or decrease in 2010? Calculate accounts payable turnover.
   How many days does it take Amazon.com, Inc. to pay an average account payable? Comment on the length of the period in days.
2. Examine Note 9—Income Taxes—in the Notes to Consolidated Financial Statements. Income tax provision is another title for income tax expense. What was Amazon.com, Inc.'s income tax provision in 2010? How much did the company pay in federal income taxes? How much was income taxes payable as of December 31, 2010? In general, why were these amounts different? (Challenge)
3. Did Amazon.com, Inc., borrow more or pay off more long-term debt during 2010? How can you tell? (Challenge)
4. Examine Note 6—Commitments and Contingencies—in the Notes to Consolidated Financial Statements. Describe some of Amazon.com, Inc.'s commitments and contingent liabilities as of December 31, 2010. Are any of these amounts included in the numbers in the balance sheet?
5. How would you rate Amazon.com, Inc.'s overall debt position—risky, safe, or average? Compute three ratios at December 31, 2010 and 2009 that answers this question.

Focus on Analysis: | RadioShack Corporation

(*Learning Objectives 1, 2, 3, 4, 5: Analyze current liabilities and long-term debt*) **Refer to** RadioShack Corporation's consolidated financial statements in Appendix B at the end of this book. These financial statements report a number of liabilities.

1. The current liability section of RadioShack Corporation's Consolidated Balance Sheet as of December 31, 2010, lists four different liabilities. List them and give a brief description of each.

2. RadioShack Corporation's largest single current liability is "accrued expenses and other current liabilities." Refer to Note 3 entitled "Supplemental Balance Sheet Disclosures." List the items that are included in this category and give a brief description of each.

3. Calculate accounts payable turnover, both as a ratio and in number of days. Describe what this ratio means. Also compute the following other ratios (if you have already computed them as part of your work in previous chapters, refer to them): (1) current ratio, (2) quick ratio, (3) days sales to collection for accounts receivable, and (4) inventory turnover (express in days by dividing 365 by the turnover). How do you think you would combine the information in these ratios to assess RadioShack's current debt-paying ability (Challenge)?

4. Refer to Note 5 (Indebtedness and Borrowing Facilities). What specific items are included? List them, including interest rates. Where is related interest information recorded? Are any of these amounts due currently? Which ones? How can you tell? When are the remainder due?

5. Refer to Note 13 (Commitments and Contingencies). Describe the contents of this footnote. Are any of these items included in the liabilities recorded in either the current or long-term section of the balance sheet? Why or why not?

6. Compute the company's debt ratio, leverage ratio, and times-interest-earned ratio. Would you evaluate RadioShack Corporation as risky, safe, or average in terms of these ratios?

7. Access RadioShack Corporation's most recent financial statements from its Web site (www. radioshack.com). You will find a link called "investor relations" at the bottom of the website, which will lead you to the latest financial statements filed with the SEC. What has happened to RadioShack's debt position since the end of 2010?

Group Projects

Project 1. Consider three different businesses:

1. A bank
2. A magazine publisher
3. A department store

For each business, list all of its liabilities—both current and long-term. Then compare the three lists to identify the liabilities that the three businesses have in common. Also identify the liabilities that are unique to each type of business.

Project 2. Alcenon Corporation leases the majority of the assets that it uses in operations. Alcenon prefers operating leases (versus capital leases) in order to keep the lease liability off its balance sheet and maintain a low debt ratio.

Alcenon is negotiating a 10-year lease on an asset with an expected useful life of 15 years. The lease requires Alcenon to make 10 annual lease payments of $20,000 each, with the first payment due at the beginning of the lease term. The leased asset has a market value of $135,180. The lease agreement specifies no transfer of title to the lessee and includes no bargain purchase option.

Write a report for Alcenon's management to explain what conditions must be present for Alcenon to be able to account for this lease as an operating lease.

For online homework, exercises, and problems that provide you with immediate feedback, please visit **www.myaccountinglab.com**.

MyAccountingLab

Quick Check Answers

1. *a*

2. *c*

3. *a*

4. *c* [900 × 0.02 × $45 = warranty expense of $810; repaired $45 × 5 = $225; year-end liability = $585 ($810 − $225)]

5. *e*

6. *c*

7. *a*

8. *a*

9. *a*

10. *b*

11. *c*

12. *c* ($96,602 × 0.08 × 6/12 = $3,864)

13. *c* [Int. exp. = $3,864 − Int. payment = $3,750] =114

14. *d* ($100,000 × 0.075 = $7,500)

15. *a* (See Amortization Schedule)

Date	Interest Payment	Interest Expense	Discount Amortize	Bond Carry Amt.
1/1/2013				$96,602
7/1/2013	$3,750	$3,864	$114	96,716
1/1/2014	3,750	3,869	119	96,835

16. *b* {$96,602 + [($100,000 − $96,602) × 1/10] = $96,942}

10

Stockholders' Equity

SPOTLIGHT: RadioShack Corporation

Your parents have given you a $500 gift card from "The Shack" for your birthday. What will you buy: a high-definition wide screen TV? a digital camera? a new cell phone with an extended service plan for additional text messaging time? If you can catch a sale, maybe you can get several items for this amount. We have featured **RadioShack Corporation** in several places earlier in this text, so by now you're probably familiar with the company. If not, you soon will be. Interestingly, outside of its core business operations (consumer electronics), RadioShack's largest single cash outlay in 2010 was to repurchase its own stock!

In this chapter we'll show you how to account for the issuance of corporate capital stock to investors. We'll also cover the other elements of stockholders' equity—Additional Paid-in Capital, Retained Earnings, and Treasury Stock, plus dividends and stock splits. By the time you finish this chapter, you may be ready to drop into The Shack for a shopping spree. Or you may want to go out and buy some RadioShack Corporation stock. On the next page, you'll find the company's consolidated balance sheet as of December 31, 2010. ●

© Dwayne Newton/Photo Edit

		RadioShack Corporation and Subsidiaries Consolidated Balance Sheets		
			December 31,	
		(in millions, except for share amounts)*	2010	2009
		Assets		
		Current assets:		
		Cash and cash equivalents	$ 569.4	$ 908.2
		Accounts and notes receivable, net	377.5	322.5
		Inventories	723.7	670.6
		Other current assets	108.1	114.4
		Total current assets	1,778.7	2,015.7
		Property, plant, and equipment, net	274.3	282.3
		Goodwill, net	41.2	38.9
		Other assets, net	81.2	92.4
		Total assets	$2,175.4	$2,429.3
		Liabilities and Stockholders' Equity		
		Current liabilities:		
		Current maturities of long-term debt	$ 308.0	$ —
		Accounts payable	272.4	262.9
		Accrued expenses and other current liabilities	318.0	360.7
		Income taxes payable	9.7	30.9
		Total current liabilities	908.1	654.5
		Long-term debt, excluding current maturities	331.8	627.8
		Other non-current liabilities	93.0	98.7
		Total liabilities	1,332.9	1,381.0
		Commitments and contingencies		
	1	Stockholders' equity:		
	2	Preferred stock, no par value, 1,000,000 shares authorized;		
		Series A junior participating, 300,000 shares designated and none issued	—	—
	3	Common stock, $1 par value, 650,000,000 shares authorized;		
		146,033,000 and 191,033,000 shares issued, respectively	146.0	191.0
	4	Additional paid-in capital	147.3	161.8
	5	Retained earnings	1,502.5	2,323.9
	6	Treasury stock, at cost; 40,260,000 and 65,806,000 shares, respectively	(949.0)	(1,621.9)
	7	Accumulated other comprehensive loss	(4.3)	(6.5)
	8	Total stockholders' equity	842.5	1,048.3
		Total liabilities and stockholders' equity	$2,175.4	$2,429.3

*The accompanying notes are an integral part of these consolidated financial statements.

Chapters 4 to 9 discussed accounting for assets and liabilities. By this time, you should be familiar with all the assets and liabilities listed on RadioShack Corporation's consolidated balance sheet. **Let's focus now on RadioShack Corporation's stockholders' equity.** In this chapter we discuss some of the decisions a company faces when

- ▶ issuing stock
- ▶ buying back its stock, and
- ▶ paying dividends.

In addition, we discuss the factors that influence evaluation of profitability in relation to stockholders' investment.

Let's begin with the organization of a corporation.

1 **Explain** the features of a corporation

2 **Account** for the issuance of stock

3 **Show** how treasury stock affects a company

4 **Account** for retained earnings, dividends, and splits

5 **Use** stock values in decision making

6 **Report** equity transactions in the financial statements

Learning Objectives

Explain The Features of a Corporation

Anyone starting a business must decide how to organize the company. Corporations differ from proprietorships and partnerships in several ways.

1 **Explain** the features of a corporation

Separate Legal Entity. A corporation is a business entity formed under state law. It is a distinct entity—an artificial person that exists apart from its owners, the **stockholders**, or **shareholders**. The corporation has many of the rights that a person has. For example, a corporation may buy, own, and sell property. Assets and liabilities in the business belong to the corporation and not to its owners. The corporation may enter into contracts, sue, and be sued.

Nearly all large companies, such as RadioShack, **Toyota**, and **Wal-Mart**, are corporations. Their full names may include *Corporation* or *Incorporated* (abbreviated *Corp.* and *Inc.*) to indicate that they are corporations—like RadioShack Corporation and Williams-Sonoma, Inc., for example. Corporations can also use the word *Company*, such as Ford Motor Company.

Continuous Life and Transferability of Ownership. Corporations have *continuous lives* regardless of changes in their ownership. The stockholders of a corporation may buy more of the stock, sell the stock to another person, give it away, or bequeath it in a will. The transfer of the stock from one person to another does not affect the continuity of the corporation. In contrast, proprietorships and partnerships terminate when their ownership changes.

Limited Liability. Stockholders have **limited liability** for the corporation's debts. They have no personal obligation for corporate liabilities. The most that a stockholder can lose on an investment in a corporation's stock is the cost of the investment. Limited liability is one of the most attractive features of the corporate form of organization. It enables corporations to raise more capital from a wider group of investors than proprietorships and partnerships can. By contrast, proprietors and partners are personally liable for all the debts of their businesses.[1]

Separation of Ownership and Management. Stockholders own the corporation, but the *board of directors*—elected by the stockholders—appoints officers to manage the business. Thus, stockholders may invest $1,000 or $1 million in the corporation without having to manage it.

Management's goal is to maximize the firm's value for the stockholders. But the separation between owners and managers may create problems. Corporate officers may run the business for their own benefit and not for the stockholders. For example, the CEO of **Tyco Corporation** was accused of looting Tyco of $600 million. The CFO of **Enron Corporation** set up outside partnerships and paid himself millions to manage the partnerships—unknown to Enron stockholders. Both men went to prison.

Corporate Taxation. Corporations are separate taxable entities. They pay several taxes not borne by proprietorships or partnerships, including an annual franchise tax levied by the state. The franchise tax keeps the corporate charter in force. Corporations also pay federal and state income taxes.

[1] Unless the business is organized as a limited-liability company (LLC) or a limited-liability partnership (LLP).

Corporate earnings are subject to **double taxation** on their income to the extent they are distributed to shareholders in the form of dividends.

▶ First, corporations pay income taxes on their corporate income.
▶ Then stockholders pay income tax on the cash dividends received from corporations. Proprietorships and partnerships pay no business income tax. Instead, the business' tax falls solely on the owners.

Government Regulation. Because stockholders have only limited liability for corporation debts, outsiders doing business with the corporation can look no further than the corporation if it fails to pay. To protect a corporation's creditors and stockholders, both federal and state governments monitor corporations. The regulations mainly ensure that corporations disclose the information that investors and creditors need to make informed decisions. Accounting provides much of this information.

Exhibit 10-1 summarizes the advantages and disadvantages of the corporate form of business organization.

EXHIBIT 10-1 | Advantages and Disadvantages of a Corporation

Advantages	Disadvantages
1. Can raise more capital than a proprietorship or partnership can	1. Separation of ownership and management
2. Continuous life	2. Corporate taxation
3. Ease of transferring ownership	3. Government regulation
4. Limited liability of stockholders	

Organizing a Corporation

The creation of a corporation begins when its organizers, called the *incorporators*, obtain a charter from the state. The charter includes the authorization for the corporation to issue a certain number of shares of stock. A share of stock is the basic unit of ownership for a corporation. The incorporators

▶ pay fees,
▶ sign the charter,
▶ file documents with the state, and
▶ agree to a set of **bylaws**, which act as the constitution for governing the company.

The corporation then comes into existence.

Ultimate control of the corporation rests with the stockholders who elect a **board of directors** that sets company policy and appoints officers. The board elects a **chairperson**, who usually is the most powerful person in the organization. The chairperson of the board of directors often has the title chief executive officer (CEO). The board also designates the **president**, who is the chief operating officer (COO) in charge of day-to-day operations. Most corporations also have vice presidents in charge of sales, manufacturing, accounting and finance (the chief financial officer, or CFO), and other key areas. Exhibit 10-2 shows the authority structure in a corporation.

Stockholders' Rights

Ownership of stock entitles stockholders to four basic rights, unless a specific right is withheld by agreement with the stockholders:

1. *Vote.* The right to participate in management by voting on matters that come before the stockholders. This is the stockholder's sole voice in the management of the corporation. A stockholder gets one vote for each share of stock owned.

2. *Dividends.* The right to receive a proportionate part of any dividend. Each share of stock in a particular class receives an equal dividend.

EXHIBIT 10-2 | Authority Structure of a Corporation

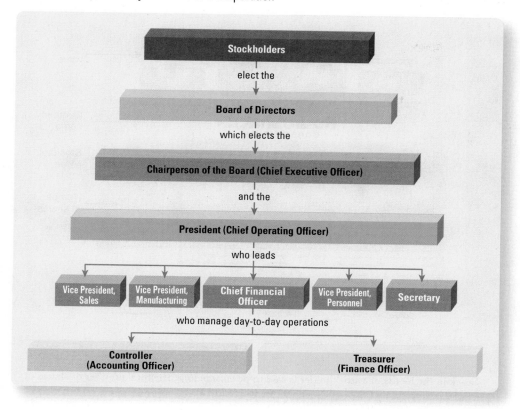

3. *Liquidation.* The right to receive a proportionate share of any assets remaining after the corporation pays its liabilities in liquidation. Liquidation means to go out of business, sell the assets, pay all liabilities, and distribute any remaining cash to the owners.

4. *Preemption.* The right to maintain one's proportionate ownership in the corporation. Suppose you own 5% of a corporation's stock. If the corporation issues 100,000 new shares, it must offer you the opportunity to buy 5% (5,000) of the new shares. This right, called the *preemptive right*, is usually withheld from the stockholders.

Stockholders' Equity

As we saw in Chapter 1, **stockholders' equity** represents the stockholders' ownership interest in the assets of a corporation. Stockholders' equity is divided into two main parts:

1. **Paid-in capital**, also called **contributed capital**. This is the amount of stockholders' equity the stockholders have contributed to the corporation. Paid-in capital includes the stock accounts and any additional paid-in capital.

2. **Retained earnings**. This is the amount of stockholders' equity the corporation has earned through profitable operations and has not used for dividends.

Corporations report stockholders' equity by source. They report paid-in capital separately from retained earnings because most states prohibit the declaration of cash dividends from paid-in capital. Thus, cash dividends are declared from retained earnings.

The owners' equity of a corporation is divided into shares of **stock**. A corporation issues *stock certificates* to its owners when the company receives their investment in the business—usually cash. Because stock represents the corporation's capital, it is often called *capital stock*. The basic unit of capital stock is a *share*. A corporation may issue a stock certificate for any number of shares—1, 100, or any other number—but the total number of *authorized* shares is limited by charter. Exhibit 10-3 shows an actual stock certificate for RadioShack Corporation common stock.

EXHIBIT 10-3 | RadioShack Corporation Stock Certificate

Stock in the hands of a stockholder is said to be *outstanding*. The total number of shares of stock outstanding at any time represents 100% ownership of the corporation.

Classes of Stock

Corporations issue different types of stock to appeal to a variety of investors. The stock of a corporation may be either

- ▶ common or preferred, and
- ▶ par or no-par.

Common and Preferred. Every corporation issues **common stock**, the basic form of capital stock. Unless designated otherwise, the word *stock* is understood to mean "common stock." Common stockholders have the four basic rights of stock ownership, unless a right is specifically withheld. The common stockholders are the owners of the corporation. They stand to benefit the most if the corporation succeeds because they take the most risk by investing in common stock.

Preferred stock gives its owners certain advantages over common stockholders. Preferred stockholders receive dividends before the common stockholders and they also receive assets before the common stockholders if the corporation liquidates. Owners of preferred stock also have the four basic stockholder rights, unless a right is specifically denied. Companies may issue different classes of preferred stock (Class A and Class B or Series A and Series B, for example). Each class of stock is recorded in a separate account. The most preferred stockholders can expect to earn on their investments is a fixed dividend.

Preferred stock is a hybrid between common stock and long-term debt. Like interest on debt, preferred stock pays a fixed dividend. But unlike interest on debt, the dividend is not required to be paid unless the board of directors declares the dividend. Also, companies have no obligation to pay back true preferred stock. Preferred stock that must be redeemed (paid back) by the corporation is a liability masquerading as a stock.

Preferred stock is rare. A recent survey of 600 corporations revealed that only 9% of them had preferred stock (Exhibit 10-4 on the following page). In contrast, all corporations have common stock. The balance sheet of RadioShack Corporation (p. 582) shows that the company has a million shares of Series A preferred stock authorized, but none of this stock has ever been issued—300,000 shares have been "designated." The stock is also labeled "junior participating."

EXHIBIT 10-4 | Preferred Stock

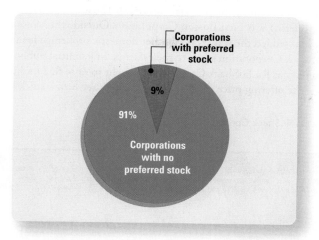

The term "participating" means that both preferred and common shareholders would share in dividend distributions on these shares if they are ever issued. We will explain the meanings of the other terms later.

Exhibit 10-5 shows some of the similarities and differences among common stock, preferred stock, and long-term debt.

EXHIBIT 10-5 | Comparison of Common Stock, Preferred Stock, and Long-Term Debt

	Common Stock	Preferred Stock	Long-Term Debt
1. Obligation to repay principal	No	No	Yes
2. Dividends/interest	Dividends are not tax-deductible	Dividends are not tax-deductible	Interest expense is tax-deductible
3. Obligation to pay dividends/interest	Only after declaration	Only after declaration	At fixed rates and dates

Par Value and No-Par. Stock may be par-value stock or no-par stock. **Par value** is an arbitrary amount assigned by a company to a share of its stock. Most companies set the par value of their common stock low to avoid legal difficulties from issuing their stock below par. Most states require companies to maintain a minimum amount of stockholders' equity for the protection of creditors, and this minimum is often called the corporation's *legal capital*. For corporations with par-value stock, **legal capital** is the par value of the shares issued.

The par value of **PepsiCo** common stock is $0.0166 (1 2/3 cents) per share. **Best Buy's, Southwest Airlines'**, and **RadioShack's** common stock (p. 582) all carry a par value of $1 per share.

No-par stock does not have par value. **RadioShack Corporation's** Series A preferred stock is designated as no-par stock. Some no-par stock has a **stated value**, which makes it similar to par-value stock. The stated value is an arbitrary amount similar to par value. In a recent survey, only 9% of the companies had no-par stock outstanding. Apple, Inc., Krispy Kreme Doughnuts, and Sony all have no-par stock.

Account for the Issuance of Stock

Large corporations such as **RadioShack Corporation, PepsiCo**, and **Microsoft** need huge quantities of money to operate. Corporations may sell stock directly to the stockholders or use the service of an *underwriter*, such as the investment banking firms **UBS** and **Goldman Sachs**. Companies often advertise the issuance of their stock to attract investors. The *Wall Street Journal* is the most popular medium for such advertisements, which are also called *tombstones*.

Account for the issuance of stock

Exhibit 10-6 is a reproduction of an announcement in the *Wall Street Journal* when the company instituted a hypothetical initial public offering (IPO). The lead underwriter of RadioShack Corporation's public offering was First Boston Corporation. Outside the United States, Credit Suisse First Boston Limited led the way. Several other domestic brokerage firms and investment bankers sold RadioShack Corporation stock to their clients. In its initial public offering (Exhibit 10-6), assume that RadioShack Corporation sought to raise $62 million of capital (6.2 million shares at the offering price of $10 per share). Let's see how a stock issuance works.

EXHIBIT 10-6 | Announcement of Public Offering of RadioShack Corporation Stock (Adapted)

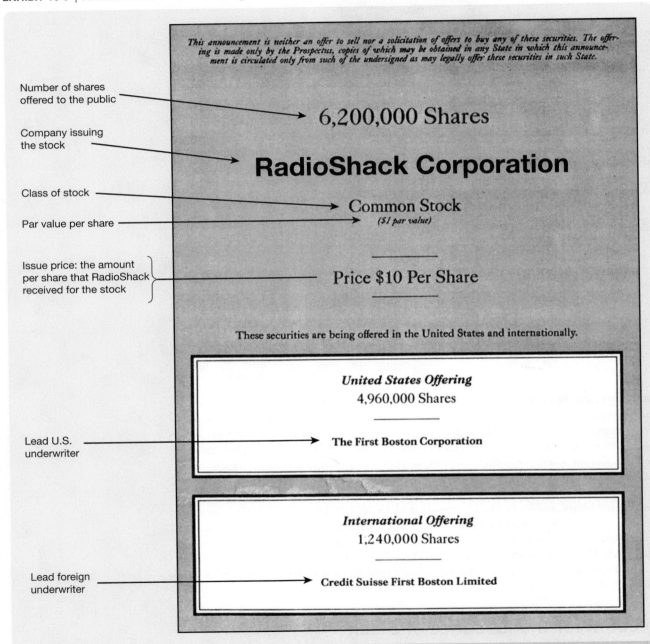

Common Stock

Common Stock at Par. Suppose RadioShack Corporation's common stock had carried a par value equal to its issuance price of $10 per share. The entry for issuance of 6.2 million shares of stock at par would be as follows:

Jan 8	Cash (6,200,000 × $10)	62,000,000	
	Common Stock		62,000,000
	To issue common stock.		

RadioShack Corporation's assets and stockholders' equity increase by the same amount.

Assets	=	Liabilities	+	Stockholders' Equity
+ 62,000,000	=	0		+ 62,000,000

Common Stock Above Par. Most corporations set par value low and issue common stock for a price above par. Rather than $10 as in the assumed example above, RadioShack Corporation's common stock has a par value of $1 per share. The $9 difference between issue price ($10) and par value ($1) is additional paid-in capital. Both the par value of the stock and the additional amount are part of paid-in capital.

Because the entity is dealing with its own stockholders, a sale of stock is not gain, income, or profit to the corporation. This situation illustrates one of the fundamentals of accounting:

> **A company neither earns a profit nor incurs a loss when it sells its stock to, or buys its stock from, its own stockholders.**

With par value of $1, RadioShack Corporation's actual entry to record the issuance of common stock looked something like this:

Jul 23	Cash (6,200,000 × $10)	62,000,000	
	Common Stock (6,200,000 × $1)		6,200,000
	Paid-in Capital in Excess of Par—Common		
	(6,200,000 × $9)		55,800,000
	To issue common stock.		

Both assets and equity increase by the same amount.

Assets	=	Liabilities	+	Stockholders' Equity
+ 62,000,000	=	0		+ 6,200,000
				+ 55,800,000

Another title for Paid-in capital in excess of par—common is Additional paid-in capital, as used by RadioShack Corporation (p. 582, line 4.) At the end of the year, RadioShack could report stockholders' equity on its balance sheet as follows (figures assumed):

Stockholders' Equity	
Common stock, $1 par, 650 million shares authorized, 6.2 million shares issued	$ 6,200,000
Additional paid-in capital	55,800,000
Total paid-in capital	62,000,000
Retained earnings	338,790
Total stockholders' equity	$62,338,790

All the transactions in this section include a receipt of cash by the corporation as it issues *new* stock. The transactions we illustrate are different from those reported in the daily news. In those transactions, one stockholder sold stock to another investor. The corporation doesn't record those transactions because they were between two outside parties.

STOP & THINK...

Examine RadioShack Corporation's consolidated balance sheet at December 31, 2010 (p. 582). Answer these questions about RadioShack Corporation's actual stock transactions:

(1) What was RadioShack Corporation's total paid-in capital at December 31, 2010?

(2) How many shares of common stock had RadioShack Corporation issued through the end of 2010?

(3) What was the average issue price of the RadioShack Corporation common stock that the company had issued through the end of 2010?

Answers:

		December 31, 2010
(1)	Total paid-in capital (in millions)	$146 + $147.3 = $293.3
(2)	Number of shares of common stock issued (in millions)	146

(3)
$$\text{Average issue price of common stock through the end of 2010} = \frac{\text{Total received from issuance of common stock}}{\text{Common shares issued}} = \frac{\$146 + \$147.3 = \$293.3}{146}$$
$$= \$2.01 \text{ per share}$$

RadioShack Corporation has issued its common stock at an average price of $2.01 per share.

No-Par Common Stock. To record the issuance of no-par stock, the company debits the asset received and credits the stock account for the cash value of the asset received. Suppose Apple, Inc., issues 916 million shares of no-par common stock for $10,668 million. Apple's stock issuance entry is as follows (in millions):

Aug 14	Cash	10,668	
	Common Stock		10,668
	To issue no-par common stock.		

Assets	=	Liabilities	+	Stockholders' Equity
+10,668	=	0		+ 10,668

Apple's charter authorizes the company to issue 1,800 million shares of no-par stock, and the company has approximately $37,169 million in retained earnings and ($46) of accumulated other comprehensive loss. Apple, Inc., reports stockholders' equity on the balance sheet as follows (in millions):

Stockholders' Equity	
(in millions)	
Common stock, no par, 1,800 shares authorized, 916 shares issued	$10,668
Retained earnings	37,169
Accumulated other comprehensive (loss)	(46)
Total stockholders' equity	$47,791

You can see that a company with true no-par stock has no Additional Paid-in Capital account.

No-Par Common Stock with a Stated Value. Accounting for no-par stock with a stated value is identical to accounting for par-value stock. The excess over stated value is credited to Additional Paid-in Capital.

Common Stock Issued for Assets Other Than Cash. When a corporation issues stock and receives assets other than cash, the company records the assets received at their current market value and credits the stock and additional paid-in capital accounts accordingly. The assets' prior book values aren't relevant because the stockholder will demand stock equal to the market value of the asset given. On November 12, Kahn Corporation issued 15,000 shares of its $1 par common stock for equipment worth $4,000 and a building worth $120,000. Kahn's entry is as follows:

Nov 12	Equipment	4,000	
	Building	120,000	
	Common Stock (15,000 × $1)		15,000
	Paid-in Capital in Excess of Par—Common		
	($124,000 – $15,000)		109,000
	To issue no-par common stock in exchange for equipment		
	and a building.		

Assets and equity both increase by $124,000.

Assets	=	Liabilities	+	Stockholders' Equity
+ 4,000				+ 15,000
+ 120,000	=	0		+ 109,000

Common Stock Issued for Services. Sometimes a corporation will issue shares of common stock in exchange for services rendered, either by employees or outsiders. In this case, no cash is exchanged. However, the transaction is recognized at fair market value. The corporation usually recognizes an expense for the fair market value of the services rendered. Common stock is increased for its par value (if any), and additional paid-in capital is increased for any difference. For example, assume that Kahn Corporation engages an attorney to represent the company on a legal matter. The attorney bills the corporation $25,000 for services, and agrees to accept 2,500 shares of $1 par common stock, rather than cash, in settlement of the fee. The fair market value of the stock is $10 per share. The journal entry to record the transaction is as follows:

Legal Expense	25,000	
Common Stock		2,500
Paid-in Capital in Excess of Par—Common ($25,000 – $2,500)		22,500

In this case, retained earnings (stockholders' equity) is eventually decreased (through legal expense) by $25,000, and paid-in capital (stockholders' equity) is increased for the same amount.

A Stock Issuance for Other Than Cash Can Create an Ethical Challenge

Generally accepted accounting principles require a company to record its stock at the fair market value of whatever the corporation receives in exchange for the stock. When the corporation receives cash, there is clear evidence of the value of the stock because cash is worth its face amount. But when the corporation receives an asset other than cash, the value of the asset can create an ethical challenge.

A computer whiz may start a new company by investing in computer software. The software may be market-tested or it may be new. The software may be worth millions, or it may be worthless. The corporation must record the asset received and the stock given with a journal entry such as the following:

Software	500,000	
Common Stock		500,000
Issued stock in exchange for software.		

If the software is really worth $500,000, the accounting records are okay. But if the software is new and untested, the assets and equity may be overstated.

Suppose your computer-whiz friend invites you to invest in the new business and shows you this balance sheet:

Gee-Whiz Computer Solutions, Inc.			
Balance Sheet			
December 31, 2012			
Assets		**Liabilities**	
Computer software	$500,000		$ -0-
		Stockholders' Equity	
		Common stock	500,000
Total assets	$500,000	Total liabilities and equity	$500,000

Companies like to report large asset and equity amounts on their balance sheets. That makes them look prosperous and creditworthy. Gee-Whiz looks debt-free and appears to have a valuable asset. Will you invest in this new business? Here are two takeaway lessons:

► Some accounting values are more solid than others.
► Not all financial statements mean exactly what they say—unless they are audited by independent CPAs.

Preferred Stock

Accounting for preferred stock follows the same pattern we illustrated for common stock. When a company issues preferred stock, it credits Preferred Stock at its par value, with any excess credited to Paid-in Capital in Excess of Par—Preferred.

There may be separate accounts for paid-in capital in excess of par for preferred and common stock, but not necessarily. Some companies combine paid-in capital in excess of par from both preferred and common stock transactions into one account. Accounting for no-par preferred follows the pattern for no-par common stock. When reporting stockholders' equity on the balance sheet, a corporation lists its accounts in this order:

► Preferred stock
► Common stock
► Additional paid-in capital
► Retained earnings

as illustrated for RadioShack Corporation on page 582.

In Chapter 9, we saw how to account for convertible bonds payable (p. 540). Companies also issue convertible preferred stock. The preferred stock is usually convertible into the company's common stock at the discretion of the preferred stockholders, as the price of the common stock, as well as its dividend, rises to an attractive level in the future. Here are some representative journal entries for convertible preferred stock, using the following assumed amounts:

► Convertible preferred stock $1 par, 50,000 shares issued at par value

2012	Cash	50,000	
	Convertible Preferred Stock		50,000
	Issued convertible preferred stock.		

► Converted preferred stock to common stock at the rate of 6.25 to 1 (8,000 shares of $1 par value common stock issued in exchange for 50,000 shares of preferred stock)

2012	Convertible Preferred Stock	50,000	
	Common Stock		8,000
	Paid-in Capital in Excess of Par—Common		42,000
	Investors converted preferred into common.		

As you can see, we merely remove Preferred Stock from the books and give the new Common Stock the prior book value of the preferred.

MID-CHAPTER SUMMARY PROBLEM

1. Test your understanding of the first half of this chapter by deciding whether each of the following statements is true or false.

   a. The policy-making body in a corporation is called the board of directors.

   b. The owner of 100 shares of preferred stock has greater voting rights than the owner of 100 shares of common stock.

   c. Par-value stock is worth more than no-par stock.

   d. Issuance of 1,000 shares of $5 par-value stock at $12 increases contributed capital by $12,000.

   e. The issuance of no-par stock with a stated value is fundamentally different from issuing par-value stock.

   f. A corporation issues its preferred stock in exchange for land and a building with a combined market value of $200,000. This transaction increases the corporation's owners' equity by $200,000 regardless of the assets' prior book values.

   g. Preferred stock is a riskier investment than common stock.

2. Adolfo Company has two classes of common stock. Only the Class A common stockholders are entitled to vote. The company's balance sheet included the following presentation:

Stockholders' Equity	
Capital stock:	
Class A common stock, voting, $1 par value,	
authorized and issued 1,260,000 shares	$ 1,260,000
Class B common stock, nonvoting, no par value,	
authorized and issued 46,200,000 shares	11,000,000
	12,260,000
Additional paid-in capital	2,011,000
Retained earnings	872,403,000
	$886,674,000

▶ Requirements

a. Record the issuance of the Class A common stock. Use the Adolfo account titles.

b. Record the issuance of the Class B common stock. Use the Adolfo account titles.

c. How much of Adolfo's stockholders' equity was contributed by the stockholders? How much was provided by profitable operations? Does this division of equity suggest that the company has been successful? Why or why not?

d. Write a sentence to describe what Adolfo's stockholders' equity means.

▶ Answers

1. a. True **b.** False **c.** False **d.** True **e.** False **f.** True **g.** False

2. a.

Cash		3,271,000	
Class A Common Stock			1,260,000
Additional Paid-in Capital			2,011,000
To record issuance of Class A common stock.			

b.

Cash		11,000,000	
Class B Common Stock			11,000,000
To record issuance of Class B common stock.			

c. Contributed by the stockholders: $14,271,000 ($12,260,000 + $2,011,000). Provided by profitable operations: $872,403,000.

This division suggests that the company has been successful because most of its stockholders' equity has come from profitable operations.

d. Adolfo's stockholders' equity of $886,674,000 means that the company's stockholders own $886,674,000 of the business's assets.

Authorized, Issued, and Outstanding Stock

It is important to distinguish among three distinctly different numbers of a company's stock. The following examples use RadioShack Corporation's actual data from page 582.

▶ **Authorized stock** is the maximum number of shares the company can issue under its charter. As of December 31, 2010, RadioShack Corporation was authorized to issue 650 million shares of common stock.

▶ **Issued stock** is the number of shares the company has issued to its stockholders. This is a cumulative total from the company's beginning up through the current date, less any shares permanently retired. As of December 31, 2009, RadioShack Corporation had issued 191,033,000 shares. In 2010, the corporation purchased and permanently retired 45 million shares. Therefore, as of December 31, 2010, RadioShack Corporation had 146,033,000 shares of its common stock issued. The company's share repurchase program is discussed later.

▶ **Outstanding stock** is the number of shares that the stockholders own (that is, the number of shares outstanding in the hands of the stockholders). Outstanding stock is issued stock minus treasury stock. At December 31, 2010, RadioShack Corporation had 105,773,000 shares of common stock outstanding, computed as follows:

Issued shares (line 3)	146,033,000
Less: Treasury shares (line 6)	(40,260,000)
Outstanding shares	105,773,000

Now let's learn about treasury stock.

Show How Treasury Stock Affects a Company

A company's own stock that it has issued and later reacquired is called **treasury stock.**[2] In effect, the corporation holds this stock in its treasury. Many public companies spend millions of dollars each year to buy back their own stock. Corporations purchase their own stock for several reasons:

1. The company has issued all its authorized stock and needs some stock for distributions to employees under stock purchase plans or compensation plans.

2. The business wants to increase net assets by buying its stock low and hoping to resell it for a higher price.

3. Management wants to avoid a takeover by an outside party.

4. Management wants to increase its reported earnings per share (EPS) of common stock (net income/number of common shares outstanding). Purchasing shares removes them from outstanding shares, thus decreasing the denominator of this fraction and increasing EPS. We cover the computation of EPS in more depth in Chapter 11.

5. Management uses a share repurchase program as a way to return excess cash to shareholders, in a manner similar to a dividend.

How is Treasury Stock Recorded?

Treasury stock is recorded at cost (the market value of the stock on the date of the purchase) without regard to the stock's par value. Treasury stock is a *contra stockholders' equity* account. Therefore, the treasury stock account carries a debit balance, the opposite of the other equity accounts. It is reported beneath the retained earnings account on the balance sheet as a negative amount.

To understand the way treasury stock transactions work, it is helpful to analyze the changes that occur in the treasury stock account during the year. Let's start with RadioShack Corporation's stockholders' equity at the end of the previous year, December 31, 2009 (we use rounded amounts in millions, except for shares):

RadioShack Corporation and Subsidiaries **Stockholders' Equity** **December 31, 2009**	
(in millions)	
Preferred stock	$ -0-
Common stock	191
Additional paid-in capital	162
Retained earnings	2,324
Treasury stock (65,806,000 shares)	(1,622)
Accumulated other comprehensive loss	(7)
Total stockholders' equity	$1,048

Notice that, up to the end of 2009, RadioShack Corporation had spent $1,622,000,000 to repurchase 65,806,000 shares of its own stock throughout the company's history. The average price it has paid for its shares through the years has been about $24.65 ($1,622,000,000/65,806,000).

Repurchasing treasury stock provides a way for public companies to return cash to shareholders other than through dividends. The disadvantage to the shareholder of a share repurchase plan is that, in order to receive cash, the shareholder has to surrender (dilute) ownership in the company.

---

[2]In this text, we illustrate the *cost* method of accounting for treasury stock because it is used most widely. Other methods are presented in intermediate accounting courses.

Note 6 of RadioShack Corporation's 2010 financial statements gives more information about the company's share repurchase program:

> **(Adapted) Accelerated Share Repurchase Program:** ... in August 2010, we entered into an accelerated share repurchase program with two investment banks to repurchase shares of our common stock under our approved share repurchase program. On August 24, 2010, we paid $300 million to the investment banks in exchange for an initial delivery of 11.7 million shares to us. At the conclusion of the ASR program, we received an additional 3.2 million shares. The 14.9 million shares delivered to us was based on the average daily volume weighted average price of our common stock over a period beginning immediately after the effective date of the ASR agreements and ending on November 2, 2010.

The footnote reflects that the company paid $300 million to purchase 14.9 million shares. This figures to $20.14 per share ($300,000,000 ÷ 14,900,000). The details of such a complicated transaction are beyond the scope of this textbook. Over a period of time, the company actually acquired a total of 19.8 million shares of treasury stock for $398.8 million. The entry to record the aggregate of these purchases is as follows:

2010			
Aug 24	Treasury Stock	398,800,000	
	Cash		398,800,000
	Purchased treasury stock.		

Assets	=	Liabilities	+	Stockholders' Equity
− 398,800,000	=	0		− 398,800,000

Notice that treasury stock is recorded at cost, which is the market price of the stock on the day that RadioShack Corporation purchased it. The financial statement impact of the transaction is decreased cash as well as stockholders' equity.

Retirement of Stock

A corporation may purchase its own stock and *retire* it by canceling the stock certificates. Retired stock cannot be reissued. In RadioShack Corporation's case, the company's officers and board of directors decided it was very unlikely that many of its repurchased treasury shares would ever be reissued, and that the balance in the treasury stock account was too high. The company decided to retire 45 million of its treasury shares, thus permanently canceling them. This impacted common stock, additional paid-in-capital, retained earnings, and treasury stock accounts in the following way:

	Debit	Credit
Common stock	45,000,000	
− 45 million shares		
Additional paid-in capital	17,900,000	
Retained earnings	1,001,000,000	
Treasury stock		1,063,900,000
− 45 million shares		
Retired 45 million shares of stock held in treasury.		

Assets	Liabilities	Stockholder's Equity
		− 1,063,900,000
		+ 1,063,900,000

Notice that although the individual accounts within stockholders' equity were impacted in significant ways, the net effect on the accounting equation was zero. Neither total assets nor total liabilities was affected, and stockholders' equity was both increased and decreased by the same amount, so the net impact on stockholders' equity was also zero.

Resale of Treasury Stock

Reselling treasury stock for cash grows assets and equity exactly as issuing new stock does. The sale increases assets and equity by the full amount of cash received. A company *never records gains or losses on transactions involving its own treasury stock*. Rather, amounts received in excess of amounts originally paid for treasury stock are recorded as additional paid-in capital, thus bypassing the income statement. If amounts received from resale of treasury stock were less than amounts originally paid, the difference would be debited to paid-in capital to the extent of that balance, and after that, to retained earnings. RadioShack did not resell any of its treasury stock in 2010, but suppose that it had resold 100,000 shares of treasury stock for $30 per share. Further assume that the average cost of treasury shares is $27 per share. RadioShack Corporation would have recorded this sale of treasury stock as follows:

2010				
Jul 22	Cash		3,000,000	
	Treasury Stock			2,700,000
	Additional Paid-in Capital			300,000
	Sold treasury stock.			

Assets	=	Liabilities	+	Stockholders' Equity
+ 3,000,000	=	0		+ 2,700,000
				+ 300,000

Treasury Stock for Employee Compensation

Sometimes companies supplement employee salaries by granting them shares of stock rather than cash. In 2010, RadioShack Corporation issued 300,000 of its treasury shares in conjunction with an employee stock option and compensation plan. The entry the company made was as follows:

	Debit	Credit
Compensation expense	11,100,000	
Treasury stock		7,800,000
Additional paid-in capital		3,300,000
To record stock-based compensation plan.		

Now let's take a look at RadioShack Corporation's Stockholders' Equity as of December 31, 2010. For now, focus only on the treasury stock account:

RadioShack Corporation and Subsidiaries Stockholders' Equity December 31, 2010	
(in millions)	
Preferred stock	$ -0-
Common stock	146
Paid-in capital in excess of par	147
Retained earnings	1,503
Less Treasury stock (at cost) 40,260,000 shares	(949)
Accumulated other comprehensive loss	(4)
Total stockholders' equity	$ 843

After treasury stock transactions for 2010 have been recorded, the new number of treasury shares is 40,260,000.[3] The balance in the treasury stock account is $949,000,000. The new average purchase price of treasury shares is about $23.57 ($949 million ÷ 40.26 million).

Summary of Treasury-Stock Transactions

The types of treasury-stock transactions we have reviewed are as follows:

- ▶ Buying treasury stock. Assets and equity *decrease* by an amount equal to the cost of treasury stock purchased.
- ▶ Reselling treasury stock. Assets and equity *increase* by an amount equal to the sale price of the treasury stock sold.
- ▶ Retiring treasury stock, thus removing it from both common stock and from the treasury.
- ▶ Reissuing treasury stock for employee compensation. Expenses are increased, treasury stock is decreased, and additional paid-in capital is either increased or decreased for the difference.

Account for Retained Earnings, Dividends, and Splits

The Retained Earnings account carries the balance of the business's net income, less its net losses and less any declared dividends that have been accumulated over the corporation's lifetime. *Retained* means "held onto." Successful companies grow by reinvesting back into the business the assets they generate through profitable operations. RadioShack Corporation is an example. Take another look at its stockholders' equity as of December 31, 2010 (p. 582). Notice that the Retained Earnings account ($1502.5 billion) is the largest account balance in stockholders' equity as of the end of 2010. In fact, because historically the company has spent so much money on treasury stock, retained earnings actually *exceeds* total stockholders' equity ($842.5 million) as of the end of 2010.

Account for retained earnings, dividends, and splits

The Retained Earnings account is not a reservoir of cash for paying dividends to the stockholders. In fact, the corporation may have a large balance in Retained Earnings but not have enough cash to pay a dividend. Cash and Retained Earnings are two entirely separate accounts with no particular relationship. Retained Earnings says nothing about the company's cash balance.

---

[3]There is a slight difference in the computation of the number of shares from the balance sheet total due to rounding.

A *credit* balance in Retained Earnings is normal, indicating that the corporation's lifetime earnings exceed lifetime losses and dividends. A *debit* balance in Retained Earnings arises when a corporation's lifetime losses and dividends exceed lifetime earnings. Called a **deficit**, this amount is subtracted to determine total stockholders' equity. In a recent survey, 15.5% of companies had a retained earnings deficit (Exhibit 10-7).

EXHIBIT 10-7 | Percentage of Companies with Positive Retained Earnings, Deficits

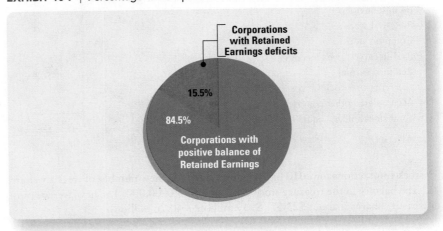

Should the Company Declare and Pay Cash Dividends?

A **dividend** is a distribution by a corporation to its stockholders, usually based on earnings. Dividends usually take one of three forms:

- ▶ Cash
- ▶ Stock
- ▶ Non-cash assets

In this section we focus on cash dividends and stock dividends because non-cash dividends are rare. For a non-cash asset dividend, debit Retained Earnings and credit the asset (for example, Long-Term Investment) for the current market value of the asset given.

Cash Dividends

Most dividends are cash dividends. Finance courses discuss how a company decides on its dividend policy. Accounting tells a company if it can pay a dividend. To do so, a company must have both

- ▶ enough retained earnings   and   ▶ enough cash to *pay*
  to *declare* the dividend,   the dividend.

A corporation declares a dividend before paying it. Only the board of directors has the authority to declare a dividend. The corporation has no obligation to pay a dividend until the board declares one, but once declared, the dividend becomes a legal liability of the corporation. There are three relevant dates for dividends (using assumed amounts):

1. **Declaration date, *June 19.*** On the declaration date, the board of directors announces the dividend. Declaration of the dividend creates a liability for the corporation. Declaration is recorded by debiting Retained Earnings and crediting Dividends Payable. Assume a $50,000 dividend.

Jun 19	Retained Earnings[4]	50,000	
	Dividends Payable		50,000
	Declared a cash dividend.		

---

[4]In the early part of this book, we debited a Dividends account to clearly identify the purpose of the payment. From here on, we follow the more common practice of debiting the Retained Earnings account for dividend declarations.

Liabilities increase, and stockholders' equity decreases.

Assets	=	Liabilities	+	Stockholders' Equity
0	=	+ 50,000		− 50,000

2. **Date of record, July 1.** As part of the declaration, the corporation announces the record date, which follows the declaration date by a few weeks. The stockholders on the record date will receive the dividend. There is no journal entry for the date of record.

3. **Payment date, July 10.** Payment of the dividend usually follows the record date by a week or two. Payment is recorded by debiting Dividends Payable and crediting Cash.

Jul 10	Dividends Payable	50,000	
	Cash		50,000
	Paid cash dividend.		

Both assets and liabilities decrease. The corporation shrinks.

Assets	=	Liabilities	+	Stockholders' Equity
− 50,000	=	− 50,000		

The net effect of a dividend declaration and its payment, as shown in steps 1, 2, and 3, is a decrease in assets and a corresponding decrease in stockholders' equity.

Analyzing the Stockholder's Equity Accounts

By knowing accounting, you can look at a company's comparative year-to-year financial statements and tell a lot about what the company did during the current year. For example, RadioShack Corporation reported the following for Retained earnings (in millions):

	December 31,	
	2010	2009
Retained earnings...............	$1,503	$2,324

What do these figures tell you about RadioShack Corporation's results of operations during 2010—was it a net income or a net loss? How can you tell? Remember that

► net income is the only item that increases retained earnings;
► net losses decrease retained earnings;
► dividends decrease retained earnings; and
► other adjustments to retained earnings are usually relatively minor and relatively rare.

In most cases, if you know the amount of either net income or dividends, but not both, and if you know both beginning and ending balances of retained earnings, you can figure out the amount you don't know by analyzing the Retained earnings account.

Let's analyze RadioShack Corporation's Retained earnings account for the year ended December 31, 2010. As shown previously, the balance of Retained earnings was $2,324 on December 31, 2009. Net income, according to the company's consolidated statement of income, was $206.1 million. If there were no other changes in Retained earnings besides dividends, how much in dividends did the company pay?

If you know accounting, you can compute RadioShack Corporation's dividend declarations during 2010, as follows (in thousands):

Retained earnings			
		Beg bal	2,324
Dividends	x	Net income	206
		End bal	1,503

Dividends (x) would have been $1,027 ($2,324 + $206 − x) = $1,503; x = $1,027. It really helps to be able to use accounting in this way!

Unfortunately, in RadioShack Corporation's case, 2010 wasn't that simple. The retirement of treasury stock, described in the previous section, resulted in a $1,001 million reduction in Retained earnings. When we factor in that decrease, our $1,027 difference calculated above reduces to the true amount of dividend of about $26 million.

Therefore, an analysis of RadioShack's ending balance in Retained earnings as of December 31, 2010, is as follows (in thousands):

Retained earnings			
Retirement of stock	1,001	Beg bal	2,324
Dividends	26	Net income	206
		End bal	1,503

Dividends on Preferred Stock

When a company has issued both preferred and common stock, the preferred stockholders receive their dividends first. The common stockholders receive dividends only if the total dividend is large enough to pay the preferred stockholders first.

Avant Garde, Inc., has 100,000 shares of $1.50 preferred stock outstanding in addition to its common stock. The $1.50 designation means that the preferred stockholders receive an annual cash dividend of $1.50 per share. In 2012, Avant Garde declares an annual dividend of $500,000. The allocation to preferred and common stockholders is as follows:

Preferred dividend (100,000 shares × $1.50 per share)............	$150,000
Common dividend (remainder: $500,000 − $150,000)	350,000
Total dividend..	$500,000

If Avant Garde declares only a $200,000 dividend, preferred stockholders receive $150,000, and the common stockholders get the remainder, $50,000 ($200,000 − $150,000).

Two Ways to Express the Dividend Rate on Preferred Stock. Dividends on preferred stock are stated either as a

▶ percent of par value   or   ▶ dollar amount per share.

For example, preferred stock may be "6% preferred," which means that owners of the preferred stock receive an annual dividend equal to 6% of the stock's par value. If par value is $100 per share, preferred stockholders receive an annual cash dividend of $6 per share (6% of $100). Alternatively, the preferred stock may be "$3 preferred," which means that the preferred stockholders receive an annual dividend of $3 per share regardless of the stock's par value. The dividend rate on no-par preferred stock is stated in a dollar amount per share.

Dividends on Cumulative and Noncumulative Preferred Stock. The balance sheet classification of preferred stock, as well as the allocation of dividends, may be complex if the preferred stock is *cumulative*. Why? Corporations sometimes fail to pay a dividend to preferred stockholders. This is called *passing the dividend*, and the passed dividends are said to be *in arrears*. The owners of **cumulative preferred stock** must receive all dividends in arrears plus the current year's dividend before any dividends go to the common stockholders. In this sense, cumulative dividends almost take on the flavor of accrued interest on long-term debt, but not quite. Although cumulative dividends must be paid before other dividends, they must still be declared by the company's board of directors. *In most states, preferred stock is cumulative unless it is specifically labeled as noncumulative.*

Here's an example of how cumulative dividends work. Let's assume that the preferred stock of Avant Garde, Inc., is cumulative. Suppose Avant Garde passed the preferred dividend of $150,000 in 2011. Before paying dividends to common in 2012, Avant Garde must first pay preferred dividends of $150,000 for both 2011 and 2012—a total of $300,000. On September 6, 2012, Avant Garde declares a $500,000 dividend. The entry to record the declaration is as follows:

Sep 6	Retained Earnings	500,000	
	Dividends Payable, Preferred ($150,000 × 2)		300,000
	Dividends Payable, Common ($500,000 – $300,000)		200,000
	To declare a cash dividend.		

If the preferred stock is *noncumulative*, the corporation is not obligated to pay dividends in arrears—until the board of directors declares the dividend.

Stock Dividends

A **stock dividend** is a proportional distribution by a corporation of its own stock to its stockholders. Stock dividends increase the stock account and decrease Retained Earnings. Total equity is unchanged, and no asset or liability is affected.

The corporation distributes stock dividends to stockholders in proportion to the number of shares they already own. If you own 300 shares of RadioShack Corporation common stock and the corporation distributes a 10% common stock dividend, you get 30 (300 × 0.10) additional shares. You would then own 330 shares of the stock. All other RadioShack Corporation stockholders would also receive 10% more shares, leaving all stockholders' ownership unchanged.

In distributing a stock dividend, the corporation gives up no assets. Why, then, do companies issue stock dividends? A corporation may choose to distribute stock dividends for these reasons:

1. *To continue dividends but conserve cash.* A company may need to conserve cash and yet wish to continue dividends in some form. So the corporation may distribute a stock dividend. Stockholders pay no income tax on stock dividends.

2. *To reduce the per-share market price of its stock.* Distribution of a stock dividend usually causes the stock's market price to fall because of the increased number of outstanding shares that result from it. The objective is to make the stock less expensive and therefore attractive to more investors.

Generally accepted accounting principles (GAAP) label a stock dividend of 25% or less as *small* and suggest that the dividend be recorded at the market value of the shares distributed. Suppose RadioShack Corporation declared a 10% common stock dividend on December 31, 2010. At the time, RadioShack Corporation had approximately 146,000,000 shares of common stock outstanding, and the corporation's stock was trading for $10 per share. RadioShack Corporation would record this stock dividend as follows:

2010			
Dec 31	Retained earnings[5] (146,000,000 shares of common outstanding × 0.10 stock dividend × $10 market value per share of common)	146,000,000	
	Common stock (146,000,000 × 0.10 × $1.00 per value per share)		14,600,000
	Additional paid-in capital		131,400,000
	Distributed a 10% stock dividend.		

The accounting equation clearly shows that a stock dividend has no effect on total assets, liabilities, or equity. The increases in equity offset the decreases, and the net effect is zero.

Assets	=	Liabilities	+	Stockholders' Equity
0	=	0		− 146,000,000
				+ 14,600,000
				+ 131,400,000

GAAP identifies stock dividends above 25% as *large* and permits large stock dividends to be recorded at par value. For a large stock dividend, therefore, RadioShack Corporation would debit Retained earnings and credit Common stock for the par value of the shares distributed in the dividend.

Stock Splits

A **stock split** is an increase in the number of shares of stock authorized, issued, and outstanding, coupled with a proportionate reduction in the stock's par value. For example, if the company splits its stock 2 for 1, the number of outstanding shares is doubled and each share's par value is halved. A stock split, like a large stock dividend, decreases the market price of the stock—with the intention of making the stock more attractive in the market. Most leading companies in the United States—including **IBM**, **PepsiCo**, and **Best Buy**—have split their stock.

Assume the market price of a share of Best Buy common stock is approximately $50 per share. Assume that Best Buy wishes to decrease the market price to approximately $25 per share. Best Buy can split its common stock 2 for 1, and the stock price will fall to around $25. A 2-for-1 stock split means that

▶ the company will have twice as many shares of stock authorized, issued, and outstanding after the split as it had before.

▶ each share's par value will be cut in half.

---

[5]Many companies debit Additional Paid-in Capital for their stock dividends.

Before the split, Best Buy had approximately 500 million shares of $0.10 (10 cent) par common stock issued and outstanding. Compare Best Buy's stockholders' equity before and after a 2-for-1 stock split:

Best Buy Co., Inc., Stockholders' Equity (Adapted)

Before 2-for-1 Stock Split	(In millions)	After 2-for-1 Stock Split	(In millions)
Common stock, $0.10 par, 1,000 shares authorized, 500 shares issued	$ 50	Common stock, $0.05 par, 2,000 shares authorized, 1,000 shares issued	$ 50
Additional paid-in capital	643	Additional paid-in capital	643
Retained earnings	4,304	Retained earnings	4,304
Other equity	260	Other	260
Total stockholders' equity	$5,257	Total stockholders' equity	$5,257

All account balances are the same after the stock split as before. Only three Best Buy items are affected:

► Par value per share drops from $0.10 to $0.05.
► Shares *authorized* double from 1,000 to 2,000 (both in millions).
► Shares *issued* double from 500 to 1,000 (both in millions).

Total equity doesn't change, nor do any assets or liabilities.

Summary of the Effects on Assets, Liabilities, and Stockholders' Equity

We've seen how to account for the basic stockholders' equity transactions:

► Issuance of stock—common and preferred (pp. 587–593)
► Purchase and sale of treasury stock (pp. 596–599)
► Cash dividends (pp. 600–603)
► Stock dividends and stock splits (pp. 603–605)

How do these transactions affect assets, liabilities, and equity? Exhibit 10-8 provides a helpful summary.

EXHIBIT 10-8 | Effects of Stock Transactions

Transaction	Assets	=	Liabilities	+	Stockholders' Equity
			Effect on Total		
Issuance of stock—common and preferred	Increase		No effect		Increase
Purchase of treasury stock	Decrease		No effect		Decrease
Sale of treasury stock	Increase		No effect		Increase
Declaration of cash dividend	No effect		Increase		Decrease
Payment of cash dividend	Decrease		Decrease		No effect
Stock dividend—large and small	No effect		No effect		No effect*
Stock split	No effect		No effect		No effect

*The stock accounts increase and retained earnings decrease by offsetting amounts that net to zero.

Use Stock Values in Decision Making

5

Use stock values in decision making

The business community measures *stock values* in various ways, depending on the purpose of the measurement. These values include market value, redemption value, liquidation value, and book value.

Market, Redemption, Liquidation, and Book Value

A stock's **market value**, or *market price*, is the price for which a person can buy or sell 1 share of the stock. Market value varies with the corporation's net income, financial position, and future prospects, and with general economic conditions. *In almost all cases, stockholders are more concerned about the market value of a stock than any other value.*

RadioShack Corporation's stock price has been quoted recently at $15.93 per share. Therefore, if RadioShack Corporation were issuing 1 million shares of its common stock, it would receive cash of $15,930,000 (1,000,000 shares × $15.93 per share). This is the market value of the stock RadioShack Corporation issued.

Preferred stock that requires the company to redeem the stock at a set price is called **redeemable preferred stock**. The company is *obligated* to redeem (pay to retire) the preferred stock. Therefore, redeemable preferred stock is really not stockholders' equity. Instead, it's a liability. The price the corporation agrees to pay for the stock, set when the stock is issued, is called the **redemption value**. **Liquidation value** is the amount that a company must pay a preferred stockholder in the event the company liquidates (sells out) and goes out of business.

The **book value** per share of common stock is the amount of owners' equity on the company's books for each share of its stock. If the company has only common stock outstanding, its book value is computed by dividing total shareholders' equity by the number of shares of common stock *outstanding*. Recall that *outstanding* stock is *issued* stock minus *treasury* stock. For example, a company with common stockholders' equity of $150,000 and 5,000 shares of common stock outstanding has a book value of $30 per share ($150,000 ÷ 5,000 shares).

If the company has both preferred and common outstanding, the preferred stockholders have the first claim to owners' equity. Preferred stock often has a specified redemption value. The preferred equity is its redemption value plus any cumulative preferred dividends in arrears. Book value per share of common is then computed as follows:

$$\text{Book value per share of common stock} = \frac{\text{Total stockholders' equity} - \text{Preferred equity}}{\text{Number of shares of common stock outstanding}}$$

Crusader Corporation's balance sheet reports the following amounts:

Stockholders' Equity	
Preferred stock, 5%, $100 par, 400 shares issued, redemption value $130 per share	$ 40,000
Common stock, $10 par, 5,500 shares issued	55,000
Additional paid-in capital—common	72,000
Retained earnings	88,000
Treasury stock—common, 500 shares at cost	(15,000)
Total stockholders' equity	$240,000

Cumulative preferred dividends are in arrears for four years (including the current year). Crusader's preferred stock has a redemption value of $130 per share. The book-value-per-share computations for Crusader Corporation are as follows:

Preferred Equity	
Redemption value (400 shares × $130)	$52,000
Cumulative dividends ($40,000 × 0.05 × 4 years)	8,000
Preferred equity	$60,000*

Common Equity	
Total stockholders' equity	$240,000
Less preferred equity	(60,000)
Common equity	$180,000
Book value per share [$180,000 ÷ 5,000 shares outstanding (5,500 shares issued minus 500 treasury shares)]	$ 36.00

*If the preferred stock had no redemption value, then preferred equity would be $40,000 + preferred dividends in arrears.

Some investors search for stocks whose market price is below book value. They believe this indicates a good buy. Financial analysts often shy away from companies with a stock price at or below book value. To these investors, such a company is in trouble. As you can see, not all investors agree on a stock value. In fact, wise investors base their decisions on more than a single ratio. In Chapter 13 you'll see the full range of financial ratios, plus more analytical techniques.

ROE: Relating Profitability to Stockholder Investment

Investors search for companies whose stocks are likely to increase in value. They're constantly comparing companies. But a comparison of RadioShack Corporation with a start-up company is not meaningful. RadioShack Corporation's profits run into the millions, far exceeding a new company's net income. In addition, management of the company has spent years investing in assets and managing both borrowed resources and stockholders' invested capital. Does this automatically make RadioShack Corporation a better investment? Not necessarily. To compare profitability of companies of different size, investors use some standard profitability measures, including

- ▶ return on assets and
- ▶ return on equity.

DuPont analysis, discussed earlier in Chapters 7 and 9, provides a convenient and meaningful way to analyze the various elements of profitability, as shown in the following diagram:

ROA			×	Leverage Ratio	=	ROE
Net Profit Margin	×	Asset Turnover	×	Leverage Ratio	=	Return on Equity
$\dfrac{\text{Net income}}{\text{Net sales}}$	×	$\dfrac{\text{Net sales}}{\text{Average total assets}}$	×	$\dfrac{\text{Average total assets}}{\text{Average common stockholders' equity}}$	=	$\dfrac{\text{Net income}}{\text{Average common stockholders' equity}}$

The left-hand side of the diagram shows that **rate of return on total assets** or **return on assets** (**ROA**) is the product of two drivers: *net profit* and *asset turnover*. Net profit measures how effectively the company has earned revenue while controlling costs. Asset turnover measures how efficiently the company has managed its assets. We discussed these ratios as well as strategies that management uses to improve them in Chapter 7 (pp. 428–430). In Chapter 9 (p. 543), we introduced the the *leverage ratio,* or *equity multiplier,* that shows the impact of the use of debt, or leverage, to magnify

ROA. Together, the three ratios combine to measure **Rate of return on common stockholders' equity**, or **Return on equity (ROE)**, in the last column on the right-hand side of the diagram.

ROE shows the relationship between net income and common stockholders' equity. Return on equity is computed only on common stock because the return to preferred stockholders is usually limited to a specified dividend (for example, 5%).

The numerator of ROE is net income minus preferred dividends, if any. The denominator is *average common stockholders' equity*—total stockholders' equity minus preferred equity, if any. Since most companies do not have preferred stock, adjustments for preferred dividends and preferred equity are usually not necessary.

Let's use the DuPont analysis model to analyze RadioShack Corporation's ROE as of December 31, 2010 (see the consolidated statements of income on page 2 (Chapter 1) for net income and net sales, and the consolidated balance sheets on page 582, for total assets and common stockholders' equity):

	ROA		×	Leverage Ratio	=	ROE
Net Profit Margin	×	Asset Turnover	×	Leverage Ratio	=	Return on Equity
$\dfrac{\text{Net income}}{\text{Net sales}}$	×	$\dfrac{\text{Net sales}}{\text{Average total assets}}$	×	$\dfrac{\text{Average total assets}}{\text{Average common stockholders' equity}}$	=	$\dfrac{\text{Net income}}{\text{Average common stockholders' equity}}$
$\dfrac{206}{4,472}$	×	$\dfrac{4,472}{2,302}$	×	$\dfrac{2,302}{945}$	=	$\dfrac{206}{945}$
$\{4.6\%\}$	×	$\{1.94\}$	×	$\{2.44\}$	=	$\{21.8\%\}$
	$\{\text{ROA} = 8.92\%\}$					

RadioShack Corporation earned $206 million on $4,472 million in sales in 2010, for a net profit margin of 4.6%. Each dollar of sales has resulted in 4.6 cents of net profit. The company's asset turnover was 1.94, meaning that it earned $1.94 in sales for each average dollar invested in total assets. A leverage ratio of 2.44 to 1 means that the company owns $2.44 of assets for each dollar of stockholders' equity invested. Average total liabilities are $1,357 ($2,302 − $945), so the debt ratio for the company is about 59% ($1,357/$2,302). The leverage ratio of 2.44, multiplied by ROA of 8.92%, magnifies profitability on shareholder investment to 21.8%.

Are these returns strong, weak, or somewhere in between? To answer that question, it is necessary to have other information, such as

▶ comparative returns for RadioShack Corporation for prior years and
▶ comparative returns for other companies in the same industry.

For example, the following diagram compares RadioShack Corporation's 2010 and 2009 ROE. It also compares RadioShack Corporations 2010 ROE with that of a competitor, **Best Buy Co, Inc.**

	Net Profit Margin	×	Asset Turnover	×	Leverage Ratio	=	Return on Equity
RadioShack 2010	4.6%	×	1.94	×	2.44	=	21.8%
RadioShack 2009	4.8%	×	1.83	×	2.45	=	21.5%
Best Buy 2010	2.5%	×	2.78	×	2.54	=	17.7%

In comparison with 2009, RadioShack Corporations' ROE is about the same. Its profit margin in 2010 was slightly lower than 2009, but asset turnover was slightly higher, which means the company earned slightly more in sales per dollar invested (thus, was more efficient) in 2010 than 2009. The leverage ratio remained about the same over the two years. In comparison with Best Buy Co., Inc., RadioShack Corporation's ROE was higher, mostly due to a higher net profit margin (4.6% compared with 2.5%).

Although Best Buy's asset turnover was higher (signaling higher efficiency), and its leverage ratio was also slightly higher (meaning it was making slightly greater use of borrowed money), these were not enough to compensate for a lower net profit margin percentage compared to that of RadioShack.

What is a good rate of return on total assets? Ten percent is considered a strong benchmark in most industries. However, rates of return on assets vary by industry, because the components of ROA are different across industries. Some high-technology companies earn much higher returns than do utility companies, groceries, and manufacturers of consumer goods such as toothpaste and paper towels. Companies that are efficient, generating a large amount of sales per dollar of assets invested, or companies that can differentiate their products and earn higher margins on them, have higher ROA than companies that do not have these attributes.

You can see by studying the DuPont model that, whenever ROA is positive, ROE is always higher than ROA because of the leverage multiplier. This also makes sense from an economic standpoint. Stockholders take a lot more investment risk than creditors, so the stockholders demand that ROE exceed ROA. They expect the return on their investment to exceed the amount they have to pay their creditors for borrowed funds. Investors and creditors use ROE in much the same way they use ROA—to compare companies. The higher the rate of return, the more successful the company. In many industries, 15% is considered a good ROE.

The Decision Guidelines at the end of the chapter (p. 611) offer suggestions for what to consider when investing in stock. You will also use all of these ratios more in Chapter 13.

Report Equity Transactions in the Financial Statements

The details of transactions impacting the various accounts in stockholders' equity are reported on the statement of stockholders' equity, which is covered in Chapter 11. In this section, we will show how stockholders' equity transactions are reported on the statement of cash flows as well as on the balance sheet.

⑥

Report equity transactions in the financial statements

Statement of Cash Flows

Many of the transactions we've covered are reported on the statement of cash flows. Equity transactions are *financing activities* because the company is dealing with its owners. Financing transactions that affect both cash and equity fall into three main categories:

CASH FLOW

▶ Issuance of stock
▶ Treasury stock
▶ Dividends

Issuances of Stock. RadioShack Corporation issued no common or preferred stock in 2010.

Treasury Stock. During 2010, RadioShack Corporation purchased treasury stock and reported the payment as a financing activity.

Dividends. Most mature companies, including RadioShack Corporation, pay cash dividends to their stockholders. Dividend payments are a type of financing transaction because the company is paying its stockholders for the use of their money. Stock dividends are not reported on the statement of cash flows because the company pays no cash for them.

In Exhibit 10-9, cash payments for purchase of treasury stock and dividends appear as negative amounts, denoted by parentheses. Issuance of stock would appear as a positive amount.

EXHIBIT 10-9 | RadioShack Corporation's Financing Activities Related to Stockholders' Equity

Cash Flows from Financing Activities	(In millions)
Purchase of treasury stock...........................	(399)
Payment of dividends	(26)

Reporting Stockholders' Equity on the Balance Sheet

Businesses may report stockholders' equity in a way that differs from our examples. We use a detailed format in this book to help you learn all the components of stockholders' equity.

One of the most important skills you will take from this course is the ability to understand the financial statements of real companies. Exhibit 10-10 presents a side-by-side comparison of our general teaching format and the format you are likely to encounter in real-world balance sheets, such as RadioShack Corporation's. All amounts are assumed for this illustration.

EXHIBIT 10-10 | Formats for Reporting Stockholders' Equity

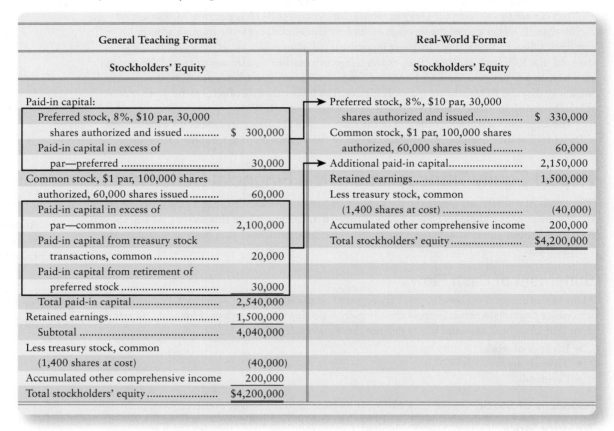

General Teaching Format		Real-World Format	
Stockholders' Equity		**Stockholders' Equity**	
Paid-in capital:		Preferred stock, 8%, $10 par, 30,000	
Preferred stock, 8%, $10 par, 30,000		shares authorized and issued	$ 330,000
shares authorized and issued	$ 300,000	Common stock, $1 par, 100,000 shares	
Paid-in capital in excess of		authorized, 60,000 shares issued	60,000
par—preferred	30,000	Additional paid-in capital	2,150,000
Common stock, $1 par, 100,000 shares		Retained earnings	1,500,000
authorized, 60,000 shares issued	60,000	Less treasury stock, common	
Paid-in capital in excess of		(1,400 shares at cost)	(40,000)
par—common	2,100,000	Accumulated other comprehensive income	200,000
Paid-in capital from treasury stock		Total stockholders' equity	$4,200,000
transactions, common	20,000		
Paid-in capital from retirement of			
preferred stock	30,000		
Total paid-in capital	2,540,000		
Retained earnings	1,500,000		
Subtotal	4,040,000		
Less treasury stock, common			
(1,400 shares at cost)	(40,000)		
Accumulated other comprehensive income	200,000		
Total stockholders' equity	$4,200,000		

In general,

▶ Preferred stock comes first and is usually reported as a single amount.

▶ Common stock lists par value per share, the number of shares authorized, and the number of shares issued. The balance of the Common stock account is determined as follows:

> Common stock = Number of shares *issued* × Par value per share

▶ Additional paid-in capital combines Paid-in capital in excess of par plus Paid-in capital from treasury stock transactions plus Paid-in capital from retirement of preferred stock. Additional paid-in capital belongs to the common stockholders.

▶ Outstanding stock equals issued stock minus treasury stock.

▶ Retained earnings comes after the paid-in capital accounts.

▶ Treasury stock is reported, usually at cost, as a deduction.

► Many companies like RadioShack Corporation (p. 582) report Accumulated other comprehensive income as a final addition (or loss as a deduction). This account includes accumulated unrealized gains and losses from sales of available-for-sale securities, plus foreign currency translation adjustments resulting from consolidation of foreign subsidiaries, which are discussed in Chapter 8. The statement of other comprehensive income is discussed further in Chapter 11.

DECISION GUIDELINES

INVESTING IN STOCK

Suppose you've saved $5,000 to invest. You visit a nearby **Edward Jones** office, where the broker probes for your risk tolerance. Are you investing mainly for dividends or for growth in the stock price? You must make some key decisions.

Investor Decision	Guidelines
Which category of stock to buy for:	
• A safe investment?	Preferred stock is safer than common, but for even more safety, invest in high-grade corporate bonds or government securities.
• Steady dividends?	Cumulative preferred stock. However, the company is not obligated to declare preferred dividends, and the dividends are unlikely to increase.
• Increasing dividends?	Common stock, as long as the company's net income is increasing and the company has adequate cash flow to pay a dividend after meeting all obligations and other cash demands.
• Increasing stock price?	Common stock, but again only if the company's net income and cash flow are increasing.
How to identify a good stock to buy?	There are many ways to pick stock investments. One strategy that works reasonably well is to invest in companies that consistently earn higher rates of return on assets and on equity than competing firms in the same industry. Also, select industries that are expected to grow.

END-OF-CHAPTER SUMMARY PROBLEM

1. The balance sheet of Trendline Corp. reported the following at December 31, 2012. The company has no transactions that produce other comprehensive income or loss.

Stockholders' Equity	
Preferred stock, 4%, $10 par, 10,000 shares authorized and issued (redemption value, $110,000)	$100,000
Common stock, no-par, $5 stated value, 100,000 shares authorized, 50,000 shares issued	250,000
Paid-in capital in excess of par or stated value:	
Common stock	239,500
Retained earnings	395,000
Less: Treasury stock, common (1,000 shares)	(8,000)
Total stockholders' equity	$976,500

▶ Requirements

a. Is the preferred stock cumulative or noncumulative? How can you tell?

b. What is the total amount of the annual preferred dividend?

c. How many shares of common stock are outstanding?

d. Compute the book value per share of the common stock. No preferred dividends are in arrears, and Trendline has not yet declared the 2012 dividend.

2. Use the following accounts and related balances to prepare the classified balance sheet of Whitehall, Inc., at September 30, 2012. Use the account format of the balance sheet.

Common stock, $1 par, 50,000 shares authorized, 20,000 shares issued	$ 20,000	Long-term note payable	$ 80,000
		Inventory	85,000
Dividends payable	4,000	Property, plant, and equipment, net	226,000
Cash	9,000	Accounts receivable, net	23,000
Accounts payable	28,000	Preferred stock, $3.75, no-par, 10,000 shares authorized, 2,000 shares issued	24,000
Paid-in capital in excess of par—common	115,000		
Treasury stock, common, 1,000 shares at cost	6,000	Accrued liabilities	3,000
		Retained earnings	75,000

▶ **Answers**

1. a. The preferred stock is cumulative because it is not specifically labeled otherwise.

b. Total annual preferred dividend: $4,000 ($100,000 × 0.04).

c. Common shares outstanding: 49,000 (50,000 issued − 1,000 treasury).

d. Book value per share of common stock:

Common:	
Total stockholders' equity	$976,500
Less stockholders' equity allocated to preferred	(114,000)*
Stockholders' equity allocated to common	$862,500
Book value per share ($862,500 ÷ 49,000 shares)	$17.60

*Redemption value	$110,000
Cumulative dividend ($100,000 × 0.04)	4,000
Stockholders' equity allocated to preferred	$114,000

2.

Whitehall, Inc.
Balance Sheet
September 30, 2012

Assets			Liabilities		
Current			Current		
Cash	$ 9,000		Account payable		$ 28,000
Accounts receivable, net	23,000		Dividends payable		4,000
Inventory	85,000		Accrued liabilities		3,000
Total current assets	117,000		Total current liabilities		35,000
Property, plant, and equipment, net	226,000		Long-term note payable		80,000
			Total liabilities		115,000
			Stockholders' Equity		
			Preferred stock, $3.75, no par,		
			10,000 shares authorized,		
			2,000 shares issued	$ 24,000	
			Common stock, $1 par,		
			50,000 shares authorized,		
			20,000 shares issued	20,000	
			Paid-in capital in excess of		
			par—common	115,000	
			Retained earnings	75,000	
			Treasury stock, common,		
			1,000 shares at cost	(6,000)	
			Total stockholders' equity		228,000
			Total liabilities and		
Total assets	$343,000		stockholders' equity		$343,000

REVIEW | Stockholders' Equity

Quick Check (Answers are given on page 649.)

1. Danzig Company is authorized to issue 70,000 shares of $2 par common stock. On November 30, 2012, Danzig issued 10,000 shares at $22 per share. Danzig's journal entry to record these facts should include a

   a. credit to Common Stock for $20,000.
   b. debit to Common Stock for $220,000.
   c. credit to Paid-in Capital in Excess of Par for $220,000.
   d. Both a and c

Questions 2–5 use the following account balances of McQuaide Co. at August 31, 2012:

Dividends Payable........................	$ 22,500	Cash...	$124,000
Preferred Stock, $100 par.............	150,000	Common Stock, $1 par	200,000
Paid-in Capital in Excess of Par—		Retained Earnings	400,000
Common.................................	100,000		

2. How many shares of common stock has McQuaide issued?

   a. 124,000   c. 300,000
   b. 200,000   d. Some other amount

3. McQuaide's total paid-in capital at August 31, 2012, is

   a. $427,500.   c. $827,500.
   b. $100,000.   d. $450,000.

4. McQuaide's total stockholders' equity as of August 31, 2012, is

   a. $951,500.   c. $850,000.
   b. $450,000.   d. $827,500.

5. What would McQuaide's total stockholders' equity be if McQuaide had $25,000 of treasury stock?

   a. $951,500   c. $827,500
   b. $825,000   d. $450,000

6. Tops Corporation purchased treasury stock in 2012 at a price of $22 per share and resold the treasury stock in 2013 at a price of $42 per share. What amount should Tops report on its income statement for 2013?

   a. $20 gain per share   c. $42 gain per share
   b. $22 gain per share   d. $0

7. The stockholders' equity section of a corporation's balance sheet reports

	Discount on Bonds Payable	Treasury Stock
a.	Yes	No
b.	No	No
c.	Yes	Yes
d.	No	Yes

8. The purchase of treasury stock
   a. decreases total assets and decreases total stockholder's equity.
   b. decreases total assets and increases total stockholders' equity.
   c. increases one asset and decreases another asset.
   d. has no effect on total assets, total liabilities, or total stockholders' equity.

9. When does a cash dividend become a legal liability?
   a. On date of payment
   b. It never becomes a liability because it is paid.
   c. On date of declaration
   d. On date of record

10. When do dividends increase stockholders' equity?

    a. Never
    b. On date of payment

    c. On date of declaration
    d. On date of record

11. Elm Tree Mall, Inc., has 3,000 shares of 5%, $40 par cumulative preferred stock and 140,000 shares of $1 par common stock outstanding. At the beginning of the current year, preferred dividends were four years in arrears. Elm Tree's board of directors wants to pay a $1.50 cash dividend on each share of outstanding common stock in the current year. To accomplish this, what total amount of dividends must Elm Tree declare?

    a. $210,000
    b. $234,000

    c. $240,000
    d. Some other amount

12. Stock dividends
    a. have no effect on total stockholders' equity.
    b. are distributions of cash to stockholders.
    c. reduce the total assets of the company.
    d. increase the corporation's total liabilities.

13. What is the effect of a stock dividend and a stock split on total assets?

	Stock dividend	Stock split
a.	No effect	No effect
b.	Decrease	No effect
c.	Decrease	Decrease
d.	No effect	Decrease

14. A 2-for-1 stock split has the same effect on the number of shares being issued as a

    a. 200% stock dividend.
    b. 50% stock dividend.

    c. 20% stock dividend.
    d. 100% stock dividend.

15. The numerator for computing the rate of return on total assets is
    a. gross margin.
    b. net income.
    c. net income minus preferred dividends.
    d. net income plus depreciation expense.

16. The denominator for computing the rate of return on equity is
    a. average common stockholders' equity.
    b. average total assets.
    c. net sales.
    d. net income.

Accounting Vocabulary

authorized stock (p. 595) Maximum number of shares a corporation can issue under its charter.

board of directors (p. 584) Group elected by the stockholders to set policy for a corporation and to appoint its officers.

book value (of a stock) (p. 606) Amount of owners' equity on the company's books for each share of its stock.

bylaws (p. 584) Constitution for governing a corporation.

chairperson (p. 584) Elected by a corporation's board of directors, usually the most powerful person in the corporation.

common stock (p. 586) The most basic form of capital stock. The common stockholders own a corporation.

contributed capital (p. 585) The amount of stockholders' equity that stockholders have contributed to the corporation. Also called *paid-in capital*.

cumulative preferred stock (p. 603) Preferred stock whose owners must receive all dividends in arrears before the corporation can pay dividends to the common stockholders.

deficit (p. 600) Debit balance in the Retained Earnings account.

dividend (p. 600) Distribution (usually cash) by a corporation to its stockholders.

double taxation (p. 584) Corporations pay income taxes on corporate income. Then, the stockholders pay personal income tax on the cash dividends that they receive from corporations.

DuPont analysis (p. 607) A detailed approach to measuring rate of return on equity (ROE), calculated as follows: Net profit margin (net income before taxes/net sales) × total asset turnover (net sales/ average total assets) × leverage ratio (average total assets/average stockholders' equity). The first two components of the model comprise return on assets (ROA).

issued stock (p. 595) Number of shares a corporation has issued to its stockholders.

legal capital (p. 587) Minimum amount of stockholders' equity that a corporation must maintain for the protection of creditors. For corporations with par-value stock, legal capital is the par value of the stock issued.

limited liability (p. 583) No personal obligation of a stockholder for corporation debts. A stockholder can lose no more on an investment in a corporation's stock than the cost of the investment.

liquidation value (p. 606) The amount a corporation must pay a preferred stockholder in the event the company liquidates and goes out of business.

market value (of a stock) (p. 606) Price for which a person could buy or sell a share of stock.

outstanding stock (p. 595) Stock in the hands of stockholders.

paid-in capital (p. 585) The amount of stockholders' equity that stockholders have contributed to the corporation. Also called *contributed capital*.

par value (p. 587) Arbitrary amount assigned by a company to a share of its stock.

preferred stock (p. 586) Stock that gives its owners certain advantages, such as the priority to receive dividends before the common stockholders and the priority to receive assets before the common stockholders if the corporation liquidates.

president (p. 584) Chief operating officer in charge of managing the day-to-day operations of a corporation.

rate of return on common stockholders' equity (p. 608) Net income minus preferred dividends, divided by average common stockholders' equity. A measure of profitability. Also called *return on equity*.

rate of return on total assets (p. 607) Net income divided by average total assets. This ratio measures a company's success in using its assets to earn income for the persons who finance the business. Also called *return on assets*.

redeemable preferred stock (p. 606) A corporation reserves the right to buy an issue of stock back from its shareholders, with the intent to retire the stock.

redemption value (p. 606) The price a corporation agrees to eventually pay for its redeemable preferred stock, set when the stock is issued.

retained earnings (p. 585) The amount of stockholders' equity that the corporation has earned through profitable operation of the business and has not given back to stockholders.

return on assets (ROA) (p. 607) Another name for *rate of return on total assets*.

return on equity (ROE) (p. 608) Another name for *rate of return on common stockholders' equity*.

shareholders (p. 583) Persons or other entities that own stock in a corporation. Also called *stockholders*.

stated value (p. 587) An arbitrary amount assigned to no-par stock; similar to par value.

stock (p. 585) Shares into which the owners' equity of a corporation is divided.

stock dividend (p. 603) A proportional distribution by a corporation of its own stock to its stockholders.

stockholder (p. 583) A person who owns stock in a corporation. Also called a *shareholder*.

stockholders' equity (p. 585) The stockholders' ownership interest in the assets of a corporation.

stock split (p. 604) An increase in the number of authorized, issued, and outstanding shares of stock coupled with a proportionate reduction in the stock's par value.

treasury stock (p. 596) A corporation's own stock that it has issued and later reacquired.

ASSESS YOUR PROGRESS

Short Exercises

S10-1 (*Learning Objective 1: Explain advantages and disadvantages of a corporation*) What are two main advantages that a corporation has over a proprietorship and a partnership? What are two main disadvantages of a corporation?

S10-2 (*Learning Objective 1: Describe the authority structure in a corporation*) Consider the authority structure in a corporation, as diagrammed in Exhibit 10-2.
1. What group holds the ultimate power in a corporation?
2. Who is the most powerful person in the corporation? What's the abbreviation of this person's title?
3. Who's in charge of day-to-day operations? What's the abbreviation of this person's title?
4. Who's in charge of accounting and finance? What's the abbreviation of this person's title?

S10-3 (*Learning Objective 1: Describe characteristics of preferred and common stock*) Answer the following questions about the characteristics of a corporation's stock:
1. Who are the real owners of a corporation?
2. What privileges do preferred stockholders have over common stockholders?
3. Which class of stockholders reaps greater benefits from a highly profitable corporation? Explain.

S10-4 (*Learning Objective 1: Explain how to organize a corporation*) Jessica Johnson and Claudia Stein are opening a Submarine's deli. Johnson and Stein need outside capital, so they plan to organize the business as a corporation. They come to you for advice. Write a memorandum informing them of the steps in forming a corporation. Identify specific documents used in this process, and name the different parties involved in the ownership and management of a corporation.

S10-5 (*Learning Objective 2: Describe the effect of a stock issuance on paid-in capital*) ARM received $48,000,000 for the issuance of its stock on May 14. The par value of the ARM stock was only $48,000. Was the excess amount of $47,952,000 a profit to ARM? If not, what was it?

Suppose the par value of the ARM stock had been $4 per share, $8 per share, or $14 per share. Would a change in the par value of the company's stock affect ARM's total paid-in capital? Give the reason for your answer.

S10-6 (*Learning Objective 2: Issue stock—par value stock and no-par stock*) At fiscal year-end 2012, Hana Printer and Delightful Doughnuts reported these adapted amounts on their balance sheets (amounts in millions):

Hana Printer:		
Common stock, $0.01 par value, 2,700 shares issued		$ 27
Additional paid-in capital		17,800

Delightful Doughnuts:		
Common stock, no par value, 66 shares issued		$ 298

Assume each company issued its stock in a single transaction. Journalize each company's issuance of its stock, using its actual account titles. Explanations are not required.

S10-7 (*Learning Objective 2: Issue stock to finance the purchase of assets*) This short exercise demonstrates the similarity and the difference between two ways to acquire plant assets.

Case A—Issue stock and buy the assets in separate transactions:

Hampton, Inc., issued 17,000 shares of its $25 par common stock for cash of $850,000. In a separate transaction, Hampton used the cash to purchase a building for $590,000 and equipment for $260,000. Journalize the two transactions.

Case B—Issue stock to acquire the assets in a single transaction:

Hampton, Inc., issued 17,000 shares of its $25 par common stock to acquire a building valued at $590,000 and equipment worth $260,000. Journalize this transaction.

Compare the balances in all the accounts after making both sets of entries. Are the account balances similar or different?

S10-8 (*Learning Objective 2: Prepare the stockholders' equity section of a balance sheet*) The financial statements of Ridgeview Employment Services, Inc., reported the following accounts (adapted, with dollar amounts in thousands except for par value):

Paid-in capital in excess of par	$193	Total revenues......................	$1,370
Other stockholders' equity (negative)........	(27)	Accounts payable	460
Common stock, $0.01 par		Retained earnings................	643
800 shares issued..................................	8	Other current liabilities	2,562
Long-term debt	23	Total expenses......................	812

Prepare the stockholders' equity section of Ridgeview's balance sheet. Net income has already been closed to Retained Earnings.

S10-9 (*Learning Objectives 2, 5: Use stockholders' equity data*) Refer to the data in S10-8. Using only year-end figures rather than averages, compute the following for Ridgeview Employment Services:

  a. Net income
  b. Total liabilities
  c. Total assets (use the accounting equation)
  d. Net profit ratio
  e. Asset turnover
  f. Leverage ratio
  g. Return on equity

What additional information do you need before you can use this data to make decisions?

S10-10 (*Learning Objective 3: Account for the purchase and sale of treasury stock*) Gellman Marketing Corporation reported the following stockholders' equity at December 31 (adapted and in millions):

Common stock..................................	$ 256
Additional paid-in capital.................	286
Retained earnings.............................	2,190
Treasury stock..................................	(690)
Total stockholders' equity................	$2,042

During the next year, Gellman Marketing purchased treasury stock at a cost of $22 million and resold treasury stock for $15 million (this treasury stock had cost Gellman Marketing $4 million). Record the purchase and resale of Gellman Marketing's treasury stock. Overall, how much did stockholders' equity increase or decrease as a result of the two treasury stock transactions?

S10-11 (*Learning Objective 3: Explain purchase of treasury stock to fight off a takeover of the corporation*) Karen Knox Exports, Inc., is located in Clancy, New Mexico. Knox is the only company with reliable sources for its imported gifts. The company does a brisk business with specialty stores such as Neiman Marcus. Knox's recent success has made the company a prime target for a takeover. An investment group in Alberton is attempting to buy 52% of Knox's outstanding stock against the wishes of Knox's board of directors. Board members are convinced that the Alberton investors would sell the most desirable pieces of the business and leave little of value.

At the most recent board meeting, several suggestions were advanced to fight off the hostile takeover bid. The suggestion with the most promise is to purchase a huge quantity of treasury stock. Knox has the cash to carry out this plan.

▶ Requirements

1. Suppose you are a significant stockholder of Karen Knox Exports, Inc. Write a memorandum to explain to the board how the purchase of treasury stock would make it difficult for the Alberton group to take over Knox. Include in your memo a discussion of the effect that purchasing treasury stock would have on stock outstanding and on the size of the corporation.
2. Suppose Knox management is successful in fighting off the takeover bid and later sells the treasury stock at prices greater than the purchase price. Explain what effect these sales will have on assets, stockholders' equity, and net income.

S10-12 (*Learning Objective 4: Account for cash dividends*) Greenwood Corporation earned net income of $85,000 during the year ended December 31, 2012. On December 15, Greenwood declared the annual cash dividend on its 8% preferred stock (20,000 shares with total par value of $200,000) and a $0.15 per share cash dividend on its common stock (40,000 shares with total par value of $400,000). Greenwood then paid the dividends on January 4, 2013.

Journalize the following for Greenwood Corporation:

a. Declaring the cash dividends on December 15, 2012
b. Paying the cash dividends on January 4, 2013

Did Retained Earnings increase or decrease during 2012? By how much?

S10-13 (*Learning Objective 4: Divide cash dividends between preferred and common stock*) Sterling Garde, Inc., has 90,000 shares of $1.35 preferred stock outstanding in addition to its common stock. The $1.35 designation means that the preferred stockholders receive an annual cash dividend of $1.35 per share. In 2012, Sterling Garde declares an annual dividend of $500,000. The allocation to preferred and common stockholders is as follows:

Preferred dividend, (90,000 shares × $1.35 per share).............	$121,500
Common dividend (remainder: $500,000 − $121,500)	378,500
Total dividend...	$500,000

Answer these questions about Sterling Garde's cash dividends.

1. How much in dividends must Sterling Garde declare each year before the common stockholders receive any cash dividends for the year?
2. Suppose Sterling Garde, Inc., declares cash dividends of $550,000 for 2012. How much of the dividends goes to preferred? How much goes to common?
3. Is Sterling Garde's preferred stock cumulative or noncumulative? How can you tell?
4. Sterling Garde, Inc., passed the preferred dividend in 2011 and 2012. Then in 2013, Sterling Garde declares cash dividends of $1,600,000. How much of the dividends goes to preferred? How much goes to common?

S10-14 (*Learning Objective 4: Record a small stock dividend*) Payne Bancshares has 18,000 shares of $4 par common stock outstanding. Suppose Payne distributes an 8% stock dividend when the market value of its stock is $20 per share.

1. Journalize Payne's distribution of the stock dividend on May 11. An explanation is not required.
2. What was the overall effect of the stock dividend on Payne's total assets? On total liabilities? On total stockholders' equity?

S10-15 (*Learning Objective 5: Compute book value per share*) Copperhead, Inc., has the following stockholders' equity:

Preferred stock, 1%, $12 par,	
35,000 shares authorized and issued.................................	$ 420,000
Common stock, $8 par, 100,000 shares authorized,	
67,000 shares issued	536,000
Additional paid-in capital...	2,140,000
Retained earnings..	1,800,000
Less treasury stock, common (1,400 shares at cost)	(49,000)
Total stockholders' equity......................................	$4,847,000

That company has passed its preferred dividends for three years including the current year. Compute the book value per share of the company's common stock.

S10-16 (*Learning Objective 5: Compute and explain return on assets and return on equity*) Give the DuPont model formula for computing (a) rate of return on total assets (ROA) and (b) rate of return on common stockholders' equity (ROE). Then answer these questions about the rate-of-return computations.

1. Explain the meaning of the component driver ratios in the computation of ROA.
2. What impact does the leverage ratio have on ROA?
3. Under what circumstances will ROE be higher than ROA? Under what circumstances would ROE be lower than ROA?

S10-17 (*Learning Objective 5: Compute return on assets and return on equity for a leading company*) POLA Corporation's 2012 financial statements reported the following items, with 2011 figures given for comparison (adapted and in millions).

	2012	2011
Balance Sheet		
Total assets	¥10,632	¥9,523
Total liabilities	¥ 7,414	¥6,639
Total stockholders' equity (all common)	3,218	2,884
Total liabilities and equity	¥10,632	¥9,523
Income Statement		
Revenues and other income	¥ 7,632	
Operating expense	7,289	
Interest expense	31	
Other expense	194	
Net income	¥ 118	

Use the DuPont model to compute POLA's return on assets and return on common equity for 2012. Evaluate the rates of return as strong or weak. What additional information would be helpful in making this decision? ¥ is the symbol for the Japanese yen.

S10-18 (*Learning Objectives 1, 2, 5: Explain the features of a corporation's stock*) Graham Corporation is conducting a special meeting of its board of directors to address some concerns raised by the stockholders. Stockholders have submitted the following questions. Answer each question.

1. Why are common stock and retained earnings shown separately in the shareholders' equity section of the balance sheet?
2. Abby Adams, a Graham shareholder, proposes to transfer some land she owns to the company in exchange for shares of the company stock. How should Graham Corporation determine the number of shares of our stock to issue for the land?
3. Preferred shares generally are preferred with respect to dividends and in the event of our liquidation. Why would investors buy our common stock when preferred stock is available?
4. What does the redemption value of our preferred stock require us to do?
5. One of our stockholders owns 200 shares of Graham stock and someone has offered to buy her shares for their book value. Our stockholder asks us the formula for computing the book value of her stock.

S10-19 (*Learning Objective 6: Measure cash flows from financing activities*) During 2012, Granite Corporation earned net income of $5.1 billion and paid off $2.9 billion of long-term notes payable. Granite raised $1.6 billion by issuing common stock, paid $3.9 billion to purchase treasury stock, and paid cash dividends of $1.9 billion. Report Granite's *cash flows from financing activities* on the statement of cash flows for 2012.

Exercises

All of the A and B exercises can be found within MyAccountingLab, an online homework and practice environment. Your instructor may ask you to complete these exercises using MyAccountingLab.

MyAccountingLab

Group A

E10-20A (*Learning Objectives 2, 6: Account for issuance of stock; report stockholders' equity*) Hambrick Sales, Inc., is authorized to issue 170,000 shares of common stock and 5,000 shares of preferred stock. During its first year, the business completed the following stock issuance transactions:

Aug 19	Issued 10,000 shares of $5.00 par common stock for cash of $12.00 per share.
Nov 3	Issued 1,000 shares of $4.00 no par preferred stock for $49,000 cash.
11	Received inventory valued at $14,000 and equipment with market value of $11,000 for 3,900 shares of the $5.00 par common stock.

▶ Requirements

1. Journalize the transactions. Explanations are not required.
2. Prepare the stockholders' equity section of Hambrick Sales' balance sheet. The ending balance of retained earnings is a deficit of $42,000.

E10-21A (*Learning Objectives 2, 6: Account for issuance of stock; prepare the stockholders' equity section of a balance sheet*) Colonel Sporting Goods is authorized to issue 18,000 shares of common stock. During a two-month period, Colonel completed these stock-issuance transactions:

Apr	23	Issued 3,000 shares of $1.00 par common stock for cash of $14.50 per share.
	12	Received inventory valued at $14,000 and equipment with market value of $44,000 for 3,200 shares of the $1.00 par common stock.

▶ Requirement

1. Prepare the stockholders' equity section of Colonel Sporting Goods' balance sheet for the transactions given in this exercise. Retained Earnings has a balance of $48,000. Journal entries are not required.

E10-22A (*Learning Objective 2: Measure paid-in capital of a corporation*) Excursion Publishing was recently organized. The company issued common stock to an attorney who provided legal services worth $20,000 to help organize the corporation. Excursion also issued common stock to an inventor in exchange for his patent with a market value of $81,000. In addition, Excursion received cash both for the issuance of 8,000 shares of its preferred stock at $70 per share and for the issuance of 16,000 of its common shares at $6 per share. During the first year of operations, Excursion earned net income of $70,000 and declared a cash dividend of $26,000. Without making journal entries, determine the total paid-in capital created by these transactions.

E10-23A (*Learning Objectives 3, 6: Show how treasury stock affects a company; prepare the stockholders' equity section of a balance sheet*) Casey Software had the following selected account balances at December 31, 2012 (in thousands, except par value per share).

Inventory...	$ 720	Common stock, $0.25 par		
Property, plant, and		per share, 900 shares		
equipment, net	860	authorized, 400 shares		
Paid-in capital in excess of par	903	issued	$ 100	
Treasury stock,		Retained earnings...............	2,200	
90 shares at cost........................	1,035	Accounts receivable, net......	1,100	
Accumulated other	(732)*	Notes payable	1,274	
comprehenive income (loss)........				

*Debit balance

▶ Requirements

1. Prepare the stockholders' equity section of Casey's balance sheet (in thousands).
2. How can Casey have a larger balance of treasury stock than the sum of Common Stock and Paid-in Capital in Excess of Par?

E10-24A (*Learning Objectives 2, 3: Account for issuance of stock; show how treasury stock transactions affect stockholders' equity*) Journalize the following transactions of Alameda Productions:

Jan	21	Issued 1,800 shares of $1.25 par common stock at $13 per share.
Jun	23	Purchased 500 shares of treasury stock at $15 per share.
Jul	12	Sold 400 shares of treasury stock at $22 per share.

What was the overall effect of these transactions on Alameda's stockholders' equity?

E10-25A (*Learning Objectives 2, 3, 4: Account for issuance of stock; show how treasury stock affects a company; account for dividends*) At December 31, 2012, Blumenthal Corporation reported the stockholders' equity accounts shown here (with dollar amounts in millions, except per-share amounts).

Common stock $3.00 par value per share, 2,400 million shares issued...............	$ 7,200
Capital in excess of par value...............	7,200
Retained earnings.................................	290
Treasury stock, at cost	(80)
Total stockholders' equity................	$14,610

Blumenthal's 2013 transactions included the following:

a. Net income, $450 million
b. Issuance of 22 million shares of common stock for $14.00 per share
c. Purchase of 9 million shares of treasury stock for $18 million
d. Declaration and payment of cash dividends of $32 million

▶ Requirement

1. Journalize Blumenthal's transactions in b, c, and d. Explanations are not required.

E10-26A (*Learning Objective 6: Report stockholders' equity after a sequence of transactions*) Use the Blumenthal Corporation data in Exercise 10-25A to prepare the stockholders' equity section of the company's balance sheet at December 31, 2013.

E10-27A (*Learning Objectives 2, 3, 4, 6: Infer transactions from a company's comparative stockholders' equity*) Omicron Products Company reported the following stockholders' equity on its balance sheet:

Stockholders' Equity (Dollars and shares in millions)	December 31,	
	2013	2012
Preferred stock—$1.00 par value; authorized 70 shares; Convertible Preferred Stock; issued and outstanding: 2013 and 2012—8 and 16 shares, respectively	$ 8	$ 16
Common stock—$5 per share par value; authorized 1,100 shares; issued: 2013 and 2012—400 and 300 shares, respectively	2,000	1,500
Additional paid-in capital	2,800	1,950
Retained earnings	6,260	4,996
Treasury stock, common—at cost 2013—19 shares; 2012—14 shares	(342)	(60)
Total stockholders' equity	10,726	8,402
Total liabilities and stockholders' equity	$51,323	$47,202

▶ Requirements

1. What caused Omicron's preferred stock to decrease during 2013? Cite all possible causes.
2. What caused Omicron's common stock to increase during 2013? Identify all possible causes.
3. How many shares of Omicron's common stock were outstanding at December 31, 2013?
4. Omicron's net income during 2013 was $1,470 million. How much were Omicron's dividends during the year?
5. During 2013, Omicron sold no treasury stock. What average price per share did Omicron pay for the treasury stock that the company purchased during the year?

E10-28A (*Learning Objective 4: Compute dividends on preferred and common stock*) Superb Manufacturing, Inc., reported the following:

Stockholders' Equity		
Preferred stock, cumulative, $1.00 par, 6%, 90,000 shares issued	$	90,000
Common stock, $0.30 par, 9,130,000 shares issued		2,739,000

Superb Manufacturing has paid all preferred dividends through 2009.

▶ Requirement

1. Compute the total amounts of dividends to both preferred and common for 2012 and 2013 if total dividends are $90,000 in 2012 and $270,000 in 2013.

E10-29A (*Learning Objectives 4, 6: Record a stock dividend and report stockholders' equity*) The stockholders' equity for Dairy Place Drive-Ins (DP) on December 31, 2012, follows:

Stockholders' Equity	
Common stock, $0.30 par, 2,600,000 shares authorized, 600,000 shares issued	$ 180,000
Paid-in capital in excess of par—common	614,400
Retained earnings	7,177,000
Accumulated other comprehensive income (loss)	(200,000)
Total stockholders' equity	$7,771,400

On April 16, 2013, the market price of DP common stock was $20 per share. Assume DP distributed an 18% stock dividend on this date.

▶ Requirements

1. Journalize the distribution of the stock dividend.
2. Prepare the stockholders' equity section of the balance sheet after the stock dividend.
3. Why is total stockholders' equity unchanged by the stock dividend?
4. Suppose DP had a cash balance of $580,000 on April 17, 2013. What is the maximum amount of cash dividends DP can declare?

E10-30A (*Learning Objectives 2, 3, 4: Measure the effects of stock issuance, dividends, and treasury-stock transactions*) Identify the effects—both the direction and the dollar amount—of these assumed transactions on the total stockholders' equity of Townsend Corporation. Each transaction is independent.

a. Declaration of cash dividends of $76 million.
b. Payment of the cash dividend in (a).
c. A 20% stock dividend. Before the dividend, 72 million shares of $1.00 par common stock were outstanding; the market value was $3.875 at the time of the dividend.

d. A 40% stock dividend. Before the dividend, 72 million shares of $1.00 par common stock were outstanding; the market value was $14.25 at the time of the dividend.

e. Purchase of 1,700 shares of treasury stock (par value $1.00) at $3.25 per share.

f. Sale of 800 shares of the treasury stock for $6.00 per share. Cost of the treasury stock was $3.25 per share.

g. A 2-for-1 stock split. Prior to the split, 72 million shares of $1.00 par common stock were outstanding.

E10-31A *(Learning Objectives 4, 6: Account for a stock split; report stockholders' equity after a stock split)* Ace Corp. had the following stockholders' equity at January 31 (dollars in millions, except par value per share):

Stockholders' Equity	
Common stock, $1.80 par, 500 million shares authorized, 425 million shares issued	$ 765
Additional paid-in capital	324
Retained earnings	2,391
Accumulated other comprehensive income (loss)	(143)
Total stockholders' equity	$3,337

On March 2, Ace split its $1.80 par common stock 2-for-1.

▶ Requirement

1. Prepare the stockholders' equity section of the balance sheet immediately after the split.

E10-32A *(Learning Objective 5: Measure book value per share of common stock)* The balance sheet of Basket Rug Company reported the following:

Redeemable preferred stock, 5%, $70 par value, redemption value $35,000; outstanding 400 shares...............	$ 28,000
Common stockholders' equity:	
5,000 shares issued and outstanding	80,000
Total stockholders' equity..	$108,000

▶ Requirements

1. Compute the book value per share for the common stock, assuming all preferred dividends are fully paid up (none in arrears).

2. Compute the book value per share of the common stock, assuming that three years' cumulative preferred dividends, including the current year, are in arrears.

3. Basket Rug's common stock recently traded at a market price of $12.85 per share. Does this mean that Basket Rug's stock is a good buy at $12.85?

E10-33A (*Learning Objective 5: Evaluate profitability*) Lofty Inns reported these figures for 2013 and 2012 (in millions):

	2013	2012
Balance sheet		
Total assets	$27,000	$18,400
Common stock and additional paid-in capital	43	389
Retained earnings	11,525	16,523
Other stockholders' equity	(3,008)	(9,300)
Income statement		
Net sales	$30,500	$28,200
Operating income	4,022	3,819
Net income	2,100	1,546

▶ Requirements

1. Use DuPont analysis to compute Lofty's return on assets and return on common stockholders' equity for 2013.
2. Do these rates of return suggest strength or weakness? Give your reason.
3. What additional information do you need to make the decision in (2)?

E10-34A (*Learning Objective 5: Evaluate profitability*) California Company included the following items in its financial statements for 2012, the current year (amounts in millions):

Payment of long-term debt..........	$17,045	Dividends paid......................	$	235
Proceeds from issuance		Net sales:		
of common stock....................	8,420	Current year......................		60,000
Total liabilities:		Preceding year..................		55,000
Current year-end....................	32,319	Net income:		
Preceding year-end	38,023	Current year......................		1,884
Total stockholders' equity:		Preceding year..................		1,997
Current year-end....................	23,479	Operating income:		
Preceding year-end	14,035	Current year......................		9,980
Borrowings.............................	6,580	Preceding year..................		4,008

▶ Requirements

1. Use DuPont analysis to compute California's return on assets and return on common equity during 2012 (the current year). California has no preferred stock outstanding.
2. Do the company's rates of return look strong or weak? Give your reason.
3. What additional information do you need to make the decision in (2)?

E10-35A (*Learning Objective 6: Report cash flows from financing activities*) Use the California Company data in Exercise E10-34A to show how the company reported cash flows from financing activities during 2012 (the current year). List items in descending order from largest to smallest dollar amount.

Group B

E10-36B (*Learning Objectives 2, 6: Account for issuance of stock; report stockholders' equity*)
Pryor Sales, Inc., is authorized to issue 190,000 shares of common stock and 10,000 shares of preferred stock. During its first year, the business completed the following stock issuance transactions:

Jul	19	Issued 12,000 shares of $4.00 par common stock for cash of $12.00 per share.
Oct	3	Issued 600 shares of $3.00 no-par preferred stock for $62,000 cash.
	11	Received inventory valued at $16,000 and equipment with market value of $8,500 for 3,600 shares of the $4.00 par common stock.

▶ Requirements

1. Journalize the transactions. Explanations are not required.
2. Prepare the stockholders' equity section of Pryor Sales' balance sheet. The ending balance of retained earnings is a deficit of $40,000.

E10-37B (*Learning Objectives 2, 6: Account for issuance of stock; prepare the stockholders' equity section of a balance sheet*) Captain Sporting Goods is authorized to issue 13,000 shares of common stock. During a two-month period, Captain completed these stock-issuance transactions:

Jul	23	Issued 3,200 shares of $1.00 par common stock for cash of $13.00 per share.
	12	Received inventory valued at $13,000 and equipment with market value of $48,000 for 3,000 shares of the $1.00 par common stock.

▶ Requirement

1. Prepare the stockholders' equity section of Captain Sporting Goods' balance sheet for the transactions given in this exercise. Retained Earnings has a balance of $49,000. Journal entries are not required.

E10-38B (*Learning Objective 2: Measure paid-in capital of a corporation*) Time Travel Publishing was recently organized. The company issued common stock to an attorney who provided legal services worth $25,000 to help organize the corporation. Time Travel also issued common stock to an inventor in exchange for his patent with a market value of $76,000. In addition, Time Travel received cash both for the issuance of 1,000 shares of its preferred stock at $120 per share and for the issuance of 16,000 shares of its common shares at $8 per share. During the first year of operations, Time Travel earned net income of $60,000 and declared a cash dividend of $25,000. Without making journal entries, determine the total paid-in capital created by these transactions.

E10-39B (*Learning Objectives 3, 6: Show how treasury stock affects a company; prepare the stockholders' equity section of a balance sheet*) Sagebrush Software had the following selected account balances at December 31, 2012 (in thousands, except par value per share):

Inventory	$ 652	Common stock, $2.25 par	
Property, plant, and		per share, 1,000 shares	
equipment, net	859	authorized, 280 shares	
Paid-in capital in excess of par	900	issued	$ 630
Treasury stock,		Retained earnings	2,260
140 shares at cost	1,540	Accounts receivable, net	1,200
Accumulated other		Notes payable	1,188
comprehensive income (loss)	(727)*		

*Debit balance

▶ Requirements

1. Prepare the stockholders' equity section of Sagebrush Software's balance sheet (in thousands).
2. How can Sagebrush have a larger balance of treasury stock than the sum of Common Stock and Paid-in Capital in Excess of Par?

E10-40B (*Learning Objectives 2, 3: Account for issuance of stock; show how treasury stock transactions affect stockholders' equity*) Journalize the following assumed transactions of Ambient Productions:

Feb 22	Issued 1,800 shares of $1.75 par common stock at $5 per share.
Jun 25	Purchased 400 shares of treasury stock at $14 per share.
Jul 9	Sold 300 shares of treasury stock at $22 per share.

What was the overall effect of these transactions on Ambient's stockholders' equity?

E10-41B (*Learning Objectives 2, 3, 4: Account for issuance of stock; show how treasury stock affects a company; account for dividends*) At December 31, 2012, Northern Corporation reported the stockholders' equity accounts shown here (with dollar amounts in millions, except per-share amounts).

Common stock $4.00 par value per share,	
2,300 million shares issued	$ 9,200
Paid-in capital in excess of par value	4,600
Retained earnings	265
Treasury stock, at cost	(40)
Total stockholders' equity	$14,025

Northern's 2013 transactions included the following:

a. Net income, $444 million
b. Issuance of 10 million shares of common stock for $11 per share
c. Purchase of 1 million shares of treasury stock for $10 million
d. Declaration and payment of cash dividends of $28 million

▶ Requirement

1. Journalize Northern's transactions in b, c, and d. Explanations are not required.

E10-42B (*Learning Objective 6: Report stockholders' equity after a sequence of transactions*) Use the Northern Corporation data in Exercise 10-41B to prepare the stockholders' equity section of the company's balance sheet at December 31, 2013.

E10-43B (*Learning Objectives 2, 3, 4, 6: Infer transactions from a company's comparative stockholders' equity*) Zeta Products Company reported the following stockholders' equity on its balance sheet:

Stockholders' Equity (Dollars and shares in millions)	December 31, 2013	December 31, 2012
Preferred stock—$1.00 par value; authorized 20 shares; Convertible Preferred Stock; issued and outstanding: 2013 and 2012—4 and 8 shares, respectively	$ 4	$ 8
Common stock—$1 per share par value; authorized 1,500 shares; issued: 2013 and 2012—200 and 100 shares, respectively	200	100
Additional paid-in capital	1,400	650
Retained earnings	6,280	5,075
Treasury stock, common—at cost 2013—20 shares; 2012—10 shares	(400)	(160)
Total stockholders' equity	7,484	5,673
Total liabilities and stockholders' equity	$48,484	$42,673

▶ Requirements

1. What caused Zeta's preferred stock to decrease during 2013? Cite all possible causes.
2. What caused Zeta's common stock to increase during 2013? Identify all possible causes.
3. How many shares of Zeta's common stock were outstanding at December 31, 2013?
4. Zeta's net income during 2013 was $1,375 million. How much were Zeta's dividends during the year?
5. During 2013, Zeta sold no treasury stock. What average price per share did Zeta pay for the treasury stock that the company purchased during the year?

E10-44B (*Learning Objective 4: Compute dividends on preferred and common stock*) Majestic Manufacturing, Inc., reported the following:

Stockholders' Equity	
Preferred stock, cumulative, $2.00 par, 8%, 70,000 shares issued	$ 140,000
Common stock, $0.15 par, 9,070,000 shares issued	1,360,500

Majestic Manufacturing has paid all preferred dividends through 2009.

▶ Requirement

1. Compute the total amounts of dividends to both preferred and common for 2012 and 2013 if total dividends are $120,000 in 2012 and $144,000 in 2013.

E10-45B (*Learning Objectives 4, 6: Record a stock dividend and report stockholders' equity*) The stockholders' equity for Perfect Desserts Drive-Ins (PD) on December 31, 2012, follows:

Stockholders' Equity	
Common stock, $0.75 par, 2,700,000 shares authorized, 500,000 shares issued	$ 375,000
Paid-in capital in excess of par—common	512,000
Retained earnings	7,100,000
Accumulated comprehensive income (loss)	(195,000)
Total stockholders' equity	$7,792,000

On July 13, 2013, the market price of PD common stock was $17 per share. Assume PD distributed a 25% stock dividend on this date.

▶ Requirements

1. Journalize the distribution of the stock dividend.
2. Prepare the stockholders' equity section of the balance sheet after the stock dividend.
3. Why is total stockholders' equity unchanged by the stock dividend?
4. Suppose PD had a cash balance of $600,000 on July 14, 2013. What is the maximum amount of cash dividends PD can declare?

E10-46B (*Learning Objectives 2, 3, 4: Measure the effects of stock issuance, dividends, and treasury-stock transactions*) Identify the effects—both the direction and the dollar amount—of these assumed transactions on the total stockholders' equity of Triton Corporation. Each transaction is independent.

a. Declaration of cash dividends of $75 million.
b. Payment of the cash dividend in (a).
c. A 25% stock dividend. Before the dividend, 69 million shares of $1.00 par common stock were outstanding; the market value was $9.885 at the time of the dividend.
d. A 40% stock dividend. Before the dividend, 69 million shares of $1.00 par common stock were outstanding; the market value was $18.50 at the time of the dividend.
e. Purchase of 1,800 shares of treasury stock (par value $1.00) at $4.00 per share.
f. Sale of 800 shares of the treasury stock for $8.00 per share. Cost of the treasury stock was $4.00 per share.
g. A 2-for-1 stock split. Prior to the split, 69 million shares of $1.00 par common stock were outstanding.

E10-47B (*Learning Objectives 4, 6: Account for a stock split; report stockholders' equity after a stock split*) Solartech Corp. had the following stockholders' equity at May 31 (dollars in millions, except par value per share):

Stockholders' Equity	
Common stock, $1.20 par, 900 million shares authorized, 400 million shares issued	$ 480
Additional paid-in capital	324
Retained earnings	2,394
Accumulated other comprehensive income (loss)	(150)
Total stockholders' equity	$3,048

On July 3, Solartech split its $1.20 par common stock 3-for-1.

▶ Requirement

1. Prepare the stockholders' equity section of the balance sheet immediately after the split.

E10-48B (*Learning Objective 5: Measure book value per share of common stock*) The balance sheet of Beecham Rug Company reported the following:

Redeemable preferred stock, 6%, $90 par value, redemption value $25,000; outstanding 200 shares................	$18,000
Common stockholders' equity:	
4,000 shares issued and outstanding	60,000
Total stockholders' equity	$78,000

▶ Requirements

1. Compute the book value per share for the common stock, assuming all preferred dividends are fully paid up (none in arrears).
2. Compute the book value per share of the common stock, assuming that three years' cumulative preferred dividends, including the current year, are in arrears.
3. Beecham Rug's common stock recently traded at a market price of $11.00 per share. Does this mean that Beecham Rug's stock is a good buy at $11.00?

E10-49B (*Learning Objective 5: Evaluate profitability*) Lexington Inns reported these figures for 2013 and 2012 (in millions):

	2013	2012
Balance sheet		
Total assets	$15,702	$13,728
Common stock and additional paid-in capital	80	680
Retained earnings	11,519	16,499
Other stockholders' equity	(3,005)	(9,095)
Income statement		
Net sales	$25,500	$27,500
Operating income	4,025	3,813
Net income	1,500	1,550

▶ Requirements

1. Use DuPont analysis to compute Lexington's return on assets and return on common stock-holders' equity for 2013.
2. Do these rates of return suggest strength or weakness? Give your reason.
3. What additional information do you need to make the decision in (2)?

E10-50B (*Learning Objective 5: Evaluate profitability*) Easton Company included the following items in its financial statements for 2012, the current year (amounts in millions):

Payment of long-term debt..........	$17,200	Dividends paid......................	$ 195
Proceeds from issuance		Net sales:	
of common stock.....................	8,405	Current year......................	65,000
Total liabilities:		Preceding year..................	62,000
Current year-end.....................	32,309	Net income:	
Preceding year-end..................	38,033	Current year......................	2,200
Total stockholders' equity:		Preceding year..................	1,995
Current year-end.....................	23,471	Operating income:	
Preceding year-end..................	14,037	Current year......................	9,125
Borrowings.................................	6,585	Preceding year..................	4,002

▶ Requirements

1. Use DuPont analysis to compute Easton's return on assets and return on common equity during 2012 (the current year). Easton has no preferred stock outstanding.
2. Do the company's rates of return look strong or weak? Give your reason.
3. What additional information do you need to make the decision in (2)?

E10-51B (*Learning Objective 6: Report cash flows from financing activities*) Use the Easton data in Exercise E10-50B to show how the company reported cash flows from financing activities during 2012 (the current year). List items in descending order from largest to smallest dollar amount.

Quiz

Test your understanding of stockholders' equity by answering the following questions. Select the best choice from among the possible answers given.

Q10-52 Which of the following is a characteristic of a corporation?
a. No income tax
b. Mutual agency
c. Limited liability of stockholders
d. Both a and b

Q10-53 Home Team, Inc., issues 280,000 shares of no-par common stock for $15 per share. The journal entry is which of the following?

a.	Cash	4,200,000	
	Common Stock		280,000
	Gain on the Sale of Stock		3,920,000
b.	Cash	4,200,000	
	Common Stock		4,200,000
c.	Cash	4,200,000	
	Common Stock		560,000
	Paid-in Capital in Excess of Par		3,640,000
d.	Cash	280,000	
	Common Stock		280,000

Q10-54 Par value
a. is established for a share of stock after it is issued.
b. represents the original selling price for a share of stock.
c. is an arbitrary amount that establishes the legal capital for each share.
d. may exist for common stock but not for preferred stock.
e. represents what a share of stock is worth.

Q10-55 The paid-in capital portion of stockholders' equity does not include
a. Paid-in Capital in Excess of Par Value.
b. Common Stock.
c. Preferred Stock.
d. Retained Earnings.

Q10-56 Preferred stock is least likely to have which of the following characteristics?
a. Preference as to dividends
b. The right of the holder to convert to common stock
c. Preference as to assets on liquidation of the corporation
d. Extra liability for the preferred stockholders

Q10-57 Which of the following classifications represents the most shares of common stock?
a. Issued shares
b. Outstanding shares
c. Authorized shares
d. Treasury shares
e. Unissued shares

Use the following information for Questions Q10-58 to Q10-60:
These account balances at December 31 relate to Aqua Sport, Inc.:

Accounts Payable	$ 51,400	Paid-in Capital in Excess	
Accounts Receivable	81,950	of Par—Common	$260,000
Common Stock	313,000	Preferred Stock, 10%, $100 Par	81,000
Treasury Stock	5,700	Retained Earnings	71,600
Bonds Payable	3,900	Notes Receivable	12,300

Q10-58 What is total paid-in capital for Aqua Sport, Inc.?
a. $659,700
b. $648,300
c. $725,600
d. $654,000
e. None of the above

Q10-59 What is total stockholders' equity for Aqua Sport, Inc.?
a. $719,900
b. $725,600
c. $731,300
d. $654,000
e. None of the above

Q10-60 Aqua Sport's net income for the period is $119,300 and beginning common stockholders' equity is $681,200. Calculate Aqua Sport's return on common stockholders' equity.
a. 16.8%   c. 18.9%
b. 18.1%   d. 17.0%

Q10-61 A company paid $26 per share to purchase 500 shares of its common stock as treasury stock. The stock was originally issued at $10 per share. The journal entry to record the purchase of the treasury stock is which of the following?

a.	Treasury Stock	5,000	
	Paid-in Capital in Excess of Par	8,000	
	Cash		13,000
b.	Common Stock	13,000	
	Cash		13,000
c.	Treasury Stock	13,000	
	Cash		13,000
d.	Treasury Stock	5,000	
	Retained Earnings	8,000	
	Cash		13,000

Q10-62 When treasury stock is sold for less than its cost, the entry should include a debit to
a. Gain on Sale of Treasury Stock.   c. Retained Earnings.
b. Loss on Sale of Treasury Stock.   d. Paid-in Capital in Excess of Par.

Q10-63 A company purchased 100 shares of its common stock at $49 per share. It then sells 75 of the treasury shares at $58 per share. The entry to sell the treasury stock includes a
a. credit to Cash for $4,350.
b. credit to Paid-in Capital, Treasury Stock for $675.
c. credit to Treasury Stock for $4,350.
d. debit to Retained Earnings for $675.
e. credit to Retained Earnings for $900.

Q10-64 Stockholders are eligible for a dividend if they own the stock on the date of
a. issuance.
b. record.
c. payment.
d. declaration.

Q10-65 Toni's Foods has outstanding 300 shares of 2% preferred stock, $100 par value; and 1,900 shares of common stock, $20 par value. Toni's declares dividends of $18,200. The correct entry is which of the following?

a.	Dividends Payable, Preferred	600	
	Dividends Payable, Common	17,600	
	Cash		18,200
b.	Retained Earnings	18,200	
	Dividends Payable, Preferred		600
	Dividends Payable, Common		17,600
c.	Dividends Expense	18,200	
	Cash		18,200
d.	Retained Earnings	18,200	
	Dividends Payable, Preferred		9,100
	Dividends Payable, Common		9,100

Q10-66 A corporation has 50,000 shares of 1% preferred stock outstanding. Also, there are 50,000 shares of common stock outstanding. Par value for each is $100. If a $450,000 dividend is paid, how much goes to the preferred stockholders?
a. None
b. $4,500
c. $50,000
d. $450,000
e. $30,000

Q10-67 Assume the same facts as in question 66. What is the amount of dividends per share on common stock?
a. $4.50
b. $11.00
c. $8.00
d. $9.00
e. None of these

Q10-68 Which of the following is *not* true about a 10% stock dividend?
a. Total stockholders' equity remains the same.
b. Paid-in Capital increases.
c. Par value decreases.
d. Retained Earnings decreases.
e. The market value of the stock is needed to record the stock dividend.

Q10-69 A company declares a 5% stock dividend. The debit to Retained Earnings is an amount equal to

a. the book value of the shares to be issued.
b. the excess of the market price over the original issue price of the shares to be issued.
c. the par value of the shares to be issued.
d. the market value of the shares to be issued.

Q10-70 Which of the following statements is *not* true about a 3-for-1 stock split?

a. Total stockholders' equity increases.
b. Par value is reduced to one-third of what it was before the split.
c. Retained Earnings remains the same.
d. The market price of each share of stock will decrease.
e. A stockholder with 10 shares before the split owns 30 shares after the split.

Q10-71 Blue Company's net income and net sales are $38,000 and $900,000, respectively, and average total assets are $250,000. What is Blue's return on assets?

a. 15.2%
b. 27.8%
c. 17.2%
d. 4.2%

Problems

MyAccountingLab

All of these A and B problems can be found within MyAccountingLab (MAL), an online homework and practice environment. Your instructor may ask you to complete these problems using MyAccountingLab.

Group A

P10-72A ***(Learning Objectives 2, 6: Account for stock issuance; report stockholders' equity)*** The partners who own Jefferson Canoes Co. wished to avoid the unlimited personal liability of the partnership form of business, so they incorporated as Jefferson Canoes, Inc. The charter from the state of Nevada authorizes the corporation to issue 110,000 shares of $8 par common stock. In its first month, Jefferson Canoes completed the following transactions:

Mar 6	Issued 700 shares of common stock to the promoter for assistance with issuance of the common stock. The promotional fee was $14,700. Debit Organization Expense.
9	Issued 8,000 shares of common stock to Jim Jefferson and 20,000 shares to John Jefferson in return for cash equal to the stock's market value of $21 per share. The Jeffersons were partners in Jefferson Canoes Co.
26	Issued 1,400 shares of common stock for $21 cash per share.

► Requirements

1. Record the transactions in the journal.
2. Prepare the stockholders' equity section of the Jefferson Canoes, Inc., balance sheet at March 31. The ending balance of Retained Earnings is $65,000.

P10-73A ***(Learning Objectives 6: Report stockholders' equity)*** Doorman Corp. has the following stockholders' equity information:

Doorman's charter authorizes the company to issue 7,000 shares of 10% preferred stock with par value of $140 and 750,000 shares of no-par common stock. The company issued 1,400 shares of the preferred stock at $140 per share. It issued 187,500 shares of the common stock for a total of $516,000. The company's retained earnings balance at the beginning of 2012 was $74,000, and net income for the year was $98,000. During 2012, Doorman declared the specified dividend on preferred and a $0.25 per-share dividend on common. Preferred dividends for 2011 were in arrears.

► Requirement

1. Prepare the stockholders' equity section of Doorman Corp.'s balance sheet at December 31, 2012. Show the computation of all amounts. Journal entries are not required.

P10-74A (*Learning Objectives 2, 3, 4: Show the effects of stock issuance, treasury stock, and dividend transactions on stockholders' equity*) Fresh Produce Foods, Inc., is authorized to issue 3,750,000 shares of $5.00 par common stock.

In its initial public offering during 2012, Fresh Produce issued 360,000 shares of its $5.00 par common stock for $5.50 per share. Over the next year, Fresh Produce's stock price increased, and the company issued 400,000 more shares at an average price of $9.50.

During 2014, the price of Fresh Produce's common stock dropped to $7.50, and Fresh Produce purchased 59,000 shares of its common stock for the treasury. After the market price of the common stock rose in 2015, Fresh Produce sold 45,000 shares of the treasury stock for $10.00 per share.

During the five years 2012 to 2017, Fresh Produce earned net income of $940,000 and declared and paid cash dividends of $245,000. Stock dividends of $441,630 were distributed to the stockholders in 2013, with $315,450 credited to common stock and $126,180 credited to additional paid-in capital. At December 31, 2017, total assets of the company are $14,500,000, and liabilities add up to $8,017,500.

► Requirement

1. Show the computation of Fresh Produce's total stockholders' equity at December 31, 2017. Present a detailed computation of each element of stockholders' equity. Use the end-of chapter summary problem on pages 612–613 to format your answer.

P10-75A (*Learning Objectives 2, 4: Analyze stockholders' equity and dividends of a corporation*) Reliable Outdoor Furniture Company included the following stockholders' equity on its year-end balance sheet at February 28, 2013:

Stockholders' Equity	
Preferred stock, 7.5% cumulative—par value $15 per share; authorized 110,000 shares in each class	
Class A—issued 80,000 shares	$ 1,200,000
Class B—issued 92,000 shares...............................	1,380,000
Common stock—$10 par value:................................	
authorized 2,000,000 shares,	
issued 270,000 shares.................................	2,700,000
Additional paid-in capital—common	5,570,000
Retained earnings...	8,360,000
	$19,210,000

► Requirements

1. Identify the different issues of stock that Reliable Outdoor Furniture Company has outstanding.
2. Give the summary entries to record issuance of all the Reliable stock. Assume that all the stock was issued for cash. Explanations are not required.
3. Suppose Reliable passed its preferred dividends for three years. Would the company have to pay those dividends in arrears before paying dividends to the common stockholders? Give your reason.
4. What amount of preferred dividends must Reliable declare and pay each year to avoid having preferred dividends in arrears?
5. Assume that preferred dividends are in arrears for 2012. Journalize the declaration of an $830,000 dividend on February 28, 2013. An explanation is not required.

P10-76A (*Learning Objectives 2, 3, 4: Account for stock issuance, dividends, and treasury stock*)
Paris Jewelry Company reported the following summarized balance sheet at December 31, 2012:

Assets	
Current assets..	$ 33,700
Property and equipment, net	108,700
Total assets..	$142,400
Liabilities and Equity	
Liabilities	$ 37,000
Stockholders' equity:	
$0.40 cumulative preferred stock, $20 par, 800 shares issued ...	16,000
Common stock, $8 par, 6,100 shares issued.........................	48,800
Paid-in capital in excess of par	17,600
Retained earnings...	23,000
Total liabilities and equity...	$142,400

During 2013, Paris completed these transactions that affected stockholders' equity:

Feb	13	Issued 5,300 shares of common stock for $10 per share.
Jun	7	Declared the regular cash dividend on the preferred stock.
	24	Paid the cash dividend.
Aug	9	Distributed a 10% stock dividend on the common stock. Market price of the common stock was $14 per share.
Oct	26	Reacquired 800 shares of common stock as treasury stock, paying $15 per share.
Nov	20	Sold 100 shares of the treasury stock for $17 per share.

▶ Requirements

1. Journalize Paris' transactions. Explanations are not required.
2. Report Paris' stockholders' equity at December 31, 2013. Net income for 2013 was $27,000.

P10-77A (*Learning Objectives 3, 4: Measure the effects of dividend and treasury-stock transactions on a company*) Assume Frozen Foods of Maine, Inc., completed the following transactions during 2012, the company's 10th year of operations:

Feb	3	Issued 11,000 shares of common stock ($3.00 par) for cash of $275,000.
Mar	19	Purchased 2,400 shares of the company's own common stock at $20 per share.
Apr	24	Sold 1,100 shares of treasury common stock for $34 per share.
Aug	15	Declared a cash dividend on the 12,000 shares of $0.90 no-par preferred stock.
Sep	1	Paid the cash dividends.
Nov	22	Distributed a 10% stock dividend on the 98,000 shares of $3.00 par common stock outstanding. The market value of the common stock was $22 per share.

▶ Requirement

1. Analyze each transaction in terms of its effect on the accounting equation of Frozen Foods of Maine, Inc.

P10-78A (*Learning Objectives 4, 5: Prepare a corporation's balance sheet; measure profitability*)
The following accounts and related balances of Bluebird Designers, Inc., as of December 31, 2012, are arranged in no particular order.

Cash....................................	$ 45,000	Interest expense..........................	$ 16,300
Accounts receivable, net...............	25,000	Property, plant, and	
Paid-in capital in excess		equipment, net.......................	359,000
of par—common.......................	53,800	Common stock, $2 par,	
Accrued liabilities..........................	22,000	500,000 shares authorized,	
Long-term note payable...............	97,000	110,000 shares issued.............	220,000
Inventory......................................	89,000	Prepaid expenses.......................	14,000
Dividends payable.........................	9,000	Common stockholders'	
Retained earnings..........................	?	equity, December 31, 2011....	220,000
Accounts payable..........................	135,000	Net income.................................	90,000
Trademarks, net...........................	9,000	Total assets,	
Goodwill.......................................	18,000	December 31, 2009................	500,000
		Treasury stock,	
		8,000 shares at cost................	23,000
		Net sales.....................................	750,000

▶ Requirements

1. Prepare Bluebird's classified balance sheet in the account format at December 31, 2012.
2. Use DuPont analysis to compute rate of return on total assets and rate of return on common stockholders' equity for the year ended December 31, 2012.
3. Do these rates of return suggest strength or weakness? Give your reason. What additional information might help you make your decision?

P10-79A (*Learning Objective 6: Analyze the statement of cash flows*) The statement of cash flows of Spirit, Inc., reported the following for the year ended December 31, 2012:

Cash flows from financing activities (amounts in millions)	
Cash dividends paid..	$(1,832)
Issuance of common stock at par value.................................	1,512
Proceeds from issuance of long-term notes payable...............	57
Purchases of treasury stock..	(3,100)
Payments of long-term notes payable....................................	(161)

▶ Requirement

1. Make the journal entry that Spirit would use to record each of these transactions.

Group B

P10-80B (*Learning Objectives 2, 6: Account for stock issuance; report stockholders' equity*) The partners who own Ameen Canoes Co. wished to avoid the unlimited personal liability of the partnership form of business, so they incorporated as Ameen Canoes, Inc. The charter from the state of Mississippi authorizes the corporation to issue 150,000 shares of $20 par common stock. In its first month, Ameen Canoes completed the following transactions:

Jan	6	Issued 100 shares of common stock to the promoter for assistance with issuance of common stock. The promotional fee was $3,000. Debit Organization Expense.
	9	Issued 7,000 shares of common stock to Al Ameen and 11,000 shares to Arnold Ameen in return for cash equal to the stock's market value of $30 per share. The Ameens were partners inAmeen Canoes Co.
	26	Issued 900 shares of common stock for $30 cash per share.

▶ Requirements

1. Record the transactions in the journal.
2. Prepare the stockholders' equity section of Ameen Canoes, Inc., balance sheet at January 31. The ending balance of Retained Earnings is $80,000.

P10-81B (*Learning Objective 6: Report stockholders' equity*) Callman Corp. has the following stockholders' equity information:

Callman's charter authorizes the company to issue 10,000 shares of 6% preferred stock with par value of $90 and 750,000 shares of no-par common stock. The company issued 2,000 shares of the preferred stock at $90 per share. It issued 75,000 shares of the common stock for a total of $517,000. The company's retained earnings balance at the beginning of 2012 was $78,000, and net income for the year was $95,000. During 2012, Callman declared the specified dividend on preferred and a $0.90 per-share dividend on common. Preferred dividends for 2011 were in arrears.

▶ Requirement

1. Prepare the stockholders' equity section of Callman Corp.'s balance sheet at December 31, 2012. Show the computation of all amounts. Journal entries are not required.

P10-82B (*Learning Objectives 2, 3, 4: Show the effects of stock issuance, treasury stock, and dividend transactions on stockholders' equity*) Healthy Living Foods, Inc., is authorized to issue 4,250,000 shares of $1.00 par common stock.

In its initial public offering during 2012, Healthy Living issued 390,000 shares of its $1.00 par common stock for $5.50 per share. Over the next year, Healthy Living's stock price increased, and the company issued 460,000 more shares at an average price of $8.50.

During 2014, the price of Healthy Living's common stock dropped to $6.00, and Healthy Living purchased 58,000 shares of its common stock for the treasury. After the market price of the common stock rose in 2015, Healthy Living sold 30,000 shares of the treasury stock for $10.00 per share.

During the five years 2012 to 2017, Healthy Living earned net income of $1,200,000 and declared and paid cash dividends of $350,000. Stock dividends of $712,800 were distributed to the stockholders in 2013, with $79,200 credited to common stock and $633,600 credited to additional paid-in capital. At December 31, 2017, total assets of the company are $14,400,000, and liabilities add up to $7,543,000.

▶ Requirement

1. Show the computation of Healthy Living's total stockholders' equity at December 31, 2017. Present a detailed computation of each element of stockholders' equity. Use the end-of-chapter summary problem on pages 612–613 to format your answer.

P10-83B (*Learning Objectives 2, 4: Analyze stockholders' equity and dividends of a corporation*)
Bentley Outdoor Furniture Company included the following stockholders' equity on its year-end balance sheet at February 28, 2013:

Stockholders' Equity	
Preferred stock, 6.0% cumulative—par value $25 per share authorized 140,000 shares in each class	
Class A—issued 80,000 shares	$ 2,000,000
Class B—issued 90,000 shares....................................	2,250,000
Common stock—$5 par value:...	
authorized 1,400,000 shares,	
issued 240,000 shares.....................................	1,200,000
Additional paid-in capital—common	5,560,000
Retained earnings...	8,350,000
	$19,360,000

▶ Requirements

1. Identify the different issues of stock that Bentley Outdoor Furniture Company has outstanding.
2. Give the summary entries to record issuance of all the Bentley stock. Assume that all the stock was issued for cash. Explanations are not required.
3. Suppose Bentley passed its preferred dividends for three years. Would the company have to pay these dividends in arrears before paying dividends to the common stockholders? Give your reasons.
4. What amount of preferred dividends must Bentley declare and pay each year to avoid having preferred dividends in arrears?
5. Assume that preferred dividends are in arrears for 2012. Journalize the declaration of an $840,000 dividend on February 28, 2013. An explanation is not required.

P10-84B (*Learning Objectives 2, 3, 4: Account for stock issuance, dividends, and treasury stock*)
Madrid Jewelry Company reported the following summarized balance sheet at December 31, 2012:

Assets	
Current assets...	$ 34,500
Property and equipment, net	101,300
Total assets..	$135,800
Liabilities and Equity	
Liabilities	$ 37,500
Stockholders' equity:	
$0.30 cumulative preferred stock, $10 par,	
700 shares issued.................................	7,000
Common stock, $8 par, 5,900 shares issued..............	47,200
Paid-in capital in excess of par	18,100
Retained earnings.....................................	26,000
Total liabilities and equity..	$135,800

During 2013, Madrid completed the following transactions that affected stockholders' equity:

Feb	13	Issued 5,700 shares of common stock for $11 per share.
Jun	7	Declared the regular cash dividend on the preferred stock.
	24	Paid the cash dividend.
Aug	9	Distributed a 5% stock dividend on the common stock. Market price of the common stock was $14 per share.
Oct	26	Reacquired 200 shares of common stock as treasury stock, paying $18 per share.
Nov	20	Sold 100 shares of the treasury stock for $19 per share.

▶ **Requirements**

1. Journalize Madrid's transactions. Explanations are not required.
2. Report Madrid's stockholders' equity at December 31, 2013. Net income for 2013 was $22,000.

P10-85B *(Learning Objectives 3, 4: Measure the effects of dividend and treasury-stock transactions on a company)* Assume ABC Cupcakes of Montana, Inc., completed the following transactions during 2012, the company's 10th year of operations:

Feb	3	Issued 10,000 shares of common stock ($3.00 par) for cash of $280,000.
Mar	19	Purchased 2,700 shares of the company's own common stock at $24 per share.
Apr	24	Sold 1,400 shares of treasury stock for $26 per share.
Aug	15	Declared a cash dividend on the 16,000 shares of $0.50 no-par preferred stock.
Sep	1	Paid the cash dividends.
Nov	22	Distributed a 20% stock dividend on the 94,000 shares of $3.00 par common stock outstanding. The market value of the common stock was $25 per share.

▶ **Requirement**

1. Analyze each transaction in terms of its effect on the accounting equation of ABC Cupcakes of Montana, Inc.

P10-86B *(Learning Objectives 4, 5: Prepare a corporation's balance sheet; measure profitability)* The following accounts and related balances of Dove Designers, Inc., as of December 31, 2012, are arranged in no particular order.

Cash	$53,000	Interest expense	$ 16,200
Accounts receivable, net	27,000	Property, plant, and	
Paid-in capital in excess		equipment, net	355,000
of par—common	75,600	Common stock, $2 par,	
Accrued liabilities	25,000	1,250,000 shares authorized,	
Long-term note payable	95,000	118,000 shares issued	236,000
Inventory	98,000	Prepaid expenses	14,000
Dividends payable	6,000	Common stockholders'	
Retained earnings	?	equity, December 31, 2011	233,000
Accounts payable	130,000	Net income	71,000
Trademarks, net	3,000	Total assets,	
Goodwill	18,000	December 31, 2011	495,000
		Treasury stock, common,	
		8,000 shares at cost	25,000
		Net sales	800,000

▶ **Requirements**

1. Prepare Dove's classified balance sheet in the account format at December 31, 2012.
2. Use DuPont analysis to compute rate of return on total assets and rate of return on common stockholders' equity for the year ended December 31, 2012.
3. Do these rates of return suggest strength or weakness? Give your reason. What additional information might help you make your decision?

P10-87B *(Learning Objective 6: Analyze the statement of cash flows)* The statement of cash flows of Cooper, Inc., reported the following for the year ended December 31, 2012:

Cash flows from financing activities (amounts in millions)	
Cash dividends paid	$(1,790)
Issuance of common stock at par value	1,498
Proceeds from issuance of long-term notes payable	51
Purchases of treasury stock	(3,020)
Payments of long-term notes payable	(159)

▶ Requirement

1. Make the journal entry that Cooper would use to record each of these transactions.

Challenge Exercises and Problem

E10-88 *(Learning Objectives 2, 3, 4: Reconstruct transactions from the financial statements)*

I-9 Networking Solutions began operations on January 1, 2012, and immediately issued its stock, receiving cash. I-9's balance sheet at December 31, 2012, reported the following stockholders' equity:

Common stock, $1 par	$ 56,000
Additional paid-in capital	394,400
Retained earnings	41,000
Treasury stock, 500 shares	(2,000)
Total stockholders' equity	$489,400

During 2012, I-9

- **a.** issued stock for $8 per share.
- **b.** purchased 800 shares of treasury stock, paying $4 per share.
- **c.** resold some of the treasury stock.
- **d.** declared and paid cash dividends.

▶ Requirement

1. Journalize all of I-9's stockholders' equity transactions during the year. I-9's entry to close net income to Retained Earnings was as follows:

Revenues	177,000	
Expenses		112,000
Retained Earnings		65,000

E10-89 *(Learning Objective 6: Report financing activities on the statement of cash flows)* Use the I-9 Networking Solutions data in Exercise 10-88 to show how the company reported cash flows from financing activities during 2012.

E10-90 *(Learning Objectives 2, 3, 4: Account for issuance of stock and treasury stock; explain the changes in stockholders' equity)* Orbit Corporation reported the following stockholders' equity data (all dollars in millions except par value per share):

| | December 31, | |
	2012	2011
Preferred stock	$ 606	$ 738
Common stock, $1 par value	900	885
Additional paid-in capital	1,496	1,466
Retained earnings	20,661	19,104
Treasury stock, common	(2,800)	(2,640)

Orbit earned net income of $2,920 during 2012. For each account except Retained Earnings, one transaction explains the change from the December 31, 2011, balance to the December 31, 2012, balance. Two transactions affected Retained Earnings. Give a full explanation, including the dollar amount, for the change in each account.

E10-91 *(Learning Objectives 2, 3, 4: Account for issuance of stock, treasury stock, and other changes in stockholders' equity)* Smiley Site, Inc., ended 2012 with 10 million shares of $1 par common stock issued and outstanding. Beginning additional paid-in capital was $9 million, and retained earnings totaled $44 million.

- ▶ In April 2013, Smiley Site issued 9 million shares of common stock at a price of $2 per share.
- ▶ In June, the company distributed a 10% stock dividend at a time when Smiley Site's common stock had a market value of $12 per share.
- ▶ Then in September, Smiley Site's stock price dropped to $1 per share and the company purchased 9 million shares of treasury stock.
- ▶ For the year, Smiley Site earned net income of $24 million and declared cash dividends of $13 million.

▶ Requirement

1. Complete the following tabulation to show what Smiley Site should report for stockholders' equity at December 31, 2013. Journal entries are not required.

(Amounts in millions)	Common Stock	+	Additional Paid-In Capital	+	Retained Earnings	−	Treasury Stock	=	Total Equity
Balance, Dec 31, 2012......................	$10		$9		$44		0		$63
Issuance of stock									
Stock dividend....................................									
Purchase of treasury stock.................									
Net income...									
Cash dividends...................................									
Balance, Dec 31, 2013......................									

P10-92 (*Learning Objective 5: Analyze information from stockholders' equity*) The stockholders' equity of All-Star Uniforms as of December 31, 2012 and 2011 follows:

	2012	2011
Common stock, 2,000,000 shares authorized,		
1,000,000 and 950,000 shares issued, respectively	$ 100,000	$ 95,000
Paid-in capital in excess of par	39,980,000	37,905,000
Paid-in capital-treasury stock transactions	55,000	50,000
Retained earnings	67,000,000	60,000,000
Treasury stock, at cost, 20,000 and 25,000 shares, respectively	(792,000)	(990,000)
Total stockholders' equity	$106,343,000	$97,060,000

▶ Requirements

1. What is the par value of the common stock?
2. How many shares of common stock were outstanding at the end of 2012?
3. As of December 31, 2012, what was the average price that stockholders paid for all common stock when issued?
4. Prepare a summary journal entry to record the change in common stock during the year.
5. What was the average price that stockholders paid for the common stock issued in 2012?
6. What was the average price paid by All-Star for the treasury stock?
7. Prepare a summary journal entry to record the change in treasury stock during the year.
8. Assuming net income for 2012 was $10,000,000, prepare a summary journal entry to record the dividends declared during 2012.

APPLY YOUR KNOWLEDGE

Decision Cases

Case 1. (*Learning Objectives 2, 6: Evaluate alternative ways of raising capital*) Nate Smith and Darla Jones have written a computer program for a video game that may rival PlayStation and Xbox. They need additional capital to market the product, and they plan to incorporate their business. Smith and Jones are considering alternative capital structures for the corporation. Their primary goal is to raise as much capital as possible without giving up control of the business. Smith and Jones plan to receive 50,000 shares of the corporation's common stock in return for the net assets of their old business. After the old company's books are closed and the assets are adjusted to current market value, Smith's and Jones' capital balances will each be $25,000.

The corporation's plans for a charter include an authorization to issue 10,000 shares of preferred stock and 500,000 shares of $1 par common stock. Smith and Jones are uncertain about the most desirable features for the preferred stock. Prior to incorporating, Smith and Jones are discussing their plans with two investment groups. The corporation can obtain capital from outside investors under either of the following plans:

 + *Plan 1.* Group 1 will invest $80,000 to acquire 800 shares of 6%, $100 par nonvoting, preferred *stock*.
 + *Plan 2.* Group 2 will invest $55,000 to acquire 500 shares of $5, no-par preferred stock and $35,000 to acquire 35,000 shares of common stock. Each preferred share receives 50 votes on matters that come before the stockholders.

▶ Requirements

Assume that the corporation is chartered.
1. Journalize the issuance of common stock to Smith and Jones. Debit each person's capital account for its balance.

2. Journalize the issuance of stock to the outsiders under both plans.
3. Assume that net income for the first year is $120,000 and total dividends are $30,000. Prepare the stockholders' equity section of the corporation's balance sheet under both plans.
4. Recommend one of the plans to Smith and Jones. Give your reasons. (Challenge)

Case 2. (*Learning Objective 4: Analyze cash dividends and stock dividends*) **United Parcel Service (UPS), Inc.,** had the following stockholders' equity amounts on December 31, 2012 (adapted, in millions):

Total assets	$65,503
Total liabilities	54,033
Stockholders' equity	11,470
Net income, as reported, for 2012................	979

During 2012, UPS paid a cash dividend of $0.715 per share. Assume that, after paying the cash dividends, UPS distributed a 10% stock dividend. Assume further that the following year UPS declared and paid a cash dividend of $0.65 per share.

Suppose you own 10,000 shares of UPS common stock, acquired three years ago, prior to the 10% stock dividend. The market price of UPS stock was $61.02 per share before the stock dividend.

▶ Requirements

1. How does the stock dividend affect your proportionate ownership in UPS? Explain.
2. What amount of cash dividends did you receive last year? What amount of cash dividends will you receive after the above dividend action?
3. Assume that immediately after the stock dividend was distributed, the market value of UPS's stock decreased from $61.02 per share to $55.473 per share. Does this decrease represent a loss to you? Explain.
4. Suppose UPS announces at the time of the stock dividend that the company will continue to pay the annual $0.715 *cash* dividend per share, even after distributing the *stock* dividend. Would you expect the market price of the stock to decrease to $55.473 per share as in Requirement 3? Explain.

Case 3. (*Learning Objectives 2, 3, 4, 5: Evaluate financial position and profitability*) At December 31, 2000, **Enron Corporation** reported the following data (condensed in millions):

Common stock and additional paid-in capital; 1,135 shares issued..............	$ 278
Retained earnings...	9,457
Total stockholders' equity..	$9,735

During 2001, Enron restated company financial statements for 1997 to 2000, after reporting that some data had been omitted from those prior-year statements. Assume that the startling events of 2001 included the following:

+ Several related companies should have been, but were not, included in the Enron statements for 2000. These companies had total assets of $5,700 million, liabilities totaling $5,600 million, and net losses of $130 million.
+ In January 2001, Enron's stockholders got the company to give them $2,000 million of 12% long-term notes payable in return for their giving up their common stock. Interest is accrued at year-end.

Take the role of a financial analyst. It is your job to analyze Enron Corporation and rate the company's long-term debt.

► Requirements

1. Measure Enron's expected net income for 2001 two ways:
   a. Assume 2001's net income should be the same as the amount of net income that Enron actually reported for 2000. (Given)
   b. Recompute expected net income for 2001, taking into account the new developments of 2001. (Challenge)
   c. Evaluate Enron's likely trend of net income for the future. Discuss why this trend is developing. Ignore income tax. (Challenge)
2. Write Enron's accounting equation two ways:
   a. As actually reported at December 31, 2000
   b. As adjusted for the events of 2001 (Challenge)
3. Measure Enron's debt ratio as reported at December 31, 2000, and again after making the adjustments for the events of 2001.
4. Based on your analysis, make a recommendation to the Debt-Rating Committee of Moody's Investor Services. Would you recommend upgrading, downgrading, or leaving Enron's debt rating undisturbed (currently, it is "high-grade"). (Challenge)

Ethical Issues

Ethical Issue 1. *Note:* This case is based on a real situation. George Campbell paid $50,000 for a franchise that entitled him to market Success Associates software programs in the countries of the European Union. Campbell intended to sell individual franchises for the major language groups of western Europe—German, French, English, Spanish, and Italian. Naturally, investors considering buying a franchise from Campbell asked to see the financial statements of his business.

Believing the value of the franchise to be greater than $50,000, Campbell sought to capitalize his own franchise at $500,000. The law firm of McDonald & LaDue helped Campbell form a corporation chartered to issue 500,000 shares of common stock with par value of $1 per share. Attorneys suggested the following chain of transactions:

a. A third party borrows $500,000 and purchases the franchise from Campbell.
b. Campbell pays the corporation $500,000 to acquire all its stock.
c. The corporation buys the franchise from the third party, who repays the loan.

In the final analysis, the third party is debt-free and out of the picture. Campbell owns all the corporation's stock, and the corporation owns the franchise. The corporation balance sheet lists a franchise acquired at a cost of $500,000. This balance sheet is Campbell's most valuable marketing tool.

► Requirements

1. What is the ethical issue in this situation?
2. Who are the stakeholders to the suggested transaction?
3. Analyze this case from the following standpoints: (a) economic, (b) legal, (c) ethical. What are the consequences to each stakeholder?
4. How should the transaction be reported?

Ethical Issue 2. St. Genevieve Petroleum Company is an independent oil producer in Baton Parish, Louisiana. In February, company geologists discovered a pool of oil that tripled the company's proven reserves. Prior to disclosing the new oil to the public, St. Genevieve quietly bought most of its stock as treasury stock. After the discovery was announced, the company's stock price increased from $6 to $27.

► Requirements

1. What is the ethical issue in this situation? What accounting principle is involved?
2. Who are the stakeholders?
3. Analyze the facts from the following standpoints: (a) economic, (b) legal, and (c) ethical. What is the impact to each stakeholder?
4. What decision would you have made?

Focus on Financials: | Amazon.com, Inc.

(Learning Objectives 2, 3, 5: Analyze common stock, retained earnings, return on equity, and return on assets) **Amazon.com's** consolidated financial statements appear in Appendix A at the end of this book.

1. Refer to the Consolidated Balance Sheets and Note 7 (Stockholders' Equity). Describe the classes of stock that Amazon.com, Inc., has authorized. How many shares of each class have been issued? How many are outstanding as of December 31, 2010?

2. Refer to the Consolidated Balance Sheets and the Consolidated Statements of Stockholders' Equity. (Note: The Statement of Stockholders' Equity is discussed in detail in Chapter 11, pages 664 through 666.) How many shares of treasury stock did the company purchase during the year ended December 31, 2010? What was the cost of the treasury stock? How much per share?

3. Examine Amazon.com's consolidated statement of stockholders' equity. Analyze the change that occurred in the company's Retained Earnings account during the year ended December 31, 2010. Can you trace the change to any of its other financial statements? Is this a good thing or a bad thing?

4. Use DuPont analysis to compute Amazon.com's return on equity and return on assets for 2010. Pick a company that is a competitor of Amazon.com. Also compute these ratios for the competitor. Which ratios are similar? Which are different? Which company do you think is more profitable? Explain.

Focus on Analysis: | RadioShack Corporation

(Learning Objectives 2, 3, 4: Analyze treasury stock and retained earnings) This case is based on the consolidated financial statements of **RadioShack Corporation** given in Appendix B at the end of this book. In particular, this case uses RadioShack Corporation's consolidated statement of shareholders' equity for the year 2010.

1. As of the end of December 31, 2010, how many shares of common stock does RadioShack Corporation have authorized? Issued? Outstanding?

2. During 2010, RadioShack Corporation purchased treasury stock. How many shares did it purchase? How much did it pay for the stock? What was the average price paid per share? Compare the price it paid for these shares with the market price of the company's stock today (RadioShack's trading symbol is RSH). Does it look like the company got a "good deal" on the purchase of its stock? Why do you think RadioShack purchased the shares? (Challenge)

3. Did RadioShack Corporation issue any new shares of common stock during 2010? Briefly explain the reasons. (Challenge)

4. Prepare a T-account to show the beginning and ending balances, plus all the activity in Retained Earnings for 2010.

Group Project in Ethics

The global economic recession that started in 2007, and that persists in certain sectors, has impacted every business, but it was especially hard on banks, automobile manufacturing, and retail companies. Banks were largely responsible for the recession. Some of the biggest banks made excessively risky investments collateralized by real estate mortgages, and many of these investments soured when the real estate markets collapsed. When banks had to write these investments down to market values, the regulatory authorities notified them that they had inadequate capital ratios on their balance sheets to operate. Banks stopped loaning money. Because stock prices were depressed, companies could not raise capital by selling stock. With both debt and stock financing frozen, many businesses had to close their doors.

Fearing collapse of the whole economy, the central governments of the United States and several European nations loaned money to banks to prop up their capital ratios and keep them open. The government also loaned massive amounts to the largest insurance company in the United States (AIG), as well as to General Motors and Chrysler, to help them stay in business. When asked why, many in government replied "these businesses were too important to fail." In several cases, the U.S. government has taken an "equity stake" in some banks and businesses by taking preferred stock in exchange for the cash infusion.

Because of the recession, corporate downsizing has occurred on a massive scale throughout the world. While companies in the retail sector provide more jobs than the banking and automobile industry combined, the government has not chosen to "bail out" any retail businesses. Each company or industry mentioned in this book has pared down plant and equipment, laid off employees, or restructured operations. Some companies have been forced out of business altogether. Unemployment in the United States persists at above 9 percent.

▶ Requirements

1. Identify all the stakeholders of a corporation. A *stakeholder* is a person or a group who has an interest (that is, a stake) in the success of the organization.
2. Do you believe that some entities are "too important to fail?" Should the federal government help certain businesses to stay afloat during economic recessions and allow others to fail?
3. Identify several measures by which a company may be considered deficient and in need of downsizing. How can downsizing help to solve this problem?
4. Debate the bailout issue. One group of students takes the perspective of the company and its stockholders, and another group of students takes the perspective of the other stakeholders of the company (the community in which the company operates and society at large).
5. What is the problem with the government taking an equity position such as preferred stock in a private enterprise?

For online homework, exercises, and problems that provide you with immediate feedback, please visit **www.myaccountinglab.com**.

MyAccountingLab

Quick Check Answers

1. *a* (10,000 shares × $2 = $20,000)
2. *b* ($200,000/$1 par = 200,000 shares)
3. *d* ($150,000 + $100,000 + $200,000)
4. *c* ($150,000 + $100,000 + $200,000 + $400,000)
5. *b* ($850,000 − $25,000)
6. *d* [No gain or loss (for the income statement) on treasury stock transactions]
7. *d*
8. *a*
9. *c*
10. *a*
11. *c* [First, annual preferred dividend = $6,000 (3,000 × $40 × 0.05)]. Five years of preferred dividends must be paid (four in arrears plus the current year). [($6,000 × 5) + (140,000 × $1.50 per share common dividend) = $240,000]
12. *a*
13. *a*
14. *d*
15. *b*
16. *a*

The Income Statement, the Statement of Comprehensive Income, & the Statement of Stockholders' Equity

11

SPOTLIGHT: The Gap, Inc: A Global Icon Adapts to Changing Markets

The Gap, Inc., is a leading international specialty retailer with a strong portfolio of casual apparel, accessories, and personal care products for men, women, and children under The Gap, Old Navy, Banana Republic, Piperlime and Althea brands. The Gap, Inc., is truly a case study in how even a strong company has to adapt to changing market conditions in order to prosper in a highly competitive global economy. For several years in the past, the company encountered "top line" (revenue) headwinds due to strategic marketing and merchandising mistakes. In addition, at the end of 2008, a global recession caused revenues, as well as profit from operations, to plummet. The company responded with a renewed commitment to serve the needs of customers while delivering "quality earnings and long-term value to shareholders." The Gap, Inc., began adding stores in China, the world's largest developing economy with a huge and growing middle class, as well as in fashion-conscious Italy. The company also began adding to its online sales capability. The results from fiscal 2010 show that the company is finally but slowly returning to growth in sales and profitability. When you finish this chapter, you will have a better understanding of earnings quality and how you can use a company's income statement to estimate it. ●

This chapter rounds out your coverage of the corporate income statement. After studying this chapter, you will have seen all the types of items that typically appear on an income statement. You'll study the components of *net income from operations*, which is the basis for many analysts' predictions about companies' future operations, as well as their current values. You'll learn how conducting international business transactions in foreign currencies impacts net income. You'll also learn about earnings per share, the most often-mentioned statistic in business. Finally, you'll learn about the statement of stockholders' equity, of which a component is the analysis of changes in other comprehensive income as well as changes in retained earnings. The knowledge you get from this chapter will help you analyze financial statements and use the information in decision making.

We begin with a basic question: How do we evaluate the quality of a company's earnings? The term *quality of earnings* refers to the characteristics of an earnings number that make it most useful for decision making.

1. **Evaluate** quality of earnings

2. **Account** for foreign-currency gains and losses

3. **Account** for other items on the income statement

4. **Compute** earnings per share

5. **Analyze** the statement of comprehensive income and the statement of stockholders' equity

6. **Differentiate** management's and auditors' responsibilities in financial reporting

Learning Objectives

Evaluate Quality of Earnings

A corporation's net income, or net earnings (including earnings per share), receives more attention than any other single item in the financial statements. To stockholders, the larger the net income, the greater the likelihood of dividends. In addition, a steady and upward trend in *persistent* earnings generally translates sooner or later to a higher stock price.

Suppose you are considering investing in either the stock of **The Gap, Inc.,** or Brand X Superstore. How do you make the decision? A knowledgeable investor will want to assess each company's **earnings quality.** The higher the quality of earnings in the current period as compared to its recent past, the more likely it is that the company is executing a successful business strategy to generate healthy earnings in the future, which is a key component in its stock price.

There are many components of earnings quality. Among the most prominent are (1) proper revenue and expense recognition, (2) high and persistently improving gross margin/sales ratio, (3) low operating expenses compared to sales, and (4) high and persistently improving operating earnings/sales ratio. To explore the makeup and the quality of earnings, let's examine its various sources. Exhibit 11-1 shows the Consolidated Statements of Earnings of The Gap, Inc., for fiscal years 2010, 2009, and 2008. We'll use these statements as a basis for our discussion of earnings quality.

1

Evaluate quality of earnings

Revenue Recognition

The first component of earnings quality, and the top line of the income statement, is proper recognition of net revenue, or *net sales.* You learned about revenue in Chapters 3 through 5. The *revenue principle,* discussed in Chapter 3 (p. 138), states that, under accrual accounting, revenue should

EXHIBIT 11-1 | The Gap, Inc., Consolidated Statements of Income

The Gap, Inc.
Consolidated Statements of Income

	Fiscal Year		
($ and shares in millions except per share amounts)	2010	2009	2008
1 Net sales	$14,664	$14,197	$14,526
2 Cost of goods sold and occupancy expenses	8,775	8,473	9,079
3 Gross profit	5,889	5,724	5,447
4 Operating expenses	3,921	3,909	3,899
5 Operating income	1,968	1,815	1,548
6 Interest expense (reversal)	(8)	6	1
7 Interest income	(6)	(7)	(37)
8 Income before income taxes	1,982	1,816	1,584
9 Income taxes	778	714	617
10 Net Income	$ 1,204	$ 1,102	$ 967
11 Weighted-average number of shares—basic	636	694	716
12 Weighted-average number of shares—diluted	641	699	719
13 Earnings per share—basic	$ 1.89	$ 1.59	$ 1.35
14 Earnings per share—diluted	$ 1.88	$ 1.58	$ 1.34
15 Cash dividends declared and paid per share	$ 0.40	$ 0.34	$ 0.34

be recognized when it is *earned*—that is, when the selling business has fulfilled its obligation to either deliver the product or the service to the customer. In recognizing revenue, several important events usually have to occur: (1) The seller delivers the product or service to the customer, (2) the customer takes both possession and ownership of the product or service, and (3) the seller either collects cash or is reasonably assured of collecting the cash in the near future. In Chapter 4 (pp. 252–253), you learned about the importance of internal controls over the processes by which revenue is recognized and by which cash collections are entered into the accounting system. In Chapter 5 (pp. 289–290), you learned that net sales is the difference between gross sales and reductions made by sales returns and sales discounts. You also learned that credit sales, or sales on account, have to go through the process of collection, that some will ultimately not be collectible, and that a company must make allowances for doubtful accounts. You studied the concept of *free on board* (FOB) terms, which governs the issue of who owns the goods during the shipment process, and therefore the timing of revenue. You must understand all of these concepts in order to grasp the meaning of proper revenue recognition.

Proper revenue recognition in a retail business like The Gap, Inc., is relatively straightforward. As explained in its Notes to Consolidated Financial Statements, The Gap, Inc., recognizes revenue as well as related cost of goods sold at the time customers receive the products. In the stores, revenue is recognized at the registers when the customers receive and pay for merchandise. For online sales (which comprise about 9% of the total), the company has to estimate how long it takes the merchandise to reach customers by mail or courier. For both over-the-counter and Internet sales, the company estimates an allowance for returns and deducts it from gross sales to report *net sales*.

Let's examine Exhibit 11-1 and analyze the trend in The Gap's net sales revenue (in millions, line 1). Notice that, over the past three years, net sales for the company have followed a see-saw pattern. From 2008 to 2009, net sales declined from $14,526 to $14,197 (about 2.3%). Then, in 2010, net sales climbed back to $14,664 (3.3% over 2009). Same-store sales, a key factor in growth for retail stores, increased in 2010 for all Gap, Inc., companies except its flagship stores,

The Gap. Competition from other specialty retailers as well as the frenetic pace of specialty fashion retailing and a global recession all contributed to the "top line" jigsaw pattern. As a rule, markets tend to react negatively to volatility in revenue trends. The Gap, Inc.'s stock price, like that of other specialty retailers, has been no exception, fluctuating from a low of below $10 per share to a high of above $26 per share over the two-year period.

The FASB and IASB have reached agreement on a new standard, to be issued in 2012, that will bring the revenue recognition standards of the two bodies into much closer harmony and consistency than existed under previous standards. The new proposed standard, discussed in Chapter 3, has no impact on the material covered in this course, since the standards for revenue recognition in the retail industry were already closely aligned globally. You may cover the new standard in more detail in later accounting courses.

with Revenue

Research has shown that roughly half of all financial statement fraud over the past two decades has involved improper revenue recognition.[1] Following are several of the more significant revenue recognition issues involving fraud from the SEC's files:

▶ **Recognizing revenue prematurely (before it is earned).** One of the common fraud techniques is **channel stuffing**, where a company may ship inventory to regular customers in excess of amounts ordered. **Bristol-Myers Squibb**, a global pharmaceuticals company, was sued by the SEC in 2004 for channel stuffing during 2000 and 2001. The company allegedly stuffed its distribution channels with excess inventory near the end of every quarter in amounts sufficient to meet company sales targets (tied to executive bonuses), overstating revenue by about $1.5 billion. The company paid a civil fine of $100 million and established a $50 million fund to compensate shareholders for their losses.[2]

▶ **Providing incentives for customers to purchase more inventory than is needed**, in exchange for future discounts and other benefits.

▶ **Reporting revenue when significant services are still to be performed or goods delivered.**

▶ **Reporting sales to fictitious or nonexistent customers.** This may include falsified shipping and inventory records.

Cost of Goods Sold and Gross Profit (Gross Margin)

After revenue, the next two important components in earnings quality are cost of goods sold and resulting gross profit. Before we get to these components, however, it is important to emphasize that, just as it is important to avoid premature or improper revenue recognition, it is equally important to make sure that *all expenses are accurately, completely, and transparently included* in the computation of net income. We saw with the example of the WorldCom fraud in Chapter 7 what can happen when a company manipulates reported earnings by deliberately understating expenses. Without the integrity that comes through full and complete disclosures of all existing expenses, and without recognizing those expenses against the revenues they are incurred to earn, trends in earnings are at best meaningless, and at worst, downright misleading.

Cost of Goods Sold. Covered in Chapter 6, cost of goods sold represents the direct cost of the goods sold to customers. In the case of The Gap, Inc., cost of goods sold also includes the cost of occupying the space used to sell the product, or store rent. As shown on line 2 of

---

[1]*CPA Letter* (February 2003). American Institute of Certified Public Accountants. See www.aicpa.org/pubs/cpaltr/feb2003/financial.htm.
[2]Accounting and Auditing Enforcement Release No. 2075, August 4, 2004. *Securities and Exchange Commission v. Bristol-Myers Squibb Company*, 04-3680 DNJ (2004). See www.sec.gov/news/press/2004-105.htm.

Exhibit 11-1, cost of goods sold and occupancy expenses represents the largest single operating expense for The Gap, Inc. Cost of goods sold as a percentage of sales fell from about 63% in 2008 to about 60% in 2009 and 2010. In general, assuming cost of goods sold is accurately measured each period, steadily decreasing cost of goods sold as a percentage of net sales revenue is regarded as a sign of increasing earnings quality.

Gross Profit (Gross Margin). Gross profit (gross margin) represents the difference between net sales and cost of goods sold. Conversely with steadily decreasing cost of goods sold, steadily increasing gross profit as a percentage of net sales revenue is considered a sign of increasing earnings quality. For The Gap, Inc., gross profit increased from about 37.5% ($5,447/$14,526) in 2008 to about 40% ($5,724/$14,197) in 2009 and again in 2010 ($5,889/$14,664). This represents a positive trend, for the same reasons noted above.

Operating and Other Expenses

As implied in the title, operating expenses are the ongoing expenses incurred by the entity, other than direct expenses for merchandise and other costs directly related to sales. The largest operating expenses generally include salaries, wages, utilities, and supplies. Again, given that the entity takes care to accurately measure operating expenses, the lower these costs are relative to sales, the more efficiently and, therefore, the more profitably, we can assume management is operating the business. As shown in line 4 of Exhibit 11-1, operating expenses of The Gap, Inc., have followed a rather stable pattern in relation to sales over the three-year period. From fiscal 2008 to fiscal 2010, operating expenses increased from $3,899 to $3,921, while revenue grew from $14,526 to $14,664. This kept operating expenses consistently in the range of 26.8% to 27.5% of net sales. When companies are having revenue difficulties, it is wise to try to trim fat from operations by cutting back on costs. The trick is knowing when and how much to cut, because indiscriminate cost cutting can erode perceived quality of the company's product or service, further damaging the bottom line.

Operating Income (Earnings)

Given the integrity that comes with accuracy and transparency of reported revenues and expenses, a trend of high and persistently improving operating earnings in relation to net sales reflects increasing earnings quality. Operating income is a function of all of its individual ingredients: revenue, cost of goods sold, gross margin, and operating expenses. For The Gap, Inc., the trend in income from operations (line 5 of Exhibit 11-1) has turned consistently positive only in the past three years, showing a 17.2% [($1,815/$1,548) − 1.0] jump in 2009 and another 8.4% [($1,968/$1,815) − 1.0] increase in 2010. It is troubling that 2010's rate of increase in operating income was less than half that of 2009, which raises doubts as to whether the company can continue to improve its operating earnings over the long-term. As a matter of fact, if you analyzed these trends for the three years preceding 2008, you would see that the company's growth rate in operating earnings has traditionally been rather erratic.

Account for Foreign-Currency Gains and Losses

2

Account for foreign-currency gains and losses

International transactions are common in many businesses and can significantly influence reported earnings. Manufacturing of all kinds of products has migrated to places such as China, India, and Southeast Asia, where labor and materials are less costly. Transportation and communications systems, as well as manufacturing processes, have improved to the point at which it has become convenient and cost effective for retailers to purchase virtually all items for resale from companies in these developing countries. According to The Gap, Inc.'s annual report, the company purchases nearly all of its inventories from sources outside the United States. Sometimes those purchases are made in currencies other than U.S. dollars, such as Chinese yuan. The Gap, Inc., owns and operates stores in Canada, the United Kingdom, France, Ireland, Japan, China, and Italy. In addition, it has franchise agreements with unaffiliated companies to operate Gap and Banana Republic Stores in many other countries around the world.

Dollars Versus Foreign Currency

Assume The Gap, Inc., ships clothing and accessories to Republica, an unaffiliated franchise operation with stores in Mexico City, Monterrey, Guadalajara, and Cancun, Mexico. The sale can be made in dollars or in pesos. If Republica agrees to pay in dollars, The Gap, Inc., avoids the complication of dealing in a foreign currency, and the transaction is the same as selling at a Banana Republic store in San Francisco. But suppose Republica orders 1 million pesos (approximately $90,000) worth of inventory from The Gap, Inc. Further, suppose that Republica requests to pay in pesos, and The Gap, Inc., agrees to receive pesos instead of dollars.

The Gap, Inc., will need to convert the pesos to dollars, so the transaction poses a challenge. What if the peso weakens before The Gap, Inc., collects from the Mexican chain? In that case, The Gap, Inc., will not collect as many dollars as expected. The following example shows how to account for **foreign-currency exchange rate** gains and losses.

The Gap, Inc., sells goods to Republica for a price of 1 million pesos on July 28. On that date, a peso is worth $0.086. One month later, on August 28, the peso has weakened against the dollar so that a peso is worth only $0.083. The Gap, Inc., receives 1 million pesos from Republica on August 28, but the dollar value of The Gap, Inc.'s cash receipt is $3,000 less than expected. The Gap, Inc., ends up earning less than hoped for on the transaction. The following journal entries show how The Gap, Inc., would account for these transactions:

Jul 28	Accounts Receivable—Republica (1,000,000 pesos × $0.086)	86,000	
	Sales Revenue		86,000
	Sale on account.		

Aug 28	Cash (1,000,000 pesos × $0.083)	83,000	
	Foreign-Currency Transaction Loss	3,000	
	Accounts Receivable—Republica		86,000
	Collection on account.		

If The Gap, Inc., had required Republica to pay at the time of the sale, The Gap, Inc., would have received pesos worth $86,000. But by selling on account, The Gap, Inc., exposed itself to foreign-currency exchange risk. The Gap, Inc., therefore had a $3,000 *foreign-currency transaction loss* when it received $3,000 less cash than expected. If the peso had increased in value relative to the dollar, The Gap, Inc., would have had a *foreign-currency transaction gain.*

When a company holds a receivable denominated in a foreign currency, it wants the foreign currency to strengthen so that it can be converted into more dollars. Unfortunately, that did not occur for The Gap, Inc., on the sale in this example.

Purchasing in a foreign currency also exposes a company to foreign-currency exchange risk. To illustrate, assume The Gap, Inc., buys a shipment of watches from Excel, Ltd., a Swiss company. The price is 20,000 Swiss francs. On September 15, The Gap, Inc., receives the goods, and the Swiss franc is quoted at $1.15. When The Gap, Inc., pays two weeks later, the Swiss franc has weakened against the dollar—to $1.10. The Gap, Inc., would record the purchase and payment as follows:

Sep 15	Inventory (20,000 Swiss francs × $1.15)	23,000	
	Accounts Payable—Excel, Ltd.		23,000
	Purchase on account.		

Sep 29	Accounts Payable—Excel, Ltd.	23,000	
	Cash (20,000 Swiss francs × $1.10)		22,000
	Foreign-Currency Transaction Gain		1,000
	Payment on account.		

The Swiss franc could have strengthened against the dollar, and The Gap, Inc., would have had a foreign-currency transaction loss. A company with a payable denominated in a foreign currency wants the dollar to get stronger: The payment then costs fewer dollars.

Reporting Foreign-Currency Gains and Losses on the Income Statement

The foreign-currency transaction gain account holds gains on transactions settled in a foreign currency. Likewise, the foreign-currency transaction loss account holds losses on transactions conducted in foreign currencies. Report the *net amount* of these two accounts on the income statement as Other Revenues and Gains, or Other Expenses and Losses, as the case may be. For example, assuming the two transactions we just described were the only two during the year, The Gap, Inc., would combine its $3,000 foreign-currency loss and the $1,000 gain and report the net loss of $2,000 on the income statement as follows:

Other Expenses and Losses:	
Foreign-currency transaction loss, net	$2,000

These gains and losses fall into the "Other" category because they arise from buying and selling foreign currencies, not from the company's main business. The Gap, Inc.'s foreign-currency losses amounted to less than $3 million in 2010, according to financial statement footnotes.

Should We Hedge Our Foreign-Currency-Transaction Risk?

One way for U.S. companies to avoid foreign-currency transaction losses is to insist that international transactions be settled in dollars. This requirement puts the burden of currency translation on the foreign party. But this approach may alienate customers and decrease sales. Another way for a company to protect itself is by hedging. **Hedging** enables the entity to protect itself from losing money in one transaction by engaging in a counterbalancing transaction.

A U.S. company selling goods to be collected in Mexican pesos expects to receive a fixed number of pesos. If the peso is losing value, the U.S. company would expect the pesos to be worth fewer dollars than the amount of the receivable—an expected-loss situation, as we saw for The Gap, Inc.

The U.S. company may have accumulated payables in a foreign currency, such as The Gap, Inc.'s payable to the Swiss company. Losses on pesos may be offset by gains on Swiss francs. Most companies do not have equal amounts of receivables and payables in foreign currency. To obtain a more precise hedge, companies can buy *futures contracts*. These are contracts for foreign currencies to be received in the future. Futures contracts can create a payable to exactly offset a receivable, and vice versa. Many companies that do business internationally, such as The Gap, Inc., use hedging techniques.

Account for Other Items on the Income Statement

Interest Expense and Interest Income

3

Account for other items on the income statement

Covered in Chapters 5, 8, and 9, respectively, interest income represents the return earned on invested money, and interest expense represents the cost of borrowed money. As shown in lines 6 and 7 of Exhibit 11-1, these amounts are very nominal for The Gap, Inc., in comparison with income from operations. Because of reversals of certain transactions in 2010, interest expense actually carried a credit balance, reclassifying it to interest income, increasing the total interest income from $8 million to $14 million for 2010. These amounts indicate that The Gap, Inc., is conducting business in 2010 virtually debt-free on both the receivable and payable sides of the balance sheet.

Corporate Income Taxes

The next important ingredient of earnings is corporate income tax expense, which must be subtracted to arrive at net income. The current maximum federal income tax rate for corporations is 35%. In addition, state income taxes run about 5% in many states. The Gap, Inc.'s fiscal 2010 income tax provision (expense) of $778 amounts to about 39.3% of earnings before income taxes. Thus, we use a rate of 40% to approximate income taxes in our illustrations that follow.

To account for income tax, the corporation measures

▶ *income tax expense*, an expense on the income statement. Income tax expense helps measure net income.

▶ *income tax payable*, a current liability on the balance sheet. Income tax payable is the amount of tax to be paid to the government based on the company's income tax return.

Accounting for income tax follows the principles of accrual accounting. Suppose at the end of fiscal 2012 The Gap, Inc., reports net income before tax (also called **pretax accounting income**) of $1 billion. As we saw previously, The Gap, Inc.'s combined income tax rate is close to 40%. To start this discussion, assume income tax expense and income tax payable are the same. Then on February 1, 2013, the end of its 2012 fiscal year, The Gap, Inc., would record income tax for the year as follows (amounts in millions):

2013	(In millions)		
Feb 1	Income Tax Expense ($1,000 × 0.40)	400	
	Income Tax Payable		400
	Recorded income tax for the year.		

The Gap, Inc.'s financial statements for fiscal 2012 would report these figures (partial, in millions):

Income statement (in millions)		Balance sheet (in millions)	
Income before income tax	$1,000	Current liabilities:	
Income tax expense	(400)	Income tax payable	$400
Net income.................................	$ 600		

In general, income tax expense and income tax payable can be computed as follows:

Income tax *expense*	=	Income before income tax (from the *income statement*)	×	Income tax rate		Income tax *payable*	=	Taxable income (from the *income tax return* filed with the IRS)	×	Income tax rate

The income statement and the income tax return are entirely separate documents:

▶ The *income statement* reports the results of operations.

▶ The *income tax return* is filed with the Internal Revenue Service (IRS) to measure how much tax to pay the government.

For most companies, income tax expense and income tax payable differ. Some revenues and expenses affect income differently for accounting and for tax purposes. The most common difference between accounting income and **taxable income** occurs when a corporation uses straight-line depreciation in its financial statements and accelerated depreciation for the tax return.

Continuing with the The Gap, Inc., illustration, suppose for fiscal 2012 that it had

▶ pretax accounting income of $1 billion on its income statement, and

▶ taxable income of $800 million on its income tax return.

Taxable income is less than accounting income because The Gap, Inc., uses

▶ straight-line depreciation for accounting purposes (say $100 million), and

▶ accelerated depreciation for tax purposes (say $300 million).

The Gap, Inc., would record income tax for fiscal 2012 as follows (dollar amounts in millions and an income tax rate of 40%):

2013	(In millions)		
Feb 1	Income Tax Expense ($1,000 × 0.40)	400	
	Income Tax Payable ($800 × 0.40)		320
	Deferred Tax Liability		80
	Recorded income tax for the year.		

Deferred Tax Liability is usually long-term.

The Gap, Inc.'s financial statements for fiscal 2012 will report the following:

Income statement (in millions)		Balance sheet (in millions)	
Income before income tax	$1,000	Current liabilities:	
Income tax expense	(400)	Income tax payable	$320
Net income	$ 600	Long-term liabilities:	
		Deferred tax liability	80*

*The beginning balance of Deferred tax liability was zero.

In March 2013, The Gap, Inc., would pay income tax payable of $320 million because this is a current liability. The deferred tax liability can be paid later.

For a given year, Income Tax Payable can exceed Income Tax Expense. This occurs when, because of differences in revenue and expenses for book and tax purposes, taxable income exceeds book income. When that occurs, the company debits a Deferred Tax Asset. The remainder of this topic is reserved for a more advanced course.

Effective tax planning, both by in-house tax staff, and externally, through the counsel of the company's independent outside accountants and attorneys, can help lower the company's tax burden and can contribute substantially to improved operating profits.

Which Income Number Predicts Future Profits?

How is income from continuing operations used in investment analysis? Suppose Kimberly Kuhl, an analyst with **Morgan Stanley**, is estimating the value of The Gap, Inc.'s common stock. Kuhl believes that The Gap, Inc., can earn annual income each year equal to its income from ongoing (continuing) operations after tax—$1,204 million for The Gap, Inc.

To estimate the value of The Gap, Inc.'s common stock, financial analysts use a method similar to that described in Chapter 8 to determine the present value of The Gap, Inc.'s stream of future income. Ms. Kuhl must use some interest rate to compute the present value. Assume that an appropriate interest rate (*i*) for the valuation of The Gap, Inc., is 8%. This rate is often based on the company's **weighted-average cost of capital** (WACC), which is a measure of the average returns that creditors and investors demand from the company. WACC is a major focus in corporate finance courses, so we do not discuss it, or how it is computed, in detail. However, you should know that WACC is influenced by the risk that a company might not be able to sustain a certain rate of return into the indefinite future. The higher the risk associated with an investment, the higher the rate of return demanded by investors and creditors, and vice versa. This rate is also called an **investment capitalization rate** because it is used to estimate the value of an investment. Assuming the capitalization rate is reasonable, the computation of the estimated value of the stock of The Gap, Inc., is

$$\text{Estimated value of The Gap, Inc., common stock} = \frac{\text{Estimated annual income in the future}}{\text{Investment capitalization rate}} = \frac{\$1,204 \text{ million}}{0.08} = \$15.05 \text{ billion}$$

Kuhl thus estimates that The Gap, Inc., as a company is worth $15.05 billion. She then computes the company's market capitalization based on its most recent stock price. The Gap, Inc.'s balance sheet at January 29, 2011, reports that the company has 588 million shares of common stock outstanding. The market price of The Gap, Inc., common stock at the beginning of February 2011 is $19.27 per share. The current market value of The Gap, Inc., as a company (market capitalization) as of that date is thus

Current market value of the company	=	Number of shares of common stock outstanding	×	Current market price per share
$11.33 billion	=	588 million	×	$19.27

The investment decision rule is

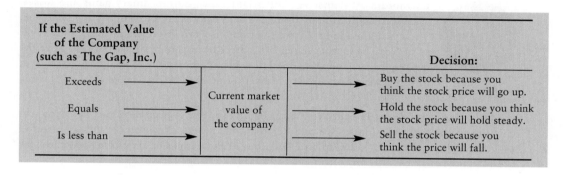

In this case,

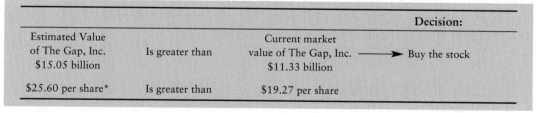

*$15.05 billion/588 million = $25.60

Kuhl believes The Gap, Inc.'s stock price should rise above its current market value of $19.27 to somewhere in a range near $25. Based on this analysis, Morgan Stanley would recommend that investors buy The Gap, Inc., common stock. Tracking the stock over time will reveal whether Morgan Stanley's decision is correct. In late May, 2011, shares of The Gap, Inc. were selling for about $23. As of this date, it appears that Morgan Stanley made a good decision, although the shares had not reached the price that Morgan Stanley predicted. You should use caution in making these types of estimates, because they do not include information about the company that might emerge at a later time, or other market uncertainties. In reality, such estimates are only educated guesses. It is very difficult to predict stock price trends. Although some experts have better track records than others, even the experts often don't predict stock prices accurately!

Discontinued Operations

Most large companies engage in several lines of business. For example, The Gap, Inc., owns The Gap stores, its mid-line store; as well as **Old Navy**, its less-expensive lines; **Banana Republic**, its upscale lines; and **Piperlime**, a specialty line of women's shoes and handbags. **General Electric** makes household appliances and jet engines and owns **NBC**, the media network. We call each identifiable part of a company a *segment* of the business.

A company may sell or discontinue a segment of its business. This did not happen to The Gap, Inc., during 2008 through 2010, the fiscal years covered in Exhibit 11-1. However, during fiscal 2007, The Gap, Inc., closed its Forth and Towne stores, which were designed to appeal to women 35 and older. The discontinuance of a business segment, either through sale or closure, is viewed as a one-time transaction. The Gap, Inc.'s income statement for 2007 (not shown in Exhibit 11-1) reported the loss from the closure of Forth and Towne stores under the heading Discontinued Operations. The loss was reported net of the income tax benefit that the company received from being allowed to deduct the loss on its corporate income tax return. All gains and losses from discontinued operations are shown "net of tax"—that is, the income tax expense (or savings) from the gain (or loss) is subtracted from the item before reporting it in the income statement. *Financial analysts typically do not include discontinued operations in predictions of future corporate income because the discontinued segments will not continue to generate income for the company.*

Extraordinary Items: An IFRS Difference **Extraordinary gains and losses**, also called **extraordinary items**, are both *unusual* for the company and *infrequent*. These gains and losses, like those from discontinued operations, are shown "net of tax" on the income statement. Losses from natural disasters (such as earthquakes, floods, and tornadoes) and the expropriation of company assets by a foreign government are extraordinary. The Gap, Inc., had no extraordinary items on its income statement for fiscal year 2010.

Gains and losses due to lawsuits, restructuring, and the sale of plant assets are *not* extraordinary items. These gains and losses are considered normal business occurrences and are reported as Other Gains and Losses. The Gap, Inc., had none of these items on its income statement for fiscal 2010.

International Financial Reporting Standards (IFRS) do not give special treatment to extraordinary items. Instead, items that are "unusual" in nature or "infrequent" in occurrence are combined with operating income and expenses on the income statement. The result of U.S. companies' adoption of IFRS will be that extraordinary items will eventually disappear from the income statement. In fact, due to the narrow definition, extraordinary items are very rare even under current U.S. GAAP.

Accounting Changes

Companies sometimes change from one accounting method to another, such as from double-declining-balance (DDB) to straight-line depreciation, or from first-in, first-out (FIFO) to average cost for inventory. An accounting change makes it difficult to compare one period with preceding periods. Without detailed information, investors can be misled into thinking that the current year is better or worse than the preceding year, when in fact the only difference is a change in the accounting method.

Two types of accounting changes are most relevant to introductory accounting:

a. *Changes in accounting estimates* include changing the estimated life of a building or equipment and the collectibility of receivables. For these changes, companies report amounts for the *current and future* periods on the new basis. There is no looking back to the past. A change in depreciation method is treated as a change in estimate.

b. *Changes in accounting principles* include most changes in accounting methods, such as from FIFO to average cost for inventory and from one method to another for a revenue or an expense. For these changes, the company reports figures for all periods presented in the income statement—*past as well as current*—on the new basis. The company *retrospectively restates* (looks back and restates) all prior-period amounts that are presented for comparative purposes with the current year, as though the new accounting method had been in effect all along. This lets investors compare all periods that are presented on the same accounting basis. If an accounting change impacts periods prior to the earliest one presented in the current income statement, an adjustment to retained earnings must be made.

Compute Earnings Per Share

The final segment of the income statement reports **earnings per share** (EPS), which is the amount of a company's net income per share of its *outstanding common stock*. EPS is a key measure of a business's success because it shows how much income the company earned for each share of stock. Stock prices are quoted at an amount per share, and investors buy a certain number of shares. EPS is used to help determine the value of a share of stock. EPS is computed as follows:

Compute earnings per share

$$\text{Earnings per share} = \frac{\text{Net income} - \text{Preferred dividends}}{\text{Weighted-average number of shares of common stock outstanding}}$$

The corporation lists its various sources of income separately: continuing operations, discontinued operations, and so on. It also lists the EPS figure for each element of net income. Consider the EPS of The Gap, Inc. The final section of Exhibit 11-1 (lines 11 through 14) shows how companies report EPS. Notice that two EPS computations are made: one for "basic" (the currently outstanding shares) and one for "diluted" (which takes into account potential increases in outstanding shares). Companies must first compute a weighted-average number of shares outstanding. This computation, which is beyond the scope of this textbook, takes into account the changes that might occur in the number of shares outstanding during the year from such things as treasury stock purchases or reissuances. According to Exhibit 11-1, The Gap, Inc., has a "basic" weighted average of 636 million shares of common stock outstanding as of the end of fiscal 2010.

11	Weighted-average number of shares—basic......................................	636
13	Earnings per share—basic ($1,204/636)	$1.88

Effect of Preferred Dividends on Earnings per Share. Recall that EPS is earnings per share of *common* stock. But the holders of preferred stock have first claim on dividends. Therefore, preferred dividends must be subtracted from net income to compute EPS. Preferred dividends are not subtracted from discontinued operations or extraordinary items.

Suppose that The Gap, Inc., had 10,000,000 shares of preferred stock outstanding, each with a $1.00 dividend. The Gap, Inc.'s annual preferred dividends would be $10,000,000 (10,000,000 × $1.00). The $10,000,000 is subtracted from each income subtotal, resulting in the following EPS amounts (recall that The Gap, Inc., has a weighted average of 636 million shares of common stock outstanding):

Basic earnings per share of common stock (636 weighted-average
shares outstanding) (in millions): ($1,204 − $10)/636 .... $1.88

Earnings per Share Dilution. Some corporations have convertible preferred stock, which may be exchanged for common stock. For example, The Gap, Inc., is authorized to issue 30 million shares of preferred stock, which is convertible into shares of its current common stock. The company has not yet issued any of these shares, but could, at some date in the future. When preferred is converted to common, the EPS is *diluted*—reduced—because more common shares are divided into net income. Corporations with complex capital structures present two sets of EPS figures:

▶ EPS based on actual outstanding common shares (*basic* EPS)

▶ EPS based on outstanding common shares plus the additional shares that can arise from conversion of the preferred stock into common (*diluted* EPS)

The Gap, Inc.'s weighted-average diluted number of shares as of January 29, 2011 (the end of fiscal 2010) is 641 million. Therefore, the EPS on a diluted basis is reduced by about $0.01 per share to account for the additional shares outstanding on a diluted basis (line 14 of Exhibit 11-1). The computations for diluted EPS are similar to those illustrated previously for basic EPS.

What Should You Analyze to Gain an Overall Picture of a Company?

Two key figures used in financial analysis are

- ▶ net income (or income from continuing operations), and
- ▶ cash flow from operations.

For a given period, The Gap, Inc.'s net income and net cash flow from operating activities may chart different paths. Accounting income arises from the accrual process as follows:

> Total revenues and gains − Total expenses and losses = Net income (or Net loss)

As we have seen, revenues and gains are recorded when they occur, regardless of when the company receives or pays cash.

Net cash flow, on the other hand, is based solely on cash receipts and cash payments. During 2012, a company may have a hefty net income. But the company may have weak cash flow because it cannot collect from customers. The reverse may also be true: The company may have abundant cash but little income.

The income statement and the cash flows statement often paint different pictures of the company. Which statement provides better information? Neither: Both statements are needed, along with the balance sheet and statement of stockholders' equity, for an overall view of the business. In Chapter 12 we'll cover the statement of cash flows in detail.

Correcting Retained Earnings

Occasionally a company records a revenue or an expense incorrectly. If the error is corrected in a later period, the balance of Retained Earnings is wrong until corrected. Corrections to Retained Earnings for errors of an earlier period are called **prior-period adjustments**. The prior-period adjustment appears on the statement of retained earnings.

Assume that NPR Corporation recorded 2012 income tax expense as $30,000, but the correct amount was $40,000. This error understated expenses by $10,000 and overstated net income by $10,000. The government sent a bill in 2013 for the additional $10,000, and this alerted NPR to the mistake.

This accounting error requires a prior-period adjustment. Prior-period adjustments are not reported on the income statement because they relate to an earlier accounting period. This prior-period adjustment would appear on the statement of retained earnings, as shown in Exhibit 11-2, with all amounts assumed:

EXHIBIT 11-2 │ Effects of Prior-Period Adjustments

NPR Corporation Statement of Retained Earnings Year Ended December 31, 2013	
Retained earnings balance, December 31, 2012, as originally reported	$390,000
Prior-period adjustment—debit to correct error in recording income tax expense of 2012	(10,000)
Retained earnings balance, December 31, 2012, as adjusted	380,000
Net income for 2013	110,000
	490,000
Dividends for 2013	(40,000)
Retained earnings balance, December 31, 2013	$450,000

Analyze the Statement of Comprehensive Income and the Statement of Stockholders' Equity

Reporting Comprehensive Income

All companies report net income or net loss on their income statements. As we saw in Chapter 8, companies with unrealized gains and losses on certain investments and foreign-currency translation adjustments also report another income figure. **Comprehensive income** is the company's change in total stockholders' equity from all sources other than from the owners of the business. Comprehensive income includes net income plus

▶ unrealized gains (losses) on available-for-sale investments, and

▶ foreign-currency translation adjustments.

5

Analyze the statement of comprehensive income and the statement of stockholders' equity

These types of other comprehensive income were discussed in Chapter 8. There are others, but discussion of them is reserved for later courses.

Items of comprehensive income, other than net income, do not enter into the determination of earnings per share.

Exhibit 11-3 on page 664 presents Comprehensive Income as part of the Consolidated Statement of Stockholders' Equity of The Gap, Inc., as of January 29, 2011 (end of fiscal 2010). Comprehensive Income is listed in the far right column. Notice that it includes net income of $1,204 million from the income statement in Exhibit 11-1 (line 10), plus a foreign-currency translation adjustment (net of taxes) of $37 million. The other two adjustments pertain to changes in fair value of derivative financial instruments [($31) + $24], which are a type of available-for-sale investment. Both of these items are also shown net of taxes.

For accounting periods ending after November 15, 2011, comprehensive income for a company must be presented either alone in a separate **statement of comprehensive income** or combined with net income into a unified statement of comprehensive income, rather than as a part of the statement of stockholders' equity. Therefore, after November 15, 2011, everything we see in lines 3 through 5 in the far right column of Exhibit 11-3 will be presented either in a separate statement, or be combined with net income into a Statement of Comprehensive Income. The Gap, Inc.'s unified Consolidated Statement of Comprehensive Income, including both net income and other comprehensive income, for the year ended January 29, 2011 (fiscal 2010), would appear as follows:

The Gap, Inc. Consolidated Statement of Comprehensive Income Year Ended January 29, 2011	
(in millions)	
Net income:	
Net sales	$14,664
Cost of goods sold and occupancy expenses	8,775
Gross profit	5,889
Operating expenses	3,921
Operating income	1,968
Interest income	14
Income before income taxes	1,982
Income taxes	778
Net Income*	1,204
Other comprehensive income:	
Foreign currency translation, net of tax ($6)	37
Change in fair value of derivative financial instruments, net of tax ($19)	(31)
Reclassification adjustment for realized losses on derivative financial instruments, net of tax benefit of $14	24
Comprehensive income	1,234

*Earnings per share: (identical to Exhibit 11-1)

EXHIBIT 11-3 | Statement of Stockholders' Equity

THE GAP, INC.
Consolidated Statement of Stockholders' Equity

| ($ and shares in millions except per share amounts) | Common stock | | Additional Paid-in Capital | Retained Earnings | Accumulated Other Comprehensive Income | Treasury Stock | | Total | Comprehensive Income |
	Shares	Amount				Shares	Amount		
1. Balance at January 30, 2010	1,106	55	2,935	10,815	155	(430)	(9,069)	4,891	
2. Net income				1,204				1,204	$1,204
3. Foreign currency translation, net of tax $(6)					37			37	37
4. Change in fair value of derivative financial instruments, not of tax benefit of $(19)					(31)			(31)	(31)
5. Reclassification adjustment for realized losses on derivative financial instruments, net of tax benefit of $14					24			24	24
6. Repurchases of common stock						(96)	(1,956)	(1,956)	
7. Reissuance of treasury stock pursuant to stock option and other stock award plans, net of shares withheld for employee taxes			(89)			8	159	70	
8. Tax benefit exercise of stock options and vesting of stock units			11					11	
9. Share-based compensation, net of estimated forfeitures			82					82	
10. Cash dividends				(252)				(252)	
11. Balance at January 29, 2011	1,106	$55	$2,939	$11,767	$185	(518)	$(10,866)	$4,080	$1,234

The unified version of the statement (shown) would include all revenues and expenses that are a part of net income, followed by items of other comprehensive income (gains and losses on available-for-sale securities, foreign currency translation adjustments, and other items, shown net of tax). The earnings per share section would be then be added, and would be identical to that shown in Exhibit 11-1. *Items of other comprehensive income do not impact earnings per share.* This change will harmonize U.S. GAAP reporting practices for comprehensive income with those prescribed by IFRS.

The separate statement (not shown) would begin with net income ($1,204) and then only list items of other comprehensive income, as well as total comprehensive income.

Reporting Stockholders' Equity

The **statement of stockholders' equity** reports the reasons for all the changes in the stockholders' equity section of the balance sheet during the period.

Take another look at Exhibit 11-3, the Consolidated Statement of Stockholders' Equity for The Gap, Inc. Study its format. There is a column for each element of equity, starting with Common Stock on the left. The second column from the far right reports the total. The top row (line 1) reports beginning balances as of January 30, 2010, taken from the prior period's statement of stockholders' equity. The rows then report the various transactions that affected equity, starting

EXHIBIT 11-4 | The Gap, Inc., Consolidated Balance Sheet (Partial)

The Gap, Inc.
Consolidated Balance Sheet (Partial)
January 29, 2011

(In millions)	
Total assets..	$ 7,065
Total liabilities	$ 2,985
Stockholders' equity:	
Common stock, $0.05 par, shares issued—1,106, shares outstanding—588	55
Additional paid-in capital	2,939
Retained earnings	11,767
Accumulated other comprehensive income	185
Treasury stock, 518 shares...	(10,866)
Total stockholders' equity...	4,080
Total liabilities and stockholders' equity	$ 7,065

with net income (line 2). The statement ends with the January 29, 2011, balances (line 11). All the amounts on the bottom line appear on the ending balance sheet, given in Exhibit 11-4.

Let's examine the changes in The Gap, Inc.'s stockholders' equity during fiscal 2010.

Net Income (Line 2). During fiscal 2010, The Gap, Inc., earned net income (net earnings) of $1,204 million, which increased Retained Earnings. Trace net income from the Consolidated Statements of Income (Exhibit 11-1, p. 652) to the Consolidated Statement of Stockholders' Equity (Exhibit 11-3).

Accumulated Other Comprehensive Income (Lines 3 through 5).
Accumulated Other Comprehensive Income summarizes the history of changes to stockholders' equity brought about by elements of comprehensive income other than net income (see discussion on page 663).

At January 30, 2010, The Gap, Inc. had Accumulated Other Comprehensive Income from previous years of $155 million (line 1). During fiscal 2010, it made a foreign-currency translation adjustment that increased accumulated other comprehensive income by $37 million (line 3). Also, during fiscal 2010, the company recorded an unrealized loss of $31 million from the change in fair value of derivative financial instruments (available-for-sale) and made another positive adjustment of $24 million to reclassify realized losses from these investments. Thus, the net addition to accumulated other comprehensive income is $30 million (the sum of lines 3 through 5). The company ended fiscal 2010 with accumulated other comprehensive income of $185 million ($155 million + $30 million).

As discussed earlier, for periods ending after November 15, 2011, companies will be required to present a separate statement of comprehensive income for each reporting period. Since the details of additions and deductions to comprehensive income will then be presented in that statement, there is no need for them to appear as separate additions or deductions to accumulated other comprehensive income in the statement of stockholders' equity. Rather, only the current year's *net change in comprehensive income other than net income* ($1,234 − $1,204 = $30) will be shown as a lump sum incremental change (either an addition or a deduction) to accumulated other comprehensive income. Net income or net loss (as shown in Exhibit 11-1) will continue to appear as an addition to or a deduction from retained earnings in the statement of stockholders' equity, as shown in Exhibit 11-3.

Treasury Stock Transactions (Lines 6 and 7).
The company repurchased 96 million shares of its own stock for $1.956 billion in fiscal 2010, resulting in a reduction to total stockholders' equity. It then reissued 8 million shares for $70 million, resulting in a reduction in treasury stock in the amount of $159 million and a reduction in additional paid-in capital of $89 million.

Stock-Based Compensation (Lines 8 and 9). The company compensated employees in connection with the exercise of employee stock options. Although no additional shares were issued, this had a total impact of $93 million on stockholders' equity. We discussed the use of stock in employee compensation briefly in Chapter 10. Further discussion of this topic is beyond the scope of this text.

Declaration of Cash Dividends (Line 10). The Gap, Inc., declared cash dividends of $0.40 per share in fiscal 2010. This resulted in a reduction in retained earnings of $252 million. The per-share impact is shown on line 15 in Exhibit 11-1.

Differentiate Management's and Auditors' Responsibilites in Financial Reporting

Management's Responsibility

⑥

Differentiate management's and auditors' responsibilities in financial reporting

Management issues a report on internal control over financial reporting, along with the company's financial statements. Exhibit 11-5 is an excerpt from the report of management for The Gap, Inc.

Management declares its responsibility for the internal controls over financial reporting in accordance with the Securities Exchange Act of 1934. Management also states that it has conducted an assessment of internal controls over financial reporting based on the framework established by the Committee of Sponsoring Organizations (COSO) of the Treadway Commission and has concluded that, as of January 29, 2011, internal controls over financial reporting are effective. In addition, management states that the internal controls of the company have been audited by the company's outside auditors, and refers to their report, an excerpt of which is contained in Exhibit 11-6 in the next section.

Auditor Report

The Securities Exchange Act of 1934 requires companies that issue their stock publicly to file audited financial statements with the SEC. Companies engage outside auditors who are certified public accountants to examine their financial statements as well as their internal controls over financial reporting. The independent auditors decide whether the company's financial statements comply with GAAP. They must also decide whether the internal controls of the company meet certain standards. They then issue a combined audit report on both the financial statements and the company's system of internal controls over financial reporting. Exhibit 11-6 contains this report for The Gap, Inc., and its subsidiaries as of January 29, 2011.

The audit report is addressed to the board of directors and stockholders of the company. A partner of the auditing firm signs the firm's name to the report. In this case, the auditing firm is the San Francisco office of **Deloitte & Touche, LLP** (limited liability partnership).

EXHIBIT 11-5 | Statement of Management's Responsibility

Management is responsible for establishing and maintaining an adequate system of internal control over financial reporting. Management conducted an assessment of internal control over financial reporting based on the framework established by the Committee of Sponsoring Organizations of the Treadway Commission in *Internal Control—Integrated Framework*. Based on the assessment, management concluded that, as of January 29, 2011, our internal control over financial reporting is effective. The Company's internal control over financial reporting as of January 29, 2011, has been audited by Deloitte & Touche, LLP, an independent registered public accounting firm, as stated in its report, which is included herein.

EXHIBIT 11-6 | Independent Auditors' Report

To the Board of Directors and Stockholders of The Gap, Inc.

We have audited the accompanying consolidated balance sheets of The Gap, Inc., and subsidiaries (the "Company") as of January 29, 2011, and January 30, 2010, and the related consolidated statements of earnings, stockholders' equity, and cash flows for each of the three fiscal years in the period ended January 29, 2011. We also have audited the Company's internal control over financial reporting as of January 29, 2010, based on criteria established by *Internal Control—Integrated Framework* issued by the Committee of Sponsoring Organizations of the Treadway Commission. The Company's management is responsible for these financial statements, for maintaining effective internal control over financial reporting, and for its assessment of the effectiveness of internal control over financial reporting, included in the accompanying Management's Report on Internal Control over Financial Reporting. Our responsibility is to express an opinion on these financial statements and opinion on the Company's internal control over financial reporting based on our audits.

We conducted our audits in accordance with the standards of the Public Company Accounting Oversight Board (United States). Those standards require that we plan and perform the audit to obtain reasonable assurance about whether the financial statements are free from material misstatements and whether effective internal control over financial reporting was maintained in all material respects...We believe that our audits provide a reasonable basis for our opinions.

A company's internal control over financial reporting is a process designed by, or under the supervision of, the company's...financial officers...and effected by the Company's board of directors...to provide reasonable assurance regarding the reliability of financial reporting and the preparation of financial statements...in accordance with generally accepted accounting principles.

Because of the inherent limitations of internal control over financial reporting, including the possibility of collusion or improper management override of controls, material misstatements due to error or fraud may not be prevented or detected on a timely basis. Also, projections of any evaluation of the effectiveness of internal control over financial reporting to future periods are subject to the risk that the controls may become inadequate because of changes in conditions, or that the degree of compliance with the policies or procedures may deteriorate.

In our opinion, the consolidated financial statement referred to above present fairly, in all material respects, the financial position of The Gap, Inc., and subsidiaries as of January 29, 2011, and January 30, 2010, and the results of their operations and their cash flows for each of the three years in the period ended January 29, 2011, in conformity with accounting principles generally accepted in the United States of America. Also, in our opinion, the Company maintained, in all material respects, effective internal control over financial reporting as of January 29, 2011, based on the criteria established in *Internal Control—Integrated Framework* issued by the Committee of Sponsoring Organizations of the Treadway Commission.

/s/ Deloitte & Touche, LLP

San Francisco, California

March 28, 2011

The combined audit report on financial statements and internal control over financial reporting typically contains five paragraphs:

▶ The first paragraph identifies the audited financial statements as well as the company being audited. It also states the responsibility of the company's management as well as the auditor's responsibilities.

▶ The second paragraph describes how the audit was performed in accordance with generally accepted auditing standards of the Public Company Accounting Oversight Board (an independent regulatory body with SEC oversight). These are the standards used by auditors as the benchmark for evaluating audit quality.

► The third paragraph describes in detail what a system of internal controls is, noting that it should be designed to provide reasonable assurance that transactions are recorded to permit preparation of financial statements that are fairly presented in conformity with GAAP.

► The fourth paragraph describes inherent limitations in the system of internal controls and notes that, at best, the system of internal controls can only provide reasonable assurance that financial statements are fairly presented.

► The fifth paragraph expresses the auditor's combined opinion on both the fairness of financial statements, in all material respects, in conformity with GAAP, and the effectiveness of the company's internal controls over financial reporting. Deloitte & Touche, LLP, is expressing an **unqualified (clean) opinion** on both the fairness of the financial statements and the effectiveness of The Gap, Inc.'s internal controls. The unqualified opinion is the highest statement of assurance that an independent certified public accountant can express.

The independent audit adds credibility to the financial statements of a company as well as to its system of internal controls. It is no accident that financial reporting and auditing are more advanced in the United States than anywhere else in the world and that U.S. capital markets are the envy of the world.

DECISION GUIDELINES

USING THE INCOME STATEMENT AND RELATED NOTES IN INVESTMENT ANALYSIS

Suppose you've completed your studies, taken a job, and been fortunate to save $10,000. Now you are ready to start investing. These guidelines provide a framework for using accounting information for investment analysis.

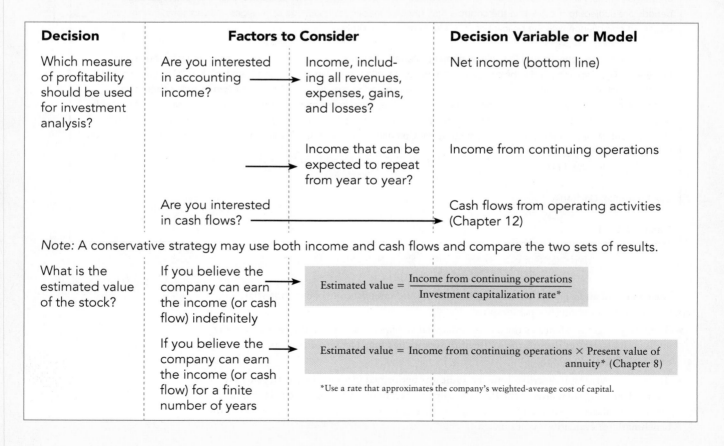

Decision	Factors to Consider		Decision Variable or Model
Which measure of profitability should be used for investment analysis?	Are you interested in accounting income? →	Income, including all revenues, expenses, gains, and losses?	Net income (bottom line)
	→	Income that can be expected to repeat from year to year?	Income from continuing operations
	Are you interested in cash flows? ───────→		Cash flows from operating activities (Chapter 12)

Note: A conservative strategy may use both income and cash flows and compare the two sets of results.

What is the estimated value of the stock?	If you believe the company can earn the income (or cash flow) indefinitely →	$$\text{Estimated value} = \frac{\text{Income from continuing operations}}{\text{Investment capitalization rate*}}$$
	If you believe the company can earn the income (or cash flow) for a finite number of years →	$$\text{Estimated value} = \text{Income from continuing operations} \times \text{Present value of annuity* (Chapter 8)}$$

*Use a rate that approximates the company's weighted-average cost of capital.

Decision	Factors to Consider		Decision Variable or Model
How does risk affect the value of the stock?	If the investment is high risk ⟶	Increase the investment capitalization rate	
	If the investment is low risk ⟶	Decrease the investment capitalization rate	

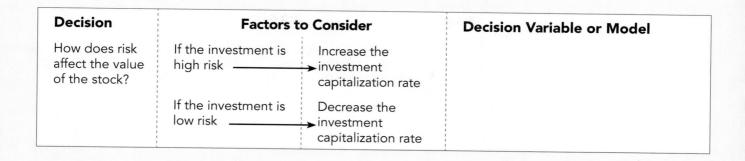

END-OF-CHAPTER SUMMARY PROBLEM

The following information was taken from the ledger of Maxim, Inc.:

Prior-period adjustment— credit to Retained Earnings	$ 5,000	Treasury stock, common (5,000 shares at cost)	$ 25,000
Gain on sale of plant assets	21,000	Selling expenses	78,000
Cost of goods sold	380,000	Common stock, no par,	
Income tax expense (saving):		45,000 shares issued	180,000
Continuing operations	32,000	Sales revenue	620,000
Discontinued operations	8,000	Interest expense	30,000
Extraordinary gain	10,000	Extraordinary gain	26,000
Preferred stock, 8%, $100 par,		Income from discontinued	
500 shares issued	50,000	operations	20,000
Dividends	16,000	Loss due to lawsuit	11,000
Retained earnings, beginning, as originally reported	103,000	General expenses	62,000

▶ Requirement

1. Prepare a single-step income statement (with all revenues and gains grouped together) and a statement of retained earnings for Maxim, Inc., for the current year ended December 31, 2012. Include the earnings-per-share presentation and show computations. Assume no changes in the stock accounts during the year.

► Answers

Maxim, Inc.
Income Statement
Year Ended December 31, 2012

Revenue and gains:		
Sales revenue..		$620,000
Gain on sale of plant assets..		21,000
Total revenues and gains		641,000
Expenses and losses:		
Cost of goods sold	$380,000	
Selling expenses	78,000	
General expenses	62,000	
Interest expense	30,000	
Loss due to lawsuit	11,000	
Income tax expense..	32,000	
Total expenses and losses		593,000
Income from continuing operations..		48,000
Discontinued operations, $20,000, less income tax, $8,000		12,000
Income before extraordinary item		60,000
Extraordinary gain, $26,000, less income tax, $10,000		16,000
Net income..		$ 76,000
Earnings per share:*		
Income from continuing operations		
[($48,000 − $4,000)/40,000 shares]		$ 1.10
Income from discontinued operations		
($12,000/40,000 shares)...		0.30
Income before extraordinary item		
[($60,000 − $4,000)/40,000 shares]		1.40
Extraordinary gain ($16,000/40,000 shares)............................		0.40
Net income [($76,000 − $4,000)/40,000 shares]....................		$ 1.80

*Computations:

$$EPS = \frac{Income - Preferred\ dividends}{Common\ shares\ outstanding}$$

Preferred dividends: $50,000 × 0.08 = $4,000
Common shares outstanding:
    45,000 shares issued − 5,000 treasury shares = 40,000 shares outstanding

Maxim, Inc.
Statement of Retained Earnings
Year Ended December 31, 2012

Retained earnings balance, beginning, as originally reported	$103,000
Prior-period adjustment—credit	5,000
Retained earnings balance, beginning, as adjusted	108,000
Net income for current year	76,000
	184,000
Dividends for current year	(16,000)
Retained earnings balance, ending	$168,000

REVIEW | The Income Statement

Quick Check (Answers are given on page 696.)

1. The quality of earnings suggests that
   a. income from continuing operations is better than income from one-time transactions.
   b. continuing operations and one-time transactions are of equal importance.
   c. stockholders want the corporation to earn enough income to be able to pay its debts.
   d. net income is the best measure of the results of operations.

2. Which statement is true?
   a. Extraordinary items are part of discontinued operations.
   b. Extraordinary items are combined with continuing operations on the income statement.
   c. Discontinued operations are a separate category on the income statement.
   d. All of the above are true.

3. Kelley Corporation earned $6.39 per share of its common stock. Suppose you capitalize Kelley's income at 9%. How much are you willing to pay for a share of Kelley stock?
   a. $6.39   c. $100.00
   b. $57.51   d. $71.00

4. The following is a selected portion of Mod Style's income statement.

		Year Ended	
	2013	2012	2011
Income (loss) from continuing operations	$(20,000)	$61,000	$160,000
Income (loss) from discontinued operations	(17,000)	(1,500)	500
Net income (loss)	$(37,000)	$59,500	$160,500
Earnings (loss) per share from continuing operations:			
Basic..	$ (0.40)	$ 1.20	$ 2.76
Earnings (loss) per share from discontinued operations:			
Basic..	$ (0.34)	$ (0.03)	$ 0.01
Earnings (loss) per share:			
Basic..	$ (0.74)	$ 1.17	$ 2.77

Mod Style has no preferred stock outstanding. How many shares of common stock did Mod Style have outstanding during fiscal year 2013?
   a. 27,027 shares   c. 50,000 shares
   b. 51,000 shares   d. 92,500 shares

5. You are taking a vacation to Italy, and you buy euros for $1.50. On your return, you cash in your unused euros for $1.20. During your vacation,
   a. the euro rose against the dollar.   c. the dollar rose against the euro.
   b. the euro gained value.   d. the dollar lost value.

6. Baylor County, Texas, purchased earth-moving equipment from a Canadian company. The cost was $1,400,000 Canadian, and the Canadian dollar was quoted at $0.97. A month later, Baylor County paid its debt, and the Canadian dollar was quoted at $0.98. What was Baylor County's cost of the equipment?
   a. $14,000   c. $1,414,000
   b. $1,372,000   d. $1,358,000

7. Why is it important for companies to report their accounting changes to the public?
   a. Accounting changes affect dividends, and investors want dividends.
   b. Some accounting changes are more extraordinary than others.
   c. It is important for the results of operations to be compared between periods.
   d. Most accounting changes increase net income, and investors need to know why the increase in net income occurred.

8. Other comprehensive income
   a. affects earnings per share.
   b. has no effect on income tax.
   c. includes unrealized gains and losses on available-for-sale investments.
   d. includes extraordinary gains and losses.

9. Go Home Systems earned income before tax of $180,000. Taxable income was $150,000, and the income tax rate was 32%. Go Home recorded income tax with this journal entry:

a.	Income Tax Payable	57,600	
	Income Tax Expense		48,000
	Deferred Tax Liability		9,600
b.	Income Tax Expense	48,000	
	Income Tax Payable		48,000
c.	Income Tax Expense	57,600	
	Income Tax Payable		57,600
d.	Income Tax Expense	57,600	
	Income Tax Payable		48,000
	Deferred Tax Liability		9,600

10. Deferred Tax Liability is usually

	Type of Account	Reported on the
a.	Long-term	Balance sheet
b.	Short-term	Income statement
c.	Long-term	Income statement
d.	Short-term	Statement of stockholders' equity

11. The main purpose of the statement of stockholders' equity is to report
    a. comprehensive income.
    b. results of operations.
    c. financial position.
    d. reasons for changes in the equity accounts.

12. An auditor report by independent accountants
    a. ensures that the financial statements are error-free.
    b. gives investors assurance that the company's financial statements conform to GAAP.
    c. gives investors assurance that the company's stock is a safe investment.
    d. is ultimately the responsibility of the management of the client company.

Accounting Vocabulary

channel stuffing (p. 653) A type of financial statement fraud that is accomplished by shipping more to customers (usually around the end of the year) than they ordered, with the expectation that they may return some or all of it. The objective is to record more revenue than the company has actually earned with legitimate sales and shipments.

clean opinion (p. 668) An *unqualified opinion*.

comprehensive income (p. 663) A company's change in total stockholders' equity from all sources other than from the owners of the business.

earnings per share (EPS) (p. 661) Amount of a company's net income per share of its outstanding common stock.

earnings quality (p. 651) The characteristics of an earnings number that make it most useful for decision making. The degree to which earnings are an accurate reflection of underlying economic events for both revenues and expenses, and the

extent to which earnings from a company's core operations are improving over time. Assuming that revenues and expenses are measured accurately, high-quality earnings are reflected in steadily improving sales and steadily declining costs over time, so that income from continuing operations follows a high and improving pattern over time.

extraordinary gains and losses (p. 660) Also called *extraordinary items*, these gains and losses are both unusual for the company and infrequent.

extraordinary items (p. 660) An *extraordinary gain or loss*.

foreign-currency exchange rate (p. 655) The measure of one country's currency against another country's currency.

hedging (p. 656) To protect oneself from losing money in one transaction by engaging in a counterbalancing transaction.

investment capitalization rate (p. 658) An earnings rate used to estimate the value of an investment in stock.

pretax accounting income (p. 657) Income before tax on the income statement.

prior-period adjustment (p. 662) A correction to beginning balance of retained earnings for an error of an earlier period.

statement of comprehensive income (p. 663) A statement showing all of the changes in stockholders' equity during a period other than transactions with owners. The statement of comprehensive income includes net income as well as other comprehensive income, such as gains/losses on available-for-sale securities and foreign currency translation adjustments.

statement of stockholders' equity (p. 664) Reports the changes in all categories of stockholders' equity during the period.

taxable income (p. 657) The basis for computing the amount of tax to pay the government.

unqualified (clean) opinion (p. 668) An audit opinion stating that the financial statements are reliable.

weighted-average cost of capital (p. 658) The combined rate of return expected for a company by its creditors and investors. In general, the higher the risk associated with the company, the greater the expected returns by creditors and investors.

ASSESS YOUR PROGRESS

Short Exercises

S11-1 (*Learning Objective 1: Evaluate quality of earnings*) Research has shown that over 50% of financial statement frauds are committed by companies that improperly recognize revenue. What does this mean? Describe the most common ways companies improperly recognize revenue.

S11-2 (*Learning Objective 1: Evaluate quality of earnings*) Study the 2012 income statement of Original Imports, Inc., and answer these questions about the company:

Original Imports, Inc.
Consolidated Statement of Operations (Adapted)

			Year Ended	
(In thousands except per share amounts)			2012	2011
1	Net sales		$1,825,425	$1,806,475
	Operating costs and expenses:			
2	Cost of sales (including buying and store occupancy costs)		1,121,490	1,045,580
3	Selling, general, and administrative expenses		549,850	526,150
4	Depreciation and amortization		55,275	48,450
			1,726,615	1,620,180
5	Operating income (loss)		98,810	186,295
	Nonoperating (income) and expenses:			
6	Interest and investment income		(2,625)	(2,710)
7	Interest expense		1,725	1,630
			(900)	(1,080)
8	Income (loss) from continuing operations before income taxes		99,710	187,375
9	Provision (benefit) for income taxes		36,684	69,615
10	Income (loss) from continuing operations		63,026	117,760
11	Discontinued operations:			
12	Income (loss) from discontinued operations		(2,400)	280
13	Net income (loss)		$ 60,626	$ 118,040
	Earnings (loss) per share from continuing operations:			
14	Basic		$ 0.39	$ 1.62
	Earnings (loss) per share from discontinued operations:			
15	Basic		$ (0.03)	$ 0.00
	Earnings (loss) per share:			
16	Basic		$ 0.36	$ 1.62

1. How much gross profit did Original earn on the sale of its products in 2012? How much was income from continuing operations? Net income?
2. At the end of 2012, what dollar amount of net income would most sophisticated investors use to predict Original's net income for 2013 and beyond? Name this item, give its amount, and state your reason.

S11-3 (*Learning Objective 1: Prepare a complex income statement*) Amazing Way, Inc., reported the following items, listed in no particular order at December 31, 2012 (in thousands):

Other gains (losses)	$(19,000)	Extraordinary gain	$ 3,000
Net sales revenue...................	181,000	Cost of goods sold.................	73,000
Loss on discontinued		Operating expenses	55,000
operations	13,000	Accounts receivable...............	21,000

Income tax of 35% applies to all items.

Prepare Amazing Way's income statement for the year ended December 31, 2012. Omit earnings per share.

S11-4 (*Learning Objective 1: Value a company's stock*) For fiscal year 2012, Mango Computer, Inc., reported net sales of $19,323 million, net income of $1,997 million, and no significant discontinued operations, extraordinary items, or accounting changes. Earnings per share was $2.20. At a capitalization rate of 5%, how much should one share of Mango stock be worth? Compare your estimated stock price with the market price of $94.02 as quoted in the newspaper. Based on your estimated market value, should you buy, hold, or sell Mango stock?

S11-5 (*Learning Objective 2: Account for foreign-currency gains and losses*) Suppose Cola Corp. sells soft drink syrup to a Russian company on September 12. Cola Corp. agrees to accept 200,000 Russian rubles. On the date of sale, the ruble is quoted at $0.34. Cola Corp. collects half the receivable on October 18 when the ruble is worth $0.30. Then on November 15, when the foreign-exchange rate of the ruble is $0.36, Cola Corp. collects the final amount.

Journalize these three transactions for Cola Corp.

S11-6 (*Learning Objective 2: Account for foreign-currency gains and losses*) Boat Belting sells goods for 900,000 Mexican pesos. The foreign-exchange rate for a peso is $0.094 on the date of sale. Boat Belting then collects cash on April 24 when the exchange rate for a peso is $0.099. Record Boat's cash collection.

Boat Belting buys inventory for 21,000 Swiss francs. A Swiss franc costs $1.12 on the purchase date. Record Boat Belting's payment of cash on October 25, when the exchange rate for a Swiss Franc is $1.14.

In these two scenarios, which currencies strengthened? Which currencies weakened?

S11-7 (*Learning Objectives 1, 3: Evaluate quality of earnings, use other information on an income statement*) Jamison Cruise Lines, Inc., reported the following income statement for the year ended December 31, 2012:

	Millions
Operating revenues	$95,500
Operating expenses	84,100
Operating income..	11,400
Other revenue (expense), net	1,000
Income from continuing operations......................................	12,400
Discontinued operations, net of tax......................................	1,100
Net income..	$13,500

▶ Requirements

1. Were Jamison's discontinued operations more like an expense or revenue? How can you tell?
2. Should the discontinued operations of Jamison be included in or excluded from net income? State your reason.

3. Suppose you are working as a financial analyst and your job is to predict Jamison's net income for 2013 and beyond. Which item from the income statement will you use for your prediction? Identify its amount. Why will you use this item?

S11-8 (*Learning Objective 3: Account for a corporation's income tax*) Apex Marine, Inc., had income before income tax of $117,000 and taxable income of $91,000 for 2012, the company's first year of operations. The income tax rate is 30%.

1. Make the entry to record Apex Marine's income taxes for 2012.
2. Show what Apex Marine will report on its 2012 income statement starting with income before income tax. Also show what Apex Marine will report for current and long-term liabilities on its December 31, 2012, balance sheet.

S11-9 (*Learning Objective 4: Compute earnings per share*) Return to the Amazing Way data in Short Exercise 11-3. Amazing Way had 10,000 shares of common stock outstanding during 2012. Amazing Way declared and paid preferred dividends of $6,000 during 2012.

Report Amazing Way's earnings per share on the income statement. (Round all calculations to two decimal places.)

S11-10 (*Learning Objective 5: Report comprehensive income*) Use the Amazing Way data in Short Exercise S11-3. In addition, Amazing Way had unrealized gains of $1,100 on investments and a $2,400 foreign-currency translation adjustment (a gain) during 2012. Both amounts are net of tax. Start with Amazing Way's net income from S11-3 and show how the company could report other comprehensive income on its 2012 financial statements.

Should Amazing Way report earnings per share for other comprehensive income? State why or why not.

S11-11 (*Learning Objective 4: Interpret earnings-per-share data*) Baxter Motor Company has preferred stock outstanding and issued additional common stock during the year.

1. Give the basic equation to compute earnings per share of common stock for net income.
2. List the income items for which Baxter must report earnings-per-share data.
3. What makes earnings per share so useful as a business statistic?

S11-12 (*Learning Objective 5: Report a prior-period adjustment*) iLife, Inc., was set to report the following statement of retained earnings for the year ended December 31, 2012:

iLife, Inc. Statement of Retained Earnings Year Ended December 31, 2012	
Retained earnings, December 31, 2011	$ 70,000
Net income for 2012	85,000
Dividends for 2012	(29,000)
Retained earnings, December 31, 2012	$126,000

Before issuing its 2012 financial statements, iLife learned that net income of 2011 was overstated by $18,000. Prepare iLife's 2012 statement of retained earnings to show the correction of the error—that is, the prior-period adjustment.

S11-13 (*Learning Objective 5: Analyze comprehensive income and the statement of stockholders' equity*) Use the statement of stockholders' equity to answer the following questions about Osborn Electronics Corporation:

Osborn Electronics Corporation
Statement of Stockholders' Equity
For the Year Ended December 31, 2012

		Common Stock $10 Par	Additional Paid-in Capital	Retained Earnings	Treasury Stock	Accumulated Other Comprehensive Income	Total Stockholders' Equity
1	Balance, December 31, 2011	$100,000	$ 80,000	$185,000	$(21,000)	$ 5,000	$ 349,000
2	Issuance of stock	200,000	1,180,000				1,380,000
3	Net income			70,000			70,000
4	Cash dividends			(20,000)			(20,000)
5	Stock dividends—10%	30,000	42,000	(72,000)			0
6	Purchase of treasury stock				(8,000)		(8,000)
7	Sale of treasury stock		10,000		3,000		13,000
8	Other comprehensive income					19,000	19,000
9	Balance, December 31, 2012	$330,000	$1,312,000	$163,000	$(26,000)	$24,000	$1,803,000

1. How much cash did the issuance of common stock bring in during 2012?
2. What was the effect of the stock dividends on Osborn's retained earnings? On total paid-in capital? On total stockholders' equity? On total assets?
3. What was the cost of the treasury stock that Osborn purchased during 2012? What was the cost of the treasury stock that Osborn sold during the year? For how much did Osborn sell the treasury stock during 2012?
4. How much was Osborn's net income?
5. Osborne re-valued available-for-sale investments during the year, resulting in an unrealized gain of $9,000. They also consolidated a foreign subsidiary, resulting in a currency translation gain of $10,000. How much was comprehensive income? How much should be added to Osborne's Accumulated Other Comprehensive Income?

S11-14 (*Learning Objective 6: Differentiate responsibility for financial statements*) The annual report of Westminster Computer, Inc., included the following:

Management's Annual Report on Internal Control over Financial Reporting
The Company's management is responsible for establishing and maintaining adequate control over financial reporting [....] Management conducted an evaluation of the effectiveness of the Company's internal control over financial reporting [....] Based on this evaluation, management has concluded that the Company's internal control over financial reporting was effective as of September 30, 2012....

Report of Independent Registered Public Accounting Firm
The Board of Directors and Shareholders
Westminster Computer, Inc.:

We have audited the accompanying consolidated balance sheets of Westminster Computer, Inc., and subsidiaries (the Company) as of September 30, 2012, and September 30, 2011, and the related consolidated statements of operations, shareholders' equity, and cash flows for each of the years in the three-year period ended September 30, 2012. These consolidated financial statements are the responsibility of the Company's management. Our responsibility is to express an opinion on these consolidated financial statements based on our audits.

We conducted our audits in accordance with the standards of the Public Company Accounting Oversight Board (United States)....

In our opinion, the consolidated financial statements referred to above present fairly, in all material respects, the financial position of the Company as of September 30, 2012, and September 30, 2011, and the results of its operations and its cash flows for each of the years in the three-year period ended September 30, 2012, in conformity with accounting principles generally accepted in the United States of America.

SLMA LLP

Aurora, Colorado
December 28, 2012

1. Who is responsible for Westminster's financial statements?
2. By what accounting standards are the financial statements prepared?
3. Identify one concrete action that Westminster management takes to fulfill its responsibility for the reliability of the company's financial information.
4. Which entity gave an outside, independent opinion on the Westminster financial statements? Where was this entity located, and when did it release its opinion to the public?
5. Exactly what did the audit cover? Give names and dates.
6. By what standards did the auditor conduct the audit?
7. What was the auditor's opinion of Westminster's financial statements?

Exercises

All of the A and B exercises can be found within MyAccountingLab, an online homework and practice environment. Your instructor may ask you to complete these exercises using MyAccountingLab.

MyAccountingLab

Group A

E11-15A (*Learning Objective 1: Prepare and use a complex income statement; prepare a statement of comprehensive income*) Suppose Dupree Cycles, Inc., reported a number of special items on its income statement. The following data, listed in no particular order, came from Dupree's financial statements (amounts in thousands):

Income tax expense (savings):			Net sales..	$13,000
Continuing operations..................	$285		Foreign-currency translation	
Discontinued operations...............	64		gain..	310
Extraordinary loss........................	(2)		Extraordinary loss...............................	12
Unrealized gain on			Income from discontinued operations	320
available-for-sale investments.......	39		Dividends declared and paid	650
Short-term investments....................	45		Total operating expenses......................	12,200

▶ **Requirements**

1. Show how the Dupree Cycles, Inc., income statement for the year ended September 30, 2012, should appear. Omit earnings per share.
2. Prepare the Statement of Comprehensive Income for Dupree Cycles, Inc., for the year ended September 30, 2012.

E11-16A *(Learning Objectives 1, 4: Prepare an income statement; compute earnings per share; evaluate a company as an investment)* The Moran Book Company accounting records include the following for 2012 (in thousands):

Other revenues	$ 1,700
Income tax expense—extraordinary gain	800
Income tax expense—income from continuing operations............	4,040
Extraordinary gain..	2,000
Sales revenue..	106,000
Total operating expenses..	97,600

▶ **Requirements**

1. Prepare Moran Book's single-step income statement for the year ended December 31, 2012, including EPS. Moran had 1,200 thousand shares of common stock and no preferred stock outstanding during the year.
2. Assume investors capitalize Moran Book's earnings from continuing operations at 9%. Estimate the price of one share of the company's stock.

E11-17A *(Learning Objective 1: Use income data for investment analysis)* During 2012, Resource, Inc., had sales of $7.16 billion, operating profit of $2.70 billion, and net income of $3.70 billion. EPS was $4.50. On June 9, 2013, one share of Resource's common stock was priced at $54.20 on the New York Stock Exchange.

What investment capitalization rate did investors appear to be using to determine the value of one share of Resource stock? The formula for the value of one share of stock uses EPS in the calculation.

E11-18A *(Learning Objective 2: Account for foreign-currency gains and losses)* Assume that Twitter Stores completed the following foreign-currency transactions:

Jun	9	Purchased DVD players as inventory on account from Moshu, a Japanese company. The price was 600,000 yen, and the exchange rate of the yen was $0.0087.
Jul	18	Paid Moshu when the exchange rate was $0.0076.
	22	Sold merchandise on account to Le Fleur, a French company, at a price of 30,000 euros. The exchange rate was $1.17.
	28	Collected from Le Fleur when the exchange rate was $1.14.

▶ **Requirements**

1. Journalize these transactions for Twitter. Focus on the gains and losses caused by changes in foreign-currency rates. (Round your answers to the nearest whole dollar.)
2. On June 10, immediately after the purchase, and on July 23, immediately after the sale, which currencies did Twitter want to strengthen? Which currencies did in fact strengthen? Explain your reasoning.

E11-19A *(Learning Objective 3: Account for income tax by a corporation)* During 2012, the Martell Heights Corp. income statement reported income of $500,000 before tax. The company's income tax return filed with the IRS showed taxable income of $440,000. During 2012, Martell Heights was subject to an income tax rate of 40%.

▶ Requirements

1. Journalize Martell Heights' income taxes for 2012.
2. How much income tax did Martell Heights have to pay for the year 2012?
3. At the beginning of 2012, Martell Heights' balance of Deferred Tax Liability was $32,000. How much Deferred Tax Liability did Martell Heights report on its balance sheet at December 31, 2012?

E11-20A *(Learning Objective 4: Compute earnings per common share)* Palace Loan Company's balance sheet reports the following:

Preferred stock, $20 par value, 2%, 11,000 shares issued	$ 220,000
Common stock, $2.50 par, 1,100,000 shares issued....................	2,750,000
Treasury stock, common, 120,000 shares at cost	480,000

During 2012, Palace earned net income of $6,200,000. Compute Palace's earnings per common share (EPS) for 2012. (Round EPS to two decimal places.)

E11-21A *(Learning Objective 4: Compute and use earnings per share)* Prep Holding Company operates numerous businesses, including motel, auto rental, and real estate companies. 2012 was interesting for Prep, which reported the following on its income statement (in millions):

Net revenues	$3,802
Total expenses and other...	3,227
Income from continuing operations............................	575
Discontinued operations, net of tax..............................	82
Income before extraordinary item, net of tax	657
Extraordinary gain, net of tax......................................	6
Net income...	$ 663

During 2012, Prep had the following (in millions, except for par value per share):

Common stock, $0.02 par value, 900 shares issued	$ 18
Treasury stock, 300 shares at cost..	(3,542)

▶ Requirement

1. Show how Prep should report earnings per share for 2012. (Round EPS to the nearest cent.)

E11-22A *(Learning Objective 5: Report a prior-period adjustment on the statement of retained earnings)* Clean, Inc., a household products chain, reported a prior-period adjustment in 2012. An accounting error caused net income of 2011 to be understated by $15 million. Retained earnings at December 31, 2011, as previously reported, was $346 million. Net income for 2012 was $93 million, and 2012 dividends were $60 million.

▶ Requirement

1. Prepare the company's statement of retained earnings for the year ended December 31, 2012. How does the prior-period adjustment affect Clean's net income for 2012?

E11-23A (*Learning Objective 5: Prepare a statement of stockholders' equity*) At December 31, 2012, Mendonca Mall, Inc., reported stockholders' equity as follows:

Common stock, $0.50 par, 500,000 shares authorized, 350,000 shares issued	$ 175,000
Additional paid-in capital..	900,000
Retained earnings...	620,000
	$1,695,000

During 2013, Mendonca Mall completed these transactions (listed in chronological order):

a. Declared and issued a 9% stock dividend on the outstanding stock. At the time, Mendonca Mall stock was quoted at a market price of $22 per share.
b. Issued 2,300 shares of common stock at the price of $15 per share.
c. Net income for the year, $350,000.
d. Declared cash dividends of $182,000.

▶ Requirement

1. Prepare Mendonca Mall, Inc.'s statement of stockholders' equity for 2013.

E11-24A (*Learning Objective 5: Use a company's statement of stockholders' equity*) Revere Water Company reported the following items on its statement of shareholders' equity for the year ended December 31, 2012:

	$3.50 Par Common Stock	Additional Paid-in Capital	Retained Earnings	Accumulated Other Comprehensive Income	Total Shareholders' Equity
Balance, December 31, 2011	$395	$1,505	$4,700	$8	$6,608
Net earnings..			1,050		
Other comprehensive income				1	
Issuance of stock	140	70			
Cash dividends....................................			(80)		
Balance, December 31, 2012					

1. Determine the December 31, 2012, balances in Revere Water's shareholders' equity accounts and total shareholders' equity on this date.
2. Revere Water's total liabilities on December 31, 2012, are $7,400. What is Revere Water's debt ratio on this date?
3. Was there a profit or a loss for the year ended December 31, 2012? How can you tell?
4. At what price per share did Revere Water issue common stock during 2012?

Group B

E11-25B (*Learning Objective 1: Prepare and use a complex income statement; prepare a statement of comprehensive income*) Suppose Whitney Cycles, Inc., reported a number of special items on its income statement. The following data, listed in no particular order, came from Whitney's financial statements (amounts in thousands):

Income tax expense (savings):		Net sales..	$13,600
Continuing operations..................	$290	Foreign-currency translation	
Discontinued operations..............	56	gain...	350
Extraordinary loss........................	(1)	Extraordinary loss...................................	13
Unrealized gain on		Income from discontinued operations	280
available-for-sale investments.......	36	Dividends declared and paid	640
Short-term investments...................	35	Total operating expenses........................	12,700

1. Show how the Whitney Cycles, Inc., income statement for the year ended September 30, 2012, should appear. Omit earnings per share.
2. Prepare the Statement of Comprehensive Income for Whitney Cycles, Inc., for the year ended September 30, 2012.

E11-26B (*Learning Objectives 1, 4: Prepare an income statement; compute earnings per share; evaluate a company as an investment*) The Bergeron Book Company's accounting records include the following for 2012 (in thousands):

Other revenues	$ 1,500
Income tax expense—extraordinary gain	640
Income tax expense—income from continuing operations	4,920
Extraordinary gain	1,600
Sales revenue	108,000
Total operating expenses	97,200

▶ Requirements

1. Prepare Bergeron Book's single-step income statement for the year ended December 31, 2012, including EPS. Bergeron Book had 800 thousand shares of common stock and no preferred stock outstanding during the year.
2. Assume investors capitalize Bergeron Book earnings from continuing operations at 8%. Estimate the price of one share of the company's stock.

E11-27B (*Learning Objective 1: Use income data for investment analysis*) During 2012, Beta, Inc., had sales of $6.86 billion, operating profit of $2.20 billion, and net income of $3.40 billion. EPS was $4.80. On May 11, 2013, one share of Beta's common stock was priced at $54.30 on the New York Stock Exchange.

What investment capitalization rate did investors appear to be using to determine the value of one share of Beta stock? The formula for the value of one share of stock uses EPS in the calculation.

E11-28B (*Learning Objective 2: Account for foreign-currency gains and losses*) Assume that Better Buy Stores completed the following foreign-currency transactions:

May 9	Purchased DVD players as inventory on account from Toyita, a Japanese company. The price was 400,000 yen, and the exchange rate of the yen was $0.0083.
Jun 18	Paid Toyita when the exchange rate was $0.0078.
22	Sold merchandise on account to Bon Appetit, a French company, at a price of 10,000 euros. The exchange rate was $1.17.
28	Collected from Bon Appetit when the exchange rate was $1.11.

▶ Requirements

1. Journalize these transactions for Better Buy. Focus on the gains and losses caused by changes in foreign-currency rates. (Round your answers to the nearest whole dollar.)
2. On May 10, immediately after the purchase, and on June 23, immediately after the sale, which currencies did Better Buy want to strengthen? Which currencies did in fact strengthen? Explain your reasoning.

E11-29B (*Learning Objective 3: Account for income tax by a corporation*) During 2012, Campbell Heights Corp.'s income statement reported income of $300,000 before tax. The company's income tax return filed with the IRS showed taxable income of $260,000. During 2012, Campbell Heights was subject to an income tax rate of 25%.

▶ Requirements

1. Journalize Campbell Heights' income taxes for 2012.
2. How much income tax did Florimax Heights have to pay for the year 2012?
3. At the beginning of 2012, Florimax Heights' balance of Deferred Tax Liability was $38,000. How much Deferred Tax Liability did Florimax Heights report on its balance sheet at December 31, 2012?

E11-30B (*Learning Objective 4: Compute earnings per share*) Hampton Loan Company's balance sheet reports the following:

Preferred stock, $80 par value, 8%, 11,000 shares issued	$ 880,000
Common stock, $2.50 par, 1,500,000 shares issued.....................	3,750,000
Treasury stock, common, 100,000 shares at cost	900,000

During 2012, Hampton earned net income of $5,900,000. Compute Hampton's earnings per common share (EPS) for 2012. (Round EPS to two decimal places.)

E11-31B (*Learning Objective 4: Compute and use earnings per share*) Plato Holding Company operates numerous businesses, including motel, auto rental, and real estate companies. 2012 was interesting for Plato, which reported the following on its income statement (in millions):

Net revenues	$3,800
Total expenses and other...	3,217
Income from continuing operations...............................	583
Loss from discontinued operations,	
net of tax savings	(87)
Income before extraordinary item, net of tax	496
Extraordinary gain, net of tax.......................................	4
Net income..	$ 500

During 2012, Plato had the following (in millions, except for par value per share):

Common stock, $0.25 par value, 1,000 shares issued	$ 250
Treasury stock, 200 shares at cost...	(3,600)

▶ Requirement

1. Show how Plato should report earnings per share for 2012. (Round EPS to the nearest cent.)

E11-32B (*Learning Objective 5: Report a prior-period adjustment on the statement of retained earnings*) Dwelling, Inc., a household products chain, reported a prior-period adjustment in 2012. An accounting error caused net income of 2011 to be overstated by $16 million. Retained earnings at December 31, 2011, as previously reported, was $345 million. Net income for 2012 was $91 million, and 2012 dividends were $64 million.

▶ Requirement

1. Prepare the company's statement of retained earnings for the year ended December 31, 2012. How does the prior-period adjustment affect Dwelling's net income for 2012?

E11-33B (*Learning Objective 5: Prepare a statement of stockholders' equity*) At December 31, 2012, Rondeau Mall, Inc., reported stockholders' equity as follows:

Common stock, $1.50 par, 700,000 shares authorized, 310,000 shares issued	$ 465,000
Additional paid-in capital.......................................	500,000
Retained earnings..	640,000
	$1,605,000

During 2013, Rondeau Mall completed these transactions (listed in chronological order):

a. Declared and issued a 5% stock dividend on the outstanding stock. At the time, Rondeau Mall stock was quoted at a market price of $20 per share.
b. Issued 1,900 shares of common stock at the price of $15 per share.
c. Net income for the year, $346,000.
d. Declared cash dividends of $187,000.

► Requirement

1. Prepare Rondeau Mall, Inc.'s statement of stockholders' equity for 2013.

E11-34B (*Learning Objective 5: Use a company's statement of stockholders' equity*) Wave Water Company reported the following items on its statement of shareholders' equity for the year ended December 31, 2012:

	$3 Par Common Stock	Additional Paid-in Capital	Retained Earnings	Accumulated Other Comprehensive Income	Total Shareholders' Equity
Balance, December 31, 2011.............	$375	$2,225	$4,200	$12	$6,812
Net earnings.......................................			990		
Other comprehensive income				3	
Issuance of stock	120	240			
Cash dividends....................................			(69)		
Balance, December 31, 2012.............					

► Requirements

1. Determine the December 31, 2012, balances in Wave Water's shareholders' equity accounts and total shareholders' equity on this date.
2. Wave Water's total liabilities on December 31, 2012, are $7,800. What is Wave Water's debt ratio on this date?
3. Was there a profit or a loss for the year ended December 31, 2012? How can you tell?
4. At what price per share did Wave Water issue common stock during 2012?

Quiz

Test your understanding of the corporate income statement and the statement of stockholders' equity by answering the following questions. Select the best choice from among the possible answers given.

Q11-35 What is the best source of income for a corporation?
a. Prior-period adjustments
b. Continuing operations
c. Discontinued operations
d. Extraordinary items

Q11-36 Leslie's Lotion Company reports several earnings numbers on its current-year income statement (parentheses indicate a loss):

Gross profit	$165,000	Income from continuing operations	$ 40,000
Net income	41,000	Extraordinary gains	11,000
Income before income tax	78,000	Discontinued operations	(10,000)

How much net income would most investment analysts predict for Leslie's to earn next year?
a. $40,000
b. $38,000
c. $71,000
d. $30,000

Q11-37 Return to the preceding question. Suppose you are evaluating Leslie's Lotion Company stock as an investment. You require an 8% rate of return on investments, so you capitalize Leslie's earnings at 8%. How much are you willing to pay for all of Leslie's stock?
a. $2,062,500
b. $975,000
c. $512,500
d. $500,000

Q11-38 Boston Systems purchased inventory on account from Megaplex. The price was ¥140,000, and a yen was quoted at $0.0091. Boston paid the debt in yen a month later when the price of a yen was $0.0092. Boston
a. recorded a Foreign-Currency Transaction Gain of $14.
b. debited Inventory for $1,288.
c. debited Inventory for $1,274.
d. None of the above

Q11-39 One way to hedge a foreign-currency transaction loss is to
a. pay debts as late as possible.
b. pay in the foreign currency.
c. offset foreign-currency inventory and plant assets.
d. collect in your own currency.

Q11-40 Foreign-currency transaction gains and losses are reported on the
a. balance sheet.
b. income statement.
c. statement of cash flows.
d. consolidation work sheet.

Q11-41 Earnings per share is *not* reported for
a. discontinued operations.
b. extraordinary items.
c. comprehensive income.
d. continuing operations.

Q11-42 Copycat Corporation has income before income tax of $110,000 and taxable income of $100,000. The income tax rate is 30%. Copycat's income statement will report net income of
a. $30,000.
b. $33,000.
c. $77,000.
d. $107,000.

Q11-43 Copycat Corporation in the preceding question must immediately pay income tax of
a. $77,000.
b. $30,000.
c. $33,000.
d. $70,000.

Q11-44 Use the Copycat Corporation data in question 43. At the end of its first year of operations, Copycat's deferred tax liability is

a. $27,000.

b. $11,000.

c. $3,000.

d. $19,000.

Q11-45 Which of the following items is most closely related to prior-period adjustments?

a. Retained earnings

b. Earnings per share

c. Preferred stock dividends

d. Accounting changes

Q11-46 Examine the statement of stockholders' equity of Wellington Electronics Corporation. What was the market value of each share of the stock that Wellington gave its stockholders in the stock dividend?

Wellington Electronics Corporation
Statement of Stockholders' Equity
Year Ended December 31, 2012

	Common Stock $4 Par	Additional Paid-in Capital	Retained Earnings	Treasury Stock	Accumulated Other Comprehensive Income	Total Stockholders' Equity
1 Balance, December 31, 2011	$ 40,000	$ 110,000	$170,000	$(27,000)	$ (3,000)	$ 290,000
2 Issuance of stock	80,000	1,060,000				1,140,000
3 Net income			140,000			140,000
4 Cash dividends			(21,000)			(21,000)
5 Stock dividend—10%	12,000	66,000	(78,000)			0
6 Purchase of treasury stock				(6,000)		(6,000)
7 Sale of treasury stock		7,000		1,000		8,000
8 Other comprehensive income					11,000	11,000
9 Balance, December 31, 2010	$132,000	$1,243,000	$211,000	$(32,000)	$ 8,000	$1,562,000

a. $26

b. $39,000

c. $3,000

d. $52

Q11-47 Which statement is true?

a. The Public Company Oversight Board evaluates internal controls.

b. GAAP governs the form and content of the financial statements.

c. Management audits the financial statements.

d. Independent auditors prepare the financial statements.

Problems

All of the A and B problems can be found within MyAccountingLab, an online homework and practice environment. Your instructor may ask you to complete these problems using MyAccountingLab.

MyAccountingLab

Group A

P11-48A *(Learning Objectives 1, 4: Prepare a complex income statement, including earnings per share; evaluate quality of earnings)* The following information was taken from the records of Crowley Cosmetics, Inc., at December 31, 2012:

Prior-period adjustment—			Dividends on common stock	$ 26,000
debit to Retained Earnings	$ 7,000		Interest expense	23,000
Income tax expense (saving):			Gain on lawsuit settlement	7,000
Continuing operations	27,300		Dividend revenue	13,000
Income from discontinued			Treasury stock, common	
operations	5,600		(3,000 shares at cost)	15,000
Extraordinary loss	(11,570)		General expenses	71,900
Loss on sale of plant assets	11,000		Sales revenue	540,000
Income from discontinued			Retained earnings, beginning,	
operations	14,000		as originally reported	196,000
Preferred stock, 8%, $30 par,			Selling expenses	82,000
3,000 shares issued	90,000		Common stock, no par,	
Extraordinary loss	29,000		24,000 shares authorized	
Cost of goods sold	304,000		and issued	360,000

▶ Requirements

1. Prepare Crowley Cosmetics' single-step income statement, which lists all revenues together and all expenses together, for the fiscal year ended December 31, 2012. Include earnings-per-share data.
2. Evaluate income for the year ended December 31, 2012. Crowley's top managers hoped to earn income from continuing operations equal to 13% of sales.

P11-49A *(Learning Objective 5: Preparing a statement of retained earnings)* Use the data in Problem P11-48A to prepare the Crowley Cosmetics statement of retained earnings for the year ended December 31, 2012. Use the Statement of Retained Earnings for Maxim, Inc., in the End-of-Chapter Summary Problem as a model.

P11-50A *(Learning Objective 1: Use income data to make an investment decision)* Crowley Cosmetics in Problem P11-48A holds significant promise for carving a niche in its industry. A group of Irish investors is considering purchasing the company's outstanding common stock. Crowley's stock is currently selling for $22 per share.

A *BetterLife Magazine* story predicted the company's income is bound to grow. It appears that Crowley can earn at least its current level of income for the indefinite future. Based on this information, the investors think that an appropriate investment capitalization rate for estimating the value of Crowley's common stock is 10%. How much will this belief lead the investors to offer for Crowley Cosmetics? Will Crowley's existing stockholders be likely to accept this offer? Explain your answers.

P11-51A *(Learning Objective 2: Account for foreign-currency gains or losses)* Suppose Gray Corporation completed the following international transactions:

May	1	Sold inventory on account to Giorgio, the Italian automaker, for €80,000. The exchange rate of the euro was $1.35, and Giorgio demands to pay in euros.
	10	Purchased supplies on account from a Canadian company at a price of Canadian $51,000. The exchange rate of the Canadian dollar was $0.76, and the payment will be in Canadian dollars.
	17	Sold inventory on account to an English firm for 144,000 British pounds. Payment will be in pounds, and the exchange rate of the pound was $1.91.
	22	Collected from Giorgio. The exchange rate is €1 = $1.38.
Jun	18	Paid the Canadian company. The exchange rate of the Canadian dollar is $0.75.
	24	Collected from the English firm. The exchange rate of the British pound was $1.88.

▶ Requirements

1. Record these transactions in Gray's journal and show how to report the transaction gain or loss on the income statement.
2. How will what you learned in this problem help you structure international transactions?

P11-52A (*Learning Objectives 1, 3, 4: Evaluate quality of earnings; compute earnings per share; estimate the price of a stock*) Capital Experts, Ltd., (CEL) specializes in taking underperforming companies to a higher level of performance. CEL's capital structure at December 31, 2011, included 14,000 shares of $2.25 preferred stock and 115,000 shares of common stock. During 2012, CEL issued common stock and ended the year with 123,000 shares of common stock outstanding. Average common shares outstanding during 2012 were 119,000. Income from continuing operations during 2012 was $235,000. The company discontinued a segment of the business at a loss of $69,000, and an extraordinary item generated a gain of $46,000. All amounts are after income tax.

▶ Requirements

1. Compute CEL's earnings per share. Start with income from continuing operations.
2. Analysts believe CEL can earn its current level of income for the indefinite future. Estimate the market price of a share of CEL common stock at investment capitalization rates of 9%, 11%, and 13%. Which estimate presumes an investment in CEL is the most risky? How can you tell?

P11-53A (*Learning Objectives 3, 4, 5: Prepare an income statement; compute earnings per share; prepare a statement of comprehensive income*) John Holland, accountant for Sunny Pie Foods, was injured in an auto accident. While he was recuperating, another inexperienced employee prepared the following income statement for the fiscal year ended June 30, 2012:

Sunny Pie Foods, Inc.		
Income Statement		
June 30, 2012		
Revenue and gains:		
Sales		$894,000
Paid-in capital in excess of par—common		11,000
Total revenues and gains		905,000
Expenses and losses:		
Cost of goods sold	$400,000	
Selling expenses	102,000	
General expenses	92,000	
Sales returns	20,000	
Unrealized loss on available-for-sale investments	10,000	
Dividends paid	16,000	
Sales discounts	14,000	
Income tax expense	29,000	
Total expenses and losses		683,000
Income from operations		222,000
Other gains and losses:		
Extraordinary gain	36,000	
Loss on discontinued operations	(25,000)	
Total other gains (losses)		11,000
Net income		$233,000
Earnings per share		$ 23.30

The individual *amounts* listed on the income statement are correct. However, some *accounts* are reported incorrectly, and some accounts do not belong on the income statement at all. Also, income tax (30%) has not been applied to all appropriate figures. Sunny Pie Foods issued 17,000 shares of common stock back in 2004 and held 7,000 shares as treasury stock all during the fiscal year 2012.

► Requirement

1. Prepare a corrected Statement of Comprehensive Income for Sunny Pie Foods for the fiscal year ended June 30, 2012. Include net income, which lists all revenues together and all expenses together, as well as other comprehensive income, net of tax. After calculating comprehensive income, prepare the earnings-per-share section of the statement.

P11-54A (*Learning Objective 3: Account for a corporation's income tax*) The accounting (not the income tax) records of Mahoney Publications, Inc., provide the income statement for 2012.

	2012
Total revenue	$900,000
Expenses:	
Cost of goods sold	$470,000
Operating expenses	260,000
Total expenses before tax	730,000
Pretax accounting income	$170,000

Taxable income for 2012 includes these modifications from pretax accounting income:

a. Additional taxable income of $16,000 earned in 2013 but taxed in 2012
b. Additional depreciation expense of $45,000 for MACRS tax depreciation in 2012

The income tax rate is 40%.

► Requirements

1. Compute Mahoney's taxable income for 2012.
2. Journalize the corporation's income taxes for 2012.
3. Prepare the corporation's income statement for 2012.

P11-55A (*Learning Objective 5: Analyze a statement of stockholders' equity*) Fabulous Food Specialties, Inc., reported the following statement of stockholders' equity for the year ended October 31, 2012:

	Fabulous Food Specialties, Inc. Statement of Stockholders' Equity For the Year Ended October 31, 2012				
(In millions)	Common Stock	Additional Paid-in Capital	Retained Earnings	Treasury Stock	Total
Balance, October 31, 2011	$430	$1,640	$ 904	$(115)	$2,859
Net income			480		480
Cash dividends			(190)		(190)
Issuance of stock (200 shares)	100	120			220
Stock dividend	106	127	(233)		—
Sale of treasury stock		11		7	18
Balance, October 31, 2012	$636	$1,898	$ 961	$(108)	$3,387

► Requirements

Answer these questions about Fabulous Food Specialties' stockholders' equity transactions.

1. The income tax rate is 40%. How much income before income tax did Fabulous Food Specialties report on the income statement?
2. What is the par value of the company's common stock?
3. At what price per share did Fabulous Food Specialties issue its common stock during the year?
4. What was the cost of treasury stock sold during the year? What was the selling price of the treasury stock sold? What was the increase in total stockholders' equity?
5. Fabulous Food Specialties' statement of stockholders' equity lists the stock transactions in the order in which they occurred. What was the percentage of the stock dividend? (Round to the nearest percentage.)

Group B

P11-56B (*Learning Objectives 1, 4: Prepare a complex income statement, including earnings per share; evaluate quality of earnings*) The following information was taken from the records of Shaw Cosmetics, Inc., at December 31, 2012:

Prior-period adjustment—		Dividends on common stock	$26,000
debit to Retained Earnings	$ 9,000	Interest expense	25,000
Income tax expense (saving):		Gain on lawsuit settlement	10,000
Continuing operations	25,950	Dividend revenue	16,000
Income from discontinued		Treasury stock, common	
operations	8,000	(5,000 shares at cost)	15,000
Extraordinary loss	(13,500)	General expenses	81,000
Loss on sale of plant assets	15,000	Sales revenue	570,000
Income from discontinued		Retained earnings, beginning,	
operations	20,000	as originally reported	197,000
Preferred stock, 6%, $30 par,		Selling expenses	93,000
1,000 shares issued	30,000	Common stock, no par,	
Extraordinary loss	34,000	30,000 shares authorized	
Cost of goods sold	316,000	and issued	390,000

► Requirements

1. Prepare Shaw Cosmetics' single-step income statement, which lists all revenues together and all expenses together, for the fiscal year ended December 31, 2012. Include earnings-per-share data.
2. Evaluate income for the year ended December 31, 2012. Shaw's top managers hoped to earn income from continuing operations equal to 11% of sales.

P11-57B (*Learning Objective 5: Prepare a statement of retained earnings*) Use the data in Problem P11-56B to prepare the Shaw Cosmetics statement of retained earnings for the year ended December 31, 2012. Use the Statement of Retained Earnings for Maxim, Inc., in the End-of-Chapter Summary Problem as a model.

P11-58B (*Learning Objective 1: Use income data to make an investment decision*) Shaw Cosmetics in Problem P11-56B holds significant promise for carving a niche in its industry. A group of Irish investors is considering purchasing the company's outstanding common stock. Shaw's stock is currently selling for $18 per share.

A *Better Life Magazine* story predicted the company's income is bound to grow. It appears that Shaw can earn at least its current level of income for the indefinite future. Based on this information, the investors think that an appropriate investment capitalization rate for estimating the value of Shaw's common stock is 7%. How much will this belief lead the investors to offer for Shaw Cosmetics? Will Shaw's existing stockholders be likely to accept this offer? Explain your answers.

P11-59B *(Learning Objective 2: Account for foreign-currency gains or losses)* Suppose Blanco Corporation completed the following international transactions:

May	1	Sold inventory on account to Aromando, the Italian automaker, for €70,000. The exchange rate of the euro was $1.33, and Aromando demands to pay in euros.
	10	Purchased supplies on account from a Canadian company at a price of Canadian $54,000. The exchange rate of the Canadian dollar was $0.72, and the payment will be in Canadian dollars.
	17	Sold inventory on account to an English firm for 140,000 British pounds. Payment will be in pounds, and the exchange rate of the pound was $1.93.
	22	Collected from Aromando. The exchange rate is €1 = $1.36.
Jun	18	Paid the Canadian company. The exchange rate of the Canadian dollar is $0.71.
	24	Collected from the English firm. The exchange rate of the British pound was $1.90.

▶ Requirements

1. Record these transactions in Blanco's journal and show how to report the transaction gain or loss on the income statement.
2. How will what you learned in this problem help you structure international transactions?

P11-60B *(Learning Objectives 1, 3, 4: Evaluate quality of earnings; compute earnings per share; estimate the price of a stock)* Better Experts Ltd. (BEL) specializes in taking underperforming companies to a higher level of performance. BEL's capital structure at December 31, 2011, included 10,000 shares of $2.25 preferred stock and 120,000 shares of common stock. During 2012, BEL issued common stock and ended the year with 126,000 shares of common stock outstanding. Average common shares outstanding during 2012 were 123,000. Income from continuing operations during 2012 was $219,000. The company discontinued a segment of the business at a loss of $65,000, and an extraordinary item generated a gain of $49,000. All amounts are after income tax.

▶ Requirements

1. Compute BEL's earnings per share. Start with income from continuing operations.
2. Analysts believe BEL can earn its current level of income for the indefinite future. Estimate the market price of a share of BEL common stock at investment capitalization rates of 6%, 8%, and 10%. Which estimate presumes an investment in BEL is the most risky? How can you tell?

P11-61B *(Learning Objectives 3, 4, 5: Prepare an income statement; compute earnings per share; prepare a statement of comprehensive income)* Jackson Hallstead, accountant for Confection Pies, was injured in an auto accident. While he was recuperating, another inexperienced employee prepared the following income statement for the fiscal year ended June 30, 2012:

Confection Pies, Inc.
Income Statement
June 30, 2012

Revenue and gains:			
Sales			$904,000
Paid-in capital in excess of par—common			15,000
Total revenues and gains			919,000
Expenses and losses:			
Cost of goods sold		$383,000	
Selling expenses		103,000	
General expenses		90,000	
Sales returns		21,000	
Unrealized loss on available-for-sale investments		14,000	
Dividends paid		16,000	
Sales discounts		12,000	
Income tax expense		33,000	
Total expenses and losses			672,000
Income from operations			247,000
Other gains and losses:			
Extraordinary gain		44,000	
Loss on discontinued operations		(28,000)	
Total other gains (losses)			16,000
Net income			$263,000
Earnings per share			$ 13.15

The individual *amounts* listed on the income statement are correct. However, some *accounts* are reported incorrectly, and some accounts do not belong on the income statement at all. Also, income tax (30%) has not been applied to all appropriate figures. Confection Pies issued 28,000 shares of common stock back in 2004 and held 8,000 shares as treasury stock all during the fiscal year 2012.

▶ Requirement

1. Prepare a corrected Statement of Comprehensive Income for Confection Pies for the fiscal year ended June 30, 2012. Include net income, which lists all revenues together and all expenses together, as well as other comprehensive income, net of tax. After calculating comprehensive income, prepare the earnings-per-share section of the statement.

P11-62B (*Learning Objective 3: Account for a corporation's income tax*) The accounting (not the income tax) records of Johnson Publications, Inc., provide the income statement for 2012.

	2012
Total revenue	$850,000
Expenses:	
Cost of goods sold	$470,000
Operating expenses	240,000
Total expenses before tax	710,000
Pretax accounting income	$140,000

Taxable income for 2012 includes these modifications from pretax accounting income:

a. Additional taxable income of $14,000 earned in 2013 but taxed in 2012.
b. Additional depreciation expense of $25,000 for MACRS tax depreciation in 2012.

The income tax rate is 32%.

▶ Requirements

1. Compute Johnson's taxable income for 2012.
2. Journalize the corporation's income taxes for 2012.
3. Prepare the corporation's income statement for 2012.

P11-63B (*Learning Objective 5: Analyze a statement of stockholders' equity*) Fall River Specialties, Inc., reported the following statement of stockholders' equity for the year ended October 31, 2012:

	Fall River Specialties, Inc. Statement of Stockholders' Equity For the Year Ended October 31, 2012				
(In millions)	Common Stock	Additional Paid-in Capital	Retained Earnings	Treasury Stock	Total
Balance, October 31, 2011	$470	$1,610	$911	$(118)	$2,873
Net income			350		350
Cash dividends			(195)		(195)
Issuance of stock (40 shares)	80	100			180
Stock dividend	55	69	(124)		—
Sale of treasury stock		12		7	19
Balance, October 31, 2012	$605	$1,791	$942	$(111)	$3,227

▶ Requirements

Answer these questions about Fall River Specialties' stockholders' equity transactions.

1. The income tax rate is 30%. How much income before income tax did Fall River Specialties report on the income statement?
2. What is the par value of the company's common stock?
3. At what price per share did Fall River Specialties issue its common stock during the year?
4. What was the cost of treasury stock sold during the year? What was the selling price of the treasury stock sold? What was the increase in total stockholders' equity?
5. Fall River Specialties' statement of stockholders' equity lists the stock transactions in the order in which they occurred. What was the percentage of the stock dividend? (Round to the nearest percentage).

Challenge Exercise and Problem

E11-64 (*Learning Objectives 1, 5: Explain and analyze accumulated other comprehensive income*) Brown-Box Retail Corporation reported shareholders' equity on its balance sheet at December 31, 2013 as follows:

	Brown-Box Retail Balance Sheet (Partial) December 31, 2013	
(dollar amounts in millions)		
Shareholder's Equity:		
Common stock, $0.10 par value—		
1,200 million shares authorized,		$ 50
500 million shares issued		1,098
Additional paid-in capital		6,100
Retained earnings		(?)
Accumulated other comprehensive (loss)		(80)
Less: Treasury stock, at cost		

▶ Requirements

1. Identify the two components that typically make up accumulated other comprehensive income.
2. For each component of accumulated other comprehensive income, describe the event that can cause a *positive* balance. Also describe the events that can cause a *negative* balance for each component.
3. At December 31, 2012, Brown-Box Retail's accumulated other comprehensive loss was $57 million. Then during 2013, Brown-Box Retail had a positive foreign-currency translation adjustment of $25 million and an unrealized loss of $15 million on available-for-sale investments. What was Brown-Box Retail's balance of accumulated other comprehensive income (loss) at December 31, 2013?

P11-65 (*Learning Objectives 1, 2, 4, 5: Analyze how various transactions affect the income statement and EPS*) Aerostar, Inc., operates as a retailer of casual apparel. A recent, condensed income statement for Aerostar follows:

Income Statement
For the Year Ended January 31, 2012

Sales revenue		$2,400,000
Operating expenses:		
Cost of goods sold	$1,500,000	
Selling and administrative expenses	500,00	2,000,000
Operating income		400,000
Other revenue (expenses)		50,000
Income before tax		450,000
Income tax expense (40% tax rate)		180,000
Net income		$ 270,000
Earnings per share (50,000 shares)		$ 5.40

▶ Requirements

1. Assume that the following transactions were inadvertently omitted at the end of the year. Using the categories in the table, indicate the effect of each of the transactions on each category. (Use + for increase, − for decrease, and NE for no effect). Provide dollar amounts for each column except Earnings per Share.

Transaction	Operating Income	Income Before Tax	Net Income	Earnings per Share
Unadjusted balances	400,000	450,000	270,000	
a.				
b.				
c.				
d.				
e.				
f.				
g.				
h.				
i.				
Totals				

a. Purchased inventory on account from a German company. The price was 100,000 euros. The exchange rate of the euro was $1.47.
b. Sold inventory on account, $120,000 (cost of inventory, $75,000).
c. Corrected a $50,000 overstatement of depreciation expense from a previous year.
d. Paid the German company for the inventory purchased when the exchange rate was $1.50.
e. Distributed 5,000 shares in a 10% stock dividend. The market value of the stock was $50.
f. Recorded additional administrative expense, $5,000.
g. Recorded interest earned, $20,000.
h. Declared dividends on preferred stock, $50,000.
i. Issued additional 5,000 shares of common stock, $260,000.

2. Determine the amount of Operating Income, Income Before Tax, Net Income, and Earnings Per Share after recording these transactions.

APPLY YOUR KNOWLEDGE

Decision Cases

Case 1. (*Learning Objective 1: Evaluate quality of earnings*) Prudhoe Bay Oil Co. is having its initial public offering (IPO) of company stock. To create public interest in its stock, Prudhoe Bay's chief financial officer has blitzed the media with press releases. One, in particular, caught your eye. On November 19, Prudhoe Bay announced unaudited earnings per share (EPS) of $1.19—up 89% from last year's EPS of $0.63. An 89% increase in EPS is outstanding!

Before deciding to buy Prudhoe Bay stock, you investigated further and found that the company omitted several items from the determination of unaudited EPS, as follows:

▶ Unrealized loss on available-for-sale investments, $0.06 per share
▶ Gain on sale of building, $0.05 per share
▶ Prior-period adjustment, increase in retained earnings, $1.10 per share
▶ Restructuring expenses, $0.29 per share
▶ Loss on settlement of lawsuit begun five years ago, $0.12 per share
▶ Lost income due to employee labor strike, $0.24 per share
▶ Income from discontinued operations, $0.09 per share

Wondering how to treat these "special items," you called your stockbroker at **Merrill Lynch**. She thinks that these items are nonrecurring and outside Prudhoe Bay's core operations. Furthermore, she suggests that you ignore the items and consider Prudhoe Bay's earnings of $1.19 per share to be a good estimate of long-term profitability.

▶ Requirement

1. What EPS number will you use to predict Prudhoe Bay's future profits? Show your work, and explain your reasoning for each item.

Case 2. (*Learning Objective 1: Evaluate quality of earnings*) Mike Magid Toyota is an automobile dealership. Magid's annual report includes Note 1—Summary of Significant Accounting Policies as follows:

> **Income Recognition**
>
> **Sales are recognized when cash payment is received or, in the case of credit sales, which represent the majority of . . . sales, when a down payment is received and the customer enters into an installment sales contract. These installment sales contracts . . . are normally collectible over 36 to 60 months. . . .**
>
> **Revenue from auto insurance policies sold to customers are recognized as income over the life of the contracts.**

Bay Area Nissan, a competitor of Mike Magid Toyota, includes the following note in its Summary of Significant Accounting Policies:

> ### Accounting Policies for Revenues
>
> Sales are recognized when cash payment is received or, in the case of credit sales, which represent the majority of . . . sales, when the customer enters into an installment sales contract. Customer down payments are rare. Most of these installment sales contracts are normally collectible over 36 to 60 months. . . . Revenue from auto insurance policies sold to customers are recognized when the customer signs an insurance contract. Expenses are recognized over the life of the insurance contracts.

Suppose you have decided to invest in an auto dealership, and you've narrowed your choices to Magid and Bay Area. Which company's earnings are of higher quality? Why? Will their accounting policies affect your investment decision? If so, how? Mention specific accounts in the financial statements that will differ between the two companies. (Challenge)

Ethical Issue

The income statement of Royal Bank of Singapore reported the following results of operations:

Earnings before income taxes and extraordinary gain	$187,046
Income tax expense	72,947
Earnings before extraordinary gain	114,099
Extraordinary gain, net of income tax	419,557
Net earnings	$533,656

Suppose Royal Bank's management, in violation of International Financial Reporting Standards (IFRS), had reported the company's results of operations in this manner:

Earnings before income taxes	$847,111
Income tax expense	352,651
Net earnings	$494,460

▶ Requirements

1. Identify the ethical issue in this situation.
2. Who are the stakeholders?
3. Evaluate the issue from the standpoint of (a) economic, (b) legal or regulatory, and (c) ethical dimensions. What are the possible effects on all stakeholders you identified?
4. Put yourself in the position of the controller of the bank. Your boss, the CEO, tries to pressure you to make the disclosure that violates IFRS. What would you do? What are the potential consequences?

Focus on Financials: | Amazon.com, Inc.

(*Learning Objective 1: Evaluate quality of earnings; evaluate an investment*) Refer to the **Amazon.com, Inc.**, consolidated financial statements in Appendix A at the end of this book.

1. Amazon.com, Inc.'s consolidated statements of operations do not mention income from continuing operations. Why not? Focus your attention on the company's Consolidated Statements of Operations for the three years ended December 31, 2010, as well as the footnotes to financial statements and other materials. What clues do you find that help you evaluate the quality of Amazon.com, Inc.'s earnings?

2. Assume the role of an investor. Suppose you are determining the price to pay for a share of Amazon.com, Inc., stock. Assume you are considering three investment capitalization rates that depend on the risk of an investment in Amazon.com: 5%, 6%, and 7%. Compute your estimated value of a share of Amazon.com, Inc., stock, using each of the three capitalization rates. Which estimated value would you base your investment strategy on if you rate Amazon.com, Inc., risky? If you consider Amazon.com, Inc., a safe investment? Use basic earnings per share for 2010.

3. Go to Amazon.com's Web site and compare your computed estimates to its actual stock price. Which of your prices is most realistic? (Challenge)

Focus on Analysis: | RadioShack Corporation

(*Learning Objective 1: Evaluate quality of earnings; evaluate an investment*) This case is based on the **RadioShack Corporation** consolidated financial statements in Appendix B at the end of this book.

1. Focus on the company's Consolidated Statements of Income for the three years ended December 31, 2010, as well as Note 2 summarizing the company's significant accounting policies. What is your evaluation of the quality of RadioShack Corporation's earnings? Explain how you formed your opinion.

2. At the end of 2010, how much would you have been willing to pay for one share of RadioShack Corporation's stock if you had rated the investment as high risk? As low risk? Use even-numbered investment capitalization rates in the range of 4%–10% for your analysis, and use basic earnings per share for continuing operations.

3. Go to RadioShack Corporation's Web site and get the current price of a share of its common stock. Which value that you estimated in Requirement 2 is closest to the company's actual stock price? (Challenge)

Group Project

Select a company and research its business. Search the Internet for articles about this company. Obtain its latest available annual report from the company's Web site or from www.sec.gov. Use the link entitled "Search for Company Filings."

▶ Requirements

1. Based on your group's analysis, come to class prepared to instruct the class on six interesting facts about the company that can be found in its financial statements and the related notes. Your group can mention only the obvious, such as net sales or total revenue, net income, total assets, total liabilities, total stockholders' equity, and dividends, in conjunction with other terms. Once you use an obvious item, you may not use that item again.

2. The group should write a paper discussing the facts that it has uncovered. Limit the paper to two double-spaced word-processed pages.

MyAccountingLab

For online homework, exercises, and problems that provide you with immediate feedback, please visit **www.myaccountinglab.com**.

Quick Check Answers

1. *a*	5. *c*	11. *d*
2. *c*	6. *d* ($1,400,000 × $0.97)	12. *b*
3. *d* ($6.39/.09)	7. *c*	
4. *c* (($37,000)/(.74)) (rounding causes slight differences for computations of other lines)	8. *c*	
	9. *d*	
	10. *a*	

12 The Statement of Cash Flows

SPOTLIGHT: Google: The Ultimate Answer Machine

What Internet search engine do you use? It's probably Google, the world's largest search engine. Google was created by Larry Page and Sergey Brin when they were students at Stanford University. From small beginnings, Google has grown to become a global technology leader that has helped transform the way people connect with information. The company generates revenue primarily by delivering cost-effective online advertising. Google maintains an index of billions of Web pages, which it makes freely available via its search engine to anyone with an Internet connection. Google stock has been a "hit" on Wall Street since its initial public offering (IPO). Recently, a share of Google, Inc., traded between $500 and $600 per share.

The beauty of Google is that it's so easy to use. Access the Internet at www.google.com, and you can simply enter what you want to find in the search box. You get a whole list of helpful Web sites. The world is literally at your fingertips. Google may be the ultimate answer machine, and lately, it has become a cash machine as well! In 2010, its cash flow from operations exceeded its net income by more than $3.4 billion, and the company finished the year with $13.6 billion in cash on the books! ●

© David Grossman/Photo Researchers, Inc.

Google, Inc.
Consolidated Statement of Cash Flows (Adapted, In millions)
Year Ended December 31, 2010

Cash flows from operating activities:		
Net income	$ 8,505	
Adjustments to reconcile net income to net cash		
provided by operating activities:		
Depreciation and amortization	1,396	
Stock-based compensation, net of taxes	1,291	
Change in assets and liabilities, net of acquired businesses:		
Accounts receivable	(1,129)	
Other current assets	(414)	
Accounts payable	272	
Accrued expenses and other liabilities	745	
Unearned revenue	325	
Income taxes payable	102	
Other, net	(12)	
Net cash provided by operating activities		$11,081
Cash flows from investing activities:		
Purchases of property and equipment	$ (4,018)	
Purchases of investments	(45,055)	
Sales of investments	39,460	
Acquisitions of other companies	(1,067)	
Net cash used in investing activities		(10,680)
Cash flows from financing activities (net)		3,050
Other, net		(19)
Net increase (decrease) in cash and cash equivalents		3,432
Cash and cash equivalents at beginning of year		10,198
Cash and cash equivalents at end of year		$13,630

In preceding chapters, we covered cash flows as they related to various topics: receivables, plant assets, and so on. **In this chapter, we show you how to prepare and use the statement of cash flows.** We begin with the statement format used by the vast majority of companies, the *indirect method*. We end with the alternate format of the statement of cash flows, the *direct method*, which is used by a minority of companies but is considered more informative by many. After working through this chapter, you will be able to analyze the cash flows of actual companies using both approaches.

This chapter has three distinct sections:

▶ Introduction, beginning on this page
▶ Preparing the Statement of Cash Flows: Indirect Method, page 702
▶ Preparing the Statement of Cash Flows: Direct Method, page 716

The introduction applies to all the cash-flow topics. Professors who wish to cover only the indirect method can assign the first two parts of the chapter. Those interested only in the direct method can proceed from the introduction, which ends on page 701, to the direct method, on page 716.

1 **Identify** the purposes of the statement of cash flows

2 **Distinguish** among operating, investing, and financing activities

3 **Prepare** a statement of cash flows by the indirect method

4 **Prepare** a statement of cash flows by the direct method

Learning Objectives

Identify the Purposes of the Statement of Cash Flows

The balance sheet reports financial position, and balance sheets from two periods show whether cash increased or decreased. But that doesn't tell _why_ the cash balance changed. The income statement reports net income and offers clues about cash, but the income statement doesn't tell _why_ cash increased or decreased. We need a third financial statement.

The **statement of cash flows** reports **cash flows**—cash receipts and cash payments—in other words, where cash came from (receipts) and how it was spent (payments). The statement covers a span of time and therefore is dated "Year Ended December 31, 2012" or "Month Ended June 30, 2012." Exhibit 12-1 illustrates the relative timing of the four basic statements.

The statement of cash flows serves these purposes:

1. **Predicts future cash flows.** Past cash receipts and payments are reasonably good predictors of future cash flows.

2. **Evaluates management decisions.** Businesses that make wise decisions prosper, and those that make unwise decisions suffer losses. The statement of cash flows reports how managers got cash and how they used cash to run the business.

3. **Determines ability to pay dividends and interest.** Stockholders want dividends on their investments. Creditors demand interest and principal on their loans. The statement of cash flows reports on the ability to make these payments.

4. **Shows the relationship of net income to cash flows.** Usually, high net income leads to an increase in cash, and vice versa. But cash flow can suffer even when net income is high.

On a statement of cash flows, _cash_ means more than just cash in the bank. It includes **cash equivalents**, which are highly liquid short-term investments that can be converted into cash immediately. Examples include money-market accounts and investments in U.S. Government securities. Throughout this chapter, the term _cash_ refers to cash and cash equivalents.

1 **Identify** the purposes of the statement of cash flows

EXHIBIT 12-1 | Timing of the Financial Statements

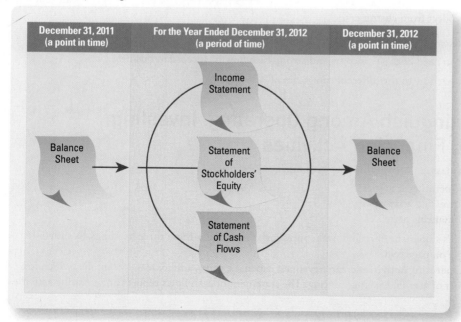

How's Your Cash Flow? Telltale Signs of Financial Difficulty

Companies want to earn net income because profit measures success. Without net income, a business sinks. There will be no dividends, and the stock price suffers. High net income attracts investors, but you can't pay bills with net income. That requires cash.

A company needs both net income and strong cash flow. Income and cash flow usually move together because net income generates cash. Sometimes, however, net income and cash flow take different paths. To illustrate, consider Fastech Company:

Fastech Company
Income Statement
Year Ended December 31, 2012

Sales revenue	$100,000
Cost of goods sold	30,000
Operating expenses	10,000
Net income	$ 60,000

Fastech Company
Balance Sheet
December 31, 2012

Cash	$ 3,000	Total current liabilities	$ 50,000
Receivables	37,000	Long-term liabilities	20,000
Inventory	40,000		
Plant assets, net	60,000	Stockholders' equity	70,000
Total assets	$140,000	Total liabilities and equity	$140,000

What can we glean from Fastech's income statement and balance sheet?

▶ Fastech is profitable. Net income is 60% of revenue. Fastech's profitability looks outstanding.
▶ The current ratio is 1.6, and the debt ratio is only 50%. These measures suggest little trouble in paying bills.
▶ But Fastech is on the verge of bankruptcy. Can you spot the problem? Can you see what is causing the problem? Three trouble spots leap out to a financial analyst.

1. The cash balance is very low. Three thousand dollars isn't enough cash to pay the bills of a company with sales of $100,000.

2. Fastech isn't selling inventory fast enough. Fastech turned over its inventory only 0.75 times during the year. As we saw in Chapter 6, inventory turnover rates of 3–8 times a year are common. A turnover ratio of 0.75 times means that it takes Fastech far too long to sell its inventory, and that delays cash collections.

3. Fastech's days' sales in receivables ratio is 135 days. Very few companies can wait that long to collect from customers.

The takeaway lesson from this discussion is this:

▶ You need both net income and strong cash flow to succeed in business.

Let's turn now to the different categories of cash flows.

Distinguish Among Operating, Investing, and Financing Activities

Distinguish
among operating, investing, and financing activities

A business engages in three types of business activities:

▶ Operating activities
▶ Investing activities
▶ Financing activities

Google's statement of cash flows reports cash flows under these three headings, as shown for Google on page 698.

Operating activities create revenues, expenses, gains, and losses—*net income*, which is a product of accrual basis accounting. The statement of cash flows reports on operating activities.

Operating activities are the most important of the three categories because they reflect the core of the organization. *A successful business must generate most of its cash from operating activities.*

Investing activities increase and decrease *long-term assets*, such as computers, land, buildings, equipment, and investments in other companies. Purchases and sales of these assets are investing activities. Investing activities are important, but they are less critical than operating activities.

Financing activities obtain cash from investors and creditors. Issuing stock, borrowing money, buying and selling treasury stock, and paying cash dividends are financing activities. Paying off a loan is another example. Financing cash flows relate to *long-term liabilities* and *stockholders' equity*. They are the least important of the three categories of cash flows, and that's why they come last. Exhibit 12-2 shows how operating, investing, and financing activities relate to the various parts of the balance sheet.

EXHIBIT 12-2 │ How Operating, Investing, and Financing Activities Affect the Balance Sheet

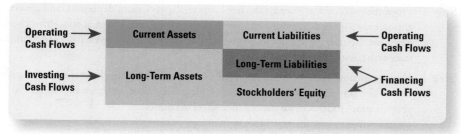

Examine Google's statement of cash flows on page 698. Focus on the final line of each section: Operating, Investing, and Financing. Google has very strong cash flows. During 2010, Google's operating activities provided about $11.1 billion of cash. Google invested $ 10.7 billion and received about $3.1 billion in financing. These figures show that

▶ *operations* are Google's largest source of cash.
▶ the company is *investing* in the future.
▶ other companies and individuals are willing to *finance* Google by lending to and investing in the company.

Two Formats for Operating Activities

There are two ways to format operating activities on the statement of cash flows:

▶ **Indirect method**—reconciles from net income to net cash provided by operating activities. (pp. 702–716)
▶ **Direct method**—reports all cash receipts and cash payments from operating activities. (pp. 716–726)

The two methods use different computations, but they produce the same figure for cash from *operating activities*. The two methods do not affect *investing* or *financing activities*. The following table summarizes the differences between the indirect and direct methods:

Indirect Method		Direct Method	
Net income......................................	$600	Collections from customers..........	$2,000
Adjustments:		*Deductions:*	
Depreciation, etc.	300	Payments to suppliers, etc.	(1,100)
Net cash provided by		Net cash provided by	
operating activities	$900	operating activities	$ 900

— same —

We begin with the indirect method because the vast majority of companies use it.

Prepare a Statement of Cash Flows by the Indirect Method

To illustrate the statement of cash flows, we use **The Roadster Factory, Inc. (TRF)**, a dealer in auto parts for sports cars. Proceed as follows to prepare the statement of cash flows by using the indirect method:

Step 1 Lay out the template as shown in Part 1 of Exhibit 12-3. The exhibit is comprehensive. The diagram in Part 2 (p. 703) gives a visual picture of the statement.

Step 2 Use the balance sheet to determine the increase or decrease in cash during the period. The change in cash is the "check figure" for the statement of cash flows. Exhibit 12-4 (p. 704) gives The Roadster Factory's (TRF's) comparative balance sheets, with cash highlighted. TRF's cash decreased by $8,000 during 2012. *Why* did cash decrease? The statement of cash flows will provide the answer.

Step 3 From the income statement, take net income, depreciation, depletion, and amortization expense, and any gains or losses on the sale of long-term assets. Print these items on the statement of cash flows. Exhibit 12-5 (p. 704) gives TRF's income statement, with relevant items highlighted.

Step 4 Use the income statement and balance sheet data to prepare the statement of cash flows. The statement of cash flows is complete only after you have explained the year-to-year changes in all the balance sheet accounts.

EXHIBIT 12-3 | Part 1: Template of the Statement of Cash Flows: Indirect Method

The Roadster Factory, Inc. (TRF)
Statement of Cash Flows
Year Ended December 31, 2012

Cash flows from operating activities:
 Net income
  Adjustments to reconcile net income to net cash provided by operating activities:
  + Depreciation/depletion/amortization expense
  + Loss on sale of long-term assets
  − Gain on sale of long-term assets
  − Increases in current assets other than cash
  + Decreases in current assets other than cash
  + Increases in current liabilities
  − Decreases in current liabilities
   Net cash provided by (used for) operating activities

Cash flows from investing activities:
 + Sales of long-term assets (investments, land, building, equipment, and so on)
 − Purchases of long-term assets
 + Collections of notes receivable
 − Loans to others
  Net cash provided by (used for) investing activities

Cash flows from financing activities:
 + Issuance of stock
 + Sale of treasury stock
 − Purchase of treasury stock
 + Borrowing (issuance of notes or bonds payable)
 − Payment of notes or bonds payable
 − Payment of dividends
  Net cash provided by (used for) financing activities

Net increase (decrease) in cash during the year:
 + Cash at December 31, 2011
 = Cash at December 31, 2012

Go to "Cash Flows from Operating Activities" in Exhibit 12-6 on page 705.

EXHIBIT 12-3 │ Part 2: Positive and Negative Items on the Statement of Cash Flows: Indirect Method

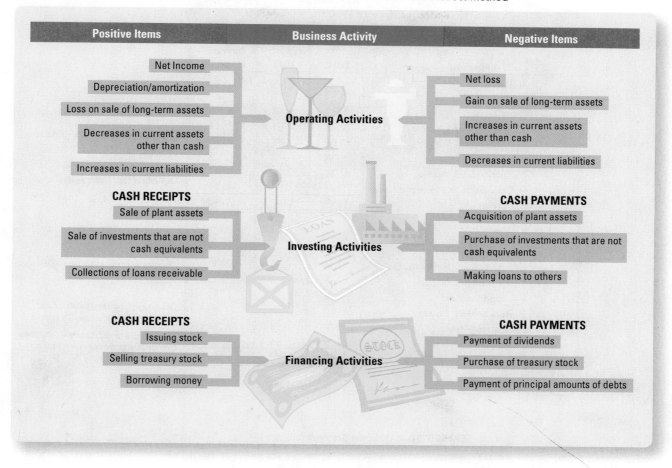

Cash Flows from Operating Activities

> **Operating activities are related to the transactions that make up net income.**

The operating section of the Statement of Cash Flows (Exhibit 12-6) begins with the net income, taken from the income statement (Exhibit 12-5), and is followed by "Adjustments to reconcile net income to net cash provided by operating activities." Let's discuss these adjustments.

Ⓐ **Depreciation, Depletion, and Amortization Expenses.** These expenses are added back to net income to convert net income to cash flow. Let's see why. Depreciation is recorded as follows:

Depreciation Expense	18,000	
Accumulated Depreciation		18,000

Depreciation has no effect on cash. But depreciation, like all other expenses, decreases net income. Therefore, to convert net income to cash flows, we add depreciation back to net income. The add-back cancels the earlier deduction.

EXHIBIT 12-4 | Comparative Balance Sheets

The Roadster Factory, Inc. (TRF)
Comparative Balance Sheets
December 31, 2012 and 2011

(In thousands)	2012	2011	Increase (Decrease)	
Assets				
Current:				
Cash	$ 34	$ 42	$ (8)	
Accounts receivable	96	81	15	Changes in current assets—*Operating*
Inventory	35	38	(3)	
Prepaid expenses	8	7	1	
Notes receivable	21	—	21	Changes in noncurrent assets—*Investing*
Plant assets, net of depreciation	343	219	124	
Total	$537	$387	$150	
Liabilities				
Current:				
Accounts payable	$ 91	$ 57	$ 34	
Salary and wage payable	4	6	(2)	Changes in current liabilities—*Operating*
Accrued liabilities	1	3	(2)	
Long-term debt	160	77	83	Changes in long-term liabilities and paid-in capital accounts—*Financing*
Stockholders' Equity				
Common stock	162	158	4	
Retained earnings	119	86	33	Changes due to net income—*Operating* Change due to dividends—*Financing*
Total	$537	$387	$150	

EXHIBIT 12-5 | Income Statement

The Roadster Factory, Inc. (TRF)
Income Statement
Year Ended December 31, 2012

	(In thousands)	
Revenues and gains:		
Sales revenue	$303	
Interest revenue	2	
Gain on sale of plant assets	8	
Total revenues and gains		$313
Expenses:		
Cost of goods sold	$150	
Salary and wage expense	56	
Depreciation expense	18	
Other operating expense	17	
Income tax expense	15	
Interest expense	7	
Total expenses		263
Net income		$ 50

EXHIBIT 12-6 | Statement of Cash Flows—Operating Activities—Indirect Method

	The Roadster Factory, Inc. (TRF) Statement of Cash Flows (Indirect Method) For the Year Ended December 31, 2012	(In thousands)	
	Cash flows from operating activities:		
	Net income		$50
	Adjustments to reconcile net income to net cash provided by operating activities:		
Ⓐ	Depreciation	$ 18	
Ⓑ	Gain on sale of plant assets	(8)	
Ⓒ	Increase in accounts receivable	(15)	
	Decrease in inventory	3	
	Increase in prepaid expenses	(1)	
	Increase in accounts payable	34	
	Decrease in salary and wage payable	(2)	
	Decrease in accrued liabilities	(2)	27
	Net cash provided by operating activities		$77

Example: Suppose you had only two transactions, a $1,000 cash sale and depreciation expense of $300. Cash flow from operations is $1,000, and net income is $700 ($1,000 – $300). To go from net income ($700) to cash flow ($1,000), we add back the depreciation ($300). Depletion and amortization are treated like depreciation.

Ⓑ **Gains and Losses on the Sale of Assets.** Sales of long-term assets are *investing* activities, and there's often a gain or loss on the sale. On the statement of cash flows, the gain or loss is an adjustment to net income. Exhibit 12-6 includes an adjustment for a gain. During 2012, The Roadster Factory sold equipment for $62,000. The book value was $54,000, so there was a gain of $8,000.

The $62,000 cash received from the sale is an investing activity (Exhibit 12-7), and the $62,000 includes the $8,000 gain. Net income also includes the gain, so we must subtract the gain from net cash provided by operations, so that it may be added to the net book value of equipment removed in the investing section ($54,000 + $8,000 = $62,000). (We explain investing activities in the next section.)

A loss on the sale of plant assets also creates an adjustment in the operating section. Since the cash received from the sale of a long-term asset at a loss is less than the asset's book value, the amount of cash received reflects the loss. Losses are deducted from net income. Therefore, in order to show the amount of cash received from the sale of the asset in the investments section, losses are *added back* to net income to compute cash flow from operations.

Ⓒ **Changes in the Current Asset and Current Liability Accounts.** Most current assets and current liabilities result from operating activities. For example, accounts receivable result from sales, inventory relates to cost of goods sold, and so on. Changes in the current accounts are adjustments to net income on the cash flow statement. The reasoning follows:

1. *An increase in another current asset decreases cash.* It takes cash to acquire assets. Suppose you make a sale on account. Accounts receivable are increased, but cash isn't affected yet. Exhibit 12-4 (p. 704) reports that during 2012, The Roadster Factory's Accounts Receivable increased by $15,000. To compute cash flow from operations, we must subtract the $15,000 increase in Accounts Receivable, as shown in Exhibit 12-6. The reason is

this: We have *not* collected this $15,000 in cash. Similar logic applies to all the other current assets. If they increase, cash decreases.

2. **A decrease in another current asset increases cash.** Suppose TRF's Accounts Receivable balance decreased by $4,000. Cash receipts caused Accounts Receivable to decrease, so we add decreases in Accounts Receivable and the other current assets to net income.

3. **A decrease in a current liability decreases cash.** Payment of a current liability decreases both cash and the liability, so we subtract decreases in current liabilities from net income. In Exhibit 12-6, the $2,000 decrease in Accrued Liabilities is *subtracted* to compute net cash provided by operations.

4. **An increase in a current liability increases cash.** The Roadster Factory's Accounts Payable increased. That can occur only if cash was not spent to pay this debt. Cash payments are therefore less than expenses, and TRF has more cash on hand. Thus, increases in current liabilities increase cash.

Evaluating Cash Flows from Operating Activities. Let's step back and evaluate The Roadster Factory's operating cash flows during 2012. TRF's operations provided net cash flow of $77,000. This amount exceeds net income, which is one sign of a healthy company. Now let's examine TRF's investing and financing activities, as reported in Exhibit 12-7.

EXHIBIT 12-7 | Statement of Cash Flows—Indirect Method

The Roadster Factory, Inc. (TRF) Statement of Cash Flows (Indirect Method) For the Year Ended December 31, 2012		
	(In thousands)	
Cash flows from operating activities:		
Net income		$ 50
Adjustments to reconcile net income to net cash provided by operating activities:		
Ⓐ Depreciation	$ 18	
Ⓑ Gain on sale of plant assets	(8)	
Increase in accounts receivable	(15)	
Decrease in inventory	3	
Ⓒ Increase in prepaid expenses	(1)	
Increase in accounts payable	34	
Decrease in salary and wage payable	(2)	
Decrease in accrued liabilities	(2)	27
Net cash provided by operating activities		77
Cash flows from investing activities:		
Acquisition of plant assets	$(196)	
Loan to another company	(21)	
Proceeds from sale of plant assets	62	
Net cash used for investing activities		(155)
Cash flows from financing activities:		
Proceeds from issuance of long-term debt	$ 94	
Proceeds from issuance of common stock	4	
Payment of long-term debt	(11)	
Payment of dividends	(17)	
Net cash provided by financing activities		70
Net (decrease) in cash		$ (8)
Cash balance, December 31, 2011		42
Cash balance, December 31, 2012		$ 34

Cash Flows from Investing Activities

> Investing activities affect long-term assets, such as Plant Assets, Investments, and Notes Receivable. Increases in these accounts represent purchases of these assets and are offset by decreases to cash. Decreases to these accounts represent sales of these assets and are offset by increases to cash.

Most of the data come from the balance sheet.

Computing Purchases and Sales of Plant Assets. Companies keep a separate account for each plant asset. But for computing cash flows, it is helpful to combine all the plant assets into a single summary account. Also, we subtract accumulated depreciation and use the net figure. It's easier to work with a single plant asset account.

To illustrate, observe that The Roadster Factory's

- ▶ balance sheet reports beginning plant assets, net of accumulated depreciation, of $219,000. The ending balance is $343,000 (Exhibit 12-4).
- ▶ income statement shows depreciation expense of $18,000 and an $8,000 gain on sale of plant assets (Exhibit 12-5).

TRF's purchases of plant assets total $196,000 (take this amount as given; see Exhibit 12-7). How much, then, are the proceeds from the sale of plant assets? First, we must determine the book value of the plant assets sold, as follows:

Plant Assets, Net									
Beginning balance	+	Acquisitions	−	Depreciation	−	Book value of assets sold	=	Ending balance	
$219,000	+	$196,000	−	$18,000	−	−X	=	$343,000	
						−X	=	$343,000 − $219,000 − $196,000 + $18,000	
						X	=	$54,000	

The sale proceeds are $62,000, determined as follows:

Sale proceeds	=	Book value of assets sold	+	Gain	−	Loss
X	=	$54,000	+	$8,000	−	$0
X	=	$62,000				

Trace the sale proceeds of $62,000 to the statement of cash flows in Exhibit 12-7. The Plant Assets T-account provides another look at the computation of the book value of the assets sold.

Plant Assets, Net			
Beginning balance	219,000	Depreciation	18,000
Acquisitions	196,000	Book value of assets sold	54,000
Ending balance	343,000		

If the sale resulted in a loss of $3,000, the sale proceeds would be $51,000 ($54,000 − $3,000), and the statement of cash flows would report $51,000 as a cash receipt from this investing activity.

Computing Purchases and Sales of Investments, and Loans and Collections. The cash amounts of investment transactions can be computed in the manner illustrated for plant assets. Investments are easier because there is no depreciation, as shown in the following equation:

Investments (amounts assumed for illustration only)					
Beginning balance	+ Purchases	−	Book value of investments sold	=	Ending balance
$100,000	+ $50,000		−X	=	$140,000
			−X	=	$140,000 − $100,000 − $50,000
			X	=	$10,000

The Investments T-account provides another look (amounts assumed).

Investments			
Beginning balance	100,000		
Purchases	50,000	Book value of investments sold	10,000
Ending balance	140,000		

The Roadster Factory has a long-term receivable, and the cash flows from loan transactions on notes receivable can be determined as follows (data from Exhibit 12-4):

Notes Receivable					
Beginning balance	+	New loans made	− Collections	=	Ending balance
$0	+	X	−0	=	$21,000
		X		=	$21,000

Notes Receivable			
Beginning balance	0		
New loans made	21,000	Collections	0
Ending balance	21,000		

Exhibit 12-8 summarizes the cash flows from investing activities, highlighted in color.

Cash Flows from Financing Activities

Financing activities affect liabilities and stockholders' equity, such as Notes Payable, Bonds Payable, Long-Term Debt, Common Stock, Paid-in Capital in Excess of Par, and Retained Earnings. Most of the data come from the balance sheet. Increases in these accounts are offset by increases in cash. Decreases in these accounts are offset by decreases in cash.

Computing Issuances and Payments of Long-Term Debt. The beginning and ending balances of Long-Term Debt, Notes Payable, or Bonds Payable come from the balance sheet. If either new issuances or payments are known, the other amount can be computed. Assume that

EXHIBIT 12-8 | Computing Cash Flows from Investing Activities

Receipts

From sale of plant assets	Beginning plant assets, net	+	Acquisition cost	−	Depreciation	−	Book value of assets sold	=	Ending plant assets, net
	Cash received	=	Book value of assets sold	+ or −	Gain on sale Loss on sale				
From sale of investments	Beginning investments	+	Purchase cost of investments	−	Cost of investments sold	=	Ending investments		
	Cash received	=	Cost of investments sold	+ or −	Gain on sale Loss on sale				
From collection of notes receivable	Beginning notes receivable	+	New loans made	−	Collections	=	Ending notes receivable		

Payments

For acquisition of plant assets	Beginning plant assets, net	+	Acquisition cost	−	Depreciation	−	Book value of assets sold	=	Ending plant assets, net
For purchase of investments	Beginning investments	+	Purchase cost of investments	−	Cost of investments sold	=	Ending investments		
For new loans made	Beginning notes receivable	+	New loans made	−	Collections	=	Ending notes receivable		

proceeds from the Roadster Factory's new debt issuances (represented as an increase in cash) total $94,000 (take this amount as given in Exhibit 12-7). Debt payments (represented by a decrease in cash) are computed by performing an analysis of the Long-Term Debt account (see Exhibit 12-4).

Long-Term Debt (Notes Payable, Bonds Payable)

Beginning balance	+	Issuance of new debt	−	Payments of debt	=	Ending balance
$77,000	+	$94,000		−X	=	$160,000
				−X	=	$160,000 − $77,000 − $94,000
				X	=	$11,000

Long-Term Debt

		Beginning balance	77,000
Payments	11,000	Issuance of new debt	94,000
		Ending balance	160,000

Computing Issuances of Stock and Purchases of Treasury Stock.

These cash flows can be determined from the stock accounts. For example, cash received from issuing common stock is computed from Common Stock and Capital in Excess of Par. We use a single summary Common Stock account as we do for plant assets. The Roadster Factory data are as follows:

Common Stock

Beginning balance	+	Issuance of new stock	=	Ending balance
$158,000	+	$4,000	=	$162,000

Common Stock	
Beginning balance	158,000
Issuance of new stock	4,000
Ending balance	162,000

Increases in common stock and related additional paid-in capital are represented by offsetting increases in cash.

The Roadster Factory has no treasury stock, but cash flows from purchasing treasury stock can be computed as follows (using assumed amounts):

Treasury Stock (amounts assumed for illustration only)					
Beginning balance	+	Purchase of treasury stock	=	Ending balance	
$16,000	+	$3,000	=	$19,000	

Treasury Stock	
Beginning balance	16,000
Purchase of treasury stock	3,000
Ending balance	19,000

Increases (purchases) of treasury stock are represented by offsetting decreases in cash. If treasury stock is reissued for cash, the decrease in treasury stock is offset by an increase in cash.

Computing Dividend Declarations and Payments. If dividend declarations and payments are not given elsewhere, they can be computed. For The Roadster Factory, this computation is as follows:

Retained Earnings						
Beginning balance	+	Net income	−	Dividend declarations and payments	=	Ending balance
$86,000	+	$50,000		−X	=	$119,000
				−X	=	$119,000 − $86,000 − $50,000
				X	=	$17,000

The T-account also shows the dividend computation. Dividends paid, represented by decreases in retained earnings, are offset by decreases in cash.

Retained Earnings			
Dividend declarations and payments	17,000	Beginning balance	86,000
		Net income	50,000
		Ending balance	119,000

Exhibit 12-9 summarizes the cash flows from financing activities, highlighted in color.

EXHIBIT 12-9 | Computing Cash Flows from Financing Activities

Receipts

From borrowing—issuance of long-term debt (notes payable)	Beginning long-term debt (notes payable)	+ Cash received from issuance of long-term debt	− Payment of debt =	Ending long-term debt (notes payable)
From issuance of stock	Beginning stock	+ Cash received from issuance of new stock	=	Ending stock

Payments

Of long-term debt	Beginning long-term debt (notes payable)	+ Cash received from issuance of long-term debt	− Payment of debt =	Ending long-term debt (notes payable)
To purchase treasury stock	Beginning treasury stock + Purchase cost of treasury stock = Ending treasury stock			
Of dividends	Beginning retained earnings + Net income − Dividend declarations and payments = Ending retained earnings			

STOP & THINK. . .

Classify each of the following as an operating activity, an investing activity, or a financing activity as reported on the statement of cash flows prepared by the *indirect* method.

a. Issuance of stock
b. Borrowing long-term
c. Sales revenue
d. Payment of dividends
e. Purchase of land
f. Purchase of treasury stock

g. Paying bonds payable
h. Interest expense
i. Sale of equipment
j. Cost of goods sold
k. Purchase of another company
l. Making a loan

Answers:

a. Financing
b. Financing
c. Operating
d. Financing
e. Investing
f. Financing

g. Financing
h. Operating
i. Investing
j. Operating
k. Investing
l. Investing

Non-Cash Investing and Financing Activities

Companies make investments that do not require cash. They also obtain financing other than cash. Our examples have included none of these transactions. Now suppose The Roadster Factory issued common stock valued at $300,000 to acquire a warehouse. TRF would journalize this transaction as follows:

Warehouse Building	300,000	
Common Stock		300,000

This transaction would not be reported as a cash payment because TRF paid no cash. But the investment in the warehouse and the issuance of stock are important. These non-cash investing and financing activities can be reported in a separate schedule under the statement of cash flows. Exhibit 12-10 illustrates non-cash investing and financing activities (all amounts are assumed).

EXHIBIT 12-10 | Non-Cash Investing and Financing Activities

	Thousands
Non-cash investing and financing activities:	
Acquisition of building by issuing common stock	$300
Acquisition of land by issuing note payable	70
Payment of long-term debt by issuing common stock	100
Total non-cash investing and financing activities	$470

Now let's apply what you've learned about the statement of cash flows prepared by the indirect method.

MID-CHAPTER SUMMARY PROBLEM

Lucas Corporation reported the following income statement and comparative balance sheets, along with transaction data for 2012:

Lucas Corporation
Income Statement
Year Ended December 31, 2012

Sales revenue		$662,000
Cost of goods sold		560,000
Gross profit		102,000
Operating expenses		
Salary expenses	$46,000	
Depreciation expense— equipment	7,000	
Amortization expense— patent	3,000	
Rent expense	2,000	
Total operating expenses		58,000
Income from operations		44,000
Other items:		
Loss on sale of equipment		(2,000)
Income before income tax		42,000
Income tax expense		16,000
Net income		$ 26,000

Lucas Corporation
Comparative Balance Sheets
December 31, 2012 and 2011

Assets	2012	2011	Liabilities	2012	2011
Current:			Current:		
Cash and equivalents	$ 19,000	$ 3,000	Accounts payable	$ 35,000	$ 26,000
Accounts receivable	22,000	23,000	Accrued liabilities	7,000	9,000
Inventories	34,000	31,000	Income tax payable	10,000	10,000
Prepaid expenses	1,000	3,000	Total current liabilities	52,000	45,000
Total current assets	76,000	60,000	Long-term note payable	44,000	—
Long-term investments	18,000	10,000	Bonds payable	40,000	53,000
Equipment, net	67,000	52,000	**Owners' Equity**		
Patent, net	44,000	10,000	Common stock	52,000	20,000
			Retained earnings	27,000	19,000
			Less: Treasury stock	(10,000)	(5,000)
Total assets	$205,000	$132,000	Total liabilities and equity	$205,000	$132,000

Transaction Data for 2012:

Purchase of equipment	$ 98,000	Issuance of long-term note payable	
Payment of cash dividends	18,000	to purchase patent	$ 37,000
Issuance of common stock to		Issuance of long-term note payable to	
retire bonds payable	13,000	borrow cash	7,000
Purchase of long-term investment	8,000	Issuance of common stock for cash	19,000
Purchase of treasury stock	5,000	Sale of equipment (book value, 76,000)	74,000

Requirement

1. Prepare Lucas Corporation's statement of cash flows (indirect method) for the year ended December 31, 2012. Follow the four steps outlined below. For Step 4, prepare a T-account to show the transaction activity in each long-term balance sheet account. For each plant asset, use a single account, net of accumulated depreciation (for example: Equipment, Net).

   Step 1 Lay out the template of the statement of cash flows.

   Step 2 From the comparative balance sheets, determine the increase in cash during the year, $16,000.

   Step 3 From the income statement, take net income, depreciation, amortization, and the loss on sale of equipment to the statement of cash flows.

   Step 4 Complete the statement of cash flows. Account for the year-to-year change in each balance sheet account.

▶ Answer

Lucas Corporation Statement of Cash Flows Year Ended December 31, 2012		
Cash flows from operating activities:		
Net income		$ 26,000
Adjustments to reconcile net income to		
net cash provided by operating activities:		
Depreciation	$ 7,000	
Amortization	3,000	
Loss on sale of equipment	2,000	
Decrease in accounts receivable	1,000	
Increase in inventories	(3,000)	
Decrease in prepaid expenses	2,000	
Increase in accounts payable	9,000	
Decrease in accrued liabilities	(2,000)	19,000
Net cash provided by operating activities		45,000
Cash flows from investing activities:		
Purchase of equipment	$(98,000)	
Sale of equipment	74,000	
Purchase of long-term investment	(8,000)	
Net cash used for investing activities		(32,000)
Cash flows from financing activities:		
Issuance of common stock	$ 19,000	
Payment of cash dividends	(18,000)	
Issuance of long-term note payable	7,000	
Purchase of treasury stock	(5,000)	
Net cash provided by financing activities		3,000
Net increase in cash		16,000
Cash balance, December 31, 2011		3,000
Cash balance, December 31, 2012		$ 19,000
Non-cash investing and financing activities:		
Issuance of long-term note payable to purchase patent		$ 37,000
Issuance of common stock to retire bonds payable		13,000
Total non-cash investing and financing activities		$ 50,000

Long-Term Investments		
Bal	10,000	
	8,000	
Bal	18,000	

Equipment, Net		
Bal	52,000	
	98,000	76,000
		7,000
Bal	67,000	

Patent, Net		
Bal	10,000	
	37,000	3,000
Bal	44,000	

Long-Term Note Payable		
		Bal	0
			37,000
			7,000
		Bal	44,000

Bonds Payable		
		Bal	53,000
	13,000	
		Bal	40,000

Common Stock		
		Bal	20,000
			13,000
			19,000
		Bal	52,000

Retained Earnings		
		Bal	19,000
	18,000		26,000
		Bal	27,000

Treasury Stock		
Bal	5,000	
	5,000	
Bal	10,000	

Prepare a Statement of Cash Flows by the Direct Method

④

Prepare a statement of cash flows by the direct method

The Financial Accounting Standards Board (FASB) and the International Accounting Standards Board (IASB) prefer the direct method of reporting operating cash flows because it provides clearer information about the sources and uses of cash. However, only a very small percentage of companies use this method because it requires more computations than the indirect method. Investing and financing cash flows are unaffected by the operating cash flows.

To illustrate the statement of cash flows, we use The Roadster Factory, Inc. (TRF), a dealer in auto parts for sports cars. To prepare the statement of cash flows by the direct method, proceed as follows:

Step 1 Lay out the template of the statement of cash flows by the direct method, as shown in Part 1 of Exhibit 12-11. Part 2 (p. 718) gives a visual presentation of the statement.

Step 2 Use the balance sheet to determine the increase or decrease in cash during the period. The change in cash is the "check figure" for the statement of cash flows. The Roadster Factory's comparative balance sheets show that cash decreased by $8,000 during 2012 (Exhibit 12-4, p. 704). *Why* did cash decrease during 2012? The statement of cash flows explains.

Step 3 Use the available data to prepare the statement of cash flows. The Roadster Factory's transaction data appear in Exhibit 12-12 on page 718. These transactions affected both the income statement (Exhibit 12-5, p. 704) and the statement of cash flows. Some transactions affect one statement and some affect the other. For example, sales (item 1) are reported on the income statement. Cash collections (item 2) go on the statement of cash flows. Other transactions, such as interest expense and payments (item 12), affect both statements. *The statement of cash flows reports only those transactions with cash effects* (those with an asterisk in Exhibit 12-12). Exhibit 12-13 (on p. 719) gives The Roadster Factory's statement of cash flows for 2012.

EXHIBIT 12-11 | Part 1: Template of the Statement of Cash Flows—Direct Method

The Roadster Factory, Inc. (TRF)
Statement of Cash Flows
Year Ended December 31, 2012

Cash flows from operating activities:
Receipts:
   Collections from customers
   Interest received on notes receivable
   Dividends received on investments in stock
     Total cash receipts
Payments:
   To suppliers
   To employees
   For interest
   For income tax
     Total cash payments
Net cash provided by (used for) operating activities
Cash flows from investing activities:
   Sales of long-term assets (investments, land, building, equipment, and so on)
− Purchases of long-term assets
+ Collections of notes receivable
− Loans to others
Net cash provided by (used for) investing activities
Cash flows from financing activities:
   Issuance of stock
+ Sale of treasury stock
− Purchase of treasury stock
+ Borrowing (issuance of notes or bonds payable)
− Payment of notes or bonds payable
− Payment of dividends
Net cash provided by (used for) financing activities
Net increase (decrease) in cash during the year
+ Cash at December 31, 2011
= Cash at December 31, 2012

Cash Flows from Operating Activities

Operating cash flows are listed first because they are the most important. Exhibit 12-13 shows that The Roadster Factory is sound; operating activities were the largest source of cash.

Cash Collections from Customers. Both cash sales and collections of accounts receivable are reported on the statement of cash flows as "Collections from customers . . . $288,000" in Exhibit 12-13.

Cash Receipts of Interest and Dividends. The income statement reports interest revenue and dividend revenue. Only the cash receipts of interest and dividends appear on the statement of cash flows—$2,000 of interest received in Exhibit 12-13.

Payments to Suppliers. Payments to suppliers include all expenditures for inventory and operating expenses except employee pay, interest, and income taxes. *Suppliers* are those entities that provide inventory and essential services. For example, a clothing store's suppliers may include **Tommy Hilfiger, Adidas,** and **Ralph Lauren.** Other suppliers provide advertising, utilities, and office supplies. Exhibit 12-13 shows that The Roadster Factory paid suppliers $133,000.

EXHIBIT 12-11 | Part 2: Cash Receipts and Cash Payments on the Statement of Cash Flows—Direct Method

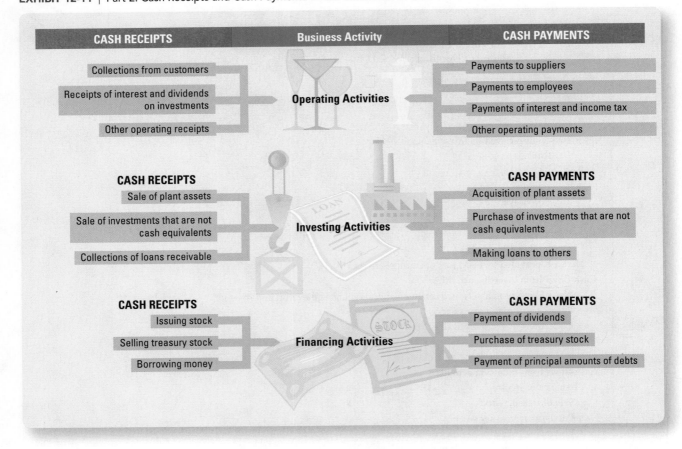

EXHIBIT 12-12 | Summary of the Roadster Factory's 2012 Transactions

Operating Activities
1. Sales on credit, $303,000
*2. Collections from customers, $288,000
*3. Interest revenue and receipts, $2,000
4. Cost of goods sold, $150,000
5. Purchases of inventory on credit, $147,000
*6. Payments to suppliers, $133,000
7. Salary and wage expense, $56,000
*8. Payments of salary and wages, $58,000
9. Depreciation expense, $18,000
10. Other operating expense, $17,000
*11. Income tax expense and payments, $15,000
*12. Interest expense and payments, $7,000

Investing Activities
*13. Cash payments to acquire plant assets, $196,000
*14. Loan to another company, $21,000
*15. Proceeds from sale of plant assets, $62,000, including $8,000 gain

Financing Activities
*16. Proceeds from issuance of long-term debt, $94,000
*17. Proceeds from issuance of common stock, $4,000
*18. Payment of long-term debt, $11,000
*19. Declaration and payment of cash dividends, $17,000

*Indicates a cash flow to be reported on the statement of cash flows.
Note: Income statement data are taken from Exhibit 12-16, page 722.

EXHIBIT 12-13 | Statement of Cash Flows—Direct Method

The Roadster Factory, Inc. (TRF)
Statement of Cash Flows (Direct Method)
For Year Ended December 31, 2012

	(In thousands)	
Cash flows from operating activities:		
Receipts:		
Collections from customers	$ 288	
Interest received	2	
Total cash receipts		$ 290
Payments:		
To suppliers	$(133)	
To employees	(58)	
For income tax	(15)	
For interest	(7)	
Total cash payments		(213)
Net cash provided by operating activities		77
Cash flows from investing activities:		
Acquisition of plant assets	$(196)	
Loan to another company	(21)	
Proceeds from sale of plant assets	62	
Net cash used for investing activities		(155)
Cash flows from financing activities:		
Proceeds from issuance of long-term debt	$ 94	
Proceeds from issuance of common stock	4	
Payment of long-term debt	(11)	
Payment of dividends	(17)	
Net cash provided by financing activities		70
Net (decrease) in cash		(8)
Cash balance, December 31, 2011		42
Cash balance, December 31, 2012		$ 34

Payments to Employees. This category includes salaries, wages, and other forms of employee pay. Accrued amounts are excluded because they have not yet been paid. The statement of cash flows reports only the cash payments of $58,000.

Payments for Interest Expense and Income Tax Expense. Interest and income tax payments are reported separately. The Roadster Factory paid cash for all its interest and income taxes. Therefore, the same amount goes on the income statement and the statement of cash flows. These payments are operating cash flows because the interest and income tax are expenses.

Depreciation, Depletion, and Amortization Expense

These expenses are *not* listed on the direct-method statement of cash flows because they do not affect cash.

Cash Flows from Investing Activities

Investing is critical because a company's investments affect the future. Large purchases of plant assets signal expansion. Meager investing activity means the business is not growing.

Purchasing Plant Assets and Investments and Making Loans to Other Companies. These cash payments acquire long-term assets. The Roadster Factory's first investing activity in Exhibit 12-13 is the purchase of plant assets ($196,000). TRF also made a $21,000 loan and thus got a note receivable.

Proceeds from Selling Plant Assets and Investments and from Collecting Notes Receivable. These cash receipts are also investing activities. The sale of the plant assets needs explanation. The Roadster Factory received $62,000 cash from the sale of plant assets, and there was an $8,000 gain on this transaction. What is the appropriate amount to show on the cash flow statement? It is $62,000, the cash received from the sale, not the $8,000 gain.

Investors are often critical of a company that sells large amounts of its plant assets. That may signal an emergency. For example, problems in the airline industry have caused some companies to sell airplanes to generate cash.

Cash Flows from Financing Activities

Cash flows from financing activities include the following:

Proceeds from Issuance of Stock and Debt (Notes and Bonds Payable). Issuing stock and borrowing money are two ways to finance a company. In Exhibit 12-13, The Roadster Factory received $4,000 when it issued common stock. TRF also received $94,000 cash when it issued long-term debt (such as a note payable) to borrow money.

Payment of Debt and Purchasing the Company's Own Stock. Paying debt (notes payable) is the opposite of borrowing. TRF reports long-term debt payments of $11,000. The purchase of treasury stock is another example of a use of cash.

Payment of Cash Dividends. Paying cash dividends is a financing activity, as shown by The Roadster Factory's $17,000 payment in Exhibit 12-13. A *stock* dividend has no effect on Cash and is *not* reported on the cash flow statement.

Non-Cash Investing and Financing Activities

Companies make investments that do not require cash. They also obtain financing other than cash. Our examples thus far have included none of these transactions. Now suppose that The Roadster Factory issued common stock valued at $300,000 to acquire a warehouse. TRF would journalize this transaction as follows:

Warehouse Building	300,000	
Common Stock		300,000

This transaction would not be reported as a cash payment because TRF paid no cash. But the investment in the warehouse and the issuance of stock are important. These non-cash investing and financing activities can be reported in a separate schedule under the statement of cash flows. Exhibit 12-14 illustrates non-cash investing and financing activities (all amounts are assumed).

EXHIBIT 12-14 | Non-Cash Investing and Financing Activities

	Thousands
Non-cash investing and financing activities:	
Acquisition of building by issuing common stock	$300
Acquisition of land by issuing note payable	70
Payment of long-term debt by issuing common stock	100
Total non-cash investing and financing activities	$470

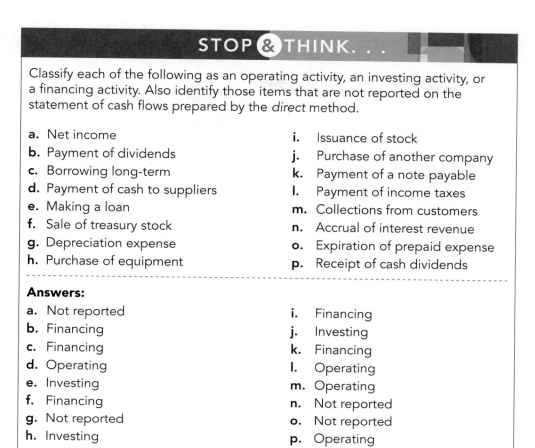

STOP & THINK...

Classify each of the following as an operating activity, an investing activity, or a financing activity. Also identify those items that are not reported on the statement of cash flows prepared by the *direct* method.

a. Net income
b. Payment of dividends
c. Borrowing long-term
d. Payment of cash to suppliers
e. Making a loan
f. Sale of treasury stock
g. Depreciation expense
h. Purchase of equipment

i. Issuance of stock
j. Purchase of another company
k. Payment of a note payable
l. Payment of income taxes
m. Collections from customers
n. Accrual of interest revenue
o. Expiration of prepaid expense
p. Receipt of cash dividends

Answers:

a. Not reported
b. Financing
c. Financing
d. Operating
e. Investing
f. Financing
g. Not reported
h. Investing

i. Financing
j. Investing
k. Financing
l. Operating
m. Operating
n. Not reported
o. Not reported
p. Operating

Now let's see how to compute the operating cash flows by the direct method.

Computing Operating Cash Flows by the Direct Method

To compute operating cash flows by the direct method, we use the income statement and the *changes* in the balance sheet accounts. Exhibit 12-15 diagrams the process. Exhibit 12-16 is The Roadster Factory's income statement, and Exhibit 12-17 shows the comparative balance sheets.

EXHIBIT 12-15 | Direct Method of Computing Cash Flows from Operating Activities

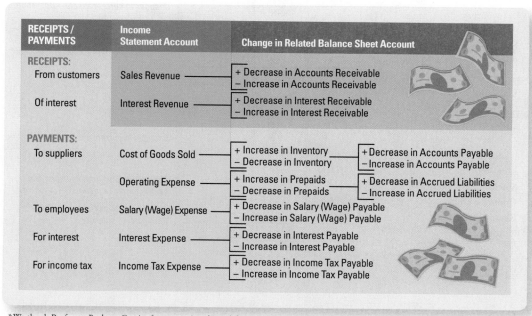

EXHIBIT 12-16 │ Income Statement

The Roadster Factory, Inc. (TRF)
Income Statement
Year Ended December 31, 2012

			(In thousands)	
Revenues and gains:				
	Sales revenue	$303		
	Interest revenue	2		
	Gain on sale of plant assets	8		
	Total revenues and gains		$313	
Expenses:				
	Cost of goods sold	$150		
	Salary and wage expense	56		
	Depreciation expense	18		
	Other operating expense	17		
	Income tax expense	15		
	Interest expense	7		
	Total expenses		263	
Net income			$ 50	

EXHIBIT 12-17 │ Comparative Balance Sheets

The Roadster Factory, Inc. (TRF)
Comparative Balance Sheets
December 31, 2012 and 2011

(In thousands)	2012	2011	Increase (Decrease)	
Assets				
Current:				
Cash	$ 34	$ 42	$ (8)	⎫
Accounts receivable	96	81	15	⎬ Changes in current assets—*Operating*
Inventory	35	38	(3)	
Prepaid expenses	8	7	1	⎭
Notes receivable	21	—	21	⎫ Changes in noncurrent assets—*Investing*
Plant assets, net of depreciation	343	219	124	⎬
Total	$537	$387	$150	
Liabilities				
Current:				
Accounts payable	$ 91	$ 57	$ 34	⎫
Salary and wage payable	4	6	(2)	⎬ Changes in current liabilities—*Operating*
Accrued liabilities	1	3	(2)	⎭
Long-term debt	160	77	83	⎫ Changes in long-term liabilities and
Stockholders' Equity				⎬ paid-in capital accounts—*Financing*
Common stock	162	158	4	⎭
Retained earnings	119	86	33	⎬ Change due to net income—*Operating*
				Change due to dividends—*Financing*
Total	$537	$387	$150	

Computing Cash Collections from Customers. Collections start with sales revenue (an accrual basis amount). The Roadster Factory's income statement (Exhibit 12-16) reports sales of $303,000. Accounts receivable increased from $81,000 at the beginning of the year to $96,000 at year-end, a $15,000 increase (Exhibit 12-17). Based on those amounts, Cash Collections equal $288,000, as follows. We must solve for cash collections (X):

Accounts Receivable							
Beginning balance	+	Sales	−	Collections	=	Ending balance	
$81,000	+	$303,000		−X	=	$96,000	
				−X	=	$96,000 − $81,000 − $303,000	
				X	=	$288,000	

The T-account for Accounts Receivable provides another view of the same computation.

Accounts Receivable			
Beginning balance	81,000		
Sales	303,000	Collections	288,000
Ending balance	96,000		

Accounts Receivable increased, so collections must be less than sales.

All collections of receivables are computed this way. Let's turn now to cash receipts of interest revenue. In our example, The Roadster Factory earned interest revenue and collected cash of $2,000. The amounts of interest revenue and cash receipts of interest often differ, and Exhibit 12-15 shows how to make this computation.

Computing Payments to Suppliers. This computation includes two parts:
▶ Payments for inventory
▶ Payments for operating expenses (other than interest and income tax)

Payments for inventory are computed by converting cost of goods sold to the cash basis. We use Cost of Goods Sold, Inventory, and Accounts Payable. First, we must solve for purchases. All the amounts come from Exhibits 12-16 and 12-17.

Cost of Goods Sold							
Beginning inventory	+	Purchases	−	Ending inventory	=	Cost of goods sold	
$38,000	+	X	−	$35,000	=	$150,000	
		X			=	$150,000 − $38,000 + $35,000	
		X			=	$147,000	

Now we can compute cash payments for inventory (Y), as follows:

Accounts Payable							
Beginning balance	+	Purchases	−	Payments for inventory	=	Ending balance	
$57,000	+	$147,000		−Y	=	$91,000	
				−Y	=	$91,000 − $57,000 − $147,000	
				Y	=	$113,000	

The T-accounts show where the data come from. Start with Cost of Goods Sold.

Cost of Goods Sold			
Beg inventory	38,000	End inventory	35,000
Purchases	147,000		
Cost of goods sold	150,000		

Accounts Payable			
Payments for inventory	113,000	Beg bal	57,000
		Purchases	147,000
		End bal	91,000

Accounts Payable increased, so payments for inventory are less than purchases.

Computing Payments for Operating Expenses. Payments for operating expenses other than interest and income tax are computed from three accounts: Prepaid Expenses, Accrued Liabilities, and Other Operating Expenses. All The Roadster Factory data come from Exhibits 12-16 and 12-17.

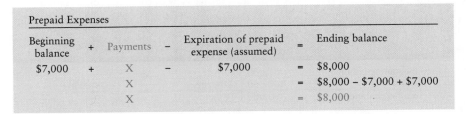

Prepaid Expenses							
Beginning balance	+	Payments	−	Expiration of prepaid expense (assumed)	=	Ending balance	
$7,000	+	X	−	$7,000	=	$8,000	
		X			=	$8,000 − $7,000 + $7,000	
		X			=	$8,000	

Accrued Liabilities						
Beginning balance	+	Accrual of expense at year-end (assumed)	−	Payments	=	Ending balance
$3,000	+	$1,000		−X	=	$1,000
				−X	=	$1,000 − $3,000 − $1,000
				X	=	$3,000

Other Operating Expenses						
Accrual of expense at year-end	+	Expiration of prepaid expense	−	Payments	=	Ending balance
$1,000	+	$7,000		X	=	$17,000
				X	=	$17,000 − $1,000 − $7,000
				X	=	$9,000
			Total payments for operating expenses		=	$8,000 + $3,000 + $9,000
					=	$20,000

The T-accounts give another picture of the same data.

Prepaid Expenses			
Beg bal	7,000	Expiration of prepaid expense	7,000
Payments	8,000		
End bal	8,000		

Accrued Liabilities			
Payment	3,000	Beg bal	3,000
		Accrual of expense at year-end	1,000
		End bal	1,000

Other Operating Expenses		
Accrual of expense at year-end	1,000	
Expiration of prepaid expense	7,000	
Payments	9,000	
End bal	17,000	

Total payments for operating expenses = $20,000($8,000 + $3,000 + $9,000)

Now we can compute Payments to Suppliers as follows:

Payments to suppliers	=	Payments for inventory	+	Payments for operating expenses
$133,000	=	$113,000	+	$20,000

Computing Payments to Employees.

It is convenient to combine all payments to employees into one account, Salary and Wage Expense. We then adjust the expense for the change in Salary and Wage Payable, as shown here:

Salary and Wage Payable

Beginning balance	+	Salary and wage expense	−	Payments	=	Ending balance
$6,000	+	$56,000		−X	=	$4,000
				−X	=	$4,000 − $6,000 − $56,000
				X	=	$58,000

Salary and Wage Payable

	Beginning balance	6,000
Payments to employees 58,000	Salary and wage expense	56,000
	Ending balance	4,000

Computing Payments of Interest and Income Taxes.

The Roadster Factory's expense and payment amounts are the same for interest and income tax, so no analysis is required. If the expense and the payment differ, the payment can be computed as shown in Exhibit 12-15.

Computing Investing and Financing Cash Flows

Investing and financing activities are explained on pages 707–711. These computations are the same for both the direct and the indirect methods.

STOP & THINK. . .

Fidelity Company reported the following for 2012 and 2011 (in millions):

At December 31,	2012	2011
Receivables, net.........................	$3,500	$3,900
Inventory....................................	5,200	5,000
Accounts payable	900	1,200
Income taxes payable	600	700

Year Ended December 31,	2012
Revenues	$23,000
Cost of goods sold.......................	14,100
Income tax expense	900

Based on these figures, how much cash did
- Fidelity collect from customers during 2012?
- Fidelity pay for inventory during 2012?
- Fidelity pay for income taxes during 2012?

Answers

		Beginning receivables	+	Revenues	−	Collections	=	Ending receivables
Collections from customers	= $23,400:	$3,900	+	$23,000	−	$23,400	=	$3,500

		Cost of goods sold	+	Increase in inventory	+	Decrease in accounts payable	=	Payments
Payments for inventory	= $14,600:	$14,100	+	($5,200 − $5,000)	+	($1,200 − $900)	=	$14,600

		Beginning income taxes payable	+	Income tax expense	−	Payment	=	Ending income taxes payable
Payment of income taxes	= $1,000:	$700	+	$900	−	$1,000	=	$600

Measuring Cash Adequacy: Free Cash Flow

Throughout this chapter, we have focused on cash flows from operating, investing, and financing activities. Some investors want to know how much cash a company can "free up" for new opportunities. **Free cash flow** is the amount of cash available from operations after paying for planned investments in plant assets. Free cash flow can be computed as follows:

$$\text{Free cash flow} = \frac{\text{Net cash provided}}{\text{by operating activities}} - \frac{\text{Cash payments earmarked for}}{\text{investments in plant assets}}$$

PepsiCo, Inc., uses free cash flow to manage its operations. Suppose PepsiCo expects net cash inflow of $2.3 billion from operations. Assume PepsiCo plans to spend $1.9 billion to modernize its bottling plants. In this case, PepsiCo's free cash flow would be $0.4 billion ($2.3 billion − $1.9 billion). If a good investment opportunity comes along, PepsiCo should have $0.4 billion to invest in the other company. **Shell Oil Company** also uses free-cash-flow analysis. A large amount of free cash flow is preferable because it means that a lot of cash is available for new investments. The Decision Guidelines that follow show some ways to use cash-flow and income data for investment and credit analysis.

DECISION GUIDELINES

INVESTORS' AND CREDITORS' USE OF CASH-FLOW AND RELATED INFORMATION

Jan Childres is a private investor. Through years of experience she has devised some guidelines for evaluating both stock investments and bond investments. Childres uses a combination of accrual-accounting data and cash-flow information. Here are her decision guidelines for both investors and creditors.

INVESTORS

Questions	Factors to Consider	Financial Statement Predictor/Decision Model*
1. How much in dividends can I expect to receive from an investment in stock?	Expected future net income	Income from continuing operations**
	Expected future cash balance	Net cash flows from (in order) ▶ operating activities ▶ investing activities ▶ financing activities
	Future dividend policy	Current and past dividend policy
2. Is the stock price likely to increase or decrease?	Expected future net income	Income from continuing operations**
	Expected future cash flows from operating activities	Income from continuing operations** Net cash flow from operating activities
3. What is the future stock price likely to be?	Expected future income from	
	▶ continuing operations, and	$$\text{Expected future price of a share of stock} = \frac{\text{Expected future earnings per share**}}{\text{Investment capitalization rate**}}$$
	▶ net cash flow from operating activities	$$\text{Expected future price of a share of stock} = \frac{\text{Net cash flow from operations per share}}{\text{Investment capitalization rate**}}$$

CREDITORS

Question	Factors to Consider	Financial Statement Predictor
Can the company pay the interest and principal at the maturity of a loan?	Expected future net cash flow from operating activities	Income from continuing operations** Net cash flow from operating activities

*There are many other factors to consider in making these decisions. These are some of the more common.

**See Chapter 11.

END-OF-CHAPTER SUMMARY PROBLEM

Adeva Health Foods, Inc., reported the following comparative balance sheets for 2012 and 2011 and the income statement for 2012.

Adeva Health Foods, Inc.
Comparative Balance Sheets
December 31, 2012 and 2011

	2012	2011
Cash	$ 19,000	$ 3,000
Accounts receivable	22,000	23,000
Inventories	34,000	31,000
Prepaid expenses	1,000	3,000
Equipment, net	90,000	79,000
Intangible assets	9,000	9,000
	$175,000	$148,000
Accounts payable	$ 14,000	$ 9,000
Accrued liabilities	16,000	19,000
Income tax payable	14,000	12,000
Notes payable	45,000	50,000
Common stock	31,000	20,000
Retained earnings	64,000	40,000
Treasury stock	(9,000)	(2,000)
	$175,000	$148,000

Adeva Health Foods, Inc.
Income Statement
Year Ended December 31, 2012

Sales revenue	$190,000
Gain on sale of equipment	6,000
Total revenue and gains	196,000
Cost of goods sold	85,000
Depreciation expense	19,000
Other operating expenses	36,000
Total expenses	140,000
Income before income tax	56,000
Income tax expense	18,000
Net income	$ 38,000

Assume that **Berkshire Hathaway** is considering buying Adeva. Berkshire Hathaway requests the following cash-flow data for 2012. There were no non-cash investing and financing activities.

a. Collections from customers.

b. Cash payments for inventory.

c. Cash payments for operating expenses.

d. Cash payment for income tax.

e. Cash received from the sale of equipment. Adeva paid $40,000 for new equipment during the year.

f. Issuance of common stock.

g. Issuance of notes payable. Adeva paid off $20,000 during the year.

h. Cash dividends. There were no stock dividends.

Provide the requested data. Show your work.

▶ **Answers**

a. Analyze Accounts Receivable (let X = Collections from customers):

Beginning	+	Sales	−	Collections	=	Ending
$23,000	+	$190,000	−	X	=	$22,000
				X	=	$191,000

b. Analyze Inventory and Accounts Payable (let X = Purchases, and let Y = Payments for inventory):

Beginning Inventory	+	Purchases	−	Ending Inventory	=	Cost of Goods Sold
$31,000	+	X	−	$34,000	=	$85,000
		X			=	$88,000

Beginning Accounts Payable	+	Purchases	−	Payments	=	Ending Accounts Payable
$9,000	+	$88,000	−	Y	=	$14,000
				Y	=	$83,000

c. Start with Other Operating Expenses, and adjust for the changes in Prepaid Expenses and Accrued Liabilities:

Other Operating Expenses	− Decrease in Prepaid Expenses	+ Decrease in Accrued Liabilities	=	Payments for Operating Expenses
$36,000	− $2,000	+ $3,000	=	$37,000

d. Analyze Income Tax Payable (let X = Payment of income tax):

Beginning	+	Income Tax Expense	−	Payments	=	Ending
$12,000	+	$18,000	−	X	=	$14,000
				X	=	$16,000

e. Analyze Equipment, Net (let X = Book value of equipment sold. Then combine with the gain or loss to compute cash received from the sale.):

Beginning	+	Acquisitions	–	Depreciation	–	Book Value Sold	=	Ending
$79,000	+	$40,000	–	$19,000	–	X	=	$90,000
						X	=	$10,000

Cash Received from Sale	=	Book Value Sold	+	Gain on Sale
$16,000	=	$10,000	+	$6,000

f. Analyze Common Stock (let X = Issuance):

Beginning	+	Issuance	=	Ending
$20,000	+	X	=	$31,000
		X	=	$11,000

g. Analyze Notes Payable (let X = Issuance):

Beginning	+	Issuance	–	Payment	=	Ending
$50,000	+	X	–	$20,000	=	$45,000
		X			=	$15,000

h. Analyze Retained Earnings (let X = Dividends):

Beginning	+	Net Income	–	Dividends	=	Ending
$40,000	+	$38,000	–	X	=	$64,000
				X	=	$14,000

REVIEW | Statement of Cash Flows

Quick Check (Answers are given on page 770.)

1. All except which of the following activities are reported on the statement of cash flows?
   a. Investing activities
   b. Operating activities
   c. Marketing activities
   d. Financing activities

2. Activities that create long-term liabilities are usually
   a. operating activities.
   b. financing activities.
   c. investing activities.
   d. non-cash investing and financing activities.

3. Activities affecting long-term assets are
   a. operating activities.
   b. marketing activities.
   c. financing activities.
   d. investing activities.

4. In 2012, MLL Corporation borrowed $90,000, paid dividends of $26,000, issued 12,000 shares of stock for $20 per share, purchased land for $25,000, and received dividends of $10,000. Net income was $120,000, and depreciation for the year totaled $11,000 Accounts receivable increased by $10,000. How much should be reported as net cash provided by operating activities by the indirect method?

a. $121,000

b. $115,000

c. $131,000

d. $420,000

5. Activities that obtain the cash needed to launch and sustain a company are

a. financing activities.

b. income activities.

c. marketing activities.

d. investing activities.

6. The exchange of stock for land would be reported as which of the following?

a. Exchanges are not reported on the statement of cash flows.

b. Non-cash investing and financing activities

c. Financing activities

d. Investing activities

Use the following Georgia Company information for questions 7–10.

Net income..	$40,000	Increase in accounts payable	$ 9,000
Depreciation expense	15,000	Acquisition of equipment	25,000
Payment of dividends	1,000	Sale of treasury stock	6,000
Increase in accounts receivable......................	3,000	Payment of long-term debt	13,000
Collection of long-term notes receivable..........	11,000	Proceeds from sale of land..........	42,000
Loss on sale of land..	10,000	Decrease in inventories...............	6,000

7. Under the indirect method, net cash provided by operating activities would be

a. $94,000.

b. $97,000.

c. $77,000.

d. $71,000.

8. Net cash provided by (used for) investing activities would be

a. $94,000.

b. $71,000.

c. $28,000.

d. $(97,000).

9. Net cash provided by (used for) financing activities would be

a. $5,000.

b. $1,000.

c. $(8,000).

d. $94,000.

10. The cost of land must have been

a. $42,000.

b. $52,000.

c. $5,000.

d. Cannot be determined from the data given

11. Cold Cup Ice Cream began the year with $30,000 in accounts receivable and ended the year with $16,000 in accounts receivable. If sales for the year were $575,000, the cash collected from customers during the year amounted to

a. $589,000.

b. $605,000.

c. $591,000.

d. $561,000.

12. Berkshire Farms, Ltd., made sales of $680,000 and had cost of goods sold of $440,000. Inventory decreased by $25,000, and accounts payable decreased by $12,000. Operating expenses were $195,000. How much was Berkshire Farms' net income for the year?
    a. $20,000
    b. $33,000
    c. $240,000
    d. $45,000

13. Use the Berkshire Farms data from question 12. Accounts payable relates solely to the purchase of inventory. How much cash did Berkshire Farms pay for inventory during the year?
    a. $20,000
    b. $452,000
    c. $440,000
    d. $427,000

Accounting Vocabulary

cash equivalents (p. 699) Highly liquid short-term investments that can be converted into cash immediately.

cash flows (p. 699) Cash receipts and cash payments (disbursements).

direct method (p. 701) Format of the operating activities section of the statement of cash flows; lists the major categories of operating cash receipts (collections from customers and receipts of interest and dividends) and cash disbursements (payments to suppliers, to employees, for interest and income taxes).

financing activities (p. 701) Activities that obtain from investors and creditors the cash needed to launch and sustain the business; a section of the statement of cash flows.

free cash flow (p. 726) The amount of cash available from operations after paying for planned investments in plant assets.

indirect method (p. 701) Format of the operating activities section of the statement of cash flows; starts with net income and reconciles to cash flows from operating activities.

investing activities (p. 701) Activities that increase or decrease the long-term assets available to the business; a section of the statement of cash flows.

operating activities (p. 700) Activities that create revenue or expense in the entity's major line of business; a section of the statement of cash flows. Operating activities affect the income statement.

statement of cash flows (p. 699) Reports cash receipts and cash payments classified according to the entity's major activities: operating, investing, and financing.

ASSESS YOUR PROGRESS

Short Exercises

S12-1 (*Learning Objective 1: Explain the purposes of the statement of cash flows*) State how the statement of cash flows helps investors and creditors perform each of the following functions:

   a. Predict future cash flows
   b. Evaluate management decisions

S12-2 (*Learning Objective 1: Explain the purposes of the statement of cash flows*) Bryant, Inc., has experienced an unbroken string of nine years of growth in net income. Nevertheless, the company is facing bankruptcy. Creditors are calling all of Bryant's loans for immediate payment, and the cash is simply not available. It is clear that the company's top managers overemphasized profits and gave too little attention to cash flows.

Write a brief memo, in your own words, to explain to the managers of Bryant, Inc., the purposes of the statement of cash flows.

S12-3 (*Learning Objective 2: Evaluate operating cash flows—indirect method*) Examine the statement of cash flows of Mirror, Inc.

Mirror, Inc.
Consolidated Statement of Cash Flows (Adapted, In millions)
Year Ended December 31, 2012

Cash flows from operating activities:		
Net income	$ 786	
Adjustment to reconcile net income to net cash		
used in operating activities:		
Depreciation and amortization	222	
Change in assets and liabilities, net of acquired businesses:		
Accounts receivable	(470)	
Other current assets	(160)	
Accounts payable	(78)	
Accrued expenses and other liabilities	(238)	
Unearned revenue	25	
Income taxes payable	(266)	
Other, net	26	
Net cash used in operating activities		(153)
Cash flows from investing activities:		
Purchase of property and equipment	$ (1,593)	
Purchase of investments	(21,282)	
Sale of investments	19,286	
Acquisitions of other companies	(363)	
Net cash used in investing activities		(3,952)
Cash flows from financing activities:		
Proceeds from the issuance of common stock, net	$ 835	
Other, net	378	
Net cash provided by financing activities		1,213
Other, net		18
Net increase (decrease) in cash and cash equivalents		(2,874)
Cash and cash equivalents at beginning of year		4,155
Cash and cash equivalents at end of year		$ 1,281

Suppose Mirror's operating activities *provided*, rather than *used*, cash. Identify three things under the indirect method that could cause operating cash flows to be positive.

S12-4 (*Learning Objectives 1, 2: Use cash-flow data to evaluate performance*) Top managers of Harmony Inns are reviewing company performance for 2012. The income statement reports a 20% increase in net income over 2011. However, most of the increase resulted from a gain on insurance proceeds from fire damage to a building. The balance sheet shows a large increase in receivables. The cash flows statement, in summarized form, reports the following:

Net cash used for operating activities	$(71,500)
Net cash provided by investing activities	43,000
Net cash provided by financing activities	36,000
Increase in cash during 2012	$ 7,500

Write a memo giving Harmony Inns' managers your assessment of 2012 operations and your outlook for the future. Focus on the information content of the cash flows data.

S12-5 (*Learning Objective 3: Report cash flows from operating activities—indirect method*)
Incredible America Transportation (IAT) began 2012 with accounts receivable, inventory, and prepaid expenses totaling $48,000. At the end of the year, IAT had a total of $49,000 for these

current assets. At the beginning of 2012, IAT owed current liabilities of $36,000, and at year-end current liabilities totaled $40,000.

Net income for the year was $81,000. Included in net income were a $9,000 loss on the sale of land and depreciation expense of $4,000.

Show how IAT should report cash flows from operating activities for 2012. IAT uses the *indirect* method.

S12-6 *(Learning Objective 2: Distinguish among operating, financing, and investing activities — indirect method)* Smith Clinic, Inc., is preparing its statement of cash flows (*indirect* method) for the year ended March 31, 2012. Consider the following items in preparing the company's statement of cash flows. Identify each item as an operating activity—addition to net income (O+) or subtraction from net income (O–), an investing activity (I), a financing activity (F), or an activity that is not used to prepare the cash flows statement by the indirect method (N). Place the appropriate symbol in the blank space.

	a. Increase in accounts payable
	b. Purchase of equipment
	c. Decrease in prepaid expense
	d. Collection of cash from customers
	e. Net income
	f. Retained earnings
	g. Payment of dividends
	h. Decrease in accrued liabilities
	i. Issuance of common stock
	j. Gain on sale of building
	k. Loss on sale of land
	l. Depreciation expense
	m. Increase in inventory
	n. Decrease in accounts receivable

S12-7 *(Learning Objective 3: Prepare operating cash flows—indirect method)* Eldred Corporation accountants have assembled the following data for the year ended June 30, 2012:

Net income..............................	$?	Cost of goods sold....................	$114,000
Payment of dividends	5,500	Other operating expenses.........	39,000
Proceeds from the issuance		Purchase of equipment	37,000
of common stock	15,000	Increase in current liabilities.....	11,000
Sales revenue...........................	222,000	Payment of note payable	29,000
Increase in current assets		Proceeds from sale of land........	31,000
other than cash	32,000	Depreciation expense	6,000
Purchase of treasury stock........	8,000		

Prepare the *operating activities section* of Eldred's statement of cash flows for the year ended June 30, 2012. Eldred uses the *indirect* method for operating cash flows.

S12-8 *(Learning Objective 3: Prepare a statement of cash flows—indirect method)* Use the data in Short Exercise 12-7 to prepare Eldred Corporation's statement of cash flows for the year ended June 30, 2012. Eldred uses the *indirect* method for operating activities.

S12-9 (*Learning Objective 3: Compute investing cash flows*) Motorvehicles of Philadelphia, Inc., reported the following financial statements for 2012:

Motorvehicles of Philadelphia, Inc.
Income Statement
Year Ended December 31, 2012

(In thousands)	
Service revenue	$720
Cost of goods sold	350
Salary expense	60
Depreciation expense	10
Other expenses	180
Total expenses	600
Net income	$120

Motorvehicles of Philadelphia, Inc.
Comparative Balance Sheets
December 31, 2012 and 2011

(In thousands)					
Assets	**2012**	**2011**	**Liabilities**	**2012**	**2011**
Current:			Current:		
Cash	$ 26	$ 12	Accounts payable	$ 51	$ 48
Accounts receivable	56	48	Salary payable	24	22
Inventory	72	87	Accrued liabilities	13	16
Prepaid expenses	7	6	Long-term notes payable	63	57
Long-term investments	52	75			
Plant assets, net	222	180	**Stockholders' Equity**		
			Common stock	47	36
			Retained earnings	237	229
Total	$435	$408	Total	$435	$408

Compute the following investing cash flows: (Enter all amounts in thousands.)

a. Acquisitions of plant assets (all were for cash). Motorvehicles of Philadelphia sold no plant assets.
b. Proceeds from the sale of investments. Motorvehicles of Philadelphia purchased no investments.

S12-10 (*Learning Objective 3: Compute financing cash flows*) Use the Motorvehicles of Philadelphia data in Short Exercise 12-9 to compute the following: (Enter all amounts in thousands.)

a. New borrowing or payment of long-term notes payable. Motorvehicles of Philadelphia had only one long-term note payable transaction during the year.
b. Issuance of common stock or retirement of common stock. Motorvehicles of Philadelphia had only one common stock transaction during the year.
c. Payment of cash dividends (same as dividends declared).

S12-11 (*Learning Objective 4: Compute operating cash flows—direct method*) Use the Motorvehicles of Philadelphia data in Short Exercise 12-9 to compute the following: (Enter all amounts in thousands.)

a. Collections from customers
b. Payments for inventory

S12-12 (*Learning Objective 4: Compute operating cash flows—direct method*) Use the Motorvehicles of Philadelphia data in Short Exercise 12-9 to compute the following: (Enter all amounts in thousands).

    a. Payments to employees
    b. Payments of other expenses

S12-13 (*Learning Objective 4: Prepare a statement of cash flows—direct method*) Paloma Horse Farm, Inc., began 2012 with cash of $100,000. During the year, Paloma earned service revenue of $594,000 and collected $580,000 from customers. Expenses for the year totaled $410,000, with $400,000 paid in cash to suppliers and employees. Paloma also paid $144,000 to purchase equipment and a cash dividend of $46,000 to stockholders. During 2012, Paloma borrowed $22,000 by issuing a note payable. Prepare the company's statement of cash flows for the year. Format operating activities by the *direct* method.

S12-14 (*Learning Objective 4: Computing operating cash flows—direct method*) Medford Golf Club, Inc., has assembled the following data for the year ended September 30, 2012:

Cost of goods sold............................	$106,000	Payment of dividends..........................	$ 9,000
Payments to suppliers.......................	112,000	Proceeds from issuance	
Purchase of equipment.....................	22,000	of common stock......................	15,000
Payments to employees.....................	66,000	Sales revenue..	235,000
Payment of note payable	17,000	Collections from customers................	202,000
Proceeds from sale of land................	46,000	Payment of income tax.......................	9,000
Depreciation expense	10,000	Purchase of treasury stock.................	5,400

Prepare the *operating activities section* of Medford Golf Club, Inc.'s statement of cash flows for the year ended September 30, 2012. Medford uses the *direct* method for operating cash flows.

S12-15 (*Learning Objective 4: Preparing a statement of cash flows—direct method*) Use the data in Short Exercise 12-14 to prepare Medford Golf Club, Inc.'s statement of cash flows for the year ended September 30, 2012. Medford uses the *direct* method for operating activities.

Exercises

MyAccountingLab

> All of the A and B exercises can be found within MyAccountingLab, an online homework and practice environment. Your instructor may ask you to complete these exercises using MyAccountingLab.

Group A

E12-16A (*Learning Objectives 2, 3: Distinguish among operating, investing, and financing activities for the statement of cash flows—indirect method*) McTaggart-Hicks Investments specializes in low-risk government bonds. Identify each of McTaggart-Hicks transactions as operating (O), investing (I), financing (F), non-cash investing and financing (NIF), or a transaction that is not reported on the statement of cash flows (N). Indicate whether each item increases (+) or decreases (−) cash. The *indirect* method is used for operating activities.

☐	a.	Sale of long-term investment
☐	b.	Issuance of long-term note payable to borrow cash
☐	c.	Increase in prepaid expenses
☐	d.	Payment of cash dividend
☐	e.	Loss of sale of equipment
☐	f.	Decrease in merchandise inventory
☐	g.	Acquisition of equipment by issuance of note payable
☐	h.	Increase in accounts payable
☐	i.	Amortization of intangible assets
☐	j.	Net income
☐	k.	Payment of long-term debt
☐	l.	Accrual of salary expense
☐	m.	Cash sale of land
☐	n.	Purchase of long-term investment
☐	o.	Acquisition of building by cash payment
☐	p.	Purchase of treasury stock
☐	q.	Issuance of common stock for cash
☐	r.	Decrease in accrued liabilities
☐	s.	Depreciation of equipment

E12-17A (*Learning Objectives 2, 3: Distinguish among operating, investing, and financing activities for the statement of cash flows—indirect method*) Indicate whether each of the following transactions affects an operating activity, an investing activity, a financing activity, or a non-cash investing and financing activity.

a.	Depreciation Expense	16,000		h.	Cash	74,000	
	Accumulated Depreciation		16,000		Accounts Receivable	13,000	
b.	Treasury Stock	12,000			Service Revenue		87,000
	Cash		12,000	i.	Bonds Payable	70,000	
c.	Land	123,000			Cash		70,000
	Cash		123,000	j.	Cash	110,000	
d.	Equipment	28,000			Common Stock		17,000
	Cash		28,000		Capital in Excess of Par		93,000
e.	Salary Expense	36,000		k.	Dividends Payable	25,000	
	Cash		36,000		Cash		25,000
f.	Furniture and Fixtures	36,000		l.	Loss on Disposal of Equipment	2,000	
	Cash		36,000		Equipment, Net		2,000
g.	Building	235,000		m.	Cash	10,000	
	Note Payable, Long-Term		235,000		Long-Term Investment		10,000

E12-18A (*Learning Objective 3: Compute cash flows from operating activities—indirect method*) The accounting records of Mid West Distributors, Inc., reveal the following:

Net income..	$10,000	Depreciation.....................................	$12,000
Collection of dividend revenue..........	7,300	Increase in current liabilities...........	15,000
Payment of interest............................	17,000	Increase in current assets	
Sales revenue.....................................	206,000	other than cash	25,000
Gain on sale of land	20,000	Payment of dividends.....................	7,300
Acquisition of land	38,000	Payment of income tax...................	4,000

▶ Requirement

1. Compute cash flows from operating activities by the *indirect* method. Use the format of the operating activities section of Exhibit 12-6. Also evaluate the operating cash flow of Mid West Distributors. Give the reason for your evaluation.

E12-19A (*Learning Objective 3: Compute cash flows from operating activities—indirect method*)
The accounting records of Michigan Fur Traders include these accounts:

Cash				Accounts Receivable				Inventory			
Dec 1	100,000			Dec 1	5,000			Dec 1	6,000		
Receipts	526,000	Payments	438,000	Receipts	528,000	Collections	526,000	Purchases	451,000	Cost of Sales	448,000
Dec 31	188,000			Dec 31	7,000			Dec 31	9,000		

Equipment				Accumulated Deprec.—Equipment				Accounts Payable			
Dec 1	181,000					Dec 1	60,000			Dec 1	14,500
Acquisition	10,000					Depreciation	9,000	Payments	331,000	Purchases	451,000
Dec 31	191,000					Dec 31	69,000			Dec 31	134,500

Accrued Liabilities				Retained Earnings			
		Dec 1	19,000	Quarterly		Dec 1	67,000
Payments	29,000	Receipts	25,000	Dividend	19,000	Net Income	10,000
		Dec 31	15,000			Dec 31	58,000

▶ Requirement

1. Compute Michigan's net cash provided by (used for) operating activities during December. Use the *indirect* method. Do you see any potential problems in Michigan's cash flows from operations? How can you tell?

E12-20A (*Learning Objective 3: Preparing the statement of cash flows—indirect method*)
The income statement and additional data of Bolton Travel Products, Inc., follow:

Bolton Travel Products, Inc.
Income Statement
Year Ended December 31, 2012

Revenues:		
Service revenue	$237,000	
Dividend revenue	8,700	$245,700
Expenses:		
Cost of goods sold	100,000	
Salary expense	59,000	
Depreciation expense	28,000	
Advertising expense	2,900	
Interest expense	2,100	
Income tax expense	14,000	206,000
Net income		$ 39,700

Additional data:

a. Acquisition of plant assets was $130,000. Of this amount, $75,000 was paid in cash and $55,000 by signing a note payable.
b. Proceeds from sale of land totaled $25,000.
c. Proceeds from issuance of common stock totaled $50,000.
d. Payment of long-term note payable was $16,000.
e. Payment of dividends was $11,000.

f. From the balance sheets:

	December 31,	
	2012	2011
Current assets:		
Cash	$125,000	$50,800
Accounts receivable	41,000	57,000
Inventory	94,000	73,000
Prepaid expenses	9,200	8,700
Current liabilities:		
Accounts payable	$32,000	$18,000
Accrued liabilities	82,000	57,000

► Requirements

1. Prepare Bolton's statement of cash flows for the year ended December 31, 2012, using the *indirect* method.
2. Evaluate Bolton's cash flows for the year. In your evaluation, mention all three categories of cash flows and give the reason for your evaluation.

E12-21A (*Learning Objective 3: Evaluate a statement of cash flows—indirect method*) Consider three independent cases for the cash flows of Building Blocks Corp. For each case, identify from the statement of cash flows how Building Blocks Corp. generated the cash to acquire new plant assets. Rank the three cases from the most healthy financially to the least healthy.

	Case A	Case B	Case C
Cash flows from operating activities:			
Net income	$ 25,000	$ 25,000	$ 25,000
Depreciation and amortization	11,000	11,000	11,000
Increase in current assets	(27,000)	(2,000)	(14,000)
Decrease in current liabilities	(12,000)	(5,000)	(1,000)
	(3,000)	29,000	21,000
Cash flows from investing activities:			
Acquisition of plant assets	(102,000)	(102,000)	(102,000)
Sales of plant assets	11,000	46,000	111,000
	(91,000)	(56,000)	9,000
Cash flows from financing activities:			
Issuance of stock	119,000	76,000	18,000
Payment of debt	(27,000)	(47,000)	(28,000)
	92,000	29,000	(10,000)
Net increase (decrease) in cash	$ (2,000)	$ 2,000	$ 20,000

E12-22A (*Learning Objectives 3, 4: Compute investing and financing amounts for the statement of cash flows*) Compute the following items for the statement of cash flows:

a. Beginning and ending Plant Assets, Net, are $99,000 and $92,000, respectively. Depreciation for the period was $11,000, and purchases of new plant assets were $23,000. Plant assets were sold at a $7,000 gain. What were the cash proceeds of the sale?
b. Beginning and ending Retained Earnings are $37,000 and $74,000, respectively. Net income for the period was $61,000, and stock dividends were $14,000. How much were cash dividends?

E12-23A (*Learning Objective 4: Compute cash flows from operating activities—direct method*) The accounting records of Best Pharmaceuticals, Inc., reveal the following:

Payment of salaries and wages	$32,000	Net income	$40,000
		Payment of income tax	16,000
Depreciation	23,000	Collection of dividend	
Decrease in current liabilities	18,000	revenue	12,000
		Payment of interest	20,000
Increase in current assets other than cash	21,000	Cash sales	55,000
		Gain on sale of land	7,000
Payment of dividends	9,000	Acquisition of land	25,000
Collection of accounts receivable	95,000	Payment of accounts payable	50,000

▶ Requirement

1. Compute cash flows from operating activities by the *direct* method. Also evaluate Best's operating cash flow. Give the reason for your evaluation.

E12-24A (*Learning Objective 4: Identify items for the statement of cash flows—direct method*) Selected accounts of Jessie Antiques show the following:

Salary Payable

		Beginning bal	8,000
Payments	23,000	Salary expense	21,000
		Ending bal	6,000

Buildings

Beginning bal	60,000	Depreciation	15,000
Acquisitions	90,000	Book value of building sold	89,000*
Ending bal	46,000		

*Sale price was $112,500.

Notes Payable

		Beginning bal	176,000
Payments	50,000	Issuance of note payable for cash	56,000
		Ending bal	182,000

▶ Requirement

1. For each account, identify the item or items that should appear on a statement of cash flows prepared by the *direct* method. State where to report the item.

E12-25A (*Learning Objective 4: Prepare the statement of cash flows—direct method*) The income statement and additional data of One Stop, Inc., follow:

One Stop, Inc. Income Statement Year Ended June 30, 2012		
Revenues:		
Sales revenue	$275,000	
Dividend revenue	7,500	$282,500
Expenses:		
Cost of goods sold	106,000	
Salary expense	50,000	
Depreciation expense	28,000	
Advertising expense	12,500	
Interest expense	1,000	
Income tax expense	10,500	208,000
Net income		$ 74,500

Additional data:

a. Collections from customers are $20,000 more than sales.
b. Payments to suppliers are $1,200 less than the sum of cost of goods sold plus advertising expense.
c. Payments to employees are $1,800 less than salary expense.
d. Dividend revenue, interest expense, and income tax expense equal their cash amounts.
e. Acquisition of plant assets is $213,000. Of this amount, $133,000 is paid in cash and $80,000 by signing a long-term note payable.
f. Proceeds from sale of land total $28,000.
g. Proceeds from issuance of common stock total $33,000.
h. Payment of long-term note payable is $13,000.
i. Payment of dividends is $7,000.
j. Cash balance, June 30, 2011, was $10,000.

► Requirements

1. Prepare One Stop, Inc.'s statement of cash flows and accompanying schedule of non-cash investing and financing activities. Report operating activities by the *direct* method.
2. Evaluate One Stop's cash flows for the year. In your evaluation, mention all three categories of cash flows and give the reason for your evaluation.

E12-26A (*Learning Objective 4: Compute amounts for the statement of cash flows—direct method*) Compute the following items for the statement of cash flows:

a. Beginning and ending Accounts Receivable are $21,000 and $17,000, respectively. Credit sales for the period total $66,000. How much are cash collections from customers?
b. Cost of goods sold is $81,000. Beginning Inventory was $30,000, and ending Inventory balance is $31,000. Beginning and ending Accounts Payable are $8,000 and $11,000, respectively. How much are cash payments for inventory?

Group B

E12-27B (*Learning Objectives 2, 3: Distinguish among operating, investing, and financing activities for the statement of cash flows—indirect method*) Carter-Pierce Investments specializes in low-risk government bonds. Identify each of Carter-Pierce's transactions as operating (O), investing (I), financing (F), non-cash investing and financing (NIF), or a transaction that is not reported on the statement of cash flows (N). Indicate whether each item increases (+) or decreases (−) cash. The *indirect* method is used for operating activities.

	a. Acquisition of building by cash payment
	b. Decrease in merchandise inventory
	c. Depreciation of equipment
	d. Decrease in accrued liabilities
	e. Payment of cash dividend
	f. Purchase of long-term investment
	g. Issuance of long-term note payable to borrow cash
	h. Increase in prepaid expenses
	i. Accrual of salary expense
	j. Acquisition of equipment by issuance of note payable
	k. Sale of long-term investment
	l. Issuance of common stock for cash
	m. Increase in accounts payable
	n. Amortization of intangible assets
	o. Loss on sale of equipment
	p. Payment of long-term debt
	q. Cash sale of land
	r. Purchase of treasury stock
	s. Net income

E12-28B (*Learning Objectives 2, 3: Distinguish among operating, investing, and financing activities for the statement of cash flows—indirect method*) Indicate whether each of the following transactions affects an operating activity, an investing activity, a financing activity, or a non-cash investing and financing activity.

a.	Cash	61,000		g.	Equipment	11,000	
	Common Stock		10,000		Cash		11,000
	Capital in Excess of Par		51,000	h.	Dividends Payable	13,000	
b.	Furniture and Fixtures	18,000			Cash		13,000
	Cash		18,000	i.	Salary Expense	14,000	
c.	Cash	52,000			Cash		14,000
	Accounts Receivable	11,000		j.	Building	105,000	
	Service Revenue		63,000		Note Payable—Long-Term		105,000
d.	Cash	7,000		k.	Treasury Stock	12,000	
	Long-Term Investment		7,000		Cash		12,000
e.	Loss on Disposal of Equipment	1,000		l.	Depreciation Expense	5,000	
	Equipment, Net		1,000		Accumulated Depreciation		5,000
f.	Land	15,000		m.	Bonds Payable	35,000	
	Cash		15,000		Cash		35,000

E12-29B (*Learning Objective 3: Compute cash flows from operating activities—indirect method*) The accounting records of South Central Distributors, Inc., reveal the following:

Net income..	$ 42,000	Depreciation.................................	$ 6,000
Collection of dividend revenue..........	7,100	Decrease in current liabilities..........	25,000
Payment of interest............................	12,000	Increase in current assets	
Sales revenue.....................................	307,000	other than cash....................	29,000
Gain on sale of land..........................	26,000	Payment of dividends....................	7,700
Acquisition of land...........................	35,000	Payment of income tax...................	14,000

▶ Requirement

1. Compute cash flows from operating activities by the *indirect* method. Use the format of the operating activities section of Exhibit 12-6. Also evaluate the operating cash flow of South Central Distributors. Give the reason for your evaluation.

E12-30B (*Learning Objective 3: Compute cash flows from operating activities—indirect method*) The accounting records of Ashby Fur Traders include these accounts:

Cash				Accounts Receivable				Inventory			
Aug 1	80,000			Aug 1	8,000			Aug 1	6,000		
Receipts	418,000	Payments	450,000	Receipts	522,000	Collections	418,000	Purchases	433,000	Cost of Sales	333,000
Aug 31	48,000			Aug 31	112,000			Aug 31	106,000		

Equipment			Accumulated Deprec.—Equipment				Accounts Payable			
Aug 1	181,000				Aug 1	45,000			Aug 1	15,000
Acquisition	4,000			Depreciation	5,000	Payments	334,000	Purchases	433,000
Aug 31	185,000				Aug 31	50,000			Aug 31	114,000

Accrued Liabilities				Retained Earnings			
		Aug 1	14,000	Quarterly		Aug 1	63,000
Payments	35,000	Receipts	30,000	Dividend	20,000	Net Income	25,000
		Aug 31	9,000			Aug 31	68,000

▶ Requirement

1. Compute Ashby's net cash provided by (used for) operating activities during August. Use the *indirect* method. Do you see any potential problems in Ashby's cash flows from operations? How can you tell?

E12-31B (*Learning Objective 3: Prepare the statement of cash flows—indirect method*) The income statement and additional data of Breen Travel Products, Inc., follow:

Breen Travel Products, Inc.
Income Statement
Year Ended December 31, 2012

Revenues:		
Service revenue	$283,000	
Dividend revenue	8,700	$291,700
Expenses:		
Cost of goods sold	96,000	
Salary expense	54,000	
Depreciation expense	27,000	
Advertising expense	4,300	
Interest expense	2,100	
Income tax expense	6,000	189,400
Net income		$102,300

Additional data:

a. Acquisition of plant assets was $200,000. Of this amount, $160,000 was paid in cash and $40,000 by signing a note payable.
b. Proceeds from sale of land totaled $23,000.

c. Proceeds from issuance of common stock totaled $60,000.
d. Payment of long-term note payable was $13,000.
e. Payment of dividends was $10,000.
f. From the balance sheets:

	December 31,	
	2012	2011
Current assets:		
Cash	$150,000	$138,900
Accounts receivable	44,000	57,000
Inventory	104,000	72,000
Prepaid expenses	9,500	8,300
Current liabilities:		
Accounts payable	$ 38,000	$ 23,000
Accrued liabilities	11,000	24,000

▶ Requirements

1. Prepare Breen's statement of cash flows for the year ended December 31, 2012, using the *indirect* method.
2. Evaluate Breen's cash flows for the year. In your evaluation, mention all three categories of cash flows and give the reason for your evaluation.

E12-32B (*Learning Objective 3: Evaluate a statement of cash flows—indirect method*) Consider three independent cases for the cash flows of Texas Tires Corp. For each case, identify from the statement of cash flows how Texas Tires Corp. generated the cash to acquire new plant assets. Rank the three cases from the most healthy financially to the least healthy.

	Case A	Case B	Case C
Cash flows from operating activities:			
Net income	$ 14,000	$ 14,000	$ 14,000
Depreciation and amortization	17,000	17,000	17,000
Increase in current assets	(1,000)	(7,000)	(3,000)
Decrease in current liabilities	(3,000)	(27,000)	(4,000)
	27,000	(3,000)	24,000
Cash flows from investing activities:			
Acquisition of plant assets	(141,000)	(141,000)	(141,000)
Sales of plant assets	148,000	28,000	47,000
	7,000	(113,000)	(94,000)
Cash flows from financing activities:			
Issuance of stock	26,000	149,000	104,000
Payment of debt	(38,000)	(28,000)	(45,000)
	(12,000)	121,000	59,000
Net increase (decrease) in cash	$ 22,000	$ 5,000	$ (11,000)

E12-33B (*Learning Objectives 3, 4: Compute investing and financing amounts for the statement of cash flows*) Compute the following items for the statement of cash flows:

a. Beginning and ending Plant Assets, Net, are $125,000 and $115,000, respectively. Depreciation for the period was $19,000, and purchases of new plant assets were $45,000. Plant assets were sold at a $10,000 gain. What were the cash proceeds of the sale?
b. Beginning and ending Retained Earnings are $44,000 and $69,000, respectively. Net income for the period was $61,000, and stock dividends were $10,000. How much were cash dividends?

E12-34B (*Learning Objective 4: Compute cash flows from operating activities—direct method*) The accounting records of Jasmine Pharmaceuticals, Inc., reveal the following:

Payment of salaries		Net income	$50,000
and wages	$ 31,000	Payment of income tax	20,000
Depreciation	27,000	Collection of dividend	
Increase in current		revenue	14,000
liabilities	20,000	Payment of interest	13,000
Increase in current assets		Cash sales	36,000
other than cash	24,000	Gain on sale of land	3,000
Payment of dividends	12,000	Acquisition of land	38,000
Collection of accounts		Payment of accounts	
receivable	105,000	payable	55,000

▶ Requirement

1. Compute cash flows from operating activities by the *direct* method. Also evaluate Jasmine's operating cash flow. Give the reason for your evaluation.

E12-35B (*Learning Objective 4: Identify items for the statement of cash flows—direct method*) Selected accounts of Ainsley Antiques show the following:

Salary Payable

		Beginning bal	11,000
Payments	15,000	Salary expense	32,000
		Ending bal	28,000

Buildings

Beginning bal	75,000	Depreciation	17,000
Acquisitions	116,000	Book value of building sold	88,000*
Ending bal	86,000		

*Sale price was $120,000.

Notes Payable

		Beginning bal	183,000
Payments	54,000	Issuance of note payable for cash	68,000
		Ending bal	197,000

▶ Requirement

1. For each account, identify the item or items that should appear on a statement of cash flows prepared by the *direct* method. State where to report the item.

E12-36B (*Learning Objective 4: Prepare the statement of cash flows—direct method*) The income statement and additional data of Value World, Inc., follow:

Value World, Inc. Income Statement Year Ended September 30, 2012		
Revenues:		
Sales revenue	$255,000	
Dividend revenue	9,500	$264,500
Expenses:		
Cost of goods sold	101,000	
Salary expense	43,000	
Depreciation expense	27,000	
Advertising expense	10,500	
Interest expense	2,200	
Income tax expense	11,500	195,200
Net income		$ 69,300

Additional data:

a. Collections from customers are $25,000 less than sales.
b. Payments to suppliers are $1,600 more than the sum of cost of goods sold plus advertising expense.
c. Payments to employees are $2,400 more than salary expense.
d. Dividend revenue, interest expense, and income tax expense equal their cash amounts.
e. Acquisition of plant assets is $209,000. Of this amount, $109,000 is paid in cash and $100,000 by signing a long-term note payable.
f. Proceeds from sale of land total $27,000.
g. Proceeds from issuance of common stock total $93,000.
h. Payment of long-term note payable is $17,000.
i. Payment of dividends is $9,000.
j. Cash balance, September 30, 2011, was $10,000.

▶ Requirements

1. Prepare Value World, Inc.'s statement of cash flows and accompanying schedule of non-cash investing and financing activities. Report operating activities by the *direct* method.
2. Evaluate Value World's cash flows for the year. In your evaluation, mention all three categories of cash flows and give the reason for your evaluation.

E12-37B (*Learning Objective 4: Compute amounts for the statement of cash flows—direct method*) Compute the following items for the statement of cash flows:

a. Beginning and ending Accounts Receivable are $23,000 and $27,000, respectively. Credit sales for the period total $67,000. How much are cash collections from customers?
b. Cost of goods sold is $80,000. Beginning Inventory balance is $29,000, and ending Inventory balance is $24,000. Beginning and ending Accounts Payable are $9,000 and $14,000, respectively. How much are cash payments for inventory?

Quiz

Test your understanding of the statement of cash flows by answering the following questions. Select the best choice from among the possible answers given.

Q12-38 Paying off bonds payable is reported on the statement of cash flows under
a. financing activities.
b. non-cash investing and financing activities.
c. operating activities.
d. investing activities.

Q12-39 The sale of inventory for cash is reported on the statement of cash flows under
a. investing activities.
b. non-cash investing and financing activities.
c. operating activities.
d. financing activities.

Q12-40 Selling equipment is reported on the statement of cash flows under
a. financing activities.
b. non-cash investing and financing activities.
c. operating activities.
d. investing activities.

Q12-41 Which of the following terms appears on a statement of cash flows—indirect method?
a. Collections from customers
b. Depreciation expense
c. Payments to suppliers
d. Cash receipt of interest revenue

Q12-42 On an indirect method statement of cash flows, an increase in a prepaid insurance would be
a. deducted from net income.
b. added to increases in current assets.
c. added to net income.
d. included in payments to suppliers.

Q12-43 On an indirect method statement of cash flows, an increase in accounts payable would be
a. added to net income in the operating activities section.
b. reported in the financing activities section.
c. deducted from net income in the operating activities section.
d. reported in the investing activities section.

Q12-44 On an indirect method statement of cash flows, a gain on the sale of plant assets would be
a. reported in the investing activities section.
b. ignored, since the gain did not generate any cash.
c. deducted from net income in the operating activities section.
d. added to net income in the operating activities section.

Q12-45 Select an activity for each of the following transactions:
1. Paying cash dividends is a/an _____ activity.
2. Receiving cash dividends is a/an _____ activity.

Q12-46 Photosmart Camera Co. sold equipment with a cost of $18,000 and accumulated depreciation of $6,000 for an amount that resulted in a gain of $4,000. What amount should Photosmart report on the statement of cash flows as "proceeds from sale of plant assets"?
a. $16,000
b. $12,000
c. $8,000
d. Some other amount

Questions 47–55 use the following data. Solomon Corporation formats operating cash flows by the *indirect* method.

Solomon's Income Statement for 2012

Sales revenue	$170,000	
Gain on sale of equipment	10,000*	$180,000
Cost of goods sold	112,000	
Depreciation	7,500	
Other operating expenses	24,000	143,500
Net income		$ 36,500

*The book value of equipment sold during 2012 was $20,000.

Solomon's Comparative Balance Sheets at the end of 2012

	2012	2011		2012	2011
Cash	$ 3,000	$ 2,000	Accounts payable	$ 7,000	$ 8,000
Accounts receivable	6,000	11,000	Accrued liabilities	5,000	1,000
Inventory	8,000	7,000	Common stock	24,000	12,000
Plant and equipment, net	95,000	67,000	Retained earnings	76,000	66,000
	$112,000	$87,000		$112,000	$87,000

Q12-47 How many items enter the computation of Solomon's net cash provided by operating activities?
a. 2
b. 5
c. 3
d. 7

Q12-48 How do Solomon's accrued liabilities affect the company's statement of cash flows for 2012?
a. Increase in cash provided by operating activities
b. They don't because the accrued liabilities are not yet paid
c. Increase in cash used by financing activities
d. Increase in cash used by investing activities

Q12-49 How do accounts receivable affect Solomon's cash flows from operating activities for 2012?
a. Decrease in cash provided by operating activities
b. Increase in cash provided by operating activities
c. They don't because accounts receivable result from investing activities
d. Decrease in cash used by investing activities

Q12-50 Solomon's net cash provided by operating activities during 2012 was
a. $41,000.
b. $47,000.
c. $38,000.
d. $44,000.

Q12-51 How many items enter the computation of Solomon's net cash flow from investing activities for 2012?
a. 5
b. 3
c. 2
d. 7

Q12-52 The book value of equipment sold during 2012 was $20,000. Solomon's net cash flow from investing activities for 2012 was

a. net cash used of $38,000.

b. net cash used of $47,000.

c. net cash used of $44,000.

d. net cash used of $25,500.

Q12-53 How many items enter the computation of Solomon's net cash flow from financing activities for 2012?

a. 3

b. 7

c. 2

d. 5

Q12-54 Solomon's largest financing cash flow for 2012 resulted from (Assume no stock dividends were distributed.)

a. sale of equipment.

b. purchase of equipment.

c. payment of dividends.

d. issuance of common stock.

Q12-55 Solomon's net cash flow from financing activities for 2012 was (Assume no stock dividends were distributed.)

a. net cash used of $25,500.

b. net cash provided of $12,000.

c. net cash provided of $42,000.

d. net cash used of $14,500.

Q12-56 Credit sales totaled $750,000, accounts receivable increased by $60,000, and accounts payable decreased by $40,000. How much cash did the company collect from customers?

a. $690,000

b. $810,000

c. $730,000

d. $750,000

Q12-57 Income Tax Payable was $5,000 at the end of the year and $2,600 at the beginning. Income tax expense for the year totaled $58,900. What amount of cash did the company pay for income tax during the year?

a. $56,500

b. $58,900

c. $61,300

d. $61,500

Problems

> All of the A and B problems can be found within MyAccountingLab, an online homework and practice environment. Your instructor may ask you to complete these problems using MyAccountingLab.

MyAccountingLab

Group A

P12-58A (*Learning Objectives 2, 3: Prepare an income statement, balance sheet, and statement of cash flows—indirect method*) Modern Automobiles of Denver, Inc., was formed on January 1, 2012. The following transactions occurred during 2012:

On January 1, 2012, Modern issued its common stock for $280,000. Early in January, Modern made the following cash payments:

a. $120,000 for equipment

b. $136,000 for inventory (four cars at $34,000 each)

c. $23,000 for 2012 rent on a store building

In February, Modern purchased nine cars for inventory on account. Cost of this inventory was $414,000 ($46,000 each). Before year-end, Modern paid $124,200 of this debt. Modern uses the FIFO method to account for inventory.

During 2012, Modern sold seven autos for a total of $490,000. Before year-end, Modern collected 90% of this amount.

The business employs four people. The combined annual payroll is $100,000, of which Modern owes $3,000 at year-end. At the end of the year, Modern paid income tax of $15,000.

Late in 2012, Modern declared and paid cash dividends of $16,000.

For equipment, Modern uses the straight-line depreciation method, over five years, with zero residual value.

▶ Requirements

1. Prepare Modern Automobiles of Denver, Inc.'s income statement for the year ended December 31, 2012. Use the single-step format, with all revenues listed together and all expenses together.
2. Prepare Modern's balance sheet at December 31, 2012.
3. Prepare Modern's statement of cash flows for the year ended December 31, 2012. Format cash flows from operating activities by using the *indirect* method.

P12-59A (*Learning Objectives 2, 4: Prepare an income statement, balance sheet, and statement of cash flows—direct method*) Use the Modern Automobiles of Denver, Inc., data from Problem 12-58A.

▶ Requirements

1. Prepare Modern's income statement for the year ended December 31, 2012. Use the single-step format, with all revenues listed together and all expenses together.
2. Prepare Modern's balance sheet at December 31, 2012.
3. Prepare Modern's statement of cash flows for the year ended December 31, 2012. Format cash flows from operating activities by using the *direct* method.

P12-60A (*Learning Objectives 2, 3: Prepare the statement of cash flows—indirect method*) Stellar Software Corp. has assembled the following data for the years ending December 31, 2012 and 2011.

	December 31,	
	2012	**2011**
Current Accounts:		
Current assets:		
Cash and cash equivalents	$85,500	$43,000
Accounts receivable	42,300	64,600
Inventories	34,600	79,000
Prepaid expenses	3,200	2,100
Current liabilities:		
Accounts payable	$ 9,100	$55,700
Income tax payable	28,600	16,300
Accrued liabilities	15,300	7,800

Transaction Data for 2012:

Acquisition of land by issuing		Purchase of treasury stock.....	$14,500
long-term note payable	$204,000	Loss on sale of equipment	4,000
Stock dividends	31,600	Payment of cash dividends	18,100
Collection of loan..................	10,000	Issuance of long-term note	
Depreciation expense	25,000	payable to borrow cash.....	34,800
Purchase of building..............	105,000	Net income..........................	57,000
Retirement of bonds payable		Issuance of common stock	
by issuing common stock	75,000	for cash	39,000
Purchase of long-term		Proceeds from sale of	
investment........................	45,400	equipment	12,700
		Amortization expense..........	4,200

▶ Requirement

1. Prepare Stellar Software Corp.'s statement of cash flows using the *indirect* method to report operating activities. Include an accompanying schedule of non-cash investing and financing activities.

P12-61A (*Learning Objectives 2, 3: Prepare the statement of cash flows—indirect method*)
The comparative balance sheets of Mystic Movie Theater Company at June 30, 2012, and 2011, reported the following:

	June 30,	
	2012	2011
Current assets:		
Cash and cash equivalents	$39,000	$22,000
Accounts receivable	14,800	22,200
Inventories	63,400	60,700
Prepaid expenses	3,700	1,600
Current liabilities:		
Accounts payable	$58,200	$55,200
Accrued liabilities	36,800	26,800
Income tax payable	9,500	10,500

Mystic Movie Theater's transactions during the year ended June 30, 2012, included the following:

Acquisition of land		Sale of long-term investment....	$13,600
by issuing note payable	$102,000	Depreciation expense	15,500
Amortization expense............	3,000	Cash purchase of building.....	50,000
Payment of cash dividend......	31,000	Net income............................	56,000
Cash purchase of		Issuance of common	
equipment.........................	56,700	stock for cash	8,000
Issuance of long-term note		Stock dividend......................	10,000
payable to borrow cash.....	44,000		

▶ Requirements

1. Prepare Mystic Movie Theater Company's statement of cash flows for the year ended June 30, 2012, using the *indirect* method to report cash flows from operating activities. Report non-cash investing and financing activities in an accompanying schedule.
2. Evaluate Mystic Movie Theater's cash flows for the year. Mention all three categories of cash flows and give the reason for your evaluation.

P12-62A (*Learning Objectives 2, 3: Prepare the statement of cash flows—indirect method*)
The 2012 and 2011 comparative balance sheets and 2012 income statement of Summer Time
Supply Corp. follow:

	December 31, 2012	December 31, 2011	Increase (Decrease)
Summer Time Supply Corp. Comparative Balance Sheets			
Current assets:			
Cash and cash equivalents	$ 67,200	$ 1,900	$ 65,300
Accounts receivable	54,700	45,000	9,700
Inventories	53,400	52,200	1,200
Prepaid expenses	2,400	5,000	(2,600)
Plant assets:			
Land	49,200	30,800	18,400
Equipment, net	52,900	49,600	3,300
Total assets	$279,800	$184,500	$ 95,300
Current liabilities:			
Accounts payable	$ 35,500	$ 26,900	$ 8,600
Salary payable	24,000	13,100	10,900
Other accrued liabilities	22,100	23,700	(1,600)
Long-term liabilities:			
Notes payable	49,000	30,000	19,000
Stockholders' equity:			
Common stock, no-par	89,000	64,000	25,000
Retained earnings	60,200	26,800	33,400
Total liabilities and stockholders' equity	$279,800	$184,500	$ 95,300

Summer Time Supply Corp.
Income Statement
Year Ended December 31, 2012

Revenues:		
Sales revenue		$441,000
Expenses:		
Cost of goods sold	$185,500	
Salary expense	76,700	
Depreciation expense	16,100	
Other operating expense	50,000	
Interest expense	24,100	
Income tax expense	28,500	
Total expenses		380,900
Net income		$ 60,100

Summer Time Supply had no non-cash investing and financing transactions during 2012. During
the year, there were no sales of land or equipment, no payment of notes payable, no retirements of
stock, and no treasury stock transactions.

► Requirements

1. Prepare the 2012 statement of cash flows, formatting operating activities by using the *indirect* method.
2. How will what you learned in this problem help you evaluate an investment?

P12-63A (*Learning Objectives 2, 4: Prepare the statement of cash flows—direct method*) Use the Summer Time Supply Corp. data from Problem 12-62A.

► Requirements

1. Prepare the 2012 statement of cash flows by using the *direct* method.
2. How will what you learned in this problem help you evaluate an investment?

P12-64A (*Learning Objectives 2, 4: Prepare the statement of cash flows—direct method*) Landry Furniture Gallery, Inc., provided the following data from the company's records for the year ended March 31, 2012:

  a. Credit sales, $600,000
  b. Loan to another company, $12,300
  c. Cash payments to purchase plant assets, $82,100
  d. Cost of goods sold, $292,200
  e. Proceeds from issuance of common stock, $8,000
  f. Payment of cash dividends, $48,500
  g. Collection of interest, $4,800
  h. Acquisition of equipment by issuing short-term note payable, $16,200
  i. Payments of salaries, $79,000
  j. Proceeds from sale of plant assets, $22,800, including $6,700 loss
  k. Collections on accounts receivable, $406,000
  l. Interest revenue, $4,000
  m. Cash receipt of dividend revenue, $4,500
  n. Payments to suppliers, $368,400
  o. Cash sales, $171,600
  p. Depreciation expense, $60,000
  q. Proceeds from issuance of note payable, $20,200
  r. Payments of long-term notes payable, $71,000
  s. Interest expense and payments, $13,400
  t. Salary expense, $77,200
  u. Loan collections, $12,500
  v. Proceeds from sale of investments, $8,900, including $2,400 gain
  w. Payment of short-term note payable by issuing long-term note payable, $66,000
  x. Amortization expenses, $6,600
  y. Income tax expense and payments, $38,000
  z. Cash balance: March 31, 2011, $100,000; March 31, 2012, $46,600

► Requirements

1. Prepare Landry Furniture Gallery, Inc.'s statement of cash flows for the year ended March 31, 2012. Use the *direct* method for cash flows from operating activities. Include an accompanying schedule of non-cash investing and financing activities.
2. Evaluate 2012 from a cash-flows standpoint. Give your reasons.

P12-65A (*Learning Objectives 2, 3, 4: Prepare the statement of cash flows—direct and indirect methods*) To prepare the statement of cash flows, accountants for Dora Electric Company have summarized 2012 activity in two accounts as follows:

Cash

Beginning bal	9,100	Payments on accounts payable	399,700
Sale of long-term investment	21,500	Payments of dividends	27,400
Collections from customers	661,200	Payments of salaries and wages	134,900
Issuance of common stock	61,000	Payments of interest	29,200
Receipts of dividends	17,500	Purchase of equipment	31,100
		Payments of operating expenses	34,000
		Payment of long-term note payable	41,400
		Purchase of treasury stock	19,000
		Payment of income tax	18,400
Ending Bal	35,200		

Common Stock

Beginning bal	56,600
Issuance for cash	61,000
Issuance to acquire land	80,300
Issuance to retire note payable	22,000
Ending bal	219,900

Dora's 2012 income statement and balance sheet data follow:

Dora Electric Company
Income Statement
Year Ended December 31, 2012

Revenues:		
Sales revenue		$679,100
Dividend revenue		17,500
Total revenue		696,600
Expenses and losses:		
Cost of goods sold	$348,200	
Salary and wage expense	142,800	
Depreciation expense	19,300	
Other operating expense	43,900	
Interest expense	28,300	
Income tax expense	16,000	
Loss on sale of investments	27,400	
Total expenses and losses		625,900
Net income		$ 70,700

Dora Electric Company
Selected Balance Sheet Data
December 31, 2012

	Increase (Decrease)
Current assets:	
Cash and cash equivalents	$ 26,100
Accounts receivable	17,900
Inventories	59,700
Prepaid expenses	600
Long-term investments	(48,900)
Equipment, net	11,800
Land	80,300
Current liabilities:	
Accounts payable	8,200
Interest payable	(900)
Salary payable	7,900
Other accrued liabilities	10,500
Income tax payable	(2,400)
Long-term note payable	(63,400)
Common stock	163,300
Retained earnings	43,300
Treasury stock	(19,000)

▶ Requirements

1. Prepare the statement of cash flows of Dora Electric Company for the year ended December 31, 2012, using the *direct* method to report operating activities. Also prepare the accompanying schedule of non-cash investing and financing activities.

2. Use Dora's 2012 income statement and balance sheet to prepare a supplementary schedule of cash flows from operating activities by using the *indirect* method.

P12-66A *(Learning Objectives 2, 3, 4: Prepare the statement of cash flows—indirect and direct methods)* The comparative balance sheets of Susan Saboda Design Studio, Inc., at June 30, 2012 and 2011, and transaction data for fiscal 2012, are as follows:

Susan Saboda Design Studio Comparative Balance Sheets			
	June 30,		Increase
	2012	2011	(Decrease)
Current assets:			
Cash	$ 28,600	$ 12,200	$ 16,400
Accounts receivable	59,000	22,100	36,900
Inventories	78,400	40,400	38,000
Prepaid expenses	1,500	2,300	(800)
Long-term investment	20,400	2,700	17,700
Equipment, net	74,700	73,800	900
Land	49,700	92,800	(43,100)
	$312,300	$246,300	$ 66,000
Current liabilities:			
Notes payable, short-term	$ 13,800	$ 18,700	$ (4,900)
Accounts payable	46,400	40,400	6,000
Income tax payable	13,400	15,100	(1,700)
Accrued liabilities	66,500	3,100	63,400
Interest payable	3,500	2,300	1,200
Salary payable	800	2,900	(2,100)
Long-term note payable	47,100	94,000	(46,900)
Common stock	69,300	51,200	18,100
Retained earnings	51,500	18,600	32,900
	$312,300	$246,300	$ 66,000

Transaction data for the year ended June 30, 2012, follows:

a. Net income, $70,600
b. Depreciation expense on equipment, $13,300
c. Purchased long-term investment, $17,700
d. Sold land for $36,400, including $6,700 loss
e. Acquired equipment by issuing long-term note payable, $14,200
f. Paid long-term note payable, $61,100
g. Received cash for issuance of common stock, $13,200
h. Paid cash dividends, $37,700
i. Paid short-term note payable by issuing common stock, $4,900

▶ Requirements

1. Prepare the statement of cash flows of Susan Saboda Design Studio, Inc., for the year ended June 30, 2012, using the *indirect* method to report operating activities. Also prepare the accompanying schedule of non-cash investing and financing activities. All current accounts except Notes payable, short term result from operating transactions.
2. Prepare a supplementary schedule showing cash flows from operations by the *direct* method. The accounting records provide the following: collections from customers, $228,600; interest received, $1,400; payments to suppliers, $98,400; payments to employees, $30,700; payments for income tax, $13,200; and payment of interest, $4,400.

Group B

P12-67B (*Learning Objectives 2, 3: Prepare an income statement, balance sheet, and statement of cash flows—indirect method*) Classic Automobiles of Cedar Grove, Inc., was formed on January 1, 2012. The following transactions occurred during 2012:

On January 1, 2012, Classic issued its common stock for $430,000. Early in January, Classic made the following cash payments:

  a. $160,000 for equipment
  b. $234,000 for inventory (six cars at $39,000 each)
  c. $18,000 for 2012 rent on a store building

In February, Classic purchased four cars for inventory on account. Cost of this inventory was $192,000 ($48,000 each). Before year-end, Classic paid $76,800 of this debt. Classic uses the FIFO method to account for inventory.

During 2012, Classic sold seven vintage autos for a total of $504,000. Before year-end, Classic collected 50% of this amount.

The business employs two people. The combined annual payroll is $60,000, of which Classic owes $9,000 at year-end. At the end of the year, Classic paid income tax of $22,000.

Late in 2012, Classic declared and paid cash dividends of $18,000.

For equipment, Classic uses the straight-line depreciation method, over five years, with zero residual value.

▶ Requirements

  1. Prepare Classic Automobiles of Cedar Grove, Inc.'s income statement for the year ended December 31, 2012. Use the single-step format, with all revenues listed together and all expenses together.
  2. Prepare Classic's balance sheet at December 31, 2012.
  3. Prepare Classic's statement of cash flows for the year ended December 31, 2012. Format cash flows from operating activities by using the *indirect* method.

P12-68B (*Learning Objectives 2, 4: Prepare an income statement, balance sheet, and statement of cash flows—direct method*) Use the Classic Automobiles of Cedar Grove, Inc., data from Problem 12-67B.

▶ Requirements

  1. Prepare Classic's income statement for the year ended December 31, 2012. Use the single-step format, with all revenues listed together and all expenses together.
  2. Prepare Classic's balance sheet at December 31, 2012.
  3. Prepare Classic's statement of cash flows for the year ended December 31, 2012. Format cash flows from operating activities by using the *direct* method.

P12-69B (*Learning Objectives 2, 3: Prepare the statement of cash flows—indirect method*) Galvin Software Corp. has assembled the following data for the year ended December 31, 2012:

	December 31,	
	2012	2011
Current Accounts:		
Current assets:		
Cash and cash equivalents	$85,600	$10,000
Accounts receivable	44,900	64,700
Inventories	39,000	78,000
Prepaid expenses	3,000	2,200
Current liabilities:		
Accounts payable	58,100	55,400
Income tax payable	28,400	16,300
Accrued liabilities	15,400	7,000

Transaction Data for 2012:

Acquisition of land by issuing		Purchase of treasury stock	$12,100
long-term note payable	$203,000	Gain on sale of equipment.....	8,000
Stock dividends	40,100	Payment of cash dividends	19,000
Collection of loan..................	10,600	Issuance of long-term note	
Depreciation expense	21,000	payable to borrow cash.....	50,600
Purchase of building..............	134,000	Net income..........................	61,000
Retirement of bonds payable		Issuance of common stock	
by issuing common stock	80,000	for cash	52,000
Purchase of long-term		Proceeds from sale of	
investment.........................	45,200	equipment	12,900
		Amortization expense..........	4,600

▶ Requirement

1. Prepare Galvin Software Corp.'s statement of cash flows using the *indirect* method to report operating activities. Include an accompanying schedule of non-cash investing and financing activities.

P12-70B (*Learning Objectives 2, 3: Prepare the statement of cash flows—indirect method*) The comparative balance sheets of Moynihan Movie Theater Company at September 30, 2012 and 2011, reported the following:

	September 30,	
	2012	2011
Current assets:		
Cash and cash equivalents	$ 40,400	$14,500
Accounts receivable	14,300	21,800
Inventories	63,500	60,600
Prepaid expenses	16,700	6,000
Current liabilities:		
Accounts payable	$57,700	$55,800
Accrued liabilities	24,100	17,100
Income tax payable	15,300	10,300

Moynihan's transactions during the year ended September 30, 2012, included the following:

Acquisition of land		Sale of long-term investment....	$12,300
by issuing note payable	$104,000	Depreciation expense	16,000
Amortization expense............	8,000	Cash purchase of building.....	44,000
Payment of cash dividend......	25,000	Net income...........................	56,000
Cash purchase of		Issuance of common	
equipment........................	62,200	stock for cash...................	12,000
Issuance of long-term note		Stock dividend......................	13,000
payable to borrow cash.....	45,000		

▶ Requirements

1. Prepare Moynihan Movie Theater Company's statement of cash flows for the year ended September 30, 2012, using the *indirect* method to report cash flows from operating activities. Report non-cash investing and financing activities in an accompanying schedule.
2. Evaluate Moynihan's cash flows for the year. Mention all three categories of cash flows and give the reason for your evaluation.

P12-71B (*Learning Objectives 2, 3: Prepare the statement of cash flows—indirect method*)
The 2012 and 2011 comparative balance sheets and 2012 income statement of Perfect Supply Corp. follow:

Perfect Supply Corp.
Comparative Balance Sheets

	December 31, 2012	December 31, 2011	Increase (Decrease)
Current assets:			
Cash and cash equivalents	$ 47,500	$ 5,000	$42,500
Accounts receivable	61,000	60,000	1,000
Inventories	65,200	52,200	13,000
Prepaid expenses	2,500	1,000	1,500
Plant assets:			
Land	48,400	32,600	15,800
Equipment, net	64,100	49,100	15,000
Total assets	$288,700	$199,900	$88,800
Current liabilities:			
Accounts payable	$ 35,400	$ 28,000	$ 7,400
Salary payable	32,000	36,500	(4,500)
Other accrued liabilities	22,800	24,100	(1,300)
Long-term liabilities:			
Notes payable	58,000	30,000	28,000
Stockholders' equity:			
Common stock, no-par	88,500	64,300	24,200
Retained earnings	52,000	17,000	35,000
Total liabilities and stockholders' equity	$288,700	$199,900	$88,800

Perfect Supply Corp.
Income Statement
Year Ended December 31, 2012

Revenues:		
Sales revenue		$441,000
Expenses:		
Cost of goods sold	$185,300	
Salary expense	76,900	
Depreciation expense	15,000	
Other operating expense	50,200	
Interest expense	24,800	
Income tax expense	29,100	
Total expenses		381,300
Net income		$ 59,700

Perfect Supply had no non-cash investing and financing transactions during 2012. During the year, there were no sales of land or equipment, no payment of notes payable, no retirements of stock, and no treasury stock transactions.

▶ Requirements

1. Prepare the 2012 statement of cash flows, formatting operating activities by using the *indirect* method.
2. How will what you learned in this problem help you evaluate an investment?

P12-72B (*Learning Objectives 2, 4: Prepare the statement of cash flows—direct method*) Use the Perfect Supply Corp. data from Problem P12-71B.

▶ Requirements

1. Prepare the 2012 statement of cash flows by using the *direct* method.
2. How will what you learned in this problem help you evaluate an investment?

P12-73B (*Learning Objectives 2, 4: Prepare the statement of cash flows—direct method*) Fashion Furniture Gallery, Inc., provided the following data from the company's records for the year ended December 31, 2012:

    a. Credit sales, $522,000
    b. Loan to another company, $8,900
    c. Cash payments to purchase plant assets, $77,000
    d. Cost of goods sold, $403,000
    e. Proceeds from issuance of common stock, $10,000
    f. Payment of cash dividends, $48,200
    g. Collection of interest, $4,900
    h. Acquisition of equipment by issuing short-term note payable, $16,300
    i. Payments of salaries, $78,000
    j. Proceeds from sale of plant assets, $23,000, including $6,600 loss
    k. Collections on accounts receivable, $333,000
    l. Interest revenue, $1,800
    m. Cash receipt of dividend revenue, $4,000
    n. Payments to suppliers, $299,400
    o. Cash sales, $171,800
    p. Depreciation expense, $49,800
    q. Proceeds from issuance of note payable, $24,500
    r. Payments of long-term notes payable, $57,000
    s. Interest expense and payments, $13,800

t. Salary expense, $74,900

u. Loan collections, $8,500

v. Proceeds from sale of investments, $9,500, including $2,200 gain

w. Payment of short-term note payable by issuing long-term note payable, $94,000

x. Amortization expenses, $6,600

y. Income tax expense and payments, $36,000

z. Cash balance: December 31, 2011, $100,000; December 31, 2012, $70,900

▶ Requirements

1. Prepare Fashion Furniture Gallery, Inc.'s statement of cash flows for the year ended December 31, 2012. Use the *direct* method for cash flows from operating activities. Include an accompanying schedule of non-cash investing and financing activities.

2. Evaluate 2012 from a cash-flows standpoint. Give your reasons.

P12-74B (*Learning Objectives 2, 3, 4: Prepare the statement of cash flows—direct and indirect methods*) To prepare the statement of cash flows, accountants for Rosie Electric Company have summarized 2012 activity in two accounts as follows:

Cash

Beginning bal	44,300	Payments on accounts payable	399,000
Sale of long-term investment	32,400	Payments of dividends	27,800
Collections from customers	661,500	Payments of salaries and wages	143,900
Issuance of common stock	47,300	Payments of interest	27,000
Receipts of dividends	16,900	Purchase of equipment	31,100
		Payments of operating expenses	34,300
		Payment of long-term note payable	41,000
		Purchase of treasury stock	26,300
		Payment of income tax	18,600
Ending Bal	53,400		

Common Stock

		Beginning bal	56,600
		Issuance for cash	47,300
		Issuance to acquire land	52,000
		Issuance to retire note payable	24,000
		Ending bal	179,900

Rosie's 2012 income statement and balance sheet data follow:

Rosie Electric Company
Income Statement
Year Ended December 31, 2012

Revenues:		
Sales revenue		$634,000
Dividend revenue		16,900
Total revenue		650,900
Expenses and losses:		
Cost of goods sold	$347,500	
Salary and wage expense	151,500	
Depreciation expense	18,600	
Other operating expense	23,500	
Interest expense	28,700	
Income tax expense	15,200	
Loss on sale of investments	16,500	
Total expenses and losses		601,500
Net income		$ 49,400

Rosie Electric Company
Selected Balance Sheet Data
December 31, 2012

	Increase (Decrease)
Current assets:	
Cash and cash equivalents	$ 9,100
Accounts receivable	(27,500)
Inventories	59,700
Prepaid expenses	400
Long-term investments	(48,900)
Equipment, net	12,500
Land	52,000
Current liabilities:	
Accounts payable	8,200
Interest payable	1,700
Salary payable	7,600
Other accrued liabilities	(10,400)
Income tax payable	(3,400)
Long-term note payable	(65,000)
Common stock	123,300
Retained earnings	21,600
Treasury stock	(26,300)

▶ Requirements

1. Prepare the statement of cash flows of Rosie Electric Company for the year ended December 31, 2012, using the *direct* method to report operating activities. Also prepare the accompanying schedule of non-cash investing and financing activities.

2. Use Rosie's 2012 income statement and balance sheet to prepare a supplementary schedule of cash flows from operating activities by using the *indirect* method.

P12-75B (*Learning Objectives 2, 3, 4: Prepare the statement of cash flows—indirect and direct methods*) The comparative balance sheets of Lesley Leary Design Studio, Inc., at June 30, 2012 and 2011, and transaction data for fiscal 2012, are as follows:

		June 30,		Increase
		2012	2011	(Decrease)
Current assets:				
Cash		$ 28,600	$ 18,500	$ 10,100
Accounts receivable		48,000	31,700	16,300
Inventories		68,700	50,200	18,500
Prepaid expenses		1,900	2,700	(800)
Long-term investment		10,000	5,200	4,800
Equipment, net		74,700	73,600	1,100
Land		33,100	89,900	(56,800)
		$265,000	$271,800	$ (6,800)
Current liabilities:				
Notes payable, short-term		$ 13,800	$19,200	$ (5,400)
Accounts payable		39,500	40,900	(1,400)
Income tax payable		13,500	15,000	(1,500)
Accrued liabilities		20,700	9,600	11,100
Interest payable		3,300	2,800	500
Salary payable		4,500	4,900	(400)
Long-term note payable		38,400	84,100	(45,700)
Common stock		65,400	51,800	13,600
Retained earnings		65,900	43,500	22,400
		$265,000	$271,800	$ (6,800)

Lesley Leary Design Studio
Comparative Balance Sheets

Transaction data for the year ended June 30, 2012, follows:

a. Net income, $60,500
b. Depreciation expense on equipment, $13,900
c. Purchased long-term investment, $4,800
d. Sold land for $50,400, including $6,400 loss
e. Acquired equipment by issuing long-term note payable, $15,000
f. Paid long-term note payable, $60,700
g. Received cash for issuance of common stock, $8,200
h. Paid cash dividends, $38,100
i. Paid short-term note payable by issuing common stock, $5,400

▶ Requirements

1. Prepare the statement of cash flows of Lesley Leary Design Studio, Inc., for the year ended June 30, 2012, using the *indirect* method to report operating activities. Also prepare the accompanying schedule of non-cash investing and financing activities. All current accounts except Notes payable, short-term, result from operating transactions.
2. Prepare a supplementary schedule showing cash flows from operations by the *direct* method. The accounting records provide the following: collections from customers, $232,600; interest received, $1,600; payments to suppliers, $130,300; payments to employees, $29,500; payments for income tax, $13,500; and payment of interest, $5,800.

Challenge Exercises and Problem

E12-76 (*Learning Objectives 3, 4: Compute cash-flow amounts*) Rodeo Drive, Inc., reported the following in its financial statements for the year ended May 31, 2012 (in thousands):

	2012	2011
Income Statement		
Net sales	$25,118	$21,543
Cost of sales	18,162	15,333
Depreciation	268	227
Other operating expenses	3,885	4,283
Income tax expense	537	488
Net income	$ 2,266	$ 1,212
Balance Sheet		
Cash and equivalents	$ 13	$ 10
Accounts receivable	597	612
Inventory	3,100	2,833
Property and equipment, net	4,345	3,431
Accounts payable	1,549	1,368
Accrued liabilities	939	636
Income tax payable	198	190
Long-term liabilities	477	466
Common stock	518	443
Retained earnings	4,374	3,783

► Requirement

1. Determine the following cash receipts and payments for Rodeo Drive, Inc., during 2012: (Enter all amounts in thousands.)
    a. Collections from customers
    b. Payments for inventory
    c. Payments for other operating expenses
    d. Payment of income tax
    e. Proceeds from issuance of common stock
    f. Payment of cash dividends

E12-77 (*Learning Objective 3: Use the balance sheet and the statement of cash flows together*) Craftsman Specialties reported the following at December 31, 2012 (in thousands):

	2012	2011
From the comparative balance sheet:		
Property and equipment, net	$10,600	$9,640
Long-term notes payable	4,400	3,000
From the statement of cash flows:		
Depreciation	$ 1,910	
Capital expenditures	(4,175)	
Proceeds from sale of property and equipment	820	
Proceeds from issuance of long-term note payable	1,220	
Payment of long-term note payable	(140)	
Issuance of common stock	385	

► Requirement

1. Determine the following items for Craftsman Specialties during 2012:
   a. Gain or loss on the sale of property and equipment
   b. Amount of long-term debt issued for something other than cash

P12-78 (*Learning Objectives 2, 3: Prepare a balance sheet from a statement of cash flows*)
The December 31, 2011, Balance Sheet and the 2012 Statement of Cash Flows for Snow, Inc.,
follow:

<table>
<tr><td colspan="2" align="center">**Snow, Inc.**
Balance Sheet
December 31, 2011</td></tr>
<tr><td>**Assets:**</td><td></td></tr>
<tr><td>Cash</td><td>$ 11,000</td></tr>
<tr><td>Accounts receivable (net)</td><td>92,000</td></tr>
<tr><td>Inventory</td><td>103,000</td></tr>
<tr><td>Prepaid expenses</td><td>6,000</td></tr>
<tr><td>Land</td><td>69,000</td></tr>
<tr><td>Machinery and equipment (net)</td><td>59,000</td></tr>
<tr><td>Total</td><td>$340,000</td></tr>
<tr><td>**Liabilities:**</td><td></td></tr>
<tr><td>Accounts payable</td><td>$ 66,000</td></tr>
<tr><td>Unearned revenue</td><td>1,000</td></tr>
<tr><td>Income taxes payable</td><td>4,000</td></tr>
<tr><td>Long-term debt</td><td>75,000</td></tr>
<tr><td>**Total liabilities**</td><td>$146,000</td></tr>
<tr><td>**Stockholders' equity:**</td><td></td></tr>
<tr><td>Common stock, no par</td><td>$ 26,000</td></tr>
<tr><td>Retained earnings</td><td>168,000</td></tr>
<tr><td>Total stockholders' equity</td><td>$194,000</td></tr>
<tr><td>Total liabilities and stockholders' equity</td><td>$340,000</td></tr>
</table>

Snow, Inc.
Statement of Cash Flows
Year Ended December 31, 2012

Cash flows from operating activities:		
Net income		$18,000
Adjustments to reconcile net income to net cash		
provided by operating activities:		
Depreciation	$16,000	
Loss on sale of equipment	15,000	
Gain on sale of land	(6,000)	
Change in assets and liabilities:		
Accounts receivable	10,000	
Inventory	(7,000)	
Prepaid expenses	1,000	
Accounts payable	12,000	
Taxes payable	(2,500)	
Unearned revenue	1,500	40,000
Net cash provided by operating activities		$58,000
Cash flows from investing activities:		
Purchase of equipment	(25,000)	
Sale of equipment	9,000	
Sale of land	11,000	
Net cash used for investing activities		(5,000)
Cash flows from financing activities:		
Repayment of long-term debt	(16,000)	
Issuance of common stock	20,000	
Dividends paid (dividends declared, $7,000)	(5,000)	
Net cash provided by financing activities		(1,000)
Increase (decrease) in cash		52,000
Cash balance, December 31, 2011		11,000
Cash balance, December 31, 2012		$63,000

▶ Requirement

1. Prepare the December 31, 2012, balance sheet for Snow, Inc.

APPLY YOUR KNOWLEDGE

Decision Cases

Case 1. (*Learning Objective 3: Prepare and use the statement of cash flows to evaluate operations*) The 2012 income statement and the 2012 comparative balance sheet of T-Bar-M Camp, Inc., have just been distributed at a meeting of the camp's board of directors. The directors raise a fundamental question: Why is the cash balance so low? This question is especially troublesome since 2012 showed record profits. As the controller of the company, you must answer the question.

T–Bar–M Camp, Inc.
Income Statement
Year Ended December 31, 2012

(In thousands)	
Revenues:	
Sales revenue	$436
Expenses:	
Cost of goods sold	$221
Salary expense	48
Depreciation expense	46
Interest expense	13
Amortization expense	11
Total expenses	339
Net income	$ 97

T–Bar–M Camp, Inc.
Comparative Balance Sheets
December 31, 2012 and 2011

(In thousands)	2012	2011
Assets:		
Cash	$ 17	$ 63
Accounts receivable, net	72	61
Inventories	194	181
Long-term investments	31	0
Property, plant, and equipment	369	259
Accumulated depreciation	(244)	(198)
Patents	177	188
Totals	$ 616	$ 554
Liabilities and owners' equity:		
Accounts payable	$ 63	$ 56
Accrued liabilities	12	17
Notes payable, long-term	179	264
Common stock, no par	149	61
Retained earnings	213	156
Totals	$ 616	$ 554

▶ Requirements

1. Prepare a statement of cash flows for 2012 in the format that best shows the relationship between net income and operating cash flow. The company sold no plant assets or long-term investments and issued no notes payable during 2012. There were *no* non-cash investing and financing transactions during the year. Show all amounts in thousands.
2. Answer the board members' question: Why is the cash balance so low? Point out the two largest cash payments during 2012. (Challenge)
3. Considering net income and the company's cash flows during 2012, was it a good year or a bad year? Give your reasons.

Case 2. *(Learning Objectives 1, 2: Use cash-flow data to evaluate an investment)* Applied Technology, Inc., and Four-Star Catering are asking you to recommend their stock to your clients. Because Applied and Four-Star earn about the same net income and have similar financial positions, your decision depends on their statements of cash flows, summarized as follows:

	Applied		Four–Star	
Net cash provided by operating activities:		$ 30,000		$ 70,000
Cash provided by (used for) investing activities:				
Purchase of plant assets	$(20,000)		$(100,000)	
Sale of plant assets	40,000	20,000	10,000	(90,000)
Cash provided by (used for) financing activities:				
Issuance of common stock		—		30,000
Paying off long-term debt		(40,000)		—
Net increase in cash		$ 10,000		$10,000

Based on their cash flows, which company looks better? Give your reasons. (Challenge)

Ethical Issue

Columbia Motors is having a bad year. Net income is only $37,000. Also, two important overseas customers are falling behind in their payments to Columbia, and Columbia's accounts receivable are ballooning. The company desperately needs a loan. The Columbia board of directors is considering ways to put the best face on the company's financial statements. Columbia's bank closely examines cash flow from operations. Daniel Peavey, Columbia's controller, suggests reclassifying as long-term the receivables from the slow-paying clients. He explains to the board that removing the $80,000 rise in accounts receivable from current assets will increase net cash provided by operations. This approach may help Columbia get the loan.

▶ Requirements

1. Using only the amounts given, compute net cash provided by operations, both without and with the reclassification of the receivables. Which reporting makes Columbia look better?
2. Identify the ethical issue(s).
3. Who are the stakeholders?
4. Analyze the issue from the (a) economic, (b) legal, and (c) ethical standpoints. What is the potential impact on all stakeholders?
5. What should the board do?
6. Under what conditions would the reclassification of the receivables be considered ethical?

Focus on Financials: | Amazon.com, Inc.

(Learning Objectives 1, 2, 3, 4: Use the statement of cash flows) Use **Amazon.com, Inc.'s** consolidated statement of cash flows along with the company's other consolidated financial statements, all in Appendix A at the end of the book, to answer the following questions.

▶ Requirements

1. By which method does Amazon.com, Inc., report cash flows from operating activities? How can you tell?

2. Suppose Amazon.com, Inc., reported net cash flows from operating activities by using the direct method. Compute the following amounts for the year ended December 31, 2010 (ignore the statement of cash flows, and use only Amazon.com, Inc.'s income statement and balance sheet).

   a. Collections from vendors, customers, and others. Use the information in Note 1—Description of Business and Accounting Policies. Prepare a T-account for Gross Accounts Receivable. Prepare another T-account for Allowance for Doubtful Accounts. Calculate the beginning and ending gross amounts of gross accounts receivable by adding the beginning and ending balances of allowance for doubtful accounts ($72 million and $72 million, respectively) to the net accounts receivable at both the beginning and end of the year. Assume that all sales are on account. Also assume that the company uses the percentage of net sales method for estimating doubtful accounts expense, and that the company estimates this amount at 0.5%.

   b. Payments to suppliers. Amazon.com, Inc., calls its Cost of Goods Sold "Cost of Sales." For this computation, use the format provided in Exhibit 12-15. Assume all inventory is purchased on account, and that all cash payments to suppliers are made from accounts payable.

   c. Refer to Note 3—Fixed Assets. Prepare a T-account for Gross Fixed Assets and another T-account for Accumulated Depreciation. Fill in the beginning balances as supplied in Note 3. Analyze all activity in the fixed assets and accumulated depreciation accounts for 2010. In your analysis, make the following assumptions. Refer to the supplemental cash flow information at the bottom of the cash flow statement. Assume that both fixed asset acquisitions acquired under capital leases and fixed assets acquired under build-to-suit leases were non-cash financing and investing activities. Assume that, of the $568 million for depreciation and amortization (operating section of cash flow statement), $400 million is for depreciation expense. Prepare journal entries for (a) acquisition of leased equipment under capital leases, (b) acquisition of fixed assets for cash, (c) depreciation expense for fixed assets, and (d) for retirement of fixed assets. What is the gain or loss on retirement of fixed assets? Where would this gain or loss be reported? (Challenge)

   d. Evaluate 2010 for Amazon.com, Inc., in terms of net income, total assets, stockholders' equity, cash flows from operating activities, and overall results. Be specific. (Challenge)

Focus on Analysis: | RadioShack Corporation

(*Learning Objectives 1, 2, 3, 4: Analyze cash flows*) Refer to the **RadioShack Corporation**, consolidated financial statements in Appendix B at the end of this book. Focus on the year ended December 31, 2010.

1. What is RadioShack Corporation's main source of cash? Is this good news or bad news to RadioShack managers, stockholders, and creditors? What is RadioShack Corporation's main use of cash? Is this good news or bad news? Discuss your reasoning.

2. Explain briefly the three most significant differences between net cash provided by operations and net income.

3. Did RadioShack Corporation buy or sell more fixed assets during 2010 than in previous years? How can you tell?

4. Identify the largest two items in the financing activities section of the Consolidated Statement of Cash Flows. Explain the company's probable reasoning behind these two expenditures.

5. Evaluate RadioShack Corporation's overall performance for 2010 in terms of cash flows. Be as specific as you can. What other information would be helpful to you in making your evaluation (Challenge)?

Group Projects

Project 1. Each member of the group should obtain the annual report of a different company. Select companies in different industries. Evaluate each company's trend of cash flows for the most recent two years. In your evaluation of the companies' cash flows, you may use any other information that is publicly available—for example, the other financial statements (income statement, balance sheet, statement of stockholders' equity, and the related notes) and news stories from magazines and newspapers. Rank the companies' cash flows from best to worst and write a two-page report on your findings.

Project 2. Select a company and obtain its annual report, including all the financial statements. Focus on the statement of cash flows and, in particular, the cash flows from operating activities. Specify whether the company uses the direct method or the indirect method to report operating cash flows. As necessary, use the other financial statements (income statement, balance sheet, and statement of stockholders' equity) and the notes to prepare the company's cash flows from operating activities by using the *other* method.

MyAccountingLab

> For online homework, exercises, and problems that provide you with immediate feedback, please visit **www.myaccountinglab.com**.

Quick Check Answers

1. *c*
2. *b*
3. *d*
4. *c* ($120,000 + $11,000)
5. *a*
6. *b*
7. *c* ($40,000 + $15,000 − $3,000 + $10,000 + $9,000 + $6,000)
8. *c* ($11,000 − $25,000 + $42,000)
9. *c* (− $1,000 + $6,000 − $13,000)
10. *b* ($42,000 + $10,000)
11. *a* ($30,000 + $575,000 − $16,000)
12. *d* ($680,000 − $440,000 − $195,000)
13. *d* ($440,000 − $25,000 + $12,000)

13 Financial Statement Analysis

SPOTLIGHT: How Well is Amazon.com Doing?

Throughout this book we have shown how to account for the financial position, results of operations, and cash flows of companies such as **Apple, Inc.**, **Starbucks**, **PepsiCo**, **Southwest Airlines**, and **Google.** Only one aspect of the course remains: financial statement analysis. In this chapter, we analyze the financial statements of Amazon.com, one of the book's focus companies, whose annual report is in Appendix A, using horizontal and vertical analysis. In the second half of the chapter, we illustrate financial statement analysis of Apple, Inc., using the ratios covered in previous chapters of the text.

Amazon.com is the largest virtual supermarket on the globe. Since its inception as mostly a bookseller in 1995, the company has become synonymous with Internet retailing, expanding its lines of merchandise to cover almost every conceivable consumer item. Amazon.com's most famous recent product is the Kindle, an integrated information retrieval system developed by an Amazon subsidiary, which has revolutionized the way people access books, newspapers, magazines, blogs, and other digital media. You may even be reading this page on your Kindle reader! If you look a little closer at the company's website (www.amazon.com), however, you will discover that it offers perhaps the world's biggest selection of merchandise: books; movies, music, and games; computer hardware and software; electronics; home and garden supplies; grocery, health, and beauty products; children's toys and apparel; adult apparel; sports and recreational gear; and auto and industrial tools. In fact, it is hard to think of any consumer item Amazon.com does not sell at competitive prices! How well has Amazon.com been performing during the most severe economic recession in 70 years? We can answer that question by financial statement analysis. We begin with the analysis of Amazon.com, Inc.'s comparative consolidated statements of

© Ken James/Landov Media

operations for the years ended December 31, 2010, 2009, and 2008. In 2010, Amazon.com earned revenues of about $34.2 billion. Is that positive or negative news? One of several things we can do to answer that question is compare 2010 results to 2009 and 2008. We also need to compare Amazon.com's results with those of some of its competitors. ●

Amazon.com, Inc.
Consolidated Statements of Operations
Year Ended December 31

(In millions, except per share data)	2010	2009	2008
Net sales	$34,204	$24,509	$19,166
Cost of sales	26,561	18,978	14,896
Gross profit	7,643	5,531	4,270
Operating expenses:			
Fulfillment	2,898	2,052	1,658
Marketing	1,029	680	482
Technology and content	1,734	1,240	1,033
General and administrative	470	328	279
Other operating expense (income), net	106	102	(24)
Total operating expenses	6,237	4,402	3,428
Income from operations	1,406	1,129	842
Interest income	51	37	83
Interest expense	(39)	(34)	(71)
Other income (expense), net	79	29	47
Total non-operating income (expense)	91	32	59
Income before income taxes	1,497	1,161	901
Provision for income taxes	(352)	(253)	(247)
Equity-method investment activity, net of tax	7	(6)	(9)
Net income	$ 1,152	$ 902	$ 645
Basic earnings per share	$ 2.58	$ 2.08	$ 1.52
Diluted earnings per share	$ 2.53	$ 2.04	$ 1.49

This chapter covers the basic tools of financial analysis. The first part of the chapter shows how to evaluate Amazon.com from year to year and how to compare Amazon.com to other companies that are in the same lines of business. For this comparison, we use a retail competitor, **Wal-Mart Stores, Inc.**, a company that operates in both the Internet and store-front retail sectors. The second part of the chapter discusses the most widely used financial ratios. You have seen most of these ratios in earlier chapters. However, we have yet to use all of them in a comprehensive analysis of a company. By studying all these ratios together,

▸ you will learn the basic tools of financial analysis.
▸ you will enhance your business education.

Regardless of your chosen field—marketing, management, finance, entrepreneurship, or accounting—you will find these analytical tools useful as you move through your career.

① **Perform** horizontal analysis

② **Perform** vertical analysis

③ **Prepare** common-size financial statements

④ **Analyze** the statement of cash flows

⑤ **Use** ratios to make business decisions

⑥ **Use** other measures to make investment decisions

Investors and creditors cannot evaluate a company by examining only one year's data. This is why most financial statements are comparative, that is, they cover at least two periods, like Amazon.com's Consolidated Statements of Operations that begins this chapter. In fact, most financial analysis covers trends of 3 to 10 years. Since one of the goals of financial analysis is to predict the future, it makes sense to start by mapping the trends of the past. This is particularly true of income statement data such as net sales and net income.

The graphs in Exhibit 13-1 show Amazon.com's three-year trend of net sales and income from operations.

EXHIBIT 13-1 | Comparative Sales and Income from Operations for Amazon.com (2008–2010)

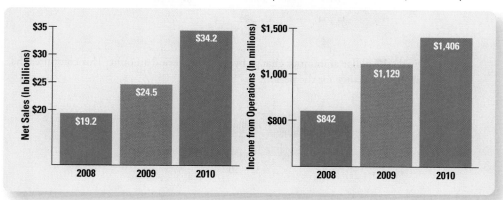

Amazon.com's net sales and income from operations (see Chapter 11 for discussion) both increased at a healthy pace during 2009 and 2010. In fact, sales and income from operations have been on a steady increase for the past six years. These are good signs, because they may point the way to growth in company value in future years. How would you predict Amazon.com's net sales and income from operations for 2011 and beyond? Based on the past, assuming similar economic conditions and management strategy, you would probably continue to extend the net sales line and the income from operations line upward. Let's examine some financial analysis tools. We begin with horizontal analysis.

Perform Horizontal Analysis

Many decisions hinge on the trend of revenues, expenses, income from operations, and so on. Have revenues increased from last year? By how much? Suppose net sales have increased by $50,000. Considered alone, this fact is not very helpful, but knowing the long-term *percentage change* in net sales helps a lot. It's better to know that net sales have increased by 20% than to know that the increase is $50,000. It's even better to know that percentage increases in net sales for the past several years have been rising year over year.

①

Perform horizontal analysis

The study of percentage changes from year to year is called **horizontal analysis**. Computing a percentage change takes two steps:

1. Compute the dollar amount of the change from one period (the base period) to the next.

2. Divide the dollar amount of change by the base-period amount.

Illustration: Amazon.com, Inc.

Horizontal analysis is illustrated for Amazon.com, Inc., as follows (using the 2009 and 2010 figures, dollars in millions):

	2010	2009	Increase (Decrease) Amount	Increase (Decrease) Percentage
Net sales...............	$34,204	$24,509	$9,695	39.6%

Amazon.com's net sales increased by 39.6% during 2010, computed as follows:

Step 1 Compute the dollar amount of change from 2009 to 2010:

2010		2009		Increase
$34,204	−	$24,509	=	$9,695

Step 2 Divide the dollar amount of change by the base-period amount. This computes the percentage change for the period:

$$\text{Percentage change} = \frac{\text{Dollar amount of change}}{\text{Base-year amount}}$$

$$= \frac{\$9,695}{\$24,509} = 39.6\%$$

Exhibits 13-2 and 13-3 (on page 775 and 776, respectively) are detailed horizontal analysis for Amazon.com, Inc. The comparative Consolidated Statements of Operations show that net sales increased by 39.6% during 2010. In addition, Amazon.com's net income on the bottom line grew by 27.7%. Why the difference? Amazon.com was successful in increasing net sales by a healthy percentage. However, cost of sales and other operating expenses increased at 40% and 41.7%, respectively. Gross profit increased by 38.2%, and income from operations increased by only 24.5%. In the operating expense category, every expense except one category (other) grew at a faster pace than net sales. Non-operating income items turned in a 184% positive change. The provision for income taxes increased by 39.1%. The result was a 27.7% increase in net income after taxes, which is good news for shareholders. However, Amazon.com's management may need to keep a closer eye on expenses in the future to help keep profits growing at a healthy pace.

Studying changes in balance sheet accounts can enhance our total understanding of the current and long-term financial position of the entity. Let's look at a few balance sheet changes. First, cash increased by a healthy 9.7% in 2010, and marketable securities increased by 70.6%. These changes indicate that the company's liquidity has significantly improved. Inventories and accounts receivable increased by large amounts (47.5% and 60.6%, respectively), faster than net sales (39.6%). Accounts payable also increased by more than net sales (43.6%), indicating that the company's payments of short-term debt are not quite keeping pace with its overall rate of growth in net sales. Overall, current assets and current liabilities increased at roughly the same rate (40.3% and 40.8%, respectively). Net working capital (current assets − current liabilities) grew from $2,433 to $3,375 in fiscal 2010.

EXHIBIT 13-2 | Comparitive Consolidated Statements of Operations—Horizontal Analysis

Amazon.com, Inc.
Consolidated Statements of Operations
Year Ended December 31

(In millions, except per share data)	2010	2009	Increase (Decrease)	
			Amount	Percentage
Net sales	$34,204	$24,509	$9,695	39.6
Cost of sales	26,561	18,978	$7,583	40.0%
Gross profit	7,643	5,531	$2,112	38.2%
Operating expenses:				
Fulfillment	2,898	2,052	$ 846	41.2%
Marketing	1,029	680	$ 349	51.3%
Technology and content	1,734	1,240	$ 494	39.8%
General and administrative	470	328	$ 142	43.3%
Other operating expense (income), net	106	102	$ 4	3.9%
Total operating expenses	6,237	4,402	$1,835	41.7%
Income from operations	1,406	1,129	$ 277	24.5%
Interest income	51	37	$ 14	37.8%
Interest expense	(39)	(34)	$ (5)	14.7%
Other income (expense), net	79	29	$ 50	172.4%
Total non-operating income (expense)	91	32	$ 59	184.4%
Income before income taxes	1,497	1,161	$ 336	28.9%
Provision for income taxes	(352)	(253)	$ (99)	39.1%
Equity-method investment activity, net of tax	7	(6)	$ 13	216.7%
Net income	$ 1,152	$ 902	$ 250	27.7%
Basic earnings per share	$ 2.58	$ 2.08	$ 0.50	24.0%

The aggregate impact of these changes in the current section of the balance sheet indicates that the company grew its working capital substantially during 2010. Fixed assets, net (property, plant and equipment) increased by over 87%, indicating that the company is growing significantly by investing in long-term assets. Long-term liabilities, which consist largely of amounts borrowed to finance international operations, as well as debt related to capital lease obligations, increased by 31% during the year. There were no changes in either common stock or treasury stock during 2010. The major reason for the increase in additional paid-in capital ($589 million, or 10.3%) was stock-based compensation and issuance of employee benefit plan stock. Finally, net income of $1,152 million increased retained earnings by 670% during 2010! Overall, it appears that 2010 was a very good year for Amazon.com, Inc., while other companies (especially retailers) were struggling to survive.

STOP & THINK. . .

Examine Exhibits 13-2 and 13-3. Which items had the largest percentage fluctuations during 2010? Should these fluctuations cause concern? Explain your reasoning.

Answer:

On the Consolidated Statements of Operations, the category Equity-method investment activity increased most (217%). The very small dollar amount makes this account immaterial. The category Other Income and Expense also had a large percentage increase (172.4%). According to Note 1 of the financial statements, this consists mostly of net gains on the sale of marketable securities, as well as foreign currency transaction gains and losses. These are not particularly a cause for concern. They are a necessary part of doing business for a company like Amazon. However, they could possibly reverse in future periods, producing losses in this category. On the comparative Consolidated Balance Sheets, marketable securities increased by 70.6%, indicating that the company generated excess cash from operations, investing the cash in trading securities. Inventories and accounts receivable (net) also increased, indicating growth in current and anticipated sales volume. The company's investment in fixed assets almost doubled. Current and long-term liabilities grew significantly as well. All of these changes are signs of a healthy and growing company.

EXHIBIT 13-3 | Comparative Consolidated Balance Sheets—Horizontal Analysis

Amazon.com, Inc.
Consolidated Balance Sheets
Year Ended December 31

(In millions, except per share data)	2010	2009	Increase (decrease) Amount	Increase (decrease) Percentage
Assets				
Current assets:				
Cash and cash equivalents	$ 3,777	$ 3,444	$ 333	9.7%
Marketable securities	4,985	2,922	2,063	70.6%
Inventories	3,202	2,171	1,031	47.5%
Accounts receivable, net and other	1,587	988	599	60.6%
Deferred tax assets	196	272	(76)	−27.9%
Total current assets	13,747	9,797	3,950	40.3%
Fixed assets, net	2,414	1,290	1,124	87.1%
Deferred tax assets	22	18	4	22.2%
Goodwill	1,349	1,234	115	9.3%
Other assets	1,265	1,474	(209)	−14.2%
Total assets	$18,797	$13,813	$4,984	36.1%
Liabilities and Stockholders' Equity				
Current liabilities:				
Accounts payable	$ 8,051	$ 5,605	$2,446	43.6%
Accrued expenses and other	2,321	1,759	562	31.9%
Total current liabilities	10,372	7,364	3,008	40.8%
Long-term liabilities	1,561	1,192	369	31.0%
Commitments and contingencies				
Stockholders' equity:				
Preferred stock, $0.01 par value:				
Authorized shares—500				
Issued and outstanding shares—none				
Common stock, $0.01 par value:				
Authorized shares—5,000				
Issued shares—445 and 431				
Outstanding shares—428 and 416	5	5	—	0.0%
Treasury stock, at cost	(600)	(600)	—	0.0%
Additional paid-in capital	6,325	5,736	589	10.3%
Accumulated other comprehensive income (loss)	(190)	(56)	(134)	239.3%
Retained earnings	1,324	172	1,152	669.8%
Total stockholders' equity	6,864	5,257	1,607	30.6%
Total liabilities and stockholders' equity	$18,797	$13,813	$4,984	36.1%

Trend Percentages

Trend percentages are a form of horizontal analysis. Trends indicate the direction a business is taking. How have revenues changed over a five-year period? What trend does net income show? These questions can be answered by trend percentages over a representative period, such as the most recent five years.

Trend percentages are computed by selecting a base year whose amounts are set equal to 100%. The amount for each following year is stated as a percentage of the base amount. To compute a trend percentage, divide an item for a later year by the base-year amount.

$$\text{Trend \%} = \frac{\text{Any year \$}}{\text{Base year \$}} \times 100$$

Recall that, in Chapter 11, we established that income from continuing operations is often viewed as the primary measure of a company's earnings quality. This is because operating income represents a company's best predictor of the future net inflows from its core business units. Income from operations is often used in estimating the current value of the business.

Amazon.com, Inc., showed income from operations for 2006–2010 years as follows:

(In millions)	2010	2009	2008	2007	2006	(Base)
Income from operations	$1,406	$1,129	$842	$655	$389	

We want to calculate a trend for the period 2006 through 2010. The first year in the series (2006) is set as the base year. Trend percentages are computed by dividing each succeeding year's amount by the 2006 amount. The resulting trend percentages follow (2006 = 100%):

	2010	2009	2008	2007	2006	(Base)
Income from operations	361	290	216	168	100	

In 2007, operating income took a 68% jump, relative to the base year, and it took another 48% jump in 2008. It took a 74% jump in 2009, and another 71% in 2010, relative to the base year. The cause for these results is the tremendous growth occurring in online sales, in addition to Amazon. com's very successful business model. The relative convenience and lower cost of shopping from home as opposed to traveling to the store have made Internet sales boom.

You can perform a trend analysis on any item you consider important. Trend analysis using income statement data is widely used for predicting the future.

Horizontal analysis highlights changes over time. However, no single technique gives a complete picture of a business.

Perform Vertical Analysis

Vertical analysis shows the relationship of a financial-statement item to its base, which is the 100% figure. All items on the particular financial statement are reported as a percentage of the base. For the income statement, total revenue (sales) is usually the base. Suppose that under normal conditions a company's net income is 8% of revenue. A drop to 6% may cause the company's stock price to fall.

2 **Perform** vertical analysis

Illustration: Amazon.com, Inc.

Exhibit 13-4 shows the vertical analysis of Amazon.com, Inc.'s Consolidated Statements of Operations. In this case,

$$\text{Vertical analysis \%} = \frac{\text{Each income statement item}}{\text{Net sales (revenue)}}$$

EXHIBIT 13-4 | Comparative Consolidated Statements of Operations—Vertical Analysis

Amazon.com, Inc.
Consolidated Statements of Operations
Year Ended December 31

(In millions, except per share data)	2010	% of total	2009	% of total
Net sales	$34,204	100.0%	$24,509	100.0%
Cost of sales	26,561	77.7%	18,978	77.4%
Gross profit	7,643	22.3%	5,531	22.6%
Operating expenses:				
Fulfillment	2,898	8.5%	2,052	8.4%
Marketing	1,029	3.0%	680	2.8%
Technology and content	1,734	5.1%	1,240	5.1%
General and administrative	470	1.4%	328	1.3%
Other operating expense (income), net	106	0.3%	102	0.4%
Total operating expenses	6,237	18.2%	4,402	18.0%
Income from operations	1,406	4.1%	1,129	4.6%
Interest income	51	0.1%	37	0.2%
Interest expense	(39)	−0.1%	(34)	−0.1%
Other income (expense), net	79	0.2%	29	0.1%
Total non-operating income (expense)	91	0.3%	32	0.1%
Income before income taxes	1,497	4.4%	1,161	4.7%
Provision for income taxes	(352)	−1.0%	(253)	−1.0%
Equity-method investment activity, net of tax	7	0.0%	(6)	0.0%
Net income	$ 1,152	3.4%	$ 902	3.7%

(Note: Slight differences exist in computation of percentages vs. sums of percentages due to rounding.)

For Amazon.com, Inc., in 2010, the vertical-analysis percentage for cost of sales is 77.7% ($26,561/$34,204), up by 0.3% from 77.4% in 2009. Therefore, the company's gross margin percentage declined from 22.6% to 22.3% over the year. Operating expenses for fulfillment, marketing, and general and administrative were up, as a percentage of net sales, in 2010. As a category, operating expenses increased from 18.0% to 18.2% of net sales. This increase, along with a 0.3% increase in cost of goods sold, caused income from operations to decline by 0.5% as a percentage of sales.

Exhibit 13-5 on the following page shows the vertical analysis of Amazon.com's Consolidated Balance Sheets. The base amount (100%) is total assets for each year. The vertical analysis of Amazon.com's balance sheet reveals several things about Amazon.com's financial position at December 31, 2010, relative to 2009:

▶ While cash increased by 9.7% from 2009 (Exhibit 13-3, p. 776), it declined as a percentage of total assets from 24.9% to 20.1%. At the same time, marketable (likely trading) securities increased as a percentage of total assets from 21.2% to 26.5%. This shows that Amazon.com, Inc., invested a higher proportion of its excess cash in short-term investments in 2010, expecting to earn a higher return than it would have earned on interest-bearing cash accounts. Generally, this is a smart move.

▶ Inventories as a percentage of total assets increased from 15.7% to 17.0%, indicating that inventory turnover is declining, because sales (and related cost of sales) are not increasing as fast as inventories are. Accounts receivable as a percentage of total assets increased from 7.2% to 8.4%, reflecting an increase in net credit sales activity. Overall, current assets make up a larger percentage of total assets in 2010 (73.1%) than in 2009 (70.9%).

▶ The company's debt to total assets (55.2% + 8.3% = 63.5%) increased slightly in 2010 from 61.9% in 2009. This was wholly accounted for by a proportionate increase in accounts payable. However, these debt ratios are still totally within reasonable limits for a retail concern, as pointed out in earlier chapters. Amazon.com, Inc., remained a very healthy company from the standpoint of both liquidity and leverage in 2010.

EXHIBIT 13-5 | Comparative Consolidated Balance Sheets—Vertical Analysis

Amazon.com, Inc.
Consolidated Balance Sheets
Year Ended December 31

(In millions, except per share data)	2010	Percentage of total assets	2009	Percentage of total assets
Assets				
Current assets:				
Cash and cash equivalents	$ 3,777	20.1%	$ 3,444	24.9%
Marketable securities	4,985	26.5%	2,922	21.2%
Inventories	3,202	17.0%	2,171	15.7%
Accounts receivable, net and other	1,587	8.4%	988	7.2%
Deferred tax assets	196	1.0%	272	2.0%
Total current assets	13,747	73.1%	9,797	70.9%
Fixed assets, net	2,414	12.8%	1,290	9.3%
Deferred tax assets	22	0.1%	18	0.1%
Goodwill	1,349	7.2%	1,234	8.9%
Other assets	1,265	6.7%	1,474	10.7%
Total assets	$18,797	100.0%	$13,813	100.0%
Liabilities and Stockholders' Equity				
Current liabilities:				
Accounts payable	$ 8,051	42.8%	$ 5,605	40.6%
Accrued expenses and other	2,321	12.3%	1,759	12.7%
Total current liabilities	10,372	55.2%	7,364	53.3%
Long-term liabilities	1,561	8.3%	1,192	8.6%
Commitments and contingencies				
Stockholders' equity:				
Preferred stock, $0.01 par value:				
Authorized shares—500				
Issued and outstanding shares—none				
Common stock, $0.01 par value:				
Authorized shares—5,000				
Issued shares—445 and 431				
Outstanding shares—428 and 416	5	0.0%	5	0.1%
Treasury stock, at cost	(600)	0.0%*	(600)	−4.3%
Additional paid-in capital	6,325	33.6%	5,736	41.5%
Accumulated other comprehensive income (loss)	(190)	−1.0%	(56)	−0.4%
Retained earnings	1,324	7.0%	172	1.2%
Total stockholders' equity	6,864	36.5%	5,257	38.1%
Total liabilities and stockholders' equity	$18,797	100.0%	$13,813	100.0%

Note: Slight differences exist in computation of percentages vs. sums of percentages due to rounding.

Prepare Common-Size Financial Statements

Exhibits 13-4 and 13-5 can be modified to report only percentages (no dollar amounts). Such financial statements are called **common-size statements**. In order to perform vertical analysis, you must first convert the financial statements to common-size format.

On a common-size income statement, each item is expressed as a percentage of the revenue (net sales) amount. Total revenue is therefore the *common size*. In the balance sheet, the common size is total assets. A common-size financial statement aids the comparison of different companies because all amounts are stated in percentages, thus expressing the financial results of each comparative company in terms of a common denominator.

Prepare common-size financial statements

STOP & THINK. . .

Calculate the common-size percentages for the following income statement:

Net sales..................................	$150,000
Cost of goods sold..................	60,000
Gross profit.............................	90,000
Operating expense..................	40,000
Operating income...................	50,000
Income tax expense................	15,000
Net income.............................	$ 35,000

Answer:

Net sales..................................	100%	(= $150,000 ÷ $150,000)
Cost of goods sold..................	40	(= $ 60,000 ÷ $150,000)
Gross profit.............................	60	(= $ 90,000 ÷ $150,000)
Operating expense..................	27	(= $ 40,000 ÷ $150,000)
Operating income...................	33	(= $ 50,000 ÷ $150,000)
Income tax expense................	10	(= $ 15,000 ÷ $150,000)
Net income.............................	23%	(= $ 35,000 ÷ $150,000)

Benchmarking

Benchmarking compares a company to some standard set by others. The goal of benchmarking is improvement. Suppose you are a financial analyst for **Goldman Sachs**, a large investment bank. You are considering investing in one of two different retailers, say Amazon.com, Inc., or Wal-Mart Stores, Inc. A direct comparison of these companies' financial statements is not meaningful, in part because Wal-Mart, Inc., is so much larger than Amazon.com. However, you can convert the companies' income statements to common size and compare the percentages. This comparison is meaningful, as we shall see.

Benchmarking Against a Key Competitor

Exhibit 13-6 presents the common-size income statements of Amazon.com, Inc., benchmarked against Wal-Mart Stores, Inc. The companies are not exactly comparable because of differences in their business models. For example, Wal-Mart has physical stores as well as online retail services. However, if you look at their Web sites, the two companies are very similar, organized in much the same way. They are close enough to illustrate the value of common-size vertical analysis. In this comparison, the results of the two companies are strikingly similar. Amazon.com's cost of sales is 2.5% higher than Wal-Mart's, but its operating expenses are about a percentage point lower. Their net incomes as a percentage of net sales are very similar. Of course, Wal-Mart comes out far ahead in terms of total earnings because of its sheer size ($16.4 billion vs. $1.15 billion for Amazon.com).

EXHIBIT 13-6 | Common-Size Income Statements Benchmarked Against Competitor

Amazon.com, Inc.
Common-Size Income Statement for Comparison with Key Competitor (Adapted)
Year Ended During 2010

	Amazon.com	Wal-Mart
Net sales	100.0%	100.0%
Cost of sales	77.7%	75.2%
Operating expenses	18.2%	19.3%
Other expenses (income), net	0.7%	1.6%
Net income	3.4%	3.9%

Analyze the Statement of Cash Flows

This chapter has focused on the income statement and balance sheet. We may also perform horizontal and vertical analyses on the statement of cash flows. To continue our discussion of its role in decision making, let's use Exhibit 13-7, the comparative Consolidated Statements of Cash Flows of Amazon.com, Inc. We have modified the statements somewhat to illustrate selected horizontal and vertical percentage changes.

Analyze the state-ment of cash flows.

EXHIBIT 13-7 | Amazon.com, Inc., Comparative Consolidated Statements of Cash Flows

Amazon.com, Inc.
Comparative Consolidated Statements of Cash Flows (Adapted) (USD $)
Year Ended December 31

(In millions, except per share data)	2010	2009	% Chg.
CASH AND CASH EQUIVALENTS, BEGINNING OF PERIOD	$3,444	$2,769	+ 24.4%
OPERATING ACTIVITIES:			
Net income	1,152	902	
Adjustments to reconcile net income to net cash from operating activities:			
Depreciation and amortization	568	378	
Stock-based compensation	424	341	
Other operating expense (income), net	106	103	
Losses (gains) on sales of marketable securities, net	−2	−4	
Other expense (income), net	−79	−15	
Deferred income taxes	4	81	
Excess tax benefits from stock-based compensation	−259	−105	
Changes in operating assets and liabilities:			
Inventories	−1,019	−531	
Accounts receivable, net and other	−295	−481	
Accounts payable	2,373	1,859	
Accrued expenses and other	740	300	
Additions to unearned revenue	687	1,054	
Amortization of previously unearned revenue	−905	−589	
Net cash provided by (used in) operating activities	3,495	3,293	+ 6.1%
Operating cash as % of net income	303%	365%	
INVESTING ACTIVITIES:			
Purchases of fixed assets, including software and website development	−979	−373	+ 162%
Acquisitions, net of cash acquired, and other	−352	−40	+ 780%
Sales of marketable securities and investments	4,250	1,966	+ 116%
Purchases of marketable securities and investments	−6,279	−3890	+ 61%
Net cash provided by (used in) investing activities	−3,360	−2,337	+ 44%
FINANCING ACTIVITIES:			
Excess tax benefits from stock-based compensation	259	105	
Proceeds from long-term debt and other	143	87	
Repayments of long-term debt and capital leases	−221	−472	
Net cash provided by (used in) financing activities	181	−280	
Foreign-currency effect on cash and cash equivalents	17	−1	
Net increase in cash and cash equivalents	333	675	
CASH AND CASH EQUIVALENTS, END OF PERIOD	3,777	3,444	
SUPPLEMENTAL CASH FLOW INFORMATION:			
Cash paid for interest	11	32	
Cash paid for income taxes	75	48	
Fixed assets acquired under capital leases	405	147	
Fixed assets acquired under build-to-suit leases	172	188	

For both 2010 and 2009, net cash provided by operating activities was the major source of cash for the company. Also, for both 2010 and 2009, net cash provided by operating activities exceeded net income by over 200%. Both of these relationships are signs of a healthy company.

The next thing to notice is how the company has used the cash it has generated mostly from operations. Focus on the investing activities section, which normally shows a net use of cash. Total investing activities are up by 44% in 2010. Purchases of fixed assets have increased by several multiples year over year. This is a signal that the company is plowing cash back into the business, and that excess cash generated from operations is being invested for future use. These are also signs of financial strength from a cash-flow perspective.

Analysts may find the statement of cash flows as helpful for spotting weakness as for gauging success. Why? Because a *shortage* of cash can throw a company into bankruptcy, but lots of cash doesn't ensure success. Let's look at the cash flow statement of Unix Corporation. See if you can find signals of cash-flow weakness.

Unix Corporation Statement of Cash Flows Year Ended June 30, 2012		
(In millions)		
Operating activities:		
Net income		$ 35,000
Adjustments for non-cash items:		
Depreciation	$ 14,000	
Net increase in current assets other than cash	(24,000)	
Net increase in current liabilities	8,000	(2,000)
Net cash provided by operating activities		33,000
Investing activities:		
Sale of property, plant, and equipment	$ 91,000	
Net cash provided by investing activities		91,000
Financing activities:		
Borrowing	$ 22,000	
Payment of long-term debt	(90,000)	
Purchase of treasury stock	(9,000)	
Payment of dividends	(23,000)	
Net cash used for financing activities		(100,000)
Increase (decrease) in cash		$ 24,000

Unix Corporation's statement of cash flows reveals the following:

► Net cash provided by operating activities is less than net income. That's strange. Ordinarily, net cash provided by operating activities exceeds net income because of the add-back of depreciation and amortization. The increases in current assets and current liabilities should cancel out over time. For Unix Corporation, current assets increased far more than current liabilities during the year. This may be harmless. But it may signal difficulty in collecting receivables or selling inventory. Either event will cause trouble.

► The sale of plant assets is Unix's major source of cash. This is okay if this is a one-time situation. Unix may be shifting from one line of business to another, and it may be selling off old assets. But if the sale of plant assets is the major source of cash for several periods, Unix will face a cash shortage. A company can't sell off its plant assets forever. Soon it will go out of business.

▶ The only strength shown by the statement of cash flows is that Unix paid off more long-term debt than it borrowed. This will improve the debt ratio and Unix's credit standing.

In summary, here are some cash-flow signs of a healthy company:

▶ Operations are the major *source* of cash (not a *use* of cash).

▶ Investing activities include more purchases than sales of long-term assets.

▶ Financing activities are not dominated by borrowing.

MID-CHAPTER SUMMARY PROBLEM

Perform a horizontal analysis and a vertical analysis of the comparative income statement of Hard Rock Products, Inc., which makes metal detectors. State whether 2012 was a good year or a bad year, and give your reasons.

Hard Rock Products, Inc.
Comparative Income Statements
Years Ended December 31, 2012 and 2011

	2012	2011
Total revenues	$275,000	$225,000
Expenses:		
Cost of goods sold	194,000	165,000
Engineering, selling, and administrative expenses	54,000	48,000
Interest expense	5,000	5,000
Income tax expense	9,000	3,000
Other expense (income)	1,000	(1,000)
Total expenses	263,000	220,000
Net income	$ 12,000	$ 5,000

▶ Answer

The horizontal analysis shows that total revenues increased 22.2%. This was greater than the 19.5% increase in total expenses, resulting in a 140% increase in net income.

Hard Rock Products, Inc.
Horizontal Analysis of Comparative Income Statements
Years Ended December 31, 2012 and 2011

	2012	2011	Increase (Decrease) Amount	Percent
Total revenues	$275,000	$225,000	$50,000	22.2%
Expenses:				
Cost of goods sold	194,000	165,000	29,000	17.6
Engineering, selling, and administrative expenses	54,000	48,000	6,000	12.5
Interest expense	5,000	5,000	—	—
Income tax expense	9,000	3,000	6,000	200.0
Other expense (income)	1,000	(1,000)	2,000	—*
Total expenses	263,000	220,000	43,000	19.5
Net income	$ 12,000	$ 5,000	$ 7,000	140.0%

*Percentage changes are typically not computed for shifts from a negative to a positive amount and vice versa.

The vertical analysis shows decreases in the percentages of net sales consumed by the cost of goods sold (from 73.3% to 70.5%) and by the engineering, selling, and administrative expenses (from 21.3% to 19.6%). Because these two items are Hard Rock's largest dollar expenses, their percentage decreases are quite important. The relative reduction in expenses raised 2012 net income to 4.4% of sales, compared with 2.2% the preceding year. The overall analysis indicates that 2012 was significantly better than 2011.

Hard Rock Products, Inc.
Vertical Analysis of Comparative Income Statements
Years Ended December 31, 2012 and 2011

	2012 Amount	Percent	2011 Amount	Percent
Total revenues	$275,000	100.0 %	$225,000	100.0 %
Expenses:				
Cost of goods sold	194,000	70.5	165,000	73.3
Engineering, selling, and administrative expenses	54,000	19.6	48,000	21.3
Interest expense	5,000	1.8	5,000	2.2
Income tax expense	9,000	3.3	3,000	1.4**
Other expense (income)	1,000	0.4	(1,000)	(0.4)
Total expenses	263,000	95.6	220,000	97.8
Net income	$ 12,000	4.4 %	$ 5,000	2.2 %

**Number rounded up.

Use Ratios to Make Business Decisions

5

Use ratios to make business decisions

Ratios are a major tool of financial analysis. We have discussed the use of many ratios in financial analysis in various chapters throughout the book. A ratio expresses the relationship between various types of financial information. In this section, we review how ratios are computed and used to make business decisions, using Apple, Inc., which was our spotlight company in Chapter 2.

Many companies include ratios in a special section of their annual reports. Exhibit 13-8 shows a summary of selected data from previous Apple, Inc., annual reports. Financial Web sites such as www.yahoofinance.com and www.googlefinance.com report many of these ratios.

EXHIBIT 13-8 | Financial Summary: Apple, Inc.

Apple, Inc.

Results of operations (dollar amounts in millions)	FY 2010	FY 2009	FY 2008
Net sales			
Domestic	$28,633	$22,325	$20,893
International	36,592	20,580	16,598
Total net sales	65,225	42,905	37,491
Gross margin	25,684	17,222	13,197
Gross margin as percent of net sales	39	40	35
Operating income	18,385	11,740	8,327
Operating income as percent of net sales	28	27	22
Net income after provision for income taxes	14,013	8,235	6,119
Net income as percent of sales	21	19	16
Earnings per weighted-average common share, basic	$ 15.41	$9.22	$6.94
Return on average stockholders' equity	35.30%	23.80%	27.20%
Financial position (dollar amounts in millions)			
Current assets	$41,678	$31,555	$30,006
Current liabilities	20,722	11,506	11,361
Working capital	20,956	20,049	18,645
Current ratio	2.01	2.74	2.64
Quick ratio	1.50	2.33	1.95
Total assets	75,183	47,501	36,171
Total liabilities	27,392	15,861	13,874
Debt ratio	0.36	0.33	0.38

The ratios we discuss in this chapter are classified as follows:

1. Measuring ability to pay current liabilities

2. Measuring turnover and cash conversion

3. Measuring leverage: overall ability to pay debts

4. Measuring profitability

5. Analyzing stock as an investment

You will find the skills you have acquired in earlier courses helpful when performing financial analysis using software like Microsoft Excel as you work on the problems related to this section. Packages such as Excel make computation of financial ratios a breeze. However, interpretation of what the ratios mean and use of the ratios to make decisions takes more time and effort! Now, let's analyze Apple, Inc.

How do you determine whether a company's performance has been strong or weak, based on its current period ratios? You can only make that decision if you have the following ratios to compare the current period against: (1) prior-year ratios; and (2) industry comparables, either in the form of an industry average or the ratios of a strong competitor. In the case of all the ratios in the following sections, we compare Apple's current-year ratios with (1) its prior years' ratios and (2) ratios for the industry (if available) or ratios of one of Apple, Inc.'s competitors.

Measuring Ability to Pay Current Liabilities

Working capital is defined as follows:

Working capital = Current assets − Current liabilities

Working capital measures the ability to pay current liabilities with current assets. In general, the larger the working capital, the better the ability to pay debts. Recall that capital is total assets minus total liabilities. Working capital is like a "current" version of total capital. Consider two companies with equal working capital:

	Company	
	Jones	Smith
Current assets......................	$100,000	$200,000
Current liabilities	50,000	150,000
Working capital	$ 50,000	$ 50,000

Both companies have working capital of $50,000, but Jones' working capital is as large as its current liabilities. Smith's working capital is only one-third as large as current liabilities. Jones is in a better position because its working capital is a higher percentage of current liabilities. As shown in Exhibit 13-8, Apple, Inc.'s working capital as of September 25, 2010 (the end of its 2010 fiscal year), was $20,956 million. This compares with $20,049 million and $18,645 million at the end of its 2009 and 2008 fiscal years, respectively. In comparison, the working capital of Dell, Inc., a strong competitor of Apple, Inc,, as of the end of its 2010 fiscal year was $17,538 million. Apple, Inc., appears to be in a very strong position from the standpoint of working capital. But the picture is incomplete. Let's look at two key ratios that help tell the rest of the story.

Current Ratio. The most common ratio evaluating current assets and current liabilities is the **current ratio**, which is current assets divided by current liabilities. As discussed in Chapter 3, the current ratio measures the ability to pay current liabilities with current assets. Exhibit 13-9 and Exhibit 13-10 show the Consolidated Statements of Operations and the Consolidated Balance Sheets of Apple, Inc.

EXHIBIT 13-9 | Comparative Consolidated Statements of Operations—Apple, Inc.

Apple, Inc.
Consolidated Statements of Operations (USD $)
12 Months Ended

(In millions, except share data in thousands, unless otherwise specified)	Sep 25, 2010	Sep 26, 2009	Sep 27, 2008
Net sales	$ 65,225	$ 42,905	$ 37,491
Cost of sales	39,541	25,683	24,294
Gross margin	25,684	17,222	13,197
Operating expenses:			
Research and development	1,782	1,333	1,109
Selling, general, and administrative	5,517	4,149	3,761
Total operating expenses	7,299	5,482	4,870
Operating income	18,385	11,740	8,327
Other income and expense	155	326	620
Income before provision for income taxes	18,540	12,066	8,947
Provision for income taxes	4,527	3,831	2,828
Net income	$ 14,013	$ 8,235	$ 6,119
Earnings per common share:			
Basic	$ 15.41	$ 9.22	$ 6.94
Diluted	$ 15.15	$ 9.08	$ 6.78
Shares used in computing earnings per share:			
Basic	909,461	893,016	881,592
Diluted	924,712	907,005	902,139

EXHIBIT 13-10 | Comparative Consolidated Balance Sheets—Apple, Inc.

Apple, Inc.
Consolidated Balance Sheets (USD $)
12 Months Ended

(In millions)	Sep 25, 2010	Sep 26, 2009
Current assets:		
Cash and cash equivalents	$11,261	$ 5,263
Short-term marketable securities	14,359	18,201
Accounts receivable, less allowance of $55 and $52 respectively	5,510	3,361
Inventories	1,051	455
Deferred tax assets	1,636	1,135
Vendor non-trade receivables	4,414	1,696
Other current assets	3,447	1,444
Total current assets	41,678	31,555
Long-term marketable securities	25,391	10,528
Property, plant, and equipment, net	4,768	2,954
Goodwill	741	206
Acquired intangible assets, net	342	247
Other assets	2,263	2,011
Total assets	75,183	47,501
Current liabilities:		
Accounts payable	12,015	5,601
Accrued expenses	5,723	3,852
Deferred revenue	2,984	2,053
Total current liabilities	20,722	11,506
Deferred revenue—non-current	1,139	853
Other non-current liabilities	5,531	3,502
Total liabilities	27,392	15,861
Commitments and contingencies		
Shareholders' equity:		
Common stock, no par value, 1,800,000,000 shares authorized, 915,970,050 and 899,805,500 shares issued and outstanding, respectively	10,668	8,210
Retained earnings	37,169	23,353
Accumulated other comprehensive (loss)/income	(46)	77
Total shareholders' equity	47,791	31,640
Total liabilities and shareholders' equity	$75,183	$47,501

Using figures from Exhibit 13-10, current ratios of Apple, Inc., at September 25, 2010, and September 26, 2009, follow, along with the average for the computer manufacturing industry:

		Apple, Inc.'s Current Ratio		Industry
Formula		2010	2009	Average
Current ratio =	$\dfrac{\text{Current assets}}{\text{Current liabilities}}$	$\dfrac{\$41,678}{\$20,722} = 2.01$	$\dfrac{\$31,555}{\$11,506} = 2.74$	1.30

Although still strong, Apple, Inc.'s current ratio decreased significantly during 2010, from 2.74 to 2.01. Further examination of current assets and current liabilities in Exhibit 13-10 shows that current liabilities almost doubled during 2010, while current assets increased by about 32%. Accounts payable more than doubled. It will be necessary to dig into the footnotes further to discover why the company allowed this to happen. This is not necessarily a bad thing, especially since the current ratio is well within the bounds of what is considered healthy from the standpoint of the ability to pay current liabilities. In general, a higher current ratio indicates a stronger financial position. Apple, Inc., certainly has more than sufficient current assets to maintain its operations. Apple's current ratio of 2.01 compares quite favorably with the current ratios of the industry as well as with two well-known competitors:

Company	Current Ratio
Dell, Inc..	1.49
Hewlett-Packard Company................	1.09

Note: These figures show that ratio values vary widely from one industry to another.

What is an acceptable current ratio? The answer depends on the industry. The norm for companies in most industries is around 1.50, as reported by the Risk Management Association. Apple, Inc.'s current ratio of 2.01 is better than average.

Quick (Acid-test) Ratio. As discussed in Chapter 5, the **quick (acid-test) ratio** tells us whether the entity could pass the acid test of paying all its current liabilities if they came due immediately (quickly). The quick ratio uses a narrower base to measure liquidity than the current ratio does.

To compute the quick ratio, we add cash, short-term investments, and accounts receivable (net of allowances), and divide by current liabilities. Inventory and prepaid expenses are excluded because they are less liquid. A business may be unable to convert inventory to cash immediately.

Using the information in Figure 13-10, Apple, Inc.'s quick ratios for 2010 and 2009 follow:

Formula	Apple, Inc.'s Quick Ratio		Industry Average
	2010	2009	
Quick ratio = $\dfrac{\text{Cash} + \text{Short-term investments} + \text{Net current receivables}}{\text{Current liabilities}}$	$\dfrac{\$11,261 + \$14,359 + \$5,510}{\$20,722} = 1.50$	$\dfrac{\$5,263 + \$18,201 + \$3,361}{\$11,506} = 2.33$	0.80

Like the current ratio, the company's quick ratio deteriorated somewhat during 2010 but is still significantly better than the industry average. Compare Apple, Inc.'s quick ratio with the values of its leading competitors:

Company	Quick (Acid-Test) Ratio
Dell, Inc..	1.07
Hewlett-Packard Company................	0.65

A quick ratio of 0.90 to 1.00 is acceptable in most industries. How can many retail companies like Wal-Mart function with low quick ratios? Because they price their inventories to turn over (sell) quickly and because they collect most of the revenues in cash. This points us to the next group of ratios, which measure turnover.

Measuring Turnover and the Cash Conversion Cycle

The ability to sell inventory and collect receivables, as well as pay accounts payable, is the lifeblood of any retail, wholesale, or manufacturing concern. In this section, we discuss three ratios that measure this ability—inventory turnover, accounts receivable turnover, and accounts payable turnover—as well as the relationship between them, called the *cash conversion cycle*.

Inventory Turnover.   Companies generally strive to sell their inventory as quickly as possible. The faster inventory sells, the sooner cash comes in.

Inventory turnover, discussed in Chapter 6, measures the number of times a company sells its average level of inventory during a year. A fast turnover indicates ease in selling inventory; a low turnover indicates difficulty. A value of 6 means that the company's average level of inventory has been sold six times during the year, and that's usually better than a turnover of three times. But too high a value can mean that the business is not keeping enough inventory on hand, which can lead to lost sales if the company can't fill orders. Therefore, a business strives for the most *profitable* rate of turnover, not necessarily the *highest* rate.

To compute inventory turnover, divide cost of goods sold by the average inventory for the period. We use the cost of goods sold—*not sales*—in the computation because both cost of goods sold and inventory are stated *at cost*. Apple, Inc.'s inventory turnover for 2010 is as follows:

Formula	Apple, Inc.'s Inventory Turnover	Competitor (Dell, Inc.)
Inventory turnover $= \dfrac{\text{Cost of goods sold}}{\text{Average inventory}}$	$\dfrac{\$39,541}{\$753} = 52.5$	35.8
Days' inventory outstanding (DIO) $= \dfrac{365}{\text{Turnover}}$	$\dfrac{365}{52.5} = 7$ days	10 days

Cost of goods sold comes from the Consolidated Statement of Operations (Exhibit 13-9). Average inventory is the average of beginning ($455) and ending inventory ($1,051). (See the balance sheet, Exhibit 13-10.) If inventory levels vary greatly from month to month, you should compute the average by adding the 12 monthly balances and dividing the sum by 12.

Inventory turnover varies widely with the nature of the business. For example, Apple's inventory turned over 52.5 times in 2010! On a daily basis (days inventory outstanding), that means once every 7 days (365/52.5)! In 2009, Apple, Inc.'s inventory turned over 53.3 times. Dell, Inc.'s inventory turnover for 2010 was 35.8 times (once every 10 days). Hewlett-Packard Company's inventory turned over 10.33 times in 2010 (once every 35 days). Computer manufacturers purposely keep very low inventory levels because of their ability to manufacture inventory quickly and because technology is subject to rapid obsolescence. **YUM! Brands**, owner of fast food restaurants Pizza Hut, Taco Bell, KFC, and Long John Silver's, has an inventory turnover ratio of 29 times per year because food spoils so quickly. **Williams-Sonoma, Inc.**, on the other hand, turns its inventory over only about 3.7 times per year. Williams-Sonoma keeps enough inventory on hand for customers to make their selections.

To evaluate inventory turnover, compare the ratio over time as well as with industry averages or competitors. A sharp decline suggests the need for corrective action.

Accounts Receivable Turnover.

Accounts receivable turnover measures the ability to collect cash from customers. In general, the higher the ratio, the better. However, a receivable turnover that is too high may indicate that credit is too tight, and that may cause a company to lose sales to good customers.

To compute accounts receivable turnover, divide net sales (assumed all on credit) by average net accounts receivable. The ratio tells how many times during the year average receivables were turned into cash. Apple, Inc.'s accounts receivable turnover ratio for 2010 was as follows:

Formula	Apple, Inc.'s Accounts Receivable Turnover	Competitor (Dell, Inc.)
Accounts receivable turnover $= \dfrac{\text{Net sales}}{\text{Average net accounts receivable}}$	$\dfrac{\$65,225}{\$4,436} = 14.7$	8.1
Days' sales outstanding (DSO) (or days'-sales-in-receivables) $= \dfrac{365}{\text{Turnover}}$	$\dfrac{365}{14.7} = 25$ days	45 days

Net sales comes from Exhibit 13-9. Average net accounts receivable (Exhibit 13-10) is figured by adding beginning ($ 3,361) and ending receivables ($ 5,510), then dividing by 2. If accounts receivable vary widely during the year, compute the average by using the 12 monthly balances. Apple, Inc., collected its average accounts receivable 14.7 times during 2010. The comparable ratio for Apple, Inc., for 2009 was 14.8 times. Dell, Inc.'s accounts receivable turnover for 2010 was 8.1.

Apple, Inc's accounts receivable turnover of 14.7 times per year is much faster than the industry average. Apple owns and operates a large number of retail stores, and much of its sales are for cash, which makes the receivables balance very low relative to the sales balance.

Days' Sales in Receivables. Businesses must convert accounts receivable to cash. All else being equal, the lower the receivable balance, the better the cash flow.

The *days' sales outstanding (DSO)* or **days'-sales-in-receivables** ratio, discussed in Chapter 5, shows how many days' sales remain in Accounts Receivable. Days' sales in receivables can be calculated two different ways, each of which produces the identical result. First, if you have already calculated receivables turnover (see the previous section), simply divide the turnover into 365. For Apple, Inc., days' sales in receivables works out to 24.8 (rounded to 25) days (365/14.7). The second way to compute the ratio, described in Chapter 5, merely works from a different angle, by a two-step process:

1. Divide net sales by 365 days to figure average daily sales.

2. Divide average net receivables by average daily sales.

The data to compute this ratio for Apple, Inc., are taken from the 2010 income statement (Exhibit 13-9) and balance sheet (Exhibit 13-10):

Formula		Apple, Inc.'s Days' Sales in Accounts Receivable	Competitor (Dell, Inc.)
Days' sales outstanding (DSO) or days' sales in receivables:			
1. Average daily sales $=$	$\dfrac{\text{Net sales}}{\text{365 days}}$	$\dfrac{\$65,225}{\text{365 days}} = \$178.7$	
2. Convert average daily sales to DSO $=$	$\dfrac{\text{Average net accounts receivable}}{\text{Average daily sales}}$	$\dfrac{\$4,436}{\$178.7} = 25$ days	45 days

In comparison, Dell, Inc.'s DSO in 2010 was 45 days (365/8.1 turnover). Dell owns far fewer retail outlets and sells fewer products than Apple.

Accounts payable turnover. Discussed in Chapter 9, *accounts payable turnover* measures the number of times per year that the entity pays off its accounts payable. To compute accounts payable turnover, divide cost of goods sold by average accounts payable. For Apple, Inc., this ratio is as follows:

Formula		Apple, Inc.'s Accounts Payable Turnover	Competitor (Dell, Inc.)
Accounts payable turnover $=$	$\dfrac{\text{Cost of goods sold}}{\text{Average accounts payable}}$	$\dfrac{\$39,541}{\$8,808} = 4.49$	3.71
Days' payable outstanding (DPO) $=$	$\dfrac{365}{\text{Turnover}}$	$\dfrac{365}{4.49} = 81$ days	98 days

On average, Apple, Inc., pays off its accounts payable 4.49 times per year, which is about every 81 days. To convert accounts payable turnover to days' payable outstanding (DPO), divide the turnover into 365 (365 ÷ 4.49 = 81 days). In comparison, Dell, Inc.'s accounts payable turnover is 3.71 times per year, or about every 98 days.

Cash conversion cycle. By expressing the three turnover ratios in days, we can compute a company's **cash conversion cycle** as follows:

Formula		Apple, Inc.'s Cash Conversion Cycle	Competitor (Dell, Inc.)
Cash conversion cycle	= DIO + DSO − DPO	7 + 25 − 81 = −49 days	−43 days
where DIO	= Days' inventory outstanding		
DSO	= Days' sales outstanding		
DPO	= Days' payable outstanding		

At first glance, a negative amount for the cash conversion cycle looks odd. What does it mean? Apple, Inc., is in the enviable position of being able to sell inventory and collect from its customers 49 days before it has to pay its suppliers who provided the parts and materials to produce those inventories. This means that Apple can stock less inventory and hold onto cash longer than other companies. It also helps explain why the company could afford to keep over $14 billion in short-term marketable securities (Exhibit 13-10), to "sop up" its excess cash, using it to make still more money while waiting to pay off suppliers. Apple's competitor, Dell, Inc., has a similar situation, with a cash conversion cycle of −43 days. Amazon.com, featured earlier in this chapter, also has a negative cash conversion cycle of about −31 days, whereas Barnes & Noble, a competitor of Amazon.com's, has a positive number because it has a much slower inventory turnover ratio than Amazon.com. Retail companies that have a more "normal" inventory turnover (about four times per year, or about every 90 days) have cash conversion cycles in the range of 30 to 60 days, depending on how long it takes to collect from customers. The cash conversion cycle for service-oriented businesses consists only of (DSO − DPO) because service businesses typically do not carry inventory.

Measuring Leverage: Overall Ability to Pay Debts

The ratios discussed so far relate to current assets and current liabilities. They measure the ability to sell inventory, collect receivables, and pay current bills. Two indicators of the ability to pay total liabilities are the *debt ratio* and the *times-interest-earned ratio*.

Debt Ratio. Suppose you are a bank loan officer and you have received loan applications for $500,000 from two similar companies. The first company already owes $600,000, and the second owes only $250,000. Which company gets the loan? Company 2 may look like the stronger candidate, because it owes less.

This relationship between total liabilities and total assets is called the **debt ratio**. Discussed in Chapters 3 and 9, the debt ratio tells us the proportion of assets financed with debt. A debt ratio of 1 reveals that debt has financed all the assets. A debt ratio of 0.50 means that debt finances half the assets. The higher the debt ratio, the greater the pressure to pay interest and principal. The lower the debt ratio, the lower the company's credit risk.

The debt ratios for Apple, Inc., in 2010 and 2009 follow:

Formula	Apple, Inc.'s Debt Ratio		Competitor (Dell, Inc.)
	2010	2009	
Debt ratio = $\dfrac{\text{Total liabilities}}{\text{Total assets}}$	$\dfrac{\$27,392}{\$75,183}$ = 0.36	$\dfrac{\$15,861}{\$47,501}$ = 0.33	0.80

This is an extremely low debt ratio, because of Apple, Inc.'s unusually healthy cash position described in the previous section. Notice that Dell, Inc., has a much higher debt ratio than Apple, Inc. The Risk Management Association reports that the average debt ratio for most companies ranges around 0.62, with relatively little variation from company to company. However, companies in certain industries such as airlines usually have higher debt ratios. The debt ratio is related to the leverage ratio discussed in the next section, which is used in DuPont analysis to compute return on assets and return on equity.

Times-Interest-Earned Ratio. Analysts use a second ratio—the **times-interest-earned ratio** (introduced in Chapter 9)—to relate income to interest expense. To compute the times-interest-earned ratio, divide income from operations (operating income) by interest expense. This ratio measures the number of times operating income can *cover* interest expense and is also called the *interest-coverage ratio*. A high ratio indicates ease in paying interest; a low value suggests difficulty.

Formula	Apple, Inc.'s Times-Interest-Earned Ratio		Competitor (Dell, Inc.)
	2010	2009	
Times-interest-earned ratio $= \dfrac{\text{Income from operations}}{\text{Interest expense}}$	N/A	N/A	41.4

It is not possible to compute the times-interest-earned ratio for Apple, Inc., for one simple reason: The company has no interest-bearing debt. Why should it borrow money and pay interest, with so much cash on the balance sheet and the ability to generate cash from sales 49 days before having to pay creditors? From Exhibit 13-10, notice that $20 billion of the total $27 billion in liabilities is current, which is usually non-interest bearing. In addition, an examination of the financial statement footnotes reveals that, of the $5.5 billion of "other non-current liabilities" none are interest bearing. Although Apple, Inc.'s competitor, Dell, Inc., has a relatively high debt ratio (0.80), its times-interest-earned ratio is quite high (41.4), meaning that Dell, Inc., is quite capable of servicing its interest payments. In contrast, in Chapter 9, we studied the financial statements of Southwest Airlines, with 5.9 times interest coverage, and United Continental with only 1.2 times interest coverage. In summary, the judgment about the adequacy of interest coverage, like so many other factors of financial statement analysis, is very much dependent on the industry, as well as the company being studied.

Measuring Profitability

The fundamental goal of business is to earn a profit, and so the ratios that measure profitability are reported widely.

Gross (Profit) Margin. In Chapter 6, we defined gross margin as net sales – cost of goods sold. That is, gross margin is the amount of profit that the entity makes from merely selling a product before other operating costs are subtracted. In Chapter 11, we emphasized that a persistently improving gross margin is one important element of earnings quality. Let's look at Apple, Inc.'s gross margin percentages:

Formula	Apple, Inc.'s Gross Margin		Competitor (Dell, Inc.)
	2010	2009	
Gross Margin % $= \dfrac{\text{Gross margin}}{\text{Net sales}}$	39.4%	40.1%	18.5%

Apple is known as *the* innovator in the technology field. The company is constantly inventing new technology that everyone literally stands in line to purchase! Do you remember the last time you visited an Apple store (perhaps when a new version of the iPhone was introduced)? How much were you willing to pay for your new iPhone, iPad, or iMac? Do you remember how crowded the store was? As we discussed in Chapter 7, because of the creative talents of their people, some companies have been able to adopt a "product differentiation" business strategy, which allows them to sell their products for more than their competitors. When everyone wants the product, they are usually willing to pay more for it. Although Apple's gross margin of 39.3% in 2010 is slightly less than the 40.1% it earned in 2009, this is quite an impressive number, and is higher than any competitor. In contrast, Dell, Inc., with an 18.5% gross margin, is known as a low-cost provider of computer equipment. Dell sells a lot of products, but it is usually not the first to introduce new products, so it has to sell products for lower prices, thus lowering its gross margin.

Operating Income (Profit) Percentage. Operating income (profit) percentage is net income from operations as a percentage of net sales. It is an important statistic, because it measures the percentage of profit earned from each sales dollar in a company's core business operations. In Chapter 11, we pointed out that a persistently high operating income compared to net sales is an important determinant of earnings quality. The first component of high operating earnings is a high gross margin percentage. After that, maximizing operating income depends on keeping operating costs as low as possible, given the level of desired product quality and customer service. Apple, Inc.'s operating income percentages, compared with Dell, Inc., follow:

Formula	Apple, Inc.'s Operating Income %		Competitor (Dell, Inc.)
	2010	2009	
Operating Income % $= \dfrac{\text{Operating Income}}{\text{Net sales}}$	28.2%	27.4%	5.6%

Apple is far ahead of the competition on earnings from its core operations, and the company is also improving steadily over prior years.

DuPont Analysis. In Chapters 7 (pp. 428–430) and 10 (pp. 607–609), we introduced **DuPont analysis**, which is a detailed analysis of rate of return on total assets (ROA) and rate of return on common stockholders' equity (ROE). It might prove valuable to re-read those pages before you proceed with the following material. In Exhibit 13-11, we review the basic driver ratios for DuPont analysis to provide a template for the analysis by component that follows.

EXHIBIT 13-11 | DuPont Analysis Model

ROA			×	Leverage ratio (Equity multiplier)	=	ROE
Rate of return on sales (Net profit margin)	×	Asset turnover	×	Leverage ratio (Equity multiplier)	=	Return on equity (ROE)
$\dfrac{\text{Net income}}{\text{Net sales}}$	×	$\dfrac{\text{Net sales}}{\text{Average total assets}}$	×	$\dfrac{\text{Average total assets}}{\text{Average common stockholders' equity}}$	=	$\dfrac{\text{Net income}}{\text{Average common stockholders' equity}}$

Notice that the ultimate goal of DuPont analysis is to explain the rate of return on common stockholders' equity in a detailed fashion (far right hand column) by breaking it down into its component elements: rate of return on sales, asset turnover, and leverage. The first two components of the model combine to give rate of return on total assets (ROA). When the last component (leverage) is combined into the model, it produces (by cross cancellation) rate of return on common stockholders' equity (ROE). We now explain each component of the model, using figures for Apple, Inc., to illustrate.

Rate of Return (Net Profit Margin) on Sales. In business, *return* refers to profitability. Consider the **rate of return on net sales**, or simply *return on sales* (ROS). (The word *net* is usually omitted for convenience.) In Chapter 7, we referred to this ratio as *net profit margin*. The initial element of DuPont analysis, this ratio shows the percentage of each sales dollar earned as net income. The return-on-sales ratios for Apple, Inc. are as follows:

Formula	Apple, Inc.'s Rate of Return on Sales		Competitor (Dell, Inc.)
	2010	2009	
Rate of return on sales (Net profit margin) $= \dfrac{\text{Net income}}{\text{Net sales}}$	$\dfrac{\$14,013}{\$65,225} = 21.5\%$	$\dfrac{\$8,235}{\$42,905} = 19.2\%$	4.3%

Companies strive for a high rate of return on sales. The higher the percentage, the more profit is being generated by sales dollars. Apple, Inc.'s return on sales is astoundingly high in 2010

(21.5%) and is over two percentage points higher than it was in 2009. Compare Apple, Inc.'s rate of return on sales to the rates of some leading companies:

Company	Rate of Return on Sales
FedEx.....................	5.6%
PepsiCo.................	11.9%
Intel.......................	14.1%
Dell, Inc................	4.3%

Asset turnover. As discussed in Chapter 7, **asset turnover** measures the amount of net sales generated for each dollar invested in assets. As such, it is a measure of how efficiently management is operating the company. Companies with high asset turnover tend to be more productive than companies with low asset turnover. Let's examine Apple, Inc.'s asset turnover for 2010 compared with 2009, and then compare it to competitor Dell, Inc.'s asset turnover.

	Formula	Apple, Inc.'s Asset Turnover		Competitor
		2010	2009	(Dell, Inc.)
Asset turnover =	Net sales	$65,225	$42,905	
	Average total Assets	$61,342 = 1.063	$41,836 = 1.026	1.7

Compared to Dell, Apple has invested more in assets per dollar of sales. This is often the case with innovative companies, as opposed to companies that focus on low cost. To make major product innovations requires a significant investment in both tangible and intangible assets. So, while Apple, Inc., is significantly more profitable than Dell, Inc., it is less efficiently managed, at least by this measure.

Rate of Return on Total Assets (ROA). Having computed the "driver ratios" (rate of return on net sales and asset turnover), we are now prepared to combine them into the first two elements of DuPont analysis to compute **rate of return on assets** (ROA) as follows:

Rate of return on assets (ROA)	Apple, Inc.'s ROA		Competitor
	2010	2009	(Dell, Inc.)
Rate of return on sales*	21.5%	19.2%	4.3%
×	×	×	×
Asset turnover	1.063	1.026	1.7
=	=	=	=
ROA	22.9%	19.7%	7.3%

Again, the raw figures for our computations are based on income and asset figures from Exhibits 13-9 and 13-10, but the component ratios are based on the previous two illustrations. We see from these computations that for Apple, Inc., ROA is driven principally by its high profitability based on product differentiation, rather than efficiency. In contrast, Dell, Inc.'s ROA is based more on efficiency than profitability. Dell is a low-margin provider of basic computer technology, and as the low-cost provider, it is more efficient, generating more sales per dollar invested in total assets than Apple.

Leverage (Equity Multiplier) Ratio. The final element of DuPont analysis is **leverage**, which measures the impact of debt financing on profitability. You learned in Chapters 9 and 10 that it can be advantageous to use borrowed capital to finance a business. Earlier, we expressed the debt ratio as the ratio of total liabilities to total assets. The **leverage ratio**, or equity multiplier, measures the proportion of each dollar of assets financed with stockholders' equity. Since total assets – stockholders' equity = total liabilities, the leverage ratio is a way of inversely expressing the debt ratio—it merely looks at financing from the other side of the fundamental accounting equation. Let's examine Apple, Inc.'s leverage ratios for 2010 and 2009, compared with that of its competitor, Dell, Inc.

---

*Some analysts use net income before interest expense to compute ROA, since interest expense measures the return earned by creditors who provide the portion of total assets for which the company has used borrowed capital.

	Formula	Apple, Inc.'s Leverage Ratios		Competitor (Dell, Inc.)
		2010	2009	
Leverage ratio =	$\dfrac{\text{Average total assets}}{\text{Average common stockholders' equity}}$	$\dfrac{\$61,342}{\$39,715} = 1.545$	$\dfrac{\$41,836}{\$26,968} = 1.551$	5.39

As we pointed out in a previous section, Apple, Inc., has a comparatively low debt ratio (36% and 33% for 2010 and 2009, respectively). This translates to very low leverage ratios for Apple, Inc. (1.545 and 1.551 for 2010 and 2009, respectively). In comparison, Dell, Inc., has a comparatively high debt ratio (80% for 2010). Therefore, Dell uses much more borrowed capital than equity capital to finance its operations, and its leverage ratio is much higher (5.39).

Rate of Return on Common Stockholders' Equity (ROE).

A popular measure of profitability is **rate of return on common stockholders' equity**, often shortened to *return on equity* (ROE). Also discussed in Chapter 10, this ratio shows the relationship between net income and common stockholders' investment in the company—how much income is earned for every $1 invested.

To compute this ratio, first subtract preferred dividends, if any, from net income to measure income available to the common stockholders. Then divide income available to common by average common equity during the year. Common equity is total equity minus preferred equity. The 2010 return on common stockholders' equity for Apple, Inc., is as follows[†]:

	Formula	Apple, Inc.'s 2010 Rate of Return on Common Stockholders' Equity	Competitor (Dell, Inc.)
Rate of return on common stockholders' equity =	$\dfrac{\text{Net income} - \text{Preferred dividends}}{\text{Average common stockholders' equity}}$	$\dfrac{\$14,013 - \$0}{\$39,715} = 35.3\%$	39.3%

[†]Note: Because of rounding, this computation is slightly different [35.28%] than the product of ROA and leverage using DuPont analysis model [22.9% × 1.545 = 35.38%].)

Now observe something interesting: Apple has beaten its closest competitor (Dell, Inc.) on virtually every measure so far, right? But here we see that Dell's ROE (39.3%) is substantially higher than Apple, Inc.'s ROE (35.3%). How can this be? If we hadn't considered the impact of leverage, we might have missed it. By using DuPont analysis to analyze the final components of ROE, we see it right away:

Rate of Return on Stockholders' Equity (ROE)	Apple, Inc.'s ROE		Competitor (Dell, Inc.)
	2010	2009	
ROA	22.9%	19.7%	7.3%
×	×	×	×
Leverage ratio	1.545	1.551	5.39
=	=	=	=
ROE	(rounded) 35.3%	(rounded) 30.6%	39.3%

Apple, Inc., is by far the more profitable company. However, Dell, Inc., is more highly leveraged than Apple, having an 80% debt ratio and a leverage ratio of $5.39 of assets per dollar of stockholders' equity. Thus, the detailed analysis provided by the DuPont model gives far more information on which to judge the quality of earnings than just the ROE ratio alone.

To be sure, use of leverage is often a good thing, as long as it is kept within reasonable limits. The practice of using leverage is called **trading on the equity**. Companies like Dell that finance operations with debt are said to *leverage* their positions.

As we pointed out in Chapter 10, leverage can hurt ROE as well as help. If revenues drop, debts still must be paid. Therefore, leverage is a double-edged sword. It increases profits during good times but also compounds losses during bad times.

Apple, Inc.'s ROE is slightly less than Dell's, but it exceeds that of **General Electric**, **Google**, and **Starbucks**.

Company	Rate of Return on Common Equity
General Electric..................	11.5%
Google	19.2%
Starbucks	27.8%

Earnings per Share of Common Stock. Discussed in Chapters 9 and 11, *earnings per share of common stock*, or simply **earnings per share** (EPS), is the amount of net income earned for each share of outstanding *common* stock. EPS is the most widely quoted of all financial statistics. It's the only ratio that appears on the income statement.

Earnings per share is computed by dividing net income available to common stockholders by the average number of common shares outstanding during the year. Preferred dividends are subtracted from net income because the preferred stockholders have a prior claim to their dividends. Apple, Inc., has no preferred stock and thus has no preferred dividends. The firm's EPS for 2010 and 2009 follows (based on Exhibit 13-9):

		Apple, Inc.'s Earnings per Share (Basic)	
	Formula	2010	2009
Earnings per share of common stock	$= \dfrac{\text{Net income} - \text{Preferred dividends (in thousands)}}{\text{Average number of shares of common stock outstanding (in thousands)}}$	$\dfrac{\$14{,}013{,}000 - \$0}{909{,}461} = \$15.41$	$\dfrac{\$8{,}235{,}000 - \$0}{893{,}016} = \$9.22$

Apple, Inc.'s EPS increased 67% during 2010, and that's good news. That's more than double the percentage increase in EPS from 2008 to 2009 ($9.22 vs. $6.94). Such huge increases in earnings have certainly had an impact on the company's stock price. Apple, Inc., stockholders have been enjoying huge appreciation in their investment for several years. In mid-2011, the stock was selling for over $320 per share! That's tremendous appreciation if you had purchased the stock five years ago, when the stock was selling for less than $100 per share. But is it still a good buy at this price? That's the relevant question a prospective stockholder wants to know. The next section gives you some information on how analysts make this decision.

Analyzing Stock as an Investment

Investors buy stock to earn a return on their investment. This return consists of two parts: (1) gains (or losses) from selling the stock and (2) dividends.

Price/Earnings Ratio (Multiple). The **price/earnings ratio** (**multiple**) is the ratio of common stock price to earnings per share. This ratio, abbreviated P/E, appears in *The Wall Street Journal* stock listings and online. It shows the market price of $1 of earnings.

Calculations for the P/E ratios of Apple, Inc., follow. The market price of Apple's common stock was $292.32 at September 25, 2010 (the end of its 2010 fiscal year), and $182.37 at September 26, 2009 (the end of its 2009 fiscal year). Stock prices can be obtained from a company's Web site or various other financial Web sites.

		Apple, Inc.'s Price/Earnings Ratio	
	Formula	2010	2009
P/E ratio $=$	$\dfrac{\text{Market price per share of common stock}}{\text{Earnings per share}}$	$\dfrac{\$292.32}{\$15.41} = 19.0$	$\dfrac{\$182.37}{\$9.22} = 19.8$

Given Apple, Inc.'s 2010 P/E ratio of 19.0, we would say that the company's stock is selling at 19 times earnings. Each $1 of Apple's earnings is worth $19 to the stock market. Stocks trade in ranges, and public companies report updated EPS quarterly. These earnings are annualized and projected for the upcoming year (quarterly earnings multiplied by 4). Since Apple's yearly earnings were reported in 2010, its stock has traded in the range of $235 to $365 per share. As of June 22, 2011, the latest quarterly (annualized) EPS for Apple, Inc., was $20.99, and the stock closed at $322.61. As of June 22, 2011, therefore, the P/E Ratio for Apple, Inc., was 15.37. You can see by this that P/E ratios fluctuate daily. Certainly reported earnings play a role in these fluctuations. However, market prices of stocks are based on consensus estimations of what may happen in the future—business cycles, government policies, new product announcements, foreign trade deals, currency fluctuations, even the health of key company executives may significantly impact the estimates. Markets run on sentiment and are very difficult to predict. Some analysts study past trends in P/E multiples and try to estimate future trading ranges. If the P/E multiple of a particular stock drifts toward the low end of a range, and if its projected earnings are increasing, it means that the price of the stock is becoming more attractive, which is a signal to buy. As P/E multiples drift higher, given projected earnings, the stock becomes too expensive, and the analyst would recommend "hold" or "sell." Based on the difference between the P/E multiples in September 2010 and June 2011, assuming no predicted bad news for the economy, the industry, or the company, analysts might say that a current P/E multiple of 15.37 makes Apple, Inc., an attractive buy at $322.61 per share. With projected yearly EPS of $20.99 per share, if the P/E climbs back up to 19, as it was in September 2010, Apple's stock price could climb to almost $400 per share. Would you buy it?

Dividend Yield. **Dividend yield** is the ratio of dividends per share of stock to the stock's market price. This ratio measures the percentage of a stock's market value returned annually to the stockholders as dividends. Although dividends are never guaranteed, some well-established companies have continued to pay dividends even through turbulent economic times. *Preferred* stockholders pay special attention to this ratio because they invest primarily to receive dividends. However, certain companies such as General Electric, **Merck Pharmaceuticals**, or IBM also pay attractive dividends on their common stock. In periods of low interest rates on certificates of deposit or money-market funds, dividend-paying stocks become more attractive alternatives for conservative investors.

Apple, Inc., has never paid dividends on its common stock, and the company has never authorized any preferred stock. Dividends are relatively rare in the technology industry. However, **International Business Machines (IBM)** has paid cash dividends each quarter for years, and shareholders have come to expect them. IBM paid annual dividends of $3.00 per share in 2011. The 50-day moving average market price of the company's common stock was $167.29 in mid-2011. Therefore, the firm's dividend yield on its common stock was as follows:

Formula	Dividend Yield on IBM Common Stock
	Mid-2011
Dividend yield on common stock* $= \dfrac{\text{Dividend per share of common stock}}{\text{Market price per share of common stock}}$	$\dfrac{\$3.00}{\$167.29} = 0.018$

*Dividend yields may also be calculated for preferred stock.

An investor who buys IBM common stock for $167.29 can expect to receive around 1.8% of the investment annually in the form of cash dividends. You might think that's a very low rate, but compared to current yields on certificates of deposit or bonds, it's pretty attractive. Dividend yields vary widely. They are generally higher for older, established firms (such as **Procter & Gamble** and General Electric) and lower to non-existent for young, growth-oriented companies.

Book Value per Share of Common Stock. **Book value per share of common stock** is simply common stockholders' equity divided by the number of shares of common stock outstanding. Common equity equals total equity less preferred equity. Apple, Inc., has no preferred stock outstanding. Calculations of its book value per share of common follow. Numbers are based on Exhibit 13-9 and Exhibit 13-10, using weighted-average number of shares outstanding.

		Book Value per Share of Apple, Inc. Common Stock	
Formula (figures in thousands)		2010	2009
Book value per share of common stock =	$\dfrac{\text{Total stockholders' equity} - \text{Preferred equity}}{\text{Weighted-average number of shares of common stock outstanding (basic)}}$	$\dfrac{\$47{,}791{,}000 - \$0}{909{,}461} = \$52.55$	$\dfrac{\$31{,}640{,}000 - \$0}{893{,}016} = \$35.43$

Book value per share indicates the recorded accounting amount for each share of common stock outstanding. Many experts believe book value is not useful for investment analysis because it bears no relationship to market value and provides little information beyond what's reported on the balance sheet. But some investors base their investment decisions on book value. For example, some investors rank stocks by the ratio of market price per share to book value per share. The lower the ratio, the more attractive the stock. These investors are called "value" investors, as contrasted with "growth" investors, who focus more on trends in net income.

What does the outlook for the future look like for Apple, Inc? If the company can stay on the same path it has followed for the past several years, it looks bright. Its earnings per share are solid, and its ROS and ROA lead the industry. ROE for Apple is second to a competitor that is highly leveraged, so in comparison, Apple still looks preferable. From the standpoint of liquidity and leverage, the company is in stellar shape. It has a negative cash conversion cycle, meaning that it sells out inventory and collects cash weeks before accounts payable are due. It has no interest-bearing debt, and virtually no long-term debt. The company's recent P/E ratio of 15.37 is relatively low. Beyond that, Apple is one of the most innovative companies in the world, continually putting out personal electronics products that everyone wants. All of these factors make Apple, Inc., stock look like a good investment.

The Limitations of Ratio Analysis

Business decisions are made in a world of uncertainty. As useful as ratios are, they aren't a cure-all. Consider a physician's use of a thermometer. A reading of 102.0° Fahrenheit tells a doctor that something is wrong with the patient but doesn't indicate what the problem is or how to cure it.

In financial analysis, a sudden drop in the current ratio signals that *something* is wrong, but it doesn't identify the problem. A manager must analyze the figures to learn what caused the ratio to fall. A drop in current assets may mean a cash shortage or that sales are slow. The manager must evaluate all the ratios in the light of factors such as increased competition or a slowdown in the economy.

Legislation, international affairs, scandals, and other factors can turn profits into losses. To be useful, ratios should be analyzed over a period of years to consider all relevant factors. Any one year, or even any two years, may not represent the company's performance over the long term. The investment decision, whether in stocks, bonds, real estate, cash, or more exotic instruments, depends on one's tolerance for risk, and risk is the one factor that is always a certainty!

Use Other Measures to Make Investment Decisions

6

Use other measures to make investment decisions

Economic Value Added (EVA®)

The top managers of **Coca-Cola**, **Quaker Oats**, and other leading companies use **economic value added (EVA®)** to evaluate operating performance. EVA® combines accounting and finance to measure whether operations have increased stockholder wealth. EVA® can be computed as follows:

$$\text{EVA}^{\circledR} = \text{Net income} + \text{Interest expense} - \text{Capital charge}$$

$$\text{Capital charge} = \left(\begin{array}{c} \text{(Beginning balances)} \\ \text{Notes} + \begin{array}{c} \text{Current} \\ \text{maturities} \\ \text{of long-} \\ \text{term debt} \end{array} + \begin{array}{c} \text{Long-term} \\ \text{debt} \end{array} + \begin{array}{c} \text{Stockholders'} \\ \text{equity} \end{array} \end{array} \right) \times \begin{array}{c} \text{Cost of} \\ \text{capital} \end{array}$$

All amounts for the EVA® computation, except the cost of capital, come from the financial statements. The **weighted-average cost of capital**, discussed earlier in Chapter 11, is a weighted average of the returns demanded by the company's stockholders and lenders. Cost of capital varies with the company's level of risk. For example, stockholders would demand a higher return from a start-up company than from Amazon.com, Inc., because the new company is untested and therefore riskier. Lenders would also charge the new company a higher interest rate because of its greater risk. Thus, the new company has a higher cost of capital than Amazon.com, Inc.

The cost of capital is a major topic in finance classes. In the following discussions, we assume a value for the cost of capital (such as 10%, 12%, or 15%) to illustrate the computation of EVA®.

The idea behind EVA® is that the returns to the company's stockholders (net income) and to its creditors (interest expense) should exceed the company's capital charge. The **capital charge** is the amount that stockholders and lenders *charge* a company for the use of their money. A positive EVA® amount suggests an increase in stockholder wealth, and so the company's stock should remain attractive to investors. If EVA® is negative, stockholders will probably be unhappy with the company and sell its stock, resulting in a decrease in the stock's price. Different companies tailor the EVA® computation to meet their own needs.

Let's apply EVA® to Amazon.com, Inc. The company's EVA® for 2010 (see Exhibit 13-2 and Exhibit 13-3 for inputs) can be computed as follows, using net income before taxes (NIBT), and assuming an 8% cost of capital (dollars in millions):

					(Beginning balances)						
Amazon.com, Inc.'s EVA® =	NIBT	+	Interest expense	−	Short-term borrowings	+	Long-term debt	+	Stockholders' equity	×	Cost of capital
=	$1,497	+	$39	−	[($0	+	$1,192	+	$5,257)	×	0.08]
=	$1,536			−			$6,449			×	0.08
=	$1,536			−					$516		
=				$1,020							

By this measure, Amazon.com, Inc.'s operations added $1,020 million of value to its stockholders' wealth during 2010 after meeting the company's capital charge. This performance is considered strong.

Red Flags in Financial Statement Analysis

Recent accounting scandals have highlighted the importance of *red flags* in financial analysis. The following conditions may mean a company is very risky.

► *Earnings Problems.* Have income from continuing operations and net income decreased for several years in a row? Has income turned into a loss? This may be okay for a company in a cyclical industry, such as an airline or a home builder, but a company such as Amazon.com, Inc., may be unable to survive consecutive loss years.

► *Decreased Cash Flow.* Cash flow validates earnings. Is net cash provided by operations consistently lower than net income? Are the sales of plant assets a major source of cash? If so, the company may be facing a cash shortage.

► *Too Much Debt.* How does the company's debt ratio compare to that of major competitors and to the industry average? If the debt ratio is much higher than average, the company may be unable to pay debts during tough times. As we saw earlier, Apple, Inc.'s debt ratio of 36% in 2010 (while still high) was much better than Dell's 80% debt ratio.

► *Inability to Collect Receivables.* Are days' sales in receivables growing faster than for other companies in the industry? A cash shortage may be looming. Apple, Inc.'s cash collections from customers are very strong.

▶ *Buildup of Inventories.* Is inventory turnover slowing down? If so, the company may be unable to move products, or it may be overstating inventory as reported on the balance sheet. Recall from the cost-of-goods-sold model that one of the easiest ways to overstate net income is to overstate ending inventory. Apple, Inc., has no problem here.

▶ *Trends of Sales, Inventory, and Receivables.* Sales, receivables, and inventory generally move together. Increased sales lead to higher receivables and require more inventory in order to meet demand. Strange movements among these items may spell trouble. Apple, Inc.'s relationships look normal.

Efficient Markets

An **efficient capital market** is one in which market prices fully reflect all information available to the public. Because stock prices reflect all publicly accessible data, it can be argued that the stock market is efficient. Market efficiency has implications for management action and for investor decisions. It means that managers cannot fool the market with accounting gimmicks. If the information is available, the market as a whole can set a "fair" price for the company's stock.

Suppose you are the president of Anacomp Corporation. Reported earnings per share are $4, and the stock price is $40—so the P/E ratio is 10. You believe Anacomp's stock is underpriced. To correct this situation, you are considering changing your depreciation method from accelerated to straight-line. The accounting change will increase earnings per share to $5. Will the stock price then rise to $50? Probably not; the company's stock price will probably remain at $40 because the market can understand the accounting change. After all, the company merely changed its method of computing depreciation. There is no effect on Anacomp's cash flows, and the company's economic position is unchanged. An efficient market interprets data in light of their true underlying meaning.

In an efficient market, the search for "underpriced" stock is fruitless unless the investor has relevant *private* information. But it is unlawful as well as unethical to invest on the basis of *inside* information. An appropriate strategy seeks to manage risk, diversify investments, and minimize transaction costs. Financial analysis helps mainly to identify the risks of various stocks and then to manage the risk.

The Decision Guidelines feature summarizes the most widely used ratios.

DECISION GUIDELINES

USING RATIOS IN FINANCIAL STATEMENT ANALYSIS

Lane and Kay Collins operate a financial services firm. They manage other people's money and do most of their own financial-statement analysis. How do they measure companies' ability to pay bills, sell inventory, collect receivables, and so on? They use the standard ratios we have covered throughout this book.

Ratio	Computation	Information Provided
Measuring ability to pay current liabilities:		
1. Current ratio	$$\frac{\text{Current assets}}{\text{Current liabilities}}$$	Measures ability to pay current liabilities with current assets
2. Quick (acid-test) ratio	$$\frac{\text{Cash} + \dfrac{\text{Short-term}}{\text{investments}} + \dfrac{\text{Net current}}{\text{receivables}}}{\text{Current liabilities}}$$	Shows ability to pay all current liabilities if they come due immediately

Ratio	Computation	Information Provided
Measuring turnover and cash conversion:		
3. Inventory turnover and days' inventory outstanding (DIO)	$$\text{Inventory turnover} = \frac{\text{Cost of goods sold}}{\text{Average inventory}}$$ $$\text{Days' inventory outstanding (DIO)} = \frac{365}{\text{Inventory turnover}}$$	Indicates saleability of inventory—the number of times a company sells its average level of inventory during a year
4. Accounts receivable turnover	$$\frac{\text{Net credit sales}}{\text{Average net accounts receivable}}$$	Measures ability to collect cash from credit customers
5. Days' sales in receivables or days' sales outstanding (DSO)	$$\frac{\text{Average net accounts receivable}}{\text{Average daily sales}}$$ or $$\frac{365}{\text{Accounts receivable turnover}}$$	Shows how many days' sales remain in Accounts Receivable—how many days it takes to collect the average level of receivables
6. Payables turnover and days' payable outstanding (DPO)	$$\text{Accounts payable turnover} = \frac{\text{Cost of goods sold}}{\text{Average accounts payable}}$$ $$\text{Days' payable outstanding (DPO)} = 365/\text{Accounts payable turnover}$$	Shows how many times a year accounts payable turn over, and how many days it takes the company to pay off accounts payable
7. Cash conversion cycle	$$\text{Cash conversion cycle} = \text{DIO} + \text{DSO} - \text{DPO}$$ where DIO = Days' inventory outstanding DSO = Days' sales outstanding DPO = Days' payable outstanding	Shows overall liquidity by computing the total days it takes to convert inventory to receivables and back to cash, less the days to pay off creditors
Measuring ability to pay long-term debt:		
8. Debt ratio	$$\frac{\text{Total liabilities}}{\text{Total assets}}$$	Indicates percentage of assets financed with debt
9. Times-interest-earned ratio	$$\frac{\text{Income from operations}}{\text{Interest expense}}$$	Measures the number of times operating income can cover interest expense
Measuring profitability:		
10. Gross margin %	$$\frac{\text{Gross margin}}{\text{Net sales}}$$	Shows the percentage of profit that a company makes from merely selling the product, before any other operating costs are subtracted
11. Operating income %	$$\frac{\text{Income from operations}}{\text{Net sales}}$$	Shows the percentage of profit earned from each dollar in the company's core business, after operating costs have been subtracted

Ratio	Computation	Information Provided
12. DuPont model	Exhibit 13-11	A detailed analysis of return on assets (ROA) and return on common stockholders' equity (ROE)
13. Rate of return on net sales	$$\frac{\text{Net income}}{\text{Net sales}}$$	Shows the percentage of each sales dollar earned as net income
14. Asset turnover	$$\frac{\text{Net sales}}{\text{Average total assets}}$$	Measures the amount of net sales generated for each dollar invested in assets
15. Rate of return on total assets	Rate of return on total assets (ROA) DuPont method: Rate of return on net sales $\times$ Asset turnover $\quad$ or $\quad \dfrac{\text{Net income}}{\text{Average total assets}}$	Measures how profitably a company uses its assets
16. Leverage ratio	$$\frac{\text{Average total assets}}{\text{Average common stockholders' equity}}$$	Otherwise known as the *equity multiplier*, measures the ratio of average total assets to average common stockholders' equity
17. Rate of return on common stockholders' equity	Rate of return on common stockholders' equity (ROE) DuPont method: ROA $\times$ Leverage ratio $\quad$ or $\quad \dfrac{\text{Net income} - \text{preferred dividends}}{\text{Average common stockholders' equity}}$	Measures how much income is earned for every dollar invested by the company's common shareholders
18. Earnings per share of common stock	$$\frac{\text{Net income} - \text{Preferred dividends}}{\text{Average number of shares of common stock outstanding}}$$	Measures the amount of net income earned for each share of the company's common stock outstanding

Analyzing stock as an investment:

Ratio	Computation	Information Provided
19. Price/earnings ratio	$$\frac{\text{Market price per share of common stock}}{\text{Earnings per share}}$$	Indicates the market price of $1 of earnings
20. Dividend yield	$$\frac{\text{Dividend per share of common (or preferred) stock}}{\text{Market price per share of common (or preferred) stock}}$$	Shows the percentage of a stock's market value returned as dividends to stockholders each period
21. Book value per share of common stock	$$\frac{\text{Total stockholders' equity} - \text{Preferred equity}}{\text{Number of shares of common stock outstanding}}$$	Indicates the recorded accounting amount for each share of common stock outstanding

END-OF-CHAPTER SUMMARY PROBLEM

The following financial data are adapted from the annual reports of Lampeer Corporation:

Lampeer Corporation
Four-Year Selected Financial Data
Years Ended January 31, 2012, 2011, 2010, and 2009

Operating Results*	2012	2011	2010	2009
Net Sales	$13,848	$13,673	$11,635	$9,054
Cost of goods sold and occupancy expenses excluding depreciation and amortization	9,704	8,599	6,775	5,318
Interest expense	109	75	45	46
Income from operations	338	1,445	1,817	1,333
Net earnings (net loss)	(8)	877	1,127	824
Cash dividends	76	75	76	77
Financial Position				
Merchandise inventory	1,677	1,904	1,462	1,056
Total assets	7,591	7,012	5,189	3,963
Current ratio	1.48:1	0.95:1	1.25:1	1.20:1
Stockholders' equity	3,010	2,928	2,630	1,574
Average number of shares of common stock outstanding (in thousands)	860	879	895	576

*Dollar amounts are in thousands.

▶ Requirement

1. Compute the following ratios for 2010 through 2012, and evaluate Lampeer's operating results. Are operating results strong or weak? Did they improve or deteriorate during the three-year period? Your analysis will reveal a clear trend.

   a. Inventory turnover (assume occupancy expenses are included in cost of goods sold)
   b. Gross margin (profit) percentage
   c. Operating income (profit) percentage
   d. Rate of return on sales
   e. Asset turnover
   f. Rate of return on assets
   g. Leverage ratio
   h. Rate of return on stockholders' equity
   i. Times interest earned
   j. Earnings per share

▶ Answer

		2012	2011	2010
a.	Inventory turnover	$\dfrac{\$9,704}{(\$1,677 + \$1,904)/2} = 5.4$ times	$\dfrac{\$8,599}{(\$1,904 + \$1,462)/2} = 5.1$ times	$\dfrac{\$6,775}{(\$1,462 + \$1,056)/2} = 5.4$ times
b.	Gross profit percentage	$\dfrac{\$13,848 - \$9,704}{\$13,848} = 29.9\%$	$\dfrac{\$13,673 - \$8,599}{\$13,673} = 37.1\%$	$\dfrac{\$11,635 - \$6,775}{\$11,635} = 41.8\%$
c.	Operating income percentage	$\dfrac{\$338}{\$13,848} = 2.4\%$	$\dfrac{\$1,445}{\$13,673} = 10.6\%$	$\dfrac{\$1,817}{\$11,635} = 15.6\%$
d.	Rate of return on sales	$\dfrac{\$(8)}{\$13,848} = (0.06)\%$	$\dfrac{\$877}{\$13,673} = 6.4\%$	$\dfrac{\$1,127}{\$11,635} = 9.7\%$
e.	Asset turnover	$\dfrac{\$13,848}{(\$7,591 + \$7,012)/2} = 1.897$	$\dfrac{\$13,673}{(\$7,012 + \$5,189)/2} = 2.241$	$\dfrac{\$11,635}{(\$5,189 + \$3,963)/2} = 2.543$
*f.	Rate of return on assets	$(0.06)\% \times 1.897 = (.114\%)$	$6.4\% \times 2.241 = 14.3\%$	$9.7\% \times 2.543 = 24.7\%$
g.	Leverage ratio	$\dfrac{\$7,301.50}{(\$3,010 + \$2,928)/2} = 2.459$	$\dfrac{\$6,100.50}{(\$2,928 + \$2,630)/2} = 2.195$	$\dfrac{\$4,576}{(\$2,630 + \$1,574)/2} = 2.176$
*h.	Rate of return on stockholders' equity	$(.114)\% \times 2.459 = (0.3\%)$	$14.3\% \times 2.195 = 31.4\%$	$24.7\% \times 2.176 = 53.7\%$
i.	Times-interest-earned ratio	$\dfrac{\$338}{\$109} = 3.1$ times	$\dfrac{\$1,445}{\$75} = 19.3$ times	$\dfrac{\$1,817}{\$45} = 40.4$ times
j.	Earnings per share	$\dfrac{\$(8)}{860} = \$(0.01)$	$\dfrac{\$877}{879} = \$1.00$	$\dfrac{\$1,127}{895} = \$1.26$

* Used DuPont model in Exhibit 13-11.

Evaluation: During this period, Lampeer's operating results deteriorated on all these measures except inventory turnover. The gross profit percentage is down sharply, as are the times-interest-earned ratio and all the return measures. From these data it is clear that Lampeer could sell its merchandise, but not at the markups the company enjoyed in the past. The final result, in 2012, was a net loss for the year. This yielded a negative ROA, and because of leverage, an even more negative ROE.

REVIEW | Financial Statement Analysis

Quick Check (Answers are given on pages 843–844.)

Analyze Renda Company's financial statements by answering the questions that follow. Renda owns a chain of restaurants.

Renda Company Consolidated Statements of Income (Adapted) Years Ended December 31, 2012 and 2011		
(In millions, except per share data)	2012	2011
Revenues		
Sales by Company-operated restaurants	$17,100	11,800
Revenues from franchised and affiliated restaurants	4,800	3,900
Total revenues	21,900	15,700
Food and paper (Cost of goods sold)	5,130	3,304
Payroll and employee benefits	3,800	3,500
Occupancy and other operating expenses	3,300	3,400
Franchised restaurants—occupancy expenses	947	845
Selling, general, and administrative expenses	1,825	1,720
Other operating expense, net	525	830
Total operating expenses	15,527	13,599
Operating income	6,373	2,101
Interest expense	340	350
Other nonoperating expense, net	92	63
Income before income taxes	5,941	1,688
Income tax expense	2,376	675
Net income	$ 3,565	$ 1,013
Per common share basic:		
Net income	$ 5.09	$ 1.69
Dividends per common share	$ 0.65	$ 0.40

Renda Company
Consolidated Balance Sheets
December 31, 2012 and 2011

(In millions, except per share data)	2012	2011
Assets		
Current assets:		
Cash and equivalents	$ 605	$ 420
Accounts and notes receivable	760	920
Inventories, at cost, not in excess of market	110	160
Prepaid expense and other current assets	570	390
Total current assets	2,045	1,890
Other assets:		
Investments in affiliates	1,160	1,019
Goodwill, net	1,790	1,520
Miscellaneous	970	1,090
Total other assets	3,920	3,629
Property and equipment:		
Property and equipment, at cost	28,710	26,400
Accumulated depreciation and amortization	(8,800)	(7,700)
Net property and equipment	19,910	18,700
Total assets	$25,875	$24,219
Liabilities and Stockholders' Equity		
Current liabilities:		
Accounts payable	$ 610	$ 615
Income taxes	75	17
Other taxes	230	190
Accrued interest	195	192
Accrued restructuring and restaurant closing costs	125	325
Accrued payroll and other liabilities	924	715
Current maturities of long-term debt	386	305
Total current liabilities	2,545	2,359
Long-term debt	8,700	9,700
Other long-term liabilities and minority interests	670	560
Deferred income taxes	995	995
Total liabilities	$12,910	$13,614
Stockholders' equity:		
Preferred stock, no par value; authorized—140.0 million shares; issued—none	—	—
Common stock, $0.01 par value; authorized—2.0 billion shares; issued—1,300 million shares	13	13
Additional paid-in capital	465	1,479
Unearned ESOP compensation	(88)	(97)
Retained earnings	22,910	19,800
Accumulated other comprehensive income (loss)	(845)	(1,600)
Common stock in treasury, at cost; 400 and 420 million shares	(9,490)	(8,990)
Total stockholders' equity	12,965	10,605
Total liabilities and stockholders' equity	$25,875	$24,219

1. Horizontal analysis of Renda's income statement for 2012 would show which of the following for Selling, General, and Administrative expenses?

a. 0.94

b. 1.06

c. 0.08

d. None of the above

2. Vertical analysis of Renda's income statement for 2012 would show which of the following for Selling, General, and Administrative expenses (use total revenues as the base)?

  a. 0.118

  b. 0.083

  c. 0.107

  d. None of the above

3. Which item on Renda's income statement has the most favorable trend during 2011–2012?

  a. Net income

  b. Payroll and employee benefits

  c. Food and paper costs

  d. Total revenues

4. On Renda's common-size balance sheet for 2012, Goodwill would appear as

  a. up by 17.8%.

  b. 0.069.

  c. 8.17% of total revenues.

  d. $1,790 million.

5. A good benchmark for Renda Company would be

  a. Volvo.

  b. Microsoft.

  c. Whataburger.

  d. all of the above.

6. Renda's inventory turnover for 2012 was

  a. 15 times.

  b. 38 times.

  c. 91 times.

  d. 61 times.

7. Renda's quick (acid-test) ratio at the end of 2012 was

  a. 2.24

  b. 0.54

  c. 0.80.

  d. 0.05.

8. Renda's average collection period for accounts and notes receivables is

  a. 14 days.

  b. 1 day.

  c. 2 days.

  d. 32 days.

9. The average debt ratio for most companies is around 0.61. Renda's total debt position looks

  a. risky.

  b. safe.

  c. middle-ground.

  d. Cannot tell from the financials

10. Renda's return on total revenues for 2012 is

  a. 13.78%.

  b. $5.09.

  c. $1.16.

  d. 16.3%.

11. Renda's return on stockholders' equity for 2012 is

  a. 16.3%.

  b. 13.78%.

  c. $3,565 million.

  d. 30.3%.

12. On May 31, 2012, Renda's common stock sold for $26 per share. At that price, how much did investors say $1 of the company's net income was worth?

  a. $5.11

  b. $26.00

  c. $.14

  d. $1.00

13. On May 31, 2012, Renda's common stock sold for $26 per share, and dividends per share were $0.65. Compute Renda's dividend yield during 2012.

  a. 0.7%

  b. 6.5%

  c. 2.5%

  d. 5.7%

14. How much EVA® did Renda generate for investors during 2012? Assume the cost of capital was 10%.

  a. $4,220 million

  b. $1.700 million

  c. $3,905 million

  d. $3,565 million

Accounting Vocabulary

accounts receivable turnover (p. 789) Measures a company's ability to collect cash from credit customers. To compute accounts receivable turnover, divide net credit sales by average net accounts receivable.

acid-test ratio (p. 788) Ratio of the sum of cash plus short-term investments plus net current receivables to total current liabilities. Tells whether the entity can pay all its current liabilities if they come due immediately. Also called the *quick ratio*.

asset turnover (p. 794) The dollars of sales generated per dollar of assets invested. Formula is Net sales ÷ Average total assets.

benchmarking (p. 780) The comparison of a company to a standard set by other companies, with a view toward improvement.

book value per share of common stock (p. 797) Common stockholders' equity divided by the number of shares of common stock outstanding. The recorded amount for each share of common stock outstanding.

capital charge (p. 799) The amount that stockholders and lenders charge a company for the use of their money. Calculated as (Notes payable + Loans payable + Long-term debt + Stockholders' equity) × Cost of capital.

cash conversion cycle (p. 791) The number of days it takes to convert cash into inventory, inventory to receivables, and receivables back into cash, after paying off payables. The formula is Days inventory outstanding + Days sales outstanding – Days payables outstanding.

common-size statement (p. 779) A financial statement that reports only percentages (no dollar amounts).

current ratio (p. 786) Current assets divided by current liabilities. Measures a company's ability to pay current liabilities with current assets.

days' sales in receivables (p. 790) Ratio of average net accounts receivable to one day's sales. Indicates how many days' sales remain in Accounts Receivable awaiting collection. Also called the *collection period* and *days sales outstanding*.

debt ratio (p. 791) Ratio of total liabilities to total assets. States the proportion of a company's assets that is financed with debt.

dividend yield (p. 797) Ratio of dividends per share of stock to the stock's market price per share. Tells the percentage of a stock's market value that the company returns to stockholders as dividends.

DuPont analysis (p. 793) Detailed method of analyzing rate of return on common stockholders' equity. Rate of return on sales × Asset turnover × Leverage = Return on average common stockholders' equity.

earnings per share (EPS) (p. 796) Amount of a company's net income earned for each share of its outstanding common stock.

economic value added (EVA®) (p. 798) Used to evaluate a company's operating performance. EVA combines the concepts of accounting income and corporate finance to measure whether the company's operations have increased stockholder wealth. EVA = Net income + Interest expense – Capital charge.

efficient capital market (p. 800) A capital market in which market prices fully reflect all information available to the public.

horizontal analysis (p. 774) Study of percentage changes in comparative financial statements.

inventory turnover (p. 789) Ratio of cost of goods sold to average inventory. Indicates how rapidly inventory is sold.

leverage (p. 794) Earning more income on borrowed money than the related interest expense, thereby increasing the earnings for the owners of the business. Also called *trading on the equity*.

leverage ratio (p. 794) Ratio of average total assets to average common stockholders' equity. Measures the proportion of average total assets actually owned by the stockholders.

price/earnings ratio (p. 796) Ratio of the market price of a share of common stock to the company's earnings per share. Measures the value that the stock market places on $1 of a company's earnings.

quick ratio (p. 788) Another name for the *acid-test ratio*.

rate of return on common stockholders' equity (p. 795) Net income minus preferred dividends, divided by average common stockholders' equity. A measure of profitability. Also called *return on equity*. Also can be computed with DuPont analysis.

rate of return on net sales (p. 793) Ratio of net income to net sales. A measure of profitability. Also called *return on sales*.

rate of return on assets (p. 794) Net income divided by average total assets. This ratio measures a company's success in using its assets to earn income for the persons who finance the business. Also called *return on total assets*. *Can also be computed using the first two elements of DuPont analysis (rate of return on net sales × asset turnover).*

times-interest-earned ratio (p. 792) Ratio of income from operations to interest expense. Measures the number of times that operating income can cover interest expense. Also called the *interest-coverage ratio*.

trading on the equity (p. 795) Another name for *leverage*.

trend percentages (p. 777) A form of horizontal analysis that indicates the direction a business is taking.

vertical analysis (p. 777) Analysis of a financial statement that reveals the relationship of each statement item to a specified base, which is the 100% figure.

weighted average cost of capital (p. 799) A weighted average of the returns demanded by the company's stockholders and lenders. Often referred to as the *weighted-average cost of capital (WACC)*.

working capital (p. 785) Current assets minus current liabilities; measures a business's ability to meet its short-term obligations with its current assets. Also called *net working capital*.

ASSESS YOUR PROGRESS

Short Exercises

S13-1 *(Learning Objective 1: Perform horizontal analysis of revenues and net income)* Verifine Corporation reported the following amounts on its 2012 comparative income statements:

(In thousands)	2012	2011	2010
Revenues........................	$10,289	$10,045	$9,449
Total expenses...............	5,915	5,238	5,100

Perform a horizontal analysis of revenues and net income—both in dollar amounts and in percentages—for 2012 and 2011.

S13-2 *(Learning Objective 1: Perform trend analysis of sales and net income)* Witkum, Inc., reported the following sales and net income amounts:

(In thousands)	2012	2011	2010	2009
Sales...........................	$9,960	$9,260	$8,790	$8,590
Net income................	670	500	480	445

Show Witkum's trend percentages for sales and net income. Use 2009 as the base year.

S13-3 *(Learning Objective 2: Perform vertical analysis to correct a cash shortage)* McCormick Software reported the following amounts on its balance sheets at December 31, 2012, 2011, and 2010:

	2012	2011	2010
Cash.....................................	$ 23,200	$ 15,600	$ 14,340
Receivables, net..................	34,800	20,800	23,900
Inventory.............................	266,800	197,600	148,180
Prepaid expenses	34,800	41,600	33,460
Property, plant, and equipment, net	220,400	244,400	258,120
Total assets	$580,000	$520,000	$478,000

Sales and profits are high. Nevertheless, McCormick is experiencing a cash shortage. Perform a vertical analysis of McCormick Software's assets at the end of years 2012, 2011, and 2010. Use the analysis to explain the reason for the cash shortage.

S13-4 *(Learning Objective 3: Compare common-size income statements of two companies)* Craft, Inc., and Kleen Corporation are competitors. Compare the two companies by converting their condensed income statements to common size.

(In millions)	Craft	Kleen
Net sales...	$17,800	$7,569
Cost of goods sold..	10,573	4,965
Selling and administrative expenses................	4,895	1,521
Interest expense...	53	23
Other expenses...	89	38
Income tax expense..	730	250
Net income...	$ 1,460	$ 772

Which company earned more net income? Which company's net income was a higher percentage of its net sales? Explain your answer.

S13-5 *(Learning Objective 5: Evaluate the trend in a company's current ratio)* Examine the financial data of Stephens Corporation.

Year Ended December 31	2012	2011	2010
Operating Results			
Net income..	$ 250	$ 340	$ 342
Per common share......................................	$1.37	$1.68	$1.99
Percent of sales..	19.9%	17.9%	19.3%
Return on average stockholders' equity...............	21.0	18.0	19.0
Financial Position			
Current assets..	$ 590	$ 497	$ 445
Current liabilities	$ 362	$ 333	$ 339
Working capital	$ 228	$ 164	$ 106
Current ratio..	1.63	1.49	1.31

Show how to compute Stephens current ratio for each year 2010 through 2012. Is the company's ability to pay its current liabilities improving or deteriorating?

S13-6 *(Learning Objective 5: Evaluate a company's quick (acid-test) ratio)* Use the Allstott, Inc., balance sheet data on the following page.

1. Compute Allstott, Inc.'s quick (acid-test) ratio at December 31, 2012 and 2011.
2. Use the comparative information from the table on the bottom of page 811 for Baker, Inc., Colvin Company, and Dunn Companies Limited. Is Allstott, Inc.'s quick (acid-test) ratio for 2012 and 2011 strong, average, or weak in comparison?

Allstott, Inc.
Balance Sheets (Adapted)
December 31, 2012 and 2011

(Dollar amounts in millions)	2012	2011	Increase (Decrease) Amount	Increase (Decrease) Percentage
Assets				
Current assets:				
Cash and cash equivalents	$1,200	$ 900	$ 300	33.3 %
Short-term investments	6	70	(64)	(91.4)
Receivables, net	240	250	(10)	(4.0)
Inventories	96	81	15	18.5
Prepaid expenses and other assets	243	363	(120)	(33.1)
Total current assets	1,785	1,664	121	7.3
Property, plant, and equipment, net	3,611	3,376	235	7.0
Intangible assets	1,011	878	133	15.1
Other assets	828	722	106	14.7
Total assets	$7,235	$6,640	$ 595	9.0 %
Liabilities and Stockholders' Equity				
Current liabilities:				
Accounts payable	$ 1,000	$ 900	$ 100	11.1 %
Income tax payable	39	61	(22)	(36.1)
Short-term debt	118	111	7	6.3
Other	70	73	(3)	(4.1)
Total current liabilities	1,227	1,145	82	7.2
Long-term debt	3,500	2,944	556	18.9
Other liabilities	1,117	1,036	81	7.8
Total liabilities	5,844	5,125	719	14.0
Stockholders' equity:				
Common stock	2	2	—	—
Retained earnings	1,543	1,689	(146)	(8.6)
Accumulated other comprehensive (loss)	(154)	(176)	22	12.6
Total stockholders' equity	1,391	1,515	(124)	(8.2)
Total liabilities and stockholders' equity	$7,235	$6,640	$ 595	9.0 %

Company	Quick (acid-test) Ratio
Baker, Inc. (Utility)...	0.71
Calvin Company (Department store)......................	1.01
Dunn Companies Limited (Grocery store)..............	1.05

S13-7 (*Learning Objective 5: Compute and evaluate turnover and the cash conversion cycle*) Use the Allstott 2012 income statement that follows and the balance sheet from Short Exercise 13-6 to compute the following:

Allstott, Inc.
Statements of Income (Adapted)
Year Ended December 31, 2012 and 2011

(Dollar amounts in millions)	2012	2011
Revenues	$9,500	$9,309
Expenses:		
Food and paper (Cost of goods sold)	2,509	2,644
Payroll and employee benefits	2,138	2,211
Occupancy and other operating expenses	2,413	2,375
General and administrative expenses	1,217	1,148
Interest expense	184	117
Other expense (income), net	19	(34)
Income before income taxes	1,020	848
Income tax expense	285	267
Net income	$ 735	$ 581

a. Allstott's rate of inventory turnover and days inventory outstanding for 2012
b. Days' sales in average receivables (days sales outstanding) during 2012 (Round dollar amounts to one decimal place.)
c. Accounts payable turnover and days payables outstanding
d. Length of cash conversion cycle in days

Do these measures look strong or weak? Give the reason for your answer.

S13-8 (*Learning Objective 5: Measure ability to pay long-term debt*) Use the financial statements of Allstott, Inc., in Short Exercises 13-6 and 13-7.

1. Compute the company's debt ratio at December 31, 2012.
2. Compute the company's times-interest-earned ratio for 2012. For operating income, use income before both interest expense and income taxes. You can simply add interest expense back to income before taxes.
3. Is Allstott's ability to pay liabilities and interest expense strong or weak? Comment on the value of each ratio computed for questions 1 and 2.

S13-9 (*Learning Objective 5: Measure profitability using DuPont*) Use the financial statements of Allstott, Inc., in Short Exercises 13-6 and 13-7 to compute these profitability measures for 2012. Show each computation.

a. Rate of return on sales
b. Asset turnover
c. Rate of return on total assets.
d. Leverage (equity multiplier) ratio
e. Rate of return on common stockholders' equity
f. Is Allstott, Inc.'s profitability strong, medium, or weak?

S13-10 (*Learning Objective 5: Compute EPS and the price/earnings ratio*) The annual report of Feeney Cars, Inc., for the year ended December 31, 2012, included the following items (in millions):

Preferred stock outstanding, 3%	$700
Net income..	$600
Number of shares of common stock outstanding	700

1. Compute earnings per share (EPS) and the price/earnings ratio for Feeney Cars' stock. Round to the nearest cent. The price of a share of Feeney Car stock is $11.83.
2. How much does the stock market say $1 of Feeney Cars' net income is worth?

S13-11 (*Learning Objective 5: Use ratio data to reconstruct an income statement*) A skeleton of Westview Country Florist's income statement appears as follows (amounts in thousands):

Income Statement	
Net sales	$7,300
Cost of goods sold	(a)
Selling expenses	1,520
Administrative expenses	330
Interest expense	(b)
Other expenses	156
Income before taxes	1,042
Income tax expense	(c)
Net income	$ (d)

Use the following ratio data to complete Westview Country Florist's income statement:

a. Inventory turnover was 3 (beginning inventory was $800; ending inventory was $772).
b. Rate of return on sales (after income taxes) is 0.09.

S13-12 (*Learning Objective 5: Use ratio data to reconstruct a balance sheet*) A skeleton of Westview Country Florist's balance sheet appears as follows (amounts in thousands):

Balance Sheet			
Cash	$ 60	Total current liabilities	$2,100
Receivables	(a)	Long-term debt	(e)
Inventories	774	Other long-term liabilities	920
Prepaid expenses	(b)		
Total current assets	(c)		
Plant assets, net	(d)	Common stock	180
Other assets	2,375	Retained earnings	2,701
Total assets	$6,700	Total liabilities and equity	$ (f)

Use the following ratio data to complete Westview Country Florist's balance sheet:

a. Debt ratio is 0.57.
b. Current ratio is 1.20.
c. Quick (acid-test) ratio is 0.20.

S13-13 (*Learning Objective 5: Analyze a company based on its ratios*) Take the role of an investment analyst at Cole Binder. It is your job to recommend investments for your client. The only information you have is the following ratio values for two companies in the graphics software industry.

Ratio	Tower.org	Graphics Imaging
Days' sales in receivables............................	41	48
Inventory turnover...................................	7	11
Gross profit percentage	67%	58%
Net income as a percent of sales...............	12%	13%
Times interest earned	19	13
Return on equity.....................................	35%	30%
Return on assets.....................................	14%	19%

Write a report to the Cole Binder investment committee. Recommend one company's stock over the other. State the reasons for your recommendation.

S13-14 (*Learning Objective 6: Measure economic value added*) Compute economic value added (EVA®) for Lazeren Software. The company's cost of capital is 3%. Net income was $755 thousand, interest expense $401 thousand, beginning long-term debt $620 thousand, and beginning stockholders' equity was $3,010 thousand. Round all amounts to the nearest thousand dollars.

Should the company's stockholders be happy with the EVA®?

Exercises

> All of the A and B exercises can be found within MyAccountingLab, an online homework and practice environment. Your instructor may ask you to complete these exercises using MyAccountingLab.

Group A

E13-15A (*Learning Objective 1: Compute year-to-year changes in working capital*) What were the dollar amount of change and the percentage of each change in Blueberry Lane Lodge's working capital during 2012 and 2011? Is this trend favorable or unfavorable?

	2012	2011	2010
Total current assets	$330,000	$280,000	$260,000
Total current liabilities	155,000	140,000	130,000

E13-16A (*Learning Objective 1: Perform horizontal analysis of an income statement*) Prepare a horizontal analysis of the comparative income statements of McMahon Music Co. Round percentage changes to the nearest one-tenth percent (three decimal places).

McMahon Music Co. Comparative Income Statements Years Ended December 31, 2012 and 2011		
	2012	**2011**
Total revenue	$1,077,000	$917,000
Expenses:		
Cost of goods sold	$477,000	$408,750
Selling and general expenses	287,000	265,000
Interest expense	23,500	13,500
Income tax expense	105,500	84,650
Total expenses	893,000	771,900
Net income	$184,000	$145,100

E13-17A (*Learning Objective 1: Compute trend percentages*) Compute trend percentages for Peak Valley Sales & Service's total revenue and net income for the following five-year period, using year 0 as the base year. Round to the nearest full percent.

(In thousands)	Year 4	Year 3	Year 2	Year 1	Year 0
Total revenue	$1,400	$1,242	$1,093	$1,001	$1,024
Net income	180	117	105	99	86

Which grew faster during the period, total revenue or net income?

E13-18A (*Learning Objective 2: Perform vertical analysis of a balance sheet*) Putt Golf Company has requested that you perform a vertical analysis of its balance sheet to determine the component percentages of its assets, liabilities, and stockholders' equity.

Putt Golf Company
Balance Sheet
December 31, 2012

Assets	
Total current assets	$ 42,000
Property, plant, and equipment, net	206,000
Other assets	40,000
Total assets	$288,000
Liabilities	
Total current liabilities	$ 47,000
Long-term debt	107,000
Total liabilities	154,000
Stockholders' Equity	
Total stockholders' equity	134,000
Total liabilities and stockholders' equity	$288,000

E13-19A (*Learning Objective 3: Prepare a common-size income statement*) Prepare a comparative common-size income statement for McMahon Music Co., using the 2012 and 2011 data of Exercise 13-16A and rounding to four decimal places.

E13-20A (*Learning Objective 4: Analyze the statement of cash flows*) Identify any weaknesses revealed by the statement of cash flows of New York Apple Farms, Inc.

New York Apple Farms, Inc.
Statement of Cash Flows
For the Current Year

Operating activities:		
Net income		$ 67,100
Add (subtract) noncash items:		
Depreciation	$ 11,250	
Net increase in current assets other than cash	(53,500)	
Net decrease in current liabilities		
exclusive of short-term debt	(19,750)	(62,000)
Net cash provided by operating activities		5,100
Investing activities:		
Sale of property, plant, and equipment		124,200
Financing activities:		
Issuance of bonds payable	$ 117,050	
Payment of short-term debt	(180,525)	
Payment of long-term debt	(89,025)	
Payment of dividends	(39,500)	
Net cash used for financing activities		(192,000)
Increase (decrease) in cash		$ (62,700)

E13-21A *(Learning Objective 5: Compute ratios; evaluate turnover, liquidity, and current debt-paying ability)* The financial statements of Family News, Inc., include the following items:

	2012	2011	2010
Balance sheet:			
Cash	$ 53,000	$ 89,000	
Short-term investments	17,000	21,000	
Net receivables	77,000	80,000	55,000
Inventory.....................................	90,000	72,000	60,000
Prepaid expenses...........................	8,000	6,000	
Total current assets	245,000	268,000	
Accounts Payable.........................	65,000	55,000	50,000
Total current liabilities.................	131,000	90,000	
Income statement:			
Net credit sales	$494,000	$502,000	$480,000
Cost of goods sold	276,000	280,000	254,000

▶ Requirements

1. Compute the following ratios for 2012 and 2011:
   a. Current ratio
   b. Quick (acid test) ratio
   c. Inventory turnover and days' inventory outstanding (DIO)
   d. Accounts receivable turnover
   e. Days' sales in average receivables or days' sales outstanding (DSO)
   f. Accounts payable turnover and days' payable outstanding (DPO)
   g. Cash conversion cycle (in days)

(When computing days, round your answer to the nearest whole number.)

2. Evaluate the company's liquidity and current debt-paying ability for 2012. Has it improved or deteriorated from 2011?
3. As a manager of this company, what would you try to improve next year?

E13-22A (*Learning Objective 6: Analyze the ability to pay liabilities*) Branson Furniture Company has requested that you determine whether the company's ability to pay its current liabilities and long-term debts improved or deteriorated during 2012. To answer this question, compute the following ratios for 2012 and 2011: (Round your answers to two decimal places.)

a. Working capital
b. Current ratio
c. Quick (acid-test) ratio
d. Debt ratio
e. Times-interest-earned ratio

Summarize the results of your analysis in a written report.

	2012	2011
Cash	$ 50,000	$ 49,000
Short-term investments.................	28,000	27,000
Net receivables.............................	115,000	128,000
Inventory.......................................	240,000	268,000
Prepaid expenses	22,000	8,000
Total assets...................................	510,000	540,000
Total current liabilities	207,000	262,000
Long-term debt	97,000	174,000
Income from operations	301,000	150,000
Interest expense...........................	41,000	42,000

E13-23A (*Learning Objective 5: Analyze profitability*) Compute return on sales (ROS), asset turnover (AT), return on assets (ROA), leverage (L), return on common stockholders' equity (ROE), gross profit (GP), operating income percentage (OI), and earnings per share (EPS), to measure the ability to earn profits for Prairies Decor, Inc., whose comparative income statements follow (use DuPont analysis for ROA and ROE and round each component ratio to three decimals; for other ratio computations, round to two decimals):

Prairies Decor, Inc.
Comparative Income Statements
Years Ended December 31, 2012 and 2011

	2012	2011
Net sales	$250,000	$199,000
Cost of goods sold	123,000	102,000
Gross profit	127,000	97,000
Selling and general expenses	55,000	51,000
Income from operations	72,000	46,000
Interest expense	14,000	18,000
Income before income tax	58,000	28,000
Income tax expense	20,000	10,000
Net income	$ 38,000	$ 18,000

Additional data:

	2012	2011	2010
Total assets...	$310,000	$305,000	$300,000
Common stockholders' equity.................	$196,000	$194,000	$192,000
Preferred dividends..................................	$ 2,000	$ 1,000	$ 0
Average common shares outstanding during the year	15,000	14,000	13,000

Did the company's operating performance improve or deteriorate during 2012?

E13-24A (*Learning Objectives 5, 6: Evaluate a stock as an investment*) Evaluate the common stock of Tristan Distributing Company as an investment. Specifically, use the three common stock ratios to determine whether the common stock increased or decreased in attractiveness during the past year. (Round calculations and your final answer to three decimal places.)

	2012	2011
Net income...	$ 84,000	$ 93,000
Dividends to common	28,000	17,000
Total stockholders' equity at year-end................	575,000	500,000
(includes 90,000 shares of common stock)		
Preferred stock, 10%..	115,000	115,000
Market price per share of common stock at year-end	$ 23.50	$ 15.50

E13-25A (*Learning Objective 6: Use economic value added to measure corporate performance*) Two companies with different economic-value-added (EVA®) profiles are Emerson Oil Pipeline Incorporated and Farmer Bank Limited. Adapted versions of the two companies' financial statements are presented here (in millions):

	Emerson Oil Pipeline, Inc.	Farmer Bank Limited
Balance sheet data:		
Total assets	$ 4,331	$13,403
Interest-bearing debt	$ 1,244	$ 7
All other liabilities............................	2,550	2,575
Stockholders' equity.........................	537	10,821
Total liabilities and equity................	$ 4,331	$13,403
Income statement data:		
Total revenue	$10,772	$ 4,000
Interest expense................................	83	1
Net income..	$ 200	$ 1,706

▶ Requirements

1. Before performing any calculations, which company do you think represents the better investment? Give your reason.
2. Compute the EVA® for each company and then decide which company's stock you would rather hold as an investment. Assume that both companies' cost of capital is 11.0%.

Group B

E13-26B (*Learning Objective 1: Compute year-to-year changes in working capital*) What were the dollar amount of change and the percentage of each change in Cobb Hill Lodge's working capital during 2012 and 2011? Is this trend favorable or unfavorable?

	2012	2011	2010
Total current assets	$60,000	$230,000	$250,000
Total current liabilities	20,000	115,000	125,000

E13-27B (*Learning Objective 1: Perform horizontal analysis of an income statement*) Prepare a horizontal analysis of the comparative income statements of McCracken Music Co. Round percentage changes to the nearest one-tenth percent (three decimal places).

McCracken Music Co. Comparative Income Statements Years Ended December 31, 2012 and 2011		
	2012	**2011**
Total revenue	$844,000	$934,000
Expenses:		
Cost of goods sold	$404,000	$400,000
Selling and general expenses	234,000	263,000
Interest expense	9,300	12,000
Income tax expense	84,000	86,000
Total expenses	731,300	761,000
Net income	$112,700	$173,000

E13-28B (*Learning Objective 1: Compute trend percentages*) Compute trend percentages for Maple Valley Sales & Service's total revenue and net income for the following five-year period, using year 0 as the base year. Round to the nearest full percent.

(In thousands)	Year 4	Year 3	Year 2	Year 1	Year 0
Total revenue	$1,428	$1,219	$1,043	$1,001	$1,022
Net income	129	125	101	95	90

Which grew faster during the period, total revenue or net income?

E13-29B (*Learning Objective 2: Perform vertical analysis of a balance sheet*) Drive Golf Company has requested that you perform a vertical analysis of its balance sheet to determine the component percentages of its assets, liabilities, and stockholders' equity.

Drive Golf Company
Balance Sheet
December 31, 2012

Assets	
Total current assets	$ 33,000
Property, plant, and equipment, net	199,000
Other assets	37,000
Total assets	$269,000
Liabilities	
Total current liabilities	$ 48,000
Long-term debt	102,000
Total liabilities	150,000
Stockholders' Equity	
Total stockholders' equity	119,000
Total liabilities and stockholders' equity	$269,000

E13-30B (*Learning Objective 3: Prepare a common-size income statement*) Prepare a comparative common-size income statement for McCracken Music Co. using the 2012 and 2011 data of Exercise 13-27B and rounding to four decimal places.

E13-31B (*Learning Objective 4: Analyze the statement of cash flows*) Identify any weaknesses revealed by the statement of cash flows of Florida Oranges, Inc.

Florida Oranges, Inc.
Statement of Cash Flows
For the Current Year

Operating activities:		
Net income		$ 95,000
Add (subtract) noncash items:		
Depreciation	$ 32,000	
Net increase in current assets other than cash	(65,000)	
Net decrease in current liabilities		
exclusive of short-term debt	(44,000)	(77,000)
Net cash provided by operating activities		18,000
Investing activities:		
Sale of property, plant, and equipment		151,000
Financing activities:		
Issuance of bonds payable	$ 110,000	
Payment of short-term debt	(186,000)	
Payment of long-term debt	(101,000)	
Payment of dividends	(56,000)	
Net cash used for financing activities		(233,000)
Increase (decrease) in cash		$ (64,000)

E13-32B (*Learning Objective 5: Compute ratios; evaluate turnover, liquidity, and current debt-paying ability*) The financial statements of Alliance News, Inc., include the following items:

	2012	2011	2010
Balance sheet:			
Cash	$ 39,000	$ 45,000	
Short-term investments	12,000	23,000	
Net receivables	73,000	76,000	60,000
Inventory	91,000	77,000	62,000
Prepaid expenses	11,000	5,000	
Total current assets	226,000	226,000	
Accounts payable	70.000	55,000	50,000
Total current liabilities	133,000	94,000	
Income statement:			
Net credit sales	$491,000	$504.000	
Cost of goods sold	277,000	282,000	

▶ Requirements

1. Compute the following ratios for 2012 and 2011:
   a. Current ratio
   b. Quick (acid test) ratio
   c. Inventory turnover and days' inventory outstanding (DIO)
   d. Accounts receivable turnover
   e. Days' sales in average receivables or days' sales outstanding (DSO)
   f. Accounts payable turnover and days' payable outstanding (DPO)
   g. Cash conversion cycle (in days)

(When computing days, round your answer to the nearest whole number.)

2. Evaluate the company's liquidity and current debt-paying ability for 2012. Has it improved or deteriorated from 2011?
3. As a manager of this company, what would you try to improve next year?

E13-33B (*Learning Objective 5: Analyze the ability to pay liabilities*) Evensen Furniture Company has requested that you determine whether the company's ability to pay its current liabilities and long-term debts improved or deteriorated during 2012. To answer this question, compute the following ratios for 2012 and 2011. (Round your answers to two decimal places.)

   a. Working capital
   b. Current ratio
   c. Quick (acid-test) ratio
   d. Debt ratio
   e. Times-interest-earned ratio

Summarize the results of your analysis in a written report.

	2012	2011
Cash	$ 40,000	$ 50,000
Short-term investments	31,000	6,000
Net receivables	121,000	129,000
Inventory	238,000	267,000
Prepaid expenses	15,000	5,000
Total assets	570,000	540,000
Total current liabilities	237,000	151,000
Long-term debt	87,000	255,000
Income from operations	250,000	199,000
Interest expense	40,000	40,000

E13-34B (*Learning Objective 5: Analyze profitability*) Compute return on sales (ROS), asset turnover (AT), return on assets (ROA), leverage (L), return on common stockholders' equity (ROE), gross profit (GP), operating income percentage (OI), and earnings per share (EPS), to measure the ability to earn profits for Cavalier Decor, Inc., whose comparative income statements follow (use DuPont analysis for ROA and ROE and round each component ratio to three decimals; for other ratio computations, round to two decimals):

Cavalier Decor, Inc. Comparative Income Statements Years Ended December 31, 2012 and 2011		
	2012	**2011**
Net sales	$350,000	$290,000
Cost of goods sold	175,000	148,000
Gross profit	175,000	142,000
Selling and general expenses	100,000	94,000
Income from operations	75,000	48,000
Interest expense	13,000	10,000
Income before income tax	62,000	38,000
Income tax expense	22,000	13,000
Net income	$ 40,000	$ 25,000

Additional data:

	2012	2011	2010
Total assets..	$400,000	$396,000	$394,000
Common stockholders' equity.................	$149,000	$140,000	$131,000
Preferred dividends...................................	$ 11,000	$ 9,000	$ 7,000
Average common shares outstanding during the year	20,000	15,000	5,000

Did the company's operating performance improve or deteriorate during 2012?

E13-35B (*Learning Objectives 5, 6: Evaluate a stock as an investment*) Evaluate the common stock of Orville Distributing Company as an investment. Specifically, use the three common stock ratios to determine whether the common stock increased or decreased in attractiveness during the past year. (Round calculations and your final answer to three decimal places.)

	2012	2011
Net income...	$ 143,000	$ 97,000
Dividends to common	23,000	19,000
Total stockholders' equity at year-end................	550,000	500,000
(includes 90,000 shares of common stock)		
Preferred stock, 6%...	170,000	110,000
Market price per share of common		
stock at year-end	$ 21.50	$ 16.25

E13-36B (*Learning Objective 6: Use economic value added to measure corporate performance*)
Two companies with different economic-value-added (EVA®) profiles are Karin Oil Pipeline,
Inc., and Larson Bank Limited. Adapted versions of the two companies' financial statements are
presented here (in millions):

(In millions)	Karin Oil Pipeline, Inc.	Larson Bank Limited
Balance sheet data:		
Total assets	$ 4,353	$14,200
Interest-bearing debt	$ 1,246	$ 17
All other liabilities............................	2,800	2,605
Stockholders' equity	307	11,578
Total liabilities and equity................	$ 4,353	$14,200
Income statement data:		
Total revenue	$10,807	$ 3,697
Interest expense.................................	77	8
Net income...	$ 195	$ 1,496

▶ Requirements

1. Before performing any calculations, which company do you think represents the better
   investment? Give your reason.
2. Compute the EVA® for each company and then decide which company's stock you would
   rather hold as an investment. Assume that both companies' cost of capital is 12.5%. (Round
   your EVA® calculation to the nearest whole number.)

Quiz

Use the Buffalo Bell Corporation financial statements that follow to answer questions 13-37 through 13-48.

			December 31,	
Buffalo Bell Corporation **Consolidated Statements of Financial Position** **(In millions)**			**2012**	**2011**
Assets:				
Current Assets				
Cash and cash equivalents			$ 4,333	$ 4,226
Accounts and notes receivable			3,400	2,403
Short-term investments			845	520
Inventories, at cost			433	411
Prepaid expense and other current assets			1,638	1,226
Total current assets			10,649	8,786
Property and equipment, net			1,555	907
Investments			6,804	5,199
Other non-current assets			303	155
Total assets			$19,311	$15,047
Liabilities and stockholders' equity:				
Current liabilities				
Accounts payable			$ 7,708	$ 6,009
Accrued and other liabilities			3,676	3,033
Total current liabilities			11,384	9,042
Long-term debt			304	305
Other non-current liabilities			1,701	1,179
Total liabilities			13,389	10,526
Stockholders' equity				
Preferred stock and capital in excess of $0.02 par value; shares issued and outstanding: none			—	—
Common stock and capital in excess of $0.05 par value; shares authorized: 6,000; shares issued: 2,163 and 1,903, respectively			7,803	7,001
Treasury stock, at cost: 183 and 123 shares, respectively			(6,444)	(4,401)
Retained earnings			4,676	1,990
Other comprehensive loss			(79)	(25)
Other			(34)	(44)
Total stockholders' equity			5,922	4,521
Total liabilities and stockholders' equity			$19,311	$15,047

Buffalo Bell Corporation
Consolidated Statements of Income
(In millions, except per share amounts)

	Year ended December 31,		
	2012	2011	2010
Net Revenue	$42,666	$35,220	$31,111
Cost of goods sold	35,147	29,255	25,492
Gross profit	7,519	5,965	5,619
Operating expenses:			
Selling, general, and administrative	3,341	3,250	2,985
Research, development, and engineering	544	553	536
Special charges	—	—	512
Total operating expenses	3,885	3,803	4,033
Operating income	3,634	2,162	1,586
Investment and other income (loss), net	153	196	(30)
Income before income taxes	3,787	2,358	1,556
Income tax expense	1,136	940	472
Net income	$ 2,651	$ 1,418	$ 1,084
Earnings per common share:			
Basic	$ 1.41	$ 0.95	$ 0.37

Q13-37 During 2012, Buffalo Bell's total assets

a. increased by 28.3%.

b. increased by $1,420 million.

c. both a and b.

d. increased by 22.1%.

Q13-38 Buffalo Bell's current ratio at year end 2012 is closest to

a. $1,420.

b. 0.9.

c. 22.1.

d. 1.2.

Q13-39 Buffalo Bell's quick (acid-test) ratio at year-end 2012 is closest to

a. 0.75.

b. $8,578 million.

c. 0.45.

d. 0.68.

Q13-40 What is the largest single item included in Buffalo Bell's debt ratio at December 31, 2012?

a. Cash and cash equivalents

b. Common Stock

c. Accounts payable

d. Investments

Q13-41 Using the earliest year available as the base year, the trend percentage for Buffalo Bell's net revenue during 2012 was

a. 121%.

b. up by 21.1%

c. 137%.

d. up by $11,555 million.

Q13-42 Buffalo Bell's common-size income statement for 2012 would report cost of goods sold as

a. 137.9%.

b. $35,147 million.

c. up by 20.1%.

d. 82.4%.

Q13-43 Buffalo Bell's days' sales in average receivables during 2012 was

a. 137.9 days.

b. 20.1 days.

c. 35 days.

d. 25 days.

Q13-44 Buffalo Bell's inventory turnover during fiscal year 2012 was

a. $35,147.

b. very slow.

c. 83 times.

d. 137.9 times.

Q13-45 Buffalo Bell's long-term debt bears interest at 11%. During the year ended December 31, 2012, Bell's times-interest-earned ratio was

a. 137.9 times.

b. $35,147.

c. 108 times.

d. 20.1 times.

Q13-46 Buffalo Bell's trend of return on sales is

a. worrisome.

b. declining.

c. stuck at 22.1%.

d. improving.

Q13-47 How many shares of common stock did Buffalo Bell have outstanding, on average, during 2012? Hint: Compute earnings per share.

a. 1,880 million

b. 137.9 million

c. 20.1 million

d. 35,147 million

Q13-48 Book value per share of Buffalo Bell's common stock outstanding at December 31, 2012, was

a. 137.9.

b. $35,147.

c. $2.99.

d. 20.1.

Problems

Group A

P13-49A (*Learning Objectives 1, 5: Compute trend percentages, return on sales, asset turnover, and ROA, and compare with industry*) Net sales, net income, and total assets for Aaron Shipping, Inc., for a five-year period follow:

(In thousands)	2012	2011	2010	2009	2008
Net sales	$900	$400	$352	$314	$296
Net income	50	39	46	37	24
Total assets	308	269	252	231	209

▶ Requirements

1. Compute trend percentages for each item for 2009 through 2012. Use 2008 as the base year and round to the nearest percent.
2. Compute the rate of return on net sales for 2010 through 2012, rounding to three decimal places. Explain what this means.
3. Compute asset turnover for 2010 through 2012. Explain what this means.
4. Use DuPont analysis to compute rate of return on average total assets (ROA) for 2010 through 2012.
5. How does Aaron Shipping's return on net sales for 2012 compare with previous years? How does it compare with that of the industry? In the shipping industry, rates above 5% are considered good, and rates above 7% are outstanding.
6. Evaluate Aaron Shipping, Inc.'s ROA for 2012, compared with previous years, and against a 15% benchmark for the industry.

P13-50A (*Learning Objectives 3, 5: Prepare common-size statements; analyze profitability; make comparisons with the industry*) Top managers of O'Hare Products, Inc., have asked for your help in comparing the company's profit performance and financial position with the average for the industry. The accountant has given you the company's income statement and balance sheet and also the following data for the industry:

O'Hare Products, Inc.
Income Statement Compared with Industry Average
Year Ended December 31, 2012

	O'Hare	Industry Average
Net sales	$960,000	100.0%
Cost of goods sold	662,400	57.3
Gross profit	297,600	42.7
Operating expenses	220,800	29.4
Operating income	76,800	13.3
Other expenses	9,600	2.5
Net income	$ 67,200	10.8%

O'Hare Products, Inc.
Balance Sheet Compared with Industry Average
December 31, 2012

	O'Hare	Industry Average
Current assets	$292,000	72.1%
Fixed assets, net	72,800	19.0
Intangible assets, net	14,000	4.8
Other assets	21,200	4.1
Total	400,000	100.0%
Current liabilities	188,000	47.2%
Long-term liabilities	84,000	21.0
Stockholders' equity	128,000	31.8
Total	$400,000	100.0%

▶ Requirements

1. Prepare a common-size income statement and balance sheet for O'Hare Products. The first column of each statement should present O'Hare Products' common-size statement, and the second column should show the industry averages.
2. For the profitability analysis, compare O'Hare Products' (a) ratio of gross profit to net sales, (b) ratio of operating income to net sales, and (c) ratio of net income to net sales with the industry averages. Is O'Hare Products' profit performance better or worse than the average for the industry?
3. For the analysis of financial position, compute O'Hare Products' (a) ratios of current assets and current liabilities to total assets and (b) ratio of stockholders' equity to total assets. Compare these ratios with the industry averages. Is O'Hare Products' financial position better or worse than the average for the industry?

P13-51A (*Learning Objective 4: Use the statement of cash flows for decision making*) You are evaluating two companies as possible investments. The two companies, which are similar in size, are commuter airlines that fly passengers up and down the West Coast. All other available information has been analyzed, and your investment decision depends on the statements of cash flows.

Blue Yonder Airlines
Statements of Cash Flows
Years Ended November 30, 2013 and 2012

	2013		2012	
Operating activities:				
Net income (net loss)		$(63,000)		$160,000
Adjustments for non-cash items:				
Total		79,000		(13,000)
Net cash provided by operating activities		16,000		147,000
Investing activities:				
Purchase of property, plant,				
and equipment	$ (67,000)		$(140,000)	
Sale of long-term investments	58,000		9,000	
Net cash provided by (used for)				
investing activities		(9,000)		(131,000)
Financing activities:				
Issuance of short-term notes payable	$ 198,000		$ 218,000	
Payment of short-term notes payable	(246,000)		(183,000)	
Payment of cash dividends	(51,000)		(92,000)	
Net cash provided by financing activities		(99,000)		(57,000)
Increase (decrease) in cash		$(92,000)		$ (41,000)
Cash balance at beginning of year		106,000		147,000
Cash balance at end of year		$ 14,000		$106,000

Horizon, Inc.
Statements of Cash Flows
Years Ended September 30, 2013 and 2012

	2013		2012	
Operating activities:				
Net income		$ 264,000		$ 193,000
Adjustments for non-cash items:				
Total		67,000		79,000
Net cash provided by operating activities		331,000		272,000
Investing activities:				
Purchase of property, plant,				
and equipment	$(395,000)		$(610,000)	
Sale of property, plant, and equipment	69,000		119,000	
Net cash used for investing activities		(326,000)		(491,000)
Financing activities:				
Issuance of long-term notes payable	$ 198,000		$ 131,000	
Payment of short-term notes payable	(95,000)		(26,000)	
Net cash provided by financing activities		103,000		105,000
Increase (decrease) in cash		$ 108,000		$ (114,000)
Cash balance at beginning of year		176,000		290,000
Cash balance at end of year		$ 284,000		$ 176,000

► Requirement

1. Discuss the relative strengths and weaknesses of Blue Yonder Airlines and Horizon, Inc. Conclude your discussion by recommending one of the companies' stocks as an investment.

P13-52A *(Learning Objective 5: Compute effects of business transactions on selected ratios)* Financial statement data of Shawsworth Engineering include the following items:

Cash	$ 23,000	Accounts payable	$107,000
Short-term investments	36,000	Accrued liabilities	35,000
Accounts receivable, net	87,000	Long-term notes payable	163,000
Inventories	141,000	Other long-term liabilities	33,000
Prepaid expenses	4,000	Net income	95,000
Total assets	675,000	Number of common	
Short-term notes payable	42,000	shares outstanding	51,000

► Requirements

1. Compute Shawsworth's current ratio, debt ratio, and earnings per share. (Round all ratios to two decimal places.)
2. Compute the three ratios after evaluating the effect of each transaction that follows. Consider each transaction *separately*.

   a. Borrowed $ 120,000 on a long-term note payable
   b. Issued 15,000 shares of common stock, receiving cash of $364,000
   c. Paid short-term notes payable, $24,000
   d. Purchased merchandise of $46,000 on account, debiting Inventory
   e. Received cash on account, $15,000

P13-53A *(Learning Objective 5: Use ratios to evaluate a stock investment)* Comparative financial statement data of Hamden Optical Mart follow:

Hamden Optical Mart **Comparative Income Statements** Years Ended December 31, 2012 and 2011		
	2012	2011
Net sales	$687,000	$595,000
Cost of goods sold	375,000	276,000
Gross profit	312,000	319,000
Operating expenses	129,000	142,000
Income from operations	183,000	177,000
Interest expense	37,000	45,000
Income before income tax	146,000	132,000
Income tax expense	36,000	51,000
Net income	$110,000	$ 81,000

Hamden Optical Mart
Comparative Balance Sheets
December 31, 2012 and 2011

	2012	2011	2010*
Current assets:			
Cash	$ 45,000	$ 49,000	
Current receivables, net	212,000	158,000	$200,000
Inventories	297,000	281,000	181,000
Prepaid expenses	4,000	29,000	
Total current assets	558,000	517,000	
Property, plant, and equipment, net	285,000	277,000	
Total assets	$843,000	$794,000	700,000
Accounts payable	150,000	105,000	112,000
Other current liabilities	135,000	188,000	
Total current liabilities	$285,000	$293,000	
Long-term liabilities	243,000	231,000	
Total liabilities	528,000	524,000	
Common stockholders' equity, no par	315,000	270,000	199,000
Total liabilities and stockholders' equity	$843,000	$794,000	

*Selected 2010 amounts.

Other information:

1. Market price of Hamden common stock: $102.17 at December 31, 2012, and $77.01 at December 31, 2011
2. Common shares outstanding: 18,000 during 2012 and 17,500 during 2011
3. All sales on credit

▶ Requirements

1. Compute the following ratios for 2012 and 2011:
   a. Current ratio
   b. Quick (acid-test) ratio
   c. Receivables turnover and days sales outstanding (DSO) (round to the nearest whole day)
   d. Inventory turnover and days inventory outstanding (DIO) (round to the nearest whole day)
   e. Accounts payable turnover and days payable outstanding (DPO) (round to the nearest whole day)
   f. Cash conversion cycle (in days)
   g. Times-interest-earned ratio
   h. Return on assets (use DuPont analysis)
   i. Return on common stockholders' equity (use DuPont analysis)
   j. Earnings per share of common stock
   k. Price/earnings ratio

2. Decide whether (a) Hamden's financial position improved or deteriorated during 2012 and (b) the investment attractiveness of Hamden's common stock appears to have increased or decreased.

3. How will what you learned in this problem help you evaluate an investment?

P13-54A (*Learning Objectives 5, 6: Use ratios to decide between two stock investments; measure economic value added*) Assume that you are considering purchasing stock as an investment. You have narrowed the choice to CDRom.com and Web Stores and have assembled the following data.

Selected income statement data for the current year:

	CDRom.com	Web Stores
Net sales (all on credit).................	$601,000	$523,000
Cost of goods sold.........................	455,000	382,000
Income from operations	95,000	76,000
Interest expense............................	—	11,000
Net income....................................	68,000	39,000

Selected balance sheet and market price data at *end* of current year:

	CDRom.com	Web Stores
Current assets:		
Cash	$ 31,000	$ 36,000
Short-term investments	7,000	11,000
Current receivables, net	182,000	165,000
Inventories...	208,000	184,000
Prepaid expenses...	15,000	14,000
Total current assets	443,000	410,000
Total assets..	984,000	927,000
Total current liabilities	368,000	332,000
Total liabilities	665,000	710,000
Preferred stock, 6%, $100 par...............................		20,000
Common stock, $1 par (150,000 shares).................	150,000	
$5 par (10,000 shares)....................		50,000
Total stockholders' equity	319,000	217,000
Market price per share of common stock	$ 4.95	$ 64.26

Selected balance sheet data at *beginning* of current year:

	CDRom.com	Web Stores
Balance sheet:		
Current receivables, net...	$144,000	$192,000
Inventories	204,000	198,000
Total assets...	841,000	912,000
Long-term debt	—	307,000
Preferred stock, 6%, $100 par...............................		20,000
Common stock, $1 par (150,000 shares)................	150,000	
$5 par (10,000 shares).................		50,000
Total stockholders' equity.......................................	263,000	217,000

Your strategy is to invest in companies that have low price/earnings ratios but appear to be in good shape financially. Assume that you have analyzed all other factors and that your decision depends on the results of ratio analysis.

▶ Requirements

1. Compute the following ratios for both companies for the current year and decide which company's stock better fits your investment strategy.
   a. Quick (acid-test) ratio
   b. Inventory turnover
   c. Days' sales in average receivables

    d. Debt ratio

    e. Times-interest-earned ratio

    f. Return on common stockholders' equity

    g. Earnings per share of common stock

    h. Price/earnings ratio

2. Compute each company's economic-value-added (EVA®) measure and determine whether the companies' EVA®s confirm or alter your investment decision. Each company's cost of capital is 12%.

Group B

P13-55B (*Learning Objectives 1, 5: Compute trend percentages, return on sales, asset turnover, and ROA, and compare with industry*) Net sales, net income, and total assets for Azbell Shipping, Inc., for a five-year period follow:

(In thousands)	2012	2011	2010	2009	2008
Net sales.....................	$700	$618	$325	$309	$299
Net income.................	41	39	41	34	27
Total assets	300	262	253	223	201

▶ Requirements

1. Compute trend percentages for each item for 2009 through 2012. Use 2008 as the base year and round to the nearest percent.
2. Compute the rate of return on net sales for 2010 through 2012, rounding to three decimal places. Explain what this means.
3. Compute asset turnover for 2010 through 2012. Explain what this means.
4. Use DuPont analysis to compute rate of return on average total assets (ROA) for 2010 through 2012.
5. How does Azbell Shipping's return on net sales compare with previous years? How does it compare with that of the industry? In the shipping industry, rates above 5% are considered good, and rates above 7% are outstanding.
6. Evaluate Azbell Shipping, Inc.'s ROA for 2012, compared with previous years, and against a 15% benchmark for the industry.

P13-56B (*Learning Objectives 3, 5: Prepare common-size statements; analyze profitability; make comparisons with the industry*) Top managers of Gilligan Products, Inc., have asked for your help in comparing the company's profit performance and financial position with the average for the industry. The accountant has given you the company's income statement and balance sheet and also the following data for the industry:

Gilligan Products, Inc. Income Statement Compared with Industry Average Year Ended December 31, 2012		
	Gilligan	**Industry Average**
Net sales	$800,000	100.0%
Cost of goods sold	552,000	57.3
Gross profit	248,000	42.7
Operating expenses	184,000	29.4
Operating income	64,000	13.3
Other expenses	4,000	2.5
Net income	$ 60,000	10.8%

<table>
<tr><th colspan="3">Gilligan Products, Inc.
Balance Sheet Compared with Industry Average
December 31, 2012</th></tr>
<tr><th></th><th>Gilligan</th><th>Industry Average</th></tr>
<tr><td>Current assets</td><td>$377,600</td><td>72.1%</td></tr>
<tr><td>Fixed assets, net</td><td>113,920</td><td>19.0</td></tr>
<tr><td>Intangible assets, net</td><td>19,200</td><td>4.8</td></tr>
<tr><td>Other assets</td><td>129,280</td><td>4.1</td></tr>
<tr><td>Total</td><td>$640,000</td><td>100.0%</td></tr>
<tr><td></td><td></td><td></td></tr>
<tr><td>Current liabilities</td><td>$300,800</td><td>47.2%</td></tr>
<tr><td>Long-term liabilities</td><td>134,400</td><td>21.0</td></tr>
<tr><td>Stockholders' equity</td><td>204,800</td><td>31.8</td></tr>
<tr><td>Total</td><td>$640,000</td><td>100.0%</td></tr>
</table>

► Requirements

1. Prepare a common-size income statement and balance sheet for Gilligan Products. The first column of each statement should present Gilligan Products' common-size statement, and the second column should show the industry averages.

2. For the profitability analysis, compare Gilligan Products' (a) ratio of gross profit to net sales, (b) ratio of operating income to net sales, and (c) ratio of net income to net sales with the industry averages. Is Gilligan Products' profit performance better or worse than the average for the industry?

3. For the analysis of financial position, compare Gilligan Products' (a) ratios of current assets and current liabilities to total assets and (b) ratio of stockholders' equity to total assets with the industry averages. Is Gilligan Products' financial position better or worse than the average for the industry?

P13-57B (*Learning Objective 4: Use the statement of cash flows for decision making*) You are evaluating two companies as possible investments. The two companies, which are similar in size, are commuter airlines that fly passengers up and down the West Coast. All other available information has been analyzed, and your investment decision depends on the statements of cash flows.

Smooth Airlines
Statements of Cash Flows
Years Ended May 31, 2013 and 2012

		2013		2012
Operating activities:				
Net income (net loss)		$(105,000)		$214,000
Adjustments for non-cash items:				
Total		118,000		(44,000)
Net cash provided by operating activities		13,000		170,000
Investing activities:				
Purchase of property, plant, and				
equipment	$ (94,000)		$(147,000)	
Sale of long-term investments	98,000		29,000	
Net cash provided by (used for)				
investing activities		4,000		(118,000)
Financing activities:				
Issuance of short-term notes payable	$ 149,000		$ 185,000	
Payment of short-term notes payable	(256,000)		(134,000)	
Payment of cash dividends	(67,000)		(106,000)	
Net cash used for financing activities		(174,000)		(55,000)
Increase (decrease) in cash		$(157,000)		$ (3,000)
Cash balance at beginning of year		168,000		171,000
Cash balance at end of year		$ 11,000		$168,000

Mountain, Inc.
Statements of Cash Flows
Years Ended May 31, 2013 and 2012

		2013		2012
Operating activities:				
Net income		$ 201,000		$ 147,000
Adjustments for non-cash items				
Total		92,000		66,000
Net cash provided by operating activities		293,000		213,000
Investing activities:				
Purchase of property, plant, and equipment	$(448,000)		$(630,000)	
Sales of property, plant, and equipment	87,000		113,000	
Net cash used for investing activities		(361,000)		(517,000)
Financing activities:				
Issuance of long-term notes payable	$ 244,000		$ 168,000	
Payment of short-term notes payable	(107,000)		(16,000)	
Net cash provided by financing activities		137,000		152,000
Increase (decrease) in cash		$ 69,000		$(152,000)
Cash balance at beginning of year		135,000		287,000
Cash balance at end of year		$ 204,000		$ 135,000

► Requirement

1. Discuss the relative strengths and weaknesses of Smooth and Mountain. Conclude your discussion by recommending one of the companies' stocks as an investment.

P13-58B (*Learning Objective 5: Compute effects of business transactions on selected ratios*) Financial statement data of Eastland Engineering include the following items:

Cash	$ 30,000	Accounts payable	$107,000
Short-term investments..............	32,000	Accrued liabilities......................	31,000
Accounts receivable, net............	86,000	Long-term notes payable...........	163,000
Inventories	147,000	Other long-term liabilities	31,000
Prepaid expenses	5,000	Net income...............................	91,000
Total assets	673,000	Number of common	
Short-term notes payable...........	48,000	shares outstanding	50,000

► Requirements

1. Compute Eastland's current ratio, debt ratio, and earnings per share. (Round all ratios to two decimal places.)
2. Compute the three ratios after evaluating the effect of each transaction that follows. Consider each transaction *separately*.

   a. Borrowed $110,000 on a long-term note payable
   b. Issued 20,000 shares of common stock, receiving cash of $368,000
   c. Paid short-term notes payable, $30,000
   d. Purchased merchandise of $48,000 on account, debiting Inventory
   e. Received cash on account, $24,000

P13-59B (*Learning Objective 5: Use ratios to evaluate a stock investment*) Comparative financial statement data of Panfield Optical Mart follow:

Panfield Optical Mart
Comparative Income Statements
Years Ended December 31, 2012 and 2011

	2012	2011
Net sales	$686,000	$592,000
Cost of goods sold	380,000	281,000
Gross profit	306,000	311,000
Operating expenses	127,000	148,000
Income from operations	179,000	163,000
Interest expense	30,000	50,000
Income before income tax	149,000	113,000
Income tax expense	38,000	45,000
Net income	$111,000	$ 68,000

Panfield Optical Mart
Comparative Balance Sheets
December 31, 2012 and 2011

		2012	2011	2010*
Current assets:				
Cash		$ 32,000	$ 82,000	
Current receivables, net		217,000	157,000	$200,000
Inventories		297,000	284,000	188,000
Prepaid expenses		7,000	29,000	
Total current assets		553,000	552,000	
Property, plant, and equipment, net		283,000	271,000	
Total assets		$836,000	$823,000	701,000
Accounts Payable		150,000	105,000	112,000
Other current liabilities		135,000	187,000	
Total current liabilities		$285,000	$292,000	
Long-term liabilities		240,000	233,000	
Total liabilities		525,000	525,000	
Common stockholders' equity, no par		311,000	298,000	199,000
Total liabilities and stockholders' equity		$836,000	$823,000	

*Selected 2010 amounts.

Other information:

1. Market price of Panfield common stock: $94.38 at December 31, 2012, and $85.67 at December 31, 2011
2. Common shares outstanding: 15,000 during 2012 and 10,000 during 2011
3. All sales on credit

▶ Requirements

1. Compute the following ratios for 2012 and 2011:
   a. Current ratio
   b. Quick (acid-test) ratio
   c. Receivables turnover and days' sales outstanding (DSO) (round to nearest whole day)
   d. Inventory turnover and days' inventory outstanding (DIO) (round to nearest whole day)
   e. Accounts payable turnover and days' payable outstanding (DPO) (round to nearest whole day).
   f. Cash conversion cycle (in days)
   g. Times-interest-earned ratio
   h. Return on assets (use DuPont analysis)
   i. Return on common stockholders' equity (use DuPont analysis)
   j. Earnings per share of common stock
   k. Price/earnings ratio

2. Decide whether (a) Panfield's financial position improved or deteriorated during 2012 and (b) the investment attractiveness of Panfield's common stock appears to have increased or decreased.

3. How will what you learned in this problem help you evaluate an investment?

P13-60B (*Learning Objectives 5, 6: Use ratios to decide between two stock investments; measure economic value added*)   Assume that you are considering purchasing stock as an investment. You have narrowed the choice to Topline.com and E-shop Stores and have assembled the following data.

Selected income statement data for current year:

	Topline.com	E-Shop Stores
Net sales (all on credit).................	$598,000	$518,000
Cost of goods sold........................	452,000	382,000
Income from operations	95,000	69,000
Interest expense............................	—	11,000
Net income	63,000	37,000

Selected balance sheet and market price data at the *end* of the current year:

	Topline.com	E-Shop Stores
Current assets:		
Cash	$ 28,000	$ 36,000
Short-term investments	9,000	11,000
Current receivables, net	187,000	166,000
Inventories...	219,000	186,000
Prepaid expenses...	15,000	13,000
Total current assets	458,000	412,000
Total assets	984,000	935,000
Total current liabilities	371,000	340,000
Total liabilities	663,000	700,000
Preferred stock: 8%, $150 par		30,000
Common stock, $1 par (100,000 shares)..............	100,000	
$5 par (10,000 shares)................		50,000
Total stockholders' equity	321,000	235,000
Market price per share of common stock	$ 6.93	$ 58.82

Selected balance sheet data at the *beginning* of the current year:

	Topline.com	E-Shop Stores
Balance sheet:		
Current receivables, net...........................	$143,000	$194,000
Inventories	212,000	199,000
Total assets..	853,000	913,000
Long-term debt	—	310,000
Preferred stock, 8%, $150 par		30,000
Common stock, $1 par (100,000 shares)................	100,000	
$5 par (10,000 shares)................		50,000
Total stockholders' equity.......................	259,000	219,000

Your strategy is to invest in companies that have low price/earnings ratios but appear to be in good shape financially. Assume that you have analyzed all other factors and that your decision depends on the results of ratio analysis.

▶ Requirements

1. Compute the following ratios for both companies for the current year and decide which company's stock better fits your investment strategy.
   a. Quick (acid-test) ratio
   b. Inventory turnover
   c. Days' sales in average receivables

d. Debt ratio

e. Times-interest-earned ratio

f. Return on common stockholders' equity

g. Earnings per share of common stock

h. Price/earnings ratio

2. Compute each company's economic-value-added (EVA®) measure and determine whether the companies' EVA®s confirm or alter your investment decision. Each company's cost of capital is 6%.

Challenge Exercises and Problem

E13-61 (*Learning Objectives 2, 3, 5: Use ratio data to reconstruct a company's balance sheet*)
The following data (dollar amounts in millions) are taken from the financial statements of Number 1 Industries, Inc.:

Total liabilities	$12,500
Total current assets	$13,500
Accumulated depreciation	$ 1,600
Debt ratio...	50%
Current ratio	1.50

▶ Requirement

1. Complete the following condensed balance sheet. Report amounts to the nearest million dollars.

	(In millions)
Current assets...	
Property, plant, and equipment................................	
Less: Accumulated depreciation.....................	
Total assets	
Current liabilities	
Long-term liabilities	
Stockholders' equity..	
Total liabilities and stockholders' equity	

E13-62 (*Learning Objectives 2, 3, 5: Use ratio data to reconstruct a company's income statement*)
The following data (dollar amounts in millions) are from the financial statements of Valley Corporation:

Average stockholders' equity...............................	$5,400
Interest expense..	$ 800
Operating income as a percent of sales................	25%
Rate of return on stockholders' equity	10%
Income tax rate	40%

▶ Requirement

1. Complete the following condensed income statement. Report amounts to the nearest million dollars.

Sales..	
Operating expense..................	
Operating income...................	
Interest expense......................	
Pretax income	
Income tax expense...............	
Net income............................	

P13-63 (*Learning Objectives 1, 2, 3, 4: Use trend percentages, common-size percentages, and ratios to reconstruct financial statements*) An incomplete comparative income statement and balance sheet for Amherst Corporation follow:

Amherst Corporation
Comparative Income Statements
Years Ended December 31, 2013 and 2012

	2013	2012
Sales revenue	$2,100,000	$2,000,000
Cost of goods sold	?	1,400,000
Gross profit	?	600,000
Operating expense	?	400,000
Operating income	?	200,000
Interest expense	40,000	40,000
Income before income tax	?	160,000
Income tax expense (30%)	?	48,000
Net Income	?	$ 112,000

Amherst Corporation
Comparative Income Statements
Years Ended December 31, 2013 and 2012

	2013	2012
ASSETS		
Current:		
Cash	$?	$ 30,000
Accounts receivable, net	?	135,000
Inventory	?	180,000
Total current assets	?	345,000
Plant and equipment, net	?	555,000
Total assets	$?	$900,000
LIABILITIES		
Current liabilities	$160,000	$140,000
10% Bonds payable	?	400,000
Total liabilities	?	540,000
STOCKHOLDERS' EQUITY		
Common stock, $5 par	?	220,000
Retained earnings	?	140,000
Total stockholders' equity	?	360,000
Total liabilities and stockholders' equity	$?	$900,000

▶ Requirement

1. Using the ratios, common-size percentages, and trend percentages given, complete the income statement and balance sheet for Amherst for 2013. Additional information:

Additional information:	2013	2012
Common size cost of goods sold %:	65%	70%
Common size common stock %:	30%	24.4%
Trend percentage, Operating income	135%	100%
Asset turnover	2	
Accounts receivable turnover	14	
Quick (acid-test) ratio	1.25	
Current ratio	2.75	
Return on equity (DuPont model)	32.2%	

APPLY YOUR KNOWLEDGE

Decision Cases

Case 1. (*Learning Objectives 5, 6: Assess the effects of transactions on a company*) Suppose **Time Warner, Inc.**, is having a bad year in 2012, as the company has incurred a $4.9 billion net loss. The loss has pushed most of the return measures into the negative column, and the current ratio dropped below 1.0. The company's debt ratio is still only 0.27. Assume top management of Time Warner is pondering ways to improve the company's ratios. In particular, management is considering the following transactions:

1. Sell off the cable television segment of the business for $30 million (receiving half in cash and half in the form of a long-term note receivable). Book value of the cable television business is $27 million.
2. Borrow $100 million on long-term debt.
3. Purchase treasury stock for $500 million cash.
4. Write off one-fourth of goodwill carried on the books at $128 million.
5. Sell advertising at the normal gross profit of 60%. The advertisements run immediately.
6. Purchase trademarks from **NBC**, paying $20 million cash and signing a one-year note payable for $80 million.

▶ Requirements

1. Top management wants to know the effects of these transactions (increase, decrease, or no effect) on the following ratios of Time Warner:
   a. Current ratio
   b. Debt ratio
   c. Times-interest-earned ratio (measured as [net income + interest expense]/interest expense)
   d. Return on equity
   e. Book value per share of common stock

2. Some of these transactions have an immediately positive effect on the company's financial condition. Some are definitely negative. Others have an effect that cannot be judged as clearly positive or negative. Evaluate each transaction's effect as positive, negative, or unclear. (Challenge)

Case 2. (*Learning Objectives 5, 6: Analyze the effects of an accounting difference on the ratios*)
Assume that you are a financial analyst. You are trying to compare the financial statements of
Caterpillar, Inc., with those of **CNH Global**, an international company that uses international
financial reporting standards (IFRS). Caterpillar, Inc., uses the last-in, first-out (LIFO) method
to account for its inventories. IFRS does not permit CNH Global to use LIFO. Analyze the
effect of this difference in accounting method on the two companies' ratio values. For each ratio
discussed in this chapter, indicate which company will have the higher (and the lower) ratio value.
Also identify those ratios that are unaffected by the FIFO/LIFO difference. Ignore the effects of
income taxes, and assume inventory costs are increasing. Then, based on your analysis of the ratios,
summarize your conclusions as to which company looks better overall.

Case 3. (*Learning Objectives 2, 5: Identify action to cut losses and establish profitability*) Suppose
you manage Outward Bound, Inc., a Vermont sporting goods store that lost money during the
past year. To turn the business around, you must analyze the company and industry data for the
current year to learn what is wrong. The company's data follow:

Outward Bound, Inc.
Common-Size Balance Sheet Data

	Outward Bound	Industry Average
Cash and short-term investments	3.0%	6.8%
Trade receivables, net	15.2	11.0
Inventory	64.2	60.5
Prepaid expenses	1.0	0.0
Total current assets	83.4%	78.3%
Fixed assets, net	12.6	15.2
Other assets	4.0	6.5
Total assets	100.0%	100.0%
Notes payable, short-term, 12%	17.1%	14.0%
Accounts payable	21.1	25.1
Accrued liabilities	7.8	7.9
Total current liabilities	46.0	47.0
Long-term debt, 11%	19.7	16.4
Total liabilities	65.7	63.4
Common stockholders' equity	34.3	36.6
Total liabilities and stockholders' equity	100.0%	100.0%

Outward Bound, Inc. Common-Size Income Statement Data		
	Outward Bound	Industry Average
Net sales	100.0%	100.0%
Cost of sales	(68.2)	(64.8)
Gross profit	31.8	35.2
Operating expense	(37.1)	(32.3)
Operating income (loss)	(5.3)	2.9
Interest expense	(5.8)	(1.3)
Other revenue	1.1	0.3
Income (loss) before income tax	(10.0)	1.9
Income tax (expense) saving	4.4	(0.8)
Net income (loss)	(5.6)%	1.1%

▶ Requirement

1. On the basis of your analysis of these figures, suggest four courses of action Outward Bound might take to reduce its losses and establish profitable operations. Give your reason for each suggestion. (Challenge)

Ethical Issue

Turnberry Golf Corporation's long-term debt agreements make certain demands on the business. For example, Turnberry may not purchase treasury stock in excess of the balance of retained earnings. Also, long-term debt may not exceed stockholders' equity, and the current ratio may not fall below 1.50. If Turnberry fails to meet any of these requirements, the company's lenders have the authority to take over management of the company.

Changes in consumer demand have made it hard for Turnberry to attract customers. Current liabilities have mounted faster than current assets, causing the current ratio to fall to 1.47. Before releasing financial statements, Turnberry management is scrambling to improve the current ratio. The controller points out that the company owns an investment that is currently classified as long-term. The investment can be classified as either long-term or short-term, depending on management's intention. By deciding to convert an investment to cash within one year, Turnberry can classify the investment as short-term—a current asset. On the controller's recommendation, Turnberry's board of directors votes to reclassify long-term investments as short-term.

▶ Requirements

1. What is the accounting issue in this case? What ethical decision needs to be made?
2. Who are the stakeholders?
3. Analyze the potential impact on the stakeholders from the following standpoints: (a) economic, (b) legal, and (c) ethical.
4. Shortly after the financial statements are released, sales improve; so, too, does the current ratio. As a result, Turnberry management decides not to sell the investments it had reclassified as short term. Accordingly, the company reclassifies the investments as long term. Has management acted unethically? Give the reasoning underlying your answer.

Focus on Financials: | Amazon.com, Inc.

(*Learning Objectives 4, 5, 6: Compute standard financial ratios; use the statement of cash flows; measure liquidity and profitability; analyze stock as an investment*) Use the consolidated financial statements and the data in **Amazon.com, Inc.'s** annual report (Appendix A at the end of the book) to evaluate the company's comparative performance for 2010 versus 2009. Use all the ratio analysis tools described in this chapter. Does the company appear to be improving or declining in the following dimensions?

► Requirements

1. The ability to pay its current liabilities
2. The ability to sell inventory and collect receivables. Accounts receivable balance as of December 31, 2008, was $827; inventory balance as of December 31, 2008, was $1,399.
3. The ability to pay long-term debts
4. Profitability (Use DuPont analysis). Total assets as of December 31, 2008, were $8,314. Total stockholders' equity as of December 31, 2008, was $2,672.
5. Cash flows from operations
6. The potential of the company's stock as a long-term investment. Use year-end stock prices, when applicable, as found on investment Web sites such as www.googlefinance.com. (Challenge)

Focus on Analysis: | RadioShack Corporation

(Learning Objectives 1, 5: Analyze trend data; compute the standard financial ratios and use them to make decisions) Use the RadioShack Corporation consolidated financial statements in Appendix B at the end of this book to address the following questions.

1. Perform a trend analysis of RadioShack Corporation's net sales, gross profit, operating income, and net income. Use 2008 as the base year, and compute trend figures for 2008 through 2010.
2. Find RadioShack Corporation's annual report for 2011 at www.sec.gov. Also perform research at a popular investment Web site such as www.msnmoney.com or www.finance.yahoo.com to update the information from part 1. (Challenge)
3. What in your opinion is the company's outlook for the future? Would you buy the company's stock as an investment? Why or why not? (Challenge)

Group Projects

Project 1. Select an industry you are interested in, and use the leading company in that industry as the benchmark. Then select two other companies in the same industry. For each category of ratios in the Decision Guidelines feature on pages 800–802, compute at least two ratios for all three companies. Write a two-page report that compares the two companies with the benchmark company.

Project 2. Select a company and obtain its financial statements. Convert the income statement and the balance sheet to common size and compare the company you selected to the industry average. **Risk Management Association's** *Annual Statement Studies,* **Dun & Bradstreet's** *Industry Norms & Key Business Ratios,* and **Prentice Hall's** *Almanac of Business and Industrial Financial Ratios* by Leo Troy, publish common-size statements for most industries. You will find these and other resources in your campus library and on the Internet.

For online homework, exercises, and problems that provide you with immediate feedback, please visit **www.myaccountinglab.com**.

MyAccountingLab

Quick Check Answers

1. *b* ($1,825/$1,720)
2. *b* ($1,825/$21,900)
3. *a*
4. *b* ($1,790/$25,875)
5. *c*

6. $b\left[\dfrac{\$5,130}{(\$160 + \$110)/2}\right]$
   $= 38\ times$

7. $b\ [(\$605 + \$760)/\$2,545$
   $= 0.54]$

8. $a\left[\dfrac{\$760 + \$920/2}{\$21,900/365}\right]$
   $= 14\ days$

9. *b*

10. d ($3,565/$21,900 = .163)

11. $d\left[\dfrac{\$3,565}{\$12,965 + \$10,605/2}\right]$ = .303

12. a ($26/$5.09)

13. c ($0.65/$26)

14. a [$5,941 + $340 − ($305 + $9,700 + $10,605) × 0.10] = $4,220

Comprehensive Financial Statement Analysis Project

The objective of this exercise is to develop your ability to perform a comprehensive analysis on a set of financial statements. Obtain a copy of the 2011 annual report (10-K) of Target Stores from either www.sec.gov or www.investors.target.com.

▶ Requirement 1

Basic Information (provide sources)
   a. Using a site such as www.hoovers.com or www.finance.yahoo.com, research the discount variety store industry. List two competitors of Target.
   b. Describe Target's business and risk factors.
   c. List three Target brands.
   d. What is Target's largest asset? Largest liability?
   e. How many shares of common stock are authorized? Issued? Outstanding?
   f. Did Target repurchase any shares of common stock during the year? If so, how many?
   g. When does Target record revenue?
   h. What inventory method does Target use?
   i. What was Target's bad debt expense for the year?
   j. Does Target have any business interests in foreign countries? Explain your answer.

▶ Requirement 2

Evaluate profitability. Using information you have learned in the text and elsewhere, evaluate Target's profitability for 2011 compared with 2010. In your analysis, you should compute the following ratios and then comment on what those ratios indicate.
   a. Rate of return sales
   b. Asset turnover
   c. Return on assets (DuPont model)
   d. Leverage ratio
   e. Return on equity (DuPont model)
   f. Gross margin (Exclude credit card revenues from this calculation.)
   g. Earnings per share (show computation)
   h. Book value per share

▶ Requirement 3

Evaluate the company's ability to sell inventory, collect receivables, and pay debts during 2011 and 2010. In your analysis, you should compute the following ratios and then comment on what those ratios indicate. (Since the 2011 annual report only includes the balance sheet for 2011 and 2010, you will need to look up the 10-K for 2010 for information about 2009 inventory and accounts receivable.)
   a. Inventory turnover
   b. Receivables turnover
   c. Cash collection cycle
   d. Current ratio
   e. Quick (acid-test) ratio
   f. Debt ratio
   g. Times interest earned

▶ Requirement 4

Evaluate Target's cash flow.

 a. For 2011, what are Target's two main sources of cash?
 b. Is Target's cash flow from operations greater than or less than net income? What is the primary cause of the difference?
 c. For 2011, what is the primary source of cash from investing activities? Is this the same as in 2010 and 2009? If not, state the primary source(s) of cash from investing activities in 2010 and 2009.
 d. For 2011, what is the primary source of cash from financing activities? Is this the same as in 2010 and 2009? If not, state the primary source(s) of cash from financing activities in 2010 and 2009.
 e. What trend(s) do you detect from this analysis?

▶ Requirement 5

Other financial analysis.

 a. Compute common-size percentages for sales, gross profit, operating income, and net income for 2009–2011. Comment on your results.
 b. Find the selected financial date in the 10-K where Target reports selected information since 2005. Compute trend percentages, using 2005 as the base year, for total revenues and net earnings. Comment on your results.

▶ Requirement 6

Evaluate Target stock as an investment. Express your evaluation in terms of a "buy," "hold," or "sell" decision. State your reasons.

 a. What was the closing market price of Target stock on the balance sheet date, January 28, 2012?
 b. Compute the price-earnings ratio using your EPS calculation and the market price you just determined.
 c. Express your evaluation in terms of a "buy," "hold," or "sell" decision. State your reasons. In retrospect, would your decision of the date of the financial statements have been a wise one? State your reasons.

2 0 1 0

A N N U A L   R E P O R T

AMAZON.COM, INC.

PART I

Item 1. *Business*

This Annual Report on Form 10-K and the documents incorporated herein by reference contain forward-looking statements based on expectations, estimates, and projections as of the date of this filing. Actual results may differ materially from those expressed in forward-looking statements. See Item 1A of Part I—"Risk Factors."

Amazon.com, Inc. was incorporated in 1994 in the state of Washington and reincorporated in 1996 in the state of Delaware. Our principal corporate offices are located in Seattle, Washington. We completed our initial public offering in May 1997 and our common stock is listed on the Nasdaq Global Select Market under the symbol "AMZN."

As used herein, "Amazon.com," "we," "our" and similar terms include Amazon.com, Inc. and its subsidiaries, unless the context indicates otherwise.

General

Amazon.com opened its virtual doors on the World Wide Web in July 1995 and offers Earth's Biggest Selection. We seek to be Earth's most customer-centric company for three primary customer sets: consumers, sellers, and enterprises. In addition, we generate revenue through other marketing and promotional services, such as online advertising, and co-branded credit card agreements.

We have organized our operations into two principal segments: North America and International. See Item 8 of Part II, "Financial Statements and Supplementary Data—Note 10—Segment Information." See Item 7 of Part II, "Management's Discussion and Analysis of Financial Condition and Results of Operations—Results of Operations—Supplemental Information" for supplemental information about our net sales.

Consumers

We serve consumers through our retail websites, and focus on selection, price, and convenience. We design our websites to enable millions of unique products to be sold by us and by third parties across dozens of product categories. We also manufacture and sell the Kindle e-reader. We strive to offer our customers the lowest prices possible through low everyday product pricing and free shipping offers, including through membership in Amazon Prime, and to improve our operating efficiencies so that we can continue to lower prices for our customers. We also provide easy-to-use functionality, fast and reliable fulfillment, and timely customer service.

We fulfill customer orders in a number of ways, including through the U.S. and international fulfillment centers and warehouses that we operate, through co-sourced and outsourced arrangements in certain countries, and through digital delivery. We operate customer service centers globally, which are supplemented by co-sourced arrangements. See Item 2 of Part I, "Properties."

Sellers

We offer programs that enable sellers to sell their products on our websites and their own branded websites and to fulfill orders through us. We are not the seller of record in these transactions, but instead earn fixed fees, revenue share fees, per-unit activity fees, or some combination thereof.

Enterprises

We serve developers and enterprises of all sizes through Amazon Web Services ("AWS"), which provides access to technology infrastructure that enables virtually any type of business.

Competition

Our businesses are rapidly evolving and intensely competitive. Our current and potential competitors include: (1) physical-world retailers, publishers, vendors, distributors, manufacturers, and producers of our products; (2) other online e-commerce and mobile e-commerce sites, including sites that sell or distribute digital content; (3) a number of indirect competitors, including media companies, web portals, comparison shopping websites, and web search engines, either directly or in collaboration with other retailers; (4) companies that provide e-commerce services, including website development, fulfillment, and customer service; (5) companies that provide infrastructure web services or other information storage or computing services or products; and (6) companies that design, manufacture, market, or sell digital media devices. We believe that the principal competitive factors in our retail businesses include selection, price, and convenience, including fast and reliable fulfillment. Additional competitive factors for our seller and enterprise services include the quality, speed, and reliability of our services and tools. Many of our current and potential competitors have greater resources, longer histories, more customers, and greater brand recognition. They may secure better terms from suppliers, adopt more aggressive pricing and devote more resources to technology, infrastructure, fulfillment, and marketing. Other companies also may enter into business combinations or alliances that strengthen their competitive positions.

Intellectual Property

We regard our trademarks, service marks, copyrights, patents, domain names, trade dress, trade secrets, proprietary technologies, and similar intellectual property as critical to our success, and we rely on trademark, copyright and patent law, trade-secret protection, and confidentiality and/or license agreements with our employees, customers, partners, and others to protect our proprietary rights. We have registered, or applied for the registration of, a number of U.S. and international domain names, trademarks, service marks, and copyrights. Additionally, we have filed U.S. and international patent applications covering certain of our proprietary technology. We have licensed in the past, and expect that we may license in the future, certain of our proprietary rights to third parties.

Seasonality

Our business is affected by seasonality, which historically has resulted in higher sales volume during our fourth quarter, which ends December 31. We recognized 38%, 39%, and 35% of our annual revenue during the fourth quarter of 2010, 2009, and 2008.

Employees

We employed approximately 33,700 full-time and part-time employees at December 31, 2010. However, employment levels fluctuate due to seasonal factors affecting our business. Additionally, we utilize independent contractors and temporary personnel to supplement our workforce, particularly on a seasonal basis. Although we have works councils and statutory employee representation obligations in certain countries, our employees are not represented by a labor union and we consider our employee relations to be good. Competition for qualified personnel in our industry has historically been intense, particularly for software engineers, computer scientists, and other technical staff.

Available Information

Our investor relations website is www.amazon.com/ir and we encourage investors to use it as a way of easily finding information about us. We promptly make available on this website, free of charge, the reports that we file or furnish with the Securities and Exchange Commission ("SEC"), corporate governance information (including our Code of Business Conduct and Ethics), and select press releases and social media postings.

Report of Ernst & Young LLP, Independent Registered Public Accounting Firm

The Board of Directors and Shareholders
Amazon.com, Inc.

We have audited the accompanying consolidated balance sheets of Amazon.com, Inc. as of December 31, 2010 and 2009, and the related consolidated statements of operations, stockholders' equity, and cash flows for each of the three years in the period ended December 31, 2010. These financial statements are the responsibility of the Company's management. Our responsibility is to express an opinion on these financial statements based on our audits.

We conducted our audits in accordance with the standards of the Public Company Accounting Oversight Board (United States). Those standards require that we plan and perform the audit to obtain reasonable assurance about whether the financial statements are free of material misstatement. An audit includes examining, on a test basis, evidence supporting the amounts and disclosures in the financial statements. An audit also includes assessing the accounting principles used and significant estimates made by management, as well as evaluating the overall financial statement presentation. We believe that our audits provide a reasonable basis for our opinion.

In our opinion, the financial statements referred to above present fairly, in all material respects, the consolidated financial position of Amazon.com, Inc. at December 31, 2010 and 2009, and the consolidated results of its operations and its cash flows for each of the three years in the period ended December 31, 2010, in conformity with U.S. generally accepted accounting principles.

We also have audited, in accordance with the standards of the Public Company Accounting Oversight Board (United States), Amazon.com, Inc.'s internal control over financial reporting as of December 31, 2010, based on criteria established in Internal Control—Integrated Framework issued by the Committee of Sponsoring Organizations of the Treadway Commission and our report dated January 27, 2011 expressed an unqualified opinion thereon.

/s/ Ernst & Young LLP

Seattle, Washington
January 27, 2011

AMAZON.COM, INC.

CONSOLIDATED STATEMENTS OF CASH FLOWS
(in millions)

	Year Ended December 31,		
	2010	**2009**	**2008**
CASH AND CASH EQUIVALENTS, BEGINNING OF PERIOD	$ 3,444	$ 2,769	$ 2,539
OPERATING ACTIVITIES:			
Net income	1,152	902	645
Adjustments to reconcile net income to net cash from operating activities:			
Depreciation of fixed assets, including internal-use software and website development, and other amortization	568	378	287
Stock-based compensation	424	341	275
Other operating expense (income), net	106	103	(24)
Losses (gains) on sales of marketable securities, net	(2)	(4)	(2)
Other expense (income), net	(79)	(15)	(34)
Deferred income taxes	4	81	(5)
Excess tax benefits from stock-based compensation	(259)	(105)	(159)
Changes in operating assets and liabilities:			
Inventories	(1,019)	(531)	(232)
Accounts receivable, net and other	(295)	(481)	(218)
Accounts payable	2,373	1,859	812
Accrued expenses and other	740	300	247
Additions to unearned revenue	687	1,054	449
Amortization of previously unearned revenue	(905)	(589)	(344)
Net cash provided by (used in) operating activities	3,495	3,293	1,697
INVESTING ACTIVITIES:			
Purchases of fixed assets, including internal-use software and website development	(979)	(373)	(333)
Acquisitions, net of cash acquired, and other	(352)	(40)	(494)
Sales and maturities of marketable securities and other investments	4,250	1,966	1,305
Purchases of marketable securities and other investments	(6,279)	(3,890)	(1,677)
Net cash provided by (used in) investing activities	(3,360)	(2,337)	(1,199)
FINANCING ACTIVITIES:			
Excess tax benefits from stock-based compensation	259	105	159
Common stock repurchased	—	—	(100)
Proceeds from long-term debt and other	143	87	98
Repayments of long-term debt and of capital and financing leases	(221)	(472)	(355)
Net cash provided by (used in) financing activities	181	(280)	(198)
Foreign-currency effect on cash and cash equivalents	17	(1)	(70)
Net increase in cash and cash equivalents	333	675	230
CASH AND CASH EQUIVALENTS, END OF PERIOD	$ 3,777	$ 3,444	$ 2,769
SUPPLEMENTAL CASH FLOW INFORMATION:			
Cash paid for interest	$ 11	$ 32	$ 64
Cash paid for income taxes	75	48	53
Fixed assets acquired under capital leases	405	147	148
Fixed assets acquired under build-to-suit leases	172	188	72
Conversion of debt	—	—	605

See accompanying notes to consolidated financial statements.

AMAZON.COM, INC.

CONSOLIDATED STATEMENTS OF OPERATIONS
(in millions, except per share data)

	Year Ended December 31,		
	2010	2009	2008
Net sales	$34,204	$24,509	$19,166
Operating expenses (1):			
Cost of sales	26,561	18,978	14,896
Fulfillment	2,898	2,052	1,658
Marketing	1,029	680	482
Technology and content	1,734	1,240	1,033
General and administrative	470	328	279
Other operating expense (income), net	106	102	(24)
Total operating expenses	32,798	23,380	18,324
Income from operations	1,406	1,129	842
Interest income	51	37	83
Interest expense	(39)	(34)	(71)
Other income (expense), net	79	29	47
Total non-operating income (expense)	91	32	59
Income before income taxes	1,497	1,161	901
Provision for income taxes	(352)	(253)	(247)
Equity-method investment activity, net of tax	7	(6)	(9)
Net income	$ 1,152	$ 902	$ 645
Basic earnings per share	$ 2.58	$ 2.08	$ 1.52
Diluted earnings per share	$ 2.53	$ 2.04	$ 1.49
Weighted average shares used in computation of earnings per share:			
Basic	447	433	423
Diluted	456	442	432

(1) Includes stock-based compensation as follows:

Fulfillment	$ 90	$ 79	$ 61
Marketing	27	20	13
Technology and content	223	182	151
General and administrative	84	60	50

See accompanying notes to consolidated financial statements.

AMAZON.COM, INC.

CONSOLIDATED BALANCE SHEETS
(in millions, except per share data)

	December 31,	
	2010	**2009**
ASSETS		
Current assets:		
Cash and cash equivalents	$ 3,777	$ 3,444
Marketable securities	4,985	2,922
Inventories	3,202	2,171
Accounts receivable, net and other	1,587	988
Deferred tax assets	196	272
Total current assets	13,747	9,797
Fixed assets, net	2,414	1,290
Deferred tax assets	22	18
Goodwill	1,349	1,234
Other assets	1,265	1,474
Total assets	$18,797	$13,813
LIABILITIES AND STOCKHOLDERS' EQUITY		
Current liabilities:		
Accounts payable	$ 8,051	$ 5,605
Accrued expenses and other	2,321	1,759
Total current liabilities	10,372	7,364
Long-term liabilities	1,561	1,192
Commitments and contingencies		
Stockholders' equity:		
Preferred stock, $0.01 par value:		
Authorized shares—500		
Issued and outstanding shares—none	—	—
Common stock, $0.01 par value:		
Authorized shares—5,000		
Issued shares—468 and 461		
Outstanding shares—451 and 444	5	5
Treasury stock, at cost	(600)	(600)
Additional paid-in capital	6,325	5,736
Accumulated other comprehensive income (loss)	(190)	(56)
Retained earnings	1,324	172
Total stockholders' equity	6,864	5,257
Total liabilities and stockholders' equity	$18,797	$13,813

See accompanying notes to consolidated financial statements.

AMAZON.COM, INC.
CONSOLIDATED STATEMENTS OF STOCKHOLDERS' EQUITY
(in millions)

	Common Stock Shares	Common Stock Amount	Treasury Stock	Additional Paid-In Capital	Accumulated Other Comprehensive Income (Loss)	Retained Earnings (Accumulated Deficit)	Total Stockholders' Equity
Balance at December 31, 2007	416	$ 4	$(500)	$3,063	$ 5	$(1,375)	$1,197
Net income	—	—	—	—	—	645	645
Foreign currency translation losses, net of tax	—	—	—	—	(127)	—	(127)
Change in unrealized losses on available-for-sale securities, net of tax	—	—	—	—	(1)	—	(1)
Comprehensive income							517
Unrecognized excess tax benefits from stock-based compensation	—	—	—	(8)	—	—	(8)
Exercise of common stock options and conversion of debt	14	—	—	624	—	—	624
Repurchase of common stock	(2)	—	(100)	—	—	—	(100)
Excess tax benefits from stock-based compensation	—	—	—	154	—	—	154
Stock-based compensation and issuance of employee benefit plan stock	—	—	—	288	—	—	288
Balance at December 31, 2008	428	4	(600)	4,121	(123)	(730)	2,672
Net income	—	—	—	—	—	902	902
Foreign currency translation gains net of tax	—	—	—	—	62	—	62
Change in unrealized gains on available-for-sale securities, net of tax	—	—	—	—	4	—	4
Amortization of unrealized loss on terminated Euro Currency Swap, net of tax	—	—	—	—	1	—	1
Comprehensive income							969
Exercise of common stock options	7	—	—	19	—	—	19
Issuance of common stock for acquisition activity	9	1	—	1,144	—	—	1,145
Excess tax benefits from stock-based compensation	—	—	—	103	—	—	103
Stock-based compensation and issuance of employee benefit plan stock	—	—	—	349	—	—	349
Balance at December 31, 2009	444	5	(600)	5,736	(56)	172	5,257
Net income	—	—	—	—	—	1,152	1,152
Foreign currency translation gains net of tax	—	—	—	—	(137)	—	(137)
Change in unrealized gains on available-for-sale securities, net of tax	—	—	—	—	3	—	3
Comprehensive income							1,018
Exercise of common stock options	7	—	—	16	—	—	16
Excess tax benefits from stock-based compensation	—	—	—	145	—	—	145
Stock-based compensation and issuance of employee benefit plan stock	—	—	—	428	—	—	428
Balance at December 31, 2010	451	$ 5	$(600)	$6,325	$(190)	$ 1,324	$6,864

See accompanying notes to consolidated financial statements.

40

AMAZON.COM, INC.

NOTES TO CONSOLIDATED FINANCIAL STATEMENTS

Note 1—DESCRIPTION OF BUSINESS AND ACCOUNTING POLICIES

Description of Business

Amazon.com opened its virtual doors on the World Wide Web in July 1995 and offers Earth's Biggest Selection. We seek to be Earth's most customer-centric company for three primary customer sets: consumers, sellers, and enterprises. We serve consumers through our retail websites and focus on selection, price, and convenience. We also manufacture and sell the Kindle e-reader. We offer programs that enable sellers to sell their products on our websites and their own branded websites and to fulfill orders through us. We serve developers and enterprises of all sizes through Amazon Web Services ("AWS"), which provides access to technology infrastructure that enables virtually any type of business. In addition, we generate revenue through other marketing and promotional services, such as online advertising, and co-branded credit card agreements.

We have organized our operations into two principal segments: North America and International. See "Note 10—Segment Information."

Principles of Consolidation

The consolidated financial statements include the accounts of the Company, its wholly-owned subsidiaries, and those entities in which we have a variable interest and are the primary beneficiary. Intercompany balances and transactions have been eliminated.

Use of Estimates

The preparation of financial statements in conformity with U.S. GAAP requires estimates and assumptions that affect the reported amounts of assets and liabilities, revenues and expenses, and related disclosures of contingent liabilities in the consolidated financial statements and accompanying notes. Estimates are used for, but not limited to, determining the selling price of products and services in multiple element revenue arrangements and determining the lives of these elements, incentive discount offers, sales returns, vendor funding, stock-based compensation, income taxes, valuation of investments and inventory, collectability of receivables, valuation of acquired intangibles and goodwill, depreciable lives of fixed assets and internally-developed software, and contingencies. Actual results could differ materially from those estimates.

Earnings per Share

Basic earnings per share is calculated using our weighted-average outstanding common shares. Diluted earnings per share is calculated using our weighted-average outstanding common shares including the dilutive effect of stock awards as determined under the treasury stock method.

The following table shows the calculation of diluted shares (in millions):

	Year Ended December 31,		
	2010	**2009**	**2008**
Shares used in computation of basic earnings per share	447	433	423
Total dilutive effect of outstanding stock awards (1)	9	9	9
Shares used in computation of diluted earnings per share	456	442	432

(1) Calculated using the treasury stock method, which assumes proceeds are used to reduce the dilutive effect of outstanding stock awards. Assumed proceeds include the unrecognized deferred compensation of stock awards, and assumed tax proceeds from excess stock-based compensation deductions.

Cash and Cash Equivalents

We classify all highly liquid instruments with an original maturity of three months or less at the time of purchase as cash equivalents.

Inventories

Inventories, consisting of products available for sale, are accounted for using primarily the FIFO method, and are valued at the lower of cost or market value. This valuation requires us to make judgments, based on currently-available information, about the likely method of disposition, such as through sales to individual customers, returns to product vendors, or liquidations, and expected recoverable values of each disposition category.

We provide fulfillment-related services in connection with certain of our sellers' programs. Third party sellers maintain ownership of their inventory, regardless of whether fulfillment is provided by us or the third party sellers, and therefore these products are not included in our inventories.

Accounts Receivable, Net, and Other

Included in "Accounts receivable, net, and other" on our consolidated balance sheets are amounts primarily related to vendor and customer receivables. At December 31, 2010 and 2009, vendor receivables, net, were $763 million and $495 million, and customer receivables, net, were $561 million and $341 million.

Allowance for Doubtful Accounts

We estimate losses on receivables based on known troubled accounts and historical experience of losses incurred. The allowance for doubtful customer and vendor receivables was $72 million and $72 million at December 31, 2010 and 2009.

Internal-use Software and Website Development

Costs incurred to develop software for internal use and our websites are capitalized and amortized over the estimated useful life of the software. Costs related to design or maintenance of internal-use software and website development are expensed as incurred. For the years ended 2010, 2009, and 2008, we capitalized $213 million (including $38 million of stock-based compensation), $187 million (including $35 million of stock-based compensation), and $187 million (including $27 million of stock-based compensation) of costs associated with internal-use software and website development. Amortization of previously capitalized amounts was $184 million, $172 million, and $143 million for 2010, 2009, and 2008.

Depreciation of Fixed Assets

Fixed assets include assets such as furniture and fixtures, heavy equipment, technology infrastructure, internal-use software and website development. Depreciation is recorded on a straight-line basis over the estimated useful lives of the assets (generally two years for assets such as internal-use software, three years for our technology infrastructure, five years for furniture and fixtures, and ten years for heavy equipment). Depreciation expense is classified within the corresponding operating expense categories on our consolidated statements of operations.

Leases and Asset Retirement Obligations

We categorize leases at their inception as either operating or capital leases. On certain of our lease agreements, we may receive rent holidays and other incentives. We recognize lease costs on a straight-line basis without regard to deferred payment terms, such as rent holidays that defer the commencement date of required payments. Additionally, incentives we receive are treated as a reduction of our costs over the term of the agreement. Leasehold improvements are capitalized at cost and amortized over the lesser of their expected useful life or the non-cancellable term of the lease.

We establish assets and liabilities for the estimated construction costs incurred under build-to-suit lease arrangements to the extent we are involved in the construction of structural improvements or take construction risk prior to commencement of a lease. Upon occupancy of facilities under build-to-suit leases, we assess whether these arrangements qualify for sales recognition under the sale-leaseback accounting guidance. If we continue to be the deemed owner, the facilities are accounted for as financing leases.

We establish assets and liabilities for the present value of estimated future costs to retire long-lived assets at the termination or expiration of a lease. Such assets are depreciated over the lease period into operating expense, and the recorded liabilities are accreted to the future value of the estimated retirement costs.

Goodwill

We evaluate goodwill for impairment annually or more frequently when an event occurs or circumstances change that indicate that the carrying value may not be recoverable. We test goodwill for impairment by first comparing the book value of net assets to the fair value of the reporting units. If the fair value is determined to be less than the book value, a second step is performed to compute the amount of impairment as the difference between the estimated fair value of goodwill and the carrying value. We estimate the fair value of the reporting units using discounted cash flows. Forecasts of future cash flows are based on our best estimate of future net sales and operating expenses, based primarily on estimated category expansion, pricing, market segment share and general economic conditions.

We conduct our annual impairment test as of October 1 of each year, and have determined there to be no impairment for any of the periods presented. There were no events or circumstances from the date of our assessment through December 31, 2010 that would impact this conclusion.

See "Note 4—Acquisitions, Goodwill, and Acquired Intangible Assets."

Other Assets

Included in "Other assets" on our consolidated balance sheets are amounts primarily related to marketable securities restricted for longer than one year, the majority of which are attributable to collateralization of bank guarantees and debt related to our international operations; acquired intangible assets, net of amortization; deferred costs; certain equity investments; and intellectual property rights, net of amortization.

Investments

We generally invest our excess cash in investment grade short- to intermediate-term fixed income securities and AAA-rated money market funds. Such investments are included in "Cash and cash equivalents," or "Marketable securities" on the accompanying consolidated balance sheets, classified as available-for-sale, and reported at fair value with unrealized gains and losses included in "Accumulated other comprehensive income (loss)."

Equity investments are accounted for using the equity method of accounting if the investment gives us the ability to exercise significant influence, but not control, over an investee. The total of these investments in equity-method investees, including identifiable intangible assets, deferred tax liabilities and goodwill, is classified on our consolidated balance sheets as "Other assets." Our share of the investees' earnings or losses, amortization of the related intangible assets, and related gains or losses, if any, are classified as "Equity-method investment activity, net of tax" on our consolidated statements of operations.

Equity investments without readily determinable fair values for which we do not have the ability to exercise significant influence are accounted for using the cost method of accounting and classified as "Other assets" on our consolidated balance sheets. Under the cost method, investments are carried at cost and are adjusted only for other-than-temporary declines in fair value, certain distributions, and additional investments.

Equity investments that have readily determinable fair values are classified as available-for-sale and included in "Marketable securities" in our consolidated balance sheet and are recorded at fair value with unrealized gains and losses, net of tax, included in "Accumulated other comprehensive loss."

We periodically evaluate whether declines in fair values of our investments below their book value are other-than-temporary. This evaluation consists of several qualitative and quantitative factors regarding the severity and duration of the unrealized loss as well as our ability and intent to hold the investment until a forecasted recovery occurs. Additionally, we assess whether we have plans to sell the security or it is more likely than not we will be required to sell any investment before recovery of its amortized cost basis. Factors considered include quoted market prices; recent financial results and operating trends; implied values from any recent transactions or offers of investee securities; credit quality of debt instrument issuers; other publicly available information that may affect the value of our investments; duration and severity of the decline in value; and our strategy and intentions for holding the investment.

Long-Lived Assets

Long-lived assets, other than goodwill, are reviewed for impairment whenever events or changes in circumstances indicate that the carrying amount of the assets might not be recoverable. Conditions that would necessitate an impairment assessment include a significant decline in the observable market value of an asset, a significant change in the extent or manner in which an asset is used, or any other significant adverse change that would indicate that the carrying amount of an asset or group of assets may not be recoverable.

For long-lived assets used in operations, impairment losses are only recorded if the asset's carrying amount is not recoverable through its undiscounted, probability-weighted future cash flows. We measure the impairment loss based on the difference between the carrying amount and estimated fair value. Long-lived assets are considered held for sale when certain criteria are met, including when management has committed to a plan to sell the asset, the asset is available for sale in its immediate condition, and the sale is probable within one year of the reporting date. Assets held for sale are reported at the lower of cost or fair value less costs to sell. Assets held for sale were not significant at December 31, 2010 or 2009.

Accrued Expenses and Other

Included in "Accrued expenses and other" at December 31, 2010 and 2009 were liabilities of $503 million and $347 million for unredeemed gift certificates. We reduce the liability for a gift certificate when it is applied to an order. If a gift certificate is not redeemed, we recognize revenue when it expires or, for a certificate without an expiration date, when the likelihood of its redemption becomes remote, generally two years from the date of issuance.

Unearned Revenue

Unearned revenue is recorded when payments are received in advance of performing our service obligations and is recognized over the service period. Current unearned revenue is included in "Accrued expenses and other" and non-current unearned revenue is included in "Long-term liabilities" on our consolidated balance sheets. Current unearned revenue was $461 million and $511 million at December 31, 2010 and 2009. Non-current unearned revenue was $34 million and $201 million at December 31, 2010 and 2009.

Income Taxes

Income tax expense includes U.S. and international income taxes. Except as required under U.S. tax law, we do not provide for U.S. taxes on our undistributed earnings of foreign subsidiaries that have not been previously taxed since we intend to invest such undistributed earnings indefinitely outside of the U.S. Undistributed earnings of foreign subsidiaries that are indefinitely invested outside of the U.S were $1.6 billion at December 31, 2010. Determination of the unrecognized deferred tax liability that would be incurred if such amounts were repatriated is not practicable.

Deferred income tax balances reflect the effects of temporary differences between the carrying amounts of assets and liabilities and their tax bases and are stated at enacted tax rates expected to be in effect when taxes are actually paid or recovered.

Deferred tax assets are evaluated for future realization and reduced by a valuation allowance to the extent we believe a portion will not be realized. We consider many factors when assessing the likelihood of future realization of our deferred tax assets, including our recent cumulative earnings experience and expectations of future taxable income and capital gains by taxing jurisdiction, the carry-forward periods available to us for tax reporting purposes, and other relevant factors. We allocate our valuation allowance to current and long-term deferred tax assets on a pro-rata basis.

We utilize a two-step approach to recognizing and measuring uncertain tax positions (tax contingencies). The first step is to evaluate the tax position for recognition by determining if the weight of available evidence indicates it is more likely than not that the position will be sustained on audit, including resolution of related appeals or litigation processes. The second step is to measure the tax benefit as the largest amount which is more than 50% likely of being realized upon ultimate settlement. We consider many factors when evaluating and estimating our tax positions and tax benefits, which may require periodic adjustments and which may not accurately forecast actual outcomes. We include interest and penalties related to our tax contingencies in income tax expense.

Fair Value of Financial Instruments

Fair value is defined as the price that would be received to sell an asset or paid to transfer a liability in an orderly transaction between market participants at the measurement date. To increase the comparability of fair value measures, the following hierarchy prioritizes the inputs to valuation methodologies used to measure fair value:

Level 1—Valuations based on quoted prices for identical assets and liabilities in active markets.

Level 2—Valuations based on observable inputs other than quoted prices included in Level 1, such as quoted prices for similar assets and liabilities in active markets, quoted prices for identical or similar assets and liabilities in markets that are not active, or other inputs that are observable or can be corroborated by observable market data.

Level 3—Valuations based on unobservable inputs reflecting our own assumptions, consistent with reasonably available assumptions made by other market participants. These valuations require significant judgment.

We measure the fair value of money market funds and equity securities based on quoted prices in active markets for identical assets or liabilities. All other financial instruments were valued based on quoted market prices of similar instruments and other significant inputs derived from or corroborated by observable market data.

Revenue

We recognize revenue from product sales or services rendered when the following four criteria are met: persuasive evidence of an arrangement exists, delivery has occurred or services have been rendered, the selling price is fixed or determinable, and collectability is reasonably assured. Revenue arrangements with multiple deliverables are divided into separate units and revenue is allocated using estimated selling prices if we do not have vendor-specific objective evidence or third-party evidence of the selling prices of the deliverables. Also, see "Recent Accounting Pronouncements" below.

We evaluate whether it is appropriate to record the gross amount of product sales and related costs or the net amount earned as commissions. Generally, when we are primarily obligated in a transaction, are subject to inventory risk, have latitude in establishing prices and selecting suppliers, or have several but not all of these indicators, revenue is recorded at the gross sales price. If we are not primarily obligated, and do not have latitude in establishing prices, amounts earned are determined using a fixed percentage, a fixed-payment schedule, or a combination of the two, we generally record the net amounts as commissions earned.

Product sales and shipping revenues, net of promotional discounts, rebates, and return allowances, are recorded when the products are shipped and title passes to customers. Retail sales to customers are made pursuant to a sales contract that provides for transfer of both title and risk of loss upon our delivery to the carrier. Return allowances, which reduce product revenue, are estimated using historical experience. Revenue from product sales and services rendered is recorded net of sales and consumption taxes. Amounts received in advance for subscription services, including amounts received for Amazon Prime and other membership programs, are deferred and recognized as revenue over the subscription term.

We periodically provide incentive offers to our customers to encourage purchases. Such offers include current discount offers, such as percentage discounts off current purchases, inducement offers, such as offers for future discounts subject to a minimum current purchase, and other similar offers. Current discount offers, when accepted by our customers, are treated as a reduction to the purchase price of the related transaction, while inducement offers, when accepted by our customers, are treated as a reduction to purchase price based on estimated future redemption rates. Redemption rates are estimated using our historical experience for similar inducement offers. Current discount offers and inducement offers are presented as a net amount in "Net sales."

Commissions and per-unit fees received from sellers and similar amounts earned through other seller sites are recognized when items are sold by sellers and our collectability is reasonably assured. We record an allowance for estimated refunds on such commissions using historical experience.

Shipping Activities

Outbound shipping charges to customers are included in "Net sales." Outbound shipping-related costs are included in "Cost of sales."

Cost of Sales

Cost of sales consists of the purchase price of consumer products and content sold by us, inbound and outbound shipping charges, and packaging supplies. Shipping charges to receive products from our suppliers are included in inventory cost, and recognized as "Cost of sales" upon sale of products to our customers. Payment processing and related transaction costs, including those associated with seller transactions, are classified in "Fulfillment" on our consolidated statements of operations.

Vendor Agreements

We have agreements to receive cash consideration from certain of our vendors, including rebates and cooperative marketing reimbursements. We generally consider amounts received from our vendors as a reduction of the prices we pay for their products and, therefore, record such amounts as a reduction of the cost of inventory we buy from them. Vendor rebates are typically dependent upon reaching minimum purchase thresholds. We evaluate the likelihood of reaching purchase thresholds using past experience and current year forecasts. When volume rebates can be reasonably estimated, we record a portion of the rebate as we make progress towards the purchase threshold.

When we receive direct reimbursements for costs incurred by us in advertising the vendor's product or service, the amount we receive is recorded as an offset to "Marketing" on our consolidated statements of operations.

Fulfillment

Fulfillment costs represent those costs incurred in operating and staffing our fulfillment and customer service centers, including costs attributable to buying, receiving, inspecting, and warehousing inventories; picking, packaging, and preparing customer orders for shipment; payment processing and related transaction costs, including costs associated with our guarantee for certain seller transactions; and responding to inquiries from customers. Fulfillment costs also include amounts paid to third parties that assist us in fulfillment and customer service operations.

Marketing

Marketing costs consist primarily of targeted online advertising, television advertising, public relations expenditures; and payroll and related expenses for personnel engaged in marketing, business development, and selling activities. We pay commissions to participants in our Associates program when their customer referrals result in product sales and classify such costs as "Marketing" on our consolidated statements of operations. We also participate in cooperative advertising arrangements with certain of our vendors, and other third parties.

Advertising and other promotional costs, are expensed as incurred, and were $890 million, $593 million, and $420 million in 2010, 2009, and 2008. Prepaid advertising costs were not significant at December 31, 2010 and 2009.

Technology and Content

Technology and content expenses consist principally of payroll and related expenses for employees involved in application development, category expansion, editorial content, buying, merchandising selection, and systems support, as well as costs associated with the compute, storage and telecommunications infrastructure used internally and supporting AWS.

Technology and content costs are expensed as incurred, except for certain costs relating to the development of internal-use software and website development, including software used to upgrade and enhance our websites and applications supporting our business, which are capitalized and amortized over two years.

General and Administrative

General and administrative expenses consist of payroll and related expenses for employees involved in general corporate functions, including accounting, finance, tax, legal, and human relations, among others; costs associated with use by these functions of facilities and equipment, such as depreciation expense and rent; professional fees and litigation costs; and other general corporate costs.

Stock-Based Compensation

Compensation cost for all stock-based awards expected to vest is measured at fair value on the date of grant and recognized over the service period. The fair value of restricted stock units is determined based on the number of shares granted and the quoted price of our common stock. Such value is recognized as expense over the service period, net of estimated forfeitures, using the accelerated method. The estimation of stock awards that will ultimately vest requires judgment, and to the extent actual results or updated estimates differ from our current estimates, such amounts will be recorded as a cumulative adjustment in the period estimates are revised. We consider many factors when estimating expected forfeitures, including employee class, economic environment, and historical experience.

Other Operating Expense (Income), Net

Other operating expense (income), net, consists primarily of intangible asset amortization expense, expenses related to legal settlements, and certain gains and losses on the sale of assets.

Other Income (Expense), Net

Other income (expense), net, consists primarily of gains and losses on sales of marketable securities and foreign currency transaction gains and losses.

Foreign Currency

We have internationally-focused websites for the United Kingdom, Germany, France, Japan, Canada, China, and Italy. Net sales generated from internationally-focused websites, as well as most of the related expenses directly incurred from those operations, are denominated in the functional currencies of the resident countries. The functional currency of our subsidiaries that either operate or support these international websites is the same as the local currency. Assets and liabilities of these subsidiaries are translated into U.S. Dollars at period-end exchange rates, and revenues and expenses are translated at average rates prevailing throughout the period. Translation adjustments are included in "Accumulated other comprehensive income (loss)," a separate component of stockholders' equity, and in the "Foreign currency effect on cash and cash equivalents," on our consolidated statements of cash flows. Transaction gains and losses including intercompany transactions denominated in a currency other than the functional currency of the entity involved are included in "Other income (expense), net" on our consolidated statements of operations. In connection with the remeasurement of intercompany balances, we recorded losses of $70 million in 2010, and gains of $5 million, and $23 million in 2009 and 2008.

Recent Accounting Pronouncements

In June 2009, the Financial Accounting Standards Board ("FASB") issued ASU 2009-17, *Improvements to Financial Reporting by Enterprises Involved With Variable Interest Entities*, which provides authoritative guidance on the consolidation of variable interest entities. The new guidance requires a qualitative approach to identifying a controlling financial interest in a variable interest entity ("VIE"), and requires ongoing assessment of whether an entity is a VIE and whether an interest in a VIE makes the holder the primary beneficiary of the VIE. We adopted this guidance on January 1, 2010. Adoption did not have a material impact on our consolidated financial statements.

On January 1, 2010, we prospectively adopted ASU 2009-13, which amends Accounting Standards Codification ("ASC") Topic 605, Revenue Recognition. Under this standard, we allocate revenue in arrangements with multiple deliverables using estimated selling prices if we do not have vendor-specific objective evidence or third-party evidence of the selling prices of the deliverables. Estimated selling prices are management's best estimates of the prices that we would charge our customers if we were to sell the standalone elements separately.

Sales of our Kindle e-reader are considered arrangements with multiple deliverables, consisting of the device, 3G wireless access and delivery for some models, and software upgrades. Under the prior accounting standard, we accounted for sales of the Kindle ratably over the average estimated life of the device. Accordingly, revenue and associated product cost of the device through December 31, 2009, were deferred at the time of sale and recognized on a straight-line basis over the two year average estimated economic life.

As of January 2010, we account for the sale of the Kindle as multiple deliverables. The revenue related to the device, which is the substantial portion of the total sale price, and related costs are recognized upon delivery. Revenue related to 3G wireless access and delivery and software upgrades is amortized over the average life of the device, which remains estimated at two years.

Because we have adopted ASU 2009-13 prospectively, we are recognizing $508 million throughout 2010 and 2011 for revenue previously deferred under the prior accounting standard.

In January 2010, the FASB issued ASU 2010-6, *Improving Disclosures About Fair Value Measurements*, which requires reporting entities to make new disclosures about recurring or nonrecurring fair-value measurements including significant transfers into and out of Level 1 and Level 2 fair-value measurements and information on purchases, sales, issuances, and settlements on a gross basis in the reconciliation of Level 3 fair-value measurements. ASU 2010-6 is effective for annual reporting periods beginning after December 15, 2009, except for Level 3 reconciliation disclosures which are effective for annual periods beginning after December 15, 2010. The adoption of ASU 2010-6 did not have a material impact on our consolidated financial statement disclosures.

Note 2—CASH, CASH EQUIVALENTS, AND MARKETABLE SECURITIES

As of December 31, 2010 and 2009 our cash, cash equivalents, and marketable securities primarily consisted of cash, U.S. and foreign government and agency securities, AAA-rated money market funds and other investment grade securities. Such amounts are recorded at fair value. The following table summarizes, by major security type, our assets that are measured at fair value on a recurring basis and are categorized using the fair value hierarchy (in millions):

| | December 31, 2010 | | | |
	Cost or Amortized Cost	Gross Unrealized Gains	Gross Unrealized Losses	Total Estimated Fair Value
Cash	$ 613	$—	$—	$ 613
Level 1 securities:				
Money market funds	1,882	—	—	1,882
Equity securities	2	—	(1)	1
Level 2 securities:				
Foreign government and agency securities	2,152	7	(1)	2,158
U.S. government and agency securities	3,746	11	(1)	3,756
Corporate debt securities	457	3	(1)	459
Asset-backed securities	32	1	—	33
Other fixed income securities	17	—	—	17
	$8,901	$ 22	$ (4)	8,919
Less: Long-term restricted cash, cash equivalents, and marketable securities (1)				(157)
Total cash, cash equivalents, and marketable securities				$8,762

---

(1)   We are required to pledge or otherwise restrict a portion of our cash, cash equivalents, and marketable securities as collateral for standby letters of credit, guarantees, debt, and real estate lease agreements. We classify cash and marketable securities with use restrictions of twelve months or longer as non-current "Other assets" on our consolidated balance sheets. See "Note 6—Commitments and Contingencies."

The following table summarizes gross gains and gross losses realized on sales of available-for-sale marketable securities (in millions):

| | Year Ended December 31, | | |
	2010	2009	2008
Realized gains	$5	$ 4	$9
Realized losses	4	—	7

The following table summarizes contractual maturities of our cash equivalent and marketable fixed-income securities as of December 31, 2010 (in millions):

	Amortized Cost	Estimated Fair Value
Due within one year	$5,973	$5,976
Due after one year through five years	2,312	2,329
	$8,285	$8,305

Note 3—FIXED ASSETS

Fixed assets, at cost, consisted of the following (in millions):

| | December 31, | |
	2010	2009
Gross Fixed Assets (1):		
Fulfillment and customer service	$ 778	$ 551
Technology infrastructure	1,240	551
Internal-use software, content, and website development	487	398
Other corporate assets	491	137
Construction in progress	260	278
Gross fixed assets	3,256	1,915
Accumulated Depreciation (1):		
Fulfillment and customer service	211	202
Technology infrastructure	316	178
Internal-use software, content, and website development	255	207
Other corporate assets	60	38
Total accumulated depreciation	842	625
Total fixed assets, net	$2,414	$1,290

(1) Excludes the original cost and accumulated depreciation of fully-depreciated assets.

Depreciation expense on fixed assets was $552 million, $384 million, and $311 million which includes amortization of fixed assets acquired under capital lease obligations of $164 million, $88 million, and $50 million for 2010, 2009, and 2008. Gross assets remaining under capital leases were $818 million, and $430 million at December 31, 2010 and 2009. Accumulated depreciation associated with capital leases was $331 million and $184 million at December 31, 2010 and 2009.

We capitalize construction in progress and record a corresponding long-term liability for lease agreements where we are considered the owner during the construction period for accounting purposes, including portions of our Seattle, Washington, corporate office space that we do not currently occupy. The buildings which we have not yet occupied are scheduled to be completed between 2011 and 2013.

For buildings that are under build-to-suit lease arrangements, where we have taken occupancy during the year ended December 31, 2010, we determined that we continue to be the deemed owner. These arrangements do not qualify for sales recognition under the sale-leaseback accounting guidance due principally to our significant investment in tenant improvements. As a result, the buildings in the amount of $189 million have been reclassified within "Fixed assets" from "Construction in progress" to "Other corporate assets" and are being depreciated over the shorter of their useful lives or the related lease terms. The long-term construction obligation has been reclassified within "Long-term liabilities" from "Construction liability" to "Long-term financing lease obligations" with amounts payable during the next 12 months recorded as "Accrued expenses and other."

Note 4—ACQUISITIONS, GOODWILL, AND ACQUIRED INTANGIBLE ASSETS

2010 Acquisition Activity

In 2010, we acquired certain companies for an aggregate purchase price of $228 million, resulting in goodwill of $111 million and acquired intangible assets of $91 million. The primary reasons for these acquisitions were to expand our customer base and sales channels. The purchase price was allocated to the tangible assets and intangible assets acquired and liabilities assumed based on their estimated fair values on the acquisition date, with the remaining unallocated purchase price recorded as goodwill. The fair value assigned to identifiable intangible assets acquired has been determined primarily by using the income and cost approach. Purchased identifiable intangible assets are amortized on a straight-line or accelerated basis over their respective useful lives.

The acquired companies were consolidated into our financial statements starting on their respective acquisition dates. The financial effect of these acquisitions, individually and in the aggregate, was not material to our consolidated financial statements. Pro forma results of operations have not been presented because the effects of these business combinations, individually and in the aggregate, were not material to our consolidated results of operations.

Note 6—COMMITMENTS AND CONTINGENCIES

Commitments

We have entered into non-cancellable operating, capital and financing leases for equipment and office, fulfillment center, and data center facilities. Rental expense under operating lease agreements was $225 million, $171 million, and $158 million for 2010, 2009, and 2008.

The following summarizes our principal contractual commitments, excluding open orders for inventory purchases that support normal operations, as of December 31, 2010:

| | Year Ended December 31, | | | | | | |
| | 2011 | 2012 | 2013 | 2014 | 2015 | Thereafter | Total |
				(in millions)			
Operating and capital commitments:							
Debt principal and interest	$ 54	$ 95	$101	$—	$—	$ —	$ 250
Capital leases, including interest	235	168	85	15	8	—	511
Financing lease obligations, including interest (1) ...	16	16	17	18	18	186	271
Operating leases	244	227	192	179	148	563	1,553
Other commitments (2) (3)	107	105	76	65	72	789	1,214
Total commitments	$656	$611	$471	$277	$246	$1,538	$3,799

(1) Relates to the 590,000 square feet of occupied corporate office space under build-to-suit lease arrangements
(2) Includes the estimated timing and amounts of payments for rent, operating expenses, and tenant improvements associated with approximately 1.11 million square feet of corporate office space currently being developed under build-to-suit leases and which we anticipate occupying in 2011 to 2013. The amount of space available and our financial and other obligations under the lease agreements are affected by various factors, including government approvals and permits, interest rates, development costs and other expenses and our exercise of certain rights under the lease agreements. See "Note 3—Fixed Assets" for a discussion of these leases.
(3) Excludes $213 million of tax contingencies for which we cannot make a reasonably reliable estimate of the amount and period of payment, if any.

Pledged Securities

We have pledged or otherwise restricted $160 million and $303 million in 2010 and 2009 of our cash and marketable securities as collateral for standby and trade letters of credit, guarantees, debt related to our international operations, as well as real estate leases. We classify cash and marketable securities with use restrictions of twelve months or longer as non-current "Other assets" on our consolidated balance sheets.

Inventory Suppliers

During 2010, no vendor accounted for 10% or more of our inventory purchases. We generally do not have long-term contracts or arrangements with our vendors to guarantee the availability of merchandise, particular payment terms, or the extension of credit limits.

Legal Proceedings

The Company is involved from time to time in claims, proceedings and litigation, including the following:

In March 2009, Discovery Communications, Inc. filed a complaint against us for patent infringement in the United States District Court for the District of Delaware. The complaint alleges that our Kindle e-reader infringes a patent owned by Discovery purporting to cover an "Electronic Book Security and Copyright Protection System" (U.S. Patent No. 7,298,851) and seeks monetary damages, a continuing royalty sufficient to compensate Discovery for any future infringement, treble damages, costs and attorneys fees. In May 2009, we filed counterclaims and an additional lawsuit in the United States District Court for the Western District of Washington against Discovery alleging infringement of several patents owned by Amazon and requesting a declaration that several Discovery patents, including the one listed above, are invalid and unenforceable. We dispute the allegations of wrongdoing and intend to vigorously defend ourselves in this matter.

In May 2009, Big Baboon, Inc. filed a complaint against us for patent infringement in the United States District Court for the Central District of California. The complaint alleges, among other things, that our third-party selling and payments technology infringes a patent owned by Big Baboon, Inc. purporting to cover an "Integrated Business-to-Business Web Commerce and Business Automation System" (U.S. Patent No. 6,115,690) and seeks injunctive relief, monetary damages, treble damages, costs and attorneys fees. We dispute the allegations of wrongdoing and intend to vigorously defend ourselves in this matter.

In December 2009, Nazomi Communications, Inc. filed a complaint against us for patent infringement in the United States District Court for the Eastern District of Texas. The complaint alleges, among other things, that the processor core in our Kindle e-reader infringes two patents owned by Nazomi purporting to cover "Java virtual machine hardware for RISC and CISC processors" and "Java hardware accelerator using microcode engine" (U.S. Patent Nos. 7,080,362 and 7,225,436) and seeks monetary damages, injunctive relief, costs and attorneys fees. We dispute the allegations of wrongdoing and intend to vigorously defend ourselves in this matter.

In February 2010, Texas OCR Technologies LLC filed a complaint against us for patent infringement in the United States District Court for the Eastern District of Texas. The complaint alleged, among other things, that our Search Inside the Book feature infringes a patent owned by Texas OCR Technologies purporting to cover a "Methodology for Displaying Search Results Using Character Recognition" (U.S. Patent No. 6,363,179) and sought monetary damages, costs and attorneys fees. In January 2011, we settled this litigation on terms that include a nonexclusive license to the patent in suit and, accordingly, the lawsuit has been dismissed with prejudice.

In May 2010, Sharing Sound LLC filed a complaint against us for patent infringement in the United States District Court for the Eastern District of Texas. The complaint alleged, among other things, that our website technology infringes a patent licensed by the plaintiffs purporting to cover a "Distribution of Musical Products by a Website Vendor Over the Internet" (U.S. Patent No. 6,233,682) and sought monetary damages, injunctive relief, costs and attorneys fees. In January 2011, we settled this litigation on terms that include a nonexclusive license to the patent in suit and, accordingly, we expect the lawsuit to be dismissed with prejudice.

In July 2010, Positive Technologies Inc. filed a complaint against us for patent infringement in the United States District Court for the Eastern District of Texas. The complaint alleges, among other things, that certain of our products, including our Kindle e-reader, infringe three patents owned by the plaintiff purporting to cover a "DC Integrating Display Driver Employing Pixel Status Memories" (U.S. Patent Nos. 5,444,457, 5,627,558 and 5,831,588) and seeks monetary damages, injunctive relief, costs and attorneys fees. We dispute the allegations of wrongdoing and intend to vigorously defend ourselves in this matter.

In July 2010, the Federal Trade Commission staff informed us that it was considering whether to recommend enforcement proceedings against us for advertising and selling certain textile fiber products as "bamboo" when they are made of rayon manufactured from bamboo, in violation of the Textile Fiber Product Identification Act, the FTC Act, and the regulations promulgated there under. We do not believe we have violated these laws and regulations and are cooperating voluntarily with the Commission's inquiry.

Other Contingencies

In September 2010, the State of Texas issued an assessment of $269 million for uncollected sales taxes for the period from December 2005 to December 2009, including interest and penalties through the date of the assessment. The State of Texas is alleging that we should have collected sales taxes on applicable sales transactions during those years. We believe that the State of Texas did not provide a sufficient basis for its assessment and that the assessment is without merit. We intend to vigorously defend ourselves in this matter.

Depending on the amount and the timing, an unfavorable resolution of this matter could materially affect our business, results of operations, financial position, or cash flows.

See also "Note 9—Income Taxes."

Note 7—STOCKHOLDERS' EQUITY

Preferred Stock

We have authorized 500 million shares of $0.01 par value Preferred Stock. No preferred stock was outstanding for any period presented.

Common Stock

Common shares outstanding plus shares underlying outstanding stock awards totaled 465 million, 461 million, and 446 million, at December 31, 2010, 2009 and 2008. These totals include all vested and unvested stock-based awards outstanding, before consideration of estimated forfeitures.

Stock Repurchase Activity

In January 2010, our Board of Directors authorized a program to repurchase up to $2 billion of our common stock, which replaces the Board's prior authorization. We did not repurchase any of our common stock in 2010 or 2009. We repurchased 2.2 million shares of common stock for $100 million in 2008 under the $1 billion repurchase program authorized by our Board of Directors in February 2008.

Note 8—OTHER COMPREHENSIVE INCOME (LOSS)

The components of other comprehensive income (loss) are as follows:

	Year Ended December 31,		
	2010	**2009**	**2008**
	(in millions)		
Net income	$1,152	$902	$ 645
Net change in unrealized gains/losses on available-for-sale securities:			
Unrealized gains (losses), net of tax of $(2), $(2), and $0	5	7	—
Reclassification adjustment for losses (gains) included in net income, net of tax effect of $0, $1, and $1	(2)	(3)	(1)
Net unrealized gains (losses) on available for sale securities	3	4	(1)
Foreign currency translation adjustment, net of tax effect of $29, $0, and $3	(137)	62	(127)
Other	—	1	—
Other comprehensive income (loss)	(134)	67	(128)
Comprehensive income	$1,018	$969	$ 517

Balances within accumulated other comprehensive income (loss) are as follows:

	December 31,	
	2010	**2009**
	(in millions)	
Net unrealized losses on foreign currency translation, net of tax	$(203)	$(66)
Net unrealized gains on available-for-sale securities, net of tax	13	10
Total accumulated other comprehensive income (loss)	$(190)	$(56)

Note 9—INCOME TAXES

In 2010, 2009, and 2008 we recorded net tax provisions of $352 million, $253 million, and $247 million. A majority of this provision is non-cash. We have current tax benefits and net operating losses relating to excess stock-based compensation that are being utilized to reduce our U.S. taxable income. As such, cash taxes paid, net of refunds, were $75 million, $48 million, and $53 million for 2010, 2009, and 2008.

Item 9.   *Changes in and Disagreements with Accountants On Accounting and Financial Disclosure*

None.

Item 9A.   *Controls and Procedures*

Evaluation of Disclosure Controls and Procedures

We carried out an evaluation required by the 1934 Act, under the supervision and with the participation of our principal executive officer and principal financial officer, of the effectiveness of the design and operation of our disclosure controls and procedures, as defined in Rule 13a-15(e) of the 1934 Act, as of December 31, 2010. Based on this evaluation, our principal executive officer and principal financial officer concluded that, as of December 31, 2010, our disclosure controls and procedures were effective to provide reasonable assurance that information required to be disclosed by us in the reports that we file or submit under the 1934 Act is recorded, processed, summarized, and reported within the time periods specified in the SEC's rules and forms and to provide reasonable assurance that such information is accumulated and communicated to our management, including our principal executive officer and principal financial officer, as appropriate to allow timely decisions regarding required disclosures.

Management's Report on Internal Control over Financial Reporting

Management is responsible for establishing and maintaining adequate internal control over financial reporting, as defined in Rule 13a-15(f) of the 1934 Act. Management has assessed the effectiveness of our internal control over financial reporting as of December 31, 2010 based on criteria established in Internal Control—Integrated Framework issued by the Committee of Sponsoring Organizations of the Treadway Commission. As a result of this assessment, management concluded that, as of December 31, 2010, our internal control over financial reporting was effective in providing reasonable assurance regarding the reliability of financial reporting and the preparation of financial statements for external purposes in accordance with generally accepted accounting principles. Ernst & Young has independently assessed the effectiveness of our internal control over financial reporting and its report is included below.

Changes in Internal Control Over Financial Reporting

There were no changes in our internal control over financial reporting during the quarter ended December 31, 2010 that materially affected, or are reasonably likely to materially affect, our internal control over financial reporting.

Limitations on Controls

Our disclosure controls and procedures and internal control over financial reporting are designed to provide reasonable assurance of achieving their objectives as specified above. Management does not expect, however, that our disclosure controls and procedures or our internal control over financial reporting will prevent or detect all error and fraud. Any control system, no matter how well designed and operated, is based upon certain assumptions and can provide only reasonable, not absolute, assurance that its objectives will be met. Further, no evaluation of controls can provide absolute assurance that misstatements due to error or fraud will not occur or that all control issues and instances of fraud, if any, within the Company have been detected.

2010 ANNUAL REPORT

THE SHACK IS SERIOUSLY CONNECTED.

RadioShack.

Report of Independent Registered Public Accounting Firm

To the Board of Directors and Stockholders of RadioShack Corporation:

In our opinion, the consolidated financial statements listed in the accompanying index present fairly, in all material respects, the financial position of RadioShack Corporation and its subsidiaries at December 31, 2010 and 2009, and the results of their operations and their cash flows for each of the three years in the period ended December 31, 2010 in conformity with accounting principles generally accepted in the United States of America. Also in our opinion, the Company maintained, in all material respects, effective internal control over financial reporting as of December 31, 2010, based on criteria established in *Internal Control - Integrated Framework* issued by the Committee of Sponsoring Organizations of the Treadway Commission (COSO). The Company's management is responsible for these financial statements, for maintaining effective internal control over financial reporting and for its assessment of the effectiveness of internal control over financial reporting, included in Management's Report on Internal Control over Financial Reporting appearing under Item 9A. Our responsibility is to express opinions on these financial statements and on the Company's internal control over financial reporting based on our integrated audits. We conducted our audits in accordance with the standards of the Public Company Accounting Oversight Board (United States). Those standards require that we plan and perform the audits to obtain reasonable assurance about whether the financial statements are free of material misstatement and whether effective internal control over financial reporting was maintained in all material respects. Our audits of the financial statements included examining, on a test basis, evidence supporting the amounts and disclosures in the financial statements, assessing the accounting principles used and significant estimates made by management, and evaluating the overall financial statement presentation. Our audit of internal control over financial reporting included obtaining an understanding of internal control over financial reporting, assessing the risk that a material weakness exists, and testing and evaluating the design and operating effectiveness of internal control based on the assessed risk. Our audits also included performing such other procedures as we considered necessary in the circumstances. We believe that our audits provide a reasonable basis for our opinions.

A company's internal control over financial reporting is a process designed to provide reasonable assurance regarding the reliability of financial reporting and the preparation of financial statements for external purposes in accordance with generally accepted accounting principles. A company's internal control over financial reporting includes those policies and procedures that (i) pertain to the maintenance of records that, in reasonable detail, accurately and fairly reflect the transactions and dispositions of the assets of the company; (ii) provide reasonable assurance that transactions are recorded as necessary to permit preparation of financial statements in accordance with generally accepted accounting principles, and that receipts and expenditures of the company are being made only in accordance with authorizations of management and directors of the company; and (iii) provide reasonable assurance regarding prevention or timely detection of unauthorized acquisition, use, or disposition of the company's assets that could have a material effect on the financial statements.

Because of its inherent limitations, internal control over financial reporting may not prevent or detect misstatements. Also, projections of any evaluation of effectiveness to future periods are subject to the risk that controls may become inadequate because of changes in conditions, or that the degree of compliance with the policies or procedures may deteriorate.

/s/ PricewaterhouseCoopers LLP

Fort Worth, Texas
February 22, 2011

RADIOSHACK CORPORATION AND SUBSIDIARIES

Consolidated Statements of Income

| | Year Ended December 31, | | | | | |
| | 2010 | | 2009 | | 2008 | |
(In millions, except per share amounts)	Dollars	% of Revenues	Dollars	% of Revenues	Dollars	% of Revenues
Net sales and operating revenues	$ 4,472.7	100.0%	$ 4,276.0	100.0%	$ 4,224.5	100.0%
Cost of products sold (includes depreciation amounts of $7.7 million, $9.2 million and $11.2 million, respectively)	2,462.1	55.0	2,313.5	54.1	2,301.8	54.5
Gross profit	2,010.6	45.0	1,962.5	45.9	1,922.7	45.5
Operating expenses:						
Selling, general and administrative	1,554.7	34.8	1,507.9	35.3	1,509.8	35.7
Depreciation and amortization	76.5	1.7	83.7	2.0	87.9	2.1
Impairment of long-lived assets	4.0	0.1	1.5	--	2.8	0.1
Total operating expenses	1,635.2	36.6	1,593.1	37.3	1,600.5	37.9
Operating income	375.4	8.4	369.4	8.6	322.2	7.6
Interest income	2.6	--	4.8	0.1	14.6	0.3
Interest expense	(41.9)	(0.9)	(44.1)	(1.0)	(34.9)	(0.8)
Other loss	--	--	(1.6)	--	(2.4)	--
Income before income taxes	336.1	7.5	328.5	7.7	299.5	7.1
Income tax expense	130.0	2.9	123.5	2.9	110.1	2.6
Net income	$ 206.1	4.6%	$ 205.0	4.8%	$ 189.4	4.5%
Net income per share:						
Basic	$ 1.71		$ 1.63		$ 1.47	
Diluted:	$ 1.68		$ 1.63		$ 1.47	
Shares used in computing net income per share:						
Basic	120.5		125.4		129.0	
Diluted	122.7		126.1		129.1	

The accompanying notes are an integral part of these consolidated financial statements.

RADIOSHACK CORPORATION AND SUBSIDIARIES

Consolidated Balance Sheets

	December 31,	
(In millions, except for share amounts)	2010	2009
Assets		
Current assets:		
Cash and cash equivalents	$ 569.4	$ 908.2
Accounts and notes receivable, net	377.5	322.5
Inventories	723.7	670.6
Other current assets	108.1	114.4
Total current assets	1,778.7	2,015.7
Property, plant and equipment, net	274.3	282.3
Goodwill, net	41.2	38.9
Other assets, net	81.2	92.4
Total assets	$ 2,175.4	$ 2,429.3
Liabilities and Stockholders' Equity		
Current liabilities:		
Current maturities of long-term debt	$ 308.0	$ --
Accounts payable	272.4	262.9
Accrued expenses and other current liabilities	318.0	360.7
Income taxes payable	9.7	30.9
Total current liabilities	908.1	654.5
Long-term debt, excluding current maturities	331.8	627.8
Other non-current liabilities	93.0	98.7
Total liabilities	1,332.9	1,381.0
Commitments and contingencies		
Stockholders' equity:		
Preferred stock, no par value, 1,000,000		
shares authorized:		
Series A junior participating, 300,000 shares designated and none issued	--	--
Common stock, $1 par value, 650,000,000 shares authorized;		
146,033,000 and 191,033,000 shares issued, respectively	146.0	191.0
Additional paid-in capital	147.3	161.8
Retained earnings	1,502.5	2,323.9
Treasury stock, at cost; 40,260,000 and 65,806,000 shares, respectively	(949.0)	(1,621.9)
Accumulated other comprehensive loss	(4.3)	(6.5)
Total stockholders' equity	842.5	1,048.3
Total liabilities and stockholders' equity	$ 2,175.4	$ 2,429.3

The accompanying notes are an integral part of these consolidated financial statements.

RADIOSHACK CORPORATION AND SUBSIDIARIES

Consolidated Statements of Cash Flows

(In millions)	Year Ended December 31,		
	2010	2009	2008
Cash flows from operating activities:			
Net income	$ 206.1	$ 205.0	$ 189.4
Adjustments to reconcile net income to net cash			
provided by operating activities:			
Depreciation and amortization	84.2	92.9	99.1
Amortization of discount on convertible notes	15.0	13.8	5.0
Impairment of long-lived assets	4.0	1.5	2.8
Stock-based compensation	9.9	12.1	12.8
Deferred income taxes	12.0	7.6	11.7
Other non-cash items	12.7	0.8	18.7
Changes in operating assets and liabilities:			
Accounts and notes receivable	(39.9)	(79.6)	15.2
Inventories	(60.4)	(34.7)	93.6
Other current assets	(3.6)	(2.8)	(8.7)
Accounts payable, accrued expenses, income taxes payable and other	(85.0)	29.2	(165.0)
Net cash provided by operating activities	155.0	245.8	274.6
Cash flows from investing activities:			
Additions to property, plant and equipment	(80.1)	(81.0)	(85.6)
Acquisition of Mexican subsidiary, net of cash acquired	--	(0.2)	(42.0)
Other investing activities	0.1	0.4	3.3
Net cash used in investing activities	(80.0)	(80.8)	(124.3)
Cash flows from financing activities:			
Purchases of treasury stock	(398.8)	--	(111.3)
Payments of dividends	(26.5)	(31.3)	(31.3)
Changes in cash overdrafts	7.5	2.2	(16.8)
Proceeds from exercise of stock options	4.0	0.7	--
Repayments of borrowings	--	(43.2)	(5.0)
Issuance of convertible notes	--	--	375.0
Convertible notes issuance costs	--	--	(9.4)
Purchase of convertible notes hedges	--	--	(86.3)
Sale of common stock warrants	--	--	39.9
Net cash (used in) provided by financing activities	(413.8)	(71.6)	154.8
Net (decrease) increase in cash and cash equivalents	(338.8)	93.4	305.1
Cash and cash equivalents, beginning of period	908.2	814.8	509.7
Cash and cash equivalents, end of period	$ 569.4	$ 908.2	$ 814.8
Supplemental cash flow information:			
Interest paid	$ 26.6	$ 30.3	$ 26.5
Income taxes paid	136.7	122.4	123.2

The accompanying notes are an integral part of these consolidated financial statements.

RADIOSHACK CORPORATION AND SUBSIDIARIES

Consolidated Statements of Stockholders' Equity and Comprehensive Income

(In millions)	Shares at December 31,			Dollars at December 31,		
	2010	2009	2008	2010	2009	2008
Common stock						
Beginning of year	191.0	191.0	191.0	$ 191.0	$ 191.0	$ 191.0
Retirement of treasury stock	(45.0)	--	--	(45.0)	--	--
Beginning and end of year	146.0	191.0	191.0	$ 146.0	$ 191.0	$ 191.0
Treasury stock						
Beginning of year	(65.8)	(65.9)	(59.9)	$ (1,621.9)	$ (1,625.9)	$ (1,516.5)
Purchase of treasury stock	(19.8)	--	(6.1)	(398.8)	--	(111.3)
Issuance of common stock	0.1	0.1	0.1	2.7	3.1	1.9
Retirement of treasury stock	45.0	--	--	1,063.9	--	--
Exercise of stock options	0.2	--	--	5.1	0.9	--
End of year	(40.3)	(65.8)	(65.9)	$ (949.0)	$ (1,621.9)	$ (1,625.9)
Additional paid-in capital						
Beginning of year				$ 161.8	$ 152.5	$ 108.4
Issuance of common stock				(4.4)	(1.7)	(1.3)
Exercise of stock options				(1.9)	(0.2)	--
Stock-based compensation				9.6	11.2	11.7
Retirement of treasury stock				(17.8)	--	--
Conversion option of convertible notes				--	--	76.9
Purchase of convertible notes hedges				--	--	(86.3)
Tax benefit from purchase of convertible notes hedges				--	--	3.2
Sale of common stock warrants				--	--	39.9
End of year				$ 147.3	$ 161.8	$ 152.5
Retained earnings						
Beginning of year				$ 2,323.9	$ 2,150.2	$ 1,992.1
Net income				206.1	205.0	189.4
Retirement of treasury stock				(1,001.0)	--	--
Cash dividends declared				(26.5)	(31.3)	(31.3)
End of year				$ 1,502.5	$ 2,323.9	$ 2,150.2
Accumulated other comprehensive loss						
Beginning of year				$ (6.5)	$ (7.0)	$ (5.3)
Other comprehensive income (loss)				2.2	0.5	(1.7)
End of year				$ (4.3)	$ (6.5)	$ (7.0)
Total stockholders' equity				$ 842.5	$ 1,048.3	$ 860.8
Comprehensive income						
Net income				$ 206.1	$ 205.0	$ 189.4
Other comprehensive income (loss), all net of tax:						
Foreign currency translation adjustments				2.4	1.1	(2.5)
Pension adjustments				(0.2)	(0.5)	0.8
Amortization of gain on cash flow hedge				--	(0.1)	--
Other comprehensive income (loss)				2.2	0.5	(1.7)
Comprehensive income				$ 208.3	$ 205.5	$ 187.7

The accompanying notes are an integral part of these consolidated financial statements.

NOTE 1 – DESCRIPTION OF BUSINESS

RadioShack Corporation was incorporated in Delaware in 1967. Throughout this report, the terms "our," "we," "us" and "RadioShack" refer to RadioShack Corporation, including its subsidiaries. We primarily engage in the retail sale of consumer electronics goods and services through our RadioShack store chain.

U.S. RADIOSHACK COMPANY-OPERATED STORES

At December 31, 2010, we operated 4,486 U.S. company-operated stores under the RadioShack brand located throughout the United States, as well as in Puerto Rico and the U.S. Virgin Islands. These stores are located in strip centers and major shopping malls, as well as individual storefronts. Each location carries a broad assortment of both name brand and private brand consumer electronics products.

Our product lines are categorized into seven platforms. Our wireless platform includes postpaid and prepaid wireless handsets and communication devices such as scanners and GPS products. Our accessory platform includes home entertainment, wireless, music, computer, video game and GPS accessories; media storage; power adapters; digital imaging products and headphones. Our modern home platform includes home audio and video end-products, personal computing products, residential telephones, and Voice over Internet Protocol products. Our personal electronics platform includes digital cameras, digital music players, toys, satellite radios, video gaming hardware, camcorders, and general radios. Our power platform includes general and special purpose batteries and battery chargers. Our technical platform includes wire and cable, connectivity products, components and tools, and hobby products. We also provide consumers access to third-party services such as prepaid wireless airtime and extended service plans in our service platform.

KIOSKS

At December 31, 2010, we operated 1,267 kiosks located throughout most of the United States. These kiosks are located inside Target and Sam's Club stores. These locations, which are not RadioShack-branded, offer primarily wireless handsets with activation of third-party wireless services.

In February 2009, we signed a contract extension with Sam's Club through March 31, 2011, with a transition period ending June 30, 2011, to continue operating kiosks in certain Sam's Club locations. As of December 31, 2010, we operated 417 of these kiosks. This transition will begin on April 1, 2011, and conclude on June 30, 2011, with the assignment to Sam's Club of all kiosks operated by the Company in Sam's Club stores. As part of the terms of the contract, we assigned the operation of 22 and 66 kiosk locations to Sam's Club in 2010 and 2009, respectively.

In April 2009 we agreed with Sprint to cease our arrangement to jointly operate the Sprint-branded kiosks in operation at that date. This agreement allowed us to operate these kiosks under the Sprint name for a reasonable period of time, allowing us to transition the kiosks to a new format. In August 2009, we transitioned these kiosks to multiple wireless carrier RadioShack-branded locations. Most of these locations are now managed and reported as extensions of existing RadioShack company-operated stores located in the same shopping malls.

In the fourth quarter of 2009, we commenced a test rollout of kiosk locations in approximately 100 Target stores. In the third quarter of 2010, we signed a multi-year agreement to operate kiosk locations in certain Target stores ("Target Mobile"). We operated 850 Target Mobile locations at December 31, 2010. We plan to operate Target Mobile locations in approximately 1,450 Target stores by June 30, 2011.

OTHER

In addition to the reportable segments discussed above, we have other sales channels and support operations described as follows:

Dealer Outlets: At December 31, 2010, we had a network of 1,207 RadioShack dealer outlets, including 34 located outside of North America. Our North American outlets provide name brand and private brand products and services, typically to smaller communities. These independent dealers are often engaged in other retail operations and augment their businesses with our products and service offerings. Our dealer sales derived outside of the United States are not material.

RadioShack.com: Products and information are available through our commercial website *www.radioshack.com*. Online customers can purchase, return or exchange various products available through this website. Additionally, certain products ordered online may be picked up, exchanged or returned at RadioShack stores.

International Operations: As of December 31, 2010, there were 211 company-operated stores under the RadioShack brand, nine dealers, and one distribution center in Mexico. Prior to December 2008, these operations were overseen by a joint venture in which we were a slightly less than 50% minority owner with Grupo Gigante, S.A.B. de C.V. In December 2008, we increased our ownership of this joint venture to 100%.

Support Operations:
Our retail stores, along with our kiosks and dealer outlets, are supported by an established infrastructure. Below are the major components of this support structure.

Distribution Centers - At December 31, 2010, we had four U.S. distribution centers shipping to our U.S. retail locations and dealer outlets. One of these distribution centers also serves as a fulfillment center for our online customers. Additionally, we have a distribution center that ships fixtures to our U.S. company-operated stores and kiosks.

RadioShack Technology Services ("RSTS") - Our management information system architecture is composed of a distributed, online network of computers that links all stores, customer channels, delivery locations, service centers, credit providers, distribution facilities and our home office into a fully integrated system. Each store has its own server to support the point-of-sale ("POS") system. The majority of our U.S. company-operated stores and kiosks communicate through a broadband network, which provides efficient access to customer support data. This design also allows store management to track daily sales and inventory at the product or sales associate level. RSTS provides the majority of our programming and systems analysis needs.

RadioShack Global Sourcing ("RSGS") - RSGS serves our wide-ranging international import/export, sourcing, evaluation, logistics and quality control needs. RSGS's activities support our name brand and private brand businesses.

Consumer Electronics Manufacturing - We operate two manufacturing facilities in the United States and one in China. These three manufacturing facilities employed approximately 1,800 people as of December 31, 2010. We manufacture a variety of products, primarily sold through our retail outlets, including telephones, antennas, wire and cable products, and a variety of "hard-to-find" parts and accessories for consumer electronics products.

NOTE 2 – SUMMARY OF SIGNIFICANT ACCOUNTING POLICIES

Basis of Presentation: The consolidated financial statements include the accounts of RadioShack Corporation and all majority-owned domestic and foreign subsidiaries. All intercompany accounts and transactions are eliminated in consolidation.

Use of Estimates: The preparation of financial statements in accordance with accounting principles generally accepted in the United States requires us to make estimates and assumptions that affect the reported amounts of assets and liabilities, related revenues and expenses, and the disclosure of gain and loss contingencies at the date of the financial statements and during the periods presented. We base these estimates on historical results and various other assumptions believed to be reasonable, all of which form the basis for making estimates concerning the carrying values of assets and liabilities that are not readily available from other sources. Actual results could differ materially from those estimates.

Cash and Cash Equivalents: Cash on hand in stores, deposits in banks and all highly liquid investments with a maturity of three months or less at the time of purchase are considered cash and cash equivalents. We carry our cash equivalents at cost, which approximates fair value because of the short maturity of the instruments. The weighted average annualized interest rates were 0.4% and 0.3% at December 31, 2010 and 2009, respectively, for cash equivalents totaling $462.1 million and $820.5 million, respectively. We maintain zero balance cash disbursement accounts with certain banks. Outstanding checks in excess of deposits with these banks totaled $49.1 million and $41.6 million at December 31, 2010 and 2009, respectively, and are classified as accounts payable in the Consolidated Balance Sheets. Changes in these overdraft amounts are reported in the Consolidated Statements of Cash Flows as a financing activity.

Accounts Receivable and Allowance for Doubtful Accounts: Concentrations of credit risk with respect to customer and dealer receivables are limited due to the large number of customers, dealers and their location in many different geographic areas of the country. We establish an allowance for doubtful accounts based on factors surrounding the credit risk of specific customers, historical trends and other information. Historically, such losses, in the aggregate, have not exceeded our expectations. Account balances are charged against the allowance when we believe it is probable that the receivable will not be recovered. We have concentration of credit risk from service providers in the wireless telephone industry, primarily Sprint, AT&T, T-Mobile and Verizon. The average payment term for these receivable balances is approximately 45 days.

Inventories: Our inventories are stated at the lower of cost (principally based on average cost, which approximates FIFO) or market value and are comprised primarily of finished goods. Included in the cost of the inventories are in-bound freight expenses to our distribution centers, out-bound freight expenses to our retail outlets, and other direct costs relating to merchandise acquisition and distribution. Also included in the cost of inventory are certain vendor allowances that are not a reimbursement of specific, incremental and identifiable costs to promote a vendor's products. If the calculated net realizable value of the inventory is determined to be less than the recorded cost, a provision is made to reduce the carrying amount of the inventory.

Property, Plant and Equipment: We state our property, plant and equipment at cost, less accumulated depreciation and amortization. Depreciation and amortization are calculated using the straight-line method over the following useful lives: 10-40 years for buildings; 2-15 years for furniture, fixtures, equipment and software; leasehold improvements are amortized over the shorter of the terms of the underlying leases, including certain renewal periods, or the estimated useful lives of the improvements. Major additions and betterments that substantially extend the useful life of an asset are capitalized and depreciated. Expenditures for normal maintenance and repairs are charged directly to expense as incurred.

Capitalized Software Costs: We capitalize qualifying costs related to the acquisition or development of internal-use software. Capitalization of costs begins after the conceptual formulation stage has been completed. Capitalized costs are amortized over the estimated useful life of the software, which ranges between three and five years. The unamortized balance of capitalized software costs at December 31, 2010 and 2009, was $55.3 million and $46.6 million, respectively. Amortization of computer software was approximately $11.9 million, $15.1 million and $21.1 million in 2010, 2009 and 2008, respectively.

Impairment of Long-Lived Assets: We review long-lived assets (primarily property, plant and equipment) held and used, or to be disposed of, for impairment whenever events or changes in circumstances indicate that the net book value of the asset may not be recoverable. Recoverability is assessed based on estimated undiscounted cash flows from the useful asset. If the carrying amount of an asset is not recoverable, we recognize an impairment loss equal to the amount by which the carrying amount exceeds fair value. We estimate fair value based on projected future discounted cash flows. Our policy is to evaluate long-lived assets for impairment at a store level for retail operations.

Leases: For lease agreements that provide for escalating rent payments or free-rent occupancy periods, we recognize rent expense on a straight-line basis over the non-cancelable lease term and certain option renewal periods that appear to be reasonably assured at the inception of the lease term. The lease term commences on the date we take possession of or control the physical use of the property. Deferred rent is included in other current liabilities in the Consolidated Balance Sheets.

Goodwill and Intangible Assets: Goodwill represents the excess of the purchase price over the fair value of net assets acquired. Goodwill and intangible assets with indefinite useful lives are reviewed at least annually for impairment (and in interim periods if certain events occur indicating that the carrying value of goodwill and intangible assets may be impaired). We estimate fair values utilizing valuation methods such as discounted cash flows and comparable market valuations. We have elected the fourth quarter to complete our annual goodwill impairment test. As a result of the fourth quarter impairment analyses, we determined that no impairment charges to goodwill were required.

The changes in the carrying amount of goodwill by segment were as follows for the years ended December 31, 2010 and 2009:

(In millions)	U.S. RadioShack Stores	Kiosks	Other	Total
Balances at December 31, 2008				
Goodwill	$ 2.8	$ 18.6	$ 35.4	$ 56.8
Accumulated impairment losses	--	(18.6)	(1.5)	(20.1)
	2.8	--	33.9	36.7
Purchase accounting adjustments				
related to acquisition of RadioShack de Mexico	--	--	0.3	0.3
Foreign currency translation adjustment	--	--	1.9	1.9
Balances at December 31, 2009				
Goodwill	2.8	18.6	37.6	59.0
Accumulated impairment losses	--	(18.6)	(1.5)	(20.1)
	2.8	--	36.1	38.9
Acquisition of dealer	0.1	--	--	0.1
Foreign currency translation adjustment	--	--	2.2	2.2
Balances at December 31, 2010				
Goodwill	2.9	18.6	39.8	61.3
Accumulated impairment losses	--	(18.6)	(1.5)	(20.1)
	$ 2.9	$ --	$ 38.3	$ 41.2

Self-Insurance: We are self-insured for certain claims relating to workers' compensation, automobile, property, employee health care, and general and product liability claims, although we obtain third-party insurance coverage to limit our exposure to these claims. We estimate our self-insured liabilities using historical claims experience and actuarial assumptions followed in the insurance industry. Although we believe we have the ability to reasonably estimate losses related to claims, it is possible that actual results could differ from recorded self-insurance liabilities.

Income Taxes: Income taxes are accounted for using the asset and liability method. Deferred taxes are recognized for the tax consequences of temporary differences by applying enacted statutory tax rates applicable to future years to differences between the financial statement carrying amounts and the tax bases of existing assets and liabilities. The effect on deferred taxes of a change in tax rates is recognized in income in the period that includes the enactment date. In addition, we recognize future tax benefits to the extent that such benefits are more likely than not to be realized. Income tax expense includes U.S. and international income taxes, plus the provision for U.S. taxes on undistributed earnings of international subsidiaries not deemed to be permanently invested.

Revenue Recognition: Our revenue is derived principally from the sale of name brand and private brand products and services to consumers. Revenue is recognized, net of an estimate for customer refunds and product returns, when persuasive evidence of an arrangement exists, delivery has occurred or services have been rendered, the

sales price is fixed or determinable, and collectability is reasonably assured.

Certain products, such as wireless telephone handsets, require the customer to use the services of a third-party service provider. The third-party service provider pays us an upfront commission and, in some cases, a monthly recurring residual amount based upon the ongoing arrangement between the service provider and the customer. Our sale of an activated wireless telephone handset is the single event required to meet the delivery criterion for both the upfront commission and the residual revenue. Upfront commission revenue, net of estimated service deactivations, is generally recognized at the time an activated wireless telephone handset is sold to the customer at the point-of-sale. Based on our extensive history in selling activated wireless telephone handsets, we have been able to establish reliable deactivation estimates. Recurring residual income is recognized as earned under the terms of our contracts with the service providers, which is typically as the service provider bills its customer, generally on a monthly basis. Sales of wireless handsets and the related commissions and residual income constitute more than 40 percent of our total revenue. Our three largest third-party wireless service providers are Sprint, AT&T, and T-Mobile.

Cost of Products Sold: Cost of products sold primarily includes the total cost of merchandise inventory sold, direct costs relating to merchandise acquisition and distribution (including depreciation and excise taxes), costs of services provided, in-bound freight expenses to our distribution centers, out-bound freight expenses to our retail outlets, physical inventory valuation adjustments and losses, customer shipping and handling charges, and certain vendor allowances (see "Vendor Allowances" below).

Vendor Allowances: We receive allowances from third-party service providers and product vendors through a variety of promotional programs and arrangements as a result of purchasing and promoting their products and services in the normal course of business. We consider vendor allowances received to be a reduction in the price of a vendor's products or services and record them as a component of inventory until the product is sold, at which point we record them as a component of cost of products sold unless the allowances represent reimbursement of specific, incremental and identifiable costs incurred to promote a vendor's products and services. In this case, we record the vendor reimbursement when earned as an offset to the associated expense incurred to promote the applicable products and/or services.

Advertising Costs: Our advertising costs are expensed the first time the advertising takes place. We receive allowances from certain third-party service providers and product vendors that we record when earned as an offset to advertising expense incurred to promote the applicable products and/or services only if the allowances represent reimbursement of specific, incremental and identifiable costs (see "Vendor Allowances" above). Advertising expense was $206.1 million, $193.0 million and $214.5 million for the years ended December 31, 2010, 2009 and 2008, respectively.

Stock-Based Compensation: We measure all employee stock-based compensation awards using a fair value method and record this expense in the consolidated financial statements. Our stock-based compensation relates to stock options, restricted stock awards, and other equity-based awards issued to our employees and directors. On the date that an award is granted, we determine the fair value of the award and recognize the compensation expense over the requisite service period, which typically is the period over which the award vests.

Fair Value Measurements: Certain assets and liabilities are required to be measured at fair value either on a recurring or non-recurring basis. We estimate fair values based on one or more of the following valuation techniques: the market approach (comparable market prices), the income approach (present value of future income or cash flow), or the cost approach (cost to replace the service capacity of an asset or replacement cost). See Note 12 - "Fair Value Measurements" for additional disclosures of our fair value measurements.

Derivative Instruments and Hedging Activities: We recognize all financial instruments that qualify for derivative instrument accounting at fair value in the Consolidated Balance Sheets. Changes in the fair value of derivative financial instruments that qualify for hedge accounting are recorded in stockholders' equity as a component of comprehensive income or as an adjustment to the carrying value of the hedged item. Changes in fair values of derivatives not qualifying for hedge accounting are reported in earnings.

We maintain internal controls over our hedging activities, which include policies and procedures for risk assessment and the approval, reporting and monitoring of all derivative financial instrument activities. We monitor our hedging positions and creditworthiness of our counter-parties and do not anticipate losses due to our counter-parties' nonperformance. We do not hold or issue derivative financial instruments for trading or speculative purposes. To qualify for hedge accounting, derivatives must meet defined correlation and effectiveness criteria, be designated as a hedge and result in cash flows and financial statement effects that substantially offset those of the position being hedged.

Foreign Currency Translation: The functional currency of substantially all operations outside the U.S. is the applicable local currency. Translation gains or losses related to net assets located outside the United States are included as a component of accumulated other comprehensive (loss) income and are classified in the stockholders' equity section of the accompanying Consolidated Balance Sheets.

Reclassifications: Certain amounts in the December 31, 2009 and 2008, financial statements have been reclassified to conform to the December 31, 2010, presentation. These reclassifications had no effect on net income or total stockholders' equity as previously reported.

New Accounting Standards: In June 2009, the FASB issued new accounting guidance to improve financial reporting by companies involved with variable interest entities and to provide more relevant and reliable information to users of financial statements. This guidance was effective for fiscal years beginning after November 15, 2009. We adopted this guidance effective January 1, 2010, and the adoption had no effect on our consolidated financial statements.

NOTE 3 – SUPPLEMENTAL BALANCE SHEET DISCLOSURES

Accounts and Notes Receivable, Net: As of December 31, 2010 and 2009, we had the following accounts and notes receivable outstanding in the accompanying Consolidated Balance Sheets:

	December 31,	
(In millions)	2010	2009
Receivables from vendors and service providers, net	$ 291.0	$ 247.5
Trade accounts receivable	57.6	49.1
Other receivables	30.3	27.7
Allowance for doubtful accounts	(1.4)	(1.8)
Accounts and notes receivable, net	$ 377.5	$ 322.5

Receivables from vendors and service providers relate to earned wireless activation commissions, rebates, residual income, promotions, marketing development funds and other payments from our third-party service providers and product vendors, after taking into account estimates for service providers' customer deactivations and non-activations, which are factors in determining the amount of wireless activation commissions and residual income earned.

The change in the allowance for doubtful accounts is as follows:

	December 31,		
(In millions)	2010	2009	2008
Balance at the beginning of the year	$ 1.8	$ 1.5	$ 2.5
Provision for bad debts included in selling, general and administrative expense	0.1	0.4	0.6
Uncollected receivables written off, net	(0.5)	(0.1)	(1.6)
Balance at the end of the year	$ 1.4	$ 1.8	$ 1.5

Other Current Assets, Net:

	December 31,	
(In millions)	2010	2009
Deferred income taxes	$ 61.4	$ 68.8
Other	46.7	45.6
Total other current assets, net	$ 108.1	$ 114.4

Property, Plant and Equipment, Net:

	December 31,	
(In millions)	2010	2009
Land	$ 2.4	$ 2.4
Buildings	55.7	55.2
Furniture, fixtures, equipment and software	673.5	663.2
Leasehold improvements	362.8	360.9
Total PP&E	1,094.4	1,081.7
Less accumulated depreciation and amortization	(820.1)	(799.4)
Property, plant and equipment, net	$ 274.3	$ 282.3

Other Assets, Net:

	December 31,	
(In millions)	2010	2009
Notes receivable	$ 9.6	$ 10.0
Deferred income taxes	45.9	53.1
Other	25.7	29.3
Total other assets, net	$ 81.2	$ 92.4

Accrued Expenses and Other Current Liabilities:

	December 31,	
(In millions)	2010	2009
Payroll and bonuses	$ 60.0	$ 68.7
Insurance	65.0	75.9
Sales and payroll taxes	41.4	41.9
Rent	36.5	36.8
Advertising	26.9	31.4
Gift card deferred revenue	19.5	19.4
Other	68.7	86.6
Total accrued expenses and other current liabilities	$ 318.0	$ 360.7

Other Non-Current Liabilities:

	December 31,	
(In millions)	2010	2009
Deferred compensation	$ 34.6	$ 33.1
Liability for unrecognized tax benefits	36.6	35.1
Other	21.8	30.5
Total other non-current liabilities	$ 93.0	$ 98.7

NOTE 4 – ACQUISITIONS

RadioShack de Mexico: In December 2008, we acquired the remaining interest (slightly more than 50%) of our Mexican joint venture - RadioShack de Mexico, S.A. de C.V. - with Grupo Gigante, S.A.B. de C.V. We now own 100% of this subsidiary, which consisted of 200 RadioShack-branded stores and 14 dealers throughout Mexico at the time of acquisition. The purchase price was $44.9 million, which consisted of $42.2 million in cash paid and transaction costs, net of cash acquired, plus $2.7 million in assumed debt. The acquisition was accounted for using the purchase method of accounting in accordance with the FASB's accounting guidance for business combinations. The purchase price allocation resulted in an excess of purchase price over net tangible assets acquired of $35.5 million, all of which was attributed to goodwill. The goodwill is not subject to amortization for book purposes but rather an annual test for impairment. The premium we paid in excess of the fair value of the net assets acquired was based on the established business in Mexico and our ability to expand our business in Mexico and possibly other countries. The goodwill is not deductible for tax purposes. Results of the acquired business have been included in our operations since December 1, 2008.

NOTE 5 – INDEBTEDNESS AND BORROWING FACILITIES

Long-Term Debt:

(In millions)	December 31, 2010	December 31, 2009
Five year 2.5% unsecured convertible notes due in 2013	$ 375.0	$ 375.0
Ten-year 7.375% unsecured note payable due in 2011	306.8	306.8
Other	1.0	1.0
	682.8	682.8
Unamortized debt discounts and other costs	(44.2)	(59.4)
Basis adjustment due to interest rate swaps	1.2	4.4
	639.8	627.8
Less current portion of:		
Notes payable	306.8	--
Unamortized basis adjustment and other costs	1.2	--
	308.0	--
Total long-term debt	$ 331.8	$ 627.8

Long-term borrowings outstanding at December 31, 2010, mature as follows:

(In millions)	Long-Term Borrowings
2011	$ 306.8
2012	--
2013	375.0
2014	1.0
2015	--
2016 and thereafter	--
Total	$ 682.8

2013 Convertible Notes: In August 2008, we issued $375 million principal amount of convertible senior notes due August 1, 2013, (the "2013 Convertible Notes") in a private offering to qualified institutional buyers under Securities and Exchange Commission ("SEC") Rule 144A. The 2013 Convertible Notes were issued at par and bear interest at a rate of 2.50% per annum. Interest is payable semiannually, in arrears, on February 1 and August 1.

Each $1,000 of principal of the 2013 Convertible Notes is initially convertible, under certain circumstances, into 41.2414 shares of our common stock (or a total of approximately 15.5 million shares), which is the equivalent of $24.25 per share, subject to adjustment upon the occurrence of specified events set forth under terms of the 2013 Convertible Notes. Upon conversion, we would pay the holder the cash value of the applicable number of shares of our common stock, up to the principal amount of the note. Amounts in excess of the principal amount, if any (the "excess conversion value"), may be paid in cash or in stock, at our option. Holders may convert their 2013 Convertible Notes into common stock on the net settlement basis described above at any time from May 1, 2013, until the close of business on July 29, 2013, or if, and only if, one of the following conditions has been met:

- During any calendar quarter, and only during such calendar quarter, in which the closing price of our common stock for at least 20 trading days in the period of 30 consecutive trading days ending on the last trading day of the preceding calendar quarter exceeds 130% of the conversion price per share of common stock in effect on the last day of such preceding calendar quarter

- During the five consecutive business days immediately after any 10 consecutive trading day period in which the average trading price per $1,000 principal amount of 2013 Convertible Notes was less than 98% of the product of the closing price of the common stock on such date and the conversion rate on such date

- We make specified distributions to holders of our common stock or specified corporate transactions occur

The 2013 Convertible Notes were not convertible at the holders' option at any time during 2010 or 2009.

Holders who convert their 2013 Convertible Notes in connection with a change in control may be entitled to a make-whole premium in the form of an increase in the conversion rate. In addition, upon a change in control, liquidation, dissolution or delisting, the holders of the 2013 Convertible Notes may require us to repurchase for cash all or any portion of their 2013 Convertible Notes for 100% of the principal amount of the notes plus accrued and unpaid interest, if any. As of December 31, 2010, none of the conditions allowing holders of the 2013 Convertible Notes to convert or requiring us to repurchase the 2013 Convertible Notes had been met.

In connection with the issuance of the 2013 Convertible Notes, we entered into separate convertible note hedge transactions and separate warrant transactions with respect to our common stock to reduce the potential dilution upon conversion of the 2013 Convertible Notes (collectively referred to as the "Call Spread Transactions"). The convertible note hedges and warrants will generally have the effect of increasing the economic conversion price of the 2013 Convertible Notes to $36.60 per share of our common stock, representing a 100% conversion premium based on the closing price of our common stock on August 12, 2008. See Note 6 - "Stockholders' Equity," for more information on the Call Spread Transactions.

Because the principal amount of the 2013 Convertible Notes will be settled in cash upon conversion, the 2013 Convertible Notes will only affect diluted earnings per share when the price of our common stock exceeds the conversion price (initially $24.25 per share). We will include the effect of the additional shares that may be issued from conversion in our diluted net income per share calculation using the treasury stock method.

When accounting for the 2013 Convertible Notes, we apply accounting guidance related to the accounting for convertible debt instruments that may be settled in cash upon conversion. This guidance requires us to account separately for the liability and equity components of our convertible notes in a manner that reflects our nonconvertible debt borrowing rate when interest cost is recognized in subsequent periods. This guidance requires bifurcation of a component of the debt, classification of that component in equity, and then accretion of the resulting discount on the debt as part of interest expense being reflected in the income statement.

Accordingly, we recorded an adjustment to reduce the carrying value of our 2013 Convertible Notes by $73.0 million and recorded this amount in stockholders' equity. This adjustment was based on the calculated fair value of a similar debt instrument in August 2008 (at issuance) that did not have an associated equity component. The annual interest rate calculated for a similar debt instrument in August 2008 was 7.6%. The resulting discount is being amortized to interest expense over the remaining term of the convertible notes. The carrying value of the 2013 Convertible Notes was $330.8 million and $315.8 million at December 31, 2010 and 2009, respectively. We recognized interest expense of $9.4 million in both 2010 and 2009 related to the stated 2.50% coupon. We recognized non-cash interest expense of $15.0 million, $13.8 million, and $5.0 million in 2010, 2009 and 2008, respectively, for the amortization of the discount on the liability component.

Debt issuance costs of $7.5 million were capitalized and are being amortized to interest expense over the term of the 2013 Convertible Notes. Unamortized debt issuance costs were $3.7 million at December 31, 2010. Debt issuance costs of $1.9 million were related to the equity component and were recorded as a reduction of additional paid-in capital.

For federal income tax purposes, the issuance of the 2013 Convertible Notes and the purchase of the convertible note hedges are treated as a single transaction whereby we are considered to have issued debt with an original issue discount. The amortization of this discount in future periods is deductible for tax purposes.

NOTE 6 – STOCKHOLDERS' EQUITY

2005 Share Repurchase Program: In February 2005, our Board of Directors approved a share repurchase program with no expiration date authorizing management to repurchase up to $250 million of our common stock in open market purchases. During 2008, we repurchased approximately 0.1 million shares or $1.4 million of our common stock under this program. As of December 31, 2008, there were no further share repurchases authorized under this program.

2008 Share Repurchase Program: In July 2008, our Board of Directors approved a share repurchase program with no expiration date authorizing management to repurchase up to $200 million of our common stock. During the third quarter of 2008, we repurchased 6.0 million shares or $110.0 million of our common stock under this program. As of December 31, 2008, there was $90.0 million available for share repurchases under this program.

In August 2009, our Board of Directors approved a $200 million increase in this share repurchase program. As of December 31, 2009, $290 million of the total authorized amount was available for share repurchases under this program.

In August 2010, our Board of Directors approved an increase in this share repurchase program from $400 million to $610 million with $500 million available for share repurchases under this program. In November 2010, we completed a $300 million accelerated share repurchase ("ASR") program that we entered into in August 2010, which is further discussed below. We repurchased 14.9 million shares under the ASR program. In addition, after the conclusion of the ASR program in November 2010, we repurchased $98.6 million worth of shares in the open market, representing 4.9 million shares. As of December 31, 2010, $101.4 million of the total authorized amount was available for share repurchases under this program.

Accelerated Share Repurchase Program: As mentioned above, in August 2010, we entered into an accelerated share repurchase program with two investment banks to repurchase shares of our common stock under our approved share repurchase program. On August 24, 2010, we paid $300 million to the investment banks in exchange for an initial delivery of 11.7 million shares to us. At the conclusion of the ASR program, we received an additional 3.2 million shares. The 14.9 million shares delivered to us was based on the average daily volume weighted average price of our common stock over a period beginning immediately after the effective date of the ASR agreements and ending on November 2, 2010.

Dividends Declared: We declared an annual dividend of $0.25 per share in November of 2010, 2009 and 2008. The dividends were paid in December of each year.

NOTE 12 – FAIR VALUE MEASUREMENTS

Assets and Liabilities Measured at Fair Value on a Recurring Basis

(In millions)	Fair Value of Assets (Liabilities)	Basis of Fair Value Measurements		
		Quoted Prices in Active Markets for Identical Items (Level 1)	Significant Other Observable Inputs (Level 2)	Significant Unobservable Inputs (Level 3)
As of December 31, 2010				
Derivatives Not Designated as Hedging Instruments:				
Interest rate swaps [1] [2]	$1.9	--	$1.9	--
As of December 31, 2009				
Derivatives Not Designated as Hedging Instruments:				
Interest rate swaps [1] [3]	$5.3	--	$5.3	--

(1)   These interest rate swaps serve as economic hedges on our 2011 Notes

(2)   Included in other current assets

(3)   Included in other assets, net

The FASB's accounting guidance utilizes a fair value hierarchy that prioritizes the inputs to the valuation techniques used to measure fair value into three broad levels:

- Level 1: Observable inputs such as quoted prices (unadjusted) in active markets for identical assets or liabilities
- Level 2: Inputs, other than quoted prices, that are observable for the asset or liability, either directly or indirectly; these include quoted prices for similar assets or liabilities in active markets and quoted prices for identical or similar assets or liabilities in markets that are not active
- Level 3: Unobservable inputs that reflect the reporting entity's own assumptions

The fair values of our interest rate swaps are the estimated amounts we would have received to settle the agreements. Other financial instruments not measured at fair value on a recurring basis include cash and cash equivalents, accounts receivable, accounts payable, accrued liabilities, and long-term debt. With the exception of long-term debt, the financial statement carrying amounts of these items approximate their fair values due to their short-term nature. Estimated fair values for long-term debt have been determined using recent trading activity and/or bid/ask spreads.

Carrying amounts and the related estimated fair value of our debt financial instruments are as follows:

(In millions)	December 31, 2010		December 31, 2009	
	Carrying Amount	Fair Value	Carrying Amount	Fair Value
Total debt	$ 639.8	$ 713.1	$ 627.8	$ 740.2

The fair values of our 2013 Convertible Notes and 2011 Notes at December 31, 2010, were $400.7 million and $311.4 million, respectively, compared with $422.5 million and $316.7, respectively, at December 31, 2009.

NOTE 13 – COMMITMENTS AND CONTINGENCIES

Lease Commitments: We lease rather than own most of our facilities. Our lease agreements expire at various dates through 2025. Some of these leases are subject to renewal options and provide for the payment of taxes, insurance and maintenance. Our retail locations comprise the largest portion of our leased facilities. These locations are primarily in major shopping malls and shopping centers owned by other companies. Some leases are based on a minimum rental plus a percentage of the store's sales in excess of a stipulated base figure (contingent rent). Certain leases contain escalation clauses. We also lease a distribution center in Mexico and our corporate headquarters. Additionally, we lease automobiles and information systems equipment.

Future minimum rent commitments at December 31, 2010, under non-cancelable operating leases (net of immaterial amounts of sublease rent income), are included in the following table.

(In millions)	Operating Leases
2011	$ 196.7
2012	140.1
2013	93.7
2014	60.1
2015	39.1
2016 and thereafter	33.2
Total minimum lease payments	$ 562.9

Litigation: On October 10, 2008, the Los Angeles County Superior Court granted our second Motion for Class Decertification in the class action lawsuit of *Brookler v. RadioShack Corporation*. Plaintiffs' claims that we violated California's wage and hour laws relating to meal periods were originally certified as a class action on February 8, 2006. Our first Motion for Decertification of the class was denied on August 29, 2007. After a California Appellate Court's favorable decision in the similar case of *Brinker Restaurant Corporation v. Superior Court*, we again sought class decertification. Based on the California Appellate Court's decision in *Brinker*, the trial court granted our second motion. The plaintiffs in *Brookler* have appealed this ruling. Due to the unsettled nature of California state law regarding the employers' standard of liability for meal periods, we and the *Brookler* plaintiffs requested that the California appellate court stay its ruling on the plaintiffs' appeal of the class decertification ruling, pending the California Supreme Court's decision in *Brinker*. The appellate court denied this joint motion and then heard oral arguments for this matter on August 5, 2010. On August 26, 2010, the Court of Appeals reversed the trial court's decertification of the class, and our Petition for Rehearing was denied on September 14, 2010. On September 28, 2010, we filed a Petition for Review with the California Supreme Court, which is currently pending. The outcome of this action is uncertain and the ultimate resolution of this matter could have a material adverse effect on our financial position, results of operations, and cash flows in the period in which any such resolution is recorded.

ITEM 9A. CONTROLS AND PROCEDURES.

Evaluation of Disclosure Controls and Procedures

We have established a system of disclosure controls and other procedures that are designed to ensure that information required to be disclosed by us in the reports that we file or submit under the Exchange Act, is recorded, processed, summarized and reported within the time periods specified by the SEC's rules and forms, and that such information is accumulated and communicated to management, including our Chief Executive Officer and Chief Financial Officer, as appropriate to allow timely decisions regarding required disclosure. An evaluation of the effectiveness of the design and operation of our disclosure controls and procedures (as defined in Rule 13a-15(e) under the Exchange Act) was performed as of the end of the period covered by this annual report. This evaluation was performed under the supervision and with the participation of management, including our CEO and CFO.

Based upon that evaluation, our CEO and CFO have concluded that these disclosure controls and procedures were effective.

Management's Report on Internal Control Over Financial Reporting

Our management is responsible for establishing and maintaining adequate internal control over financial reporting, as such term is defined in Exchange Act Rule 13a-15(f). Under the supervision and with the participation of our management, including our CEO and CFO, we conducted an evaluation of the effectiveness of our internal control over financial reporting based on the framework in "Internal Control – Integrated Framework" issued by the Committee of Sponsoring Organizations of the Treadway Commission. Based on our evaluation under the framework in "Internal Control – Integrated Framework," our management concluded that our internal control over financial reporting was effective as of December 31, 2010. The effectiveness of our internal control over financial reporting as of December 31, 2010, has been audited by PricewaterhouseCoopers LLP, an independent registered public accounting firm, as stated in their report which is included herein.

Changes in Internal Controls

There were no changes in our internal control over financial reporting that occurred during our last fiscal quarter that have materially affected, or are reasonably likely to materially affect, our internal control over financial reporting.

ITEM 9B. OTHER INFORMATION.

None.

APPENDIX C

Typical Charts of Accounts for Different Types of Businesses

A Simple Service Corporation

Assets	Liabilities	Stockholders' Equity
Cash	Accounts Payable	Common Stock
Accounts Receivable	Notes Payable, Short-Term	Retained Earnings
Allowance for Uncollectible Accounts	Salary Payable	Dividends
Notes Receivable, Short-Term	Wages Payable	
Interest Receivable	Payroll Taxes Payable	**Revenues and Gains**
Supplies	Employee Benefits Payable	Service Revenue
Prepaid Rent	Interest Payable	Interest Revenue
Prepaid Insurance	Unearned Service Revenue	Gain on Sale of Land (Furniture,
Notes Receivable, Long-Term	Notes Payable, Long-Term	Equipment, or Building)
Land		
Furniture		**Expenses and Losses**
Accumulated Depreciation—Furniture		Salary Expense
Equipment		Payroll Tax Expense
Accumulated Depreciation—Equipment		Employee Benefits Expense
Building		Rent Expense
Accumulated Depreciation—Building		Insurance Expense
		Supplies Expense
		Uncollectible Account Expense
		Depreciation Expense—Furniture
		Depreciation Expense—Equipment
		Depreciation Expense—Building
		Property Tax Expense
		Interest Expense
		Miscellaneous Expense
		Loss on Sale (or Exchange) of Land (Furniture, Equipment, or Building)

A Service Partnership

Same as service corporation, except for owners' equity

Owners' Equity

Partner 1, Capital
Partner 2, Capital
.
.
.
Partner N, Capital

Partner 1, Drawing
Partner 2, Drawing
.
.
.
Partner N, Drawing

A Complex Merchandising Corporation

Assets	Liabilities	Stockholders' Equity

Assets

Cash
Short-Term Investments
Accounts Receivable
Allowance for Uncollectible
 Accounts
Notes Receivable, Short-Term
Interest Receivable
Inventory
Supplies
Prepaid Rent
Prepaid Insurance
Notes Receivable, Long-Term
Investments in Subsidiaries
Investments in Stock
 (Available-for-Sale
 Securities)
Investments in Bonds (Held-to-
 Maturity Securities)
Other Receivables, Long-Term
Land
Land Improvements
Furniture and Fixtures
Accumulated Depreciation—
 Furniture and Fixtures
Equipment
Accumulated Depreciation—
 Equipment
Buildings
Accumulated Depreciation—
 Buildings
Franchises
Patents
Leaseholds
Goodwill

Liabilities

Accounts Payable
Notes Payable, Short-Term
Current Portion of Bonds
 Payable
Salary Payable
Wages Payable
Payroll Taxes Payable
Employee Benefits Payable
Interest Payable
Income Tax Payable
Unearned Sales Revenue
Notes Payable, Long-Term
Bonds Payable
Lease Liability
Minority Interest

Stockholders' Equity

Preferred Stock
Paid-in Capital in Excess of
 Par—Preferred
Common Stock
Paid-in Capital in Excess of
 Par—Common
Paid-in Capital from Treasury
 Stock Transactions
Paid-in Capital from
 Retirement of Stock
Retained Earnings
Unrealized Gain (or Loss)
 on Investments
Foreign Currency Translation
 Adjustment
Treasury Stock

Revenues and Gains

Sales Revenue
Interest Revenue
Dividend Revenue
Equity-Method Investment
 Revenue
Unrealized Holding Gain on
 Trading Investments
Gain on Sale of Investments
Gain on Sale of Land
 (Furniture and Fixtures,
 Equipment, or Buildings)
Discontinued Operations—
 Gain
Extraordinary Gains

Expenses and Losses

Cost of Goods Sold
Salary Expense
Wage Expense
Commission Expense
Payroll Tax Expense
Employee Benefits Expense
Rent Expense
Insurance Expense
Supplies Expense
Uncollectible Account Expense
Depreciation Expense—Land
 Improvements
Depreciation Expense—
 Furniture and Fixtures
Depreciation Expense—
 Equipment
Depreciation Expense—
 Buildings
Organization Expense
Amortization Expense—
 Franchises
Amortization Expense—
 Leaseholds
Amortization Expense—
 Goodwill
Income Tax Expense
Unrealized Holding Loss on
 Trading Investments
Loss on Sale of Investments
Loss on Sale (or Exchange) of
 Land (Furniture and
 Fixtures, Equipment, or
 Buildings)
Discontinued Operations—
 Loss
Extraordinary Losses

A Manufacturing Corporation

Same as merchandising corporation, except for assets

Assets

Inventories:
 Materials Inventory
 Work-in-Process Inventory
 Finished Goods Inventory
Factory Wages
Factory Overhead

Summary of Generally Accepted Accounting Principles (GAAP)

Every technical area has professional associations and regulatory bodies that govern the practice of the profession. Accounting is no exception. In the United States, generally accepted accounting principles (GAAP) are written by the Financial Accounting Standards Board (FASB). The FASB has seven full-time members and a large staff. An independent organization with no government or professional affiliation, the FASB is subject to oversight by the Financial Accounting Foundation (FAF), which selects its members and funds its work. In order to ensure impartiality, FASB members are required to sever all ties to previous firms and institutions that they may have served prior to joining the FASB. Each member is appointed for a five-year term and is eligible for one additional five-year term.

FASB pronouncements are called *Statements of Financial Accounting Standards*. Once issued, these pronouncements are added to the *Accounting Standards Codification*™, which is the single source of authoritative nongovernmental U.S. GAAP. The codification organizes the many pronouncements that constitute U.S. GAAP–each of which specifies how to measure and report a particular type of business event or transaction–into a consistent, searchable format. GAAP is the "accounting law of the land." In the same way that our laws draw authority from their acceptance by the people, GAAP depends on general acceptance by the business community. Throughout this book, we refer to GAAP as the proper way to measure and report business activity.

In 2002, the FASB and the International Accounting Standards Board (IASB) announced a convergence project, whereby both bodies agreed to combine international financial reporting standards (IFRS) and U.S. GAAP into one set of global, compatible, high-quality standards. All new FASB and IASB standards written since that time have been written to measure and report various types of business activities in compatible (if not identical) ways. However, some differences between the two sets of standards still exist. Those differences are discussed in Appendix E.

The U.S. Congress has given the Securities and Exchange Commission (SEC), a government organization that regulates the trading of investments, ultimate responsibility for establishing accounting rules for companies that are owned by the general investing public. However, the SEC has delegated much of its rule-making power to the FASB. Exhibit D-1 outlines the flow of authority for developing GAAP.

EXHIBIT D-1 | Flow of Authority for Developing GAAP

| United States Congress | Securities and Exchange Commission | Financial Accounting Standards Board | Pronouncements that make up generally accepted accounting principles (GAAP) |

The Objective of Financial Reporting

The basic objective of financial reporting is to provide information that is useful in making investment and lending decisions. The FASB believes that accounting information can be useful in decision making only if it is *relevant* and if it *faithfully represents* economic reality.

Relevant information is useful in making predictions and for evaluating past performance–that is, the information has feedback value. For example, PepsiCo's disclosure of the profitability of each of its lines of business is relevant for investor evaluations of the company. To be relevant, information must be timely. To faithfully represent, the information must be complete, neutral (free from bias), and without material error (accurate). Accounting information must focus on the *economic substance* of a transaction, event, or circumstance, which may or may not always be the same as its legal form. Faithful representation makes the information *reliable* to users. Exhibit 1-3 on page 7 of Chapter 1 presents the objective of accounting, its fundamental and enhancing qualitative characteristics, and as its constraints. These characteristics and constraints combine to shape the concepts and principles that make up GAAP. Exhibit D-2 summarizes the assumptions, concepts, and principles that accounting has developed to provide useful information for decision making.

EXHIBIT D-2 | Summary of Important Accounting Concepts, Principles, and Financial Statements

Assumptions, Concepts, Principles, and Financial Statements	Quick Summary	Text Reference
Assumptions and Concepts		
Entity assumption	Accounting draws a boundary around each organization to be accounted for.	Chapter 1, page 8
Continuity (going-concern) assumption	Accountants assume the business will continue operating for the foreseeable future.	Chapter 1, page 8
Stable-monetary-unit assumption	Accounting information is expressed primarily in monetary terms that ignore the effects of inflation.	Chapter 1, page 9
Time-period concept	Ensures that accounting information is reported at regular intervals.	Chapter 3, page 138
Materiality	A constraint of accounting. Accountants perform strictly proper accounting only for items that are significant to the company's financial statements.	Chapter 1, page 6
Cost	A constraint of accounting, meaning that the cost of producing information should not exceed the expected benefits to users.	Chapter 1, page 7
Principles		
Historical cost principle	Assets, services, revenues, and expenses are recorded at their actual historical cost.	Chapter 1, page 8
Revenue principle	Tells accountants when to record revenue (only after it has been earned) and the amount of revenue to record (the cash value of what has been received).	Chapter 3, page 138, and Chapter 11
Expense recognition (matching) principle	Directs accountants to (1) identify and measure all expenses incurred during the period and (2) match the expenses against the revenues earned during the period. The goal is to measure net income.	Chapter 3, page 139
Consistency principle	Businesses should use the same accounting methods from period to period.	Chapter 6, page 353
Disclosure principle	A company's financial statements should report enough information for outsiders to make informed decisions about the company.	Chapter 6, page 353
Financial Statements		
Balance sheet	Assets = Liabilities + Owners' Equity at a point in time.	Chapter 1
Income statement	Revenues and gains − Expenses and losses = Net income or net loss for the period	Chapters 1 and 11
Statement of cash flows	Cash receipts − Cash payments = Increase or decrease in cash during the period, grouped under operating, investing, and financing activities	Chapters 1 and 12
Statement of Comprehensive Income	Net income (from income statement) + Other comprehensive income − Other comprehensive loss = Comprehensive income	Chapter 11
Statement of retained earnings	Beginning retained earnings + Net income (or − Net loss) − Dividends = Ending retained earnings	Chapters 1 and 11
Statement of stockholders' equity	Shows the reason for the change in each stockholders' equity account, including retained earnings.	Chapter 11
Financial statement notes	Provide information that cannot be reported conveniently on the face of the financial statements. The notes are an integral part of the statements.	Chapter 11

APPENDIX E

Summary of Differences Between U.S. GAAP and IFRS Cross Referenced to Chapter

The following table describes some of the current differences between U.S. generally accepted accounting principles (GAAP) and International Financial Reporting Standards (IFRS) that relate to topics (by chapter) covered in this textbook. The U.S. Securities and Exchange Commission (SEC) has adopted a timetable whereby U.S. public companies may adopt IFRS by 2015. Because of a global economic recession and a crisis in the financial markets, a significant number of informed persons believe that this time table may be delayed. Nevertheless, most people believe that the integration of GAAP and IFRS will eventually become a reality. The last column of the table explains what could happen if the U.S. GAAP of today were to switch to IFRS as they currently exist. This will help you assess the impact of these changes on U.S. financial statements.

Accounts	Topic	U.S. GAAP Position	IFRS Position	Implications of Switch to IFRS
Inventory and Cost of Goods Sold Chapter 6	Inventory costing	Companies can choose to use LIFO inventory costing, if desired. A large portion of U.S. companies currently use LIFO for its tax benefits.	LIFO is not allowed under any circumstances.	LIFO could be eliminated. Companies could still choose to use FIFO, average, or specific identification methods.
	Lower-of-cost-or market (LCM)	Market is usually determined to be replacement cost. LCM write-downs cannot be reversed.	Market is always net realizable value (fair market value). LCM write-downs can be reversed under certain conditions.	LCM write-downs may become less common, as selling prices are usually greater than replacement costs. Some write-downs might be reversed over time.
Property, Plant, and Equipment Chapter 7	Asset impairment and revaluation	If long-term assets are impaired, they are written down. Write-downs may not be reversed.	Long-term assets may be written up or down, based on fair market value (appraisals). Adjustments may be potentially reversed.	The cost principle might not apply to long-term assets as strongly. Assets could be evaluated by independent appraisers and adjusted either up or down.
	Depreciation	Assets are depreciated by classes (i.e., buildings, equipment, etc.).	Assets are depreciated by component (much more detailed than by classes).	Much more detailed records would have to be kept over depreciation.
Research and Development Chapter 7	Development costs	All research and development costs are expensed. Only exception is for computer software development costs, which can be capitalized and amortized over future sales revenues.	All research is expensed, but all development costs are capitalized and amortized over future sales revenues.	Standards already developed by U.S. GAAP might be extended to apply to all development costs, not just computer software development.
Intangible Assets Chapter 7	Capitalization and recognition of intangible assets on balance sheet	Only recognized when purchased. Internally developed not recognized.	Recognized if future benefit is probable and reliably measurable (same criteria as recognition of contingencies). May be purchased or internally developed.	More intangible assets could be recognized on balance sheet. Adjusted for amortization or impairment over time.
Contingent Liabilities Chapter 9	Recording of contingent liabilities	Accrued (recorded in journal entry) if probable and reliably measurable. Contingent liabilities that are possible are disclosed in notes to financial statements.	Both probable and possible contingent liabilities are recorded in journal entries.	More liabilities will likely be recorded, regardless of the outcome of proposals being studied by FASB and IASB.

Accounts	Topic	U.S. GAAP Position	IFRS Position	Implications of Switch to IFRS
Contingent Liabilities Chapter 9	Disclosure of contingencies	The FASB has proposed that the standard for disclosure of loss contingencies be increased to include all such matters that are expected to be resolved in the near term (i.e., within the next year) and that could have a severe impact (higher than material, disruptive to the business). In addition, the proposal requires a quantitative tabular reconciliation of accrued loss contingencies that includes increases or decreases in such amounts during the most recent year.	IASB is studying its present requirements with a view to increase required disclosures in the next few years.	More liabilities will likely be recorded, regardless of the outcome of proposals being studied by the FASB and IASB.
Lease Liabilities Chapter 9	Classification of leases	FASB and IASB have issued a joint exposure draft that would eliminate virtually all operating leases. The present value of all future payments on leased assets would be capitalized under the category of "right to use" assets. The related obligations would be reported as "future lease payment" long-term liabilities. As of this publication, the exposure draft is still being debated.	Same as U.S. GAAP Position.	More leases could be classified as capital leases, resulting in more frequent recognition of long-term assets as well as long-term liabilities.
Revenue Chapter 11	Revenue recognition	Until recently, U.S. GAAP allowed many different ways to recognize revenues, depending on the industry and type of contract. However, the FASB and IASB have recently issued a joint exposure draft of a standard that greatly eliminates differences, requiring an entity to recognize revenue when it transfers goods or services to a customer in the amount of consideration it expects to receive from the customer. For the retail industry (largely featured in this book), U.S. GAAP and IFRS for revenue recognition were already essentially identical.	Revenue recognition based mainly on a single standard that contains general principles applied to different types of transactions.	The new standard will standardize the way in which revenues are recognized, resulting in changes in the timing of revenue recognition.
Extraordinary Items Chapter 11	Recording of extraordinary items	Allows separate disclosure of extraordinary items (unusual in nature and infrequent in occurrence) after income from continuing operations. The use of extraordinary items, although allowed, is extremely rare under U.S. GAAP.	Extraordinary items do not have special treatment. Even "unusual and infrequent" items are reported in income from continuing operations.	Extraordinary items may disappear from the income statement, to be reclassified as "ordinary" revenues and expenses.
Interest Revenue and Interest Expense Chapter 12	Indirect method cash flows statement presentation

Direct method cash flows statement presentation | Interest revenue and interest expense are part of net income, and as such are included in operating activities (as part of net income) on an indirect method cash flows statement. Interest is not reported under investing activities. | Interest revenue and interest expense are removed from net income (as an adjustment, similar to the adjustment for depreciation expense) in the operating activities section of the indirect method cash flows statement. Interest income is reported under financing activities, and interest expense is reported under investing activities for both direct and indirect methods. | Interest revenue and interest expense reclassified to different sections of the cash flows statement. |

Company Index

Glindex A Combined Glossary and Subject Index

A

Above par common stock, 589–590

Accelerated depreciation method. A depreciation method that writes off a relatively larger amount of the asset's cost nearer the start of its useful life than the straight-line method does, 410–411

Account. The record of the changes that have occurred in a particular asset, liability, or stockholders' equity during a period. The basic summary device of accounting, 61–62. *See also* Accounts

Account format. A balance-sheet format that lists assets on the left and liabilities and stockholders' equity on the right, 164

Account numbers, list of, 85–86

Accounting. The information system that measures business activities, processes that information into reports and financial statements, and communicates the results to decision makers, 3. *See also* Assumptions; Accounting decisions; Accounting equation; Accounting information

Accounting principles, 6
  changing methods of, 660
  financial, 4
  management, 4
  vs. bookkeeping, 3

Accounting decisions, 25

Accounting equation. The most basic tool of accounting: Assets = Liabilities + Owners' Equity, 11–12

Accounting errors, correcting, 61, 84–85

Accounting estimates, changes in, 660

Accounting information
  accuracy of, 6
  comparability of, 7
  completeness of, 6
  disclosure of, 6
  enhancing qualitative characteristics, 7
  flow of, 78–83
  freedom from bias, 6
  global, 9–10
  and internal control, 239
  material, 6
  on economic substance, 6
  relevance, 6, 8
  understandability of, 7
  verifiability of, 7–8
  users of, 4

Accounting principles
  changes in, 660
  fair value, 9–10, 29–30
  faithful representation, 6
  historical value, 8–9, 31
  generally accepted accounting principles (GAAP), 6–7, 9–10, 31

Accounts. *See also* Adjustments to entries
  adjusting, 140–142

analyzing, 84
asset accounts, 61
chart of, 85–86
formulas for, 86
impact of transactions on, 73–75
liabilities accounts, 61
normal balance of, 86
permanent, 162
posted to ledger, 82
stockholders' equity accounts, 62
temporary, 162
types of, 61
uncollectible, 293–295, 298

Accounts payable, 61, 518

Accounts payable turnover. The number of times per year a company pays off its accounts payable, 519, 790

Accounts receivable, 61

Accounts receivable turnover. Measures a company's ability to collect cash from credit customers. To compute accounts receivable turnover, divide net credit sales by average net accounts receivable, 307, 789–790

Accrual. An expense or a revenue that occurs before the business pays or receives cash. An accrual is the opposite of a deferral, 142

Accrual accounting. Accounting that records the impact of a business event as it occurs, regardless of whether the transaction affected cash, 136–137
  and cash flows, 137
  ethical issues in, 140

Accrued expense. An expense incurred but not yet paid in cash. Also called *accrued liability*, 19, 62, 146–148, 521

Accrued liability. A liability for an expense that has not yet been paid by the company. Also called *accrued expense*, 62, 146–148, 521

Accrued revenue. A revenue that has been earned but not yet received in cash, 148–149

Accumulated benefit obligation, 546

Accumulated depreciation. The cumulative sum of all depreciation expense from the date of acquiring a plant asset, 18–19, 145–146

Accumulated depreciation account,145–146

Accumulated other comprehensive income, 665

Acid-test ratio. Ratio of the sum of cash plus short-term investments plus net current receivables to total current liabilities. Tells whether the entity can pay all its current liabilities if they come due immediately. Also called the *quick ratio*, 306, 788

Adjusted trial balance. A list of all the ledger accounts with their adjusted balances, 153–154

Adjustments to entries
  accruals, 142
  accrued expenses, 146–148
  accrued revenues, 148–149
  deferrals, 141

U

U. S. Securities and Exchange Commission (SEC), 4, 9

Uncollectible accounts, writing off, 298

Uncollectible-account expense. Cost to the seller of extending credit. Arises from the failure to collect from credit customers. Also called *doubtful-account expense* or *bad-debt expense*, 294

Underfunded benefit plan, 547

Underwriter. Organization that purchases the bonds from an issuing company and resells them to its clients or sells the bonds for a commission, agreeing to buy all unsold bonds, 529, 587

Unearned revenue. A liability created when a business collects cash from customers in advance of earning the revenue. The obligation is to provide a product or a service in the future, 148–151, 522–523

  on the balance sheet, 526

Unit of output, of plant assets, 409

Units-of-production (UOP) method. Depreciation method by which a fixed amount of depreciation is assigned to each unit of output produced by the plant asset, 409–410

Unqualified (clean) opinion. An audit opinion stating that the financial statements are reliable, 668

Unrealized gains and losses, 285, 470

Unsecured bonds, 529

Useful life of a depreciable asset, 416–417

V

Vertical analysis. Analysis of a financial statement that reveals the relationship of each statement item to a specified base, which is the 100% figure, 777–778

W

Wages, 521, 717, 725

Warranty, 523

  estimated warranty payable, 523–524

  expense of, 523

Weak currency. A currency whose exchange rate is falling relative to that of other nations, 482

Weighted average cost of capital (WACC). A weighted average of the returns demanded by the company's stockholders and lenders. The combined rate of return expected for a company by its creditors and investors. In general, the higher the risk associated with the company, the greater the expected returns by creditors and investors, 658, 799, 808

Weighted-average-method. Another name for the *average-cost method*, 346–347

  effect on cost of goods sold, 348–349

  effect on gross profit, 348–349

Working capital. Current assets minus current liabilities; measures a business's ability to meet its short-term obligations with its current assets. Also called *net working capital*, 166, 785–786

Writing off uncollectible accounts, 298